The Routledge Handbook of Sociophonetics covers the field comprehensively. Each chapter contains an extensive literature review and an example of empirical research on its topic. These features make this book an essential reference for anyone embarking on sociophonetic research of any kind.

Erik R. Thomas, *North Carolina State University, USA*

THE ROUTLEDGE HANDBOOK OF SOCIOPHONETICS

The Routledge Handbook of Sociophonetics is the definitive guide to sociophonetics. Offering a practical and accessible survey of an unparalleled range of theoretical and methodological perspectives, this is the first handbook devoted to sociophonetic research and applications of sociophonetics within and beyond linguistics. It defines what sociophonetics is as a field and offers views of what sociophonetics might become. Split into three sections, this book:

- examines the suprasegmental, segmental, and subsegmental units that sociophoneticians study;
- reveals the ways that sociophoneticians create knowledge and solve problems across a range of theoretical and practical applications;
- explores sociophonetic traditions around the world in spoken and signed languages;
- includes case studies that demonstrate sociophonetic research in action, which will support and inspire readers to conduct their own projects.

This handbook is an indispensable resource for researchers, undergraduate and graduate students in sociophonetics, as well as researchers and students in sociolinguistics, phonetics, phonology, language variation and change, cognitive linguistics, psycholinguistics, speech pathology, and language teaching—and indeed any area of study where phonetics and phonology interact with social factors and forces.

Christopher Strelluf is an associate professor of linguistics at the University of Warwick. His research interests include sociophonetics, language variation and change, and dialectology.

ROUTLEDGE HANDBOOKS IN LINGUISTICS

Routledge Handbooks in Linguistics provide overviews of a whole subject area or sub-discipline in linguistics, and survey the state of the discipline including emerging and cutting edge areas. Edited by leading scholars, these volumes include contributions from key academics from around the world and are essential reading for both advanced undergraduate and postgraduate students.

THE ROUTLEDGE HANDBOOK OF COGNITIVE LINGUISTICS
Edited by Xu Wen and John R. Taylor

THE ROUTLEDGE HANDBOOK OF THEORETICAL AND EXPERIMENTAL SIGN LANGUAGE RESEARCH
Edited by Josep Quer, Roland Pfau, and Annika Herrmann

THE ROUTLEDGE HANDBOOK OF LANGUAGE AND PERSUASION
Edited by Jeanne Fahnestock and Randy Allen Harris

THE ROUTLEDGE HANDBOOK OF SEMIOSIS AND THE BRAIN
Edited by Adolfo M. García and Agustín Ibáñez

THE ROUTLEDGE HANDBOOK OF LINGUISTIC PRESCRIPTIVISM
Edited by Joan C. Beal, Morana Lukač, and Robin Straaijer

THE ROUTLEDGE HANDBOOK OF EXPERIMENTAL LINGUISTICS
Edited by Sandrine Zufferey and Pascal Gygax

THE ROUTLEDGE HANDBOOK OF SOCIOPHONETICS
Edited by Christopher Strelluf

Further titles in this series can be found online at www.routledge.com/series/RHIL

THE ROUTLEDGE
HANDBOOK OF
SOCIOPHONETICS

Edited by Christopher Strelluf

Routledge
Taylor & Francis Group

LONDON AND NEW YORK

Designed cover image: © Getty Images | Kateryna Kovarzh

First published 2024
by Routledge
4 Park Square, Milton Park, Abingdon, Oxon OX14 4RN

and by Routledge
605 Third Avenue, New York, NY 10158

Routledge is an imprint of the Taylor & Francis Group, an informa business

British Library Cataloguing-in-Publication Data
A catalogue record for this book is available from the British Library

Library of Congress Cataloging-in-Publication Data
Names: Strelluf, Christopher, editor.
Title: The Routledge handbook of sociophonetics / edited by Christopher Strelluf.
Description: Abingdon, Oxon ; New York, NY : Routledge, 2023. |
Series: Routledge handbooks in linguistics |
Includes bibliographical references and index. |
Summary: "The Routledge Handbook of Sociophonetics is the
definitive guide to sociophonetics. Offering a practical and accessible
survey of an unparalleled range of theoretical and methodological
perspectives, this is the first handbook devoted to sociophonetic
research and applications of sociophonetics within and beyond
linguistics. It defines what sociophonetics is as a field and offers views of what
sociophonetics might become"– Provided by publisher.
Identifiers: LCCN 2023015644 (print) | LCCN 2023015645 (ebook) |
ISBN 9780367472795 (hardback) | ISBN 9781032562414 (paperback) |
ISBN 9781003034636 (ebook)
Subjects: LCSH: Sociophonetics. | LCGFT: Essays.
Classification: LCC P40.5.P48 R68 2023 (print) |
LCC P40.5.P48 (ebook) | DDC 306.44–dc23/eng/20230616
LC record available at https://lccn.loc.gov/2023015644
LC ebook record available at https://lccn.loc.gov/2023015645

ISBN: 978-0-367-47279-5 (hbk)
ISBN: 978-1-032-56241-4 (pbk)
ISBN: 978-1-003-03463-6 (ebk)

DOI: 10.4324/9781003034636

Typeset in Times New Roman
by Newgen Publishing UK

CONTENTS

Contents

CONTRIBUTORS

Yoshiyuki Asahi is a Professor of Sociolinguistics in the Department of Research at National Institute for Japanese Language and Linguistics. He completed his PhD at Osaka University in 2004. He works on language variation and change through dialect contact. He is the author of *Saharin-ni nokosareta nihongo Karafuto hōgen* [A Japanese dialect of Karafuto in Sakhalin, Russia] (Meiji Shoin, 2012) and *Nyūtaun kotoba no keisei-ni kansuru shakaigengogakuteki kenkyū* [A sociolinguistic study on the formation of a new town koine] (Hituzi Syobo, 2008), and the editor of *Handbook of Japanese sociolinguistics* (De Gruyter Mouton, 2022).

Mary Baltazani is a Phonetician who is interested in speech prosody, particularly intonation and its interaction with timing and prosodic phrasing, as well as segmental phonetics, especially vowel systems and rhotic variation. Her research has focused on the role of prosody in pragmatics and in language processing, as well as the historical and social aspects of intonational variation. She is a researcher at the Phonetics Laboratory, University of Oxford, and received her PhD from the University of California, Los Angeles. She is currently leading a project on the diachronic effects of language contact on intonational patterns.

Amelia A. Becker is a postdoctoral researcher in the Wheelock College of Education & Human Development at Boston University. Her research focuses on the phonetics and phonology of American Sign Language and their interaction with iconicity. She is currently studying how deaf children leverage iconicity and phonological neighborhood density in their acquisition of ASL signs.

Charles Boberg is a Professor of Linguistics at McGill University in Montreal. He is co-author, with William Labov and Sharon Ash, of the *Atlas of North American English* (Mouton de Gruyter, 2006) and author of *The English language in Canada* (Cambridge University Press, 2010). He recently co-edited the *Handbook of dialectology* (Wiley, 2018) with John Nerbonne and Dominic Watt. His current research focuses on variation and change in Canadian English, as well as on accent variation in North American film and television. His most recent book is *Accent in North American film and television: A sociophonetic analysis* (Cambridge University Press, 2021).

Silvia Calamai is a Professor of Linguistics at the University of Siena. She is a member of the CLARIN Legal Issues Committee and the CLARIN-IT Committee. She is coordinating two projects on oral archives ("Voices from Ravensbrueck," CLARIN ERIC, and "Gra.fo reloaded," Regione Toscana 2022–2024). She is on the scientific committee of the Historical Archive of the Arezzo psychiatric hospital and on the board of *Sonorités Bulletin de l'AFAS Association française des détenteurs de documents audiovisuels et sonores*. Her main research interests are sociophonetics, oral archives, and dialectology. She discovered neglected oral archives, for which she received the attention of press and media. She is among the first researchers working on linguicism in Italian society.

Maria Candea is a Professor in French Sociolinguistics at Université Sorbonne Nouvelle, Paris, mainly working in French sociophonetics. She is a member of the editorial boards of the journals *Langage et société* and *GLAD!*. Her publications often deal with linguistic ideologies; on the one hand, they look at speech and voice perception, especially phonostyles and the gendered voice, and on the other hand, they focus on the description of various accents in contemporary French. She is also interested in applied sociophonetics, particularly in policies against pronunciation-based discrimination.

Christopher Carignan is a Phonetician specializing in the articulation and acoustics of speech production, as well as computational method development for investigating the relationship between speech articulation and acoustics. Carignan is currently a Senior Lecturer in Speech Science, Director of the MSc Language Sciences Programme, and Leader of the Dynamics of the Articulation, Acoustics and Processing of Speech (DAAPS) Lab in the department of Speech, Hearing, and Phonetic Sciences at University College London.

Whitney Chappell is a 2019 Fulbright Scholar, a 2020–2021 Lutcher Brown Distinguished Professor, and an Associate Professor of Hispanic linguistics at the University of Texas at San Antonio. Her research focuses on sociophonetic variation in the Spanish-speaking world, and her work has been published in venues like *Language Variation and Change* and *Studies in Second Language Acquisition*, among many others. Her edited volumes explore *Spanish socio-historical linguistics: Isolation and contact* (co-edited with Bridget Drinka; John Benjamins, 2021) and *Recent advances in the study of Spanish sociophonetic perception* (John Benjamins, 2019).

Alida Chevalier holds a PhD from the University of Cape Town. She is currently a member of the academic staff at 2U Cape Town and was till recently affiliated with UCT as a research officer in linguistics attached to Rajend Mesthrie's research chair. Her research interests include sociophonetics, sociolinguistics, language variation and change including automated vowel analysis, and statistics for linguistics. Her publications include book chapters and articles, including a chapter in the book *English in multilingual South Africa* (edited by R. Hickey; Cambridge University Press, 2020) and an article in *Language Variation and Change* (2015).

Eleanor Chodroff is an Assistant Professor in Computational Linguistics at the University of Zurich and holds associate status with the Department of Language and Linguistic Science at the University of York. She received her PhD in Cognitive Science from Johns Hopkins University. Her research focuses on the phonetics–phonology interface, cross-talker and cross-linguistic phonetic variation, speech prosody, and speech perception. A recurring theme in her research is the use of large spoken corpora to advance linguistic theory.

Felicity Cox is a Professor in the Linguistics Department at Macquarie University, Sydney. She is an Australian Research Council Future Fellow and has published widely on the phonetics and phonology of Australian English. Her work at the interface between speech science, culture and identity, informs theories of sociophonetic variation and sound change. She is President of the Australasian Speech Science and Technology Association and co-author of *Australian English: Pronunciation and Transcription* (with Janet Fletcher; Cambridge University Press, 2017).

Justin Davidson is an Associate Professor of Hispanic Linguistics and Romance Linguistics at the University of California, Berkeley. His research agenda in sociophonetics is guided by questions that primarily address language variation and language change in contact situations, specifically as linked to the empirical assessment of contact-induced linguistic change, incorporating a variety of linguistic frameworks and methodologies. His work appears across several journal, book, and handbook venues, including the *Journal of Sociolinguistics*, *Sibilants in Spanish: Diachronic and sociolinguistic analysis* (edited by Eva Núñez-Méndez; Routledge, 2021), and the *Manual of Romance phonetics and phonology* (edited by Christoph Gabriel et al.; De Gruyter, 2022).

Lisa Davidson is a Professor in the Linguistics Department at New York University. Her research interests include the phonetics and sociophonetics of voice quality, the production of connected speech, and the perception and production of non-native phonotactics. She is currently the General Editor of *Laboratory Phonology* and the director of the Phonetics and Phonology Lab at NYU.

Marianna Di Paolo is an Emeritus Associate Professor in the departments of Anthropology and of Linguistics, University of Utah; a Research Associate at the National Museum of Natural History (the Smithsonian); and Director of the Shoshoni Language Project https://shoshoniproj ect.utah.edu/. She was the founding Chair of the University of Utah's Department of Linguistics. Her publications include *Sociophonetics: A student's guide* (co-edited with Malcah Yaeger-Dror; Routledge, 2010), *Languages and dialects in the US: Focus on diversity and linguistics* (co-edited with Arthur K. Spears; Routledge, 2014), "Phonation differences and the phonetic content of the tense-lax contrast in Utah English," and "The Peripatetic History of ME *ɛ:".

Gerard Docherty is a Professor of Phonetics at Griffith University, Brisbane. A common strand through his research has been a focus on quantitative acoustic analysis of aspects of speech with a view to enhancing understanding of the nature of social-indexical phonetic variability and its implications for phonetic theory. While much of his work has focused on typical adult speakers, he has also investigated the acquisition of speech sound patterning in children and the nature of speech in populations of speakers with atypical speech production. He is currently a Co-Investigator (with Catherine Travis and Ksenia Gnevsheva; both ANU) on an Australian Research Council-funded Discovery Project, "Voices of Regional Australia: The Linguistic Patterning of Local Attachment."

Bronwen G. Evans is an Associate Professor in the Department of Speech, Hearing & Phonetic Sciences at University College London. She completed undergraduate and postgraduate degrees at Cambridge and Newcastle universities, before graduating with a PhD in Experimental Phonetics from University College London. Her work combines theory and methodologies from the disciplines of sociophonetics, experimental phonetics, and speech perception to investigate how speakers use variation to signal identity and how listeners adapt to and use this information in perception. She works with a range of languages and speakers, including monolingual and multilingual speech communities, children, and adults.

Silvia Filippi is a PhD student in psychological sciences. Her main research interests are economic inequality and wealth redistribution. She focuses on the antecedents of support for wealth redistribution and on the role of linguistic frames in shaping people attitudes towards progressive taxation and tax compliance. She is also interested in topics related to employees' well-being, work–life balance, and new forms of organizational governance, such as self-managing organizations.

Jami N. Fisher is the Director of the American Sign Language and Senior Lecturer in Foreign Languages in the Department of Linguistics at the University of Pennsylvania, a position she has held since 2005. She is a native ASL user and CODA (Child of Deaf Adults), born and raised in Philadelphia. She has a BA in English and Education from Colby College, an MS Ed in Education, Culture, and Society and an EdD in Higher Education from University of Pennsylvania's Graduate School of Education. Her current academic interests include finding ways to integrate meaningful, collaborative, community-based activities into ASL and Deaf Studies coursework as well as documenting and analyzing the Philadelphia variety of American Sign Language.

Magdalena Formanowicz is an Associate Professor at the Center for Research on Social Relations, SWPS University in Warsaw. Her research focuses on social cognition and language and relies on a multimethod approach that incorporates experimental studies and analyses of large textual data to investigate language pertinent to discrimination and intergroup relations. She is also interested in dehumanization and agency.

Paul Foulkes is a Professor in the Department of Language and Linguistic Science at the University of York. He holds an MA, MPhil, and PhD from the University of Cambridge (Churchill College). His interests lie mainly in sociophonetics, forensic speech science, and child language development, with a particular interest in understanding how sociophonetic variation is learned, stored cognitively, and accessed in speech production.

Christina García is an Associate Professor of Spanish and Linguistics at Saint Louis University. Her research interests include phonetic variation of the Spanish-speaking world, sociophonetic perception, and L2 pronunciation acquisition. Her work has been published in journals such as *Language Variation and Change*, *Studies in Hispanic and Lusophone Linguistics*, and *Spanish in Context*, and she co-edited with Rosario Gómez and Erin O'Rourke the volume *Ecuadorian Spanish in the 21st century: Historical and contemporary perspectives* (Cambridge Scholars Publishing, 2022).

Ksenia Gnevsheva is a Senior Lecturer in Linguistics at the Australian National University, Canberra. Her main research interest lies at the intersection of sociophonetics and second language acquisition. Her current work focuses on sociolinguistic variation in bilingual speakers in production and perception.

Julie A. Hochgesang is a Professor of Linguistics at Gallaudet University. She is a deaf linguist who specializes in phonetics and phonology of signed languages, documentation (including fieldwork and corpora) of signed languages, and ethics of working with signed language communities. Hochgesang also works towards making linguistics accessible to the communities, especially the ASL communities, sharing multimodal products via social media and digital repositories. She has contributed to ongoing efforts to create accessible collections for the ASL communities, most notably as an active maintainer of the ASL Signbank. Her most recent ASL documentation projects include the "Philadelphia Signs Project," "Motivated Look at Indicating Verbs in ASL (MoLo)," and "Documenting the Experiences of the ASL communities in the time of COVID-19" (O5S5 - ASL name derived from ASL variants for "Document COVID").

Stamatina Katsiveli is a Sociolinguist and Conversation Analyst who specializes in the relationship between language, gender, sexuality, and nation. She completed her PhD in linguistics at Queen Mary University of London in 2021. Her work has been published in the *Journal of Pragmatics* and *Gender and Language*, among other venues. She is currently an Instructor in the Department of Communication at Deree–The American College of Greece.

Tyler Kendall is a Professor of Linguistics at the University of Oregon. He works on the corpus-based and sociophonetic study of language variation and change and has developed software and other infrastructure for the language sciences. He is the creator of the Sociolinguistic Archive and Analysis Project (SLAAP) and the Corpus of Regional African American Language (CORAAL), as well as the NORM website for vowel plotting and normalization and the Vowels.R package. His books include *Speech rate, pause, and sociolinguistic variation: Studies in corpus sociophonetics* (Palgrave Macmillan, 2013) and, with Valerie Fridland, *Sociophonetics* (Cambridge University Press, 2021).

Ghada Khattab is a Professor in Phonetics and Phonology in the School of Education, Communication and Language Sciences at Newcastle University. She obtained her BA in English Language at the American University of Beirut and her MA and PhD in Linguistics from the University of Leeds. Ghada specializes in Arabic phonetics and phonology, sociolinguistics, second language phonology, and phonological development in monolingual and multilingual contexts.

Erez Levon is a Professor of Sociolinguistics and Director of the Center for the Study of Language and Society at the University of Bern. His work draws on quantitative, qualitative, and experimental methods to examine how people produce and perceive socially meaningful patterns of variation in language. He has conducted research on these topics in Israel/Palestine, the United States, the United Kingdom, Brazil, and South Africa.

Margaret Maclagan holds an adjunct position as an Associate Professor in the School of Psychology, Speech and Hearing at the University of Canterbury in Christchurch. She is a member of the New Zealand Institute of Language, Brain and Behaviour. Before her retirement she taught language acquisition and language analysis, including phonetic analysis, to speech-language pathology students. Her research interests include sound change over time in New Zealand English and in te reo Māori, and language change over time in people living with dementia.

Toby Macrae is a Theme Leader (Language Learning Across the Lifespan) in the New Zealand Institute of Language, Brain and Behaviour and a Senior Lecturer in the School of Psychology, Speech and Hearing at the University of Canterbury in Christchurch. His areas of interest include assessment and treatment of childhood speech and language disorders, and languages and dialects spoken by minority populations, including te reo Māori (New Zealand) and African American English. Toby is a qualified and American Speech-Language-Hearing Association-certified speech-language pathologist with experience working with children in the education system in New Zealand and in private practice in New Zealand and in the United States.

Kenjirō Matsuda is a Professor of Linguistics at Kobe Shoin Women's University, Kobe. He studied at Sophia University and obtained his PhD at University of Pennsylvania. His major works include: "Dissecting analogical leveling quantitatively: A case of innovative potential form in Tōkyō Japanese" (*Language Variation and Change*, 1993), *Variable zero-marking of (o) in Tōkyō Japanese* (Technical Report, Institute for Research in Cognitive Sciences, University of Pennsylvania, 1995), "Constant Rate Hypothesis, age-grading, and apparent time construct" (*Penn Working Papers in Linguistics*, 2003), and "The birth and diffusion of group languages in the National Diet" (*Proceedings of Methods XVI*, 2020).

Rajend Mesthrie is an Emeritus Professor of Linguistics at the University of Cape Town. His interests are in General Linguistics with special emphasis on historical linguistics, language contact, dialectology, and sociolinguistics. He was President of the Linguistics Society of Southern Africa (2002–2009) and President of the International Congress of Linguists (2013–2018). Amongst his book publications are *Language in indenture: A sociolinguistic history of Bhojpuri-Hindi in South Africa* (Routledge, 1992; reprint edition 2019), *Language in South Africa* (ed., Cambridge University Press, 2002), and *Youth language practices & urban language contact in Africa* (ed., with Ellen Hurst-Harosh and Heather Brookes; Cambridge University Press, 2021). He is an elected honorary life member of the Linguistic Society of America.

Aurélie Nardy is an Assistant Professor at Université Grenoble Alpes. Her fields of interest are oral language development with a particular focus on the relationship between social context, taken in a broad sense, and the diversity of language uses, notably sociophonetic variants. More specifically, she is interested in language development and its links with child-directed speech (within the family and at school), peer interactions, and sociological factors.

Ichiro Ota is a Professor of Sociolinguistics at Kagoshima University. He studied sociolinguistics at Seinan Gakuin University and University of Essex. His current research interests include variation and change in regional dialect and language in the media. His major works are: "Tonal variation of Kagoshima Japanese and its relevant factors" (*ICUWPL* 10, 2020), "Media models, 'the shelf', and stylistic variation in East and West. Rethinking the influence of the media on language variation" (with Jane Stuart-Smith, 2014), and "The media influence on language change in Japanese sociolinguistic context" (with Shoji Takano, 2014).

Erin O'Rourke studies language contact issues related to Spanish and indigenous languages. Adopting a sociophonetic approach, she has examined variation at the segmental and suprasegmental levels. She earned her PhD from the University of Illinois Urbana-Champaign, and is currently Associate Professor of Spanish Linguistics at the University of Alabama. The overall goal of her research is to observe how sound systems develop and change, how social and linguistic factors contribute to the development of variation, and the role of bilinguals in that process.

Margaret E.L. Renwick is an Associate Professor of Linguistics at the University of Georgia, having received her PhD at Cornell University in 2012. She studies vowels and consonants, in English and the Romance languages, to understand how phonological contrasts are implemented phonetically and how they vary across locations, time, and social groups. Her research projects are rooted in laboratory phonology, an approach which integrates experimental methods with more abstract linguistic representations of sound structure.

Yolandi Ribbens-Klein holds a PhD from the University of Cape Town and has worked on diverse sociolinguistic research projects, the majority of these focusing on language variation and change in Afrikaans and South African Englishes. She is specifically interested in the intersection of sociophonetic variation and the embodied performances of identities, ideologies, and senses of place and belonging in multilingual societies. Her approach is interdisciplinary and she draws on sociology, phenomenology, human geography, and decolonial and feminist studies. She has till recently held the position of Research Officer within Rajend Mesthrie's research chair, after spending two years in a postdoctoral position at the University of Duisburg-Essen.

Scott Sadowsky is a Professor of Linguistics at the Universidad de Cartagena. His research focuses on socioeconomic, ethnic, and sex-based language variation and change, principally through the lens of sociophonetics, language contact, and corpus linguistics, with a focus on Spanish and Mapudungun. His most recent projects include the Sociolinguistic Speech Corpus of Chilean Spanish (www.corpora.pro) and Sound Comparisons: Mapudungun (soundcomparisons.com/Mapudungun).

Koen Sebregts is an Assistant Professor of English linguistics at Utrecht University. His research areas are laboratory phonology and sociophonetics, with a particular interest in sound changes in progress.

James N. Stanford is a Professor and Chair of Linguistics at Dartmouth College in Hanover, New Hampshire. He is co-editor of *Language Variation and Change*, associate editor of *Asia-Pacific Language Variation*, co-editor of *Variation in indigenous minority languages* (with Dennis Preston; John Benjamins, 2009), and author of *New England English: Large-scale acoustic sociophonetics and dialectology* (Oxford University Press, 2019).

Joseph A. Stanley is an Assistant Professor in the Linguistics Department at Brigham Young University. His research focuses on documenting change and variation in Western and Southern American Englishes with current projects based around English in Georgia, Utah, and Idaho. He also works on quantitative methods and data visualization in sociophonetic research.

Christopher Strelluf is an Associate Professor of Linguistics at the University of Warwick. His research interests include sociophonetics, language variation and change, and dialectology. He is author of *Speaking from the Heartland: The Midland vowel system of Kansas City* (Duke University Press, 2018) and, with Matthew J. Gordon, *The origins of Missouri English: A historical sociophonetic analysis* (Lexington, forthcoming).

Caterina Suitner is an Associate Professor at the University of Padova, where she teaches Persuasion and Social Influence, Work and Organizational Psychology, and Social Network Analysis. She is currently Editor-in-Chief of *European Journal of Social Psychology*. Her research focuses on the relationship between social cognition and language, with particular attention to the role of para-semantic linguistic features and their role in attitude formation (e.g., trust in vaccines) and belief in fake news, social inequality, and gender issues.

Shoji Takano is a Professor of Sociolinguistics at Hokusei Gakuen University, Sapporo. He obtained his MA at University of Wisconsin-Madison and his PhD degree at the University of Arizona. His research interests include language change in real time, sociophonetics, language and identity, and discourse-pragmatic variation. He has recently published "Lifespan 'changes from above' in the standardization of Japanese regional dialects: Levels of grammar, lexical properties and community characteristics" (*Language Variation and Change*, 2021) and "A sociophonetic approach to variation in Japanese pitch realizations: Region, age, gender, and stylistic parameters" (with Ichiro Ota; *Asia-Pacific Language Variation*, 2017).

Meredith Tamminga is an Associate Professor of Linguistics at the University of Pennsylvania, where she also completed her PhD and is currently serving as Graduate Chair. Her research is in sociolinguistics and its intersections with psycholinguistics and language change, using both experimental and corpus methods. She directs the Language Variation & Cognition Lab and is one of the lead researchers on the Philadelphia Signs Project.

Weijie Tan is a PhD student at the University of Macau. Her current research interests include language variation and change, sociophonetics, and the cognitive process of language production and perception and the relationship between them.

Tracey Toefy holds a PhD from the University of Cape Town and is a member of faculty at the University of Pretoria's Gordon Institute of Business Science. She teaches in the areas of business communication, strategy, research methodology, and writing. She is the academic head of the Postgraduate Diploma in Business Administration, and the course lead for the Strategic Implementation core module on the Master of Business Administration degree. Her research interests are focused at the intersection of language, strategy, and communication.

Gisela Tomé Lourido is a Lecturer in Sociophonetics in the School of Languages, Cultures and Societies at the University of Leeds. She completed undergraduate and postgraduate degrees at Universidade da Coruña and University College London (UCL) and graduated with a PhD in Speech, Hearing and Phonetic Sciences from UCL. Her research uses eye-tracking and other behavioral methods to investigate accent variation in speech perception and production in bilingual and monolingual populations. She has mainly worked on Galician, English, and the documentation of the phonetics and phonology of Mehri and Shehret, two endangered Modern South Arabian Languages.

Danielle Turton is a Senior Lecturer in Sociolinguistics at Lancaster University. Her research considers variation and change in English from a phonological perspective. She has a particular interest in consonantal and vocalic variation in Northern English. Her PhD and much subsequent work focuses on laterals, bringing together perspectives from articulatory phonetics, theoretical phonology, and variationist sociolinguistics under one approach.

Hans Van de Velde is a Senior Researcher at Fryske Akademy, Leeuwarden and Chair of Sociolinguistics at Utrecht University. He became fascinated by variation in Dutch /r/ during his

PhD dissertation, and co-founded the 'r-atics workshop series. His research focuses on laboratory sociolinguistics, and he is responsible for the development of language tools for Frisian.

Roeland van Hout is a Professor Emeritus of the Radboud University Nijmegen. He has been a professor in sociolinguistics, dialectology, research methodology, and applied linguistics. His articles have appeared in leading language journals. He has a special interest in statistical aspects of empirical language research.

Paul Warren is a Professor of Linguistics at Victoria University of Wellington, where his teaching and research is in psycholinguistics, phonetics (including the pronunciation of New Zealand English), and laboratory phonology. His publications include *Introducing psycholinguistics* (Cambridge University Press, 2012) and *Uptalk: The phenomenon of rising intonation* (Cambridge University Press, 2016). He is a founding member of the Association for Laboratory Phonology.

Dominic Watt is a Professor of English Linguistics at Universität Vechta. His research interests are in forensic linguistics and phonetics, multimodal speech perception, sociophonetics, language and identity studies, and dialectology. He is a member of the Accent Bias in Britain research group, and undertakes forensic speech analysis consultancy work on a regular basis. His publications include *The handbook of dialectology* (co-editors Charles Boberg and John Nerbonne; Wiley, 2018), *Language and identities* (with Carmen Llamas; Edinburgh University Press, 2010), and *English accents and dialects* (with Arthur Hughes and Peter Trudgill; Hodder Education, 2012).

Bruce Wileman has specialized in the sociophonetics of South African English and holds a PhD from the University of Cape Town, where he also completed a postdoctoral fellowship. His primary research interests include vowel quality and voice quality variation in South African English, as well as prosodic variation. His earlier research work investigated and documented regional variation in vowel quality in White South African English. His more recent academic work has focused on ethnolinguistic variation in voice quality in South African English. He has till recently worked as a voice developer for Cerence, a company specializing in providing innovative automotive voice and AI solutions.

Marta Witkowska is a Social Psychologist specializing in intergroup relations and social cognition. She holds a PhD from the Center for Research on Prejudice at the University of Warsaw. Her research there lay at the intersection of political psychology and intergroup relations, and it showed the impact of social perception related to others' morality on intergroup attitudes in post-conflict areas. Currently, at the Center for Research on Social Relations, SWPS University of Social Sciences and Humanities in Warsaw, she studies the language of agency and its relation to psychological phenomena such as collective action, well-being, and persuasion.

Cathryn Yang is a Program Faculty Member of the Linguistics Department at Payap University in Chiang Mai. Her research focuses on ongoing and diachronic tone change, with an emphasis on tonal reconstruction in the Ngwi languages of southwest China. She is the author of *Lalo dialects across time and space: Subgrouping, dialectometry, and intelligibility* (ANU Asia-Pacific Linguistics, 2015).

Georgia Zellou is a Linguist specializing in phonetics and laboratory phonology. She serves as an Associate Professor in the Linguistics Department at UC Davis. She has received several awards, grants, and fellowships, including from the National Science Foundation and Amazon and she was a Fulbright research scholar in France. In 2019, she received the Chancellor's Award for Excellence in Undergraduate Mentoring and she was also named a UC Davis Dean's Fellow in 2020. She was co-director of the 2019 LSA Linguistic Institute. In 2020, she was named a Fellow of the Linguistic Society of America.

Jingwei Zhang is an Assistant Professor at the Department of Chinese Language and Literature, Faculty of Arts and Humanities in the University of Macau. Her research interests include language variation and change, sociophonetics, and psycholinguistics.

OVERVIEW

Christopher Strelluf

This handbook provides a definitive view of sociophonetics. It defines what sociophonetics is as a field, and offers views of what sociophonetics might become.

It is organized into three sections. The first, "Units of Analysis," examines the suprasegmental, segmental, and subsegmental features that sociophoneticians study. The second, "Applications," explores some of the ways sociophoneticians are leveraging their work to create knowledge and solve problems across a range of theoretical and practical domains. The third, "Sociophonetics Around the World," gives a glimpse of some sociophonetic traditions beyond the Global North English speech communities that form a large portion of the sociophonetic literature.

This handbook is intentionally designed to describe the current state of sociophonetics while also innovating it. It casts a wide net for coverage. Each section includes chapters on topics that have been extensively researched in sociophonetics for several decades, as well as chapters on topics that are—at least so far—relatively niche areas of investigation. This approach is intended to map the well-known landscapes of sociophonetics and inspire exploration of newer territories. The handbook also avoids a division that underlies much sociophonetic research (and specializations of researchers) between studies of production and studies of perception, as each chapter explores relevant research in production, perception, and the interfaces between them. To the extent that bifurcations between production and perception can be avoided, this handbook should encourage work across the totality of the human sociophonetic faculty.

The *Routledge Handbook of Sociophonetics* is also constructed to innovate the genre of the handbook. In addition to the expected summaries and syntheses of canonical and innovative research, each chapter includes a case study to exemplify sociophonetic research in action. Conceptually, the inclusion of case studies is grounded in sociophonetics' ethos as an empirical, data-driven science. While the distillations of a field by its leading experts remain the most important contribution of this handbook, case studies acknowledge the understanding—and fun—that comes from being guided by an expert through the compilation and exploration of a dataset to create knowledge. Authors take a range of approaches to case studies—in some instances offering entirely new research and in others revisiting prior work, and with some case studies being very brief and others serving as the bulk of chapter content. In all instances, though, case studies provide insights into the ways sociophonetics is done and the discoveries sociophoneticians can achieve, and will be engaging and accessible to new students and established scholars alike.

I am indebted to the authors who shared their expertise and vision to build this handbook—and who did so, moreover, while their lives and work were upended during the global COVID-19 pandemic. I also thank the editorial board members—John H. Esling, Paul Foulkes, Jane Stuart-Smith, Meghan Sumner, and Erik R. Thomas—who agreed to guide the handbook's design and to review chapters. I am especially grateful to Erik, John, and Paul for shouldering substantial review responsibilities, and for mentoring and supporting me as I learned the process of editing a project of this scale. Carmen Llamas and Perry R. Hinton also kindly reviewed chapters. The successes of this handbook are obviously due to the generous contributions of the authors, reviewers, and editorial board members. Where there are gaps in coverage—and inevitably, if frustratingly, there are certainly such gaps—I hope these will inspire future work to continue to sharpen the picture of the field.

Finally, on behalf of all contributors to this handbook, I acknowledge the uncounted language users who contributed the tens of millions of datapoints that comprise our collective knowledge of sociophonetics.

1

SOCIOPHONETICS AND THE SOCIOLINGUISTIC-PHONETIC INTERFACE

A radical introduction

Christopher Strelluf

The emergence of "sociophonetics"

Foulkes & Docherty (2006:410) trace the label "sociophonetics" to Denise Deshaies-Lafontaine's 1974 doctoral thesis. In the five decades since the names of the linguistic subdisciplines of phonetics and sociolinguistics were blended, a rich research tradition has emerged.

Sociophonetics benefits from an extensive meta-disciplinary literature. Foulkes & Docherty's (2006) article was included in a special issue of the *Journal of Phonetics* edited by Stefanie Jannedy and Jennifer Hay, which can now be recognized as having been published near the beginning of a period of intense activity by researchers to recognize, reflect upon, and codify sociophonetics as a distinctive set of theories, methodologies, and findings. A few years earlier, Thomas's (2002:189) chapter on instrumental phonetics in the first edition of the *Handbook of language variation and change* had noted that the "melding of sociolinguistics and phonetics is sometimes referred to as 'sociophonetics'" (and symbolic of the rapid growth in recognition of sociophonetics in the years that would follow, Thomas's 2013 chapter in the second edition of that handbook was revised and retitled, "sociophonetics"). In 2005, Marinna Di Paolo and Malcah Yaeger-Dror hosted the first "Best practices in sociophonetics" workshop, which would become an annual staple of the New Ways of Analyzing Variation (NWAV) conference. Hay & Drager's (2007) review of sociophonetics appeared in the *Annual Review of Anthropology*. The focus of the Laboratory Phonology 11 conference in 2008 was "Phonetic detail in the lexicon," and papers from the conference subtheme on socio-indexical knowledge were collected and edited by Jen Hay and Paul Warren as the first issue of the journal *Laboratory Phonology*, with several contributions being framed explicitly as sociophonetic and all exemplifying sociophonetic lines of inquiry. In 2010, Scuola Normale Superiore in Pisa hosted the international workshop "Sociophonetics, at the crossroads of speech variation, processing and communication," the proceedings of which were published as Calamai, Celata & Ciucci (2012) and inspired the collection Celata & Calamai (2014).

Three milestone book-length explorations of sociophonetics were published in the months just before and after the Pisa workshop: Preston & Niedzielski (2010), Di Paolo & Yaeger-Dror

DOI: 10.4324/9781003034636-1

(2011), and Thomas (2011). Along with Celata & Calamai (2014), these books remain essential to every sociophonetician's library. Preston & Niedzielski's reader presents a sample of research into a remarkably wide-ranging set of subsegmental, segmental, and suprasegmental sociophonetic variables (mostly in English but also with excursions into Dutch, French, Japanese, and Spanish, as well as in non-US/UK Englishes and children's language) in ways that anticipate many of the recent advances that are celebrated in the present handbook. Di Paolo & Yaeger-Dror's "student's guide" (which they note emerged largely from the NWAV workshops) is also impressive in its range of coverage, which is offered as accessible overviews of methods for collecting and measuring sociophonetic data. While technological and theoretical advances in the field leave some aspects of their book feeling dated, my anecdotal experience using Di Paolo & Yaeger-Dror (2011) in teaching is that its presentation is so accessible, and the principles and advice it offers are so fundamental, that students who are new to sociophonetics prefer it over other available texts. In practical terms, the biggest limitation of Di Paolo & Yaeger-Dror (2011) might be that it is not currently available in a digital format; creating such a format might extend its shelf-life and help introduce another generation of emerging sociophoneticians to the field. On the other hand, Thomas's (2011) textbook shows no hints of its age. Because Thomas exhaustively details measurement and analytic techniques—including presenting about 200 figures, tables, and equations—the book remains a resource that a sociophonetician of any level of experience can turn to for guidance on exploring sociophonetic variation. Moreover, Thomas's approach was not only to report the current state of sociophonetic research at the time he was writing, but also to identify potential sites of sociophonetic variability that were not yet being examined, and then to digest the landscape of phonetic research to introduce techniques that might be leveraged in sociophonetics. As a result, many of the recent and exciting innovations reported in this handbook reflect techniques and respond to calls for inquiry that initially appeared in Thomas (2011). Indeed, the textbook offers methods and research questions that have yet to be pursued by sociophoneticians. Scholars who wish to be early methodological innovators in sociophonetics can still look to Thomas (2011) for inspiration.

The sociophonetics library continues to be expanded and enriched by entries such as Chappell (2019), Watson (2021), and Kendall & Fridland (2021). Chapter-length overviews of sociophonetics also routinely appear in the handbooks and encyclopedias of other linguistic disciplines and subdisciplines. Excellent examples include Foulkes, Scobbie & Watt (2010) in the *Handbook of phonetic sciences*; Docherty & Mendoza-Denton (2011) and Scobbie et al. (2011) in the *Oxford handbook of laboratory phonology;* Baranowski (2013) in the *Oxford handbook of sociolinguistics*; Thomas (2013) in the *Handbook of language variation and change*; Podesva & Kajino (2014) in the *Handbook of language, gender, and sexuality*; Thomas (2019) in the *Routledge handbook of phonetics*; Drager & Kettig (2021) in the *Cambridge handbook of phonetics*; and Docherty (2022) in the *Oxford research encyclopedia of linguistics*. Collections like the special issue of *Linguistics Vanguard* on "Current methodological innovations in sociophonetics" edited by Pharao & Fabricius (2020) offer further insights into the field—as of course do the many presentations of sociophonetic research that now regularly appear at major conferences like NWAV or the International Congress of Phonetic Sciences and the many sociophonetic journal articles, book chapters, and books that appear in print each year.

The rapid and robust growth of a meta-literature of sociophonetics reflects the energy and enthusiasm with which sociophoneticians have pursued linguistic insight, and the influence of their insights into the human language faculty. The chapters in this handbook represent another milestone in the meta-literature of sociophonetics—collecting, building upon, and advancing the shared knowledge that sociophoneticians have created across a diverse and nuanced range of units of analysis, applications, and global language varieties. They complement the other disciplinary syntheses sociophoneticians have produced, providing students and scholars with incredibly rich resources to understand what sociophonetics is and does, and what sociophonetics may become and might do.

Because so many excellent overviews of sociophonetics are already available, and because the chapters in this handbook so richly describe sociophonetics from the perspectives of some of the best scholars in the field, this introductory chapter will avoid either general summaries of sociophonetic research or summaries of the chapters in this handbook. Instead, it will attempt to draw on the insights of the meta-literature of sociophonetics to consider the place of sociophonetics in linguistic science and the ways that sociophonetic research is conceptualized. In doing so, it seeks to build upon the tremendous advances in sociophonetics in recent decades—culminating so far in the chapters of this handbook—to point out directions for the next developmental stages of sociophonetics.

What is sociophonetics?

Sociophonetics is routinely defined as the interface between sociolinguistics and phonetics. This "interface" is represented as the area of overlap in the Venn diagram in Figure 1.1. Figure 1.1 also overlays two labels that are not widely used—"phonetic sociolinguistics" and "sociolinguistic phonetics"—and places these at either end of the space encapsulated by sociophonetics. The sociophonetic zone is itself shaded in Figure 1.1 as a gradient transition from sociolinguistics to phonetics.

While the blending of sociolinguistics and phonetics is intuitively straightforward, the scholars who have done most to define, demonstrate, and advance sociophonetics take a range of positions on the relationship between sociolinguistics and phonetics within that overlapping space, on how extensive the overlap between sociolinguistics and phonetics is, on what falls within the overlapping space, and on the extent to which the overlapping space is itself differentiated from either sociolinguistics or phonetics. In this section, I will advocate for conceptualizing sociophonetics philosophically and disciplinarily according to the model depicted by Figure 1.1, which reflects the conventional view of sociophonetics as a space of overlap between sociolinguistics and phonetics, while also—by depicting that overlap as a gradient and transitional space—presenting a more expansive and less circumscribed view of what "counts" as sociophonetic data and sociophonetic research. This model maximizes the body of datasets, historical findings, methodologies, and theories that sociophoneticians can engage with, provides a vocabulary for mapping scholars' contributions and approaches along a continuum from sociolinguistics to phonetics, and implies a

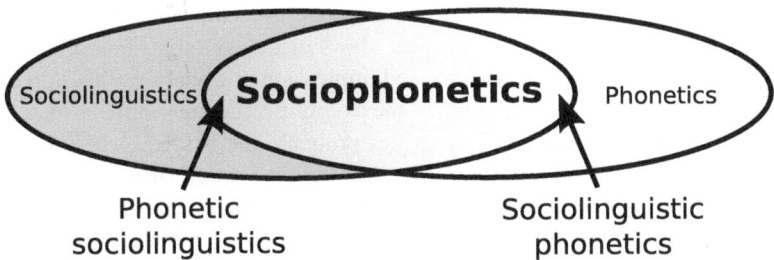

Figure 1.1 Venn diagram of sociophonetics as the interface between sociolinguistics and phonetics

space at the core of sociophonetics where research generates its maximally unique and important contributions to knowledge of the language faculty.

Differing conceptualizations of sociophonetics show up at broad levels of disciplinary positioning. Preston & Niedzielski's (2010:3) introduction to *A reader in sociophonetics*, for instance, frames sociophonetics as a sub-branch of sociolinguistics, while the same book's back-cover summary defines sociophonetics as a sub-branch of phonetics. Baranowski (2013:403) takes a "modest view of sociophonetics as a tool contributing to our understanding of the nature of language variation and change," and suggests that "it remains to be seen whether sociophonetics develops into a separate discipline, with its own questions and standards of proof, or whether it continues to mark a methodological approach within variationist sociolinguistics." Foulkes, Scobbie & Watts (2010) take an expansive view of sociophonetics, arguing that the increasingly wide-reaching subdisciplinary engagements, theorical commitments, and empirical contributions of sociophonetics are indicative of sociophonetics being an independent discipline (704), and one "which is beginning to lay claim to be a core phonetic science" (737). Drager & Kettig (2021:560) take an even broader view, listing, for instance, the Harvard Dialect Survey as an example of a survey used by sociophoneticians, even though the project extensively collected judgments of lexical and morphosyntactic variables and limited phonetic and phonological data largely to judgments about pronunciations. Thomas's (2013:108) overview suggests a moment of "transformation from being seen as a methodological approach to becoming a theoretical discipline with links to cognitive and neuro-linguistic sciences," which "can and should alter the direction of sociolinguistics as a whole."

Disagreements over what "sociophonetics" is (as an area of research) extend to questions over what is "sociophonetic" (as a dataset). In other words, what types of data "count" as sociophonetic data, rather than being sociolinguistic or phonetic? The loosest possible definition would see any sociolinguistic study that deals with phonetic or phonological variables as being within the purview of sociophonetics, along with any phonetic or phonological study that acknowledges effects of social factors on datasets. Such a broad definition would expand the disciplinary history of sociophonetics deep into the origins of language research. Docherty summarizes:

> Many topics investigated under the sociophonetics banner have been a long-standing focus for researchers who would not necessarily classify their work as such. Social-indexical phonetic variation has featured strongly in work on dialectology, in studies of historical phonological change and the consequences of language/variety contact, and, above all, in work since the 1960s on sociolinguistics […].
>
> Docherty 2022:2

Chapters in this handbook explore the historical place of sociophonetics in dialectology (Watt, Renwick & Stanley) and in theories of sound change associated especially with William Labov (Boberg). But scholars routinely take more circumspect views of the data that should be labeled "sociophonetic," in particular excluding the auditory and impressionistic analyses that dominated dialectology and sociolinguistics until the beginning of the twenty-first century in favor of acoustic and articulatory techniques. Thomas (2011:1–2) provides probably the best-known summary of this position. Baranowski (2013:403) similarly notes that sociophonetics "usually implies the use of instrumental techniques"; Podesva & Kajino (2014:103) juxtapose sociophonetics and variationist sociolinguistics by saying that the former deals in scalar variables and the latter in categorical variables; and Docherty (2022:5) presupposes instrumental measurements marking sociophonetics as distinct from sociolinguistics, for example by describing instrumental studies of consonants extending understanding of social-indexical variation "as opposed to the auditory impressionistic methods that tended to be prevalent within sociolinguistic studies of consonants." This focus on instrumental measurement filters sociophonetics on the basis of its "phonetic" component, with auditorily coded data being considered to have been measured with insufficient precision to qualify as valid by phoneticians.

Data may also be filtered on the basis of whether social predictors of phonetic or phonological variability are sufficiently sociolinguistic. Foulkes & Docherty (2006:409), for instance, intuitively exclude from sociophonetics variation which is "largely explicable with reference to articulatory constraints and/or the natural laws of aerodynamics and acoustics operating within the vocal tract," the latter of which will, to some extent, be correlated with social factors—for instance when anatomical tendencies in vocal tract length and vocal fold thickness result in male adults producing lower f0 than female children. Foulkes & Docherty (2006:411) point out, though, that there may "be no clear dividing line between learned and non-learned behavior or between arbitrary and non-arbitrary phonetic variation." They give the example "that male-female differences emerge in children's speech well before the onset of puberty produces large differences in vocal tract sizes." Accordingly, they set a low bar for counting data as sufficiently sociolinguistic:

> In light of this, we will use the term sociophonetic to cover any instance of variation where the indexed factor is at least partly socially constructed and, therefore, cannot be fully explained by universal principles such as those of aerodynamics and acoustics.
>
> Foulkes & Docherty 2006:412

Kendall & Fridland (2021:7) differentiate sociophonetic data specifically from variationist sociolinguistic data. They indicate that variationist sociolinguistics tends to be characterized by studies of categorical variables, by datasets drawn primarily from conversational interview recordings, and by emphasis on understanding social factors as predictors of language change. By contrast, in sociophonetics, variables are primarily continuous, datasets from conversational recordings are complemented by data collected in controlled and laboratory settings, and cognitive and perceptual factors are more theoretically and methodologically central. Additionally, Kendall & Fridland point out the ostensibly analytic difference that sociophonetics is focused on sound systems, while variationist sociolinguistics encompasses syntactic and discursive variability.

Broadly speaking, the chapters in this handbook reflect the characteristics outlined in relatively restrictive definitions of sociophonetics. The vast majority of the sources cited as demonstrating, defining, and expanding sociophonetic intersections with phonetic units of analysis, theoretical and practical applications, and traditions in language varieties around the world report instrumental (and overwhelmingly acoustic) data. The case studies that exemplify sociophonetic approaches exclusively employ instrumental methods. To varying degrees, some chapters exclude noninstrumental data, either on empirical principles of quality (e.g., Sadowsky) or by beginning coverage near the turn of the millennium (e.g., Zhang, Tan & Strelluf) when advances in personal computing revolutionarily expanded access to acoustic analysis. Likewise, chapters in this volume highlight unique contributions to knowledge of the cognitive and perceptual apparati, particularly through the theoretical lens of exemplar theory (e.g., Cox & Docherty; Warren) and through models of sound change that depend on the processing of co-articulation (e.g., Carignan & Zellou). And wherever they are available, chapters synthesize findings from laboratory and other experimentally elicited datasets.

There is value, however, in conceptualizing these characteristic emphases as reflections of the state-of-the-art of sociophonetics, rather than as constitutive rules for research that can be counted as sociophonetic. Intuitively, Kendall & Fridland's (2021) observation that sociophonetics is limited to the domain of sound seems the surest differentiator of sociophonetics from other fields, but to be precise this more directly distinguishes sociophonetics from approaches such as socio-pragmatics and socio-syntax rather than from variationist sociolinguistics. Even here, boundaries will not be absolute as the phonetic and phonological domains will inherently interact with other aspects of the language faculty, as exemplified (illustratively, not exhaustively) by Yaeger-Dror et al.'s (2010) examination of f0 contours in morphosyntactic negation, Acton's (2022) aligning of sociophonetic variation with signaling Gricean Utterer's Intent, and Levon's (2016) identification of relational work in clause-final rising intonation. Indeed, Drager & Kettig's (2021:551) introductory definition of sociophonetics specifies investigation of "socially conditioned phonetic and morphological variation." Still, it is trivially true that there are studies that are sociolinguistic without being sociophonetic because they do not deal with phonetic or phonological data.

Additional discriminators of sociophonetic research from sociolinguistics, phonetics, and other areas of inquiry are arguably more circumstantial than constitutive, though. This is especially the case with the emphasis in sociophonetic research on instrumentally measured data over auditorily coded data. The growth in research positioned as "sociophonetic" since the start of the twenty-first century has coincided with (or been driven by) widespread access to the capability to conduct acoustic analysis. The turn to acoustic analysis was unquestionably a quantum leap forward for sociophonetic methodologies, theories, and discoveries. As Thomas synthesizes in the context of dialectology, acoustic measurements

> permit more precision than auditory coding, they reduce variability among practitioners, they facilitate replicability of studies, and, as Docherty & Foulkes (1999) note, they allow investigation of variables that cannot be coded by ear.
>
> Thomas 2018:314

Increased precision and the reduction of "variability among practitioners" are strikingly important in looking at data collected before the widespread adoption of instrumental techniques, especially in the case of phonetic variants that were transcribed by fieldworkers during large-scale linguistic atlas projects in Europe and the United States through much of the 1900s. These projects are wrought with fieldworker-specific differences, such as the "McDavid distribution" identified by Kretzschmar (1992), where the common source of features of interviewees' language is that they were interviewed by Raven McDavid (see Chambers 2018:276). Even more problematic are cases where a fieldworker mischaracterized a phonetic or phonological feature of an area because their own phonology differed from that of the area where they were working—the incorrect mapping of the vowels in LOT and THOUGHT as being merged in the US city of Providence, Rhode Island in the *Linguistic Atlas of the North East* offers a well-known example (see Labov, Ash & Boberg 2006:228).

On the other hand, Foulkes, Scobbie & Watt (2010:730) point out that "acoustic data are not inherently superior to data derived from careful auditory analysis." Most compellingly, they note that auditorily coded data benefit from being "processed through the best normalization mechanism yet developed: the human ear and perceptual system." The value of the careful auditory judgments of trained phoneticians is further enhanced by the increased reliance on technologies that automatically extract acoustic measurements from recordings which, as Cox & Docherty (this volume) warn, can lead to "black box" analyses where no human actually listens to the speech.

There is good reason, then, to understand instrumental and auditory analyses as different from each other (and of course to acknowledge instrumental analysis as superior in important ways) but not to limit sociophonetics exclusively to instrumental analysis while leaving auditory analysis to sociolinguistics. Moreover, the emphasis in sociophonetics on instrumental data does not clearly differentiate sociophonetics from sociolinguistics, so much as it reflects a chronological fact that sociophonetics came to be widely adopted as a methodological label at the same time that (or because) acoustic analysis became widely accessible. In other words, it is a historical fact that studies dealing with phonetic and phonological variables were generally labeled "sociolinguistic" when technological and methodological realities meant that most researchers could only compile data from impressionistic or auditory judgments. Then acoustic analysis came to predominate sociolinguistic analysis of phonetic and phonological variables, and as that happened (and, likely to an extent, because it happened) the label "sociophonetic" also came to be widely used by researchers. To say that sociolinguistics and sociophonetics are differentiated by the use of auditory data in the former and instrumental data in the latter implies that the fields diverged, so that sociolinguistics continued to rely on auditory analysis while sociophonetics relied on instrumental techniques. But in fact it is rare to encounter projects labeled as "sociolinguistic" that rely on auditory analysis in today's conferences and journals. So, the opposition is not between auditory sociolinguistic research and instrumental sociophonetic research, but between sociolinguistic examinations of phonetic variables before and after instrumental methods came to be widely available. The emphasis on instrumental measurement in sociophonetics is, then, a reflection of the momentous availability of instrumental techniques to sociophoneticians, rather than a definitive characteristic of sociophonetics.

Similarly, the focus in sociophonetics on continuous variables also reflects a fact about the common practices of sociophoneticians rather than a constitutive requirement. The instrumental methods that have been central to sociophonetic studies of speech production during the twenty-first century generally return continuous data, so sociophoneticians have often reported or modeled data continuously. However, it has also been frequent practice to discretize continuous instrumental data into categorical data, as in Labov, Ash & Boberg's (2006) various thresholds for the positions of vowels along acoustic continua, or Stuart-Smith, Lawson & Scobbie's (2014) categorizations of articulations of rhoticization. Similarly, perceptual experiments ubiquitously treat variables categorically, constructing stimuli by substituting a small number of discrete variants for each other, such as splicing either [θ] or [f] into a recording (Levon & Fox 2014) or presenting a vowel to hearers that is either centralized, canonical, or "ultra-low" (Niedzielski 1999).

The centrality of laboratory experiments in sociophonetics also reflects, to an extent, a fact that some phonetic and phonological variables lend themselves to experimentation better than many variables in other linguistic domains. The amenability of stops and fricatives to being spliced into continuous speech (Levon & Fox 2014), to vowel formants being synthesized along continua (Niedzielski 1999), and to f0, duration, and intensity being manipulated (D'Onofrio & Eckert 2021) all present pathways to creating experimental stimuli. However, sociolinguists have shown that categorical variables in nonphonetic/phonological linguistic domains—such as Squires's (2014) mouse-tracking study of cognitive processing of nonstandard and unlikely subject-verb agreement patterns in connection with visual representations of socioeconomic class—readily contribute to sociolinguistic knowledge outside phonetics and phonology.

In short, while the meta-literature of sociophonetics has, to varying degrees, carved out distinctive spaces for sociophonetics (particularly from sociolinguistics), there is room to allow for some fuzziness in the interface between sociolinguistics and phonetics. In the context of this handbook that celebrates the remarkable scope and productivity of sociophonetic research, such fuzziness allows as much research as possible to "count" as sociophonetic. Essential to this (as suggested by the gradient shading in Figure 1.1) is conceptualizing the interface between sociolinguistics and phonetics as a continuum from sociolinguistics to phonetics rather than as a discrete space from either. At the sociolinguistic extreme of this continuum, I have offered the label "phonetic sociolinguistics," which would encompass sociolinguistic studies that examine phonetic or phonological variables but do so in ways that would not necessarily pass muster among phoneticians. At the phonetic end of the continuum, "sociolinguistic phonetics" provides a label for studies that are primarily phonetic in nature but also account for socio-categorical factors as predictors of phonetic production and perception. A survey of current phonetic research would raise the challenge that this definition is so broad that almost no phonetic research would be excluded from the umbrella of sociophonetics, but this is a reflection of the growth of recognition of the centrality of social factors to the language faculty rather than a problem of terminological looseness.

This gradient conceptualization of sociophonetics accommodates the deep view of the field's history that Docherty (2022:2) notes some scholars take. For instance, Fischer's (1958) study of variation between [n] and [ŋ] among New England school children would be phonetic sociolinguistics and Peterson & Barney's (1952) documentation of vocalic formant values in a sample of US men, women, and children would be sociolinguistic phonetics, and both would be early sociophonetic approaches (see Kendall & Fridland [2021:97–99, 152] for discussion of these works as foundational to modern sociophonetic theory). Anachronistically, such studies pre-date the advent of sociolinguistics as a field of inquiry. However, given that the methods and findings of these works specifically influenced the early work of Labov (1963, 1966) and Labov, Yaeger & Steiner (1972), and given that a liberal view of the remit of sociophonetics would include much of Labov's foundational sociolinguistic work under its scope, this disciplinary history positions sociolinguistics and sociophonetics (accurately, I think) as fields that grew up together. Indeed, perhaps it would be most accurate to say that Labov's studies in Martha's Vineyard and New York City popularized sociophonetics as a research approach, and that sociolinguistics later branched off from sociophonetics as scholars transferred sociophonetic methods to nonphonetic/phonological variables in morphosyntax, discourse, and other domains of linguistics.

At the center of the sociophonetic continuum is a core space occupied by research that maximally draws on sociolinguistic and phonetic science. Work from this core space creates the greatest potential to shed light on human language in uniquely sociophonetic ways, and serves as the gold standard of sociophonetic research—which more restrictive definitions of sociophonetics are seeking to highlight as the primary focus of the field. It is this core sociophonetic space that answers Erik Thomas's calls for sociophonetics to "alter the direction of sociolinguistics as a whole" (2013:108) and "to be brought to bear on the other major question of linguistics, how language is structured in the brain/mind" (2011:310). The following section argues that sociophonetics achieves these goals by leading research toward a fourth wave of variationist sociolinguistics.

Sociophonetics and the fourth wave of variationist sociolinguistics

Penelope Eckert's (2012) historicization of three "waves" of variationist sociolinguistics has become central to the ways that sociolinguists conceptualize and position their work (see Hall-Lew, Moore & Podesva 2021; Levon & Katsiveli this volume). In her model, sociolinguistics is characterized by three partly successive and frequently interacting waves, which differ fundamentally in the ways that social factors and motivations are operationalized as predictors of variation, in the ways that linguists approach and engage with language users, and in the relationships between language users and their performance of linguistic variation. The first wave centers on sociological surveys, especially of formal speech communities such as cities, and examines linguistic variation as an outcome of language users' membership in macro-level social categories and in response to ideologies with regard to linguistic variables within their speech community. These are typified by surveys of urban speech communities, with the most famous example being Labov's (1966) New York City study. The second wave emphasizes ethnographic studies of informal speech communities such as neighborhoods, schools, and groups of workers, and examines variation as a consequence of language users' membership within these local communities and their engagement with other language users within the same community or in other communities. These are perhaps best represented by Milroy's network studies in Belfast. The third wave focuses especially on individuals, often as members of local communities of practice such as friendship groups or workers in a specific profession, and examines variation as a consequence of language users selecting variants from a pool of locally meaningful options as part of a broader set of stylistic practices that coalesce to project personae. Bucholtz's (1996) study of members of a friendship group of "nerd girls" in a high school, and of each girl's relative engagement with and rejection of linguistic features that are in broader use in the high school and surrounding speech community, exemplifies third-wave approaches.

Unsurprisingly, given the sociolinguistic component of sociophonetics, sociophonetic approaches are entwined with the theoretical perspectives and commitments of Eckert's waves. This is visible in some of the landmark overviews of sociophonetics, including the work of Foulkes & Docherty (2006), who generally frame the social factors that interact with sociophonetic variation as first-wave macro-level categories; of Hay & Drager (2007), who explore sociophonetics in the context of second-wave ethnography (including proposing a form of laboratory ethnography); and of Podesva & Kajino (2014), who highlight sociophonetic variation being operationalized by individuals to construct third-wave personae. Chapters in this handbook similarly reflect varying alignments of sociophonetic studies with the waves model. Sadowsky, for instance, typologizes sociophonetic studies of Spanish according to the three waves, and chapters on fricatives (Chappell, García & Davidson), Japanese (Matsuda et al.), and intonation (O'Rourke & Baltazani) highlight the recent importance of third-wave sociolinguistics in those areas of inquiry. Many chapters note the likely importance of third-wave perspectives in future work.

A model of three semi-sequential waves in a vibrant and active research field naturally suggests that, eventually, there will be a fourth wave. Proposals for the focus of a fourth wave have no doubt been proffered elsewhere. Allan Bell, for instance, in a talk at the 2016 meeting of NWAV titled, "A brief history of style, and its contribution to 21st-century sociolinguistic theory," suggested that conceptualizations of style had moved into a fourth phase that simultaneously accounted for (third-wave) speaker agentivity and (first- and second-wave) external forces acting on speakers. Because shifts in the first three phases of style were part of Eckert's third wave, Bell's fourth phase of style might implicitly signal the emergence of a fourth wave of variationist sociolinguistics.

However, I posit that a fourth wave of variationist sociolinguistics is, in fact, already well established, and that it is most strongly attested and advanced by the sociophonetic outputs from the core of the interface between sociolinguistics and phonetics. These are studies that, as Thomas (2011:2) puts it, "converge on the goal of understanding the cognitive and diachronic aspects of language," and they do so specifically by probing and revealing the ways that socio-indexicalities and phonetic inputs and outputs interact with the human brain. In this view, the fourth wave explores the intersections between sociolinguistic variation and human cognition, and sociophonetic studies—particularly those that have advanced exemplar-based models of language acquisition, storage, and change—have been at the crest of this wave.

Foulkes & Docherty (2006) firmly linked sociophonetics with exemplar theory. In the context of phonological knowledge, exemplar theory posits that people store memories of every string of phonetic units (i.e., every word) they encounter, as well as a memory of their encounter of each word (i.e., who uttered it and in what context). In Pierrehumbert's (2003) influential model, people extrapolate from these stored memories to build abstract representations of the allophones in their language based on probabilistic calculations of the distributions of these exemplars. Meta-disciplinary overviews of sociophonetics frequently align in arguing that exemplar theory is validated in sociophonetic datasets (e.g., Hay & Drager 2007; Foulkes, Scobbie & Watt 2010; Docherty & Mendoza-Denton 2011; Scobbie et al. 2011; Thomas 2011, 2013, 2019; see also Foulkes 2010; Docherty & Foulkes 2014), as do chapters in this volume that take up questions of sociophonetics and cognition (e.g., Cox & Docherty; Evans & Tomé Lourido; Gnevsheva; Khattab & Foulkes; Watt, Renwick & Stanley; Warren).

Exemplar theory finds natural support from sociophonetics because much of the field's data are, in fact, a sample of ambient language that language users encounter and must draw upon to build their language. In a sense, when a sociophonetician builds a model of their data, they mirror the modeling that exemplar theory posits a language learner must do to build their own language. This point is illustrated in Figure 1.2, which plots normalized single-point estimates of the first two formants of utterances of /æ/ where the vowel occurs in words before an oral obstruent (TRAP) or nasal continuant (TAN), produced during conversational speech by married couple Robert and Mary, and their daughter Madison. (See Strelluf 2018 for a full description of the dataset.) Dashed lines in each F1/F2 plot provide a common point of reference.

The points plotted in Figure 1.2 are typical of datasets generated by automated extraction of acoustic features of vowels. While such datasets are routinely explored to characterize phonetic and phonological developments in language varieties (e.g., Madison produces TRAP tokens relatively backer than her parents do, and with greater separation from TAN; see Strelluf 2018), at a broader conceptual level, these plots offer a snapshot of the phonetic inputs that Madison must have used to build her own language. As her mother and father spoke to her and around her throughout her childhood, they would have produced many words containing /æ/. Any given feature of these productions (such as the simplistic "central tendency" that single-point F1/F2 estimates are meant to indicate) would have varied radically across these productions. Yet, through this radical variability, distributional probabilities emerge for productions of /æ/. The vowel plots in Figure 1.2, then, enable general characterizations of Robert's, Mary's, and Madison's TRAP systems, and they mirror the process that, according to exemplary theory, baby Madison's brain would have followed to calculate positional allophones for productions of /æ/ in her language. Moreover, as Madison identifies differences in distributions in her mother's language compared with her father's, and in the language productions of other people around her, she would build further models for /æ/ for different people, for people with shared sets of traits, and for different social situations and semantic and semiotic contexts. Such categorical information would effectively function like predictor variables in sociophonetic studies—from the macro-level categories of the first wave to projections of affect in the third wave (cf. Eckert 2011). In short, by exhaustively capturing, reporting, and modeling phonetic features of a language, sociophoneticians are depicting the real-world phonetic inputs that children encounter during language acquisition and analyzing these inputs in ways that mirror exemplar theory's model of cognitive processes of acquisition.

Differences between the language Madison acquired from Mary and Robert and the language Madison produces then offers insights into how Madison must be building her own language rather than simply replicating the language she is surrounded by. As Foulkes & Docherty (2006:430–431), Foulkes (2010), and Docherty & Foulkes (2014) describe, as children's social identities emerge, children may assign different weightings to exemplars that align or disalign with social and ideational categories. They will also continue to store new exemplars from their

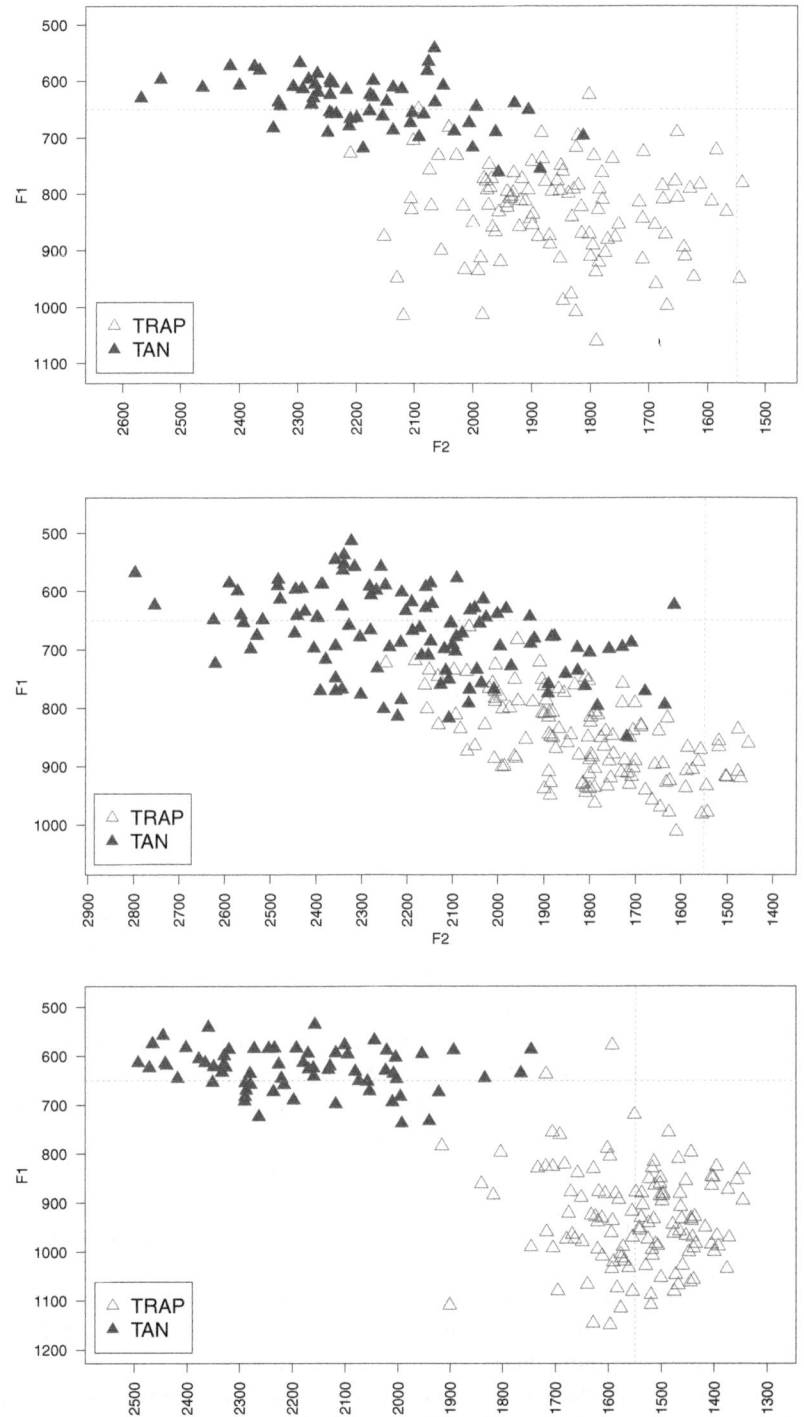

Figure 1.2   Single-point measurements of F1 and F2 in utterances of TRAP and LOT vowels by three members of a family: Robert (top), Mary (middle), Madison (bottom)

broader community, which might include innovative variants of peers as they enter childhood and adolescent networks (and indeed these exemplars might be assigned enhanced weighting, given the importance of peer over family networks at some phases of childhood).

While exemplar theory is an especially compelling model for language cognition that explains and is explained by observations of sociophonetic datasets, the fundamental value of sociophonetic datasets to explain cognitive linguistic processes remains even without commitments to exemplar theory per se. William Labov, for instance, occasionally challenges exemplar theory on the basis of observations about sound changes in progress. In Labov (2006:508–513) he argues that lexically driven accounts of language acquisition would predict that sound changes would proceed on a word-by-word basis, but that processes such as mergers and chain shifts tend to occur uniformly across phonemes (or in specific allophonic environments, such as vowels before /ɹ/ in many Englishes). In Labov (2010:46, 84, elsewhere), he further suggests that exemplar theory would predict local advantage in recognizing words affected by an ongoing sound change and—while acknowledging that such an advantage is identified in Hay, Warren & Drager (2006)—such local recognition advantages do not appear in North American English speech communities. Despite questioning exemplar theory, however, Labov's models of the processes of transmission and incrementation depend on children's probabilistic modeling of distributions of allophones, and in particular on whether children process productions at the periphery of distributions as outliers (and dismiss them from their calculations of phonetic and phonemic targets) or as valid priors that factor into their calculations of targets (for further discussion, see, e.g., Labov 1994:580–588, 2001:446–497, 2010:140–145).

The unifying insight of sociophonetic data, then, whether viewed through the lens of exemplar theory or other processes of statistical modeling, is that observable data and analytic processes for making sense of it may reflect cognitive processes for building language. These insights are revolutionary for acknowledging facts about linguistic variability and the human experience of linguistic variability, and positing that human language must be built through the experience of variability rather than in spite of it.

These interrelationships of phonetic variability, phonological knowledge, social knowledge, and cognition are dramatically reinforced by laboratory experiments that reveal that the cognitive processing of objectively present phonetic inputs is shaped by expectations about the social characteristics of the people who are believed to be the sources of those inputs. Canonical studies highlight that hearers will hear or mishear dialectally salient variables in order to match their expectations about speakers' dialects (Niedzielski 1999; Hay, Warren & Drager 2006) or hear speakers differently based on subtle cultural cues (Hay & Drager 2010). It is uncontroversial that the neural networks that constitute the human brain are built, structured, and restructured by learning, and it has been a core tenet of Chomskyan linguistics that the language faculty is a biological component of the human brain. As such, to the extent that sociophonetic and sociolinguistic variability build language, sociophonetic and sociolinguistic variability build the brain. This positions the brain as a natural site for new horizons in examining the sociolinguistic-phonetic interface.

That the fourth wave of variationist sociolinguistics would be sited in the brain and cognition is a logical progression of Eckert's Three Waves model. At a simplistic level, the first three waves progress from large communities to individuals. The fourth wave moves into individuals' brains. Disciplinarily, the fourth wave also reflects a continuation of relationships between broader theoretical and methodological trends and theoretical advances in sociolinguistics and sociophonetics. The first three waves reflect the sequential influence in academia and society more generally of sociological surveys (first wave), ethnography (second wave), and performativities (third wave).

Table 1.1 Schematic of four waves of sociophonetics and variationist sociolinguistics

Wave	Theoretical perspective	Primary research site	Core methodology	Fundamental research question
First	Sociophonetic variation is a consequence of membership in demographic categories and navigation of community attitudes toward variants.	Formal community	Sociological survey	How do language and society construct each other?
Second	Sociophonetic variation is a consequence of membership in networks, and of roles and relationships within and between networks.	Embedded community	Ethnographic survey	How do language and local networks construct each other?
Third	Sociophonetic variation is enacted as part of a range of locally situated identity construction and projection strategies.	Community of practice	Case study	How do language and individuals construct each other?
Fourth	Sociophonetic variation drives the construction of the language faculty, and outputs of language faculty generate sociophonetic variation.	The brain	Laboratory experiment; big data corpus	How do language and the human brain construct each other?

The fourth wave reflects the increased knowledge of human cognition and the new frontiers of knowledge attained through computational modeling of massive datasets, including those underlying artificial intelligence and its applications in natural language processing and production.

As such, it is natural that sociophonetics would alter "the direction of sociolinguistics" (Thomas 2013:108) by revealing "how language is structured in the brain/mind" (Thomas 2011:310). This unique contribution has ushered in a fourth wave of variationist sociolinguistics. Production-focused fourth-wave studies draw on massive sociophonetic corpora to model the sociophonetic inputs to the language faculty, and perception-focused fourth-wave studies examine the role of sociophonetic variability in language and social processing and storage. Table 1.1 compares the four waves.

Doing things with sociophonetics

Kendall & Fridland (2021:212) conclude their volume *Sociophonetics* by acknowledging "a deeply applied and public-facing thread" running through sociolinguistics and sociophonetics. Among other examples of applications of sociophonetics, they note Purnell, Idsardi & Baugh's (1999) anti-racist work to uncover housing discrimination resulting from phonetic features associated with ethnicities and to identify the minuscule amount of phonetic information from which hearers can make determinations about speaker race. Kendall & Fridland point to this as an example of the potential for sociophonetics to be leveraged for social justice. They further urge that "advances in sociophonetics can naturally benefit other allied fields, such as forensic phonetics and speech pathology, and sociophoneticians should actively pursue ways to collaborate with scholars and practitioners in fields like these."

This ethos is reflected in the design of this handbook, with Section 2 ("Applications") highlighting not only intersections between sociophonetics and various scholarly lines of inquiry, but also between sociophonetics and professional and practical outcomes. These range from moral imperatives such as reducing language prejudice (Witkowska et al.) to therapeutic applications (Macrae & Maclagan) to preservation of cultural and linguistic heritage (Calamai; Di Paolo).

It is worth remembering that the scholars who built the foundations of sociophonetics have positioned research-for-good as an obligation. Articulations of this obligation include Labov's (1982:172–173) "principle of error correction" and "principle of the debt incurred" and Wolfram's (1993:227) "principle of linguistic gratuity." At a more general level, recognizing the relatively marginal position of linguistics in most universities and in the public consciousness, Mark Liberman argues that it is essential that linguists bring visibility to their work through public engagement and impact if linguistics is to survive as a scholarly endeavor (Zimmer 2012). Such pragmatic factors add a layer of existential urgency to the ethical imperative for sociophoneticians to contribute to justice and well-being.

The contributors to this handbook who work most directly in applying sociophonetics for practical and social good, though, also reveal the challenges of doing so. This is perhaps clearest in Macrae & Maclagan's work on speech language therapy, which simultaneously describes the value of sociophonetically informed practices while also showing the practical limits of sociophonetics in real-world contexts, where students and practitioners must negotiate major physical trauma and quality-of-life issues, and are routinely under-resourced and limited in the treatment they can provide.

The insights shared in these application chapters point toward a need for focused conversations among sociophoneticians about the types of value that sociophonetics can provide in applied and public-facing contexts. Practical applications of phonetics might offer models for sociophoneticians' strategies. In the context of phonetics and language pedagogy, for instance, Munro & Derwing (2019) differentiate between "applied phonetics" and "phonetics applied." The latter describes knowledge of phonetics being used to support local practice (e.g., in an English language classroom, a teacher might describe articulatory characteristics of [θ] to help learners physically create the consonant). The former approach deals with more global and theoretical considerations such as (in the context of language teaching) "what to teach, how to teach, and when to do so" (Munro & Derwing 2019:475).

Parallel conceptualizations of "sociophonetics applied" and "applied sociophonetics" might offer sociophoneticians frames for thinking about the ways their work contributes to fields like speech language therapy or forensic sciences. Documenting the spread of TH-fronting among children in a speech community, for instance, might give a speech language therapist a datapoint to consider in their evaluation of whether a child who produces [f] for /θ/ has a speech deficit or is participating in linguistic innovation (see Macrae & Maclagan this volume)—this would be sociophonetics applied. Hypothesizing that an ear witness in a court trial involving a bomb threat would be unlikely to recognize a segmental distinction in the voice of the caller because their own dialect is likely to have merged the segments might provide a forensic phonetician a pathway to test the veracity of testimony against evidence—this would be applied sociophonetics. Such a differentiation could create space for sociophoneticians to identify precisely the ways their work might be positioned in applied and public-facing contexts, with sociophonetics applied providing relatively modest and supportive inputs and applied sociophonetics potentially pointing toward more substantial changes in practices and approaches.

A distinction between sociophonetics applied and applied sociophonetics suggests an approach to new considerations of doing meaningful good with sociophonetics. It is undoubtedly important that sociophoneticians seek outcomes for their work that make the people's lives better and society more just. Thinking meta-strategically about how we achieve these outcomes is likely to be an important part of this process.

Sociophonetic tools

The expertise shared in this handbook reveals sociophonetics' ethos for discovering and innovating ways to analyze sociophonetic variation. Thomas (2011:51–53, 87–88) summarizes some of the instrumental techniques available for studying the physiology of sociophonetic variation, including electropalatography, electromyography, X-ray microbeams, magnetic resonance imaging, ultra-sound, electroencephalograms, positron emission tomography, and functional magnetic resonance imaging. Carignan & Zellou (this volume) add tools in the context of exploring and quantifying nasality, including fibroscopy, cinefluorography, nasographs, velotrace, pneumotachographs, and nasometry. Electromagnetic articulometry has also been shown to yield articulatory insights (e.g., Harrington, Kleber & Reubold 2011; Carignan 2013). Majors & Gordon (2008) demonstrated the utility of video recording for measuring externally visible features such as lip spread and rounding, and such techniques offer exciting prospects for exploring a widening pool of embodied phonetic gestures including movement (Voigt, Podesva & Jurafsky 2014), smile (Aubergé & Cathiard 2003; Podesva et al. 2015), and jaw setting (Pratt & D'Onofrio 2017). Conceivably, "embodied" sociophonetics could further lead to measurements of physical gestures that are increasingly distal from the vocal tract but could be correlated with sociophonetic productions, such as facial expressions, arm movements, and posture (cf. Kita, Alibali & Chu 2017). While such a broad conceptualization might seem to expand the purview of sociophonetics vacuously into semiotic and communicative spaces that are not "phonetic," it also acknowledges the fact that phonetic perception draws on visual information; this is established famously in the "McGurk effect" (McGurk & MacDonald 1976), and Sebregts, van Hout & Van de Velde (this volume) cite recent research showing that hearers interpret visible labial gestures to differentiate *r* variants.

Measurement of embodied phonetics should also draw attention to the sociophonetics of visual, manual, and tactile language modes. Becker et al. (this volume) describe emergent instrumental techniques in signed languages, including infrared-based motion capture systems and cybergloves that measure manual articulations. Innovations in measuring manual articulations further suggest that breakthroughs in phonetic instrumentation might be most likely to come as sociophoneticians increasingly explore datasets from languages that are not, in particular, spoken English, and where the most exciting features differ from those of more widely studied spoken languages. This is illustrated by this handbook's chapters on Chinese (Zhang, Tan & Strelluf) and Japanese (Matsuda et al.), where the semantic importance of suprasegmental features in those languages has driven innovation in analyses of f0 and prosody. Neck-surface accelerometers, for instance, offer potential for measuring glottal actions with a device that is relatively cheap to build and comfortable for participants to wear during normal activity (Mehta, Van Stan & 2016), but may be most likely to gain traction in languages where scholars are especially interested in actions of the larynx. More generally, it seems plausible that the increasing ubiquity of wearable devices that measure biological functions will further increase the pool of physiological functions that might be tied to sociophonetic variation, as well as the availability of instruments to measure those functions and the normalness for people to be measured by such instruments.

As exciting as continued innovation in instrumental techniques is, the chapters of this handbook also make it imminently clear that the (now remarkably banal) acoustic analysis of recorded speech and capture of responses to stimuli will remain core methodologies of sociophonetics. The impact on sociophonetics and linguistics more broadly of (often free) software capable of constructing complex experiments (e.g., PsychoPy; Peirce et al. 2019), extracting acoustic features (e.g., Praat; Boersma & Weenink 2023), compiling massive corpora (see chapter 8 of Kendall & Fridland 2021 for a recent and accessible overview of software suites), and calculating sophisticated statistical models (e.g., R; R Core Team 2022) cannot be overstated. These technologies have democratized sociophonetics by facilitating research in low-resource contexts and among new students and scholars that would have been restricted to specialist laboratories just a few decades ago. They also facilitate collection of data from participants in relatively comfortable, naturalistic settings and experiences, and arguably reflect the most important features of language experience (i.e., the sound waves that are measured in acoustic analysis are primary inputs to hearers).

Almost certainly, among the most exciting innovations in sociophonetics going forward will be those that continue to enhance the ability of researchers to collect data through these core instrumental approaches. Given commercially driven advances in natural language processing and production, these will include improvements in automated speech transcription and processing and the extraction of valid measurements of speech, as well as methods for building perceptual stimuli through artificial intelligence. They will also increasingly expand to support languages beyond English (and, indeed, beyond "mainstream" Englishes of North America and the British Isles; see Mesthrie et al. this volume) and other globally dominant varieties. To the extent that such resources become available to researchers working in a range of financial, institutional, and linguistic contexts, they will further the democratizing force of innovations such as Praat. As Becker et al. (this volume) note, technologies paralleling those that automate analysis of oral-aural languages must also be developed.

Computational innovation will also feature centrally in the perspective I have labeled "fourth-wave" sociophonetics. To varying extents depending on commitments, exemplar theory assigns tremendous storage capacities and statistical capabilities to the human brain, rendering the language faculty remarkably similar to the processes used to train and refine computational natural language processing and production. The centrality of exemplar theory specifically and of computational processing of sociophonetic variation and variability in much fourth-wave sociophonetic research makes it likely that tools like support vector machines and deep neural networks might become increasingly central to understanding the ways that the human brain is built by sociophonetic variation and, in turn, builds sociophonetic variation.

The field will also benefit from innovations that are less techy. Sociophonetic research around the world, for instance, will be facilitated by development within language varieties of frameworks equivalent to J.C. Wells's (1982) lexical sets for English. Contributors to this handbook frequently make use of Wells lexical sets when writing about English vocalic variables. These allow sociophoneticians to refer to, for example, words containing the BATH vowel as sharing common historical links across Englishes, despite differences across Englishes in whether BATH is a separate phoneme from TRAP, in the phonetic quality of productions of BATH, and in the inventory of words that are assigned to BATH. They offer a remarkable shorthand for scholars working and thinking across Englishes, and complement transcription conventions that highlight other features phonetically and phonologically, including phonemic notation /ɑ/, phonetic notation [ɑ], sociolinguistic variable notation (ɑ), and (again in the case of Englishes) binary notation /æh/ (see Boberg this volume). The continued growth and enrichment of sociophonetics around the world will undoubtedly lead to new ways for scholars of varieties to conceptualize, document, analyze, and communicate the features of those varieties, and it will be exciting to see the understandings that will emerge through these innovations.

Conclusion

The Routledge handbook of sociophonetics presents a remarkable snapshot of the state-of-the-art of sociophonetics. The experts who have written its chapters show how much sociophonetics has contributed to our knowledge of the human experience of language and through language, and how much more sociophonetics is likely to contribute. They show that sociophonetics has become central to our understanding of the language faculty. I hope this introduction makes a compelling case that sociophonetics has, in fact, been central to sociolinguistics and phonetics for much longer than the label "sociophonetics" has been in wide use, and that continued exploration across the continuum of the sociolinguistic-phonetic interface will continue to push the frontiers of our knowledge of language, society, and cognition.

References

Acton, Eric K. 2022. Sociophonetics, semantics, and intention. *Journal of Linguistics* 58(3). 465–494. https://doi.org/10.1017/S0022226721000475

Aubergé, Véronique & Marie Cathiard. 2003. Can we hear the prosody of smile? *Speech Communication* 40(1–2). 87–97. https://doi.org/10.1016/S0167-6393(02)00077-8

Baranowski, Maciej. 2013. Sociophonetics. In Robert Bayley, Richard Cameron & Ceil Lucas (eds.), *The Oxford handbook of sociolinguistics*, 403–424. Oxford University Press. https://doi.org/10.1093/oxfordhb/9780199744084.013.0020

Boberg, Charles, John Nerbonne & Dominic Watt (eds.). 2018. *The handbook of dialectology*. Wiley.

Boersma, Paul & David Weenink. 2023. *Praat: Doing phonetics by computer* [Computer program], ver. 6.3.08. www.praat.org/

Bucholtz, Mary. 1999. "Why be normal?": Language and identity practices in a community of nerd girls. *Language in Society* 28(2). 203–223. https://doi.org/10.1017/S0047404599002043

Calamai, Silvia & Chiara Celata (eds.). 2014. *Advances in sociophonetics*. John Benjamins.

Calamai, Silvia, Chiara Celata & Luca Ciucci (eds.). 2012. *Proceedings of "Sociophonetics, at the crossroads of speech variation, processing and communication" (Pisa, December 14–15, 2010)*. Edizioni della Normale.

Carignan, Christopher. 2013. *When nasal is more than nasal: The oral articulation of nasal vowels in two dialects of French*. PhD dissertation, University of Illinois at Urbana-Champaign.

Chambers, J.K. 2018. Written dialect surveys. In Boberg, Nerbonne & Watt, 268–283. https://doi.org/10.1002/9781118827628.ch15

Chappell, Whitney. 2019. *Recent advances in the study of Spanish sociophonetic perception*. John Benjamins.

Cohn, Abigail C., Cécile Fougeron & Marie K. Huffman (eds.). 2011. *The Oxford handbook of laboratory phonology*. Oxford University Press.

Deshaies-Lafontaine, Denise. 1974. *A socio-phonetic study of a Québec French community: Trois-Rivièrs*. PhD thesis, University College London.

Di Paolo, Marianna & Malcah Yaeger-Dror (eds.). 2011. *Sociophonetics: A student's guide*. Routledge.

Docherty, Gerard J. 2022. Sociophonetics. In *Oxford research encyclopedia of linguistics*. Oxford University Press. https://doi.org/10.1093/acrefore/9780199384655.013.752

Docherty, Gerard J. & Paul Foulkes. 1999. Derby and Newcastle: Instrumental phonetics and variationist studies. In Paul Foulkes & Gerard J. Docherty (eds.), *Urban voices: Accent studies in the British Isles*, 47–71. Arnold.

Docherty, Gerard J. & Paul Foulkes. 2014. An evaluation of usage-based approaches to the modelling of sociophonetic variability. *Lingua* 142. 42–56. https://doi.org/10.1016/j.lingua.2013.01.011

Docherty, Gerard J. & Norma Mendoza-Denton. 2011. Speaker-related variation-sociophonetic factors. In Cohn, Fougeron & Huffman, 42–60. https://doi.org/10.1093/oxfordhb/9780199575039.013.0004

D'Onofrio, Annette & Penelope Eckert. 2021. Affect and iconicity in phonological variation. *Language in Society* 50(1). 29–51. https://doi.org/10.1017/S0047404520000871

Drager, Katie & Thomas Kettig. 2021. Sociophonetics. In Rachael-Anne Knight & Jane Setter (eds.), *The Cambridge handbook of phonetics*, 551–577. https://doi.org/10.1017/9781108644198.023

Eckert, Penelope. 2011. Where does the social stop? In Frans Gregersen, Jeffrey K. Parrott & Pia Quist (eds.), *Language variation–European perspectives III: Selected papers from the 5th International Conference on Language Variation in Europe (ICLaVE 5), Copenhagen, June 2009*, 13–30. John Benjamins.

Eckert, Penelope. 2012. Three waves of variation study: The emergence of meaning in the study of sociolinguistic variation. *Annual Review of Anthropology* 41. 87–100. https://doi.org/10.1146/annurev-anthro-092611-145828

Fischer, John L. 1958. Social influences on the choice of a linguistic variant. *Word* 14(1). 47–56. https://doi.org/10.1080/00437956.1958.11659655

Foulkes, Paul. 2010. Exploring social-indexical knowledge: A long past but a short history. *Laboratory Phonology* 1(1). 5–39. https://doi.org/10.1515/labphon.2010.003

Foulkes, Paul & Gerard J. Docherty. 2006. The social life of phonetics and phonology. *Journal of Phonetics* 34(4). 409–438. https://doi.org/10.1016/j.wocn.2005.08.002

Foulkes, Paul, James M. Scobbie & Dominic Watt. 2010. Sociophonetics. In William J. Hardcastle, John Laver & Fiona E. Gibbon (eds.), *The handbook of phonetic sciences*, 703–754. Blackwell.

Hall-Lew, Lauren, Emma Moore & Robert J. Podesva (eds.). 2021. *Social meaning and linguistic variation: Theorizing the third wave*. Cambridge University Press.

Harrington, Jonathan, Felicitas Kleber & Ulrich Reubold. 2011. The contributions of the lips and the tongue to the diachronic fronting of high back vowels in Standard Southern British English. *Journal of the International Phonetic Association* 41(2). 137–156. https://doi.org/10.1017/S0025100310000265

Hay, Jennifer & Katie Drager. 2007. Sociophonetics. *Annual Review of Anthropology* 36. 89–103. https://doi.org/10.1146/annurev.anthro.34.081804.120633

Hay, Jennifer & Katie Drager. 2010. Stuffed toys and speech perception. *Linguistics* 48(4). 865–892. https://doi.org/10.1515/ling.2010.027

Hay, Jennifer, Paul Warren & Katie Drager. 2006. Factors influencing speech perception in the context of a merger-in-progress. *Journal of Phonetics* 34(4). 458–484. https://doi.org/10.1016/j.wocn.2005.10.001

Jannedy, Stefanie & Jennifer Hay (eds.). 2006. Modelling sociophonetic variation [Special issue]. *Journal of Phonetics* 34(4).

Katz, William F. & Peter F. Assmann (eds.). 2019. *The Routledge handbook of phonetics.* Routledge.

Kendall, Tyler & Valerie Fridland. 2021. *Sociophonetics*. Cambridge University Press.

Kita, Sotaro, Martha W. Alibali & Mingyuan Chu. 2017. How do gestures influence thinking and speaking? The Gesture-for-Conceptualization Hypothesis. *Psychological Review* 124(3). 245–266. https://doi.org/10.1037/rev0000059

Kretzschmar, William A. Jr. 1992. Interactive computer mapping for the Linguistic Atlas of the Middle and South Atlantic States. In Joan H. Hall, Nick Doane & Dick Ringler (eds.), *Old English and new: Studies in language and linguistics in honor of Frederic G. Cassidy*, 400–414. Garland.

Labov, William. 1963. The social motivation of a sound change. *Word* 19(3). 273–309. https://doi.org/10.1080/00437956.1963.11659799

Labov, William. 1966. *The social stratification of English in New York City*. Center for Applied Linguistics.

Labov, William. 1982. Objectivity and commitment in linguistic science. *Language in Society* 11(2).165–201. https://doi.org/10.1017/S0047404500009192

Labov, William. 1994. *Principles of linguistic change,* vol. 1, *Internal factors.* Blackwell.

Labov, William. 2001. *Principles of linguistic change,* vol. 2, *Social factors.* Blackwell.

Labov, William. 2006. A sociolinguistic perspective on sociophonetic research. *Journal of Phonetics* 34(4). 500–515. https://doi.org/10.1016/j.wocn.2006.05.002

Labov, William. 2010. *Principles of linguistic change,* vol. 3, *Cognitive and cultural factors*. Wiley.

Labov, William, Sharon Ash & Charles Boberg. 2006. *The atlas of North American English: Phonetics, phonology, and sound change: A multimedia reference tool.* De Gruyter.

Labov, William, Malcah Yaeger & Richard Steiner. 1972. *A quantitative study of sound change in progress.* US Regional Survey.

Levon, Erez. 2016. Gender, interaction and intonational variation: The discourse functions of High Rising Terminals in London. *Journal of Sociolinguistics* 20(2). 133–163. https://doi.org/10.1111/josl.12182

Levon, Erez & Sue Fox. 2014. Social salience and the sociolinguistic monitor: A case study of ING and TH-fronting in Britain. *Journal of English Linguistics* 42(3). 185–217. https://doi.org/10.1177/0075424214531487

Majors, Tivoli & Matthew J. Gordon. 2008. The [+spread] of the Northern Cities Shift. *University of Pennsylvania Working Papers in Linguistics* 14(2). Article 14. https://repository.upenn.edu/pwpl/vol14/iss2/14

McGurk, Harry & John MacDonald. 1976. Hearing lips and seeing voices. *Nature* 264. 746–748. https://doi.org/10.1038/264746a0

Mehta, Daryush D., Jarrad H. Van Stan & Robert E. Hillman. 2016. Relationships between vocal function measures derived from an acoustic microphone and a subglottal neck-surface accelerometer. *IEEE/ACM Transactions on Audio, Speech, and Language Processing* 24(4). 659–668. https://doi.org/10.1109/TASLP.2016.2516647

Milroy, Lesley. 1980. *Language and social networks*. Blackwell.

Munro, Murray J. & Tracey M. Derwing. 2019. Phonetics and second language teaching research. In Katz & Assmann, 473–495.

Niedzielski, Nancy. 1999. The effect of social information on the perception of sociolinguistic variables. *Journal of Language and Social Psychology* 18(1). 62–85. https://doi.org/10.1177/0261927X9901 8001005

Peirce, Jonathan, Jeremy R. Gray, Sol Simpson, Michael MacAskill, Richard Höchenberger, Hiroyuki Sogo, Erik Kastman & Jonas Kristoffer Lindeløv. 2019. PsychoPy2: Experiments in behavior made easy. *Behavior Research Methods* 51(1). https://doi.org/10.3758/s13428-018-01193-y

Peterson, Gordon E. & Harold L. Barney. 1952. Control methods used in a study of vowels. *Journal of the Acoustical Society of America* 24(2). 175–184. https://doi.org/10.1121/1.1906875

Pharao, Nicolai & Anne H. Fabricius (eds.). 2020. Innovative methods in sociophonetics. *Linguistic Vanguard* 6(S1).

Pierrehumbert, Janet B. 2003. Phonetic diversity, statistical learning, and acquisition of phonology. *Language and Speech* 46(2–3). 115–156. https://doi.org/10.1177/00238309030460020501

Podesva, Robert J., Patrick Callier, Rob Voigt & Dan Jurafsky. 2015. The connection between smiling and GOAT fronting: Embodied affect in sociophonetic variation. In Scottish Consortium for ICPhS 2015 (ed.), *Proceedings of the 18th International Congress of Phonetic Sciences*, Paper 343. University of Glasgow.

Podesva, Robert J. & Sakiko Kajino. 2014. Sociophonetics, gender, and sexuality. In Susan Ehrlich, Miriam Meyerhoff & Janet Holmes (eds.), *Handbook of language, gender, and sexuality*, 103–122. https://doi.org/10.1002/9781118584248.ch5

Pratt, Teresa & Annette D'Onofrio. 2017. Jaw setting and the California Vowel Shift in parodic performance. *Language in Society* 46(3). 283–312. https://doi.org/10.1017/S0047404517000227

Preston, Dennis R. & Nancy Niedzielski (eds.). 2010. *A reader in sociophonetics*. De Gruyter Mouton.

Purnell, Thomas, William Idsardi & John Baugh. 1999. Perceptual and phonetic experiments on American English dialect identification. *Journal of Language and Social Psychology* 18(1). 10–30. https://doi.org/10.1177/0261927X99018001002

R Core Team. 2022. *R: A language and environment for statistical computing*. R Foundation for Statistical Computing. www.R-project.org

Scobbie, James M., Jane Stuart-Smith, Natasha Warner, Paul Warren & Jennifer Hay. 2011. Experimental design and data collection: Socially stratified sampling in laboratory-based phonological experimentation, Methods for studying spontaneous speech, Methods and experimental design for studying sociophonetic variation. In Cohn, Fougeron & Huffman, 607–642. https://doi.org/10.1093/oxfordhb/9780199575 039.013.0021

Squires, Lauren. 2014. Processing, evaluation, knowledge: Testing the perception of English subject–verb agreement variation. *Journal of English Linguistics* 42(2). 144–172. https://doi.org/10.1177/007542421 4526057

Strelluf, Christopher. 2018. *Speaking from the Heartland: The Midland vowel system of Kansas City* [Publication of the American Dialect Society 103]. Duke University Press.

Stuart-Smith, Jane, Eleanor Lawson & James M. Scobbie. 2014. Derhoticisation in Scottish English: A sociophonetic journey. In Celata & Calamai, 59–96. https://doi.org/10.1075/silv.15.03stu

Thomas, Erik R. 2002. Instrumental phonetics. In J.K. Chambers, Peter Trudgill & Natalie Schilling-Estes, *The handbook of language variation and change*, 1st edn., 168–200. Wiley. https://doi.org/10.1002/9780470756591.ch7

Thomas, Erik R. 2011. *Sociophonetics: An introduction*. Palgrave.

Thomas, Erik R. 2013. Sociophonetics. In J.K. Chambers & Natalie Schilling (eds.), *The handbook of language variation and change*, 2nd edn., 108–127. Wiley. https://doi.org/10.1002/9781118335598.ch5

Thomas, Erik R. 2018. Acoustic phonetic dialectology. In Boberg, Nerbonne & Watt, 314–329. https://doi.org/10.1002/9781118827628.ch18

Thomas, Erik R. 2019. Innovations in sociophonetics. In Katz & Assmann, 448–472.

Voigt, Rob, Robert J. Podesva & Dan Jurafsky. 2014. Speaker movement correlates with prosodic indicators of engagement. *Proceedings of Speech Prosody 2014.* 70–74. https://doi.org/10.21437/SpeechProsody.2014-2

Watson, Kevin. 2021. *English sociophonetics.* Edinburgh University Press.

Wells, J. C. 1982. *Accents of English.* 3 vols. Cambridge University Press.

Wolfram, Walt. 1993. Ethical considerations in language awareness programs. *Issues in Applied Linguistics* 4(2). 225–255. https://doi.org/10.5070/L442030813

Yaeger-Dror, Malcah, Tania Granadillo, Shoji Takano & Lauren Hall-Lew. 2010. The sociophonetics of prosodic contours on NEG in three language communities: Teasing apart sociolinguistic and phonetic influences on speech. In Preston & Niedzielski, 133–175.

Zimmer, Benjamin. 2012. Audio feature: New microscopes, new telescopes: A conversation with Mark Liberman about the uncertain future of linguistics. *American Speech* 87(1). https://doi.org/10.1215/00031283-1599977

SECTION 1

Units of analysis

2

SOCIOPHONETICS AND INTONATION

A proposal for socioprosodics

Erin O'Rourke and Mary Baltazani

Introduction

Intonation refers to the modulation of parameters such as the fundamental frequency of the voice (f0), duration, and intensity, over domains such as the phrase and the utterance. It delineates phrases and encodes different kinds of meaning, including semantic, pragmatic, affective, and social. The focus of this chapter is the social meaning of intonation as an index of regional or social differences which have been documented in many languages.

Fine-grained differences in the synchronization of f0 turning points with segmental material have been shown to be perceptually salient in distinguishing between different tunes such as declaratives and questions (Arvaniti, Ladd & Mennen 2006), and additional attention has been paid to the social factors that may contribute to the variation within these tunes. Sociophonetic approaches to the study of intonation have been developed recently and are beginning to emerge as a focused area of inquiry.

In our survey we have found a number of articles that investigate the effect of some sociolinguistic factor on intonation, for example gender, age, level of education, or social status, but in most of these articles the sociolinguistic aspect is incidental rather than programmatic. That is, the main focus is variation in intonation rather than what we would like to term "socioprosodics."

The phrase "socio-prosodic variation" does appear in Yaeger-Dror & Fagyal (2011) in their discussion of best practices in prosodic analysis. The hyphenated use of the term demonstrates the juxtaposition of fields that are beginning to be recognized as related concepts. This trend of marrying social factors with intonation is also present, albeit to a lesser degree, from the reverse direction of sociolinguists or sociophoneticians who incidentally also consider intonation, among other factors (see Eckert 2019:765–777). We view socioprosodics as a nascent field, in the sense that there is an increasing trend among scholars of intonation to delve into social factors as a source of variability, or among variationists and sociophoneticians to research intonational components of speech. We believe that pointing out the common ground covered by these so far disparate areas of study and placing them under the same umbrella allows for comparison and dialogue between them. This in turn can lead to further insights about sources of intonation variation on the one hand and the social indexicality of intonation on the other.

DOI: 10.4324/9781003034636-3

Research on prosody and sociophonetics has flourished in separate but parallel directions. Within phonetics, there has been an increasing focus on prosody. As early as the 6th International Congress of Phonetic Sciences (ICPhS) in 1967, a quarter of the papers presented (53 out of 213) were on prosody and this trend increased to 41.8 percent (214 out of 511) in the 17th ICPhS, 44 years later (Šturm 2015). As for sociophonetics, after the 1990s a growing number of sociophonetic studies have appeared and there are collections of studies, journal special issues, handbooks, and textbooks dedicated to this area of research.

Socioprosodics as a new field needs to follow the trajectory of the significant amount of work being done at the segmental level. Here are a few examples of recent collections that have appeared in the past ten years with no or very little content on intonation, which may be due in part to some of the challenges we note in this chapter. We offer these remarks merely as a recognition of the status quo, rather than a critique of any one volume or line of research. The *Oxford handbook of sociolinguistics* (Bayley, Cameron & Lucas 2013) contains two paragraphs on intonation within its literature review of sociophonetics, the *Routledge handbook of phonetics* (Katz & Assmann 2019) one page. In more specialized volumes, such as *Advances in sociophonetics* (Celata & Calamai 2014), there is examination of consonantal variation without mention of intonation (see also Díaz-Campos, Lacorte & Muñoz-Basols 2021). The *Handbook of language variation and change* (Chambers & Schilling 2013) contains, within Thomas (2013), two paragraphs on the challenges in studying variation within intonation and a short discussion of dialectal differences reported in intonation. As late as the *Oxford handbook of language prosody* (Gussenhoven & Chen 2020), there is no separate chapter on work that could be considered socioprosodic. In the 18th ICPhS held in 2015 (Scottish Consortium for ICPhS 2015), 13 of the 770 papers presented (1.7 percent) were on socioprosodics in the more than 20 sessions devoted to sociophonetics and prosody. In the 10th International Conference on Speech Prosody in 2020 (Minematsu 2020), three out of 208 papers covered socioprosodics. The 2021 New Ways of Analyzing Variation (NWAV49) conference had nine sessions on sociophonetics, and one on prosody. Across the conference 11 papers would be considered to fall within the domain of socioprosodics.

However, we have yet to see a combination of these two recognized as one field. As recently as 2020, the literature on what we term "socioprosodics" has not been examined closely. In what follows, we review work that has appeared either within sociolinguistics or within the phonetics/phonology of intonation which could be characterized as socioprosodic research, in the sense that it is either essentially sociolinguistic work that also examines intonation to a lesser or greater degree, or that it is essentially work on intonation variation that also examines some social factors that contribute to this variation. "Socioprosodic" is used (provisionally) hereafter as a term to cover this range of approaches and perspectives. We will also frequently juxtapose approaches taken by sociolinguists with approaches taken by prosodists to highlight areas where these two approaches converge or differ.

Adopting the term socioprosodics is also a deliberate choice for another reason, to avoid the use of "sociophonetics of intonation," which we believe is imprecise in at least two ways. One way is that intonation has both continuously varying characteristics, its phonetics, as well as categorically varying ones, its phonology (Ladd 1996, 2008; Gussenhoven 2004). Another reason is that socioprosodics extends beyond intonation, to interlinked phenomena of pitch modulation, speech rate, rhythm, and lexical tone, to name a few. The focus of this chapter is intonation. More detailed treatments of other aspects of socioprosodics can be found in other chapters of this volume (see Davidson; Stanford & Yang; and Kendall). In what follows, we will employ the term socioprosodics in reference to this potentially emergent field even though we recognize that the work we discuss (which we consider to contribute to the field) has been conducted before said field has fully formed.

Socioprosodic theory

Central research questions

A field is defined to some extent by the questions it addresses, along with the methodologies employed to approach them. Works by Labov (1966, 2001), Tagliamonte (2006, 2011, 2015), and others (e.g., Foulkes & Docherty 1999; Silva-Corvalán 2001; Chambers 2003; Trudgill 2011; Eckert 2012, 2019; Silva-Corvalán & Enrique-Arias 2017) demonstrate the types of questions and approaches used within sociolinguistics. Socioprosodics, and the study of intonation as part of that, may have the following questions, among others, of central interest:

1) How does intonation vary according to social factors within a speech community?
2) Are intonation features used differently among social groups to express the same meaning?
3) Is any observed intonation variation stable or indicative of a change in progress?
4) How do individual speakers operationalize intonation to construct and navigate their social identities?

A significant amount of work on intonation has been conducted up to this point in many of these areas such that there is now a growing wealth of literature to be drawn upon for looking at socio-linguistic variation within intonation. Socioprosodics may also complement research at segmental levels (e.g., Sóskuthy & Stuart-Smith 2020; Stuart-Smith 2020) and provide opportunities for intersection with other areas such as word recognition, vocal quality, and f0 range (e.g., Kim & Sumner 2017; Esling et al. 2019; Signorello et al. 2020; Gold et al. 2021).

Congosto Martín & Morgenthaler (2019:326), recognizing the momentum of the field, bring together nine studies related to languages in contact in a special issue on prosody, and note that "sociolinguistic implications should be taken into consideration since they may affect differently the acquisition, use, prestige, stigmatization, and contextualization of the language." In the issue, one of the papers, titled "Prosody: A feature of languages or a feature of speakers?" brings into focus the presiding empirical question, indicating that "prosody is the convergence point of lin-guistic information, on the one hand, and sociolinguistic and geolectal information, on the other" (Muñiz-Cachón 2019:464).

Key theories and frameworks

We approach our discussion on socioprosodics in part by how it relates to the field of sociolinguistics. Bell (2016:401–402) recognizes the importance of Eckert's "three waves" model (2012, 2019) of variationist sociolinguistics, which moves from an initial focus on language variation within social categories, to the use of ethnographic approaches to define categories, to the foregrounding of style in the expression of variation. Importantly, socioprosodics has the potential to be studied adopting the approaches from each of these waves, although the fact that it still remains (a small) niche speaks to the degree of development that is needed in the field. This delay in develop-ment is also at least in some part due to challenges in analyzing intonation and intonational vari-ation. These challenges include speed and reliability of transcription methods (Pitrelli, Beckman

& Hirschberg 1994), the issue of mapping many pragmatic interpretations to one form and vice versa (Baltazani, Gryllia & Arvaniti 2020), the fact that a number of phonetic parameters encode intonational meaning beyond f0 (Arvaniti 2020), as well as the different frameworks employed for intonation analysis, as described below.

Traditionally intonation has been analyzed within different frameworks and a distinction is frequently made between the so-called "configurations" versus "targets" models (for more details, see Ladd 1996, 2008; Prieto 2003; Gussenhoven 2004; Arvaniti & Ladd 2009; Xu et al. 2015). In the British School of intonation (e.g., O'Connor & Arnold 1973), the units of analysis are f0 configurations—trajectories such as rise, fall, rise-fall, thought to be melodic units, and phonetic detail such as the precise alignment between tones and segments is lacking. Other configurational frameworks employ a phonetic approach to the analysis of intonation which focuses on the phonetic detail but lacks phonological abstraction (e.g., Fujisaki & Ohno 1995; Xu 2005).

The model of intonational analysis which seems to be the most widely used today is the Autosegmental-Metrical (AM) approach (Pierrehumbert 1980; Ladd 1996, 2008). In this framework, the units of intonational analysis are H and L tones which are independent from segments (thus the "autosegmental" part of the AM label) and which are associated with tone-bearing units in the segmental string, such as stressed syllables or phrase edges, prosodic heads, or boundaries of metrical constituents respectively (hence the "metrical" part of the AM label). Unlike the configurations models mentioned above, AM combines phonological theory (i.e., categorical contrasts between different tones or tone combinations such as L*, H*+L over the same segmental string associated with differences in meaning) with phonetic realization rules (i.e., the same phonological category, e.g., H*+L, may have a different phonetic realization depending on the context).

Some, but not all of the socioprosodic work covered in this chapter is cast within the AM framework. Other work uses more phonetic prosody metrics, which are global measures of f0, such as pitch range, pitch level, and "dynamism." Typically in such studies, no intonational analysis of prosodic structure is given in terms of f0 tunes, tonal inventory, or prosodic phrasing. This methodological difference in intonational analysis makes comparisons of results and typological generalizations difficult.

Questions addressed in literature

The social meaning of variation in intonation has been approached by some researchers through demographic traits of speaker communities, such as age, gender, dialect, and socioeconomic status (e.g., Fletcher, Grabe & Warren 2005; Warren 2014). Others aim to describe the intraspeaker use of intonation as an index of a social attitude or a persona (e.g., Podesva 2011).

An important question that we believe should be addressed in socioprosodics regards the methods best suited to study variation. The lack of such a unified methodological approach and its consequences have been noted before. For example, Queen (2001:57) attributes the dearth of studies on intonation in language contact to the difference of methodological frameworks between phonological studies of intonation, which mostly employ controlled laboratory experiments, and sociolinguistic studies of language contact, which rely typically on natural speech and observational data: "Because these differences may be epistemological as well as methodological, bringing together such divergent strands of research presents a formidable task, which is, nonetheless, crucial for understanding the phenomena at hand." This tension between the need for quantifiable measurements of controlled experiments on one hand and socially appropriate observational studies of behavior on the other exists beyond the realm of language contact to all aspects of socioprosodics.

The role of language contact on intonation change and the mechanisms through which this is achieved are among the most frequent research questions. Several mechanisms have been explored, which have been borrowed from the literature on contact in other grammatical levels. These include "direct transfer" (i.e., of features from L1 to L2 through "imperfect" learning), "fusion" (mixing of two systems into one that differs from those used by monolinguals), "accommodation" (adopting characteristics used in one social group of speakers by another), "borrowing," "convergence," and "divergence" (see Sankoff 2013 for discussion of potential results of language contact), though it is still unclear what the definitions of these terms are, regarding intonation, and which characteristics of intonation they target (for discussion see, e.g., Roseano et al. 2015; Mascaró & Roseano 2020; also for a discussion of convergence vs. borrowing, see Colantoni & Gurlekian 2004 or Mennen 2004). Further questions on language contact involve the direction of transfer—that is, from native (L1) to non-native (L2) or the reverse, whether there are specific borrowability scales whereby some intonational characteristics are more prone to change than others (Kireva 2016:246), what factors facilitate change, such as genetic and typological similarity between languages, intensity of contact, attitudes towards L2, as well as how well the effects of historical contact survive after contact ceases.

A special case of language contact, New Englishes, has brought into focus questions about whether and to what degree individual postcolonial varieties progress towards endonormativity in developing, using, and publicly sanctioning their own distinctive linguistic forms (Meer & Fuchs 2022). One hypothesis examined in this literature is that after the establishment of political independence, speakers of these varieties increasingly adopt and produce local forms of English even in formal contexts, such that the emerging New English variety is "recognizably distinct" from the former (British) colonial standard in a number of respects (Schneider 2007:50–51) and also that these local forms are viewed positively (2007:49).

Apart from the small-scale studies mentioned so far, in the new millennium several large-scale studies have appeared which have created online corpora and intonational atlases, such as the *Interactive atlas of Romance intonation* (Prieto, Borràs-Comes & Roseano 2010–2014), *AMPER* (Martínez Celdrán et al. 2003–2020), and the *IViE* corpus (Grabe 2004). Studies like these concentrate on typological and dialectometric questions, incorporating social aspects beyond dialect and gender in their exploration of intonational variability, thus contributing to the field's knowledge of socioprosodics.

Questions within third-wave approaches to variation explore style as intraspeaker variation rather than the more traditional view of style as interspeaker variation (e.g., Podesva, Roberts & Campbell-Kibler 2002; Fagyal & Stewart 2011; Podesva 2011; Fine 2019a; Holliday, Bishop & Kuo 2020). Style in this sense expresses a fluid construction of identity which depends on communicative context. For example, researchers have examined the connection between f0 contour patterns and the expression of more- versus less-animated personas (Podesva 2011) or between f0 height and personas expressing different sexual orientation (Fine 2019a).

Several interesting questions arise in connection to the perception of intonation in socioprosodics, although the perceptual side of socioprosodic research is lagging behind research on production. In general, there is an imbalance in the amount of research devoted to specific questions within broader questions. More work has been done in socioprosodics through essentialist views of interspeaker social categories such as gender, dialect (crossed with socioeconomic status), and ethnic background (e.g., contact studies, bilingualism, L2) than through intraspeaker third-wave approaches such as social networks, sexual orientation, and expression of gender identity.

Prominent methods and approaches

Despite the different methodological approaches between sociolinguists and prosodists outlined above, lately there is a trend towards bridging the gap in at least one respect, that is, between natural/conversational speech and controlled speech by combining tasks that elicit controlled, semi-spontaneous, and naturally occurring speech (e.g., Grabe, Post & Nolan 2001; Vella 2003; Elordieta & Calleja 2005; Aly 2017; Bleorțu & Cuevas Alonso 2017; Correa 2017; Baltazani, Przedlacka & Coleman 2019). Collection methods include sociolinguistic interviews (Barrera-Tobón 2013; Romera & Elordieta 2013; McLarty 2018), Map Task dialogues (Queen 2001; Grabe & Post 2002; Dalton & Ní Chasaide 2003, 2005; Grice & Savino 2003; Fletcher, Grabe & Warren 2005; Simonet 2008; Savino 2012; Henriksen 2013; Hellmuth 2014), story-builder cards (Queen 2001; Muntendam & Torreira 2016; Fenton, Bustin & Muntendam 2020), Discourse Completion Tasks (Prieto & Roseano 2010; Astruc, Vanrell & Prieto 2016; Fernández Rei 2016; Kireva 2016; Aly 2017; Gryllia, Baltazani & Arvaniti 2018), retelling of a familiar story (Grabe, Post & Nolan 2001; Barnes & Michnowicz 2013; Stewart 2015; Takano & Ota 2017), and interactive card games (Lai & Gooden 2018a, 2018b). Despite the frequent warning against lab-controlled speech and the recommendation for spontaneous speech, systematic comparisons of the two are few (for examples of comparisons, see, e.g., Silverman et al. 1992 on rising contours in American English; Blaauw 1995 on Dutch; Face 2003 on Spanish; Serra 2009 on Brazilian Portuguese; Barnes & Michnowicz 2015 on Veneto-Spanish contact; Peng et al. 2005 on comparisons across dialects of Mandarin and code-switching).

One area where differences do exist between prosodists and sociolinguists is in which features of intonation are measured. We focus on acoustic approaches to measurement of intonation which involve measuring the fundamental frequency (f0) of the pitch contour and how that relates to the segmental material. While these approaches are most frequently used currently, we recognize that prior approaches included auditory coding (e.g., Bolinger 1972) and that other nonacoustic instrumental approaches are also beginning to appear (e.g., articulatory analyses of intonation, Katsika et al. 2020). On one hand, prosodists typically attend to phonological aspects of intonation and their local, fine-grained, contextually influenced phonetic realization, such as alignment (the temporal synchronization of tones with segmental tone-bearing units), scaling (the absolute f0 value of particular tones), downstepping (the scaling of tones relative to preceding ones), or truncation and compression of tones due to tonal crowding. These measures have been used to examine intonational variability due to dialects, socioeconomic status, and bilingual speech. For instance, Fletcher, Grabe & Warren (2005) examine the high rising terminal (HRT) tune which accompanies syntactically marked declarative utterances as well as yes/no questions in Australian and New Zealand English. They present data on HRT in Australian English which show that the use is not only found in speech of young adolescent females (where it was associated with low prestige varieties and was stigmatized) but has extended to both genders and "it is often used as a floor-holding device" (2005:399) (for other studies using such intonational measures to examine intonational variability, see Guy et al. 1986 for HRT in Australian English; Grabe et al. 2000 for British English varieties; van Heuven & Haan 2000 for Dutch; Atterer & Ladd 2004 for German varieties; Warren 2005 for HRT in New Zealand English; Vion & Colas 2006 for French; Arvaniti & Garding 2007 for American English varieties; Baird 2015 for K'ichee'-Spanish bilinguals; Maxwell & Payne 2018 for Indian Englishes).

On the other hand, sociolinguists often employ global phonetic metrics of f0, which can be thought of as more "traditional" in the sense that they predate the advent of the AM framework and sometimes even the advent of sociolinguistics (e.g., Mysak 1959, investigating differences in such global measures between age groups; McGlone & Hollien 1963, looking into differences in pitch range among women after puberty, which does not vary significantly, even in advanced age groups). These include speech rate and variation in intensity (Rodero Antón 2013), global pitch range over a whole utterance (e.g., Henton 1995; Podesva 2011; Fine 2019b), phonetically defined pitch movements (Stanford 2010; Fagyal & Stewart 2011; Fine 2019b), pitch variability around the pitch mean and "dynamism" (Henton 1995; Stanford 2010; Lee & Van Lancker Sidtis 2017; Meer & Fuchs 2022). In a number of these studies no correlation has been possible between the continuous/global phonetic intonation measures and the sociolinguistic variables, which may indicate that such coarse-grained measures are not appropriate and should be counterbalanced with more fine-grained measures, such as those within the AM framework.

A similar imbalance between prosodists and sociolinguists relates to the social factors employed to account for intonational variation, with the former lagging behind in their adoption of the latest theoretical developments in sociolinguistics. With some exceptions, many phonological papers on intonation only included sex, dialect, and level of education (e.g., Martínez Celdrán et al. 2003–2020; Prieto, Borràs-Comes & Roseano 2010–2014; Clopper & Smiljanic 2011; Gabriel, Feldhausen & Pešková 2011; Barrera-Tobón 2013; Stewart 2015; Muntendam & Torreira 2016). Lately, however, studies have included more nuanced divisions in the sociolinguistic variables they examine as explanatory factors of intonational variation, such as intensity of language contact (Kireva 2016; van Buren 2017; Kaminskaïa 2018; Baltazani, Przedlacka & Coleman 2020; Elordieta & Romera 2020), race or ethnic identity (Lipski 2010; Holliday 2016; Fenton, Bustin & Muntendam 2020; Elordieta & Romera 2020), social prestige (Colantoni & Gurlekian 2004; Enbe & Tobin 2008; Lleó & Gabriel 2011) or stigmatization (Hualde & Schwegler 2008), social networks (Miller 2007; Correa 2017; McLarty 2018), and social distance (Astruc, Vanrell & Prieto 2016). On the other hand, the social attributes that sociolinguists explore as indices of intonational variation include differences in social category membership, such as gender and sexuality (Podesva 2011; Fine 2019a), generation (Stanford 2010), or political stance (Holliday, Bishop & Kuo 2020), but also changes in style which express the adoption of different personas (Gaudio 1994; Fagyal & Stewart 2011; Podesva 2011; Yaeger-Dror et al. 2010; Slobe 2018; Fine 2019a, 2019b; Holliday, Bishop & Kuo 2020).

The methodology and measures employed in socioprosodics also depend on the specific field of a study. For example, dialectometry, a quantitative method which measures phonetic distance between segments, has been extended to intonation with measurements of f0 alignment and scaling to illuminate historical trajectories in intonation (Sullivan 2011) and to characterize intonation differences between varieties within Romance (e.g., Martínez Celdrán et al. 2003–2020; Moutinho et al. 2011; Roseano, Elvira-García & Fernández-Planas 2017; Elvira-García et al. 2018). Intonational variability has also been the basis of atlases, using parallel corpora which facilitate cross-linguistic comparisons and also include sociolinguistic variables beyond dialect, such as gender, age, and education level (e.g., Prieto & Roseano 2009–2013 for Spanish; Prieto, Borràs-Comes & Roseano 2010–2014 for Romance).

The diachronic development of intonation frequently concentrates on generational differences, using apparent- or real-time data from contemporary (Mzemba 2014 for French-English contact; Lee & Jongman 2015 for Korean; Fenton, Bustin & Muntendam 2020 for Afro-Peruvian Spanish) or archival (Pešková et al. 2012 for Porteño Spanish; McLarty 2018 for African American vs. European American English; Baltazani, Przedlacka & Coleman 2019 for Greek-Turkish historical contact) sources. Most of these studies employ AM methods for intonational analysis, while Baltazani, Przedlacka & Coleman (2019) additionally use mathematical modeling of f0 contours.

Pragmatic meanings (see House 2006 for a review) can confound sociolinguistic analysis (Milroy & Gordon 2003:185; Foulkes, Scobbie & Watt 2010:721). Some researchers prefer the use of read speech or map tasks, where the pragmatic interpretation is controlled (e.g., Grabe et al. 2000; Grabe & Post 2002; Dalton & Ní Chasaide 2003; Grabe 2004; Dalton & Ní Chasaide 2005), while others code for pragmatic function in corpora. For example, Stirling et al. (2001) investigated the interplay between prosody and discourse structure in the ANDOSL Australian map task corpus, where the level of familiarity between participants in the map task varied between "known" and "unknown" and the role of each participant varied between "instruction-giver" and "instruction-follower" (see also Fletcher & Harrington 2001; McGregor & Palethorpe 2008; Ritchart & Arvaniti 2014).

Larger-scale studies spanning more than one variety of a language are typically conducted by prosodists and frequently employ a multilayered corpus approach, with recordings of read utterances controlled for parameters of interest, narrative retelling of a story, map task (e.g., Grabe, Post & Nolan 2001 for intonational variation in English; Hellmuth 2014, 2020 for variation in Arabic), or variations of these. Further tasks in large-scale projects (e.g., AMPER [Martínez Celdrán et al. 2003–2020]; IARI [Prieto, Borràs-Comes & Roseano 2010–2014]) include Discourse Completion Tasks (DCT), interviews, and what is called a "textual elicitation corpus,"—that is, acted laboratory speech sentences (Romano, Lai & Roullet 2005). The DCT is a common method in intonation studies (e.g., Vanrell, Feldhausen & Astruc 2018) which consists of presenting a daily-life situation to which the speaker is expected to produce an utterance they would use in a target tune, for example a statement or a question. Frequently f0 measurements in such studies are time-normalized and converted to semitones (e.g., Lai & Gooden 2018a; Baltazani, Przedlacka & Coleman 2019).

In comparison, within studies of sociolinguistics and style, several factors have been examined as sociolinguistic reasons for intonational patterns, such as prestige and politeness (Enbe & Tobin 2008), and gender, sexuality, and expressive affect (Podesva 2011; Henriksen 2013; Esposito 2020). Additionally, formal versus informal speech style as well as interlocutor (e.g., human vs. computer screen) have been investigated. Some examples include using gap tasks where participants are asked to fill empty speech bubbles in drawings of characters in different situations (Henriksen 2013), differences between friendly phone calls and recordings versus newscasts (e.g., Kato 2001; Yaeger-Dror, Hall-Lew & Deckert 2002; Takano 2008), societal norms of power and solidarity (Brown & Gilman 1960; Watts 2003), stylized genres such as story-telling, telephone speech, sports reporting, and political or religious speeches (Liberman & McLemore 1992; Hirschberg 2000), and speech stances, such as informative, supportive, remedial, and self-protective (Yaeger-Dror, Hall-Lew & Deckert 2003).

Finally, in perception studies addressing language or dialect discrimination (e.g., Gooskens 1997 and van Bezooijen & Gooskens 1999 for Dutch and English; Peters et al. 2002 for varieties of German; van Leyden 2004 for Orkney and Shetland English; Gooskens 2005 for Norwegian), or perceived distance between intonational patterns of distinct dialects or languages (e.g., Gili-Fivela 2012; Simon et al. 2012; Fernández Planas et al. 2013), speech is frequently manipulated, resynthesized, or low-pass filtered to remove segmental information. Forced-choice and discrimination tasks are used and distance matrices are created, based on confusion matrices, which are further submitted to cluster analysis. The open-guise technique (versus the more common matched-guise technique) of using a single speaker known to style-shift is discussed in Holliday & Villarreal (2020).

Perception studies from a bilingual perspective have examined the impact of intonation and code-switching on the perception of some characteristic, for example narrow focus, via manipulation of H tone (or "peak") alignment and H tone scaling (or "peak height") (Olson & Ortega-Llebaria 2010). The encoding of politeness in intonation is usually examined through pitch height and range in connection with politeness, friendliness, or deference ratings. For example, Gryllia, Baltazani & Arvaniti (2018) found that Greek wh-questions ended in a higher final boundary tone when the interlocutors were nonsolidary and when there was a power difference between them, whether the speaker was inferior or superior to the addressee (see also Goodwin, Goodwin & Yaeger-Dror 2002 for Hispanic and African American elementary school girls; Chen, Gussenhoven & Rietveld 2004 for Dutch and English; Orozco 2008, 2010 for Mexican Spanish; Winter & Grawunder 2011, 2012 and Brown et al. 2014 for Korean; Devís Herraiz & Cantero Serena 2014 for Catalan; Brown et al. 2015 for Korean, Japanese, German, and Russian).

Summary

In this section we have focused on both phonological and sociolinguistic approaches to the study of intonation, each of which in turn incorporates the other as a secondary consideration. However, it is this juxtaposition that demonstrates the range of perspectives encompassed by socioprosodics.

Socioprosodic insights

Variation across dialects and social groups

Geographic differences in intonation have often been studied in tandem with segmental variation. Advances in intonation dialect research have led to the development of large online databases, which typically include multiple speakers from a large number of locations. These speakers are sometimes differentiated according to social factors such as gender, education, or social class, and may be monolingual or bilingual speakers of a given dialect depending on the corpus. However, the emphasis is on uncovering dialectal differences. Beyond these, a notable amount of intonation studies has included first-wave social factors such as gender, age, and education/socioeconomic status (e.g., Moreno Fernández 1999 on Peninsular [Alcalá] Spanish; Froemming 2020 for Ecuadorian [Cuenca] Spanish).

Of the social factors, gender has received the most attention. Females show greater use of final H% and a richer inventory of pitch contours over males in prepared TED talks (Huang & Zhang 2019). More instances of uptalk (final rises) by females compared to males were found in speech in game shows (Linneman 2013 for English; Vergara 2015 for Spanish), with some discourse functions of uptalk having similar frequency of use in both groups ("showing camaraderie" and "softening a command") and some being used more by males ("holding the floor") and females ("flirting"). In Standard Southern British English, among adolescents, H% boundary tones are more frequent among females than males (Jiang 2011; see also Nance, Kirkham & Groarke 2018 for analysis of gender effects in Liverpool English intonation). In Belfast English, considering the indexicality of intonation, Lowry (2011:226) concludes, "the direct association is between expressiveness and nuclear falls, and only indirectly between nuclear falls and females." Lowry's (2011) work aligns with third-wave sociolinguistics by not taking social category as the defining characteristic of the prosodic behavior a priori, but rather starting from the intentionality of the speaker to be more expressive, after which correspondences related to gender are observed. Reed (2016, 2020) recasts geographic space as an aspect of identity by looking at the local orientation or "rootedness" of speakers to a region as expressed through their use of intonation patterns.

Some intonation studies include information regarding participants (age, gender, education level, or social class) with no specific socioprosodic research question to be explored, but rather hold one or more variables constant (for example, only reporting data from females or members of the same age group—e.g., Willis 2003; Elordieta & Calleja 2005; Alvord 2010). While this may not afford any immediate claims to social factors for the given study, this information is still important since it allows for comparison with subsequent research. Beyond a binary gender distinction between male/female speakers, there are studies that connect intonation with other gender identification, such as Queer identity (Shar 2018) which shed further light on the ways speakers may leverage intonation in connection with gender performativities.

Fewer studies focus specifically on age differences within a given dialect. No clear intonation differences due to age group were found in Mexican Spanish sociolinguistic interviews by male and female speakers from the lower social class who were distributed evenly between three age groups (Martín Butragueño 2004). Differences are reported in post-focus compression (PFC) between younger, mid-age, and older age groups who were sequential Southern Min-Mandarin bilinguals (Chen, Xu & Guion-Anderson 2015). Some age-related intonation differences are also reported between young children, mid-age and older adults in Argentinian Spanish (Enbe & Tobin 2008).

Bilinguals and language contact: Historical or synchronic perspective

In bilingualism research, transfer is sometimes reported from the direction of the dominant/majority to the non-dominant/minority language (e.g., Kaminskaïa 2018; Lai & Gooden 2018a; Kim & Repiso-Puigdelliura 2021), sometimes in the reverse direction (e.g., Elordieta 2003; Colantoni & Gurlekian 2004; O'Rourke 2004, 2005; Elordieta & Calleja 2005; Gabriel, Feldhausen & Pešková 2011; Baird 2015; Lai & Gooden 2018b; Maxwell & Payne 2018), and sometimes in both (Bullock 2009; Queen 2012; Kireva 2016). To our knowledge, no typology of intonational changes exists yet, but Kireva (2016:246) proposed a hierarchy of features more (to less) likely to change: "Prenuclear accents > Focus markers > Nuclear configurations > Prosodic phrasing > IP-final lengthening."

Few typological discussions exist on intonation contact outcomes (e.g., divergence, convergence, transfer, interference, shift, borrowing) and how these outcomes relate to observations for other levels of grammar (but see Gooden 2022 for a review of intonation in Creole languages). However, a number of studies have appeared which discuss the effect of contact on the intonation of single languages. For example, Colantoni & Gurlekian (2004) discuss phonetic convergence in peak alignment as the result of Argentinian-Italian contact in Porteño Spanish, a term that McMahon (2004) rejects, in favor of "borrowing," on the grounds that convergence describes bi-directional change, while the change in Porteño involves one-way transfer from Italian to the dominant Argentinian Spanish. Colantoni & Gurlekian opt against "borrowing" because the term usually refers to transfer from a majority to a minority language, not the direction found in Porteño. The need for clear terminological definitions suitable for intonational empirical data emerges from the dialogue between these two papers, "without presupposing they will be similar to the mechanisms of contact-induced change on segments" (McMahon 2004:122).

Some intonational effects of language contact are phonological, as has been reported in Queen (2012), who found that a Turkish-like terminal rise contrasts with a German-like one in Turkish-German bilinguals in Germany, differing in alignment, slope (how fast f0 rises or falls), and pragmatic interpretation from each other (and from those of monolinguals). On the basis of this evidence, Queen (2012) argues that there is no intonational attrition found in Turkish-German bilinguals, who instead have added German phonological categories to their intonational repertoire. Similarly, no attrition of French is found among heritage speakers in Pennsylvania, who, in addition to the French, have also adopted additional pitch accents from the dominant English (Bullock 2009)—but compare with Mzemba (2014, 2016), who finds increasingly more English-like patterns among younger speakers.

The mechanism of code-switching has been studied in a number of papers in relation to intonational contact and social factors. For example, in Pijal Media Lengua, a Quichua-Spanish mixed language, this mechanism is connected with the predominance of Quichua intonation patterns (Stewart 2015). In code-switching between Occitan and Southern French, more conservative speakers use the Occitan rising-falling pattern with higher frequency while less conservative speakers adopt the standard French pattern (Sichel-Bazin, Buthke & Meisenburg 2012). Differences in pitch accent category in the intonation of adult monolingual Spanish speakers who recently adopted L2 Majorcan Catalan prosodic patterns were attributed to a desire by immigrant L1 Spanish speakers for approval by the native Majorcans (Romera & Elordieta 2013). L1 influences are documented in L2 English termed "World Englishes," such as Cameroon English (Simo Bobda 2004), Nigerian English (Gut 2005; Gussenhoven & Udofot 2010), South African English (Zerbian 2013), and Indian English (Maxwell 2014; Maxwell & Payne 2018).

On the phonetic side, peak alignment differences are reported between contact and noncontact varieties of the same language. The monolingual Spanish late prenuclear peak alignment differs from early peak alignment in contact varieties of Spanish with languages that are either typologically similar, for example, Venetian (Barnes & Michnowicz 2015), English (Alvord 2006, 2010; Barrera-Tobón 2013; Aly 2017; Kim & Repiso-Puigdelliura 2021), and Italian (Colantoni & Gurlekian 2004; Colantoni 2011), or typologically different, such as Basque (Elordieta 2003; Elordieta & Calleja 2005), Quechua (O'Rourke 2004, 2005), Yucatec Maya (Michnowicz & Barnes 2013), and K'ichee' Mayan (Baird 2015). Evidently, typological distance between the source and receiving languages is not a determinant of change, contrary to reports made about typological distance for other aspects of grammar (e.g., Thomason 2008). Several other factors need to be explored to account for such variation, as argued in O'Rourke (2006), who reports that Peruvian Spanish speakers employ level and upstepped prenuclear peaks both in Lima and Cusco, such that several factors (linguistic, pragmatic, and sociolinguistic) may "explain this use in Peruvian Spanish" (2006:72).

Peak alignment differences do not correlate neatly with geographic variety but have been attributed to sociolinguistic factors such as language dominance. For example, Canadian French in contact with dominant English in Ontario displays later peak alignment than French in Québec and Vendée where English is nondominant (Kaminskaïa 2018). A strong sense of ethnolinguistic Venetian Italian identity is documented as a factor regulating early peak alignment for younger speakers in Chipilo Spanish in Mexico, which distinguishes them from the mainstream Mexican culture (Barnes & Michnowicz 2013). Different intonational patterns among younger generations which serve as identity markers are also cited for Cuban-American speakers in Miami (Alvord 2010), Spanish-English bilinguals in New York City (Barrera-Tobón 2013), and Argentinian-Italian speakers of Porteño (Pešková et al. 2012).

In Afro-Peruvian Spanish, females and older speakers use more delayed peaks and falling tones in prenuclear position compared to males and younger speakers (Fenton, Bustin & Muntendam 2020). In Palenquero, a Spanish-based creole language mixed with the African language Kikongo spoken in Colombia, conservative older-generation speakers use invariant HL word-level contours (Hualde & Schwegler 2008) while younger speakers have generalized the use of an emphatic upstepped final high tone to nonemphatic contexts (Lipski 2010); see also Hernandez (2020) for the effects of age, gender, and language dominance on the intonation of Galician-Spanish bilinguals.

Uptalk in monolingual Mexican Spanish speakers differs phonetically from that of heritage Spanish speakers in the United States; Kim & Repiso-Puigdelliura (2021) found that English-dominant heritage speakers produced higher final rises, smaller pitch excursions, and a flatter slope than monolinguals and less English-dominant speakers. The monolingual uptalk pattern was attributed in Mexican Spanish to a *fresa* elitist style (see also Holguín-Mendoza 2011; Martínez Gómez 2018), while the heritage uptalk pattern was ascribed to influence from English. Peak alignment differences have been detected in nuclear pitch accents of Cuba-born Spanish speakers in Miami between code-switched and monolingual utterances, as well as between the code-switched utterances of Miami-born speakers who produce more English-like pitch accents (e.g., H*) and the Cuba-born ones who prefer the Spanish-like L+H* accent (Aly 2017). Higher H scaling and larger pitch span have been reported in the nondominant language of K'ichee' Mayan-Spanish bilinguals, attributed to the bilinguals' uncertainty or lower confidence in their less-dominant language (Baird 2019).

Unlike the intonational effects of synchronic contact, there is still scarce evidence regarding how long these persist after contact has ceased. The intonational effects of Italian immigration to Argentina from 1830 to 1950, mentioned above, are still present today (Colantoni & Gurlekian 2004; Gabriel, Feldhausen & Pešková 2011; Pešková et al. 2012). Similar lasting effects have been reported for the influence of Turkish on Asia Minor Greek heritage speakers, whose contact with Turkish ceased in 1923 (Baltazani, Przedlacka & Coleman 2019, 2020; Baltazani et al. 2023). There are also reports of present effects of past Afro-Spanish contact (Rao & Sessarego 2016, 2018; Fenton, Bustin & Muntendam 2020) and African-English contact (McLarty 2018). Hualde (2003) presents a diachronic reconstruction of intonational patterns of a proto-language in Romance, using Occitan as an intermediate step in the development of prosody, bridging the gap between French on one hand and Ibero- and Italo-Romance on the other.

Perception and pragmatics

Perceptual studies have explored which listener characteristics are associated with perceptual differences in intonation. In some studies, characteristics such as gender, race, political affiliation, or bilingual background were not found to be significant. For example, higher peaks in manipulated tokens were associated with Black compared to non-Black speech, regardless of listener characteristics (Holliday & Villarreal 2018, 2020) and narrow focus was perceived with the manipulation of peak height and alignment in code-switched utterances (Olson & Ortega-Llebaria 2010). In other studies, listener characteristics did contribute to differences in the perception of intonation. Female listeners judged the high-ending wh-question contours of female talkers (but not male ones) as more polite than the low-ending ones (Arvaniti, Baltazani & Gryllia 2014). The listeners' exposure to non-Salerno dialects was one factor affecting their interpretation of biased questions in Salerno Italian (Orrico & D'Imperio 2020).

Other questions explored in perceptual experiments include whether intonational features are associated with social characteristics and whether these features carry enough information for dialect or language discrimination. Based on prosody alone, English listeners were able to identify dialects of their own language whereas Dutch listeners were not (van Bezooijen & Gooskens 1999), and in Shetland and Orkney speech, peak alignment strongly correlated with dialect classification (van Leyden 2004). In Nijmegen Dutch, pitch variation is strongly associated with dominance, willpower, and self-confidence, but not with education and social position (van Bezooijen 1988). Significant differences in perception of transgender male-to-female speakers were found, with rising contours and larger pitch range being perceived as female (Hancock, Colton & Douglas 2014).

The indexical function of intonation and the assigned social meaning of sociolinguistic stereo-types has been explored in the upper-class *fresa* speech style in Mexico where audio clips of uptalk were matched more with photos of stereotypical *fresa* style compared to other photos (Martínez Gómez 2018). Similarly, the interpretation of a sentence-final contour in French as a question or a statement depended on visual cues from the dialect region, that is, a Corsican or Parisian newspaper (Portes & German 2019). Social cues affected the interpretation of final rises in New Zealand English as declaratives or questions, such as whether a SQUARE diphthong preceding the rise was realized as an [iə] or an [eə] (typical of younger or older speakers respectively), indicating a link between older speakers' preference for both [eə] and non-rising statements (Warren 2017).

Intonational variation in Greek was related to politeness (operationalized as levels of power, solidarity, and familiarity) in a DCT where listeners judged rising wh-questions as more polite than falling ones (Gryllia, Baltazani & Arvaniti 2018). Rising Catalan yes/no questions were more likely to encode high-cost offers and requests (which require more politeness) than falling patterns (Astruc, Vanrell & Prieto 2016). Women produced polite requests in Mexican Spanish with a high boundary and wider pitch range more frequently than men (Orozco 2008). Preschool children used intonational and visual cues to interpret rising questions as polite and falling ones as impolite (Hübscher, Wagner & Prieto 2020; see also Brown & Prieto 2017 for the prosodic study of (im) politeness).

This discussion of politeness is just a portion of the work that can be conducted on pragmatics, social factors, and intonation within a socioprosodic framework (see Wharton 2012; Clark 2017; Hirschberg 2017 for overviews of pragmatics and intonation/prosody; see Armstrong & Prieto 2015; Tomlinson, Gotzner & Bott 2017; Baltazani, Gryllia & Arvaniti 2020 for recent experi-mental work on pragmatics and intonation).

Style

Intonational variation connected to race has been reported between mainstream US English and African American Language (AAL), which contains more pitch accents (McLarty 2018), more fre-quent use of L+H* pitch accents (Holliday 2016; McLarty 2018), different types of boundary tones (McLarty 2018; Holliday 2019), and a different inventory of tones (Gooden 2009; Thomas 2015). Not all these characteristics of AAL were confirmed when race was combined with style (Holliday, Bishop & Kuo 2020) and the only association found was between the frequency of L+H* pitch accents and a politician's (Barack Obama's) alignment with an AAL-like intonational pattern to express disapproval of a proposition. In political speech, intonational differences have been found to signal a politician's stance for or against specific issues (Mendoza-Denton & Jannedy 2011) as well as a combination of a politician's ethnicity, stance, and affect (Holliday, Bishop & Kuo 2020). Ethnicity combined with age determined the response of Hmong-American speakers in Minnesota to an interviewer (Stanford 2010). Older men style-shifted into an "authoritative voice" (using increased pitch, pitch variance, and acoustic intensity), whereas women and younger men did not use this speech style. In Japanese, younger generations across different dialects use flatter overall pitch contours (Takano & Ota 2017).

Perceived group membership (in-group vs. out-group) with the addressee often conditions prosodic variation. Fagyal & Stewart (2011) report that while neutral intonation was used with all groups, a marked intonation contour (connected with working-class youth vernacular in contact with immigrant languages) was reserved to members of the peer group. Formality and prestige are associated with f0 variation, with Belfast English speakers adopting falling pitch accents in formal settings, emulating the prestige variety of British English, but rising pitch accents typically found in both interrogatives and declaratives are associated with informal contexts in the local vernacular (Lowry 2002).

Style has been examined more extensively in studies with a sociolinguistic background. Examination of newscasters' style showed more use of the middle 50 percent and highest quartile of their pitch range, a lower minimum f0 and more L+H* pitch accents compared to non-newscasters (Rodero Antón 2013). Female newscasters had a lower maximum f0 and larger f0 standard deviation than non-news counterparts. Style is treated recently as an intraspeaker fluid construction of identity which changes throughout an individual's communicative context (e.g., Podesva, Roberts & Campbell-Kibler 2002; Fagyal & Stewart 2011; Podesva 2011; Slobe 2018; Fine 2019b; Holliday, Bishop & Kuo 2020) rather than as the more traditional view of style as interspeaker variation which is a function of attention paid to speech in the formality–informality axis (e.g., Labov 1966). In Podesva (2011), style was associated with salience: the least frequent f0 contour patterns, viewed as more salient, were used for indexing social meaning, and more extreme f0 values conveyed more "animated" personas.

In the same vein of fluid construction of identity, Fine (2019a) demonstrated correlations between style and variation in f0 height and range between personas expressing different sexual orientations. The results on the effect of sexual orientation on intonation, though, give a mixed picture. No significant difference in f0 min, max, and pitch range were reported between gay and non-gay speakers (Podesva, Roberts & Campbell-Kibler 2002) and no significant correlations emerged between pitch range and variability with listener ratings of men's speech such as "gay" versus "straight" and "masculine" versus "effeminate" (Gaudio 1994). On the other hand, there are reports that lesbian women had significantly lower mean f0 and less pitch variation than heterosexual women (Camp 2009; van Borsel, Vandaele & Corthals 2013).

CASE STUDY   Gender, language dominance, and attitude in intonation

Intonation has been shown to vary across dialects and due to language contact. Recent studies have also begun to consider other contributing factors such as attitude and degree of contact (Elordieta & Romera 2020) and language dominance (Hernandez 2020). In the present study, the intonation of read declaratives in Peruvian Spanish is compared according to gender, language dominance (in Spanish versus Quechua), and linguistic attitudes. The aim is to determine if and how these factors contribute to differences in intonation features.

Peruvian Spanish dialects have traditionally been divided according to highland Andean versus lowland coastal regions (Escobar 1978), with the Amazon as another area in need of investigation (Fafulas 2020, Jara et al. 2023). In addition, Quechua-influenced speech is recognized within the speech communities and has been remarked upon in the literature (Escobar 2011). Some prosodic features in Peruvian Spanish have been analyzed for their influence from Quechua, such as pretonic-aligned peaks or lack of downstep (O'Rourke 2004, 2006; Muntendam & Torreira 2016).

Methods

The participants were 19 speakers, ages 20–34, including 4 (3M, 1F) from Lima and 15 from Cusco (9M, 6F), representing coastal and highland varieties respectively. Each participant read a series of ten pronominal question-and-answer pairs twice. Responses were declaratives with utterance-final narrow focus which contained between three and six stressed syllables and varied according to syllable type and lexical stress pattern (O'Rourke 2020).

The alignment and height of peaks were measured in Praat (Boersma & Weenink 2021). Non-final peaks appearing during the stressed syllable were considered tonic-aligned (TA), while those occurring after the stressed syllable were counted as delayed (Del). Peak-to-peak height differences greater than 7 Hz were considered to be downstepped (Down), whereas differences less than 7 Hz as well as higher subsequent peaks (i.e., level or upstepped) were noted as a suspension of downstep (Spnd) (Klatt 1973; O'Rourke 2006). In all, 1197 prenuclear peaks and 1191 peak pairs were analyzed for alignment and height.

In many (if not most) cases, these peaks may be preceded by a low tone, which has not been the focus here. This bitonal accent would include either a tonic-aligned peak, L+H* or a delayed peak, L+<H* (see Figure 2.1; Hualde & Prieto 2016). While delayed and downstepped peaks are typical in Spanish under broad focus conditions, aligned and upstepped peaks are found in non-neutral contexts, such as in contrastive focus (Prieto & Roseano 2010). Cross-linguistic and cross-dialectal issues arise when these tonic-aligned or upstepped peaks signal marked conditions in one variety but a more neutral interpretation or meaning in another. Elicited utterances are shown in Figure 2.2, with examples of delayed and downstepped peaks on the left and tonic-aligned and upstepped peaks on the right.

To measure language dominance, a modification of the Bilingualism Language Profile (Birdsong, Gertken & Amengual 2012) or mBLP was used which included three modules weighted so that each contributed a third to the overall score: language history (120 points; weighted 0.539), language use (50 points; 1.29), and language proficiency (24 points; 2.69).

Participants' distribution according to dominance is shown in Figure 2.3a, where values from 0 to 194 indicate Spanish-dominance and values from 0 to −194 indicate Quechua-dominance. All Lima Spanish speakers scored at 194 and are shown as Spanish monolinguals. Spanish-dominant speakers

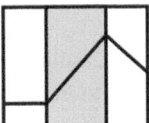 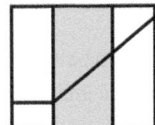

Figure 2.1   Bitonal pitch accents with tonic-aligned and delayed peaks
Figure 2.1a (left)   L+H*
Figure 2.1b (right)   L+<H*

Source: Hualde & Prieto 2016

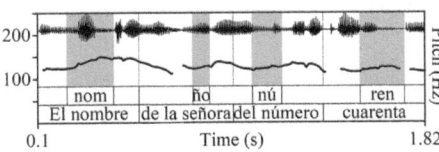 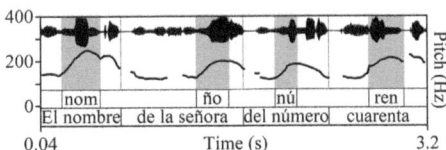

Figure 2.2   Sample utterance 'El nombre de la señora del número cuarenta es Gabriela' ("The name of the woman of the number forty (apartment) is Gabriela") with stressed syllables in separate tier
Figure 2.2a (left)   Lima male monolingual Spanish speaker
Figure 2.2b (right)   Cusco male Quechua-Spanish bilingual

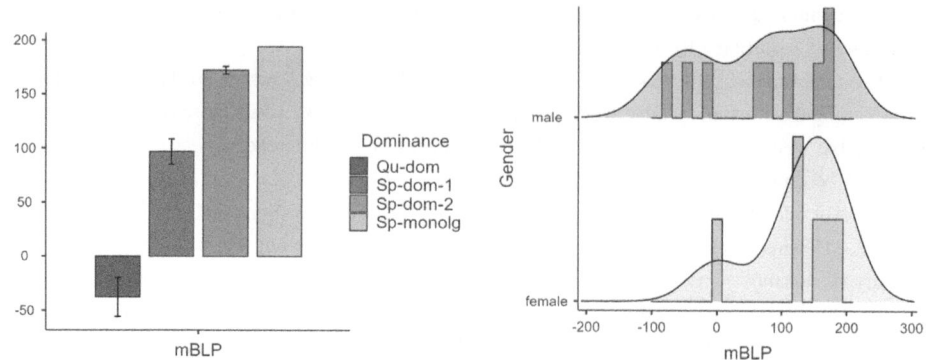

Figure 2.3 Participants' distribution as measured by a modification of the Bilingualism Language
Profile (mBLP)
Figure 2.3a (left)   by dominance (all speakers)
Figure 2.3b (right)   by gender (Cusco speakers)

are subdivided into those closer to the Spanish monolinguals and those with more intermediate values.
Cusco participants' dominance by gender is shown in Figure 2.3b. Statistical analysis and graphs were
created in jamovi (Selker et al. 2022) in R (R Core Team 2022).

Participants also completed a language history questionnaire and responded to a short attitude survey. Since the language attitude statements were about promotion of language use and language planning, these were analyzed separately from the mBLP. The statements can be subdivided
by theme: Castilianization (or a move towards use of Spanish and other Indo-European languages),
Maintenance, and Expansion of indigenous languages:

1) It is better that everyone speaks Spanish in order to be able to communicate better. [Castilianization]
2) It is important to maintain the autochthonous languages (like Quechua or Aymara) in the places
where they are spoken. [Maintenance]
3) Quechua (or Aymara) should be taught to all children, including those in Lima, in order to be able
to communicate better with people who speak Quechua (or Aymara). [Expansion]

Responses were scored as "No"=1, "Not sure/It's complicated"=2, and "Yes"=3. Ratings with low
scores were considered weak support, intermediate ratings as mid-range support, and high scores as
strong support for a given attitude statement. All participants showed nearly categorical support for
maintenance, so these will not be further discussed.

Results

Contingency tables for alignment and height were created with the independent variable (IV) being
either gender (male, female), language dominance (Qu-dom, Sp-dom-1, Sp-dom-2, Sp-ML), or attitude (weak, mid, strong). A Chi-square test of independence was calculated for each of the tables, along
with a Cramer's V Effect Size in cases where significance was found. The results are summarized in
Table 2.1.

Table 2.1 Results of Chi-square analysis according to alignment and height.

IV	Chi-square, Alignment (TA, Del)	Effect Size	Chi-square, Height (Spnd, Down)	Effect size
Gender	X^2 (1, 1197) = 1.46, p = .227		X^2 (1, 1191) = 16.2, p = <.001	.118
Dominance (3)	X^2 (2, 1197) = 28.1, p = <.001	.207	X^2 (2, 1191) = 6.85, p = .033	.0758
Dominance (4)	X^2 (3, 1197) = 55.7, p = <.001	.216	X^2 (3, 1191) = 6.96, p = .073	
Attitude–Cast.	X^2 (2, 1197) = 28.1, p = <.001	.153	X^2 (2, 1191) = 5.19, p = .075	
Attitude–Expa.	X^2 (2, 1197) = 17.0, p = <.001	.119	X^2 (2, 1191) = 0.375, p = .829	

Analysis of the speaker characteristics shows the following. Regarding gender, males produced more suspended peaks than expected. Analysis of dominance showed that Spanish-dominant speakers produced more TA peaks compared to Spanish monolinguals, and that Quechua-dominant speakers produced more suspended peaks than expected. Those with strong support of Castilianization showed more use of delayed peaks, an unmarked feature common in other Spanish varieties, whereas weak and mid-range support groups showed greater than expected TA. Mid-range support of expansion also showed greater than expected TA. Medium effect sizes (.2–.4) are found for alignment by dominance, whereas small effect sizes (.1–.2) are found for alignment by attitude and height by gender.

Discussion

This case study has found different intonation features to be significant depending on which social factor is considered: gender was significant for peak height, attitude for peak alignment, and dominance for both features. Attitude statements more directly related to the speaker's identity as in the BLP may reveal larger effects. Nonetheless, strong support of Castilianization showed greater instances of delayed peaks. Analysis of social factors in combination with linguistic factors may provide a more complete picture of the variation present in a speech community, along with a direction of potential change.

CASE STUDY   Historical intonation and contact in Asia Minor Greek

This study investigates the diachronic development of the continuation rise tune in a variety of Greek originating in the area of Cappadocia in Asia Minor: Asia Minor Greek (AMG), where Turkish was the dominant language. AMG and Turkish speakers cohabited for eight centuries until 1923 when under the Convention Concerning the Exchange of Greek and Turkish Populations, two million people were forcibly displaced, based on religion: 1.5 million Anatolian Christians to Greece and half a million Hellenic Muslims to Turkey.

A continuation rise is a phrase with an H tone on its right boundary, indicating the speaker has not finished speaking. The f0 movement from the nucleus to the end of the phrase has a different shape in the two languages: in Turkish it is a rise-fall-rise, with an H*+L accent before the H boundary

(Figure 2.4a; see also Ipek & Jun 2014); in Athenian it is a simple rise, with an L* accent before the H boundary (Figure 2.4b; see also Arvaniti & Baltazani 2005).

The first-generation AMG speakers in the analysis were born in Turkey prior to 1923, while second-generation speakers, born in Greece, no longer had contact with Turkish. These speakers are bi- or multi-dialectal, in AMG local Greek varieties and Standard Modern Greek as spoken in Athens (Janse 2009; Karatsareas 2011).

The study hypothesizes that the continuation rise tune in AMG differs from Athenian and resembles Turkish and, further, that intonation patterns of AMG speakers born before 1923 in Turkey (AMGgen1) resemble Turkish more than those of the second generation of AMG speakers born in Greece (AMGgen2). See Baltazani, Przedlacka & Coleman (2019, 2020), and Baltazani et al. 2023 for fuller exploration of these data.

Methods

The analysis was based on data from pre-existing natural speech corpora of contemporary and archival recordings from the 1930s produced by 24 speakers (Athenian: 3F, 4M, μ age = 46.2y; AMGgen1: 3F, 5M; AMGgen2: 1F, 2M; Turkish: 4F, 2M, μ age = 33.7y) and comprises 1127 continuation rise tokens (443 Athenian, 355 AMGgen1, 187 AMGgen2, 142 Turkish). The comparisons in the four groups (Athenian, Turkish, AMGgen1, AMGgen2) were quantified by a combination of tools: a) modeling the shape of the f0 contour employing Functional Data Analysis (for details, see Baltazani, Przedlacka & Coleman 2019; Baltazani et al. 2023); and b) mainstream Autosegmental-Metrical (Pierrehumbert 1980, Ladd 2008) f0 alignment with segmental landmarks.

For the alignment comparison among the four groups, the L tone was chosen as a common landmark in Athenian and Turkish. This is expected to occur after the end of the nuclear vowel in Turkish but before the end of the nuclear vowel in Athenian (see Figure 2.4). Similarity of the AMG tunes to Athenian or Turkish was measured through the shape characteristics of the f0 curves and through the alignment details of the trough with the stressed syllable.

Results

Results show that most first-generation AMG speakers produced continuation rises with two modes of trough alignment: one "late," Turkish-like pattern of trough alignment well after the nuclear vowel end and one "early," Athenian-like pattern within the nuclear vowel (Figure 2.5).

As shown in Figure 2.6, comparison of the trough alignment in the four groups (Athenian, Turkish, AMGgen1, AMGgen2) reveals a distribution with two modes of alignment in the first-generation AMG speakers.

The histograms of trough alignment P(t) in AMG generations 1 and 2 were modeled as a weighted sum of Gaussian probability density functions with means (μ) and standard deviations (s) estimated from the Athenian and Turkish controls, and weights w1 and w2:

$$P(t)AMG = w1 \text{ probdf}(t, \mu Ath, \tfrac{1}{2}sAth) + w2 \text{ probdf}(t, \mu Tur, \tfrac{1}{2}s \text{ Tur})$$

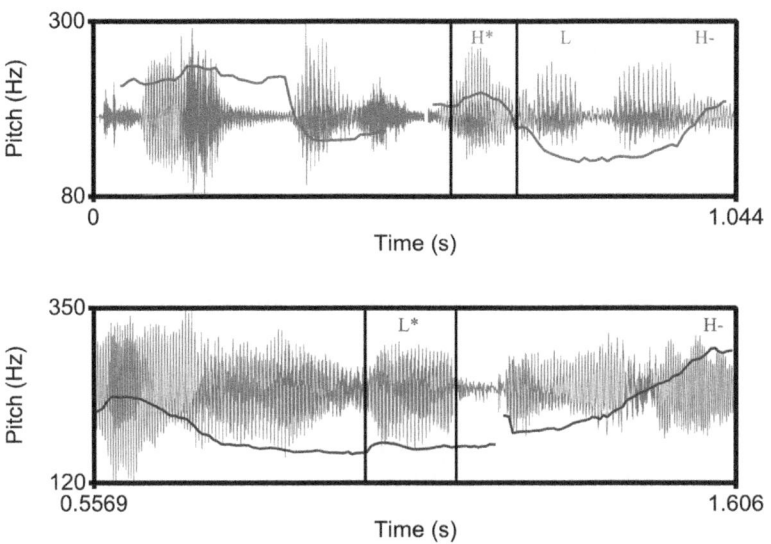

Figure 2.4   Representative examples of the continuation rise tune
Figure 2.4a (top)   Turkish [maˈsaja oˈ**tur**madan] 'Before sitting at the table'
Figure 2.4b (bottom)   Athenian [erɣaˈ**zot**ane] '(she was) working'

Note. Here and in Figure 2.5, rectangles indicate the nuclear vowel, transcribed in bold.

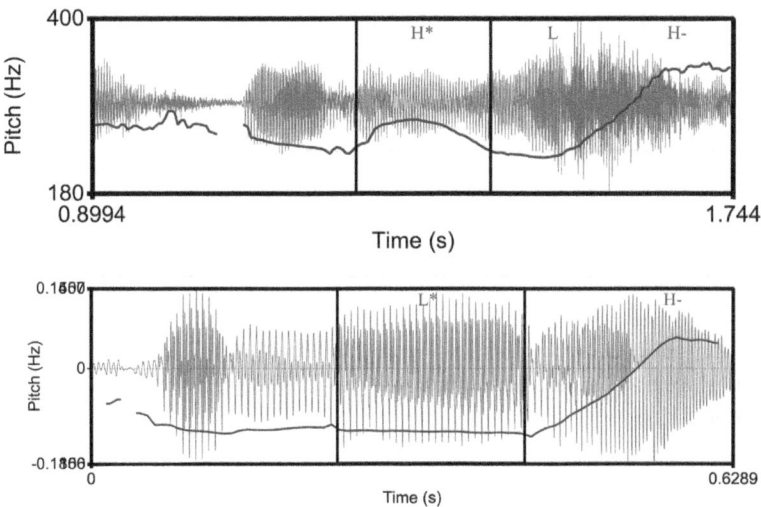

Figure 2.5   Examples from AMGgen1 speakers producing a continuation rise
Figure 2.5a (top)   Turkish-like [istoˈ**ria**] '…story…'
Figure 2.5b (bottom)   Athenian-like [taˈ**meri**] 'The places'

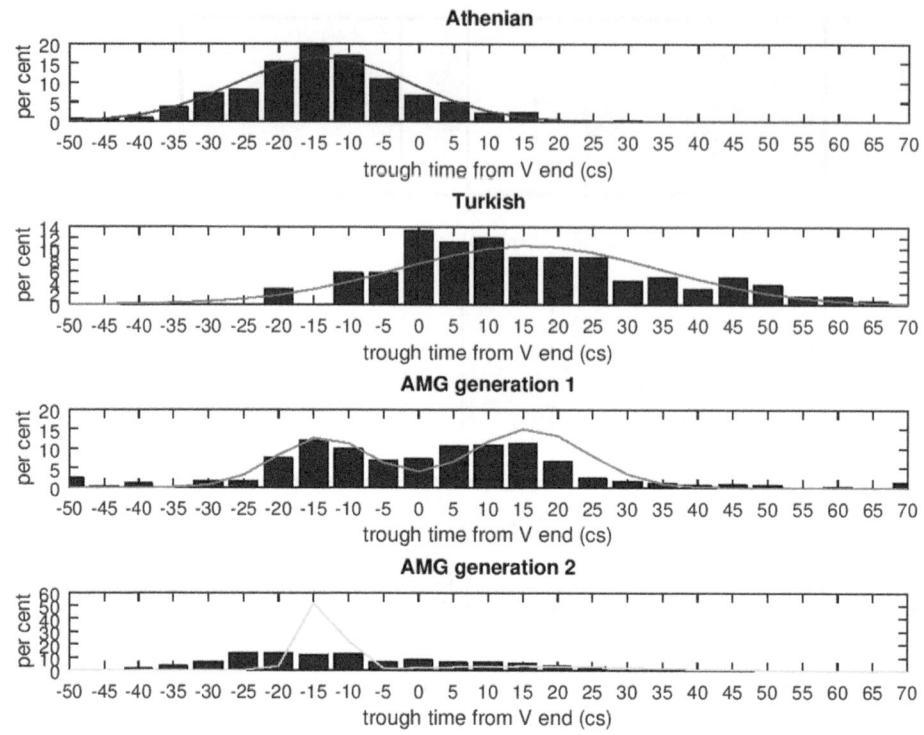

Figure 2.6   Distribution of trough time with respect to V end, which is represented as 0 in the x-axis

Table 2.2 Weights of the Athenian and Turkish components of the AMG histograms

	AMGgen1	*AMGgen2*
w1 (Athenian)	0.44237	0.78817
w2 (Turkish)	0.55763	0.21183

These models are shown as overlaid lines in Figure 2.6. Table 2.2 shows that in AMGgen1 the Athenian and Turkish components are both strong, whereas in AMGgen2 the Athenian component strongly predominates.

Discussion

The analysis confirmed that the shape of the "early alignment" utterances patterned with that of Athenian and the "late alignment" ones patterned with Turkish, indicating a heavy influence of Turkish. A diminishing proportion of Turkish pattern tokens was found in the second generation, with a shift towards a higher frequency of Athenian-type variants, suggesting intergenerational change. The bimodality also suggests code-mixing, as first-generation speakers alternated between the Athenian and the Turkish pattern. To understand more about the nature of these variants, the intonation of later generations needs to be examined (see Baltazani et al. 2023).

The future for socioprosodics

In this chapter we have presented an overview of research at the intersections of sociophonetics and intonation. Relevant literature was found in many different fields of study, including language variation and change, bilingualism, and language contact. In addition, we have noted how sociophonetics and intonation has been treated with relation to perception, pragmatics, and style. Our case studies showcase synchronic and diachronic approaches to examining sociolinguistic variation of intonation as a result of language contact.

We have proposed the term socioprosodics to describe what we see as a nascent field with potential for development in many directions. We believe and hope that raising awareness of common research goals in the scientific community of socioprosodics will lead to the adoption of comparable analytical tools in a way similar to the spread of AM methods for intonation studies in the past three decades. An analytical consensus of this kind will lead to advances in the field of socioprosodics and more generally in our understanding of the role that social factors play in intonation variability. Our wish is that this chapter will promote greater dialogue between scholars in the field of socioprosodics, and in doing so we may see the field grow and contribute to linguistic research as a whole. We hope that more typological generalizations (e.g., Kireva 2016; Mascaró & Roseano 2020) will emerge regarding the social effects on intonational change and variability.

References

Alvord, Scott M. 2006. *Spanish intonation in contact: The case of Miami Cuban bilinguals*. PhD dissertation, University of Minnesota.

Alvord, Scott M. 2010. Variation in Miami Cuban Spanish interrogative intonation. *Hispania* 93(2). 235–255. www.jstor.org/stable/25703434

Aly, Ann M. 2017. Code-switching in Miami Cuban Spanish: A preliminary study of suprasegmental effects. In Alejandro Cuza (ed.), *Cuban Spanish dialectology: Variation, contact and change*, 41–57. Georgetown University Press.

Armstrong, Meghan E. & Pilar Prieto. 2015. The contribution of context and contour to perceived belief in polar questions. *Journal of Pragmatics* 81. 77–92. https://doi.org/10.1016/j.pragma.2015.03.006

Armstrong, Meghan E., Nicholas Henriksen & Maria del Mar Vanrell (eds.). 2016. *Intonational grammar in Ibero-Romance: Approaches across linguistic subfields*. John Benjamins.

Aronoff, Mark (ed.). 2020. *Oxford research encyclopedia of linguistics*. Oxford University Press.

Arvaniti, Amalia. 2020. The phonetics of prosody. In Aronoff. https://doi.org/10.1093/acrefore/9780199384655.013.411

Arvaniti, Amalia & Mary Baltazani. 2005. Intonational analysis and prosodic annotation of Greek spoken corpora. In Jun, 84–117.

Arvaniti, Amalia, Mary Baltazani & Stella Gryllia. 2014. The pragmatic interpretation of intonation in Greek wh-questions. In Campbell, Gibbon & Hirst, 1144–1148.

Arvaniti, Amalia & Gina Garding. 2007. Dialectal variation in the rising accents of American English. In Jennifer Cole & José Ignacio Hualde (eds.), *Papers in Laboratory Phonology* 9. 547–576. De Gruyter Mouton.

Arvaniti, Amalia & D. Robert Ladd. 2009. Greek wh-questions and the phonology of intonation. *Phonology* 26(1). 43–74. https://doi.org/10.1017/S0952675709001717

Arvaniti, Amalia, D. Robert Ladd & Ineke Mennen. 2006. Tonal association and tonal alignment: Evidence from Greek polar questions and contrastive statements. *Language and Speech* 49(4). 421–450. https://doi.org/10.1177/00238309060490040101

Astruc, Lluïsa, Maria del Mar Vanrell & Pilar Prieto. 2016. Cost of the action and social distance affect the selection of question intonation in Catalan. In Armstrong, Henriksen & Vanrell, 93–114.

Atterer, Michaela & D. Robert Ladd. 2004. On the phonetics and phonology of "segmental anchoring" of F0: Evidence from German. *Journal of Phonetics* 32(2). 177–197. https://doi.org/10.1016/S0095-4470(03)00039-1

Baird, Brandon O. 2015. Pre-nuclear peak alignment in the Spanish of Spanish-K'ichee' (Mayan) bilinguals. In Erik W. Willis, Pedro M. Butragueño & Esther Herrera Zendejas (eds.), *Proceedings of the 6th Conference on Laboratory Approaches to Romance Phonology*, 163–174. Cascadilla Proceedings Project.

Baird, Brandon O. 2019. Language-specific pitch ranges among simultaneous K'ichee'-Spanish bilinguals. In Calhoun et al., 2675–2679.

Baltazani, Mary, Stella Gryllia & Amalia Arvaniti. 2020. The intonation and pragmatics of Greek wh-questions. *Language and Speech* 63(1). 56–94. https://doi.org/10.1177/0023830918823236

Baltazani, Mary, Joanna Przedlacka & John Coleman. 2019. Intonation in contact: Asia Minor Greek and Turkish. In Calhoun et al., 1665–1669.

Baltazani, Mary, Joanna Przedlacka & John Coleman. 2020. Intonation of Greek—Turkish contact: A real-time diachronic study. In Minematsu, 730–734. http://doi.org/10.21437/SpeechProsody.2020-149

Baltazani, Mary, Joanna Przedlacka, Özlem Ünal-Logačev, Pavel Logačev & John Coleman. 2023. Intonation of Greek in contact with Turkish: A diachronic study. *Language Variation and Change* 34(3). 271–303. https://doi.org/10.1017/S0954394522000126

Barnes, Hilary & Jim Michnowicz. 2013. Peak alignment in semi-spontaneous bilingual Chipilo Spanish. In Ana M. Carvalho & Sara Beaudrie (eds.), *Selected proceedings of the 6th Workshop on Spanish Sociolinguistics*, 109–122. Cascadilla Proceedings Project.

Barnes, Hilary & Jim Michnowicz. 2015. Broad focus declaratives in Veneto-Spanish bilinguals: Peak alignment and language contact. *Studies in Hispanic and Lusophone Linguistics* 8(1). 35–57. https://doi.org/10.1515/shll-2015-0002

Barrera-Tobón, Carolina. 2013. *Contact-induced changes in word order and intonation in the Spanish of New York City bilinguals*. PhD dissertation, City University of New York.

Bayley, Robert, Richard Cameron & Ceil Lucas (eds.). 2013. *The Oxford handbook of sociolinguistics*. Oxford University Press.

Beasley, T. Mark & Randall E. Schumacker. 1995. Multiple regression approach to analyzing contingency tables: Post hoc and planned comparison procedures. *Journal of Experimental Education* 64(1). 79–93. https://doi.org/10.1080/00220973.1995.9943797

Bell, Allan. 2016. Succeeding waves: Seeking sociolinguistic theory for the twenty-first century. In Nikolas Coupland (ed.), *Sociolinguistics: Theoretical debates*, 391–414. Cambridge University Press.

Birdsong, David, Libby M. Gertken & Mark Amengual. 2012. *Bilingual Language Profile: An easy-to-use instrument to assess bilingualism*. COERLL, University of Texas at Austin. https://sites.la.utexas.edu/bilingual/

Blaauw, Eleonora. 1995. *On the perceptual classification of spontaneous and read speech*. LEd.

Bleorțu, Cristina & Miguel Cuevas Alonso. 2017. Towards an interactional perspective of Spanish prosody: Guidelines for analyzing intonation. *Revue Roumaine de Linguistique* 62(1). 77–98.

Boersma, Paul & David Weenink 2021. *Praat: Doing phonetics by computer* [Computer program]. www.praat.org/

Bolinger, Dwight. 1972. Accent is predictable (if you're a mind-reader). *Language* 48(3). 633–644. https://doi.org/10.2307/412039

Brown, Lucien & Pilar Prieto. 2017. (Im)politeness: Prosody and gesture. In Jonathan Culpeper, Michael Haugh & Dániel Kádár (eds.), *The Palgrave handbook of linguistic (im)politeness*, 357–359. Palgrave.

Brown, Lucien, Bodo Winter, Kaori Idemaru & Sven Grawunder. 2014. Phonetics and politeness: Perceiving Korean honorific and non-honorific speech through phonetic cues. *Journal of Pragmatics* 66. 45–60. https://doi.org/10.1016/j.pragma.2014.02.011

Brown, Lucien, Bodo Winter, Kaori Idemaru & Sven Grawunder. 2015. The sound of honorific language: How speech indexes social meaning in Korean, Japanese, German and Russian. Paper presented at the International Pragmatics Conference (IPrA).

Brown, Roger & Albert Gilman. 1960. The pronouns of power and solidarity. In Thomas A. Sebeok (ed.), *Style in language*, 253–276. MIT Press.

Bullock, Barbara E. 2009. Prosody in contact in French: A case study from a heritage variety in the USA. *International Journal of Bilingualism* 13(2). 165–194. https://doi.org/10.1177/1367006909339817

Calhoun, Sasha, Paola Escudero, Marija Tabain & Paul Warren (eds.). 2019. *Proceedings of the 19th International Congress of Phonetic Sciences, Melbourne, Australia 2019*. Australasian Speech Science and Technology Association.

Camp, Margaret. 2009. *Japanese lesbian speech: Sexuality, gender identity, and language*. PhD dissertation, University of Arizona.

Campbell, Nick, Dafydd Gibbon & Daniel Hirst (eds.). 2014. *Proceedings of 7th International Conference on Speech Prosody*. International Speech Communication Association.

Celata, Chiara & Silvia Calamai. 2014. *Advances in sociophonetics*. John Benjamins.

Chambers, J.K. 2003. *Sociolinguistic theory: Linguistic variation and its social significance*. Blackwell.

Chambers, J.K. & Natalie Schilling (eds.). 2013. *The handbook of language variation and change*. Wiley-Blackwell.

Chen, Aoju, Carlos Gussenhoven & Toni Rietveld. 2004. Language-specificity in the perception of paralinguistic intonational meaning. *Language and Speech* 47(4). 311–349. https://doi.org/10.1177/00238309040470040101

Chen, Ying, Yi Xu & Susan Guion-Anderson. 2015. Prosodic realization of focus in bilingual production of Southern Min and Mandarin. *Phonetica* 71(4). 249–270. https://doi.org/10.1159/000371891

Clark, Brady. 2017. Pragmatics and intonation. In Aronoff. https://doi.org/10.1093/acrefore/9780199384655.013.208

Clopper, Cynthia G. & Rajka Smiljanic. 2011. Effects of gender and regional dialect on prosodic patterns in American English. *Journal of Phonetics* 39(2). 237–245. https://doi.org/10.1016/j.wocn.2011.02.006

Colantoni, Laura. 2011. Broad-focus declaratives in Argentine Spanish contact and non-contact varieties. In Christoph Gabriel & Conxita Lleó (eds.), *Intonational phrasing in Romance and Germanic: Cross-linguistic and bilingual studies*, 183–212. John Benjamins.

Colantoni, Laura & Jorge Gurlekian. 2004. Convergence and intonation: Historical evidence from Buenos Aires Spanish. *Bilingualism: Language and Cognition* 7(2). 107–119. https://doi.org/10.1017/S1366672890 4001488

Congosto Martín, Yolanda & Laura Morgenthaler. 2019. Prosodic issues in language contact situations. *Spanish in Context* 16(3). 323–328. https://doi.org/10.1075/sic.00044.con

Correa, José A. 2017. Intonation in Palenquero Creole and Palenquero Spanish (Colombia). In Armin Schwegler, Bryan Kirschen & Graciela Maglia (eds.), *Orality, identity, and resistance in Palenque (Colombia): An interdisciplinary approach*, 245–267. John Benjamins.

Dalton, Martha & Ailbhe Ní Chasaide. 2003. Modelling intonation in three Irish dialects. In Daniel Recasens, Maria-Josep Solé & Joaquín Romero (eds.), *Proceedings of the 15th International Congress of Phonetic Sciences* 1, 1073–1076. Causal Productions.

Dalton, Martha & Ailbhe Ní Chasaide. 2005. Tonal alignment in Irish dialects. *Language and Speech* 48(4). 441–464. https://doi.org/10.1177/00238309050480040501

Devís Herraiz, Empar & Francisco José Cantero Serena. 2014. The intonation of mitigating politeness in Catalan. *Journal of Politeness Research* 10. 127–149. https://doi.org/10.1515/pr-2014-0006

Díaz-Campos, Manuel, Manel Lacorte & Javier Muñoz-Basols (eds.). 2021. *The Routledge handbook of variationist approaches to Spanish*. Routledge.

Eckert, Penelope. 2012. Three waves of variation study: The emergence of meaning in the study of sociolinguistic variation. *Annual Review of Anthropology* 41. 87–100. https://doi.org/10.1146/annurev-anthro-092 611-145828

Eckert, Penelope. 2019. The limits of meaning: Social indexicality, variation, and the cline of interiority. *Language* 95(4). 751–776. https://doi.org/10.1353/lan.2019.0072

Elordieta, Gorka. 2003. The Spanish intonation of speakers of a Basque pitch-accent dialect. *Catalan Journal of Linguistics* 2. 67–95. https://doi.org/10.5565/rev/catjl.44

Elordieta, Gorka & Nagore Calleja. 2005. Microvariation in accentual alignment in Basque Spanish. *Language and Speech* 48(4). 397–439. https://doi.org/10.1177/00238309050480040401

Elordieta, Gorka & Magdalena Romera. 2020. The influence of social factors on the prosody of Spanish in contact with Basque. *International Journal of Bilingualism* 25(1). 286–317. https://doi.org/10.1177/13670 06920952867

Elvira-García, Wendy, Simone Balocco, Paolo Roseano & Ana M. Fernández-Planas. 2018. ProDis: A dialectometric tool for acoustic prosodic data. *Speech Communication* 97. 9–18. https://doi.org/10.1016/j.specom.2017.12.013

Enbe, Claudia & Yishai Tobin. 2008. Sociolinguistic variation in the intonation of Buenos Aires Spanish. *Sociolinguistic Studies* 1(3). 347–382. https://doi.org/10.1558/sols.v1i3.347

Escobar, Alberto. 1978. *Variaciones sociolingüísticas del castellano del Perú* [Peru Problema 18]. Instituto de Estudios Peruanos.

Escobar, Anna María. 2011. Spanish in contact with Quechua. In Manuel Díaz-Campos (ed.), *The handbook of Hispanic sociolinguistics*, 323–352. Wiley-Blackwell.

Esling, John H., Scott R. Moisik, Allison Benner & Lise Crevier-Buchman. 2019. *Voice quality: The laryngeal articulator model*. Cambridge University Press. https://doi.org/10.1017/9781108696555

Esposito, Lewis. 2020. Linking gender, sexuality, and affect: The linguistic and social patterning of phrase-final posttonic lengthening. *Language Variation and Change* 32(2). 191–216. https://doi.org/10.1017/S0954394520000095

Face, Timothy L. 2003. Intonation in Spanish declaratives: Differences between lab speech and spontaneous speech. *Catalan Journal of Linguistics* 2. 115–131. https://doi.org/10.5565/rev/catjl.46

Fafulas, Stephen (ed.). 2020. *Amazonian Spanish: Language contact and evolution*. John Benjamins.

Fagyal, Zsuzsanna & Christopher Stewart. 2011. Prosodic style-shifting in preadolescent peer-group interactions in a working-class suburb of Paris. In Friederike Kern & Margret Selting (eds.), *Ethnic styles of speaking in European metropolitan areas*, 75–99. John Benjamins.

Fenton, Elyssa, Amy Bustin & Antje Muntendam. 2020. The intonation of broad focus declaratives in Afro-Peruvian Spanish: Findings from two elicitation tasks. *Studies in Hispanic and Lusophone Linguistics* 13(1). 1–49. https://doi.org/10.1515/shll-2020-2024

Fernández Planas, Ana María, Paolo Roseano, Josefa Dorta Luis & Eugenio Martínez Celdrán. 2013. ¿Continuidad prosódica en diferentes puntos de la Romania? El caso de algunas interrogativas. In Emili Casanova Herrero & Cesáreo Calvo Rigual (eds.), *Actas del XXVI Congreso Internacional de Lingüística y de Filología Románicas*, 588–599. Walter de Gruyter.

Fernández Rei, Elisa. 2016. Dialectal, historical and sociolinguistic aspects of Galician intonation. *Dialectologia: Revista electrònica* VI. 147–169.

Fine, Julia Coombs. 2019a. Performing graysexuality: A segmental and prosodic analysis of three voices employed in the construction of the graysexual self. *Journal of Language and Sexuality* 8(1). 1–29. https://doi.org/10.1075/jls.18003.coo

Fine, Julia Coombs. 2019b. 'They just had such a sweet way of speaking': Constructed voices and prosodic styles in Kodiak Alutiiq. *Language & Communication* 67. 1–15. https://doi.org/10.1016/j.langcom.2018.12.002

Fletcher, Janet & Jonathan Harrington. 2001. High-rising terminals and fall-rise tunes in Australian English. *Phonetica* 58(4). 215–229. https://doi.org/10.1159/000046176

Fletcher, Janet, Esther Grabe & Paul Warren. 2005. Intonational variation in four dialects of English: The high rising tune. In Jun, 390–409.

Foulkes, Paul & Gerard J. Docherty (eds.). 1999. *Urban voices: Accent studies in the British Isles*. Arnold.

Foulkes, Paul, James M. Scobbie & Dominic Watt. 2010. Sociophonetics. In William J. Hardcastle, John Laver & Fiona E. Gibbon (eds.), *The handbook of phonetic sciences*, 703–754. Blackwell.

Froemming, Brenda JoAnn Stelter. 2020. *The intonation patterns of broad focus declaratives in the spontaneous speech of Cuenca, Ecuador: A Sp_ToBI and sociolinguistic analysis*. PhD dissertation, University of Wisconsin-Madison.

Fujisaki, Hiroya & Sumio Ohno. 1995. Analysis and modeling of fundamental frequency contours of English utterances. In *Proceedings of the 4th European Conference on Speech Communication and Technology (Eurospeech 1995)*, 985–988.

Gabriel, Christoph, Ingo Feldhausen & Andrea Pešková. 2011. Prosodic phrasing in Porteño Spanish. In Conxita Lleó & Christoph Gabriel (eds.), *Intonational phrasing in Romance and Germanic: Cross-linguistic and bilingual studies*, 153–182. John Benjamins.

Gaudio, Rudolf P. 1994. Sounding gay: Pitch properties in the speech of gay and straight men. *American Speech* 69(1). 30–57. https://doi.org/10.2307/455948

Gili Fivela, Barbara. 2012. Testing the perception of L2 intonation. In Maria Grazia Busà & Antonio Stella (eds.), *Methodological perspectives on second language prosody: Papers from ML2P 2012*, 17–30. CLEUP.

Gold, Erica, Christin Kirchhübel, Kate Earnshaw & Sula Ross. 2021. Regional variation in British English voice quality. *English World-Wide* 43(1). 96–123. https://doi.org/10.1075/eww.20007.gol

Gooden, Shelome. 2009. Authentically Black, bona fide Pittsburgher: A first look at intonation in African American women's language in Pittsburgh. In Sonja L. Lanehart (ed.), *African American Women's Language: Discourse, education, and identity*, 142–164. Cambridge Scholars Publishing.

Gooden, Shelome. 2022. Intonation and prosody in Creole languages: An evolving ecology. *Annual Review of Linguistics* 8(1). 343–364. https://doi.org/10.1146/annurev-linguistics-031120-124320

Goodwin, Marjorie Harness, Charles Goodwin & Malcah Yaeger-Dror. 2002. Multi-modality in girls' game disputes. *Journal of Pragmatics* 34(10–11). 1621–1649. https://doi.org/10.1016/S0378-2166(02)00078-4

Gooskens, Charlotte. 1997. *On the role of prosodic and verbal information in the perception of Dutch and English language varieties.* PhD dissertation, Katholieke Universiteit Nijmegen.

Gooskens, Charlotte. 2005. How well can Norwegians identify their dialects? *Nordic Journal of Linguistics* 28(1). 37–60. https://doi.org/10.1017/S0332586505001319

Grabe, Esther. 2004. Intonational variation in urban dialects of English spoken in the British Isles. In Peter Gilles & Jörg Peters (eds.), *Regional variation in intonation*, 9–31. Niemeyer.

Grabe, Esther & Brechtje Post. 2002. Intonational variation in the British Isles. In *Proceedings of the Speech Prosody 2002 Conference, 11–13 April 2002*, 343–346. Laboratoire Parole et Langage.

Grabe, Esther, Brechtje Post & Francis Nolan. 2001. Modelling intonational Variation in English: The IViE system. In Stanislaw Puppel & Grazyna Demenko (eds.), *Proceedings of Prosody 2000*, 51–58. Adam Mickiewicz University.

Grabe, Esther, Brechtje Post, Francis Nolan & Kimberley Farrar. 2000. Pitch accent realization in four varieties of British English. *Journal of Phonetics* 28(2). 161–185. https://doi.org/10.1006/jpho.2000.0111

Grice, Martine & Michelina Savino. 2003. Map tasks in Italian: Asking questions about given, accessible and new information. *Catalan Journal of Linguistics* 2. 153–180. https://doi.org/10.5565/rev/catjl.48

Gryllia, Stella, Mary Baltazani & Amalia Arvaniti. 2018. The role of pragmatics and politeness in explaining prosodic variability. In Klessa et al., 158–162. https://doi.org/10.21437/SpeechProsody.2018-32

Gussenhoven, Carlos. 2004. *The phonology of tone and intonation.* Cambridge University Press.

Gussenhoven, Carlos & Aoju Chen (eds.). 2020. *The Oxford handbook of language prosody.* Oxford University Press.

Gussenhoven, Carlos & Inyang Udofot. 2010. Word melodies vs. pitch accents: A perceptual evaluation of terracing contours in British and Nigerian English. In Mark Hasegawa-Johnson (ed.), *Proceedings of Speech Prosody 2010*, Paper 015.

Gut, Ulrike. 2005. Nigerian English prosody. *English World-Wide* 26(2). 153–177. https://doi.org/10.1075/eww.26.2.03gut

Guy, Gregory, Barbara Horvath, Julia Vonwiller, Elaine Daisley & Inge Rogers. 1986. An intonational change in progress in Australian English. *Language in Society* 15. 23–52. https://doi.org/10.1017/S004740450 0011635

Hancock, Adrienne, Lindsey Colton & Fiacre Douglas. 2014. Intonation and gender perception: Applications for transgender speakers. *Journal of Voice* 28(2). 203–209. https://doi.org/10.1016/j.jvoice.2013.08.009

Hellmuth, Sam. 2014. Dialectal variation in Arabic intonation: Motivations for a multi-level corpus approach. In Samira Farwaneh & Hamid Ouali (eds.), *Perspectives on Arabic linguistics XXV–XXVI*, 63–89. John Benjamins.

Hellmuth, Sam. 2020. Contact and variation in Arabic intonation. In Christopher Lucas & Stefano Manfredi (eds.), *Arabic and contact-induced change*, 583–601. Language Science Press. https://doi.org/10.5281/zenodo.3744553

Henriksen, Nicholas. 2013. Style, prosodic variation, and the social meaning of intonation. *Journal of the International Phonetic Association* 43(2). 153–193. https://doi.org/10.1017/S0025100313000054

Henton, Caroline G. 1995. Pitch dynamism in female and male speech. *Language & Communication* 15(1). 43–51. https://doi.org/10.1016/0271-5309(94)00011-Z

Hernandez, Erika M. 2020. *The effects of bilingualism on intonation in Galician and Spanish.* PhD dissertation, Florida State University.

Hirschberg, Julia. 2000. A corpus-based approach to the study of speaking style. In Merle Horne (ed.), *Prosody: Theory and experiment: Studies presented to Gösta Bruce*, 335–350. Kluwer Academic.

Hirschberg, Julia. 2017. Pragmatics and prosody. In Yan Huang (ed.), *The Oxford handbook of pragmatics*, 532–549. Oxford University Press.

Holguín Mendoza, Claudia. 2011. *Language, gender, and identity construction: Sociolinguistic dynamics in the borderlands.* PhD dissertation, University of Illinois Urbana-Champaign.

Holliday, Nicole. 2016. *Intonational variation, linguistic style, and the Black/biracial experience.* PhD dissertation, New York University.

Holliday, Nicole. 2019. Variation in question intonation in the corpus of regional African American language. *American Speech* 94(1). 110–130. https://doi.org/10.1215/00031283-7308038

Holliday, Nicole, Jason Bishop & Grace Kuo. 2020. Prosody and political style: The case of Barack Obama and the L+H* pitch accent. In Minematsu, 670–674. https://doi.org/10.21437/SpeechProsody.2020-137

Holliday, Nicole & Daniel Villarreal. 2018. How black does Obama sound now? Testing listener judgments of intonation in incrementally manipulated speech. *University of Pennsylvania Working Papers in Linguistics* 24(2). 55–66. https://repository.upenn.edu/pwpl/vol24/iss2/8

Holliday, Nicole & Dan Villarreal. 2020. Intonational variation and incrementality in listener judgments of ethnicity. *Laboratory Phonology* 11(1). 3. http://doi.org/10.5334/labphon.229

House, Jill. 2006. Constructing a context with intonation. *Journal of Pragmatics* 38(10). 1542–1558. https://doi.org/10.1016/j.pragma.2005.07.005

Hualde, José I. 2003. Remarks on the diachronic reconstruction of intonational patterns in Romance with special attention to Occitan as a bridge language. *Catalan Journal of Linguistics* 2. 181–205. https://doi.org/10.5565/rev/catjl.49

Hualde, José I. & Pilar Prieto. 2016. Towards an International Prosodic Alphabet (IPrA). *Laboratory Phonology* 7(1). 1–25. https://doi.org/10.5334/labphon.11

Hualde, José Ignacio & Armin Schwegler. 2008. Intonation in Palenquero. *Journal of Pidgin and Creole Languages* 23(1). 1–31. https://doi.org/10.1075/jpcl.23.1.02hua

Huang, Yunjie & Yi Zhang. 2019. Intonation and gender difference: A gender-based analysis of intonational features in the talk show. *International Journal of Arts and Commerce* 8(7). 67–83.

Hübscher, Iris, Laura Wagner & Pilar Prieto. 2020. Three-year-olds infer polite stance from intonation and facial cues. *Journal of Politeness Research* 16(1). 85–110. https://doi.org/10.1515/pr-2017-0047

Ipek, Canan & Sun-Ah Jun. 2014. Distinguishing phrase-final and phrase-medial high tone on finally stressed words in Turkish. In Nick Campbell, Dafydd Gibbon & Daniel J. Hirst (eds.), *Proceedings 7th Speech Prosody International Conference*, 393–397. Trinity College Dublin.

Janse, Mark. 2009. Greek-Turkish language contact in Asia Minor. *Études Helléniques/Hellenic Studies* 17(1). 37–54. http://hdl.handle.net/1854/LU-517623

Jara, Margarita, Roberto Zariquiey, Pilar M. Valenzuela & Anna María Escobar (eds.). 2023. *Spanish diversity in the Amazon: Dialect and language contact perspectives.* Brill.

Jiang, Hongliu. 2011. Gender difference in English intonation. In Wai Sum Lee & Eric Zee (eds.), *Proceedings of the 17th International Congress of Phonetic Sciences.* 974–977. City University of Hong Kong.

Jun, Sun-Ah (ed.). 2005. *Prosodic typology: The phonology of intonation and phrasing.* Oxford University Press.

Jun, Sun-Ah. (ed.). 2014. *Prosodic typology II: The phonology and intonation of phrasing.* Oxford University Press.

Kaminskaïa, Svetlana. 2018. Peaks and valleys of a stress group in three geographically distant varieties of French in contact and non-contact settings. In Klessa et al., 138–142. https://doi.org/10.21437/speechprosody.2018-28

Karatsareas, Petros. 2011. *A study of Cappadocian Greek nominal morphology from a diachronic and dialectological perspective.* PhD dissertation, University of Cambridge.

Kato, Akiko. 2001. *Interlanguage variation in pitch and forms of English negatives: The case of Japanese speakers of English.* PhD dissertation, University of Arizona.

Katsika, Argyro, Jiyoung Jang, Jelena Krivokapić, Louis Goldstein & Elliot Saltzman. 2020. The role of focus in accentual lengthening in American English: Kinematic analyses. In Minematsu, 275–279. https://doi.org/10.21437/SpeechProsody.2020-56

Katz, William F. & Peter F. Assmann (eds.). 2019. *The Routledge handbook of phonetics.* Routledge.

Kim, Ji Young & Gemma Repiso-Puigdelliura. 2021. Keeping a critical eye on majority language influence: The case of uptalk in Heritage Spanish. *Languages* 6(1). 13. https://doi.org/10.3390/languages6010013

Kim, Seung Kyung & Meghan Sumner. 2017. Beyond lexical meaning: The effect of emotional prosody on spoken word recognition. *Journal of the Acoustical Society of America* 142(1). EL49–EL55. https://doi.org/10.1121/1.4991328

Kireva, Elena. 2016. *Prosody in Spanish-Portuguese contact*. PhD dissertation, University of Hamburg.

Klatt, Dennis H. 1973. Discrimination of fundamental frequency contours in synthetic speech: Implications for models of pitch perception. *Journal of the Acoustical Society of America* 53(1). 8–16. https://doi.org/10.1121/1.1913333

Klessa, Katarzyna, Jolanta Bachan, Agnieszka Wagner, Maciej Karpiński & Daniel Śledziński (eds.). 2018. *Proceedings of the 9th International Conference on Speech Prosody 2018*. International Speech Communication Association.

Labov, William. 1966. *The social stratification of English in New York City*. Center for Applied Linguistics.

Labov, William. 2001. *Principles of linguistic change*, vol. 2, *Social factors.* Blackwell.

Ladd, D. Robert. 1996. *Intonational phonology*. Cambridge University Press.

Ladd, D. Robert. 2008. *Intonational phonology*, 2nd edn. Cambridge University Press. https://doi.org/10.1017/CBO9780511808814

Lai, Li-Fang & Shelome Gooden. 2018a. Intonation in contact: Mandarin influence in Yami. In Klessa et al., 952–956. https://doi.org/10.21437/SpeechProsody.2018-192

Lai, Li-Fang & Shelome Gooden. 2018b. Tonal hybridization in Yami-Mandarin contact. *Proceedings from Sixth International Symposium on Tonal Aspects of Languages*. 32–36. https://doi.org/10.21437/TAL.2018-7

Lee, Binna & Diana Van Lancker Sidtis. 2017. The bilingual voice: Vocal characteristics when speaking two languages across speech tasks. *Speech, Language and Hearing* 20(3). 174–185. https://doi.org/10.1080/2050571X.2016.1273572

Lee, Hyunjung & Allard Jongman. 2015. Acoustic evidence for diachronic sound change in Korean prosody: A comparative study of the Seoul and South Kyungsang dialects. *Journal of Phonetics* 50. 15–33. https://doi.org/10.1016/j.wocn.2015.01.003

Liberman, Mark & Cynthia McLemore. 1992. Structure and intonation of business telephone openings. *The Penn Review of Linguistics* 16. 68–83.

Linneman, Thomas J. 2013. Gender in *Jeopardy!* Intonation variation on a television game show. *Gender & Society* 27(1). 82–105. https://doi.org/10.1177/0891243212464905

Lipski, John M. 2010. Pitch polarity in Palenquero: A possible locus of H tone. In Sonia Colina, Antxon Olarrea & Ana Maria Carvalho (eds.), *Romance linguistics 2009: Selected papers from the 39th Linguistic Symposium on Romance Languages (LSRL), Tucson, Arizona, March 2009*, 111–128. John Benjamins.

Lleó, Conxita & Christoph Gabriel (eds.). 2011. *Intonational phrasing in Romance and Germanic: Cross-linguistic and bilingual studies*. John Benjamins.

Lowry, Orla. 2002. The stylistic variation of nuclear patterns in Belfast English. *Journal of the International Phonetic Association* 32(1). 33–42. https://doi.org/10.1017/S0025100302000130

Lowry, Orla. 2011. Belfast intonation and speaker gender. *Journal of English Linguistics* 39(3). 209–232. https://doi.org/10.1177/0075424210380053

Martín Butragueño, Pedro. 2004. Circumflex configurations in the intonation of Mexican Spanish. *Revista de Filología Española* 84. 347–373. https://doi.org/10.3989/rfe.2004.v84.i2.111

Martínez Celdrán, Eugenio, Ana M. Fernández Planas, Lourdes Romera Barrios & Paolo Roseano (coords.). 2003–2020. *Atlas multimèdia de la prosòdia de l'espai romànic*. http://stel.ub.edu/labfon/amper/cast/index_ampercat.html

Martínez Gómez, Rebeca. 2018. *Fresa style in Mexico: Sociolinguistic stereotypes and the variability of social meanings*. PhD dissertation, University of New Mexico.

Mascaró, Ignasi & Paolo Roseano. 2020. Intonational variation in Minorcan Catalan: Towards a prosodic change? *Lingua* 243. 102871. https://doi.org/10.1016/j.lingua.2020.102871

Maxwell, Olga. 2014. *The intonational phonology of Indian English: An autosegmental-metrical analysis based on Bengali and Kannada English*. PhD dissertation, University of Melbourne.

Maxwell, Olga & Elinor Payne. 2018. Pitch accent types and tonal alignment of the accentual rise in Indian English(es). In Klessa et al., 942–946.

McGlone, Robert E. & Harry Hollien. 1963. Vocal pitch characteristics of aged women. *Journal of Speech and Hearing Research* 6. 164–172. https://doi.org/10.1044/jshr.0602.164

McGregor, Jeannette & Sallyanne Palethorpe. 2008. High rising tunes in Australian English: The communicative function of L* and H* pitch accent onsets. *Australian Journal of Linguistics* 28(2). 171–193. https://doi.org/10.1080/07268600802308766

McLarty, Jason. 2018. African American language and European American English intonation variation over time in the American South. *American Speech* 93(1). 32–78. https://doi.org/10.1215/00031283-6904032

McMahon, April. 2004. Prosodic change and language contact. *Bilingualism: Language and Cognition* 7(2). 121–123. https://doi.org/10.1017/S136672890400152X

Meer, Philipp & Robert Fuchs. 2022. The Trini Sing-Song: Sociophonetic variation in Trinidadian English prosody and differences to other varieties. *Language and Speech* 65(4). 923–957. https://doi.org/10.1177/0023830921998404

Mendoza-Denton, Norma & Stefanie Jannedy. 2011. Semiotic layering through gesture and intonation: A case study of complementary and supplementary multimodality in political speech. *Journal of English Linguistics* 39(3). 265–299. https://doi.org/10.1177/0075424211405941

Mennen, Ineke. 2004. Bi-directional interference in the intonation of Dutch speakers of Greek. *Journal of Phonetics* 32. 543–563. https://doi.org/10.1016/j.wocn.2004.02.002

Michnowicz, Jim & Hilary Barnes. 2013. A sociolinguistic analysis of pre-nuclear peak alignment in Yucatan Spanish. In Chad Howe, Sarah E. Blackwell & Margaret Lubbers Quesada (eds.), *Selected Proceedings of the 15th Hispanic Linguistics Symposium*, 221–235. Cascadilla Proceedings Project.

Miller, Jessica. 2007. *Swiss French prosody: Intonation, rate, and speaking style in the Vaud Canton.* PhD dissertation, University of Illinois Urbana-Champaign.

Milroy, Lesley & Matthew J. Gordon. 2003. *Sociolinguistics: Method and interpretation.* Blackwell.

Minematsu, Nobuaki (ed.). 2020. *Proceedings of Speech Prosody 2020.* International Speech Communication Association.

Moreno Fernández, Francisco. 1999. Aspectos sociolingüísticos de la entonación en el español de Alcalá de Henares (Madrid): A propósito de dos enunciados interrogativos. In Amparo Morales, Julia Cardona, Humberto López Morales & Eduardo Forastieri (eds.), *Estudios de lingüística hispánica: Homenaje a María Vaquero*, 348–371. Universidad de Puerto Rico.

Moutinho, Lurdes de Castro, Rosa Lídia Coimbra, Albert Rilliard & Antonio Romano. 2011. Mesure de la variation prosodique diatopique en portugais européen. *Estudios de Fonética Experimental* 20. 33–55.

Muñiz-Cachón, Carmen. 2019. Prosody: A feature of languages or a feature of speakers? Asturian and Castilian in the center of Asturias. *Spanish in Context* 16(3). 462–474. https://doi.org/10.1075/sic.00047.mun

Muntendam, Antje G. & Francisco Torreira. 2016. Focus and prosody in Spanish and Quechua. In Armstrong, Henriksen & Vanrell, 69–90.

Mysak, Edward D. 1959. Pitch and duration characteristics of older males. *Journal of Speech and Hearing Research* 2. 46–54. https://doi.org/10.1044/jshr.0201.46

Mzemba, Diverson. 2014. Language contact and intonation: The case of three generations of Francophones in Peace River Region, Alberta. *Cahiers Linguistiques d'Ottawa/ Ottawa Papers in Linguistics* 39. 1–17. http:// doi.org/10.13140/2.1.1605.8881

Mzemba, Diverson, 2016. Intonation et contact de langues: Le cas de l'intonation du français parlé à Rivière-La-Paix, Alberta. *Electronic Thesis and Dissertation Repository.* 4063. https://ir.lib.uwo.ca/etd/4063

Nance, Claire, Sam Kirkham & Eve Groarke. 2018. Studying intonation in varieties of English: Gender and individual variation in Liverpool. In Natalie Braver & Sandra Jansen (eds.), *Sociolinguistics in England*, 275–295. Palgrave.

O'Connor, Joseph D. & Gordon F. Arnold. 1973. *Intonation of colloquial English.* Longman.

O'Rourke, Erin. 2004. Peak placement in two regional varieties of Peruvian Spanish intonation. In Julie Auger, J. Clancy Clements & Barbara S. Vance (eds.), *Contemporary approaches to Romance linguistics: Selected papers from the 33rd Linguistic Symposium on Romance Languages (LSRL), Bloomington, Indiana, April 2003,* 321–341. John Benjamins.

O'Rourke, Erin. 2005. *Intonation and language contact: A case study of two varieties of Peruvian Spanish.* PhD dissertation, University of Illinois Urbana-Champaign.

O'Rourke, Erin. 2006. The direction of inflection: Downtrends and uptrends in Peruvian Spanish broad focus declaratives. In Manuel Díaz-Campos (ed.), *Selected Proceedings of the 2nd Conference on Laboratory Approaches to Spanish Phonetics and Phonology*, 62–74. Cascadilla Proceedings Project.

O'Rourke, Erin. 2020. Peak alignment and downstep revisited: Language contact and gender in Peruvian Spanish intonation. Paper presented at Intonation, Language Contact and Social Factors (ILCSF), Bilbao, Spain.

Olson, Daniel & Marta Ortega-Llebaria. 2010. The perceptual relevance of code switching and intonation in creating narrow focus. In Marta Ortega-Llebaria (ed.), *Selected proceedings of the 4th Conference on Laboratory Approaches to Spanish Phonology*, 57–68. Cascadilla Proceedings Project.

Orozco, Leonor. 2008. Peticiones corteses y factores prosódicos. In Pedro Martín Butragueño & Esther Herrera (eds.), *Fonología instrumental: Patrones fónicos y variación*, 335–356. El Colegio de México.

Orozco, Leonor. 2010. *Estudio sociolingüístico de la cortesía en tratamientos y peticiones: Datos de Guadalajara*. PhD dissertation, El Colegio de México.

Orrico, Riccardo & Mariapaola D'Imperio. 2020. Individual empathy levels affect gradual intonation-meaning mapping: The case of biased questions in Salerno Italian. *Laboratory Phonology* 11(1). 12. https://doi.org/10.5334/labphon.238

Peng, Shu-hui, Marjorie K.M. Chan, Chiu-yu Tseng, Tsan Huang, Ok Joo Lee & Mary E. Beckman. 2005. Towards a pan-Mandarin system for prosodic transcription. In Jun, 230–270.

Pešková, Andrea, Ingo Feldhausen, Elena Kireva & Christoph Gabriel. 2012. Diachronic prosody of a contact variety: Analyzing Porteño Spanish spontaneous speech. In Kurt Braunmüller & Christoph Gabriel (eds.), *Multilingual individuals and multilingual societies*, 365–389. John Benjamins.

Peters, Jörg, Peter Gilles, Peter Auer & Margret Selting. 2002. Identification of regional varieties by intonational cues: An experimental study on Hamburg and Berlin German. *Language and Speech* 45(2). 115–138. https://doi.org/10.1177/00238309020450020201

Pierrehumbert, Janet B. 1980. *The phonology & phonetics of English intonation*. PhD dissertation, MIT.

Pitrelli, John F., Mary E. Beckman & Julia Hirschberg. 1994. Evaluation of prosodic transcription labeling reliability in the ToBI framework. In *International Conference on Spoken Language Processing*, 123–126. http://doi.org/10.21437/ICSLP.1994-34

Podesva, Robert J. 2011. Salience and the social meaning of declarative contours: Three case studies of Gay professionals. *Journal of English Linguistics* 39(3). 233–264. https://doi.org/10.1177/0075424211405161

Podesva, Robert J., Sarah J. Roberts & Kathryn Campbell-Kibler. 2002. Sharing resources and indexing meanings in the production of Gay styles. In Kathryn Campbell-Kibler, Robert J. Podesva, Sarah J. Roberts & Andrew Wong (eds.), *Language and sexuality: Contesting meaning in theory and practice*, 175–189. CSLI Publications.

Portes, Cristel & James Sneed German. 2019. Implicit effects of regional cues on the interpretation of intonation by Corsican French listeners. *Laboratory Phonology* 10(1). 22. https://doi.org/10.5334/labphon.162

Prieto, Pilar. 2003. Teorías lingüísticas de la entonación. In Pilar Prieto (ed.), *Teorías de la entonación*, 13–34. Ariel.

Prieto, Pilar & Paolo Roseano (coords.). 2009–2013. *Atlas interactivo de la entonación del español*. http://prosodia.upf.edu/atlasentonacion/

Prieto, Pilar & Paolo Roseano (eds.). 2010. *Transcription of intonation of the Spanish language*. Lincom Europa.

Prieto, Pilar, Joan Borràs-Comes & Paolo Roseano (coords.). 2010–2014. *Interactive Atlas of Romance Intonation*. http://prosodia.upf.edu/iari/

Queen, Robin. 2001. Bilingual intonation patterns: Evidence of language change from Turkish-German bilingual children. *Language in Society* 30(1). 55–80. https://doi.org/10.1017/S0047404501001038

Queen, Robin. 2012. Turkish-German bilinguals and their intonation: Triangulating evidence about contact-induced language change. *Language* 88(4). 791–816. https://doi.org/10.1353/LAN.2012.0078

R Core Team. 2022. *R: A language and environment for statistical computing*. R Foundation for Statistical Computing. www.R-project.org

Rao, Rajiv & Sandro Sessarego. 2016. On the intonation of Afro-Bolivian Spanish declaratives: Implications for a theory of Afro-Hispanic creole genesis. *Lingua* 174. 45–64. https://doi.org/10.1016/J.LINGUA.2015.12.006

Rao, Rajiv & Sandro Sessarego. 2018. The intonation of Chota Valley Spanish: Contact-induced phenomena at the discourse-phonology interface. *Studies in Hispanic and Lusophone Linguistics* 11(1). 163–192. https://doi.org/10.1515/shll-2018-0006

Reed, Paul. 2016. *The sociophonetics of Appalachian English: Identity, intonation, and monophthongization*. PhD dissertation, University of South Carolina.

Reed, Paul. 2020. Inter-and intra-regional variation in intonation: An analysis of rising pitch accents and root-edness. *Journal of the Acoustical Society of America* 147(1). 616–626. https://doi.org/10.1121/10.0000576

Ritchart, Amanda & Amalia Arvaniti. 2014. The form and use of uptalk in Southern California English. In Campbell, Gibbon & Hirst, 331–335.

Rodero Antón, Emma. 2013. Peculiar styles when narrating the news: The intonation of radio news bulletins. *Estudios sobre el mensaje periodístico* 19(1). 519–532. https://doi.org/10.5209/rev_ESMP.2013.v19.n1.42536

Romano, Antonio, Jean-Pierre Lai & Stefania Roullet. 2005. La méthodologie AMPER. Géolinguistique, Projet AMPER–Atlas Multimédia Prosodique de l'Espace Roman.

Romera, Magdalena & Gorka Elordieta. 2013. Prosodic accommodation in language contact: Spanish intonation in Majorca. *International Journal of the Sociology of Language* 2013. 127–151. https://doi.org/10.1515/ijsl-2013-0026

Roseano, Paolo, Ana Ma Fernández Planas, Wendy Elvira-García & Eugenio Martínez Celdrán. 2015. Contacto lingüístico y transferencia prosódica: El caso del alguerés. *Dialectologia et Geolinguistica* 23. 95–123. https://doi.org/10.1515/dialect-2015-0006

Roseano, Paolo, Wendy Elvira-García & Ana Ma Fernández-Planas. 2017. Calcu-Dista: A tool for dialectometric analysis of intonational variation. *Revista de Lingüística Teórica y Aplicada Concepción* 55(2). 63–87. https://doi.org/10.4067/S0718-48832017000200063

Sankoff, Gillian. 2013. Linguistic outcomes of bilingualism. In Chambers & Schilling, 501–514.

Savino, Michelina. 2012. The intonation of polar questions in Italian: Where is the rise? *Journal of the International Phonetic Association* 42(1). 23–48. https://doi.org/10.1017/S002510031100048X

Schneider, Edgar W. 2007. *Postcolonial English: Varieties around the world.* Cambridge University Press.

The Scottish Consortium for ICPhS 2015 (ed.). 2015. *Proceedings of the 18th International Congress of Phonetic Sciences.* University of Glasgow.

Selker, Ravi, Jonathon Love, Damian Dropmann & Victor Moreno. 2022. jmv: The "jamovi" analyses. R package version 2.3.4. https://CRAN.R-project.org/package=jmv

Serra, Carolina. 2009. *Realização e percepção de fronteiras prosódicas no Português do Brasil: Fala espontânea e leitura.* PhD dissertation, Universidade Federal do Rio de Janeiro.

Shar, Elizabeth. 2018. *Expressing gender and Queer identity with intonation: Variation amongst masculine, neutral, and feminine aligning AFAB Queer speakers in DC.* PhD dissertation, Georgetown University.

Sichel-Bazin, Rafèu, Carolin Buthke & Trudel Meisenburg. 2012. Language contact and prosodic interference: Nuclear configurations in Occitan and French statements of the obvious. In Qiuwu Ma, Hongwei Ding & Daniel Hirst (eds.), *Speech Prosody 2012, Sixth International Conference.* 414–417. ISCA Archive.

Signorello, Rosario, Didier Demolin, Nathalie Henrich Bernardoni, Bruce R. Gerratt, Zhaoyan Zhang & Jody Kreiman. 2020. Vocal fundamental frequency and sound pressure level in charismatic speech: A cross-gender and language study. *Journal of Voice* 34(5). 808.e1–808.e13. https://doi.org/10.1016/j.jvoice.2019.04.007

Silva-Corvalán, Carmen. 2001. *Sociolingüística y pragmática del español.* Georgetown University Press.

Silva-Corvalán, Carmen & Andrés Enrique-Arias. 2017. *Sociolingüística y pragmática del español: Segunda edición.* Georgetown University Press.

Silverman, Kim, Eleonora Blaauw, Judith Spitz & John F. Pitrelli. 1992. A prosodic comparison of spontaneous speech and read speech. In *Proceedings of the 2nd International Conference on Spoken Language Processing (ICSLP 1992),* 1299–1302. http://doi.org/10.21437/ICSLP.1992-349

Simo Bobda, Augustin. 2004. Cameroon English: Phonology. In Bernd Kortmann & Edgar Schneider (eds.) with Kate Burridge, Rajend Mesthrie & Clive Upton, *A handbook of varieties of English: A multimedia reference tool,* 885–901. Mouton de Gruyter.

Simon, Anne Catherine, Philippe Hambye, Alice Bardiaux & Philippe Boula de Mareüil. 2012. Caractéristiques des accents régionaux en français: Que nous apprennent les approches perceptives? In Anne Catherine Simon (ed.), *La variation prosodique régionale en français,* 27–40. De Boeck supérieur.

Simonet, Miguel. 2008. *Language contact in Majorca: An experimental sociophonetic approach.* PhD dissertation, University of Illinois Urbana-Champaign.

Slobe, Tyanna. 2018. Style, stance, and social meaning in mock white girl. *Language in Society* 47(4). 541–567. https://doi.org/10.1017/S004740451800060X

Sóskuthy, Márton & Jane Stuart-Smith. 2020. Voice quality and coda /r/ in Glasgow English in the early 20th century. *Language Variation and Change* 32(2). 133–157. https://doi.org/10.1017/S0954394520000071

Stanford, James N. 2010. Gender, generations, and nations: An experiment in Hmong American discourse and sociophonetics. *Language Communication* 30(4). 285–296. https://doi.org/10.1016/j.langcom.2010.05.002

Stewart, Jesse. 2015. Intonation patterns in Pijal Media Lengua. *Journal of Language Contact* 8(2). 223–262. https://doi.org/10.1163/19552629-00802003

Stirling, Lesley, Janet Fletcher, Ilana Mushin & Roger Wales. 2001. Representational issues in annotation: Using the Australian map task corpus to relate prosody and discourse structure. *Speech Communication* 33(1–2). 113–134. https://doi.org/10.1016/S0167-6393(00)00072-8

Stuart-Smith, Jane. 2020. Changing perspectives on /s/ and gender over time in Glasgow. *Linguistics Vanguard* 6(s1): 20180064. https://doi.org/10.1515/lingvan-2018-0064

Šturm, Pavel. 2015. International Phonetic Congresses: The shift in research practices and areas of interest over 44 years. In Scottish Consortium for ICPhS 2015, Paper 182.

Sullivan, Jennifer N. 2011. *Approaching intonational distance and change*. PhD dissertation, University of Edinburgh.

Tagliamonte, Sali A. 2006. *Analysing sociolinguistic variation*. Cambridge University Press.

Tagliamonte, Sali A. 2011. *Variationist sociolinguistics: Change, observation, interpretation*. Wiley-Blackwell.

Tagliamonte, Sali A. 2015. *Making waves: The story of variationist sociolinguistics*. Wiley.

Takano, Shoji. 2008. Variation in prosodic focus of the Japanese negative "nai": Issues of language specificity, interactive style and register. In Kimberly Jones & Tsuyishi Ono (eds.), *Style shifting in Japanese*, 285–327. John Benjamins.

Takano, Shoji & Ichiro Ota. 2017. A sociophonetic approach to variation in Japanese pitch realizations: Region, age, gender and stylistic parameters. *Asia-Pacific Language Variation* 3(1). 5–40. https://doi.org/10.1075/aplv.3.1.02tak

Thomas, Erik R. 2013. Sociophonetics. In Chambers & Schilling, 108–127.

Thomas, Erik R. 2015. Prosodic features of African American English. In Sonja Lanehart (ed.), *The Oxford handbook of African American Language*, 420–438. Oxford University Press.

Thomason, Sarah. 2008. Social and linguistic factors as predictors of contact-induced change. *Journal of Language Contact* 2(1). 42–56. https://doi.org/10.1163/000000008792525381

Tomlinson, John M., Jr., Nicole Gotzner & Lewis Bott. 2017. Intonation and pragmatic enrichment: How intonation constrains ad hoc scalar inferences. *Language and Speech* 60(2). 200–223. https://doi.org/10.1177/0023830917716101

Trudgill, Peter. 2011. *Sociolinguistic typology: Social determinants of linguistic complexity*. Oxford University Press.

van Bezooijen, Renée. 1988. The relative importance of pronunciation, prosody, and voice quality for the attribution of social status and personality characteristics. In Roeland van Hout & Uus Knops (eds.), *Language attitudes in the Dutch language area*, 85–104. De Gruyter Mouton.

van Bezooijen, Renée & Charlotte Gooskens. 1999. Identification of language varieties: The contribution of different linguistic levels. *Journal of Language and Social Psychology* 18(1). 31–48. https://doi.org/10.1177/0261927X99018001003

Van Borsel, John, Jana Vandaele & Paul Corthals. 2013. Pitch and pitch variation in lesbian women. *Journal of Voice* 27(5). 656.e13–656.e16. https://doi.org/10.1016/j.jvoice.2013.04.008

van Buren, Jackelyn. 2017. *Cuasi nomás Inglés: Prosody at the crossroads of Spanish and English in 20th century New Mexico*. PhD dissertation, University of New Mexico.

van Heuven, Vincent J. & Judith Haan. 2000. Phonetic correlates of statement versus question intonation in Dutch. In Antonis Botinis (ed.), *Intonation: Analysis, modelling and technology*, 119–144. Kluwer.

van Leyden, Klaske. 2004. *Prosodic characteristics of Orkney and Shetland dialects: An experimental approach*. PhD dissertation, Leiden University.

Vanrell, Maria del Mar, Ingo Feldhausen & Lluïsa Astruc. 2018. The discourse completion task in Romance prosody research: Status quo and outlook. In Ingo Feldhausen, Jan Fliessbach & Maria del Mar Vanrell (eds.), *Methods in prosody: A Romance language perspective*, 191–227. Language Science Press.

Vella, Alexandra. 2003. Language contact and Maltese intonation. In Kurt Braunmüller & Gisella Ferraresi (eds.), *Aspects of multilingualism in European language history*, 261–283. John Benjamins.

Vergara, Daniel. 2015. Uptalk in Spanish dating shows? *University of Pennsylvania Working Papers in Linguistics* 21(2). 185–196. https://repository.upenn.edu/pwpl/vol21/iss2/21

Vion, Monique & Annie Colas. 2006. Pitch cues for the recognition of yes-no questions in French. *Journal of Psycholinguistic Research* 35(5). 427–445. https://doi.org/10.1007/s10936-006-9023-x

Warren, Paul. 2005. Patterns of late rising in New Zealand English: Intonational variation or intonational change? *Language Variation and Change* 17(2). 209–230. https://doi.org/10.1017/S095439450 505009X

Warren, Paul. 2014. Sociophonetic and prosodic influences on judgements of sentence type. In Jennifer Hay & Emma Parnell (eds.), *Proceedings of the 15th Australasian International Conference on Speech Science and Technology*, 185–188. ASSTA.

Warren, Paul. 2017. The interpretation of prosodic variability in the context of accompanying sociophonetic cues. *Laboratory Phonology* 8(1). 11. https://doi.org/10.5334/labphon.92

Watts, Richard J. 2003. *Politeness*. Cambridge University Press.

Wharton, Tim. 2012. *Pragmatics and prosody*. In Keith Allan & Kasia M. Jaszczolt (eds.), *The Cambridge handbook of pragmatics*, 567–585. Cambridge University Press.

Willis, Erik Wayne. 2003. *The intonational system of Dominican Spanish: Findings and analysis*. PhD dissertation, University of Illinois Urbana-Champaign.

Winter, Bodo & Sven Grawunder. 2011. The polite voice in Korean: Searching for acoustic correlates of *contaymal* and *panmal*. *Japanese/Korean Linguistics* 19. 419–431.

Winter, Bodo & Sven Grawunder. 2012. The phonetic profile of Korean formal and informal speech registers. *Journal of Phonetics* 40(6). 808–815. https://doi.org/10.1016/j.wocn.2012.08.006

Xu, Yi. 2005. Speech melody as articulatorily implemented communicative functions. *Speech Communication* 46. 220–251. https://doi.org/10.1016/j.specom.2005.02.014

Xu, Yi, Albert Lee, Santitham Prom-on & Fang Liu. 2015. Explaining the PENTA model: A reply to Arvaniti and Ladd. *Phonology* 32(3). 505–535. https://doi.org/10.1017/S0952675715000299

Yaeger-Dror, Malcah & Zsuzsanna Fagyal. 2011. Analyzing prosody: Best practices for the analysis of prosody. In Marianna Di Paolo & Malcah Yaeger-Dror (eds.), *Sociophonetics: A student's guide*, 119–130. Routledge.

Yaeger-Dror, Malcah, Tania Granadillo, Shoji Takano & Lauren Hall-Lew. 2010. The sociophonetics of prosodic contours on NEG in three language communities: Teasing apart sociolinguistic and phonetic influences on speech. In Dennis R. Preston & Nancy Niedzielski (eds.), *A reader in sociophonetics*, 133–176. De Gruyter Mouton.

Yaeger-Dror, Malcah, Lauren Hall-Lew & Sharon Deckert. 2002. It's not or isn't it?: Using large corpora to determine the influences on contraction strategies. *Language Variation and Change* 14(1). 79–118. https://doi.org/10.1017/S0954394502141044

Yaeger-Dror, Malcah, Lauren Hall-Lew & Sharon Deckert. 2003. Situational variation in prosodic strategies. In Charles F. Meyers & Pepi Leistyna (eds.), *Corpus analysis: Language structure and language use*, 209–224. Rodopi.

Zerbian, Sabine. 2013. Prosodic marking of narrow focus across varieties of South African English. *English World-Wide* 34(1). 26–47. https://doi.org/10.1075/eww.34.1.02zer

3

SOCIOPHONETICS AND SPEECH RATE AND PAUSE

Tyler Kendall

Introduction

The growth of sociophonetics has coincided with an increased focus on aspects of prosody from sociolinguistic perspectives. Prosody includes a wide range of suprasegmental features in language, including the topics of this chapter: speech rate, sometimes referred to as tempo, and pausing. Other prosodic phenomena include rhythm and stress, as well as intonation (O'Rourke & Baltazani this volume), the melody of speech. At first mention, speech rate and pause may appear two very different areas of prosody. However, they are united in several ways: in the ways that they can contribute to understanding processes of language variation and change and the interfaces between language and cognition, in their combined influence on listeners' perceptions of talkers, and in the methodologies used to examine them.

Measures of speech rate encompass the speed at which different linguistic units, typically syllables, are produced. In this way, rate phenomena are related and relatable to other areas of prosody, such as rhythm, as well as segmental properties like duration. Silent pauses represent the absence of speech and are both a normal part of speech timing—since speech always alternates with silence—but also can relate to disfluency phenomena or aspects of discourse such as turn-management. Both disfluent (silent and filled, like *uh* and *um*) pauses and fluent pauses have been of interest to researchers working to understand the cognitive processes underlying language production. While speech rate and pause are different core phenomena with different—it would seem—sources within speech production processes, they appear to be related in their effects on the listener. Perceptions, and attitudes, about speech rates are a function not just of the actual rate at which a speaker produces syllables of speech but of a confluence of timing features that contribute together to a percept of a "fast talker" or a "slow talker." Methodologically, both speech rate and pause are united in being measurable from similar source data, since both involve measures of temporal duration and frequencies of occurrence.

DOI: 10.4324/9781003034636-4

Why should sociophoneticians care about speech rate and pause? In 2013, I argued that

> Rate of speech and pause are ubiquitous features of human language. Every utterance by every speaker of every language (even sign languages) can be characterized as having a particular rate of production and by being in relation to some intervals of silence.
>
> Kendall 2013:8

This was one part of the motivation in my earliest interests in speech rate and pause. In terms purely of data analysis, there is no hunting for data or searching corpora for relevant instances of the phenomena. They are everywhere. This plethora of data is not just a methodological benefit in making data easy to come by, but allows for greater comparison between speakers and communities than most any other feature in speech. Further, and more importantly for substantive sociolinguistic questions, "notions of rate differences are central to popular beliefs about dialect difference" (2013:16). That is, much popular discourse about language and dialect differences hinges on notions involving tempo (for instance, popular notions that Spanish is faster than English, e.g., Devlin 2021, or character types like the fast-talking used-car salesman). Speech rate and pause also bridge between topics of interest in the domain of the socio- and topics related to cognition and the processing of language. For over a half-century, pauses and features related to rate have played important roles in probing the nature of language production (Maclay & Osgood 1959; Goldman-Eisler 1968). It should also be noted that speech rate and pause are features of great relevance to approaches to language in the articulatory phonology framework (Browman & Goldstein 1992), which places a central focus on speech timing (see Turk & Shattuck-Hufnagel 2020). This chapter does not draw much from work in this related area, but we should note that speech rate, pause, and other speech timing features provide opportunities to bridge between sociophonetic interests and the growing body of work in articulatory phonology and its extensions (again see Turk & Shattuck-Hufnagel 2020).

Despite all this, and despite a growing range of work on speech rate and pause across allied disciplines, including not just the areas just mentioned, but also work in speech pathology and in forensic domains, research on speech rate and pause within sociophonetics has remained somewhat peripheral; much less work has been done on these features than on several other areas of prosody, like rhythm and intonation. In this chapter I hope to show that speech rate and pause represent areas of great opportunity for sociophonetics, both for advancing knowledge about key sociophonetic topics and for building bridges between sociophonetics and allied areas. Drawing in particular from my own studies (Kendall 2009, 2013), this chapter reviews recent sociophonetic and allied work on these two sets of features, and further considers the important role that these features can play as independent variables in the analysis of other sociophonetic phenomena. The chapter also exemplifies analyses of these features through some brief explorations of data from the Corpus of Regional African American Language (CORAAL; Kendall & Farrington 2020a), a public spoken language corpus providing speech along with accurately time-aligned orthographic transcripts from several communities. But first we start by further defining notions of rate and pause and describing more of what this chapter will cover.

Defining speech rate

In general terms, "speech rate" or "speech tempo" refers simply to the amount of spoken material produced over some span of time. As such, this can encompass a wide range of specific measures, from "speaking rate," a term often used to describe a broad measure of rate, including disfluencies and pauses, to what is commonly referred to as "articulation rate," the number of syllables produced in a span of uninterrupted speech, excluding disfluencies and pauses. Measures can also be computed over different spans of time. Articulation rate measures, which again are exclusive of pauses, tend to be measures within prosodic utterances of some sort and reported in terms of syllables per second, although studies might also investigate articulation rate within individual words or other prosodic units smaller than utterances or intonational phrases. Speaking rate, on the other hand, is often used as a global measure, over, for instance, an entire passage of speech. Sometimes speaking rate is reported in words per minute and other times syllables per minute.

Articulation rates are known to be variable within utterances, with phrase-final lengthening typically slowing the rates towards the ends of utterances (Turk & Shattuck-Hufnagel 2007; Thomas & Kendall 2019) and anticipatory shortening increasing the rates in longer utterances (Bishop & Kim 2018). Dankovičová asked about the "domain" of articulation rate "within which it varies systematically," finding that

> This domain is the intonation phrase and the pattern of variation is a slowing down throughout the phrase. The analysis also showed that the slowing down is non-linear; it is rather gradual across non-final words, with the last word within the phrase being significantly slower than any other proceeding words within the same phrase.
>
> Dankovičová 2001:65

Kendall (2013) considers these definitions and literatures more thoroughly, and readers are referred to that work for a more in-depth review of the literature. An important point for general purposes is that different studies implement measures of speech rate in different ways and this can make it surprisingly difficult to compare quantitative results across studies. Further, since measures of rate are computed from other, more basic/direct measures (numbers of syllables or words divided by some unit of time), rates can sometimes be directly, that is, mathematically, transposable to other measures, such as average syllable length. In other cases, however, different underlying techniques can lead similar-sounding data to be impossible to compare. That is, just because two studies present data on articulation rates in syllables per second does not mean that those measures are directly relatable. For instance, studies vary in terms of which utterances are included in an analysis or whether hesitation phenomena like filled pauses are excised from their data and this can have large ramifications on the emerging patterns, despite the fact that studies may appear to examine rates as measured in the same way (see Jacewicz, Fox & Wei 2010:845–846; Kendall 2013:33–34).

A large-scale analysis of articulation rates I conducted in Kendall (2013) identified the non-linear influence of utterance length on articulation rates as depicted in Figure 3.1. The shortest utterances have the slowest rates, but there is rapid increase in articulation rates as utterance lengths increase from one to about five syllables. This is, at least in large part, due to the fact that many short utterances in natural discourse are produced slowly for pragmatic and turn-management reasons ("Well …") or involve disfluencies ("The—(pause) the reason is …"). Further, phrase-final lengthening affects shorter utterances more than longer utterances since a larger proportion of the syllables are affected in shorter utterances (Kendall 2013:95). Thus, it is clear that different definitions of utterances and different analyst decisions about what kinds of utterances to include in an analysis will have a major impact on the resultant patterns.

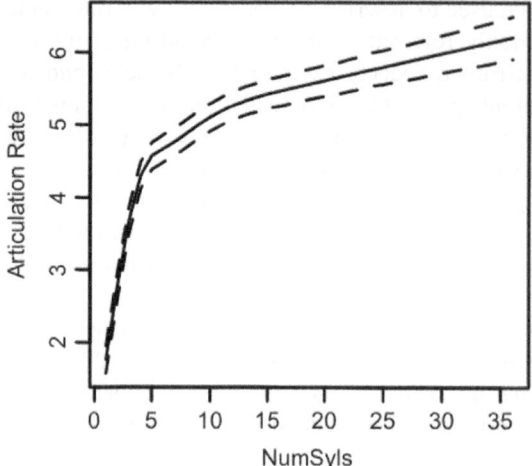

Figure 3.1   Model results for effect of utterance length (in syllables; NumSyls) on utterance articulation
rates, from ~30,000 measurements from 159 American English speakers

Source: Kendall 2013:Figure 5.3. Reproduced with permission of Palgrave Macmillan

Defining pause

Similar to speech rate, terminology around pauses can also include or exclude a wide range of
phenomena. Many studies of pauses, including the bulk of my own, focus on silent pauses, breaks
in the flow of speech, and it is naturally these pauses that align with speech rate in analytic terms.
Silent pauses can be examined in terms of their duration or their frequency. Pauses can also be
examined as within-speaker phenomena—within individual speakers' turns of talk—or as properties of the larger discourse (as in Mendoza-Denton's 1995 study of the role of pauses between
speakers' turns in the Anita Hill–Clarence Thomas hearings). Within an individual speaker's
speech we might also be interested in fluent (or "grammatical") pauses, silences occurring at structural, phrasal, or clausal boundaries, and/or pauses that fall in non-grammatical locations, as evidence of disfluencies like speech errors or repairs.

An issue of importance in studying pauses is the threshold values used to delimit which pauses
are deemed relevant in an analysis. It is quite common for studies to isolate pauses for analysis
using low threshold values of 100 milliseconds or 250 milliseconds, ignoring shorter silences
than these. Acoustic analysis software has made the detection and measurement of very short
pauses possible. Some of the studies I conducted in Kendall (2013) included pauses as short as 60
milliseconds in the data analyzed. Pauses of very short durations at some point overlap with articulatory silences, such as stop-gaps (periods of no or minimal acoustic energy due to the occlusion
of the vocal passage), and thus analysts have to make decisions about trade-offs between types of
errors—missing actual pauses due to a threshold that is too high or including some silences that
are "of a different sort" due to a threshold that is too low. Some studies of pauses have taken less
categorical approaches to thresholds. For instance, Redford (2013) used a variable threshold criteria depending on syllabic context of each pause.

While low threshold criteria are often discussed in research reports, fewer studies have described
explicit criteria for the high thresholds set for selecting pauses for analysis. Is a 1-second pause
the same phenomena as a 500-millisecond pause? What about a 5-second pause? Especially in

the conversational kinds of talk examined in much sociolinguistic research, external distractions and non-vocal activities can contribute substantially to silences during talk. Pauses are not just the result of the cognitive processes underlying language and speech production. In Kendall (2013) I included pauses up to 5 seconds in duration in many of the analyses, but found that relatively few pauses (2.4 percent of the pause dataset) were longer than 2 seconds in duration. In fact, that study, as well as others, identified that pauses distribute in a log-normal distribution with the bulk of the distribution near the low threshold used in the analysis. (See Kendall 2013:§6.3 for an in-depth exploration of silent pause duration distributions. This indicates that pause distributions should be analyzed according to this log-normal distribution, either log-transforming the data for analysis or using statistical techniques that are designed for log-normal data.)

Related to the importance of pauses as potential markers of disfluency, a small but growing body of work has investigated filled pauses—sounds (or words) like *uh*, *um*, and *er*. Filled pauses are interesting as indicators of language production processes and as related to discourse markers of other, less pause-y sorts (e.g., Clark & Fox Tree 2002). It is also notable that recent sociolinguistic studies have shown that filled pauses demonstrate interesting and important patterns of variation and change (e.g., Fruehwald 2016; Wieling et al. 2016; Erker & Bruso 2017). This chapter will only touch on filled pauses, focusing—as has much of the sociophonetic pause literature—on silent pauses.

Finally, it should be noted that speech breathing is an area related to pausing examined in the larger literature in the speech sciences (e.g., Grosjean & Collins 1979; Winkworth et al. 1995; McFarland 2001; Kallay, Mayr & Redford 2019). This work certainly has much to offer the larger understanding of pausing and speech timing, but breathing patterns in speech appear to be somewhat far afield from typical sociophonetic interests and I do not cover this area of work further in this chapter.

Studies of speech rate and pause

Speech rate and pause have been studied across a wide range of areas in linguistics and the speech sciences, and interest in these features spans more than a half-century of scientific engagement. The majority of studies have approached these features from perspectives outside of sociophonetics but many have still shed valuable insights relevant to sociophonetic interests. Some recent studies have examined these features specifically from sociophonetic perspectives.

Kendall (2009, 2013) represents one of the largest series of sociolinguistically oriented studies on speech rate and pause. My projects sought to leverage the large collection of orthographically transcribed sociolinguistic interview recordings housed in the Sociolinguistic Archive and Analysis Project (SLAAP; see Kendall 2009) to conduct an early "corpus-based sociophonetic" study. SLAAP's data and annotation structure, which is based on a finely accurate time-aligned transcription at the utterance level, lent itself to automatic extraction of temporal information. Coupled with automated syllable-counting procedures, which can be quite accurate even for languages like English with poor sound–spelling correspondences, speech rate measures are relatively easy to extract and analyze once one has accurately time-aligned and transcribed speech. Silent pauses can be extracted even more easily from such data, as they are represented in the transcript structure as the spans of time between utterances.

Figure 3.2a displays a short excerpt (8.35 seconds) of an interview from the Corpus of Regional African American Language, exemplifying a time-aligned transcription format. In the example, an intrasentential pause (of 610 milliseconds in duration) is highlighted. Figure 3.2b shows an analysis page in the SLAAP archive for the line "yeah we were older, but" in the

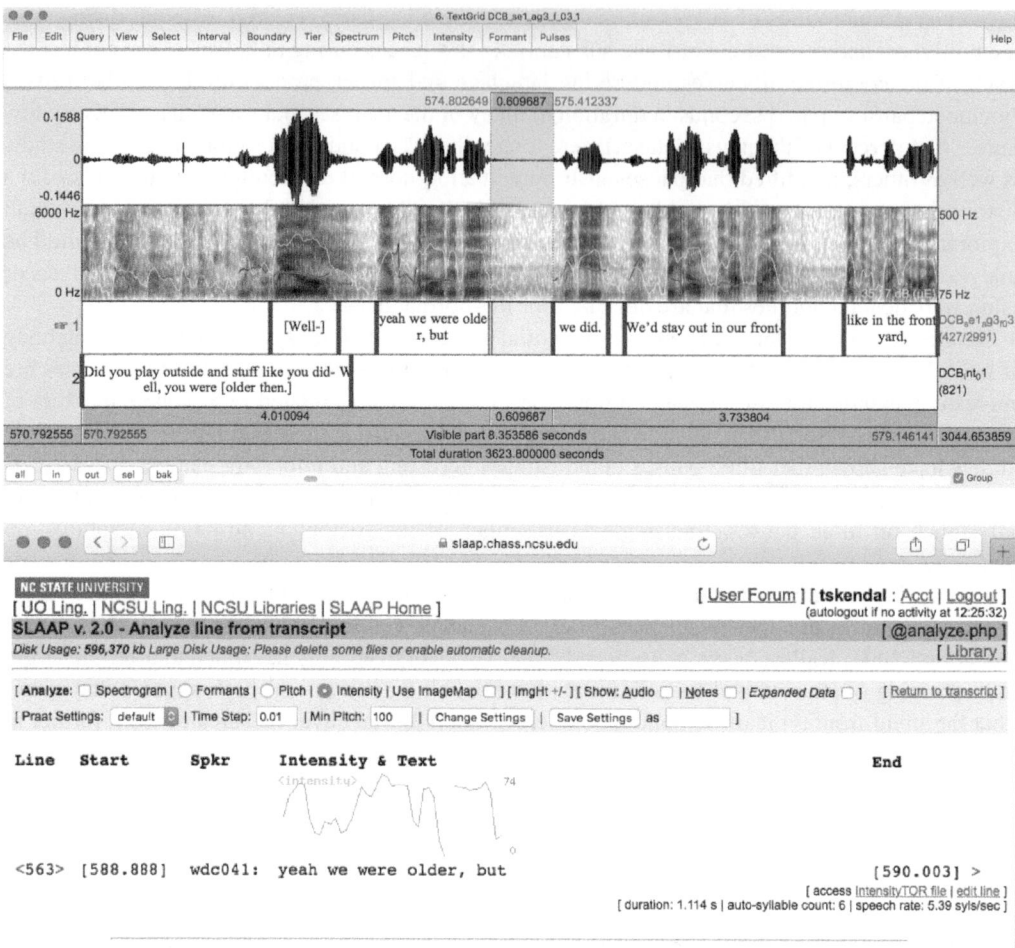

Figure 3.2 Excerpt of interview (DCB_se1_ag3_f_03) from CORAAL
Figure 3.2a (top) Praat screenshot with time-aligned transcription
Figure 3.2b (bottom) SLAAP screenshot

SLAAP version of the same recording. (SLAAP houses slightly different versions of the audio files from the public CORAAL files. The timestamps are slightly different between the two examples because SLAAP's files include some audio that is trimmed from the publicly available corpus files. wdc041 is SLAAP's speaker code for the speaker labeled DCB_se1_ag3_f_03 in the public CORAAL materials.) SLAAP's software automatically counts the syllables for each transcribed utterance and computes articulation rate, as shown in the bottom right portion of Figure 3.2b. (A syllable counter function for English in R [R Core Team 2022], based on the one used in Kendall 2013, is available at http://lingtools.uoregon.edu/coraal/explorer/examp les.php.)

Leveraging the data and data model just described, my studies in Kendall (2009, 2013) investigated a range of questions of sociolinguistic interest about speech rate and pause. Some aspects of the project focused on purely methodological questions, such as how mixed-effect

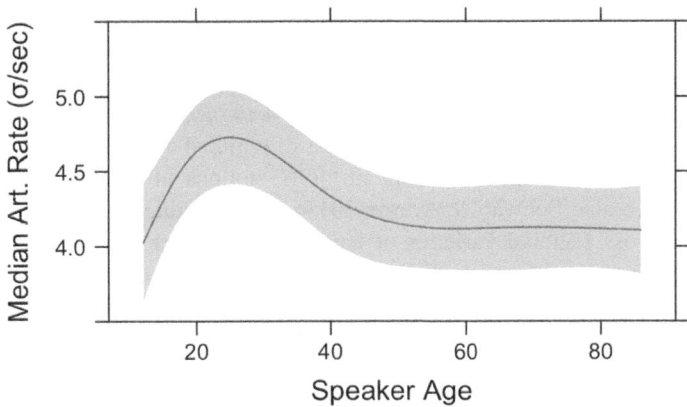

Figure 3.3   Age-graded pattern for articulation rate, modeled from conversational interview speech of 159
American English speakers

Source: Kendall 2013:Figure 5.8 (adapted). Reproduced with permission of Palgrave Macmillan

regression models of individual utterance-level articulation rate data compare to fixed-effect models of speaker central tendencies, and how many measurements are needed to gain a robust central tendency for a speaker. Other investigations focused on social predictors for speech rate and pause, finding that speakers' gender, ethnicity, and age significantly contribute to their timing patterns. In my main analysis for articulation rate (Kendall 2013:ch. 5), for instance, males are found to speak significantly faster than females, European Americans speak faster than speakers from other ethnic backgrounds, and age exhibited a curvilinear, age-graded pattern. This age pattern, modeled from the speech of 159 speakers in that dataset, is shown in Figure 3.3.

While pauses appear to play a major role in listeners' perceptions of speech rate, investigations of pause patterns have tended to find fewer social correlates than studies of articulation rate. Analyses in Kendall (2013), for instance, identified significant gender and regional patterns for pause durations, with males realizing longer pauses than females and speakers from Ohio realizing shorter pauses than speakers from the Southern communities in the study. These data also show some temporal consistency within speakers, such that speakers with faster articulation rates and fewer pauses also tended to have shorter pauses. However, the models for pause durations in the study fit the data much less well than the models for articulation rates, leading me to observe:

> We can, I think, interpret this outcome as roughly in line with the views of pause and articulation rate in the literature reviewed earlier, such as the work by Goldman-Eisler, Kowal, O'Connell, Feldstein, and others. The finding that articulation rate is quite socially mediated leaves less room for its variability to relate to cognitive aspects of speech production. Pause, on the other hand, does not appear to be (very) socially influenced and, as such, there is more space for its variability to relate potentially to cognitive and speech production processes.
>
> Kendall 2013:120

The data for these studies came from several original data collection projects across a number of regional sites in the United States (communities across the state of North Carolina and a community in Texas in the South, samples from parts of Ohio in the Midwest, a sample from Washington DC in the Mid-Atlantic), and a part of the studies' focus included probing the stereotype that Southerners talk more slowly than speakers from other US dialects. Findings were somewhat supportive with, for example, speakers from Ohio realizing significantly faster articulation rates and significantly shorter pause durations than speakers from central North Carolina (Kendall 2013:ch. 5). However, the data showed as much within-region variation within the South as cross-regional difference, ultimately mitigating any broad conclusions about the robustness of regional differences.

Perhaps related to the prominence of speech timing in "folk" notions of dialect difference (Niedzielski & Preston 2010; see also Schwab & Avanzi 2015), several other researchers have investigated rate differences across regional varieties of languages. Jacewicz et al. (2009) and Jacewicz, Fox & Wei (2010) examined English dialect differences in articulation rate across regions in the United States, and Clopper & Smiljanic (2015) investigated rate and silent pause duration and frequency in the context of the perception of the temporal organization of six US regional dialects. These studies, which set up more straightforward (i.e., intentional) regional comparisons than my own studies found relatively strong support for regional differences, with Southern US speakers in both studies showing slower articulation rates than other regions. Clopper & Smiljanic (2015) also found Southerners to exhibit longer pauses. However, other studies that also used controlled comparisons across regions, such as Ray & Zahn (1990), did not find significant regional patterns. English has not been the only language studied in this way, with, for instance, studies on regional (and national) differences in Dutch (Verhoeven et al. 2004; Quené 2008) and in French (Schwab & Avanzi 2015) finding regional differences in speech rates in their data, while a recent study of South Korean found no regional differences across a large sample of regionally distributed speakers (Lee et al. 2017). Whether or not articulation rate differences do show gross (i.e., substantial or persistent) regional patterns remains a question for future work. It may also ultimately be one that interacts too much with speech style and interactional factors to allow for such broad generalizations.

One area of complexity for speech timing studies—which I would argue can usefully be analogized to other phenomena like vowel variation—relates to questions about stylistic variability, context effects, and whether the samples of read and elicited speech used by many studies are comparable to natural conversational speech (or even to the elicited speech samples used by other studies). A number of studies have examined stylistic differences in speech samples directly. For instance, Hirose & Kawanami (2002) compared rate patterns in read speech and dialogues in Japanese and found the dialogue speech to be characterized by a dynamic ("acceleration-deacceleration") pattern not found in their read speech. Jacewicz et al. (2009) collected read sentence productions and short informal speech samples in their production study, finding persistent patterns where the read speech was produced more slowly than the spontaneous speech. In terms of social factors and style, Jacewicz, Fox & Wei (2010), examining the same data using more sophisticated statistical methods, identified similar regional patterns across both read and spontaneous speech but noted that gender and age-related patterns differed somewhat between the read and spontaneous speech. My own studies in Kendall (2013) did not compare read speech to spontaneous speech from the same individuals. However, my analyses of speech rate in reading passages collected for the Vowels in America project (Fridland & Kendall 2022) identified regional patterns, such that Western US speakers produced faster read speech than Northern and Southern US speakers, with Southerners realizing the slowest read speech, but it simultaneously uncovered patterns that appear to be specific to the style of the readings, including a significant pattern where participants speeded up their speech towards the end of the reading passage (Kendall 2013:ch. 4). Ultimately, it seems to me that speech timing is manipulated by speakers in potentially idiosyncratic ways when they are asked to produce laboratory speech or to read materials for an inquisitive linguist. Some participants produce such speech in a pedantic or reading-to-a-child style, while others read it as quickly as they possibly can (sometimes with monotonic or otherwise flattened intonational patterns). These observations led me to a primary interest in speech timing as it is realized in natural, conversational speech, the focus of the majority of my own speech timing studies.

From the perspective of Eckert's (2012) three waves model of sociolinguistic inquiry, we can note that the bulk of the studies just mentioned have approached patterns of variation and change in articulation rate from first-wave perspectives, asking how macro-social categories like region, age, and gender relate to variability in articulation rate. It is clear, however, that both articulation rate and pause represent features with great potential for the construction and performance of different kinds of identities and can certainly be put to work for more fluid social purposes. Schnoebelen (2009, 2010), for instance, explored indexical fields related to articulation rate (2009) and also how patterns of speech timing, like rate, work to convey affective states like "action readiness" (2010). Speech rate and pause also naturally tie in to work on discourse and talk-in-interaction. Many of my (Kendall 2009, 2013) investigations were motivated by prior work identifying different cultural conventions regarding silence in speech (e.g., Philips 1976; Lehtonen & Sajavaara 1985; Tannen 1985, 2000) and the importance of rate and pause features in discourse analysis and conversation analysis (e.g., Mendoza-Denton's 1995 study of the Anita Hill–Clarence Thomas hearings). Unfortunately, not much work has followed up on these connections to investigate the dynamic social meanings conveyed/negotiated through speech rate variation and the interfaces between talk-in-interaction and sociophonetic interests in areas such as language variation and change.

While my studies in Kendall (2013) were explicitly corpus-based and not ethnographic by design, I also investigated interactional patterns, like accommodation effects, in the data. Interactional patterns were notable for articulation rates, and complicate the notion that the gender, ethnicity, and age patterns described earlier are inherent or essential to particular social groups. Rather the patterns are better understood as socially constructed and functions of interactional routines rather than properties of specific groups—an observation that is congruent with other modern sociolinguistic theorizing (e.g., Bucholtz & Hall 2005; Eckert 2008). The age-graded pattern shown in Figure 3.3 could be as much a function of the fact that the sociolinguistic interviews were typically led by interviewers in their late twenties as they are of the speakers' own ages (Kendall 2013:119–120). Findings in the Kendall (2013) study also indicate that speakers talk faster when they are interviewed by someone of the same ethnicity as themselves and that speakers talk significantly more slowly when they are interviewed by a female interviewer in comparison to a male interviewer. It makes some sense that interview participants might be more comfortable when being interviewed by a stranger of similar age and ethnic background as themselves in comparison to someone more socially distant, but it is less obvious what drives the gender pattern with interviewers. Of course, the observation I just made is based on the tenuous premise that "comfortable" speech is faster speech, which itself needs empirical examination. After all, it cannot be that "fast speech" is comfortable, but rather that some range of speech rates are associated with speaker comfort, with particularly slow speech and particularly fast speech being marked in various and nonessential ways.

While the literature just surveyed bears on common sociophonetic interests, and some of the studies just discussed were explicitly framed as sociophonetic inquiries, many of the studies on speech rate and pause have approached these phenomena from speech and hearing science and applied perspectives, in particular in areas of speech pathology. Nonetheless, many of these studies have findings of interest to sociophonetics. For example, Robb, Maclagan & Chen (2004) compared speech rates between New Zealand English (NZE) and American English groups (finding that the NZE group realized significantly faster speech) to support the important argument that clinical work on the assessment and treatment of speech timing disorders needs to be sensitive to differences between varieties (see also Macrae & Maclagan this volume). Van Borsel & De Maesschalck (2008) examined gendered patterns in speech rates with the goal of providing guidance for clinicians working with transexual individuals (the study did not find significant differences between its groups of cis male, cis female, and trans female speakers). In fact, investigations in speech rate and pause have a long history in areas like clinical psychology, driven by a search for measures in speech that might be straightforwardly extracted and correlated with other psychological phenomena (such as "comfort" or, more commonly, depression; Teasdale et al. 1980; Siegman & Boyle 1993). It is also the case that speech rate and pause have been of interest in computational linguistics and natural language processing domains for their importance in automated speech recognition and for generating natural-sounding speech synthesis (e.g., Barbosa & Bailly 1994; Zellner 1998; Hirose & Kawanami 2002). Further, work on assessing nonnative speech (e.g., "scoring" speech proficiency for educational assessments) has long included measures of rates, pauses, and other disfluencies (e.g., Chen et al. 2018). Finally, quite a bit of work, relatively speaking, has examined speech rate and pause from forensic perspectives. For instance, Kunzel (1997) explored several temporal measures across three speech styles (semi-spontaneous interview speech, spontaneous conversation speech, and read speech in a voice-line-up style) with the goal of establishing some production and perception benchmarks for forensic purposes. McDougall & Duckworth (2018) examined a range of disfluencies in two speech styles (stimulated police interviews and phones calls with "accomplices") for 20 male Standard Southern British English (SSBE) speakers, identifying constituent patterns within speakers and suggesting that these patterns could be useful for forensic speaker comparison. And, returning briefly to filled pauses, Hughes, Wood & Foulkes (2016) acoustically analyzed the filled pauses of SSBE speakers, arguing for the value of filled pauses for forensic speaker comparison. As in other areas of sociophonetic research, such as the much more expansive literature on vowel variation, the intersection of sociophonetic and forensic research, as well as speech pathology, represent opportunities for convergence between fields.

Many of the studies focused explicitly on speech rate and pause, as indicated in this review, have focused on the analysis of production data. A deeper dive than can fit in this chapter will uncover some work on areas in perception, for instance Koreman's (2006) study of the perception of speech rate in spontaneous German speech and Quené's (2007) study of just-noticeable differences for speech tempo. Similarly, work on the perception and processing of prosody often intersects interests in speech rate and pause with other prosodic phenomena. As does, of course, other areas of language production research. As introduced earlier, phenomena like phrase-final lengthening relate closely to articulation rate variation. The duration of speech segments, such as vowels (see Fridland, Kendall & Farrington 2014), also has natural connections to rate, since ultimately speech rate is a function involving the duration of speech segments. Other aspects of prosody, like rhythm and stress, also relate to speech rate and pause both in terms of speech production and speech perception. For instance, Duez (1985, 1993) investigated the perception of pauses and showed that several prosodic cues beyond the attributes of the pauses themselves play a role in hearers' percepts of pauses; the presence of lengthened vowel duration alone can lead a listener to "hear" a pause, even without silence.

Filled pauses have also been studied with interesting outcomes. In a now classic and somewhat controversial study, Clark & Fox Tree (2002) proposed that the English filled pauses *uh* and *um* are, like other words, used by speakers in conversation to signal particular, conventionalized meanings, with *uh* signaling a brief delay and *um* a "major" delay. (Kendall 2013:§6.5 finds some support for this, showing that silent pauses co-occurring with *uh* and *um* are longer than silent pauses not co-occurring with filled pauses, and that silent pauses adjacent to *um* are longer than those adjacent to *uh*). Recent work, by Fruehwald (2016) and Weiling et al. (2016), has demonstrated that filled pauses change over time and exhibit other sociolinguistic patterns, such as differences related to speaker gender. Studies have also looked closely at the acoustics of filled pauses (e.g., Hughes, Wood & Foulkes 2016; de Boer & Heeren 2020), an undertaking with obvious relation to sociophonetic work. It is clear that future research on filled pauses will be able to shed important insights into sociophonetic, as well as other cognitive, questions about language.

Speech rate and pause as predictors of other phenomena

While this chapter has so far focused on studies of speech rate and pause, where these features are the overarching interest in sociophonetic, or related, studies, it is also the case that speech rate and pause play important roles as predictors of other sociophonetically important phenomena. It is perhaps here that speech rate and pause hold the most promise for upcoming work in sociophonetics, and we now turn to survey some of the ways that these and related factors have been and can be used as important parts of other, broader sociophonetic inquiries.

It is well known that the articulation of many speech features are functions of speech rate and/or durational aspects of the speech. Reduction phenomena, where phonetic and phonological features are produced with "incomplete articulatory gestures or fewer segments" (Ernestus & Warner 2011:253) relative to their canonical forms, are ubiquitous in natural, conversational speech. The speed of articulation is a major (but not the sole) factor underlying reduction. Not all sociolinguistic variables involve processes related to reduction (see Eckert & Labov 2017; Vaughn & Kendall 2019), but many do. It would seem important that speech rate measures be considered in analyses of these features, whether as a core part of one's interest or, more simply, as nuisance/control variables to help uncover the other patterns associated with the variable of interest. In some cases, the influence of articulation rate may be more a function of unit duration for some features (e.g., vowels), but in other cases rate itself may indeed be an important linguistic predictor. For instance, Farrington (2019) found that a local measure of speech rate (calculated as the number of vowels produced per second within a seven-word window around the analyzed word) was a significant predictor in his study of final /d/ deletion. Thus, it would seem prudent to include measures of rate as potential predictors in studies on a wide range of variable phenomena.

The inclusion of pauses as potential independent variables in sociolinguistic analyses has a longer history, at least in some traditions of work. Coronal stop deletion (CSD; also examined as t/d deletion or consonant cluster reduction) is among the most studied variables in the variationist sociolinguistic tradition (e.g., Guy 1980; Wolfram, Childs & Torbert 2000; Tagliamonte & Temple 2005; Guy, Hay & Walker 2008; Hazen 2011). The major linguistic factor influencing patterns of deletion is the phonological environment following the cluster containing the coronal stop. The presence of a following pause, as opposed to a vowel or consonant, is regularly found to be an important factor in CSD patterns, with different varieties showing different pre-pausal patterns (e.g., Wolfram, Childs & Torbert 2000). More recently, Tanner, Sonderegger & Wagner (2017) examined pause duration as a measurable proxy for prosodic boundary strength, itself an indicator of speech production planning, and found support for their hypothesis that longer pauses represent larger breaks in phonological planning and thus reduce the effect of upcoming consonants on rates of deletion.

As mentioned above, early research on pausing was largely in the service of using temporal phenomena to provide insights into larger questions about language production processes. Goldman-Eisler's (1968) classic book, *Psycholinguistics: Experiments in spontaneous speech*, reviewed her experimental work on pauses in spontaneous speech in order to probe how speakers produce language. A long line of research by herself and contemporaries led Goldman-Eisler to conclude that

> Pausing during the act of generating spontaneous speech is a highly variable phenomenon which is symptomatic of individual differences, sensitive to the pressure of social inter-action and to the requirements of verbal tasks and diminishing with learning, i.e. with the reduction in the spontaneity of the process.
>
> Goldman-Eisler 1968:15

Studies by other research groups over the years (see Kowal & O'Connell 1980; Crown & Feldstein 1985; Levelt 1989; Kircher et al. 2004) have added support to the understanding that pauses can be examined as indicative of underlying processes during speech and language production. This, it has seemed to me, raises interesting possibilities for hypothesis generation and testing related to questions of great importance to sociolinguistics. For instance, speech rate and pause measures provide opportunities to explore notions like Tamminga, MacKenzie & Embick's (2016) distinction between sociostylistic, internal linguistic, and psychophysiological conditioning factors underlying individual speakers' patterns of variable usage.

My own studies of speech rate and pause have been particularly influenced by a project undertaken by Goldman-Eisler and her colleagues. As a part of their interest in studying the role of pausing during speech planning in spontaneous speech, Henderson, Goldman-Eisler & Skarbek (1966) developed a visualization technique that both allows for a graphical presentation of speech timing as well as several quantitative measures derived from the technique. Following Levelt (1989), I have called this visualization method "Henderson graphing" and one of its important derivatives a "Henderson slope" measure. Figure 3.4 displays a sample Henderson graph, generated

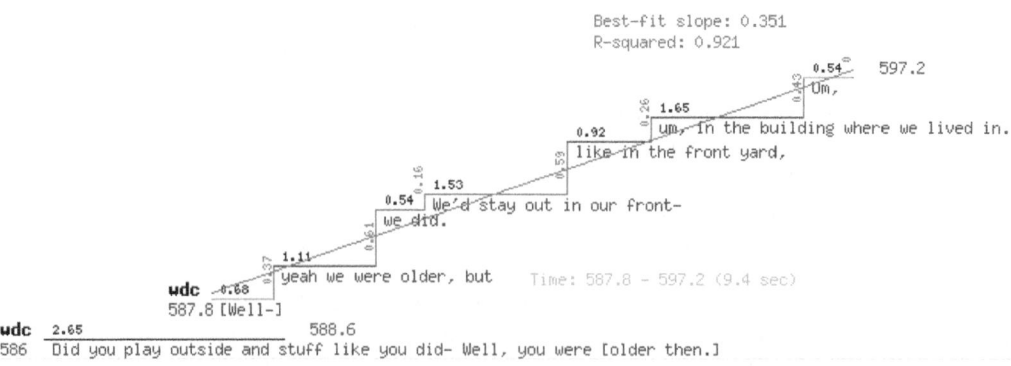

Figure 3.4   Henderson graph example for an excerpt of an interview (DCB_se1_ag3_f_03)

in SLAAP, for the same interview from CORAAL used for exemplification in Figures 3.2a and 3.2b. The example graph shows two speaker turns: a single utterance by the interviewer, followed by a longer turn by the interviewee (containing the speech displayed earlier in Figures 3.2a and 3.2b). The long turn by the interviewee, with its alternation of utterances and pauses, demonstrates the Henderson graph method, with a resultant slope value of 0.337.

As a part of my larger project investigating speech rate and pause patterns as sociolinguistically variable phenomena, I also asked how these temporal features can be used to predict other variable features and argued that the Henderson graph provides useful opportunities, and specific measures, for testing a range of questions about how speech timing and (dis)fluency relate to patterns of language variation. In Kendall (2009:ch. 10), I used Henderson graphs to explore the hypothesis that speech timing measures could gradiently capture the "performance" of traditional dialect features among younger speakers in Newfoundland, Canada, for whom the features are less integrated in their vernaculars ("vernacular," in the sense of Labov 2006[1996]:86, "a technical term to signify the language first acquired by the language learner controlled perfectly, and used primarily among intimate friends and family members"). In Kendall (2013:ch. 8) I used Henderson graph-based measures to quantify and test more general notions about channel cues to speech style (e.g., Labov 1972:94–99). In both studies, changes in Henderson slopes were significantly predictive of speaker's sociolinguistic variable use. Kendall & Thomas (2019) used Henderson slopes, as well as articulation rates, as independent measures for a close analysis of variation in variable (ING) (*talking* as *talkin'*) in a study of Mexican American English, finding that the timing measures help to establish underlying differences between Anglo and Mexican American forms for (ING).

CASE STUDY   Speech rate and pause in the Corpus of Regional African American Language

To exemplify some sociophonetic research questions and interesting phenomena related to speech rate and pause, we now turn, briefly, to explore data available from the Corpus of Regional African American Language (CORAAL; Kendall & Farrington 2020a). CORAAL is a publicly available corpus of over 100 hours of sociolinguistic interview recordings collected with African Americans from several communities and time points. We focus here on two complementary research questions:

RQ1: Are there regional and/or gender-based differences in speech rates and pause durations in CORAAL?

RQ2: Beyond macro-social factors, do properties of the interlocutors influence speech rates in the CORAAL data?

R code to explore and replicate the analyses here is available at http://lingtools.uoregon.edu/coraal/explorer/examples.php. The analyses and findings are not meant to be specific to African American Language (AAL) or any specific variety—or even to represent a comprehensive analysis of CORAAL—but rather seek to exemplify the kinds of questions that can usefully be asked of speech rate and pause from a sociophonetic perspective.

Since much sociophonetically related interest in speech timing has probed questions about regional differences, we start an empirical foray by asking whether this factor, region, as well as the macro-social factor of speaker gender, corresponds to statistically significant differences in articulation rate and pause durations among the speakers available in CORAAL. To examine regional differences, we take advantage of the structure of CORAAL, using the DCB component with its sample of speakers from Washington, DC, the PRV component, a sample of speakers from a rural community in central North Carolina, the ATL component, a sample of speakers living in Atlanta, Georgia, and the ROC component, a sample of speakers from Rochester, a city in western New York state. Due to the Great Migration, the twentieth-century mass relocation of African Americans from the (mostly rural) South to the (mostly urban) North, Washington, DC and Princeville have some regional connections among African Americans, despite Washington, DC being a major city, the capital of the United States, in the Mid-Atlantic, while Princeville is a small, rural community in the Southern state of North Carolina. Rochester, on the other hand, is expected to be more regionally distinct (see Farrington 2019 and King 2018 for deeper consideration of AAL in Rochester). Atlanta is a major city in the Southeastern United States with a diverse African American community. The speakers included in the ATL sample represent a friendship network, with speakers of more varying backgrounds than other CORAAL components (see Kendall & Farrington 2020b). Thus, the Atlanta sample also might be expected to show differences from Washington, DC.

(These four components were the contemporary components available at the time of first writing this chapter [CORAAL ver. 2020.05]; additional regional supplements are available as of more recent versions, but to keep these examples relatively streamlined the analyses here stick to these four components. Readers can easily adjust the R code available to expand the analysis to more recently released CORAAL components.)

Methods

To probe the two social factors—region and gender—in CORAAL, utterances and within-turn silent pauses were extracted from CORAAL using the R version of the CORAAL transcripts (available from http://lingtools.uoregon.edu/coraal/explorer/). Transcripts and speaker metadata were downloaded and processed using R. Utterances were selected for analysis based on a few general criteria. Utterances were removed from the dataset for analysis if they contained annotations showing overlapping speech, non-verbal noises (like laughter or coughing), or were shorter than 200 milliseconds (since such short utterances often consist of false starts or other disfluencies). Pauses were selected as the within-turn silences that separate utterances in the transcripts. Turns are defined as stretches of speech and silence by the same speaker, without interruptions or overlapping speech. Thus, only silent pauses separated by speech by the same speaker were included. Pauses within turns that were over five minutes in duration were excluded from consideration. Syllables were counted for each utterance using the script mentioned earlier, based on Kendall (2013), and articulation rate was calculated for each utterance by dividing the syllable count by the utterance duration. Pause durations, measured in milliseconds, were natural log transformed. The data were then trimmed, on a per-speaker basis, to remove all articulation rates outside of two standard deviations from each speaker's mean rate and all pauses outside of two standard deviations from each speaker's mean log pause duration. This trimming follows common practice meant to remove outlying values from the dataset; of course one could keep them in if interested in the more extreme values.

For purposes of the present analysis, utterance length was (natural) log transformed and this logged syllable count is used as a linear predictor. For the pause analysis, in order to test an intuition that pause durations may be contingent on the overall length of the turn in which they occur (with the hypothesis that longer turns would include longer pauses, since speakers have to do more speech planning within longer turns), a measure of turn duration is included in the analysis. In order to decouple the duration of a pause and the duration of its turn (since the turn's duration includes the pause's duration), the pause duration of each pause was subtracted from its turn duration measure. Turn durations were then converted to milliseconds, natural log transformed, and centered around their mean for modeling. Linear mixed-effect models were then applied to the utterance-level articulation rate and individual pause data to determine the best model accounting for the influence of the factors of interest. The articulation rate model tested the logged number of syllables in the utterance along with speaker's region (as characterized by CORAAL component) and gender. The pause duration model tested the logged duration (in milliseconds) of the turn containing the pause along with speaker's region and gender.

Results

The articulation rate model identifies the expected and strongly significant relationship between (log) syllable length and articulation rate (est. = 0.96, $p < 0.0001$). It also identifies a strong gender effect, such that males have higher rates than females (est. = 0.26, $p < 0.01$). The regional factor, the CORAAL component, arises as marginally significant ($p = 0.080$), with the Atlanta, Georgia speakers showing the slowest rates, but not quite reaching significance in comparison to Washington, DC (est. = −0.27, $p = 0.058$). The silent pause duration model identifies a significant relationship between the length of a silent pause and the overall duration of the speaker's turn (est. = 0.02, $p < 0.0001$). The model did not identify significance for speaker gender, but did identify that CORAAL component is a significant factor in pause duration ($p < 0.01$), as is the interaction between CORAAL component and turn duration ($p < 0.01$). The models' predictions for CORAAL component and the other significant factors, with confidence intervals, are shown for articulation rate, in Figure 3.5a, and pause, in Figure 3.5b.

Interestingly, in answer to RQ1, the models show that the Washington, DC and Princeville speakers are similar in having both faster articulation rates and longer pauses than the Atlanta and Rochester speakers. The log-transformed utterance length effect on articulation rate is interpreted here as comparable to the nonlinear relationship between utterance length and articulation rate described in prior work, although further testing would need to be done to determine what exact curvilinear model fits the relationship best. The turn length effect on silent pause duration also warrants further consideration. The main effect in the model supports the notion that longer turns of talk require longer pauses from speakers, although a host of other explanations are possible. The interaction between corpus component and the turn duration effect on pause duration shows that the positive correlation is robust across the data, but the different slopes suggest that the relationship has social components and cannot be purely cognitive.

The analysis to this point has followed traditional (i.e., first-wave) variationist methods in searching for correlations between macro-social categories and speakers' language patterns. As discussed earlier, evidence (such as in Kendall 2013) suggests that speech timing is not just a property of speakers divorced from the social and discourse contexts in which the data are collected. Using metadata available in CORAAL—in particular information about the interviewers' genders and about the interviewers' relationships with the interviewees—we can briefly expand on the prior analysis, to ask whether the patterns uncovered (and presented in Figure 3.5a) tell the whole story. For sake of space, we only focus on articulation rate here, and just on how these two factors impact the articulation rate analysis. It goes, I think, without saying that many additional factors would be worth considering in a full analysis,

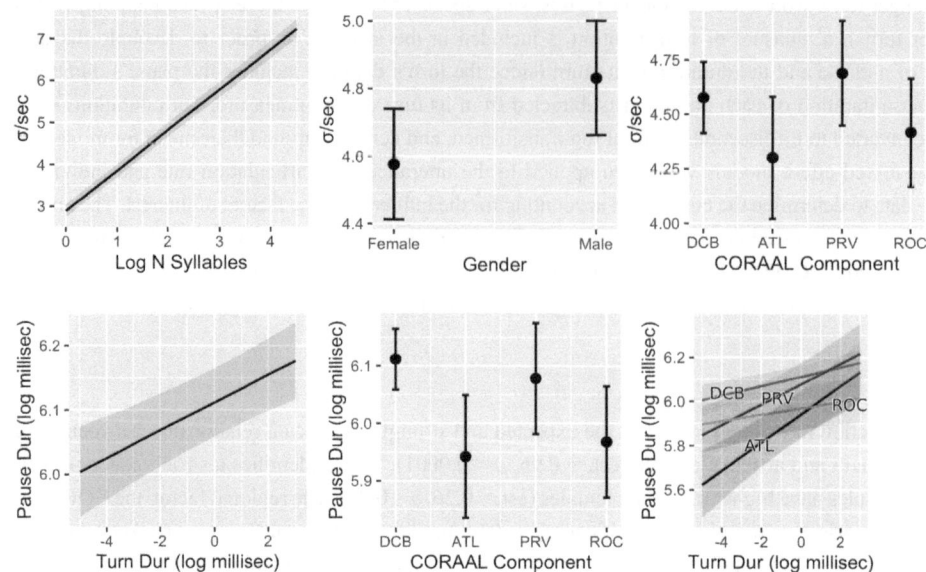

Figure 3.5   Model predictions
Figure 3.5a (top row)   Articulation rate model
Figure 3.5b (bottom row)   Pause duration model

including the actual articulation rates and other speech timing characteristics of the interviewers (Kendall 2013:§7.3), as would considerations that look closely at the discourse contexts themselves.

Accordingly, the model for articulation rate was expanded by testing the two additional factors, the gender of the interviewer (cisgender female or male) and the relationship between the interviewer and interviewee (close relationship, acquaintance, or no prior relationship). Model criticism determined that both of these factors improved the model, and that with these factors included the best models do not include the CORAAL component.

Considering all two-way interactions, modeling also determined that interactions between the speaker's gender and the interviewer's gender ($p < 0.05$) and the interviewer's gender and relationship with the interviewee ($p < 0.01$) were significant. Results from this new model are displayed in Figure 3.6. Responding to RQ2, the patterns indicate that while males speak faster than females (as identified in Figure 3.5b), the pattern is accentuated among speakers who were interviewed by males: males have faster rates and females slower rates in the interviews conducted by male fieldworkers. Further, close relationships between interviewer and interviewee appear to lead to much slower articulation rates when the interviewer is male (note the relatively flat pattern in Figure 3.6 for speakers with female interviewers).

Discussion

It is hoped that these short empirical investigations pique readers' interest in these features, and high-light the ways that speech rate and pause can be used to investigate a range of questions at the nexus of

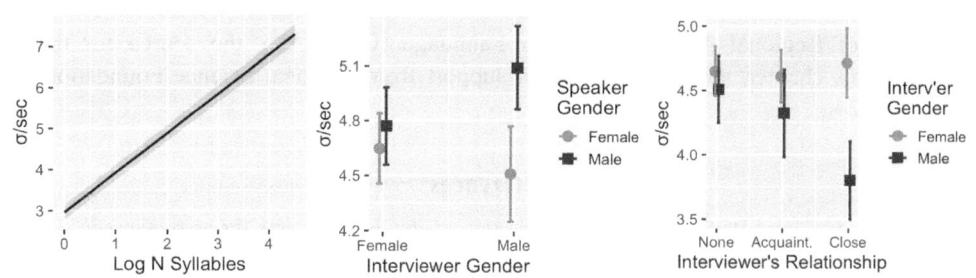

Figure 3.6　Model predictions from articulation rate model once interviewer gender and relationship with the interviewee are taken into consideration

language, cognition, and society. I hesitate to offer strong explanations for these substantive patterns in this short treatment, particularly with regard to RQ2. That speakers speak more slowly with male interviewers with whom they have close relationships could of course be a function of the particular interactions and particular identities captured in the corpus (interviewer genders and relationships with interviewees differ widely across components, as detailed in the CORAAL metadata), but it also could be telling about other aspects of the interviews. My own experiences overseeing students doing socio-linguistic interviews for class projects has highlighted for me that often the most hesitant and awkward interviews are those done by students with their very close friends. Maybe a similar pattern is the case here.

In any case, the larger point here is that this analysis highlights the ways that sociophonetic variables can be driven not only by the social attributes of speakers but by their interlocutors and the contexts of the data collection. More work is clearly needed to interrogate the durability of and roots for patterns like these. And returning to the emphasis on speech rate and pause as predictors for other sociolinguistic phenomena, these patterns further suggest that measures like speech rate and attributes of pauses can be useful "channel cues" relating to other, more global aspects of speech.

Looking ahead

As I hope to have shown in this chapter, speech rate, pause, and other aspects of speech timing present exciting opportunities for sociophonetics to uncover new insights into the relationships linking language, cognition, and society. I have reviewed a sampling of work that has probed sociolinguistic patterns related to these features. Much of what I have covered here (and in my own previous work) has focused on relatively macro-social (first-wave) aspects of sociophonetic patterns regarding speech rate and pause. It is without doubt that a finer ethnographic focus on speech timing as well as investigations that include discourse analytic approaches can fur-ther our understanding of how and why speakers modulate their rates of speech and pause patterns. The short empirical investigations included here just scratch the surface for what one could investigate in a spoken language corpus like CORAAL and are meant to whet readers' appetites for further sociophonetic investigation into speech timing. Many questions remain on the horizon for the field when it comes to speech rate, pause, and other even less well studied aspects of prosody.

Acknowledgments

The Corpus of Regional African American Language (CORAAL), the source for the data explored in this chapter, was developed with support from National Science Foundation grant # BCS-1358724.

References

Barbosa, Plínio & Gérard Bailly. 1994. Characterisation of rhythmic patterns for text-to-speech synthesis. *Speech Communication* 15(1–2). 127–137. https://doi.org/10.1016/0167-6393(94)90047-7

Bishop, Jason & Boram Kim. 2018. Anticipatory shortening: Articulation rate, phrase length, and lookahead in speech production. *Proceedings on Speech Prosody 2018*. 235–239. https://doi.org/10.21437/Speech Prosody.2018-48

Browman, Catherine P. & Louis Goldstein. 1992. Articulatory phonology: An overview. *Phonetica* 49(3–4). 155–180. https://doi.org/10.1159/000261913

Bucholtz, Mary & Kira Hall. 2005. Identity and interaction: A sociocultural linguistic approach. *Discourse Studies* 7(4–5). 585–614. https://doi.org/10.1177/1461445605054407

Chen, Lei, Klaus Zechner, Su-Youn Yoon, Keelan Evanini, Xinhao Wang, Anastassia Loukina, Jidong Tao, Lawrence Davis, Chong Min Lee, Min Ma, Robert Mundkowsky, Chi Lu, Chee Wee Leong & Binod Gyawali. 2018. Automated scoring of nonnative speech using the SpeechRater[SM] v. 5.0 engine. Research Report No. RR-18-10. https://doi.org/10.1002/ets2.12198

Clark, Herbert H. & Jean Fox Tree. 2002. Using *uh* and *um* in spontaneous speaking. *Cognition* 84(1). 73–111. https://doi.org/10.1016/s0010-0277(02)00017-3

Clopper, Cynthia G. & Rajka Smiljanic. 2015. Regional variation in temporal organization in American English. *Journal of Phonetics* 49. 1–15. https://doi.org/10.1016/j.wocn.2014.10.002

Crown, Cynthia & Stanley Feldstein. 1985. Psychological correlates of silence and sound in conversational interaction. In Tannen & Saville-Troike, 31–54.

Dankovičová, Jana. 2001. *The linguistic basis of articulation rate variation.* Hector.

de Boer, Meike & Willemijn Heeren. 2020. Cross-linguistic filled pause realization: The acoustics of *uh* and *um* in native Dutch and non-native English. *Journal of the Acoustical Society of America* 148(6). 3612–3622. https://doi.org/10.1121/10.0002871

Devlin, Thomas M. 2021, Oct. 6. Are some spoken languages faster than others? *Babbel Magazine*. www.bab bel.com/en/magazine/language-speed

Duez, Danielle. 1985. Perception of silent pauses in spontaneous speech. *Language and Speech* 28(4). 377–389. https://doi.org/10.1177/002383098502800403

Duez, Danielle. 1993. Acoustic correlates of subjective pauses. *Journal of Psycholinguistic Research* 22(1). 21–39. https://doi.org/10.1007/BF01068155

Eckert, Penelope. 2008. Variation and the indexical field. *Journal of Sociolinguistics* 12(4). 453–476. https://doi.org/10.1111/j.1467-9841.2008.00374.x

Eckert, Penelope. 2012. Three waves of variation study: The emergence of meaning in the study of sociolinguistic variation. *Annual Review of Anthropology* 41. 87–100. https://doi.org/10.1146/annurev-anthro-092 611-145828

Eckert, Penelope & William Labov. 2017. Phonetics, phonology and social meaning. *Journal of Sociolinguistics* 21(4). 467–496. https://doi.org/10.1111/josl.12244

Erker, Daniel & Joanna Bruso. 2017. *Uh, bueno, em …*: Filled pauses as a site of contact-induced change in Boston Spanish. *Language Variation and Change* 29(2). 205–244. https://doi.org/10.1017/S095439451 7000102

Ernestus, Mirjam & Natasha Warner. 2011. An introduction to reduced pronunciation variants. *Journal of Phonetics* 39(3). 253–260. https://doi.org/10.1016/S0095-4470(11)00055-6

Farrington, Charlie. 2019. *Language variation and the Great Migration: Regionality and African American language.* PhD Dissertation, University of Oregon.

Fridland, Valerie & Tyler Kendall. 2022. Managing sociophonetic data in a study of regional variation. In Andrea Berez-Kroeker, Bradley McDonnell, Eve Koller & Lauren Collister (eds.), *Open handbook of linguistic data management*, 237–247. MIT Press. https://doi.org/10.7551/mitpress/12200.003.0023

Fridland, Valerie, Tyler Kendall & Charlie Farrington. 2014. Durational and spectral differences in American English vowels: Dialect variation within and across regions. *Journal of the Acoustical Society of America* 136(1). 341–349. https://doi.org/10.1121/1.4883599

Fruehwald, Josef. 2016. Filled pause choice as a sociolinguistic variable. *University of Pennsylvania Working Papers in Linguistics* 22(2). Article 6.

Goldman-Eisler, Frieda. 1968. *Psycholinguistics: Experiments in spontaneous speech*. Academic Press.

Grosjean, François & Maryann Collins. 1979. Breathing, pausing and reading. *Phonetica* 36(2). 98–114. https://doi.org/10.1159/000259950

Guy, Gregory. 1980. Variation in the group and the individual: The case of final stop deletion. In William Labov (ed.), *Locating language in time and space*. Academic Press. 1–36.

Guy, Gregory, Jennifer Hay & Abby Walker. 2008. Phonological, lexical, and frequency factors in coronal stop deletion in early New Zealand English. Paper presented at Laboratory Phonology 11, Wellington, NZ.

Hazen, Kirk. 2011. Flying high above the social radar: Coronal stop deletion in modern Appalachia. *Language Variation and Change* 23(1). 105–137. https://doi.org/10.1017/S0954394510000220

Henderson, Alan, Frieda Goldman-Eisler & Andrew Skarbek. 1966. Sequential temporal patterns in spontaneous speech. *Language and Speech* 9(4). 207–216. https://doi.org/10.1177/002383096600900402

Hirose, Keikichi & Hiromichi Kawanami. 2002. Temporal rate change of dialogue speech in prosodic units as compared to read speech. *Speech Communication* 36(1–2). 97–111. https://doi.org/10.1016/S0167-6393(01)00028-0

Hughes, Vincent, Paul Foulkes & Sophie Wood. (2016). Strength of forensic voice comparison evidence from the acoustics of filled pauses. *International Journal of Speech, Language and the Law* 23(1). 99–132. https://doi.org/10.1558/ijsll.v23i1.29874

Jacewicz, Ewa, Robert Allen Fox, Caitlin O'Neill & Joseph Salmons. 2009. Articulation rate across dialect, age, and gender. *Language Variation and Change* 21(2). 233–256. https://doi.org/10.1017/S0954394509990093

Jacewicz, Ewa, Robert Allen Fox & Lai Wei. 2010. Between-speaker and within-speaker variation in speech tempo of American English. *Journal of the Acoustical Society of America* 128(2). 839–850. https://doi.org/10.1121/1.3459842

Kallay, Jeffrey E., Ulrich Mayr & Melissa A. Redford. 2019. Characterizing the coordination of speech production and breathing. In Sasha Calhoun, Paola Escudero, Marija Tabain & Paul Warren (eds.), *Proceedings of the 19th International Congress of Phonetic Sciences, Melbourne, Australia 2019*, 1412–1416.

Kendall, Tyler. 2009. *Speech rate, pause, and linguistic variation: An examination through the Sociolinguistic Archive and Analysis Project*. PhD dissertation, Duke University.

Kendall, Tyler. 2013. *Speech rate, pause and sociolinguistic variation: Studies in corpus sociophonetics*. Palgrave Macmillan.

Kendall, Tyler & Charlie Farrington. 2020a. *The Corpus of Regional African American Language*, ver. 2020.05. Online Resources for African American Language Project. http://oraal.uoregon.edu/coraal

Kendall, Tyler & Charlie Farrington. 2020b. *CORAAL user guide*, ver. 2020.05. Online Resources for African American Language Project. http://lingtools.uoregon.edu/coraal/userguide

Kendall, Tyler & Erik R. Thomas. 2019. Variable (ING). In Thomas, 171–197.

King, Sharese. 2018. *Exploring social and linguistic diversity across African Americans from Rochester, New York*. PhD dissertation, Stanford University.

Kircher, Tilo T., Michael J. Brammer, Willem Levelt, Mathias Bartels & Philip K. McGuire. 2004. Pausing for thought: Engagement of left temporal cortex during pauses in speech. *NeuroImage* 22(1). 84–90. https://doi.org/10.1016/j.neuroimage.2003.09.041

Koreman, Jacques. 2006. Perceived speech rate: The effects of articulation rate and speaking style in spontaneous speech. *Journal of the Acoustical Society of America* 119(1). 582–596. https://doi.org/10.1121/1.2133436

Kowal, Sabine & Daniel O'Connell. 1980. Pausological research at Saint Louis University. In Hans W. Dechert & Manfred Raupach (eds.), *Temporal variables in speech: Studies in honour of Frieda Goldman-Eisler*, 61–66. Mouton.

Kunzel, Hermann J. 1997. Some general phonetic and forensic aspects of speaking tempo. *Forensic Linguistics* 4(1). 48–83. https://doi.org/10.1558/ijsll.v4i1.48

Labov, William. 2006 [1996]. *The social stratification of English in New York City*, 2nd edn. Cambridge University Press. [1st edn., Center for Applied Linguistics, 1966.]

Labov, William. 1972. *Sociolinguistic patterns*. University of Pennsylvania Press.

Lee, Nara, Jiyoung Shin, Doyoung Yoo & KyungWha Kim. 2017. Speech rate in Korean across region, gender and generation. *Phonetics and Speech Sciences* 9(1). 7–39. https://doi.org/10.13064/KSSS.2017.9.1.027

Lehtonen, Jaako & Kari Sajavaara. 1985. The silent Finn. In Tannen & Saville-Troike, 193–201.

Levelt, Willem. 1989. *Speaking: From intention to articulation*. MIT Press.

Maclay, Howard & Charles E. Osgood. 1959. Hesitation phenomena in spontaneous English speech. *Word* 15(1) 19–44. https://doi.org/10.1080/00437956.1959.11659682

McDougall, Kirsty & Martin Duckworth. 2018. Individual patterns of disfluency across speaking styles: a forensic phonetic investigation of Standard Southern British English. *International Journal of Speech, Language and the Law* 25(2). 205–230. https://doi.org/10.1558/ijsll.37241

McFarland, David H. 2001. Respiratory markers of conversational interaction. *Journal of Speech, Language, and Hearing Research* 44(1). 128–143. https://doi.org/10.1044/1092-4388(2001/012)

Mendoza-Denton, Norma. 1995. Pregnant pauses: Silence and authority in the Anita Hill-Clarence Thomas hearings. In Kira Hall & Mary Bucholtz (eds.), *Gender articulated: Language and the socially constructed self*, 51–66. Routledge.

Niedzielski, Nancy A. & Dennis R. Preston. 2010. *Folk linguistics*. De Gruyter. https://doi.org/10.1515/9783110803389

Philips, Susan. 1976. Some sources of cultural variability in the regulation of talk. *Language in Society* 5(1). 81–95. https://doi.org/10.1017/S0047404500006862

Quené, Hugo. 2007. On the just noticeable difference for tempo in spontaneous speech. *Journal of Phonetics* 35(3). 353–362. https://doi.org/10.1016/j.wocn.2006.09.001

Quené, Hugo. 2008. Multilevel modeling of between-speaker and within-speaker variation in spontaneous speech tempo. *Journal of the Acoustical Society of America* 123(2). 1104-1113. https://doi.org/10.1121/1.2821762

R Core Team. 2022. *R: A language and environment for statistical computing*. R Foundation for Statistical Computing. www.R-project.org

Ray, George B. & Christopher J. Zahn. 1990. Regional speech rates in the United States: A preliminary analysis. *Communication Research Reports* 7(1). 34–37. https://doi.org/10.1080/08824099009359851

Redford, Melissa A. 2013. A comparative analysis of pausing in child and adult storytelling. *Applied Psycholinguistics* 34(3). 569–589. https://doi.org/10.1017/S0142716411000877

Robb, Michael, Margaret Maclagan & Yang Chen. 2004. Speaking rates of American and New Zealand varieties of English. *Clinical Linguistics and Phonetics* 18(1). 1–15. https://doi.org/10.1080/0269920031000105336

Schnoebelen, Tyler. 2009. The social meaning of tempo. Unpublished manuscript.

Schnoebelen, Tyler. 2010. Variation in speech tempo: Capt. Kirk, Mr. Spock, and all of us in between. Paper presented at New Ways of Analyzing Variation 39 [NWAV39], San Antonio, TX.

Schwab, Sandra & Mathieu Avanzi. 2015. Regional variation and articulation rate in French. *Journal of Phonetics* 48. 96–105. https://doi.org/10.1016/j.wocn.2014.10.009

Siegman, Aron W. & Stephen Boyle. 1993. Voices of fear and anxiety and sadness and depression: the effects of speech rate and loudness on fear and anxiety and sadness and depression. *Journal of Abnormal Psychology* 102(3). 430–437. https://doi.org/10.1037/0021-843X.102.3.430

Tagliamonte, Sali A. & Rosalind A.M. Temple. 2005. New perspectives on an ol' variable: (t, d) in British English. *Language Variation and Change* 17(3). 281–302. https://doi.org/10.1017/S0954394505050118

Tamminga, Meredith, Laurel MacKenzie & David Embick. 2016. The dynamics of variation in individuals. *Linguistic Variation* 16(2). 300–336. https://doi.org/10.1075/lv.16.2.06tam

Tannen, Deborah. 1985. Silence: Anything but. In Tannen & Saville-Troike, 93–111.

Tannen, Deborah. 2000. "Don't just sit there–interrupt!": Pacing and pausing in conversational style. *American Speech* 75(4). 393–395. https://doi.org/10.1215/00031283-75-4-393

Tannen, Deborah & Muriel Saville-Troike (eds.). 1985. *Perspectives on silence*. Ablex.

Tanner, James, Morgan Sonderegger & Michael Wagner. 2017. Production planning and coronal stop deletion in spontaneous speech. *Laboratory Phonology* 8(1). 15. https://doi.org/10.5334/labphon.96

Teasdale, John D., Sarah J. Fogarty & J. Mark G. Williams. 1980. Speech rate as a measure of short-term variation in depression. *British Journal of Social and Clinical Psychology* 19(3). 271–278. https://doi.org/10.1111/j.2044-8260.1980.tb00353.x

Thomas, Erik R. 2019. *Mexican American English: Substrate influence and the birth of an ethnolect*. Cambridge University Press.

Thomas, Erik R. & Tyler Kendall. 2019. Prosody. In Thomas, 215–242.

Turk, Alice E. & Stefanie Shattuck-Hufnagel. 2007. Multiple targets of phrase-final lengthening in American English words. *Journal of Phonetics* 35(4). 445–472. https://doi.org/10.1016/j.wocn.2006.12.001

Turk, Alice E. & Stephanie Shattuck-Hufnagel. 2020. *Speech timing: Implications for theories of phonology, phonetics, and speech motor control.* Oxford University Press.

Van Borsel, John & Dorothy De Maesschalck. 2008. Speech rate in males, females, and male-to-female transsexuals. *Clinical Linguistics and Phonetics* 22(9). 679–685. https://doi.org/10.1080/0269920080 1976695

Vaughn, Charlotte & Tyler Kendall. 2019. Stylistically coherent variants: Cognitive representation of social meaning. *Revista de Estudos da Linguagem* 27(4). 1787–1830. http://dx.doi.org/10.17851/ 2237-2083.27.4.1787-1830

Verhoeven, Jo, Guy De Pauw & Hanne Kloots. 2004. Speech rate in a pluricentric language: A comparison between Dutch in Belgium and the Netherlands. *Language and Speech* 47(3). 297–308. https://doi.org/ 10.1177/00238309040470030401

Wieling, Martijn, Jack Grieve, Gosse Bouma, Josef Fruehwald, John Coleman & Mark Liberman. 2016. Variation and change in the use of hesitation markers in Germanic languages. *Language Dynamics and Change* 6(2). 199–234. https://doi.org/10.1163/22105832-00602001

Winkworth, Alison L., Pamela J. Davis, Roger D. Adams & Elizabeth Ellis. 1995. Breathing patterns during spontaneous speech. *Journal of Speech, Language, and Hearing Research* 38(1). 124–144. https://doi.org/ 10.1044/jshr.3801.124

Wolfram, Walt, Becky Childs & Benjamin Torbert. 2000. Tracing language history through consonant cluster reduction: Comparative evidence from isolated dialects. *Southern Journal of Linguistics* 24(1). 17–40.

Zellner, Brigitte. 1998. Fast and slow speech rate: A characterisation for French. *Proceedings of the 5th International Conference on Spoken Language Processing* 7 [ICSLP]. 3159–3163.

4

SOCIOPHONETICS AND TONE

The world of sociotonetics

James N. Stanford and Cathryn Yang

Introduction

The majority of the world's languages have tone or pitch-accent systems (Yip 2002:17), yet these important suprasegmental phenomena are under-represented in sociophonetics (Stanford 2008; Thomas 2019). A tonal language is a language "where word meanings or grammatical categories (such as tense) are dependent on pitch level" (Crystal 2003:466). As Yip explains,

> In all languages vowel height and consonantal place of articulation are central to conveying the meanings of words, and so we do not usually categorize languages as being "vowel-height languages" or "place-of-articulation languages." Tone is different in that only a subset of languages (albeit a rather large subset!) make use of it this way.
>
> Yip 2002:1

In tonal languages with lexical tone, lexemes that are identical on the segmental level can have different meanings due to phonemically contrastive pitch. For example, in Mandarin Chinese, the word *ma* can be pronounced with four different tones: high-level tone *mā* means 'mother,' rising tone *má* means 'hemp,' dipping tone *mǎ* means 'horse,' and falling *mà* means 'to scold.' Such pitch patterns are often accompanied by voice qualities as well, such as the creaky voice that sometimes appears phonetically with dipping tone *mǎ*. Moreover, in some tone languages such as Vietnamese (Nguyen & Edmondson 1998), voice quality may be phonemically intermixed with tonal categories. In fact, some Vietnamese tone researchers report that creaky and breathy voice qualities are the primary perceptual cues for certain tones, rather than pitch (Pham 2003).

In addition to lexical tone, grammatical tone is found in languages where tone plays a role in marking morphological or syntactic features (Yip 2002:105–129). For example, tones are used for some tense distinctions in many Bantu languages (Hyman 2017), and various other types of morphological tone are found in other tonal languages. A growing subfield of interest for grammatical tone researchers is "tonosyntax," in which syntactic contrasts are marked by tonal properties at the phrasal level (Heath & McPherson 2013).

Among the diverse topics in tonal research, this chapter focuses on "sociotonetics" (Stanford 2008), which is a subfield located at the intersection between acoustic tone phonetics (e.g.,

DOI: 10.4324/9781003034636-5

Zhu 1999) and quantitative variationist sociolinguistics (e.g., Labov 1966, 1994–2010). Unlike tone phonetics (tonetics), with its focus on the phonetic detail of a small number of speakers, sociotonetics focuses on interspeaker and intraspeaker variation. As with most other variationist research, sociotonetics looks at the level of community, ideally sampling from dozens or more speakers representing a range of testable social categories for correlation, as well as speech styles and social meaning of tone variables. Thus, the overall goal of sociotonetics is to expand variationist sociolinguistic research into the vast, understudied realms of tonal variation and change.

The examples of sociotonetics research in this chapter will focus on lexical tone since that is the most well-developed area where acoustic sociophonetic methods have been applied to tonal phenomena. But we also note that pitch-accent languages can also be examined using many of the techniques described in this chapter. In languages considered to have pitch-accent systems, such as Japanese, a lexeme has an identifiable syllable marked for prominence with pitch. For example, Kerswill's (1994) work on Norwegian includes a variationist study of pitch-accent features that are coded auditorily and then quantified for correlation with social factors.

The wide-open field of sociotonetics

As sociolinguists venture beyond commonly studied languages (Nagy & Meyerhoff 2008; Stanford & Preston 2009; Meyerhoff 2017), they are encountering less commonly studied sociophonetic variables. Tone is one of these understudied variables that make sociotonetics a "wide-open field." Thomas explains:

> Because sociophoneticians have predominantly set their sights on Western languages, it is unsurprising that little instrumental work has been conducted on variation in lexical tone […] most work on tonal variation continues to rely on auditory transcription, and acoustic work on lexical tone is clearly a wide-open field.
>
> Thomas 2019:455

Many sociophonetics textbooks, edited collections, handbook chapters, and so on give little or no attention to tonal languages, even as they cover many other topics like segmental variation, intonation, timing, and voice quality. Notable exceptions are Thomas (2011:189–192), which covers lexical tone as a sociophonetic variable, and two collections that include chapters and articles on sociotonetics (Zellou, Yu & DiCanio 2022; Asahi, D'Arcy & Kerswill forthcoming). Other aspects of suprasegmental variation, such as intonation and voice quality, have received a good amount of attention in sociophonetics (e.g., Yaeger-Dror et al. 2010; Di Paolo & Yaeger-Dror 2011; Takano & Ota 2017; Holliday 2021; O'Rourke & Baltazani this volume; Davidson this volume), but variationist work on lexical tone is far less common. The overall paucity of published work in sociotonetics means that there are many opportunities for researchers to do pioneering work in this highly promising research area.

Researchers began to apply variationist sociolinguistic methods to tone variation in the early 2000s (e.g., Bauer, Cheung & Cheung 2003; Hildebrandt 2004; Zhang 2005). Stanford (2008) coined the term sociotonetics, emphasizing the need for such quantitative variationist tone research involving relatively large sets of speakers and diverse demographic categories of age, social class, and so on, as well as multiple speech styles. These early studies and those that followed have focused on questions regarding the social meaning of tone variables, tone change-in-progress, and the role of contact in tone change. The bulk of sociotonetic research has focused on major tone languages such as Cantonese, Mandarin, and Thai, but there is growing interest in the sociotonetics of lesser-studied languages—for example, Lili Wu (Shi, Chen & Mous 2020) and Lahu (Yang et al. 2022). Data elicitation in early studies was usually limited to the citation form of the tone (i.e., the tone of a monosyllabic word uttered in isolation), but recent technological advances have enabled the acoustic analysis of tone in a wider range of speech styles. In this way, sociotonetics researchers can apply the many existing principles of sociolinguistics to tone, and test whether they are relevant for tone as a sociophonetic variable.

Methods in sociotonetics

As sociotonetics is a relatively new subfield, we give considerable space to methodological issues when dealing with tone, with the aim of encouraging more sociophoneticians to dive into this exciting research area.

Normalization

The primary instrument of analysis in sociotonetics is an audio recording of a speaker's voice that is then analyzed for f0—the fundamental frequency or "singing frequency" of the speaker, often using autocorrelation software such as the "pitch-tracking" feature in Praat (Boersma & Weenink 2022). Technically, f0 is the acoustic correlate of "pitch," which is an auditory or perceptual quality of sound. But since sociotonetics primarily involves these acoustic phonetic measurements and since many software packages loosely use the term "pitch" to refer to f0, we follow this practice as well. We primarily discuss work that has focused on pitch as the salient cue in a tonal system, but we also note areas for further research with respect to voice quality.

Different speech samples will have different voice pitches and different speaking rates, so it is necessary to normalize both for time and for pitch in order to analyze inter- or intra-speaker variation (Stanford 2008:420–424). Time normalization is a relatively straightforward process of setting up a "normalized time" range that it is based on the duration of a syllable, such as a percentage scale (0–100 percent) of syllable duration (e.g., Steed & Rose 2009) or related scales (Stanford 2008). Pitch samples are typically taken at 10 msec intervals (the Praat default), and so it is a matter of taking those sample points and normalizing them in terms of percentage of total duration for the given syllable. Some languages have contrastive vowel length or differences in duration according to syllable type, and the researcher should take these structural differences into consideration when normalizing. For example, checked syllables (the traditional term in East Asian linguistics for syllables ending in –p, –t, or –k), are often "clipped," that is, shorter than unchecked syllables (ending in a vowel or nasal). In Sui, for example, the syllable *kam* is longer than the checked syllable *kap.* There are multiple ways to handle this, and it depends on the goals of the research. If duration is a key variable in question, then researchers would avoid time normalization. If pitch is the key variable, as is typically the case in sociotonetics, then researchers could time-normalize their checked syllables based on the average duration of checked syllables in the sample, and unchecked syllables normalized according to average duration of unchecked syllables. Some researchers conduct two separate analyses, one for checked syllables and one for unchecked syllables (e.g., Zhang, Zhang & Xu 2019).

Pitch normalization is more challenging. Zhu (1999:46–56) examines six approaches: *z*-scores, fraction of range, proportion of range, ratio of log semitone distances, log *z*-scores, and log proportion of range. Zhang (2018) goes even further to review 16 different pitch-normalization methods. While there are strengths and weaknesses to each method, Zhang concludes that semitone conversion is the most effective way to normalize f0 for sociotonetic research goals. Likewise, Zhu (1999:75) observes that even when speakers have widely different pitch ranges in raw Hertz (Hz, a linear scale), these sharp differences are normalized away when converted to semitones (a logarithmic scale). In his study, female speakers of Shanghai Chinese had a range of 115 Hz versus only 71 Hz for male speakers (see also Ross, Edmondson & Seibert 1986:289), yet these differences are virtually eliminated when converted to semitones: 9.5 semitones and 9.6 semitones in range for female and male speakers, respectively. Semitones and other logarithmic methods are more in line with human audition, which perceives pitch in a logarithmic rather than linear manner. For example, Traunmüller & Eriksson (1995) find that listeners perceive male and female pitch ranges to be the equivalent when they are the same in semitones, regardless of their raw Hz values.

The semitone scale is easy to understand in comparison to musical notes. A semitone is a musical half-step, such as the change in pitch from the musical note D to D#. Thus, there are 12 semitones in an octave. A one-octave difference increases the frequency by a factor of 2, so music-ally this means that the distance in semitones from the well-known piano key middle C (C4) to the next C above it (C5) is 12 semitones or 12 musical half-steps, and this is twice the frequency in Hz (261.63 Hz for C4 versus 523.26 Hz for C5). It turns out that in careful speech styles most languages' tone systems occupy about one octave, or 12 semitones (see below). Individual speakers can of course utilize intonational effects that may change this range, and casual speech styles may compress this range considerably (Stanford 2016). Standard Hz-to-semitone conver-sion formulae are available in Praat's public documentation.

As Zhang (2018) points out, some f0 normalization methods set each speaker's tone range to be the same. This is a logical step when trying to set up the data in a way that makes it possible to con-duct cross-speaker comparisons, but one problem with this approach is that range itself may turn out to be an important sociolinguistic variable in some situations. Yang et al.'s (2019) sociotonetic study of Yangliu Lalo, an endangered Tibeto-Burman language, showed differences in range as a function of speaker age, gender, and language use: young, female speakers who used Lalo infre-quently showed more compression of tone range compared to other speakers. In such cases, using speaker-specific mean f0 (as in Yang et al. 2021; see also Zhang 2018) or speaker-specific mean f0 for a mid-level tone (as in Yang et al. 2019) as the reference level when converting to semitones is the better option.

Segmental environment

Tone production is influenced by a myriad of articulatory mechanisms and constraints, and these internal constraints should be included in sociotonetic analysis. The analyst needs to consider both segmental interactions as well as suprasegmental interactions, including both tone and intonation effects. In an experimental paradigm, it is possible to control for many of these phonetic factors— for example, by narrowing the scope to targets with the same type of syllable-initial consonant. In sociotonetics, however, where natural speech is prioritized as much as possible, datasets will contain a mix of initial consonants, vowels, and prosodic environments, and therefore may not be perfectly balanced for all combinations of phonetic factors. Nonetheless, since spontaneous speech will remain of crucial interest in sociotonetics, sociotoneticians will have to thoughtfully consider how to deal with internal constraints in their statistical modeling.

It is well known that there are a number of different types of f0 perturbations due to the effect of a preceding consonant (typically located in the syllable onset). See Xu (2019:Fig. 12.3) for a detailed view of these effects. Since voiced sonorants do not inhibit vibration of the vocal folds (Gussenhoven 2004:7), they are often used as a reference level for comparison with effects of other types of consonants (e.g., Kirby & Ladd 2016). The most commonly cited effect is f0 raising after voiceless obstruents (Hombert, Ohala & Ewan 1979; Kirby & Ladd 2016). The magnitude of this effect, however, may be language-specific and interact with context. Kirby (2018) found that the raising effect of voiceless aspirated stops was greater in non-tonal Khmer versus tonal Central Thai and Vietnamese. In the tonal languages, the effect was more visible in citation form versus connected speech and in high tone contexts versus low tone contexts. To handle possible prevocalic consonant effects, sociotoneticians may choose to enter onset consonant type as a factor in their statistical modeling (e.g., "onset" with three levels: voiceless obstruent, voiced obstruent, and sonorant, as in Yang et al. 2021). It is also common to discard f0 measurements during the first 10 percent of the vowel (e.g., Zhang 2014).

Contrasts in the features of consonants can also produce significant timing "gaps" in the pitch track, and sociotoneticians need to keep this in mind when extracting or analyzing pitch data. For example, the f0 track of the syllable *ma* begins with the sonorant initial, but the f0 track for syllables like *ta* will not appear until the onset of voicing at the beginning of the vowel. While most researchers begin the measurement of f0 at the beginning of the vowel, some choose to begin measurement at the onset of voicing, which would include the f0 track during a sonorant initial consonant (e.g., Chen, Yao & Yu 2018).

Much less is known about f0 perturbations due to postvocalic consonants, even though glottal consonants /ʔ/ and /h/ in postvocalic positions are implicated as triggers in the process of tonogenesis (Haurdicourt 1954; Hombert, Ohala & Ewan 1979). Experimental results on the effect of postvocalic /ʔ/ have been mixed and may reflect language-specific implementation of glottal closure. Some languages show f0 raising before /ʔ/, as in Arabic (Hombert, Ohala & Ewan 1979), but others show no effect on f0, as in Itunyoso Trique (DiCanio 2012). f0 tends to be slightly raised before obstruents in comparison to sonorants (Gussenhoven 2004:8). As suggested above, following consonant type may be entered as a factor in the statistical modeling.

Intrinsic pitch differences in vowels can also affect sociotonetic research. Among vowel effects, high vowels tend to have higher pitch than low vowels, and such differences can affect the pitch by significant amounts, such as 1.5 semitones (Whalen & Levitt 1995:356). While a researcher could plausibly decide to limit all targeted syllables to one particular vowel, this could greatly restrict the amount of usable data, and it could have a negative effect on the naturalness of the dataset. Another approach is to include the various different vowel environments as factors in the statistical analysis, as suggested above for onsets. Such an approach to sociotonetic environments parallels the way that phonetic environments are commonly handled in vowel sociophonetics.

Prosodic environment

Tone variation in naturally occurring speech is of special interest to sociotoneticians. Most early sociotonetic studies used word-list-style data, but the development of forced aligners such as SPPAS (Bigi & Hirst 2012) and MAUS (Kisler, Reichel & Schiel 2017) has made analysis of free speech more feasible (for a review of forced aligners, see Gonzalez, Grama & Travis 2020). When dealing with free speech, there are additional phonetic environments that affect tone production. Besides the influence of neighboring segments on pitch, there is also the influence of the prosodic environment, which includes tonal and intonational contexts as well as the target's position in the word and/or phrase.

For sociotonetics, one major issue is that it takes a relatively long time to make changes to f0, compared to the amount of time for distinctions to develop at the segmental level. For vowels, Labov & Baranowski (2006) find that a duration difference of 50 ms is sufficient to make distinctions between two vowels (short vowel versus long vowel) that overlap in formant space. In contrast, Xu (2019:315) finds that it "takes about 100 ms to make even the smallest pitch change," and similar numbers are found in other literature (see review in Stanford 2016:60). Depending on the goals of the research, the researcher should consider filtering out tokens shorter than 50 ms and maybe even those that are shorter than 100 ms.

One important consequence of the relative slowness of f0 shifting is that tones tend to "spill over" into the next syllable; that is, tones often have strong carryover effects on the tone of the following syllable. As an example, Figure 4.1 (from Xu 2004) shows the effect of preceding tone on the four tones of Mandarin Chinese: H(igh), R(ising), L(ow), and F(alling). Vertical lines represent syllable boundaries; horizontally-oriented lines represent surface realizations of f0 contours. In each panel, the tonal offset of the preceding syllable determines, to some degree, the pitch level of the tonal onset of the following syllable. Preceding tone can have a large effect on the tonal contour of the following syllable. Assimilatory carryover effects have also been reported for Thai (Gandour, Potisuk & Dechongkit 1994) and other languages (for an overview, see Zhang & Liu 2011). Anticipatory effects of a following tone tend to be weaker and dissimilatory in nature (Lei 2006:105). However, Chen, Wiltshire & Li (2018) found that anticipatory and carryover effects were comparable in magnitude in Nanjing Chinese and Malaysian Hokkien. To handle potential tonal context effects on the target tone, we recommend including preceding and following tone in the statistical model (as in Yang et al. 2021).

Position in the utterance has also been found to influence tonal contour and duration in tonal languages. For example, in the complex tonal language of Yoloxóchitl Mixtec, tones in final position have longer duration and show range expansion—that is, the highest tone becomes higher and the lowest tone becomes lower (DiCanio, Benn & Castillo García 2020). Yoloxóchitl Mixtec also shows positional variation, in which rising tones are realized as level in non-final position,

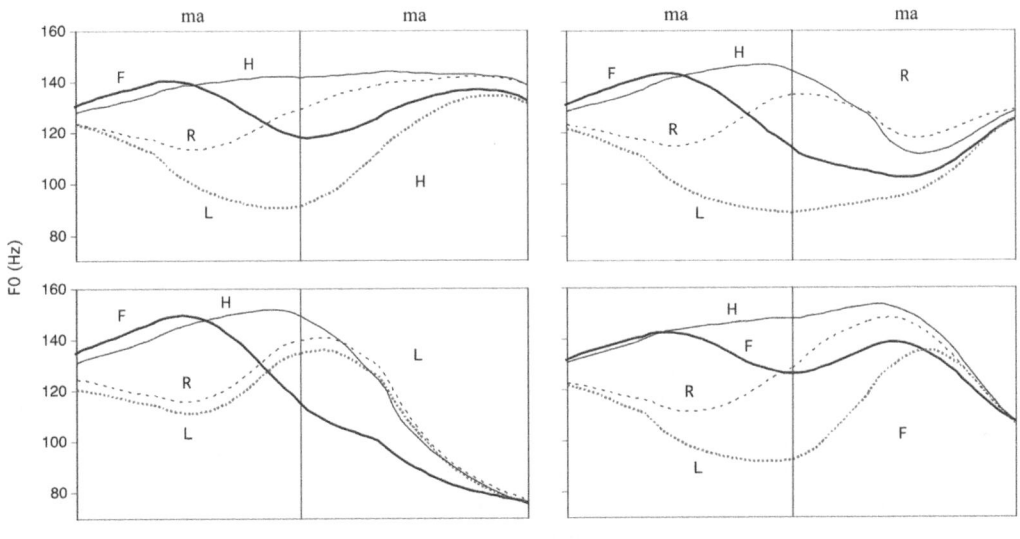

Figure 4.1 Contextual variation of Mandarin tones in mean f0 contours of *ma*
Source: Xu 2004

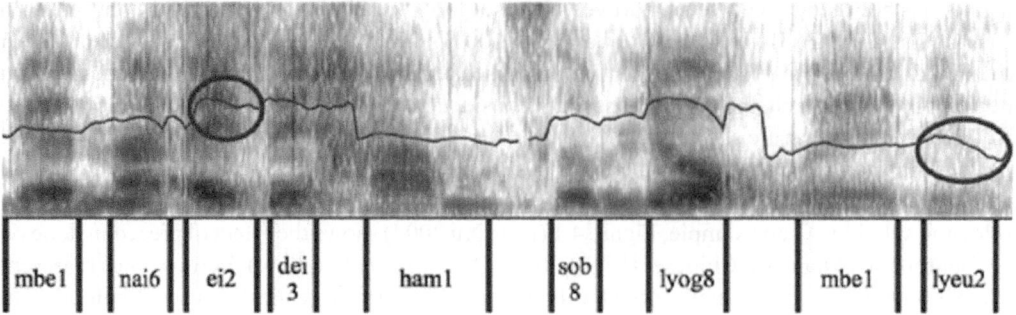

| mbe1 | nai6 | ei2 | dei 3 | ham1 | sob 8 | lyog8 | mbe1 | lyeu2 |

Figure 4.2   Challenge of declination in Sui free speech
Source: Stanford 2016: fig. 4

and declination for sentences consisting of low and mid-level tones, in which f0 gradually lowers across the utterance. Figure 4.2 illustrates the variation due to declination in free speech data from Stanford (2016). In this example from Sui conversation data, the speaker produces Tone 2 (which is a low-falling tone) at a higher f0 at the beginning of the utterance than at the end. At the beginning of the utterance, the syllable *ei* is produced much higher than the syllable *lyeu*, even though both are the same phonemic tone.

Speaking pitch range is an interesting sociolinguistic variable in the context of different speech styles. Sociolinguists examining variation at the segmental level have long known that the casual-versus-formal continuum of speech styles can be a meaningful variable in a given community. Since sociotonetic studies have mostly used more formal styles, however, this aspect of variation remains understudied. Preliminary studies such as Stanford (2016) suggest that tone range is considerably more compressed in free speech than careful speech. For Sui, tone range was approximately twice as much for careful speech versus conversation. For example, one speaker had a semitone range of 6.73 s.t. in free speech compared to 12.90 s.t. in careful speech, while another speaker had a range of 6.74 s.t. in free speech compared to 11.80 s.t. in careful speech. Note that the Sui careful speech ranges for tones are around 12 semitones, which is one octave. Xu (1999) also reports a one-octave range for speakers of Mandarin in careful speech. Xu (2019:321–322) points out that it is important to remember that the human voice has a wider range than that, typically three octaves, so there is much room left for intonational effects.

Sociotoneticians also need to be aware of the pitfalls of pitch-halving and pitch-doubling. Pitch-halving occurs when the autocorrelation method, such as Praat's pitch-tracking function, wrongly estimates the pitch at exactly half of the actual value. Since human speech is not perfectly periodic like a synthesized waveform, the autocorrelation algorithm can wrongly analyze the period as twice as large as the actual value; for example, when two periods fit inside the window, it may wrongly estimate f0 as half the real frequency. Similarly, pitch-doubling occurs when the estimate is exactly twice the actual value. These computational errors occur as Praat estimates the period of the waves and misinterprets the periodic pattern. When extracting f0 tracks manually, analysts can easily identify such aberrations in the pitch-tracking visually in the acoustic representation as sharp almost 90-degree drop-offs. It is visually evident that it is not representing the speaker's continuous voicing. Figure 4.3 shows a typical example of pitch-halving.

Manually, this can be repaired by visually and aurally noting the approximate actual pitch of the speaker's voice, such as listening to a nearby section of the recording where there is a continuous

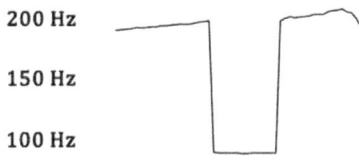

Figure 4.3   Example of pitch-halving

pitch-tracking line without pitch-halving or doubling. Suppose a speaker has a typical pitch around 280 Hz in that context. In Praat, for example, the analyst can then narrowly redefine the analysis window to be between, say, 250–350 Hz. This forces Praat or similar software to recognize the 280 Hz range as the correct pitch, rather than 140 or 560. Automated extraction software can make such adjustments as well, by detecting sudden, unnatural sharp drop-offs that likely represent pitch-halving and pitch-doubling (as in Yang et al. 2021).

Research development and trends in sociotonetics

Social meaning of tone variables

When considering the social meaning of tone, we should start with the basic question of whether lexical tone variants can carry such meaning. Is it possible that superficial variations in pitches of lexical tone are simply normalized away and ignored by speakers? There is no a priori reason to assume that every phonetic and phonological level of language can necessarily transmit social meaning through variation—though many of us sociophoneticians take this as a given. After all, subphonemic variation is the bread-and-butter of sociophonetics at the segmental level, encompassing vast amounts of dialectal and sociolectal meanings. Arguably, any phonetic variation that can be perceived is a candidate to become socially meaningful in certain circumstances, yet most of the empirical work that supports such a statement has been focused on segmental variation or else intonation, not lexical tone. How do we know that variation in lexical tone can convey social meaning and, if it does, what types of tonal variants are likely to be meaningful? A brief survey of empirical studies shows us that tone variation can convey a great deal of social meaning, and in some cases it may arguably be one of the most important indexes of certain personae or stances.

As a general rule for simple level pitches, one semitone is considered the threshold for noticeable difference (Zhang 2014; Jongman et al. 2017). In terms of percentage difference, some studies estimate that a 5–10 percent difference in f0 is the threshold for perceptible difference (Micheyl & Oxenham 2004:3040; Shattuck-Hufnagel et al. 2004:2). Based on the sociolinguistic assumptions stated above, we would therefore assume that any difference of one or more semitones (or 5–10 percent change in f0) would be a candidate to take on meaningful variation, given the appropriate social context for the variation. Since a typical tone space (in careful speech) has a range of 12 semitones, this leaves a great deal of room for perceivable variation in tone as a sociolinguistic variable.

Zhang (2005) provides one of the most well-known studies of social meaning in tone. Her study of urban Beijing speech shows that a set of phonetic variants are used to index different social identities. Standard Mandarin, also known as *Putonghua*, is based on, but not identical to, the Beijing accent. In Zhang's study, a local Beijing "smooth operator" persona is indexed by retroflex consonants, while a "cosmopolitan," "yuppie" persona is indexed by using features associated with Taiwan, Hong Kong, Singapore, and Macao. This includes tone variables. In many two-syllable words like *xiānsheng* 'mister, sir,' *piàoliang* 'pretty,' and so on, Zhang found that the "local Beijinger" persona uses a neutral tone (de-stressed and lacking a lexical tone target), while the Beijing "yuppies" were more likely to produce the full lexical tone on this second syllable—for example, *shēng* in the two-syllable word *xiānshēng,* and *liàng* in the two-syllable word *piàoliàng.* Among certain social groups in Beijing at the time of Zhang's study, the full tone carried the social meaning of an educated, international, cosmopolitan identity. Thus, Zhang effectively links tone variation to very specific social meanings and personae in that community. Zhang (2005) also found gendered variation in the use of full tones: females used full tones more than males.

Gao (2020) extends Zhang's research by asking if full tone may index femininity, specifically a "cute" feminine persona. The performance of cuteness is referred to as *sajiao* in Chinese, an innovative speech style introduced to mainland Chinese speakers through Taiwan and Hong Kong popular culture. In Gao's speech corpora study, mainland female speakers self-presenting as "cute" used full tones more frequently than female speakers who self-presented as "independent" and "strong-minded." Among "cute" speakers, full tone usage also differed by topic, with more frequent usage when talking about cosmetics compared to formal topics. In contrast, males showed infrequent full tone usage, and there was no difference in full tone usage across two social types ("outdoor" and "indoor"/"geek"). Gao suggests that full tone usage is indexing a specific persona of "cute" femininity. Both Zhang's and Gao's studies illustrate the process by which tone variables may be adopted for indexicality, in line with Silverstein's (2003) model.

Zhao (2018), in a matched-guise perception experiment with listeners from various parts of China, found that both standard use and frequent use of neutral tone were perceived as reflecting higher social status compared to infrequent use of neutral tone (in men's speech). Zhao suggests that the fact that frequent use of neutral tone, a characteristic of Beijing accent, showed no difference in status from standard use reflects the prestige that Beijing accent enjoys. Frequent use of the full tone was perceived negatively in men's speech, reflecting the association of full tone with femininity. Perceptions of women's speech showed little difference across the guises, which Zhao interprets as reflecting gender prejudice in China: while men have access to a wide range of social meanings through this tone variable, women are denied such options.

Both Zhang (2005) and Gao (2020) found that such variants are readily detectable through auditory means and coded as a binary (i.e., neutral tone or full tone), and both studies use auditorily coded tone data. Likewise, Stanford (2010) explores the social meaning of Hmong tone in an immigrant community of Hmong Americans in the Dallas/Fort Worth area of Texas, quantifying dialect contact between White Hmong and Green Mong in terms of segmental and tonal features. Auditory coding of tonal variants was sufficient to determine which speakers were using White Hmong tonal features as compared to Green Mong, which fit the goals of the study.

However, for studies where tone variables need to be examined as continuous variables, and for tone variables that are below the level of awareness of most speakers, acoustic sociophonetic methods are often crucial. One such acoustic sociophonetic study is Stanford (2008), which examines clan-based dialect differences among the Indigenous Sui language of southwest China. Stanford examines two variables: 1) Tone 6 as a high tone for some clan regions but low-rising for others; 2) Tone 1 is a low-falling for some regions but low-rising for other regions. Tone 6 variable is highly salient, and speakers are consciously aware of it enough to use it for "social work" as a second-order indexical (Silverstein 2003). When discussing dialect differences, speakers from all regions often mention words that contain Tone 6 as examples of key differences. But Tone 1 is much more subtle, and speakers rarely note it. Nonetheless, in the acoustic analysis, this subtle

Tone 1 variable shows significant dialectal contrasts for different Sui clans, primarily in terms of slope during the first one-third of the syllable, as important in acoustic sociotonetic analysis. Mean pitch is the primary correlate of variation in Tone 6, so this tone variable is examined at different points across the syllable, applying the statistical analyses to each tone token's pitch at 90 percent of syllable duration. For the subtle Tone 1 variable, the acoustic correlate that showed variation was pitch slope across the last one-third of the syllable. Thus, Stanford (2008) was able to capture clan-based sociolinguistic variation with the tools of sociotonetics.

Tone change-in-progress: Splits, mergers, and chain shifts

Observing tone change as an ongoing process in a speech community has been an abiding interest in sociotonetics. The article on Hong Kong Cantonese tones by Bauer, Cheung & Cheung (2003) is an early study that recognized the merger-in-progress of high-rising Tone 2 and low-rising Tone 5. The study examined eight speakers, all of whom were young male adults (mean age = 27 years), which limited the study to a narrow demographic range. Nonetheless, this study was innovative in its focus on variationist evidence for the merger-in-progress of the two tones. In the first experiment, the eight men read aloud characters from a randomized word list, and two of them showed possible merger of the two rising tones. In a follow-up experiment, those two men were asked to read characters representing minimal pairs. Bauer, Cheung & Cheung concluded that some speakers of Hong Kong Cantonese were likely merging Tones 2 and 5, and that tone variation in Cantonese "appears to be a potentially interesting and important sociolinguistic variable that merits more investigation" (223). They suggested that future studies should examine these tones as sociolinguistic variables in order to answer questions about the social characteristics of Cantonese speakers who may have this merger.

Further sociotonetic research on Hong Kong Cantonese not only confirmed the merger-in-progress of Tone 2 and Tone 5, but also revealed other potential ongoing mergers as well (Mok, Zuo & Wong 2013; Zhang 2019). The perception and production experiments done by Fung & Li (2019), in addition to showing a merger of Tone 2 and Tone 5 in both perception and production, also show a partial merger of Tone 3 (mid-level) and Tone 6 (low-level), in which the contrast is lost in production but maintained in perception, and a near merger between Tone 4 (low-falling) and Tone 6, in which listeners fail to discriminate between the two tones, even though they maintain a contrast in production. Studies of other dialects of Cantonese (e.g., Guangzhou, Macao, Zhuhai) show evidence of merger-in-progress at different stages (Ou 2012; Zhang 2019). Note that the above studies only examined tones in citation form. For a study of tones in conversational free speech of Hong Kong Cantonese as well as Heritage Cantonese spoken in Toronto, Canada, see Nagy, Tse & Stanford (forthcoming). Also, in Chen, Yao & Yu (2018), a longitudinal study of the public speeches of political figure C.Y. Leung reveals that Leung made his tone pairs more distinct over time, moving in the opposite direction of community trends, as he became more involved in a conservative political and language ideology.

The above studies show how tone mergers can be observed in progress, but tone splits-in-progress are less commonly observed. This is synchronic viewpoint of tone splits can potentially add significant new understanding to historical accounts of long-term changes in a tonal language, much like Weinreich, Labov & Herzog (1968) pointed out for sound change at the segmental level. One such attempt, an apparent-time study of Lili Wu tones, resulted in a conclusion that the tone split was already completed, with no generational differences observed (Shi, Chen & Mous 2020). To our knowledge, only one study has been able to investigate a tone split as an ongoing sound change in a speech community: the study of tone split-in-progress by Yang, Stanford & Yang

(2015) in Lalo, an under-described Tibeto-Burman language of southwestern China, which we summarize in our case study below.

A related question in sociotonetics is in what ways tone variation might relate to the notion of vowel chain shifts, where vowels "push" or "pull" each other in F1/F2 space, generating successive movements. A classic example is the English Great Vowel Shift that occurred near the end of the Middle English period (Trask 1996:85–87), and more recent examples include the US Northern Cities Vowel Shift (Labov, Ash & Boberg 2006:187–215). Do tones shift in this way, or do the interacting cues of voice quality, duration and so on, make tones less likely to "push" and "pull" one another in f0 space? Pittayaporn (2007, 2018) compares tonal acoustic studies of Bangkok Thai from different time periods across the twentieth century and finds phonetic changes suggestive of a tone chain shift: Tone 3 (mid-falling in the early twentieth century) is now high-falling, while Tone 4 (high-falling in the early twentieth century) is now mid rising, and Tone 5 (mid rising in the early twentieth century) is now low falling-rising. Apparent-time studies by Thepboriruk (2009, 2015) suggest that Tone 4 continues to evolve in the present day. Further sociotonetic research is needed to adequately explore the interesting issues involved in Bangkok Thai's tone chain shift-in-progress.

CASE STUDY   Observing a tone split-in-progress

This section presents a case study from sociotonetic research on Lalo (Yang, Stanford & Yang 2015) that illustrates many of the topics described in this chapter. Using a sociotonetic approach blending both production and perceptual studies, Yang, Stanford & Yang find evidence of a tone split-in-progress in Lalo. This study shows how a sociotonetic perspective provides insights not only into the social factors but also into phonological and perceptual issues involved in sound change. It also exemplifies the way that both production and perceptual work can contribute to a greater sociotonetic understanding of sound change.

Earlier acoustic analysis of Lalo tone had led to the hypothesis that Lalo's Tone 1 (high level) was undergoing a tone split (Yang 2015). Figure 4.4 provides a plot of the tone system of a 25-year-old female speaker whose Tone 1 shows phonetic effects conditioned by voicing of the syllable-initial consonant. In Tone 1 syllables with voiceless initials (including preglottalized), the pitch track is high level (the historically conservative form), but in syllables with voiced initial consonants (labeled Tone 1′), the pitch onset begins much lower and then gradually rises. Recall that there are often consonantal effects on f0 at the onset of the vowel, with higher f0 after voiceless consonants and lower after voiced. Such effects may remain stable over a long period of time, but multiple cues to the same contrast also open the door to possible sound change. In a process termed "transphonologization" (Haudricourt 1954), the original voicing contrast in consonants becomes weaker (say, through devoicing of voiced obstruents), and the accompanying cue of pitch difference becomes enhanced and perceptually salient. In the final stage, the voicing contrast is lost and is replaced by a contrast in pitch. This process is surmised to have occurred in tone splits across Asia (Edmondson & Solnit 1988). Using sociotonetic methods, the Lalo study set out to determine whether such a split could be observed in progress, rather than after the fact.

Methods

In the Lalo study, 38 native speakers from Qingyun Village participated in a production and perception experiment. Recordings of word-list data were used in the production experiment. The perceptual

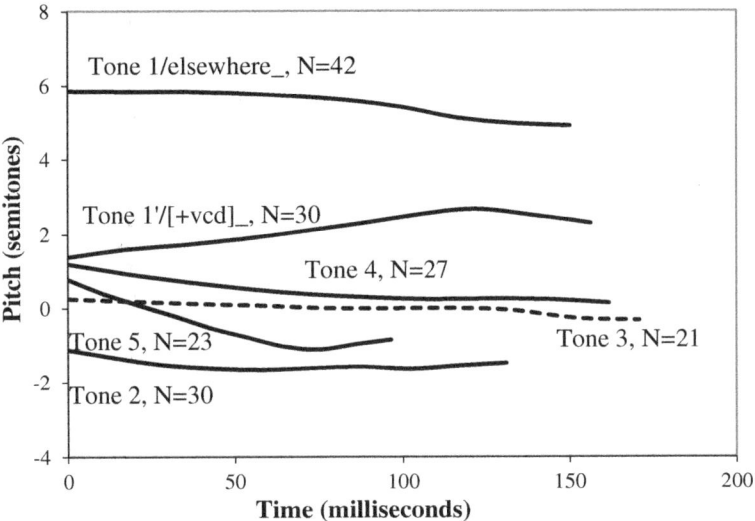

Figure 4.4 Qingyun Lalo tone system, including the Tone 1' variant after voiced initial consonants
Source: Yang 2015

study consisted of a forced-choice identification task to see whether Lalo listeners were starting to attend to pitch cues, not just segmental voicing, in identifying Tone 1 words. Participants listened to 24 audio prompts with either a voiced or voiceless obstruent initial (*pa* 'to exchange' or *ba* 'to burn'). f0 was manipulated for onset and slope. The listeners were asked to identify the word by pointing to the correct picture (Lalo does not have an orthography).

Results

The results of both experiments suggested that a tone split was indeed underway. The tone-split process is illustrated graphically by comparing acoustic analysis results from speakers at opposite ends of the demographic factors: an older man compared to a younger woman. In Figure 4.5a, the 75-year-old man's voiced-initial tone variant begins with a depressed pitch onset but then quickly rises to an early peak, thus "catching up" to the voiceless-initial variant in the first third of the syllable. In Figure 4.5b, however, the young woman's voiced-initial variant does not peak until the last half of the syllable, with the result that the two variants' pitch trajectories do not overlap for most of the syllable. Pittayaporn (2007) coined the term "peak sliding" to describe the gradual rightward sliding of a high tone target's peak over successive generations. Here the peak of the voiced-initial Tone 1 is defined as the time point when there is no statistically significant difference between the given speaker's voiced and voiceless Tone 1 tokens. When the peak's time location was examined statistically across the 38 speakers, the results showed that younger female speakers had peaks significantly later in the syllable. Results for VOT showed that more educated speakers had shorter prevoicing in their voiced stops, likely due to greater contact with Mandarin Chinese, which does not have voiced stops. Since younger speakers also tended to have higher education levels, the generational trend toward tone split

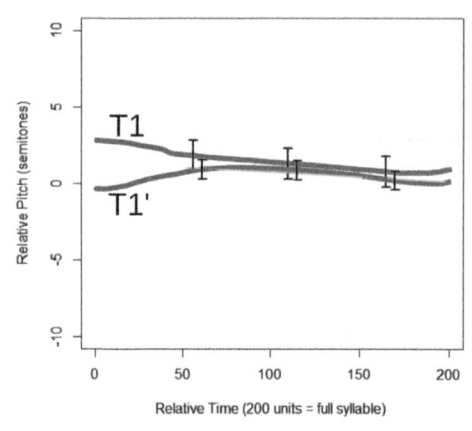 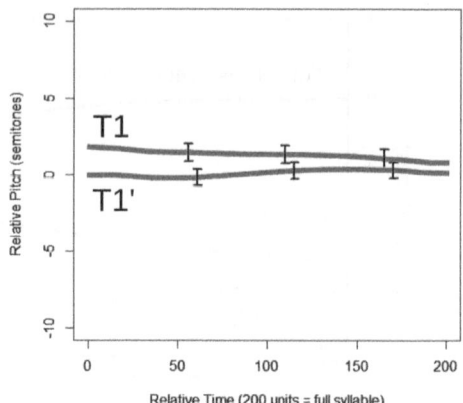

Figure 4.5   Average f0 trajectories for T1 and T1'
Figure 4.5a (left)   75-year-old male
Figure 4.5b (right)   30-year-old female

Source: Yang, Stanford & Yang 2015

is clear: as voiced obstruents become devoiced, the tone variants become increasingly distinct, eventually leading to a system where pitch rather than voicing is the main cue for the contrast, that is, a completed tone split. The logistic mixed-effect regression results matched the hypothesis that a tone split was in progress.

Discussion

Rather than only depending on consonant voicing as a cue, the results show that listeners used multiple cues to identify a word as beginning with a voiced obstruent: consonant voicing, mid f0 onset, and rising f0 contour. In cases where the prompt contained a voiceless initial, but with an onset at mid pitch and a slope between 15 Hz and 45 Hz, the majority of listeners mistakenly identified the prompt as voiced. This suggests that listeners weight the f0 onset and contour cues more heavily than voicing of the initial, which is the expected result for a tone split-in-progress. Such results are consistent with Beddor's (2009) notion of cue trading, where listeners are influenced by multiple perceptual cues during a change a progress. The results also match Pittayaporn's (2007) model of peak sliding in this type of tonal change, but we add the variationist viewpoint: With sociotonetic methods, we can observe this change in progress while it is happening, not just historically, and the specific paths of this change can be observed in fine-grained detail when correlated with social factors in the speech community.

Future of sociotonetics

Many of the world's languages are tonal, yet sociophonetics has primarily focused on segmental or intonational variables, not lexical tone or pitch accent. Although many tone languages have been studied extensively using experimental phonetic methods, such studies do not usually include questions of sociolinguistic variation. Since so few languages have been examined with sociotonetic methods, one priority is to expand the number and typology of languages studied. Expanding the scope of sociotonetics will enable researchers to develop an understanding of what types of tone variables are most likely to occur, what contextual effects should be included in the modeling, and what types of social meaning may be attached to tone variables.

Methodologically, one of the biggest challenges now facing sociotonetics is analyzing data from spontaneous speech. As we have discussed, most prior work on tone variation and change has focused on highly controlled speech styles, including citation style and sentence frames, rather than spontaneous, continuous speech. Investigating tonal variation in free speech is more complex, as segmental and prosodic environments greatly influence the tone shape, and as timing constraints cause incomplete tone excursions. Lexical tones that might be clearly contrastive in formal styles may be nearly or fully merged in spontaneous speech (Stanford 2016; Nagy, Tse & Stanford forthcoming). Nonetheless, spontaneous speech is a crucial speech style, as sociophoneticians have found for segmental and intonational variables. Thus, future research in sociotonetics needs to continue probing ways to effectively handle natural conversational data.

Acknowledgments

Special thanks to the community members who participated in these research studies and collaborated with us in these explorations of tone as a sociophonetic variable.

References

Asahi, Yoshiyuki, Alexandra D'Arcy & Paul Kerswill (eds.). Forthcoming. *Handbook of variationist sociolinguistics*. Routledge.

Bauer, Robert S., Cheung Kwan-hin & Cheung Pak-man. 2003. Variation and merger in the rising tones in Hong Kong Cantonese. *Language Variation and Change* 15(2). 211–225. https://doi.org/10.1017/S0954394503152039

Beddor, Patrice Speeter. 2009. A coarticulatory path to sound change. *Language* 85(4). 785–821. https://doi.org/10.1353/lan.0.0165

Bigi, Brigitte & Daniel Hirst. 2012. SPeech Phonetization Alignment and Syllabification (SPPAS): A tool for the automatic analysis of speech prosody. In *Proceedings on Speech Prosody 2012*, 19–22. International Speech Communication Association.

Boersma, Paul & David Weenink. 2022. *Praat: Doing phonetics by computer* [Computer program]. www.praat.org/

Chen, Si, Caroline Wiltshire & Bin Li. 2018. An updated typology of tonal coarticulation properties. *Taiwan Journal of Linguistics* 16(2). 79–114. https://doi.org/10.6519/TJL.2018.16(2).3

Chen, Ziqi, Yao Yao & Alan C.L. Yu. 2018. Changing against tone merging trends in community? The case of C.Y. Leung. In Politzer-Ahles et al., www.aclweb.org/anthology/Y18-1012

Crystal, David. 2003. *A dictionary of linguistics and phonetics*, 2nd edn. Blackwell.

Di Paolo, Marianna & Malcah Yaeger-Dror (eds.). 2011. *Sociophonetics: A student's guide*. Routledge.

DiCanio, Christian T. 2012. Coarticulation between tone and glottal consonants in Itunyoso Trique. *Journal of Phonetics* 40(1). 162–176. https://doi.org/10.1016/j.wocn.2011.10.006

DiCanio, Christian T., Joshua Benn & Rey Castillo García. 2020. Disentangling the effects of position and utterance-level declination on the production of complex tones in Yoloxóchitl Mixtec. *Language and Speech* 64(3). 515–557. https://doi.org/10.1177/0023830920939132

Edmondson, Jerold & David Solnit. 1988. *Comparative Kadai: Linguistic studies beyond Tai* [SIL International Publications in Linguistics 86]. Summer Institute of Linguistics and University of Texas.

Fung, Roxana S.Y. & Chris K.C. Lee. 2019. Tone mergers in Hong Kong Cantonese: An asymmetry of production and perception. *Journal of the Acoustical Society of America* 146(5). EL424–EL430. https:/doi.org/10.1121/1.5133661

Gandour, Jack, Siripong Potisuk & Sumalee Dechongkit. 1994. Tonal coarticulation in Thai. *Journal of Phonetics* 22(4). 477–492. https://doi.org/10.1016/S0095-4470(19)30296-7

Gao, Feier. 2020. Full tone to sound feminine: Analyzing the role of tonal variants in identity construction. *University of Pennsylvania Working Papers in Linguistics* 25(2). 41–50. https://repository.upenn.edu/pwpl/vol25/iss2/6

Gonzalez, Simon, James Grama & Catherine E. Travis. 2020. Comparing the performance of forced aligners used in sociophonetic research. *Linguistics Vanguard* 6(1). 1–13. https:/doi.org/10.1515/lingvan-2019-0058

Gussenhoven, Carlos. 2004. *The phonology of tone and intonation*. Cambridge University Press.

Haudricourt, André-Georges. 1954. De l'origine des tons en vietnamien. *Journal Asiatique* 242. 69–82.

Heath, Jeffrey & Laura McPherson. 2013. Tonosyntax and reference restriction in Dogon NPs. *Language* 89(2). 265–296. https://doi.org/10.1353/lan.2013.0020

Hildebrandt, Kristine A. 2004. *Manange tone: Scenarios of retention and loss in two communities (Nepal)*. PhD dissertation, University of California Santa Barbara.

Holliday, Nicole. 2021. Prosody and sociolinguistic variation in American Englishes. *Annual Review of Linguistics* 7. 55–68. https://doi.org/10.1146/annurev-linguistics-031220-093728

Hombert, Jean-Marie, John J. Ohala & William G. Ewan. 1979. Phonetic explanations for the development of tones. *Language* 55(1). 37–58. https://doi.org/10.2307/412518

Hyman, Larry. 2017. Bantu tone overview. *UC Berkeley Phonetics and Phonology Lab Annual Report* 13(1). 162–177. https://doi.org/10.5070/P7131040751

Jongman, Allard, Zhen Qin, Jie Zhang & Joan A. Sereno. 2017. Just noticeable differences for pitch direction, height, and slope for Mandarin and English listeners. *Journal of the Acoustical Society of America* 142(2). EL163–EL169. https://doi.org/10.1121/1.4995526

Katz, William F. & Peter F. Assman (eds.). 2019. *The Routledge handbook of phonetics*. Routledge.

Kerswill, Paul. 1994. *Dialects converging: Rural speech in urban Norway*. Clarendon Press.

Kirby, James P. 2018. Onset pitch perturbations and the cross-linguistic implementation of voicing: Evidence from tonal and non-tonal languages. *Journal of Phonetics* 71. 326–354. https://doi.org/10.1016/j.wocn.2018.09.009

Kirby, James P. & D. Robert Ladd. 2016. Effects of obstruent voicing on vowel f0: Evidence from "true voicing" languages. *Journal of the Acoustical Society of America* 140(4). 2400–2411. https://doi.org/10.1121/1.4962445

Kisler, Thomas, Uwe Reichel & Florian Schiel. 2017. Multilingual processing of speech via web services. *Computer Speech & Language* 45. 326–347. https://doi.org/10.1016/j.csl.2017.01.005

Labov, William. 1966. *The social stratification of English in New York City*. Center for Applied Linguistics.

Labov, William. 1994–2010. *Principles of linguistic change*. 3 vols. Blackwell.

Labov, William, Sharon Ash & Charles Boberg. 2006. *The atlas of North American English: Phonetics, phonology, and sound change: A multimedia reference tool*. De Gruyter.

Labov, William, & Maciej Baranowski. 2006. 50 msec. *Language Variation and Change* 18(3). 223–240. https://doi.org/10.1017/S095439450606011X

Lei, Xin. 2006. *Modeling lexical tones for Mandarin large vocabulary continuous speech recognition*. PhD dissertation, University of Washington.

Meyerhoff, Miriam. 2017. Writing a linguistic symphony: Analyzing variation while doing language documentation. *Canadian Journal of Linguistics/Revue canadienne de linguistique* 62. 1–25. https://doi.org/10.1017/cnj.2017.28

Micheyl, Christophe, & Andrew Oxenham. 2004. Sequential f0 comparisons between resolved and unresolved harmonics: no evidence for translation noise between two mechanisms. *Journal of the Acoustical Society of America* 116. 3038–3050. https://doi.org/10.1121/1.1806825

Mok, Peggy P.K., Donghui Zuo & Peggy W.Y. Wong. 2013. Production and perception of a sound change in progress: Tone merging in Hong Kong Cantonese. *Language Variation and Change* 25(3). 341–370. https://doi.org/10.1017/S0954394513000161

Nagy, Naomi & Miriam Meyerhoff. 2008. The social lives of language. In Miriam Meyerhoff & Naomi Nagy (eds.), *Social lives in language – Sociolinguistics and multilingual speech communities: Celebrating the work of Gillian Sankoff*, 1–17. John Benjamins.

Nagy, Naomi, Holman Tse & James Stanford. Forthcoming. Cantonese tone mergers in spontaneous speech. In Rajiv Rao (ed.), *Studies on the phonetics and phonology of heritage languages*. Cambridge University Press.

Nguyen, Van Loi & Jerold Edmondson. 1998. Tones and voice quality in modern northern Vietnamese: Instrumental case studies. *Mon-Khmer Studies* 28. 1–18.

Ou, Jinghua. 2012. *Tone merger in Guangzhou Cantonese*. MA thesis, Hong Kong Polytechnic University.

Pham, Andrea Hoa. 2003. The key phonetic properties of Vietnamese tone: A reassessment. In Maria-Josep Solé, Daniel Recasens & Joaquin Romero (eds.), *Proceedings of the 15th International Congress of Phonetic Sciences*, 1703–1706. Universidad Autónoma de Barcelona.

Pittayaporn, Pittayawat. 2007. Directionality of tone change. In Jürgen Trouvain & William Barry (eds.), *Proceedings of the 16th International Congress of Phonetic Sciences*, 1421–1424. Saarland University.

Pittayaporn, Pittayawat. 2018. Phonetic and systemic biases in tonal contour changes in Bangkok Thai. In Haruo Kubozono & Mikio Giriko (eds.), *Tonal change and neutralization*, 249–278. De Gruyter.

Politzer-Ahles, Stephen, Yu-Yin Hsu, Chu-Ren Huang & Yao Yao (eds.). 2018. *Proceedings of the 32nd Pacific Asia Conference on Language, Information, and Computation*. Association for Computational Linguistics.

Ross, Elliott, Jerold Edmondson & Burton Seibert. 1986. The effect of affect on various acoustic measures of prosody in tone and non-tone languages. *Journal of Phonetics* 14. 283–302. https://doi.org/10.1016/S0095-4470(19)30669-2

Shattuck-Hufnagel, Stefanie, Laura Dilley, Nanette Veilleux, Alejna Brugos & Rob Speer. 2004. f0 peaks and valleys aligned with non-prominent syllables can influence perceived prominence in adjacent syllables. In *Proceedings of Speech Prosody 2004*, 705–708.

Shi, Menghui, Yiya Chen & Maarten Mous. 2020. Tonal split and laryngeal contrast of onset consonant in Lili Wu Chinese. *Journal of the Acoustical Society of America* 147(4). 2901–2916. https://doi.org/10.1121/10.0001000.

Silverstein, Michael 2003. Indexical order and the dialectics of sociolinguistic life. *Language & Communication* 23(3). 193–229. https://doi.org/10.1016/S0271-5309(03)00013-2

Stanford, James N. 2008. A sociotonetic analysis of Sui dialect contact. *Language Variation and Change* 20(3). 409–450. https://doi.org/10.1017/S0954394508000161

Stanford, James N. 2010. The role of marriage in linguistic contact and variation: Two Hmong dialects in Texas. *Journal of Sociolinguistics* 14(1). 89–115. https://doi.org/10.1111/j.1467-9841.2009.00436.x

Stanford, James N. 2016. Sociotonetics using connected speech: A study of Sui tone variation in free-speech style. *Asia-Pacific Language Variation* 2. 48–81. https://doi.org/10.1075/aplv.2.1.02sta

Stanford, James N. & Dennis R. Preston. 2009. The lure of a distant horizon. In James Stanford and Dennis Preston (eds.), *Variation in indigenous minority Languages,* 1–20. John Benjamins.

Steed, William & Phil Rose. 2009. Same tone, different category: Linguistic-tonetic variation in the areal tone acoustics of chuqu wu. *Interspeech 2009*. 2295–2298. https://doi.org/10.21437/Interspeech.2009-650.

Takano, Shoji & Ichiro Ota. 2017. A sociophonetic approach to variation in Japanese pitch realizations. *Asia-Pacific Language Variation* 3(1). 5–40. https://doi.org/10.1075/aplv.3.1.02tak

Thepboriruk, Kanjana. 2009. Bangkok Thai tones revisited. *Journal of the Southeast Asian Linguistics Society* 3(1). 86–105.

Thepboriruk, Kanjana. 2015. *Thai in diaspora: Language and identity in Los Angeles, California*. PhD dissertation, University of Hawai'i.

Thomas, Erik R. 2011. *Sociophonetics: An introduction*. Palgrave.

Thomas, Erik R. 2019. Innovation in sociophonetics. In Katz & Assman, 448–472.

Trask, R.L. 1996. *Historical linguistics*. Arnold.

Traunmüller, Hartmut & Anders Eriksson. 1995. The frequency range of the voice fundamental in the speech of male and female adults. Unpublished manuscript.

Weinreich, Uriel, William Labov & Marvin Herzog. 1968. Empirical foundations for a theory of language change. In Winifred P. Lehmann & Yakov Malkiel (eds.), *Directions for historical linguistics: A symposium*, 95–195. University of Texas Press.

Whalen, D.H. & A.G. Levitt. 1995. The universality of intrinsic f0 of vowels. *Journal of Phonetics* 23. 349–366. https://doi.org/10.1515/9783110567502-010

Xu, Yi. 1999. Effects of tone and focus on the formation and alignment of f0 contours. *Journal of Phonetics* 27. 55–105. https://doi.org/10.1006/jpho.1999.0086

Xu, Yi. 2004. Understanding tone from the perspective of production and perception. *Language and Linguistics* 5(4). 757–797.

Xu, Yi. 2019. Prosody, tone, and intonation. In Katz & Assmann, 314–356.

Yaeger-Dror, Malcah, Tania Granadillo, Shoji Takano, Hokusei Gakuen, & Lauren Hall-Lew. 2010. The sociophonetics of prosodic contours on NEG in three language communities. In Dennis Preston & Nancy Niedzielski (eds.), *A reader in sociophonetics*, 133–175. De Gruyter.

Yang, Cathryn. 2015. *Lalo dialects across time and space: Subgrouping, dialectometry, and intelligibility.* Asia-Pacific Linguistics.

Yang, Cathryn, James Stanford & Zhengyu Yang. 2015. A sociotonetic study of Lalo tone change in progress. *Asia-Pacific Language Variation* 1(1). 52–77. https://doi.org/10.1075/aplv.1.1.03yan

Yang, Cathryn, James Stanford, Yang Liu, Jingjin Jiang, & Liufang Tang. 2019. Variation and change in the tonal space of Yangliu Lalo, an endangered language of Yunnan, China. *Linguistics of the Tibeto-Burman Area* 42(1). 2–37. https://doi.org/10.1075/ltba.18008.yan

Yang, Cathryn, Pittayawat Pittayaporn, James Kirby & Sujinat Jitwiriyanont. 2021. Change and stability in the tonal contours of King Rama IX of Thailand, 1959–1997. In Oliver Niebuhr (ed.), *Proceedings of the First International Conference on Tone and Intonation.* https://doi.org/10.21437/TAI.2021-14

Yang, Cathryn, James Stanford, Chunxia Luo & Naluo Zhang. 2022. Generational differences in the low tones of Black Lahu. *Linguistics Vanguard* 8(s5). 759–770. https://doi.org/10.1515/lingvan-2021-0099

Yip, Moira. 2002. *Tone.* Cambridge University Press.

Zellou, Georgia, Alan C.L. Yu, & Christian DiCanio (eds.). 2022. Sound change in endangered and small speech communities [Special issue]. *Linguistics Vanguard* 8(s5).

Zhang, Qing. 2005. A Chinese yuppie in Beijing: Phonological variation and the construction of a new professional identity. *Language in Society* 34(3). 431–466. https://doi.org/10.1017/S0047404505050153

Zhang, Jie & Jiang Liu. 2011. Tone sandhi and tonal coarticulation in Tianjin Chinese. *Phonetica* 68. 161–191. https://doi.org/10.1159/000333387

Zhang, Jingwei. 2014. *A sociophonetic study on tonal variation of the Wuxi and Shanghai dialects.* PhD dissertation, Utrecht University.

Zhang, Jingwei. 2018. A comparison of tone normalization methods for language variation research. In Politzer-Ahles et al. https://aclanthology.org/Y18-1095

Zhang, Jingwei. 2019. Tone mergers in Cantonese: Evidence from Hong Kong, Macao, and Zhuhai. *Asia-Pacific Language Variation* 5(1). 28–49. https://doi.org/10.1075/aplv.18007.zha

Zhang, Jingwei, Yanyong Zhang & Daming Xu. 2019. A variationist approach to tone categorization in Cantonese. *Chinese Languages and Discourse* 10(1). 1–16. https://doi.org/10.1075/cld.18008.zha

Zhao, Hui. 2018. Social meaning in the perception of neutral tone variation in *Putonghua. Asia-Pacific Language Variation* 4(2). 161–196. https://doi.org/10.1075/aplv.18003.zha.

Zhu, Xiaonong. 1999. *Shanghai tonetics.* Lincom.

5

SOCIOPHONETICS AND PHONATION

Lisa Davidson

Introduction

Phonation, in the most basic sense, typically refers to sound that is generated by the vocal folds or other structures of the larynx. The rate at which the vocal folds vibrate, typically measured in Hertz (Hz), is referred to as "fundamental frequency," or f0. "Pitch," a related term, is the perceptual correlate of fundamental frequency.

In linguistics, the primary subdivision of phonation types is often termed "modal" versus "nonmodal" phonation, where modal generally evades a precise definition and is used to indicate "ordinary voicing" (Catford 1964; Laver 1980; Kreiman & Sidtis 2011; Esling et al. 2019; Garellek 2019). Modal phonation generally assumes that the vocal folds are vibrating periodically, but it is perhaps better understood in comparison to nonmodal phonation, which refers to vocal fold vibration that is produced with adjustments to the laryngeal articulators. For example, one common nonmodal phonation is creaky voice, which is often associated with a long period between successive glottal openings (causing a low f0) that can be irregular, with low airflow, and with thickened vocal folds that can be coupled with contact by the ventricular folds, which are located just above the vocal folds (Catford 1964; Laver 1980; Gobl & Ni Chasaide 2010; Esling et al. 2019). Another nonmodal phonation, breathy voice, is produced with shortened and loosened vocal folds that can sometimes vibrate only along half the length of the glottis, such that escaping air produces noisy components in the acoustic signal (Laver 1980; Gobl & Ni Chasaide 2010; Esling et al. 2019).

Because of the independence of the source (the vocal folds) and the filter (the supralaryngeal vocal tract) (Fant 1960), different phonation types can be implemented in conjunction with the supralaryngeal articulations of most phonemes. One way in which languages can implement this relationship is to have sounds such as vowels or sonorants that lexically contrast on the basis of voice quality. That is, a vowel can be produced either with modal phonation, or with a nonmodal phonation like breathy or creaky, to change the meaning of the word (e.g., Blankenship 2002; Esposito 2010; Garellek 2012). Such uses of nonmodal phonation can also mark dialectal differences, as differences in the acoustic implementation of tense and lax vowels in New York and Utah speakers (Di Paolo & Faber 1990). Phonation can also be recruited for broader sociophonetic purposes, which is the focus of this chapter. Speakers can implement nonmodal phonation types

DOI: 10.4324/9781003034636-6

such as creaky, breathy, or falsetto to index ethnicity, race, sexuality, or gender, to distinguish them from speakers of other groups, to display affect, to communicate personality characteristics, or to impart pragmatic information.

This chapter focuses more narrowly on aspects of phonation—primarily nonmodal phonation and speaking fundamental frequency—that speakers manipulate for sociolinguistic purposes. Research has shown that speaker groups defined by gender, race, or ethnicity can employ nonmodal phonation differently than a comparison group (e.g., Mendoza-Denton 2011; Szakay 2012; Wileman 2018). Another property of phonation that can be sociolinguistically recruited is speaking fundamental frequency (SFF), which refers to the typical value of a speaker's habitual fundamental frequency. Though there is a demonstrable relationship between f0 and sex (Titze 1989; Simpson 2009), there is little evidence of a relationship between other physical characteristics such as height or weight (e.g., Hollien & Jackson 1973; Kreiman & Sidtis 2011), and speakers of any gender and body size can also raise and lower SFF much as they can implement nonmodal phonation types. Thus, research has shown that speakers of different languages can have different baseline SFFs (e.g., van Bezooijen 1995; Keating & Kuo 2012), which cannot be attributed to physical origins.

There are many ways that speakers can implement voice quality that intersect with the sociolinguistic variables that have been identified as useful in constructing identity (e.g., Bucholtz & Hall 2005), including emotion, how discourse is organized, or idiosyncratic aspects of a speakers' voice that are not due to phonation, such as nasalization. Some of these areas will be mentioned briefly in this article, but an in-depth treatment will be left to other sources that focus on those topics, such as voice register in discourse analysis (Sicoli 2010, 2015) or the expression of emotion (Gobl & Ni Chasaide 2003; Patel et al. 2011). Readers interested in the material in the current chapter should also read Podesva & Callier (2015), which focuses on how voice quality is used in the construction of identity, affect, and stance, and also briefly addresses the role voice quality plays in media, forensics, and speech technology.

Phonation as a sociolinguistic variable: Early and holistic studies

Some of the earliest work examining the use of phonation as a sociolinguistic variable was carried out by researchers in the United Kingdom who examined how location, gender (cisgender male and female), and socioeconomic status correlated with the implementation of different voice qualities. While early work relied on Catford's (1964) and Laver's (1968) phonetic categories but not instrumental work, it laid the groundwork for research in a similar vein. Trudgill (1974) describes working-class speech in Norwich English as being loud and as having creaky voice, a metallic quality, a high pitch, and a raised larynx, as compared to middle-class informants. Esling (1978a) takes a more numerical approach with speakers from Edinburgh by conducting interviews with 52 speakers and then impressionistically sorting them into 10 voice quality types (modal, creaky, harsh, whispery, breathy, and combinations of some of these). Esling observes that creaky voice is more common for the affluent speakers, while harsh voice (referring to a voice quality with a low pitch, but relatively aperiodic f0, and produced with constricted vocal folds and laryngeal structures) was found for those from a more working-class neighborhood.

One of the first studies to include analysis of spectrograms in categorizing nonmodal phonation usage is Henton & Bladon (1988), who examined the use of creak in British Received Pronunciation (RP) and Modified Northern (MN), spoken by people from Leeds who have since moved away. They find that creak is primarily used as an end-of-sentence marker, but it was more frequent in MN male speakers compared to other participants. Henton & Bladon (1985) measured the difference between the amplitude of the first and second harmonics (H1-H2) to demonstrate that cisgender female speakers of both RP and MN used breathier phonation than male speakers of both dialects. They hypothesize that the female speakers may choose this phonation because it conveys desirability to their interlocutors. Stuart-Smith (1999) likewise examined the effects of class, age, and gender (cisgender male and female) on the implementation of nonmodal phonation in Glaswegian English, showing that male Glaswegian speakers also show more creakiness than female speakers, but it does not correlate with social class.

Another type of early study is demonstrated by Pittam (1987), who examined subjective judgments of different voice qualities. Twelve Australian English speakers produced a reading passage in breathy, creaky, nasal, tense, and whispery voice. Australian and American listeners rated the voices on scales related to status and solidarity. For all listeners, male tense voice was rated as having the highest status. As for solidarity, breathy voice was rated highly for female speakers, especially older ones, and creaky and tense voice were rated as low for all speakers, but higher for male speakers than female ones. Later studies in a similar vein as Pittam (1987) have examined whether listeners appear to be sensitive to general differences in phonation in judgments of sexuality and ethnicity. For example, Levon (2007) examined a number of acoustic variables that listeners might access when making judgments about whether an English speaker is gay or straight. While the main variables in this study are sibilant duration and pitch range, a post hoc analysis of voice quality features including jitter (a measure of the variability in f0 from cycle to cycle), shimmer (a measure of variability in the amplitude of vocal fold vibration from cycle to cycle), and harmonics-to-noise ratio (HNR) show that all these values are significantly different for the gay and straight talkers in the study. Holliday & Villareal (2020), in addition to intonational variables, also measure jitter, shimmer, and HNR to investigate how listeners judge the ethnicity of English speakers. For the H* intonational peak type, a longer delay in the peak was rated as significantly more Black than a shorter delay, but only if HNR was high. For the L+H* phrases, less jitter led to higher Blackness ratings. These results suggest a complicated relationship between voice quality and intonational variables that can be used to index race or ethnicity in English.

Sociolinguistic examinations of nonmodal phonation types

In this section, we take a deeper dive into four of the nonmodal phonation types that have been most commonly examined as sociolinguistic variables: creaky, harsh and hoarse, breathy, and falsetto.

Creaky phonation

Despite early reports of greater use of creak by British cisgender male speakers (Catford 1977; Esling 1978b; Wells 1982; Henton & Bladon 1988; Stuart-Smith 1999), more recently, observations of creaky phonation have been attributed to young American (primarily white) women. For example, several popular press articles counsel women to eliminate "vocal fry" (the lay term for creaky phonation) if they hope to succeed in the workplace (Khazan 2014; Wolf 2015; Mo 2016). Despite such comments, there is not convincing evidence that young female Americans differ substantially from other speakers in the proportions of their utterances that contain creaky voice. Some studies suggest that overall women produce more syllables in read sentences or passages with creak than men do (Yuasa 2010; Wolk, Abdelli-Beruh & Slavin 2012; Abdelli-Beruh, Wolk & Slavin 2014) (though these studies mainly use perceptual, rather than acoustic, criteria to identify creak). Podesva's (2013) study of the spontaneous speech of white and Black speakers from Washington DC found greater proportions of creaky phonation for female (27 percent) than male (8 percent) speakers, regardless of their race. Others demonstrate that differences between (cisgender) men and women are either small or absent (Melvin & Clopper 2015; Abdelli-Beruh, Drugman & Red Owl 2016; Irons & Alexander 2016; Pratt 2018). A review of existing production studies examining the use of creak in varieties of English (mostly American, with one study including two British dialects) concludes that the lack of consistency in methods and results makes it very unclear what factors actually influence the prevalence of creaky phonation in English (Dallaston & Docherty 2020).

Whether or not female speakers do actually produce utterances with a greater proportion of creaky phonation, some research in communication sciences and psychology suggests that there may be negative consequences for women—but not as much for men—who use creaky phonation. Anderson et al. (2014), who tested whether creaky voice had a measurably negative effect on how listeners rated personality characteristics of speakers using vocal fry in a workplace-like setting, found that creaky tokens are given fewer positive ratings than the modal tokens in general, but listeners judge female speakers more harshly than male speakers on the stimuli containing creaky voice for the qualities of trustworthiness, competence, education, and willingness to hire.

Other studies have attempted to determine whether creaky voice is perceived to convey a particular affect. While some work suggests that creaky phonation can be associated with authoritativeness for female speakers (Yuasa 2010; Greer & Winters 2015), other studies show that creaky voice can carry a "low-energy" or "chill" connotation (Gobl & Ni Chasaide 2003; Ligon et al. 2018; Pratt 2018). For example, the communication disorders students who serve as raters in Ligon et al. (2018) apply negative adjectives to female speakers using creaky voice, such as "vain," "apathetic/disinterested," and "bored/unengaged"—though some of their participants also used adjectives like "relaxed/chill," "sophisticated," and "sexy." They speculate that women may use creaky phonation in some social situations "to avoid being called lively and aggressive, too feminine and sweet, or worse yet, insecure/hesitant" (2018:14).

One question that arises is whether physical elements factor in to whether listeners perceive creaky voice more in the speech of female speakers, or whether listeners can hear it equally in male and female speakers but only negatively evaluate it for female ones. That is, perhaps creaky phonation is more salient when compared with a speaker's SFF that is higher, as it often is for female speakers, as opposed to speakers with lower SFF. However, when Davidson (2019) presented listeners with fully modal, fully creaky, and partially creaky utterances (which started as modal and ended as creaky), listeners were nearly equally likely to identify creak in the fully and partially creaky utterances regardless of whether the speakers were male or female, or what their SFF was. While this study did not elicit subjective evaluations, it suggests that stronger negative evaluations of women are not because creak is less discernible in men.

Despite potential negative evaluations of creaky phonation, some researchers speculate that the use of creaky phonation might be nevertheless advantageous because it has the effect of lowering a speaker's f0 (Yuasa 2010; Zimman 2013, 2018; Anderson et al. 2014). Zimman (2018) observes that transgender men may employ creaky phonation to be able to access a lower pitch range if they are dissatisfied with the SFF of their voices. Davidson (2020) investigates whether listeners do hear utterances that begin as modal and end as creaky as being holistically lower in SFF than fully modal utterances, finding that this is the case for cisgender female speakers with a higher SFF (~200 Hz) but not for those with a lower SFF (~150 Hz). It is an open question as to whether this finding would apply in the same way to transgender speakers.

Sociolinguistic examinations also report that speakers can use creaky phonation to index aspects of identity related to ethnicity or sexuality, such as a hardcore Chicano gangster persona

(Mendoza-Denton 2011) or Māori English speakers in New Zealand compared to those of European descent (Szakay 2012). Levon (2015) presents a case study of a gay Orthodox Jewish man in Israel to argue that he uses creaky phonation as a way of signaling that both his homosexuality and Orthodox Jewishness are critical if conflicting aspects of his identity. Thus, creaky voice may be used relatively holistically by some speaker groups to differentiate themselves from other communities.

Harsh and hoarse voice

Besides creaky voice, two other voice qualities that involve constriction of the glottis or other laryngeal structures are harsh and hoarse voice. These are considered together here, as Esling et al. (2019) treat these two terms as referring to the same voice quality that is more constricted than creaky voice due to the addition of aryepiglottic and lower epilaryngeal tightening. Moisik (2012) examines the use of harsh voice in performances that reference racial identity, finding that primarily Black actors use harsh voice to index Blackness, especially when those same actors contrast a Black character with a white one using their own voice. Other uses of harsh voice by the actors that Moisik (2012) investigates include aggressive posturing and to indicate comedic functions. Armstrong, Henriksen & DiCanio (2015) report that some of their speakers of Peninsular Spanish narrated a picture book with a nonmodal voice quality that they believe is most consistent with hoarse voice. This judgment is based on the low value of the acoustic measurement H1-H2, which is typically associated with creaky voice, but which did not correspond to the irregular or widely spaced phonation hallmarks of creaky voice. A perception task indicated that listeners were more likely to rate the nonmodal speakers as apathetic, strong, and less intelligent. A better understanding of whether this use of hoarse voice is motivated by sociolinguistic considerations requires more participants, but this study underscores that researchers should take care when evaluating spectral measures, since they often must be corroborated by other acoustic cues to be interpreted (Garellek 2019).

Breathy voice

Breathy voice has long been observed as a voice quality with sociophonetic connotations, since vocal anatomical and modeling research has shown that cisgender female voices may be breathier for physical reasons, such as thinner vocal folds or posterior closure insufficiency that does not allow for complete closure (e.g., Titze 1989; Klatt & Klatt 1990; Schneider & Bigenzahn 2003; Simpson 2009). In phonetic comparisons of cisgender male and female speakers, greater breathiness has been reported for female speakers in a variety of languages, including British English, American English, Peninsular Spanish, German, Swedish, Czech, Danish, Dutch, and French (e.g., Henton & Bladon 1985; Klatt & Klatt 1990; Södersten & Lindestad 1990; Trittin & de Santos y Lleó 1995; Mendoza et al. 1996; Van Borsel, Janssens & De Bodt 2009; Pépiot 2014; Hejná et al. 2021). However, some authors argue that degree of breathiness may be language-specific and learned (Trittin & de Santos y Lleó 1995; Pépiot 2014), since female speakers have a smaller difference in breathiness as compared to male speakers in some languages than in others.

While breathiness in female voices may have anatomical roots, speakers can enhance its role both in crafting personal identities and in developing characters. One long-standing finding is that, cross-culturally, listeners associate breathiness with femininity. For example, in rating the femininity of Dutch vowel sounds spoken by cisgender female talkers, listeners judge the breathier vowels to be more feminine (Van Borsel, Janssens & De Bodt 2009). A study examining the perception of the speech of American English heterosexual crossdressing men who spoke in both "masculine" and "feminine mode" found that listeners rated the "feminine mode" as breathier

(Andrews & Schmidt 1997). In a study of white American female film archetypes from the 1940s–1950s, Jeong (2017) shows that actresses in "femme fatale" and "dumb blond" roles speak with breathier voices than "screwball heroines" do. This iconic use of breathiness, as well as pitch and other voice quality types, suggests that the femme fatale and dumb blond personae portray a more sexually appealing type of female character than the screwball heroine. In considering actors in Japanese, Starr (2015) describes "sweet voice" as a style of professional voice that is produced by female anime actors. The acoustic analysis indicates that sweet voice is characterized by a mix of modal and breathy voice quality, as well as lower f0 and use of "head register" (see also Ohara 2004 on breathiness and femininity in Japanese, and Matsuda et al. this volume).

Other studies suggest a possible relationship between breathiness and race/ethnicity—though it appears to be one among several variables that listeners can access. For example, American English listeners (from a variety of racial and ethnic backgrounds) are more likely to identify acoustically breathier voices as Asian American than as Black, white, or Hispanic (Newman & Wu 2011), though listeners are also sensitive to other characteristics like vowel quality and rhoticity. Studies by Erik Thomas and colleagues show nuanced differences in the importance of breathiness; whereas an acoustic analysis in McDonald & Thomas (2012) indicates that breathiness does not reliably distinguish between African and European Americans, a production study by Thomas & Reaser (2015) suggests that breathiness is a reliable correlate of African American (cisgender) male speech, but not female speech. This is consistent with a similar result that Thomas & Lass (2005) found for listeners' identification of African American versus European American male (but not female) speech. In South Africa, it is Black female speakers of South African English that have higher levels of breathiness than white female South Africans (Wileman 2018). While the research on breathiness and race/ethnicity is currently limited, it is a fruitful avenue for future research.

Falsetto voice

Falsetto has also been linked to the expression of speakers' ethnic and racial identity. Esling et al. (2019) describe falsetto as a high-pitched type of phonation that is produced when the vocal folds are stretched and thinned at the edges (see also Hollien & Michel 1968; Laver 1980). Studies of Black speakers in the United States have observed that falsetto is integral to Black identity in some communities. Some early studies suggested that falsetto was used to encourage solidarity among Black speakers (Tarone 1973; Loman 1975). More recently, Alim (2004) characterizes the falsetto used by the Californian speakers he observes as an "interrogative challenger" that occurs when speakers are in "battlin" mode, or as a declarative emphasizer, and Nielsen (2010) finds that his 14-year-old interlocutor from Washington DC uses falsetto to expressively convey oppositional alignment. Podesva (2013, 2016) also examines speakers from Washington DC, finding that falsetto is used more by the Black female speakers than by the other participants, but that the rates of falsetto for Black men are not greater than for the white speakers. Podesva (2013:442) concludes that for these Black women, "falsetto is a linguistic act of resistance to the sometimes hostile environment in which they live and work." Other work by Podesva suggests that using falsetto to convey expressiveness may in fact be a broader, conventionalized use of falsetto. In Podesva (2007), a white gay male speaker originally from Long Island, New York indexes a type of expressiveness with falsetto, as well as a diva persona, and perhaps his gay identity more broadly.

One observation about falsetto is that, perhaps more than any other voice quality, it is employed not as a diffuse characteristic of a speaker's voice, but rather to convey specific stances or pragmatic meaning. Sometimes this can be tied to an in-group identity that a speaker is trying to convey, but it also has been observed more broadly among speakers of a language. For example, speakers of Lachixío Zapotec use falsetto, rather than pronouns, to mark a respect register (Sicoli 2010, 2015). Stross (2013) describes how Tseltal Maya speakers in Chiapas, Mexico employ falsetto to indicate respect and deference, but also to communicate across distances, while Huichol speakers in Jalisco and Nayarit express excitement with falsetto.

Nonmodal phonation: Summary

Like supralaryngeal linguistic elements such as vowel quality, sibilant frequencies, or intonation, nonmodal phonation can be harnessed to create, enhance, and communicate aspects of speakers' identities. First, speakers may have a goal of contrast with other groups within their communities, or voice quality can be exploited by actors to imbue characters with a particular identity. In many cases, these implementations of voice quality are taken to be holistic, either measured in individual sounds and assumed to be generalized throughout their speech, or else broadly observed throughout speakers' utterances and not tied to specific meanings or pragmatic uses. Second, voice quality can be used to convey stances, as is demonstrated by the example that creaky voice can be implemented to suggest "low affect." It is also the case that listeners attribute affects to speakers, whether they welcome it or not (such as when creaky voice is evaluated as less intelligent.) Lastly, some voice qualities seem more amenable to being recruited for pragmatic uses, as demonstrated especially by falsetto voice, but perhaps also harsh voice when used to convey aggressive posturing. Ultimately, the ability of voice quality to spread over larger units of speech gives it a flexibility beyond phoneme-related sociophonetic elements.

CASE STUDY   Sociophonetic factors in speaking fundamental frequency

Speaking fundamental frequency (SFF) refers to whether a speaker has a relatively high- or low-pitched overall speaking voice. This case study examines the potential role of SFF in the sociolinguistic domain of beliefs about politicians to explore whether listeners use information about female politicians' pitch to make assumptions about their political affiliation.

As shown in Table 5.1, there are consistent differences in SFF between cisgender male and female speakers, but even for same-sex speakers of the same language, there can be variation in speakers' SFF ranges. While there are potentially many aspects of pitch that carry sociolinguistic import (e.g., tone, intonation, mimicry), the focus of this section is about how SFF varies across languages and how listeners evaluate properties of speakers when asked to attend to SFF.

Comparisons of SFF across many languages suggest that it is a language-specific property that must be learned by speakers, and that SFF can differ among a multilingual speaker's languages. The results shown in Table 5.1 are not comprehensive, but were chosen to sample a variety of languages. For example, results from within the same study demonstrate that while German and British speakers have a relatively low SFF for both cisgender males and females, Bulgarian and Polish speakers have a higher SFF (Andreeva et al. 2014). One reason for discrepancies among studies ostensibly reporting on the same language—other than potential hidden regional differences, or the fact that task differences can sometimes result in SFF variation (Keating & Kuo 2012; Lee & Sidtis 2017)—is that in some studies participants were recruited while living in a country where they also speak a different language, and the SFF of the language of that country could affect their native SFF.

Table 5.1 Average speaking fundamental frequencies (in Hz) reported for cisgender male and female speakers

	Male speakers	Female speakers	
American English (Black)	108.85	—	(Walton & Orlikoff 1994)
American English (Black)	127.56	256.82	(Andrianopoulos, Darrow, & Chen 2001)
American English (White)	128.31	242.06	(Andrianopoulos, Darrow & Chen 2001)
American English (White)	107.55	—	(Walton & Orlikoff 1994)
American English (ethnicity/ race not specified)	119	210	(Pépiot 2014)
American English (ethnicity/ race not specified)	102	214	(Keating & Kuo 2012)
Hindi	137.6	263.78	(Andrianopoulos, Darrow & Chen 2001)
Mandarin Chinese	154.21	295.03	(Andrianopoulos, Darrow & Chen 2001)
Mandarin Chinese	131	233	(Keating & Kuo 2012)
Polish	138	—	(Majewski, Hollien, & Zalewski 1972)
Japanese	121	238	(Terasawa, Kakita, & Hirano 1984)
French	133	234	(Pépiot 2014)
Bulgarian	154	275	(Andreeva et al. 2014)
Polish	157	259	(Andreeva et al. 2014)
German	120	206	(Andreeva et al. 2014)
British English	127	218	(Andreeva et al. 2014)

Table 5.2 Average speaking fundamental frequency (in Hz) reported for bilingual cisgender male (M) and female (F) speakers for various language pairings

	Language 1	English	Study
Korean-English* (F)	~210	~200	(Lee & Sidtis 2017)
Mandarin-English (F)	~203	~204	(Lee & Sidtis 2017)
Welsh-English (F)	217	211	(Ordin & Mennen 2017)
Welsh-English (M)	117.56	117.6	
Russian-English* (F)	208.20	190.12	(Altenberg & Ferrand 2006)
Cantonese-English (F)	174.79	182.31	(Altenberg & Ferrand 2006)
Finnish-English* (M)	M: 102.97	106.35	(Järvinen et al. 2013)
Finnish-English* (F)	F: 180.94	188.89	

The question of whether there are substantial language-specific differences may be more convincingly addressed by the studies of bilinguals who acquired both languages simultaneously or who are proficient users of both languages in their daily lives. Table 5.2 shows that for some language pairings, speakers do use distinct SFFs in the two languages that were tested. Asterisks in the first column indicate that reported differences were significant. (The results for Lee & Sidtis 2017 report only the monologue task. These numbers are approximate because they were read off from a figure.) Some authors speculate that the interrelation between femininity/masculinity and SFF may vary by language, such that high pitch and/or low pitch may be a more requisite cue to femininity or masculinity (respectively) in some languages than in others (Ohara 1992; van Bezooijen 1995). For bilingual speakers, another possible reason for cross-language difference is to distinguish between their languages in what may be a particularly acoustically salient way (Ordin & Mennen 2017). However, some authors caution that before such statements can be conclusively made, the tones that are used or the intonational patterns must be carefully controlled (Keating & Kuo 2012; Mennen, Schaeffler & Docherty 2012; Graham 2014), since it may not be that overall SFF is what differs among languages, but rather the target highs and lows of tones or intonation peaks. Taken together, these results suggest that myriad forces shape the existence of overall differences in SFF, from sociocultural considerations to intonational implementation to the materials used in eliciting speech.

While the pressure to uphold a standard of femininity or masculinity may be just a small part of determining a language-specific SFF, it nevertheless plays a role in how listeners evaluate speakers on the basis of their SFF. This idea is often related to Ohala's frequency code proposal (Ohala 1995), which claims that high pitch is cross-linguistically associated with politeness and deference, because it conveys the smallness of the person producing such an utterance. The association between pitch and sex-related characteristics has also been explored in the evolutionary biology and political psychology literature. For example, men with lower-pitched voices are perceived as more attractive or socially dominant (e.g., Feinberg et al. 2005; Wolff & Puts 2010), though Puts et al. (2007) note that the association of low pitch with social dominance may be weaker than the association with physical dominance. On the other hand, women with higher pitch are judged as more attractive (up to a certain optimal pitch) but more dominant if they have lower pitch (Collins & Missing 2003; Feinberg et al. 2008; Borkowska & Pawlowski 2011).

Another arena in which the effect of SFF on listener perceptions has been studied is political psychology. Potential voters are generally more likely to choose candidates with lower pitch (Gregory & Gallagher 2002; Klofstad, Anderson & Peters 2012; Tigue et al. 2012; Klofstad 2016), whether they are presented with manipulated versions of the same speaker's voice, or with two different speakers. Tigue et al. (2012) examine whether the scenario in which male politicians' voices are presented matters, finding that low-pitched voices are preferable in both national election and wartime scenarios. Low pitch was associated with physical prowess in both scenarios, but also took on associations with integrity in the election situation. An analysis of the speech of 51 male global presidential candidates demonstrates that there is a relatively large correlation between the SFF of the candidate and their likelihood of winning, where candidates with lower and more stable SFF won more elections (Pavela Banai, Banai & Bovan 2017).

Similar findings also apply to female politicians (Klofstad, Anderson & Peters 2012; Klofstad 2016). Interestingly, Klofstad (2016) demonstrates that the gender of the opponent may matter. In an analysis of actual 2012 races for the US Congress, lower-pitched male candidates fared worse when running against female candidates, but better when running against male candidates. One hypothesis is that compared to female politicians with higher SFF, particularly low male SFF may come across as especially aggressive. In a study examining whether the preference for a lower SFF is mediated by potential voters' political leanings, Laustsen, Petersen & Klofstad (2015) find that conservative-leaning Americans have a greater preference for deeper SFF than more liberal-leaning Americans do for male politicians, but neither group has a preference for the SFF of female politicians.

With these results from the political psychology literature as a backdrop, one question that has not yet been asked is whether SFF information predisposes potential voters to make assumptions about whether a female politician is likely to be on the political left or right. The question stems from the analogous literature on the visual appearance of politicians, which has shown that faces of actual Republican female politicians have more sex-typical facial cues than those of Democratic women, and that observers were more likely to classify faces with sex-typical cues as being Republican (Carpinella & Johnson 2013). Carpinella et al. (2016) found that Republican, but not Democratic, female politicians with more sex-typical facial features were more likely to win their Congressional races. Finally, in an experiment, potential voters from more conservative states displayed voting preferences for female candidates with gender-typical traits as compared to potential voters from more liberal states (Hehman et al. 2014).

The results predicated on visual sex-typicality present an interesting conflict for the association of SFF and a female candidate's political affiliation. On one hand, a higher SFF is considered more sex-typical (Feinberg et al. 2008), so it may be that potential voters—or at least conservative-leaning voters—will associate female politicians with a higher SFF as being Republican. On the other hand, despite preferring some sex-typical traits in female politicians, higher SFF may be in conflict with voters generally preferring lower-pitched politicians and rating them as more trustworthy and qualified (Klofstad, Anderson & Peters 2012; Tigue et al. 2012). Laustsen, Petersen & Klofstad (2015) did not find an effect of political leaning on preference for SFF in female politicians, but it is unknown whether there is any association between an assumed political orientation based on a female politician's SFF and their actual political party. That question is investigated in the study reported in the next section.

In this study, participants are asked to listen to the same sentence spoken by actual female American politicians who range in SFF from 127 Hz to 244 Hz, and are asked to guess whether the politicians are Republican or Democratic. There are several possible outcomes, informed by previous research:

1) Republican and Conservative-leaning potential voters place a greater value on higher SFF as a feminine trait, and will label higher-pitched speakers as Republicans significantly more often than Democratic-leaning voters do.

2) If a higher SFF in female speakers is considered an "attractive" quality regardless of political leaning, then participants who affiliate with a party may choose their own party for higher-pitched speakers. A corollary of this prediction is that speakers who are independent or moderate (potential "swing voters"), should not show this kind of preference for associating an "attractive" trait with a party because they do not affiliate with political parties.

3) SFF is not associated with political party per se, but rather, perhaps, with the competence/trustworthiness of the politician regardless of party, so potential voters will not distinguish between political party on the basis of SFF. Alternatively, participants on the left or right may show a preference for claiming the lower-pitched speaker as representative of their party if SFF represents desirable personality properties in a politician.

Methods

The participants were 104 (self-reported) native monolingual speakers of American English (36 females, 68 males, ages 21–63) who were recruited using Amazon Mechanical Turk (AMT). Participants were required to have an IP address in the United States to complete the study. Participants were asked to self-report their political affiliation by choosing the closest label from among the following options: liberal/progressive, Democrat, moderate, Republican, conservative, independent. To simplify the analysis below, these categories were consolidated into "left-leaning" (liberal/progressive, Democrat), "right-leaning" (conservative, Republican), "moderate," and "independent," and the participants were relatively evenly distributed among them (left: 30, right: 23, moderate: 30, independent: 21).

The stimuli for the study consist of 28 female American politicians saying the phrase "And I approve this message," which is always the second half of the federally required statement in advertising "I am/ My name is ____, and I approve this message." One sentence was chosen to eliminate the possibility that either different phonetic/phonological or semantic content would affect participants' responses. The stimuli were taken from political advertisements on YouTube from female politicians running for either the Senate or House of Representatives between 2010 and 2016. The speakers ranged in age from 36 to 66, with a mean of 54.1 years. The audio was extracted from YouTube to mp3. The target phrase was included in the stimuli only when it was spoken in isolation, and not with any background sounds or speech. The extracted utterances had a duration of 1.2–1.4 seconds and the average intensity of each sound file was set to 70 dB sound pressure level so all files were of a similar loudness.

Using Praat (Boersma & Weenink 2020), the average f0 in the utterance was calculated over the vowels and approximants [æ/ə] in *and*, [aɪə] in *I approve*, [ɹu] in *approve*, [ɪ] in *this*, and [ɛ] in *message*. The final [ə] in *message* was not measured in order to avoid including the final stage of falling declination on the calculation of SFF. The average, maximum, and minimum f0 for each speaker are shown in Table 5.3. The overall average f0 of these speakers is 174 Hz. Because the stimuli are the speech of real politicians, it was not possible to get a fully linear representation of mean f0 from the minimum to the maximum.

In addition to the test stimuli, six speech samples from different female speakers were also prepared for the practice phase. The sentence, "Fine soap saves tender skin," from the UW/NU corpus was used (Panfili et al. 2017). This corpus contains recordings of speakers from the Pacific Northwest and from

Table 5.3 Mean, minimum, and maximum f0 (in Hz) for each speaker in the stimuli

Speaker	Mean	Min.	Max.	Speaker	Mean.	Min.	Max
1	127	117	140	15	176	166	187
2	131	122	137	16	179	173	189
3	141	134	157	17	184	169	192
4	147	137	155	18	187	177	203
5	147	143	159	19	188	174	206
6	151	137	159	20	190	183	199
7	152	139	160	21	191	184	207
8	153	149	160	22	192	182	203
9	156	138	169	23	192	185	196
10	158	151	164	24	193	184	201
11	159	154	166	25	197	187	210
12	160	151	170	26	205	189	215
13	165	159	173	27	232	217	251
14	175	162	190	28	244	214	270

several cities in the US North dialect region reading sentences. The average f0 of these utterances were matched to the political stimuli, ranging from 133 Hz to 251 Hz, increasing in approximately 30 Hz intervals from the minimum to the maximum.

The experiment was conducted on AMT using the Experigen experimental platform (Becker & Levine 2013). Listeners clicked "I Accept" after reading a statement about informed consent. They were told to put on headphones and adjust the volume to a listening level that would be comfortable for them. The first screen explained that the term pitch refers to the rate of vibration of a speaker's vocal folds, and that, on average, the pitch of some talkers can either be relatively higher or lower than average. It also explained that the experiment consisted of rating each female speaker's pitch on a scale of 1 (low) to 5 (high). The next screen contained the six practice items, which were labeled in order from lowest to highest. Participants clicked on each item first from low to high and were allowed to go back and listen to them as many times as they wanted. The practice phase only involved listening; no decisions were made by the participants for this phase.

For the test phase, each of the 28 speakers was presented in a different random order to each participant. They clicked to play the item, and then were asked to rate the pitch of each item from 1 ("lowest pitch") to 5 ("highest pitch") in comparison to their knowledge of other female American English voices. They could listen to each item at most two times. Once they rated the pitch, they were asked, "Do you think this speaker is more likely to be a Democratic or a Republican candidate? If you aren't sure, it's OK to guess." Participants then chose from between a "Democratic" or "Republican" button.

After the test phase, the participants completed a demographic questionnaire which included questions about their age, their gender (male, female, nonbinary, or other), where they had lived, and what other languages they had learned and how proficient they were (in order to confirm that they were effectively monolingual). The whole study lasted about 10 minutes.

Results

The outcome for pitch rating is reported in Davidson (2018), using a subset of the data reported here. There was a strong positive correlation between rating and the mean f0 of individual speakers, and significant differences in mean f0 between all five rating categories. Findings indicate that on average an increase of 10–20 Hz led to an increase in the rating chosen from a five-point scale.

For the analysis of participants' guesses about political affiliation, a logistic mixed-effects regression using the packages lme4 (Bates et al. 2015) and lmerTest (Kuznetsova, Brockhoff & Christensen 2017) in R (R Core Team 2022) was carried out. The dependent variable was the guess about the politician's party (Democrat vs. Republican), and the fixed effects were the mean f0 for each of the 28 speakers, the participant's self-reported gender (male, female; nonbinary/other was unfortunately omitted because only two participants gave those responses), age, and political affiliation, as well as the two-way interactions that were of particular interest, including f0 mean*gender, f0 mean*age, and f0 mean*political affiliation. The baseline value for gender was female, and "independent" for political affiliation. Participant was included as a random intercept. Participants' political affiliation was sum-coded, and then the groups were later compared using a Tukey post hoc test in the multcomp package (Hothorn, Bretz & Westfall 2008).

Results for the choice of political party plotted by the average f0 over the sentence are shown in Figure 5.1. This figure shows both a violin plot and a box plot to illustrate the distribution of the

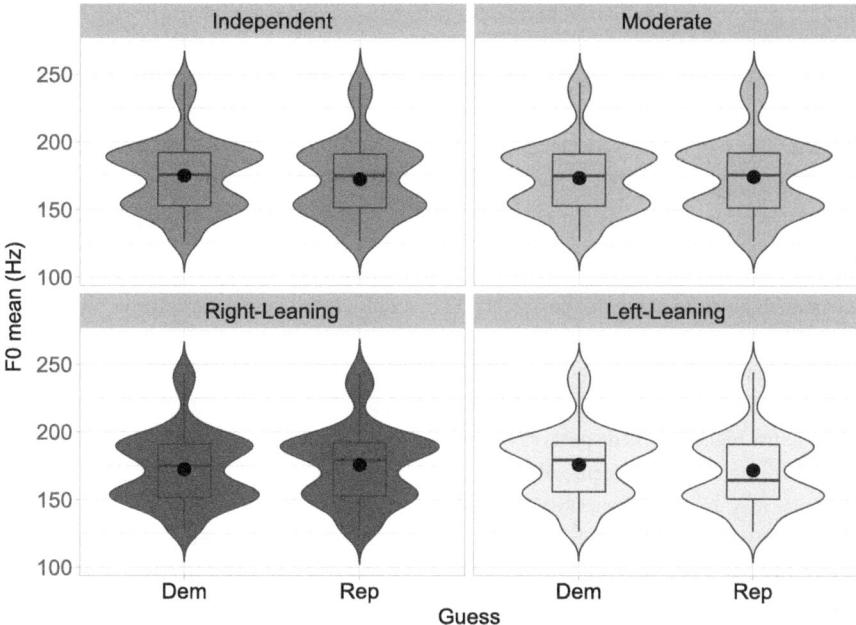

Figure 5.1   Guesses of "Democratic" or "Republican" as a function of f0 mean, divided by self-reported political affiliation of the participants

Table 5.4 Logistic regression results for participants' guesses of political affiliation

	Estimate	*Std. error*	*z value*	*Pr(>|z|)*
(Intercept)	0.190	0.446	0.425	0.6706
f0 mean	-0.001	0.002	-0.43	0.6672
Gender (male)	-0.291	0.507	-0.574	0.5658
Age	0.002	0.005	0.304	0.7612
Politics (left)	0.800	0.376	2.125	0.0335*
Politics (moderate)	-0.359	0.375	-0.956	0.3389
Politics (right)	-0.978	0.452	-2.165	0.0304*
f0 mean*male	0.002	0.003	0.82	0.4123
f0 mean:age	0.000	0.000	-1.771	0.0766
f0 mean:politics (left)	-0.004	0.002	-1.977	0.048*
f0 mean:politics (moderate)	0.002	0.002	1.077	0.2814
f0 mean:politics (right)	0.005	0.003	1.974	0.0484*

political party guesses by f0 mean. The statistical results in Table 5.4 show no significant results for f0 mean, gender, or age, but there are significant main effects for self-reported left-leaning and right-leaning political affiliation. There are also significant interactions for left-leaning and right-leaning political affiliation with f0 mean because right-leaning participants assign higher-pitched voices to Republican and left-leaning participants to Democratic. Tukey post-hoc tests confirm that the only difference for political affiliation is between left- and right-leaning participants ($\beta = -1.78$, $z = -2.61$, $p = 0.045$), with no effect for either moderate or independent participants.

The plot in Figure 5.1 illustrates that right-leaning participants were more likely to guess that the higher-pitched politicians were Republicans, whereas the left-leaning participants were more likely to guess that the same politicians were Democrats. This is evident from the bulge on the higher end of the violin plot that is bigger for different party guesses for the left- and right-leaning boxes.

Discussion

This outcome is not consistent with possibility 1) that only right-leaning participants are more likely to guess that higher-pitched female speakers are Republicans, which would have been analogous to the political psychology literature showing that Republican voters seem to prefer gender-typical visual traits in female candidates. The results are more consistent with possibility 2), that each side, left and right, "claim" the higher-pitched speakers as representing their preferred party. One explanation may be that a higher-pitched voice is generally more attractive outside of politics, so participants closer to a particular party may assume the speaker is one of "theirs." This could account for why independent and moderate voters (who could plausibly vote for either Republicans or Democrats) would not have such a preference. This explanation is complicated by the fact that not all studies show a consistent result that vocal attractiveness is correlated with higher-pitched female speakers (Zuckerman & Miyake 1993; Babel, McGuire & King 2014). If it is the case that these voices are nevertheless more attractive for other reasons, it may be due to voice quality properties such as breathiness (e.g., Xu et al. 2013). Unfortunately, because these sound clips were compressed audio extracted from YouTube they are of questionable quality for voice quality measures.

It is also notable that the opposite results were not found; participants were not more likely to claim the lower-pitched speakers for their own political party, despite the fact that studies show that voters (in general) seem to associate lower pitch with positive attributes for politicians such as trustworthiness and qualification. This suggests that the task of asking participants "Who would you vote for?" (without party information) solicits a different response than "Which political party do you think this speaker is from?", since the former question may prompt listeners to assess a political speaker's voice with regard to leadership qualities when political parties are not involved.

In summary, this case study revealed that despite previous work showing that potential voters tend to prefer deeper voices as being more trustworthy and competent, introducing information about political parties may change the way that listeners evaluate SFF. The current study showed that left-leaning participants were more likely to assume that higher-pitched female politicians were Democrats, but right-leaning participants assumed they were Republicans. This result may be more linked to vocal attractiveness than personality traits.

Going forward

Phonation is a versatile linguistic element that can be used in its various forms to create phoneme contrast, to implement tones, as intonation and prosody, pragmatically, or as a sociophonetic marker that defines identity or connotes affect. Production studies have revealed that various types of nonmodal phonation, such as creaky, breathy, harsh/hoarse, or falsetto voice, are recruited by speakers to construct identities based on their regional background, race/ethnicity, sexuality, or gender, or to convey stances or attributes such as boredom/disengagement, femininity, or aggressiveness. Some phonation types—like falsetto in particular—can be used to convey pragmatic information such as deference or excitement. From a perceptual perspective, matched-guise work comparing different voice qualities shows that listeners can use voice quality either to make guesses about race, ethnicity, sexuality, or gender, or to make assumptions about speakers whether or not such attitudes are what speakers intend to project.

SFF in modal phonation is another use of phonation that has been identified as having language-specific and sociocultural influence. Though the full picture is somewhat complicated, differences in SFF may be useful for distinguishing a multilingual speaker's languages, and there may also be gender-based differences that reflect different cultural norms about femininity and masculinity. SFF also factors into the political psychology literature, which has shown that potential voters tend to prefer deeper voices as being more trustworthy and competent. However, the case study indicates that explicitly introducing information about political parties may tap into potential voters' evaluation of vocal attractiveness rather than how SFF relates to personality traits.

As for future directions, some studies have shown the prevalence of particular voice qualities among language users within a group, but sometimes do not compare to other groups, or to the dominant language environment to ascertain how widespread a particular phonation type is, or how unique it is to the group under consideration. Going forward, more comparative work examining the same phenomenon across multiple groups would improve our understanding of how phonation interacts with sociophonetic considerations. Another avenue to pursue is the relationship between nonmodal phonation and SFF, or modal phonation. Davidson (2020) is an example of the effect of creaky phonation on the perception of the overall pitch of an utterance, but further work on how speakers may manipulate both pitch and nonmodal phonation to establish identity or create meaning would be an interesting area of research.

As sociophoneticians develop research questions, special consideration must be given to sources of data. While internet resources like YouTube, TikTok, or other streaming video may be intriguing sources of speech that is of interest to sociolinguists, it is currently unclear what effect compressed audio has on voice quality measurements like spectral tilt measures or harmonics-to-noise. Studies examining the effects of remote recording platforms such as Zoom or Skype, as well as differences between various recording devices such as computers, iPads, or mobile phones have shown that both platforms and hardware can introduce distortions to the audio signal compared to audio collected by the digital solid-state recorders and external microphones that are typically used in sociophonetic research. While f0 tends to be robust under various recording conditions (Vogel et al. 2014; Zhang et al. 2021), there are indications that other measures, including formants, spectral tilt, and noise measures can be significantly different from the uncompressed "gold standard" file and that the platform or recording device may not have uniform effects across all speech conditions under investigation (Freeman & Decker 2021; Sanker et al. 2021). Thus, researchers intending to examine sociophonetic uses of voice quality in more naturalistic samples must take care to understand whether the recording conditions are compatible with acoustic analysis.

References

Abdelli-Beruh, Nassima B., Thomas Drugman & R.H. Red Owl. 2016. Occurrence frequencies of acoustic patterns of vocal fry in American English speakers. *Journal of Voice* 30(6). 759.e711–759.e720. https://doi.org/10.1016/j.jvoice.2015.09.011

Abdelli-Beruh, Nassima B., Lesley Wolk & Dianne Slavin. 2014. Prevalence of vocal fry in young adult male American English speakers. *Journal of Voice* 28(2). 185–190. https://doi.org/10.1016/j.jvoice.2013.08.011

Alim, H. Samy. 2004. *You know my steez: An ethnographic and sociolinguistic study of styleshifting in a Black American speech community*. Duke University Press.

Altenberg, Evelyn P. & Carole T. Ferrand. 2006. Fundamental frequency in monolingual English, bilingual English/Russian, and bilingual English/Cantonese young adult women. *Journal of Voice* 20. 89–96. https://doi.org/10.1016/j.jvoice.2005.01.005

Anderson, Rindy C., Casey A. Klofstad, William J. Mayew & Mohan Venkatachalam. 2014. Vocal fry may undermine the success of young women in the labor market. *PLoS ONE, 9*(5). e97506. https://doi.org/10.1371/journal.pone.0097506

Andreeva, Bistra, Grazyna Demenko, Magdalena Wolska, Bernd Möbius, Frank Zimmerer, Jeanin Jügler, Magdalena Oleskowicz-Popiel & Jürgen Trouvain. 2014. Comparison of pitch range and pitch variation in Slavic and Germanic languages. *Proceedings of Speech Prosody 2014*. 776–780. https://doi.org/10.21437/SpeechProsody.2014-144

Andrews, Moya L. & Charles P. Schmidt. 1997. Gender presentation: Perceptual and acoustical analyses of voice. *Journal of Voice* 11(3). 307–313. https://doi.org/10.1016/S0892-1997(97)80009-4

Andrianopoulos, Mary V., Keith N. Darrow & Jie Chen. 2001. Multimodal standardization of voice among four multicultural populations: Fundamental frequency and spectral characteristics. *Journal of Voice* 15(2). 194–219. https://doi.org/10.1016/S0892-1997(01)00021-2

Armstrong, Meghan E., Nicholas Henriksen & Christian DiCanio. 2015. Sociophonetic analysis of young Peninsular Spanish women's voice quality. In Rachel Klassen, Juana M. Liceras & Elena Valenzuela (eds.), *Hispanic linguistics at the crossroads*, 293–312. John Benjamins. https://doi.org/10.1075/ihll.4.15arm

Babel, Molly, Grant McGuire & Joseph King. 2014. Towards a more nuanced view of vocal attractiveness. *PLoS ONE* 9(2). e88616. https://doi.org/10.1371/journal.pone.0088616

Bates, Douglas, Martin Mächler, Ben Bolker & Steve Walker. 2015. Fitting linear mixed-effects models using lme4. *Journal of Statistical Software* 67(1). 1–48. https://doi.org/10.18637/jss.v067.i01

Becker, Michael & Jon Levine. 2013. Experigen: An online experiment platform. http://becker.phonologist.org/experigen

Blankenship, Barbara. 2002. The timing of nonmodal phonation in vowels. *Journal of Phonetics* 30. 163–191. https://doi.org/10.1006/jpho.2001.0155

Boersma, Paul & David Weenink. 2020. *Praat: Doing phonetics by computer* [Computer program], ver. 6.1.16. www.praat.org/

Borkowska, Barbara & Boguslaw Pawlowski. 2011. Female voice frequency in the context of dominance and attractiveness perception. *Animal Behaviour* 82(1). 55–59. https://doi.org/10.1016/j.anbehav.2011.03.024

Bucholtz, Mary & Kira Hall. 2005. Identity and interaction: a sociocultural linguistic approach. *Discourse Studies* 7(4–5). 585–614. https://doi.org/10.1177/1461445605054407

Carpinella, Colleen M., Eric Hehman, Jonathan B. Freeman & Kerri L. Johnson. 2016. The gendered face of partisan politics: Consequences of facial sex typicality for vote choice. *Political Communication* 33(1). 21–38. https://doi.org/10.1080/10584609.2014.958260

Carpinella, Colleen M. & Kerri L. Johnson. 2013. Appearance-based politics: Sex-typed facial cues communicate political party affiliation. *Journal of Experimental Social Psychology* 49(1). 156–160. https://doi.org/10.1016/j.jesp.2012.08.009

Catford, J.C. 1964. Phonation types: The classification of some laryngeal components of speech production. In David Abercrombie (ed.), *In honour of Daniel Jones*, 26–37. Longmans.

Catford, J.C. 1977. *Fundamental problems in phonetics*. Indiana University Press.

Collins, Sarah A. & Caroline Missing. 2003. Vocal and visual attractiveness are related in women. *Animal Behaviour* 65(5). 997–1004. https://doi.org/10.1006/anbe.2003.2123

Dallaston, Katherine & Gerard J. Docherty. 2020. The quantitative prevalence of creaky voice (vocal fry) in varieties of English: A systematic review of the literature. *PLoS ONE* 15(3). e0229960. https://doi.org/10.1371/journal.pone.0229960

Davidson, Lisa. 2018. Perception of relative pitch of sentence-length utterances. *Journal of the Acoustical Society of America Express Letters* 144(2). EL89–EL94. https://doi.org/10.1121/1.5048636

Davidson, Lisa. 2019. The effects of pitch, gender, and prosodic context on the identification of creaky voice. *Phonetica* 76. 235–262. https://doi.org/10.1159/000490948

Davidson, Lisa. 2020. Contributions of modal and creaky voice to the perception of habitual pitch. *Language* 96(1). e22–e37. https://doi.org/doi:10.1353/lan.2020.0013.

Di Paolo, Marianna & Alice Faber. 1990. Phonation differences and the phonetic content of the tense-lax contrast in Utah English. *Language Variation and Change* 2(2). 155–204. https://doi.org/10.1017/S09543 94500000326

Esling, John. 1978a. The identification of features of voice quality in social groups. *Journal of the International Phonetic Association* 8(1–2). 18–23. https://doi.org/10.1017/S0025100300001699

Esling, John. 1978b. *Voice quality in Edinburgh: A sociolinguistic and phonetic study*. PhD thesis, University of Edinburgh.

Esling, John H., Scott R. Moisik, Allison Benner & Lise Crevier-Buchman. 2019. *Voice quality: The laryngeal articulator model*. Cambridge University Press.

Esposito, Christina M. 2010. Variation in contrastive phonation in Santa Ana Del Valle Zapotec. *Journal of the International Phonetic Association* 40(2). 181–198. https://doi.org/10.1017/S0025100310000046

Fant, Gunnar. 1960. *Acoustic theory of speech production*. Mouton.

Feinberg, David R., Lisa M. DeBruine, Benedict C. Jones & David I. Perrett. 2008. The role of femininity and averageness of voice pitch in aesthetic judgments of women's voices. *Perception* 37(4). 615–623. https://doi.org/10.1068/p5514

Feinberg, David R., B.C. Jones, A.C. Little, D.M. Burt & D.I. Perrett. 2005. Manipulations of fundamental and formant frequencies influence the attractiveness of human male voices. *Animal Behaviour* 69(3). 561–568. https://doi.org/10.1016/j.anbehav.2004.06.012

Freeman, Valerie & Paul De Decker. 2021. Remote sociophonetic data collection: Vowels and nasalization over video conferencing apps. *Journal of the Acoustical Society of America* 149(2). 1211–1223. https://doi.org/10.1121/10.0003529

Garellek, Marc. 2012. The timing and sequencing of coarticulated non-modal phonation in English and White Hmong. *Journal of Phonetics* 40. 152–161. https://doi.org/10.1016/j.wocn.2011.10.003

Garellek, Marc. 2019. The phonetics of voice. In William F. Katz & Peter F. Assmann (eds.), *The Routledge handbook of phonetics*, 75–106. Routledge.

Gobl, Christer & Ailbhe Ní Chasaide. 2003. The role of voice quality in communicating emotion, mood and attitude. *Speech Communication* 40(1). 189–212. doi: https://doi.org/10.1016/S0167-6393(02)00082-1

Gobl, Christer & Ailbhe Ní Chasaide. 2010. Voice source variation and its communicative function. In William J. Hardcastle, John Laver & Fiona E. Gibbon (eds.), *The handbook of phonetic sciences*, 2nd edn., 378–423. Wiley.

Graham, Calbert. 2014. Fundamental frequency range in Japanese and English: The case of simultaneous bilinguals. *Phonetica* 71(4). 271–295. https://doi.org/10.1159/000381627

Greer, Sarah D.F. & Stephen J. Winters. 2015. The perception of coolness: Differences in evaluating voice quality in male and female speakers. In Scottish Consortium for ICPhS 2015, Paper 883.

Gregory, Stanford W., Jr. & Timothy J. Gallagher. 2002. Spectral analysis of candidates' nonverbal vocal communication: Predicting U.S. presidential election outcomes. *Social Psychology Quarterly* 65(3). 298–308. https://doi.org/10.2307/3090125

Hehman, Eric, Colleen M. Carpinella, Kerri L. Johnson, Jordan B. Leitner & Jonathan B. Freeman. 2014. Early processing of gendered facial cues predicts the electoral success of female politicians. *Social Psychological and Personality Science* 5(7). 815–824. https://doi.org/10.1177/1948550614534701

Hejná, Míša, Pavel Šturm, Lea Tylečková & Tomáš Bořil. 2021. Normophonic breathiness in Czech and Danish: Are females breathier than males? *Journal of Voice* 35(3). 498.e491–498.e422. https://doi.org/10.1016/j.jvoice.2019.10.019

Henton, C.G. & R.A.W. Bladon. 1985. Breathiness in normal female speech: inefficiency vs. desirability. *Language & Communication* 5(3). 221–227. https://doi.org/10.1016/0271-5309(85)90012-6

Henton, Caroline G. & Anthony Bladon. (1988). Creak as a sociophonetic marker. In Larry M. Hyman & Charles N. Li (eds.), *Language, speech and mind: Studies in honor of Victoria A. Fromkin*, 3–29. Routledge.

Holliday, Nicole & Dan Villarreal. 2020. Intonational variation and incrementality in listener judgments of ethnicity. *Laboratory Phonology* 11(1). 3. https://doi.org/10.5334/labphon.229

Hollien, Harry & Bernard Jackson. 1973. Normative data on the speaking fundamental frequency characteristics of young adult males. *Journal of Phonetics* 1(2). 117–120. https://doi.org/10.1016/S0095-4470(19)31416-0

Hollien, Harry & John F. Michel. 1968. Vocal fry as a phonational register. *Journal of Speech and Hearing Research* 11(3). 600–604. https://doi.org/10.1044/jshr.1103.600

Hothorn, Torsten, Frank Bretz & Peter Westfall. 2008. Simultaneous inference in general parametric models. *Biometrical Journal* 50(3). 346–363. https://doi.org/10.1002/bimj.200810425

Irons, Sarah T. & Jessica E. Alexander. 2016. Vocal fry in realistic speech: Acoustic characteristics and perceptions of vocal fry in spontaneously produced and read speech. *Journal of the Acoustical Society of America* 140(4). 3397–3397. https://doi.org/10.1121/1.4970891

Järvinen, Kati, Anne-Maria Laukkanen & Olli Aaltonen. 2013. Speaking a foreign language and its effect on f0. *Logopedics Phoniatrics Vocology* 38. 47–51. https://doi.org/10.3109/14015439.2012.687764

Jeong, Sunwoo. 2017. Iconization of sociolinguistic variables: The case of archetypal female characters in classic Hollywood cinema. In Angelika Zirker, Matthias Bauer, Olga Fischer & Christina Ljungberg (eds.), *Dimensions of iconicity*, 263–286. John Benjamins. https://doi.org/10.1075/ill.15.15jeo

Keating, Patricia A. & Grace Kuo. 2012. Comparison of speaking fundamental frequency in English and Mandarin. *Journal of the Acoustical Society of America* 132(2). 1050–1060. https://doi.org/10.1121/1.4730893

Khazan, Olga. 2014, May 29. Vocal fry may hurt women's job prospects. *The Atlantic*. www.theatlantic.com/business/archive/2014/05/employers-look-down-on-women-with-vocal-fry/371811/

Klatt, Dennis H. & Laura C. Klatt. 1990. Analysis, synthesis, and perception of voice quality variations among female and male talkers. *Journal of the Acoustical Society of America* 87(2). 820–857. https://doi.org/10.1121/1.398894

Klofstad, Casey A. 2016. Candidate voice pitch influences election outcomes. *Political Psychology* 37(5). 725–738. https://doi.org/10.1111/pops.12280

Klofstad, Casey A., Rindy C. Anderson & Susan Peters. 2012. Sounds like a winner: Voice pitch influences perception of leadership capacity in both men and women. *Proceedings of the Royal Society B* 279. 2698–2704. https://doi.org/10.1098/rspb.2012.0311

Kreiman, Jody & Diana Sidtis. 2011. *Foundations of voice studies: An interdisciplinary approach to voice production and perception*. Wiley-Blackwell.

Kuznetsova, Alexandra, Per B. Brockhoff & Rune H.B. Christensen. 2017. lmerTest package: Tests in linear mixed effects models. *Journal of Statistical Software* 82(13). 1–26. https://doi.org/10.18637/jss.v082.i13

Laustsen, Lasse, Michael Bang Petersen & Casey A. Klofstad. 2015. Vote choice, ideology, and social dominance orientation influence preferences for lower pitched voices in political candidates. *Evolutionary Psychology* 13(3). 1–13. https://doi.org/10.1177/1474704915600576

Laver, John D.M. 1968. Voice quality and indexical information. *International Journal of Language & Communication Disorders* 3(1). 43–54. https://doi.org/10.3109/13682826809011440

Laver, John. 1980. *The phonetic description of voice quality*. Cambridge University Press.

Lee, Binna & Diana Van Lancker Sidtis. 2017. The bilingual voice: Vocal characteristics when speaking two languages across speech tasks. *Speech, Language and Hearing* 20(3). 174–185. https://doi.org/10.1080/2050571X.2016.1273572

Levon, Erez. 2007. Sexuality in context: Variation and the sociolinguistic perception of identity. *Language in Society* 36(4). 533–554. https://doi.org/10.1017/S0047404507070431

Levon, Erez. 2015. Conflicted selves: Language, religion, and same-sex desire in Israel. In Erez Levon & Ronald Beline Mendes (eds.), *Language, sexuality, and power: Studies in intersectional sociolinguistics*, 215–239. Oxford University Press.

Ligon, Claire, Carrie Rountrey, Noopur Vaidya Rank, Michael Hull & Aliaa Khidr. 2018. Perceived desirability of vocal fry among female speech communication disorders graduate students. *Journal of Voice* 33(5). P805.e821–805.e835. https://doi.org/10.1016/j.jvoice.2018.03.010

Loman, Bengt. 1975. Prosodic patterns in a Negro American dialect. In Håkan Ringbom, Alfhild Ingeberg, Ralf Norrman, Kurt Nyholm, Rolf Westman & Kay Wikberg (eds.), *Style and text: Studies presented to Nils Erik Enkvist*, 219–242. Sprakforlaget Skriptor AB.

Majewski, W., H. Hollien & J. Zalewski. 1972. Speaking fundamental frequency of Polish adult males. *Phonetica* 25(2). 119–125. https://doi.org/10.1159/000259375

McDonald, Katherine L. & Erik R. Thomas. 2012. Incorporating cepstral peak prominence as an acoustic method for assessing variation in voice quality. *Journal of the Acoustical Society of America* 132. 2088. https://doi.org/10.1121/1.4755712

Melvin, Shannon & Cynthia G. Clopper. 2015. Gender variation in creaky voice and fundamental frequency. In Scottish Consortium for ICPhS 2015, Paper 320.

Mendoza-Denton, Norma. 2011. The semiotic hitchhiker's guide to creaky voice: Circulation and gendered hardcore in a Chicana/o gang persona. *Journal of Linguistic Anthropology,* 21(2). 261–280. https://doi.org/10.1111/j.1548-1395.2011.01110.x

Mendoza, Elvira, Nieves Valencia, Juana Muñoz & Humberto Trujillo. 1996. Differences in voice quality between men and women: Use of the long-term average spectrum (LTAS). *Journal of Voice* 10(1). 59–66. https://doi.org/10.1016/S0892-1997(96)80019-1

Mennen, Ineke, Felix Schaeffler & Gerald J. Docherty. 2012. Cross-language differences in fundamental frequency range: A comparison of English and German. *Journal of the Acoustical Society of America* 131(3). 2249–2260. https://doi.org/10.1121/1.3681950

Mo, Kelsey. 2016, Nov. 1. Women should avoid using "vocal fry" in the workplace. *The State Press.* www.statepress.com/article/2016/11/spopinion-women-should-stop-using-vocal-fry-in-the-workplace

Moisik, Scott Reid. 2012. Harsh voice quality and its association with blackness in popular American media. *Phonetica* 69(4). 193–215. https://doi.org/10.1159/000351059

Newman, Michael & Angela Wu. 2011. "Do you sound Asian when you speak English?" Racial identification and voice in Chinese and Korean Americans' English. *American Speech* 86(2). 152–178. https://doi.org/10.1215/00031283-1336992

Nielsen, Rasmus. 2010. "I ain't never been charged with nothing!": The use of falsetto speech as a linguistic strategy of indignation. *University of Pennsylvania Working Papers in Linguistics* 15(2). 111–121. https://repository.upenn.edu/pwpl/vol15/iss2/13

Ohala, John J. 1995. The frequency code underlies the sound-symbolic use of voice pitch. In Leanne Hinton, Johanna Nichols & John J. Ohala (eds.), *Sound symbolism*, 325–347. Cambridge University Press.

Ohara, Yumiko. 1992. Gender-dependent pitch levels: A comparative study in Japanese and English. In Kira Hall, Mary Bucholtz & Birch Moonwoman (eds.), *Locating power: Proceedings of the Second Berkeley Women and Language Conference*, 469–477. Berkeley Women and Language Group.

Ohara, Yumiko. 2004. Prosody and gender in workplace interaction. In Shigeko Okamoto & Janet S. Shibamoto Smith (eds.), *Japanese language, gender, and ideology: Cultural models and real people*, 222–240. Oxford University Press.

Ordin, Mikhail & Ineke Mennen. 2017. Cross-linguistic differences in bilinguals' fundamental frequency ranges. *Journal of Speech, Language and Hearing Research* 60(6). 1493–1506. https://doi.org/10.1044/2016_JSLHR-S-16-0315

Panfili, L.M., J. Haywood, D.R. McCloy, P.E. Souza & R.A. Wright. 2017. *The UW/NU Corpus*, ver. 2.0. http://depts.washington.edu/phonlab/resources/pnnc/pnnc2

Patela, Sona, Klaus R. Scherer, Eva Björkner & Johan Sundberg. 2011. Mapping emotions into acoustic space: The role of voice production. *Biological Psychology* 87(1). 93–98. https://doi.org/10.1016/j.biopsycho.2011.02.010

Pavela Banai, Irena, Benjamin Banai & Kosta Bovan. 2017. Vocal characteristics of presidential candidates can predict the outcome of actual elections. *Evolution and Human Behavior* 38(3). 309–314. https://doi.org/10.1016/j.evolhumbehav.2016.10.012

Pépiot, Erwan. 2014. Male and female speech: A study of mean f0, f0 range, phonation type and speech rate in Parisian French and American English speakers. *Speech Prosody* 7. 305–309. https://doi.org/10.21437/SpeechProsody.2014-48.

Pittam, Jeffery. 1987. Listeners' evaluations of voice quality in Australian English speakers. *Language and Speech* 30(2). 99–113. https://doi.org/10.1177/002383098703000201

Podesva, Robert J. 2007. Phonation type as a stylistic variable: The use of falsetto in constructing a persona. *Journal of Sociolinguistics* 11(4). 478–504. https://doi.org/10.1111/j.1467-9841.2007.00334.x

Podesva, Robert J. 2013. Gender and the social meaning of non-modal phonation types. *Proceedings of the Annual Meeting of the Berkeley Linguistics Society* 37. https://escholarship.org/uc/item/2p22d9jk

Podesva, Robert J. 2016. Stance as a window into the language-race connection: Evidence from African American and white speakers in Washington, DC. In H. Samy Alim, John R. Rickford & Arnetha F. Ball (eds.), *Raciolinguistics: How language shapes our ideas about race*, 203–219. Oxford University Press.

Podesva, Robert J. & Patrick Callier. 2015. Voice quality and identity. *Annual Review of Applied Linguistics* 35. 173–194. https://doi.org/doi:10.1017/S0267190514000270

Pratt, Teresa. 2018. *Affective sociolinguistic style: An ethnography of embodied linguistic variation in an arts high school*. PhD dissertation, Stanford University.

Puts, David Andrew, Carolyn R. Hodges, Rodrigo A. Cárdenas & Steven J.C. Gaulin. 2007. Men's voices as dominance signals: Vocal fundamental and formant frequencies influence dominance attributions among men. *Evolution and Human Behavior* 28(5). 340–344. https://doi.org/10.1016/j.evolhumbehav.2007.05.002

R Core Team 2022. *R: A language and environment for statistical computing*. R Foundation for Statistical Computing. www.R-project.org

Sanker, Chelsea, Sarah Babinski, Roslyn Burns, Marisha Evans, Jeremy Johns, Juhyae Kim, Slater Smith, Natalie Weber & Claire Bowern. 2021. (Don't) try this at home! The effects of recording devices and software on phonetic analysis. *Language* 97(4). e360–e382. https://doi.org/10.1353/lan.2021.0075

Schneider, Berit & Wolfgang Bigenzahn. 2003. Influence of glottal closure configuration on vocal efficacy in young normal-speaking women. *Journal of Voice* 17(4). 468–480. https://doi.org/10.1067/S0892-1997(03)00065-1

Scottish Consortium for ICPhS 2015 (ed.). 2015. *Proceedings of the 18th International Congress of Phonetic Sciences*. University of Glasgow.

Sicoli, Mark A. 2010. Shifting voices with participant roles: Voice qualities and speech registers in Mesoamerica. *Language in Society* 39(4). 521–553. https://doi.org/10.1017/S0047404510000436

Sicoli, Mark A. 2015. Voice registers. In Deborah Tannen, Heidi E. Hamilton & Deborah Schiffrin (eds.), *Handbook of discourse analysis*, 105–126. Wiley.

Simpson, Adrian P. 2009. Phonetic differences between male and female speech. *Language and Linguistics Compass* 3(2). 621–640. https://doi.org/10.1111/j.1749-818X.2009.00125.x

Södersten, Maria & Per-Åke Lindestad. 1990. Glottal closure and perceived breathiness during phonation in normally speaking subjects. *Journal of Speech and Hearing Research* 33(3). 601–611. https://doi.org/10.1044/jshr.3303.601

Starr, Rebecca L. 2015. Sweet voice: The role of voice quality in a Japanese feminine style. *Language in Society* 44(1). 1–34. https://doi.org/10.1017/S0047404514000724

Stross, Brian. 2013. Falsetto voice and observational logic: Motivated meanings. *Language in Society* 42(2). 139–162. https://doi.org/10.1017/S004740451300002X

Stuart-Smith, Jane. 1999. Glasgow: Accent and voice quality. In Paul Foulkes & Gerry R. Docherty (eds.), *Urban voices: Accent studies in the British Isles*, 203–222. Arnold.

Szakay, Anita. 2012. Voice quality as a marker of ethnicity in New Zealand: From acoustics to perception. *Journal of Sociolinguistics* 16(3). 382–397. https://doi.org/10.1111/j.1467-9841.2012.00537.x

Tarone, Elaine E. 1973. Aspects of intonation in Black English. *American Speech* 48(1/2). 29–36. https://doi.org/10.2307/3087890

Terasawa, Ruriko, Yuki Kakita & Minoru Hirano. 1984. Simultaneous measurements of mean air flow rate, fundamental frequency and voice intensity. *Onseingoigaku* 25(3). 189–207. https://doi.org/10.5112/jjlp.25.189

Thomas, Erik R. & Norman J. Lass. 2005. Cues used for distinguishing African American and European American voices. *Journal of the Acoustical Society of America* 117(4). 2458. https://doi.org/10.1121/1.4809398

Thomas, Erik R. & Jeffrey Reaser. 2015. An experiment on cues used for identification of voices as African American or European American. In Michael D. Picone & Catherine Evans Davies (eds.), *New perspectives on language variety in the South: Historical and contemporary approaches*, 507–522. University of Alabama Press.

Tigue, Cara C., Diana J. Borak, Jillian J.M. O'Connor, Charles Schandl & David R. Feinberg. 2012. Voice pitch influences voting behavior. *Evolution and Human Behavior* 33(3). 210–216. https://doi.org/10.1016/j.evolhumbehav.2011.09.004

Titze, Ingo R. 1989. Physiologic and acoustic differences between male and female voices. *Journal of the Acoustical Society of America* 85. 1699–1707. https://doi.org/10.1121/1.397959

Trittin, Pamela Jean & Andrés de Santos y Lleó. 1995. Voice quality analysis of male and female Spanish speakers. *Speech Communication* 16(4). 359–368. https://doi.org/10.1016/0167-6393(95)00004-8

Trudgill, Peter. 1974. *The social differentiation of English in Norwich*. Cambridge University Press.

van Bezooijen, Renée. 1995. Sociocultural aspects of pitch differences between Japanese and Dutch women. *Language and Speech* 38(3). 253–265. https://doi.org/10.1177/002383099503800303

Van Borsel, John, Joke Janssens & Marc De Bodt. 2009. Breathiness as a feminine voice characteristic: A perceptual approach. *Journal of Voice* 23(3). 291–294. https://doi.org/10.1016/j.jvoice.2007.08.002

Vogel, Adam P., Kristin M. Rosen, Angela T. Morgan & Sheena Reilly. 2014. Comparability of modern recording devices for speech analysis: Smartphone, landline, laptop, and hard disc recorder. *Folia Phoniatrica et Logopaedica* 66(6). 244–250. https://doi.org/10.1159/000368227

Walton, Julie H. & Robert F. Orlikoff. 1994. Speaker race identification from acoustic cues in the vocal signal. *Journal of Speech, Language, and Hearing Research* 37(4). 738–745. https://doi.org/doi:10.1044/jshr.3704.738

Wells, John C. 1982. *Accents of English*, vol. 1. Cambridge University Press.

Wileman, Bruce Rory. 2018. *A sociophonetic investigation of ethnolinguistic differences in voice quality among young, South African English speakers*. PhD thesis, University of Cape Town.

Wolf, Naomi. 2015, July 24. Young women, give up the vocal fry and reclaim your strong female voice. *Guardian*. www.theguardian.com/commentisfree/2015/jul/24/vocal-fry-strong-female-voice

Wolff, Sarah E. & David A. Puts. 2010. Vocal masculinity is a robust dominance signal in men. *Behavioral Ecology and Sociobiology* 64(10). 1673–1683. https://doi.org/10.1007/s00265-010-0981-5

Wolk, Lesley, Nassima B. Abdelli-Beruh & Dianne Slavin. 2012. Habitual use of vocal fry in young adult female speakers. *Journal of Voice* 26(3). 111–116. https://doi.org/10.1016/j.jvoice.2011.04.007

Xu, Yi, Albert Lee, Wing-Li Wu, Xuan Liu & Peter Birkholz. 2013. Human vocal attractiveness as signaled by body size projection. *PLoS ONE* 8(4). e62397. https://doi.org/10.1371/journal.pone.0062397

Yuasa, Ikuko Patricia. 2010. Creaky voice: A new feminine voice quality for young urban-oriented upwardly mobile American women? *American Speech* 85(3). 315–337. https://doi.org/10.1215/00031283-2010-018

Zhang, Cong, Kathleen Jepson, Georg Lohfink & Amalia Arvaniti. 2021. Comparing acoustic analyses of speech data collected remotely. *Journal of the Acoustical Society of America* 149(6). 3910–3916. https://doi.org/10.1121/10.0005132

Zimman, Lal. 2013. Hegemonic masculinity and the variability of gay-sounding speech: The perceived sexuality of transgender men. *Journal of Language and Sexuality* 2(1). 1–39. https://doi.org/10.1075/jls.2.1.01zim

Zimman, Lal. 2018. Transgender voices: Insights on identity, embodiment, and the gender of the voice. *Language and Linguistics Compass* 12(8). e12284. https://doi.org/10.1111/lnc3.12284

Zuckerman, Miron & Kunitate Miyake. 1993. The attractive voice: What makes it so? *Journal of Nonverbal Behavior* 17(2). 119–135. https://doi.org/10.1007/BF01001960

6

SOCIOPHONETICS AND VOWELS

Felicity Cox and Gerard Docherty

Introduction

The history of scientific inquiry into how vowels vary with respect to speaker social characteristics epitomizes the breathtaking pace of theoretical, methodological, and statistical advances that have taken place in the language sciences over the past 60 years. Over that time, investigators have migrated from auditory analysis of small samples of speakers, through the use of ground-breaking analog instrumental acoustic methods such as sound spectrography, to increasingly sophisticated techniques for examining articulation, and the digital acoustic analysis of very large speech corpora that are processed automatically and interrogated through complex statistical modeling.

In this chapter we convey a flavor of this trajectory by focusing on aspects of the analysis of vowel variability—a key focus for sociophonetics. Over the last 25 years, sociophonetic research has drawn on insights, methods, and best practice from both phonetics and sociolinguistics to drive theoretical advances and methodological innovation. Combining phonetic and sociolinguistic approaches in the collection, analysis, and interpretation of data that are (at their core) social, helps us to understand the nuanced complexity of the relationship between language variation, change, and social context with heightened granularity (for recent general reviews see *inter alia* Thomas 2019; Drager & Kettig 2021; Kendall & Fridland 2021; Docherty 2022). In this chapter we focus on some of the antecedents to this work, and on how sociophonetic studies of vowels have featured prominently in the modeling of sound change, generating findings that feed directly into formulating new questions for the field. In the process we highlight issues relating to both methods and theory that have been (and continue to be) the subject of robust debate within the sociophonetic research community and which warrant further investigation.

Readers should note that the material below is inevitably skewed by the fact that sociophonetic research has overwhelmingly focused on mainstream and ethnolectal varieties of English (largely those spoken in the United Kingdom, United States, Canada, New Zealand, and Australia). While this Anglo-centric imbalance is starting to be redressed, there is still a good distance left to travel on this path. We must exercise caution in making generalizations when research is so heavily focused on one language. It is encouraging that more recent sociophonetic work on vowels explores a wider variety of languages (e.g., Mack 2010; Van der Harst et al. 2014; Barnes 2019; Omari & Jaber 2019; Gonzales & Starr 2020; Wolfswinkler & Harrington 2021; chapters in Section 3 of this volume).

DOI: 10.4324/9781003034636-7

Forerunners

One of the key antecedents to sociophonetics, dialectology (see Boberg, Nerbonne & Watt 2018), traditionally relied on auditory methods for describing variation. Investigators made use of careful transcription of speech segments (particularly vowel quality) to identify variants based on geographic space, often from the speech of older, rural, less mobile, and predominantly male informants in an effort to document archaic and recessive forms. Some though, did incorporate adolescents as drivers of change (e.g., Samuel McBurney made detailed observations of the speech, particularly the vowels, of school pupils in Australia and New Zealand in 1887, an excerpt of which appears in Ellis 1889). Early studies of Australian English vowels (e.g., Cochrane 1959) drawing on the work of Weinreich (1953) proposed that methods employed in regional dialectology could be harnessed in the study of social variation, providing a platform for more detailed phonetic analysis of variation within a broader range of communities and individuals, and in the construction of models of language change and diffusion across communities.

Once audio recordings of informants became commonplace, researchers were able to carefully document their auditory observations based upon repeated listening to recorded utterances. The work of Mitchell & Delbridge (1965), for example, identified social correlates of vowel variation amongst Australian English-speaking adolescents in a landmark survey of 7082 speakers, audio-recorded in the late 1950s by teachers in the school setting. The researchers transcribed the vowels which were examined for associations with school type, region, father's occupation, speaker's place of birth, and parents' place of birth. Auditory transcription of variable vowel realizations became a staple of the methodology deployed in early sociolinguistic research including Labov's (1963) watershed Martha's Vineyard project and a range of other pioneering studies (such as Trudgill 1972, 1974 on Norwich; Macaulay 1977 on Glasgow; Milroy 1980 on Belfast; and Horvath 1985 on Sydney).

Throughout these developments, the International Phonetic Alphabet (IPA) has provided an essential framework for auditory phonetic transcription, offering a rich taxonomy and transcriptional conventions for representing details of vowel quality. The IPA's 28 individual vowel symbols can be further refined using a range of diacritics to indicate degrees of phonetic variation such as length, rounding, fronting, retraction, raising, lowering, rhoticity, voice quality, and nasalization (Handbook of the IPA 1999). For example, in Mitchell & Delbridge (1965:83–84), the realizations of the vowel in a word like *so* were determined to comprise a wide range of different socio-stylistic alternants such as [oʊ, ɒʊ, ɛɣ, ɛʊ, ʌʊ, ʌˑʊ, ʌ̈ʊ, ʌ̈ɰ, ɔʊ, ɔy].

The IPA conventions remain an indispensable part of the analytic toolkit. While they have some well-understood limitations, such as the need for training in their use and careful calibration across transcribers, they are an essential tool for listening analytically to speech and in formulating hypotheses about the type of variability that might be present within a variety and worthy of further investigation. In practice though, they have tended to be somewhat swamped by acoustic methods offering the potential to drill down into speaker performance in greater detail, with a representation that yields a more easily quantifiable basis for capturing the multidimensional fine phonetic detail of speech data (although not without a different set of inherent limitations, some of which we discuss below).

Around the middle of the twentieth century, R.K. Potter pioneered the development of sound spectrography, an instrumental method for extracting detail of the acoustic characteristics of speech that would prove to have a seismic impact on phonetic research (Koenig, Dunn & Lacy 1946; Potter et al. 1947). The output of the spectrograph, the spectrogram, is a two-dimensional display representing time on the *x*-axis, frequency on the *y*-axis, with the amplitude of the spectral components of the signal displayed by the darkness of the output trace in a greyscale display. In the introductory paper to a volume of the *Journal of the Acoustical Society of America* dedicated to outlining the new sound spectrography, Potter shows extraordinary foresight with the following remarks:

> The pictures of sound discussed in the papers of this group will provide a consistent basis for visual imagery and illustration that should assist both thinking and exchange of thought in the many fields concerned with sounds. They should afford a common ground for discussion in all such fields now employing artificial symbols and terminology that are, in general, highly specialized.
>
> Potter 1946:2

History tells us that the development of the spectrograph revolutionized the fields of phonetics and sociolinguistics. The type of acoustic data represented in early instrumental studies endures as the primary source material for visualizing, measuring, and quantifying the phonetic features of individual utterances in the acoustic domain—albeit that the means of obtaining, processing, visualizing, and interrogating acoustic data have changed considerably in the digital age. These methods are unsurprisingly central to sociophonetic research in general, and to vowels in particular.

Acoustic analysis of vowels

The advent of sound spectrography allowed for measurement of spectral and temporal characteristics of vowels, particularly the high amplitude spectral peaks representing vocal tract resonances: the formants. As the vocal tract shape changes during speech production through articulatory movement, so too do the resonant frequencies. Formant 1 (F1) and formant 2 (F2) (broadly representative of the lowest two vocal tract resonances; see Whalen et al. 2022 for a discussion of this relationship) correlate with the phonetic dimensions of vowel height (inversely) and fronting respectively. Higher formant frequencies are more difficult to assign specific phonetic correspondence but do have speaker-specific value, particularly in forensic applications (Cavalcanti, Eriksson & Barbarosa 2021). F3 lowering is often used, in conjunction with lowering of F1 and F2, to indicate the rounding of the vowel, although vowel-specific effects make the interpretation of F3 somewhat challenging. F3 is also important in the analysis of vowels produced with degrees of accompanying rhoticity (Espy-Wilson et al. 2000). Vowels may vary not only in their spectral characteristics and corresponding changes of quality, but also in the temporal domain as exemplified by durational variation within and across vowel categories.

The relationship between acoustic and articulatory features of vowels remains a highly productive area of research and one that is central to understanding the nature of vowel variation (see, e.g., Noiray et al. 2014; Blackwood-Ximenes, Shaw & Carignan 2017; Strycharczuk & Scobbie 2017; Whalen et al. 2018; Lawson, Stuart-Smith & Rodger 2019; Ratko, Proctor & Cox 2022). The dynamic gestural properties of speech ensure that vowels are never static. Their articulatory configurations change throughout the interval in which they are realized, in the process affecting and being affected by the articulatory gestures for neighboring sounds. Individual vowels can be broadly classified as simple or complex, determined by the degree of articulatory (and hence, acoustic/spectral) dynamicity they display. Two phonological classes of vowels commonly occur in language vowel inventories: monophthongs and diphthongs (with triphthongs reported to be rare according to the UCLA Phonological Segment Inventory Database 2019). Monophthongs show reduced dynamicity compared to diphthongs, which require a level of inherent spectral change for identification (Ladefoged & Maddieson 1990). Given this partitioning of vowel types according to their dynamicity, monophthongs have been traditionally described with reference to the most acoustically stable portion of the vowel (or to an inflection point), generally at, or close to, the midpoint to provide a representation of the vowel "target." For diphthongs, on the other hand, their dynamic articulatory and auditory characteristics have often been represented with reference to two (different) targets acting as a proxy for the vowel's dynamicity.

Early acoustic phonetic researchers were constrained by the laborious processes involved in analyzing speech data using analog spectrography which required formants to be estimated by eye and measured by hand. A relatively small number of tokens and speakers could be physically processed using this method, and the dimensions of the coated paper, used with analogue spectrographic equipment, accommodated utterances of no more than 2.4 seconds in duration. As a result, investigators gravitated to the use of highly controlled contexts to facilitate data analysis. Peterson & Barney (1952) employed the /hVd/ consonantal frame for the elicitation of monophthongs and a single reference point was located during the "steady state" portion of the vowel for analysis. Peterson & Barney (1952:184) acknowledge that "the complex acoustical patterns […] are not adequately represented by a single section, but require more complex portrayal." Although it is not common for such controlled contexts to feature prominently in current literature, there remains a place for highly constrained elicitation tasks (often as an adjunct to analyses of more extensive contexts) if the aim is to provide a baseline analysis (Clopper & Pisoni 2006), to ensure careful control over production context in synchronic and diachronic analyses (see, e.g., Jacewicz, Fox & Salmons 2011; Cox & Palethorpe 2019; Liu et al. 2014), for normalization purposes (Harrington, Gubian, Stevens & Schiel 2019) or as a controlled context in perceptual experiments (Hillenbrand & Clark 2000; Penney, Cox & Szakay 2021; Szalay et al. 2021).

As the availability of tools for acoustic analysis improved, it became commonplace for vowels to be examined through the extraction of F1 and F2 measurements (albeit from a single time-slice in the case of monophthongs) allowing visualization of an acoustic "vowel space" oriented to resemble the traditional vowel chart with phonetic height (F1) on the vertical axis and fronting (F2) on the horizontal axis (see Essner 1947; Joos 1948). The acoustic vowel space is typically defined as the area demarcated by peripheral monophthongs within the system of vowels. Using these data, differences in vowel quality can be visually and statistically compared across speakers and segmental or situational contexts, and the properties of the acoustic vowel space overall can be interrogated. Formant analysis allows not only vowel target data to be examined but also the trajectory of acoustic change over the time course of the vowel, thereby enabling diphthong trajectories to be plotted as vectors within the same F1/F2 space used to visualize monophthongs.

For interspeaker comparisons of vowels, the impact of individual physiology must be considered. Due to overall differences in vocal tract length, formant frequencies from male speakers' vowels are generally lower than those of females which are in turn lower than those of children, but the extent of this difference is individual- and vowel-specific (Fant 1973; Vorperian & Kent 2007). The challenge for investigators then is to decide how best to capture social/linguistic differences while reducing the risk of these being artifactual of anatomical effects. An approach conventionally adopted is to transform primary formant measurement data to accommodate the consequences of anatomical speaker variation associated with differences in sex or age. Thus, various normalization techniques have been proposed to overcome these confounding individual speaker effects with the aim of rendering the formant values comparable. There are several techniques used to normalize vowels (see Disner 1980; Adank, Smits & van Hout 2004; Clopper 2009; Flynn 2011; Watt, Renwick & Stanley this volume for reviews), and normalization is now a routine feature of work on interspeaker vowel variability. These techniques, however, each have their merits and pitfalls, leading Thomas (2013:111) to note that "a 'perfect' normalization method does not exist." Some researchers eschew this approach preferring to account for sex-/age-based effects in their quantitative modeling rather than to manipulate their primary data through normalization (see, e.g., Hay et al. 2015), and the question of if, and how, to normalize remains a significant topic of methodological debate within the sociophonetics community (Barreda & Nearey 2018; Barreda 2021, Voeten, Heeringa & Van de Velde 2022). Caution is also suggested in work by Johnson (2005, 2006) showing that men and women "perform" gender differently in different languages and that gender cannot be simply considered a matter of vocal tract size (see Munson & Babel 2019 for a review).

Note that while methods for acoustic analysis of vowels are often depicted in juxtaposition to auditory methods, in reality they overlap substantially in that researchers using both approaches typically define their object of analysis in terms of the phoneme. Phonemic analyses of English arising from structuralist accounts of vowel systems (e.g., Trager & Smith 1951) were very influential in the early development of sociolinguistics and in the conceptual notion of the "phonological variable" that is still central to sociolinguistic work to this day (e.g., Labov 1966; Hebda 2012). A phonological variable is a segmental phonological unit acting as a reference point from which socially governed variation can be tracked in the form of different phonetic variants usually described with reference to the phonetic symbol conventions of the IPA. A much-used manifestation of this phonemic approach is Wells's (1982) "lexical set" framework designed as a shorthand way of referring to clusters of lexical items with vowel realizations that are aligned to a particular phonemic vowel category. For example, the FLEECE lexical set denotes the cluster of lexical items (such as *meat, sheep, lease, seat*) that share, in many English accents, a close front monophthongal realization, or in others (e.g., UK West Midlands, Australian English), a close front realization with a salient on-glide. This approach is also clearly predicated on a segmental phonemic analysis of the English vowel system, but with the merit of being agnostic in respect of the phonetic realization or range of realizations that might be found for a particular lexical set. The lexical set approach allows researchers to compare items within a lexical set to the realization of lexical items within other lexical sets, thereby capturing the key differences and similarities across speakers and/or accents.

The same segmental approach pervades the acoustic methods used to analyze vowel variability. While primary acoustic data may come in the form of formant values or representations of clusters of formant values within the F1/F2 axes defining the vowel space, these data are referenced to phonological categories expressed in exactly the same way as in early sociolinguistic work, and at present, typically in relation to one or more lexical sets that are the focus of a particular study. Thus, it is now not unusual to see investigators undertaking acoustic studies of phenomena such as "GOOSE-fronting" (e.g., Strycharczuk & Scobbie 2017; Jansen 2019), "TRAP-raising" (e.g., Watson et al. 2016), the "FOOT/STRUT split" (e.g., Turton & Baranowski 2021), and "HAPPY-tensing" (e.g., Harrington 2006).

While these methods have underpinned many important discoveries, it is clear (but not routinely acknowledged) that they involve making at least two important assumptions. One is that vowels can be analyzed as segmental entities comprehensively defined in terms of their discrete properties. A second is that vowel segments can be adequately differentiated in the low-dimensional space provided by either the IPA taxonomy (with its three primary dimensions of frontness, openness, and lip-rounding), or acoustic analysis (typically differentiating vowels across the two dimensions of F1 and F2 with some studies also considering F3 and/or duration). However, it is well known from experimental phonetic investigation that vowel articulations are co-articulated with adjacent sounds in a multidimensional time series of articulatory gestures resulting in the properties of individual vowels being distributed in time beyond what would conventionally be thought of as the limits of a vowel segment, and subject to being influenced by the articulation of adjacent consonants and by the vowels in adjacent syllables. Likewise, while classifying vowels and their associated auditory quality in a low-dimensional space is tractable and provides a basis for comparing vowels across speakers and languages, long-standing work on their acoustic properties shows that they are in reality a function of the overall shape and configuration of the vocal tract (as determined by the nature and type of constrictions generated by the lips, tongue, and pharyngeal constrictors) which has many more degrees of freedom and interaction than can be captured within a two- or three-dimensional representational framework.

Notwithstanding these simplifying assumptions, the basic segmental approach to the analysis of vowel variation persists and is built almost indelibly into the approach that is taken by most sociolinguistic and sociophonetic researchers. That is, the object of study for vowels is the inventory of vowel categories typically translated into the phonological variable rubric of sociolinguistics with investigators focused on tracking and quantifying the distribution of variants for each variable of interest as a function of a diverse set of social, situational, and linguistic-contextual factors.

Sociophonetic perspectives on vowels

The social dimensions along which vowels can vary within and across speech communities have been an enduring focus of sociolinguistic research since Labov (1963) first used spectrography to verify the auditory transcriptions that formed the basis of his Martha's Vineyard study where he identified socially motivated variation of /aɪ/ (PRICE) and /aʊ/ (MOUTH). Labov, Yaeger & Steiner's (1972) subsequent ground-breaking work, detailing F1/F2 vowel spaces for speakers in several varieties of English, triggered a paradigm shift in the sociolinguistic study of phonetic variation, and established the parameters of an acoustic phonetic methodology that remains in wide use today (e.g., see overview in Kendall & Fridland 2021).

Given this long-standing line of sociolinguistic inquiry (with an acoustic phonetic methodology at its heart), it is legitimate to ask what the surge in sociophonetic research since the late 1990s has added to our understanding of variation and change in the realization of vowels. Here we focus on two areas: how sociophonetics has led to enhancement of the vowel analysis toolkit, and a commentary on how sociophonetic research has begun to "join the dots" across phonetic and sociolinguistic theoretical perspectives which had previously been pursued largely independently. These two fields must be integrated if we are to develop adequate accounts of the generation and processing of social-indexical properties of speech.

As pointed out above, even the earliest work on the acoustic phonetic properties of vowels (Peterson & Barney 1952) was alert to the limitations of an exclusive focus on snapshots of F1 and F2 frequencies as the defining characteristics. Speakers have multiple degrees of freedom in forming the vocal tract shapes that are crucial to the auditory quality of vowels. In doing so they have to coordinate the realization of vowel targets with adjacent segments which may or may not call up the same articulators. All this has to be managed within a complex timing frame, itself subject to a range of influences such as prosodic modulation and whether a target vowel is phonologically long or short.

One consequence of this complexity is that the conventional representation of vowel types (e.g., in the IPA chart) as discrete points in vowel space was replaced early in the development of acoustic phonetic research by a recognition that each vowel category maps to a cloud of realizations, for example in the F1/F2-defined vowel space most typically deployed within studies of social-indexical variation. One of the principal lines of innovation that has emerged (almost by necessity) through sociophonetic research has been a diversification of the tools that researchers can deploy in interrogating the properties of vowels systems as realized in F1/F2 space and how these realizations differ across varieties of the same languages, communities of speakers, and individuals. For example, much greater use has been made of derived measures to allow for new interpretations of the relative distribution of vowel tokens; for example, the Euclidean distance in F1/F2 space between vowel tokens and a centroid reference point calculated to represent the center of gravity for a speaker's vowel system (or reference vowel category) has come to be used as a means of comparing the relative position of vowels in vowel space (e.g., Wright 2004; Harrington 2006; Docherty et al. 2019), or the use of F2-(2*F1) as a heuristic for estimating relative degrees of height and frontness (Labov, Rosenfelder & Fruehwald 2013; Grama, Travis & Gonzalez 2019). There has also been a significant focus on the development of statistical methods for capturing the degree of overlap in the realization of two adjacent vowel categories each characterized by a cloud of tokens (Nycz & Hall-Lew 2013; Kelley & Tucker 2020).

One of the most prominent areas of analytic innovation has been a range of new methods enabling researchers to move away from the conventional static representation of vowels and instead focus on dynamic properties. Building on early acoustic work of Nearey & Assman (1986), new analytic tools have been deployed to test the extent to which the dynamic characteristics of vowel realization might have a social-indexical dimension. These include measures of vowel-intrinsic spectral change (VISC; Fox & Jacewicz 2009; Jin & Liu 2013; Williams, van Leussen & Escudero 2015; Elvin, Williams & Escudero 2016; Schwartz 2021—often using the Discrete Cosine Transformation [DCT; Watson & Harrington 1999]), or a range of techniques designed to capture and contrast vowel formant trajectories such as Generalized Additive Mixed Models (GAMM; Sóskuthy 2017 and Wieling 2018 for tutorials) and Smoothing Spline Analysis of Variance (SS-ANOVA; Docherty, Gonzalez & Mitchell 2015). While this line of methodological development remains work in progress, there is a growing accumulation of findings suggesting that the degree and timing of articulatory/spectral change across a vowel (as opposed to simply the vowel "target") may be harnessed socio-indexically (see, e.g., Jacewicz & Fox 2011; Docherty et al. 2018; Kirkham et al. 2019; Sóskuthy, Hay & Brand 2019; Renwick & Stanley 2020; Stanley et al. 2021 and references therein).

Overall, these refinements of acoustic analysis methods enrich our understanding of the nature of social-indexical variability in speech performance by providing greater depth and focus to vowel analysis. As illustrated by our case study later in this chapter, the outcomes of this work demonstrate that a wider range of phonetic parameters must be considered in relation to models of variation and change, at a much more fine-grained level than has been common in previous work.

It is arguably not by chance that this greater interest in the detail of vowel realization has coincided with theoretical developments in speech production and processing that have moved sharply away from a legacy view that phonetic detail acts as a troublesome impediment to effective spoken communication. The now prevalent stance is that the generation and interpretation of phonetic detail in speech (including that which is social-indexical) are centrally implicated in speaking and listening. Theories relating to the characteristics of social-indexical phonetic properties cannot be adequately developed in isolation from what is known of the complex characteristics and constraints associated with speech production and perception, learning, cognitive processing, and representation (see Hruschka et al. 2009 and Stevens & Harrington 2014 for a broad overview). Social-indexical phonetic variation is now more routinely in the foreground of theoretical debate about the nature of human speech processing.

A key driver of this theoretical development has been the growing influence of usage-based (or exemplar-based) frameworks for modeling production, processing, and phonological representation (e.g., Bybee 2001, 2007; Pierrehumbert 2002, 2003, 2006; Khattab & Foulkes this volume; Warren this volume). A fundamental tenet of this approach is that exemplars of remembered speech are stored in memory in a multidimensional space that integrates not only phonological and phonetic detail but also a rich array of associated social and stylistic information. Importantly, exemplar-based representations are hypothesized to be continually updated as the result of an individual's experience as a listener, thereby providing a mechanism through which potential triggers for sound change can influence and ultimately modify phonological representation and production targets.

The role and nature of exemplar-based phonological representation is far from being a settled matter (e.g., Guy 2014; Docherty & Foulkes 2014; Drager & Kirtley 2016), but the significance of this theoretical stance is that it offers a framework for integrating what is known from sociolinguistic studies of the social dimensions of variation and change alongside insights from studies of speech production and processing (see also Harrington et al. 2018, Harrington, Kleber et al. 2019). This line of work has been facilitated by the availability of large-scale datasets with historical time-depth, enabling observation of change in the speech performance of individuals and communities in real time. A rich dataset of this type allows investigators to track trajectories of change providing invaluable raw material for testing various theoretical stances related to factors that might be active in driving change such as speaker age, sex, socioeconomic status (i.e., the type of macro-level social factors which are prominent in sociolinguistic work), how system-level changes, such as chain shifting and vowel merger, occur and how other factors such as lexical frequency have a role to play in change.

With respect to vowels, this theoretical backdrop has opened up new research questions relating to the extent to which variation and change is driven by functional pressures arising from the need to sustain a viable system of phonological categories underpinning lexical contrast, or by individuals' routine exposure to socially and phonologically structured vowel variability which impacts their representations and ultimately their repertoire of vowel production targets. It is clear that both sets of factors have a role to play, and the focus of research is very much on teasing out the precise nature of those contributions.

Labov, Yaeger & Steiner (1972) (following predecessors, particularly Sweet 1888; Paul 1891; Martinet 1952; Hockett 1955) highlighted the role of functional contrast, showing that vowels appeared to pattern together in change through an "ecological" process referred to as "chain shifting," often described with reference to symmetry and organization within vowel systems (see Lubowicz 2011; Gordon 2015). Chain shifting is said to occur when an initial triggering vowel change leads to a response by other vowels such that the structure of phonological contrasts is preserved (see Martinet 1952). While the notion of contrast preservation pre-dates the development of sociolinguistics, the acoustic phonetic methodology adopted by the latter, giving prominence to the visual representation of vowels in a two-dimensional F1/F2 space, has been hugely reinforcing of the basic concept, enabling investigators to track how a vowel's distribution within an F1/F2 space can change over time relative to that of another vowel. As a result, chain shifts have been widely studied (particularly in varieties of English) over the past 50 years (Labov 1994; Docherty & Watt 2001; Gordon 2011) and continue to provide important insights into factors that govern sound systems.

Chain shifts are typically described as either "push chain" or "drag chain," but parallel shifts are also found (see Cox 1999 for Australian English; Boberg 2005 for Canadian English; Brand et al. 2021 for New Zealand English). Push chains are said to occur when a vowel (or in acoustic terms, the center of gravity of a vowel's realizations in F1/F2 space) appears to move in response to being "crowded out" by an encroaching neighbor. An example is found in Maclagan & Hay (2007) who showed that the New Zealand English short front vowel TRAP continued a trajectory of raising after European settlement that resulted in further raising of its neighbor DRESS and ultimate retraction and lowering of KIT. Drag (or pull) chain describes the shift of a vowel into an acoustic space previously occupied by a neighbor that has moved further away. An example of a drag chain occurs in Australian English where DRESS has undergone lowering to enter a space previously occupied by the now lowered TRAP (Cox & Palethorpe 2008). Trudgill (2004) and Torgersen & Kerswill (2004) make a similar suggestion for English from the southeast of England. Studies also show that chain shifts can reverse (see, e.g., Cox & Palethorpe 2008; D'Onofrio 2021) and that they are not restricted to monophthongs. Sóskuthy et al. (2017) analyzed archival data from New Zealand English speakers born between 1857 and 1904 finding interdependence in diphthong change with FACE and GOAT shifting in parallel, and PRICE shifting through a push chain response to FACE (see also Cox, Palethorpe & Penney forthcoming for similar findings in Australian English diphthong change).

Chain shifting is often discussed as if it were a phenomenon that is uncontroversial with firm empirical foundations, but in reality most findings arise from varieties of a single language (English), and there is much still to be discovered about the extent to which the maintenance of functional contrast is a driving factor in system-wide changes to the configuration of vowel systems. Sociophonetic research adopting ever more refined approaches to quantifying and visualizing the realization of vowels, often in very large datasets with substantial time-depth, enables some of the basic premises of chain shifting to be tested. In particular, it facilitates close scrutiny of the unfolding of a chain shift to gain a better understanding of precisely how that unfolding occurs over time, within and across individuals and through an entire speech community.

For example, in Northern American varieties of English the low back vowel merger between THOUGHT and LOT is typically regarded as a trigger for the short front vowel chain shifts (Becker 2019; Boberg 2019). However, Nesbitt & Stanford (2021) describe an alternative sequence of changes in New England which, although resulting in similar systemic outcomes, arrive at those outcomes through a different chronology. They propose that local "sociohistorical circumstances and sociosymbolic meaning" may hold the key to understanding the detailed patterning and progression of chain shifts (Nesbitt & Stanford 2021:291). Hay et al. (2015) focus on the role of the lexicon in tracking the unfolding of a push chain in New Zealand English involving the three short front vowels (BIT, BET, BAT) as evidenced by data recorded over 130 years from over 80,000 vowel tokens produced by 549 different speakers. Their finding that low frequency lexical items led the series of changes is consistent with the view that regular sound change does not necessarily proceed uniformly through the lexicon. It also challenges one of the key predictions of exemplar-based models of change that high-frequency lexical items would be at the forefront of change. This line of work has been taken to a new level recently by Brand et al.'s (2021) study of co-variation and change in ten monophthongs in the same extensive dataset used by Hay et al. (2015). Their findings are in line with previous hypotheses regarding historical chain shifting in this variety, but they also point strongly to the need to factor in social dimensions of change (including at the level of individual speakers) in order to devise a full account of the patterns of co-variation and change identified through the dataset.

Charles Boberg's chapter in this handbook provides further discussion of the extent to which vocalic sound change is driven by structural factors as opposed to a balance of structural, social, cognitive and situational factors (see also Dinkin & Dodsworth 2017 and Harrington et al. 2018). As Brand et al. state,

> once we accept that a likely explanation for some co-variation is social, we are unable to rule out the possibility that all the co-variation we observe is of this kind. However, it seems very

likely that structural relationships play some role, perhaps seeding potential social interpret-ations, which then strengthen the emergent patterns of co-variation.

Brand et al. 2021:23

As a counterpoint to this long-standing focus investigating functional factors impacting vowel variation and change, a growing body of work has probed the role of individual speakers in shaping the properties of social-indexical variation and its interpretation. To what extent does an individual's experience of ambient phonetic variability (due to the specifics of their interactions—e.g., who they routinely talk to and how often) shape their phonological representation and the top-down information/expectations that they bring to bear in the interpretation of variability within the speech signal? These questions align with some earlier theorizing regarding the role of individual speakers in respect of phonological variation and change (Milroy 1992) but run somewhat counter to the notion of speech community norms that has been prominent within a lot of sociolinguistic work (Docherty & Mendoza-Denton 2012).

For example, research has shown, on the basis of real-time datasets, that an individual's phono-logical representation of vowels is not cast in stone once they reach adulthood. In a series of studies exploring data from Queen Elizabeth II's annual Christmas broadcasts from the 1950s to the 1980s, which ensured a stylistically controlled sample of the speech performance of the same speaker over an extended time period, Jonathan Harrington and colleagues found incrementation in several vowels (e.g., GOOSE-fronting, TRAP-lowering in Harrington, Palethorpe & Watson 2000, 2005; HAPPY-tensing in Harrington 2006) towards a less conservative model in concert with widespread community changes. Harrington et al. (2016) argue that the changes they observed may have come about through the Queen converging in speech to those she interacted with (con-sistent with the principles of exemplar modeling of phonological representation). Interestingly, in more recent work, Harrington & Reubold (2021) have shown evidence for some retrograde change in these vowels produced by Queen Elizabeth after the age of 60–65, suggesting an age-related change in the effectiveness of episodic memory for more recent exemplars and/or a predisposi-tion for older exemplars to be more "entrenched" in exemplar-based representation than more recent ones.

Individual differences have also been considered in work on historical vowel mergers. Hay, Warren & Drager (2006) in an analysis of the NEAR and SQUARE lexical set merger in New Zealand English, found that even speakers whose performance indicated a merger showed awareness of the unmerged categories. They suggest that these individuals who have acquired a full merger are exposed to other speakers for whom the merger is still in progress and can therefore use that experience to shape their responses to perceptual stimuli.

Hay, Warren & Drager's (2006) study not only sheds light on the construct of a merger, it also puts a focus on how individuals process and interpret the variation in vowel realization to which they are exposed. Alongside an increasing body of sociolinguistic work testing how diverse phon-etic parameters are associated by listeners with complex and fluid social meaning (e.g., Fridland, Bartlett & Kreuz 2004; Munson 2007; Campbell-Kibler 2011; Eckert & Labov 2017; Drager et al. 2021), a key focus for experimental sociophonetic research has been to unpack the perceptual mechanisms underpinning the initiation and actuation of sound change by examining the abun-dantly routine situation where speakers are engaged in spoken interaction with interlocutors whose phonetic patterning differs from their own.

The possibility that variation in speech production could be attended to by listeners and potentially form the trigger for a sound change was prominent in influential work by John Ohala. In Ohala's (1981, 1993) model of sound change, listeners may (occasionally) fail to make allowance for co-articulation, leading them to misinterpret a co-articulatory property of the speech signal, treating it instead as an inherent aspect of the segment produced. If this mis-interpretation then becomes part of a speaker's phonetic repertoire and is transmitted to (and taken up by) other members of the community through interaction, sound change may occur. For example, co-articulation between /æ/ and a following nasal consonant in the same syllable (as in *pan*) may result in a phonetically raised vowel compared to the same vowel preceding an oral coda (such as in *pad*) (see De Decker & Nycz 2012; Mielke, Carignan & Thomas 2017; Carignan & Zellou this volume). A listener failing to compensate for the co-articulatory nasal effect may interpret the vowel raising as inherent to the vowel itself. This raised vowel may then be internalized as a target for that vowel which is then used in production. Ohala's focus was principally on the misparsing of co-articulatory variability, but it is clear that the same process could in principle be applicable to any variability present within the signal—for example, vari-ability arising from different speech styles or situations.

Note that central to Ohala's model is that the trigger for a potential change was an interpret-ative error on the part of the listener. But if a model of phonological processing and representation does not treat phonetic detail as noise that could be erroneously misparsed, but rather as integral to processing and representation, this provides investigators with a different lens through which to consider how ambient variability might act as a trigger for sound change.

These ideas have led to a strand of work investigating the extent to which individuals uncon-sciously shift their speech towards the phonetic characteristics of their interlocutors during inter-action. While it is well established that children and adolescents typically develop the accents of those they interact with (Payne 1980; Kerswill & Williams 2005), adults too may shift in the direction of community changes (as per the study of the UK monarch referred to above) and, in the case of relocation to a different language or dialect region, adults have been shown to take on some features of the ambient dialect (see Nycz 2015 for a review). Change arising from exposure to ambient variability is hypothesized to be a critical source of new dialect formation (Trudgill 2008) and is strongly implicated in the development of new town (Kerswill & Williams 2005) and contact varieties (Cheshire et al. 2011).

It is fair to say though that evidence of individuals adjusting the realization of vowels as a direct result of exposure to a particular realization differing to that which they themselves would nor-mally use or hear is somewhat mixed. Laboratory studies provide some support, even though such studies often use socially impoverished single-word presentation of stimuli. Walker & Campbell-Kibler (2015) examined speech accommodation in a cross-dialectal shadowing task using single-word stimuli and seven vowel contexts in two Antipodean and two (different) US dialects. They compared Euclidean distance in the F1/F2 vowel space from each imitator's own productions to their productions in a shadowing task, finding that convergence to the model speaker was vowel-specific but was facilitated by increased phonetic distance between the imitator's own accent and that of the model. Generally, New Zealand shadowers converged more to US than Australian models and US shadowers converged more to New Zealand models than to the other US accents (although the pattern of results is complex).

Other research suggests that both social and automatic processes play a role in speakers con-verging in the direction of ambient phonetic properties. Babel (2010) found that New Zealand participants in a shadowing task converged towards an Australian model, concluding that speakers "cannot help accommodating, but group-identity attitudes modulate this automatic pro-cess" (453). Imitation may also be vowel-specific, with novel (or atypical) productions more readily imitated spontaneously (Babel 2010, 2012). In Babel (2010), the behavior of shadowers was affected by the perceived attractiveness (based on ratings of images) of the male spoken model, but this effect was different for males and females. Females converged more if the perceived attractiveness rating for the speaker was high, whereas males accommodated less to male voices associated with perceived attractive images. Females in general have been found to converge more than males (Babel et al. 2014). The potential power of imitation to influence sound change was demonstrated in Babel, McAuliffe & Haber (2013), finding that New Zealand English speakers (who merge the NEAR and SQUARE vowels) could under certain conditions show reduced merging of these vowels when shadowing a nonmerging speaker of Australian English. Gessinger et al. (2021) have shown that listeners can converge with both human and synthetic voices. Studies undertaken in natural settings, however, have generated results that are less clear-cut than those in laboratory settings. For example, Pardo et al. (2012) failed to find evidence of consistent automatic convergence in a study of selected vowels produced in an hVt/d context by five pairs of college roommates sampled at various points during the academic year. In contrast, Harrington, Gubian et al.'s (2019) study of the HAPPY, GOOSE, and GOAT lexical sets produced by speakers secluded for many months in an Antarctic scientific research base yielded some evidence not only for convergence within the isolated speech community but also for some collective innovation, suggesting that tracking natural performance of speakers within such isolated environment has considerable potential to shed further light on the processes of variation and change within a speech community.

Much remains to be understood about the nexus of social and automatic processes that are at play in studies of phonetic convergence of this sort. One unavoidable fact is that any automatic tendency to converge can be very effectively blocked by speakers. This is evident individually, as in the case of those who relocate to a community where a different variety is used but who resolutely retain the vowel qualities and other properties of their initial accent as an enduring marker of their identity, or collectively, as in the case of different varieties partitioned by a border which retain strongly differentiate features (vowel qualities, for example) despite routine contact and interaction between the two communities of speakers (see Watt & Llamas 2014).

In this section we have illustrated how sociophonetic research has begun to integrate knowledge and insights across areas that were previously somewhat partitioned from one another. While there is a growing number of signature sociophonetic studies deploying new analytic methods in order to shed light on the process through which socially structured variation in the signal can in some cases trigger change in an individual or across a whole speech community, our understanding of this process overall remains somewhat rudimentary. Harrington, Gubian, Stevens & Schiel (2019:3332) state that "population dynamics combined with updating speech sounds through passive listening may be insufficient to explain sound change that may well also be driven by social factors." A model of change that successfully incorporates social forces remains a challenge for the field as it attempts to construct effective models of the actuation of sound change.

New avenues and methodological challenges

Vowel analysis has been supported by tools and methodologies that have experienced rapid development, the pace of which continues to build. Present-day sociophoneticians are fortunate that easily accessible tools and analysis platforms are now publicly available for the examination of data extracted from very large corpora of natural speech. Extraction of qualitative (spectral) and quantitative (temporal) vowel parameters (from natural or laboratory speech) is relatively robust even in the face of the degraded signals that can form the raw data such as historical archival sound recordings, field recordings captured under less-than-ideal conditions, recordings from phone, online, or crowd-sourcing platforms (e.g., Leemann, Kolly & Britain 2018; Penney, Davies & Cox 2023), or in covert contexts (see Rathcke et al. 2017). The robust nature of vowel parameter extraction facilitates work involving these potentially degraded datasets, opening up new possibilities in testing theories of variation and change.

The flip side of these positive developments is that the easy accessibility of vowel analysis tools provides, in itself, something of a challenge to the field. It is routine now to find studies that are based on pre-existing and pre-analyzed datasets consisting of immense quantities of F1/F2 values for vowel tokens across large samples of speakers, and it is relatively simple to undertake a "black box" analysis of those vowels, without ever listening to them or unpacking the assumptions that have been built into their analysis. However, we would suggest that the integrity of vowel analysis hinges on researchers having a solid understanding of the complex nature of vowel articulation, the many intrinsic and contextual factors that shape the production of vowels, and how all of this maps to acoustic parameters. We would further suggest that this understanding is essential for informing study design, data integrity, analysis strategy, data wrangling and interrogation, and results interpretation.

Automatic transcription and segmentation of a large corpus of connected speech is now such an entrenched part of the process of sociophonetic research that it typically receives little more than a somewhat cursory description in most of the contemporary literature, and yet it is valuable to reflect on how some aspects of this can markedly constrain the subsequent analysis of vowels. Transcription and segmentation are typically based on a pre-defined set of phonological categories deployed in a machine-readable dictionary such as CELEX2 (Baayen et al. 1995). As discussed below, in the case of vowels, an immediate challenge for investigators is to ensure that the vowel categories are appropriate for the variety or varieties being investigated.

A second crucial consideration is the accuracy of speech segmentation. The platforms that are most often deployed for automatic segmentation, such as FAVE (Rosenfelder et al. 2014), LaBB-CAT (Fromont & Hay 2012), Montreal Forced Aligner (McAuliffe et al. 2017), and MAUS (Kisler, Reichel & Schiel 2017), use a range of different algorithms for segmenting the speech signal, but none of these provide segmentations that are as uniformly faithful to the properties of the signal as could be provided by a careful manual segmentation (see MacKenzie & Turton 2020 for more extensive examination of two aligners). In corpora of modest sizes, investigators may carry out manual correction of the segmentation, but in larger corpora, this is simply not feasible. Potential segmentation errors are important because the subsequent automatic extraction of acoustic parameters corresponding to each segment is referenced to the start and end points of that segment; for example, when formants are estimated at the vowel midpoint, when a formant trajectory is tracked from the start to the end of a vowel, or when vowel duration is the parameter under examination.

These segmentation issues are somewhat compounded by other potential sources of error that can arise in the determination of formant values. For example, while many researchers describe complex quantitative modeling of (typically) normalized F1/F2 datapoints, relatively few specify the analysis settings used to generate the F1/F2 data in the first place (and which are known to impact significantly on the measurements themselves—see Whalen et al. 2022). Even fewer make the fundamental observation that the F1/F2 measurements are estimates arising from the spectral analysis that generates them—that is, they are quantitative measures, but they are not any more objective than measures that might arise with a different set of analysis parameters, or for that matter measured by hand from a digital spectrogram. Likewise, there is a risk of error and/or bias arising from the operation of the analysis method that is built-in to automatic acoustic analysis tools. For example, FAVE-extract is specifically designed for use with American English and recommends using the Mahalanobis method to set the prediction parameters for an individual vowel's formant values. This method compares the range of formant values extracted using various parameters and returns the formant measurement with the smallest Mahalanobis distance from measurements of the same vowel set in the Atlas of North American English data (see Boberg this volume). FAVE uses the CMU Dictionary set of vowel categories. In American English, a word such as *ask* would be assigned to the TRAP vowel set. This means that formant measurements of the vowel in *ask* that are more like those of other words in the TRAP set would be selected by the algorithm. As there is currently no BATH class built into FAVE, it may be more suitable for the word *ask* to be reassigned to LOT for some other varieties of English. In this case FAVE will select candidate measurements that are more LOT-like. In other words, assumptions about the phonemic assignment of vowels entered into FAVE affect the measurements FAVE returns. It is therefore crucial for researchers to have a clear understanding of how automated processes such as these work, the relationships between lexical types and phonemic inventories in varieties being examined, and the implications these factors might have for their analyses (see Fromont & Watson 2016 and Gonzalez, Grama & Travis 2020 for further elaboration of these issues).

Once an acoustic analysis has been undertaken automatically across a corpus of transcribed and force-aligned speech, further potential sources of error need to be addressed at the point at which the corpus is interrogated in relation to the realization of one or more vowels. For example, while it is relatively straightforward to identify a set of words that are representative of a lexical set/vowel category (especially in controlled tasks like word lists and reading passages or in controlled/guided activities such as a map task [e.g., Anderson et al. 1991]), it is somewhat more challenging when working with a corpus of unscripted material where the investigator may want to work with all of the tokens of a particular category present within the corpus. For example, in samples of natural speech some vowel categories are dominated by high-frequency grammatical or discourse items that are often reduced and/or shorter in duration. For example, in conversational speech disproportionately frequent exponents of the TRAP, KIT, GOAT, PRICE, and SQUARE lexical sets are grammatical forms *that*, *it*, and *so*, discourse particle *like*, and conversational interjection *yeah*. This poses something of a challenge for investigators who have to determine whether to include such forms in the pool of tokens for a particular lexical set and how to deal with unstressed tokens where full vowels may not have been produced, for example, *that* and *it*. In some cases (e.g., FAVE) there is the option of excluding pre-determined lexical items such as grammatical words, but many investigators are not explicit in indicating how they resolve this, and fewer provide any comment on the theoretical implications of doing so or not; for example, in tracking vowel changes through time, especially within a theoretical framework in which token frequency is hypothesized to be a key factor, what are the implications of including grammatical items, or not?

The issue of what material should be included within a lexical set-defined pool of tokens for analysis brings other complications; for example, investigators need to take a stand on whether and how they will control for the prosodic context attached to the tokens for analysis (e.g., phrasal prominence), and to what extent they will make allowance for the effects of position-in-phrase or for the fact that some phonological contexts such as pre-/post-approximants generate automatic (and human) segmentation that is known to be somewhat unreliable (see for example, Strycharczuk & Scobbie 2017). In response to issues such as this, some investigators using a lexical sets analysis have refined the inventory of lexical sets because pooling all tokens under a single category does not capture the patterning that is the object of analysis; thus D'Onofrio, Pratt & Van Hofwegen (2019) in an analysis of Californian English vowel spaces elect to create new lexical sets TOE and TOO reflecting the fact that post-coronal tokens of GOAT and GOOSE respectively cannot simply be pooled with tokens in other phonological contexts; likewise Hall-Lew et al. (2015) make use of a BAN lexical set to reflect the fact that in the variety of Californian English they are investigating pre-nasal TRAP vowels need to be analyzed separately from others not in a pre-nasal environment (see also Grama, Travis & Gonzalez 2019 for Australian English).

One final caution to be deployed in relation to the automatic analysis of large corpora is the extent to which the frequencies of F1 and F2 are sufficient to capture the relevant social-indexical parameters of variability in relation to vowel realization. For example, in a study of the putative merger of tense and lax vowels in a pre-lateral phonological environment by speakers of English from Utah, Di Paolo & Faber (1990) revealed that while vowel categories may appear to be merged in F1/F2 vowel space, a difference between the merged categories was retained for some speakers in the form of variation in voice quality across the two categories concerned. The study found that, for some speakers, breathier voice quality was associated with the underlying tense category and creakier voice quality with the lax category, and furthermore that some listeners were able to access the relevant category based on voice quality differences in the absence of differences in F1/F2. See also Kettig (2016) for an account of cross-variety/-speaker differentiation in the use of secondary vowel lengthening in the TRAP vowel by speakers of British English.

While it is compelling to adopt a working assumption that the complexity of vowel realization can be boiled down to estimates of F1 and F2 that can be generated rapidly from vast amounts of automatically transcribed and segmented speech samples, cautionary notes such as those just described underscore some of the pitfalls of this commonly adopted methodology. In particular, we reinforce the point made earlier that the acoustic phonetic frameworks used most typically for analyzing vowel production are a considerable abstraction from the motor activity planned and executed by speakers in the production of vowel targets. This is perhaps one reason why there has been a growth in recent years of sociophonetic studies seeking to shed light on the more complex underpinning articulatory aspects of vowel variation. There is much scope for employing a range of articulatory techniques such as electromagnetic articulography (EMA), magnetic resonance imaging (MRI), or ultrasound in sociophonetic analysis. Relatively inexpensive ultrasound methods lend themselves particularly well to this task enabling clear visualization of a large part of the tongue contour and how its configuration changes during the production of vowels (see for example, studies by Lawson et al. 2018 and Lawson, Stuart-Smith & Rodger 2019). While acknowledging that the naturalness of speech may be impacted with a set of EMA sensors on the tongue, whilst lying in an MRI machine, or in the presence of an ultrasound probe, there is no doubt that articulatory methods such as these offer a means of shedding new light on the rich complexity of vowel variation, thereby contributing to the elaboration of more rounded accounts of sociophonetic variation.

A further feature of articulatory studies such as these is that the nature of the analysis technique dictates that studies tend to focus on the performance of relatively small numbers of speakers. This provides a useful counterbalance to the trend in acoustic sociophonetic studies to focus on ever-larger corpora of data (even meta-corpora incorporating and spanning across different subcorpora from the same language, e.g., McAuliffe et al. 2019; Tanner et al. 2020). It is clear that there are many theoretical questions (with regard to sound change, for example) that benefit from the use of such large-scale speech samples many of which incorporate extensive historical depth, but it is important to acknowledge a trade-off between the scale of the dataset and the ease with which it is possible to interrogate portions of those data in order to listen to speakers. Historically, a significant part of the discovery process at the heart of phonetic and sociophonetic research has been a careful auditory assessment of speakers' performance (often in conjunction with a spectrographic visualization) in order to formulate hypotheses about those features that might warrant further detailed quantitative investigation and perhaps further data from a more extensive sample. At a time when we are still at a relatively early stage in understanding the nature social-indexical properties of speech, it is important to ensure that this discovery process is not wholly supplanted by a rush to the analysis of automatically transcribed and segmented large-scale corpora with measurements of F1/F2 at vowel midpoints as the unique lens through which vowel production can be viewed.

CASE STUDY   Vowel inherent spectral change in Australian English /oː/ THOUGHT

In this section we demonstrate how the analysis of vowel-intrinsic spectral change (VISC; Fox & Jacewicz 2009) can reveal differences between groups of speakers that would remain opaque in analyses restricted to a target-only approach. For this case study of Australian English, we examine the vowel /oː/ from the THOUGHT lexical set and compare female speakers from two datasets collected at each end of a 20-year time span (1990s–2010s). The rationale for choosing this vowel for the case study is the finding in Cox & Palethorpe (2019) that female speakers from Adelaide (the capital city of South Australia) produced greater offglide for /oː/ (represented by a change in the trajectory of F1) than speakers from three other major Australian cities. Dynamicity of the /oː/ vowel had not been previously examined in acoustic studies of Australian English. In this case study we compare three methods for characterizing F1 and F2 of the monophthong /oː/ in an analysis of vowel change: the traditional target approach, Discrete Cosine Transform (DCT), and Generalized Additive Mixed Model (GAMM).

Methods

Participants and materials

Female participants between 15 and 29 years at the time of recording from the northern suburbs of Sydney were selected from corpora representing the 1990s and 2010s time periods. The full 1990s corpus (see Cox 2006) contains recordings of 120 (60 female, 60 male) students in their fourth year of secondary schooling with a mean age of 15.8 years. Speakers were recorded individually in a quiet room in their school using a portable Marantz CP430 cassette recorder and a Beyer M88 dynamic microphone. Cassette tapes were digitized at a sampling rate of 44.1 kHz 30 years after the original recordings were made. Fifty-three of the female speakers are included in this case study. The 2010s dataset has been selected from female speakers with a mean age of 19.6 years in the Australian Voices corpus (Cox & Palethorpe 2008: 66 speakers) and AusTalk (Burnham et al. 2011: 4 speakers). Participants recorded for all corpora (see Cox, Palethorpe & Penney forthcoming) engaged in a range of scripted and spontaneous speech tasks. For this case study, ten monophthongs /iː, ɪ, e, æ, ɐ, ɔ, oː, ʊ, ʉː, ɜː/ were extracted from words produced in sentences that were common to the 1990s and 2010s corpora.

Analysis

Selected words were automatically segmented and annotated using WEBMAUS (Kisler, Reichel & Schiel 2017) with subsequent analyses carried out using EmuR Winkelmann, Harrington & Jänsch 2017) in R (R Core Team 2022). The first four formant frequencies for each vowel were extracted using a 25 ms Blackman window, a 5 ms frame shift, and a nominal F1 of 550 Hz, using the wrassp package (Bombien, Winkelmann & Scheffers 2021) in R. Each token was checked, and misplaced boundaries or mistracked F1 and F2 were corrected, resulting in 1254 monophthongs (1990s: 569; 2010s: 685) available for analysis. F1 and F2 values measured across each vowel were extracted and normalized for duration and vowel targets were identified within the central 80% interval. For this case study we focus on the production of /oː/ in the first vowel in the word *water*, which was captured phrase-finally in the same read sentence across the two datasets.

Our DCT analysis focuses on the first two DCT coefficients: the zeroth DCT coefficient (DCT0), which models the mean of the formant trajectory, and the first DCT coefficient (DCT1), which models the direction and magnitude of the format change (i.e., the slope; Watson & Harrington 1999). For both target analysis and the DCT analyses, separate linear mixed effects regression models were fitted in R for F1 and F2 in Hertz on the full set of ten monophthongs using lme4 (Bates et al. 2015), with *p*-values calculated using afex (Singmann et al. 2022) with Kenward-Roger approximation for degrees of freedom. The formant measure at the vowel target or the relevant DCT measure was included as the dependent variable, fixed factors were vowel (/iː, ɪ, e, æ, ɐ, ɔ, oː, ʊ, ʉː, ɜː/) and time period (1990s, 2010s). An interaction between these factors was also included along with random intercepts for speaker. Pairwise comparisons were conducted with the emmeans package (Lenth 2022), using Tukey HSD corrections.

In order to explore the /oː/ vowel in more detail, a further comparison between the 1990s and 2010s data was made using GAMMs with the mgcv (Wood 2011, 2017) and itsadug (van Rij et al. 2020) packages in R. Separate models were fitted for F1 and F2 for the single /oː/ vowel. Each model included a parametric difference term for time period, a reference smooth for normalized duration, and a difference smooth for normalized duration by time period using the default of ten basis functions. A factor smooth over normalized duration by speaker was also included.

Results

The target analysis showed an interaction between vowel and time period for F1 ($F(9, 1110.17) = 27.78$, $p < .001$) and F2 ($F(9, 1108.28) = 17.62$, $p < .001$) indicating that the set of vowels varied differentially across the two datasets. However, pairwise comparisons showed no significant difference for /oː/ between the 1990s speakers and the 2010s speakers for either F1 or F2 at the target.

The DCT analyses showed a significant vowel by time period interaction for all of the models: F1 DCT0 ($F(9, 1108.88) = 28.74$, $p < .001$) and F1 DCT1 ($F(9, 1113.54) = 8.36$, $p < 0.001$); F2 DCT0 ($F(9, 1107.82) = 22.64$, $p < .001$) and F2 DCT1 ($F(9, 1112.77) = 13.84$, $p < 0.001$). Pairwise comparisons for /oː/ showed significant effects for F1 (DCT0 $p < 0.0001$; DCT1 $p < 0.01$) but not for F2. Figure 6.1 illustrates these effects.

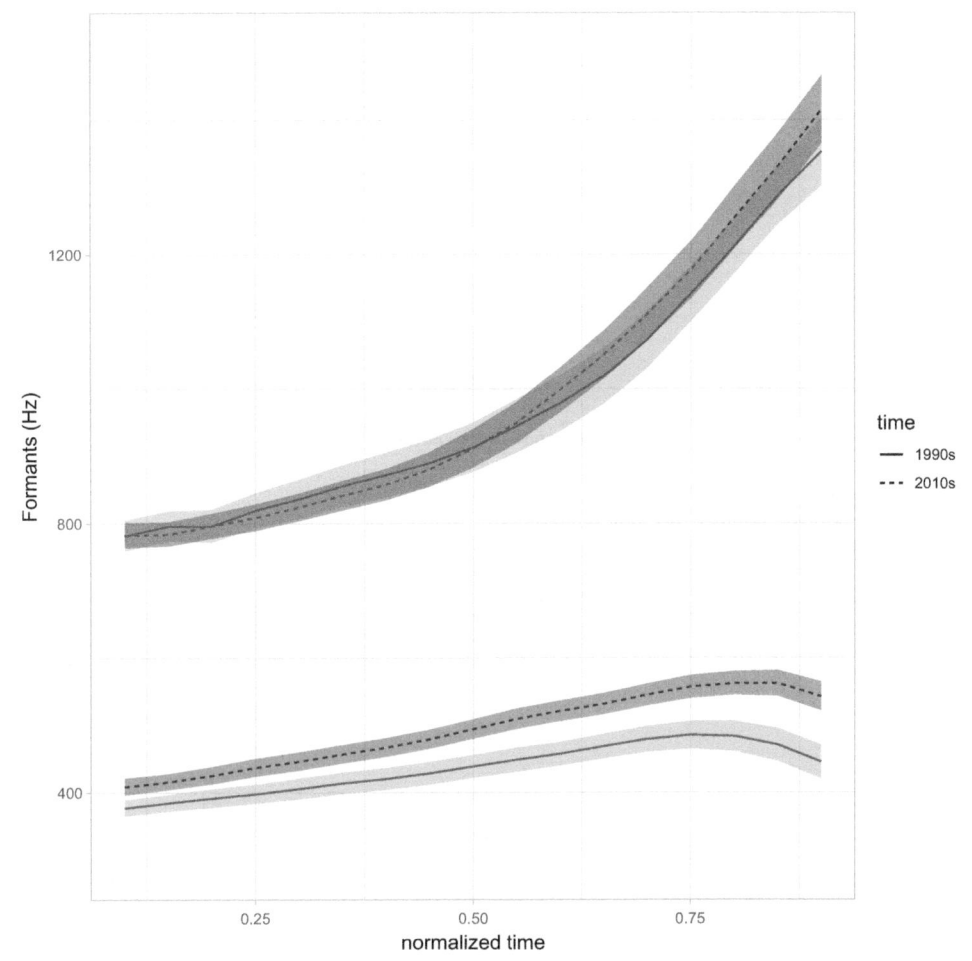

Figure 6.1 Comparison of F1 and F2 trajectories (Hz) for the vowel /oː/ produced by speakers from the 1990s and 2010s datasets

The GAMM showed a significant parametric main effect ($p < 0.001$) of time period for /oː/ for F1 and significant nonlinear differences in the trajectories between the two datasets for both formants (F1 $p < 0.001$; F2 $p < 0.05$). Figures 6.2 and 6.3 show the estimated nonlinear smooths for each time period for F1 and F2 respectively (A panels). The difference plots associated with each formant (B panels) show the sections of each trajectory where the differences are found. This is demarcated by the area between the dotted vertical lines. For F1 the entire trajectory differs between the two time periods, whereas for F2 the difference is restricted to the very end of the vowel. Error ribbons in the graphs represent 95% confidence intervals.

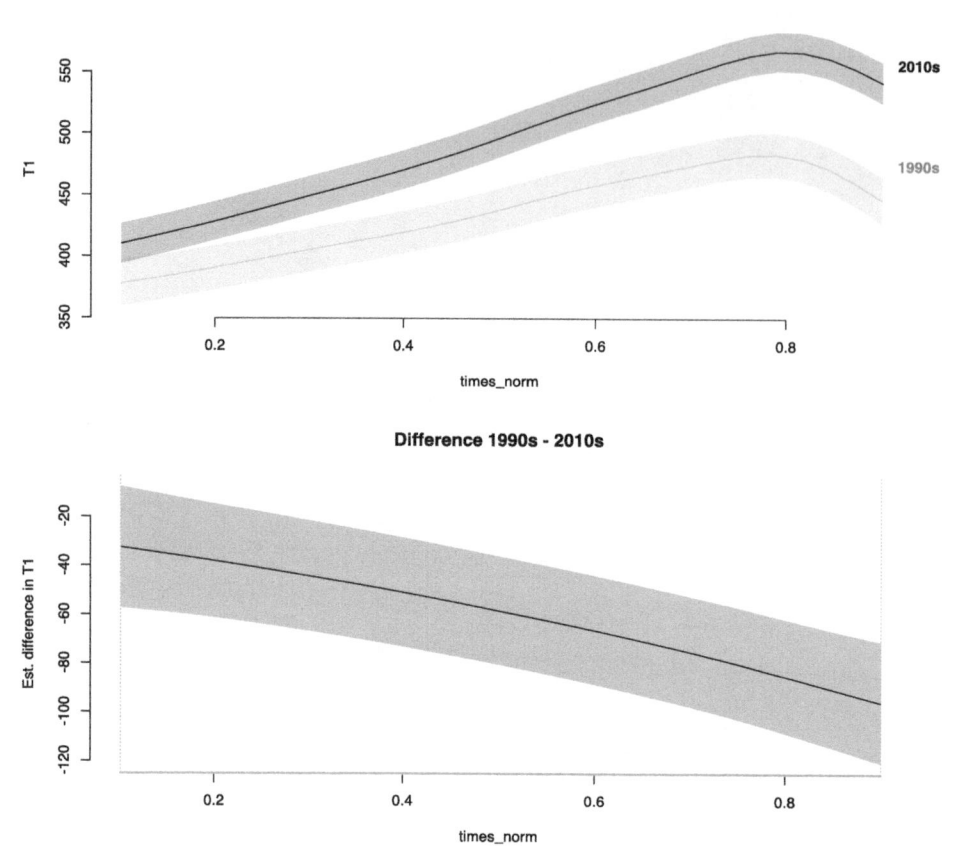

Figure 6.2   Results of GAMM nonlinear smooths (fitted values) for F1 of /oː/
Figure 6.2a (top)   by time period
Figure 6.2b (bottom)   as difference between nonlinear smooths for each time period

Discussion

This comparison between the three analytical methods shows that the target-only approach cannot capture differences between the datasets that can be illuminated when time-varying characteristics are considered. The DCT analysis was successful in demonstrating that F1 does indeed differ between the two datasets, showing that the 2010s speakers exhibited greater phonetic lowering of /oː/ as the vowel unfolds, indicating greater offglide compared to the 1990s speakers. The GAMM analysis was also able to capture this difference and, in addition, showed that the difference in F1 extended across the entire formant trajectory. The GAMM also showed an effect for F2 that was not seen in either the target or the DCT analysis, but this difference was restricted to a small section at the end of the vowel.

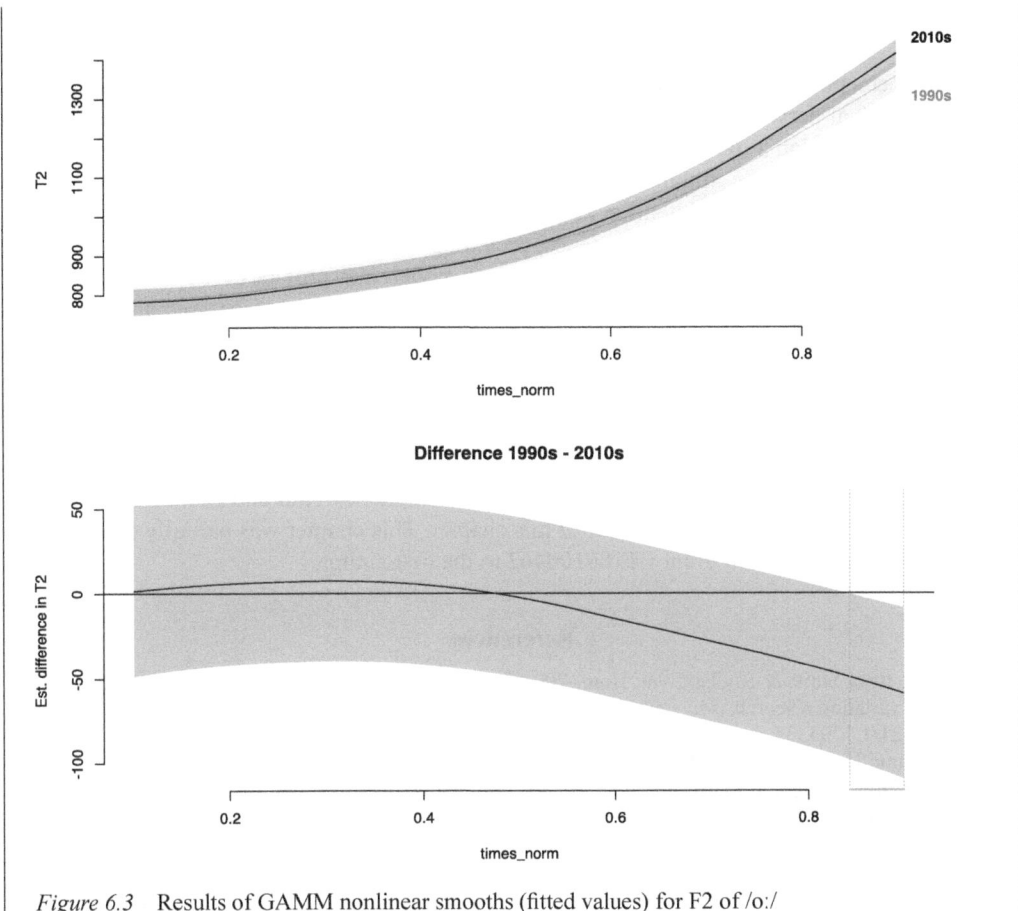

Figure 6.3   Results of GAMM nonlinear smooths (fitted values) for F2 of /oː/
Figure 6.3a (top)   by time period
Figure 6.3b (bottom)   as difference between nonlinear smooths for each time period

One potential limitation of the dynamic methods reported here is that they require time-normalization. Future larger-scale comparisons with a range of techniques such as SS-ANOVA will help sociophonetic researchers make informed decisions about the best methods for analyzing the complexity of vowel dynamicity.

Concluding comments

Given the breadth of work in the sociophonetic analysis of vowel variation and the impossibility of covering all areas of interest, we have focused on certain key topics to provide a flavor of the questions that continue to have an impact on the scientific study of social-indexical variation in vowels. An extensive array of important and vibrant areas of research have not been addressed here due to lack of space including sociophonetic analyses of understudied/under-resourced languages, the acquisition of sociophonetic variation in children, in second dialect, and second and more languages (see Evans & Tomé Lourido this volume; Gnevsheva this volume). We have also focused on speech production (particularly from English) and there is a rich emerging literature on the perception of, and attitudes towards sociophonetic variation, how fine phonetic detail indexes individual personae and stance, and a greater emphasis on languages other than English (see chapters in Section 3 of this volume).

Sociophonetics into the future will continue to incorporate insights from phonetics and sociolinguistics with increasing attention to concepts and methods from cognitive science and sociology, along with tools from computer science, providing opportunities to integrate this knowledge into new models of language variation and change. Such models may provide the key to understanding how fine-grained socio-indexical phonetic variation is used by speakers, processed and interpreted by listeners, acquired by children, and integrated into mechanisms responsible for language change.

Acknowledgments

We thank Sallyanne Palethorpe and Joshua Penney for their expertise in data checking and analysis for the case study. We would also like to thank Christopher Strelluf and Paul Foulkes for their very helpful comments on an earlier draft of this chapter. This chapter was partially supported by Australian Research Council grant FT180100462 to the first author.

References

Adank, Patti, Roel Smits & Roeland van Hout. 2004. A comparison of vowel normalization procedures for language variation research. *Journal of the Acoustical Society of America* 116(5). 3099–3107. https://doi.org/10.1121/1.1795335

Anderson, Anne H., Miles Bader, Ellen Gurman Bard, Elizabeth Boyle, Gwyneth Doherty, Simon Garrod, Stephen Isard, Jacqueline Kowtko, Jan McAllister, Jim Miller, Catherine Sotillo, Henry S. Thompson & Regina Weinert. 1991. The HCRC map task corpus. *Language and Speech.* 34(4). 351–366. https://doi.org/10.1177/002383099103400040

Baayen, R. Harald, Richard Piepenbrock & Leon Gulikers. 1995. *CELEX2 LDC96L14. Web Download.* Linguistic Data Consortium. https://doi.org/10.35111/gs6s-gm48

Babel, Molly. 2010. Dialect divergence and convergence in New Zealand English. *Language in Society* 39(4). 437–456. https://doi.org/10.1017/S0047404510000400

Babel, Molly. 2012. Evidence for phonetic and social selectivity in spontaneous phonetic imitation. *Journal of Phonetics* 40(1). 177–189. https://doi.org/10.1016/j.wocn.2011.09.001

Babel, Molly, Michael McAuliffe & Graham Haber. 2013. Can mergers-in-progress be unmerged in speech accommodation? *Frontiers in Psychology* 4(653). 1–14. https://doi.org/ 10.3389/fpsyg.2013.00653

Babel, Molly, Grant McGuire, Sophia Walters & Alice Nicholls. 2014. Novelty and social preference in phonetic accommodation. *Laboratory Phonology* 5(1). 123–150. https://doi.org/10.1515/lp-2014-0006

Barnes, Sonia. 2019. The role of social cues in the perception of final vowel contrasts in Asturian Spanish. In Whitney Chappell (ed.), *Recent Advances in the Study of Spanish Sociophonetic Perception*, 16–38. John Benjamins.

Barreda, Santiago. 2021. Perceptual validation of vowel normalization methods for variationist research. *Language Variation and Change* 33(1). 27–53. https://doi.org/10.1017/S0954394521000016

Barreda, Santiago & Terrence M. Nearey. 2018. A regression approach to vowel normalization for missing and unbalanced data *Journal of the Acoustical Society of America* 144(1). 500–520. https://doi.org/ 10.1121/1.5047742

Bates, Douglas, Martin Mächler, Ben Bolker & Steve Walker. 2015. Fitting linear mixed-effects models using lme4. *Journal of Statistical Software* 67(1). 1–48. https://doi.org/10.18637/jss.v067.i01

Becker, Kara (ed.). 2019. *The Low-Back Merger Shift: Uniting the Canadian Vowel Shift, the California Vowel Shift, and short front vowel rotations across North America* [Publication of the American Dialect Society 104]. Duke University Press.

Blackwood Ximenes, Arwen, Jason A. Shaw & Christopher Carignan. 2017. A comparison of acoustic and articulatory methods for analyzing vowel differences across dialects: Data from American and Australian English. *Journal of the Acoustical Society of America* 142. 363–377. https://doi.org/10.1121/1.4991346

Boberg, Charles. 2005. The Canadian Shift in Montreal. *Language Variation and Change* 17(2). 133–154. https://doi.org/10.1017/S0954394505050064

Boberg, Charles. 2019. The North American Low-Back-Merger Shift: A continental sound change. In Becker, 56–73. https://doi.org/10.1215/00031283-8032935

Boberg, Charles, John Nerbonne & Dominic Watt. 2018. Introduction. In Charles Boberg, John Nerbonne & Dominic Watt (eds.), *The Handbook of dialectology*, 1–15. Wiley.

Bombien, Lasse, Raphael Winkelmann & Michel Scheffers. 2021. wrassp: An R wrapper to the ASSP library, R package ver. 1.0.1. https://github.com/IPS-LMU/wrassp

Brand, James, Jen Hay, Lynn Clark, Kevin Watson & Márton Sóskuthy. 2021. Systematic co-variation of monophthongs across speakers of New Zealand English. *Journal of Phonetics* 88. 1–24. https://doi.org/10.1016/j.wocn.2021.101096

Burnham, Denis, Dominique Estival, Steven Fazio, Jette Viethen, Felicity Cox, Robert Dale, Steve Cassidy, Julien Epps, Roberto Togneri, Michael Wagner, Yuko Kinoshita, Roland Göcke, Joanne Arciuli, Marc Onslow, Trent Lewis, Andy Butcher & John Hajek. 2011. Building an audio-visual corpus of Australian English: Large corpus collection with an economical portable and replicable black box. In Piero Cosi, Renato De Mori, Giuseppe Di Fabbrizio & Roberto Pieraccini (eds.), *Interspeech 2011*. ISCA Archive.

Bybee, Joan. 2001. *Phonology and language use*. Cambridge University Press.

Bybee, Joan. 2007. *Frequency of use and the organization of language*. Oxford University Press.

Calhoun, Sasha, Paola Escudero, Marija Tabain & Paul Warren (eds.). 2019. *Proceedings of the 19th International Congress of Phonetic Sciences, Melbourne, Australia 2019*. Australasian Speech Science and Technology Association.

Campbell-Kibler, Kathryn. 2011. The sociolinguistic variant as a carrier of social meaning. *Language Variation and Change* 22(3). 423–441. https://doi.org/10.1017/S0954394510000177

Cavalcanti, Julio Cesar, Anders Eriksson & Plinio A. Barbarosa 2021. Acoustic analysis of vowel formant frequencies in genetically-related and non-genetically related speakers with implications for forensic speaker comparison. *PLoS ONE* 16(2). e0246645. https://doi.org/10.1371/journal.pone.0246645

Cheshire, Jenny, Paul Kerswill, Sue Fox & Eivind Torgersen. 2011. Contact, the feature pool and the speech community: The emergence of Multicultural London English. *Journal of Sociolinguistics* 15(2). 151–196. https://doi.org/10.1111/j.1467-9841.2011.00478.x

Clopper, Cynthia G. 2009. Computational methods for normalizing acoustic vowel data for talker differences. *Language and Linguistics Compass* 3(6). 1430–1442. https://doi.org/10.1111/j.1749-818X.2009.00165.x

Clopper, Cynthia G. & David B. Pisoni. 2006. Effects of region of origin and geographic mobility on perceptual dialect categorization. *Language Variation and Change* 18(2). 193–221. https://doi.org/10.1017/S0954394506060091

Cochrane, G. Robert. 1959. The Australian English vowels as a diasystem. *Word* 15(1). 69–88.

Cox, Felicity. 1999. Vowel change in Australian English. *Phonetica* 56(1–2). 1–27. https://doi.org/10.1159/000028438

Cox, Felicity. 2006. The acoustic characteristics of /hVd/ vowels in the speech of some Australian teenagers. *Australian Journal of Linguistics* 26(2). 147–179. https://doi.org/10.1080/07268600600885494

Cox, Felicity & Sallyanne Palethorpe. 2008. Reversal of short front vowel raising in Australian English. *Proceedings of Interspeech 2008*. 342–345. https://doi.org/10.21437/Interspeech.2008-144

Cox, Felicity & Sallyanne Palethorpe. 2019. Vowel variation in a standard context across four major Australian cities. In Calhoun et al., 577–581.

Cox, Felicity, Sallyanne Palethorpe & Joshua Penney. Forthcoming. 50 years of monophthong and diphthong shifts in Australian English. In Felicitas Kleber & Tamara Rathke (eds.), *Speech dynamics: Synchronic variation and diachronic change*. De Gruyter.

De Decker, Paul M. & Jennifer R. Nycz. 2012. Are tense [æ]s really tense? The mapping between articulation and acoustics. *Lingua* 122(7). 810–821. https://doi.org/10.1016/j.lingua.2012.01.003

Dinkin, Aaron J. & Robin Dodsworth. 2017. Gradience, allophony, and chain shifts. *Language Variation and Change* 29(1). 101–127. https://doi.org/10.1017/S0954394517000035

Di Paolo, Marianna & Alice Faber. 1990. Phonation differences and the phonetic content of the tense-lax contrast in Utah English. *Language Variation and Change* 2(2). 155–204. https://doi.org/10.1017/S09543 94500000326

Disner, Sandra Ferrari. 1980. Evaluation of vowel normalization methods. *Journal of the Acoustical Society of America* 67(1). 253–261.

Docherty, Gerard J. 2022. Sociophonetics. In M. Aronoff (ed.), *Oxford research encyclopedia of linguistics*. Oxford University Press.

Docherty, Gerard J. & Paul Foulkes. 2014. An evaluation of usage-based approaches to the modelling of sociophonetic variability. *Lingua* 142. 42–56. https://doi.org/10.1016/j.lingua.2013.01.011

Docherty, Gerard J., Paul Foulkes, Simón Gonzalez & Nathaniel Mitchell. 2018. Missed connections at the junction of sociolinguistics and speech processing. *Topics in Cognitive Science* 10(4). 759–774. https://doi.org/10.1111/tops.12375

Docherty, Gerard J., Simón Gonzalez & Nathaniel Mitchell. 2015. Static vs dynamic perspectives on the realization of vowel nucleii in West Australian English. In Scottish Consortium for ICPhS 2015, Paper 956.

Docherty, Gerard J., Simón Gonzalez, Nathaniel Mitchell & Paul Foulkes. 2019. An acoustic analysis of short front vowel realisations in the conversational style of young English speakers from Western Australia. In Calhoun et al., 1759–1763.

Docherty, Gerard J. & Norma Mendoza-Denton. 2012. Speaker-related variation–Sociophonetic factors. In Abigail C. Cohn, Cécile Fougeron & Marie K. Huffman (eds.), *The Oxford handbook of laboratory phonology*, 42–60. https://doi.org/10.1093/oxfordhb/9780199575039.013.0004

Docherty, Gerard J. & Dominic Watt. 2001. Chain shifts. In Rajend Mesthrie (ed.), *The concise encyclopedia of sociolinguistics*, 303–307. Pergamon.

D'Onofrio, Annette. 2021. Age-based perceptions of a reversing regional sound change. *Journal of Phonetics* 86. Article 101038. https://doi.org/10.1016/j.wocn.2021.101038

D'Onofrio, Annette, Teresa Pratt & Janneke Van Hofwegen. 2019. Compression in the California Vowel Shift: Tracking generational sound change in California's Central Valley. *Language Variation and Change* 31(2). 193–217. https://doi.org/10.1017/S0954394519000085

Drager, Katie, Kate Hardeman Guthrie, Rachel Schutz & Ivan Chik. 2021. Perceptions of style: A focus on fundamental frequency and perceived social characteristics. In Lauren Hall-Lew, Emma Moore & Robert J. Podesva (eds.) *Social meaning and linguistic variation: Theorizing the third wave*, 176–202. Cambridge University Press.

Drager, Katie & M. Joelle Kirtley. 2016. Awareness, salience, and stereotypes in exemplar-based models of speech production and perception. In Anna Babel (ed.), *Awareness and control in sociolinguistic research*, 1–24. Cambridge University Press.

Drager, Katie & Thomas Kettig. 2021 Sociophonetics. In Rachael-Anne Knight & Jane Setter (eds.), *The Cambridge handbook of phonetics*, 551-577. Cambridge University Press.

Eckert, Penelope & William Labov. 2017. Phonetics, phonology and social meaning. *Journal of Sociolinguistics* 21(4). 467–496. https://doi.org/10.1111/josl.12244

Ellis, Alexander J. 1889. *On early English pronunciation: Part V*. N. Trübner & Co.

Elvin, Jaydene, Daniel Williams & Paola Escudero. 2016. Dynamic acoustic properties of monophthongs and diphthongs in Western Sydney Australian English. *Journal of the Acoustical Society of America* 140(1). 576–581. https://doi.org/doi:10.1121/1.4952387

Espy-Wilson, Carol Y, Suzanne E. Boyce, Michel Jackson, Shrikanth Narayanan & Abeer Alwan. 2000. Acoustic modeling of American English /r/. *Journal of the Acoustical Society of America* 108(1). 343–356. https://doi.org/10.1121/1.429469

Essner, C. 1947. Recherche sur la structure des voyelles orales. *Archives Néerlandaises Phonétique Expérimentale* 20. 40–77.

Fant, Gunnar. 1973. *Speech sounds and features*. MIT Press.

Flynn, Nicholas. 2011. Comparing vowel formant normalisation procedures. *York Papers in Linguistics* 2(11). 1–28.

Fox, Robert & Ewa Jacewicz. 2009. Cross-dialectal variation in formant dynamics of American English vowels. *Journal of the Acoustical Society of America* 126. 2603–2618. https://doi.org/10.1121/1.3212921

Fridland, Valerie, Kathryn Bartlett & Roger Kreuz. 2004. Do you hear what I hear? Experimental measurement of the perceptual salience of acoustically manipulated vowel variants by Southern speakers in Memphis, TN. *Language Variation and Change* 16(1). 1–16. https://doi.org/10.1017/S0954394504161012

Fromont, Robert & Jennifer Hay. 2012. LaBB-CAT: An annotation store. In Paul Cook & Scott Nowson (eds.), *Proceedings of Australasian Language Technology Association Workshop*, 113–117. Australasian Language Technology Association.

Fromont, Robert & Kevin Watson. 2016. Factors influencing automatic segmental alignment of sociophonetic corpora. *Corpora* 11(3). 401–431. https://doi.org/10.3366/COR.2016.0101

Gessinger, Iona, Eran Raveh, Ingmar Steiner & Bernd Möbius. 2021. Phonetic accommodation to natural and synthetic voices: Behavior of groups and individuals in speech shadowing. *Speech Communication* 127. 43–63. https://doi.org/10.1016/j.specom.2020.12.004

Gonzales, Wilkinson Daniel Wong & Rebecca Lurie Starr. 2020. Vowel system or vowel systems? Variation in the monophthongs of Philippine Hybrid Hokkien. *Journal of Pidgin and Creole Languages* 35(2). 253–292. https://doi.org/10.1075/jpcl.00061.won

Gonzalez, Simon, James Grama & Catherine E. Travis. 2020. Comparing the performance of forced aligners used in sociophonetic research. *Linguistics Vanguard* 6(1). 1–13. https://doi.org/10.1515/lingvan-2019-0058

Gordon, Matthew J. 2011. Methodological and theoretical issues in the study of chain shifting. *Language and Linguistics Compass* 5(11). 784–794. https://doi.org/10.1111/j.1749-818X.2011.00310.x

Gordon, Matthew J. 2015. Exploring chain shifts, mergers, and near-mergers as changes in progress. In Patrick Honeybone & Joseph Salmons (eds.) *The Oxford handbook of historical phonology*, 173–190. Oxford University Press

Grama, James, Catherine E. Travis & Simon Gonzalez. 2019. Initiation, progression, and conditioning of the short-front vowel shift in Australia. In Calhoun et al., 1769–1773.

Guy, Gregory R. 2014. Linking usage and grammar: Generative phonology, exemplar theory, and variable rules. *Lingua* 142. 57–65. https://doi.org/10.1016/j.lingua.2012.07.007

Hall-Lew, Lauren, Amanda Cardoso, Yova Kemenchedjieva, Kieran Wilson, Ruaridh Purse & Julie Saigusa. 2015. San Francisco English and the California Vowel Shift. In Scottish Consortium for ICPhS 2015, Paper 591.

Handbook of the International Phonetic Association. 1999. Cambridge University Press.

Harrington, Jonathan. 2006. An acoustic analysis of 'HAPPY-tensing' in the Queen's Christmas broadcasts. *Journal of Phonetics* 34(4). 439–457. https://doi.org/10.1016/j.wocn.2005.08.001

Harrington, Jonathan, Michele Gubian, Mary Stevens & Florian Schiel. 2019. Phonetic change in an Antarctic winter. *Journal of the Acoustical Society of America* 146(5). 3327–3332. https://doi.org/10.1121/1.5130709

Harrington, Jonathan, Felicitas Kleber, Ulrich Reubold, Florian Schiel & Mary Stevens. 2018. Linking cognitive and social aspects of sound change using agent-based modeling. *Topics in Cognitive Science* 10(4). 707–728. https://doi.org/10.1111/tops.12329

Harrington, Jonathan, Felicitas Kleber, Ulrich Reubold, Florian Schiel & Mary Stevens. 2019. The phonetic basis of the origin and spread of sound change. In Katz & Assmann, 401–426.

Harrington, Jonathan, Felicitas Kleber, Ulrich Reubold & Mary Stevens. 2016. The relevance of context and experience for the operation of historical sound change. In Anna Esposito & Lakhmi Jain (eds.), *Toward robotic socially believable behaving systems*, vol. 2: *Modeling social signals*, 61–92. Springer.

Harrington, Jonathan, Sallyanne Palethorpe & Catherine Watson. 2000. Monophthongal vowel changes in Received Pronunciation: An acoustic analysis of the Queen's Christmas broadcasts. *Journal of the International Phonetic Association* 30(1/2). 63–78. https://doi.org/10.1017/S0025100300006666

Harrington, Jonathan, Sallyanne Palethorpe & Catherine Watson. 2005. Deepening or lessening the divide between diphthongs: An analysis of the Queen's annual Christmas broadcasts. In William J. Hardcastle & J. Mackenzie Beck (eds.), *A figure of speech: A Festschrift for John Laver*, 227–261. Routledge.

Harrington, Jonathan & Ulrich Reubold. 2021. Accent reversion in older adults: Evidence from the Queen's Christmas broadcasts. In Karen V. Beaman & Isabelle Buchstaller (eds.), *Language variation and language change across the lifespan*, 119–137. Routledge.

Hay, Jennifer B., Janet B. Pierrehumbert, Abby J. Walker & Patrick LaShell. 2015. Tracking word frequency effects through 130 years of sound change. *Cognition* 139. 83–91. https://doi.org/10.1016/j.cognition.2015.02.012

Hay, Jennifer, Paul Warren, Katie Drager. 2006. Factors influencing speech perception in the context of a merger-in-progress. *Journal of Phonetics* 34(4). 458–484. https://doi.org/10.1016/j.wocn.2005.10.001

Hebda, Anna. 2012. Phonological variables. In Juan Manuel Hernández-Campoy & Juan Camilo Conde-Silvestre (eds.), *The Handbook of historical sociolinguistics*, 237–252. Wiley-Blackwell.

Hillenbrand, James M. & Michael J. Clark. 2000. Some effects of duration on vowel recognition. *Journal of the Acoustical Society of America* 108(6). 3013–3022. https://doi.org/10.1121/1.1323463

Hockett, Charles F. (ed.). 1955. *A manual of phonology. International Journal of American Linguistics* 21(4). Part 1.

Horvath, Barbara. 1985. *Variation in Australian English: The sociolects of Sydney.* Cambridge University Press.

Hruschka, Daniel J., Morten H. Christiansen, Richard A. Blythe, William Croft, Paul Heggarty, Salikoko S. Mufwene, Janet Pierrehumbert & Shana Poplack. 2009. Building social cognitive models of language change. *Trends in Cognitive Sciences* 13(11). 464–469. https://doi.org/10.1016/j.tics.2009.08.008

Jacewicz, Ewa & Robert Allen Fox. 2011. Perceptual distinctiveness of vowels in relation to dialectal sound change. *Journal of the Acoustical Society of America* 129(4). 2421–2421. https://doi.org/10.1121/1.4991021

Jacewicz, Ewa, Robert Allen Fox & Joseph Salmons. 2011. Cross-generational vowel change in American English. *Language Variation and Change* 23(1). 45–86. https://doi.org/10.1017/S0954394510000219

Jansen, Sandra. 2019. Change and stability in GOOSE, GOAT and FOOT: Back vowel dynamics in Carlisle English. *English Language and Linguistics* 23(1). 1–29. https://doi.org/10.1017/S1360674317000065

Jin, Su-Hyun & Liu Chang. 2013. The vowel inherent spectral change of English vowels spoken by native and non-native speakers. *Journal of the Acoustical Society of America.* 133(5). EL363. https://doi.org/10.1121/1.4798620

Johnson, Keith. 2005. Speaker normalization. In David B. Pisoni & Robert E. Remez (eds.), *The handbook of speech perception*, 363–389. Blackwell.

Johnson, Keith. 2006. Resonance in an exemplar-based lexicon: The emergence of social identity and phonology. *Journal of Phonetics* 34(4). 485–499. https://doi.org/10.1016/j.wocn.2005.08.004

Joos, Martin. 1948. Acoustic phonetics. *Language* 24(4). 1–136.

Katz, William F. & Peter F. Assmann (eds.). 2019. *The Routledge handbook of phonetics.* Routledge.

Kelley, Matthew C. & Benjamin V. Tucker. 2020. A comparison of four vowel overlap measures. *Journal of the Acoustical Society of America* 147(1). 137–145. https://doi.org/10.1121/10.0000494

Kendall, Tyler & Valerie Fridland. 2021. *Sociophonetics.* Cambridge University Press.

Kerswill, Paul & Ann Williams. 2005. New towns and koineization: Linguistic and social correlates. *Linguistics* 43(5). 1023–1048. https://doi.org/10.1515/ling.2005.43.5.1023

Kettig, Thomas. 2016. The BAD-LAD split: Secondary /æ/-lengthening in Southern Standard British English. *Proceedings of the LSA* 1. https://doi.org/10.3765/plsa.v1i0.3732

Kirkham, Sam, Claire Nance, Bethany Littlewood, Kate Lightfoot & Eve Groarke. 2019. Dialect variation in formant dynamics: The acoustics of lateral and vowel sequences in Manchester and Liverpool English. *Journal of the Acoustical Society of America* 145(2). 784. https://doi.org/10.1121/1.5089886

Kisler, Thomas, Uwe Reichel & Florian Schiel. 2017. Multilingual processing of speech via web services. *Computer Speech & Language* 45. 326–347. https://doi.org/10.1016/j.csl.2017.01.005

Koenig, Walter, Hugh K. Dunn & L.Y. Lacy. 1946. The sound spectrograph. *Journal of the Acoustical Society of America* 18(1). 19–49. https://doi.org/10.1121/1.1916342

Labov, William. 1963. The social motivation of a sound change. *Word* 19(3). 273–309. https://doi.org/10.1080/00437956.1963.11659799

Labov, William. 1966. The linguistic variable as a structural unit. *Washington Linguistics Review* 3. 4–22.

Labov, William. 1994. *Principles of linguistic change*, vol. 1: *Internal factors.* Blackwell.

Labov, William, Ingrid Rosenfelder & Josef Fruehwald. 2013. One hundred years of sound change in Philadelphia: Linear incrementation, reversal, and reanalysis. *Language* 89(1). 30–65. https://doi.org/10.1353/lan.2013.0015

Labov, William, Malcah Yaeger & Richard Steiner. 1972. *A quantitative study of sound change in progress.* US Regional Survey.

Ladefoged, Peter & Ian Maddieson. 1990. Vowels of the world's languages. *Journal of Phonetics* 18(2). 93–122. https://doi.org/10.1016/S0095-4470(19)30396-1

Lawson, Eleanor, Jane Stuart-Smith & Lydia Rodger. 2019. A comparison of acoustic and articulatory parameters for the GOOSE vowel across British Isles Englishes. *Journal of the Acoustical Society of America* 146(6). 4363–4381. https://doi.org/10.1121/1.5139215

Lawson, Eleanor, Jane Stuart-Smith, James M. Scobbie & Satsuki Nakai. 2018. *Dynamic dialects: An articulatory web resource for the study of accents.* University of Glasgow. www.dynamicdialects.ac.uk/

Leemann, Adrian, Marie-José Kolly & David Britain. 2018. The English Dialects App: The creation of a crowdsourced dialect corpus. *Ampersand* 5. 1–17. https://doi.org/10.1016/j.amper.2017.11.001

Lenth, Russell V. 2022. *emmeans: Estimated marginal means, aka least-squares means*. R package ver. 1.8.2. https://CRAN.R-project.org/package=emmeans

Liu, Chang, Su-Hyun Jin & Chia-Tsen Chen. 2014. Durations of American English vowels by native and non-native speakers: Acoustic analyses and perceptual effects. *Language and Speech* 57(2). 238–253. https://doi.org/10.1177/0023830913501769

Lubowicz, Anna. 2011. Chain shifts. In Marc van Oostendorp, Colin J. Ewen, Elizabeth Hume & Keren Rice (eds.), *The Blackwell companion to phonology*, 1717–1735. Wiley-Blackwell.

Macaulay, Ronald K.S. 1977. *Language, social class, and education: A Glasgow study*. Edinburgh University Press.

Mack, Sara. 2010. A sociophonetic analysis of perception of sexual orientation in Puerto Rican Spanish. *Laboratory Phonology* 1(1). 41–63. https://doi.org/10.1515/labphon.2010.004

MacKenzie, Laurel & Danielle Turton. 2020. Assessing the accuracy of existing forced alignment software on varieties of British English. *Linguistics Vanguard* 6(1). 1–14. https://doi.org/10.1515/lingvan-2018-0061

Maclagan, Margaret & Jennifer Hay. 2007. Getting *fed* up with our *feet*: Contrast maintenance and the New Zealand English "short" front vowel shift. *Language Variation and Change* 19(1). 1–25. https://doi.org/10.1017/S0954394507070020

Martinet, André. 1952. Diffusion of language and structural linguistics. *Romance Philology* 6(1). 5–13.

McAuliffe, Michael, Arlie Coles, Michael Goodale, Sarah Mihuc, Michael Wagner, Jane Stuart-Smith & Morgan Sonderegger. 2019. In Calhoun et al., 1322–1326.

McAuliffe, Michael, Michaela Socolof, Sarah Mihuc, Michael Wagner & Morgan Sonderegger. 2017. Montreal Forced Aligner: Trainable text-speech alignment using Kaldi. *Proceedings of Interspeech 2017*. 498–502. https://doi.org/10.21437/Interspeech.2017-1386

Mielke, Jeff, Christopher Carignan & Erik R. Thomas. 2017. The articulatory dynamics of pre-velar and pre-nasal /æ/-raising in English: An ultrasound study. *Journal of the Acoustical Society of America* 142(1). 332–349. https://doi.org/10.1121/1.4991348

Milroy, Lesley. 1980. *Language and social networks*. Blackwell.

Milroy, James. 1992. *Linguistic variation and change: On the historical sociolinguistics of English*. Blackwell.

Mitchell, Alexander George & Arthur Delbridge. 1965. *The speech of Australian adolescents: A survey*. Angus & Robertson.

Munson, Benjamin. 2007. The acoustic correlates of perceived masculinity, perceived femininity, and perceived sexual orientation. *Language and Speech* 50(1). 125–142. https://doi.org/10.1177/00238309070500010601

Munson, Benjamin & Molly Babel. 2019. The phonetics of sex and gender. In Katz & Assmann, 499–525.

Nearey, Terrance M. & Peter F. Assmann. 1986. Modeling the role of inherent spectral change in vowel identification. *Journal of the Acoustical Society of America* 80(5). 1297–1308. https://doi.org/10.1121/1.394433

Nesbitt, Monica & James Stanford. 2021. Structure, chronology and local social meaning of a supra-local vowel shift: Emergence of the Low-Back-Merger Shift in New England. *Language Variation and Change* 33(3). 269–295. https://doi.org/10.1017/S0954394521000168

Noiray, Aude, Khalil Iskarous & D.H. Whalen. 2014. Variability in English vowels is comparable in articulation and acoustics. *Laboratory Phonology* 5(2). 271–288. https://doi.org/10.1515/lp-2014-0010

Nycz, Jennifer. 2015. Second dialect acquisition: A sociophonetic perspective. *Language and Linguistics Compass* 9(11). 469–482. https://doi.org/10.1111/lnc3.12163

Nycz, Jennifer & Lauren Hall-Lew. 2013. Best practice in measuring vowel merger. *Proceedings of Meetings on Acoustics* 20. https://doi.org/10.1121/1.4894063

Ohala, John J. 1981. The listener as a source of sound change. In Carrie S. Masek, Roberta A. Hendrick & Mary Francis Miller (eds.), *Papers from the Parasession on Language and Behavior*, 178–203. Chicago Linguistic Society.

Ohala, John J. 1993. The phonetics of sound change. In Charles Jones (ed.), *Historical linguistics: Problems and perspectives*, 237–278. Longman.

Omari, Osama & Aziz Jaber. 2019. Variation in the acoustic correlates of emphasis in Jordanian Arabic: Gender and social class. *Folia Linguistica* 53(1). 160–200. https://doi.org/10.1515/flin-2019-2007

Pardo, Jennifer S., Rachel Gibbons, Alexandra Suppes & Robert M. Krauss. 2012. Phonetic convergence in college roommates. *Journal of Phonetics* 40(1). 190–197. https://doi.org/10.1016/j.wocn.2011.10.001

Paul, Hermann. 1891. *Principles of the history of language*. Longmans.

Payne, Arvilla C. 1980. Factors controlling the acquisition of the Philadelphia dialect by out-of-state children. In William Labov (ed.), *Locating language in time and space*, 179–218. Academic Press.

Penney, Joshua, Felicity Cox & Anita Szakay. 2021. Effects of glottalisation, preceding vowel duration, and coda closure duration on the perception of coda stop voicing. *Phonetica* 78(1). 29–63. https://doi.org/10.1159/000508752

Penney, Joshua, Benjamin Davies & Felicity Cox. 2023. Assessing the validity of remote recordings captured with a generic smartphone application designed for speech research. In *Proceedings of the 18th Australasian Speech Science and Technology Conference*.

Peterson, Gordon E. & Harold L. Barney. 1952. Control methods used in a study of the vowels. *Journal of the Acoustical Society of America* 24(2). 175–184. https://doi.org/10.1121/1.1906875

Pierrehumbert, Janet B. 2002. Word-specific phonetics. In Carlos Gussenhoven and Natasha Warner (eds.), *Laboratory Phonology 7*, 101–139. Mouton de Gruyter.

Pierrehumbert, Janet B. 2003. Phonetic diversity, statistical learning, and acquisition of phonology. *Language and Speech* 46(2–3). 115–154. https://doi.org/10.1177/00238309030460020503

Pierrehumbert, Janet B. 2006. The next toolkit. *Journal of Phonetics* 34(4). 516–530. https://doi.org/10.1016/j.wocn.2006.06.003

Potter, Ralph K. 1946. Introduction to technical discussions of sound portrayal. *Journal of the Acoustical Society of America* 18(1). 1–3.

Potter, Ralph K., George A. Kopp & Harriet C. Green. 1947. *Visible speech*. Van Nostrand Company.

R Core Team. 2022. *R: A language and environment for statistical computing*. R Foundation for Statistical Computing. www.R-project.org

Rathcke, Tamara, Jane Stuart-Smith, Bernard Torsney & Jonathan Harrington. 2017. The beauty in a beast: Minimising the effects of diverse recording quality on vowel formant measurements in sociophonetic real-time studies. *Speech Communication* 86. 24–41. https://doi.org/10.1016/j.specom.2016.11.001

Ratko, Louise, Michael Proctor & Felicity Cox. 2022. Articulation of vowel length contrasts in Australian English. *Journal of the International Phonetic Association*. https://doi.org/10.1017/S0025100322000068

Renwick, Margaret E.L. & Joseph A. Stanley. 2020. Modeling dynamic trajectories of front vowels in the American South. *Journal of the Acoustical Society of America* 147. 579. https://doi.org/10.1121/10.0000549

Rosenfelder, Ingrid, Josef Fruehwald, Keelan Evanini & Jiahong Yuan. 2014. *FAVE (Forced Alignment and Vowel Extraction) Program Suite*. http://fave.ling.upenn.edu

Schwartz, Geoffrey. 2021. The phonology of vowel VISC-osity–acoustic evidence and representational implications. *Glossa* 6(1). 26. https://doi.org/10.5334/gjgl.1182

The Scottish Consortium for ICPhS 2015 (ed.). 2015. *Proceedings of the 18th International Congress of Phonetic Sciences*. University of Glasgow.

Singmann, Henrik, Ben Bolker, Jake Westfall, Frederik Aust & Mattan S. Ben-Shachar. 2022. *afex: Analysis of factorial experiments*, R package ver. 1.2-0. https://CRAN.R-project.org/package=afex

Sóskuthy, Márton. 2017. Generalised Additive Mixed Models for dynamic analysis in linguistics: A practical introduction. *arXiv*:1703.05339 [stat:AP]. https://doi.org/10.48550/arXiv.1703.05339

Sóskuthy, Márton, Jennifer Hay & James Brand. 2019. Horizontal diphthong shift in New Zealand English. In Calhoun et al., 597–601.

Sóskuthy, Márton, Jennifer Hay, Margaret Maclagan, Katie Drager & Paul Foulkes. 2017. Early New Zealand English: The closing diphthongs. In Raymond Hickey (ed.), *Listening to the past: Audio records of accents of English*, 529–561. Cambridge University Press.

Stanley, Joseph A., Margaret E.L. Renwick, Katherine Ireland Kuiper & Rachel M. Olsen. 2021. Back vowel dynamics and distinctions in Southern American English. *Journal of English Linguistics* 49(4). 389–418. https://doi.org/10.1177/0075424221104316

Stevens, Mary & Jonathan Harrington. 2014. The individual and the actuation of sound change. *Loquens* 1(1). e003. https://doi.org/10.3989/loquens

Strycharczuk, Patrycja & James M. Scobbie. 2017. Fronting of Southern British English high-back vowels in articulation and acoustics. *Journal of the Acoustical Society of America* 142(1). 322–331. https://doi.org/10.1121/1.4991010

Sweet, Henry. 1888. *A history of English sounds from the earliest period, with full word-lists (1888)*. Clarendon Press.

Szalay, Tünde, Titia Benders, Felicity Cox, Sallyanne Palethorpe & Michael Proctor. 2021. Spectral contrast reduction in Australian English /l/-final rimes. *Journal of the Acoustical Society of America* 149(2). 1183–1197. https://doi.org/10.1121/10.0003499

Tanner, James, Morgan Sonderegger, Jane Stuart-Smith & Josef Fruehwald. 2020. Toward "English" phonetics: Variability in the pre-consonantal voicing effect across English dialects and speakers. *Frontiers in Artificial Intelligence* 3 . Article 38. https://doi.org/10.3389/frai.2020.00038

Thomas, Erik R. 2013. Sociophonetics. In J.K. Chambers & Natalie Schilling-Estes. (eds.) *Handbook of language variation and change*, 2nd edn., 108– 127. Wiley-Blackwell.

Thomas, Erik R. 2019. Innovations in sociophonetics. In Katz & Assmann, 448–472.

Torgersen, Elvind & Paul Kerswill. 2004. Internal and external motivation in phonetic change: Dialect levelling outcomes for an English vowel shift. *Journal of Sociolinguistics* 8(1). 23–52. https://doi.org/10.1111/j.1467-9841.2004.00250.x

Trager, George L. & Henry Lee Smith. 1951. *An outline of English structure*. Batterburg Press.

Trudgill, Peter. 1972. Sex, covert prestige and linguistic change in the urban British English of Norwich. *Language in Society* 1(2). 179–195. https://doi.org/10.1017/S0047404500000488

Trudgill, Peter. 1974. Linguistic change and diffusion: Description and explanation in sociolinguistic dialect geography. *Language in Society* 3(2). 215–246. https://doi.org/10.1017/S0047404500004358

Trudgill, Peter. 2004. *New-dialect formation: The inevitability of colonial Englishes*. Oxford University Press.

Trudgill, Peter. 2008. Colonial dialect contact in the history of European languages: On the irrelevance of identity to new-dialect formation. *Language in Society* 37(2). 241–254. https://doi.org/10.1017/S0047404508080287

Turton, Danielle & Maciej Baranowski. 2021. Not quite the same: The social stratification and phonetic conditioning of the FOOT-STRUT vowels in Manchester. *Journal of Linguistics* 57(1). 163–201. https://doi.org/10.1017/S0022226720000122

UCLA Phonological Segment Inventory Database. 2019. Lelemi sound inventory (UPSID). In Steven Moran & Daniel McCloy (eds.), *PHOIBLE 2.0*. Max Planck Institute for the Science of Human History. http://phoible.org/inventories/view/441

Van der Harst, Sander, Hans Van de Velde & Roeland Van Hout. 2014. Variation in Standard Dutch vowels: The impact of formant measurement methods on identifying the speaker's regional origin. *Language Variation and Change* 26(2). 247–272. https://doi.org/10.1017/S0954394514000040

van Rij, Jacolien, Martijn Wieling, R. Harald Baayen & Hedderik van Rinj. 2022. *Itsadug: Interpreting time series and autocorrelated data using GAMMs*. https://CRAN.R-project.org/package=itsadug

Voeten, Cesko C., Wilbert Heeringa & Hans Van de Velde. 2022. Normalisation of nonlinearly time-dynamic vowels. *Journal of the Acoustical Society of America* 152. 2692. https://doi.org/10.1121/10.0015025

Vorperian, Houri & Raymond Kent. 2007. Vowel acoustic space development in children: A synthesis of acoustic and anatomic data. *Journal of Speech, Language, and Hearing Research* 50(6). 1510–1545. https://doi.org/10.1044/1092-4388(2007/104)

Walker, Abby & Kathryn Campbell-Kibler. 2015. Repeat what after whom? Exploring variable selectivity in a cross-dialectal shadowing task. *Frontiers in Psychology* 6. Article 546. https://doi.org/10.3389/fpsyg.2015.00546

Watson, Catherine I. & Jonathan Harrington. 1999. Acoustic evidence for dynamic formant trajectories in Australian English vowels. *Journal of the Acoustical Society of America* 106(1). 458–468. https://doi.org/10.1121/1.427069

Watson, Catherine I., Margaret A. Maclagan, Jeanette King, Ray Harlow & Peter J. Keegan. 2016. Sound change in Māori and the influence of New Zealand English. *Journal of the International Phonetic Association* 46(2). 185–218. https://doi.org/10.1017/S0025100316000025

Watt, Dominic & Carmel Llamas. 2014. *Language, borders and identity*. Edinburgh University Press.

Weinreich, Uriel. 1953. Is a structural dialectology possible? *Word* 10(2–3). 388–400. https://doi.org/10.1080/00437956.1954.11659535

Wells, J.C. 1982. *Accents of English*. Cambridge University Press.

Whalen, D.H., Wei-Rong Chen, Christine H. Shadle. 2022. Formants are easy to measure; resonances, not so much: Lessons from Klatt (1986). *Journal of the Acoustical Society of America* 152. 933. https://doi.org/10.1121/10.0013410

141

Whalen, D.H., Wei-Rong Chen, Mark, K. Tiede & Hosung Nam. 2018. Variability of articulator positions and formants across nine English vowels. *Journal of Phonetics* 68(1). 1–14. https://doi.org/10.1016/j.wocn.2018.01.003

Wieling, Martijn. 2018. Analyzing dynamic phonetic data using generalized additive mixed modeling: A tutorial focusing on articulatory differences between L1 and L2 speakers of English. *Journal of Phonetics* 70. 86–116. https://doi.org/10.1016/j.wocn.2018.03.002

Williams Daniel, Jan-Willem van Leussen & Paola Escudero. 2015. Beyond North American English: Modelling vowel inherent spectral change in British English and Dutch. In Scottish Consortium for ICPhS 2015, Paper 596.

Winkelmann, Raphael, Jonathan Harrington & Klaus Jänsch. 2017. EMU-SDMS: Advanced speech database management and analysis in R. *Computer Speech & Language* 45. 392–410. https://doi.org/10.1016/j.csl.2017.01.002

Wolfswinkler, Katrin & Jonathan Harrington. 2021. The influence of Standard German on the vowels and diphthongs of West Central Bavarian. *Journal of the International Phonetic Association*. https://doi.org/10.1017/S0025100321000232

Wood, Simon N. 2011. Fast stable restricted maximum likelihood and marginal likelihood estimation of semiparametric generalized linear models. *Journal of the Royal Statistical Society (B)* 73(1). 3–36. https://doi.org/10.1111/j.1467-9868.2010.00749.x

Wood, Simon N. 2017. *Generalized Additive Models: An introduction with R*, 2nd edn. Chapman & Hall/CRC.

Wright, Richard. 2004. Factors of lexical competition in vowel articulation. In John Local, Richard Ogden & Rosalind Temple (eds.), *Papers in laboratory phonology VI: Phonetic interpretation*, 75–87. Cambridge University Press. https://doi.org/10.1017/CBO9780511486425.005

7

SOCIOPHONETICS AND STOPS

Eleanor Chodroff and Paul Foulkes

Introduction

All languages have stop consonants. The voiceless stops /p t k/ occur in around 98 percent of languages (Moran & McCloy 2019), and "every known language has sounds similar to two of these three" (Ladefoged 2005:156). Stops are also acquired early by children learning almost any language (McLeod & Crowe 2018).

While their prevalence and early acquisition might suggest some degree of simplicity, stops are complex from a phonetic perspective. Consider the articulatory actions involved in generating a plosive. First, an active articulator is brought into contact with a passive articulator. The closure is held while pulmonic air pressure builds up behind it. Plosion occurs as the constriction is released, and the articulators then continue to move to produce the subsequent sound (or to return to rest). These supralaryngeal actions are also coordinated in time with laryngeal action to ensure, for example, that vocal fold vibration starts and ceases appropriately. The sequence of articulatory changes thus generates a complex series of aerodynamic and acoustic changes. Airflow is first channeled through an increasingly narrow cavity as the closure is formed, then air pressure builds during the hold phase before being released abruptly and generating the sudden stop "burst" as high-pressure air escapes the oral tract. Following the release there is a sudden drop in air pressure before airflow continues through a vocal tract that is changing to produce subsequent sounds. In acoustic terms we see a series of events including (depending on the precise sequence of sounds) formant transitions in a preceding voiced sound, acoustic silence during a voiceless closure or low amplitude periodic energy during a voiced one, transient(s) at the point of release, aperiodic noise as air escapes, further acoustic transitions in any subsequent sound, and ongoing changes in phonation throughout the sequence.

This physical complexity presents a wide range of opportunities for variation in the phonetic qualities of stops. Variation can be observed in the closing phase, the hold phase, the release phase, and/or in the timing relationship between supralaryngeal and laryngeal actions. From a cross-linguistic perspective, Ladefoged & Maddieson (1996:47–48) note that stops vary in their precise place of articulation, glottal state, air stream mechanism, activity at onset and offset (e.g., pre-aspiration and post-aspiration), length, and strength. Variation can be gradient (e.g., in the duration of voice onset time [VOT—the time between the release of the closure hold and the beginning

DOI: 10.4324/9781003034636-8

of periodic voicing]) or categorical (e.g., in terms of deletion, insertion, or substitution of phono-logical units). Similar patterns of variation can, in principle, be observed within and between speakers of a given language. Variation may reflect universal constraints of biology and physics, but it may also reflect systematic regional and social differences that convey indexical meaning.

In this chapter we review sources and patterns of variation in stops. We treat the terms "stops" and "plosives" as equivalent for this class of consonants, preferring to use "stops" in our work. We focus mainly on speech production, but also discuss some perceptual studies. We describe phonetic and phonological variation in stops, and explore intersections between stop variation and a range macro- and micro-level sociolinguistic factors. We then describe a case study conducted on variation across speaker sex and age as measured through VOT and spectral center of gravity (COG).

Phonetic and phonological variation in stops

This section explores research in sociophonetic variation in stops according to the three phases of stop closure: closing, hold, and release. Additionally, we review research on laryngeal coupling and VOT, as well as on common phonological alternations observed with stops.

Closing phase

The closing gesture for a stop may be executed at varying speed, and with varying coordination relative to laryngeal activity. In some circumstances—for example, if closure is relatively slow and phonation ceases prior to full closure—there may be a period in which a relatively narrow channel in the oral tract coincides with high airflow. These conditions may generate aperiodic noise at the point of constriction (i.e., pre-affrication) and/or at the glottis or throughout the vocal tract (i.e., pre-aspiration). The presence or absence of pre-aspiration can signal a phonological contrast, as in Gaelic and Icelandic. It is also common but noncontrastive in other Nordic languages (Helgason 2002; Hejná 2015; Clayton 2017), and reported as a social and/or regional feature in several languages. Pre-aspiration often patterns with speaker sex, with female speakers producing more and longer pre-aspiration than male speakers. This is the case, for example, in Nordic languages (Helgason 2002; Stölten & Engstrand 2002; Helgason & Ringen 2008), Welsh (Morris & Hejná 2020), and Newcastle English (Docherty & Foulkes 1999). Younger speakers have shorter and less intense pre-aspiration than older speakers of Gaelic (Nance & Stuart-Smith 2013).

In Greek there is debate on how the closing phase is coordinated with velic action. Voiced stops in some dialects are preceded by a nasal element, leading some scholars to treat them as prenasalized, while others treat them as sequences of nasal+homorganic stop. However, recent studies suggest that the overall duration is not increased if there is a nasal element, supporting the prenasalization interpretation (Arvaniti 2007). Prenasalization also varies by region, younger speakers produce it less than their elders, and it is less common in more casual styles.

Rate of closure varies by place of articulation. The velocity of the tongue body is typically slower than that of the tongue tip. The following vowel also influences this rate, with low vowels corresponding to faster closing rates, at least for tongue tip and tongue body closures (Löfqvist & Gracco 2002). Alveolars and velars are often influenced by adjacent sounds (front vowels leading to fronter stop articulation, and back vowels conversely leading to retraction).

Another common source of variation is found in the magnitude of the closure. While stops canonically involve complete closure, in some accents and some circumstances (e.g., certain phonological contexts or in rapid speech) the full closure is not made. Instead, speakers generate narrow but incomplete constrictions, thus producing phonetic fricatives or even approximants.

Such events are often described as one type of lenition or weakening (e.g., Lass 1984; Kirchner 2001; Gurevich 2004). Stop lenition, especially in intervocalic and noninitial positions, is reported in many languages including Spanish (Hualde 2005), Shilluk (spoken in Sudan and South Sudan; Remijsen, Ayoker & Mills 2011), and Paya Kuna (spoken in Panama and Colombia; Pike, Forster & Forster 1986). Lenition patterns frequently target a full laryngeal series (e.g., the voiced stop series in Spanish), but the propensity for lenition varies across languages, segments, and phonological contexts.

Lenition also varies socially and regionally in accents of English and Italian, among others. In Liverpool English, /k/ is stereotypically realized as [x], especially in noninitial contexts, although all stops are affected by lenition, subject to constraints of word and syllable position (Clark & Watson 2016). The lenition pattern is spreading outwards from Liverpool to surrounding areas, but with simplification in the linguistic constraints operating on some variants. Irish accents often display a fricative realization of /t/ in coda position, referred to as "slit-T" (O'Dwyer 2019). Detailed analysis shows that slit-T is usually voiceless and apico-alveolar, but a wider range of variants may be used including voiced fricatives, a laminal [s], and flaps (Skarnitzl & Rálišová 2022). In Italian, lenition of /p t k/ is characteristic of Rome, and central and southern varieties (Vietti 2019). The process is expanding, with signs that it holds a degree of prestige and signals a macro-regional identity. Lenited stops are also stereotypical of Tuscan accents (a process known as *gorgia toscana*), especially the high-status accent of Florence. Stops lenite on a continuum from fricatives to approximants, [h], and full deletion, depending on speech rate and stylistic register. The Australian language Murrinh Patha displays an unusual lenition pattern affecting /p/ and /k/ in stressed onsets, while young male speakers lenite more than other groups (Mansfield 2015).

Another contributory factor underlying variability in lenition is informativity (Cohen Priva 2017). Languages are more tolerant of lenition where the segments concerned offer relatively low information content (defined as the mean predictability of segments in context, rather than raw frequency). Such work is facilitated by corpus-based methods which allow access to the large datasets required to assess factors like predictability and frequency.

Variation in place of articulation is also well known as a regional feature in English. Dental variants of /t d/ are stereotypical of some Irish and Caribbean accents (Wells 1982). Similar but socially subtler variation is found in South Africa (Mesthrie 2012). Dental variants are common in Cape Town but not Durban, while all coronals are variably dental for broader Cape Town Coloured and Indian speakers (see Mesthrie et al. this volume). Retracted or retroflex variants are common for some speakers of British Asian accents (Kirkham 2011). In Multicultural London English, /k/ is often backed towards [q] (Fox & Torgersen 2018).

Hold phase

Once a closure is formed it may be held for varying durations. The duration of this closure, or hold, is frequently correlated with laryngeal activity. There seems to be a universal pattern in which hold duration and VOT are in an inverse correlation with respect to place of articulation. Labials have the longest hold duration and shortest VOT, while velars have a shorter hold duration and longer VOT (Byrd 1993; Maddieson 1997; Yao 2007; Phillips & Tucker 2020). In a study of American English, Yao (2007) observed some variation between individual speakers in closure duration, although [pʰ] had the longest hold for all speakers. The correlation between hold duration and VOT likely reflects the fact that phonation can initiate only when supraglottal pressure is lower than subglottal pressure. This has a direct relationship with place of articulation, as the constriction location results in different intraoral volumes. Once the closure is made, supraglottal pressure immediately begins to increase as air accumulates behind the closure. Supraglottal pressure may come to equal that of subglottal pressure, thus rendering vocal fold vibration impossible without articulatory adjustment, such as lowering the larynx, expanding the cheeks, or releasing air by lowering the velum (Westbury 1983). A larger intraoral volume corresponds to a lower baseline supraglottal pressure. In voiced stops this allows for longer vocal fold vibration during the hold, resulting in a more negative (but greater magnitude) VOT for [b] than [g]. For instance, in Lisker & Abramson's (1964) data for Puerto Rico Spanish, mean VOT for [b] was −138 ms while that for [g] was −108 ms. In voiceless stops, in which phonation must follow the hold phase, a larger intraoral volume requires more time for a rise in supraglottal pressure, resulting in a long hold duration and correspondingly shorter VOT ([p] < [k]; see further below).

Davidson (2016) offers a detailed study of stops in American English, showing that phonation from preceding sonorants frequently "bleeds" into the hold phase of stops (~80 percent of all cases), but varies in respect of word and phrase position, stress, and the type of preceding segment. A case of "bleeding" is voicing that continues from a preceding vowel into the hold phase, but decreases in intensity and ceases in the final third of the interval. Because supraglottal pressure quickly rises in stops, partial devoicing of phonologically voiced stops is common. In addition, where a phonologically voiced series is cued by zero or short VOT, many speakers in fact also occasionally or regularly use pre-voicing (Lisker & Abramson 1964; Docherty 1992). Where pre-voicing is used, phonation is often extinguished prior to release. As described above, vocal fold vibration becomes impossible if intraoral air pressure rises to equalize or exceed subglottal pressure.

In some languages duration plays an additional phonological role, where geminates (sounds with a long hold) contrast with singleton consonants (short hold). The precise timing relationship between geminate and singleton differs across and within languages. The ratio between geminate and singleton duration varies from less than 2:1 to as much as 3:1 (Khattab & Al-Tamimi 2014; see also Ham 2001; Aoyama & Reid 2006; and papers in Kubozono 2017). Ham (2001) hypothesizes that the timing ratio is larger for mora-timed than syllable-timed languages. Cues other than duration may also be used to signal the contrast. For example, vowels tend to be shorter before geminates than before singletons (Al-Tamimi & Khattab 2015). Al-Tamimi & Khattab (2018) provide a detailed discussion of voicing in the context of the singleton-geminate contrast in Lebanese Arabic, drawing on a set of 19 acoustic measures. Ultrasound studies indicate that geminates involve greater tongue raising than singletons (Percival, Kochetov & Kang 2018 on Eastern Oromo; Percival et al. 2020 on Hungarian). Closure duration is also relevant for the contrast between a full plosive and a tap; in intervocalic position, it is common for alveolar stops to reduce from plosives to taps, as in Shoshone and North American and Australasian Englishes (Gurevich 2004).

Variation in laryngeal action is also evident in many languages that have glottal stops. Although the IPA classification of [ʔ] implies that it is parallel to oral stops in terms of its articulation, it is often lenited to a period of creaky voicing rather than executed as a full glottal closure+ hold+release sequence. This is true both for languages with a contrastive /ʔ/ such as Hawai'ian (Davidson 2021) and for languages like English and German where it is allophonic (Kohler 1994; Docherty & Foulkes 1999). A full glottal closure appears most likely in word-initial position.

We can find relatively little evidence of social or regional variation in the hold phase of stops. A few studies report small differences in hold duration related to age, but this appears to be biologically rather than socially driven (Benjamin 1997). Some regional variation is found in geminate consonants, including stops. Degemination occurs in northern Italian accents. Central and southern accents observe a pattern of consonant lengthening via external sandhi in word-initial positions when preceded by a final stressed vowel or certain morphemes (Vietti 2019); for example, *tre case* 'three houses' [ˌtreˈkːaːse]. This process is called *raddoppiamento sintattico* ('syntactic doubling'). Vietti (2019) comments that this process has rarely been subject to sociolinguistic investigation. However, in Turin it appears that *raddoppiamento sintattico* is spreading among young immigrants from the Maghreb, apparently via contact with southern speakers (Boario 2009, cited by Vietti 2019). Vietti suggests it may therefore eventually become a sociolinguistic marker. Degemination is stigmatized in Veneto (Trumper & Maddalon 1990, cited by Vietti 2019). Gemination is also reported as a feature of Cypriot Greek but not standard Greek (Alexander 2014).

Bundgaard-Nielsen & O'Shannessy (2021) report an acoustic study of stops in Light Warlpiri (a mixed language spoken in the Northern Territory of Australia). Speakers show an interesting phonological development arising from contact between Warlpiri and both English and Kriol (i.e., a creole largely lexified from English). While Warlpiri has a single stop series, consisting of voiceless stops at five places of articulation, Light Warlpiri shows amalgamation of the phonological categories of both Warlpiri and English/Kriol. VOT is emerging as a contrastive feature in initial positions, while in medial position, constriction duration is the main cue for contrast. Short constriction duration is used for English and Kriol words with a phonologically voiced stop, whereas longer duration is used to signal voiceless stops.

Release phase

Stop releases (also referred to as bursts) may vary in intensity and frequency characteristics. Though Lisker (1986) identified burst intensity as a potential correlate of the voicing contrast, with voiceless stops tending to have louder bursts than voiced, research findings have been somewhat mixed. Greater intensity of voiceless than voiced stops has been found in American English (Zue 1976), Canadian English and Canadian French (Sundara, Polka & Baum 2006), European French (Sundara 2005), and P'urépecha (Zerbe 2013: fortis > lenis). However, the opposite pattern has been observed in Georgian (Vicenik 2010: voiced > voiceless) and Itunyoso Trique (DiCanio 2012: lenis > fortis). Mixed outcomes have been observed depending on place of articulation in Danish (Fischer-Jørgensen 1954). In Korean, aspirated stops have more intense bursts than lenis and fortis stops (Cho, Jun & Ladefoged 2002).

Spectral shape is commonly measured for understanding aspects of the release burst, particularly the place of articulation (Blumstein & Stevens 1979, 1980; Stevens & Blumstein 1981; Kewley-Port 1983; Bonneau, Djezzar & Laprie 1996). Labial stops have greater energy at lower frequencies (diffuse-falling spectrum), coronal stops have greater energy at higher frequencies (diffuse-rising spectrum), and dorsal stops have spectral energy concentrated in the mid-frequency range (compact spectrum). Aspects of the spectral shape can also serve as an acoustic correlate and perceptual cue to the stop voicing contrast (Chodroff & Wilson 2014). Word-initial voiceless stops have greater energy in the higher frequencies relative to voiced stops, at least for labials and coronals (American English: Halle, Hughes & Radley 1957; Zue 1976; Parikh & Loizou 2005; Chodroff & Wilson 2014; Canadian English: Sundara 2005; British English: Kirkham 2011; Dutch: van Alphen & Smits 2004; German: Harrington 2010:192; Georgian: Vicenik 2010). Moreover, listeners are sensitive to these differences in perceptual categorization of voiced and voiceless stops, at least in American English (Chodroff & Wilson 2014). The overall spectral shape is frequently summarized via metrics like the spectral peak or spectral moments (center of gravity [COG], variance or standard deviation, skewness, and kurtosis).

A few studies have considered regional or social variation in burst spectral frequency or intensity. In Derby English, impressionistic comments suggest older speakers produce lower frequency releases of /t/ and /d/, which might reflect a more retracted articulation relative to younger speakers (Docherty & Foulkes 1999:51; see also case study below). Though measures of spectral shape are commonly used for studying social variation in fricatives, only a handful of studies have examined measures such as COG for social variation in stops. Female speakers tend to have a higher COG for stops relative to male speakers in English (Sundara 2005; Chodroff & Wilson 2014). British Asian English speakers produce /t/ with a higher COG, skewness, and kurtosis, as well as a lower spectral SD, relative to British White English speakers (Kirkham 2011). The acoustic properties of release bursts also differ between female Modern Standard Greek and Cypriot Greek speakers (Themistocleous 2016). With respect to burst intensity, Kirkham (2011) found that British Asian English /t/ was marked by a greater relative burst intensity than corresponding /d/, whereas British White English speakers demonstrated the opposite pattern.

Mirroring the variation found in the closing phase, variation occurs in the release phase in terms of speed of release, and coordination relative to laryngeal activity. A slow release may generate aperiodic noise at the point of articulation (i.e., affrication or assibilation). This occurs most frequently before high vowels and /j/, and is reported, for example, in Finnish, Québecois French, Korean, Basque, Polish, and West Futuna-Aniwa (Hall & Hamann 2006). Release of the air trapped within the oral tract is usually executed by lowering the active articulator to allow the air to escape forwards, but for some speakers the release may be lateral if a lateral sound follows (cf. for some English speakers, *adder* [adə] versus *addle* [adˡɬ]) or nasal, via lowering the velum (cf. *butter* [bʌtə] versus *button* [bʌtⁿn̩]). A different type of variability in release is discussed by Wang (2019), in which contact between Jin and Mandarin in the Inner Mongolian city Hohhot is explored. The city is split into an old town and new town, the former being Jin-speaking, while the latter is populated by incomers from all over China who mainly use Mandarin as a *lingua franca*. Jin speakers typically realize the fricative element of aspirated stops /pʰ tʰ kʰ/ with a back fricative rather than glottal friction, [ˣ] (and /h/ itself as [x]). The new town speakers are developing a new contact variety, in which they converge on the [ˣ] variant. Sex and age effects were also found.

A range of factors also govern whether a coda-final stop is released (Davidson 2011). In American English, these factors include the place of articulation, the manner of the following segment, and the phonological context (word-medial, word-final, or phrase-final). Davidson (2011) also reported a strong ethnic difference, with white speakers having a higher rate of stop releases than Black speakers. Additional studies have shown that variants of /t/ specifically can also be harnessed to signal aspects of identity or persona. Podesva et al. (2015) suggest that final released [t] is used as a marker of an "articulate persona" among US politicians, while the same feature is used to construct "nerd" identity (Bucholtz 1996), Jewish identity (Benor 2001), or to "sound gay" (Podesva, Roberts & Campbell-Kibler 2001; Levon 2006). Several studies on English have also considered the release patterns of utterance-final /t/ as cues to structure conversation. For example, fully released utterance-final [t] acts as a turn-handover cue in Tyneside (Docherty et al. 1997).

Beyond final releases, other variants of /t/ have also been implicated as markers of social identity. Palatalized /t/, in combination with fronted /s/, increases percepts of gayness in Copenhagen Danish (Pharao & Maegaard 2017). In French, affricated /t/ is a stigmatized feature of *cité* (referring to low status housing) or *beur* (North African heritage) speech, but holds covert prestige due to the prevalence of these urban varieties in hip-hop (Jamin 2004; Gadet & Hambye 2014). The feature appears to have spread into Moroccan Arabic hip-hop and rap styles (Schwartz 2018).

In some cases, strong releases are generated by a temporary switch in airstream mechanism from pulmonic to glottal to produce ejectives. Ejectives are contrastive in many languages (Vicenik 2010), and are allophonic variants of voiceless pulmonic stops in other languages. For instance, they are widespread in utterance-final position for many speakers of German and British English, and occur more for /k/ than /p/ or /t/ (McCarthy & Stuart-Smith 2013; Brandt & Simpson 2021). Phonological context contributes considerably to variation in ejectives in several languages including the Mayan language Q'anjob'al (Kuang 2019), the Salish language Hul'q'umi'num' (Percival 2019), as well as Georgian and German (Brandt & Simpson 2021). Ogden (2009:163ff.) shows that ejectives also serve to structure conversation. For some speakers, releases themselves may be complex, articulated not as a single physical opening and acoustic transient but as a series of them. This phenomenon of multiple bursts is reported for English (e.g., Lavoie 2001; Yao 2007; Parveen & Goberman 2014), Hungarian (Gráczi & Kohári 2014), and Spanish (Lavoie 2001), and appears mostly to affect posterior places of articulation. /k/ in particular often displays two or three transients, though six or even more have been reported (Parveen & Goberman 2014). Various explanations have been offered for why multiple releases occur, including gradual release, additional closures being generated by the Bernoulli effect, and transients reflecting "pops" as saliva is sucked from the articulators (Foulkes, Docherty & Jones 2010:65).

Stops exert epiphenomenal effects on following vowels. The f0 at the start of a vowel is higher after a voiceless stop than after a voiced stop (Lee, Holliday & Kong 2020). The f0 difference has come to be the dominant cue over time in some languages (for example Korean; Kang & Guion 2008), leading to the emergence of tonal differences (Hombert, Ohala & Ewan 1979).

Formant transitions in vowels provide information about the place of articulation of adjacent stops. Following a labial stop, all formants rise at the onset of a following vowel, and a reverse pattern of falling formants at the end of the vowel can be observed in vowel+labial sequences. In alveolars and velars the F2 and F3 patterns vary depending on the specific vowel+consonant sequence (Kewley-Port 1982). However, F3 can be especially useful in separating velars and alveolars (Öhman 1966; Fant 1973; Cassidy & Harrington 1995). After a velar, F3 and F2 at the onset of a vowel often appear to emerge from a single point in the frequency range, giving a visual impression of a "pinch." A similar pattern occurs in vowels prior to velars.

VOT and laryngeal timing

Around 60 percent of languages display a voicing contrast between stops produced at the same place of articulation (Maddieson 2013). While the label "voicing" implies a difference in phonation, the voicing contrast frequently relates to the phonological contrast between two (or more) series of stop consonants that differ in their laryngeal realization. The label used to express this contrast varies across researchers and frameworks. These include descriptions such as voiced vs. voiceless, [±voice], [±spread glottis], and fortis vs. lenis. Though typologically rare, some languages also have three- or even four-way laryngeal contrasts. Languages with three-way contrasts include Thai (voiced vs. voiceless unaspirated vs. voiceless aspirated) and Korean (fortis vs. lenis vs. aspirated). Languages with four-way contrasts include Hindi and Urdi, among others (voiced unaspirated vs. voiced aspirated vs. voiceless unaspirated vs. voiceless aspirated). These are sometimes phonologically classified as being a two-way voicing contrast with a two-way aspiration contrast (e.g., Schertz & Khan 2020).

In stop production, supralaryngeal actions must be coordinated in time with laryngeal ones to ensure that voicing cues are appropriate for the phonological status of the stop. In principle, given their IPA descriptors, this means that voiceless stops such as /p t k/ have no vocal fold vibration during the stop articulation, while voiced stops such as /b d g/ have vocal fold vibration throughout their articulation. However, phonological /b d g/ are often cued by phonation starting more or less simultaneously with the release.

Lisker and Abramson (1964) provide benchmark VOT values to typify three prototypical categories that apply across most languages: −125 to −75 ms for pre-voiced stops (lead VOT: voicing precedes the stop release, and is thus conventionally given a negative value), 0–25 ms for unaspirated stops (short-lag VOT: a short lag exists between stop release and onset of voicing), and 60–100 ms for aspirated stops (long-lag VOT: a long lag exists between stop release and voicing). Studies differ in how exactly the boundaries of VOT are identified (Foulkes, Docherty & Jones 2010; Abramson & Whalen 2017). These three modes have largely been corroborated in cross-linguistic studies of VOT (Cho & Ladefoged 1999; Cho, Whalen & Docherty 2019; Chodroff, Golden & Wilson 2019); however, several languages also have what could be considered medium-lag VOT (e.g., Lebanese Arabic: Khattab 2003; Hebrew: Raphael et al. 1995; Japanese: Riney et al. 2007).

VOT varies substantially not only across languages, but also across individual speakers of a given language. To cite just one example, reported averages for the VOT of /t/ for mainstream American English range from 49 ms (Byrd 1993) to 98 ms (Chodroff & Wilson 2017), with further variation between speakers. VOT variation between stop categories, however, is relatively structured across both languages and individuals. As noted above, labial stop VOTs are almost always shorter than dorsal stop VOTs within the same laryngeal series (e.g., Lisker & Abramson 1964; Klatt 1975; Nearey & Rochet 1994; Chodroff, Golden & Wilson 2019). The coronal VOT value is frequently intermediate to the labial and dorsal values; however, considerable variation in its exact ranking has been reported (e.g., Suomi 1980; Gandour et al. 1986; Docherty 1992; Yao 2009; Chodroff & Wilson 2017; Chodroff, Golden & Wilson 2019).

Beyond the ordinal relationship of VOT across place of articulation (/p/ < /k/), languages and speakers also exhibit highly linear VOT relationships. Not only is the VOT of /p/ universally shorter than that of /k/, but the difference between /p/ and /k/ is very predictable regardless of whether the VOT is long or short. Across talkers and languages, the mean VOTs for [pʰ], [tʰ], and [kʰ] are highly correlated with one another: as the mean VOT for [pʰ] increases, so does the VOT for [tʰ] and [kʰ] (Chodroff & Wilson 2017; Chodroff, Golden & Wilson 2019). This particularly holds true of stop series with long-lag or lead VOT, but also to some degree for stops with short-lag VOT. This tight relationship between mean values across individuals and languages likely relates to a relatively uniform timing relationship between the laryngeal activity and the hold phase for each place of articulation (Chodroff & Wilson 2017). Moreover, listeners are sensitive to this relationship across place of articulation. After exposure to a talker producing [pʰ], listeners learn not only the characteristic VOT for [pʰ], but also that for [kʰ] (Theodore & Miller 2010). This has also been observed in phonetic imitation studies in which listeners lengthened VOT not only after exposure to a long VOT [pʰ], but also for unheard [kʰ] (Nielsen 2011). The degree to which talkers imitate VOT, however, varies across individuals (Yu, Abrego-Collier & Sonderegger 2013; Wade, Lai & Tamminga 2021).

VOT further varies in response to many factors including the height of the following vowel, prosodic position, stress, number of syllables, speaking rate, lexical frequency, and phonological neighborhood density. In general, VOT is longer before high vowels than mid or low vowels (Klatt 1975; Esposito 2002; Berry & Moyle 2011; but cf. Mortensen & Tøndering 2013). Additionally, VOT tends to be longer before tense vowels than lax vowels, for example [i u a] versus [ɪ ʊ ʌ] in English (Port & Rotunno 1979; Weismer 1979; Nearey & Rochet 1994). With respect to prosodic position, voiceless stops in phrase-initial position or with a phrasal accent tend to have lengthened

VOT relative to other positions in English (Pierrehumbert & Talkin 1992; Choi 2003; Cole et al. 2003, 2007; Chodroff & Wilson 2017) and Korean (Cho & Keating 2001, 2009), though for Dutch, prosodic strength corresponds to a shorter VOT for /t/ (Cho & McQueen 2005). For stress, VOT is longer in stressed syllables, though this difference is diminished in running speech (Lisker & Abramson 1967; Klatt 1975; Keating 1984). Word-initial voiceless stop VOT is also longer in monosyllabic words than polysyllabic words (Klatt 1975). Faster speaking rates correspond to shorter VOTs in production and perception (e.g., Summerfield 1975; Theodore, Miller & DeSteno 2009), and this effect has been confirmed with measures of speaking rate that include syllable duration (e.g., Miller, Green & Reeves 1986; Kessinger & Blumstein 1997, 1998), following vowel duration (e.g., Port & Rotunno 1979; Allen & Miller 1999; Allen, Miller & DeSteno 2003; Theodore, Miller & DeSteno 2009), and number of syllables per second (Baum & Ryan 1993). Higher frequency words are associated with shorter VOTs, at least in English word-initial stops (Yao 2009; Chodroff & Wilson 2017; Mielke & Nielsen 2018). Phonological neighborhood density also has a particular effect on voiceless stop VOT, in that VOT is enhanced for lexical items with a stop-initial competitor and overall high phonological neighborhood density (Baese-Berk & Goldrick 2009; Kirov & Wilson 2012; Fox, Reilly & Blumstein 2015; Nelson & Wedel 2017).

With regards to perception, stop VOT and the perception of the laryngeal contrast is typically used as a marquee case for categorical perception. Listeners tend to have sharp categorization boundaries along the VOT continuum that mark the laryngeal contrast (Lisker & Abramson 1967). Beyond the sharp perceptual boundary, categorical perception of VOT is also characterized by diminished perceptual discrimination between acoustically different stops that are on the same side of the perceptual boundary. Categorical perception of stop VOT has been found in listeners as young as one month of age (Eimas et al. 1971). Though the phonological encoding could be categorical, several studies have argued that perception of the laryngeal contrast is encoded gradiently. The exact location of the boundary varies by language, place of articulation, vowel context, and other acoustic properties of the signal, lexical frequency, as well as by listener (Stevens & Klatt 1974; Ganong 1980; Keating, Mikoś & Ganong 1981; Andruski, Blumstein & Burton 1994). Listeners employ multiple acoustic cues to determine stop identity, suggesting fine encoding of acoustic detail at some level of representation (Toscano & McMurray 2010). Additional evidence for gradient encoding of the acoustic signal comes from neural event-related potential measures in response to variation in VOT (Blumstein, Myers & Rissman 2005; Toscano et al. 2010).

In languages with more than a two-way laryngeal contrast, the perception of each phonation type becomes more complicated and can depend on the exact constellation of acoustic correlates that separate the phonation categories. For example, the phonetic realization of Korean's three-way laryngeal contrast makes use of both VOT and f0. For the fortis–aspirated contrast, VOT serves as the primary cue, whereas for the lenis–aspirated contrast, the relative influence of both VOT and f0 depends on the dialect. In Hindi and Urdu, listeners make use of multiple cues including the presence and degree of pre-voicing, aspiration, and voice quality (murmur or breathy voice; Schertz & Khan 2020). VOT is also a secondary cue that distinguishes emphatic from plain stops; for example, emphatic /ṭ/ has a shorter VOT than the corresponding plain /t/ in Jordanian Arabic (Khattab, Al-Tamimi & Heselwood 2006).

VOT can also vary considerably with respect to intralanguage regional variation and social variation. Regional differences have been reported in Danish (Puggaard 2021), French (Caramazza & Yeni-Komshian 1974), German (Kleber 2018), Italian (Villafaña Dalcher 2008; Vietti 2019), Korean (Cho, Jun, & Ladefoged 2002), Spanish (Michnowicz & Carpenter 2013), and Japanese (Utsugi, Sasaki & Igarashi 2013; though the evidence in this case is inconsistent).

In English, speakers of some regional accents use shorter VOT for /p t k/ than is found in Southern UK English accents. They include varieties in Scotland (Scobbie 2006; Docherty et al. 2011; Stuart-Smith et al. 2015), northern England, notably Lancashire (Wells 1982:74, 370), and South Africa (Bowerman 2008; Finn 2008; Mesthrie 2008a; van Rooy 2008). Regional varieties of English in several parts of Asia also manifest de-aspiration, presumably through the influence of other languages spoken in the respective location (Gargesh 2008; Mahboob & Ahmar 2008). Pre-voicing for /b d g/ is reported for some speakers of many languages in which the standard variety uses short lag. This includes English (e.g., Lisker & Abramson 1964; Docherty 1992). Pre-voicing varies regionally across the United States, and has been found to be used more by African Americans than Caucasians (Ryalls, Zipprer & Baldauff 1997; Herd 2020).

Variation in VOT also correlates with social factors in several studies. It is often found that female speakers produce longer aspiration than male speakers (e.g., English: Swartz 1992; Ryalls, Zipprer & Baldauff 1997; Whiteside, Henry & Dobbin 2004; Mandarin: Peng, Chen & Lee 2014; Ma et al. 2018; Hakka: Peng, Chen & Lee 2014). By contrast, male speakers produce longer unaspirated VOT (e.g., Li 2013; Peng, Chen & Lee 2014; Ma et al. 2018) and use more pre-voicing in phonologically voiced stops (e.g., Ryalls, Zipprer & Baldauff 1997 for US English; Helgason & Ringen 2008 for Swedish). Children demonstrate sex differences in VOT production along the same lines as adults (Whiteside & Marshall 2001; Whiteside, Henry & Dobbin 2004; cf. Chodroff, Bradshaw & Vivesay 2022). The exact factors which contribute to these sex and age differences are yet to be identified, although aerodynamic, physiological, and anatomical factors have all been suggested (Swartz 1992; Koenig 2001). However, the sex-based pattern is not universal. Morris, McCrea & Herring (2008) found no difference between American male and female speakers when controlling for speech rate. Li (2013) also found that the Mandarin sex difference in aspiration could be accounted for by differences in speaking rate. Moreover, it is male speakers who produce longer VOT in Florentine Italian (Piccardi 2017), Hungarian (Gósy & Ringen 2009), Korean (Oh 2011), Mandarin (Li 2013), and Serbian (Sokolovic-Perovic 2012). Thus we must infer that sociolinguistic factors must also play a role in shaping VOT production.

Differences in VOT act as indicators of ethnicity among Lebanese Australians, who use more pre-voicing and slightly shorter aspiration than comparator speakers (Clothier & Loakes 2018), while VOT patterns among Polish speakers of English appear to be linked to issues of "nationalist" versus "cosmopolitan" identity (Kozminska 2015).

There is conflicting information as to whether VOT increases or decreases as speakers age. Some studies report no age difference in VOT means (Neiman et al. 1983; Petrosino et al. 1993), whereas others report that older speakers have reliably shorter VOTs than younger speakers (e.g., Benjamin 1982; Morris & Brown 1994; Ryalls, Simon & Thomason 2004; Torre & Barlow 2009; Docherty et al. 2011; Kleinschmidt, Weatherholtz & Jaeger 2018; Ma et al. 2018). VOT differences by age are not entirely reducible to speech rate, however: in general, speech rate slows for elderly speakers and as a consequence, VOT lengthens (Stuart-Smith et al. 2015). Furthermore, Torre and Barlow (2009) outline the importance of considering sex-specific age differences. Age-related changes to the body differ by sex: changes to laryngeal structures tend to be greater in male speakers, whereas changes to the respiratory system tend to be greater in female speakers (Gorham-Rowan & Laures-Gore 2006). Increased VOT variability has also been found in both children and elderly speakers (Petrosino et al. 1993). VOT variability decreases with age up until adulthood (Zlatin & Koenigsknecht 1976; Macken & Barton 1980; Clumeck et al. 1981; Koenig 2001; Yang 2018). Effects of parental input on VOT are reported, for example, by Scobbie (2006), who found that Scottish teenagers with Shetland Island parents tended to show at least some use of the Shetland pattern, in which the voicing contrast is signaled by pre-voicing in /b d g/ versus short-lag VOT in /p t k/.

Further confounds are introduced by speech style: VOT tends to be longer in careful speech such as word-list readings, and shorter in spontaneous speech (Lisker & Abramson 1967; Baran, Laufer & Daniloff 1977). VOT is also reported to be longer for /p t k/ in some (but not all) studies of infant-directed speech (Fish et al. 2017); however, these studies have mostly been restricted to US English. Data for English /t/ from Fish et al. (2017), for example, reveal a mean of 130 ms in infant-directed speech compared to 101 ms in adult-directed speech when analyzed from words in context.

Several studies indicate that VOT can be subject to change over time. Traditional Received Pronunciation had rather shorter aspiration than its modern descendant (Hickey 2017). The standard German VOT distinction has been lost in some dialects, but the merger appears to be in the process of reversal in Bavaria and Saxony, likely due to influence from the standard dialect (Kleber 2018). In Korean, VOT for aspirated and lenis stops has increased over time, and f0 in the following vowel has emerged as an important cue to contrast (Lee, Holliday & Kong 2020). Social and regional variation is also reported for devoicing patterns in French (Temple 1999), Setswana (Duran et al. 2017), and Calabrian as spoken in Toronto (Nodari, Celata & Nagy 2019). Contact between languages has been cited to explain developments over time in VOT patterns. For example, contact with standard Spanish has led to loss of aspiration for Patagonian Welsh (Sleeper 2020), and contact with English has led to longer aspiration in Māori (Maclagan et al. 2009).

Other aspects of oral-laryngeal timing show regional and social variation. Tyneside English, for example, has a very distinctive set of local variants for intervocalic /p t k/, which are generally signaled by partial or full voicing during closure and a secondary glottal constriction and release prior to or following the release (Docherty & Foulkes 1999, 2005). The supralaryngeal constriction in these variants is often lenited. Moreover, the timing of the secondary glottal articulation varies between speakers, with older male speakers tending to produce the glottal earlier in the sequence. This in turn leads to a greater proportion of tokens with clear oral release, which for younger speakers is often masked by the secondary glottal action.

Social factors are also implicated in degree of VOT imitation and convergence. Sanchez, Miller & Rosenblum (2010) found that speakers (all female US students) modulated VOT to be more similar to their interlocutor in a speech shadowing task. The degree to which speakers converge to an interlocutor can also depend on the speaker's attitude towards the interlocutor (Abrego-Collier et al. 2011; Yu, Abrego-Collier & Sonderegger 2013). Adolescents are less likely to converge on VOT than adults (Schertz & Johnson 2022), and there is considerable individual variability in the degree of convergence (Wade, Lai & Tamminga 2021).

Finally, the production and perception of the Korean three-way stop contrast is also modulated by social factors. Relative to older Seoul listeners, younger Seoul listeners are more likely to rely on f0 than VOT for the lenis–aspirated contrast (Kang 2010); for the same contrast, Kyungsang listeners are more likely to rely on VOT than f0 than Seoul listeners (Lee, Politzer-Ahles & Jongman 2013). These perceptual patterns are largely mirrored in production (Kang & Guion 2008; Lee & Jongman 2012). Kong, Holliday, and Lee (2022) also identified more flexibility in the relative weighting of VOT and f0 for the Korean three-way stop contrast among university speakers than younger students, who were more likely to perceive the contrast in line with their local production patterns.

Phonological alternations

Stops are subject to a wide range of phonological processes in which phonetic form is affected in quantal ways, such that we might model them as segmental substitutions, deletions or additions, rather than adjustments to the gestural phases of stop production. These processes vary between and within languages, and are often linked to social differences between speaker groups. Documenting these processes comprehensively is beyond the scope of this work, and we cite just a few examples here.

Segmental substitutions (or alternations) are found in most if not all languages. For example, assimilation, which is generally anticipatory, can affect place, manner, and/or voicing (Zsiga 2011). Assimilation of place and manner is reported, for instance, in Catalan (Recasens & Mira 2015), voicing assimilation in Russian (Padgett 2002), and place assimilation in Korean (Kochetov & Pouplier 2008). As for social and regional variation, anticipatory place of articulation assimilation found in standard English appears not to occur in Durham (Kerswill 1987), which by contrast permits regressive voicing assimilation. A similar process is found in West Yorkshire, where a phrase such as *Hyde Park* may be realized as [haɪt̚ paːk] (or [haɪʔ paːk] via glottaling), although this feature seems to be receding (Whisker-Taylor & Clark 2019).

Voiced stops (and other obstruents) may be subject to devoicing in word-final position, when adjacent to voiceless consonants, and preceding a pause (for a cross-linguistic review, see Keating, Linker & Huffman 1983). Such patterns are observed, for example, in German (Wiese 2000), Wolof (Ngom 2003), and Turkish (Becker, Ketrez & Nevins 2011). Devoicing in word-initial position occurs in Japanese (Gao & Arai 2019).

One of the most salient sociolinguistic markers in Arabic is (q), referring to the variants [k g q ʔ] used for standard /q/ (Watson 2002:17; Khattab & Foulkes this volume). Variation is complex, related not only to region but to sex, age, ethnicity, and a rural–urban distinction. Regional variants typically include [g] in Jordan, Upper Egypt, and Saudi Arabia; [ʔ] in Levantine varieties and Lower Egypt; [k] in the rural West Bank; and [q] in Maghrebi, rural Syrian dialects, and amongst the Druze community in Lebanon. In Palestine, [k g ʔ] are subject to ongoing change linked to age, sex, and dialectal background (Cotter 2014). Usage patterns are further complicated by diglossia, whereby [q] is used for learned words and when speakers switch to Modern Standard Arabic. Variation in stop realization is also reported in Ewe (Noglo 2009), where fortition of /ɸ/ to [p] is an urban rather than rural marker and used more by female than male speakers. Regional variation in stop realization is also reported for Turkish (Yağlı 2018).

In English, /t/ can alternate with a range of variants depending on phonological context and accent. These variants include [ɾ d ɹ ʔ], full deletion (*must go* > [mʌs ɡəʊ]), and assimilation to following bilabials or velars (*hot coffee* > [hɒk kɒfi]). The linguistic constraints on variant patterns can be very complex. The glottal variant of /t/ in British English varies in frequency according to at least the following: word and syllable position, following segment, lexical status (more glottals are used in function words than lexical words), and lexical frequency (more glottals in more frequent words, as is typical for lenition processes) (Foulkes & Hughes forthcoming). Variants of /t/ have probably been the subject of more studies than any other consonant for English. In the United Kingdom, glottaling of /t/, particularly in intervocalic position, is associated with non-standard accents, less formal styles, and speakers of lower social status. Male speakers generally use more glottals than female speakers, as is typical of sociolinguistic changes from below (e.g., Straw & Patrick 2007; Schleef 2013; but see also Mees & Collins 1999). Intervocalic glottal variants are spreading in RP, even reaching the speech of younger royals (Shaw & Foulkes 2015).

Several recent studies have also assessed the emergence of glottal variants in US English, where the change appears to be led by young female speakers (Eddington & Brown 2021). /t/ variants can generate strong social evaluations by listeners. The glottal variant is generally stigmatized in the United Kingdom, although the stigma appears to be waning fast (Fabricius 2002). In the United States both glottals and full releases received negative evaluation (Eddington & Brown 2021); speakers who used glottal stops were viewed as less educated and less friendly, while full oral releases were judged more "rustic" and less educated. In Tyneside there is evidence that children are exposed to sociolinguistic variation differently, depending on their age and sex. Girls typically hear more standard variants of /p t k/ than boys do (Foulkes, Docherty & Watt 2005).

In North American and Australasian Englishes, intervocalic /t/ is generally realized as a tap, [ɾ]. The change towards this variant from [t] is tracked in detail for New Zealand English by Hay & Foulkes (2016), who show effects of age, sex, social class, word frequency, "word age" (i.e., words used more by younger speakers contain more of the innovative variant), repetition in discourse, and topic of conversation. In Australia, /t/ variants differ across Aboriginal and "mainstream" communities (Loakes et al. 2018).

Deletion processes occur in many languages, including Suva Rotuman (deletion of /ʔ/ in initial position; Fimone 2020), Capanahua (deletion of /ʔ/; Elias-Ulloa 2004), Persian (coda obstruent cluster simplification; Falahati Ardestani 2013), and Catalan (word-final stop deletion; Mascaró 1989). Deletion can furthermore vary socially. For example, deletion of initial /ʔ/ in Rotuman shows social variation and change in progress (Fimone 2020). Deletion occurs less for younger speakers and older female speakers, suggesting increased influence of the standard form as well as social identity factors at work.

English /t d/ deletion in word-final consonant clusters has been widely studied (Tagliamonte & Temple 2005; Raymond, Brown & Healy 2016; Baranowski & Turton 2020; MacKenzie & Tamminga 2021). Deletion is generally most common in monomorphemes (*mist*) and least common in regular past tense forms (*missed*), with irregular past tense forms (*kept*) accepting deletion at an intermediate rate. The nature of the following segment is also crucial (more deletion before consonants, less or no deletion before vowels or pause). Deletion of /t d/ is regionally and socially variable, occurring in pre-vocalic and pre-pausal positions in African American English as well as the more common pre-consonantal context observed in Anglo accents (e.g., Labov 1972). /t d/ deletion has also been studied in Jamaican creole (Patrick 2008) and Hispanic varieties in the US (e.g., Santa Ana 1992; Bayley 1994). Evidence from articulatory studies, however, suggests that complete deletion might be an auditory/acoustic rather than physical effect, with evidence that some articulatory gesture tends to remain even where there is no audible stop (Purse 2019).

Segmental addition, epenthesis, is also observed in many languages, for example in nasal+fricative sequences in Dutch and English (e.g., *prince* realized as [pɹɪnts]). Epenthesis is most common in word-final clusters (Yoo & Blankenship 2003). Epenthetic stops are shorter than phonological stops (Fourakis & Port 1986), and can therefore be analyzed as epiphenomenal, generated by mistiming of the articulatory gestures for the nasal and fricative, rather than segmental insertions. In perception experiments, Warner & Weber (2001, 2002) found that listeners were slower to identify epenthetic stops than lexical stops, especially in medial position. Epenthesis of /t/ in English shows variation both in respect of individual speaker (Yoo & Blankenship 2003) and region. Although common in many varieties, it appears not to occur in South African English (Fourakis & Port 1986).

CASE STUDY   Variation in stop VOT and COG across sex and age in Derby English

A key component of sociophonetic analysis concerns characterizing the relationship between social/ regional and phonetic/phonological variables. The latter are traditionally characterized either as segmental units, such as the use of [ʔ] for English /t/, or as a specific acoustic or articulatory dimension of a single speech sound, such as the VOT of [tʰ] or the COG of [s]. In the present study, we try to address two limitations of previous sociophonetic studies involving stops: first, that studies of VOT tend to be limited to voiceless stops, or even a single stop such as [tʰ] and, second, that spectral shape is an understudied aspect of sociophonetic variation in stops. In the present study, we examine the influence of social and linguistic factors on the phonetic realization of all six English stops [pʰ tʰ kʰ b d g] in a spontaneous speech corpus from Derby, United Kingdom. The data come from 35 native speakers, balanced by sex and age (following the categories employed in the original fieldwork). Phonetic realization is assessed via the acoustic dimensions of positive VOT and COG.

Methods

Participants

Thirty-five speakers from Derby were recorded in fieldwork conducted in 1995. The speakers were balanced across demographic factors of sex (female or male), age (younger or older), as well as professional status (broadly "working class" or "lower middle class"). The present study focuses on sex and age. Younger speakers were born between the years 1967 to 1981 and were 14–27 years of age at the time of recording. Older speakers were born between 1925 and 1957 and were 38–69 years of age at the time of recording. Factors of sex and age were counterbalanced across 32 of the 35 speakers (8 female–younger, 8 male–younger, 8 female–older, 8 male–older). Three elderly speakers (2 female, 1 male) were also recorded; these speakers were born between 1913 and 1916 and were 79–82 years of age. They are included here in the respective older speaker groups.

Procedure

Each conversation took place in self-selected dyads among the speakers (in the case of the elderly speaker group, a triad). Age and professional status were matched within each speaker group. The total speech duration per speaker ranged from 10 to 37 minutes with an average of 24 minutes of speech per speaker. Recordings were made with 46-minute Digital Audio tapes and digitized with a sampling rate of 22,050 Hz (Docherty & Foulkes 1999).

Processing

The corpus includes audio, various alignments (and, critically, a word- and phone-level alignment), along with metadata for the participants. Annotations were completed using LaBB-CAT (Fromont & Hay 2012). AutoVOT was used to identify the stop release and following vowel onset boundaries using automatic methods (Keshet, Sonderegger & Knowles 2014). The present analysis focused on word-initial, prevocalic stop consonants, [pʰ tʰ kʰ b d g]. Following Chodroff & Wilson (2017), the phone-level alignments of voiceless stop consonants were extended 31 ms beyond each pre-aligned

156

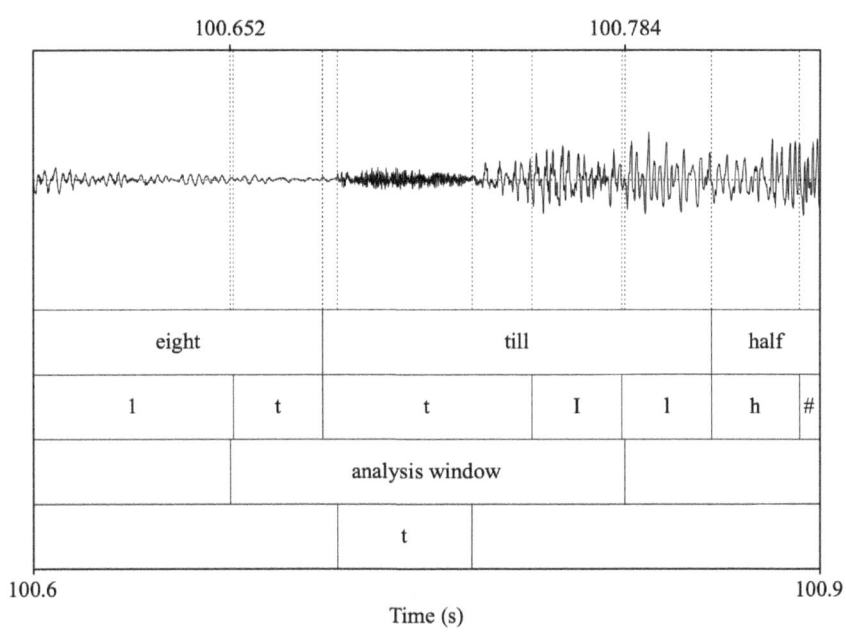

Figure 7.1a   Analysis windows submitted to AutoVOT for word-initial voiceless stop

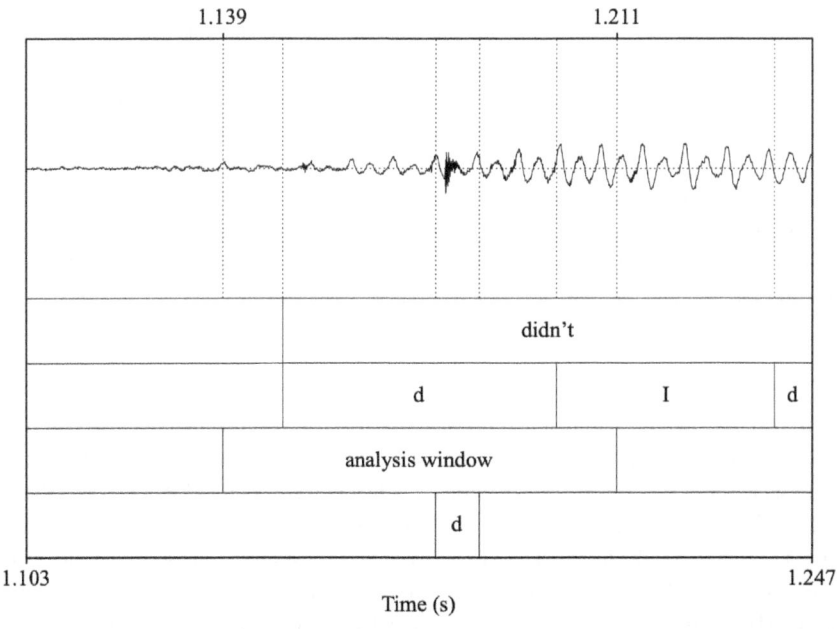

Figure 7.1b   Analysis windows submitted to AutoVOT for word-initial voiced stop

Table 7.1 Total number of tokens available for each stop category, with summary counts per speaker

Stop	Total	Median	Range
[pʰ]	1247	37	4–60
[tʰ]	1597	43	8–127
[kʰ]	2302	65	11–139
[b]	4343	126	16–272
[d]	3319	92	21–203
[g]	2989	75	18–187

boundary, and for voiced stops, 11 ms (see Figure 7.1). The minimum permissible VOT value was set to 15 ms for voiceless stops and 4 ms for voiced stops. Stops were removed if they occurred in an unfinished word or in the word *to*, due to its common reduction. A total of 16,032 stops met the initial criteria for analysis. Of these, 1610 stops (~10 percent of the corpus) were audited and corrected based on random sampling or a suspicious VOT value (e.g., excessively long or the minimum threshold). Audited stops without a release burst were removed (n = 232), leaving 15,797 stops available for analysis (see Table 7.1 for a summary of counts per stop and speaker).

Measurements

Positive VOT and COG from the initial release burst were extracted from word-initial, prevocalic stop consonants. Positive VOT was measured as the duration between the automatic or manually corrected boundaries described above. COG is the energy-weighted mean frequency of the spectrum, and was taken from a time-averaged spectrum over the initial stop burst. The smoothed spectrum was the average of seven 64-point FFT spectra that were extracted from 3 ms Hamming windows with a 1 ms window shift. The first window was centered 1 ms into the initial release (Hanson & Stevens 2003; Chodroff & Wilson 2014). If the stop was shorter than the amount of time required for the full seven windows, then the number of windows was reduced to accommodate the duration. Prior to extraction, the audio was high-pass filtered at 200 Hz and pre-emphasized above 1000 Hz (see also Forrest et al. 1988; Sundara 2005). Measurements were extracted from the manually corrected stop consonant when available.

Analysis

Variation in VOT and COG from the initial release burst was analyzed using Bayesian mixed-effects linear regressions with the brms package (Bürkner 2018) in R (R Core Team 2022). Each linear regression had the same set of predictors. All categorical predictors were sum-coded. VOT and COG were predicted from fixed effects of place of articulation, voicing, following vowel height, following vowel duration (ms), sex, age, and the full interactions between the phonological and social predictors (place, voicing, sex, and age). The model for VOT included an additional interaction between voicing and following vowel duration, as speaking rate is known to influence voiceless stop VOT more than voiced stop VOT (Kessinger & Blumstein 1997). The random effect structure included a by-participant intercept and slopes for place and voicing.

Prior distributions over fixed effects were estimated where possible using Mixer-6 VOT data from 180 speakers of American English released with Chodroff & Wilson (2018) (https://osf.io/jt5mc/). All other priors were only weakly informative. The exact model specifications, raw data, code, and model results can be found in the OSF repository (https://osf.io/6a5jq/).

Each beta coefficient can be interpreted as the deviation from the estimated mean VOT or COG in milliseconds and hertz respectively. This is because categorical predictors were sum-coded and continuous predictors were centered. Doubling the beta estimate yields the estimated contrast between binary predictors. Reliability of an effect was determined using the 95% credible interval (CI) over the marginal posterior distribution for the coefficient estimate. If the 95% CI excluded 0, we concluded that the direction of the estimate was reliable in the estimated direction.

Results

VOT

Variation in VOT by sex, age, and stop category is illustrated in Figure 7.2 and Table 7.2. The model of VOT variation revealed credible effects of several linguistic and social factors (see Figure 7.3). As expected, voiceless stops had longer VOTs than voiced stops, with the model generating the following coefficient for voicing: 16.95, 95% CI [15.90, 18.00]. This means that voiceless stops were approximately 17 ms longer than the average VOT, and voiced stops were approximately 17 ms shorter than

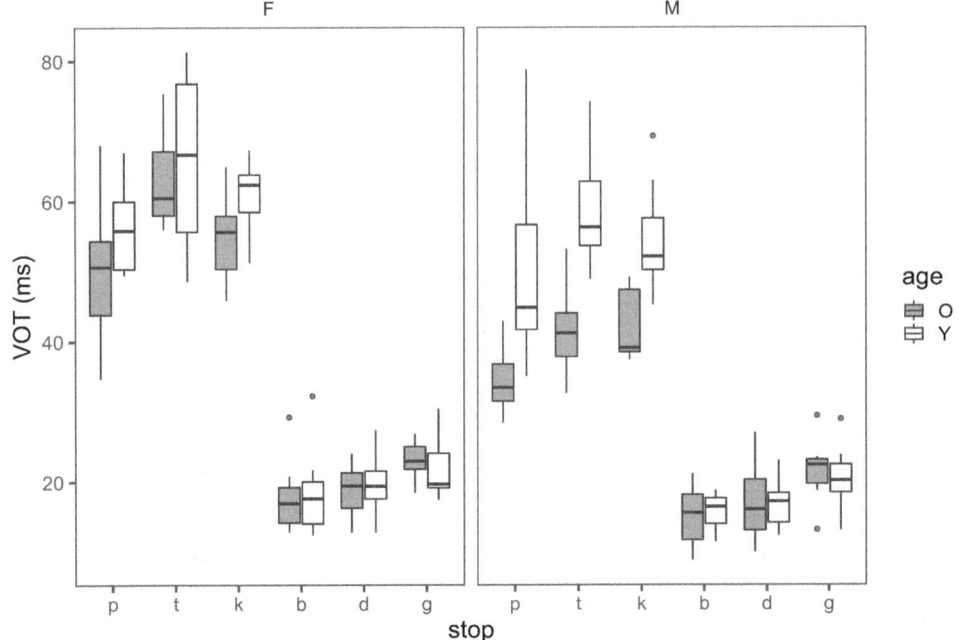

Figure 7.2   Variation in by-speaker VOT means for [pʰ tʰ kʰ b d g] across sex and age

Table 7.2 VOT means and standard deviations (ms) calculated over talker-specific means for each stop category and social group

VOT	[pʰ]	[tʰ]	[kʰ]	[b]	[d]	[g]
Younger female	57 (8)	67 (14)	63 (7)	16 (5)	17 (5)	19 (3)
Younger male	49 (14)	58 (8)	54 (8)	12 (3)	13 (3)	19 (4)
Older female	51 (10)	65 (8)	56 (6)	16 (4)	16 (3)	22 (3)
Older male	37 (9)	42 (7)	43 (7)	14 (5)	14 (5)	21 (5)

the average VOT, yielding an overall difference of 34 ms. Coronal and dorsal stops had overall longer VOTs relative to the average (coronal: 1.45, 95% CI [0.63, 2.27]; dorsal: 2.17, 95% CI [1.35, 2.94]), but this was reliably modulated by voicing. Compared to estimates from the main effects of place and voicing alone, the voicing contrast was reliably larger for coronal stops and reliably smaller for dorsal stops (coronal × voice: 2.55, 95% CI [1.83, 3.26]; dorsal × voicing: −1.05, 95% CI [−1.87, −0.21]). Longer VOTs were also observed prior to longer vowel durations, particularly for voiceless stops (vowel duration: 30.69, 95% CI [27.74, 33.70]; voicing × vowel duration: 5.49, 95% CI [2.54, 8.56]). The effect of vowel height was not reliable: VOT before high vowels was not reliably different from VOT before non-high vowels (vowel: −0.02, 95% CI [−0.48, 0.43]).

Among social factors, both sex and age reliably structured VOT variation: female speakers had longer VOTs than male speakers, and younger speakers had longer VOTs than older speakers (sex: 3.11, 95% CI [1.69, 4.51]; age: −2.81, 95% CI [−4.25, −1.33]). Moreover, the voicing contrast was credibly larger for female than male speakers, larger for younger than older speakers, and the contrast further reduced specifically for older male speakers (voicing × sex: 2.27, 95% CI [1.23, 3.31]; voicing × age: −2.56, 95% CI [−3.64, −1.48]; voicing × sex × age: 1.35, 95% CI [0.31, 2.38]). Finally, female speakers had longer VOTs for coronal stops than male speakers relative to the expected coronal stop VOT (coronal × sex: 0.82, 95% CI [0.01, 1.62]). Moreover, female speakers had an increased contrast between [tʰ] and [d] VOT relative to male speakers (coronal × voicing × sex: 0.84, 95% CI [0.13, 1.53]). No other interactions were reliable in their direction.

COG

Variation in COG by sex, age, and stop category is displayed in Figure 7.3 and Table 7.3. The model revealed credible influences of several linguistic and social factors on COG variation. As expected, COG in coronal stops was higher (by approximately 614 Hz) than the average COG, and COG in dorsal stops was approximately 323 Hz lower than the average (coronal: 614.41, 95% CI [538.06, 692.65]; dorsal: −322.72, 95% CI [−395.06, −251.31]). Voiceless stops had higher COGs than voiced COGs (voicing: 609.77, 95% CI [546.97, 673.49]); however, this was reliably modulated by place of articulation: the voicing contrast in COG was reliably enhanced between coronal stops and diminished between dorsal stops (coronal × voicing: 350.11, 95% CI [287.95, 409.82]; dorsal × voicing: −206.68, 95% CI [−267.53, −145.90]). The main effect of voicing could potentially reflect a minor influence of vocal fold vibration on voiced stops and/or increased airflow associated with voiceless stops (e.g., Zue 1976; Chodroff & Wilson 2014). Stop COG was also reliably higher before high vowels than non-high vowels (vowel: 59.35, 95% CI [32.66, 86.46]), as well as before longer vowels (i.e., slower speaking rates; vowel duration: 410.57, 95% CI [243.87, 574.50]).

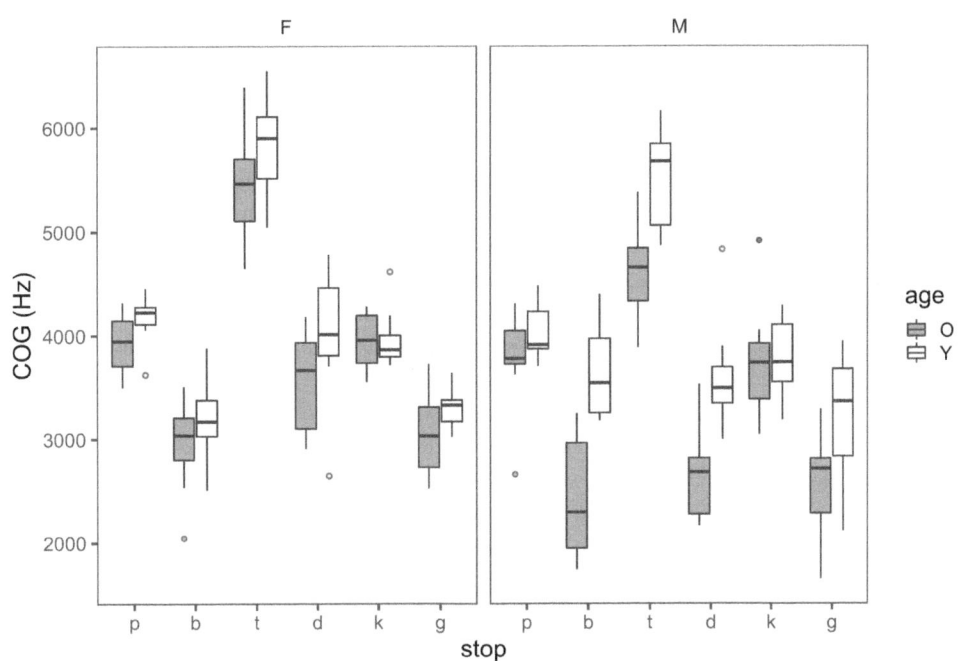

Figure 7.3 Variation in COG for [pʰ tʰ kʰ b d g] across sex and age

Table 7.3 COG means and standard deviations (Hz) calculated over talker-specific means for each stop category and social group

COG	[pʰ]	[tʰ]	[kʰ]	[b]	[d]	[g]
Younger female	4167 (254)	5836 (467)	3969 (298)	3211 (418)	4013 (678)	3295 (200)
Younger male	4030 (280)	5521 (489)	3779 (410)	3637 (456)	3622 (549)	3203 (623)
Older female	3929 (296)	5454 (493)	3954 (262)	2958 (422)	3551 (468)	3078 (427)
Older male	3793 (485)	4589 (451)	3733 (552)	2417 (551)	2689 (487)	2564 (504)

Among social factors, sex and age reliably structured COG variation, largely paralleling the VOT patterns: female speakers had higher COGs than male speakers, and younger speakers had higher COGs than older speakers (sex: 162.69, 95% CI [61.22, 260.18]; age: −235.43, 95% CI [−335.41, −134.82]). In addition, older male speakers had overall lower COGs relative to what would be expected based on the main effects of sex and age alone (sex × age: 96.98, 95% CI [1.60, 190.37]). Social factors also had large interactions with place of articulation: coronal stop COGs were particularly high across female speakers (coronal × sex: 151.76, 95% CI [72.08, 230.62]), and markedly low across older speakers (coronal × age: −104.32, 95% CI [−178.76, −28.73]). Dorsal COGs were also somewhat higher across older speakers than would be expected based on the other effects (dorsal × age: 110.28, 95% CI [41.88, 176.89]). Finally, older speakers had a greater contrast in COG between voiced and voiceless stops relative to younger speakers (voicing × age: 63.61, 95% CI [0.97, 125.61]), except between [tʰ] and [d] (coronal × voicing × age: −67.93, 95% CI [−128.06, −5.66]). No other interactions were reliable in their direction.

Discussion

Derby stop realization contains rich phonological, contextual, and—critically—social variation. Many of these effects were fully in line with expectations. With regards to phonological and contextual effects, main influences on VOT were phonological voicing, following vowel duration (as a proxy for speaking rate), and the interaction between voicing and vowel duration. The interaction between place of articulation and voicing had additional reliable influences, with VOT increasing with more posterior places of articulation. In contrast to previous studies of English, following vowel height did not reliably influence VOT (cf. Nearey & Rochet 1994). For COG, place of articulation had the largest influence on variation, as expected. But phonological voicing had a similarly large effect on realization within each place of articulation, and the interactions between place and voicing were also reliable. Notably, dorsal voiced and voiceless stops did not differ to the same degree as coronal and labial stop contrasts. This minimized effect of voicing on dorsal stops has been observed previously (e.g., Chodroff & Wilson 2014). COG was also reliably raised before high vowels, as well as before longer vowels.

For VOT, female speakers had longer VOTs than male speakers, and older speakers had shorter VOTs than younger speakers. These patterns are in keeping with previous studies on English (e.g., Swartz 1992; Ryalls, Zipprer & Baldauff 1997; Whiteside, Henry & Dobbin 2004; Ma et al. 2018). Social factors also interacted reliably with the voicing contrast (i.e., the sex × voicing and age × voicing interactions). These indicated female speakers had an overall greater voicing contrast using VOT (and higher voiceless stop VOTs) than male speakers. Furthermore, older speakers had a smaller voicing contrast than younger speakers. Minor but reliable influences of social factors were also found on the size of the voicing contrast specifically for coronal segments. Critically, interactions between social factors and place of articulation alone were again minimal, and mostly not reliable in their direction. The one exception was the finding that female speakers had slightly longer VOTs for coronal stops relative to other places of articulation. Indeed, VOT primarily reflected the voicing contrast, and the largest variation in social influence was in this particular contrast. Social factors had negligible influence on contrasts between places of articulation.

Female speakers had higher COGs than male speakers, younger speakers had higher COGs than older speakers, and older male speakers also had particularly low COGs. The low COGs observed among older speakers could reflect multiple sources; COG does primarily capture information regarding place, and therefore the lowered COG could reflect more retracted articulations for dorsals and especially coronals (the latter supporting impressionistic observation; Docherty & Foulkes 1999:51). However, it is also not immune to influences from phonetic voicing. It is possible that older speakers may also employ a higher degree of phonetic voicing among voiced stops than younger speakers. It is also possible that the lowered COG reflects a decreased lung volume among older speakers (Mead et al. 1967). Isolating these exact influences on COG, and the theoretical implications of such patterns, remains for further research.

Conclusion

In this chapter, we have reviewed variation in stop realization relating to linguistic, biological, and social factors. Social variation in stops is present along each of the phases of stop articulation including the closing phase, hold phase, and release phase. In addition, considerable work has also investigated and identified variation in the coupling between the oral and laryngeal gestures, which has most commonly been studied in terms of VOT. Regional and/or social variation is observed in several acoustic and articulatory correlates of stop production. Stops are thus potentially a very rich resource for social variation. However, our review reveals clear gaps that future research could easily fill.

VOT is one of the most widely studied phonetic dimensions of all segments. There is certainly evidence for social and individual variation in VOT, but the actual effects tend to be small and inconsistent. It is unclear how useful these are in perception. For example, even where small sex effects are observed, as far as we are aware no study has shown that listeners orient to these differences as a marker for sex. We can only speculate as to why this might be, but VOT has high variability both within and across speakers. As suggested by Kleinschmidt (2019), this contributes to it having less utility for determining social categories relative to other phonetic measures such as vowel formants. In addition, Kleinschmidt shows that social categories are less informative for determining the identity of a stop given its VOT than the identity of a vowel given its formants. We might further ask whether this point is a more general one, namely that social marking is more successful when applied to frequency-based features or discrete segmental units rather than durational features. Variation in the temporal domain certainly does contribute socio-indexical information, for example, via speech rate, rhythm, and stress. VOT might therefore contribute to variation at this level as one of many features that can vary temporally, but presumably it is less free to carry its own social value.

Moreover, VOT is not the only dimension of stop variation. As demonstrated above, stops also vary along several other dimensions. The increasing availability of large-scale speech corpora and automatic analysis tools offers tremendous scope to explore sociophonetic variation in the acoustic form of stops. Our case study, which drew on a fairly small corpus, illustrates one such approach. Further research can also draw on perceptual and articulatory measures for understanding variation in stops. Finally, as with many other sociophonetic studies, analysis of stops enables us to explore theoretical questions of fundamental importance: the structure of the lexicon, speech production and perception, and the cognitive representation of socio-indexical information.

References

Abramson, Arthur S. & Doug H. Whalen. 2017. Voice Onset Time (VOT) at 50: Theoretical and practical issues in measuring voicing distinctions. *Journal of Phonetics* 63. 75–86. https://doi.org/10.1016/j.wocn.2017.05.002

Abrego-Collier, Carissa, Julian Grove, Morgan Sonderegger & Alan C.L. Yu. 2011. Effects of speaker evaluation on phonetic convergence. In Lee & Zee, 192–195.

Alexander, K. Katarzyna. 2014. *Perception of the boundary between singleton and geminate plosives by Greek Cypriots: A sociophonetic perspective*. PhD thesis, University of York.

Allen, J. Sean & Joanne L. Miller. 1999. Effects of syllable-initial voicing and speaking rate on the temporal characteristics of monosyllabic words. *Journal of the Acoustical Society of America* 106(4). 2031–2039. http://doi.org/10.1121/1.427949

Allen, J. Sean, Joanne L. Miller & David DeSteno. 2003. Individual talker differences in voice-onset-time. *Journal of the Acoustical Society of America* 113(1). 544–552. https://doi.org/10.1121/1.1528172

Al-Tamimi, Jalal & Ghada Khattab. 2015. Acoustic cue weighting in the singleton vs. geminate contrast in Lebanese Arabic: The case of fricative consonants. *Journal of the Acoustical Society of America* 138(1). 344–360. https://doi.org/10.1121/1.4922514

Al-Tamimi, Jalal & Ghada Khattab. 2018. Acoustic correlates of the voicing contrast in Lebanese Arabic singleton and geminate stops. *Journal of Phonetics* 71. 306–325. https://doi.org/10.1016/j.wocn.2018.09.010

Andruski, Jean E., Sheila E. Blumstein & Martha Burton. 1994. The effect of subphonetic differences on lexical access. *Cognition* 52(3). 163–187. https://doi.org/10.1016/0010-0277(94)90042-6

Aoyama, Katsura & Lawrence A. Reid. 2006. Cross-linguistic tendencies and durational contrasts in geminate consonants: An examination of Guinaang Bontok geminates. *Journal of the International Phonetic Association* 36(2). 145–157. https://doi.org/10.1017/S0025100306002520

Arvaniti, Amalia. 2007. Greek phonetics: The state of the art. *Journal of Greek Linguistics* 8. 97–208. https://doi.org/10.1075/jgl.8.08arv

Baese-Berk, Melissa M. & Matthew Goldrick. 2009. Mechanisms of interaction in speech production. *Language and Cognitive Processes* 24(4). 527–554. https://doi.org/10.1080/01690960802299378

Baran, Jane A., Marsha Z. Laufer & Ray Daniloff. 1977. Phonological contrastivity in conversation: A comparative study of voice onset time. *Journal of Phonetics* 5(4). 339–350. https://doi.org/10.1016/S0095-4470(19)31204-5

Baranowski, Maciej & Danielle Turton. 2020. TD-deletion in British English: New evidence for the long-lost morphological effect. *Language Variation and Change* 32(1). 1–23. https://doi.org/10.1017/S0954394520000034

Baum, Shari R. & Laurie Ryan. 1993. Rate of speech effects in aphasia: Voice onset time. *Brain and Language* 44(4). 431–445. https://doi.org/10.1006/brln.1993.1026

Bayley, Robert. 1994. Consonant cluster reduction in Tejano English. *Language Variation and Change* 6(3). 303–326. https://doi.org/10.1017/S0954394500001708

Becker, Michael, Nihan Ketrez & Andrew Nevins. 2011. The surfeit of the stimulus: Analytic biases filter lexical statistics in Turkish laryngeal alternations. *Language* 87(1). 84–125. https://doi.org/10.1353/lan.2011.0016

Benjamin, Barbaranne J. 1982. Phonological performance in gerontological speech. *Journal of Psycholinguistic Research* 11(2). 159–167. https://doi.org/10.1007/Bf01068218

Benjamin, Barbaranne J. 1997. Speech production of normally aging adults. *Seminars in Speech and Language* 18(2). 135–141. https://doi.org/10.1055/s-2008-1064068

Benor, Sarah. 2001. The learned /t/: Phonological variation in Orthodox Jewish English. *Penn Working Papers in Linguistics* 7(3). Article 2. https://repository.upenn.edu/pwpl/vol7/iss3/2

Berry, Jeff & Maura Moyle. 2011. Covariation among vowel height effects on acoustic measures. *Journal of the Acoustical Society of America* 130(5). EL365–EL371. https://doi.org/10.1121/1.3651095

Blumstein, Sheila E., Emily B. Myers & Jesse Rissman. 2005. The perception of voice onset time: An fMRI investigation of phonetic category structure. *Journal of Cognitive Neuroscience* 17(9). 1353–1366. https://doi.org/10.1162/0898929054985473

Blumstein, Sheila E. & Kenneth N. Stevens. 1979. Acoustic invariance in speech production: Evidence from measurements of the spectral characteristics of stop consonants. *Journal of the Acoustical Society of America* 66(4). 1001–1017. https://doi.org/10.1121/1.383319

Blumstein, Sheila E. & Kenneth N. Stevens. 1980. Perceptual invariance and onset spectra for stop consonants in different vowel environments. *Journal of the Acoustical Society of America* 67(2). 648–662. https://doi.org/10.1121/1.383890

Boario, Anna. 2009. *Il raddoppiamento fonosintattico nelle varietà di parlanti adolescenti nativi e non nativi.* In Carlo Consani, P. Desideri, F. Guazzelli & C. Perta (eds.), *Alloglossie e comunità alloglotte nell'Italia contemporanea. Teorie, applicazioni e descrizioni, prospettive*, 383–398. Bulzoni. https://doi.org/10.1400/137401

Bonneau, Anne, Linda Djezzar & Yves Laprie. 1996. Perception of the place of articulation of French stop bursts. *Journal of the Acoustical Society of America* 100(1). 555–564. https://doi.org/10.1121/1.415866

Bowerman, Sean. 2008. White South African English: Phonology. In Mesthrie 2008b, 164–176.

Brandt, Erika & Adrian P. Simpson. 2021. The production of ejectives in German and Georgian. *Journal of Phonetics* 89. 101111. https://doi.org/10.1016/j.wocn.2021.101111

Bucholtz, Mary. 1996. Geek the girl: Language, femininity, and female nerds. In Natasha Warner, Jocelyn Ahlers, Leela Bilmes, Monica Oliver, Suzanne Wertheim & Melinda Chen (eds.), *Gender and belief systems: Proceedings of the Fourth Berkeley Women and Language Conference*, 119–131. Berkeley Women and Language Group.

Bundgaard-Nielsen, Rikke L. & Carmel O'Shannessy. 2021. When more is more: The mixed language Light Warlpiri amalgamates source language phonologies to form a near-maximal inventory. *Journal of Phonetics* 85. 101037. https://doi.org/10.1016/j.wocn.2021.101037

Bürkner, Paul-Christian. 2018. Advanced Bayesian multilevel modeling with the R Package brms. *The R Journal* 10(1). 395–411. https://doi.org/10.32614/rj-2018-017

Byrd, Dani. 1993. 54,000 American stops. *UCLA Working Papers in Phonetics* 83. 97–116.

Calhoun, Sasha, Paola Escudero, Marija Tabain & Paul Warren (eds.). 2019. *Proceedings of the 19th International Congress of Phonetic Sciences, Melbourne, Australia 2019*. Australasian Speech Science and Technology Association.

Caramazza, Alfonso & Grace Yeni-Komshian. 1974. Voice onset time in two French dialects. *Journal of Phonetics* 2(3). 239–245. https://doi.org/10.1016/S0095-4470(19)31274-4

Cassidy, Stephen & Jonathan Harrington. 1995. The place of articulation distinction in voiced oral stops: Evidence from burst spectra and formant transitions. *Phonetica* 52(4). 263–284. https://doi.org/10.1159/000262182

Cho, Taehong, Sun-Ah Jun & Peter Ladefoged. 2002. Acoustic and aerodynamic correlates of Korean stops and fricatives. *Journal of Phonetics* 30(2). 193–228. https://doi.org/10.1006/jpho.2001.0153

Cho, Taehong & Patricia A. Keating. 2001. Articulatory and acoustic studies on domain-initial strengthening in Korean. *Journal of Phonetics* 29(2). 155–190. https://doi.org/10.1006/jpho.2001.0131

Cho, Taehong & Patricia A. Keating. 2009. Effects of initial position versus prominence in English. *Journal of Phonetics* 37(4). 466–485. https://doi.org/10.1016/j.wocn.2009.08.001

Cho, Taehong & Peter Ladefoged. 1999. Variation and universals in VOT: Evidence from 18 languages. *Journal of Phonetics* 27(2). 207–229. http://dx.doi.org/10.1006/jpho.1999.0094

Cho, Taehong & James M. McQueen. 2005. Prosodic influences on consonant production in Dutch: Effects of prosodic boundaries, phrasal accent and lexical stress. *Journal of Phonetics* 33(2). 121–157. https://doi.org/10.1016/j.wocn.2005.01.001

Cho, Taehong, Douglas H. Whalen & Gerard J. Docherty. 2019. Voice onset time and beyond: Exploring laryngeal contrast in 19 languages. *Journal of Phonetics* 72(1). 52–65. https://doi.org/10.1016/j.wocn.2018.11.002

Chodroff, Eleanor, Leah Bradshaw & Vivian Livesay. 2022. Subsegmental representation in child speech production: Structured variability of stop consonant voice onset time in American English and Cantonese. *Journal of Child Language*. https://doi.org/10.31234/osf.io/gd9rs

Chodroff, Eleanor, Alessandra Golden & Colin Wilson. 2019. Covariation of stop voice onset time across languages: Evidence for a universal constraint on phonetic realization. *Journal of the Acoustical Society of America* 145(1). EL109–EL115. https://doi.org/10.1121/1.5088035

Chodroff, Eleanor & Colin Wilson. 2014. Burst spectrum as a cue for the stop voicing contrast in American English. *Journal of the Acoustical Society of America* 136(5). 2762–2772. https://doi.org/10.1121/1.4896470

Chodroff, Eleanor & Colin Wilson. 2017. Structure in talker-specific phonetic realization: Covariation of stop consonant VOT in American English. *Journal of Phonetics* 61. 30–47. https://doi.org/10.1016/j.wocn.2017.01.001

Chodroff, Eleanor & Colin Wilson. 2018. Predictability of stop consonant phonetics across talkers: Between-category and within-category dependencies among cues for place and voice. *Linguistics Vanguard* 4(s2). 20170047. https://doi.org/10.1515/lingvan-2017-0047

Choi, Hansook. 2003. Prosody-induced acoustic variation in English stop consonants. In Solé, Recasens & Romero, 2661–2664.

Clark, Lynn & Kevin Watson. 2016. Phonological leveling, diffusion, and divergence: /t/ lenition in Liverpool and its hinterland. *Language Variation and Change* 28(1). 31–62. https://doi.org/10.1017/S0954394515000204

Clayton, Ian. 2017. Preaspiration in Hebrides English. *Journal of the International Phonetic Association* 47(2). 155–181. https://doi.org/10.1017/S002510031700007X

Clothier, Josh & Debbie Loakes. 2018. Coronal stop VOT in Australian English: Lebanese Australians and Mainstream Australian English. In Epps et al., 13–16.

Clumeck, Harold, David Barton, Marlys A. Macken & Dorothy Huntington. 1981. The aspiration contrast in Cantonese word-initial stops: Data from children and adults. *Journal of Chinese Linguistics* 9(2). 210–225.

Cohen Priva, Uriel. 2017. Informativity and the actuation of lenition. *Language* 93(3). 569–597. https://doi.org/10.1353/lan.2017.0037

Cole, Jennifer S., Hansook Choi, Heejin Kim & Mark Hasegawa-Johnson. 2003. The effect of accent on the acoustic cues to stop voicing in Radio News speech. In Solé, Recasens & Romero, 15–18.

Cole, Jennifer S., Hansook Choi, Heejin Kim & Mark Hasegawa-Johnson. 2007. Prosodic effects on acoustic cues to stop voicing and place of articulation: Evidence from Radio News speech. *Journal of Phonetics* 35(2). 180–209. https://doi.org/10.1016/j.wocn.2006.03.004

Cotter, William M. 2014. (q) as a sociolinguistic variable in the Arabic of Gaza City. In Youssef A. Haddad & Eric Potsdam (eds.) *Perspectives on Arabic Linguistics XXVIII. Papers from the Annual Symposium on Arabic Linguistics, Gainesville, Florida*, 2014, 229–246. John Benjamins.

Davidson, Lisa. 2011. Characteristics of stop releases in American English spontaneous speech. *Speech Communication* 53(8). 1042–1058. https://doi.org/10.1016/j.specom.2011.05.010

Davidson, Lisa. 2016. Variability in the implementation of voicing in American English obstruents. *Journal of Phonetics* 54. 35–50. https://doi.org/10.1016/j.wocn.2015.09.003

Davidson, Lisa. 2021. Effects of word position and flanking vowel on the implementation of glottal stop: Evidence from Hawaiian. *Journal of Phonetics* 88. 101075. https://doi.org/10.1016/j.wocn.2021.101075

DiCanio, Christian T. 2012. The phonetics of fortis and lenis consonants in Itunyoso Trique. *International Journal of American Linguistics* 78(2). 239–272. https://doi.org/10.1086/664481

Docherty, Gerard J. 1992. *The timing of voicing in British English obstruents*. Walter de Gruyter.

Docherty, Gerard J. & Paul Foulkes. 1999. Derby and Newcastle upon Tyne: Instrumental phonetics and variationist studies. In Foulkes & Docherty, 47–71.

Docherty, Gerard J. & Paul Foulkes. 2005. Glottal variants of (t) in the Tyneside variety of English: An acoustic profiling study. In William Hardcastle & Janet Mackenzie Beck (eds.), *A figure of speech: A Festschrift for John Laver*, 173–199. Lawrence Erlbaum.

Docherty, Gerard J., Paul Foulkes, James Milroy, Lesley Milroy & David Walshaw. 1997. Descriptive adequacy in phonology: A variationist perspective. *Journal of Linguistics* 33(2). 275–310. https://doi.org/10.1017/S002222679700649X

Docherty, Gerard J., Dominic Watt, Carmen Llamas, Damien Hall & Jennifer Nycz. 2011. Variation in voice onset time along the Scottish-English Border. In Lee & Zee, 591–594.

Duran, Daniel, Jagoda Bruni, Grzegorz Dogil & Justus Roux. 2017. The social life of Setswana ejectives. In *Proceedings of Interspeech 2017*, 3787–3791. https://doi.org/10.21437/Interspeech.2017-922

Eimas, Peter D., Einar R. Siqueland, Peter Jusczyk & James Vigorito. 1971. Speech perception in infants. *Science* 171(3968). 303–306. https://doi.org/10.1126/science.171.3968.303

Elías-Ulloa, Jose. 2004. Quantity (in)sensitivity and underlying glottal-stop deletion in Capanahua. *Coyote Papers* 13. http://hdl.handle.net/10150/126614

Eddington, David Ellingson & Earl K. Brown. 2021. A production and perception study of /t/-glottalization and oral releases following glottals in the United States. *American Speech* 96(1). 78–104. https://doi.org/10.1215/00031283-8620501

Epps, Julien, Joe Wolfe, John Smith & Caroline Jones (eds.). 2018. *Proceedings of the Seventeenth Australasian International Conference on Speech Science and Technology*. Australasian Speech Science and Technology Australia.

Esposito, Anna. 2002. On vowel height and consonantal voicing effects: Data from Italian. *Phonetica* 59(4). 197–231. https://doi.org/10.1159/000068347

Fabricius, Anne. 2002. Ongoing change in modern RP: Evidence for the disappearing stigma of t-glottalling. *English World-Wide* 23(1). 115–136. https://doi.org/10.1075/eww.23.1.06fab

Falahati Ardestani, Reza. 2013. *Gradient and categorical consonant cluster simplification in Persian: An ultrasound and acoustic study*. PhD thesis, University of Ottawa.

Fant, Gunnar. 1973. *Speech sounds and features*. MIT Press.

Fimone, Wilfred. 2020. Onset glottal stop deletion in Suva Rotuman. *Asia-Pacific Language Variation* 6(2). 196–221. https://doi.org/10.1075/aplv.19016.fim

Finn, Peter. 2008. Cape Flats English: Phonology. In Mesthrie 2008b, 200–222.

Fischer-Jørgensen, Eli. 1954. Acoustic analysis of stop consonants. *Le Maître Phonétique* 32. 42–59.

Fish, Melanie S., Adriáb García-Sierra, Nairán Ramírez-Esparza & Patricia K. Kuhl. 2017. Infant-directed speech in English and Spanish: Assessments of monolingual and bilingual caregiver VOT. *Journal of Phonetics* 63. 19–34. https://doi.org/10.1016/j.wocn.2017.04.003

Forrest, Karen, Gary Weismer, Paul Milenkovic & Ronald R. Dougall. 1988. Statistical analysis of word-initial voiceless obstruents: Preliminary data. *Journal of the Acoustical Society of America* 84(1). 115–123. https://doi.org/10.1121/1.396977

Foulkes, Paul & Gerard J. Docherty (eds.) 1999. *Urban voices: Accent studies in the British Isles*. Arnold.

Foulkes, Paul, Gerard J. Docherty & Mark J. Jones. 2010. Analysing stops. In Marianna Di Paolo & Malcah Yaeger-Dror (eds.) *Sociophonetics: A student's guide*, 58–71. Routledge.

Foulkes, Paul, Gerard J. Docherty & Dominic Watt. 2005. Phonological variation in child directed speech. *Language* 81(1). 177–206. https://doi.org/10.1353/lan.2005.0018

Foulkes, Paul & Vincent Hughes. Forthcoming. Dialectological and sociolinguistic foundations of forensic speaker comparison. In Francis Nolan, Kirsty McDougall & Toby Hudson (eds.), *The Oxford handbook of forensic phonetics*. Oxford University Press.

Fourakis, Marios & Robert Port. 1986. Stop epenthesis in English. *Journal of Phonetics* 14(2). 197–221. https://doi.org/10.1016/S0095-4470(19)30658-8

Fox, Neal P., Megan Reilly & Sheila E. Blumstein. 2015. Phonological neighborhood competition affects spoken word production irrespective of sentential context. *Journal of Memory and Language* 83. 97–117. https://doi.org/10.1016/j.jml.2015.04.002

Fox, Sue & Eivind Torgersen. 2018. Language change and innovation in London: Multicultural London English. In Natalie Braber & Sandra Jansen (eds.), *Sociolinguistics in England*, 189–213. Palgrave Macmillan.

Fromont, Robert & Jennifer Hay. 2012. LaBB-CAT: An annotation store. In Felicity Cox, Katherine Demuth, Susan Lin, Kelly Miles, Sallyanne Palethorpe, Jason Shaw & Ivan Yuen (eds.), *Proceedings of the 14th Australasian International Conference on Speech Science and Technology*, 113–117. Australasian Speech Science and Technology Association Inc.

Gadet, Françoise & Philippe Hambye. 2014. Contact and ethnicity in "youth language" description: In search of specificity. In Robert Nicolaï (ed.) *Questioning language contact: Limits of contact, contact at its limits*, 183–217. Brill. https://doi.org/10.1163/9789004279056_008

Gandour, Jack, Soranee H. Petty, Rochana Dardarananda, Sumalee Dechongkit & Sunee Mukngoen. 1986. The acquisition of the voicing contrast in Thai: A study of voice onset time in word-initial stop consonants. *Journal of Child Language* 13(3). 561–572. https://doi.org/10.1017/S0305000900006887

Ganong, William F. 1980. Phonetic categorization in auditory word perception. *Journal of Experimental Psychology: Human Perception and Performance* 6(1). 110–125. https://doi.org/10.1037/0096-1523.6.1.110

Gao, Jiayin & Takayuki Arai. 2019. Plosive (de-)voicing and f0 perturbations in Tokyo Japanese: Positional variation, cue enhancement, and contrast recovery. *Journal of Phonetics* 77. 100932. https://doi.org/10.1016/j.wocn.2019.100932

Gargesh, Ravinder. 2008. Indian English: Phonology. In Mesthrie 2008b, 231–243.

Gorham-Rowan, Mary M. & Jacqueline Laures-Gore. 2006. Acoustic-perceptual correlates of voice quality in elderly men and women. *Journal of Communication Disorders* 39(3). 171–184. https://doi.org/10.1016/j.jcomdis.2005.11.005

Gósy, Mária & Catherine O. Ringen. 2009. Everything you always wanted to know about VOT in Hungarian. Paper presented at the IX International Conference on the Structure of Hungarian, Debrecen, Hungary.

Gráczi, T.E., & Kohári, A. 2014. Multiple bursts in Hungarian voiceless plosives and VOT measurements. In Susanne Fuchs, Martine Grice, Anne Hermes, Leonardo Lancia & Doris Mücke (eds.), *Proceedings of the 10th International Seminar on Speech Production (ISSP)*, 158–161.

Gurevich, Naomi. 2004. *Lenition and contrast: The functional consequences of certain phonetically conditioned sound changes*. Routledge.

Hall, Tracy A. & Silke Hamann. 2006. Towards a typology of stop assibilation. *Linguistics* 44(6). 1195–1236. https://doi.org/10.1515/LING.2006.039

Halle, Morris, George W. Hughes & Jean-Pierre A. Radley. 1957. Acoustic properties of stop consonants. *Journal of Acoustical Society of America* 29(1). 107–116. https://doi.org/10.1121/1.1908634

Ham, William H. 2001. *Phonetic and phonological aspects of geminate timing*. Routledge. https://doi.org/10.4324/9781315023755

Hanson, Helen M. & Kenneth N. Stevens. 2003. Models of aspirated stops in English. In Solé, Recasens & Romero, 783–786.

Harrington, Jonathan. 2010. *The phonetic analysis of speech corpora*. Wiley-Blackwell.

Hay, Jennifer & Paul Foulkes. 2016. The evolution of medial /t/ over real and remembered time. *Language* 92(2). 298–330. https://doi.org/10.1353/lan.2016.0036

Hejná, Michaela. 2015. *Pre-aspiration in Welsh English: A case study of Aberystwyth*. PhD thesis, University of Manchester.

Helgason, Pétur. 2002. *Preaspiration in the Nordic Languages: Synchronic and diachronic aspects*. PhD thesis, Stockholm University.

Helgason, Pétur & Catherine O. Ringen. 2008. Voicing and aspiration in Swedish stops. *Journal of Phonetics* 36(4). 607–628. https://doi.org/10.1016/j.wocn.2008.02.003

Herd, Wendy. 2020. Sociophonetic voice onset time variation in Mississippi English. *Journal of the Acoustical Society of America* 147(1). 596–605. https://doi.org/10.1121/10.0000545

Hickey, Raymond. 2017. Twentieth-century Received Pronunciation: Stop articulation. In Raymond Hickey (ed.) *Listening to the Past,* 66–84. Cambridge University Press.

Hombert, Jean-Marie, John J. Ohala & William G. Ewan. 1979. Phonetic explanations for the development of tones. *Language* 55(1). 37–58. https://doi.org/10.2307/412518

Hualde, José I. 2005. *The sounds of Spanish*. Cambridge University Press.

Jamin, Mikaël. 2004. 'Beurs' and *accent des cités*: A case study of linguistic diffusion in La Courneuve. *Contemporary French and Francophone Studies* 8(2). 169–176. https://doi.org/10.1080/102602104200 0199355

Kang, Kyoung-Ho. 2010. Generational differences in the perception of Korean stops. *Phonetics and Speech Sciences* 2(3). 3–10.

Kang, Kyoung-Ho & Susan G. Guion. 2008. Clear speech production of Korean stops: Changing phonetic targets and enhancement strategies. *Journal of the Acoustical Society of America*. 124(6). 3909–3917. https://doi.org/10.1121/1.2988292

Keating, Patricia A. 1984. Phonetic and phonological representation of stop consonant voicing. *Language* 60(2). 286–319. https://doi.org/10.2307/413642

Keating, Patricia A., Wendy Linker & Marie Huffman. 1983. Patterns in allophone distribution for voiced and voiceless stops. *Journal of Phonetics* 11(3). 277–290. https://doi.org/10.1016/ S0095-4470(19)30827-7

Keating, Patricia A., Michael J. Mikoś & William F. Ganong III. 1981. A cross-language study of range of voice onset time in the perception of initial stop voicing. *Journal of the Acoustical Society of America* 70(5). 1261–1271. https://doi.org/10.1121/1.387139

Kerswill, Paul. 1987. Levels of linguistic variation in Durham. *Journal of Linguistics* 23(1). 25–49. https:// doi.org/10.1017/S0022226700011026

Keshet, Joseph, Morgan Sonderegger & Thea Knowles. 2014. AutoVOT: A tool for automatic measurement of voice onset time using discriminative structured prediction [Computer program], ver. 0.91. https://git hub.com/mlml/autovot/.

Kessinger, Rachel H. & Sheila E. Blumstein. 1997. Effects of speaking rate on voice-onset time in Thai, French, and English. *Journal of Phonetics* 25(2). 143–168. https://doi.org/10.1006/jpho.1996.0039

Kessinger, Rachel H. & Sheila E. Blumstein. 1998. Effects of speaking rate on voice-onset time and vowel production: Some implications for perception studies. *Journal of Phonetics* 26(2). 117–128. https://doi. org/10.1006/jpho.1997.0069

Kewley-Port, Diane. 1982. Measurement of formant transitions in naturally produced stop consonant–vowel syllables. *Journal of the Acoustical Society of America* 72(2). 379–389. https://doi.org/10.1121/ 1.388081

Kewley-Port, Diane. 1983. Time-varying features as correlates of place of articulation in stop consonants. *Journal of Acoustical Society of America* 73(1). 322–335. https://doi.org/10.1121/1.388813

Khattab, Ghada. 2003. Age, input, and language mode factors in the acquisition of VOT by English-Arabic bilingual children. In Solé, Recasens & Romero, 3213–3216.

Khattab, Ghada & Jalal Al-Tamimi. 2014. Geminate timing in Lebanese Arabic: The relationship between phonetic timing and phonological structure. *Laboratory Phonology* 5(2). 231–269. https://doi.org/ 10.1515/lp-2014-0009

Khattab, Ghada, Jalal Al-Tamimi & Barry Heselwood. 2006. Acoustic and auditory differences in the /t/-/ T/ opposition in male and female speakers of Jordanian Arabic. In Sami Boudelaa (ed.) *Perspectives on Arabic Linguistics XVI*, 131–160. John Benjamins.

Kirchner, Robert. 2001. *An effort based approach to consonant lenition*. Routledge.

Kirkham, Sam. 2011. The acoustics of coronal stops in British Asian English. In Lee & Zee, 1102–1105.

Kirov, Christo & Colin Wilson. 2012. The specificity of online variation in speech production. In Naomi Miyake, David Peebles & Richard P. Cooper (eds.), *Proceedings of the 34th Annual Conference of the Cognitive Science Society*, 587–592.

Klatt, Dennis H. 1975. Voice onset time, frication, and aspiration in word-initial consonant clusters. *Journal of Speech and Hearing Research* 18(4). 686–706. https://doi.org/10.1044/jshr.1804.686

Kleber, Felicitas. 2018. VOT or quantity: What matters more for the voicing contrast in German regional varieties? Results from apparent-time analyses. *Journal of Phonetics* 71. 468–486. https://doi.org/10.1016/j.wocn.2018.10.004

Kleinschmidt, Dave F. 2019. Structure in talker variability: How much is there and how much can it help? *Language, Cognition and Neuroscience* 34(1). 43–68. https://doi.org/10.1080/23273798.2018.1500698

Kleinschmidt, Dave F., Kodi Weatherholtz & T. Florian Jaeger. 2018. Sociolinguistic perception as inference under uncertainty. *Topics in Cognitive Science* 10(4). 818–834. https://doi.org/10.1111/tops.12331

Kochetov, Alexei & Marianne Pouplier. 2008. Phonetic variability and grammatical knowledge: An articulatory study of Korean place assimilation. *Phonology* 25(3). 399–431. https://doi.org/10.1017/S0952675708001553

Koenig, Laura L. 2001. Distributional characteristics of VOT in children's voiceless aspirated stops and interpretation of developmental trends. *Journal of Speech, Language and Hearing Research* 44. 1058–1068. https://doi.org/10.1044/1092-4388(2001/084)

Kohler, Klaus J. 1994. Glottal stops and glottalization in German. *Phonetica* 51(1–3). 38–51. https://doi.org/10.1159/000261957

Kong, Eun Jong, Jeffrey J. Holliday & Hyunjung Lee. 2022. Post-adolescent changes in the perception of regional sub-phonemic variation. *Journal of Phonetics* 90. 101114. https://doi.org/10.1016/j.wocn.2021.101114

Kozminska, Kinga. 2015. Preliminary results of a sociophonetic study of VOT and Polish transnational identities in the UK. In The Scottish Consortium for ICPhS 2015 (ed.), *Proceedings of the 18th International Congress of Phonetic Sciences*, Paper 0827. University of Glasgow.

Kuang, Jianjing. 2019. Contextual variation of glottalic stops in Q'anjob'al. In Calhoun et al., 1114–1118.

Kubozono, Haruo (ed.). 2017. *The phonetics and phonology of geminate consonants*. Oxford University Press.

Labov, William. 1972. *Sociolinguistic patterns*. University of Pennsylvania Press.

Ladefoged, Peter. 2005. *Vowels and consonants*, 2nd edn. Blackwell.

Ladefoged, Peter & Ian Maddieson. 1996. *The sounds of the world's languages*. Blackwell.

Lass, Roger. 1984. *Phonology*. Cambridge University Press.

Lavoie, Lisa M. 2001. *Consonant strength: Phonological patterns and phonetic manifestations*. Garland.

Lee, Hyunjung, Jeffrey J. Holliday & Eun Jun Kong. 2020. Diachronic change and synchronic variation in the Korean stop laryngeal contrast. *Language and Linguistics Compass* 14(7). e12374. https://doi.org/10.1111/lnc3.12374

Lee, Hyunjung & Allard Jongman. 2012. Effects of tone on the three-way laryngeal distinction in Korean: An acoustic and aerodynamic comparison of the Seoul and South Kyungsang dialects. *Journal of the International Phonetic Association* 42(2). 145–169. https://doi.org/10.1017/S0025100312000035

Lee, Hyunjung, Stephen Politzer-Ahles & Allard Jongman. 2013. Speakers of tonal and non-tonal Korean dialects use different cue weightings in the perception of the three-way laryngeal stop contrast. *Journal of Phonetics* 41(2). 117–132. https://doi.org/10.1016/j.wocn.2012.12.002

Lee, Wai Sum & Eric Zee (eds.). 2011. *Proceedings of the 17th International Congress of Phonetic Sciences (ICPhS XVII)*. City University of Hong Kong.

Levon, Erez. 2006. Hearing "gay": Prosody, interpretation, and the affective judgments of men's speech. *American Speech* 81(1). 56–78. https://doi.org/10.1215/00031283-2006-003

Li, Fanfang. 2013. The effect of speakers' sex on voice onset time in Mandarin stops. *Journal of the Acoustical Society of America* 133(2). EL142. https://doi.org/10.1121/1.4778281

Lisker, Leigh. 1986. "Voicing" in English: A catalogue of acoustic features signaling /b/ versus /p/ in trochees. *Language and Speech* 29(1). 3–11. https://doi.org/10.1177/002383098602900102

Lisker, Leigh & Arthur S. Abramson. 1964. A cross-language study of voicing in initial stops: Acoustical measurements. *Word* 20(3). 384–422. https://doi.org/10.1080/00437956.1964.11659830

Lisker, Leigh & Arthur S. Abramson. 1967. Some effects of context on voice onset time in English stops. *Language and Speech* 10(1). 1–28. https://doi.org/10.1177/002383096701000101

Loakes, Debbie, Kirsty McDougall, Josh Clothier, John Hajek & Janet Fletcher. 2018. Sociophonetic variability of post-vocalic /t/ in Aboriginal and mainstream Australian English. In Epps et al., 1–4.

Löfqvist, Anders & Vincent L. Gracco. 2002. Control of oral closure in lingual stop consonant production. *Journal of the Acoustical Society of America* 111(6). 2811–2827. https://doi.org/10.1121/1.1473636

Ma, Junzhou, Xiaoxiang Chen, Yezhou Wu & Linjie Zhang. 2018. Effects of age and sex on voice onset time: Evidence from Mandarin voiceless stops. *Logopedics Phoniatrics Vocology* 43(2). 56–62. https://doi.org/10.1080/14015439.2017.1324915

Macken, Marlys A. & David Barton. 1980. The acquisition of the voicing contrast in English: A study of voice onset time in word-initial stop consonants. *Journal of Child Language* 7(1). 41–74. https://doi.org/10.1017/S0305000900007029

MacKenzie, Laurel & Meredith Tamminga. 2021. New and old puzzles in the morphological conditioning of coronal stop deletion. *Language Variation and Change* 33(2). 217–244. https://doi.org/10.1017/S0954394521000119

Maclagan, Margaret, Catherine I. Watson, Ray Harlow, Jeanette King & Peter Keegan. 2009. /u/ fronting and /t/ aspiration in Māori and New Zealand English. *Language Variation and Change* 21(2). 175–192. https://doi.org/10.1017/S095439450999007X

Maddieson, Ian. 1997. Phonetic universals. In John Laver & William J. Hardcastle (eds.), *Handbook of phonetic sciences*, 619–639. Blackwell.

Maddieson, Ian. 2013. Voicing in plosives and fricatives. In Matthew S. Dryer & Martin Haspelmath (eds.), *The world atlas of language structures online*. Max Planck Institute for Evolutionary Anthropology. http://wals.info/chapter/4

Mahboob, Ahmar & Nadra Huma Ahmar. 2008. Pakistani English: Phonology. In Mesthrie 2008b, 164–176.

Mansfield, John Basil. 2015. Consonant lenition as a sociophonetic variable in Murrinh Patha (Australia). *Language Variation and Change* 27(2). 203–225. https://doi.org/10.1017/S0954394515000046

Mascaró, Joan. 1989. On the form of segment deletion and insertion rules. *Probus* 1(1). 31–61. https://doi.org/10.1515/prbs.1989.1.1.31

McCarthy, Owen & Jane Stuart-Smith. 2013. Ejectives in Scottish English: A social perspective. *Journal of the International Phonetic Association* 43(3). 273–298. https://doi.org/10.1017/S0025100313000212

McLeod, Sharynne & Kathryn Crowe. 2018. Children's consonant acquisition in 27 languages: A cross-linguistic review. *American Journal of Speech-Language Pathology* 27(4). 1546–1571. https://doi.org/10.1044/2018_AJSLP-17-0100

Mead, Jere, James M. Turner, Peter T. Macklem & John B. Little. 1967. Significance of the relationship between lung recoil and maximum expiratory flow. *Journal of Applied Physiology* 22(1). 95–108. https://doi.org/10.1152/jappl.1967.22.1.95

Mees, Inger M. & Beverley Collins. 1999. Cardiff: A real-time study of glottalisation. In Foulkes & Docherty, 185–202.

Mesthrie, Rajend. 2008a. Indian South African English: Phonology. In Mesthrie 2008b, 188–199.

Mesthrie, Rajend (ed.). 2008b. *Varieties of English, vol. 4, Africa, South and Southeast Asia*. Mouton de Gruyter.

Mesthrie, Rajend. 2012. Ethnicity, substrate and place: The dynamics of Coloured and Indian English in five South African cities in relation to the variable (t). *Language Variation and Change* 24(3). 371–395. https://doi.org/10.1017/S0954394512000178

Michnowicz, Jim & Lindsey Carpenter. 2013. Voiceless stop aspiration in Yucatan Spanish: A sociolinguistic analysis. *Spanish in Context* 10(3). 410–437. https://doi.org/10.1075/sic.10.3.05mic

Mielke, Jeff & Kuniko Nielsen. 2018. Voice Onset Time in English voiceless stops is affected by following postvocalic liquids and voiceless onsets. *Journal of the Acoustical Society of America* 144(4). 2166–2177. https://doi.org/10.1121/1.5059493

Miller, Joanne L., Kerry P. Green & Adam Reeves. 1986. Speaking rate and segments: A look at the relation between speech production and speech perception for the voicing contrast. *Phonetica* 43(1–3). 106–115. https://doi.org/10.1159/000261764

Moran, Steven & Daniel McCloy (eds.) 2019. PHOIBLE 2.0. Max Planck Institute for the Science of Human History. http://phoible.org

Morris, Jonathan & Michaela Hejná. 2020. Pre-aspiration in Bethesda Welsh: A sociophonetic analysis. *Journal of the International Phonetic Association* 50(2). 168–192. https://doi.org/10.1017/S0025100318000221

Morris, Richard J. & William S. Brown, Jr. 1994. Age-related differences in speech variability among women. *Journal of Communication Disorders* 27(1). 49–64. https://doi.org/10.1016/0021-9924(94)90010-8

Morris, Richard J., Christopher R. McCrea & Kaileen D. Herring. 2008. Voice onset time differences between adult males and females: Isolated syllables. *Journal of Phonetics* 36(2). 308–317. https://doi.org/10.1016/j.wocn.2007.06.003

Mortensen, Johannes & John Tøndering. 2013. The effect of vowel height on voice onset time in stop consonants in CV sequences in spontaneous Danish. In Robert Eklund (ed.), *Proceedings of Fonetik*, 49–52. Linköping University.

Nance, Claire & Jane Stuart-Smith. 2013. Pre-aspiration and post-aspiration in Scottish Gaelic stop consonants. *Journal of the International Phonetic Association* 43(2). 129–152. https://doi.org/10.1017/S0025100313000042

Nearey, Terrance M. & Bernard L. Rochet. 1994. Effects of place of articulation and vowel context on VOT production and perception for French and English stops. *Journal of the International Phonetic Association* 24(1). 1–18. https://doi.org/10.1017/S0025100300004965

Neiman, Gary S., Richard J. Klich & Elaine M. Shuey. 1983. Voice onset time in young and 70-year-old women. *Journal of Speech, Language, and Hearing Research* 26(1). 118–123. https://doi.org/10.1044/jshr.2601.118

Nelson, Noah R. & Andrew Wedel. 2017. The phonetic specificity of competition: Contrastive hyperarticulation of voice onset time in conversational English. *Journal of Phonetics* 64. 51–70. https://doi.org/10.1016/j.wocn.2017.01.008

Ngom, Fallou. 2003. *Wolof*. Lincom Europa.

Nielsen, Kuniko. 2011. Specificity and abstractness of VOT imitation. *Journal of Phonetics* 39(2). 132–142. https://doi.org/10.1016/j.wocn.2010.12.007

Nodari, Rosalba, Chiara Celata & Naomi Nagy. 2019. Socio-indexical phonetic features in the heritage language context: Voiceless stop aspiration in the Calabrian community in Toronto. *Journal of Phonetics* 73. 91–112. https://doi.org/10.1016/j.wocn.2018.12.005

Noglo, Kossi. 2009. Sociophonetic variation in urban Ewe. In James N. Stanford & Dennis R. Preston (eds.), *Variation in indigenous minority languages*, 229–244. John Benjamins.

O'Dwyer, Fergus. 2019. Slit-t in Dublin English. In Juan-Andrés Villena Ponsoda, Francisco Díaz-Montesinos, Antonio-Manuel Ávila-Muñoz & Matilde Vida-Castro (eds.), *Language variation–European perspectives VII*, 161–175. John Benjamins.

Ogden, Richard A. 2009. *An introduction to English phonetics*. Edinburgh University Press.

Oh, Eunjin. 2011. Effects of speaker gender on voice onset time in Korean stops. *Journal of Phonetics* 39(1). 59–67. https://doi.org/10.1016/j.wocn.2010.11.002

Öhman, Sven E.G. 1966. Coarticulation in VCV utterances: Spectrographic measurements. *Journal of the Acoustical Society of America* 39. 151–168. https://doi.org/10.1121/1.1909864

Padgett, Jaye. 2002. Russian voicing assimilation, final devoicing, and the problem of [v]. Unpublished manuscript.

Parikh, Gaurang & Philipos C. Loizou. 2005. The influence of noise on vowel and consonant cues. *Journal of the Acoustical Society of America* 118(6). 3874–3888. https://doi.org/10.1121/1.2118407

Parveen, Sabiha & Alexander M. Goberman. 2014. Presence of stop bursts and multiple bursts in individuals with Parkinson disease. *International Journal of Speech-Language Pathology* 16(5). 456–463. https://doi.org/10.3109/17549507.2013.808702

Patrick, Peter. 2008. Creoles at the intersection of variable processes: –t,d deletion and past-marking in the Jamaican mesolect. *Language Variation and Change* 3(2). 171–189. https://doi.org/10.1017/S095439450000051X

Peng, Jui-Feng, Li-mei Chen & Chia-Cheng Lee. 2014. Voice onset time of initial stops in Mandarin and Hakka: Effect of gender. *Taiwan Journal of Linguistics* 28(9). 63–79. https://doi.org/10.6519/TJL.2014.12(1).3

Percival, Maida. 2019. Contextual variation in the acoustics of Hul'q'umi'num' ejective stops. In Calhoun et al., 3270–3274.

Percival, Maida, Tamás G. Csapó, Márton Bartók, Andrea Deme, Tekla E. Gráczi & Alexandra Markó. 2020. Ultrasound imaging of Hungarian geminates. Paper presented at UltraFest IX, Indiana University.

Percival, Maida, Alexei Kochetov & Yoonjung Kang. 2018. An ultrasound study of gemination in coronal stops in Eastern Oromo. *Proceedings of Interspeech 2018*. 1531–1535. https://doi.org/10.21437/Interspeech.2018-2512

Petrosino, Linda, Roger D. Colcord, Karen B. Kurcz & Robert J. Yonker. 1993. Voice onset time of velar stop productions in aged speakers. *Perceptual and Motor Skills* 76(1). 83–88. https://doi.org/10.2466/pms.1993.76.1.83

Pharao, Nicolai & Marie Maegaard. 2017. On the influence of coronal sibilants and stops on the perception of social meanings in Copenhagen Danish. *Linguistics* 55(5). 1141–1167. https://doi.org/10.1515/ling-2017-0023

Phillips, Audra & Benjamin Tucker. 2020. Context effects on the acoustic realization of stops and affricates in Northern Pwo Karen. *Journal of the International Phonetic Association* 52(1). 1–32. https://doi.org/10.1017/S0025100320000109

Piccardi, Duccio. 2017. Sociophonetic factors of speakers' sex differences in Voice Onset Time: A Florentine case study. In Chiara Bertini, Chiara Celata, Giovanna Lenoci, Chiara Meluzzi & Irene Ricci (eds.), *Fattori sociali e biologici nella variazione fonetica/Social and biological factors in speech variation*, 83–106. AISV. https://doi.org/10.17469/O2103AISV000005

Pierrehumbert, Janet B. & David Talkin. 1992. Lenition of /h/ and glottal stop. In Gerard J. Docherty & D. Robert Ladd (eds.), *Papers in laboratory phonology II: Gesture, segment, prosody*, 90–117. Cambridge University Press.

Pike, Eunice V., Keith Forster & Wilma J. Forster. 1986. Fortis versus lenis consonants in the Paya dialect of Kuna. In Benjamin F. Elson, (ed.), *Language in global perspective: Papers in honor of the 50th anniversary of the Summer Institute of Linguistics 1935–1985,* 451–464. Summer Institute of Linguistics.

Podesva, Robert J., Jermay Reynolds, Patrick Callier & Jessica Baptiste. 2015. Constraints on the social meaning of released /t/: A production and perception study of U.S. politicians. *Language Variation and Change* 27(1). 59–87. https://doi.org/10.1017/S0954394514000192

Podesva, Robert J., Sarah J. Roberts & Kathryn Campbell-Kibler. 2001. Sharing resources and indexing meanings in the production of gay styles. In Kathryn Campbell-Kibler, Robert J. Podesva, Sarah J. Roberts & Andrew Wong (eds.), *Language and sexuality: Contesting meaning in theory and practice,* 175–189. CSLI Publications.

Port, Robert F. & Rosemarie Rotunno. 1979. Relation between voice-onset time and vowel duration. *Journal of the Acoustical Society of America* 66(3). 654–682. https://doi.org/10.1121/1.383692

Puggaard, Rasmus. 2021. Modeling regional variation in voice onset time of Jutlandic varieties of Danish. In Hans Van de Velde, Nanna Haug Hilton & Remco Knooihuizen (eds.), *Language Variation–European Perspectives VIII*, 79–109. John Benjamins.

Purse, Ruaridh. 2019. The articulatory reality of coronal stop "deletion." In Calhoun et al., 1595–1599.

R Core Team. 2022. *R: A language and environment for statistical computing*. R Foundation for Statistical Computing. www.R-project.org

Raphael, Lawrence J., Yishai Tobin, Alice Faber, Tova Most, H. Betty Kollia & Doron Milstein. 1995. Intermediate values of voice onset time. In Fredericka Bell-Berti & Raphael J. Lawrence (eds.), *Producing speech: Contemporary issues*, 117–127. American Institute of Physics.

Raymond, William, Esther Brown & Alice Healy. 2016. Cumulative context effects and variant lexical representations: Word use and English final t/d deletion. *Language Variation and Change* 28(2). 175–202. https://doi.org/10.1017/S0954394516000041

Recasens, Daniel & Meritxell Mira. 2015. Place and manner assimilation in Catalan consonant clusters. *Journal of the International Phonetic Association* 45(2). 115–147. https://doi.org/10.1017/S0025100315000080

Remijsen, Bert, Otto G. Ayoker & Timothy Mills. 2011. Shilluk. *Journal of the International Phonetic Association* 41(1). 111–125. https://doi.org/10.1017/S0025100310000289

Riney, Timothy J., Naoyuki Takagi, Kaori Ota & Yoko Uchida. 2007. The intermediate degree of VOT in Japanese initial voiceless stops. *Journal of Phonetics* 35(3). 439–444. https://doi.org/10.1016/j.wocn.2006.01.002

Ryalls, Jack, Marni Simon & Jerry Thomason. 2004. Voice onset time production in older Caucasian- and African-Americans. *Journal of Multilingual Communication Disorders* 2(1). 61–67. https://doi.org/10.1080/14769670310000090980

Ryalls, John, Allison Zipprer & Penelope Baldauff. 1997. A preliminary investigation of the effects of gender and race on voice onset time. *Journal of Speech, Language, and Hearing Research* 40(3). 642–645. https://doi.org/10.1044/jslhr.4003.642

Sanchez, Kauyumari, Rachel M. Miller & Lawrence D. Rosenblum. 2010. Visual influences on alignment to voice onset time. *Journal of Speech, Language, and Hearing Research* 53(2). 262–272. https://doi.org/10.1044/1092-4388(2009/08-0247)

Santa Ana, A. Otto. 1992. Chicano English evidence for the exponential hypothesis: A variable rule pervades lexical phonology. *Language Variation and Change* 4. 275–289. https://doi.org/10.1017/S0954394500000818

Schertz, Jessamyn & Elizabeth K. Johnson. 2022. Voice onset time imitation in teens versus adults. *Journal of Speech, Language, and Hearing Research* 65(5). 1–12. https://doi.org/10.1044/2022_JSLHR-21-00460

Schertz, Jessamyn & Sarah Khan. 2020. Acoustic cues in production and perception of the four-way stop laryngeal contrast in Hindi and Urdu. *Journal of Phonetics* 81. 100979. https://doi.org/10.1016/j.wocn.2020.100979

Schleef, Erik. 2013. Glottal replacement of /t/ in two British capitals: Effects of word frequency and morphological compositionality. *Language Variation and Change* 25(2). 201–223. https://doi.org/10.1017/S0954394513000094

Schwartz, Sarah R. 2018. *Repping the streets, Repping the hometown: A sociophonetic analysis of dialectal variation in the Moroccan hip hop community.* MA dissertation, University of Texas at Austin.

Scobbie, James M. 2006. Flexibility in the face of incompatible English VOT systems. In Louis M. Goldstein, Douglas H. Whalen & Catherine T. Best (eds.), *Papers in laboratory phonology 8: Varieties of phonological competence*, 367–392. Mouton de Gruyter.

Shaw, Hannah & Paul Foulkes. 2015. Real time change in Prince William's speech. Paper presented at UKLVC 10, University of York.

Skarnitzl, Radek & Diana Rálišová. 2022. Phonetic variation of Irish English /t/ in the syllabic coda. *Journal of the International Phonetic Association*. https://doi.org/10.1017/S0025100321000347

Sleeper, Morgan. 2020. Contact effects on voice-onset time (VOT) in Patagonian Welsh. *Journal of the International Phonetic Association* 50(2). 153–167. https://doi.org/10.1017/S002510031800021X

Sokolovic-Perovic, Mirjana. 2012. *The voicing contrast in Serbian stops.* PhD thesis, Newcastle University.

Solé, Maria-Josep, Daniel Recasens & Joaquin Romero (eds.). 2003. *Proceedings of the 15th International Congress of Phonetic Sciences (ICPhS XV).* Causal Productions.

Stevens, Kenneth N. & Dennis H Klatt. 1974. Role of formant transitions in the voiced-voiceless distinction for stops. *Journal of the Acoustical Society of America* 55(3). 653–659. https://doi.org/10.1121/1.1914578

Stevens, Kenneth N. & Sheila E. Blumstein. 1981. The search for invariant acoustic correlates of phonetic features. In Peter D. Eimas & Joanne L. Miller (eds.), *Perspectives on the study of speech*, 1–38. Lawrence Erlbaum.

Stölten, Katrin & Olle Engstrand. 2002. Effects of sex and age in the Arjeplog dialect: A listening test and measurements of preaspiration and VOT. *Proceedings of Fonetik* 44(1). 29–32.

Straw, Michelle & Peter Patrick. 2007. Dialect acquisition of glottal variation in /t/: Barbadians in Ipswich. *Language Sciences* 29(2–3). 385–407. https://doi.org/10.1016/j.langsci.2006.12.025

Stuart-Smith, Jane, Morgan Sonderegger, Tamara Rathcke & Rachel Macdonald. 2015. The private life of stops: VOT in a real-time corpus of spontaneous Glaswegian. *Laboratory Phonology* 6(3–4). 505–549. https://doi.org/10.1515/lp-2015-0015

Summerfield, Quentin. 1975. How a full account of segmental perception depends on prosody and vice versa. In Antonie Cohen & Sibout G. Nooteboom (eds.), *Structure and process in speech perception*, 51–68. Springer.

Sundara, Megha. 2005. Acoustic-phonetics of coronal stops: A cross-language study of Canadian English and Canadian French. *Journal of the Acoustical Society of America* 118(2). 1026–1037. https://doi.org/10.1121/1.1953270

Sundara, Megha, Linda Polka & Shari Baum. 2006. Production of coronal stops by simultaneous bilingual adults. *Bilingualism: Language and Cognition* 9(1). 97–114. https://doi.org/10.1017/S1366728905002403

Suomi, Kari. 1980. *Voicing in English and Finnish stops.* PhD dissertation, University of Turku.

Swartz, Bradford L. 1992. Gender difference in voice onset time. *Perceptual and Motor Skills* 75(3). 983–992. https://doi.org/10.2466/pms.1992.75.3.983

Tagliamonte, Sali A. & Rosalind A.M. Temple. 2005. New perspectives on an ol' variable: (t, d) in British English. *Language Variation and Change* 17(3). 281–302. https://doi.org/10.1017/S0954394505050118

Temple, Rosalind A.M. 1999. Phonetic and sociophonetic conditioning of voicing patterns in the stop consonants of French. In John J. Ohala, Yoko Hasegawa, Manjari Ohala, Daniel Granville & Ashlee C. Bailey (eds.), *Proceedings of the 14th International Congress of Phonetic Sciences*, 1409–1412. San Francisco.

Themistocleous, Charalambos. 2016. The bursts of stops can convey dialectal information. *Journal of the Acoustical Society of America* 140(4). EL334–EL339. https://doi.org/10.1121/1.4964818

Theodore, Rachel M. & Joanne L. Miller. 2010. Characteristics of listener sensitivity to talker-specific phonetic detail. *Journal of the Acoustical Society of America* 128(4). 2090–2099. https://doi.org/10.1121/1.3467771

Theodore, Rachel M. & Joanne L. Miller & David DeSteno. 2009. Individual talker differences in voice-onset-time: Contextual influences. *Journal of the Acoustical Society of America* 125(6). 3974–3982. https://doi.org/10.1121/1.3106131

Torre, Peter & Jessica A. Barlow. 2009. Age-related changes in acoustic characteristics of adult speech. *Journal of Communication Disorders* 42(5). 324–333. https://doi.org/10.1016/j.jcomdis.2009.03.001

Toscano, Joseph C. & Bob McMurray. 2010. Cue integration with categories: Weighting acoustic cues in speech using unsupervised learning and distributional statistics. *Cognitive Science* 34(3). 434–464. https://doi.org/10.1111/j.1551-6709.2009.01077.x

Toscano, Joseph C., Bob McMurray, Joel Dennhardt & Steven J. Luck. 2010. Continuous perception and graded categorization: Electrophysiological evidence for a linear relationship between the acoustic signal and perceptual encoding of speech. *Psychological Science* 21(10). 1532–1540. https://doi.org/10.1177/0956797610384142

Trumper, John & Marta Maddalon. 1990. *Il problema delle varietà: L'italiano parlato nel Veneto.* In Manlio A. Cortelazzo & Alberto M. Mioni (eds.), *L'italiano Regionale. Atti del XVIII Congresso Internazionale di Studi Della Società di Linguistica Italiana,* 159–191. Bulzoni.

Utsugi, Akira, Kan Sasaki & Yosuke Igarashi. 2013. Regional variation of VOT in Ibaraki Japanese. *Proceedings of the 27th Annual Meeting of the Phonetic Society of Japan,* 199–124. https://doi.org/10.24467/onseikenkyu.17.3_88_2

van Alphen, Petra M. & Roel Smits. 2004. Acoustical and perceptual analysis of the voicing distinction in Dutch initial plosives: The role of prevoicing. *Journal of Phonetics* 32(4). 455–491. https://doi.org/10.1016/j.wocn.2004.05.001

van Rooy, Bertus. 2008. Black South African English: Phonology. In Mesthrie 2008b, 177–187.

Vicenik, Chad. 2010. An acoustic study of Georgian stop consonants. *Journal of the International Phonetic Association* 40(1). 59–92. https://doi.org/10.1017/S0025100309990302

Vietti, Alessandro. 2019. Phonological variation and change in Italian. *Oxford research encyclopedia of linguistics.* https://doi.org/10.1093/acrefore/9780199384655.013.494

Villafaña Dalcher, Christina. 2008. Consonant weakening in Florentine Italian: A cross-disciplinary approach to gradient and variable sound change. *Language Variation and Change* 20(2). 275–316. https://doi.org/10.1017/S0954394508000021

Wade, Lacey, Wei Lai & Meredith Tamminga. 2021. The reliability of individual differences in VOT imitation. *Language and Speech* 64(3). 576–593. https://doi.org/10.1177/0023830920947769

Wang, Xuan. 2019. Dialect contact across three generations: a sociophonetic analysis of variation in [pʰ tʰ kʰ, h] in a contact variety in Hohhot, China. In Calhoun et al., 2339–2343.

Warner, Natasha & Andrea Weber. 2001. Perception of epenthetic stops. *Journal of Phonetics* 29(1). 53–87. https://doi.org/10.1006/jpho.2001.0129

Warner, Natasha & Andrea Weber. 2002. Stop epenthesis at syllable boundaries. In John L. Hansen & Bryan Pellom (eds.), *Proceedings of Interspeech 7,* 1121–1124. ISCA Archive.

Watson, Janet C. 2002. *The phonology and morphology of Arabic.* Oxford University Press.

Weismer, Gary. 1979. Sensitivity of voice-onset time (VOT) measures to certain segmental features in speech production. *Journal of Phonetics* 7(2). 197–204. https://doi.org/10.1016/S0095-4470(19)31041-1

Wells, John C. 1982. *Accents of English.* 3 vols. Cambridge University Press.

Westbury, John R. 1983. Enlargement of the supraglottal cavity and its relation to stop consonant voicing. *Journal of the Acoustical Society of America* 73(4). 1322–1336. https://doi.org/10.1121/1.389236

Whisker-Taylor, Kate & Lynn Clark. 2019. Yorkshire assimilation: Exploring the production and perception of a geographically restricted variable. *Journal of English Linguistics* 47(3). 221–248. https://doi.org/10.1177/0075424219849093

Whiteside, Sandra P. & Jeni Marshall. 2001. Developmental trends in voice onset time: Some evidence for sex differences. *Phonetica* 58(3). 196–210. https://doi.org/10.1159/000056199

Whiteside, Sandra P., Luisa Henry & Rachel Dobbin. 2004. Sex differences in voice onset time: A developmental study of phonetic context effects in British English. *Journal of the Acoustical Society of America* 116(2). 1179–1183. https://doi.org/10.1121/1.1768256

Wiese, Richard. 2000. *The phonology of German.* Oxford University Press.

Yağlı, Emre. 2018. *Indexing social meaning: Sociophonetic variables and listener perceptions of Turkish.* PhD thesis, Hacettepe University.

Yang, Jing. 2018. Development of stop consonants in three-to six-year-old Mandarin-speaking children. *Journal of Child Language* 45(5). 1091–1115. https://doi.org/10.1017/S0305000918000090

Yao, Yao. 2007. Closure duration and VOT of word-initial voiceless plosives in English in spontaneous connected speech. *UC Berkeley Phonology Lab Annual Report* 3. 183–225. https://doi.org/10.5070/P71hs7h769

Yao, Yao. 2009. Understanding VOT variation in spontaneous speech. *UC Berkeley Phonology Lab Annual Report* 5. 29–43. https://doi.org/10.5070/P76dd1x6cs

Yoo, Isaiah WonHo & Barbara Blankenship. 2003. Duration of epenthetic [t] in polysyllabic American English words. *Journal of the International Phonetic Association* 33(2). 153–164. https://doi.org/10.1017/S0025100303001269

Yu, Alan C.L., Carissa Abrego-Collier & Morgan Sonderegger. 2013. Phonetic imitation from an individual-difference perspective: Subjective attitude, personality and "autistic" traits. *PloS ONE* 8(9). e74746. https://doi.org/10.1371/journal.pone.0074746

Zerbe, Alison. 2013. P'urépecha fortis v. lenis consonants. *University of Washington, Working Papers in Linguistics [UWWPL]* 31.

Zlatin, Marsha A. & Roy Koenigsknecht. 1976. Development of the voicing contrast: A comparison of voice onset time in stop perception and production. *Journal of Speech and Hearing Research* 19(1). 93–111. https://doi.org/10.1044/jshr.1901.93

Zsiga, Elizabeth C. 2011. Local assimilation. In Marc van Oostendorp, Colin Ewen, Beth Hume & Keren Rice (eds.), *The companion to phonology, vol. 3.* Wiley-Blackwell. https://doi.org/10.1002/9781444335262.wbctp0081

Zue, Victor W. 1976. *Acoustic characteristics of stop consonants: A controlled study.* PhD thesis, Massachusetts Institute of Technology.

8

SOCIOPHONETICS AND FRICATIVES

Whitney Chappell, Christina García, and Justin Davidson

Introduction

The present chapter has two main aims: first, to provide a broad overview of the sociophonetic research related to fricatives across languages and, second, to home in on a specific fricative process: the voicing of intervocalic /s/. Intervocalic /s/ voicing in Spanish (e.g., *masa* 'dough' as ['ma.za]) is considered nonstandard, yet it occurs across several distinct dialects. Some of these dialects coexist with other languages, such as Quechua and Catalan, and this language contact appears to influence the voicing process in Spanish (Davidson 2019a, 2020, 2021). In other regions, however, this process cannot be readily attributed to language contact and appears to be an endogenous phenomenon, as is the case in San José, Costa Rica (Chappell & García 2017) and Loja, Ecuador (García 2020).

Although social and linguistic variables have been found to condition intervocalic /s/ voicing somewhat differently across the Spanish-speaking world, speaker gender has consistently been identified as a significant factor. The case study provided in this chapter explores the ways in which sociolinguistic factors, with a special focus on gender, condition /s/ voicing across three dialects of Spanish—namely those spoken in Barcelona, San José, and Loja. Using percent voicing of intervocalic /s/ in conversational Spanish as our acoustic measurement across three datasets, our comparative analysis sheds light on how a single social factor can come to influence one phonetic variable across varieties of the same language. To set the stage, we first offer a broad sketch of previous sociophonetic research on fricatives. We then present our case study before offering concluding thoughts and suggesting future directions for sociophonetic research on fricatives.

Literature review

Previous sociophonetic research on fricatives

This section summarizes some of the most prominent methods, theories, research questions, and findings to have emerged in sociophonetic research on fricatives. Numerous fricative processes associated with social groups and/or social meanings take place across the world's languages, and this brief section aims to provide a broad overview of the most thoroughly researched of these

DOI: 10.4324/9781003034636-9

processes. Beginning with the acoustic measurements employed in previous research on fricatives, this section then explores some of the key debates revolving around fricatives in English, Spanish, and other languages.

Acoustic measurements are a useful tool for objectively classifying fricatives, as, for example, different places of articulation are associated with high amplitudes within specific frequency ranges. A power spectrum is generally used to capture how fricatives' acoustic energy is distributed along one or more of the four spectral moments (see Shadle & Mair 1996; Jongman, Wayland & Wong 2000; van Son & van Santen 2005). Among the measurements typically extracted from a Long Term Average Spectrum (LTAS), center of gravity (COG) is the most common in sociophonetic work on fricatives, providing a weighted average of the frequencies in the spectrum (Thomas 2016). COG is also referred to as the first spectral moment, spectral mean, or centroid (Kendall & Fridland 2021:63). The other moments include measurements of spectral variance (also known as the second spectral moment, range, or spread), which determine the range of energy concentration; skewness (the third spectral moment), which establishes how symmetrically distributed the energy is within the spectrum; and kurtosis (the fourth spectral moment), which identifies the propensity for outliers in the acoustic energy's distribution (see Gradoville, Brown & File-Muriel 2022). Some studies utilize all four spectral moments (e.g., Jannedy et al. 2010), while others use fewer moments.

Across studies, different combinations of moments have been selected for analysis. For example, Stuart-Smith (2007) incorporates COG and standard deviation in her analysis of /s/ in Glaswegian. Other scholars employ less common acoustic measurements, such as the overall intensity within the spectrum (e.g., Minnick Fox 2006), the spectral peak frequency (e.g., Jongman, Wayland & Wong 2000), the zero crossing rate (e.g., Nance & Stuart-Smith 2013; Ruch & Harrington 2014), the intensity of the third formant (e.g., Jongman, Wayland & Wong 2000), the amplitude ratio between the second formant and most prominent peak (e.g., Li, Edwards & Beckman 2007), measurements of vowel formants during transitions (Thomas 2011:104, 115), measurements of psychoacoustic spectra like peak ERB_N number (Reidy 2016), and spectral slope measures along with the dynamic range of the spectrum (Jesus & Shadle 2002).

While the vast majority of fricative research incorporates static acoustic measurements (i.e., measures either pulled from a specific point in time during a fricative's production or averaged across the fricative's duration), dynamic measures capturing time-varying change from the start to the end of the fricative's production have also been successfully integrated in sociophonetics. For example, Stuart-Smith (2020) applied Discrete Cosine Transformation (DCT) to obtain continuous trajectory shapes of both COG and spectral slope for /s/ in Glasgow English and Reidy (2016) used polynomial growth-curve analysis to differentiate spectral peak trajectories between English and Japanese fricatives.

Jesus & Shadle (2002) additionally incorporate measurements of devoicing in their work on European Portuguese fricatives, and, similarly, percent voicing is often used to classify fricatives in Spanish (Rohena-Madrazo 2015; Chappell & García 2017; Davidson 2020; García 2020). An ongoing debate in the measurement of percent voicing has been whether to treat voicing as a continuous measurement (e.g., Schmidt & Willis 2011), to partition percent voicing into categories like unvoiced/voiceless, partially voiced, and fully voiced (e.g., Campos-Astorkiza 2014), or both (e.g., Hualde & Prieto 2014). Some studies utilize Praat's voicing report (e.g., Hualde & Prieto 2014; Rohena-Madrazo 2015), while others (e.g., Campos-Astorkiza 2014; Strycharczuk et al. 2014) measure percent voicing "by hand," judging which portion of the fricative is voiced based on the waveform/spectrogram, as the voicing report can be fooled by "phantom glottal pulses" that do not correspond with voicing (Gradoville 2011:70).

Central to the debate about how to operationalize percent voicing is how much voicing is necessary for a fricative to be perceived as voiced, which has been investigated in perception studies that examine the categorization of fricatives in synthesized or manipulated stimuli. An effect of fricative duration on the perception of voicing is found in English (Cole & Cooper 1975) and Spanish (Widdison 1997), whereby longer fricatives are more likely to be perceived as voiceless. Overwhelmingly, though, the studies that manipulate multiple acoustic characteristics reveal a stronger effect of voicing duration/ratio on the perception of voicing than fricative duration, vowel duration, or VC formant transitions across languages, including English (Jongman 1989; Stevens et al. 1992; Smith 2013), Portuguese (Pape et al. 2015), and Hungarian (Bárkányi & Kiss 2021).

For place of articulation, Jongman (1989) demonstrates that fricative duration influences perception of place in English fricatives, while Mann & Soli (1991) argue that vocalic cues also affect the perception of English [s] versus [ʃ]. Other studies have compared the use of perceptual cues among speakers of different languages. For instance, Broersma (2010) finds that, when determining final fricative voicing in English stimuli, Dutch listeners use preceding vowel duration less than English listeners, showing that the perceptual cues they use in Dutch in intervocalic context are not transferred to the L2 (English) word-final context. Finally, Blecua Falgueras & Rost Bagudanch (2015) used naturally occurring variants of intervocalic /f/ in a perception experiment to establish how different realizations ([f], [f̬], [v], and [β]) are categorized phonologically, concluding that [v] can be interpreted as both /f/ and /b/. As a whole, these studies demonstrate the complexity inherent in the perception of fricatives and point to the need to consider the interconnectedness of multiple perceptual cues as listeners process and categorize auditory stimuli.

Of course, sociophonetic research on fricatives goes a step beyond acoustic analysis and phonological perception, introducing social variables with the goal of assessing how acoustic differences distinguish social groups and/or individuals. As acoustic measures reflect articulatory gesturing and positioning, acoustic data can be carefully interpreted with respect to unique articulatory configurations, and thus may also reflect physiological differences between (groups of) speakers. Acoustic measures can also be used to determine correlations between articulatory configurations and the social stratification or ideological meaning of specific features. One such feature is tongue position, for which there exists considerable variation both at inter- and intra-speaker levels. Variability in the degree of more backed or more fronted tongue position is strongly correlated with acoustic measurements such as COG and spectral peak frequency, such that higher values signal more fronted tongue positioning, whereas lower values signal more backed tongue positioning. In English and other languages, tongue positioning has been rather robustly linked to unique gender groups, with women producing /s/ as more fronted than men (Stuart-Smith 2007; Levon & Holmes-Elliot 2013; Podesva & Van Hofwegen 2014; Podesva & Van Hofwegen 2016). This gender stratification in production has in turn led to ideological associations between tongue position and femininity/masculinity, such that listeners readily associate more fronted /s/ productions as more feminine, and more backed /s/ productions as more masculine (Campbell-Kibler 2011; Mack & Munson 2012; Levon 2014; Pharao et al. 2014; Zimman 2017; Calder 2019). The combination of production and perceptual patterning of tongue position for /s/ production accordingly facilitates the treatment of /s/ as a highly gendered sociophonetic variable.

Acoustic measurements have also proven useful in analyses of Spanish /s/ weakening (e.g., *pasta* 'paste' realized as [ˈpah.ta]), a phenomenon that has been linked with a range of social meanings. Although the phenomenon has generally been explored auditorily, with listener judgments defining the boundaries of the traditional variants [s], [h], and ø (e.g., Cedergren 1973), Erker (2010), and File-Muriel & Brown (2011) suggest that instrumental measures (such as /s/

duration, COG, and voicelessness) are superior to categorical representations, accounting for more variance and more accurately reflecting nuanced patterns in the data. However, Brogan & Bolyanatz (2018) contend that instrumental measurements alone may obscure the social distribution and behavior of the variants. They find an ordinal approach to weakening that combines perceived variants and instrumental measures better captures the meaningful social distinctions in their data, simultaneously acknowledging the gradience inherent to lenition processes while also taking into account the psychological importance of the segment to speakers/listeners. Several studies have shown that the variants of /s/ evoke social meanings specific to the local communities in which they live, and a purely instrumental analysis may overlook the social significance of these ordinal categories to the population under investigation. For Mexican and Puerto Rican listeners, for example, the aspirated variant is associated with lower status and, for most listeners, greater heteronormativity, but these evaluations are filtered through regional stereotypes and listener expectations (Walker et al. 2014; Chappell 2019). Local norms can even influence the perception of the prestige variant; in Uruguay, where the "standard" [s] is negatively associated with border Spanish influenced by Portuguese, the "nonstandard" [h] is used as a marker of social prestige to evoke the cultural capital of Montevideo and the variety of Spanish spoken there (Carvalho 2006).

A range of social meanings linked to fricatives that are specific to the local context have been identified across languages, including work on interdental fricatives in Cajun and Newfoundland English (Dubois & Horvath 1998; Childs et al. 2010), h-dropping in Essex English (Cole 2020), /θ/-fronting in northern and southern British English (Schleef & Ramsammy 2013; Levon & Fox 2014), the deaffrication of /t͡ʃ/ in the Spanish of Chile and Huelva, Spain (Regan 2020b; Boomershine & Forgash 2021), rhotic assibilation and the bilabial fricative in Mexican Spanish (Rissel 1989; Robles-Puente & Vilches-Aguado 2019), and the loss of distinction between [ʃ] and [ç] in German (Jannedy & Weirich 2014). For example, Jannedy & Weirich's (2014) perception study demonstrated that listeners associate a particular merger in German (/ʃ/ and the [ç] allophone of /x/) with the Turkish German population. Although scholars have drawn on different theoretical frameworks to account for the relationship between social and linguistic factors, many recent sociophonetic studies, including those exploring fricative phenomena, have called upon indexicality to make sense of phonetic variants' social meanings (e.g., Chappell 2016). Phonetic variants that develop social meaning become signs, and the creation of a sign in turn creates orders of indexicality (Silverstein 2003), which can be thought of as points along a line of social meaning. The first order indexes a group of people, the second takes on a meaning related to this group, and the reconstrual of social meanings continues linearly in the third, fourth, fifth order, and so on, progressively taking on related social meanings. Indexical fields help capture the perpetual reconstrual of social meaning by displaying the range of possible "ideologically related meanings, any one of which can be activated in the situated use of the variable" (Eckert 2008:454).

Social meaning plays such a crucial role in linguistic variation and change that the behavior of certain fricatives seems to upend established linguistic theory. For instance, using demerger indices created for each speaker using COG, mean intensity, skewness, and variance, Regan (2020a) investigated the demerger of /s/ and /θ/ in Huelva and Lepe, Spain. Although Garde's Principle states that innovations can result in mergers but cannot demerge them (Garde 1961:38–39, as cited in Labov 1994:311–313) and, similarly, Herzog's Principle explains that "mergers expand at the expense of distinctions" (Herzog 1965, as cited in Labov 1994:313), Regan (2020a) demonstrates that under certain circumstances, such as large-scale societal changes and greater dialectal contact, /s/ and /θ/ can demerge. As a prestigious change from above, the demerger is being led by certain social groups like women, more educated individuals, younger speakers, and professionals with service-related positions.

Another widespread Spanish merger, that of /ʎ/ and /j/, has given rise to two salient and well-studied fricative processes in Argentinian and Uruguayan Spanish: *zheísmo* and *sheísmo*. Following the merger (e.g., *malla* 'mesh' and *maya* 'Maya' both became /maja/), the palatal fricative /j/ was strengthened to [ʒ] (*zheísmo*) and, in some regions like Buenos Aires, devoiced (*sheísmo*). The extent of this change in progress in Buenos Aires has been debated over the years; early studies found that devoicing was led by the lower and middle classes (Fontanella de Weinberg 1978), and more recently, Chang (2008) proposed the sound change had been completed among speakers born after 1975, who nearly categorically produced the voiceless variant across social groups. If the sound change had been completed, Rohena-Madrazo (2015) posited, the devoiced [ʃ] in Buenos Aires should behave like the voiceless /s/ in Spanish, which undergoes gradient voicing due to co-articulation. Using percent voicing to explore allophonic patterns, the comparison showed that only young, middle-class speakers produce similar voicing patterns for both fricatives, which suggests the change is complete only for this group, while other speakers continue to voice the prepalatal fricative more than /s/. This devoicing process serves as an excellent case study to evaluate different metrics of fricative voicing, which is taken up by Gradoville (2011) in his comparison of instrumental techniques and analysis of which technique best matches up with auditory coding of [ʃ] and [ʒ]. Examining fricative duration, percent voicing, harmonicity, relative intensity, and COG, Gradoville concludes that percent voicing is one of the most reliable measurements of fricative voicing.

Why the fortition of /j/ and its subsequent devoicing has taken place in River Plate Spanish and not in other varieties harkens back to the actuation problem (Weinreich, Labov & Herzog 1968). An attempt to solve the problem has centered around fricatives in recent years, namely work on /s/ retraction (e.g., *street* becomes more like [ʃtɹit]), which takes place across several varieties of English. In their work on American English, Baker, Archangeli & Mielke (2011) argue that the presence of interspeaker phonetic variation in a particular community (i.e., retractors and non-retractors) facilitates listener perception of a phonetically motivated co-articulatory phenomenon as a new production target, which can then spread socially throughout the community. However, Harrington et al.'s (2018) interactive-phonetic model, when applied to Stevens & Harrington's (2016) /s/-backing data from Australian English, contrasts with the notion that variants spread socially through a community due to preferential accommodation (Giles, Taylor & Bourhis 1973). Rather, they contend that stable phonetic biases can be converted into sound changes through more general speech properties as a result of individuals in contact with each other, a process that is more automatic in nature than social.

In addition to highlighting several different methods applied to the investigation of fricatives across languages, the studies outlined in this section have drawn attention to important ongoing debates, namely, the origination of phonetic change and the constraints that condition its social diffusion. Through this very brief literature review, we have seen that the complexities of fricative phenomena allow for a rich investigation of the interaction between social and linguistic forces.

Homing in on intervocalic /s/ voicing in Spanish

Though Spanish /s/ is most often investigated with respect to its possible aspiration or elision (Chappell 2016:361), its voicing constitutes another rich source of sociophonetic variation. Spanish voiceless alveolar [s] and voiced alveolar [z] are prescriptively found in complementary distribution for the lone alveolar fricative phoneme /s/, with [z] being restricted to contexts of a following voiced (semi)consonant (e.g., *desde* 'since/from,' *isla* 'island,' *los huecos* 'the holes,' *las hierbas* 'the herbs') as a product of regressive voicing assimilation (Hualde 2014:154–155).

In the remaining contexts, including intervocalic position, Spanish /s/ is systematically realized as [s] (e.g., *sopa* 'soup,' *casa* 'house,' *pasta* 'pasta,' *comes* 'you eat'), with [z] being described as "abnormal and sporadic" (Navarro Tomás 1918:83 [authors' translation]). Nevertheless, empirical research on Spanish /s/ across several varieties (e.g., Peninsular Spanish [Campos-Astorkiza 2014], Mexico City Spanish [Schmidt & Willis 2011], Highland Colombian Spanish [García 2013], and Quito Spanish [Strycharczuk et al. 2014]) has revealed that this categorical presence of [z] before voiced (semi)consonants and [s] everywhere else is merely an idealized characterization of the actual phonetic variability that exists in real speech, which instead boasts both voiceless and voiced productions in all contexts. As Clegg & Strong (1992:32) note, "There is no question as to the existence of the phenomena of sporadic voicing of /s/ in all positions and extensive voicing in some speech communities."

This more sporadic characterization of /s/ voicing, outside the context of a following voiced (semi)consonant (e.g., intervocalic position), is traditionally characterized as a result of endogenous or language-internal tendencies (Obaid 1973; Torreblanca 1978). Indeed, the variable voicing and devoicing of alveolar fricatives has been touted as a diachronically natural fluctuation in Romance, evidenced for example in the evolution of 'house' from Latin (/kasa/) to Old Spanish (/kaza/) to Modern Spanish (/kasa/) (Penny 2002:98–103; Hualde & Prieto 2014:111). In intervocalic contexts, the voicing of /s/ to [z] can be characterized as a product of lenition, modeled within a framework of gestural phonology (Browman & Goldstein 1989) as a consequence of conflicting laryngeal gestures for [s] (vocal fold abduction) and a following voiced vowel (vocal fold adduction), which can give rise to gestural blending that results in a single vocal fold adduction gesture that gradiently extends into the /s/ segment, yielding voiced [z] (Romero 1999; Campos-Astorkiza 2014:19; Hualde 2014:107). Faster speech rates and more casual speech styles have often been linked to greater voicing rates (Torreira & Ernestus 2012; García 2013; Strycharczuk et al. 2014; Chappell & García 2017; García 2020), corroborating the characterization of sporadic voicing in monolingual varieties of Spanish (e.g., Mexico, Spain, El Salvador, Panama [Obaid 1973; Torreblanca 1978]) as a product of language-internal articulatory lenition. Alternatively, contact-induced motivations for intervocalic Spanish [z] have been posited for Spanish in contact with Catalan (Wesch 1997; Vann 2001; Davidson 2020, 2021), English (Teschner 1996; Schmidt 2008; Menke & Face 2012; Boomershine & Stevens 2021), and varieties of Quechua (Toscano Mateus 1953; Córdova 1996; Davidson 2019a), all of which posit phonemic /z/ in the contact language as a source for transfer into Spanish on the part of Spanish bilinguals.

A series of linguistic variables has been found to consistently mediate variation in Spanish intervocalic voicing, including word position (favoring greater voicing word-finally over word-initially and/or word-medially [Chappell 2011; Davidson 2014, 2019a, 2020, 2021; Hualde & Prieto 2014; Strycharczuk et al. 2014; Chappell & García 2017]), speech rate and style (favoring greater voicing in faster, more casual speech [Torreira & Ernestus 2012; García 2013; Strycharczuk et al. 2014; Chappell & García 2017; García 2020; Davidson 2020, 2021]), and stress (favoring greater voicing across unstressed syllables [Torreira & Ernestus 2012; Davidson 2014, 2019a, 2020, 2021; Chappell & García 2017; García 2020]), whereas the effects of other linguistic variables, such as word frequency and morphological status of /s/, have been less consistent (Chappell 2011; Torreira & Ernestus 2012; Davidson 2014).

On the other hand, social variables found to condition Spanish intervocalic [z] production vary widely by variety. For some variables, such as age, the direction of effect has been consistent across the varieties that exhibit sensitivity, such as greater voicing being uniformly favored among younger speakers in the Spanish of Loja, Ecuador (García 2020) and Barcelona, Spain (Davidson 2020, 2021). For other variables, such as gender, the direction of effect varies across varieties that show sensitivity, such as greater voicing by male speakers in San José Spanish, Madrid Spanish, and Loja Spanish (Torreira & Ernestus 2012; Chappell & García 2017; García 2020), in contrast with greater voicing by female speakers in Barcelona Spanish (Davidson 2020, 2021).

As regards the social meaning and perception of Spanish intervocalic [z], matched-guise research has recently been carried out for San José Spanish (Chappell 2016), Loja Spanish (García 2019), and Barcelona Spanish (Davidson 2019b). For listeners from San José, Costa Rica, the covert attitudes associated with intervocalic [z] varied significantly by speaker gender, such that an asymmetry in its indexical field was posited whereby male speakers who use [z] are afforded positive evaluations of niceness, localness, confidence, and masculinity, whereas female speakers using [z] are only afforded negative associations of lower education and lower social class. Given the different social meanings accessible to men and women in the indexical field of [z], men are argued to employ [z] more frequently for social gain, while women avoid it to eschew the more negative qualities [z] indexes for women (Chappell 2016:371). This asymmetrical gender-based indexicality was also found for listeners in Loja, Ecuador. Negative covert associations of lower social class and unpleasantness were afforded exclusively to female speakers using intervocalic [z], while affiliations of a more highland (i.e., from Cuenca or Quito) regional origin were afforded to both male and female speakers who use intervocalic [z], where systematic /s/ voicing takes place word-finally (García 2019:146). As such, intervocalic [z] may be an incoming change in progress led by younger Loja men in greater contact with speakers from Quito and Cuenca. Finally, in Barcelona, intervocalic [z] was found to be covertly associated with positive affiliations of Catalan bilingualism and local solidarity, consistent with a change in progress from below led by Catalan-dominant young female speakers (Davidson 2019b:59, 67).

As can be readily observed from the data presented to this point, a plethora of fricative phenomena have been explored across the world's languages, and scholars have applied a range of methods and theoretical approaches to their study. Crucial to the present chapter is the fact that fricative variants often become associated with social meaning. In the specific case of intervocalic /s/ voicing in Spanish that we have highlighted, the social meaning linked with a single variant differs across varieties of the same language. This complex background sets the stage for our case study on sociophonetic variation.

CASE STUDY   Cross-dialectal comparison of intervocalic /s/ voicing in Spanish

Given the geographic extension and social variability of intervocalic /s/ voicing, the variable offers a rich landscape for possible sociolinguistic inquiry, including the interplay between language-internal and language-external factors, language variation and change, and the connection between the social perception of [z] and its usage patterns in the speech community. As a case study in the nature of sociophonetic variation in fricatives, we provide a novel comparative analysis of intervocalic /s/ voicing across datasets exploring three varieties of Spanish: Barcelona Spanish, San José Spanish, and Loja Spanish. A dialectal comparison of this nature provides fruitful insights into the nature of this fricative process and, more specifically, the ways in which the fricative process intersects with social factors. Of particular relevance for the present paper will be gender-mediated variation, which uniquely links intervocalic /s/ production across distinct Spanish-speaking communities. We seek to answer the following question: How do sociolinguistic factors such as gender ultimately account for the divergent linguistic outcomes of a single linguistic variable across three related language varieties?

Methods

The data for this case study come from semi-spontaneous interview speech from each of the three varieties. The Barcelona Spanish dataset (Davidson 2021) consists of interviews with 48 speakers of Barcelona Spanish from two age groups: 18–30 and 48–60 year olds. The participants in this dataset fall along a continuum of bilingualism ranging from those who are Catalan-dominant to those who are Spanish-dominant, and the sample is balanced in terms of how many participants come from each language dominance group. The San José Spanish dataset (Chappell & García 2017) is composed of interviews with 18 natives of the province of San José, Costa Rica, who are evenly distributed (six speakers per group) among three age groups: under 30, 30–50, and over 54 years old. Finally, the Loja Spanish dataset (García 2020 forthcoming) includes interviews with 31 natives of Loja, Ecuador, relatively balanced between three age groups: under 30, 31–45, and 45–68 years old. All of the San José and Loja participants have Spanish as their first language and, while some have studied English or another language, none consider themselves fluent in English or any other language. All three datasets are balanced for gender, with equal numbers of male and female speakers.

For the San José and Loja datasets, 60 tokens containing intervocalic /s/ were extracted from each interview after the 10-minute mark of the sociolinguistic interview portion, where possible. Token extraction began after the 10-minute mark in hopes that the interviewees would feel more comfortable with the researcher at that point. Of the 60 tokens, 20 came from each of the three word positions: word-medial (e.g., *casa* 'house'), word-final (e.g., *cas agrio* 'bitter Costa Rican guava'), and word-initial (e.g., *la sopa* 'the soup'). In the case of the Barcelona dataset, 20 tokens of intervocalic /s/ balanced for word position (word-initial vs. word-final) and stress were extracted from each interview. The token extraction in the Barcelona dataset was limited to 20 tokens per speaker, as this was the highest number of tokens offered by all speakers that provided a perfectly balanced distribution of tokens per linguistic factor cell. In total, the analysis presented here includes 915 tokens from the San José dataset, 1387 tokens from the Loja dataset, and 960 tokens from the Barcelona dataset.

Following Gradoville (2011), we measure voicing in terms of the percentage of each token's voiced duration. First, we manually delimited the boundaries of each token of /s/ by examining the waveform and spectrogram to find the points where the aperiodic noise of the fricative begins and ends and the formants of the surrounding vowels disappear and appear. With the boundaries set, the total duration of the fricative was noted. The duration of voicing was then calculated by measuring the portions of the fricative that exhibited periodicity in the waveform and a voicing bar in the spectrogram. Finally, the total voicing duration was divided by the total fricative duration, resulting in percent voicing for each token.

The social factors modeled for all three varieties are gender and age, and language dominance is also incorporated for the Barcelona dataset. The linguistic factors examined consist of word position and stress only for the Barcelona data, and also preceding/following vowel and local speech rate for the San José and Loja data. Additionally, F2 and f0 were examined in the San José analysis. In all models, percent voicing served as the dependent variable and speaker was included as a random effect. The San José and Loja analyses employ inflated beta regression with mixed effects using the package gamlss (Rigby & Stasinopoulos 2005) in R (R Core Team 2022), while the Barcelona Spanish analysis employs mixed-effects linear regression using the lmer function in the lme4 package (Bates et al. 2015). The overall results and specific results for each dataset are briefly summarized in the following section. For complete model outputs for the Barcelona, San José, and Loja data, respectively, the reader should refer to Davidson (2021:109), Chappell & García (2017:23–24), and García (2020:449).

Results

Voicing across varieties

Figure 8.1 shows histograms of percent voicing for the Barcelona, San José, and Loja datasets. What is immediately obvious in all three histograms is that percent voicing does not constitute a normal distribution. Instead, we observe roughly a bimodal distribution in which there is a peak at 100 percent voicing and another peak around 0–30 percent voicing. Another notable aspect of the histograms is that in all three datasets there are no tokens that fall in the 90–99 percent voicing range. Interestingly, this gap between 90–99 percent voicing has also been found by other scholars who examine percent voicing in Spanish /s/ (e.g., Campos-Astorkiza 2014). This may be attributable to anatomical restrictions in that there is a threshold in which the vocal folds cannot cease vibration for such a short period of time, and thus an intervocalic /s/ that is near-fully voiced becomes fully voiced by default.

Crucial to note, as well, is the fact that the distribution of percent voicing in the three varieties is quite similar in terms of its bimodality. Given that Barcelona Spanish is a contact variety and San José and Loja Spanish are not, we might have expected the distributions to differ. Instead, we see that regardless of contact status, all varieties exhibit a bimodal distribution.

In the case of the Barcelona dataset, the significant social factors conditioning voicing are language dominance, age, and gender (see Davidson 2021). Higher rates of voicing are found in progressively more Catalan-dominant speakers, younger speakers, and among female speakers. More voicing is also found in /s/ between unstressed vowels, characteristic of a lenition or reduction process. Finally, there is significantly more voicing in word-final than word-initial contexts, indeed approaching a categorical absence of fully voiced [z] tokens in word-initial contexts for the majority of speakers, which notably coincides with the site of a phonemic /s/-/z/ voicing distinction in Catalan. This effect of word position interacts with participant language dominance and age, with the strongest effect of word position being found in younger speakers and those with the most exposure to and use of Catalan.

Given the extensive and systematic use of intervocalic /s/ voicing by all Barcelona bilinguals, even those that are Spanish-dominant, this feature appears to be an important regional marker of Catalonian

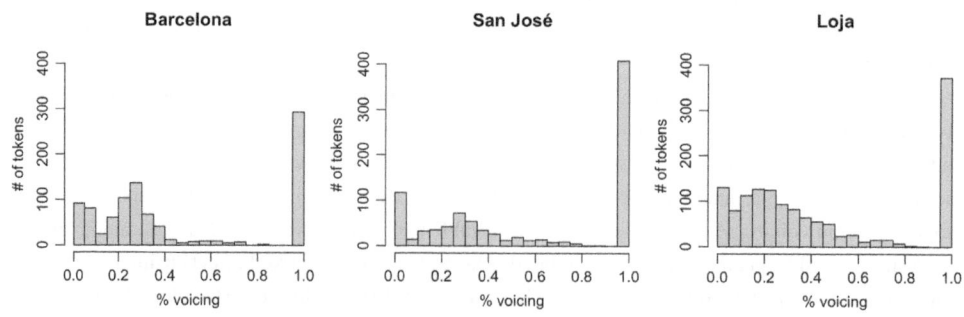

Figure 8.1 Histograms of percent voicing for Barcelona, San José, and Loja

Spanish. Furthermore, because higher rates are found in female speakers and younger speakers, this may represent a change in progress from below. Voicing in this variety lacks overt awareness and negative social stigma, which allows it to take on exclusively positive associations of a bilingual identity and solidarity, in contrast with other phonetic features, like lateral velarization, which align more closely with an overtly negative sociolinguistic stereotype (Davidson 2019b, 2022).

In San José Spanish, as in Barcelona Spanish, intervocalic [z] resembles a reduction process, as higher rates of voicing are found at higher speech rates and between unstressed vowels (see Chappell & García 2017). Additionally, there is more voicing in word-final contexts and there is no effect of preceding/following vowel in the San José data. Finally, because there is no observable effect of participant age, voicing seems to be a case of stable variation in San José Spanish as opposed to a sound change in progress, although this should be confirmed with data from more participants. Finally, both gender and physiology were found to condition intervocalic /s/ voicing in San José Spanish. Greater voicing was observed among men and speakers with larger vocal tracts, which was indirectly established through F2.

As in Barcelona and San José Spanish, voicing can be considered a reduction process in Loja, as it is favored in faster speech rates, between unstressed vowels, and when followed by a non-high vowel (see García 2020). Voicing is also favored in word-initial and final contexts, which is not immediately suggestive of reduction, but the resyllabification of word-final intervocalic /s/ to the onset of a following syllable may encourage some degree of analogical blurring at the word boundary. Social factors also serve to condition intervocalic /s/ voicing in Loja; higher voicing rates were observed among men and younger speakers, which may be indicative of a change in progress led by young men.

To summarize the findings presented thus far, the distribution of percent voicing in the three varieties is quite similar, and we see that they also share some of the same conditioning factors. Voicing in all varieties is favored between unstressed vowels, indicative of a lenition process as a result of gestural blending. On the other hand, the results for word position do differ somewhat, with voicing favored in only word-final contexts in Barcelona and San José Spanish, while it is favored in both word-final and initial contexts in Loja Spanish.

The results for age in Barcelona and Loja coincide, with more voicing among younger speakers, but the effect of age is not significant in the San José data. This suggests, based on the apparent-time construct (e.g., Bailey 2004), that intervocalic /s/ voicing may be a change in progress in Barcelona and Loja, and may represent more stable variation in San José. In all instances, social and linguistic factors work together to condition voicing, but the specific factors at play depend on the dialect. For example, language contact with Catalan has facilitated intervocalic /s/ voicing's ongoing adoption in Barcelona Spanish and heavily restricted it from word-initial contexts that in Catalan preserve a phonemic voicing distinction, while in Loja Spanish, increased contact with neighboring Highland Ecuadorian dialects that have systematic voicing has promoted the propagation of systematic voicing into the Loja community.

Effects of gender in the three varieties

Given its crossdialectal importance with regard to intervocalic /s/ voicing and to fricative processes cross-linguistically, gender merits a more thorough exploration. The particular effect of gender on intervocalic /s/ voicing differs according to the variety, with voicing favored by female speakers

Figure 8.2   Boxplot of percent voicing by gender for Barcelona, San José, and Loja

in Barcelona and, conversely, favored by male speakers in San José and Loja. To examine this difference further, Figure 8.2 displays boxplots of percent voicing by gender for each of the three varieties.

These boxplots show us that gender patterns in Barcelona and Loja are essentially mirror images of each other. In Barcelona, female speakers have a wider range of voicing with a significantly higher median voicing than male speakers, while male speakers in Loja have a wider range of voicing with a significantly higher median voicing than female speakers. On the other hand, female and male speakers in San José have similar ranges of percent voicing, but the median voicing of males is significantly higher than that of females. The different gendered patterns observed in these datasets, even for dialects where voicing appears to be led by men, suggest that the "gender effect" warrants deeper scrutiny in order to fully understand both the range of voicing and median voicing.

Discussion

Certain linguistic factors related to articulatory phenomena condition intervocalic /s/ voicing similarly across Barcelona, San José, and Loja Spanish—for example, gestural blending results in greater voicing between unstressed vowels in each variety. However, the effect of gender is markedly distinct across these dialects, with women as the predominant voicers in Barcelona and men leading voicing in Loja and San José. Furthermore, even in Loja and San José, the particular gender patterns are not identical, as both women and men in San José exhibit the full range of voicing (0–100 percent), albeit with different median percent voicing, whereas only men in Loja demonstrate this same full range of voicing.

How, then, can we account for the emergence and spread of the same phonetic innovation, which exhibits such divergent behavior, across three varieties of the same language? In addition to the phonetically motivated /s/ to [z] reduction between vowels, particularly between unstressed vowels and word-finally, several scholars have proposed that the origin of some linguistic features may be the result of physiology. For example, palatal morphology can affect individuals' realizations of the /s/-/ʃ/ contrast in German (Weirich & Fuchs 2013) and, in the case of intervocalic consonant voicing, larger vocal tracts hinder the rapid cessation of vocal fold vibration between vowels (Nadeu & Hualde 2014), resulting in greater gestural overlap in men's speech, who tend to have larger vocal tracts. In San José Spanish, vocal tract size and gender (male or female) were both found to condition intervocalic

/s/ voicing similarly, with vocal tract size offering a slightly better fit for the data in model construction (Chappell & García 2017). However, distinguishing between gender-based social motivations and physiological motivations is a tall order, as these categories tend to overlap and intersect, and other conditioning factors beyond physiology likely play a role as well. This disjuncture between physiology and productions has been identified in other aspects of articulation; for example, Fuchs et al. (2015) contend that f0 declination in German (and likely in other languages) is not purely rooted in breathing; this physiological factor appears to interact with speech style and pragmatic communicative constraints.

Although physiological explanations (men with larger vocal tracts exhibit greater voicing) and general lenition tendencies (greater reduction takes place between unstressed vowels) may account, to some extent, for the behavior of intervocalic /s/ voicing in San José and Loja Spanish, this argument is especially complicated by the Barcelona data. In Barcelona, women produce greater rates of [z], belying the notion that intervocalic /s/ voicing pervades men's speech more than women's as a consequence of having originated physiologically in male vocal tracts. Additionally, a comparison of voicing patterns in San José and Loja demonstrates differences as well, with more gradient voicing in Loja and more categorical voicing in San José.

Sociophonetic perception studies can shed light on the social meaning (or lack thereof) motivating the behavior of the same phonetic variants in different environments. Based on perception studies of intervocalic /s/, we argue that differing local societal conditions and norms give rise to the distinct gender patterns observed in our datasets. What appears to originate as a result of phonetic, physiological, or phonological factors (that is, the result of articulatory forces, the body, or bilingualism) becomes imbued with social meaning specific to the local context, instantiating three unique trajectories. In San José Spanish, /s/ voicing represents stable variation that has become associated with male speakers, whereby male speakers that use [z] are perceived as nicer, local, confident, and masculine, and female speakers using [z] are heard as less educated and from a lower social class (Chappell 2016). Accordingly, female speakers tend to avoid this variant, as its use triggers negative associations among local listeners.

By contrast, apparent-time analyses in Barcelona and Loja Spanish suggest a change in progress may be taking place. As such, the different indexical fields that are emerging for the variable in each locality influence how the change progresses and patterns in the broader social fabric. For Barcelona, the indexical field of intervocalic [z] features exclusively positive associations with bilingualism and local solidarity, which sanction its gradual adoption in the speech community, unlike other phonetic markers of Catalonian Spanish that are the topic of overt social ridicule (Davidson 2019b, 2021). In Loja, men's use of intervocalic [z] is seen as unnoteworthy and is not strongly associated with most of the social characteristics examined, while intervocalic [z] makes female speakers sound less pleasant, lower status, and younger (García 2019). Additionally, this variable serves as a marker of regional identity, with voicing being associated with neighboring Highland Ecuadorian dialects (Cuenca and Quito) that exhibit systematic voicing. García (2020) hypothesizes that young men are the leaders of this change, largely due to the fact that they are in greater contact with these highland varieties. Looking at the intersection of age and gender, she shows that the mean voicing rates of females are roughly two age groups behind those of males; in other words, it is not necessarily the case that Loja women are avoiding voicing like the San José women, but rather that they are further behind in the adoption of the incoming variant. In both communities, Barcelona and Loja, this variable is not particularly salient for naive native speakers. Regardless of its salience, the hyper-local interaction with gender still dictates unique production patterns and social meanings.

Silverstein's (2003) orders of indexicality may further clarify the directionality of the development of intervocalic [z] across these varieties: in San José, intervocalic [z] came to be associated with men and later adopted social meanings frequently associated with men in the region, including localness, confidence, and masculinity. In Barcelona, intervocalic [z] indexes a local Barcelona identity, and the variant then acquires positive associations with bilingualism and cultural pride. Unlike San José Spanish, where [z] became intertwined with masculinity and ideologically connected characteristics, essentially precluding the variant's use among women, women in Barcelona were able to harness the cultural capital of intervocalic [z], which could be used to signal their local pride and fluency in Catalan. Finally, intervocalic [z] in Loja appears to be less advanced along the linear order of indexicalities, mainly evoking evaluations of regional highland identity, and young men appear to be producing greater rates of voicing as a result of greater contact with Highland Ecuadorian Spanish speakers from places outside of Loja. In time, intervocalic [z] in Loja may become associated with other social qualities linked with Highland Ecuadorian Spanish speakers or with young men in Loja. This remains to be seen, but what is clear is that the ideologically related meanings associated with intervocalic [z] across these varieties, their indexical fields (Eckert 2008), vary as a result of the social fabric in which each variant resides and stand to be continually reinterpreted through ongoing social interactions.

The future for fricatives

This concise literature review and case study have served to grapple with the complex push and pull between social and linguistic factors in the study of fricative phenomena and, more specifically, to home in on the local societal conditions that cause a single linguistic variable to evolve distinctly in different Spanish-speaking communities. While the novel case study has offered some insight into why gender patterning is quite different across the three varieties explored, it also suggests the need for more nuance in the way that we conceptualize social factors, such as gender, that have an influence on fricative phenomena.

Based on the types of data presented in the case study, we are limited to canonical conceptualizations and discussions of gender. Undoubtedly, the future of this field and what will advance the sociophonetic study of fricatives are more "third-wave" (Eckert 2012) studies that consider the role of gender and sexuality beyond fixed social categories. Indeed, it is not only the influence of gender that should be considered as a continuum rather than a dichotomy, but other social factors as well, such as age and social class (Eckert & McConnell-Ginet 1992). Approaching gender as a dynamic entity avoids many of the problematic assumptions that go hand in hand with more traditional accounts, for example, the unmotivated combination of vastly different men and vastly different women or the inability to account for individual identities, personae, or stances in the meaning-making endeavor.

More recent work on /s/ fronting has highlighted this point; for example, drag queens in San Francisco have been shown to alter the amplitude of /s/ as they visually transform themselves using makeup, wigs, and clothing into their feminine drag personae, showing the symbiosis of linguistic and visual presentation (Calder 2019). Zimman (2017) similarly demonstrates that transgender men lower f0 in the production of /s/ as a function of how long they have been undergoing testosterone therapy, ultimately arguing for a re-theoretization of gender as a fluid kind of sociolinguistic style. The ongoing, more third-wave reconceptualization of social categories as inherently gradient will inevitably need to reconcile, on the one hand, these fluid categories as integral to the highly dynamic process of linguistic variation and identity construction at the individual level with, on the other hand, community level, aggregate patterns of language variation and change that rise above the incredible diversity of social identities and processes of meaning construction of its individual speakers.

Acknowledgments

This project was funded by the University of Texas at San Antonio's Office of the Vice President for Research and Department of Modern Languages and Literatures, the Ohio State University Office of International Affairs, and the Tinker Foundation Field Research Grant. We would like to thank Terrell Morgan and Scott Schwenter for encouraging this analysis years ago, Maricel Quintero for her assistance recruiting Costa Rican Spanish speakers, the Garcia and Samaniego families for help recruiting Loja participants, as well as Gemma de Blas, Antonio Torres, Pilar Prieto, Mireia Trenchs-Parera, Aida Martori, and Clara Cervera for their assistance in recruiting Catalonian speakers. We also extend our heartfelt gratitude to our participants, who generously shared their time and voices with us.

References

Alvord, Scott M. (ed.). 2011. *Selected proceedings of the 5th Conference on Laboratory Approaches to Romance Phonology*. Cascadilla Proceedings Project.

Bailey, Guy. 2004. Real and apparent time. In J.K. Chambers, Peter Trudgill & Natalie Schilling-Estes (eds.), *The handbook of language variation and change*, 312–332. Blackwell.

Baker, Adam, Diana Archangeli & Jeff Mielke. 2011. Variability in American English s-retraction suggests a solution to the actuation problem. *Language Variation and Change* 23. 347–374. https://doi.org/10.1017/S0954394511000135

Bárkányi, Zsuzsanna and Zoltán G. Kiss. 2021. The perception of voicing contrast in assimilation contexts in minimal pairs: evidence from Hungarian. *Acta Linguistica Academica* 68(1–2). 207–229. https://doi.org/10.1556/2062.2021.00473

Bates, Douglas, Martin Mächler, Ben Bolker & Steve Walker. 2015. Fitting linear mixed-effects models using lme4. *Journal of Statistical Software* 67(1). 1–48. https://doi.org/10.18637/jss.v067.i01.

Blecua Falgueras, Beatriz & Assumpció Rost Bagudanch. 2015. Implicaciones perceptivas de la variación: la fricativa labiodenta*l*. *Revista Española de Lingüística* 45(1). 25–44.

Boomershine, Amanda & Stephanie Forgash. 2021. Social perception of the variable realization of /t͡ʃ/ in Chile. In Manuel Díaz-Campos & Sandro Sessarego (eds.), *Aspects of Latin American Spanish dialectology: In honor of Terrell A. Morgan*, 97–124. John Benjamins.

Boomershine, Amanda & Jon Stevens. 2021. Variable /s/-voicing by heritage Spanish speakers in the United States. In Eva Núñez-Méndez (ed.), *Sibilants in Spanish: Diachronic and sociolinguistic analysis*, 192–214. Routledge.

Broersma, Mirjam. 2010. Perception of final fricative voicing: Native and nonnative listeners' use of vowel duration. *Journal of the Acoustical Society of America* 127(3). 1636–1644. https://doi.org/10.1121/1.3292996

Brogan, Franny D. & Mariška Bolyanatz. 2018. A sociophonetic account of onset /s/ weakening in Salvadoran Spanish: Instrumental and segmental analyses. *Language Variation and Change* 30(2). 203–230. https://doi.org/10.1017/S0954394518000066

Browman, Catherine P. & Louis Goldstein. 1989. Articulatory gestures as phonological units. *Phonology* 6. 201–252. https://doi.org/10.1017/S0952675700001019

Calder, Jeremy. 2019. The fierceness of fronted /s/: Linguistic rhematization through visual transformation. *Language in Society* 48(1). 38–64. https://doi.org/10.1017/S004740451800115X

Campbell-Kibler, Kathryn. 2011. Intersecting variables and perceived sexual orientation in men. *American Speech* 86(1). 52–68. https://doi.org/10.1215/00031283-1277510

Campos-Astorkiza, Rebeka. 2014. Sibilant voicing assimilation in Peninsular Spanish as gestural blending. In Marie-Hélène Côté, Éric Mathieu & Shana Poplack (eds.), *Variation within and across Romance languages*, 17–38. John Benjamins.

Carvalho, Ana Maria. 2006. Spanish (s) aspiration as a prestige marker on the Uruguayan-Brazilian border. *Spanish in Context* 3(1). 85–114. https://doi.org/10.1075/sic.3.1.07car

Cedergren, Henrietta. 1973. *The interplay of social and linguistic factors in Panama*. PhD dissertation, Cornell University.

Chang, Charles. 2008. Variation in palatal production in Buenos Aires Spanish. *UC Berkeley Phonology Lab Annual Report (2008)* 55–64. https://doi.org/10.5070/P72384g5v5

Chappell, Whitney. 2011. The intervocalic voicing of /s/ in Ecuadorian Spanish. In Jim Michnowicz & Robin Dodsworth (eds.), *Selected proceedings of the 5th Workshop on Spanish Sociolinguistics*, 57–64. Cascadilla Proceedings Project.

Chappell, Whitney. 2016. On the social perception of intervocalic /s/ voicing in Costa Rican Spanish. *Language Variation and Change* 28(3). 357–378. https://doi.org/10.1017/S0954394516000107

Chappell, Whitney. 2019. Caribeño or mexicano, profesionista or albañil? Mexican listeners' evaluations of /s/ aspiration and maintenance in Mexican and Puerto Rican voices. *Sociolinguistic Studies* 12. 367–393.

Chappell, Whitney & Christina García. 2017. Variable production and indexical social meaning: On the potential physiological origin of intervocalic /s/ voicing in Costa Rican Spanish. *Studies in Hispanic and Lusophone Linguistics* 10(1). 1–37. https://doi.org/10.1515/shll-2017-0001

Childs, Becky, Paul De Decker, Rachel Deal, Tyler Kendall, Jennifer Thorburn, Maia Williamson & Gerard Van Herk. 2010. Stop signs: The intersection of interdental fricatives and identity in Newfoundland. *University of Pennsylvania Working Papers in Linguistics* 16(2). 26–35. https://repository.upenn.edu/pwpl/vol16/iss2/5

Clegg, J. Halvor & Robert M. Strong. 1992. Assimilation of the phoneme /s/ in Spanish. In Eric L. Pederson (ed.), *Proceedings of the Deseret Language and Linguistic Society 1992 Symposium*, 31–34. Deseret Language and Linguistics Society.

Cole, Amanda. 2020. Co-variation, style and social meaning: The implicational relationship between (H) and (ING) in Debden, Essex. *Language Variation and Change* 32(3). 349–371. https://doi.org/10.1017/S0954394520000162

Cole, Ronald A. & William E. Cooper. 1975. Perception of voicing in English affricates and fricatives. *Journal of the Acoustical Society of America* 58(6). 1280–1287.

Córdova, Carlos Joaquín. 1996. Ecuador. In Manuel Alvar (ed.), *Manual de dialectología hispánica: el español de América*, 184–195. Editorial Ariel.

Davidson, Justin. 2014. A comparison of fricative voicing and lateral velarization phenomena in Barcelona: A variationist approach to Spanish in Contact with Catalan. *Romance Languages and Linguistic Theory* 6. 223–244. https://doi.org/10.1075/rllt.6.11dav

Davidson, Justin. 2019a. Intervocalic /s/ voicing in Andean Spanish: Problematizing the assessment of contact-induced change. In Gregory L. Thompson & Scott M. Alvord (eds.), *Contact, community, and connections: Current approaches to Spanish in multilingual populations*, 111–146. Vernon Press.

Davidson, Justin. 2019b. Covert and overt attitudes towards Catalonian Spanish laterals and intervocalic fricatives. In Whitney Chappell (ed.), *Recent advances in the study of Spanish sociophonetic perception*, 39–84. John Benjamins. https://doi.org/10.1075/ihll.21.03dav

Davidson, Justin. 2020. Asymmetry and directionality in Catalan-Spanish contact: Intervocalic fricatives in Barcelona and Valencia. *Languages* 5(4). 60. https://doi.org/10.3390/languages5040060

Davidson, Justin. 2021. Intervocalic /s/-voicing in Spanish in contact with Catalan. In Eva Núñez-Méndez (ed.), *Sibilants in Spanish: Diachronic and sociolinguistic analysis*, 95–127. Routledge.

Davidson, Justin. 2022. On Catalan as a minority language: The case of Catalan laterals in Barcelonan Spanish. *Journal of Sociolinguistics* 26(3). 362–385. https://doi.org/10.1111/josl.12545W

Dubois, Sylvie & Barbara M. Horvath. 1998. Let's tink about dat: Interdental fricatives in Cajun English. *Language Variation and Change* 10(3). 245–261. https://doi.org/10.1017/S0954394500001320

Eckert, Penelope. 2008. Variation and the indexical field. *Journal of Sociolinguistics* 12(4). 453–476. https://doi.org/10.1111/j.1467-9841.2008.00374.x

Eckert, Penelope. 2012. Three waves of variation study: The emergence of meaning in the study of sociolin-guistic variation. *Annual Review of Anthropology* 41. 87–100. https://doi.org/10.1146/annurev-anthro-092 611-145828

Eckert, Penelope & Sally McConnell-Ginet. 1992. Think practically and look locally: Language and gender as community-based practice. *Annual Review of Anthropology* 21. 461–490. https://doi.org/10.1146/annu rev.an.21.100192.002333

Erker, Daniel. 2010. A subsegmental approach to coda /s/ weakening in Dominican Spanish. *International Journal of the Sociology of Language* 203. 9–26. https://doi.org/10.1515/ijsl.2010.019

File-Muriel, Richard J. & Earl K. Brown. 2011. The gradient nature of s-lenition in Caleño Spanish. *Language Variation and Change* 23(2). 223–243. https://doi.org/10.1017/S0954394511000056

Fontanella de Weinberg, María Beatriz. 1978. Un cambio lingüístico en marcha: las palatales del español bonaerense. *Orbis* 27. 215–247.

Fuchs, Susanne, Caterina Petrone, Amélie Rochet-Capellan, Uwe D. Reichel & Laura L. Koenig. 2015. Assessing respiratory contributions to f0 declination in German across varying speech tasks and respira-tory demands. *Journal of Phonetics* 52. 35–45. https://doi.org/10.1016/j.wocn.2015.04.002

García, Allison. 2013. *Allophonic variation in the Spanish sibilant fricative*. PhD dissertation, University of Wisconsin-Milwaukee.

García, Christina. 2019. Social evaluation of intervocalic /s/ voicing in Ecuadorian Spanish. In Whitney Chappell (ed.), *Recent advances in the study of Spanish sociophonetic perception*, 125–152. John Benjamins. https://doi.org/10.1075/ihll.21.05gar

García, Christina. 2020. Seeds of change: Social factors conditioning intervocalic /s/ voicing in Loja, Ecuador. *Spanish in Context* 17(3). 438–463. https://doi.org/10.1075/sic.19012.gar

García, Christina. Forthcoming. Phonetic and social forces in interaction: Intervocalic /s/ voicing in Lojano Spanish. In Rosario Gómez, Erin O'Rourke & Christina García (eds.), *Ecuadorian Spanish in the 21st century: Historical and contemporary perspectives*. Cambridge Scholars Publishing.

Garde, Paul. 1961. Réflexions sur les différences phonétiques entre les langues slaves. *Word* 17(1). 34–62. https://doi.org/10.1080/00437956.1961.11659746

Giles, Howard, Donald M. Taylor & Richard Y. Bourhis. 1973. Towards a theory of interpersonal accommo-dation through speech: Some Canadian data. *Language in Society* 2. 177–192. https://doi.org/10.1017/ S0047404500000701

Gradoville, Michael S. 2011. Validity in measurements of fricative voicing: Evidence from Argentine Spanish. In Alvord, 59–74.

Gradoville, Michael S., Earl K. Brown & Richard J. File-Muriel. 2022. The phonetics of sociophonetics: Validating acoustic approaches to Spanish /s/ realization. *Journal of Phonetics* 91. https:// doi.org/10.1016/j.wocn.2021.101125

Harrington, Jonathan, Felicitas Kleber, Ulrich Reubold, Florian Schiel & Mary Stevens. 2018. Linking cog-nitive and social aspects of sound change using agent-based modeling. *Topics in Cognitive Science* 10. 707–728. https://doi.org/10.1111/tops.12329

Herzog, Marvin I. 1965. *The Yiddish language in northern Poland: Its geography and history*. Indiana University.

Hualde, José Ignacio. 2014. *Los sonidos del español*. Cambridge University Press.

Hualde, José Ignacio & Pilar Prieto. 2014. Lenition of intervocalic alveolar fricatives in Catalan and Spanish. *Phonetica* 71(2). 109–127. https://doi.org/10.1159/000368197

Jannedy, Stephanie & Melanie Weirich. 2014. Sound change in an urban setting: Category instability of the palatal fricative in Berlin. *Laboratory Phonology* 5(1). 91–122. https://doi.org/10.1515/lp-2014-0005

Jannedy, Stephanie, Melanie Weirich, Jane Brunner & Micaela Mertins. 2010. Perceptual evidence for allo-phonic variation of the palatal fricative [ç] in spontaneous Berlin German. *Journal of the Acoustical Society of America* 128(4). 2458. https://doi.org/10.1121/1.3508800

Jesus, Luis M.T. & Christine H. Shadle. 2002. A parametric study of the spectral characteristics of European Portuguese fricatives. *Journal of Phonetics* 30(3). 437–464. https://doi.org/10.1006/jpho.2002.0169

Jongman, Allard. 1989. Duration of frication noise required for identification of English fricatives. *Journal of the Acoustical Society of America* 85(4). 1718–1725. https://doi.org/10.1121/1.397961

Jongman, Allard, Ratree Wayland & Serena Wong. 2000. Acoustic characteristics of English fricatives. *Journal of the Acoustical Society of America* 108(3). 1252–1263. https://doi.org/10.1121/1.1288413

Kendall, Tyler & Valerie Fridland. 2021. *Sociophonetics*. Cambridge University Press.

Labov, William. 1994. *Principles of linguistic change*, vol. 1, *Internal factors*. Blackwell.

Levon, Erez. 2014. Categories, stereotypes, and the linguistic perception of sexuality. Language in Society 43(5). 539–566. https://doi.org/10.1017/S0047404514000554

Levon, Erez & Sue Fox. 2014. Social salience and the sociolinguistic monitor: A case study of ING and TH-fronting in Britain. *Journal of English Linguistics* 42(3). 185–217. https://doi.org/10.1177/007542421 4531487

Levon, Erez & Sophie Holmes-Elliott. 2013. East End boys and West End girls: /s/-fronting in Southeast England. *University of Pennsylvania Working Papers in Linguistics* 19(2). 111–120. https://repository. upenn.edu/pwpl/vol19/iss2/13

Li, Fangfang, Jan Edwards & Mary Beckman. 2007. Spectral measures for sibilant fricatives of English, Japanese, and Mandarin Chinese. In William J. Barry & Jürgen Trouvain (eds.), *Proceedings of the XVIth International Congress of Phonetic Sciences*, 917–920. Universität des Saarlandes.

Mack, Sara & Benjamin Munson. 2012. The influence of /s/ quality on ratings of men's sexual orientation: Explicit and implicit measures of the "gay lisp" stereotype. *Journal of Phonetics* 40(1). 198–212. https://doi.org/10.1016/j.wocn.2011.10.002

Mann, Virginia & Siegfried D. Soli. 1991. Perceptual order and the effect of vocalic context on fricative perception. *Perception & Psychophysics* 49(5). 399–411. https://doi.org/10.3758/BF03212174

Menke, Mandy & Timothy Face. 2012. Acquisition of /s/ by second language learners of Spanish. Paper presented at *Current Approaches to Spanish and Portuguese Second Language Phonology (CASPSLaP 2012)*. University of South Carolina.

Minnick Fox, Michelle Annette. 2006. *Usage-based effects in Latin American Spanish syllable-final /s/ lenition*. PhD dissertation, University of Pennsylvania.

Nadeu, Mariana and José Ignacio Hualde. 2014. Biomechanically conditioned variation at the origin of diachronic intervocalic voicing. *Language and Speech* 58(3). 351–370. https://doi.org/10.1177/002383091 4554727

Nance, Claire & Jane Stuart-Smith. 2013. Pre-aspiration and post-aspiration in Scottish Gaelic stop consonants. *Journal of the International Phonetic Association* 43(2). 129–152. https://doi.org/10.1017/ S0025100313000042

Navarro Tomás, Tomás. 1918. *Manual de pronunciación española*. Imprenta de los Sucesores de Hernando.

Obaid, Antonio H. 1973. The vagaries of the Spanish "S." *Hispania* 56(1). 60–67.

Pape, Daniel, Luis M.T. Jesus & Peter Birkholz. 2015. Intervocalic fricative perception in European Portuguese: An articulatory synthesis study. *Speech Communication* 74. 93–103. https://doi.org/10.1016/ j.specom.2015.09.001

Penny, Ralph J. 2002. *A history of the Spanish language*. Cambridge University Press.

Pharao, Nicolai, Marie Maegaard, Janus Spindler Moller & Tore Kristiansen. 2014. Indexical meanings of [s+] among Copenhagen youth: Social perception of a phonetic variant in different prosodic contexts. *Language in Society* 43. 1–31. https://doi.org/10.1017/S0047404513000857

Podesva, Robert J. & Janneke Van Hofwegen. 2014. How conservatism and normative gender constrain variation in inland California: The case of /s/. *University of Pennsylvania Working Papers in Linguistics* 20(2). 129–137. https://repository.upenn.edu/pwpl/vol20/iss2/15

Podesva, Robert J. & Janneke Van Hofwegen. 2016. /s/exuality in smalltown California: Gender normativity and the acoustic realization of /s/. In Erez Levon & Ronald Beline Mendes (eds.), *Language, sexuality, and power*, 168–188. Oxford University Press.

R Core Team. 2022. *R: A language and environment for statistical computing*. R Foundation for Statistical Computing. www.R-project.org

Regan, Brendan. 2020a. The split of a fricative merger due to dialect contact and societal changes: A sociophonetic study on Andalusian Spanish read-speech. *Language Variation and Change* 32(2). 159–190. https://doi.org/10.1017/S0954394520000113

Regan, Brendan. 2020b. Intra-regional differences in the social perception of allophonic variation: The evaluation of [tʃ] and [ʃ] in Huelva and Lepe (Western Andalucía). *Journal of Linguistic Geography* 8(2). 82–101. https://doi.org/10.1017/jlg.2020.7

Reidy, Patrick F. 2016. Spectral dynamics of sibilant fricatives are contrastive and language specific. *Journal of the Acoustical Society of America* 140(4). 2518–2529. https://doi.org/10.1121/1.4964510

Rigby, R.A. and Stasinopoulos, D.M. 2005. Generalized additive models for location, scale and shape. *Journal of the Royal Statistical Society: Series C (Applied Statistics)* 54. 507–554. https://doi.org/10.1111/ j.1467-9876.2005.00510.x

Rissel, Dorothy A. 1989. Sex, attitudes, and the assibilation of /r/ among young people in San Luis de Potosí, Mexico. *Language Variation and Change* 1(3). 269–283. https://doi.org/10.1017/S095439450 0000181

Robles-Puente, Sergio & José Jesús Vilches-Aguado. 2019. Bilabial fricatives in Mexican Spanish: A sociophonetic analysis. *Borealis: An International Journal of Hispanic Linguistics* 8(1). 143–161. https://doi.org/10.7557/1.8.1.4561

Rohena-Madrazo, Marcos. 2015. Diagnosing the completion of a sound change: Phonetic and phonological evidence for /ʃ/ in Buenos Aires Spanish. *Language Variation and Change* 27(3). 287–317. https://doi.org/10.1017/S0954394515000113

Romero, Joaquín. 1999. The effect of voicing assimilation on gestural coordination. In John J. Ohala, Yoko Hasegawa, Manjari Ohala, Daniel Granville & Ashlee C. Bailey (eds.), *Proceedings of the 14th International Congress of Phonetic Sciences*, 1793–1796. American Institute of Physics.

Ruch, Hanna & Jonathan Harrington. 2014. Synchronic and diachronic factors in the change from pre-aspiration to post-aspiration in Andalusian Spanish. *Journal of Phonetics* 45(1). 12–25. https://doi.org/10.1016/j.wocn.2014.02.009

Schleef, Erik & Michael Ramsammy. 2013. Labiodental fronting of /θ/ in London and Edinburgh: A cross-dialectal study. *English Language and Linguistics* 17(1). 25–54. https://doi.org/10.1017/S136067431 2000317

Schmidt, Lauren B. 2008. Acquisition of voice assimilation of sibilant /s/ in Spanish as a second language. Paper presented at the 10th Hispanic Linguistics Symposium, University of Western Ontario, October 19–22.

Schmidt, Lauren B. & Erik W. Willis. 2011. Systematic investigation of voicing assimilation of Spanish /s/ in Mexico City. In Alvord, 1–20.

Shadle, Christine H. & Sheila J. Mair. 1996. Quantifying spectral characteristics of fricatives. *Proceedings of the International Conference on Spoken Language Processing (ICSLP 96)*. 1517–1520.

Silverstein, Michael. 2003. Indexical order and the dialectics of sociolinguistic life. *Language & Communication* 23(3–4). 193–229. https://doi.org/10.1016/S0271-5309(03)00013-2

Smith, Bridget J. 2013. Eth and theta: A tale of two phonemes. Unpublished manuscript.

Stevens, Kenneth N., Sheila E. Blumstein, Laura Glicksman, Marth Burton & Kathleen Kurowski. 1992. Acoustic and perceptual characteristics of voicing in fricatives and fricative clusters. *Journal of the Acoustical Society of America* 91(5). 2979–3000. https://doi.org/10.1121/1.402933

Stevens, Mary & Jonathan Harrington. 2016. The phonetic origins of /s/-retraction: Acoustic and perceptual evidence from Australian English. *Journal of Phonetics* 58. 118–134. https://doi.org/10.1016/j.wocn.2016.08.003

Strycharczuk, Patrycja, Marijn Van't Veer, Martine Bruil & Kathrin Linke. 2014. Phonetic evidence on phonology-morphosyntax interactions. *Journal of Linguistics* 50(2). 403–452. https://doi.org/10.1017/S0022226713000157

Stuart-Smith, Jane. 2007. Empirical evidence for gendered speech production: /s/ in Glaswegian. In Jennifer Cole & José Ignacio Hualde (eds.), *Laboratory Phonology 9*, 65–86. De Gruyter Mouton.

Stuart-Smith, Jane. 2020. Changing perspectives on /s/ and gender over time in Glasgow. *Linguistics Vanguard* 6(1). 20180064. https://doi.org/10.1515/lingvan-2018-0064

Teschner, Richard V. 1996. *Camino oral: fonética, fonología y práctica de los sonidos del español*. McGraw-Hill.

Thomas, Erik R. 2011. *Sociophonetics: An introduction*. Palgrave.

Thomas, Erik R. 2016. Sociophonetics of consonantal variation. *Annual Review of Linguistics* 2. 95–113. https://doi.org/10.1146/annurev-linguistics-011415-040534

Torreblanca, Máximo. 1978. El fonema /s/ en la lengua española. *Hispania* 61(3). 498–503. https://doi.org/10.2307/341080

Torreira, Francisco & Mirjam Ernestus. 2012. Weakening of intervocalic /s/ in the Nijmegen Corpus of Casual Spanish. *Phonetica* 69(3). 124–148. https://doi.org/10.1159/000343635

Toscano Mateus, Humberto. 1953. *El español en el Ecuador*. Revista de Filología España, Anejo LXI.

van Son, Rob J.J.H. & Jan P.H. van Santen. 2005. Duration and spectral balance of intervocalic consonants: A case for efficient communication. *Speech Communication* 47(1–2). 100–123. https://doi.org/10.1016/j.specom.2005.06.005

Vann, Robert. 2001. El castellà catalanitzat a Barcelona: perspectives lingüístiques i culturals. *Catalan Review* 15(1). 117–131.

Walker, Abby, Christina García, Yomi Cortés & Kathryn Campbell-Kibler. 2014. Comparing social meanings across listener and speaker groups: The indexical field of Spanish /s/. *Language Variation and Change* 26(2). 169–189. https://doi.org/10.1017/S0954394514000088

Weinreich, Uriel, William Labov & Marvin Herzog. 1968. Empirical foundations for a theory of language change. In Winifred P. Lehmann & Yakov Malkiel (eds.), *Directions for historical linguistics: A symposium*, 95–195. University of Texas Press.

Weirich, Melanie & Susanne Fuchs. 2013. Palatal morphology can influence speaker-specific realizations of phonemic contrasts. *Journal of Speech, Language, and Hearing Research* 56(6). 1894–1908. https://doi.org/10.1044/1092-4388(2013/12-0217)

Wesch, Andreas. 1997. El castellano hablado de Barcelona y el influjo del catalán: esbozo de un programa de investigación. *Anuario Galego de Filoloxía* 24. 287–312.

Widdison, Kirk A. 1997. Phonetic explanations for sibilant patterns in Spanish. *Lingua* 102(4). 253–264. https://doi.org/10.1016/S0024-3841(97)00006-5

Zimman, Lal. 2017. Gender as stylistic bricolage: Transmasculine voices and the relationship between fundamental frequency and /s/. *Language in Society* 46(3). 339–370. https://doi.org/10.1017/S0047404517000070

9

SOCIOPHONETICS AND RHOTICS

Koen Sebregts, Roeland van Hout, and Hans Van de Velde

Introduction

Rhotics display a large amount of phonetic variation, and for this reason readily lend themselves to becoming sociolinguistic variables, in many language varieties. Rhotic variability has been shown to play a role in sociolinguistic variation within and between speech communities, from Labov's (2006[1966]) landmark department store study onwards. Labov's study was on a relatively coarse-grained level, involving the presence versus absence of post-vocalic *r*. Several other famous rhotic variation studies have been on a similarly coarse-grained, discrete level, such as the variation between alveolar and uvular *r*. More recently, a growing number of rhotic variation studies demonstrate that even fine phonetic detail has the potential to be picked up by speakers/listeners and utilized in socially relevant ways. Apart from the high propensity for rhotics to be synchronically variable, they are also involved in many historical and ongoing sound changes (and indeed these two types of variation are not independent of each other). Sound changes where rhotics play a role involve both those that target the rhotic itself and those where the immediate context (often, the preceding vowel) is the target. Outside of sociophonetics proper, rhotics are studied by phonologists, acquisitionists, and typologists, among others, illustrating the many relevant links between these and related fields with sociophonetics.

"All sounds are variable, but some are more variable than others," as Scobbie (2006:337) put it. The large amount of variability among the group of sounds classed as "rhotics" has been remarked upon by many linguists over the years, both in terms of trying to define or delimit the class—the question being: What is a rhotic?—and in terms of describing the synchronic patterns of variation displayed by the category, or phoneme, /r/ in various languages. These two questions of rhotic variability are rarely considered in conjunction, the former being largely a language typological concern (though not an unimportant debate for theoretical phonologists either), and the latter one for those with a more descriptive focus, from phonologists analyzing a particular pattern of allophony to sociolinguists investigating patterns of variation and change. That said, studying the phonetic and phonological particulars of rhotics runs into a problem that is likely unique to this class of sounds—that is, determining which sounds are, and which are not, included in it.

DOI: 10.4324/9781003034636-10

Even in this volume, a chapter on rhotics sits somewhat uneasily among others on phonological categories that relate directly to manners of articulation with phonetic definitions such as stops (Chodroff & Foulkes) and fricatives (Chappell, Garcia & Davidson) (although they each have a few complicated cases at the margins, of course). Even their closest cousins, the laterals (Turton), have nowhere near the definitional problems of the rhotic class.

Definitions of rhotics have been sought in the articulatory and acoustic domains, but a phonetic feature that is present in all sounds that have been given the rhotic label has so far not been found (Lindau 1985; Ladefoged & Maddieson 1996). Taps, trills, fricatives, and approximants have all been labeled rhotics in languages around the world, and there are languages where all these manners of articulation coexist as variants of a single /r/ phoneme—sometimes even produced by a single speaker (Sebregts 2015; Rennicke 2015). The lack of a phonetic property underpinning all rhotics has led phoneticians to propose that they are linked by a looser network of similarities (the Wittgensteinian "family resemblance" model of Lindau 1985), by diachronic connections (Barry 1997; Sebregts 2015), or indeed by orthographic convention (Ladefoged & Maddieson 1996). Phonologists, meanwhile, have proposed that rhotics need not be phonetically stable as long as they are phonologically so, either in terms of their abstract representation (Walsh Dickey 1997) or their outward phonological behavior, especially their role in phonotactics (Wiese 2001; Chabot 2019). It is important to note that these discussions are not only relevant for typologists and phonological theorists, but have a direct bearing on those working on processes of variation and, particularly, change, and they once again demonstrate the uniqueness of rhotics. Diachronically, of course, stops may change into fricatives, fricatives into approximants, nasals into stops; synchronically, these categories may display alternations with each other. However, if a particular speech sound in a particular language displays the articulatory and acoustic characteristics of an [s], it is rarely called into question whether that speech sound should indeed be analyzed as a fricative. Rhotics are trickier. An alveolar tap [ɾ] may be an allophone of /t/ in one language and consequently classed as a stop, and of /r/ in another, and classed as a rhotic; a [χ] may be a rhotic in one language and a fricative in another, and so on. Similarly, if a rhotic that was historically a trill or tap changes into a fricative or approximant, that change in manner of articulation does not usually lead to reassigning it to a different class.

While the above examples all concern manner of articulation, rhotics are also extremely variable in place of articulation. There are sounds classed as rhotics from labio-dental to pharyngeal, and everywhere in between. It shows that the category has fuzzy boundaries on all sides, and occasional debates come up surrounding particular members of the class. More than for other classes of sounds, rhotic classhood depends on arguments from outside the phonetic characteristics proper. As described above, these may be based on phonological behavior, historical connections, or orthography.

The large amount of rhotic variability is undoubtedly behind its potential as a sociolinguistic variable. Unlike most other consonants (and even more so than vowels) rhotics allow for a relatively large amount of intracategory modification without the danger of being misperceived. In fact, unlike the situation with vowels, relatively radical changes to *r* are possible without triggering changes to the entire consonant system. This relative realizational freedom gives ample opportunity for *r* variation to acquire indexical properties, and indeed it often does. As described below, in a number of languages particular *r* variants are associated with changes in progress. In a subset of these, it is not only the case that innovative variants are more frequently employed by a younger generation, but that several innovative variants coexist, serving to highlight diverging paths of change among social groups.

Literature review: *r*-processes and sociophonetic variation

This section highlights three processes involving *r* sounds that have recently featured prominently in the literature, and that demonstrate how important it is to study the social and the phonetic together: 1) the variation in place of articulation between apico-alveolar and uvular *r* variants, and in particular the substitution of the former by the latter; 2) the articulatory variation among approximant variants between retroflex (or "tip up") articulations and those involving a bunched tongue dorsum ("tip down"); 3) the emergence of new variants. A number of classic and recent studies on each of these processes are discussed below.

Trading places

Alveolar variants of *r* being replaced diachronically by uvular ones is a well-known historical process in a number of European languages. The questions of why and how alveolar variants of *r* come to be replaced by uvular ones have been taken up on a number of occasions by dialectologists, phoneticians, and phonologists. There is no lack of speech communities where alveolar *r* is the standard and where uvular realizations are regarded as speech defects (at least, by the wider public, if not by linguists), and indeed, children are sent to speech therapists to learn to produce an alveolar trill, or at least a tap. However, where uvular trills and fricatives have established themselves as acceptable variants, they are often seen to gradually take over as the more popular variant. This is particularly visible in Northwest Europe. In Danish, for instance, uvular and/or pharyngeal *r* variants are currently standard and dominant across dialects (Grønnum 1998). In European French and many varieties of German, including Standard German, uvular *r* is the dominant and/or standard, though alveolar realizations are still common in Swiss German (Ulbrich & Ulbrich 2007) and survives in some French dialects (Fougeron & Smith 1993). The process is ongoing in Belgian Dutch; alveolar *r* dominates and is largely considered standard, but uvular *r* is on the rise, both socially (after having previously been classed as a speech deficit) and geographically (Rogier 1994; Van de Velde 1996; Verhoeven 2005; Tops 2009; Van de Velde, Tops & van Hout 2013). In the Netherlands, meanwhile, uvular and alveolar *r* are both considered standard, the former increasingly dominant, though the situation is more complex due to the rapid rise of the coda approximant (see below). Uvular *r* is also either gaining ground in its perception as standard or has become dominant in coastal varieties of Norwegian and Southern Swedish (Muminovic & Engstrand 2001; Torp 2001). Outside of Northwest Europe, uvular *r* has established itself in Portuguese (including Brazilian Portuguese) (Mateus & d'Andrade 2000; Rennicke 2015), Puerto Rico Spanish (Lipski 1994), and Canadian (Quebec) French, which we discuss in a little more detail below. The ongoing shift from apical to dorsal variants in Quebec is well described and exemplifies a phase in the process of sound change that is well within the realm of traditional sociolinguistic study: the spreading of a sound change once it has been established as a competing variant, including an association with prestige (of particular urban centers or of particular social groups in which the change takes hold first) as a plausible explanation for its increasing adoption. At first blush it may in fact seem there is not much of particularly sociophonetic interest, although the wider sociolinguistic interest is obvious, but we will see that this first impression is mistaken.

While apical and dorsal *r* variants may have coexisted in Quebec for as long as three centuries, dorsal variants were largely confined to Eastern Quebec. In Montreal, the shift from alveolar to uvular variants being the norm (both in terms of dominance and in terms of being considered standard) took place over the course of the first three decades after the Second World War (Santerre 1978; Clermont & Cedergren 1979, as cited in Sankoff & Blondeau 2007). A number of studies have charted the ongoing change. Sankoff & Blondeau (2007) show that there is both a community-wide shift, with the incidence of uvular *r* increasing for every younger cohort, and, among a minority of individual speakers, change across the lifespan. While around two-thirds of the speakers in their panel study remained stable (most being either categorical or near-categorical alveolar or uvular *r* speakers), nine speakers, or just under a third of the sample, increased the proportion of uvular tokens among their *r* realizations between 1971 and 1984. Most of the speakers who increased their uvular *r* usage became near-categorical users of the innovative variant over this period of time. Their results for the most variable speakers suggest that there is at least some linguistic conditioning present, with prevocalic contexts favoring apical variants and uvular variants appearing alongside lenited/vocalic ones in codas. This is also the pattern found by Côté & Saint-Amant Lamy (2012) for their most variable speaker. Theirs is a study of a similar ongoing shift in Trois-Rivières, a city located between Montreal and Quebec City, indicated as the border between the apical and dorsal *r* areas in studies from the mid twentieth century (Sankoff, Blondeau & Charite 2001). The onset-coda allophony exhibited by variable speakers, in combination with the appearance of other, more lenited variants of *r* in codas, leads Sankoff & Blondeau to wonder to what extent the change conforms to established sociolinguistic patterns. Since the change from apical to dorsal *r* is in principle an abrupt change phonetically, it would not be unexpected for the phonological conditioning to be minimal—that is, for speakers to treat [r] and [ʀ] as discrete stylistic variants mainly related to levels of formality or standardness. In addition, the change is towards a high-prestige variant from the outside—a typical change from above. So if there is allophony, the more salient onset position might be expected to be the context that favors uvular *r*. Instead, the variant seems to "[creep] in through the back door" (Sankoff & Blondeau 2007:579). Here is where the specifically sociophonetic angle we identified above comes in: apart from the more generally sociolinguistic questions of prestige, and change via community versus individual shift, the question of why uvular *r* appears where it appears is of interest.

The phenomenon that precedes the gradual spread of uvular *r*— that of its spontaneous innovation by speakers of languages with a dominant alveolar *r* variant—has occasionally received attention from linguists, although it has mostly been from phoneticians, rather than sociolinguists. Here, the question is how uvular *r* variants are linked to alveolar ones to the extent that they (and not other potential substitutions) survive in the first place. A number of authors have highlighted the perceptual link between alveolar and uvular trills. For both, of course, the most obvious perceptual cue is the pattern of openings and closings, and indeed the trill frequencies of alveolar and uvular trills are relatively similar (Ladefoged, Cochran & Disner 1977; Lindau 1985; Verhoeven 1994; Tops 2009). The similarities do not stop there: as shown by Engstrand, Frid & Lindblom (2007) for alveolar and velar approximants, and Van de Velde & Demolin (2021) for alveolar and uvular trills, there are similarities in the formant transitions of alveolar and dorsal articulations (specifically, their high F3/low F4) that may increase the perceptual overlap. This suggests that a uvular trill is a good substitute for an alveolar one in cases where the latter is the norm and an individual speaker cannot produce it. Coupled with the articulatory complexity and aerodynamic precarity of alveolar trills (see, e.g., Solé 1998, 2002), the argument can be made that children simply hit upon uvular trills during the acquisition process as a substitution that works well enough (see, e.g., Sebregts 2015, although the argument goes back as far as Von Kempelen 1791 [cited in Wollock 1982]). On the other hand, there is evidence that alveolar and uvular articulations are not only linked perceptually and acoustically. Morin (2013) suggests that even articulatorily, moving from alveolar to uvular *r* does not constitute an abrupt sound change. He claims that uvular articulations (specifically, uvular approximant or fricative articulations) may arise as lenition variants of apico-alveolar trills. The argument goes back to Jespersen (1889), who states that alveolar trills have a double constriction: both the tongue tip and the tongue dorsum are raised. That many rhotic variants involve two or even three articulatory gestures is now well established, via articulatory research such as that by Delattre & Freeman (1968) on American English *r* and Proctor (2011) on Spanish and Russian *r* (though for a dissenting view see Recasens 2016). Morin's re-examination of data from Charbonneau (1971) and Santerre (1982) on Montreal French *r* leads to the same conclusion. Demolin & Van de Velde (submitted) combine the articulatory and acoustic evidence and, based on an articulatory model simulation, argue that the [r] > [ʀ] substitution is a "quantal change," in that a small displacement of the front constriction for [r] can lead to a perceptual reinterpretation as dorsal. That said, as noted above, the two trills are apparently perceptually different enough for uvulars to be recognized as "defective" in some strongly normative communities, and social factors remain crucial in explaining why and how uvular *r* has become socially acceptable or even desirable in a number of speech communities but not others. What these findings illustrate above all is how a detailed investigation that brings together sociolinguistic data and phonetic experimentation can shed new light on a phenomenon that was thought to be well-understood.

Going up or down?

A fertile strand of research into rhotic variation over the past 20 years has been driven by the development of instrumental methodologies, especially that of articulatory imaging techniques. The variation among speakers of rhotic American English was first described by Delattre & Freeman (1968) using motion X-ray. Since then, ultrasound tongue imaging in particular has shed light on the articulatory configurations involved in approximant *r* types. In addition to being much less invasive, dangerous, and costly than X-ray, ultrasound also makes it easier to analyze the dynamic dimension, currently using frame rates of 60–200 fps (Wrench & Scobbie 2011).

Explorations into the particulars of the retroflex/bunched distinction have not only been driven by methodological gains (i.e., researchers used articulatory imaging because they could), but also by theoretical interests shared by phoneticians and phonologists. One of these is the mapping between articulation and acoustics.

Delattre & Freeman (1968) describe how American English *r* had, in the years leading up to their study, been described as having two articulatory variants, a retroflex and a bunched one, the latter also known as "molar" (the dorsum is bunched up against or toward the palate with considerable bracing against the molars). Sources from the 1940s and 1950s tended to describe the retroflex variant as the dominant one. Delattre & Freeman's X-ray study dispelled both notions. They distinguish between eight different articulatory variants, rather than two, and of their 46 subjects the majority in fact had a bunched *r*. Later ultrasound studies confirmed the plethora of gestural shapes and the dominance of bunched ones. The various tongue shapes tend to remain classifiable as retroflex or bunched, or more accurately, though more broadly, as tip-up and tip-down.

Acoustically, American English *r* is characterized by a rapid dip in F3, as Delattre & Freeman's measurements confirm (they cite sources going back to 1947 for this finding). Their study enables the comparison of images of the maximal articulatory constriction with the acoustic output of this constriction. It shows that the F3 dip (and a resulting closeness of F2 and F3) are correlated with the strength of both the palato-velar and pharyngeal constrictions involved, as well as with the level of contraction in the bunched dorsum and the dorsum lowering behind it. Most crucially, no correlation is found between tongue shape (retroflex or bunched) and formant frequencies; the combined effects of the constrictions involved in both types lead to the same acoustic output. Interspeaker variation, in other words, was present at the articulatory level, but not at the acoustic (or auditory level).

That the acoustic target for American English *r* is a low F3, or possibly a close approximation or confluence of F2 and F3 has now been shown in many acoustic studies (Hagiwara 1995; Stevens 1998). In recent years, ultrasound studies have confirmed that this acoustic target can be reached in articulatorily clearly distinct ways, that speakers vary greatly individually, and that the various gestures they employ actually increase acoustic stability (Guenther et al. 1999; Zhang et al. 2003). In other words, there seems to be a two-to-one (or many-to-one) mapping of tongue shapes to formant shapes. Articulatory variation similar to that in American English has since been found for Dutch approximant *r* (Scobbie & Sebregts 2010). A reasonable assumption following from these facts may be that retroflex and bunched articulations are simply different strategies employed by individual speakers to arrive at the same acoustic result and that the articulatory variation is in itself irrelevant—both phonologically and socially. It is a reasonable assumption because it is hard to see how speakers could make social-indexical use of different articulations if the acoustic result is the same. This would both be difficult to learn (listeners have limited access to speakers' individual gestural patterns) and have low ecological power (socially relevant distinctions that are not recoverable from the acoustic output).

As far back as Delattre & Freeman's (1968) study, however, gestural configurations have displayed group differences. Dividing their speakers up by region, they find more tip-up articulations in the South and New York City, and more bunched *r* on the Pacific Coast and New England. In their case, much of the variation among their participants may relate to levels of rhoticity (the South and New York are two areas characterized by non-rhoticity), although this fails to explain the strong position of bunched *r* types in New England (also an area with non-rhotic dialects). That said, the assumption that the interspeaker variation related to gestural types is irrelevant socially, has found support from other studies that show speakers do not perceive the difference between different articulatory strategies, and that speakers mainly show idiosyncratic differences (Mielke, Baker & Archangeli 2010, 2016).

Meanwhile, studies on *r* production in Scottish English have in fact shown social factors to be relevant predictors of bunched versus retroflex articulations. Lawson, Scobbie & Stuart-Smith (2011) found that middle-class speakers in Glasgow were more likely to use bunched articulations compared to working-class speakers, whose productions were more often "tip up" (given the small number of actual retroflex articulations, this term is a more accurate characterization of the other end of the spectrum from the bunched ones). They also show an effect of gender: the male speakers among their (mostly young) participants use more tip-up variants than the female speakers. In other words, they discovered a classic sociolinguistic distribution corresponding to gender and class, with female middle-class speakers on one end and male working-class speakers at the other. They note that the bunched and retroflex variants are in fact auditorily distinct from each other, in contrast with those in American English.

Given the discussion above, this result may at first glance appear mysterious, but, as Lawson, Scobbie & Stuart-Smith (2011) point out, the different articulations are linked to different levels of *r*-reduction. A pattern of strong versus weak *r* realizations being associated with class differences had been established before (Romaine 1978). Even without going into its articulatory dimension, the variation was of particular interest because it goes against the assumption in earlier literature that middle-class speakers would tend towards the nonrhotic standard south of the border. In fact, it is working-class speakers who are becoming less rhotic. In addition, as a sound change in progress, it seems to be developing in both directions: the middle-class speakers are also becoming more "*r*-ful"—that is, using perceptually ever stronger *r* variants.

In a series of follow-up studies, the authors examine the phenomenon of derhoticization, the progressive loss of a perceptually salient *r* in coda positions, in the context of articulatory variation in a wider sense. They show the crucial role of gestural timing in the differences between the tip-up and tip-down speakers. Apart from the different tongue shapes, the gestures involved for the tip-up speakers reach their maximal articulatory targets later, often after the offset of voicing, leading to a reduced percept (or even one of deletion) (Lawson, Stuart-Smith & Scobbie 2018). Meanwhile, the middle-class, bunched-*r* speakers' relative stability of the bunched dorsum configuration leads to a stronger cue to rhoticity and a co-articulatory effect on pre-*r* vowels (merging /ɪ/, /ɛ/, and /ʌ/), which are kept apart more often by working-class speakers (Lawson, Scobbie & Stuart-Smith 2013; Stuart-Smith, Lawson & Scobbie 2014; Lawson & Stuart-Smith 2021). In other words, there are two concurrent sound changes taking place, both phonetically and sociolinguistically. In the sense of Labov (e.g., 1994), there is both a change from above and a change from below affecting Scottish English *r*. The former is led by female middle-class speakers towards stronger approximant *r* variants in all positions, the latter by working-class speakers who, in the words of Stuart-Smith, Lawson & Scobbie (2014), "are participating in long-term vernacular change from below," possibly on their way to a situation of non-rhoticity. Stuart-Smith, Lawson & Scobbie point out the potential relation between Scottish derhoticization and other sound changes (such as TH-fronting) that may be influenced by Anglo-English.

The studies on Scottish English articulatory *r* variation and derhoticization provide a wealth of detailed phonetic data to sociolinguists interested in the interplay between linguistic and social factors in sound change. Questions regarding the standard (or socially more attractive non-standard) varieties south of the border and their influence on changes in Scottish English can now be explored with direct reference to the phonetic detail involved. In fact, tracking closely how derhoticization develops (e.g., which vowel and consonantal contexts are targeted first) may provide a window on the past as well, allowing us to infer how varieties that are currently fully nonrhotic may have evolved.

Derhoticization, or at least a gradual weakening of coda-*r* can also be observed in other currently rhotic varieties of English, such as West Country English (Blaxter et al. 2019; Malarski 2021), as well as in other languages. In varieties of German, for instance, coda-*r* can vary between a uvular fricative [ʁ] and an open vowel [ɐ], with the latter considered more standard (Wiese 2000). Similarly, in varieties of Brazilian Portuguese word-final *r* may reduce to [h] or be deleted (Rennicke 2015), and in Dutch as well as Quebec French, approximant and vocalic variants occur in addition to more constricted alveolar and uvular ones (Sebregts 2015; Sankoff & Blondeau 2007). Whether the latter examples are in fact stages of progressive *r*-loss leading to non-rhoticity remains to be seen, but the tools to trace any further developments are now at hand.

Read my lips

Another recent focal point for studies of rhotics has been the emergence of new variants and their consequent spread throughout speech communities. By "new variants" we here mean speech sounds that were previously regarded as speech defects or developmental variants, and possibly not as rhotics at all. Children learning language varieties with an alveolar trill as one of the major allophones have been found to use a number of substitutions, including lateral, uvular, and pharyngeal consonants (see Sebregts 2015 for references; examples come from Czech, Estonian, Spanish, and Slovenian, among others). Some of these substitutions persist into adulthood; speakers from various languages have been reported to use lenited *r* variants as opposed to the prestige or standard forms (often apical trills or taps). While uvular trills tend to be regarded as rhotics, even if not target-like for a specific language or variety, other speech sounds may fall outside the category for native listeners; these may ultimately be rejected by the speech community and remain as idiosyncratic realizations, or they may become serviceable rhotics, thereby expanding the class. Examples of the latter are uvular fricatives, now the dominant *r* in French, and vocalic offglides such as [ə] or [ɐ], functioning as coda-*r* in German and Danish. The remainder of this section will examine another such variant: the labiodental approximant [ʋ], currently spreading in UK English.

Foulkes & Docherty (2000) trace the history of discourse around [ʋ] in academic and nonacademic works, to find that it has a long tradition of being regarded as defective speech, as well as a feature of upper-class affectation, going back as far as Dickens's *The Pickwick Papers*. It has since been used a source of ridicule in books, films, and commercials. They subsequently note an increasing number of linguistic sources from the 1970s, 1980s, and 1990s reporting [ʋ] as either newly emerging or already widespread and common variant of *r*, primarily a feature of young urban speakers, and spreading from the southeast of England. This means that in a relatively short space of time, labiodental variants have become accepted realizations of /r/ in at least some varieties of British English, and in fact have considerable social currency helping them spread to new varieties. Foulkes & Docherty's data come from Newcastle and Derby (urban centers in the northeast and East Midland areas of the UK, respectively). They show that use of [ʋ] is an incipient phenomenon in Newcastle, while it is already more established in Derby, especially among the working-class speakers in their sample. In discussing possible explanations for the rise of labiodental variants of /r/, Foulkes & Docherty consider them as part of a larger group of consonantal changes (including t-glottaling and TH-fronting) that emanate from southeastern accents and simultaneously move away from the traditional standard accent and from strongly local varieties (in other words, dialect leveling towards a prestigious, though nonstandard, reference accent).

Foulkes & Docherty (2000) used a relatively classical sociolinguistic approach. Apart from the independent variables being class, age, and location, their dependent variable is framed in terms of discrete phonetic categories in competition with each other. On the other hand, they acknowledge that their acoustic data display gradient variation, which they encode by having categories in between lingual [ɹ] and labiodental [ʋ] ("more [ʋ]-like than [ɹ]-like," and vice versa). That said, when examining the acoustic detail in their Newcastle and Derby data, they conclude that there is a qualitative difference between the [ɹ]-like and [ʋ]-like variants: the most typical acoustic correlate of post-alveolar (bunched or retroflex) realizations of /r/, a low third formant, was absent from the auditorily most labial-sounding tokens. This is despite lip-rounding itself also having a slight lowering effect on F3 (as part of a general lowering of formants, but especially F2, due to an increased front cavity). The phonetic pathway from lingual to labial *r* in these varieties of English is most likely not a purely acoustic one, but has an important articulatory component: what we have been calling "lingual" *r* here is usually described as having considerable secondary labialization, with [ɹʷ] a more apt transcription (e.g., Collins & Mees 1996). What remains underexplored, then, is the relative contribution of labialization of the lingual variants to their acoustic makeup, and the link between the labial component in them and the subsequent development of the labiodental variants. It is this kind of production–perception link that could provide another piece of the puzzle explaining the rapid uptake of the change. In recent years, more detailed phonetic studies, including those analyzing articulatory data, have indeed shed light on the interplay between the lingual and labial gestures in *r* variants. The work of King & Ferragne (2020a, 2020b) and King & Chitoran (2022) has shown that the labial gesture plays a crucial role in the acoustics of variants that retain the lingual gesture, too, and that the visual aspect is another factor that deserves highlighting.

The widely held assumption discussed above that Anglo-English (non-rhotic) *r* is generally a tip-up approximant variant is challenged by the work of King & Ferragne (2020a). They show that, in fact, non-rhotic Anglo-English speakers display gestural variation similar to that of rhotic American English speakers, including bunched variants, although the proportion of tip-up speakers is higher (similar results for New Zealand English, also nonrhotic, are reported in Heyne et al. 2020). King & Ferragne additionally note the relative absence of studies into the labial gesture which is, nonetheless, often noted as a feature of Anglo-English *r*. Their study shows that bunched realizations tend to be accompanied by more lip protrusion, and suggest that this may be a compensatory gesture in order to achieve an acoustic output sufficiently similar to that of retroflex speakers. The specifics of the labial gesture are at the same time sufficiently different from those of /w/, so that a perceptual contrast is maintained. Intriguingly, they suggest that the *r*-specific lip configuration comes from exposure to labiodental *r* speakers (an idea first put forward by Dalcher, Knight & Jones 2008, based on perception data); since labiodental *r* lacks the characteristic low F3 (acoustically present with both bunched and retroflex *r* speakers), Anglo-English listeners have come to rely more on the second formant. While this is low for [ɹʷ], it is lower still for [w], so the /r/~/w/ contrast is maintained—even if somewhat precariously.

In a separate study, King & Ferragne (2020b) show that an artificial neural network trained on images of the labial gestures in /r/ versus /w/ is able to classify these with an accuracy of over 90 percent, confirming that they are indeed significantly different. While the authors are careful not to extrapolate these results to human perceivers, their study certainly suggests that for face-to-face interactions, visual cues may be more important (and perhaps even sufficient) for the contrast. King & Chitoran (2022) take up this question using a cleverly designed study with matching and mismatching audio/visual [ɹʷ]~[w] pairs. They find that native Anglo-English speakers are indeed also near-perfect in identifying the contrast relying on visual information only. Auditory information alone, on the other hand, leads to considerable ambiguity. King & Chitoran conclude that the robustness of the visual contrast may contribute to an ongoing shift towards nonlingual variants in the future.

While King & Ferragne (2020a, 2020b) and King & Chitoran (2022) are not sociophonetic studies as such, as they are not focused on socially based variation, the suggested pathway of lingual to labial variants is an important contribution to the study of sound change. These studies shed light on mechanisms that have heretofore been inaccessible, but that are central in answering the basic sociolinguistic questions of how sound changes come to be (actuation) and spread (propagation) (Weinreich, Labov & Herzog 1968).

CASE STUDY   Dutch *r* variation

Dutch *r* variation is particularly complex, both socially and phonetically, due to the wealth of realizations possible not only across regional varieties of Dutch (Weijnen 1991; De Schutter & Taeldeman 1993, 1994; van Reenen 1994) but even within the relatively codified standard variety. For instance, all three processes described in the previous section are relevant. There is variation between alveolar and uvular *r* variants, particularly at the geographical level, both at a large scale (Netherlandic vs. Belgian Dutch) and at smaller ones (e.g., Bruges vs. Ghent Dutch). There is a relatively recent variant now rapidly spreading in the form of an approximant acoustically similar to those in varieties of English; articulatory studies have shown similar patterns to those in American and Scottish English, both in terms of gestural variation and gestural weakening. However, this only scratches the surface of the issues involved. This section first provides a brief overview of recent findings, and then turns its focus on the following questions: 1) How are the Dutch *r* variants linked, that is, what are the phonetic pathways that may have led particular variants to arise from other types of *r*? 2) How do social factors (age, gender) and geography interact with the linguistic ones, specifically the phonetic ones identified under 1)? We aim to demonstrate again how examining the phonetic detail and its social context maximizes our insight into processes of variation and change.

Methods

That Standard Dutch has a large amount of *r* variation was increasingly observed in studies from the 1990s, when Voortman (1994), Booij (1995), and Van de Velde (1996) identified five, six, and ten variants respectively. This century saw even more detailed studies into Dutch *r* expand the number of variants to 24 (Smakman 2006), though here we will discuss the data and classification used in Sebregts (2015), which recognizes an only slightly more manageable 20. Unlike the other studies mentioned above, Sebregts (2015) focused solely on the realizational variation of *r* in ten urban varieties of Dutch most accurately described as colloquial Standard Dutch—that is, morphosyntactically

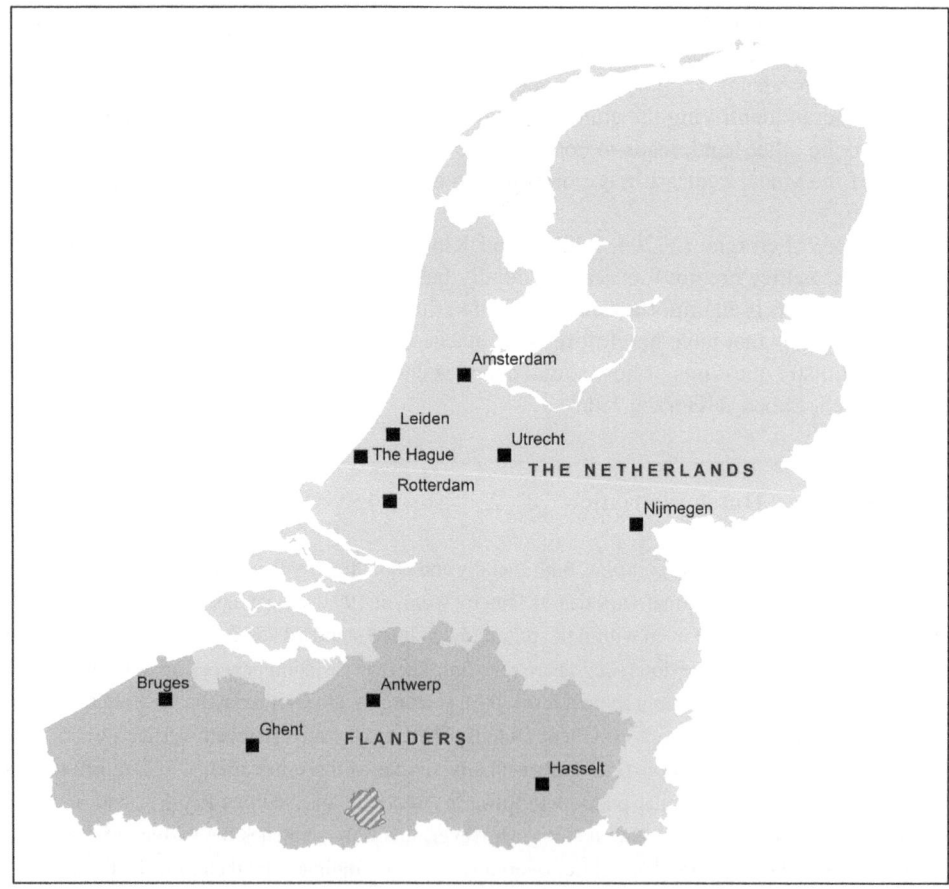

Figure 9.1   Location of the cities in the HEMA urban accent corpus within the Dutch language area

and lexically standard while allowing for variation in the sound system. Data were collected in Amsterdam, Rotterdam, The Hague, Utrecht, Nijmegen (the first four being the largest cities in the Netherlands), and Bruges, Ghent, Antwerp, and Hasselt (the largest cities in four of the five Flemish provinces in Belgium). Locations are mapped in Figure 9.1.

In each of the cities, 40 speakers, stratified by age and gender, were recorded as they participated in a picture-naming and word list reading task eliciting /r/ in a number of segmental and syllabic contexts. Recruitment was done "in the field" (i.e., by approaching patrons of cafes/restaurants in their local HEMA department store). Tokens of /r/ in the recordings were coded and transcribed by the author and Evie Tops (see Tops 2009) based on auditory and visual (spectrographic) analysis. Table 9.1 shows the twenty variants.

Results

As shown in Table 9.1, the variation concerns place of articulation (Dutch *r* can be alveolar, retroflex, palatal, or uvular) and manner (trills, taps, fricatives, approximants, and vowels coexist, as well as "zero" variants, i.e., *r*-deletion). Not all speakers use all variants. Some variants are not found in some of the urban accents at all; the number of variants per accent varies between 14 (Hasselt, The Hague) and 20 (Utrecht). Variation is also strongly constrained by the syllable context, with the number of variants found in onsets between seven and ten, while in codas it varies between 13 and 20.

Sebregts (2015) contains detailed descriptions of how the variation plays out in each city in the corpus. Figure 9.2 shows the distribution of the main six *r* categories in each Dutch (NL) and Belgian (FL) city. Place of articulation varies strongly from city to city. In Antwerp and Bruges, for instance, speakers largely use alveolar *r*, while speakers in Ghent and Nijmegen use mostly uvular variants. The token frequency of alveolar and uvular variants is most balanced in Rotterdam, Leiden, and Hasselt. However, zooming in on individual speakers reveals how this balance can have different sources; while in Hasselt, speakers tend to be either alveolar or uvular *r* speakers, a much larger number of Leiden speakers vary between the two. Manner of articulation reveals similar patterns of variation at city and individual levels, although here the major divide is the Dutch/Belgian border: while in the Belgian Dutch varieties *r* is largely consonantal (trills, taps, fricatives) in all syllable contexts, the Netherlandic ones show an allophonic pattern of consonantal variants in the onset and approximants and vowels in the coda.

Apart from larger geographical patterns and how these are shaped by individual speakers of each accent, the data also show effects of gender and age on the use of particular variants, suggesting changes in progress. For instance, in Hasselt there is an effect of age on the use of alveolar versus uvular variants, with young speakers using more uvular variants. In other words, uvular *r* seems to be gradually replacing alveolar *r*. The specific sociolinguistic situation is conducive in two ways. While the alveolar trill is the traditional prestige variant, that prestige is waning. At the same time, Hasselt is located in an area where uvular *r* has been a local vernacular form for a long time.

The more spectacular change in progress visible in the Dutch urban accent data concerns the rapid spread of what is identified as a retroflex/bunched approximant in Table 9.1. This variant marks the most salient split between the Netherlands and Flanders in the data. While virtually absent from Belgian Dutch, the retroflex/bunched approximant makes up almost 20 percent of coda tokens in Nijmegen, the

Table 9.1 *r* variants in the HEMA urban accent corpus

IPA	*Descriptive label*
r	voiced alveolar trill
r͡r̥	partially devoiced alveolar trill
r̥	voiceless alveolar trill
r͡ɹ̝	alveolar trill/tap followed by homorganic frication
ɹ̝	voiced (post)alveolar fricative
ɹ̝̊	voiceless (post)alveolar fricative
ɾ	voiced alveolar tap
ɾ̥	voiceless alveolar tap
ɹ	alveolar approximant
ʀ	uvular trill
ʀ̝	uvular fricative trill
ʁ	uvular fricative
ʁ̞	uvular approximant
ɻ	retroflex/bunched approximant
j	palatal approximant
ɛ	low-mid front vowel
ə	central vowel (schwa)
ɐ	low vowel
ØC̠	elision of /r/ with retraction of the following C
Ø	elision of /r/

Source: Sebregts 2015

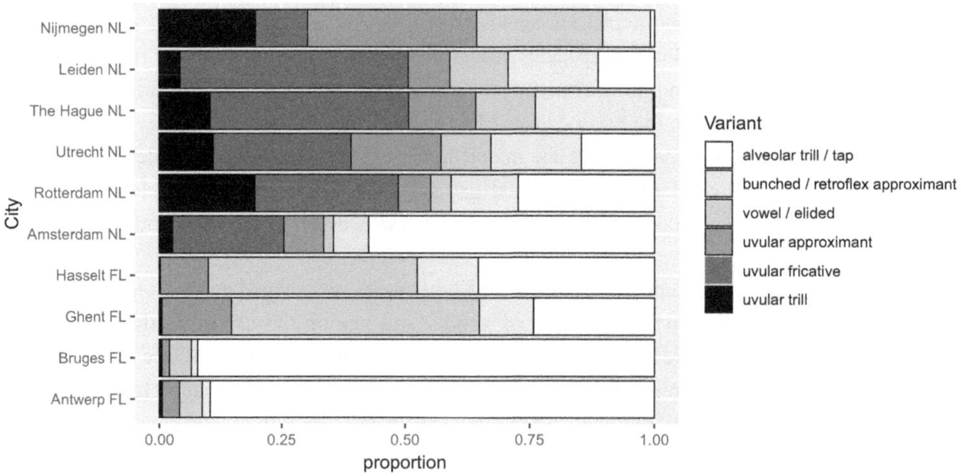

Figure 9.2 Frequency distribution of the six main *r* categories in six Dutch (NL) and four Flemish (FL) cities

Dutch city with the lowest frequency for this variant. In Leiden, on the other end of the frequency scale, this goes up to as much as 84 percent of coda-*r*. As a change in progress, it shows effects of age and gender, with young female speakers leading the way. The variant is also linguistically constrained, as it is confined to coda position. As Scobbie & Sebregts (2010) demonstrate in an articulatory study using ultrasound, this leads to complex allophonic patterns. Individual speakers combine either alveolar or uvular *r* variants in onsets with either bunched or retroflex *r* in codas, without there being an obvious articulatory connection between the two.

Discussion

The theoretical focus of Sebregts (2015) is on how the *r* variants are related to each other, a concern shared by many working on rhotics, as outlined in our introductory section. Taking off from Lindau's (1985) famous model of family resemblances among rhotics, a model of family relationships is built around the phonetic pathways that may lead certain rhotics to develop from others, through processes that are common in casual speech such as reduction/lenition, as can be seen in Figure 9.3.

The model in Figure 9.3 works through "inspecting very closely the phonetic detail of *r* sounds in connection with their linguistic distribution in a large corpus such as the urban accent data that enable the establishment of the origin of particular variants in others" (Sebregts 2015:280). An example of where this works particularly well is the development of fricative variants from trills. Based on detailed phonetic explorations such as Solé (2002), fricative *r* variants are predicted to occur due to trill failure. Trill failure itself is predicted on the basis of the articulatory complexity and aerodynamic precarity of trills, and it is even possible to predict where it is more likely to happen. For alveolar trills, specifically, the syllable coda and the segmental environment of high vowels are the most likely loci for the occurrence of fricative variants. Sebregts (2015) shows that these are indeed the contexts in which alveolar fricative variants occur most in the Dutch data, establishing the relationship between trills and fricative rhotics as one based on co-articulation and reduction. It also becomes clear, however, that these processes are not automatic and variety-independent but instead partially under control of the speaker. The relative frequencies of voiced, partially devoiced, and fully devoiced/fricated alveolar trills differ from city to city, and coda-*r* in Antwerp appears to have a more strongly devoiced/ fricated target than that in Bruges, for instance, despite strong similarities in *r* patterns at a more superficial level.

There are also cases in the Dutch *r* data where the model seems to work less well—that is, where close examination of the phonetic detail of variants in conjunction with their distributional patterns leads to counterintuitive or paradoxical results. A clear example of this is the rapid rise of retroflex/ bunched *r* in coda positions in the Netherlandic Dutch data. Here, the ultrasound study by Scobbie & Sebregts (2010) had confirmed the articulatory complexity of both the retroflex and the bunched variants subsumed under the label, each involving at least two constrictions. This makes them less clear candidates for a reduction analysis; though strictly coda variants, they are likely to be more complex than many of the onset variants used by the same speakers. This is exactly where the combination of phonetic and sociolinguistic arguments becomes crucial again: to explain the adoption and rapid spread of a gesturally complex variant, disrupting the phonetic model, we need recourse to its social status. As shown in a series of studies by Van Bezooijen and colleagues, the retroflex/bunched

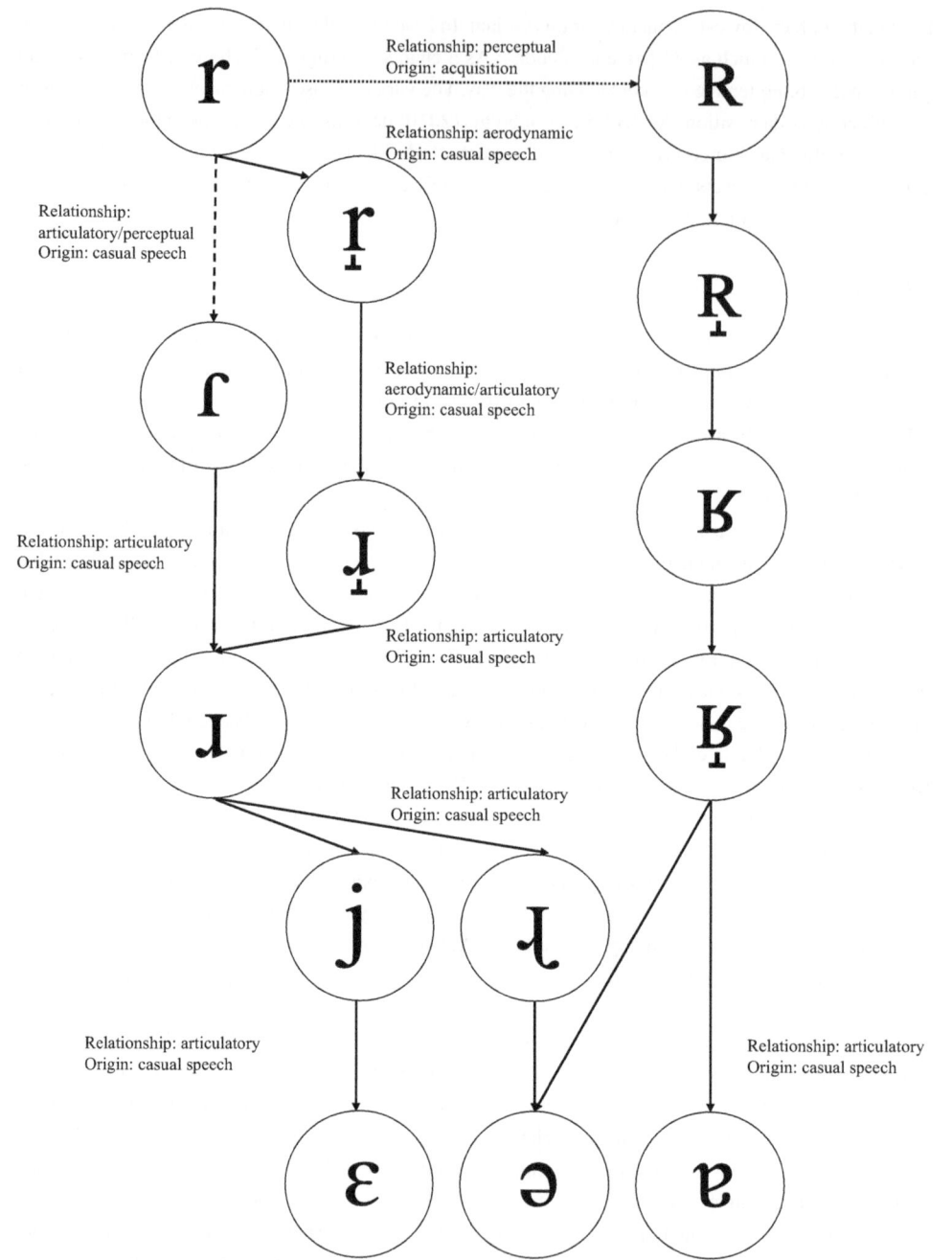

Figure 9.3   Family relationships between Dutch *r* variants, with place of articulation on the horizontal axis and manner of articulation on the vertical axis

Source: Sebregts 2015

approximant (known popularly as "Gooise r") is a high-prestige variant in the Netherlands (Bezooijen, Kroezen & van de Berg 2002; Bezooijen & van den Berg 2004; Bezooijen 2005). All in all, the situation surrounding Dutch *r* variation offers a rich testing ground for sociophonetic methodologies and, conversely, only by combining the social and the phonetic can we achieve new levels of insight in the phenomena under investigation.

The future of rhotic studies

Given the complexity of rhotics and their common and deep embedding in social and historical processes of variation and change, their study is a playground for methodological innovations and theoretical developments. The great variability and fuzzy character of rhotics indicate the necessity to improve their description in language typological databases. The present sociophonetic insights in rhotic variation are strongly based on West-Germanic (Dutch, English, and German) and Romance languages (Italian, French, Spanish, and Portuguese). These studies strongly suggest that alveolar variants and trills are over-reported and that the actual amount of variation is consistently underestimated (Anselme, Pellegrino & Dediu 2023). A structured template to describe rhotics is required, in addition to guidelines for the construction and analysis of large speech corpus data. Even for trained phoneticians it is notoriously difficult to distinguish the wide range of *r* variants, and there is a need to study *r* in large speech corpora in a wide range of languages. Hence, tools for the automatic classification of *r* variants, as well as tools for the detection of (possible) new variants in speech corpora should be developed with the help of machine learning techniques.

Another line of research should test specific hypotheses of the articulatory, aerodynamic, and acoustic characteristics of the variants and their relationship to obtain more insight in the class of rhotics. Ultrasound research has proven to be crucial in detecting more detailed articulatory gestures, but other techniques, like fMRI, articulography, or dynamic digital radiography could be explored. Measuring the acoustic and aerodynamic characteristics and visualizing in increasing detail the articulatory movements in the production of variants may uncover the contrastive spectral values and link these to articulatory gestures.

In addition to variationist quantitative studies of speech corpora, we want to argue for a more experimental approach, as proposed in laboratory sociolinguistics (Van de Velde et al. 2021). Important research tracks are the link between (variability in) production and (variability in) perception, the processing of variation in speech production and speech perception, and the acquisition of rhotic variation by both L1 and L2 speakers. Interestingly, various psycholinguistic experimental designs offer pathways for research. A promising perspective is lexically guided perceptual learning where the boundaries between two phonemes are being manipulated, for instance the boundaries between the liquids /l/ and /r/ (Scharenborg, Mitterer & McQueen 2011). Acoustic manipulations could be applied to various *r* variants, or to sounds like [χ] in Dutch that may classify as either a rhotic or a fricative.

Priming effects present another promising experimental approach. Priming research has been carried out on (ing), another classic sociolinguistic variable (White, Tamminga & Embick submitted). The alveolar and velar variants have different effects on priming words. Extending this observation to *r*, it would be relevant to know how priming processes are activated by, for example, word-final absence or presence of /r/. It would provide information on the processing of competing variants and on the way sociolinguistic variants are being stored in memory. An important research question might be whether (all) reduced variants have the same priming effect as full variants, or whether new variants differ in priming from the old ones. Priming research can be combined with eye-tracking, a very attractive way to measure processes below the level of consciousness. Techniques from social psychology like the Implicit Association Task might be instrumental in uncovering the indexical properties of the observed *r* variants (Hilton et al. 2016), but a relatively direct approach with a systematic set of words with pronunciation variants and pictures with social meanings and/or associations might work as well (see Staum Casasanto, Grondelaers & van Hout 2015).

A fascinating observation is that the observed patterns of change are mainly of a reductive nature, especially in large speech communities, resulting in a simplification of the articulatory complexity of *r* in a language variety. It is tempting to link processes of reduction to linguistic complexity and population size (Fenk-Oczlon & Pilz 2021), but at this point it is again important to realize that our insights into rhotics are mainly based on Germanic and Romance languages, and that a wider scope of languages and speech communities is needed.

References

Anselme, Rémi, François Pellegrino & Dan Dediu. 2023. What's in the *r*? A review of the usage of the *r* symbol in the illustrations of the IPA. *Journal of the International Phonetic Association*. https://doi.org/10.1017/S0025100322000238.

Barry, William J. 1997. Another R-tickle. *Journal of the International Phonetic Association* 27(1–2). 35–45. https://doi.org/10.1017/S0025100300005405

Bezooijen, Renée van. 2005. Approximant *r* in Dutch: routes and feelings. *Speech Communication* 47(1–2). 15–31. https://doi.org/10.1016/j.specom.2005.04.010

Bezooijen, Renée van, Suzan Kroezen & Rob van de Berg. 2002. Front approximant /r/: A new and vigorous change in Dutch. In Hans Broekhuis & Paula Fikkert (eds.), *Linguistics in the Netherlands 2002*, 1–11. John Benjamins. https://doi.org/10.1075/avt.19.04bez

Bezooijen, Renée van & Rob van den Berg. 2004. De Gooise r: Wie ziet er wat in en waarom? *Taal en Tongval* 56. 86–108.

Blaxter, Tam, Kate Beeching, Richard Coates, James Murphy & Emily Robinson. 2019. Each p[ɚ]son does it th[ɛː] way: Rhoticity variation and the community grammar. *Language Variation and Change* 31(1). 91–117. https://doi.org/10.1017/S0954394519000048

Booij, Geert. 1995. *The phonology of Dutch*. Clarendon.

Chabot, Alex. 2019. What's wrong with being a rhotic? *Glossa: A Journal of General Linguistics* 4(1). 38. https://doi.org/10.5334/gjgl.618

Charbonneau, René. 1971. *Étude sur les voyelles nasales du français canadien*. Presses de l'Université Laval.

Clermont, Jean & Henrietta Cedergren 1979. Les 'R' de ma mère sont perdus dans l'air. In Pierrette Thibault (ed.), *Le français parlé: études sociolinguistiques*, 13–28. Linguistic Research.

Collins, Beverly & Inger Mees. 1996. *The phonetics of English and Dutch*. Brill.

Côté, Marie-Hélène & Hugo Saint-Amant Lamy. 2012. D'un [r] à l'aut[ʁ]e: Contribution à la chute du R apical au Québec. *SHS Web of Conferences* 1. 1441–1453. https://doi.org/10.1051/shsconf/20120100187.

Dalcher, Christina Villafaña, Rachael-Anne Knight & Mark J. Jones. 2008. Cue switching in the perception of approximants: evidence from two English dialects. *University of Pennsylvania Working Papers in Linguistics* 14(2). 63–71. https://repository.upenn.edu/pwpl/vol14/iss2/9

De Schutter, Georges & Johan Taeldeman. 1993. Studies in *r*-klein I. /r/ na vocaal in onbeklemtoonde lettergreep. *Taal en Tongval* 45. 155–172.

De Schutter, Georges & Johan Taeldeman. 1994. Studies in *r*-klein II. /r/ in hoofdtonige syllabe voor medeklinker. R–zes visies op een kameleon. *Taal en Tongval* 46. 73–109.

Delattre, Pierre & Donald C. Freeman. 1968. A dialect study of American r's by x-ray motion picture. *Linguistics* 6(44). 29–68. https://doi.org/10.1515/ling.1968.6.44.29

Demolin, Didier & Hans Van de Velde. Submitted. The quantal change of alveolar [r] to uvular [r].

Engstrand, Olle, Johan Frid & Björn Lindblom. 2007. A perceptual bridge between coronal and dorsal /r/. In Maria-Josep Solé, Patrice Speeter Beddor & Manjari Ohala (eds.), *Experimental Approaches to Phonology*, 175–191. Oxford University Press.

Fenk-Oczlon, Gertraud & Jürgen Pilz. 2021. Linguistic complexity: Relationships between phoneme inventory size, syllable complexity, word and clause length, and population size. *Frontiers in Communication* 6. 626032. https://doi.org/10.3389/fcomm.2021.626032

Fougeron, Cécile & Caroline L. Smith. 1993. French: Illustrations of the IPA. *Journal of the International Phonetic Association* 23(2). 73–76. https://doi.org/10.1017/S0025100300004874

Foulkes, Paul & Gerald J. Docherty. 2000. Another chapter in the story of /r/: 'Labiodental' variants in British English. *Journal of Sociolinguistics* 4(1). 30–59. https://doi.org/10.1111/1467-9481.00102

Grønnum, Nina. 1998. Danish. *Journal of the International Phonetic Association* 28(1–2). 99–105. https://doi.org/10.1017/S0025100300006290

Guenther, Frank H., Carol Y. Espy-Wilson, Suzanne E. Boyce, Melanie L. Matthies, Majid Zandipour & Joseph S. Perkell. 1999. Articulatory tradeoffs reduce acoustic variability during American English /r/ production. *Journal of the Acoustical Society of America* 105(5). 2854–2865. https://doi.org/10.1121/1.426900

Hagiwara, Robert. 1995. *Acoustic realizations of American /r/as produced by women and men*. University of California, Los Angeles.

Heyne, Matthias, Xuan Wang, Donald Derrick, Kieran Dorreen & Kevin Watson. 2020. The articulation of /ɹ/ in New Zealand English. *Journal of the International Phonetic Association* 50(3). 366–388. https://doi.org/10.1017/S0025100318000324

Hilton, Nanna Haug, Eva Smidt, Sophie van der Meulen & Laura Rosseel. 2016. Using IAT to measure the association between [ɹ] and female speakers. Paper presented at 'r-atics5, Leeuwarden, Netherlands.

Jespersen, Otto. 1889. *The articulations of speech sounds represented by means of analphabetic symbols*. Elwert.

King, Hannah & Ioana Chitoran. 2022. Difficult to hear but easy to see: Audio-visual perception of the /r/-/w/contrast in Anglo-English. *Journal of the Acoustical Society of America* 152(1). 368–379. https://doi.org/10.1121/10.0012660

King, Hannah & Emmanuel Ferragne. 2020a. Labiodentals /r/ here to stay: Deep learning shows us why. *Anglophonia. French Journal of English Linguistics* 30. https://doi.org/10.4000/anglophonia.3424

King, Hannah & Emmanuel Ferragne. 2020b. Loose lips and tongue tips: The central role of the /r/-typical labial gesture in Anglo-English. *Journal of Phonetics* 80. 100978. https://doi.org/10.1016/j.wocn.2020.100978

Labov, William. 1994. *Principles of linguistic change, vol. 1, Internal factors*. Blackwell.

Labov, William. 2006. *The social stratification of English in New York City*. Cambridge University Press. [1st edn., Center for Applied Linguistics, 1966.]

Ladefoged, Peter, Anne Cochran & Sandra Disner. 1977. Laterals and trills. *Journal of the International Phonetic Association* 7(2). 46–54. https://doi.org/10.1017/S0025100300005636

Ladefoged, Peter & Ian Maddieson. 1996. *The sounds of the world's languages*. Blackwell.

Lawson, Eleanor, James M. Scobbie & Jane Stuart-Smith. 2011. The social stratification of tongue shape for postvocalic /r/ in Scottish English. *Journal of Sociolinguistics* 15(2). 256–268. https://doi.org/10.1111/j.1467-9841.2011.00464.x

Lawson, Eleanor, James M. Scobbie & Jane Stuart-Smith. 2013. Bunched /r/ promotes vowel merger to schwar: An ultrasound tongue imaging study of Scottish sociophonetic variation. *Journal of Phonetics* 41(3–4). 198–210. https://doi.org/10.1016/j.wocn.2013.01.004

Lawson, Eleanor & Jane Stuart-Smith. 2021. Lenition and fortition of /r/ in utterance-final position, an ultrasound tongue imaging study of lingual gesture timing in spontaneous speech. *Journal of Phonetics* 86. 101053. https://doi.org/10.1016/j.wocn.2021.101053

Lawson, Eleanor, Jane Stuart-Smith & James M. Scobbie. 2018. The role of gesture delay in coda /r/ weakening: An articulatory, auditory and acoustic study. *Journal of the Acoustical Society of America* 143. 1646–1657. https://doi.org/10.1121/1.5027833

Lindau, Mona. 1985. The story of /r/. In Victoria A. Fromkin (ed.), *Phonetic linguistics: Essays in honour of Peter Ladefoged*, 157–168. Academic Press.

Lipski, John M. 1994. *Latin American Spanish*. Longman.

Malarski, Kamil. 2021. *Loss of rhoticity in South-West England*. PhD dissertation, Uniwersytecie im. Adama Mickiewicza w Poznaniu.

Mateus, Maria Helena & Ernesto d'Andrade. 2000. *The phonology of Portuguese*. Oxford University Press.

Mielke, Jeff, Adam Baker & Diana Archangeli. 2010. Variability and homogeneity in American English /r/ allophony and /s/-retraction. In Cécile Fougeron, Barbara Kuehnert, Mariapaola D'Imperio & Nathalie Vallee (eds.), *Laboratory phonology 10*, 699–730. Walter De Gruyter. https://doi.org/10.1515/978311 0224917.5.699

Mielke, Jeff, Adam Baker & Diana Archangeli. 2016. Individual-level contact limits phonological complexity: Evidence from bunched and retroflex /r/. *Language* 92(1). 101–140. https://doi.org/10.1353/lan.2016.0019

Morin, Yves Charles. 2013. From apical [ɪ] to uvular [ʀ]: What the apico-dorsal *r* in Montreal French reveals about abrupt sound changes. In Fernando Sánchez Miret & Daniel Recasens (eds.), *Studies in phonetics, phonology and sound change in Romance*, 65–93. Lincom Europa.

Muminovic, Damra & Olle Engstrand. 2001. /r/ in some Swedish dialects: Preliminary observations. *Lund University, Department of Linguistics Working Papers* 49. 120–123.

Proctor, Michael. 2011. Towards a gestural characterization of liquids: Evidence from Spanish and Russian. *Laboratory Phonology* 2(2). 451–485. https://doi.org/10.1515/labphon.2011.017

Recasens, Daniel. 2016. What is and what is not an articulatory gesture in speech production: The case of lateral, rhotic and (alveolo)palatal consonants. *Gradus: Revista Brasileira de Fonologia de Laboratório* 1(1). 23–42. https://doi.org/10.47627/gradus.v1i1.101

Rennicke, Iiris. 2015. *Variation and change in the rhotics of Brazilian Portuguese*. PhD dissertation, University of Helsinki.

Rogier, Doreen. 1994. De verspreiding van een hooggewaardeerd taalkenmerk: De huig-R rond Gent. *Taal en Tongval* 46. 43–53.

Romaine, Suzanne. 1978. Post-vocalic /r/ in Scottish English: Sound change in progress? In Peter Trudgill (ed.), *Sociolinguistic patterns in British English*, 144–158. Edward Arnold.

Sankoff, Gillian & Hélène Blondeau. 2007. Language change across the lifespan: /r/ in Montreal French. *Language* 83(3). 560–588. https://doi.org/10.1353/lan.2007.0106

Sankoff, Gillian, Hélène Blondeau & Anne Charity. 2001. Individual roles in a real-time change. In Van de Velde & van Hout, 141–157.

Santerre, Laurent. 1978. Les /R/ montréalais en régression rapide. *Protée* 2. 117–130.

Santerre, Laurent. 1982. Des /r/ montréalais imprévisibles et inouïs. *Revue québécoise de linguistique* 12(1). 77–96.

Scharenborg, Odette, Holger Mitterer & James M. McQueen. 2011. Perceptual learning of liquids. In *Proceedings of the 12th Annual Conference of the International Speech Communication Association (Interspeech 2011)*, 149–152. ISCA.

Scobbie, James M. 2006. (R) as a variable. In Keith Brown (ed.), *Encyclopedia of language and linguistics, vol. 10*, 2nd edn., 337–344. Elsevier.

Scobbie, James M. & Koen Sebregts. 2010. Acoustic, articulatory and phonological perspectives on allophonic variation of /r/. In Rafaella Folli & Christiane Ulbrich (eds.), *Interfaces in linguistics: New research perspectives*, 131–169. Oxford University Press.

Sebregts, Koen. 2015. *The sociophonetics and phonology of Dutch r*. LOT.

Smakman, Dick. 2006. *Standard Dutch in the Netherlands. A sociolinguistic and phonetic description*. LOT.

Solé, Maria-Josep. 1998. Phonological universals: Trilling, voicing and frication. *Berkeley Linguistics Society* 42. 403–416. https://doi.org/10.3765/bls.v24i1.1238

Solé, Maria-Josep. 2002. Aerodynamic characteristics of trills and phonological patterning. *Journal of Phonetics* 30(4). 655–688. https://doi.org/10.1006/jpho.2002.0179

Staum Casasanto, Laura, Stefan Grondelaers & Roeland van Hout. 2015. Got class? Community-shared conceptualizations of social class in evaluative reactions to sociolinguistic variables. In Alexei Prikhodkine & Dennis R. Preston (eds.), *Responses to language varieties: Variability, processes and outcomes*, 157–174. John Benjamins.

Stevens, Kenneth N. 1998. *Acoustic phonetics*. MIT Press.

Stuart-Smith, Jane, Eleanor Lawson & James M. Scobbie. 2014. Derhoticisation in Scottish English. In Chiara Celata & Silvia Calamai (eds.), *Advances in sociophonetics*, 59–96. John Benjamins.

Tops, Evie. 2009. *Variatie en Verandering van de /r/ in Vlaanderen*. VUB Press.

Torp, Arne. 2001. Retroflex consonants and dorsal r—mutually excluding innovations?—On the diffusion of dorsal r in Scandinavian. In Van de Velde & van Hout, 75–90.

Ulbrich, Christiane & Horst Ulbrich. 2007. The realisation of /r/ in Swiss German and Austrian German. In *Proceedings from the 16th International Congress of Phonetic Sciences*, 1761–1764.

Van de Velde, Hans. 1996. *Variatie en verandering in het gesproken Standaard-Nederlands (1935–1993)*. Katholieke Universiteit Nijmegen.

Van de Velde, Hans & Didier Demolin. 2021. From alveolar [r] to uvular [R]: The symbiosis of dialectology, sociolinguistics, phonetics and phonology to explain sound change in progress. In Adolfo Arejita, A. (ed.), *Aniztasuna: Hizkeren berba-mintzoak*, 289–304. Euskaltzaindia.

Van de Velde, Hans, Anne-France Pinget, Cesko Voeten & Didier Demolin. 2021. Laboratory sociolinguistics. In Gitte Kristiansen, Karlien Franco, Stefano De Pascale, Laura Rosseel, & Weiwei Zhang (eds.), *Cognitive sociolinguistics revisited*, 557–571. Mouton de Gruyter. https://doi.org/10.1515/9783110733945-045

Van de Velde, Hans, Evie Tops & Roeland van Hout. 2013. The spreading of uvular [R] in Flanders. In Lorenzo Spreafico & Alessandro Vietti (eds.), *Rhotics: New data and perspectives*, 225–248. Bolzano University Press.

Van de Velde, Hans & Roeland van Hout (eds.). 2001. *'r-atics: Sociolinguistic, phonetic and phonological characteristics of /r/*. Etudes & Travaux–IVLP/ULB.

Van Reenen, Pieter. 1994. Driemaal /r/ in de Nederlandse dialecten. *Taal en Tongval* 46. 54–72.

Verhoeven, Jo. 1994. Fonetische eigenschappen van de Limburgse huig-*r*. *Taal en Tongval* 46. 9–21.

Verhoeven, Jo. 2005. Belgian Standard Dutch. *Journal of the International Phonetic Association* 35(2). 243–247. https://doi.org/10.1017/S0025100305002173

Voortman, Berber. 1994. *Regionale variatie in het taalgebruik van notabelen: Een sociolinguistisch onderzoek in Middelburg, Roermond en Zutphen*. IFOTT.

Walsh Dickey, Laura. 1997. *The phonology of liquids*. PhD thesis, University of Massachusetts.

Weijnen, Antonius Angelus. 1991. *Vergelijkende Klankleer van de Nederlandse dialecten*. SDU Uitgeverij.

Weinreich, Uriel, William Labov & Marvin Herzog. 1968. Empirical foundations for a theory of language change. In Winifred P. Lehmann & Yakov Malkiel (eds.), *Directions for historical linguistics: A symposium*, 95–195. University of Texas Press.

White, Yosiane, Meredith Tamminga & David Embick. Submitted. Methodological considerations for semantic priming studies in the auditory modality.

Wiese, Richard. 2000. *The phonology of German*. Oxford University Press.

Wiese, Richard. 2001. The unity and variation of (German) /r/. In Van de Velde & van Hout, 11–26.

Wollock, Jeffrey. 1982. Views on the decline of apical *r* in Europe: A historical study. *Folia Linguistica Historica* 3(2). 185–238. https://doi.org/10.1515/flih.1982.3.2.185

Wrench, Alan A. & James M. Scobbie. 2011. Very high frame rate ultrasound tongue imaging. In *Proceedings of the 9th International Seminar on Speech Production (ISSP)*, 155–162.

Zhang, Zhaoyan, Suzanne Boyce, Carol Espy-Wilson & Mark Tiede. 2003. Acoustic strategies for production of American English 'retroflex' /r/. In Maria-Josep Solé, Daniel Recasens & Joaquin Romero (eds.), *15th International Congress of Phonetic Sciences*, 1125–1128. ICPhS Archive.

10

SOCIOPHONETICS AND LATERALS

Danielle Turton

Introduction

Laterals are the L-like sounds of the world's languages, notable for displaying both consonant-like and vowel-like properties. From the Latin *lateralis* (literally 'belonging to the side'), laterals have closure at a point in the center of the oral tract (like a consonant) as well as the continuation of airflow down one or both sides of the tongue (like a vowel). In English, there is one phonemic lateral, the alveolar lateral approximant /l/, for example, in words like *laugh*, *fall*. Laterals have been subject to a large amount of study in sociolinguistics, phonetics, and phonology, likely due to their contextual and social variability, as well as their tendency to exhibit change over time.

This chapter summarizes existing literature on /l/ with a focus on sociophonetic research, alongside an overview of the phonetic methods used to examine variation. Whilst the focus is on English, which is the language most sociophonetic research on laterals investigates, a cross-linguistic summary is also provided. In addition, the chapter presents novel results on the sociophonetics of /l/ in a case study of Lancashire English, demonstrating some of the methods that can be used as avenues to investigate variation and change.

/l/ in English

Although English has one phonemic lateral, this is typically described as exhibiting two allophones: a "light" [l] and a "dark" [ɫ]. Syllable-based accounts of standard varieties like Received Pronunciation (RP) tend to describe the light allophone as occurring in onsets like *lovely*, and the dark allophone as occurring in codas like *pull* (e.g., Cruttenden 2014:217). In comparison to light [l], dark [ɫ] is said to have its tongue tip contact delayed, and to have a backer or even velarized tongue body (Giles & Moll 1975; Sproat & Fujimura 1993). This simple description has been illuminated by various work in sociolinguistics, phonetics, and phonology over the past few decades, showing that English /l/ is subject to vast amounts of variation not always previously accounted for in traditional descriptions. This includes full vocalization of /l/ (where the tongue tip contact may be lost altogether), phonetic gradience, morphosyntactic sensitivity, and conditioning by social factors such as age, gender, ethnicity, and social class.

DOI: 10.4324/9781003034636-11

English /l/ could be proposed to contain three broad variants forming a lenition trajectory (although see Polgárdi 2020 for an argument against /l/-darkening being a lenition process) with different varieties varying in the extent to which they display these from a phonetic and phonological perspective:

light [l] > dark [ɫ] > vocalized [w]

If dark [ɫ] is described as a delayed tongue tip gesture, vocalized [w] can be seen as the next stage of advancement on lenition trajectory whereby the tongue tip gesture is lost altogether. Although articulatory studies demonstrate that the exact nature of vocalization may vary regionally, and [w] may not be the most appropriate transcription for all of the disparate varieties which exhibit vocalization (e.g., Cockney, Philadelphian, Scottish), Ash's (1982) description of "the loss of contact between the tongue and the palate" seems to be an appropriate encapsulation across the English-speaking world. In addition, studies of some speech communities (such as some varieties of African American English) have indicated that vocalized /l/, rather than being some kind of back vocoid like [w], is actually more accurately described as complete deletion [Ø] (Labov et al. 1968; Thomas 1989; Thomas & Bailey 1998; Green 2002:120).

For the most part, studies of sociolinguistic variation in English /l/ have tended to focus on the process of vocalization, rather than darkening (e.g., Ash 1982; Horvath & Horvath 2001; Johnson & Britain 2007). This is likely due to the difficulty of measuring degree of darkness by ear, a feat which is easy for /l/-vocalization, at least the traditional kind of audible vocalization typified by accents such as Cockney (Tollfree 1999). It is also likely the case that this more extreme stage of the lenition trajectory has stronger perceptual salience, as it is more dissimilar from both the standard realization and its light counterpart. The advent of phonetic tools making more fine-grained acoustic analysis possible (Boersma & Weenink 1995) resulted in an increase in studies investigating /l/ sociophonetically from an acoustic perspective. This allowed researchers to investigate the relative lightness or darkness of /l/ on a continuum, most often using the difference between the first two formants as an acoustic correlate of darkness (lighter /l/s have a greater distance between F1 and F2; this will be explored in the context of measurements of /l/ below). These findings have been used to quantify variation in /l/ due to language-internal and external factors across varieties and within communities.

Language-internal factors

Context and morphosyntax

Word-final /l/ is the most common contextual position of study for variationists as this typically is the only position in which vocalization occurs. An exception to this is Ash (1982) in Philadelphia, who demonstrates that Philadelphia /l/ can vocalize in word-medial intervocalic tokens like *balance*, even making it near-homophonous with *bounce*. Most studies see this context as beyond the envelope of variation, focusing only on word-final vocalization. This does raise the question of defining the envelope of variation, however, as sound change may result in a progression of rule application throughout the morphosyntactic hierarchy (Turton 2014b) and a good example of this is word-final prevocalic vocalization in London. Tollfree's (1999) London data demonstrate that the youngest generation can vocalize before vowels in phrases such as *legal info*, a context which Wells (1982) had previously reported as excluded from vocalization. This demonstrates the advancement of change in the style of the life cycle of phonological processes (Bermúdez-Otero

2015; Turton 2017): a process starts its life in a phonetically favoring environment, for example, pre-pausal or pre-consonantal position, before this is reanalyzed by future generations by domain narrowing and advances into an ever-wider set of environments.

Adjacent segments

For word-final /l/s, following consonants tend to produce more vocalization than a following pause (Ash 1982), although some studies report similar effects between these two contexts (Dodsworth 2005). For /l/s in complex codas such as *help*, a hierarchy of vocalization seems to emerge from separate studies looking at place of articulation of the adjacent consonants. In the United Kingdom (Johnson & Britain 2007), the United States (Dodsworth 2005), and Australia (Horvath & Horvath 2002), a preceding velar is found to produce the most vocalization, followed by labials and then coronals: *milk > help > melt*. Although this pattern is predictable given the articulation of these segments, Ash (1982) finds no such effect in Philadelphia. Perhaps further articulatory data from Philadelphia vocalized /l/ (e.g., Purse 2020) could demonstrate if it differs considerably from vocalization in other varieties. Overall, articulatory studies of English /l/ consistently demonstrate that front vowels have a lightening effect on /l/s and back vowels have a darkening effect (Lehiste 1964; Giles & Moll 1975; Ash 1982).

Various studies consider the effects of /l/ on preceding individual vowels (e.g., Dinkin 2013; Holmes-Elliott & Smith 2018), but as Wells (1982:259) points out, perhaps the most interesting consequence of this is that /l/-vocalization may have "massive implications" for the reorganization of the vowel system in terms of conditional mergers. In the South-East of England, this happens in the back vowels, so that speakers have different versions of a merger between two or more of *pull*, *pool*, *Paul*, and possibly *pole* (reportedly the first three are merged in Southampton; Hughes, Trudgill & Watt 2012). This differs from some mergers in American English, such as that reported for Kansas City by Strelluf (2016), which primarily includes STRUT, FOOT, and GOAT, with GOOSE and THOUGHT also involved. In contrast, some /l/-vowel interactions can cause distinctions that other varieties do not have, such as the morphologically sensitive *holy–holey* distinction in RP (Sampson 1985; Halfacre 2019).

Intrusive /l/

Intrusive /l/ is relatively rare but reported for varieties with heavy vocalization, reflecting a form of phonologization or stabilization. In North America, it is found in areas such as Philadelphia and Pennsylvania more generally, where pronunciations such as *draw(l)ing* and *draw(l) it* can be heard, as well as Newark and other parts of New Jersey (Gick 2002). In the United Kingdom, this is a feature of Bristol English, to the extent that the original name of the city was Bristow (or *Brycgstow* to use the Old English spelling) before /l/ was inserted. Whereas it seems that in American English, intrusive-/l/ is a sandhi phenomenon occurring before following vowels, in Bristol it is reported as applying word-finally after a schwa, leading to the joke as reported by Wells (1982:344) about three sisters from Bristol named Idle, Evil, and Normal. Like intrusive-/r/, sandhi contexts in natural speech are extremely rare, but even so are etymologically schwa-final words in English. It is notable that Bristol is traditionally a rare remaining rhotic dialect of Anglo English (Blaxter et al. 2019), which raises interesting questions for liquid polarity (Carter & Local 2007)—the idea that a system with clearer /r/s should have darker /l/s and vice versa.

Language-external factors

Region

One of the starkest phonological differences between descriptions of the two mainstream trans-Atlantic varieties of English is that General American is said to have dark /l/ in all positions, whereas RP has some considerable difference between light word-initial *leap*-type tokens and dark word-final *peel*-type tokens (these are henceforth respectively labeled as the LEAP and PEEL lexical sets). Many phonetic studies of American English /l/ have corroborated the claim that speakers have very dark /l/s in all positions (e.g., Lehiste 1964), and this will be discussed further in the acoustic section below. Although the difference between initial and final /l/s is much smaller in American English than in a variety such as RP, most scholars still note a difference: the two contextual positions do not behave identically for most North Americans. The extent to which this represents an allophonic distinction is a topic of debate in phonetics and phonology (Sproat & Fujimura 1993; Hayes 2000; Turton 2017) which has incorporated arguments based on duration and morphological class (Yuan & Liberman 2009; Yuan & Liberman 2011; Lee-Kim, Davidson & Hwang 2013). In addition to the focus on the phonological and contextual debate, there is plenty of sociolinguistic variation within North America itself, which will be explored below.

In the British Isles, the situation seems to be much more variable in comparison to North America. Wells (1982:370) notes that in Northern England, varieties often do not show the kind of light/dark distinction found in RP and the south of England. Indeed, Taylor-Raebel (2017) puts forward the case that historical vowel breaking in the early scribal stages of Old English provides evidence for coda /l/ velarization being present in the south where breaking occurred (West Saxon, Kentish) but not so much in the North (Mercian, Northumbrian). Thus, this variation may have its roots in past millennia. Like American English, some Northern dialects have very dark /l/s in all positions, including the accents of Lancashire and Manchester (Kelly & Local 1986; Carter 2003; Beal 2008; Turton 2014a,b, 2017; Kirkham et al. 2019; Turton & Baranowski 2021), Liverpool (Knowles 1973; Turton 2017; Kirkham et al. 2019), and various locations in Yorkshire (Kelly & Local 1986; Carter 2002; Hughes, Trudgill & Watt 2012:149). Other regions of the North are traditionally claimed to be all-light, such as some areas in the North East including Newcastle, Sunderland, Durham, and Northumberland (Orton 1933; Carter 2003)—although, like many features of North East English (Watt 2002), this seems to be changing (Turton 2017). It is possible that the traditional Geordie word-final light /l/ is a feature restricted to working-class, perhaps older males today (Turton 2014a). Carlisle speakers on the west of England pattern more with the North East in having lighter /l/s (Hughes, Trudgill & Watt 2012:125), as has been found for other aspects of their sociophonetics (Jansen 2012).

Irish English speakers are notable for having very light /l/s in all positions (Jones 1966:92; Wells 1982:431; Hickey 2005:272; Hughes, Trudgill & Watt 2012:141), but sociolinguistic evidence from Derry in Northern Ireland demonstrates that this may be involved in a change in progress (McCafferty 1999:250). This could also be an effect conditioned by preceding vowel in Northern Irish varieties (Turton 2017). Linking back to North America, the Irish influence can be seen in Newfoundland, Canada through their traditionally light coda /l/s (Clarke 2010, 2012; Pierson 2016; De Decker & Mackenzie 2017). Indeed, as Clarke (2012) demonstrates, there is an ethno-religious effect in the speech community in that Irish heritage speakers show more of this light postvocalic variant. In contrast to the Irish, Scottish /l/s are very dark (Jones 1966:92), an observation which has been shown in various articulatory studies (alongside vocalization; see below). In Welsh English, /l/ may be subject to bilingualism effects (Morris 2017).

The lack of allophony in the British Isles outside of the South of England is reported in the Survey of English Dialects (Orton 1962). Mapping from these data visualizes the entirety of the North of England having light /l/ in coda position (Orton, Sanderson & Widdowson 1978; Figure 10.1 adapted from Johnson & Britain 2007). More recently, Kirkham, Turton & Leemann's (2020) analysis of the English Dialect App data (Leemann, Kolly & Britain 2018) showed that many Northern speakers did have more acoustic distance between initial and final /l/s than had been reported in some previous studies (e.g., Carter 2003; Turton 2014a). However, the authors note a social class skew; most of the speakers are young, upwardly mobile Northerners, 75 percent of whom have university degrees, which is not reflective of the general public as a whole (around a third of 18-year-olds embark on a university course in the UK; UCAS 2021). Thus, these speakers are likely speakers of General Northern English (Strycharczuk, López-Ibáñez et al. 2020), which is described as a leveled variety spoken by educated middle-class Northerners, and does not reflect the typical vernacular associated with the different areas.

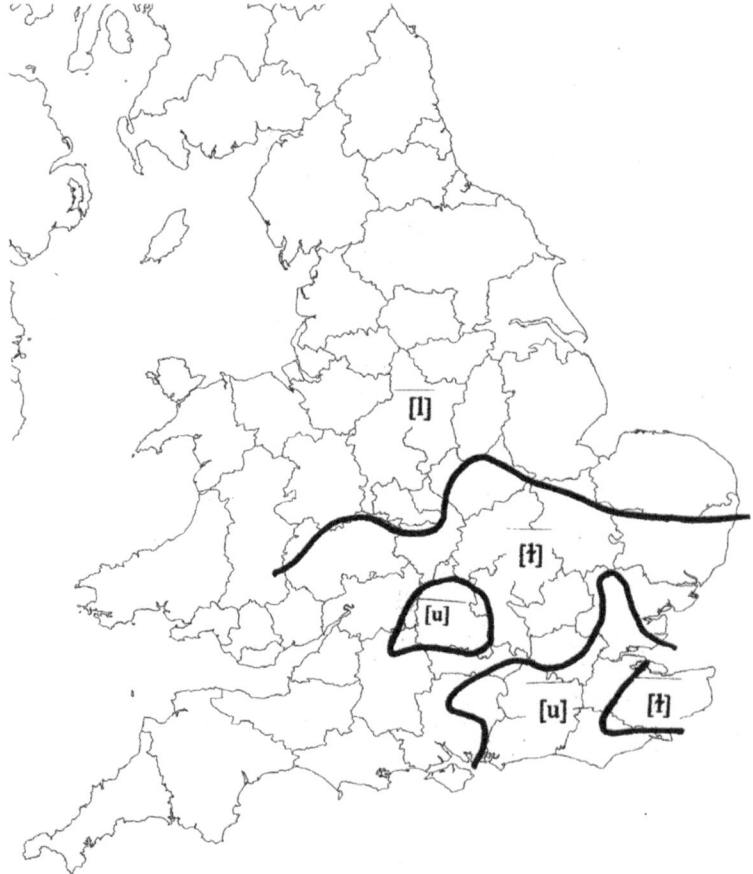

Figure 10.1 Survey of English Dialects results for word-final /l/

Source: Wyn Johnson & David Britain, L-vocalisation as a natural phenomenon: Explorations in sociophonology, *Language Sciences* 29(2). 294–315. © 2007, reprinted with permission from Elsevier

Above, we discussed /l/-vocalization as a process which can occur instead of darkness, found in disparate varieties all over the English-speaking world including the United States (Labov et al. 1968; Ash 1982; Hall-Lew & Fix 2012), Australia and New Zealand (Strycharczuk, Derrick & Shaw 2020), and the United Kingdom. In the United Kingdom, vocalization is associated with the South East of England (Wright 1989; Tollfree 1999; Przedlacka 2001; Johnson & Britain 2007; Strycharczuk & Scobbie 2020), but can also be found in Scotland (Wrench & Scobbie 2003; Scobbie & Pouplier 2010), as well as some northern areas such as Derby (Docherty & Foulkes 1999) and is mentioned passingly as a potential occurrence in Lancashire (Shorrocks 1980; Hughes, Trudgill & Watt 2012:149). /l/-vocalization has been claimed to be part of a number of urban features contributing to regional dialect leveling, typified by their presence in numerous locations throughout the UK (Britain 2009). Related to this, Johnson & Britain (2007) make the case that /l/-vocalization is phonetically natural, drawing on evidence such as that fact it is found in children of all varieties regardless of whether it persists into adulthood, as well as phonological optimality. Its presence in synchronically unconnected varieties may be further evidence of this, whilst also explaining why different varieties may display slightly different articulatory paths towards vocalization.

Age

Studies of /l/-vocalization demonstrate the most compelling evidence of the effect of age and change in progress for /l/ in the British Isles. Vocalization is reported as a change in progress in London (Tollfree 1999) and in South-Eastern English accents in general (Wells 1982; Przedlacka 2001; Johnson & Britain 2007), today even found among some RP speakers (Lindsey 2019:72). Indeed, Wells (1982:259) states that "it seems likely that it will become entirely standard in English over the course of the next century." Vocalization's status as part of a set of "urban youth norms" (Foulkes & Docherty 1999; Britain 2009) is reflected in the numerous locations it has been reported as a change in progress. On the other hand, studies of vocalization in the United States tend to find age is not a conditioning factor in variation (Ash 1982; Dodsworth, Plichta & Durian 2006; Durian 2008), although some varieties of African American English may be an exception to this.

Allophonic variation between light and dark /l/ also appears to be emerging in some varieties which historically were reported only to use one form of /l/, such as Newfoundland in Canada (Clarke 2012; Pierson 2016) and East Anglia in Britain (Wells 1982:340). It is perhaps no coincidence that this pattern tends to occur in varieties which were all-light at some point, leaving the word-final /l/ with capacity to darken. However, it does not necessarily follow that all-dark varieties cannot undergo change via different mechanisms. In Manchester, England, where initial /l/ is traditionally dark, younger speakers' already-dark /l/s are becoming even darker in apparent time (Turton & Baranowski 2021). This is something which may be happening to other all-dark varieties of the North given contemporary comparisons with old dialect data (e.g., Sheffield in Yorkshire in Stoddart, Upton & Widdowson 1999 report /l/ as all-light but Kirkham 2017 finds, at least for white speakers, /l/ is all-dark).

Gender

In British varieties, given the stark contrast between light and dark /l/s in RP and other accents of the South East, we may predict a gender preference mirroring this pattern in other areas of the country—that is, women leaning more towards the more prestigious standard. This is the case from reports in areas such as the West Midlands (Mathisen 1999) and Edinburgh (Speitel 1983), both areas which have very dark /l/s across the board. However, it seems that this tendency is over-ruled when /l/ is involved in a change in progress, which shows the usual effect of women leading (Labov 2001). London high school students show female lead in /l/-vocalization (Hudson & Holloway 1977) and, more recently in the North of England, the aforementioned change in progress towards darker /l/s in Manchester is also led by women (Turton & Baranowski 2021). One exception to this is Derby (Docherty & Foulkes 1999), where young working-class males lead in the change towards higher frequency of vocalization. Perhaps this is a difference in the level of conscious awareness. Certainly in terms of Manchester darkening, this is a change from below the level of conscious awareness. It is also likely the case that /l/-vocalization in London existed below the social radar in the early days of the sound change, despite it being more of a Cockney stereotype today—for example, Wells (1982:259) notes no marking of vocalization orthographically in *Pygmalion*'s Eliza Doolittle. In Derby, /l/-vocalization has been proposed as part of a set of urban youth norms (along with t-glottaling and TH-fronting; Britain 2009) potentially originating in London. Thus, it is possible that vocalization in Derby is a change from above the level of conscious awareness, which is why the non-standard change is male-led. This hypothesis is supported by the presence of style-shifting, which Docherty & Foulkes (1999:52) describe as "complex" because of the way it interacts with social factors such as age, gender, and class, both phonetically and phonologically.

Social class

Interestingly, darker or vocalized /l/s are features of working-class speech in several distinct varieties. This includes Manchester (Turton & Baranowski 2021) and Derby (Docherty & Foulkes 1999) in England, as well as Edinburgh (Speitel 1983) and Glasgow (Stuart-Smith 1999) in Scotland. In Newfoundland, Canada, the speech community seems to exhibit a change from below led by the second-lowest social class (Clarke 2012), in line with the curvilinear hypothesis (Labov 2001). It does seem a sharper allophony is found in the middle classes in Britain, which matches the phonetic and phonological representation found in RP. The middle-class university-educated speakers described above in Kirkham, Turton & Leemann (2020) support this observation by displaying a greater distance between initial and final /l/s than may have been described for their speech communities in the dialectological literature. In a communities-of-practice approach, Pratt (2020) demonstrates that very dark initial /l/s are utilized by a group of "tech" students (students involved with technical manual labor projects in the school) at a San Francisco high school. Pratt provides evidence that these students reflect a working-class persona in style, embodiment, and speech. Dodsworth's (2005) results potentially show us class through the lens of urban versus suburban, and she argues that lack of vocalization is a local marker of identity in the Greater Columbus area of Ohio, whilst a follow-up study of vocalization shows that this advanced stage of lenition reflects a more urban than suburban affiliation (Dodsworth, Plichta & Durian 2006). Why such an effect should be found across synchronically unconnected varieties is intriguing and Kroch's (1978:19) theory of social dialect variation comes to mind—that is, "working-class speech is more susceptible to the processes of phonetic conditioning than is the prestige dialect" and that working-class dialects tend to be "articulatorily more economical than the prestige" precisely because speakers do not subscribe to the same social pressures. Whether dark variants with their cumbersome dorsal gesture could be considered "articulatorily more economical" is a matter for debate elsewhere.

Style and stigma and identity

Variation in /l/ according to social class raises issues of speech style, of the degree to which speakers are consciously aware of /l/ variants as prestigious or stigmatized, and of whether speakers might operationalize /l/ in style-shifting. Tollfree (1999:175) notes vocalization is not stigmatized in London, although it maybe is "unconsciously suppressed" when accommodating towards the standard. Suppression of vocalization in more formal elicited styles and laboratory conditions is also reported by Hughes, Trudgill & Watt (2012) and Turton (2014a, 2014b), albeit on rare occasions. Evidence for vocalization being present in Standard Southern British English and even modern RP would support such a lack of awareness. For example, Lindsey (2019) points out that Boris Johnson, the former Prime Minister of the UK, has an elite upbringing and education, but is also an /l/-vocalizer.

Ethnicity and bilingualism

Studies within and across different ethnic groups have provided one of the most fruitful areas of investigation for the sociophonetics of /l/. Indeed, the earliest study of variation in /l/-vocalization was Labov et al.'s (1968) study of African American and Puerto Rican speakers in New York. Studies of ethnic minority groups are also an exception to the generalization that sociolinguistic investigations of /l/ focus on categorical vocalization instead of gradient approaches to darkness. Various studies have shown British South Asian speakers to display very light /l/s (Heselwood & McChrystal 2000; Sharma 2012; Kirkham 2015, 2017; Turton & Baranowski 2021) which in turn has been suggested to be an effect from languages such as Punjabi and Urdu (Naseem 2002; Stuart-Smith, Timmins & Alam 2011). In addition, Black Caribbean speakers born and raised in Manchester have lighter /l/s than their white counterparts (Turton & Baranowski 2021). It has also been proposed that this also could be a heritage effect, as lighter /l/s are found in Caribbean Englishes (Wells 1982:570). Turton & Baranowski (2021) suggest that lighter /l/s could be a feature of the new emerging multicultural youth varieties of British English cities (e.g., Cheshire et al. 2011; Drummond 2017; Gates et al. 2019).

Bilinguals in the United Kingdom contribute to this picture, with many unrelated groups showing the same pattern of lighter /l/s when compared to their white/Anglo English counterparts. Welsh-English bilinguals have lighter initial /l/s in their English than in their Welsh (Morris 2013, 2017). Young Scottish Gaelic bilinguals in Glasgow show influence from their English /l/s and may not have acquired the three-lateral system of Gaelic (Nance 2013, 2014). Lebanese Arabic and English bilinguals in Yorkshire keep their all-light Arabic and light/dark English systems largely intact (Khattab 2002, 2011) although there is some evidence of light coda /l/s which are potentially an effect of their Arabic (note that Lebanese Australian women may also exhibit lighter /l/s compared to their white counterparts; Clothier 2019).

Studies of African American speakers report a combination of patterns of darkening and vocalization which at first looks like a confound; speakers have lighter /l/s overall (Van Hofwegen 2010), but also more vocalization and even full deletion (Thomas 1989; Thomas & Bailey 1998; Green 2002:120; Durian 2008). This is easily explained when we note that varieties of African American English (AAE) have a greater distance between initial and final /l/ than mainstream American English, resulting in a pattern closer to the standard varieties of the British Isles. At its extreme, this would mean lighter /l/s in onsets but vocalization or even full deletion in codas. However, the traditional lighter AAE initial /l/s are becoming more like mainstream American English dark /l/s in apparent time (Van Hofwegen 2010), so we may see this distinction collapse in the future. Fix (2011:54) asserts that vocalization of /l/ is often used as a mimicry of AAE speakers. In her study of white women with African American friend networks, she finds the stronger the network, the higher the rate of vocalization (2011:205).

Latino New Yorkers have very clear onset /l/s (Slomanson & Newman 2004) which are characteristic of Spanish and "the most salient marker of Latino English in New York" (Newman 2010:216). In Newman (2010), although the lightest /l/ speaker is bilingual, there are some speakers at the top of the lightness continuum who speak little Spanish, demonstrating that heritage effects appear in the speech community's variety of English even for members who are not actively bilingual. This heritage effect is also what is found commonly in the UK varieties listed above.

/l/ variation cross-linguistically

Cross-linguistically, data from phonetic studies demonstrate that laterals are subject to the same extent of variation as we see in English, but sociolinguistic research is limited. The most prominent range of studies are probably on Catalan which—due to its complicated relationship as a minority language competing and coexisting with majority Spanish—has received much attention to the phonetics of its laterals (Recasens 2004; Recasens & Espinosa 2005; Simonet 2010). The velarized Catalan /l/ is subject to overt commentary as *ela catalana* 'the Catalan l' within and outside of Catalonia. Davidson (2019) argues that it constitutes a linguistic stereotype in the sense of Labov (2001). Whilst it is widely recognized that this /l/-realization transfers to L1 Catalan speakers' Spanish (e.g., Simonet 2010), more recent dedicated sociolinguistic research has demonstrated that L1 Spanish speakers in Catalonia also have darker /l/s in their Spanish when compared to speakers in Madrid (Davidson 2022), demonstrating that Catalan's status as a minority language is dubious within Catalonian urban centers of power such as Barcelona. In a study of Catalonia politicians, Blas-Arroyo (2021) demonstrates how pro-independence politicians are more likely to employ velarized /l/, which he argues indexes Catalan authenticity.

Within the minority languages of the British Isles, /l/ is well-described in comparison to other sociophonetic features. In her work with Scottish Gaelic speakers from the Isle of Lewis, Nance (2022) argues that—whilst younger generations are less acoustically distinct in the traditional three-lateral system of the language and may drop the laterality in their palatal glides—an argument for typical sound change may be problematic. She argues for an approach which pays due consideration to the fact that the local social practices around Gaelic for the older and younger generations is a better all-round predictor for change. Morris (2013) finds that /l/ is all-dark in the Welsh of speakers from North Wales, in word-initial, medial, and final positions. He notes that male speakers show the same pattern in their English, whereas females have a distinction.

Most other cross-linguistic research on /l/ shows changes in the forms associated with minority languages and dialects towards the forms associated with majority varieties. Kasstan & Müller (2017) find contact-induced change in Francoprovençal speakers, who are accommodating towards French in their use of onset cluster /l/s being palatalized. In the Viennese dialect of Austrian German, a velarized /l/ is said to have been adopted in the mid twentieth century as a result of contact with Czech immigrants in the traditional labor districts (Moosmüller et al. 2016). While men use this variant in all contextual positions, women only use velarized forms word-finally, in line with the standard. For the Uruguayan Portuguese palatal lateral /ʎ/, the standard [ʎ] is favored over nonstandard vocalized [j] (which has more stigmatized rural or working-class associations) in more formal speaking tasks, by women, by higher social classes, and among younger speakers. These findings suggest a change-from-above towards Brazilian Portuguese urban contact varieties

(Carvalho 2003; see also Bortoni-Ricardo 1985:173 for Brazilian varieties). In Arabic, /l/ is all-light and may not exhibit an alveolar gesture as typically described for languages such as English, but it may be pharyngealized or darkened in the context of emphatic consonants (Khattab 2002, 2011). In her study of Lebanese Arabic speakers, Khattab (2011) found a slight tendency for males to demonstrate emphatic context pharyngealization, but notes that a larger sociophonetic study would be required to disentangle this from other factors, such as specific variety and co-occurrence with other emphatic features.

Measuring /l/

Auditory studies

Analyzing /l/ variation by ear has been utilized by many sociolinguistic studies in the United Kingdom (Tollfree 1999; Stuart-Smith, Timmins & Tweedie 2006; Johnson & Britain 2007), the United States (Labov et al. 1968; Ash 1982; Durian 2008; Fix 2011), and Australia and New Zealand (Horvath & Horvath 2001, 2002; Borowsky 2001). These studies focus on vocalization, which is fairly simple to code auditorily. Hall-Lew & Fix (2012) report a "surprisingly high" level of intercoder reliability for their analyses of American English /l/ (whilst still cautioning that three coders is desirable over a sole coder). Analyzing the darkness of /l/ auditorily from a quantitative variationist perspective—that is, categorizing into light and dark variants—is probably best avoided. This is because of the difficulty of coding, coder bias, and the fact that darkness manifests differently between varieties. I know of no quantitative variationist studies that have done this (although see Hall-Lew & Fix 2012 for auditorily coded gradations of /l/).

Whilst coding, researchers will be looking to account for contextual information such as previous sound, following sound, position in word (e.g., simple vs. complex coda) and the position in phrase, all of which, as we have seen, have been found to predict variation in /l/ realization.

Acoustic studies

Although acoustic phonetic studies of /l/-darkness have been around for some time (e.g., Lehiste 1964), more recent advancements in the accessibility of spectrogram analyses has led to increasing numbers of sociophoneticians analyzing variation in /l/ instrumentally. Such studies most typically concern the difference between light and dark /l/, as vocalized /l/ is very difficult to distinguish from dark variants by acoustic means (Hall-Lew & Fix 2012). The primary acoustic correlate of /l/-darkness is said to be the proximity between F2 and F1. A darker /l/ has a low F2 which is close to F1. Thus, dark /l/ is characterized by a close proximity between F1 and F2, whereas light /l/ has a relatively high F2 and a low F1 (Ladefoged & Maddieson 1996; Carter 2003; Hawkins & Nguyen 2004; Gick et al. 2006). Although increased bandwidth has been associated with lateralization (Stevens & Blumstein 1994)—the presence of which is typically reduced or absent during vocalization—sociolinguists have yet to effectively quantify this to differentiate between dark and vocalized /l/. This may be a worthy avenue for future researchers.

Although RP and many varieties of British English have a much larger distinction between the first and second formants than North American English for word-initial /l/ (see Figure 10.2), most North American studies still report a robust distinction between word-initial and word-final contexts (Lehiste 1964; Nolan 1983; Olive, Greenwood & Coleman 1993; Carter 2002; Yuan & Liberman 2011; Mackenzie et al. 2018). Acoustically, some of the all-dark British English

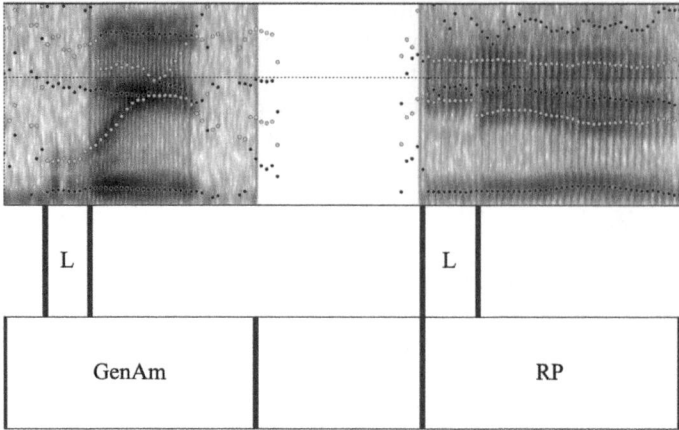

Figure 10.2   Word-initial /l/s in General American English (left, leap) and Received Pronunciation (right, Leoni)

Source: data from Turton 2014a

varieties discussed above pattern more closely with American English in that they have extremely close F1 and F2 formant trajectories.

Researchers interested in measuring /l/ by acoustic means should be aware that some have expressed concern on the reliability of such measures (Umeda 1977:846). This can be best overcome by controlling for adjacent vowels, which can have a strong conditioning effect on the /l/ (Lehiste 1964; Bladon & Al-Bamerni 1976; Nolan 1983). This perhaps explains why so few studies use spontaneous speech to measure gradient darkness (cf. Van Hofwegen 2010; Turton & Baranowski 2021), and it is certainly the case that a vast dataset is advised to effectively account for such articulatory biases by statistical means. Another methodological consideration is that of static versus dynamic measurements—that is, does the researcher rely on one point of analysis (such as the midpoint, or the midpoint of the steady state) or take measurements over the course of the /l/? On deciding whether to take static or dynamic measurements, researchers will want to consider their research questions. Dynamic measurements were once reserved for more phonetically focused studies, with those interested in investigating morphology and social factors focusing on static measurements. However, with the advent of accessible Generalized Additive Mixed Models (GAMMs; e.g., Sóskuthy 2017; Kirkham et al. 2019) it is becoming more feasible to interpret trajectory analysis through the lens of independent predictors such as social factors and linguistic factors. Nevertheless, dynamic analyses have arguably been favored in articulatory research on /l/, which we will turn to now.

Articulatory studies

Papers on the articulation of /l/ go back decades (e.g., Giles & Moll 1975) and this trend has continued into the present day both in British Englishes (Hardcastle & Barry 1989; Wright 1989; Barry 2000; Scobbie & Wrench 2003; Wrench & Scobbie 2003; Scobbie, Pouplier & Wrench 2007; Scobbie & Pouplier 2010; Turton 2017; Kirkham et al. 2019; Strycharczuk, Derrick & Shaw 2020) and in North American Englishes (Stone 1990; Sproat & Fujimura 1993; Narayanan, Alwan & Haker 1997; Gick et al. 2006; Lee-Kim, Davidson & Hwang 2013; Lin, Beddor &

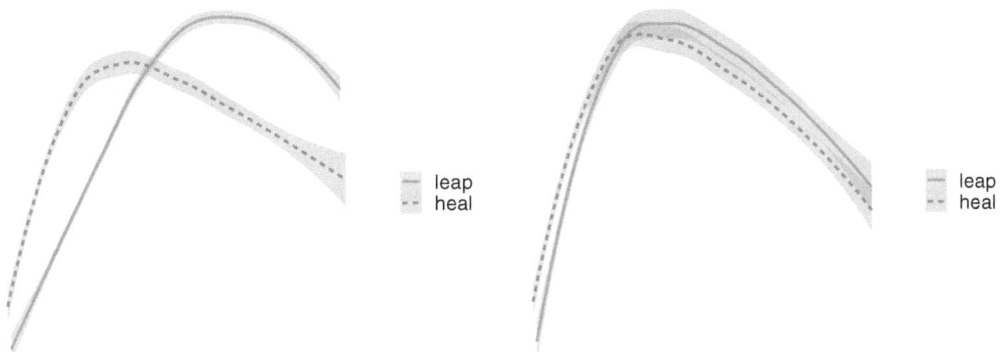

Figure 10.3 Word-initial and word-final contexts in RP (left) and Manchester (right) on ultrasound

Source: data from Turton 2014a

Coetzee 2014; De Decker & Mackenzie 2017). This is likely helped by increasing accessibility of techniques such as ultrasound tongue imaging, which is relatively cheap, noninvasive, safe, and easy to use.

The primary articulatory correlate of the difference between light and dark /l/ is said to be the amount of tongue retraction (Giles & Moll 1975), with the tongue being less retracted for light /l/ than dark /l/. In Sproat & Fujimura's (1993) influential X-ray microbeam study, the authors argue it is the relative phasing of the coronal and dorsal gestures which accounts for a light or dark /l/. The dorsal gesture lags in a lighter /l/ and leads in a darker /l/, although they explicitly reject the idea of two allophones. Note, their subjects are speakers of American English which, as has been highlighted, has much less difference between initial and final /l/s than some varieties of British English. Figure 10.3, adapted from Turton (2017), uses ultrasound tongue imaging comparisons from varieties such as RP and Manchester English to demonstrate that whilst some accents like Manchester may not have an obvious allophonic distinction, RP clearly does.

In the same manner as debates around acoustic methodologies, researchers also vary on whether they focus on static (Turton 2017) or dynamic (Lin 2011; Kirkham et al. 2019) approaches to the articulation of /l/. Strycharczuk & Scobbie's (2020) temporal approach to vocalization in Standard Southern British English using ultrasound unveils that most extreme vocalization is typified by the deletion of the tongue tip gesture, and that the temporal measure of gestural delay is a secondary manifestation of weakening. This demonstrates that a static analysis would suffice for describing a general pattern for these segments, but a temporal analysis adds detail to our understanding of these complex sounds, whilst offering a window into previously unaccounted-for mechanisms of sound change.

As discussed, studies of /l/-vocalization usually define the process as lack of contact between the tongue and the palate (Wright 1989; Wrench & Scobbie 2003; Scobbie & Pouplier 2010). This articulatory categorical "cut-off" can circumnavigate the light/dark allophonic debate some-what. That said, electropalatography studies such as Hardcastle & Barry (1989) demonstrate that vocalization can indeed have a gradient component. More recent articulatory studies of vocaliza-tion have considered degree of backness of the tongue body (Turton 2017), loss of lateralization (Strycharczuk, Derrick & Shaw 2020; Strycharczuk & Scobbie 2020), and lip-rounding (Wrench

& Scobbie 2003; Lin & Demuth 2015; Proctor et al. 2019; Szalay et al. 2019), deepening our understanding of the mechanisms of articulation further, whilst opening up new research questions for future researchers.

As technology for doing articulatory data collection and analysis improves, the promise of a tighter integration with sociolinguistic methods and easier circumnavigation of the Observer's Paradox awaits. For example, smaller ultrasound machines the size of an external hard drive means informants can be recorded in their homes, instead of in the formal lab setting. In addition, new computational methods for ultrasound analysis such as DeepLabCut (Wrench & Balch-Tomes 2022) mean that tongue tip information could more reliably be drawn from ultrasound, making it a potential alternative to the more invasive electromagnetic articulometry.

CASE STUDY   /l/ in Lancashire

Northern English varieties spoken in Lancashire are described as having dark /l/ in all positions (Beal 2008:130; Hughes, Trudgill & Watt 2012:149). Hughes, Trudgill & Watt (2012:149) note that vocalization may also occur in coda position (see also Shorrocks 1980 on Bolton). The primary focus of this case study is an acoustic analysis of /l/-darkness within the speech community of Blackburn, East Lancashire, whilst also noting that patterns of vocalization warrant further study. This section covers some of the phonetic measurements taken from novel data and presents visualizations and statistical models of observed variation.

Methods

Data are taken from spontaneous speech with 28 white speakers from Blackburn, Lancashire recorded between 2015 and 2018. Interviews were force-aligned in FAVE and formant measurements taken automatically from all /l/s across ten timepoints using a Praat script. This analysis focuses on the static midpoint only, with a view to incorporating more dynamic analysis in future studies. The contextual approach of this initial investigation is to focus on the contexts at the extremes of the potential morphology–syntax continuum: word-initial LEAP tokens and word-final PEEL tokens.

Separate mixed-effects linear regression models were created using the lmer package (Bates et al. 2015) in R (R Core Team 2022). These were run on word-initial and word-final tokens separately, with speaker and word as random effects. Contexts were separated to best analyze the neighboring segmental effects which are different for initial and final tokens (see also Turton & Baranowski 2021). All visualizations are averaged over speaker and word to account for influential or disproportionate speakers or words, as is best practice in modern spontaneous speech studies.

Table 10.1 Demographic breakdown of informants

	Younger (17–45)	*Older (49–81)*
Female	7	7
Male	7	7

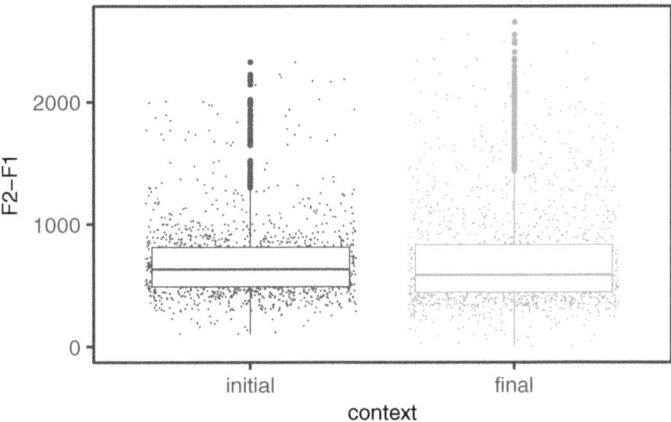

Figure 10.4   Initial vs. final /l/s in Blackburn, Lancashire

Results

Figure 10.4 shows initial versus final /l/s in Lancashire, demonstrating that there is little difference between the two contexts. Word-final prevocalic tokens (e.g., *feel it*) have been removed as a cautious approach, as we know that sometimes they behave like onsets and sometimes like codas (although it seems like that is unlikely to be of concern to us here). Note the small difference in medians in the expected direction: initial tokens are lighter than final tokens. Although it has been argued that careful laboratory data are required to ascertain the categoricity of allophonic distribution of /l/, it is not unreasonable to suggest that this small effect is potentially an epiphenomenal effect of duration (longer /l/s are darker; Sproat & Fujimura 1993; Lee-Kim, Davidson & Hwang 2013) rather than a very small acoustic reflection of allophony.

The separate linear mixed-effects models on the F2-F1 of initial and final tokens tested the following predictors: speaker gender (female vs. male); speaker age (continuous number in models, binned into 'old' and 'young' for visualization); gender*age interaction; following and preceding context (consonant, pause or vowel type); stress (primary, secondary or unstressed); /l/ duration (log transformed).

Differences between age groups were considered to see if there was any evidence of a change in progress. Recall that nearby Manchester, the closest large urban center (40 miles away from Blackburn) has recently been found to have initial /l/s changing in progress towards being darker (Turton & Baranowski 2021). There is a hint of this in Figure 10.5 which shows for the initial tokens that older speakers trend towards having lighter /l/s than younger speakers (the same direction as nearby Manchester). This does not come out as significant in the model, however, but note that the study of Manchester was a much larger representative sample of the speech community with 96 speakers over 99 years of birth. In Blackburn, final /l/s look entirely stable and this is confirmed in the model.

However, when we consider a gender–age interaction in the initial /l/s, a similar effect to that found in nearby Manchester is unveiled. This is visualized in Figure 10.6 and shows that a move towards darker /l/s in apparent time is found in the females only. This effect is confirmed by a

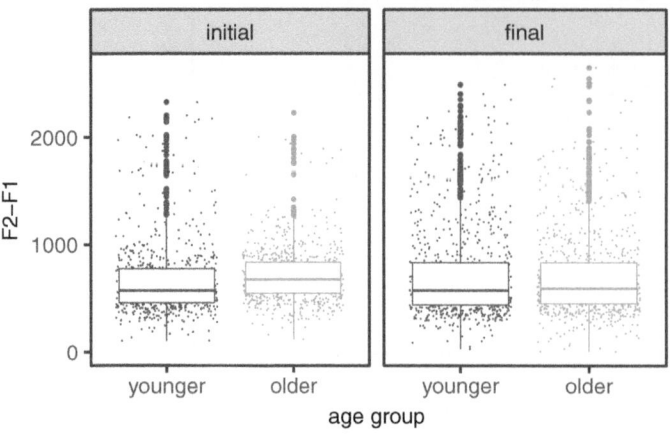

Figure 10.5   Initial and final /l/s across younger (<45) and older (>49) speakers

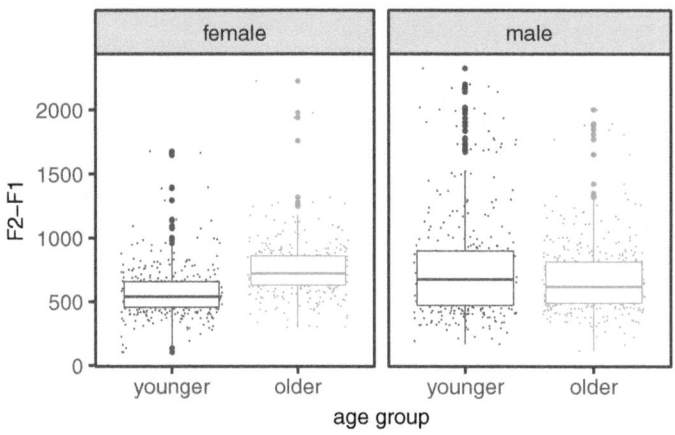

Figure 10.6   Initial /l/s across age and gender

significant addition of an age*gender effect into the initial /l/s model (by ANOVA comparison), and by separate regressions run on females and males which indicates that age is significant for females only. Thus, we may be seeing a shift to darker initial /l/s as led by females in more areas of the North of England.

In terms of nonsocial effects, preceding and following segments and contexts have strong co-articulatory effects—almost always in the expected direction—and these effects are summarized in Table 10.2. Measures of adjacent vowel height seem to fare as stronger predictors in all contexts as opposed to vowel frontness, and inclusion of height measures always results in frontness being a redundant addition to the model, as confirmed by ANOVA comparison and nonsignificant *t*-values. For word-final /l/s, the following context or height does more of the labor than the preceding context or height, and for word-initial /l/s the preceding context and height does more work. This suggests that

Table 10.2 Effects of predictors on lightness of /l/

Predictor	Effect in initial /l/ LEAP tokens	Effect in final /l/ PEEL tokens
Gender	Males are lighter than females	**Males are lighter than females**
Age	Older speakers are lighter	Older speakers are lighter
Following context	**Following vowel height: high > mid > low** from lightest to darkest	**A following low vowel has a strong darkening effect; a following pause has a lighter /l/ than a following consonant following height predictor performs better than following frontness** (by AIC)
Preceding context	**Phrase-initial /l/s are lightest** In comparison to a preceding consonant, **an adjacent low or mid vowel in the preceding word results in a darker /l/, but a high vowel results in a lighter /l/.**	**Preceding vowel height: high > mid > low** from lightest to darkest **stress: unstressed *able* are lighter than stressed *fell***
Duration	**Longer /l/s are darker**	**Longer /l/s are darker**
Age*gender (interaction)	**Females show a rate of change in progress towards being darker, males are stable**	None

Note. Significant effects in **bold**.

it is the overall phrasal context that is more important than the adjacent vowel per se. One unexpected effect was that of the preceding stress of the vowel in word-final /l/s. An unstressed preceding vowel (e.g., *able*) was lighter than a stressed preceding vowel. This effect remains when taking account of vowel height or backness, and is potentially down to the duration of the entire rime which is likely to be shorter in such environments, hence resulting in a lighter /l/.

Discussion

We have seen that Lancashire /l/s do indeed seem to be all-dark, as evidenced acoustically by a small difference between F2-F1 in all positions. In terms of social factors, it has been tentatively suggested that initial /l/ may be getting darker in apparent time and is led by females, as has been found in nearby Manchester (Turton & Baranowski 2021). Social class has not been tested here due to lack of fine-grained stratification, but should be tested in larger iterations of the dataset. In terms of contextual conditioning, LEAP tokens are lightest when they are phrase-initial (i.e., following a pause) and PEEL tokens are darker before a consonant than a pause. Predictable effects of vowel height and frontness were found, although height was the main focus of the statistical models as it had a much stronger effect. Longer /l/s are darker, as expected given the agreement of previous research.

The results so far, alongside auditory observations of the data, reveal potential avenues for future research in auditory and articulatory sociophonetics. The next step could be to investigate the extent of /l/-vocalization in coda position with an auditory analysis. Vocalization is certainly something which crops up from time to time in the interviews, although it can be rare in some speakers, and others show none whatsoever. Below, I list some passing observations on Lancashire /l/-vocalization based on casual listening to the sociolinguistic interviews:

1) It seems more common after back vowels, although not restricted to this position. *School*, *ball*, *bowl* seem to be common contexts (note THOUGHT and GOAT are merged in Blackburn anyway so the last two examples are homophones). Blackburn has some GOOSE-fronting, but no fronting before /l/, unlike other North West areas such as Manchester (Turton & Baranowski 2015).
2) The word *well* seems to be a spot for vocalization. This could be a frequency effect—this word is highly frequent in interview speech. However, it also tallies with the observation by Shorrocks (1980) that preceding /ɛ/ is an environment for vocalization in nearby Bolton.
3) Vocalization seems to occur at higher rates in some younger speakers. That said, some of our young speakers show no evidence of it. However, there is possible evidence of it being more contextually advanced in some younger speakers, for example, one of our young males has extreme vocalization after front vowels in words like *peel*.

Vocalization of /l/ in Lancashire is not a new observation, so whilst it is tempting to look at this as maybe yet another area of the British Isles which has succumbed to this "urban youth norm" (Foulkes & Docherty 1999; Britain 2009), it is more likely that this is a feature which has been around for some time. Thus, it may simply be conditioned by something other than what I have been able to investigate within the constraints of this case study, and this motivates a proper auditory analysis of the variation to disentangle potential effects of vocalization which may have been missed in the acoustics. It is worth noting that Blackburn is a rhotic dialect of Lancashire English (Turton & Lennon, under revision) which, considering previous interest in phonetics and phonology in liquid polarity as mentioned earlier for Bristol (e.g., Carter 2002; Carter & Local 2007), may be of interest in further investigations.

In terms of articulatory work, investigations using ultrasound tongue imaging or electromagnetic articulatography would allow us to engage with arguments around gestural phasing and tongue body position. We may wish to pose questions such as, if all /l/s are phonetically dark, do we see any difference in the relative phasing of gestures in initial versus final position? Extending this to consider any effects of vocalization, we might ask, how does tongue body position compare in dark versus vocalized final /l/s?

Conclusion

This chapter has provided an overview of sociophonetic studies of laterals, especially in English. We have seen how social factors such as age, gender, class, and ethnicity are predictors of both /l/-vocalization and the relative lightness or darkness of /l/ within a given speech community. We have considered examples of how researchers implement various methodologies to investigate such variation by auditory, acoustic, and articulatory means. Using an acoustic sociophonetic approach, we have also seen how these methods can be applied to novel data on /l/ from Blackburn in Lancashire, confirming a lack of any obvious allophony and potentially suggesting a change in progress towards an even darker realization in apparent time led by young females.

Looking ahead, as various studies have unveiled, /l/ is changing across the English-speaking world in socially interesting ways, and level of conscious awareness plays an intriguing role which is yet to be unveiled. Further investigation disentangling these social effects would be beneficial, particularly if we could get the articulatory insights from more relaxed settings. However, the vast majority of studies are on English, and sociolinguistic analyses of languages other than English are vital for moving forward our understanding of how this set of sound changes over time and space.

Acknowledgments

This research was funded by the Leverhulme Trust grant RPG-2020-029. I would like to thank my speakers, as well as George Bailey, Maciej Baranowski, Ricardo Bermúdez-Otero, Maya Dewhurst, Josef Fruehwald, Robert Lennon, Patrycja Strycharczuk, and the Lancaster University Phonetics Lab.

References

Ash, Sharon. 1982. *The vocalization of /l/ in Philadelphia*. PhD dissertation, University of Pennsylvania.

Barry, Martin. 2000. A phonetic and phonological investigation of English clear and dark syllabic /l/. *Bulletin de la Communication Parlée* 5. 77–88.

Bates, Douglas, Martin Mächler, Ben Bolker & Steve Walker. 2015. Fitting linear mixed-effects models using lme4. *Journal of Statistical Software* 67(1). 1–48. https://doi.org/10.18637/jss.v067.i01

Beal, Joan. 2008. English dialects in the north of England: Phonology. In Bernd Kortmann & Clive Upton (eds.), *Varieties of English*, vol. 1, *The British Isles*, 122–144. Mouton de Gruyter.

Bermúdez-Otero, Ricardo. 2015. Amphichronic explanation and the life cycle of phonological processes. In Patrick Honeybone & Joseph C. Salmons (eds.), *The Oxford handbook of historical phonology*, 374–399. Oxford University Press.

Bladon, R.A.W. & Ameen Al-Bamerni. 1976. Coarticulation resistance of English /l/. *Journal of Phonetics* 4(2). 135–150. https://doi.org/10.1016/S0095-4470(19)31234-3

Blas-Arroyo, José. 2021. Indexing political identity in the Catalonian procés: A sociophonetic approach. *Language in Society* 50(3). 411–440. https://doi.org/10.1017/S004740452000072X

Blaxter, Tam, Kate Beeching, Richard Coates, James Murphy & Emily Robinson. 2019. Each p[ɚ]son does it th[ɛː] way: Rhoticity variation and the community grammar. *Language Variation and Change* 31(1). 91–117. https://doi.org/10.1017/S0954394519000048

Boersma, Paul & David Weenink. 1995. *Praat: Doing phonetics by computer* [Computer program], ver. 3.1. www.praat.org/

Borowsky, Toni. 2001. The vocalisation of dark-l in Australian English. In David Blair & Peter Collins (eds.), *English in Australia*, 69–87. John Benjamins. https://doi.org/10.1075/veaw.g26.07bor

Bortoni-Ricardo, S.M. 1985. *The urbanization of rural dialect speakers: A sociolinguistic study in Brazil*. Cambridge University Press.

Britain, David. 2009. One foot in the grave? Dialect death, dialect contact, and dialect birth in England. *International Journal of the Sociology of Language* 2009. 121–155. https://doi.org/10.1515/IJSL.2009.019

Calhoun, Sasha, Paola Escudero, Marija Tabain & Paul Warren (eds.). 2019. *Proceedings of the 19th International Congress of Phonetic Sciences, Melbourne, Australia 2019*. Australasian Speech Science and Technology Association.

Carter, Paul. 2002. *Structured variation in British English liquids*. PhD thesis, University of York.

Carter, Paul. 2003. Extrinsic phonetic interpretation: Spectral variation in English liquids. In Richard Ogden, John Local & Rosalind Temple (eds.), *Phonetic interpretation: Papers in laboratory phonology* 6, 237–252. Cambridge University Press.

Carter, Paul & John Local. 2007. F2 variation in Newcastle and Leeds English liquid systems. *Journal of the International Phonetic Association* 37(2). 183–199. https://doi.org/10.1017/S0025100307002939

Carvalho, Ana Maria. 2003. The sociolinguistic distribution of (lh) in Uruguayan Portuguese: A case of dialect diffusion. In Silvina Montrul & Francisco Ordóñez (eds.), *Linguistic theory and language development in Hispanic languages*, 30–44. Cascadilla.

Cheshire, Jenny, Paul Kerswill, Sue Fox & Eivind Torgersen. 2011. Contact, the feature pool and the speech community: The emergence of Multicultural London English. *Journal of Sociolinguistics* 15(2). 151–196. https://doi.org/10.1111/j.1467-9841.2011.00478.x

Clarke, Sandra. 2010. *Newfoundland and Labrador English*. Edinburgh University Press.

Clarke, Sandra. 2012. Phonetic change in Newfoundland English. *World Englishes* 31(4). 503–518. https://doi.org/10.1111/j.1467-971X.2012.01777.x

Clothier, Josh. 2019. A sociophonetic analysis of /l/ darkness and Lebanese Australian ethnic identity in Australian English. In Calhoun et al., 1888–1892.

Cruttenden, Alan. 2014. *Gimson's pronunciation of English*. Routledge.

Davidson, Justin. 2019. Covert and overt attitudes towards Catalonian Spanish laterals and intervocalic fricatives. In Whitney Chappell (ed.), *Recent advances in the study of Spanish sociophonetic perception*, 39–84. John Benjamins. https://doi.org/10.1075/ihll.21.03dav

Davidson, Justin. 2022. On Catalan as a minority language: The case of Catalan laterals in Barcelonan Spanish. *Journal of Sociolinguistics* 26(3). 362–385. https://doi.org/10.1111/josl.12545W

De Decker, Paul M. & Sara Mackenzie. 2017. Tracking the phonological status of /l/ in Newfoundland English: Experiments in articulation and acoustics. *Journal of the Acoustical Society of America* 142(1). 350–362. https://doi.org/10.1121/1.4991349

Dinkin, Aaron J. 2013. What's really happening to short-a before L in Philadelphia? *American Speech* 88(1). 7–31. https://doi.org/10.1215/00031283-2322619

Docherty, Gerard J. & Paul Foulkes. 1999. Derby and Newcastle: Instrumental phonetics and variationist studies. In Foulkes & Docherty, 47–71.

Dodsworth, Robin. 2005. Attribute networking: A technique for modeling social perceptions. *Journal of Sociolinguistics* 9(2). 225–253. https://doi.org/10.1111/j.1360-6441.2005.00291.x

Dodsworth, Robin, Bartek Plichta & David Durian. 2006. An acoustic study of Columbus /l/ vocalization. Paper presented at NWAV 35, Columbus, OH.

Drummond, Rob. 2017. (Mis)interpreting urban youth language: White kids sounding Black? *Journal of Youth Studies* 20(5). 640–660. https://doi.org/10.1080/13676261.2016.1260692

Durian, David. 2008. The vocalization of /l/ in urban blue collar Columbus, OH African American Vernacular English: A quantitative sociophonetic analysis. *Ohio State University Working Papers in Linguistics* 58. 30–51.

Fix, Sonya. 2011. *"Dark-skinned white girls": Linguistic and ideological variation among white women with African American ties in the urban Midwest*. PhD dissertation, New York University.

Foulkes, Paul & Gerald J. Docherty (eds.). 1999. *Urban voices: Accent studies in the British Isles*. Arnold.

Gates, Shivonne M, Christian Ilbury, Clare Wright, Lou Harvey & James Simpson. 2019. Standard language ideology and the non-standard adolescent speaker. In Clare Wright, Lou Harvey & James Simpson (eds.), *Voices and practices in applied linguistics: Diversifying a discipline*, 109–126. White Rose University Press. https://doi.org/10.22599/BAAL1.g

Gick, Bryan. 2002. The American intrusive l. *American Speech* 77(2). 167–183. https://doi.org/10.1215/00031283-77-2-167

Gick, Bryan, Fiona Campbell, Sunyoung Oh & Linda Tamburri-Watt. 2006. Toward universals in the gestural organization of syllables: A cross-linguistic study of liquids. *Journal of Phonetics* 34(1). 49–72. https://doi.org/10.1016/j.wocn.2005.03.005

Giles, Stephen B. & Kenneth L. Moll. 1975. Cinefluorographic study of selected allophones of English /l/. *Phonetica* 31. 206–227. https://doi.org/10.1159/000259670

Green, Lisa J. 2002. *African American English: A linguistic introduction*. Cambridge University Press.

Halfacre, Caitlin. 2019. North-South dividers in privately educated speakers: A sociolinguistic study of Received Pronunciation using the FOOT-strut and TRAP-BATH distinctions in the North East and South East of England. In Calhoun et al., 2665–2669.

Hall-Lew, Lauren & Sonya Fix. 2012. Perceptual coding reliability of (L)-vocalization in casual speech data. *Lingua* 122(7). 794–809. https://doi.org/10.1016/j.lingua.2011.12.005

Hardcastle, William & William Barry. 1989. Articulatory and perceptual factors in /l/ vocalisations in English. *Journal of the International Phonetic Association* 15(2). 3–17. https://doi.org/10.1017/S0025100300002930

Hawkins, Sarah & Noël Nguyen. 2004. Influence of syllable-coda voicing on the acoustic properties of syllable-onset /l/ in English. *Journal of Phonetics* 32(2). 199–231. https://doi.org/10.1016/S0095-4470(03)00031-7

Hayes, Bruce. 2000. Gradient well-formedness in Optimality Theory. In Joost Dekkers, Frank van der Leeuw & Jeroen van de Weijer (eds.), *Optimality Theory: Phonology, syntax, and acquisition*, 88–120. Oxford University Press.

Heselwood, Barry & Louise McChrystal. 2000. Gender, accent features and voicing in Panjabi-English bilingual children. *Leeds Working Papers in Linguistics and Phonetics* 8. 45–70.

Hickey, Raymond. 2005. *Dublin English: Evolution and change*. John Benjamins.

Holmes-Elliott, Sophie & Jennifer Smith. 2018. Dressing down up north: DRESS-lowering and /l/ allophony in a Scottish dialect. *Language Variation and Change* 30(1). 23–50. https://doi.org/10.1017/S0954394517000278

Horvath, Barbara M. & Ronald J. Horvath. 2001. A multilocality study of a sound change in progress: The case of /l/ vocalization in New Zealand and Australian English. *Language Variation and Change* 13(1). 37–57. https://doi.org/10.1017/S0954394501131029

Horvath, Barbara M. & Ronald J. Horvath. 2002. The geolinguistics of /l/-vocalization in Australia and New Zealand. *Journal of Sociolinguistics* 6(3). 319–346. https://doi.org/10.1111/1467-9481.00191

Hudson, Richard & A.F. Holloway. 1977. *Variation in London English*. Final Report to the Social Sciences Research Council. Department of Phonetics & Linguistics, University College London.

Hughes, Arthur, Peter Trudgill & Dominic Watt. 2012. *English accents and dialects: An introduction to social and regional varieties of English in the British Isles*. Routledge.

Jansen, Sandra. 2012. *Language variation and change in the Cumbrian City Dialect of Carlisle*. PhD thesis, University of Duisburg-Essen.

Johnson, Wyn & David Britain. 2007. L-vocalisation as a natural phenomenon: Explorations in sociophonology. *Language Sciences* 29(2). 294–315. https://doi.org/10.1016/j.langsci.2006.12.022

Jones, Daniel. 1966. *The pronunciation of English*, 4th edn. Cambridge University Press.

Kasstan, Jonathan & Daniela Müller. 2017. (l) as a sociolinguistic variable in Francoprovençal. *International Journal of the Sociology of Language*. 249. 99–118.

Kelly, John & John Local. 1986. Long-domain resonance patterns in English. In *International Conference on Speech Input/Output; techniques and applications* [IEE Conference Publication Number 258], 304–309. Institution of Electrical Engineers.

Khattab, Ghada. 2002. /l/ production in English-Arabic bilingual speakers. *International Journal of Bilingualism* 6(3). 335–353. https://doi.org/10.1177/13670069020060030701

Khattab, Ghada. 2011. Acquisition of Lebanese Arabic and Yorkshire English /l/ by bilingual and monolingual children. In Zeki Majeed Hassan & Barry Heselwood (eds.), *Instrumental studies in Arabic phonetics*, 325–354. John Benjamins.

Kirkham, Sam. 2015. Intersectionality and the social meanings of variation: Class, ethnicity, and social practice. *Language in Society* 44(5). 629–652. https://doi.org/10.1017/S0047404515000585

Kirkham, Sam. 2017. Ethnicity and phonetic variation in Sheffield English liquids. *Journal of the International Phonetic Association* 47(1). 17–35. https://doi.org/10.1017/S0025100316000268

Kirkham, Sam, Claire Nance, Bethany Littlewood, Kate Lightfoot & Eve Groarke. 2019. Dialect variation in formant dynamics: The acoustics of lateral and vowel sequences in Manchester and Liverpool English. *Journal of the Acoustical Society of America* 145. 784–794. https://doi.org/10.1121/1.5089886

Kirkham, Sam, Danielle Turton & Adrian Leemann. 2020. A typology of laterals in twelve English dialects. *Journal of the Acoustical Society of America* 148(1). EL72–EL76. https://doi.org/10.1121/10.0001587

Knowles, Gerald O. 1973. *Scouse: The urban dialect of Liverpool*. PhD thesis, University of Leeds.

Kroch, Anthony. 1978. Toward a theory of social dialect variation. *Language in Society* 7(1). 17–36. https://doi.org/10.1017/S0047404500005315

Labov, William. 2001. *Principles of linguistic change*, vol. 2, *Social factors*. Blackwell.

Labov, William, Paul Cohen, Clarence Robins & John Lewis. 1968. *A study of the nonstandard English of Negro and Puerto Rican speakers of New York City*, vol. 1, *Phonological and grammatical analysis*. Office of Education Cooperative Research Project 3288.

Ladefoged, Peter & Ian Maddieson. 1996. *The sounds of the world's languages*. Blackwell.

Lee-Kim, Sang-Im, Lisa Davidson & Sangjin Hwang. 2013. Morphological effects on the darkness of English intervocalic /l/. *Laboratory Phonology* 4(2). 475–511. https://doi.org/10.1515/lp-2013-0015

Leemann, Adrian, Marie-José Kolly & David Britain. 2018. The English Dialects App: The creation of a crowdsourced dialect corpus. *Ampersand* 5. 1–17. https://doi.org/10.1016/j.amper.2017.11.001

Lehiste, Ilse. 1964. Acoustical characteristics of selected English consonants. *Indiana Research Center in Anthropology, Folklore, and Linguistics* 34. 10–50.

Lin, Susan. 2011. *Production and perception of prosodically varying inter-gestural timing in American English laterals*. PhD thesis, University of Michigan.

Lin, Susan, Patrice Speeter Beddor & Andries W. Coetzee. 2014. Gestural reduction, lexical frequency, and sound change: A study of post-vocalic /l/. *Laboratory Phonology* 5(1). 9–26. https://doi.org/10.1515/lp-2014-0002

Lin, Susan & Katherine Demuth. 2015. Children's acquisition of English onset and coda /l/: Articulatory evidence. *Journal of Speech, Language, and Hearing Research* 58(1). 13–27. https://doi.org/10.1044/2014_JSLHR-S-14-0041

Lindsey, Geoff. 2019. *English after RP standard British pronunciation today*. Palgrave Macmillan.

Mackenzie, Sara, Erin Olson, Meghan Clayards & Michael Wagner. 2018. North American /l/ both darkens and lightens depending on morphological constituency and segmental context. *Laboratory Phonology* 9(1). https://doi.org/10.5334/labphon.104

Mathisen, Anne. 1999. Sandwell, West Midlands: Ambiguous perspectives on gender patterns and models of change. In Foulkes & Docherty, 107–123.

McCafferty, Kevin. 1999. Derry: Between Ulster and local speech–class, ethnicity and language change. In Foulkes & Docherty, 246–264.

Moosmüller, Sylvia, Carolin Schmid & Christian H. Kasess. 2016. Alveolar and velarized laterals in Albanian and in the Viennese dialect. *Language and Speech* 59(4). 488–515. https://doi.org/10.1177/002383 0915615

Morris, Jonathan. 2013. *Sociolinguistic variation and regional minority language bilingualism: An investigation of Welsh-English bilinguals in North Wales*. PhD thesis, University of Manchester.

Morris, Jonathan. 2017. Sociophonetic variation in a long-term language contact situation:/l/-darkening in Welsh-English bilingual speech. *Journal of Sociolinguistics* 21(2). 183–207. https://doi.org/10.1111/josl.12231

Nance, Claire. 2013. *Phonetic variation, sound change, and identity in Scottish Gaelic*. PhD thesis, University of Glasgow.

Nance, Claire. 2014. Phonetic variation in Scottish Gaelic laterals. *Journal of Phonetics* 47. 1–17. https://doi.org/10.1016/j.wocn.2014.07.005

Nance, Claire. 2022. Sound change or community change? The speech community in sound change studies: a case study of Scottish Gaelic. *Linguistics Vanguard* 8(s5). 677–689. https://doi.org/10.1515/lingvan-2021-0023

Narayanan, Shrikanth S, Abeer A Alwan & Katherine Haker. 1997. Toward articulatory-acoustic models for liquid approximants based on MRI and EPG data. Part I. The laterals. *Journal of the Acoustical Society of America* 101(2). 1064–1077.m https://doi.org/10.1121/1.418030

Naseem, Tahira. 2002. Acoustic analysis of Punjabi phonemes /l/ and /n/. *CRULP Annual Student Report 2002–3* 3.

Newman, Michael. 2010. Focusing, implicational scaling, and the dialect status of New York Latino English. *Journal of Sociolinguistics* 14(2). 207–239. https://doi.org/10.1111/j.1467-9841.2010.00441.x

Nolan, Francis (ed.). 1983. *The phonetic bases of speaker recognition*. Cambridge University Press.

Olive, Joseph P., Alice Greenwood & John Coleman. 1993. *Acoustics of American English speech: A dynamic approach*. Springer Verlag.

Orton, Harold. 1933. *The phonology of a south Durham dialect: Descriptive, historical, and comparative*. Keegan Paul.

Orton, Harold. 1962. *Survey of English dialects (a): Introduction*. Routledge.

Orton, Harold, S. Sanderson & J. Widdowson (eds.). 1978. *The linguistic atlas of England*. Croom Helm.

Pierson, Rosanna. 2016. *The current state of /l/ allophony in St. John's English*. MA thesis, Memorial University of Newfoundland.

Polgárdi, Krisztina. 2020. Darkening and vocalisation of /l/ in English: An Element Theory account. *English Language & Linguistics* 24(4). 745–768. https://doi.org/10.1017/S1360674319000315

Pratt, Teresa. 2020. Embodying "tech": Articulatory setting, phonetic variation, and social meaning. *Journal of Sociolinguistics* 24(3). 328–349. https://doi.org/10.1111/josl.12369

Proctor, Michael, Rachel Walker, Caitlin Smith, Tünde Szalay, Louis Goldstein & Shrikanth Narayanan. 2019. Articulatory characterization of English liquid-final rimes. *Journal of Phonetics* 77. 100921. https://doi.org/10.1016/j.wocn.2019.100921

Przedlacka, Joanna. 2001. Estuary English and RP: Some recent findings. *Studia Anglica Posnaniensia* 36. 35–50.

Purse, Ruaridh. 2020. The envelope of variation for /l/ vocalisation in Philadelphia English. *University of Pennsylvania Working Papers in Linguistics* 25(2). 99–106. https://repository.upenn.edu/pwpl/vol25/iss2/12

R Core Team. 2022. *R: A language and environment for statistical computing*. R Foundation for Statistical Computing. www.R-project.org

Recasens, Daniel. 2004. Darkness in [l] as a scalar phonetic property: Implications for phonology and articulatory control. *Clinical Linguistics and Phonetics* 18(6–8). 593–603. https://doi.org/10.1080/026992004 10001703556

Recasens, Daniel & Aina Espinosa. 2005. Articulatory, positional and coarticulatory characteristics for clear /l/and dark /l/: Evidence from two Catalan dialects. *Journal of the International Phonetic Association* 35(1). 1–25. https://doi.org/10.1017/S0025100305001878

Sampson, Rodney. 1985. The 'GOAT split': A phonological puzzle in one variety of English. *Anglia* 103. 282–296.

Scobbie, James M., Marianne Pouplier & Alan Wrench. 2007. Conditioning factors in external sandhi: an EPG study of English /l/ vocalisation. In *Proceedings of the 16th International Congress of Phonetic Sciences, Saarland University, Saarbrücken*, 441–444.

Scobbie, James M. & Marianne Pouplier. 2010. The role of syllable structure in external sandhi: An EPG study of vocalisation and retraction in word-final English /l/. *Journal of Phonetics* 38(2). 240–259. https://doi.org/10.1016/j.wocn.2009.10.005

Scobbie, James M. & Alan A. Wrench. 2003. An articulatory investigation of word final /l/ and /l/-sandhi in three dialects of English. In Maria-Josep Solé, Daniel Recasens & Joaquin Romero, *Proceedings of the 15th International Congress of Phonetic Sciences, Barcelona, Spain*, 1871–1874. Universitat Autonoma de Barcelona.

Sharma, Devyani. 2012. Stylistic activation in ethnolinguistic repertoires. *University of Pennsylvania Working Papers in Linguistics* 18(2). Article 15. https://repository.upenn.edu/pwpl/vol18/iss2/15

Shorrocks, Graham. 1980. *A grammar of the dialect of Farnworth and District (Greater Manchester county, formerly Lancashire)*. PhD thesis, University of Sheffield.

Simonet, Miquel. 2010. Dark and clear laterals in Catalan and Spanish: Interaction of phonetic categories in early bilinguals. *Journal of Phonetics* 38(4). 663–678. https://doi.org/10.1016/j.wocn.2010.10.002

Slomanson, Peter & Michael Newman. 2004. Peer group identification and variation in New York Latino English laterals. *English World-Wide* 25(2). 199–216. https://doi.org/10.1075/eww.25.2.03slo

Sóskuthy, Márton. 2017. Generalised Additive Mixed Models for dynamic analysis in linguistics: A practical introduction. *arXiv:1703.05339*. https://doi.org/10.48550/arXiv.1703.05339

Speitel, Hans-Henning. 1983. *A sociolinguistic investigation of Edinburgh speech*. Economic Social Research Council end of grant report.

Sproat, Richard & Osamu Fujimura. 1993. Allophonic variation in English /l/ and its implications for phonetic implementation. *Journal of Phonetics* 21(3). 291–311. https://doi.org/10.1016/S0095-4470(19)31340-3

Stevens, Kenneth N. & Sheila E. Blumstein. 1994. Attributes of lateral consonants. *Journal of the Acoustical Society of America* 95. 2875. https://doi.org/10.1121/1.409455

Stoddart, Jana, Clive Upton & J. Widdowson. 1999. Sheffield dialect in the 1990s: Revisiting the concept of NORMs. In Foulkes & Docherty, 72–89.

Stone, Maureen. 1990. A three-dimensional model of tongue movement based on ultrasound and x-ray microbeam data. *Journal of the Acoustical Society of America* 87(5). 2207–2217. https://doi.org/10.1121/1.399188

Strelluf, Christopher. 2016. Overlap among back vowels before /l/ in Kansas City. *Language Variation and Change* 28(3). 379–407. https://doi.org/10.1017/S0954394516000144

Strycharczuk, Patrycja, Donald Derrick & Jason Shaw. 2020. Locating de-lateralization in the pathway of sound changes affecting coda /l/. *Laboratory Phonology* 11(1). 21. https://doi.org/10.5334/labphon.236

Strycharczuk, Patrycja, Manuel López-Ibáñez, Georgina Brown & Adrian Leemann. 2020. General Northern English. Exploring regional variation in the North of England with machine learning. *Frontiers in Artificial Intelligence* 3(48). 1–18. https://doi.org/10.3389/frai.2020.00048

Strycharczuk, Patrycja & James M. Scobbie. 2020. Gestural delay and gestural reduction: Articulatory variation in /l/-vocalisation in southern British English. In Anne Przewozny, Cécile Viollain & Sylvain Navarro, *The corpus phonology of English: Multifocal analyses of variation*, 9–29. Edinburgh University Press. https://doi.org/10.1515/9781474467018-006

Stuart-Smith, Jane. 1999. Glasgow: Accent and voice quality. In Foulkes & Docherty, 201–222.

Stuart-Smith, Jane, Claire Timmins & Farhana Alam. 2011. Hybridity and ethnic accents: A sociophonetic analysis of "Glaswasian." In Frans Gregersen, Jeffrey K. Parrott & Pia Quist (eds.), *Language variation. European perspectives III: Selected papers from the 5th International Conference on Language Variation in Europe (ICLaVE 5), Copenhagen, June 2009*, 43–57. John Benjamins.

Stuart-Smith, Jane, Claire Timmins & Fiona Tweedie. 2006. Conservation and innovation in a traditional dialect: L-vocalization in Glaswegian. *English World-Wide* 27(1). 71–87. https://doi.org/10.1075/eww.27.1.05stu

Szalay, Tünde, Titia Benders, Felicity Cox & Michael Proctor. 2019. Lingual configuration of Australian English /l/. In Calhoun et al., 2816–2820.

Taylor-Raebel, Gary. 2017. *Vocalisations evidence from Germanic*. PhD thesis, University of Essex.

Thomas, Erik R. 1989. Vowel changes in Columbus, Ohio. *Journal of English Linguistics* 22(2). 205–215. https://doi.org/10.1177/007542428902200204

Thomas, Erik R. & Guy Bailey. 1998. Parallels between vowel subsystems of African American Vernacular English and Caribbean anglophone creoles. *Journal of Pidgin and Creole Languages* 13(2). 267–296. https://doi.org/10.1075/jpcl.13.2.03tho

Tollfree, L.F. 1999. South-east London English: Discrete versus continuous modelling of consonantal reduction. In Foulkes & Docherty, 163–184.

Turton, Danielle. 2014a. *Variation in English /l/: Synchronic reflections of the life cycle of phonological processes*. PhD thesis, University of Manchester.

Turton, Danielle. 2014b. Some /l/s are darker than others: Accounting for variation in English /l/ with ultrasound tongue imaging. *Pennsylvania Working Papers in Linguistics* 20(2). https://repository.upenn.edu/pwpl/vol20/iss2/21

Turton, Danielle. 2017. Categorical or gradient? An ultrasound investigation of /l/-darkening and vocalisation in varieties of English. *Laboratory Phonology* 8(1). http://doi.org/10.5334/labphon.35

Turton, Danielle & Maciej Baranowski. 2015. Absence of a blocking r[Y]l?: The presence of /u/-fronting before /l/ in Manchester. Paper presented at UKLVC10, University of York.

Turton, Danielle & Maciej Baranowski. 2021. The sociolinguistics of /l/ in Manchester. *Linguistics Vanguard* 7(1). 20200074. https://doi.org/10.1515/lingvan-2020-0074

Turton, Danielle & Robert Lennon. Under revision. An acoustic analysis of rhoticity in Lancashire, England.

UCAS. 2021. Record levels of young people accepted into university. 7 Sept. www.ucas.com/corporate/news-and-key-documents/news/record-levels-young-people-accepted-university

Umeda, Noriko. 1977. Consonant duration in American English. *Journal of the Acoustical Society of America* 61(3). 846–858. https://doi.org/10.1121/1.381374

Van Hofwegen, Janneke. 2010. Apparent-time evolution of /l/ in one African American community. *Language Variation and Change* 22(03). 373–396. https://doi.org/10.1017/S0954394510000141

Watt, Dominic. 2002. "I don't speak with a Geordie accent, I speak, like, the northern accent": Contact-induced levelling in the Tyneside vowel system. *Journal of Sociolinguistics* 6(1). 44–63. https://doi.org/10.1111/1467-9481.00176

Wells, John C. 1982. *Accents of English*. 3 vols. Cambridge University Press.

Wrench, Alan A. & Jonathan Balch-Tomes. 2022. Beyond the edge: Markerless pose estimation of speech articulators from ultrasound and camera images using DeepLabCut. *Sensors* 22(3). 1133. https://doi.org/10.3390/s22031133

Wrench, Alan A. & James M. Scobbie. 2003. Categorising vocalisation of English /l/ using EPG, EMA and ultrasound. In Sallyanne Palethorpe & Marija Tabain (eds.), *Proceedings of the Sixth International Seminar on Speech Production*, 314–319. Macquarie Centre for Cognitive Science.

Wright, Susan. 1989. The effects of style and speaking rate on /l/-vocalisation in Local Cambridge English. *York Papers in Linguistics* 13. 355–365.

Yuan, Jiahong & Mark Liberman. 2009. Investigating /l/ variation in English through forced alignment. *Proceedings of Interspeech 2009*. 2215–2218. https://doi.org/10.21437/Interspeech.2009-630

Yuan, Jiahong & Mark Liberman. 2011. /l/ variation in American English: A corpus approach. *Journal of Speech Sciences* 1(2). 35–46. https://doi.org/10.20396/joss.v1i2.15025

11

SOCIOPHONETICS AND VOWEL NASALITY

Christopher Carignan and Georgia Zellou

Introduction

What is nasalization?

The speech process typically referred to as "nasalization" involves the articulatory lowering of the soft palate, also known as the velum. Although the primary functions of velum control are to aid in swallowing and breathing and to protect the structures of the nasal cavity, velum movement also plays a vital role in linguistic sound systems by enabling the contrast between oral phonemes (produced with a raised velum) and nasal phonemes (produced with a lowered velum). Of the languages represented in the World Atlas of Language Structures database, 98 percent utilize phonemic consonant nasality (Maddieson 2013), in which there is a complete closure in the oral cavity while the velum is lowered, and over a quarter utilize phonemic vowel nasality (Hajek 2013), in which the velum is lowered during the production of a vowel, as a phonologically contrastive feature.

Consonant nasality in particular has received considerable focus in sociophonetic research. For instance, (ING) variation—the alternation in English between velar and alveolar articulations of the final phoneme in words that end in <ing> like *running* or *talking*—has been found to vary according to a range of social and contextual factors, as well as identity practices (e.g., Labov 1966; Campbell-Kibler 2007, 2010). In this chapter, we focus instead on vowel nasalization. The complexity of vowel nasalization, due to its articulation, acoustic realization, and its perception, generates the potential for sound change and, thus, opportunity to investigate and understand socially conditioned language variation.

Lowering the velum aerodynamically and acoustically couples the nasal tract to the oropharyngeal tract via the velopharyngeal port (the gap formed by the space between the velum and the posterior pharyngeal wall), allowing air to flow into the nasal cavity and acoustic energy to radiate from the nostrils. For ease of interpretability and two-dimensional visualization, nasalization is most often illustrated using midsagittal profiles, such as the magnetic resonance images shown in Figure 11.1a–b, wherein the velum is depicted as a kind of "lever," "switch," or "trap door" that flips up and down as a mechanism to control nasalization. These simplified depictions also often characterize the nasal cavity as an empty void, for example as shown in Figure 11.1c, through

DOI: 10.4324/9781003034636-12

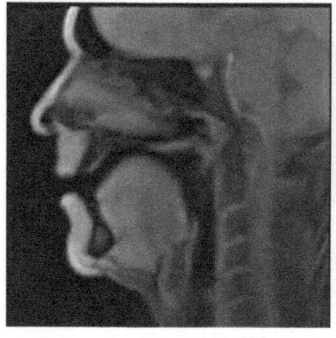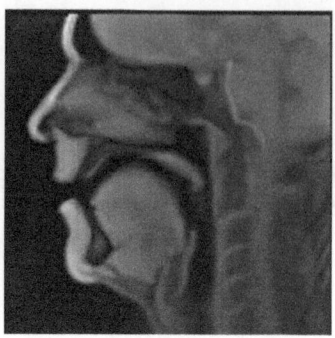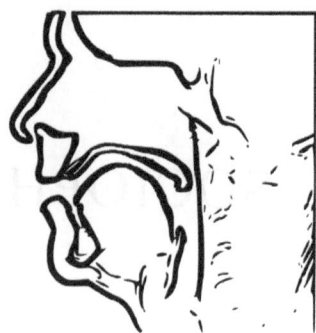

Figure 11.1   Midsagittal profiles of the oral and nasal cavity
Figure 11.1a (left)   Oral vowel, produced with a raised velum
Figure 11.1b (middle)   Nasal(ized) vowel, produced with a lowered velum
Figure 11.1c (right)   Simplified representation of vowel nasalization

which it is (unintentionally) presumed that air flows in an unimpeded manner. Yet, considering velum lowering through this simplified perspective makes it easy to neglect the truly complex nature of the physiology involved in nasalization and its effect on the acoustic speech output. In reality, controlling the height and tension of the velum and the aperture of the velopharyngeal port is a complex activity involving the interplay of multiple muscles. Far from being an empty chamber, the nasal cavity is composed of a series of curved bone shelves (conchae) and hollow cavities (sinuses) and is lined with an acoustically absorbent mucous membrane. This anatomical complexity alters airflow and acoustic transmission in equally complex ways, resulting in a wide range of modifications to the acoustic signal. For the production of vowel nasalization, in particular, these modifications include (but are not limited to) a reduction in formant amplitudes, widening of formant bandwidths, modulation of formant frequencies, shifting of spectral energy toward lower frequencies, and the addition of poles (i.e., formants) and zeros (i.e., anti-formants) to the acoustic spectrum (Fujimura & Lindqvist 1971; Maeda 1993; Feng & Castelli 1996; Chen 1997; Styler 2017; Carignan 2018c).

The multidimensional nature of vowel nasalization

Since the velum is relatively independent from other speech articulators in physiological terms, there is very little constraint on its articulation during vowel production. This gestural independence allows for potential articulatory variation in both the temporal and featural domains, variation that we will refer to loosely as "co-articulation." Co-articulation is most commonly considered in reference to variation in the temporal domain. A typical example is anticipatory co-articulation in VN sequences, where V is an oral vowel and N is a nasal consonant; in anticipation of the production of N, the velum lowers early within V, resulting in some portion of V that is phonetically nasalized due to a temporal overlap with the velum lowering gesture. In this case, a single articulatory gesture is co-produced over adjacent sounds, leading to its "shared" realization between the two segments.

Temporal co-articulation is independent from, but may co-occur with, featural co-articulation. Velum lowering may co-vary with tongue position, lip shape, pharyngeal constriction, and/or laryngeal configuration. For example, a nasal vowel may also be rounded and/or breathy, and it has been argued that this type of featural co-articulation may in fact be used to enhance linguistic contrast of nasal vowels (Carignan 2014, 2017; Garellek, Ritchart & Kuang 2016). Thus, in the case of co-articulation in the featural domain, multiple separate articulatory gestures are co-produced as features of a single segment. We use the term "articulatory co-variation" for this latter kind of co-articulation in order to distinguish it from temporal co-articulation. A growing body of research suggests that articulatory co-variation in both phonetically contextual and phonemically contrastive vowel nasalization is much more frequent and typologically prevalent than is assumed by the conventional view that nasal vowels are simply oral vowels produced with a lowered velum (Shosted 2015; Carignan 2018a).

Vowel nasalization not only has the capacity to be multidimensional in production, but also in perception. Perceptual research has suggested that the acoustic complexity arising from vowel nasalization can lead to ambiguity for listeners, particularly with regard to the percep-tual relationship between nasalization, breathy phonation, and tongue height. Breathiness on vowels has been shown to be (mis-)perceived as nasalization (Lintz & Sherman 1961; Ohala 1975; Ohala & Amador 1981; Ohala & Ohala 1992; Imatomi 2005), an effect that has been attributed to the similar acoustic effects of velopharyngeal coupling and subglottal coupling (Ohala 1974; Matisoff 1975; Garellek 2014; Carignan 2017; Johnson 2019). F1 frequency, which is typically modulated by jaw and/or tongue height, has been shown to be integrated with nasality in listeners' perception (Kingston & Macmillan 1995), leading to changes in vowel nasalization being perceived as changes in vowel quality and vice versa (Wright 1975, 1986; Beddor, Krakow & Goldstein 1986; Krakow, Beddor & Goldstein 1988). This perceptual ambiguity has been argued to be due to the similar effect that nasalization and tongue height have on F1 frequency (Chen 1971; Ohala 1974; Wright 1980; Beddor, Krakow & Goldstein 1986; Carignan 2018b,c). The potential for such ambiguity is particularly evident in cases where vowel nasalization co-occurs with breathy voicing and/or changes in tongue height—that is, the articulatory co-variation that has been shown to be typologically prevalent in vowel nasality (Shosted 2015; Garellek, Ritchart & Kuang 2016; Carignan 2018a; Cler, Perkell & Stepp 2021).

Vowel nasalization thus exemplifies a quintessential many-to-one problem of phonetics, wherein many different articulations can independently lead to a singular acoustic effect, but also a many-to-many problem, wherein in multiple co-varying articulators can give rise to myriad acoustic effects. This complex mapping between articulation and acoustics in the production of vowel nasality results in the potential for ambiguity in listeners' parsing of the original articulatory source of the effect.

Variationist approaches to nasality

A speech community naturally contains a wide range of idiolects and sound variants, known as "normal heterogeneity." Yet, a foundation of sociolinguistic research is the principle of "structured heterogeneity," wherein phonetic variation is not random or "free," but instead is systematic-ally associated with language-external factors, such as region, socioeconomic factors, prestige, gender, age, and ethnicity of the speaker, among others (Labov 1982). Variationist approaches to analyzing speech patterns traditionally have focused on differences in the articulation of single segments across speech communities (e.g., Labov, Ash & Boberg 2006). Sociophonetic work examining nasal segments has conventionally limited its coding in terms of variation between two alternations—as in studies of (ING) variation is the nasal consonants /ŋ/ and /n/. However, because of the complex relationships between the articulation, acoustics, and perception of co-articulatorily nasalized vowels, vowel nasalization provides a rich testing ground to explore more fine-grained variation in co-articulatory patterns within and across social groups.

Indeed, descriptively, there is some work that has begun to examine language-external factors that correlate with observed patterns of variation in nasal co-articulation. As a function of different social groups of speakers, differences in nasal co-articulation have been observed across generations (Zellou & Tamminga 2014) and across regional dialects (Tamminga & Zellou 2015) of American English. For example, Zellou & Tamminga (2014) examined changes over time in co-articulatory vowel nasality in both real and apparent time in Philadelphia English. They found that, for speakers who were under 25 at the time of recording, between the birth years of 1950 and 1965 there was a trend of increasing degree of co-articulatory nasalization on the vowel, then the trend reverses such that speakers born after 1965 display a trend of producing less co-articulatory nasalization. This finding demonstrates that temporal co-articulatory nasalization patterns can vary and change over time within a speech community. Co-articulatory vowel nasalization has also been observed as a socially relevant dialect variation feature. Coetzee et al. (2019) found differences in production patterns of co-articulatory vowel nasalization across different ethnic varieties of Afrikaans: White Afrikaans speakers produce heavy and extensive vowel nasalization while Kleurling speakers produce more constrained anticipatory vowel nasality patterns. Also, co-articulatory vowel nasality has been argued to contribute to differences in the patterning of /æ/-tensing in North American English (Baker, Mielke & Archangeli 2008; De Decker & Nycz 2012). Tensing patterns for some varieties are restricted to pre-nasal environments, and in other varieties the articulatory dynamics of /æ/ tensing in pre-nasal environments is distinct from the dynamics of tensing in pre-oral environments (Mielke, Carignan & Thomas 2017), suggesting that temporal co-articulation (i.e., anticipatory vowel nasalization) has given rise over time to articulatory co-variation (i.e., vowel quality modification alongside anticipatory vowel nasalization). The presence, absence, relative degree, and/or timing of this articulatory co-variation can indeed serve to characterize different dialects (Mielke, Carignan & Thomas 2017).

Speaking style is another external factor that has been shown to condition variation in vowel nasalization. Co-articulation can vary across interlocutors (Scarborough & Zellou 2013), prosodic environments (Cho, Kim & Kim 2017), and communicative contexts (Scarborough 2013; Zellou & Scarborough 2019). Some work suggests that speakers vary patterns of co-articulation for the (real or perceived) benefit of different types of interlocutors. For example, Scarborough and Zellou (2013) observed that speakers producing CVN words directed toward a real listener in a communicative task produced a greater degree of co-articulatory nasalization than those produced to an imagined hard-of-hearing individual, independent of vowel hyper-articulation and duration which were equivalent across these styles. Furthermore, different nasal co-articulation patterns have also been observed across infant- and adult-directed speech (Zellou & Scarborough 2015), and patterns of co-articulatory vowel nasalization have been shown to be imitable across speakers (Zellou, Scarborough & Nielsen 2016; Zellou, Dahan & Embick 2017). These empirical observations that co-articulation varies across and within speakers due to language-external social and communicative factors support the possibility that variations in nasal co-articulation are not arbitrary, but socially learned, socially meaningful, and potentially utilized in indexical ways.

The variation in patterns of nasalization associated with language-external factors described above might be considered as potential "changes from below" (Labov 2007). Specifically, while they appear to be learned and used in socially meaningful or relevant ways, speakers do not display explicit awareness of co-articulatory vowel nasality. Yet, co-articulatory vowel nasality might also be involved in "changes from above," in the sense that speakers are consciously aware of its variation and socially meaningful usages. For example, notions about vowel nasality surface in folk linguistic descriptions of various American English varieties, though in inconsistent and indirect ways (Preston 2011). In some cases, nasality is associated with urban speech. Cramer (2011) reports, for example, that Tennesseans attribute speech from the Northern cities, and Chicago in particular, as being particularly nasally sounding. At the same time, nasality is also applied to describe speech from rural regions. For instance, in other studies, individuals' use of the term "nasality" is associated with attributes such as "twang" or "country talk" (Trask 1996; Hall-Lew & Stephens 2012). These seemingly contradictory sociolinguistic attitudes about nasality perhaps stem from an unclear metalinguistic representation for what nasalized speech really sounds like. Labov (1994) observed that respondents used the term *nasal* to mean something like 'inappropriately nasal,' attributing it to both hyper- and hypo-nasal speech. Additional anecdotal evidence of this phenomenon is the shared knowledge that having a cold or stuffy nose affects the acoustic speech signal in predictable (if misunderstood) ways: the general lay person is aware that hyponasal speech sounds like the speaker "has a cold" and "sounds nasally," even though it is actually the lack of nasalization (more precisely, the lack of coupling of the sinuses to the nasal cavity) which helps contribute to the hypo-nasal speech of a person with a stuffy nose.

Central research questions

The empirical observations described above demonstrate that both temporal and articulatory aspects of co-articulatory vowel nasality are properties that can participate in socially motivated heterogeneity. Yet, it still remains a vastly understudied topic. How might patterns of nasality be shaped by the social world in which they are produced? This section focuses on variation in the production and perception of vowel nasality, with an emphasis on understanding how these patterns might be relevant to social structures within and across speech communities, leading to linguistic change over time.

For one, the study of nasalization can help address long-standing issues in the field of sociolinguistics. In particular, vowel nasalization can be viewed through the lens of a classical perspective on sociolinguistics to illustrate how it can provide insight into the field. Addressing how linguistic change originates, spreads, and becomes embedded in the surrounding linguistic and social systems has been a fundamental aim of sociolinguistics since Weinreich, Labov & Herzog (1968). Nasality is a rich acoustic-phonetic feature and, due to its articulatory and acoustic complexity, it presents myriad opportunities to explore the actuation and propagation of sound change. At the same time, a sociolinguistic approach to the study of nasalization can provide a better and more complete understanding of this multifaceted phenomenon. Many researchers have explored how the acoustic properties of nasalized vowels provide opportunities for phonetically motivated re-analysis. The observation that phonetic vowel nasality patterns are a learned aspect of the grammar and subject to variation opens the possibility that vowel nasality can be recruited to convey social indexicality or social meaning. Furthermore, how social structures might influence the perception of co-articulatory nasality is understudied and therefore not well understood. More broadly, how can looking at social patterns in the production and perception of nasalization inform models of speech variation, representation, and sound change?

Vowel nasalization and sociophonetic theory

Models of sound change typically assume that synchronic variation within a speech community is a necessary precursor to diachronic change. Yet, the specific mechanisms by which phonetic variation becomes phonologized vary among models. Variationist sociolinguistic theories assume phonetic variation becomes associated with social meaning (Labov 1972). It is this type of structured heterogeneity that is itself the pathway to change. Another approach argues that language-internal forces, rather than social forces, predict phonological change (e.g., Martinet 1955). These approaches vary in whether they hypothesize that the mechanisms of sound change are speaker-internal or listener-internal. With respect to co-articulatory nasalization, in particular, there are two main approaches to explaining how systematic synchronic phonetic variation leads to grammaticalized change over time. These theories propose variation and change as a function of articulatory, acoustic, or perceptual (i.e., "language-internal") factors. Yet, each of these theories explicitly considers both the speaker and listener as active agents in change. Thus, they can be investigated in tandem with social properties of individuals (both speakers and listeners), in order to provide new insights about the mechanisms of sound change.

Listener-oriented models of co-articulatory variation

Ohala's (1993) model of the listener's role in sound change provides one perspective for how the complex acoustic properties of vowel nasalization make it particularly susceptible to phono-logical re-analysis (and subsequent socially conditioned variation). As a premise, Ohala points out that there is a potentially ambiguous relationship between articulatory gestures and the resulting acoustic signal. Since listeners only have access to this acoustic signal, the process of mapping the acoustics of a nasalized vowel to the intended causal gestures might lead to discrepancies between the listener's and speaker's mental representation of a given utterance. Ohala's model lays out two types of scenarios that might occur between the speaker and listener during the production and per-ception of an utterance with nasal co-articulation. In one scenario, the speaker's mental represen-tation for a word contains an oral vowel /æ/ adjacent to a nasal coda (as in Step 1 of Figure 11.2a). Yet, due to natural and inevitable articulatory laws, the speaker produces the vowel with some degree of co-articulatory vowel nasalization (Figure 11.2a.2). Faced with the ambiguous acoustic output caused by the co-articulatory overlap, the listener has several options about how to decide what was the speaker's intended utterance (Figure 11.2a.3). One option, depicted in Figure 11.2a, is to "correct" for the speaker's performance and attribute the co-articulatory effects on the vowel to its true source, the nasal consonant. In this case, the listener's intuited mental representation for that utterance (Figure 11.2a.4) will match the speaker's.

Another possibility is that the listener does not correct for performance. Rather, the listener takes the features that are present in the acoustic output due to co-articulation, as intended by the speaker. In this case of "hypo-correction," the listener has settled on a different representation for the utterance than the speaker intended. Ohala (1993) specifically proposes that this process is

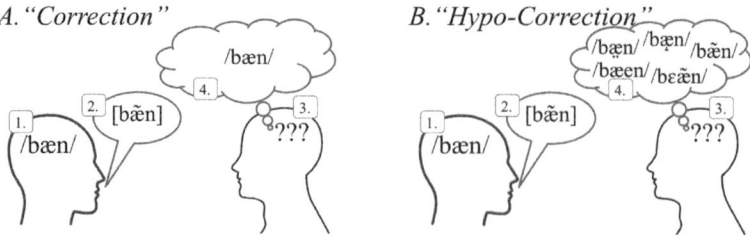

Figure 11.2 Schematics of possible listener-based mechanisms for interpreting nasal co-articulation

abrupt and leads to one type of re-analysis—for example, as /bæ̃n/. However, the hypo-correction mechanism can also be viewed in a more multifaceted way (Figure 11.2b). For example, due to the ambiguous acoustic effects of nasalization, this might include additional features that are not directly related to velum lowering, such as raised vowel articulation, a breathy vowel, or raising diphthongization (Figure 11.2b.4).

These types of hypo-corrections can explain many common sound changes observed in connection with vowel nasalization. Indeed, it has been argued that these sources of ambiguity are the driving force behind language evolution involving the diachronic emergence of breathy phonation (Blevins 2004; Igartua 2011; Garellek, Ritchart & Kuang 2016; Carignan 2017) and change in the oral quality of vowel systems (Beddor 1982; Hajek 1997; Shosted, Carignan & Rong 2012; Carignan 2018a). For example, systematic changes in vowel height have been well documented typologically as nasal vowel systems develop; high vowels tend to lower and low vowels tend to rise as vowel nasality becomes phonologized (Beddor 1982; Hajek 1997; Sampson 1999).

A notable example comes from the evolution of nasal vowels in French. Take, for example, the lowering of /i/ in the evolution of the Latin *vinum* [winum] 'wine' (where oral /i/ and nasal /n/ are heterosyllabic), to Old French *vin* [vĩn] (where [ĩ] is phonetically nasalized via assimilation to the tautosyllabic /n/), to Modern French *vin* [vɛ̃] (Sampson 1999). These are examples of perceptual and articulatory re-analysis via hypo-correction; a listener partially attributes a raised acoustic center of gravity around F1 not to the nasal lowering gesture, but instead to a lowered tongue position, an articulation that would result in the same acoustic change (i.e., a raised F1). Thus, the acoustic ambiguity of nasal vowels presents opportunities for sound change (Beddor, Krakow & Goldstein 1986; Krakow, Beddor & Goldstein 1988; Carignan 2014). Related effects have been observed in a variety of typologically diverse languages and dialects (see Carignan 2018a for a discussion of recent articulatory evidence).

Language-external factors influencing hypo-correction

Some work has begun to examine differences across individuals in hypo-correction. For instance, language experience influences the degree to which a listener compensates for patterns of nasal co-articulation in a speaker's utterance. Beddor & Krakow (1999) found that L1 speakers of Thai, who produce less extensive nasal co-articulation than L1 speakers of English do, attribute less of the co-articulatory effects to a source consonant for English vowels than native English listeners do. Yu (2013) argues that variation in socio-cognitive characteristics might lead to different patterns of perceptual compensation across individual listeners. If patterns of co-articulation in production are subject to meaningful variation both within and across speakers (Scarborough & Zellou 2013; Zellou & Tamminga 2014), it is possible that listeners have formed socio-indexical meanings for different patterns of nasal co-articulation based on experience with different types of speakers who display diverse co-articulatory patterns. One hypothesis is that listeners perceive co-articulatory detail differently depending on the sociolinguistic characteristics of the talker, which is supported by research that has shown that perception interacts with the listener's social knowledge and expectations of the speaker (e.g., Niedzielski 1999; Hay, Warren & Drager 2006; Warren this volume). Future work can explore this possibility. Work integrating both listener-oriented models (Ohala 1993) and socially mediated actuation theories (Weinreich, Labov & Herzog 1968) can elucidate the role of social factors in phonologization of nasalization.

Like Labovian approaches, the Ohalaian view posits that diachronic change stems from synchronic variation. Yet, Ohala argues that the mechanisms for change lie in the listener's act of decoding the ambiguous speech signal into a phonological representation that differs from that of the speaker. Ohala (1989) asserts that the selection of the utterance in the "pool of variation" which actually undergoes hypo-correction is ultimately random, because the misperception mechanism is accidental in nature. Yet, his model relies on the real-time dynamic between a listener and a speaker, exchanges that do not occur in a social vacuum. What if the social properties of the speaker and/or the listener play a role in the type of re-analysis that takes place? We predict this might be especially likely if the speaker and hearer belong to social groups with distinct acoustic realizations for the vowel nasality feature. For example, differences in articulatory co-variation (i.e., featural co-articulation) in vowel nasality across groups have also been observed to lead to articulatory re-analysis. Carignan (2018b) found that naïve English listeners imitated French nasal vowels with a smaller degree of nasalization, but also a concomitant raised tongue position, compared to native French speakers, while nonetheless achieving the same F1 frequency target. While this is an example of cross-language differences in nasality patterns leading to re-analysis, intralanguage differences in the realization of nasalization patterns (e.g., De Decker & Nycz 2012; Zellou & Tamminga 2014; Brotherton et al. 2019; Coetzee et al. 2019) might likewise trigger mismatches in the speaker's production target and the listener's interpretation, eventually leading to systematic variation across individuals.

The possibility that language-external factors should be considered as an additional layer in the hypo-correction mechanism was raised by Lindblom et al. (1995). They extend Ohala's model to consider the possible social or stylistic roles that the listener and, critically, the subsequent listener-turned-speaker serve in the interaction to explain when these mechanisms occur or not. In particular, they propose that listeners vary between more content-oriented (i.e., "what" is being said in an utterance) and signal-oriented (i.e., "how" the utterance is being said) modes of speech perception. In adverse listening conditions listeners might be engaged in a more "what" mode of perception. In contrast, where intelligibility is very high—for instance, when presented with high-frequency utterances or utterances spoken by a very familiar talker—listeners might adopt a "how" mode of perception. Lindblom et al. (1995) speculate that these different listening modes predict when a listener hypo-corrects for the speech signal, resulting in more attention paid to deviant phonetic variants rather than to identifying discrete word units. The Lindblom et al. proposal is one language-external extension of Ohala's model, but other approaches that consider how socio-indexical factors might influence the perception of co-articulation could be fruitful. For example, in a laboratory setting one can investigate whether, upon encountering a word, the likelihood of listeners either compensating for co-articulation or perceiving the actual acoustic properties of the vowel in context, rather than fully attributing the co-articulation to the source, can be affected by language-external factors. Ultimately, following Ohala (1993), this might affect the likelihood of a phonetic variant being noticed and undergoing hypo-correction by the listener. Such a scenario could indicate that there is a social bias in the perceptual mechanisms of sound change. Socially motivated hypo-correction for nasal co-articulation is one potential future avenue for sociophonetic work in the evolution of nasality within and across speech communities.

Speaker-oriented models of co-articulatory variation

Speaker-oriented models of speech variation can also lead us to ask questions and allow us to set up predictions about how the complexity of vowel nasalization might lead to sound change across speakers, social groups, and communities. For example, Lindblom's (1990) Hypo- and Hyper-articulation (H&H) model proposes that phonetic variation reflects a speaker's dynamic adaptation to communicative pressures. When the listening situation is ideal, the speaker can conserve articulatory effort and produce less effortful hypo-speech. When there is some impediment to communication, however, the speaker might adapt their speech to be more intelligible to the listener by hyper-articulating. In effect, the H&H model predicts that the dynamic interplay between speaker- and listener-oriented forces in a conversational interaction will influence phonetic variation.

Lindblom (1990) further makes predictions about how co-articulatory patterns will manifest in response to the trade-off between the needs of the speaker and listener. For example, the default "low cost" form of behavior by the motor system results in increased co-articulation since it facilitates production of adjacent distinct articulations, while listener-oriented hyper-speech would contain reduced co-articulation in order to maintain distinct segments. Lindblom (1990:425) nevertheless acknowledges that co-articulation might serve perception since it "does provide valuable cues" for the listener. Indeed, contrasting with Lindblom, Beddor (2009) posits that since co-articulation is perceptually informative, in the sense that it structures the speech signal to provide early and redundant information about the underlying features, it is something that speakers use in a highly controlled manner. Work done by Scarborough (2013) and Scarborough & Zellou (2013) explores how patterns of co-articulatory vowel nasalization in production might actually be listener-oriented. In contexts where there is an ostensible pressure to make speech more intelligible (e.g., for words that are more confusable due to a large number of phonological neighbors, or in high-stakes communicative tasks), Scarborough and colleagues have found that speakers produce a greater extent of nasal co-articulation than in situations with less output-oriented pressures.

Hybrid speaker/listener models of co-articulatory variation

Beddor (2009) synthesizes both the listener- and speaker-driven views to propose yet another account of co-articulatory-driven sound change involving vowel nasalization. Beddor's model is consistent with the hypo-correction proposal that listeners can phonologize the acoustic effects of nasality as a new production target (i.e., Ohala 1993), which subsequently can be reproduced by the speaker for signal-external factors (i.e., Lindblom 1990; Lindblom et al. 1995). Yet, Beddor (2009) emphasizes the perceptual import of nasal co-articulation in providing redundant and robust cues to the listener, for example, in helping the listener determine just by hearing [bĩ] that the word is *bean* not *bead* (Beddor et al. 2013; Zellou & Dahan 2019). In Beddor's model, the mechanism for sound change is not a "misperception" of co-articulation and, thus, differs crucially from Ohala. Rather, variation in the output is a product of trade-offs in production. In turn, listeners are highly sensitive to the acoustic effects of nasalization and their accurate attention to the speech signal can give rise to sound changes.

Beddor's proposal that perceptual equivalence between the multiple possible interpretations for a given utterance is the mechanism for sound change was demonstrated in her seminal 2009 study. She looked at the production and perception of words with ṼNC sequences in American English (such as *bent* and *bend*). In production, the nasal consonant shortens (or deletes) before a final voiceless oral coda, yet speakers compensate for a shortened nasal consonant by lowering their velum earlier during the vowel so that the total temporal extent of nasalization remains identical across words with voiced and voiceless oral codas. This indicates that speakers are actively maintaining the duration of nasalization present across these words, which may suggest an early stage of the phonologization of vowel nasality in American English, since the same effect has not been observed in similar sequences in, for example, German (Carignan et al. 2021). Furthermore, when rating words that were manipulated to vary in the relative duration of the nasalized portion of the vowel and the nasal consonant, American English listeners attend to the total duration of nasality across a syllable rather than the extent of nasality localized on one particular segment.

Thus, variations in the alignment of the nasalization gesture can vary and still lead to perceptually equivalent realization, for example, a VN sequence with a shortened/deleted nasal consonant and extensive co-articulatory vowel nasalization results in the percept as a VN sequence with an un-reduced nasal consonant and little co-articulatory vowel nasalization. The listener's choice in selecting which representation reflects the acoustic signal might lead to variants that are then emphasized by listener-turned-speakers.

An important aspect of this model is both the speaker's and the listener's active role in the variation: the speaker deliberately maintains the velum lowering gesture in American English (when a shorter gesture might be less effortful) and the listener detects this information before making a decision about what was said. Some experimental work demonstrates systematic differences across listeners in their perceptual decisions (Beddor 2009; Zellou 2017), which Beddor takes as evidence that "phonological grammars" vary across individuals. Since this model views individuals as agents in actively controlling their output and making decisions about the phonological form of heard utterances, it might also be extended to explore how language-external factors play a role in these processes.

Measuring vowel nasalization

In order to examine the degree and/or the timing of nasalization in production, the researcher must first decide on a method of tracking velum movement. Unlike externally visible articulators such as the lips (which can be monitored using video recording), or articulators such as the tongue that are easily accessible via the skin (which can thus be monitored using ultrasound imaging), the velum is a speech articulator that is relatively inaccessible to the researcher. In this section, we outline the various technologies and methods that have been used to observe this notoriously obscure articulator. These methods vary in how amenable they might be to sociolinguistic research, and this amenability is generally inversely related to how directly the velum movement is observed—monitoring velum movement directly involves equipment that is expensive and not easily transportable, and which may be mildly uncomfortable to the participant; measures that are indirect correlates of velum movement involve equipment that is potentially easier to transport and use, and which pose little to no discomfort to the participant.

Thus, the researcher must choose a method that strikes an appropriate balance between ease (e.g., acoustic data are easiest to collect) and accuracy (e.g., direct velum monitoring is most accurate); the particular methodological choice that strikes this balance will not be universal to all research situations, but depends on the specific needs of the researcher and the study. In this section, we present these methods in order from the most to the least direct measures of velum movement. More complete overviews of these approaches can be found in Amelot (2004; written in French) and Kochetov (2020).

Velum monitoring

The first and perhaps most intuitive approach is to monitor the velum itself, rather than the various effects that velum movement has on airflow or acoustic propagation. Techniques within this category fall into two classes of methodology: direct monitoring and indirect monitoring. Velum movement can be monitored directly using structural imaging methods, such as fibroscopy (Croft, Shprintzen & Rakoff 1981; Amelot 2004), cinefluorography (i.e., X-ray; Brichler-Labaeye 1970; Moll & Daniloff 1971), or magnetic resonance imaging (MRI). Real-time MRI video has been used to track a sagittal profile of the velum (Byrd et al. 2009; Proctor et al. 2013; Carignan et al.

2021) and to monitor the aperture of the velopharyngeal port (Martins et al. 2012; Carignan et al. 2015), and static MRI scanning has been used to obtain cross-sectional and volumetric information of the velopharyngeal port during sustained sounds with high spatial resolution (Demolin et al. 2003; Serrurier & Badin 2008). Arguably, the most direct method of monitoring velum movement is by attaching a sensor to the velum itself, which has been achieved using electromagnetic articulometry (EMA; Wrench 1999; Rossato, Badin & Bouaouni 2003) and X-ray microbeam (Condax 1982). However, physically adhering a sensor to the velum is both technically difficult and physically invasive, potentially engaging the gag reflex of the participant.

Indirect methods of monitoring velum movement have been achieved using light-sensing and pressure-sensing technologies. Ohala (1971) developed a device called a "nasograph," which consists of a light emitter and a light sensor placed inside a pliable tube. When the tube is inserted through the nasal cavity and past the velopharyngeal port such that the emitter and the sensor are located on opposite sides of the port, the total amount of emitted light received by the sensor is modulated as a function of the degree of velopharyngeal constriction on the tube; thus, the voltage of the sensor changes in inverse relation to velum height. Similar to the nasograph, the degree of velopharyngeal port opening can be measured using air pressure fluctuation instead of light fluctuation by inserting a small pliable bladder attached to a tube into the nasal cavity, such that the bulb rests inside the velopharyngeal port; as the port closes, the bulb is depressed and the subsequent pressure change is registered by a transducer connected to the other end of the tube (Moon, Kuehn & Huisman 1994; Kuehn & Moon 1998). Finally, a device called a "velotrace" was introduced by Horiguchi & Bell-Berti (1987), which consists of two levers attached to either end of a push rod. When the rod is inserted into the nasal cavity such that the internal lever rests on the top side of the velum, the external lever moves in direct relation to the physical pressure that is exerted against the internal lever as the velum closes. The position of a light-emitting diode attached to the end of the external lever is monitored by a camera, and this position is used as a correlate of velum height.

Aerodynamics

Far more common than monitoring velum movement itself is monitoring the effect that velum movement has on the flow of air through the vocal tract. The simplest and most popular way of doing this is through using pneumotachographs (pressure transducers) attached to a mesh-vented mask that the speaker wears around their nose and/or mouth; in the case of monitoring both the nose and mouth, a split mask is typically employed which creates two chambers separated by a ridge that seals against the upper lip. Venting the mask with mesh provides enough flow imped-ance to be able to calibrate the system to some known rate of flow (typically measured in cm^3/s) without appreciably interfering with the speaker's natural flow of air during speech or breathing. The rate of oral airflow is typically measured alongside the rate of nasal airflow using two separate pneumotachographs, so that the ratio/proportion of nasal airflow to total vocal tract airflow—that is, nasal airflow ÷ (nasal airflow + oral airflow)—can be calculated. Although nasal airflow can be used on its own as a measurement of the degree of nasalization, a measurement of propor-tional nasal airflow is typically preferred because it controls for variation in the overall rate of air-flow generated by the lungs (e.g., differences between louder and softer speech). However, when examining nasalization in vowels, both measurements (in particular, proportional nasal airflow) are sensitive to variation in intra-oral impedance that results from differences in tongue position/constriction. Given the same velopharyngeal aperture (i.e., the same degree of nasalization), nasal airflow will be greater for high vowels (increased lingual constriction, higher oral impedance) than for low vowels (decreased lingual constriction, lower oral impedance) because of an increase in the amount of air that is shunted through the velopharyngeal port. This, of course, is not an issue for monitoring nasal airflow in nasal consonants, where the degree of oral airflow is zero and the oral impedance is practically infinite and therefore constant. A relatively less common (and technically more complicated) aerodynamic technique is to estimate velopharyngeal aperture itself by applying the pressure-flow technique to measurements of oral pressure, nasal pressure, and nasal flow (Warren 1964; Warren & DuBois 1964).

Nasometry

Nasometry is a technology that is sometimes considered a type of aerodynamic methodology but is technically a measurement of air pressure variation (i.e., acoustic radiation) rather than a measurement of airflow. Nasometry systems consist of two directional microphones located on either side of an acoustic baffle. When the baffle is placed on the upper lip directly beneath the nose, the microphone above the baffle captures acoustic radiation from the nostrils while the microphone below the baffle captures acoustic radiation from the mouth, with minimal crosstalk between the two channels. Similar to measures of proportional nasal airflow, the degree of nasalization is typically quantified as proportional nasal energy, that is, the ratio between the amplitude captured by the nasal microphone to the summed amplitude captured by both microphones. However, Dow (2020) discusses the Differential Energy Ratio, an alternative approach to quantifying the degree of nasalization from nasometric data which are based on the global relationship between the two channels.

Although there exists a range of commercially available nasometric devices ("nasometers"), the methodological concept itself (two acoustically separated microphones) is relatively straightforward, lending itself to the innovation of solutions using readily available materials—for example, placing separate microphones (Audibert & Amelot 2011) or earbuds (Stewart & Kohlberger 2017) near a nostril and at a corner of the mouth. Like for aerodynamic measurements, nasometric measurements are sensitive to changes in intra-oral impedance and will therefore appear greater for high vowels than for low vowels. Due in part to its relatively low cost and high degree of portability, the application of nasometry to sociolinguistic and sociophonetic research has increased over recent years, in particular with regard to dialectal investigations (Awan et al. 2015; D'haeseleer et al. 2015; Kim et al. 2016; Bae et al. 2020).

Acoustics

Although the methodologies that have been mentioned above are the most direct ways of determining the magnitude and timing of nasalization, they come with a number of disadvantages. Firstly, they are the least convenient methodologies; the researcher must have access to these technologies in order to use them. In the case of large and expensive tools (e.g., MRI, EMA), this may be a considerably prohibitive disadvantage of these methods. Secondly, employing these methodologies arguably results in unnatural speech, due to the unfamiliar, intimidating, and/or potentially uncomfortable nature of the experimental surroundings, equipment, and task. Finally, these technologies can only be employed in novel studies; they cannot be applied to existing databases of speech recordings unless those recordings initially included articulatory or aerodynamic measures. For these reasons, one of the most popular methods of estimating the degree of nasalization is by using acoustic metrics that correlate with nasality.

As introduced above, when the nasal and oral tracts become coupled together during vowel nasalization the acoustic output of speech is modified in a number of complex ways compared to oral vowel production. Acoustic poles (nasal formants) and zeros (anti-formants) are introduced to the spectrum, formant frequencies shift, formant bandwidths widen, formant amplitudes decrease, and the spectrum tilts towards lower frequencies. Chen (1997) proposed two measures to capture the acoustic effects of nasalization, based on the relationship between the amplitudes of oral poles and nasal poles: A1-P0 and A1-P1, where A1 refers to the amplitude of the most prominent harmonic within F1 (the lowest-frequency oral pole) and P0 and P1 refer to the respective amplitudes of harmonics associated with the two lowest-frequency nasal poles. As the degree of nasalization increases, the amplitudes of oral poles decrease while the amplitudes of nasal poles increase. Thus, the difference between oral pole amplitudes and nasal pole amplitudes is expected to exhibit an inverse relationship with the degree of nasalization. While A1-P0 (i.e., the difference between the amplitude of the most prominent F1 harmonic and the amplitude of the lowest-frequency nasal pole) was introduced as the more robust of the two measures (and is indeed the most commonly used acoustic metric in the literature on vowel nasality), Chen (1997) noted that there are some cases where A1-P0 may fail—in particular, vowels with low F1 frequency (high vowels), for which A1 and P0 may in fact be associated with the same harmonic. Thus, for high vowels, she proposed A1-P1 as an appropriate substitute, since the frequency of P1 is expected to be much higher than the frequency range of F1 for high vowels. A1-P0 has been used to make substantial advances in our understanding of how vowel nasality is implemented across languages (Garellek, Ritchart & Kuang 2016; Khattab, Al-Tamimi & Alsiraih 2018), speakers (Kim & Kim 2019), and listeners (Zellou 2017); how it is affected both by prosodic factors (Zellou & Scarborough 2012; Cho, Kim & Kim 2017; Jang et al. 2018) and lexical factors (Scarborough 2013; Scarborough & Zellou 2013); and how it can serve as a catalyst for sound change (Beddor 2009; Zellou & Tamminga 2014).

Styler (2017) compared the efficacy of 22 acoustic features in distinguishing oral and nasal(ized) vowels in both English and French. Three features were found to be the most effective in capturing nasalization in the acoustic signal: A1-P0, F1 bandwidth, and spectral tilt. However, he observed that even these features varied considerably across vowels and speakers and between the two languages, concluding that single-measure approaches may not be reliable as universal acoustic metrics of vowel nasality, since their ability to accurately characterize vowel nasality can be idiosyncratic to a particular context. With the aim of addressing this issue and the difficulty in consistently and accurately identifying nasal poles in the acoustic spectrum (Styler 2017; Barlaz et al. 2018), Carignan (2021) proposed a method of combining a wide range of acoustic metrics with speaker-specific machine learning to create a singular, robust acoustic metric of the degree of nasalization in vowels ("Nasalization from Acoustic Features"; NAF). By using a wide range of acoustic features and speaker-specific modeling in this way, the fidelity of the resulting metric of nasality is not diminished by the fact that the accuracy of any given individual correlate may vary across different speakers and phonetic contexts. The NAF method was shown by Carignan (2021) to be more accurate than A1-P0 or A1-P1 in capturing the changing degree of nasalization over time, as well as more robust across different speakers and vowel qualities. It should be noted that the NAF method requires statistical training of specifically curated oral and nasalized vowel items and is thus most appropriate for new research studies, where these items can be included in the recording sessions as part of the study design; the NAF method can nonetheless be applied to existing datasets, provided that a phonetically balanced set of these training items can be identified in the recordings. An example of applying the NAF method to an existing dataset in order to investigate sociolinguistic patterning of vowel nasalization is detailed in our case study below.

Perceptual measures

As outlined above, listener-based models of sound change (e.g., Ohala 1993) propose that hypocorrection is a mechanism for re-analysis of the speech signal. Empirically, this has been explored using multiple different perceptual paradigms that compare listeners' responses when they hear a nasalized vowel spliced out of its original context (either in isolation or in a nonnasal consonant context) to when they hear that vowel in a nasal consonant context. The goal of such paradigms is to test under what conditions a listener displays sensitivity to co-articulatory nasalization on a vowel in the context of a nasal consonant. By observing such behavior in the laboratory, researchers can extrapolate the conditions or potential factors at play for possible re-analysis that the phonetic nasalization was an intended and inherent aspect of the vowel itself. For instance, Kawasaki (1986) asked listeners to explicitly judge whether a vowel was nasal or not. She observed that American English listeners can identify a vowel originally produced in an NVN context as nasalized when it occurs in isolation, but cannot perform that task when the vowel occurs next to a nasal segment, demonstrating that listeners compensate for acoustic effects of co-articulation when the source is present. In other words, when the nasal consonant source is present, listeners correctly identify that the acoustic effects of vowel nasalization arise from the nasal consonant, rather than incorrectly contributing those effects to the vowel.

Another way to assess perceptual sensitivity to co-articulatory vowel nasalization is by using discrimination paradigms. Krakow & Beddor (1991) presented two tokens of a word to listeners, one with an oral vowel and the other a nasalized vowel, followed by one of those vowels in isolation. Listeners decide whether the first or second token's vowel matches the isolated vowel. Evaluation of nasalized vowels in a nasal consonant context is difficult if full compensation occurs. Paired discrimination tasks lead to greater perceptual sensitivity (e.g., Beddor & Krakow 1999; Beddor, Harnsberger & Lindemann 2002). In such experiments, listeners hear two pairs of items containing vowels presented in different consonant contexts. In one pair of items the vowels are acoustically identical (e.g., oral vowels), while vowels in the second pair are acoustically different but occur in appropriate co-articulatory contexts. For example, a schematic of a trial is CVC-CVN vs. CVC-CṼN, where the oral vowels in the first three tokens are the same vowel token. The listeners' task is to indicate which pair of words has the more dissimilar-sounding vowels. The outcomes of this design can be interpreted in terms of perceptual mechanisms at play for nasality. If a listener does not compensate for nasality in the context of the nasal consonant, they will hear the vowels veridically, therefore they will choose the pair with acoustically different vowels (i.e., the second pair in the schematic). Yet, if a listener compensates, they will have a hard time deciding (compensation makes the different vowels in proper context sound the same; other vowels really are the same). Such paradigms illustrate a "laboratory" approach to observing phonetic variation and the conditions under which change might occur; the seeds of sound change can be revealed via synchronic patterns of how listeners perceptually evaluate words and sounds.

CASE STUDY   Vowel nasalization in California English

This section demonstrates a variationist approach to exploring patterns of co-articulatory nasalization across speakers. We compare speaker-normalized vowel nasalization, following the Nasalization from Acoustic Features (NAF) approach of Carignan (2021), across different vowels, genders, and regional affiliations to serve as a case study for whether co-articulatory nasalization varies due to language-internal and language-external factors.

Methods

In the current case study, a total of 40 acoustic metrics were used in speaker-specific model training and testing: 20 acoustic features of nasality outlined in Carignan (2021), and 20 Mel-frequency cepstral coefficients (MFCCs). Each of these 40 features was measured at 11 equidistant time points throughout the vowel interval. After de-correlating these features via principal components transformation, a linear regression model was created for each speaker to map the 40 de-correlated acoustic features onto vowels in CVC contexts (when the velum is assumed to be raised throughout the vowel interval) and NVN contexts (when the velum is assumed to be lowered throughout the vowel interval). Each model thus represents speaker-specific machine learning of a linear mapping between the phonetic implementation of orality/nasality and the corresponding acoustic effects. These speaker-specific models were then used to predict response scores for vowels in CVN contexts (when the velum lowers dynamically throughout the vowel interval), in order to observe the time-varying patterns of co-articulatory vowel nasalization across the vowel interval in these lexical environments.

Data were taken from a corpus of CVC, NVN, and CVN words produced by native California speakers described in Zellou, Scarborough & Kemp (2020). Thirty native speakers of American English (24 female, 6 male) participated in the production study. A subset of the word list from Zellou, Scarborough & Kemp (2020) was used here, which included 32 monosyllabic minimal pairs containing /ɛ/, /æ/, /ɑ/, and /ʌ/. Recordings were made using a Shure WH20 XLR head-mounted microphone and digitally sampled at a rate of 44 kHz in a sound-attenuated booth. Each word was repeated two times, in the carrier phrase "____ the word is ____." In total, 960 items were used in model training (32 items per speaker) and 960 items were used to generate time-varying signals of the degree of nasalization in vowels (32 items per speaker). Eight words with oral CVC structure (e.g., *dab, bob, bet, dub*) and eight words with nasalized NVN structure (e.g., *nam, mom, men, numb*) were used to train a linear NAF model for each speaker. Each speaker's fitted NAF model was then used to predict scores for 16 words with nasalized CVN structure (e.g., *ban, bon, Ben, bun*).

Results

In Figure 11.3a, we can see that co-articulatory vowel nasalization is implemented in different ways for the four vowels, suggesting that the time-varying pattern of nasalization is not purely mechanical in this variety of English. Rather, there are differences in the overall degree of nasalization (e.g., nasalization is greatest in /ɛ/), the shape of the increase of nasalization (e.g., there is a linear increase in /ɑ/, /æ/, and /ɛ/, but a non-linear increase in /ʌ/), and the timing of the increase (e.g., the increase of nasalization begins earlier in /ɑ/, /æ/, and /ɛ/ than in /ʌ/). Previous research on co-articulatory vowel nasalization in American English has not observed a conditioning factor of gender (e.g., Zellou & Tamminga 2014), and Figure 11.3b suggests that we find no such effect in these data either.

Figure 11.3c suggests that there is a difference that is conditioned by the geographic background of the speaker: the degree of vowel nasalization is greatest for the Central California speakers, least for the Southern California speakers, and between these two for the Northern California speakers. Interestingly, this difference is constrained to the beginning of the vowel interval, whereas the implementation of co-articulatory nasalization in the end of the vowel (i.e., adjacent to the nasal consonant) is the same across the three subvarieties. This suggests that there is a difference in how nasality has been phonologized in these regional varieties, since there is a difference in how nasalization is

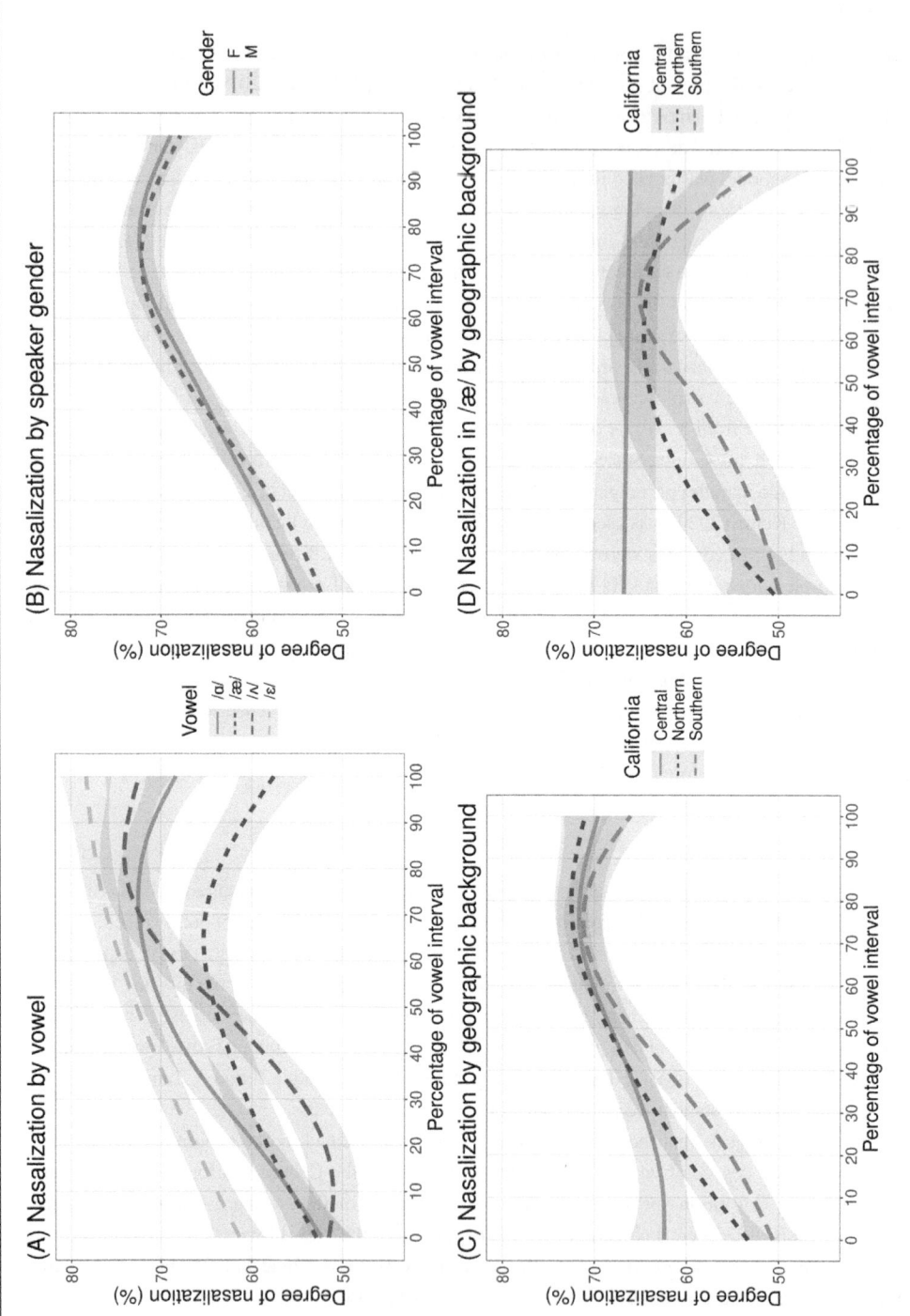

Figure 11.3 Results for an acoustic-based measurement of vowel nasalization across vowels and speakers of California English

implemented at a distance from the source itself (the nasal consonant). In other words, vowel nasalization is phonologized to the greatest extent for Central California speakers according to these patterns.

Figure 11.3d displays the separate results for /æ/, the vowel which is the primary contributor to this intervariety effect. Here, we can see that the degree of nasalization increases in a linear fashion throughout roughly the first 75 percent of the vowel interval for speakers from Northern and Southern California, but that the vowel is nasalized throughout the entire duration for speakers from Central California. The phonetic implementation of nasalization in this vowel is similar to a fully phonologized nasal vowel for Central Californians. This finding is generally consistent with, and extends, previous observations that speakers from Central California exhibit greater advancement in the phonologization of nasality in pre-nasal /æ/, relative to those from Southern California (Brotherton et al. 2019). (Though, in the previous study of /æ/, Northern Californians patterned with Central Californians. Here, we find more similar patterns for Northern and Southern California speakers.) The present results are also consistent with prior work demonstrating that patterns of nasalization in /æ/ contribute to socially relevant dialect variation in North American English (Baker, Mielke & Archangel 2008; De Decker & Nycz 2012; Mielke, Carignan & Thomas 2017).

Discussion

This case study demonstrated an application of the NAF method (Carignan 2021) for examining the acoustic properties of nasally co-articulated vowels without the need for special instrumentation. Using this method, we observed differences across vowels and speakers in both the magnitude and timing of co-articulatory vowel nasalization. Importantly, these differences were primarily revealed in the dynamics of the phonetic implementation of co-articulatory vowel nasality. In particular, we observed geographic differences at the beginning of the vowel interval (distant from the source of the co-articulation) and not at the end of the vowel interval (near to the source of the co-articulation), suggesting sociolinguistically conditioned variation in the phonologization of vowel nasality. This approach can be taken in future studies to examine variation across social groups and contexts using acoustics alone—for example, with data collected online or curated data obtained from sociolinguistic archives or broadcast recordings.

Conclusion

In this chapter, we aimed to make the case that the study of sociolinguistic patterns of vowel nasalization is a vastly understudied area. Because of the multidimensional articulatory and acoustic nature of nasality, it is a feature that generates the potential for sound change and, thus, opportunity to investigate and understand socially conditioned variation. We have laid out the most common methodological approaches for analyzing the articulation, acoustics, and perception of nasality. We also outlined prominent frameworks that account for variation, and pathways for change, in vowel nasality. These frameworks explicitly view the roles of speakers and listeners as agents of change, in communicating in a real-world context and processing speech in real time, respectively. Thus, they can be extended to make specific predictions about how variation and change in nasality is related to or triggered by social differences across people and communicative contexts.

References

Amelot, Angelique. 2004. *Etude aérodynamique, fibroscopique, acoustique et perceptive des voyelles nasales du français* [An aerodynamic, fibroscopic, acoustic and perceptual study of French nasal vowels]. PhD thesis, Université Paris III.

Audibert, Nicolas & Angelique Amelot. 2011. Comparison of nasalance measurements from accelerometers and microphones and preliminary development of novel features. *Proceedings of Interspeech 2011*. 2825–2828. https://doi.org/10.21437/Interspeech.2011-707

Awan, Shaheen N., Tim Bressmann, Bruce Poburka, Nelson Roy, Helen Sharp & Christopher Watts. 2015. Dialectical effects on nasalance: A multicenter, cross-continental study. *Journal of Speech, Language, and Hearing Research* 58(1). 69–77. https://doi.org/10.1044/2014_JSLHR-S-14-0077

Bae, Youkyung, Sue Ann S. Lee, Karl Velik, Yilan Liu, Cailynn Beck & Robert Allen Fox. 2020. Differences in nasalance and nasality perception between Texas South and Midland dialects. *Journal of the Acoustical Society of America* 147. 568–578. https://doi.org/10.1121/10.0000543

Baker, Adam, Jeff Mielke & Diana Archangeli. 2008. More velar than /g/: Consonant coarticulation as a cause of diphthongization. In Charles B. Chang & Hannah J. Haynie (eds.), *Proceedings of the 26th West Coast Conference on Formal Linguistics*, 60–68. Cascadilla Proceedings Project.

Barlaz, Marissa, Ryan Shosted, Maojing Fu & Brad Sutton. 2018. Oropharygneal articulation of phonemic and phonetic nasalization in Brazilian Portuguese. *Journal of Phonetics* 71. 81–97. https://doi.org/10.1016/j.wocn.2018.07.009

Beddor, Patrice Speeter. 1982. *Phonological and phonetic effects of nasalization on vowel height*. PhD dissertation, University of Minnesota.

Beddor, Patrice Speeter. 2009. A coarticulatory path to sound change. *Language* 85(4). 785–821, https://doi.org/10.1353/lan.0.0165

Beddor, Patrice Speeter & Rena A. Krakow. 1999. Perception of coarticulatory nasalization by speakers of English and Thai: Evidence for partial compensation. *Journal of the Acoustical Society of America* 106(5). 2868–2887. https://doi.org/10.1121/1.428111

Beddor, Patrice Speeter, James D. Harnsberger & Stephanie Lindemann. 2002. Language-specific patterns of vowel-to-vowel coarticulation: Acoustic structures and their perceptual correlates. *Journal of Phonetics* 30(4). 591–627. https://doi.org/10.1006/jpho.2002.0177

Beddor, Patrice Speeter, Rena A. Krakow & Louis M. Goldstein. 1986. Perceptual constraints and phonological change: A study of nasal vowel height. *Phonology Yearbook* 3. 197–217. https://doi.org/10.1017/S0952675700000646

Beddor, Patrice Speeter, Kevin B. McGowan, Julie E. Boland, Andries W. Coetzee & Anthony Brasher. 2013. The time course of perception of coarticulation. *Journal of the Acoustical Society of America* 133(4). 2350–2366. https://doi.org/10.1121/1.4794366

Blevins, Juliette. 2004. *Evolutionary phonology: The emergence of sound patterns*. Cambridge University Press.

Brichler-Labaeye, Catherine. 1970. *Les voyelles Françaises. Mouvements et positions articulatoires à la lumière de la radiocinématographie*. Klincksieck.

Brotherton, Chloe, Michelle Cohn, Georgia Zellou & Santiago Barreda. 2019. Sub-regional variation in positioning and degree of nasalization of /æ/ allophones in California. In Calhoun et al., 413–417.

Byrd, Dani, Stephen Tobin, Erik Bresch & Shrikanth Narayanan. 2009. Timing effects of syllable structure and stress on nasals: A real-time MRI examination. *Journal of Phonetics* 47(1). 97–110. https://doi.org/10.1016/j.wocn.2008.10.002

Calhoun, Sasha, Paula Escudero, Maria Tabain & Paul Warren (eds.). 2019. *Proceedings of the 19th International Congress of Phonetic Sciences, Melbourne, Australia 2019*. Australasian Speech Science and Technology Association.

Campbell-Kibler, Kathryn. 2007. Accent, (ING), and the social logic of listener perceptions. *American Speech* 82(1). 32–64. https://doi.org/10.1215/00031283-2007-002

Campbell-Kibler, Kathryn. 2010. The effect of speaker information on attitudes toward (ING). *Journal of Language and Social Psychology* 29(2). 214–223. https://doi.org/10.1177/0261927X09359527

Carignan, Christopher. 2014. An acoustic and articulatory examination of the "oral" in "nasal": The oral articulations of French nasal vowels are not arbitrary. *Journal of Phonetics* 46. 23–33. https://doi.org/10.1016/j.wocn.2014.05.001

Carignan, Christopher. 2017. Covariation of nasalization, tongue height, and breathiness in the realization of F1 of Southern French nasal vowels. *Journal of Phonetics* 63. 87–105. https://doi.org/10.1016/j.wocn.2017.04.005

Carignan, Christopher. 2018a. An examination of oral articulation of vowel nasality in the light of the independent effects of nasalization on vowel quality. In Alessandro Vietti, Lorenzo Spreafico, Daniela Mereu & Vincenzo Galatà (eds.), *Studi AISV IV: Speech in the Natural Context*, 19–40. Associazione Italiana Scienze della Voce. https://doi.org/10.17469/O2104AISV000002

Carignan, Christopher. 2018b. Using naïve listener imitations of native speaker productions to investigate mechanisms of listener-based sound change. *Laboratory Phonology* 9(1). 1–31. https://doi.org/10.5334/labphon.136

Carignan, Christopher. 2018c. Using ultrasound and nasalance to separate oral and nasal contributions to formant frequencies of nasalized vowels. *Journal of the Acoustical Society of America* 143(5). 2588–2601. https://doi.org/10.1121/1.5034760

Carignan, Christopher. 2021. A practical method of estimating the time-varying degree of vowel nasalization from acoustic features. *Journal of the Acoustical Society of America* 149(2). 911–922. https://doi.org/10.1121/10.0002925

Carignan, Christopher, Stefano Coretta, Jens Frahm, Jonathan Harrington, Phil Hoole, Arun Joseph, Esther Kunay & Dirk Voit. 2021. Planting the seed for sound change: Evidence from real-time MRI of velum kinematics in German. *Language* 97(2). 333–364. https://doi.org/10.1353/lan.2021.0020

Carignan, Christopher, Ryan Shosted, Maojing Fu, Zhi-Pei Liang & Brad Sutton. 2015. A real-time MRI investigation of the role of lingual and pharyngeal articulation in the production of the nasal vowel system of French. *Journal of Phonetics* 50. 34–51. https://doi.org/10.1016/j.wocn.2015.01.001

Chen, Matthew. 1971. Metarules and universal constraints on phonological theory. *Project on Linguistic Analysis, University of California, Berkeley* 13. MCI-MC56.

Chen, Marilyn. 1997. Acoustic correlates of English and French nasalized vowels. *Journal of the Acoustical Society of America* 102. 2360–2370. https://doi.org/10.1121/1.419620

Cho, Taehong, Daejin Kim & Sahyang Kim. 2017. Prosodically-conditioned fine-tuning of coarticulatory vowel nasalization in English. *Journal of Phonetics* 64. 71–89. https://doi.org/10.1016/j.wocn.2016.12.003

Cler, Gabriel J., Joseph S. Perkell & Cara E. Stepp. 2021. Oral configurations during vowel nasalization in English. *Speech Communication* 129. 17–24. https://doi.org/10.1016/j.specom.2021.02.005

Coetzee, Andries W., Patrice Speeter Beddor, Will Styler, Stephen Tobin, Ian Bekker & Daan Wissing. 2019. Producing and perceiving socially indexed coarticulation in Afrikaans. In Calhoun et al., 215–219.

Condax, I.D. 1982. X-ray microbeam study of velic movement. *Journal of the Acoustical Society of America* 71. S32. https://doi.org/10.1121/1.2019336

Cramer, Jennifer S. 2011. *The effect of borders on the linguistic production and perception of regional identity in Louisville, Kentucky*. PhD dissertation, University of Illinois.

Croft, Charles B., Robert J. Shprintzen & Saul J. Rakoff. 1981. Patterns of velopharyngeal valving in normal and cleft palate subjects: A multi-view video-endoscopic and nasendoscopic study. *Laryngoscope* 91. 265–271. https://doi.org/10.1288/00005537-198102000-00015

De Decker, Paul M. & Jennifer R. Nycz. 2012. Are tense [æ]s really tense? The mapping between articulation and acoustics. *Lingua* 122. 810–821. https://doi.org/10.1016/j.lingua.2012.01.003

Demolin, Didier, Veronique Delvaux, Thierry Metens & Alain Soquet. 2003. Determination of velum opening for French nasal vowels by magnetic resonance imaging. *Journal of Voice* 17(4). 454–467. https://doi.org/10.1067/S0892-1997(03)00036-5

D'haeseleer, Evelien, Kim Bettens, Sarah De Mets, Valerie De Moor & Kristiane Van Lierde. 2015. Normative data and dialectical effects on nasalance in Flemish adults. *Folia Phoniatrica et Logopaedica* 67(1). 42–48. https://doi.org/10.1159/000374110

Dow, Michael. 2020. A phonetic-phonological study of vowel height and nasal coarticulation in French. *Journal of French Language Studies*. 1–36. https://doi.org/10.1017/S0959269520000083.

Dryer, Matthew S. & Martin Haspelmath (eds.). 2013. *The world atlas of language structures online*. Max Planck Institute for Evolutionary Anthropology.

Feng, Gang & Eric Castelli. 1996. Some acoustic features of nasal and nasalized vowels: A target for vowel nasalization. *Journal of the Acoustical Society of America* 99(6). 3694–3706. https://doi.org/10.1121/1.414967

Ferguson, Charles A., Larry M. Hyman & John J. Ohala (eds.). 1975. *Nasálfest: Papers from a symposium on nasals and nasalization*. Stanford University Language Universals Project.

Fujimura, Osamu & Jan Lindqvist. 1971. Sweep-tone measurements of vocal-tract characteristics. *Journal of the Acoustical Society of America* 49. 541–558. https://doi.org/10.1121/1.1912385

Garellek, Marc. 2014. Voice quality strengthening and glottalization. *Journal of Phonetics* 45. 106–113. https://doi.org/10.1016/j.wocn.2014.04.001

Garellek, Marc, Amanda Ritchart & Jianjing Kuang. 2016. Breathy voice during nasality: A cross-linguistic study. *Journal of Phonetics* 59. 110–121. https://doi.org/10.1016/j.wocn.2016.09.001

Hajek, John. 1997. *Universals of sound change in nasalization.* Blackwell.

Hajek, John. 2013. Vowel nasalization. In Dryer & Haspelmath. http://wals.info/chapter/10

Hall-Lew, Lauren & Nola Stephens. 2012. Country talk. *Journal of English Linguistics* 40(3). 256–280. https://doi.org/10.1177/0075424211420568

Hay, Jennifer, Paul Warren & Katie Drager. 2006. Factors influencing speech perception in the context of a merger-in-progress. *Journal of Phonetics* 34(4). 458–484. https://doi.org/10.1016/j.wocn.2005.10.001

Horiguchi, Satoshi & Fredericka Bell-Berti. 1987. The Velotrace: A device for monitoring velar position. *Cleft Palate Journal* 24(2). 104–111.

Igartua, Ivan. 2011. La aspiración de origen nasal en la evolución fonológica del euskera: un caso de "rhinoglottophilia" [Nasal aspiration in the phonological evolution of Basque: a case of "rhinoglottophilia"]. *Anuario del Seminario de Filología Vasca "Julio de Urquijo"* 42. 171–189.

Imatomi, Setsuko. 2005. Effects of breathy voice source on ratings of hypernasality. *The Cleft Palate-Craniofacial Journal* 42(6). 641–648. https://doi.org/10.1597/03-146.1

Jang, Jiyoung, Sahyang Kim & Taehong Cho. 2018. Focus and boundary effects on coarticulatory vowel nasalization in Korean with implications for cross-linguistic similarities and differences. *Journal of the Acoustical Society of America* 144(1). EL33–EL39. https://doi.org/10.1121/1.5044641

Johnson, Sarah E. 2019. *Spontaneous nasalization: An articulatory investigation of glottal consonants in Thai.* PhD dissertation, University of Illinois.

Kawasaki, Haruko. 1986. Phonetic explanation for phonological universals: The case of distinctive vowel nasalization. In John J. Ohala & Jeri J. Jaeger (eds.), *Experimental phonology*, 81–103. Academic Press.

Khattab, Ghadda, Jalal Al-Tamimi & Wasan Alsiraih. 2018. Nasalisation in the production of Iraqi Arabic pharyngeals. *Phonetica* 75(4). 310–348. https://doi.org/10.1159/000487806

Kim, Daejin & Sahyang Kim. 2019. Coarticulatory vowel nasalization in American English: Data of individual differences in acoustic realization of vowel nasalization as a function of prosodic prominence and boundary. *Data in Brief* 27. 1–9. https://doi.org/10.1016/j.dib.2019.104593

Kim, Ha-Kyung, Xiao-meng Yu, Yan-jing Cao, Xiao-ming Liu & Zhao-Ming Huang. 2016. Dialectal and gender differences in nasalance for a Mandarin population. *Clinical Linguistics & Phonetics* 30(2). 119–130. https://doi.org/10.3109/02699206.2015.1116111

Kingston, John & Neil A. Macmillan. 1995. Integrality of nasalization and F1 in vowels in isolation and before oral and nasal consonants: A detection-theoretic application of the Garner paradigm. *Journal of the Acoustical Society of America* 97. 1261–1285. https://doi.org/10.1121/1.412169

Kochetov, Alexei. 2020. Research methods in articulatory phonetics II: Studying other gestures and recent trends. *Language and Linguistics Compass* 14(6). e12371. https://doi.org/10.1111/lnc3.12371

Krakow, Rena A. & Patrice Speeter Beddor. 1991. Coarticulation and the perception of nasality. In *Proceedings of the 12th International Congress of Phonetic Sciences*, 5. 38–41.

Krakow, Rena A., Patrice Speeter Beddor & Louis M. Goldstein. 1988. Coarticulatory influences on the perceived height of nasal vowels. *Journal of the Acoustical Society of America* 83(3). 1146–1158. https://doi.org/10.1121/1.396059

Kuehn, David P. & Jerald B. Moon. 1998. Velopharyngeal closure force and levator veli palatini activation levels in varying phonetic contexts. *Journal of Speech, Language, and Hearing Research* 41. 51–62. https://doi.org/10.1044/jslhr.4101.51

Labov, William. 1966. *The social stratification of English in New York City.* Center for Applied Linguistics.

Labov, William. 1972. *Sociolinguistic patterns.* University of Pennsylvania Press.

Labov, William. 1982. Building on empirical foundations. In Winfred P. Lehmann & Yakov Malkiel (eds.), *Perspectives on historical linguistics* [Current Issues in Linguistic Theory 24], 17–92. John Benjamins. https://doi.org/10.1075/cilt.24.06lab

Labov, William. 1994. *Principles of linguistic change*, vol. 1, *Internal factors.* Blackwell.

Labov, William. 2007. Transmission and diffusion. *Language* 83(2). 344–387. https://doi.org/10.1353/lan.2007.0082

Labov, William, Sharon Ash & Charles Boberg. 2006. *The atlas of North American English: Phonetics, phonology, and sound change: A multimedia reference tool.* De Gruyter.

Lindblom, Bjorn. 1990. Explaining phonetic variation: A sketch of the H & H theory. In William J. Hardcastle & Alain Marchal (eds.), *Speech production and speech modelling*, 403–439. Kluwer Academic Publishers.

Lindblom, Bjorn, Susan Guion, Susan Hura, Seung-Jae Moon & Raquel Willerman. 1995. Is sound change adaptive?. *Rivista di linguistica* 7. 5–36.

Lintz, Lois B. & Dorothy Sherman. 1961. Phonetic elements and perception of nasality. *Journal of Speech and Hearing Research* 4. 381–396. https://doi.org/10.1044/jshr.0404.381

Maddieson, Ian. 2013. Absence of common consonants. In Dryer & Haspelmath. http://wals.info/chapter/18

Maeda, Shinji. 1993. Acoustics of vowel nasalization and articulatory shifts in French nasal vowels. In Marie K. Huffman & Rena A. Krakow (eds.), *Nasals, nasalization, and the velum*, 147–170. Academic Press. https://doi.org/10.1016/B978-0-12-360380-7.50010-7

Martinet, André. 1955. *Economie des changements phonétiques. Traité de phonologie diachronique.* A. Francke.

Martins, Paula, Catarina Oliveira, Samuel Silva & António Teixeira. 2012. Velar movement in European Portuguese nasal vowels. In Doroteo Torre Toledano, Alfonso Ortega Giménez, António Teixeira, Joaquín González Rodríguez, Luis Hernández Gómez, Rubén San Segundo Hernández & Daniel Ramos Castro (eds.), *Proceedings of IberSpeech—VII Jornadas en Tecnología del Habla and II Iberian SLTech Workshop, Madrid, Spain*, 231–240. Springer.

Matisoff, James A. 1975. Rhinoglottophilia: The mysterious connection between nasality and glottality. In Ferguson, Hyman & Ohala, 265–287.

Mielke, Jeff, Christopher Carignan & Erik R. Thomas. 2017. The articulatory dynamics of pre-velar and pre-nasal /æ/-raising in English: An ultrasound study. *Journal of the Acoustical Society of America* 142. 332–349. https://doi.org/10.1121/1.4991348

Moll, Kenneth L. & Raymond G. Daniloff. 1971. Investigation of the timing of velar movements during speech. *Journal of the Acoustical Society of America* 50(2). 678–684. https://doi.org/10.1121/1.1912683

Moon, Jerald B., David P. Kuehn & Jessica J. Huisman. 1994. Measurement of velopharyngeal closure force during vowel production. *Cleft Palate-Craniofacial Journal* 31(5). 356–363. https://doi.org/10.1597/1545-1569_1994_031_0356_movcfd_2.3.co_2

Niedzielski, Nancy. 1999. The effect of social information on the perception of sociolinguistic variables. *Journal of Language and Social Psychology* 18(1). 62–85. https://doi.org/10.1177/0261927X99018001005

Ohala, John J. 1971. Monitoring soft palate movements in speech. *Project on linguistic analysis, University of California at Berkeley 13*. J01–J015.

Ohala, John J. 1974. Experimental historical phonology. In John M. Anderson & Charles Jones (eds.), *Historical linguistics, vol. 2*, 353–389. North-Holland.

Ohala, John J. 1975. Phonetic explanations for nasal sound patterns. In Ferguson, Hyman & Ohala, 289–316.

Ohala, John J. 1989. Sound change is drawn from a pool of synchronic variation. In Leiv E. Breivik & Ernst H. Jahr (eds.), *Language change: Contributions to the study of its causes*, 173–198. Mouton de Gruyter.

Ohala, John J. 1993. Coarticulation and phonology. *Language and speech* 36(2–3). 155–170. https://doi.org/10.1177/002383099303600303

Ohala, John J. & Mariscela Amador. 1981. Spontaneous nasalization [abstract]. *Journal of the Acoustical Society of America* 69. S54. https://doi.org/10.1121/1.386212

Ohala, John J. & Manjari Ohala. 1992. Nasals and nasalization in Hindi. Paper presented at 3rd International Symposium on Language and Linguistics: Pan-Asiatic Linguistics, Bangkok, Thailand.

Preston, Dennis R. 2011. *Perceptual dialectology: Nonlinguists' views of areal linguistics*. Foris.

Proctor, Michael, Louis Goldstein, Adam Lammert, Dani Byrd, Asterios Toutios & Shrikanth Narayanan. 2013. Velic coordination in French nasals: A real-time magnetic resonance imaging study. *Proceedings of Interspeech 2013*. 577–581. https://doi.org/10.21437/Interspeech.2013-159

Rossato, Solange, Pierre Badin & Florence Bouaouni. 2003. Velar movements in French: An articulatory and acoustical analysis of coarticulation. In Maria-Josep Solé, Daniel Recasens & Joaquín Romero (eds.), *15th International Congress of Phonetic Sciences*, 3141–3144. ICPhS Archive.

Sampson, Rodney. 1999. *Nasal vowel evolution in Romance*. Oxford University Press.

Scarborough, Rebecca. 2013. Neighborhood-conditioned patterns in phonetic detail: Relating coarticulation and hyperarticulation. *Journal of Phonetics* 41(6). 491–508. https://doi.org/10.1016/j.wocn.2013.09.004

Scarborough, Rebecca & Georgia Zellou. 2013. Clarity in communication: 'Clear' speech authenticity and lexical neighborhood density effects in speech production and perception. *Journal of the Acoustical Society of America* 134. 3793–3807. https://doi.org/10.1121/1.4824120

Serrurier, Antoine & Pierre Badin. 2008. A three-dimensional articulatory model of the velum and nasopha-ryngeal wall based on MRI and CT data. *Journal of the Acoustical Society of America* 123(4). 2335–2355. https://doi.org/10.1121/1.2875111

Shosted, Ryan. 2015. Nasal vowels are not [+nasal] oral vowels. In Jason Smith & Tabea Ihsane (eds.), *Romance Linguistics 2012*, 63–76. John Benjamins. https://doi.org/10.1075/rllt.7.05sho

Shosted, Ryan, Christopher Carignan & Panying Rong. 2012. Managing the distinctiveness of phonemic nasal vowels: Articulatory evidence from Hindi. *Journal of the Acoustical Society of America* 131. 455–465. https://doi.org/10.1121/1.3665998

Stewart, Jesse & Martin Kohlberger. 2017. Earbuds: A method for analyzing nasality in the field. *Language Documentation & Conservation* 11. 49–80.

Styler, Will. 2017. On the acoustical features of vowel nasality in English and French. *Journal of the Acoustical Society of America* 142(4). 2469–2482. https://doi.org/10.1121/1.5008854

Tamminga, Meredith & Georgia Zellou. 2015. Cross-dialectal differences in nasal coarticulation in American English. In The Scottish Consortium for ICPhS 2015 (ed.), *Proceedings of the 18th International Congress of Phonetic Sciences*, Paper 745. University of Glasgow.

Trask, R.L. 1996. *Dictionary of phonetics and phonology*. Routledge.

Warren, Donald W. 1964. Velopharyngeal orifice size and upper pharyngeal pressure-flow patterns in cleft palate speech: A preliminary study. *Plastic and Reconstructive Surgery* 34(1). 15–26. https://doi.org/10.1097/00006534-196407000-00003

Warren, Donald W. & Arthur B. DuBois. 1964. A pressure-flow technique for measuring velopharyngeal ori-fice area during continuous speech. *Cleft Palate Journal* 1(1). 52–71.

Weinreich, Uriel, William Labov & Marvin Herzog. 1968. Empirical foundations for a theory of language change. In Winifred P. Lehmann & Yakov Malkiel (eds.), *Directions for historical linguistics: A sympo-sium*, 95–195. University of Texas Press.

Wrench, Alan A. 1999. An investigation of sagittal velar movement and its correlation with lip, tongue and jaw movement. In John J. Ohala, Yoko Hasegawa, Manjari Ohala, Daniel Granville & Ashlee C. Bailey (eds.), *Proceedings of the 14th International Congress of Phonetic Sciences*, 435–438. Regents of the University of California.

Wright, James T. 1975. Effects of vowel nasalization on the perception of vowel height. In Ferguson, Hyman & Ohala, 373–388.

Wright, James T. 1980. The behavior of nasalized vowels in the perceptual vowel space. *Report of the Phonology Laboratory, University of California, Berkeley* 5. 127–163.

Wright, James T. 1986. The behavior of nasalized vowels in perceptual vowel space. In John J. Ohala & Jeri J. Jaeger (eds.), *Experimental phonology*, 45–67. Academic Press.

Yu, Alan C.L. 2013. Socio-cognitive processing and the actuation of sound change. In Alan C.L. Yu, *Origins of sound change: Approaches to phonologization*, 201–227. Oxford University Press.

Zellou, Georgia. 2017. Individual differences in the production of nasal coarticulation and perceptual com-pensation. *Journal of Phonetics* 61. 13–29. https://doi.org/10.1016/j.wocn.2016.12.002

Zellou, Georgia & Delphine Dahan. 2019. Listeners maintain phonological uncertainty over time and across words: The case of vowel nasality in English. *Journal of Phonetics* 76. 100910. https://doi.org/10.1016/j.wocn.2019.06.001

Zellou, Georgia, Delphine Dahan & David Embick. 2017. Imitation of coarticulatory vowel nasality across words and time. *Language, Cognition and Neuroscience* 32(6). 776–791. https://doi.org/10.1080/23273798.2016.1275710

Zellou, Georgia & Rebecca Scarborough. 2012. Nasal coarticulation and contrastive stress. In Zhizheng Wu, Eng Siong Chng & Haizhou Li (eds.), *Thirteenth Annual Conference of the International Speech Communication Association*, 2686–2689. International Speech Communication Association.

Zellou, Georgia & Rebecca Scarborough. 2015. Lexically conditioned phonetic variation in motherese: age-of-acquisition and other word-specific factors in infant-and adult-directed speech. *Laboratory Phonology* 6(3–4). 305–336. https://doi.org/10.1515/lp-2015-0010

Zellou, Georgia & Rebecca Scarborough. 2019. Neighborhood-conditioned phonetic enhancement of an allophonic vowel split. *Journal of the Acoustical Society of America* 145(6). 3675–3685. https://doi.org/10.1121/1.5113582

Zellou, Georgia & Meredith Tamminga. 2014. Nasal coarticulation changes over time in Philadelphia English. *Journal of Phonetics* 47. 18–35. https://doi.org/10.1016/j.wocn.2014.09.002

Zellou, Georgia, Rebecca Scarborough & Kuniko Nielsen. 2016. Phonetic imitation of coarticulatory vowel nasalization. *Journal of the Acoustical Society of America* 140(5). 3560–3575. https://doi.org/10.1121/1.4966232

Zellou, Georgia, Rebecca Scarborough & Renee Kemp. 2020. Secondary phonetic cues in the production of the nasal short-a system in California English. In Helen Meng, Bo Xu & Thomas Zheng (eds.), *Proceedings of Interspeech 2020*, 631–635. International Speech Communication Association.

SECTION 2

Applications

12

SOCIOPHONETICS AND DIALECTOLOGY

Dominic Watt, Margaret E.L. Renwick, and Joseph A. Stanley

Introduction

In this chapter we explore how the investigation of phonetic detail in speech seen through a socio-linguistic lens can inform and enhance our understanding of dialectal variation in languages. We begin by examining how sociophonetics can be considered an offshoot of dialectology, later to mature into a free-standing discipline during the late twentieth century. We next discuss the reconvergence of sociophonetics and dialectology as it became clearer that the two approaches to the study of language variation are, in combination, greater than the sum of their parts, even if their agendas may place different emphases on what should be studied, and how. We then carry out a three-part review of relevant literature, focusing first on the "socio-" element of sociophonetics, then on the "phonetics" part, and finally on "dialect," to see how these three strands have been interwoven. They lay the ground for discussion of a case study, which maps variation in the mid vowels of Standard Italian. This represents an excursion into sociophonetic dialectology outside the United Kingdom and United States, on which most of our discussion and review otherwise focus. We finally offer a reflection on where we currently stand regarding research at the meeting point of sociophonetics and dialectology, and some speculative projections about where we appear to be heading.

Let us first take a look into the past, however. Dialectology—"the study of dialect, or regional variation in language" (Boberg, Nerbonne & Watt 2018b:1)—has, for much of its history, tended to gloss over socially conditioned variability in the pronunciations of words and the segments of which they are composed. It has instead preferred to take the language habits of individual talkers (generally, older men embedded for the majority of their lives in small rural communities) to represent dialects as a whole. These observations have then been compiled into atlases enriched with maps, dictionaries, and other reference works with the aim of recording the properties of language subvarieties which were thought to be in danger of dying out. Often the goal was to provide linguists with useful insights into earlier stages of a language's development. Owing to its focus on sometimes just single exemplars of a language subvariety, however, the traditional dialectological approach has obscured the rich social and stylistic diversity present in the speech of other inhabitants in sample communities. This was done deliberately, in most cases, because deviations from the speech patterns of "traditional" speakers were thought to be symptomatic of

DOI: 10.4324/9781003034636-14

contamination of the dialect by external influences, or by innovations in the speech of younger and/or female speakers. Capturing the authentic dialect preserved by "NORMs" (nonmobile, older, rural males) in manual occupations—agriculture, fishing, artisanal manufacturing, animal husbandry, and the like—whose life histories had brought them into only limited contact with speakers of other varieties was deemed to be the best route to tracking a language's history. Consequently, we have considerably less idea of what was going on in the speech of others living contemporaneously in the same locales, necessitating a good deal more reconstruction, and frequently guesswork (cf. the critiques of orthodox dialectological research methods in Pickford 1956; Underwood 1974).

Sociophonetics, which dwells on the minutiae of speech differences between individual talkers and groups of talkers, can help us to fill in some of these blanks. It is often viewed as something of a newcomer to the study of language variation across time and space, but this perception may simply be to do with the fact that the term "sociophonetics" has a relatively short history (Foulkes, Scobbie & Watt 2010; Kendall & Fridland 2021; Strelluf this volume). Researchers in the field may place greater or lesser emphasis on the use of traditional auditory analysis methods in their investigations, but there are few sociophoneticians today who would not make use of acoustic phonetic approaches, perhaps complemented with other instrumental techniques (ultrasound-based tracking of the movements of the vocal organs, electromagnetic articulography, electroglottography, MRI vocal tract and brain imaging, etc.). The range of observation and measurement techniques is expanding constantly, providing us with an ever more detailed picture of how speech production and perception systematically vary across individuals and social groups (Di Paolo & Yaeger-Dror 2011; Thomas 2011; Watson 2020; Kendall & Fridland 2021).

If we broadly define sociophonetics to mean the study of socially and geographically conditioned variation in the pronunciation of a language, we can quite legitimately argue that the study of pronunciation variation is as old as the systematic study of other forms of language variation. A strand that we would now describe as sociophonetics has run through dialectology from the very earliest days of the discipline, which Hickey (2018) suggests could date from the late seventeenth century for English (Ray 1694). Even if dialectologists did not explicitly set out to record phonetic and phonological variation in their lexical surveys, they nevertheless often collected valuable sociophonetic data in the process. Cognates like [huːs] and [haus] 'house' are often classified as separate lexical forms. But equally they can be viewed as pronunciation alternants of the same word. So too can items which differ phonetically in multiple respects; for example, *torp* and *dorf* ('village,' in Germanic dialects) have equivalent meanings but different pronunciations, and to that extent they satisfy the definition of the "phonological variable"—the concept that lies at the heart of sociophonetic theory (see Watt 2007, 2009). Inspection of the dialect maps found in early atlases of Georg Wenker and Jules Gilliéron (see, e.g., Lameli, Kehrein & Rabanus 2010; Goebl 2018; Kretzschmar 2018) reveals a good deal about phonetic/phonological variation as well as local lexical preferences.

The sociolinguistic profiles of the informants recruited for early dialect surveys tended to be deliberately kept as uniform as possible, as we saw above. As a result, our picture of how pronunciations varied by factors like gender, social status, or speaking style is unfortunately very limited. But in many cases the motivation for these data collection projects was a perception that the traditional dialects were falling prey to the standardizing effects of mass communication and universal education. Early dialect surveys thus nevertheless provide a sense of how divergent local pronunciations were from those of other varieties that were further along the cline of standardization, and reveal how factors like proximity to major centers of population featured in the spread of innovative forms. And because the standard form of a lexeme was almost always used as the reference form by dialect surveyors, dialect pronunciations would be placed in opposition to a higher-prestige and presumably phonetically more homogeneous variety. To this extent, the early dialect atlases tell us about more than just geographical variation, even if in the absence of direct evidence we must infer a certain amount about variation within the speech communities of which the dialect surveys gave us a partial picture.

Phonetics and dialectology: Divergence and reconvergence

In some parts of the world, no systematic distinction is drawn between the terms "dialect" and "accent." This is the norm in North America, where "regional dialect" may refer just to a distinct mode of pronunciation, without necessarily implying that there are distinctive grammatical features and/or lexis as well. By contrast, in the UK tradition, linguists tend to talk about accent and dialect separately, where accent is solely to do with differences in pronunciation and sets of phonological contrasts, and dialect is a cover term for all other kinds of variation (morphological, syntactic, lexical, discoursal, etc.; Matthews 2014). The distinction is useful in situations where people may be speaking the standard dialect but using a range of different accents.

Separation of accent from dialect means that the two forms of variation can be studied in isolation, a schism assisted by the branching off of phonetics from other forms of language study during the nineteenth century. As the sound systems of major European languages came to be standardized via codification of their most desirable, highest-status accents in dictionaries and elocution guides, so phoneticians began to concern themselves more narrowly with the properties of standard varieties of languages, to the point that what held for the phonological systems of these lects was deemed to apply to the language as a whole. Accounts of the phonological system and specimen transcriptions published by the International Phonetic Association dealt almost exclusively with the pronunciation of the standard (or at any rate most prestigious) accent of the language in question. A single speaker of a standard accent was thought to be adequate as a representative of a language which might be spoken by tens of millions of people, few of whom actually used that accent themselves (see, e.g., Kohler 1990; Okada 1991; Zimmer & Orgun 1992). Treating the phonological contrasts present in a standard accent as the default sound system for that language also fed into typological studies, which as a result often made the set of shared properties between language X and language Y seem smaller than it in fact was. For example, ignoring the presence of front rounded vowels or the voiceless velar fricative /x/ in nonstandard varieties of English places English at a greater distance from other West Germanic languages like German or Dutch, and doing so amounts to distortion, even willful denial, of the facts of how languages are actually spoken (e.g., Lass 1989). Whatever motivated this unwillingness to take account of variation that could easily be observed in the field—a belief, perhaps, that readers would only really be interested in standard forms because other varieties were unimportant— the practice is plainly incompatible with the conduct of good science (see further Milroy 2006; Milroy & Milroy 2012).

Accent variation was, on this view, at best of only marginal interest, and in other ways not much more than an inconvenience. Speakers whose utterances were recorded for research purposes might be screened carefully in case they were to exhibit any deviations from the desired model. For the most part, the study of accent variation was relegated to the "special interest" bin and treated as somehow frivolous or undeserving of serious scientific inquiry. It would be decades before nonstandard accents were put on an equal footing with standard ones by academic phoneticians, in spite of the publication of occasional illustrative articles such as those of Newcastle (Tyneside) English by Jones (1911) or O'Connor (1947). Note that Jones's transcription of Tyneside speech is based on a comic song, however, while that provided by O'Connor is of a humorous, probably apocryphal, anecdote. The sense one gets here is that the phonetic profile of the variety is interesting for its curiosity value, but not a topic to be taken very seriously.

However, in more recent times much the same kind of supercilious marginalization of dialect study also went on among scholars specializing in phonological variation. The target in this case was traditional dialectology which, since the emergence of "sociolinguistic dialectology" and "urban dialectology" in the 1960s and 1970s (e.g., Labov, Yaeger & Steiner 1972), had acquired rather a poor image. Traditional dialectology, with its preoccupation with lexical variation, was said by many to have outlived its usefulness. Social and geographical mobility had fragmented the communities in which the old dialects had once been spoken, and the last remaining speakers of "genuine" dialect were dying off. Rather than focusing on the speech patterns of older, relatively immobile rural dwellers, it was argued that modern dialect study should turn its attention to the rapidly changing, socially stratified speech patterns of people living in cities (see Chambers & Trudgill 1998). Furthermore, urban centers were argued to be the nexus of linguistic innovation and change, which only later diffused into rural areas (e.g., Labov, Ash & Boberg 2006). Traditional dialectology, preoccupied with the "purity" and "authenticity" of dialects unsullied by the influence of the modern world, was criticized for being too descriptive and insufficiently theoretical. It was likened to harmless but futile hobbies such as butterfly collecting or trainspotting, rooted as it was in the nineteenth-century obsession with hierarchical classification. These criticisms are perhaps not entirely unjustified. It is true that collecting dialect words and phrases might be of only quite restricted value to the wider community of linguists, even if these items have the potential to reveal patterns of change through the processes of historical borrowing, diffusion, and leveling. And some dialectologists, many of them apparently blessed more with enthusiasm than linguistic expertise, did seem to be cataloging dialect forms effectively for the sake of doing so.

Accurate recording of localized differences in pronunciation has, however, a much broader level of generality than this, and the work of dialectologists in gathering information about fine-grained phonetic and phonological variation has provided the underpinnings of what we still believe are the mechanisms of sound change, described first by the neogrammarians and later by scholars in the structuralist tradition (e.g., Martinet 1952, 1955; Samuels 1972; Salmons & Honeybone 2015), and later still integrated into generativist phonological models such as that expounded in Chomsky & Halle (1968). Notions such as merger, split, and chain shift—some of the principal phenomena that contemporary sociophonetics seeks to model and explain—emerged from work that explicitly took variation into account, not least because older written sources predate the emergence of standard accents/dialects, and because the evidence of the operation of these processes is preserved, a little like tree-rings, in nonstandard varieties.

The rift between phonetics and dialectology that widened in the nineteenth and twentieth centuries left a gap that has only quite recently started to shrink again. Ambitious early attempts to bridge the divide by modeling language varieties in the round, such as the Tyneside Linguistic Survey (Pellowe et al. 1972), were hindered by limitations of computing power. The early dialect surveys, including the Survey of English Dialects (Orton et al. 1962–1971) or the Dictionary of American Regional English (Cassidy, Hall & Van Schneidemesser 1985), could be said to have over-generated data, much of which could only be presented in a relatively raw form in atlases and supplementary materials. Today, we face no such obstacles, and it is recognized across a much larger swath of the linguistics community that the study of dialect is every bit as methodologically rigorous as any other branch of linguistics. Indeed, thanks to its use of very large corpora and adoption of "big data" mining techniques such as crowdsourcing or scraping of vast quantities of data from apps and social media sources like Twitter and YouTube (e.g., Leemann, Kolly & Britain 2018; Kim et al. 2019), scholars in other disciplines may look to dialectology as a source of innovation for handling extremely large datasets. Increasingly, this attracts attention from specialists in fields which apparently have little to do with the study of language variation. An example is the work of James Burridge and his colleagues (e.g., Burridge & Blaxter 2020). Burridge, a mathematician specializing in probability and statistical physics, claims that the geographical distribution of dialects is contingent on simple physical principles to do with the relative likelihood of interaction between pairs of language users, and topographical features such as major rivers, mountain ranges, and coastal indentations. His simulations of the emergence of dialect boundaries in territories such as Great Britain, Italy, and the United States result in maps which are arrestingly similar to real dialect maps (Burridge 2018; Burridge et al. 2019).

Simultaneously, we see among linguists a retreat from the idea that certain language varieties are more worthy of inquiry than others. Often, the tone struck by some researchers who have chosen to focus in a new study on the properties of language X as spoken in a standard accent is faintly apologetic. This is an appropriate stance to take given the fact that standard accents are often spoken by very small minorities, for all their disproportionate visibility in the media and cultural life, though in the interests of continuity with the findings of previous studies it is understandable that scholars often instinctively stay close to the standard form, where possible. Some argue that basing a study of the phonetic/phonological properties of a language on a nonstandard variety will turn it into a dialectological or sociophonetic study, as though maintaining a focus on the standard form alone exempts the study from any such labels. The subtext might also be that orienting a study away from the standard variety will diminish the credibility of the study in some way, and could in any case lose authors a significant section of their readership. Mainstream phonetics is not yet free of the influence of this intellectual straitjacket, it would appear, but we nevertheless see plentiful encouraging signs that progress is being made in the right direction.

In the following sections we look in more detail at a number of contemporary studies of linguistic variation which exemplify the theoretical reconvergence of sociophonetics and dialectology, as well as illustrating the level of methodological sophistication that characterizes current work in the field.

A sociophonetic perspective on regional variation

The arrival of sociophonetics coincided with a relative downturn in traditional dialectological approaches, and so as we turn to recent approaches to regional variation and sociophonetics, our selections reflect work that addresses the intersections of the component parts of sociophonetics and dialectology: socio-, phonetics, and (regional) dialect. We first highlight work focused on sociolinguistics, but which considers speakers' region or dialect as a major factor. We then explore work within general phonetics that controls for, or compares across, regional varieties. Finally, we argue that with recent renewed interest in mapping and new techniques in data visualization, combined with large acoustic phonetic datasets, sociophonetics and dialectology are reunited. Going forward, we acknowledge strong biases in the linguistic features and regions represented by our discussion. From a phonetic perspective our review skews toward vowels, rather than consonants or suprasegmental phenomena—as is common in sociophonetics—and from a regional perspective, we represent varieties of US and UK English most strongly. Particularly since a full review of global regional dialectology is beyond our scope (cf. Boberg, Nerbonne & Watt 2018a), we seek to exemplify projects rich in phonetic detail that embrace cross-variety comparison and enhance our understanding of localized speech styles.

Variationist approaches to sociophonetics and regional variation

Many studies that fall under the umbrella of variationist sociolinguistics document the myriad ways a particular linguistic variant is realized among different groups of people within the same locality (typically, a city). Labov's early work set the stage for this kind of study by highlighting social variation in New York City (Labov 1966). Since then, numerous other researchers have followed his lead and have done similar work, partly to fill in the gaps on our dialectological maps. These studies are "motivated not only by a desire 'to find out' but also by a desire to record in some detail certain linguistic facts associated with a traditional dialect which might otherwise not be recorded in spite of the pioneering but necessarily less detailed efforts" of large-scale linguistic atlas projects (Trudgill 2002:32). Such studies embrace the messiness that was overlooked, and perhaps seen as a nuisance, in earlier work.

In some ways, regional variation was an important part of these studies because they describe language as it is actually used in a single geographic place—often for the first time from an acoustic, sociophonetic, and/or quantitative perspective. On the other hand, studies of a single place cannot, in isolation, explore geographic variation. In sociolinguistics, region is typically held constant so that other social variables can be explored more deeply. While early dialect surveys had wide geographic coverage but deliberately kept the demographic profiles of speakers and interviewing styles as uniform as possible, sociolinguistic studies deliberately constrain geographic coverage while exploring the effects of a spectrum of social factors on language behavior. So while they individually are not dialectological, in the sense that they do not analyze variation across broad stretches of geographic space, they collectively contribute to a growing picture of regional variation.

An example of this "patchwork" dialectology can be found in studies describing fronting of /u:/ (GOOSE). /u:/-fronting is widespread across much of the English-speaking world, and is a long-established feature of numerous varieties. In British English it has been the object of particular attention by dialectologists for several decades. Some works have described /u:/ as being fronted within a general documentation of varieties like Received Pronunciation (Henton 1983; Bauer 1985; Hawkins & Midgley 2005), Multicultural London English (Cheshire et al. 2011; Fox & Torgersen 2018), and Multicultural Manchester English (Drummond 2018), not to mention the varieties described in volumes on World Englishes (Wells 1982; Kortmann & Upton 2008). Other studies conduct focused work on /uː/ to fully document sociophonetic intricacies such as its social distribution in Southeast England (Torgersen 1997) and Carlisle (Jansen 2019), its formant trajectories in Derby (Sóskuthy et al. 2015) and Tyneside (Krug 2021), and its sociolinguistic indexicality in York (Haddican et al. 2013). Another body of research presents /uː/-fronting as evidence of more general sociolinguistic factors like the motivations for language change in Reading and Ashford (Torgersen & Kerswill 2004) and East Anglia (Trudgill 2002), regional dialect leveling in Hastings (Holmes-Elliott 2015), and the process of koineization in Milton Keynes (Kerswill & Williams 2005). While these geographically dispersed studies approach the topic of /u:/-fronting from diverse perspectives, using different methodologies and propelled by a variety of underlying motivations, they collectively paint a picture of the widespread nature of the fronting phenomenon over a large geographic area.

Another phenomenon that is well-analyzed in a series of unrelated studies is a chain shift involving the lowering and centralization of the front lax vowels in North American English. In California, the shift has been extensively documented in places like San Francisco (Hinton et al. 1987; Cardoso et al. 2016), and Santa Barbara (Janoff 2018). It has been described in detail in Canadian English as well, based on reports from Toronto (Clarke, Elms & Youssef 1995), Montreal

(Boberg 2005), Halifax (Sadlier-Brown & Tamminga 2008), St. John's (Hollett 2006), Winnipeg (Hagiwara 2006), and Vancouver (Roeder, Onosson & D'Arcy 2018). Elsewhere in North America work is patchier, but elements of this shift can be found in a variety of places and social groups. For example, though there is some shifting in /ɛ/ (DRESS) and /ɪ/ (KIT), it is /æ/ (TRAP) that is most shifted, particularly among younger women, in places like Alaska (Bowie 2020), Oregon (Becker et al. 2016), Washington (Swan 2019; Stanley 2020), Nevada (Fridland & Kendall 2017), Montana (Bar-El, Rosulek & Sprowls 2017), Missouri (Strelluf 2018), Michigan (Nesbitt, Wagner & Mason 2019), Illinois (Bigham 2010), Georgia (Stanley 2022a), Massachusetts (Stanford et al. 2019), and New York (Thiel & Dinkin 2020). For some speakers, only /æ/ and /ɛ/ are shifted; examples are Anglo women in New Mexico (Brumbaugh & Koops 2017) and Hawaiians (Kirtley et al. 2016). Among other speakers, such as Alaskan men (Bowie 2020), Idahoans (Garrison 2019), and people scattered across states like Pennsylvania, Ohio, and Texas (Thomas 2001:20–21), only /æ/ is shifting. Though the shift is described as a recent phenomenon in many regions, there is evidence in Arizona (Hall-Lew et al. 2017), Washington (Stanley 2020), Kansas (Villarreal & Kohn 2021), Ohio (Durian 2012), and North Carolina (Dodsworth & Kohn 2012) that the shift has been in motion since at least the mid-twentieth century. Despite their incomplete coverage across the continent, and their differing results, these studies collectively create a dialectological mosaic that illustrates a general trend found in North American English.

One downside to making comparisons across studies such as these is that while they occasionally directly compare the locale in question to results found in other regions, most of this research is "siloed," meaning that each is an independent study with different methods for data collection and analysis conducted by different researchers. Consequently, descriptions vary regarding the precise phonetic nuances of the phenomena being investigated. In the case of the front lax vowels in North American English, are the vowels lowering or retracting, lowering and then retracting (or vice versa), or doing both things simultaneously? Some of this apparent "regional" variation may simply be the result of methodological differences. Furthermore, at least eight different names (e.g., the "Canadian Vowel Shift," the "California Vowel Shift") are in circulation for what is likely the same underlying phenomenon (Becker 2019).

Acoustic phonetics and perception of regional varieties

While many authors frame their studies of regional and phonetic detail around social factors that condition the observed variation, another rich tradition takes region into account but sets out to address questions of more concern to researchers in general phonetics or speech acoustics. The latter strand of research is motivated by, for instance, broader theoretical and methodological questions in speech production and perception, automatic speech recognition, and phonological theory. Typically this work is based on hypothesis testing, and it acknowledges that region is expected to play a role in distinguishing speech varieties. However, the geographic or spatial aspect of variation is downplayed, and individual variation is treated as a parameter to control for.

As an illustrative example, consider the literature detailing efforts to optimize methods to normalize vowel formant data. These procedures involve various mathematical transformations of raw acoustic measurements, with the intention of maximizing the direct comparability of formant values across individual speakers. Since talker-specific variation based on anatomical/physiological or sociolinguistic sources is (generally) readily handled in human speech perception, one can argue that variability in pronunciation resulting from biological and social differences can justifiably be factored out, if the aim is to model how listeners process the speech signal (see Adank, Smits & Van Hout 2004 for an overview). That is, listeners appear mostly to have no trouble identifying a spoken vowel of a language as an exemplar of vowel phoneme X, even if its physical characteristics make it quite different from the equivalent vowel listeners would typically use themselves, and/or other reference vowel qualities that might be relevant (e.g., the vowel used by speakers of a standard variety). In perception, not only do we unconsciously factor out the large differences in formant frequencies between speakers with markedly different vocal tract lengths—for example, men versus small children—we also cope with accent-based differences which make the acoustic instantiations of a vowel category more diverse still. It is useful, therefore, to find ways of simulating how listeners might go about ignoring these often quite gross differences.

When listeners are decoding a linguistic message, they easily disregard certain types of variation in speech. However, since they can just as effortlessly detect variation that carries social meaning, it is clear that some types of interspeaker variation warrant retention and analysis. For that reason, concern developed among sociophoneticians that overly "aggressive" normalization methods might throw the baby out with the bathwater, so to speak, by eliminating regional variation worthy of linguistic description. This concern stimulated the development of a proliferation of competing methods (see Voeten, Heeringa, & Van de Velde 2022 for a recent review and comparison). Recent work such as Barreda & Nearey (2018) and Barreda (2020, 2021) has approached normalization as a procedure that "[focuses] on modeling the judgments of human listeners in response to between-speaker variation in production, rather than on modeling the variation in production itself" (Barreda 2021:24). Methods of normalization are inherently relevant to sociophonetic studies of regional variation, as a way of disentangling individual versus geographical variation.

Beyond studies focused on methods for quantitative comparison, particularly across vowel systems, regionally annotated phonetic data have been harnessed for comparative linguistic purposes. The Nationwide Speech Project (NSP; Clopper & Pisoni 2006) includes audio from 60 talkers across six United States dialect regions, joining corpora like the Santa Barbara Corpus (DuBois et al. 2000) and Buckeye Corpus (Pitt et al. 2005) as major resources mined for regionally accented sociophonetic detail within the United States. The NSP has illustrated systematic differences in major regional vowel systems (Clopper, Pisoni & De Jong 2005), and its highly controlled contents have made an ideal testbed for comparisons of speech rhythm and prosody across regional varieties (Clopper & Smiljanic 2015), which are rarely studied systematically and at scale.

Multiregion datasets are also important for investigating the interplay of dialect and speech perception. The NSP has been used to study the role of regional variation and linguistic experience in phonetic convergence (Ross et al. 2021) and speech perception via free classification tasks (Clopper & Pisoni 2006; Alcorn et al. 2020). Kendall & Fridland (2012) combine speech production tasks with phonemic categorization tasks by speakers from the US South, West, and Inland North to reveal that, at an individual level, productions of vowels involved in the regional Southern Vowel Shift can mirror perception of these vowels. Fridland, Kendall & Farrington (2014) further reveal that hearers draw on a range of spectral and durational cues simultaneously to disambiguate vowels across regional dialects. Elsewhere in the US South, regional vowel patterns have been investigated in North Carolina and compared to those from the Inland North (Wisconsin) and Midland (Ohio) regions. These three varieties differ in patterns of vowel duration (Jacewicz, Fox & Salmons 2007), formant dynamics, stop consonant voicing (Jacewicz, Fox & Lyle 2009), and fundamental frequency (Jacewicz & Fox 2018).

Studies of speech perception that are rooted in regional dialectology are increasingly relevant to phonological theory, particularly among proponents of substance-based models like exemplar theory. This line of research is inspired by findings from perceptual dialectology. A crucial starting point is Niedzielski's (1999) study in Detroit, Michigan, which illustrates the influence of linguistic stereotypes on the perceptual categorization of vowels. Listeners heard /aw/ (MOUTH) stimuli whose formant values lay along a continuum of raising towards [ʌw]. Since this raised variant is stereo-typically associated with Canadian (rather than US) speech, listeners who believed the speaker was from nearby Windsor, Ontario labeled stimuli with a greater amount of raising, compared to listeners who were told the speaker was from Detroit. This study not only shows stereotyped biases in speech perception, but also shows that listeners may be unaware of their own use of a feature—like raised /aw/, which is prevalent in Detroit. Relatedly exploiting listener awareness of regional variation in the diphthong /aɪ/ (PRICE), Plichta & Preston (2005) showed that increasingly mono-phthongal realizations are labeled as increasingly Southern within the United States. Research focused on exemplar-based models of phonology rejuvenated Niedzielski's method, showing that listeners from New Zealand select vowel variants biased toward Australian pronunciation when they see "Australian" labeled on their response sheet (Hay, Warren & Drager 2006). Such work argues that regional speech variants activate listeners' past experiences (exemplars) during speech perception, and the range of regional cue activators includes words (Sanchez, Hay & Nilson 2015) and stuffed toys (Hay & Drager 2010). Adding more nuance to these findings, Walker, Szakay & Cox (2019) observe that these effects do not apply equally in cross-dialect perception, as they show that the stuffed toys which primed New Zealanders' perceptions of vowels did not shift Australians' perceptions toward New Zealand English. These studies, which use speaker-hearers' sociophonetic knowledge as a window onto phonology and cognition, show that regional variation can help answer fundamental questions about language and the language faculty (See also Warren this volume.)

A return to mapping: Sociophonetic dialectology with Big Data

In the twenty-first century, the ease of data storage and processing (even for large audio files) combined with powerful tools for computation and data visualization in research are leading us to new frontiers in dialectology. Linguistic interviews recorded for atlas projects that have for decades languished in archives can now be digitized, transcribed, and analyzed acoustically. At the level of individual speakers, the increasing ubiquity of recording equipment—for instance, on mobile devices and laptops—has facilitated modern sociophonetic data collection on a vast scale, via dedicated apps or services like Amazon Mechanical Turk. Together, these tools and methods are allowing researchers to visualize variation in ways that hearken back to traditional dialect-ology, using maps.

In our view, mapping spoken-language variation truly draws the spirit of dialectology together with modern sociophonetic methods. Detailed regional variation can now be mapped with relative ease, including how it has changed over generational time. The following paragraphs highlight studies that illustrate historical or synchronic sociophonetic detail across regions using atlas data or corpora, and crowdsourcing or large-scale surveys. They often focus less heavily on hypothesis testing and more on visualizations, and are comfortable acknowledging individual or sub-regional variation rather than "controlling it away."

Various twentieth-century linguistic atlases were compiled using audio interviews, the contents of which were not intended to be exhaustively analyzed at the time of collection. For instance, the Linguistic Atlas of the Gulf States (LAGS; Pederson, McDaniel & Adams 1986) was recorded as semi-spontaneous interviews and conversations on reel-to-reel tape in the mid-twentieth cen-tury. Annotators combed the recordings for specific elicited lexical items, which were transcribed phonetically; the tapes' remaining contents were left untreated. In more recent times, a subset of LAGS, the Digital Archive of Southern Speech (DASS), has been digitized to .wav format (Kretzschmar et al. 2013) and fully transcribed (Kretzschmar et al. 2019). Using tools like forced alignment and automated acoustic measurements (Olsen et al. 2017), sociophonetic analysis of resulting datasets can be scaled up significantly. Removing (or at least alleviating) the bottleneck in the sociophonetic analysis pipeline can allow researchers to examine more linguistic variables in greater detail. Since linguistic atlases sample across a defined geographic area and speaker-specific information is retained, detailed phonetic data can be mapped. For instance, DASS data show subregional variation in the highly stereotyped productions of /aɪ/ found across the US South (Renwick & Stanley 2017; Olsen, Olsen & Renwick 2018). Geospatial Information System (GIS) techniques like local autocorrelation and clustering have revealed that DASS speakers' adherence to dialect features of the Southern US is highly variable, and in particular that speakers from the Mississippi River Delta diverge from them (Jones & Renwick 2022), adding to others' lexical evidence that southern Louisiana is a unique dialect area (Babington & Atwood 1961; Carver 1987).

Data from the Atlas of North American English (ANAE; Labov, Ash & Boberg 2006) have also been reanalyzed in a GIS framework, largely reproducing the ANAE's dialect boundaries but also uncovering specific lexical and phonetic characteristics that render the US Southeast highly distinct (Grieve 2013, 2014; Grieve, Speelman & Geeraerts 2013). Other cross-regional projects with a sociophonetic component include SPeech Across Dialects of English (SPADE; Sonderegger et al. 2020), which initially combined recordings principally from Glasgow (Scotland), Raleigh (North Carolina), and New England, but now includes a large number of corpora from across the United Kingdom, Canada, and United States. The data are freely available to researchers via https://spade. glasgow.ac.uk/. Results from SPADE have shown, for instance, that phonetic patterns related to stop voicing vary more across varieties than within speakers (Tanner et al. 2020). Both SPADE and DASS (Stanley et al. 2017) can be visualized interactively or analyzed, with a geographic component, via Shiny web applications (https://shiny.rstudio.com/). Recent, regionally specific efforts to digitize and analyze legacy interview data are described in Hickey (2017). A major source of sociophonetic material for African American Language (AAL) is the Corpus of Regional African American Language (CORAAL; Kendall & Farrington 2020), which includes recordings of US speakers from Washington DC, North Carolina, Atlanta, Rochester, and other sites. From a sociophonetic perspective, CORAAL has been used to explore the realization of /t,d/ in AAL across three regions (Farrington 2018).

Smartphone apps (see Hilton & Leemann 2021 and sources within) have facilitated crowd sourced data collection in Switzerland (Leemann et al. 2015; Leemann 2016; Zihlmann & Leemann 2017) and the British Isles (Leemann, Kolly & Britain 2018). Sometimes the data collection can be relatively straightforward, such as when a simple online survey is used (Stanley 2022b), or more involved, for example when a researcher guides participants through using a smartphone app over video chat (Leemann et al. 2020). Such crowd sourced techniques have been very effective in sparking the interest of the general public. Most notably, hundreds of thousands of people took a 2013 New York Times survey, which was based on questions from the Harvard Dialect Survey (Vaux & Golder 2003). Online data collection is not always conducive to obtaining the quality of sociophonetic data we would ideally wish for, but the results of Kim et al.'s (2019) study of user-submitted recordings encourage optimism. Kim et al. found that the results drawn from these speech samples are comparable to descriptions based on traditional, face-to-face methods. However, recent research suggests that videoconferencing apps are not as promising (Freeman & De Decker 2021; Calder et al. 2022). Other internet-based studies that focus on a specific linguistic variable, such as the *pin-pen* merger (Austen 2020) and prevelar raising (Stanley 2022b), or a speech community, like African Americans (Jones 2020), can collect more detailed data due to their narrowed scope. These feature-specific studies may pave the way for large-scale studies of sociophonetic variables that are undergoing changes across many varieties of English (e.g., /u:/-fronting), answering Jansen's (2019:25) call for "cross-dialectal studies of phonetic changes that seem to happen on a global scale to investigate the nature of these changes in more depth."

Consistent, nationwide studies have the added benefit of discovering unforeseen pockets of variation. Typically, when linguistic variables are unknown or not expected to vary, researchers exclude them from elicitations to trim down an already resource-heavy method. For example, the various regional Linguistic Atlas Projects used similar questionnaires, but not all words from one project were elicited in another project: the Linguistic Atlas of the Gulf States used a 104-page questionnaire while the Linguistic Atlas of the Pacific Northwest only used a 73-page one. In the Atlas of North American English, wordlists were designed to elicit words known to be variable in each region (Labov, Ash & Boberg 2006:29). By excluding some elicitation items in areas where their realization is not expected to vary, researchers are inadvertently subject to a confirmation bias and cannot verify that variation is indeed absent for a particular variable in a particular region. The patchwork approach to dialectology, which reflects the individual goals and methods of independent researchers, can sometimes lead to sampling bias as well. In such studies, linguistic features are sometimes claimed to be exclusive to one region despite a lack of evidence for the feature's absence from another region. One example of this is BEG-raising, a phenomenon wherein /ɛ/ is raised before /g/, in words like *beg*, *leg*, and *eggs*. Research is sparse on this topic and mostly confined to the Pacific Northwest and Canada, leading some to claim that it is a unique feature of those areas. However, Stanley (2022b) distributed an identical questionnaire to most parts of the United States and Canada and, as shown in Figure 12.1, found that BEG-raising is far more common than previously reported. In fact, it was found more consistently in areas like the Upper Great Plains and parts of the Midlands than in the Pacific Northwest. Since online data collection is relatively less resource-intensive than in-person methods, it is feasible to keep questionnaires consistent like this, even if it means eliciting data that are not expected to vary in a given region. Future nationwide surveys may reveal additional pockets of variation in areas that would have otherwise been overlooked.

In addition to mapping-based techniques, phonetic measurements are incorporated into analyses based in computational modeling or machine learning, which distinguish regional varieties using multiple features or dimensions simultaneously. Although we do not survey this research in detail, we argue that computational modeling of dialectology is a crucial application for sociophonetic data. This emerging area, with clear links to artificial intelligence, is represented by Heeringa, Johnson & Gooskens (2009), who compare 15 varieties of Norwegian using Levenshtein distance, which is typically applied to transcribed data (i.e., qualitative observations). Formant data corresponding to dialectal phenomena are used to create dialect groupings visualized using dendrograms and multidimensional scaling, which reflect both traditional and perceptually based classifications of the varieties. Elvira-García et al. (2018) offer an extension of this method to intonational prosody, as applied to Romance varieties. Strycharczuk et al. (2020) use machine learning, specifically a random forest analysis, to differentiate between five accents of Northern England; an appealing aspect of this paper is the use of phonetically interpretable measurements—for example, F1 and F2 values—to find vowel-specific metrics of convergence (dialect leveling) and divergence across accents. Patterns in regional datasets can also feed back into AI applications, for instance by highlighting biases against regional dialects (Tatman 2017; Tatman & Kasten 2017; Le 2021) which can be remedied by improved training data.

The studies we have reviewed are diverse but linked by their employment of rich quantitative data in addressing research questions that incorporate regional variation as an important

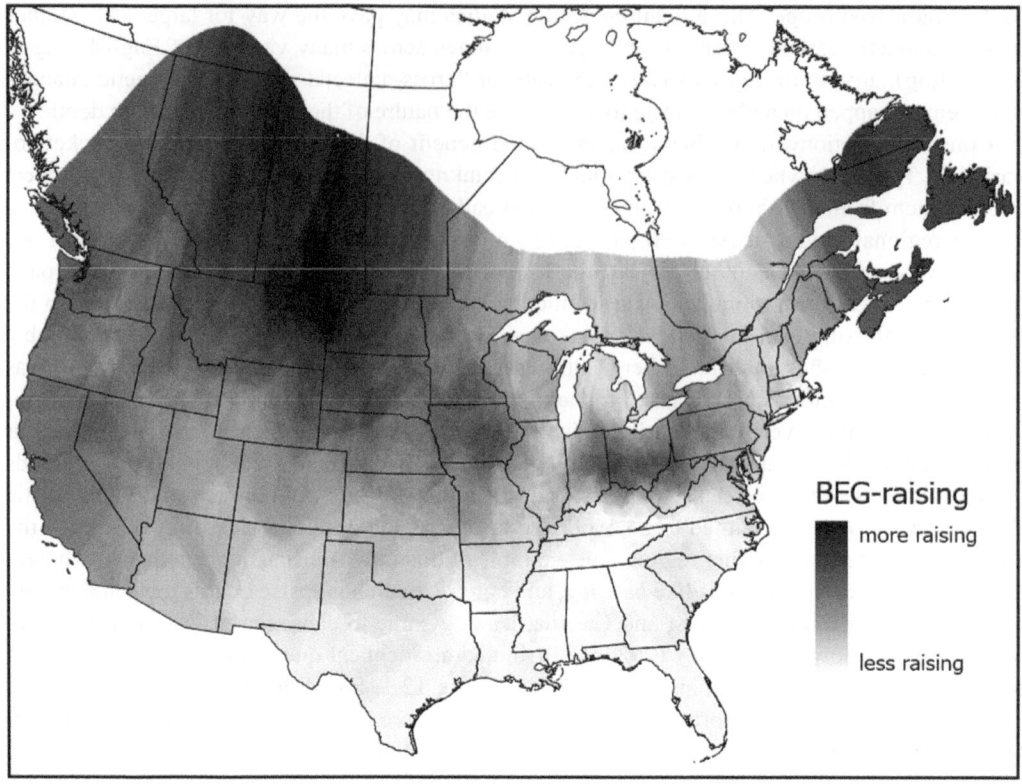

Figure 12.1 BEG-raising in North America
Source: Stanley 2022:394

conditioning factor. Depending on a study's goals, its data may be acoustic, perceptual, articulatory, or based on judgments or intuitions.

CASE STUDY Italian mid-vowel variation

In this chapter, we have highlighted studies that link sociophonetics and dialectology. In a brief case study, we draw upon our own work to illustrate some of the principles discussed above. This study maps regional and lexical variation in Standard Italian mid vowels, using acoustic phonetic data drawn from a large corpus.

This case study follows a rich tradition of dialectology in Italy, founded by Graziadio Isaia Ascoli (1873) and including the atlas of Jaberg & Jud (1928–1940) and the ongoing Atlante Linguistico Italiano project (Cugno, Rivoira & Ronco 2020). There is also growing productivity in Italian sociophonetics (see, e.g., Calamai, Celata & Ciucci 2012; Celata & Calamai 2014; Crocco 2017).

In prescriptive Standard Italian—exemplified by Florentine Italian and, to a certain extent, Roman Italian—the stressed mid vowels /e ɛ/ and /o ɔ/ contrast with one another, meaning that both the higher and lower phones can appear under the same conditions (at least, within stressed syllables). Minimal

---

pairs exist prescriptively for the front and back vowel pairs, for example, /peska/ 'fishing' versus /pɛska/ 'peach' and /foro/ 'hole' versus /fɔro/ 'forum.' However, many regional varieties deviate systematically from the standard (Canepari 1980; Bertinetto & Loporcaro 2005), and variation within individuals, cities, or regions is also documented (Canepari 1980; Renwick & Ladd 2016). Deviations typically involve influence from the phonological system of a local *dialetto*, whose vowel inventory may differ from the seven-vowel system of Standard Italian (see Maiden & Parry 1997 for an overview), or may impose phonological restrictions on mid vowel height. Syllable structure or word-stress pattern are typically relevant. Additionally, the languages of Italy developed from Latin either a "Western" system (having seven vowels, if short E and O lowered to [ɛ, ɔ], or five vowels if [e, o] raised and merged with [i, u]) or a "Sardinian" system (having five vowels) (Maiden & Parry 1997:7). This means that regional varieties of Standard Italian are influenced by *dialetti* with varying inventory sizes, and whose cognate lexical items may have different stressed vowel qualities.

Methods

The present case study draws on a large, multipurpose Italian speech corpus: CLIPS (*corpora e lessici di italiano parlato e scritto*; Leoni et al. 2007). Recorded across 15 Italian cities, it surveys 240 participants aged 18–30 who have a relatively homogeneous background with respect to socio-economic status, education level, and other social factors. All are fluent in Standard Italian as spoken in their home city, evidenced by their age and educational background (minimally a high school diploma). Previous analyses of vowels in CLIPS have focused on mid vowels, showcasing change over time in Bari (Filipponio & Cazzorla 2015), variation within Tuscany (Combei & Tordini 2017), and cross-variety differences in mid vowel distribution (Clemente, Savy & Calamai 2006).

The "read sentences" portion of CLIPS was used for the present study, including 20 sentences read aloud by each speaker, containing 272 unique words. Audio was force-aligned using the WebMAUS system (Kisler, Reichel & Schiel 2017), which has a pre-trained acoustic model for Standard Italian. Resulting Praat (Boersma & Weenink 2017) TextGrid files were hand-corrected and formant values were automatically extracted at vowel midpoint. Outliers were identified based on Mahalanobis distance (Mahalanobis 1936; Labov, Rosenfelder & Fruehwald 2013; Renwick & Stanley 2017), resulting in the exclusion of 12 percent of the dataset, and the remainder of the dataset was normalized (Lobanov 1971). To provide an estimate of vowel height unbiased by human intuition (Renwick & Ladd 2016; Nadeu & Renwick 2016), all mid vowels ($N = 66,401$) were automatically classified using k-means clustering, implemented in R (R Core Team 2022) with 100 random starts using the Hartigan & Wong (1979) algorithm. Front and back vowels were classified separately, on a city-specific basis, into a higher and lower vowel cluster; normalization is a prerequisite due to the difference in scales between raw F1 and F2 values. In this case study, two vowel heights are used for all 15 cities, to highlight regional variation, but the analysis in Renwick (2021) excludes those known to have a merger (Cagliari in Sardinia; Palermo in Sicily; and Lecce in the southern mainland).

Results

How often a word is realized with a high-mid or low-mid vowel reveals phonetic variation within and across cities. Using stressed mid vowel data from CLIPS, Figure 12.2a illustrates clustering rates of front vowels in closed syllables, a context that determines their height in some regional varieties,

Front vowel clustering in 15 Italian cities

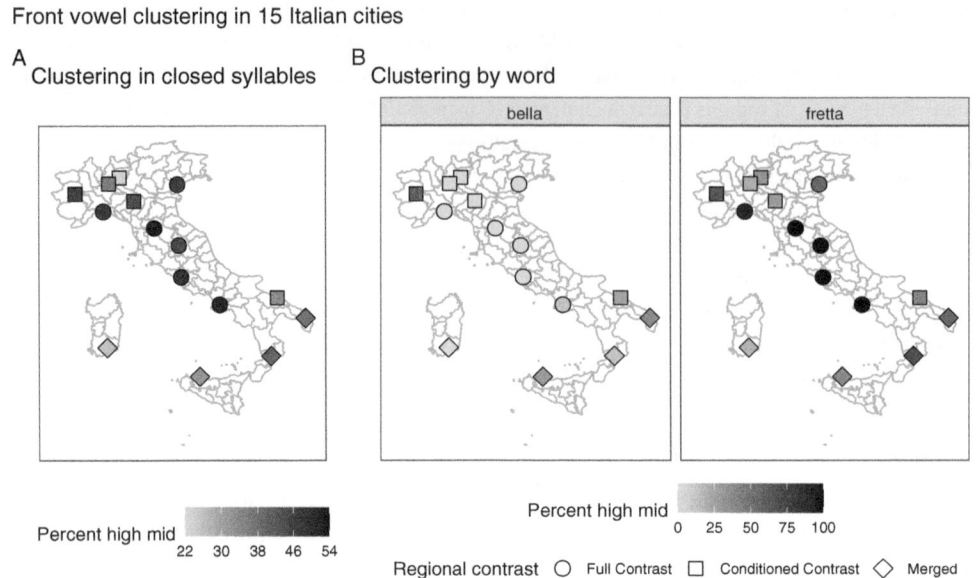

Figure 12.2   Percentage of tokens clustered as high-mid [e]

though not in the prescribed standard. In central Italian cities with fully functional mid vowel contrasts (Florence, Rome, etc.), closed-syllable tokens are high-mid approximately 50 percent of the time. In Southern cities with a merger, high-mid rates are lower (30–40 percent) for the same words. In cities with a contextually determined contrast (especially Milan and Bergamo in the North, and Bari in the Southeast), a scarcity of high-mid classifications highlights the phonological effect of syllable structure on front mid vowels.

Do these regional tendencies apply across all lexical items? Figure 12.2b reveals they do not, via clustering rates for two words with stressed <e> in a closed syllable, a context potentially favoring [ɛ]. For *bella* 'beautiful (f. sg.)', there is remarkable consistency across Northern and Central cities, which indeed have a lower vowel in this word. In *fretta* 'hurry,' however, cities diverge: a lower mid [ɛ] occurs in cities where closed syllables favor lowering (Conditioned Contrast), while cities with no conditioning (Full Contrast) prefer higher mid [e].

Discussion

These large acoustic datasets reveal regional sociophonetic variation, which may be typically obscured by analyses that focus on a standard variety. This study reiterates that even within "standard" Italian, regional variation is at play. An additional benefit of large datasets, however, is that they allow analysis of variation in specific lexical items, which can diverge from broader patterns. Although traditional dialectology also tracks individual words, this modern approach (with many tokens per city, word, speaker, etc.) gives a more nuanced view, revealing which words are most variable. These are a potential nexus for socially driven sound change.

Towards the reconvergence of sociophonetics and dialectology

New data processing and visualization techniques offer huge potential for making discoveries about the geographical distribution of linguistic forms, their diffusion or recession over time, and the mechanisms by which innovations can spread within and between communities. Ever greater unification of the methods and standards used by researchers in dialectology and sociophonetics, along with almost limitless processing power and the growing availability of unprecedentedly large and rich datasets, will equip us to study language variation and change in ways that would have seemed impossibly ambitious only a generation ago.

This fusion—or rather the reunion—of dialectology and sociophonetics may mean that before long the two fields cease to be areas of inquiry that are easily distinguished from one another. Specialisms in phonetic, grammatical, or lexical variation will undoubtedly persist, but researchers will have fewer and fewer excuses to avoid engaging with colleagues working in other areas of language variation. Such collaborative work must acknowledge the aspects of language that are fully systematic, in balance with the extensive, multidimensional variation found in naturalistic data. This approach will help us understand where linguistic competence lies, and in turn benefit linguistic theory. Highlighting the impact for phonology of embracing variation, Cohn & Renwick (2021:14) argue, "[w]e cannot limit analysis to speech patterns that can be deemed categorical and highly systematic, nor can we assume that speech communities are homogeneous." The goal of understanding how and why speakers use a language in systematically different ways is not only shared, but may also require iterative studies across multiple methods and subfields. Moreover, a growing openness to collaboration with scientists working in fields ostensibly unrelated to linguistics—experts in complexity and emergence, probability theory, population studies, or social psychology, for instance—is liable to result in valuable new insights into languages and dialects as dynamic systems with properties peculiar to themselves.

Acknowledgments

The sociophonetic analysis of Italian was prepared with support from the University of Georgia's Willson Center for Humanities & Arts.

References

Adank, Patti, Roel Smits & Roeland van Hout. 2004. A comparison of vowel normalization procedures for language variation research. *Journal of the Acoustical Society of America* 116(5). 3099–3107. https://doi.org/10.1121/1.1795335

Alcorn, Steven, Kirsten Meemann, Cynthia G. Clopper & Rajka Smiljanic. 2020. Acoustic cues and linguistic experience as factors in regional dialect classification. *Journal of the Acoustical Society of America* 147(1). 657–670. https://doi.org/10.1121/10.0000551

Ascoli, Graziadio Isaia. 1873. *Archivio glottologico italiano* 1. Periodici le Monnier.

Austen, Martha. 2020. Production and perception of the PIN-PEN merger. *Journal of Linguistic Geography* 8(2). 115–126. https://doi.org/10.1017/jlg.2020.9

Babington, Mima & E. Bagby Atwood. 1961. Lexical usage in Southern Louisiana. *Publication of the American Dialect Society* 36. 1–24. https://doi.org/10.1215/-36-1-1

Bar-El, Leora, Laura Felton Rosulek & Lisa Sprowls. 2017. Montana English and its place in the West. In Fridland et al., 107–138. https://doi.org/10.1215/00031283-4295299

Barreda, Santiago. 2020. Vowel normalization as perceptual constancy. *Language* 96(2). 224–254. https://doi.org/10.1353/lan.2020.0018

Barreda, Santiago. 2021. Perceptual validation of vowel normalization methods for variationist research. *Language Variation and Change* 33(1). 27–53. https://doi.org/10.1017/S0954394521000016

Barreda, Santiago & Terrance M. Nearey. 2018. A regression approach to vowel normalization for missing and unbalanced data. *Journal of the Acoustical Society of America* 144(1). 500–520. https://doi.org/10.1121/1.5047742

Bauer, Laurie. 1985. Tracing phonetic change in the received pronunciation of British English. *Journal of Phonetics* 13(1). 61–81. https://doi.org/10.1016/S0095-4470(19)30726-0

Becker, Kara (ed.). 2019. *The Low-Back-Merger Shift: Uniting the Canadian Vowel Shift, the California Vowel Shift, and Short Front Vowel Shifts across North America* [Publication of the American Dialect Society 104]. Duke University Press.

Becker, Kara, Anna Aden, Katelyn Best & Haley Jacobson. 2016. Variation in West Coast English: The case of Oregon. In Fridland et al., 107–134. https://10.1215/00031283-3772923

Bertinetto, Pier Marco & Michele Loporcaro. 2005. The sound pattern of Standard Italian, as compared with the varieties spoken in Florence, Milan and Rome. *Journal of the International Phonetic Association* 35(2). 131–151. https://doi.org/10.1017/S0025100305002148

Bigham, Douglas S. 2010. Correlation of the Low-Back Vowel Merger and TRAP-retraction. *Penn Working Papers in Linguistics* 15(2). Article 4. https://repository.upenn.edu/pwpl/vol15/iss2/4

Boberg, Charles. 2005. The Canadian Shift in Montreal. *Language Variation and Change* 17(2). 133–154. https://doi.org/10.1017/S0954394505050064

Boberg, Charles, John Nerbonne & Dominic Watt (eds.). 2018a. *The handbook of dialectology*. Wiley.

Boberg, Charles, John Nerbonne & Dominic Watt. 2018b. Introduction. In Boberg, Nerbonne & Watt, 1–15. https://doi.org/10.1002/9781118827628.ch0

Boersma, Paul & David Weenink. 2017. *Praat: Doing phonetics by computer* [Computer program], ver. 6.0.30. www.praat.org/

Bowie, David. 2020. English in the north: The vowels of southcentral Alaska. In Valerie Fridland, Alicia Beckford Wassink, Lauren Hall-Lew & Tyler Kendall, *Speech in the Western states*, vol. 3, *Understudied varieties* [Publication of the American Dialect Society 105], 123–143. Duke University Press. https://doi.org/10.1215/00031283-8820653

Braber, Natalie & Sandra Jansen (eds.). 2018. *Sociolinguistics in England*. Palgrave.

Brumbaugh, Susan & Christian Koops. 2017. Vowel variation in Albuquerque, New Mexico. In Fridland et al., 31–58. https://doi.org/10.1215/00031283-4295200

Burridge, James. 2018. Unifying models of dialect spread and extinction using surface tension dynamics. *Royal Society Open Science* 5(1). 171446. https://doi.org/10.1098/rsos.171446

Burridge, James & Tamsin Blaxter. 2020. Spatial evidence that language change is not neutral. *arXiv:2005.07553 [physics]*. https://doi.org/10.48550/arXiv.2005.07553

Burridge, James, Bert Vaux, Michael Gnacik & Yoana Grudeva. 2019. Statistical physics of language maps in the USA. *Physical Review E* 99(3). 032305. https://doi.org/10.1103/PhysRevE.99.032305

Calamai, Silvia, Chiara Celata & Luca Ciucci (eds.). 2012. *Sociophonetics, at the crossroads of speech variation, processing and communication*. Edizioni della Normale.

Calder, Jeremy, Rebecca Wheeler, Sarah Adams, Daniel Amarelo, Katherine Arnold-Murray, Justin Bai, Meredith Church, Josh Daniels, Sarah Gomez, Jacob Henry, Yunan Jia, Brienna Johnson-Morris, Kyo Lee, Kit Miller, Derrek Powell, Caitlin Ramsey-Smith, Sydney Rayl, Sara Rosenau & Nadine Salvador. 2022. Is Zoom viable for sociophonetic research? A comparison of in-person and online recordings for vocalic analysis. *Linguistics Vanguard*, 20200148. https://doi.org/10.1515/lingvan-2020-0148

Canepari, Luciano. 1980. *Italiano standard e pronunce regionali*. CLUEP.

Cardoso, Amanda, Lauren Hall-Lew, Yova Kementchedjhieva & Ruaridh Purse. 2016. Between California and the Pacific Northwest: The front lax vowels in San Francisco English. In Fridland et al., 33–54. https://doi.org/10.1215/00031283-3772890

Carver, Craig M. 1987. *American regional dialects: A word geography*. University of Michigan Press.

Cassidy, Frederic C., Joan Houston Hall & Luanne Van Schneidemesser. 1985. *Dictionary of American Regional English*. Belknap Press of Harvard University Press.

Celata, Chiara & Silvia Calamai. 2014. *Advances in sociophonetics*. John Benjamins.

Chambers, J.K. & Peter Trudgill. 1998. *Dialectology*, 2nd edn. Cambridge University Press.

Cheshire, Jenny, Paul Kerswill, Sue Fox & Eivind Torgersen. 2011. Contact, the feature pool and the speech community: The emergence of Multicultural London English. *Journal of Sociolinguistics* 15(2). 151–196. https://doi.org/10.1111/j.1467-9841.2011.00478.x

Chomsky, Noam & Morris Halle. 1968. *The sound pattern of English*. Harper & Row.

Clarke, Sandra, Ford Elms & Amani Youssef. 1995. The third dialect of English: Some Canadian evidence. *Language Variation and Change* 7(2). 209–228. https://doi.org/10.1017/S0954394500000995

Clemente, Giuliana, Renata Savy & Silvia Calamai. 2006. Sistemi vocalici in diatopia. In Renata Savy (ed.), *Analisi prosodica: Teorie, modelli e sistemi di annotazione. Atti del II Congresso Nazionale AISV (Salerno, 30 novembre–2 dicembre 2005)*, 439–460. EDK.

Clopper, Cynthia G. & David B. Pisoni. 2006. The Nationwide Speech Project: A new corpus of American English dialects. *Speech Communication* 48(6). 633–644. https://doi.org/10.1016/j.specom.2005.09.010

Clopper, Cynthia G., David B. Pisoni & Kenneth de Jong. 2005. Acoustic characteristics of the vowel systems of six regional varieties of American English. *Journal of the Acoustical Society of America* 118(3). 1661–1676. https://doi.org/10.1121/1.2000774

Clopper, Cynthia G. & Rajka Smiljanic. 2015. Regional variation in temporal organization in American English. *Journal of Phonetics* 49. 1–15. https://doi.org/10.1016/j.wocn.2014.10.002

Cohn, Abigail C. & Margaret E.L. Renwick. 2021. Embracing multidimensionality in phonological analysis. *Linguistic Review* 38(1). https://doi.org/10.1515/tlr-2021-2060

Combei, Claudia Roberta & Ottavia Tordini. 2017. A pilot sociophonetic study on open-mid vowels uttered by young male and female speakers of the Pisan variety. In Chiara Bertini, Chiara Celata, Giovanna Lenoci, Chiara Meluzzi & Irene Ricci (eds.), *Fattori sociali e biologici nella variazione fonetica – Social and biological factors in speech variation*, 107–126. Officinaventuno.

Crocco, Claudia. 2017. Everyone has an accent: Standard Italian and regional pronunciation. In Massimo Cerruti, Claudia Crocco & Stefania Marzo (eds.), *Towards a new standard: Theoretical and empirical studies on the restandardization of Italian*, 89–117. De Gruyter Mouton.

Cugno, Federica, Matteo Rivoira & Giovanni Ronco. 2020. L'Atlante Linguistico Italiano (ALI). *Romance Philology* 74(2). 191–216. https://doi.org/10.1484/j.rph.5.122250

Di Paolo, Marianna & Malcah Yaeger-Dror (eds.). 2011. *Sociophonetics: A student's guide*. Routledge.

Dodsworth, Robin & Mary Kohn. 2012. Urban rejection of the vernacular: The SVS undone. *Language Variation and Change* 24(2). 221–245. https://doi.org/10.1017/S0954394512000105

Drummond, Rob. 2018. The changing language of urban youth: A pilot study. In Braber & Jansen, 67–98.

Du Bois, John W., Wallace L. Chafe, Charles Meyer & Sandra A. Thompson. 2000. *Santa Barbara Corpus of Spoken American English Part 1*. Linguistic Data Consortium. https://doi.org/10.35111/s2q7-gq73

Durian, David. 2012. *A new perspective on vowel variation across the 19th and 20th centuries in Columbus, OH*. PhD dissertation, The Ohio State University.

Elvira-García, Wendy, Simone Balocco, Paolo Roseano & Ana Ma. Fernández-Planas. 2018. ProDis: A dialectometric tool for acoustic prosodic data. *Speech Communication* 97. 9–18. https://doi.org/10.1016/j.specom.2017.12.013

Farrington, Charlie. 2018. Incomplete neutralization in African American English: The case of final consonant voicing. *Language Variation and Change* 30(3). 361–383. https://doi.org/10.1017/S0954394518000145

Filipponio, Lorenzo & Sonia Cazzorla. 2015. The vowels of Bari. A comparison between local dialect and regional Italian. In Mario Vayra, Cinzia Avesani & Fabio Tamburini (eds.), *Il farsi e il disfarsi del linguaggio: Acquisizione, mutamento e distrutturazione della struttura sonora del linguaggio*, 59–71. Officinaventuno.

Foulkes, Paul, James M. Scobbie & Dominic Watt. 2010. Sociophonetics. In William J. Hardcastle, John Laver & Fiona E. Gibbon (eds.), *The handbook of phonetic sciences*, 703–754. Wiley-Blackwell.

Fox, Sue & Eivind Torgersen. 2018. Language change and innovation in London: Multicultural London English. In Braber & Jansen, 189–213.

Freeman, Valerie & Paul De Decker. 2021. Remote sociophonetic data collection: Vowels and nasalization over video conferencing apps. *Journal of the Acoustical Society of America* 149(2). 1211–1223. https://doi.org/10.1121/10.0003529

Fridland, Valerie & Tyler Kendall. 2017. Speech in the Silver State. In Fridland et al., 139–164. https://doi.org/10.1215/00031283-4295222

Fridland, Valerie, Tyler Kendall & Charlie Farrington. 2014. Durational and spectral differences in American English vowels: Dialect variation within and across regions. *Journal of the Acoustical Society of America* 136(1). 341–349. https://doi.org/10.1121/1.4883599

Fridland, Valerie, Tyler Kendall, Betsy E. Evans & Alicia Beckford Wassink (eds.). 2016. *Speech in the western states*, vol. 1, *The Pacific Coast* [Publication of the American Dialect Society 101]. Duke University Press.

Fridland, Valerie, Alicia Beckford Wassink, Tyler Kendall & Betsy E. Evans (eds.). 2017. *Speech in the western states*, vol. 2, *The mountain West* [Publication of the American Dialect Society 102]. Duke University Press.

Garrison, Arthur Scott. 2019. *Not quite Canada, definitely not California: Evidence of the Low-Back-Merger Shift in Moscow, Idaho*. Bachelor's thesis, Reed College.

Goebl, Hans. 2018. Dialectometry. In Boberg, Nerbonne & Watt 2018a, 123–142. https://doi.org/10.1002/9781118827628.ch7

Grieve, Jack. 2013. A statistical comparison of regional phonetic and lexical variation in American English. *Literary and Linguistic Computing* 28(1). 82–107. https://doi.org/10.1093/llc/fqs051

Grieve, Jack. 2014. A comparison of statistical methods for the aggregation of regional linguistic variation. In Benedikt Szmrecsanyi & Bernhard Wälchli (eds.), *Aggregating dialectology, typology, and register analysis: Linguistic variation in text and speech*, 53–88. Walter de Gruyter.

Grieve, Jack, Dirk Speelman & Dirk Geeraerts. 2013. A multivariate spatial analysis of vowel formants in American English. *Journal of Linguistic Geography* 1(1). 31–51. https://doi.org/10.1017/jlg.2013.3

Haddican, Bill, Paul Foulkes, Vincent Hughes & Hazel Richards. 2013. Interaction of social and linguistic constraints on two vowel changes in northern England. *Language Variation and Change* 25(3). 371–403. https://doi.org/10.1017/S0954394513000197

Hagiwara, Robert. 2006. Vowel production in Winnipeg. *Canadian Journal of Linguistics/Revue canadienne de linguistique* 51(2–3). 127–141. https://doi.org/10.1017/S0008413100004023

Hall-Lew, Lauren, Mirjam Eiswirth, Mary-Caitlyn Valentinsson & William Cotter. 2017. Northern Arizona vowels. In Fridland et al., 59–82. https://doi.org/10.1215/00031283-4295288

Hartigan, J.A. & M.A. Wong. 1979. A K-means clustering algorithm. *Applied Statistics* 28. 100–108. https://doi.org/10.2307/2346830

Hawkins, Sarah & Jonathan Midgley. 2005. Formant frequencies of RP monophthongs in four age groups of speakers. *Journal of the International Phonetic Association* 35(2). 183–199. https://doi.org/10.1017/S0025100305002124

Hay, Jennifer & Katie Drager. 2010. Stuffed toys and speech perception. *Linguistics* 48(4). 865–892. https://doi.org/10.1515/ling.2010.027

Hay, Jennifer, Paul Warren & Katie Drager. 2006. Factors influencing speech perception in the context of a merger-in-progress. *Journal of Phonetics* 34(4). 458–484. https://doi.org/10.1016/j.wocn.2005.10.001

Heeringa, Wilbert, Keith Johnson & Charlotte Gooskens. 2009. Measuring Norwegian dialect distances using acoustic features. *Speech Communication* 51(2). 167–183. https://doi.org/10.1016/j.specom.2008.07.006

Henton, C.G. 1983. Changes in the vowels of received pronunciation. *Journal of Phonetics* 11(4). 353–371. https://doi.org/10.1016/S0095-4470(19)30835-6

Hickey, Raymond (ed.). 2017. *Listening to the past: Audio records of accents of English*. Cambridge University Press.

Hickey, Raymond. 2018. "Yes, that's the best": Short front vowel lowering in English today: Young people across the anglophone world are changing their pronunciation of vowels according to a change which started in North America. *English Today* 34(2). 9–16. https://doi.org/10.1017/S0266078417000487

Hilton, Nanna Haug & Adrian Leemann. 2021. Editorial: Using smartphones to collect linguistic data. *Linguistics Vanguard* 7(s1). 20200132. https://doi.org/10.1515/lingvan-2020-0132

Hinton, Leanne, Birch Moonwomon, Sue Bremner, Herb Luthin, Mary Van Clay, Jean Lerner & Hazel Corcoran. 1987. It's not just the Valley Girls: A study of California English. *Proceedings of the Thirteenth Annual Meeting of the Berkeley Linguistics Society* 13. 117–128.

Hollett, Pauline. 2006. Investigating St. John's English: Real- and apparent-time perspectives. *Canadian Journal of Linguistics/Revue canadienne de linguistique* 51(2–3). 143–160. https://doi.org/10.1017/S0008413100004035

Holmes-Elliott, Sophie. 2015. *London calling: Assessing the spread of metropolitan features in the southeast*. PhD thesis, University of Glasgow. http://theses.gla.ac.uk/6374/

Jaberg, K. & Jakob Jud. 1928. *Sprach- und Sachatlas Italiens und der Südschweiz*. Ringier.

Jacewicz, Ewa & Robert Allen Fox. 2018. Regional variation in fundamental frequency of American English vowels. *Phonetica* 75. 273–309. https://doi.org/10.1159/000484610

Jacewicz, Ewa, Robert Allen Fox & Samantha Lyle. 2009. Variation in stop consonant voicing in two regional varieties of American English. *Journal of the International Phonetic Association* 39(3). 313–334. https://doi.org/10.1017/S0025100309990156

Jacewicz, Ewa, Robert Allen Fox & Joseph Salmons. 2007. Vowel duration in three American English dialects. *American Speech* 82(4). 367–385. https://doi.org/10.1215/00031283-2007-024

Janoff, Arianna. 2018. The California Vowel Shift in Santa Barbara. In Jonathan Crum (ed.), *Proceedings of the 4th Annual Linguistics Conference at UGA*, 30–49. Linguistic Society at UGA.

Jansen, Sandra. 2019. Change and stability in GOOSE, GOAT and FOOT: Back vowel dynamics in Carlisle English. *English Language & Linguistics* 23(1). 1–29. https://doi.org/10.1017/S136067431 7000065

Jones, Daniel. 1911. English: Tyneside dialect (Northumberland). *Le maître phonétique* 26. 184.

Jones, Jonathan A. & Margaret E.L. Renwick. 2022. Spatial analysis of sub-regional variation in Southern US English. *Journal of Linguistic Geography* 9(2). 1–20. https://doi.org/10.1017/jlg.2021.7

Jones, Taylor. 2020. *Variation in African American English: The Great Migration and regional differentiation*. PhD dissertation, University of Pennsylvania.

Kendall, Tyler & Charlie Farrington. 2020. *The Corpus of Regional African American Language*, ver. 2020.05. Online Resources for African American Language Project. https://oraal.uoregon.edu/coraal

Kendall, Tyler & Valerie Fridland. 2012. Variation in perception and production of mid front vowels in the US Southern Vowel Shift. *Journal of Phonetics* 40(2). 289–306. https://doi.org/10.1016/j.wocn.2011.12.002

Kendall, Tyler & Valerie Fridland. 2021. *Sociophonetics*. Cambridge University Press.

Kerswill, Paul & Ann Williams. 2005. New towns and koineization: Linguistic and social correlates. *Linguistics* 43(5). 1023–1048. https://doi.org/10.1515/ling.2005.43.5.1023

Kim, Chaeyoon, Sravana Reddy, James Stanford, Ezra Wyschogrod & Jack Grieve. 2019. Bring on the crowd! Using online audio crowdsourcing for large-scale New England dialectology and acoustic sociophonetics. *American Speech* 94(2). 151–194. https://doi.org/10.1215/00031283-7251252

Kirtley, M. Joelle, James Grama, Katie Drager & Sean Simpson. 2016. An acoustic analysis of the vowels of Hawaiʻi English. *Journal of the International Phonetic Association* 46(1). 79–97. https://doi.org/10.1017/S0025100315000456

Kisler, Thomas, Uwe Reichel & Florian Schiel. 2017. Multilingual processing of speech via web services. *Computer Speech & Language* 45. 326–347. https://doi.org/10.1016/j.csl.2017.01.005

Kohler, Klaus J. 1990. German. *Journal of the International Phonetic Association* 20(1). 48–50. https://doi.org/10.1017/S0025100300004084

Kortmann, Bernd & Clive Upton (eds.). 2008. *Varieties of English 1: The British Isles*. Mouton de Gruyter.

Kretzschmar, William A. Jr. 2018. Linguistic atlases. In Boberg, Nerbonne & Watt 2018a, 57–72. https://doi.org/10.1002/9781118827628.ch3

Kretzschmar, William A. Jr., Paulina Bounds, Jacqueline Hettel, Lee Pederson, Ilkka Juuso, Lisa Lena Opas-Hänninen & Tapio Seppänen. 2013. The Digital Archive of Southern Speech (DASS). *Southern Journal of Linguistics* 37(2). 17–38.

Kretzschmar, William A. Jr., Margaret E.L. Renwick, Lisa M. Lipani, Michael L. Olsen, Rachel M. Olsen, Yuanming Shi & Joseph A. Stanley. 2019. *Transcriptions of the Digital Archive of Southern Speech*. www.lap.uga.edu/Projects/DASS2019/

Krug, Andreas. 2021. The FLEECE and GOOSE vowels in Tyneside English: Accent levelling and morphological conditioning. *Coyote Papers* 23. 43–52. http://hdl.handle.net/10150/659841

Labov, William. 1966. *The social stratification of English in New York City*. Center for Applied Linguistics.

Labov, William, Sharon Ash & Charles Boberg. 2006. *The atlas of North American English: Phonetics, phonology, and sound change: A multimedia reference tool*. De Gruyter.

Labov, William, Ingrid Rosenfelder & Josef Fruehwald. 2013. One hundred years of sound change in Philadelphia: Linear incrementation, reversal, and reanalysis. *Language* 89(1). 30–65. https://doi.org/10.1353/lan.2013.0015

Labov, William, Malcah Yaeger & Richard Steiner. 1972. *A quantitative study of sound change in progress*. US Regional Survey.

Lameli, Alfred, Roland Kehrein & Stefan Rabanus (eds.). 2010. *Language and space: An international handbook of linguistic variation: Language mapping*. De Gruyter Mouton. https://doi.org/10.1515/978311 0219166

Lass, Roger. 1989. System-shape and the eternal return: front rounded vowels in English. *Folia linguistica historica* 23. 163–198. https://doi.org/10.1515/flih.1989.10.1-2.163

Le, Lillian. 2021. *Race and regionality on the ASpIRE ASR model*. MS thesis, University of Georgia.

Leemann, Adrian. 2016. Analyzing geospatial variation in articulation rate using crowdsourced speech data. *Journal of Linguistic Geography* 4(2). 76–96. https://doi.org/10.1017/jlg.2016.11

Leemann, Adrian, Péter Jeszenszky, Carina Steiner, Melanie Studerus & Jan Messerli. 2020. Linguistic fieldwork in a pandemic: Supervised data collection combining smartphone recordings and videoconferencing. *Linguistics Vanguard* 6(s3). 20200061. https://doi.org/10.1515/lingvan-2020-0061

Leemann, Adrian, Marie-José Kolly & David Britain. 2018. The English Dialects App: The creation of a crowdsourced dialect corpus. *Ampersand* 5. 1–17. https://doi.org/10.1016/j.amper.2017.11.001

Leemann, Adrian, Marie-José Kolly, David Britain, Ross Purves & Elvira Glaser. 2015. Documenting sound change with smartphone apps. *Journal of the Acoustical Society of America* 137(4). 2304. https://doi.org/10.1121/1.4920412

Leoni, Federico Albano, Francesco Cutugno, Renata Savy, Valentina Caniparoli, Leandro D'Anna, Ester Paone, Rosa Giordano, Olga Manfrellotti, Massimo Petrillo & Aurelio De Rosa. 2007. *Corpora e Lessici dell'Italiano Parlato e Scritto*. www.clips.unina.it/

Lobanov, Boris M. 1971. Classification of Russian vowels spoken by different speakers. *Journal of the Acoustical Society of America* 49(2B). 606–608. https://doi.org/10.1121/1.1912396

Mahalanobis, Prasanta Chandra. 1936. On the generalized distance in statistics. *Proceedings of the National Institute of Sciences of India* 2. 49–55.

Maiden, Martin & M.M. Parry. 1997. *The dialects of Italy*. Routledge.

Martinet, André. 1952. Diffusion of language and structural linguistics. *Romance Philology* 6(1). 5–13.

Martinet, André. 1955. *Économie des changements phonétiques. Traité de phonologie diachronique*. A. Francke.

Matthews, Peter. 2014. *The concise Oxford dictionary of linguistics*, 3rd edn. Oxford University Press. https://doi.org/10.1093/acref/9780199675128.001.0001

Milroy, James. 2006. The ideology of the standard language. In Carmen Llamas, Louise Mullany & Peter Stockwell (eds.), *The Routledge companion to sociolinguistics*, 133–139. Routledge.

Milroy, James & Lesley Milroy. 2012. *Authority in language: Investigating standard English*. Routledge.

Nadeu, Marianna & Margaret E.L. Renwick. 2016. Variation in the lexical distribution and implementation of phonetically similar phonemes in Catalan. *Journal of Phonetics* 58. 22–47. https://doi.org/10.1016/j.wocn.2016.05.003

Nesbitt, Monica, Suzanne Wagner & Alexander Mason. 2019. A tale of two shifts: Movement toward the Low-Back-Merger Shift in Lansing, Michigan. In Becker, 144–165. https://doi.org/10.1215/00031283-8032979

Niedzielski, Nancy. 1999. The effect of social information on the perception of sociolinguistic variables. *Journal of Language and Social Psychology* 18(1). 62–85. https://doi.org/10.1177/0261927X99018001005

O'Connor, Joseph D. 1947. The phonetic system of a dialect of Newcastle-upon-Tyne. *Le maître phonétique* 87. 6–8.

Okada, Hideo. 1991. Japanese. *Journal of the International Phonetic Association* 21(2). 94–96. https://doi.org/10.1017/S002510030000445X

Olsen, Rachel M., Michael L. Olsen & Margaret E.L. Renwick. 2018. The impact of sub-region on /aɪ/ weakening in the US South. *Proceedings of Meetings on Acoustics* 31(1). 060005. https://doi.org/10.1121/2.0000879

Olsen, Rachel M., Michael L. Olsen, Joseph A. Stanley, Margaret E.L. Renwick & William Kretzschmar. 2017. Methods for transcription and forced alignment of a legacy speech corpus. *Proceedings of Meetings on Acoustics* 30(1). 060001. https://doi.org/10.1121/2.0000559

Orton, Harold, et al. 1962–1971. *Survey of English dialects*. J. Arnold & Son.

Pederson, Lee, Susan L. McDaniel & Carol M. Adams (eds.). 1986. *Linguistic atlas of the Gulf States*. 7 vols. University of Georgia Press.

Pellowe, John, Graham Nixon, Barbara Strang & Vincent McNeany. 1972. A dynamic modelling of linguistic variation: The urban (Tyneside) linguistic survey. *Lingua* 30. 1–30. https://doi.org/10.1016/0024-3841(72)90041-1

Pickford, Glenna Ruth. 1956. American linguistic geography: A sociological appraisal. *Word* 12(2). 211–233. https://doi.org/10.1080/00437956.1956.11659600

Pitt, Mark A., Keith Johnson, Elizabeth Hume, Scott Kiesling & William Raymond. 2005. The Buckeye corpus of conversational speech: Labeling conventions and a test of transcriber reliability. *Speech Communication* 45(1). 89–95. https://doi.org/10.1016/j.specom.2004.09.001

Plichta, Bartlomiej & Dennis R. Preston. 2005. The /ay/s have it: the perception of /ay/ as a north-south stereotype in United States English. *Acta Linguistica Hafniensia* 37(1). 107–130. https://doi.org/10.1080/03740463.2005.10416086

R Core Team. 2022. *R: A language and environment for statistical computing*. R Foundation for Statistical Computing. www.R-project.org

Ray, John. 1694. *A collection of English words not generally used*. Christopher Wilkinson [Reprinted in 1969 by The Scholar Press].

Renwick, Margaret E.L. 2021. Mid vowel variation and contrast in regional Standard Italian. In Fernando Sánchez-Miret & Daniel Recasens (eds.), *Proceedings of the 4th Workshop on Sound Change*. Lincom Europa.

Renwick, Margaret E.L. & D. Robert Ladd. 2016. Phonetic distinctiveness vs. lexical contrastiveness in non-robust phonemic contrasts. *Laboratory Phonology* 7(1). 19. https://doi.org/10.5334/labphon.17

Renwick, Margaret E.L. & Joseph A. Stanley. 2017. Static and dynamic approaches to vowel shifting in the Digital Archive of Southern Speech. *Proceedings of Meetings on Acoustics* 30(1). 060003. https://doi.org/10.1121/2.0000582

Roeder, Rebecca V., Sky Onosson & Alexandra D'Arcy. 2018. Joining the western region: Sociophonetic shift in Victoria. *Journal of English Linguistics* 46(2). 87–112. https://doi.org/10.1177/0075424217753987

Ross, John P., Kevin D. Lilley, Cynthia G. Clopper, Jennifer S. Pardo & Susannah V. Levi. 2021. Effects of dialect-specific features and familiarity on cross-dialect phonetic convergence. *Journal of Phonetics* 86. 101041. https://doi.org/10.1016/j.wocn.2021.101041

Sadlier-Brown, Emily & Meredith Tamminga. 2008. The Canadian Shift: Coast to coast. In S. Jones (ed.), *Proceedings of the 2008 annual conference of the Canadian Linguistic Association*.

Salmons, Joseph & Patrick Honeybone. 2015. Structuralist historical phonology: Systems in segmental change. In Patrick Honeybone & Joseph Salmons (eds.), *The Oxford handbook of historical phonology*, 32–46. Oxford University Press.

Samuels, M.L. 1972. *Linguistic evolution: With special reference to English*. Cambridge University Press.

Sanchez, Kauyumari, Jennifer Hay & Elissa Nilson. 2015. Contextual activation of Australia can affect New Zealanders' vowel productions. *Journal of Phonetics* 48. 76–95. https://doi.org/10.1016/j.wocn.2014.10.004

Sonderegger, Morgan, Jane Stuart-Smith, James Tanner, Vanna Willerton, Rachel Macdonald & Jeff Mielke. 2020. SPADE – Speech Across Dialects of English. OSF. https://doi.org/10.17605/OSF.IO/4JFRM

Sóskuthy, Márton, Paul Foulkes, Bill Haddican, Jen Hay & Vincent Hughes. 2015. Word-level distributions and structural factors codetermine GOOSE fronting. In The Scottish Consortium for ICPhS 2015 (ed.), *Proceedings of the 18th International Congress of Phonetic Sciences*, Paper 1001. University of Glasgow.

Stanford, James N., Monica Nesbitt, James King & Sebastian Turner. 2019. Pioneering a dialect shift in the Pioneer Valley: Evidence for the Low-Back-Merger Shift in Western Massachusetts. Paper presented at the New Ways of Analyzing Variation 48 [NWAV48], Eugene, Oregon.

Stanley, Joseph A. 2020. *Vowel dynamics of the Elsewhere Shift: A sociophonetic analysis of English in Cowlitz County, Washington*. PhD dissertation, University of Georgia.

Stanley, Joseph A. 2022a. A comparison of turn-of-the-century and turn-of-the-millennium speech in Georgia. In Joseph A. Stanley (ed.), *Proceedings of the 6th Annual Linguistics Conference at UGA*. Linguistics Society at UGA.

Stanley, Joseph A. 2022b. Regional patterns in prevelar raising. *American Speech* 97(3). 374–411. https://doi.org/10.1215/00031283-9308384

Stanley, Joseph A., William A. Kretzschmar, Margaret E.L. Renwick, Michael L. Olsen & Rachel M. Olsen. 2017. *Gazetteer of Southern vowels*. http://lap3.libs.uga.edu/u/jstanley/vowelcharts/

Strelluf, Christopher. 2018. *Speaking from the Heartland: The Midland vowel system of Kansas City* [Publication of the American Dialect Society 103]. Duke University Press.

Strycharczuk, Patrycja, Manuel López-Ibáñez, Georgina Brown & Adrian Leemann. 2020. General Northern English: Exploring regional variation in the north of England with machine learning. *Frontiers in Artificial Intelligence* 3. Article 48. https://doi.org/10.3389/frai.2020.00048

Swan, Julia Thomas. 2019. The Low-Back-Merger Shift in Seattle, Washington, and Vancouver, British Columbia. In Becker, 74–99. https://doi.org/10.1215/00031283-8032946

Tanner, James, Morgan Sonderegger, Jane Stuart-Smith & Josef Fruehwald. 2020. Toward "English" phonetics: Variability in the pre-consonantal voicing effect across English dialects and speakers. *Frontiers in Artificial Intelligence* 3. Article 38. https://doi.org/10.3389/frai.2020.00038

Tatman, Rachael. 2017. Gender and dialect bias in YouTube's automatic captions. *Proceedings of the First ACL Workshop on Ethics in Natural Language Processing*. 53–59. https://10.18653/v1/W17-1606

Tatman, Rachael & Conner Kasten. 2017. Effects of talker dialect, gender & race on accuracy of Bing speech and YouTube automatic captions. *Proceedings of Interspeech 2017*. 934–938. https:// doi.org/10.21437/Interspeech.2017-1746

Thiel, Anja & Aaron J. Dinkin. 2020. Escaping the TRAP: Losing the Northern Cities Shift in real time. *Language Variation and Change* 32(3). 373–398. https://doi.org/10.1017/S0954394520000137

Thomas, Erik R. 2001. *An acoustic analysis of vowel variation in New World English* [Publication of the American Dialect Society 85]. Duke University Press.

Thomas, Erik R. 2011. *Sociophonetics: An introduction.* Palgrave.

Torgersen, Eivind. 1997. *Some phonological innovations in southeastern British English.* MA dissertation, University of Bergen.

Torgersen, Eivind & Paul Kerswill. 2004. Internal and external motivation in phonetic change: Dialect levelling outcomes for an English vowel shift. *Journal of Sociolinguistics* 8(1). 23–53. https://doi.org/10.1111/j.1467-9841.2004.00250.x

Trudgill, Peter. 2002. *Sociolinguistic variation and change.* Georgetown University Press.

Underwood, Gary N. 1974. American English dialectology: Alternatives for the Southwest. *International Journal of the Sociology of Language* 1974(2). 19–40. https://doi.org/10.1515/ijsl.1974.2.19

Vaux, Bert & Scott Golder. 2003. *The Harvard dialect survey.* Harvard University Linguistics Department.

Villarreal, Dan & Mary Kohn. 2021. Local meanings for supralocal change: Perceptions of TRAP backing in Kansas. *American Speech* 96(1). 45–77. https://doi.org/10.1215/00031283-8186897

Voeten, Cesko C., Wilbert Heeringa & Hans Van de Velde. 2022. Normalization of nonlinearly time-dynamic vowels. *Journal of the Acoustical Society of America* 152. 2692. https://doi.org/10.1121/10.0015025

Walker, Michael, Anita Szakay & Felicity Cox. 2019. Can kiwis and koalas as cultural primes induce perceptual bias in Australian English speaking listeners? *Laboratory Phonology* 10(1). 7. https://doi.org/10.5334/labphon.90

Watson, Kevin. 2020. *English sociophonetics.* Edinburgh University Press.

Watt, Dominic. 2007. Variation and the variable. In Carmen Llamas, Louise Mullany & Peter Stockwell (eds.), *The Routledge companion to sociolinguistics*, 3–11. Routledge.

Watt, Dominic. 2009. The linguistic variable. In Siobhan Chapman & Christopher Routledge (eds.), *Key ideas in linguistics and the philosophy of language*, 119–120. Edinburgh University Press.

Wells, John C. 1982. *Accents of English.* 3 vols. Cambridge University Press.

Zihlmann, Urban B. & Adrian Leemann. 2017. /l/-vocalisation in Lucerne Swiss German dialects: A sociophonetic analysis using big data. In Malte Belz, Christine Mooshammer, Susanne Fuchs, Stefanie Jannedy, Oksana Rasskazova & Marzena Zygis (eds.), *Proceedings of the Conference on Phonetics & Phonology in German-speaking countries (P&P13)*, 201–204. Leibniz-Zentrum Allgemeine Sprachwissenschaft und Humboldt-Universität zu Berlin.

Zimmer, Karl & Orhan Orgun. 1992. Turkish. *Journal of the International Phonetic Association* 22(1–2). 43–45. https://doi.org/10.1017/S0025100300004588

13

SOCIOPHONETICS AND SOUND CHANGE

Charles Boberg

Introduction

This chapter discusses the sociophonetic study of sound change, focusing especially on the work of William Labov and his colleagues, which deals primarily with sound change in North American English. After situating the sociolinguistic approach to sound change in relation to the traditional historical linguistic approach, the chapter examines the apparent-time method of studying sound change in progress; the application of acoustic phonetics to the study of vowel shifts and mergers; and the use of sociophonetic methods to address theoretical questions relating to the lexical, social, and geographic diffusion of sound change. It concludes by reviewing a case study involving the author's own use of an archive of film and television speech to study sound change over eight decades of real time, which can be compared with previous apparent-time analyses.

Many of the sound changes to be discussed here relate to regional and social variation in language, because of the close connection between variation and change that will be discussed below: synchronic variation results from the diachronic changes that gave rise to it and frequently involves further changes that are still in progress. Given the context of the present volume, this chapter will focus its review of previous research on studies that involve analyses of change over time.

In any discussion of sound change it is necessary to adopt a system for notating the sounds involved, particularly at the broad or phonemic level of transcription (for the narrow or phonetic level the International Phonetic Alphabet [IPA] is the standard system). Given this chapter's focus on the work of Labov, the "binary notation" system used throughout his work is adopted here. Binary notation offers several advantages over other conventions in the context of studying vocalic sound change—in particular, by explicitly reflecting the structural organization of the English vowel system and by facilitating diachronic, pandialectal comparison of vowels (see rationale in Labov 1991:7, 12–14; Labov, Ash & Boberg 2006:11–15; Boberg 2021:90–92). As a guide to binary notation, on the first use in this chapter of any phoneme from Labov's system, the corresponding keyword from Wells's (1982) lexical sets is also provided—for example, /ay/ (PRICE).

DOI: 10.4324/9781003034636-15

Historical linguistic and sociolinguistic approaches to sound change

Languages undergo many types of change involving sounds. These include changes in the number or type of phonemic contrasts in the phonology of the language; changes in phonological patterns like phonotactic constraints, stress contours, or morphophonemic alternations; changes in the sounds that occur in individual words or sets of phonologically related words (known as phonemic incidence); and changes in the phonetic quality of phonemes. In historical linguistics, "sound change" normally means only the last of these: general changes at the level of phonetic features— place and manner of consonants, height and advancement of vowels, and so on—that apply to phonemes, either in particular phonetically defined environments (conditioned changes) or in all the words and environments in which a phoneme occurs (unconditioned changes). In the classic view of sound change, the unit of change is the phoneme, not the word or a grammatical context.

Sound change is a constant process in all speech communities. It reflects the influence of both physical and mental economy, causing sounds to weaken or assimilate to one another, as well as functional factors like the comprehensibility of speech, the symmetry of phoneme inventories and the tolerance versus avoidance of homophony. Though these factors give rise to common patterns of sound change seen across many languages and historical periods, the particular sound changes that arise in any given community at a particular point in time are widely variable, even when the inputs are identical, as in communities that speak the same language. When sound changes that arise in one community do not spread to others, because of geographic or social barriers to communication, the result is dialect divergence. Over hundreds or thousands of years, an accumulation of sound changes, along with grammatical, lexical, and other changes, causes dialects to diverge to the point where they are no longer mutually intelligible, at which point they attain the status of separate but historically or "genetically" related languages.

A frequently cited example of this process is the historical development of Latin, first into regional dialects of popular Latin spoken in different locations across the Roman Empire, then into separate languages like French, Italian, and Spanish. Much of the difference between these languages reflects the operation of different sound changes in each. At a broader level, Latin itself was only one of many genetically related languages spoken across Europe and parts of Asia that developed in a similar way from a common ancestor called Proto-Indo-European (PIE), spoken about 6000 years ago in or near the Caucasus or Pontic-Caspian steppe region of southern Russia. Beyond the Romance languages, others in the Indo-European family include Farsi, Greek, Hindi, Russian, and Germanic languages like English, German, and Swedish. These are all very distantly related through sound change.

The most famous example of a sound change underlying the divergence of languages into related subfamilies is Grimm's Law, or the First Germanic Consonant Shift, by which the stop consonants of PIE shifted their articulation in the Germanic subfamily. This established a series of "systematic correspondences," by which the sounds in one language or subfamily are related to those of another. By Grimm's Law, PIE voiceless stops became voiceless fricatives in Germanic, voiced stops became voiceless (replacing the original voiceless stops), and aspirated voiced stops became plain voiced stops (replacing the original voiced stops). This correspondence is often illustrated with the example of PIE */p/, which remains /p/ in Latin words like *pater*, *pēs/pedis*, and *piscis* (and in other Indo-European languages), but becomes /f/ in the Germanic languages, as in the English equivalents *father*, *foot*, and *fish*. Note that all three words (and many others) show the identical sound correspondence (p:f), indicating that the change has happened at the level of the phoneme, not at the level of the lexicon, operating differently in each word; the individual words are merely instances of a general change at the phonemic level. A group of nineteenth-century historical linguists called the Neogrammarians noted that changes like this tended to be absolutely regular in their application. Even apparent exceptions to the rule were found to be systematic, governed by phonetic factors, prompting them to declare that sound change is regular and suffers no exceptions (Osthoff & Brugmann 1878), a dictum that came to be known as the "Neogrammarian hypothesis."

This hypothesis was of crucial importance because of its role in the larger goal of the Neogrammarians, which was the reconstruction of the prehistoric ancestral languages from which today's families of related languages developed. While the development of Latin into the Romance languages could be observed within the historical record, the split of PIE into Latin, Germanic, and other subfamilies occurred well before it. Our knowledge of these prehistoric linguistic ancestors therefore depends mostly on "comparative reconstruction"—the examination of systematic correspondences in the sounds of a set of potentially related languages and the proposal of a set of hypothetical original sounds from which the attested sounds might have developed by means of regular sound changes in each language. This method can only work if the sound changes involved are assumed to be regular, affecting each instance of the original sound in the same way. If sound changes potentially operate selectively or variably, affecting two or more instances of the same phoneme in different ways, there is no way to assert with any confidence that a systematic correspondence among attested languages developed from any single original sound in the proto-language.

Given the interest of historical linguists in reconstruction of the linguistic past, they tended to take a retrospective view of sound change as a process completed long ago, rather than as an ongoing process today. Changes like Grimm's Law were assumed to be not only lexically regular, affecting all environmentally similar instances of the phoneme in identical ways, but phonetically gradual, occurring in small increments over a period of many decades or even centuries. In the Great English Vowel Shift, for instance, the [i:] of Middle English, in PRICE words (still heard in French *prix*, the source of the English word *price*), became the [ai] of modern English, a low diphthong, but this shift from the high-front to the low-central sector of the vowel space happened not as a discrete change from one vowel to the other, as when modern speakers of English alternate between the two pronunciations of *either* (with the FLEECE vowel or the PRICE vowel), but as a gradual shift with many phonetically intermediate stages, in which the nucleus of the diphthong would have had a mid-central quality between [i:] and [ai], still audible in some English dialects. Neogrammarians therefore assumed that sound change was too gradual to be observed as it was happening. Like the movement of a shadow over the course of a sunny day, reflecting the rotation of the earth, the result of sound change could be noted after the passage of sufficient time, but the process itself could not be observed. Representative of this view is Bloomfield (1933:347), who proclaims, "The process of linguistic change has never been directly observed; we shall see that such observation, with our present facilities, is inconceivable." This assumption put the mechanism of sound change—how it operates phonetically and spreads across both sets of words and groups of speakers—beyond the reach of investigation.

The traditional view of sound change, and of language change more generally, was challenged by Weinreich, Labov & Herzog (1968), who asserted that a shift in focus from change in the past to change in progress today could produce the data needed to explore the mechanism of sound change. Such a shift, however, required a rejection of the dichotomy that Saussure (1916) had established between diachrony and synchrony (historical and theoretical linguistics) and between *langue* and *parole* (the supposedly homogeneous "language" of the speech community and the heterogeneous "speech" of individual people in particular contexts), the latter division later adopted by Chomsky (1965:4) as the "competence-performance" distinction. Chomsky's view was that the individual and contextual variability of performance, which he believed to be random and unsystematic—and therefore theoretically inconsequential—was a barrier to the development of general theories of linguistic competence, which should be built on the intuitions of native speakers about grammaticality; these intuitions were presumably uniform across a speech community, allowing for mutual comprehensibility. By contrast, Labov's sociolinguistic studies of variation and change in the English of Martha's Vineyard (1963) and New York City (1966) had observed a pattern he called "orderly heterogeneity": individual speakers and contexts do exhibit variation, but far from being random and therefore theoretically meaningless it is systematically correlated with social identity and attention to speech. This suggests that variability is in fact part of competence, or what native speakers "know" about their language, and should therefore be included in linguistic study rather than set aside as unimportant.

In particular, Weinreich, Labov & Herzog (1968) reasoned that language changes spread gradually through the communities they affect. Rather than being adopted by all speakers at the same time, innovative forms compete with older forms in gradually shifting proportions. This competition has three possible outcomes: 1) the innovative form eventually pushes out the older form; 2) the older form reasserts itself and the innovation is ultimately rejected; or 3) diachronically stable variation is established between them. No matter which outcome occurs, the implication of the necessary period of competition between newer and older forms is that at least some of the variation we observe in contemporary speech is linked to changes in progress, as the synchronic manifestation of diachronic processes. As Weinreich, Labov & Herzog (1968:188) conclude, "Not all variability and heterogeneity in language structure involves change; but all change involves variability and heterogeneity." Moreover, "Linguistic and social factors are closely interrelated in the development of language change" (ibid.), or, as Labov (1972:3) says, "one cannot understand the development of a language change apart from the social life of the community in which it occurs [... because] social pressures are continually operating on language, not from some remote point in the past, but as an immanent social force acting in the living present."

Studying sociolinguistic variation therefore allows us to observe language change as it is still in progress, rather than centuries after its completion, affording a view of its mechanism that was hidden from traditional historical linguistics. We have virtually no information about the social context of the prehistoric sound changes involved in Grimm's Law and even our knowledge of the social context of the Great English Vowel Shift is constrained by centuries of temporal separation and limited data. By contrast, both linguistic and social data on changes in progress today are abundant. The sociolinguistic study of these data reveals not only the linguistic mechanism of sound change, indicating how it progresses phonetically and spreads through the set of forms it affects, but its geographic and social mechanisms, indicating how and why changes diffuse across space and through the social structure of the speech community. This insight forms the theoretical basis of the modern sociophonetic study of sound change.

Labov's sociophonetic studies of the 1960s: Apparent- and real-time analysis in Martha's Vineyard and New York City

The first major sociophonetic study to proceed on this theoretical basis was Labov's (1963, 1972:1–42) investigation of "the social motivation of a sound change" on the island of Martha's Vineyard, off the coast of Massachusetts (though Labov cites earlier work by Gauchat 1905 and Hermann 1929 as precedents for his approach). The sound change in question was a local version of what later came to be known as Canadian Raising (Chambers 1973): the occurrence of mid or non-low nuclei in the low diphthongs /aw/ (MOUTH) and /ay/ (PRICE) before voiceless obstruents.

Raising of /ay/, at least, was a traditional feature of local speech, observed three decades earlier by Kurath et al. (1939–1943), whereas raising of /aw/ had not been previously noted (Labov 1972:10–11). Labov's anecdotal observations suggested that raising of /ay/ was increasing and spreading to /aw/, a change he hoped to explain by examining its social context. The Martha's Vineyard economy and social structure were undergoing a transition from a traditional reliance on fishing and farming to a modern reliance on tourism, particularly on summer vacationers from the mainland, some of whom were taking up long-term residence, a trend resented by some of the locals. Labov hypothesized that the strengthening of local phonetic features might be linked to a desire among some islanders to emphasize their local status by differentiating themselves linguistically from the summer people.

He interviewed 69 islanders, using a lexical questionnaire, attitudinal questions, and a reading passage, and measured the extent and frequency of raising in their speech. This was assessed with a four-point auditory scale, ranging from low to mid nuclear quality. He verified his scale by carrying out an acoustic analysis of 80 instances of /ay/ spoken by seven participants and comparing the acoustic data with his auditory judgments, finding that they corresponded closely. To obtain a measure of change in progress, following Gauchat (1905), he divided his sample into age cohorts, reasoning that an ongoing change would likely be more advanced among younger members of the community. Such a pattern would allow him to observe the progress of sound change in "apparent time" (Labov 1972:133, 163), as reflected in synchronic generational differences in the frequency of the innovative variant. Labov found that raising of both /ay/ and /aw/ was increasing by regular generational increments up to the youngest generation of participants in their teens and twenties, who showed a reversal of the trend, with a recession to half of the level attained by those aged 31–45 (1972:22). For an explanation for this pattern he turned to his attitudinal data, finding that those who raised the most had positive attitudes towards local island identity and tended to dominate the middle-aged groups, whereas the youngest group contained a mix of positively- and negatively-oriented individuals, the latter not yet having had an opportunity to move to the mainland (1972:31–32).

The observation of change in apparent time relies on a hypothesis that speech habits, after being acquired during childhood, are stable across the adult lifespan so that the speech of successive generations reflects successive periods of acquisition. Speakers in their thirties reflect the language of 20 years ago, those in their seventies the language of 60 years ago, and so on. An alternative hypothesis is that speech habits can change over adult lifetimes, so that generational differences may instead represent the effects of aging, a pattern known as "age-grading." Labov (1972:163, 275) is careful to acknowledge this possibility, admitting that conclusions about change in progress in apparent time can only be confirmed by reference to data on the same variable at an earlier point in "real time." In the case of diphthong raising on Martha's Vineyard, these data were available in the records of the Linguistic Atlas of New England (Kurath et al. 1939–1943) and did confirm his apparent-time analysis.

Labov's second major study of the 1960s examined five phonetic variables in New York City English: vocalization of /r/, raising of /eh/ (BATH, here labeled /æh/) and /oh/ (THOUGHT-CLOTH), and stopping of /th/ and /dh/ (/θ/ and /ð/). The data were gathered by means of 264 rapid and anonymous interactions with department store employees, focused on observing their production of /r/ in response to a question about goods located on the *fou(r)th floo(r)*, and sociolinguistic interviews with about 160 residents of Manhattan's Lower East Side.

As with the Martha's Vineyard study, analysis was primarily auditory, though a few acoustic analyses were carried out to better illustrate the character of the vocalic variables. Here again, earlier records of New York City English were available to support apparent-time analyses, though the emphasis in this study was more on contemporary sociolinguistic variation than on change in progress. Where they were examined, apparent-time patterns indicated a recession rather than an advance of traditional features of New York City English, most notably of /r/ vocalization, though in this case age interacted with social class: among higher-status speakers, restoration of /r/ was strongest among the youngest group, whereas among the middle-status speakers it was strongest in the middle-aged group (Labov 1972:59). This suggests some degree of post-acquisition change, as middle-aged speakers in the center of the social spectrum become maximally sensitive to the overtly prestigious social value of innovative variants modeled by the youngest members of higher-status social groups.

Acoustic sociophonetic study of sound change:
Labov, Yaeger & Steiner (1972)

The limited use of acoustic analysis that Labov initiated in the Martha's Vineyard and New York City studies was greatly expanded, to an international scale (including both US and British varieties), by Labov, Yaeger & Steiner (1972). Their study, familiarly known as "LYS," marks the real beginning of modern acoustic sociophonetics.

LYS uses formant analysis (then much more laborious than it is today) to study sound change in progress in the speech of 245 individuals, focusing on both vocalic chain shifts and phonemic mergers in vowel production. The sample is drawn mostly from sociolinguistic surveys of New York City and Detroit, but also includes "exploratory" datasets from other "northern cities" (Chicago and Buffalo), Philadelphia, the Outer Banks of North Carolina, Atlanta, central Texas and other parts of the Southwest, as well as London and Norwich in England. Apparent-time analyses, backed up by earlier records for real-time comparison, are used to establish the diachronic patterns in the data, but the discussion focuses more on the linguistic aspects of sound change (how changes proceed phonetically and through lexical sets and how they respond to the structure of vowel systems) than on the social aspects (correlations with age and other social attributes of speakers).

Most of the themes of Labov's later writing on sound change, to be reviewed below, first appear in LYS. Among these are the structure of the vowel space, including the role of peripherality in establishing shift trajectories and vocalic subsystems; abstract rules versus lower-level processes (e.g., tensing versus raising of /æh/ in New York City); the role of detailed phonetic conditioning in the progress of vowel shifts; the general principles of chain shifting (which are credited to Sweet 1888); the particular patterns of chain shifting later called the Northern Cities and Southern Vowel Shifts; the theory and study of mergers and near mergers; and the contrast between discrete versus continuous change, or the question of phonetic gradualness.

The adoption of acoustic formant analysis as the primary means of measuring vowel quality in LYS allowed these questions to be addressed with a greater level of precision and objectivity and established a new methodological norm for future work in sociophonetics. Following the observation of Peterson & Barney (1952) that the quality of English vowels could be reliably characterized by measurement of the frequency of the first two formants in the vocalic nucleus, LYS used single-point nuclear measurements to assess both movement and overlap (presence or absence of phonemic contrast) of vowels in a two-dimensional acoustic space. The quantitative nature of these data not only made them more precise and objective than the qualitative data produced by auditory analysis, overcoming problems of listener bias and the limitations of phonetic notation, but supported more sophisticated sociophonetic analysis using multivariate statistics. Some recent studies, such as Fridland, Kendall & Farrington (2014), Mielke, Carignan & Thomas (2017), and

Farrington, Kendall & Fridland (2018), have moved beyond the single-point measurements of LYS to analyze dynamic aspects of vowel quality, such as duration and glide trajectory, that reflect aspects of sound change beyond shifts in nuclear position. Nevertheless, while some dynamic measures like vocalic lengthening, shortening, monophthongization, and diphthongization clearly play an important role in certain sound changes and in listeners' perception of regional accents, subsequent work by Labov and his colleagues, discussed below, confirmed that nuclear quality is the primary dimension of sound change in North American English. In most cases, single nuclear measurements, taken at the point that best represents the articulatory target or central tendency of the vowel, capture the most important regional and social accent differences between speakers.

The social mechanisms of sound change: Sex and social class in Philadelphia

The research that produced LYS coincided with Labov's move from Columbia University in New York City, where he had completed his graduate studies under Uriel Weinreich, to the University of Pennsylvania in Philadelphia, where he began a new program of acoustic sociophonetic research on the sound changes underway in that city, "since it appeared that almost all of the Philadelphia vowels were in motion, and all of the basic patterns of chain shifting found in English and French could also be located in Philadelphia" (Labov 1980:254–255).

The Philadelphia neighborhood study involved in-person sociolinguistic interviews with 113 residents and telephone interviews with 60 more. Recordings of the interviews were subjected to acoustic analysis, producing 150–200 measurements per person, then to multivariate statistical analysis, to determine the individual and combined effects of age, sex, social class, social mobility, ethnicity, neighborhood, communication patterns, and knowledge of other languages on the phonetic measures. This analysis produced age coefficients for each phonetic variable, indicating the extent and direction of its movement through the formant space over apparent time, as well as its correlation with social factors. Labov found particularly strong age coefficients for the raising and fronting of /aw/ and /æh/; the raising and fronting of /ey/ (FACE) and raising of /ay/ before voiceless consonants; the fronting of /uw/ (GOOSE); and the centralization of /ow/ (GOAT). These all represent what Labov (1972:178) labels "changes from below," associated with local rather than global prestige and operating below the level of social awareness. Among them, he determined that the most robust showed a curvilinear rather than monotonic correlation with socioeconomic class, with the most advanced speakers located near the center of the social spectrum, particularly in "the highest sections of the working class" (Labov 1980:260), rather than at either extreme. This social model of sound change was further refined in Labov (1990) by an analysis of the interaction of sex and social class, which confirmed the results of previous research showing that women generally lead changes in progress, so that the leaders of the sound changes underway in Philadelphia were found more specifically to be women in the interior social classes (see also Labov 2001).

Resolving the Neogrammarian controversy: Labov (1981)

Another application of the new sociophonetic data on Philadelphia English was toward a resolution of the long-standing controversy about the nature of sound change. As discussed above, the Neogrammarian view and the standard assumption in mainstream historical linguistics was that sound change is phonetically gradual but lexically abrupt, affecting all words simultaneously. This was challenged by an opposite view, that sound change is phonetically abrupt but lexically gradual, involving discrete changes from one sound to another that proceed one or a few words at a time, often leaving behind a residue of unchanged forms. The latter position was tradition-ally favored by dialectologists, who found evidence for it in their maps of regional variation and proclaimed that "every word has its own history." It received more recent support from a study of changes in the membership of Chinese tone classes by Chen & Wang (1975), who called it "lex-ical diffusion."

Labov (1981) reconciled these theories by showing that both are correct, as they relate to different types of change. Neogrammarian regularity is seen in the operation of simple phonetic rules, like the centralization or fronting of back-up-gliding vowels. When he examined homophones like *two* and *too*, or *know* and *no*, which are lexically different but phonemically identical, he found that the members of such pairs behaved identically with respect to GOOSE- and GOAT-fronting. This provided strong evidence for sound change involving systematic, regular modification of the quality of a phoneme, affecting all instances of that phoneme in a given phonetic environment, regardless of nonphonetic factors like lexical identity, frequency, or grammatical status.

Lexical diffusion, by contrast, is seen in more abstract changes, like shifts across subsystems, as when short-a words in the lax /æ/ word class are reassigned to the tense /æh/ word class in Philadelphia's version of the Mid-Atlantic split short-a system. Here, nonphonetic factors, like grammatical and lexical status, do play a role, producing exceptions that cannot be explained in Neogrammarian terms: the name *Ann(e)* is tense but the article *an* is lax; the adjectives *mad*, *bad*, and *glad* are tense but *sad* is lax; the nouns *pan* and *(tin) can* are tense, but the past-tense verbs *ran* and *began* and the modal verb *(I) can* are lax. Moreover some words, like *planet*, *damage*, and *manage*, were found to vary in their assignment, which was subject to ongoing change. Rather than increments of phonetically gradual but lexically regular change along a spectrum of advancement, these words show alternations between assignments to what are, for Philadelphians, two separate word classes based on phonemically distinct developments of short-a. Just as most North Americans can decide whether the first vowel of *either* and *neither* is FLEECE or PRICE, native speakers of Philadelphia English can decide whether the a-sound of *planet* or *giraffe* is lax or tense. However, once the short-a in a given word has become phonologically tense, it is subject to a phonetic rule of raising that shows Neogrammarian regularity, applying to all lexical instances of tense /æh/, with the extent of raising conditioned by purely phonetic rather than lexical or other factors.

Principles of sound change and the Atlas of North American English

LYS is not widely accessible today, but its main theoretical contributions are presented more suc-cinctly in Labov (1991), which asks the question, "How do dialects of English differ?" They differ in many ways at several levels of structure, of course, but Labov argues that the most important differences, in terms of how English speakers both recognize and project regional identity, involve what dialectologists have traditionally called "accent"—phonetic differences in the quality of phonemes, particularly vowels, which result from sound change, particularly chain shifts and phonemic splits and mergers.

His analysis establishes six principles of chain shifting and shifts across vocalic subsystems:

1. Peripheral (long or tense) vowel nuclei rise;
2. Nonperipheral (lax or short) nuclei fall;
3. Back vowels move to the front;
4. Low nonperipheral vowels become peripheral;
5. High peripheral vowels become nonperipheral before peripheral glides;
6. Peripherality is defined relative to the vowel system as a whole.

The Southern Vowel Shift, for example, begins with a shift of /ay/ from the subsystem of front-up-gliding long vowels with nonperipheral nuclei to the subsystem of long monophthongal vowels with peripheral nuclei (Principle 4). This opens the way for the nonperipheral nuclei of /ey/ and /iy/ (FLEECE) to fall towards the former position of /ay/ according to Principle 2. Another shift across subsystems happens when /e/ (DRESS) and /i/ (KIT) exchange positions with /ey/ and /iy/, respectively, becoming peripheral and therefore subject to Principle 1, whereby they shift upwards, developing in-glides. In an apparently unrelated development, the back-up-gliding long vowels—/uw/, /ow/, and /aw/—all shift forward in the South, according to Principle 3.

Labov next establishes two "pivotal conditions" that underlie many of the more superficial phonetic changes that produce accent differences in North American English: the contrastive status of /æ/ and /æh/ in the low-front and of /o/ (LOT) and /oh/ in the low-back quadrant of the vowel space. In the Inland North, for instance, /æ/ and /æh/ are a single tense phoneme on the front peripheral track, but /o/ and /oh/ are distinct. An upward shift of /æ-æh/, in accordance with Principle 1, allows the low-back distinction to be maintained by a forward shift of /o/ toward the low-front position occupied by /æ/ in the split short-a system of New York City (where /æ/ and /æh/ are separate phonemes). In New York, by contrast, where low-front /æ/ blocks forward movement of /o/, the low-back distinction is instead reinforced by raising /oh/ along the rear periphery, parallel to raising of /æh/ in the front. Raising of /æ-æh/ and fronting of /o/ are shown to be the initial stages of the Northern Cities Vowel Shift, found throughout the Inland North from Chicago to western New York State. They initiate a pull chain, in which /oh/ descends to low-back position (where /o/ used to be), /ʌ/ (STRUT) retracts toward /oh/, /e/ retracts toward /ʌ/, and /i/ descends toward /e/ (see Eckert 1988, 1989 for an examination of these shifts in Detroit English).

Finally, Labov states two general principles governing merger: that mergers expand at the expense of oppositions and that mergers initiate pull shifts and inhibit push shifts. These introduce a discussion of what he calls the "Third Dialect," a provisional grouping of regions where the low-back vowels are merged (e.g., *cot* and *caught* are homophones): northern New England, western Pennsylvania, the American West, and all of Canada. Most of these also display a merger of /æ/ and /æh/. Labov suggests that the extra space created by the back and front mergers makes the Third Dialect comparatively stable, lacking the active chain shifts observed in the North, South, and other regions. Subsequent research on Canadian English by Clarke, Elms & Youssef (1995), however, together with earlier research on California English by Luthin (1987) and Hinton et al. (1987), showed that Third Dialect regions in fact display their own vowel shifts. Some of these, like the fronting of back vowels in California, are shared with the South, but the Canadian data inspired the designation of a Canadian Vowel Shift that appeared to be a response to the low-back merger, exemplifying Labov's second principle of mergers: the extra space in the low-central sector of the vowel space created by the merger of /o/ and /oh/ in low-back position encourages a retraction of /æ-æh/ toward that position (noted in Canadian English by Esling & Warkentyne 1993 and in California English by Moonwomon 1991). This retraction in turn initiates a pull shift, in which /i/ and /e/ fall toward the previous position of /æ-æh/. The principles governing chain shifting and mergers are further discussed in Labov (1994).

Labov (1991) provided the theoretical and analytical framework for what became the culmination of that research tradition: the Atlas of North American English (ANAE; Labov, Ash & Boberg 2006; for other multiregional acoustic phonetic surveys, see Thomas 2001; Clopper, Pisoni & de Jong 2005). Like previous dialect atlases, the ANAE sought to identify regional differences in speech, but its regional analysis was based on participation in ongoing sound change, particularly vocalic mergers, splits, and chain shifts, rather than on static or recessive features like traditional local vocabulary. Sampling focused on the urban majority, rather than on the rural populations favored by earlier dialectology as more representative of traditional dialects, and included a mix of ages and social backgrounds, to allow for sociolinguistic analysis within each region. Unlike traditional face-to-face fieldwork, interviews for the ANAE were carried out over the telephone, allowing for comparatively rapid collection of a continental sample of 762 participants, and were audio-recorded, allowing for acoustic analysis of a subset of 439 participants. Elicitation involved a mix of formal methods, like minimal pairs (*cot* and *caught*, etc.) to assess phonemic oppositions, and conversation prompts to stimulate spontaneous speech.

Acoustic analysis involved the measurement of F1 and F2 at a single point in the nuclei of vowels bearing primary lexical and phrasal stress, to assess the maximal approach of each token towards its articulatory target and avoid the effects of centralization in non-primary-stress contexts. The resulting data are displayed in maps showing the regional distribution of both phonemic status (particularly the low-back merger) and phonetic quality (particularly the major chain shifts identified in previous research). Multivariate regression analysis supported conclusions about ongoing change over apparent time, while acoustic data were used to construct isoglosses delimiting dialect regions. The latter include the South, defined as the region where /ay/ is generally monophthongal, initiating the Southern Shift described in Labov (1991); the Inland North, the territory of the Northern Cities Shift along the American side of the Great Lakes; New England, a region with considerable internal diversity; the Mid-Atlantic region, focused on the metropolitan dialects of New York City and Philadelphia where short-a is split into lax and tense phonemes; the Midland, a transition zone showing varying influence from neighboring regions; the West, characterized by the low-back merger and a "nasal" short-a system (/æ-æh/ is fronted and raised only and always before front nasals); and Canada, included for the first time in a major American dialect study, which was found to be generally similar to the West but was distinguished from the Inland North by the Canadian Shift and from the Midland and West by Canadian Raising.

Transmission and diffusion of sound change: Labov (2007)

Building on his resolution of the Neogrammarian controversy, ANAE data allowed Labov (2007) to examine another theoretical dichotomy in historical linguistics: the distinction between transmission and diffusion in the propagation of sound change. As in his earlier work, he points out that there is solid evidence for both types of change but makes a principled distinction between them. Transmission involves children learning local sound patterns from their parents and peers, including a trajectory of sound change modeled on a comparison of younger and older speakers, and advancing that change incrementally in each generation. Because children are expert language learners, these patterns can include relatively abstract, complex aspects of grammar, like the highly irregular Mid-Atlantic short-a split. This is faithfully acquired through transmission from local parents to children, but not by children with non-local parents, let alone by adults, whose language learning skills are considerably diminished by the time they encounter new patterns through contact with other communities. Transmitted sound changes advance by means of local or covert prestige and cause divergence among the communities in which they occur, as each community exhibits independent changes.

Not all communities are isolated from each other, however, and when they come into cultural contact through trade, migration, conquest, or other external developments, linguistic features can diffuse from one dialect to another, based on the global or overt prestige attached to them or to the dialect or speech community in which they originate. Because such contact usually involves adult populations, diffused features tend to be simple, non-structural elements of language—most commonly loanwords, pronunciations of individual words, or superficial, nonstructural sound changes like GOOSE-fronting or, in Europe, the backing of /r/ from apical to uvular.

To illustrate this restriction, Labov uses ANAE data to examine the geographic distribution of the short-a system of New York City, whose historical influence is seen in several regions across the country. He finds that the lexical distribution of tense and lax vowels loses complexity more or less in proportion to distance from New York City: the most faithful versions occur nearby in New Jersey, whereas the short-a systems of Albany (NY), Cincinnati, and New Orleans are progressively simplified, resolving themselves into single-phoneme systems with a phonetically conditioned range of allophones. The ANAE also showed the Northern Cities Shift to have diffused from Chicago to St. Louis, traditionally a Midland city, but this diffusion involved only isolated elements of the shift (individual sound changes affecting single vowels), rather than the structurally integrated chain shift, which is only found intact in the Inland North itself, as a local change transmitted from parents to children.

Testing the apparent-time model: /r/ in Montreal French

The backing of /r/ from apical to uvular is a simple sound change that is easily diffused, spreading from Paris across regions of France and even across languages, affecting the /r/ of German and Danish. This change has also been occurring more recently in Canada, where it was examined in Montreal French by Sankoff & Blondeau (2007). They observed it in a panel study with data from two points in time. The frequency of dorsal (uvular) /r/ was assessed in the speech of 120 participants in 1971 and then reassessed in a subset of 32 of them in 1984. This enabled Sankoff & Blondeau to test the assumption of the apparent-time model that phonology remains stable over the lifetimes of adult speakers, allowing the speech of older generations to represent the state of the language when they acquired it as children. An apparent-time analysis of the 1971 data showed a strong generational trend, with dorsal /r/ increasing from less than 10 percent among older speakers to over 70 percent among teens. When restudied in 1984, the majority of the 1971 speakers (20) displayed a stable frequency of dorsal /r/, but a minority (9) showed a significant increase, some advancing from variable to categorical use. As this pattern involves a shift toward greater use of the innovative feature present in the community, Sankoff & Blondeau (2007) label it "change across the lifespan," thereby distinguishing it from age-grading, which normally involves a rejection of apparently innovative features in older adulthood, thereby neutralizing the apparent change at the community level.

As there is strong evidence for a critical period in language acquisition and languages do, universally, change over time, at least some age-related linguistic variation must represent change in progress at the community level, as assumed by the apparent-time model, and it should be emphasized that most of Sankoff & Blondeau's participants did exhibit stable usage over the thirteen years between the studies, thereby supporting the model. Moreover, while age-grading always remains a possibility that can only be dismissed with real-time data from earlier studies, lifespan change is not incompatible with the apparent-time model; a shift of older adults toward the innovative form simply accelerates the change at the community level, rather than counteracting it. The middle-aged and older adults who participate in this acceleration are presumably those with a positive attitude to innovative youth speech, or greater exposure to it, possibly reflecting participation in parent–child or teacher–student relationships.

Recent sociophonetic work on sound change in North American English

The ANAE offered the first continental view of sound change and phonetic and phonological variation in North American English. This view included analyses of a number of specific sound changes in each of a dozen regions, but could not possibly provide the detailed view that might emerge from more locally focused studies. One of the aims of the atlas was therefore to inspire such research in the future. Many sociophoneticians across the continent have taken up this challenge in a wide range of recent studies, examining a diverse set of sound changes from several different theoretical and methodological perspectives. This is a much larger body of research than could possibly be exhaustively reviewed here. Some common themes have nevertheless emerged and, in the interest of pointing readers to examples of the research on each of them, a brief and necessarily selective bibliography is offered here.

First, the ANAE found that while some of the sound changes it examined showed strong age coefficients indicating change in progress in apparent time, others were slowing down, some had reached completion—becoming stable regional features rather than changes in progress—and still others were receding or reversing, as the local prestige once attached to them gave way to the global prestige attached to trans-regional features diffusing from other communities, leading to dialect convergence. Several subsequent studies of sound change have offered evidence of the weakening of regional patterns. Among these are Nagy & Irwin (2010), Wood (2011), and Stanford (2019) in New England; Becker (2014a,b), Becker & Wong (2010), Mather (2012), and Haddican et al. (2022) in New York City; Labov, Rosenfelder & Fruehwald (2013) and Labov et al. (2016) in Philadelphia; Thiel & Dinkin (2021) in Upstate New York; Driscoll and Lape (2015) in Syracuse, New York; Wagner et al. (2016) in Lansing, Michigan; McCarthy (2011), D'Onofrio & Benheim (2019), and D'Onofrio (2021) in Chicago; Dodsworth & Kohn (2012) in North Carolina; and Prichard (2010) in Atlanta.

The geographic expansion of the low-back merger, an illustration of Labov's above-cited first principle of mergers, could also be seen as a convergent sound change and has attracted recent attention from sociophoneticians in many locations, following the earlier work of Herold (1990) in northeastern Pennsylvania. Representative studies include those of Hall-Lew (2013) in California; Majors (2005) and Gordon (2006) in Missouri; Irons (2007) in Kentucky; Johnson (2010) in southeastern New England; Doernberger & Cerny (2008) in Miami; Bigham (2010) in Illinois; Thomas (2010) in eastern Ohio; Benson, Fox & Balkman (2011) in northwestern Wisconsin; Dinkin (2011) in Upstate New York; and Stanford (2019:203, 223) in Boston and northeastern New England. Fridland, Kendall & Farrington (2014) investigate the role of duration in the merger, while Kendall & Fridland (2017) examine the effect of the merger on vowel perception.

Labov's second principle of mergers suggests a causal structural connection between the low-back merger and the lowering and/or retraction of short front vowels dubbed the Low-Back-Merger Shift (LBMS) by the contributors to Becker (2019). In Canada, where the LBMS was formerly known as the Canadian Shift, studies include those by Boberg (2005) in Montreal; Boberg (2008, 2010:225–241, 2011) across Canada; Hoffman (2010), Roeder & Jarmasz (2010), and Roeder (2012) in Toronto; Swan (2016) in Vancouver; Kettig & Winter (2017) in Montreal; and Roeder, Onosson & D'Arcy (2018) in Victoria. In the United States, where the LBMS was formerly known as the California Shift, among other labels, studies include those by Eckert (2008), Podesva (2011), Kennedy & Grama (2012), Podesva et al. (2015), D'Onofrio (2015), and D'Onofrio, Pratt & Van Hofwegen (2019) in California; by Bigham (2010), Durian (2012), Becker et al. (2016), and

Strelluf (2018) in other parts of the American West and Midwest; by Nesbitt and Stanford (2021) in New England; and by Jacewicz, Fox & Salmons (2011a, 2011b) in a comparison of Wisconsin, Ohio, and North Carolina. Boberg (2019) presents cross-border data showing identical versions of the shift among Canadian and American students.

Another set of studies examines a phonetically opposite development of /æ/ to that in the LBMS: fronting and raising before voiced velars, in words like *bag*, *flag*, *hang*, and *thanks*, to a mid-front quality like that of /ey/. This was first documented in Milwaukee by Zeller (1997) and examined over a wider northwestern region, including most of Canada, in the ANAE (Labov, Ash & Boberg 2006:181–182). Now often called "BAG-raising," it has been studied more recently by Bauer & Parker (2008), Purnell (2008), and Benson, Fox & Balkman (2011) in the American Upper Midwest; by Boberg (2008), Rosen & Skriver (2015), and Roeder, Onosson & D'Arcy (2018) in western Canada; by Wassink (2015), Becker et al (2016), McLarty, Kendall & Farrington (2016), Stanley (2018), and Freeman (2021) in the American Pacific Northwest; by Swan (2020) across the international border between Vancouver and Seattle; and in a wider international sample using ultrasound by Mielke, Carignan & Thomas (2017).

Still another sound change examined in recent research on North American English is the Canadian Raising of /ay/ that was the focus of Labov's study of Martha's Vineyard (1963). This was shown in the ANAE to occur across a wide northern region of the United States, from the Upper Midwest through the Great Lakes region to the Mid-Atlantic region and parts of New England (Labov, Ash & Boberg 2006:114, 205–206), but now appears to be strengthening and expanding to new regions, as documented by the contributors to Davis & Berkson (2021).

Finally, though research on vocalic changes has continued to dominate recent sociophonetic work on sound change, at least one consonantal change has also attracted recent attention: the retraction of /s/ in /sCr-/ clusters, especially /str-/, in words like *stress*, *street*, *strike*, *strong*, and *destroy* (so that these sound like "shtress," etc.). This change was not observed by the ANAE, but is investigated in Columbus, Ohio, by Durian (2007), in Philadelphia English by Gylfadottir (2015), in Australian English by Stevens & Harrington (2016), in North Carolina English by Wilbanks (2017), and across several dialects by Stuart-Smith et al. (2019). Another conson-antal change on the horizon in American English is the spread of glottal replacement of post-vocalic or coda /t/ (Eddington & Channer 2010), which parallels, in some ways, major sound changes affecting /t/ and other stops in other Englishes around the world (Chodroff & Foulkes this volume).

Sociophonetic studies of sound change beyond North American English

The length of this chapter does not permit a discussion of the sociophonetic study of sound change outside the North American tradition initiated by Labov, even in other English-speaking regions, let alone in other languages (for an application of Labov's approach by one of his early collaborators to vowel shifts in Quebec French, see Yaeger-Dror 1994, 1996; also MacKenzie & Sankoff 2010). The subject is nevertheless actively pursued beyond North America. Of the many studies that could be cited, influential examples include those of Williams & Kerswill (1999), Watt (2002), Harrington, Kleber & Reubold (2008), Cheshire et al. (2011), and Stuart-Smith et al. (2013) on British English; Hickey (1999, 2005) on Irish English; Cox (1999), Gordon & Maclagan (2001), Horvath & Horvath (2001), and Hay, Warren & Drager (2006) on Australian and New Zealand English; and Mesthrie (2010) on South African English.

CASE STUDY   **The sociophonetics of sound change in North American film and television speech**

The preceding discussion shows that most sociophonetic studies of sound change, including the ANAE, have used an apparent-time model to analyze synchronic evidence of change in progress. This is most effective when real-time data are available for comparison, but these are often difficult to find. When they do exist, for instance in the records of dialect atlases compiled in the early twentieth century, they are often of limited quantity and quality and subject to doubts arising from methodological issues such as transcriptional practice and accuracy. A much larger source of real-time data on sound change over the twentieth century is available in the archive of speech recorded for mass media such as film and television. These present their own potential problems of artificiality and selective representation, which vary according to the source, but the possibility of tracking change over several decades of real time by analyzing mass media speech has been clearly demonstrated by several studies, such as the analysis of fricative devoicing in Dutch radio speech by Van de Velde, Gerritsen & van Hout (1996), or of the recession of /r/ vocalization in American film speech by Elliott (2000a,b).

Methods

Taking Elliott's work as a model, I recently carried out an acoustic analysis of 180 North American film and television performances, spanning eight decades from the beginning of sound film in the 1930s to the first decade of the present century, to look for real-time evidence of the sound changes identified by the apparent-time analysis of the ANAE. Initial reports on this project, which I call "Accent in North American Film and Television" (AINAFT), appeared in Boberg (2018, 2020); the complete analysis is presented in Boberg (2021).

AINAFT is primarily an acoustic study of vowel production, focusing on phonemic contrast, allophonic patterns, and phonetic quality. It is based on F1/F2 measures of 120,288 vowels, equivalent to the acoustic dataset of the ANAE. This makes an average of 668 tokens per actor, twice as many as the ANAE, but for half as many individuals. Following the ANAE method, nuclear quality was measured at a single point in the nucleus, representing each vowel's closest approach to its target, with analysis restricted to syllables bearing primary lexical and phrasal stress. Unlike in the ANAE, however, the "first pass" analysis was performed automatically in Praat, by a script that used measurement points I had selected and marked on a point tier; careful inspection of the resulting values in an Excel spreadsheet often revealed clearly erroneous or questionable formant values, which were rechecked in Praat "by hand" and corrected where necessary. Phonemic and allophonic contrasts were assessed with t-tests. Auditory analysis was used to record the presence or absence of glides (on /ay/ in Southern States and African American English) and of /r/ constriction; the latter analysis was based on an average of 109 tokens per actor. The progress of sound change over real time was measured with Pearson correlations between phonetic measures and performance year and with t-tests comparing mean values of performances from the early and late periods, before and after the mid-1960s. The most robust diachronic patterns were combined into an aggregate index of sound change used to identify the most innovative and conservative performances and the most important differences between the early and late periods were displayed on a vowel chart.

Synchronic variation was also examined in relation to biological sex, region (New York City, the South, the Inland North, and Canada), and ethnic identity (actors of European American, African American, Latino, Asian North American, and Indigenous ancestry). Mean phonetic values for each of the regional and ethnic groups were compared with the rest of the dataset to identify the most important phonetic and phonological differences between them. An index was then developed for each group, combining its most distinctive phonetic features, which was used to identify the individual performances that are most and least representative of the group. The vowel systems of the most representative individuals were then displayed in vowel charts for detailed analysis.

Results

Focusing on the subset of performances without a strong regional or ethnic identity, the main diachronic analysis identifies an overall shift from an eastern standard in the early period, based on the middle-class speech of the New York City region, to a western standard in the late period, based on the middle-class speech of Los Angeles and, more broadly, the western United States. In particular, the AINAFT dataset reveals ten sound changes that have combined, over the last eight decades, to produce what the book labels modern General North American English (GNAE), the type of regionally and ethnically unmarked speech now heard in most mass media contexts (Boberg 2021:143–144, 299):

1) Increasing constriction of post-vocalic /r/, with the mean frequency rising from 56 percent in the early period to 98 percent in the late;
2) A tendency toward the Low-Back Merger, with the mean Cartesian difference between /o/ and /oh/ shrinking from 288 Hz in the early period to 197 Hz in the late;
3) The rise of a "nasal" short-a system, replacing the older Mid-Atlantic split short-a system, with the mean Cartesian distance between /æ-æh/ and /æN-æhN/, its allophone before front nasal consonants, more than doubling, from 125 to 276 Hz;
4) An increase in the raising and fronting of /æG/, the allophone of short-a before voiced velar consonants, with the mean Cartesian distance between /æ-æh/ and /æG/ doubling, from 119 to 231 Hz;
5) Retraction of /e/ and /æ-æh/ in the Low-Back-Merger Shift, with mean F2 values decreasing from 1826 to 1761 Hz for /e/ and from 1777 to 1734 Hz for /æ-æh/;
6) Fronting or centralization of the back-up-gliding vowels /iw/ (e.g., *cue, few, music*), /uw/, /ow/, and /aw/, with their mean F2 values increasing from 1582 to 1687, 1340 to 1471, 1193 to 1230, and 1473 to 1577 Hz, respectively;
7) Reversal of the relative advancement of /uw/ and /æ-æh/, a measure called the Index of Phonetic Innovation, with /uw/ now farther forward than /æ-æh/ for many younger actors;
8) An increase in Canadian Raising of /ayT/, with the mean Cartesian distance between /ay/ and /ayT/, its allophone before voiceless obstruents, increasing from 71 to 110 Hz;
9) Conditioned neutralization of the contrast between /æ/ and /ey/ before intervocalic /r/, with the mean F1 distance between /æ/ and /ær/, its prerhotic allophone in words like *carry*, *arrow*, and *charity*, increasing from 53 to 172 Hz, as /ær/ separates from /æ/ and rises to merge with /eyr/ (SQUARE); and

10) Other changes connected with the rise in /r/ constriction, like the retraction of syllabic /r/ (NURSE), from a mean F2 of 1529 to 1405 Hz, the raising of /ahr/ (START), from a mean F1 of 829 to 773 Hz, and the raising of /owr-ohr/ (FORCE-NORTH), from a mean F1 of 626 to 571 Hz.

Discussion

This analysis concludes that

> a comparison of these sound changes with previous sociolinguistic and dialectological research on the general population found a close correspondence between the two datasets in every case [...]: real-time patterns in film and television speech do match the apparent-time patterns observed in recent studies of the private speech of ordinary people, indicating a tight connection between the two types of speech.
>
> Boberg 2021:300

Further convergence with the results of previous research on the general population emerges from the analysis of sex differences in a composite index of five phonetic variables, which finds that "all the most important sound changes are led by women, both individually and at the aggregate level" (2021:301). The phonetic character of modern GNAE is established with a set of mean formant measures for 45 word classes (2021:145–148). Like many of the previous studies discussed in this chapter, the analysis of film and television speech in Boberg (2021) demonstrates the link between synchronic phonetic variation and diachronic sound change. It also supports the conclusion of several regional studies that local sound patterns are giving way to a trans-regional continental standard, a trend led by young women—though in this respect its focus on mass media speech may exaggerate this tendency, a possibility that could be examined in future research on the relationship between popular and mass media speech.

Future directions for the sociophonetic study of sound change

This chapter has traced the development of the sociophonetic approach to the study of sound change from its beginnings in Labov's work of the 1960s to its culmination in the ANAE, and beyond, to many more recent studies inspired by the ANAE or pursuing novel directions of their own. It has focused especially on the application of sociophonetic data to important theoretical questions of historical linguistics and sociolinguistics, including the relationship between diachronic change and synchronic variation and the lexical, geographic, and social diffusion of sound change. Despite the achievements of the research reviewed here, many questions remain for future research. For instance, the preceding discussion has dealt mostly with studies of vowel production in English, which have dominated past research, whereas considerably less sociophonetic work has been done on changes involving consonants, perception, and languages other than English, all of which have the potential to broaden our understanding of sound change.

The most notable future direction, however, is likely to be the trend toward automation of acoustic analysis. It remains to be seen how our understanding of sound change will be modified or enlarged by new computational methods that allow for the rapid analysis of far larger sociophonetic datasets than was previously possible: whether such studies will merely confirm with a great deal more data what we already know, or take us in genuinely new directions. My own experience with acoustic analysis—in the ANAE, which was entirely "by hand," with AINAFT, which was partly automated, and on the Low-Back-Merger Shift, reported in Boberg (2019), which was fully automated with forced alignment—suggests a note of caution for those who wish to reap the undoubted benefits of the greater quantitative and statistical power facilitated by computational approaches (see also Cox & Docherty this volume). This caution is best expressed in the methodological discussion of AINAFT, in reference to the process of error-checking and correcting "by hand" the formant data produced by automated analysis:

The frequency of needed corrections depended on the sound quality of the original source and the .wav file made from it and on the characteristics of the actor's voice ([…] the high, breathy voices of some actresses were especially problematic), but typical rates ranged from 10 to 25 percent of the tokens analyzed for each actor. In no case could the initial, automated analysis, performed with constant parameters across all tokens, be considered accurate: careful error-checking and manual correction of at least some tokens was required for every actor. Computerized acoustic analysis is tremendously useful in sociophonetic research and recent advances in computational methods have greatly increased the speed with which such analyses can be performed, but the experience of carrying out the 180 acoustic analyses in this project clearly indicates that the accuracy of acoustic analysis depends on three factors that have nothing to do with computational methods: careful listening, familiarity with the accent being analyzed and a solid understanding of both acoustic and articulatory phonetics.

Boberg 2021:102

There is, not surprisingly, a trade-off between quantity and quality, between statistical power and individual accuracy, and between an overarching view of large-scale aggregate patterns and a more intimate understanding (and possibly enjoyment) of how each person pronounces each token. The desired balance between these competing advantages is a matter for each researcher to determine.

References

Bauer, Matt & Frank Parker. 2008. /æ/-raising in Wisconsin English. *American Speech* 83(4). 403–431. https://doi.org/10.1215/00031283-2008-029

Becker, Kara. 2014a. (r) we there yet? The change to rhoticity in New York City English. *Language Variation and Change* 26(2). 141–168. https://doi.org/10.1017/S0954394514000064

Becker, Kara. 2014b. The social motivations of reversal: Raised BOUGHT in New York City English. *Language in Society* 43(4). 395–420. https://doi.org/10.1017/S0047404514000372

Becker, Kara (ed.). 2019. *The Low-Back-Merger Shift: Uniting the Canadian Vowel Shift, the California Vowel Shift, and Short Front Vowel Shifts across North America* [Publication of the American Dialect Society 104]. Duke University Press.

Becker, Kara, Anna Aden, Katelyn Best & Haley Jacobson. 2016. Variation in West Coast English: The case of Oregon. In Fridland et al., 107–134.

Becker, Kara & Amy Wing-mei Wong. 2010. The short-a system of New York City English: An update. *University of Pennsylvania Working Papers in Linguistics* 15(2). Article 3. https://repository.upenn.edu/pwpl/vol15/iss2/3/

Benson, Erica J., Michael J. Fox & Jared Balkman. 2011. *The bag that Scott bought*: The low vowels in northwest Wisconsin. *American Speech* 86(3). 271–311. https://doi.org/10.1215/00031283-1503910

Bigham, Douglas S. 2010. Correlation of the Low-Back Vowel Merger and TRAP-retraction. *Penn Working Papers in Linguistics* 15(2). Article 4. https://repository.upenn.edu/pwpl/vol15/iss2/4

Bloomfield, Leonard. 1933. *Language*. University of Chicago Press.

Boberg, Charles. 2005. The Canadian Shift in Montreal. *Language Variation and Change* 17(2). 133–154. https://doi.org/10.1017/S0954394505050064

Boberg, Charles. 2008. Regional phonetic differentiation in Standard Canadian English. *Journal of English Linguistics* 36(2). 129–154. https://doi.org/10.1177/0075424208316648

Boberg, Charles. 2010. *The English language in Canada: Status, history and comparative analysis*. Cambridge University Press.

Boberg, Charles. 2011. Reshaping the vowel system: An index of phonetic innovation in Canadian English. *Penn Working Papers in Linguistics* 17(2). 20–29. https://repository.upenn.edu/pwpl/vol17/iss2/4

Boberg, Charles. 2018. New York City English in film: Phonological change in reel time. *American Speech* 93(2). 153–185. https://doi.org/10.1215/00031283-6926135

Boberg, Charles. 2019. A closer look at the Short Front Vowel Shift in Canada. *Journal of English Linguistics* 47(2). 91–119. https://doi.org/10.1177/0075424219831353

Boberg, Charles. 2020. Diva diction: Hollywood's leading ladies and the rise of General American English. *American Speech* 95(4). 441–484. https://doi.org/10.1215/00031283-8221002

Boberg, Charles. 2021. *Accent in North American film and television: A sociophonetic analysis*. Cambridge University Press.

Chambers, J.K. 1973. Canadian Raising. *Canadian Journal of Linguistics* 18(2). 113–135. https://doi.org/10.1017/S0008413100007350

Chen, Matthew & William S.-Y. Wang. 1975. Sound change: Actuation and implementation. *Language* 51(2). 255–281. https://doi.org/10.2307/412854

Cheshire, Jenny, Paul Kerswill, Sue Fox & Eivind Torgersen. 2011. Contact, the feature pool and the speech community: The emergence of Multicultural London English. *Journal of Sociolinguistics* 15(2). 151–196. https://doi.org/10.1111/j.1467-9841.2011.00478.x

Chomsky, Noam. 1965. *Aspects of the theory of syntax*. MIT Press.

Clarke, Sandra, Ford Elms & Amani Youssef. 1995. The third dialect of English: Some Canadian evidence. *Language Variation and Change* 7(2). 209–228. https://doi.org/10.1017/S0954394500000995

Clopper, Cynthia G., David B. Pisoni & Kenneth de Jong. 2005. Acoustic characteristics of the vowel systems of six regional varieties of American English. *Journal of the Acoustical Society of America* 118(3). 1661–1676. https://doi.org/10.1121/1.2000774

Cox, Felicity. 1999. Vowel change in Australian English. *Phonetica* 56(1–2). 1–27. https://doi.org/10.1159/000028438

Davis, Stuart & Kelly Berkson (eds.). 2021. *American Raising* [Publication of the American Dialect Society 106]. Duke University Press.

Dinkin, Aaron J. 2011. Weakening resistance: Progress toward the low back merger in New York State. *Language Variation and Change* 23(3). 315–345. https://doi.org/10.1017/S0954394511000147

Dodsworth, Robin & Mary Kohn. 2012. Urban rejection of the vernacular: The SVS undone. *Language Variation and Change* 24(2). 221–245. https://doi.org/10.1017/S0954394512000105

Doernberger, Jeremy & Jacob Cerny. 2008. The low back merger in Miami. *University of Pennsylvania Working Papers in Linguistics* 14(2). Article 3. https://repository.upenn.edu/pwpl/vol14/iss2/3

D'Onofrio, Annette. 2015. Persona-based information shapes linguistic perception: Valley Girls and California vowels. *Journal of Sociolinguistics* 19(2). 241–256. https://doi.org/10.1111/josl.12115

D'Onofrio, Annette. 2021. Age-based perceptions of a reversing regional sound change. *Journal of Phonetics* 86. Article 101038. https://doi.org/10.1016/j.wocn.2021.101038

D'Onofrio, Annette, & Jaime Benheim. 2019. Contextualizing reversal: Local dynamics of the Northern Cities Shift in a Chicago community. *Journal of Sociolinguistics* 24(4). 469–491. https://doi.org/10.1111/josl.12398

D'Onofrio, Annette, Teresa Pratt & Janneke Van Hofwegen. 2019. Compression in the California Vowel Shift: Tracking generational sound change in California's Central Valley. *Language Variation and Change* 31(2). 193–217. https://doi.org/10.1017/S0954394519000085

Driscoll, Anna & Emma Lape. 2015. Reversal of the Northern Cities Shift in Syracuse, New York. *University of Pennsylvania Working Papers in Linguistics* 21(2). Article 6. https://repository.upenn.edu/pwpl/vol21/iss2/6

Durian, David. 2007. Getting [ʃ]tronger every day?: More on urbanization and the socio-geographic diffusion of (str) in Columbus, OH. *University of Pennsylvania Working Papers in Linguistics* 13(2). Article 6. https://repository.upenn.edu/pwpl/vol13/iss2/6

Durian, David. 2012. *A new perspective on vowel variation across the 19th and 20th centuries in Columbus, OH*. PhD dissertation, The Ohio State University.

Eckert, Penelope. 1988. Adolescent social structure and the spread of linguistic change. *Language in Society* 17(2). 183–207. https://doi.org/10.1017/S0047404500012756

Eckert, Penelope. 1989. The whole woman: Sex and gender differences in variation. *Language Variation and Change* 1(3). 245–267. https://doi.org/10.1017/S095439450000017X

Eckert, Penelope. 2008. Where do ethnolects stop? *International Journal of Bilingualism* 12(1-2). 25–42. https://doi.org/10.1177/13670069080120010301

Eddington, David & Caitlin Channer. 2010. American English has go? a lo? of glottal stops: Social diffusion and linguistic motivation. *American Speech* 85(3). 338–351. https://doi.org/10.1215/00031283-2010-019

Elliott, Nancy C. 2000a. *A sociolinguistic study of rhoticity in American film speech from the 1930s to the 1970s*. PhD Dissertation, Indiana University.

Elliott, Nancy C. 2000b. Rhoticity in the accents of American film actors: A sociolinguistic study. *Voice and Speech Review* 1(1). 103–130. https://doi.org/10.1080/23268263.2000.10761390

Esling, John H. & Henry J. Warkentyne. 1993. Retracting of /æ/ in Vancouver English. In Sandra Clarke (ed.), *Focus on Canadian English*, 229–246. John Benjamins.

Farrington, Charlie, Tyler Kendall & Valerie Fridland. 2018. Vowel dynamics in the Southern Vowel Shift. *American Speech* 93(2). 186–222. https://doi.org/10.1215/00031283-6926157

Foulkes, Paul & Gerard J. Docherty (eds.). 1999. *Urban voices: Accent studies in the British Isles*. Routledge.

Freeman, Valerie. 2021. Vague eggs and tags: Prevelar merger in Seattle. *Language Variation and Change* 33(1). 57–80. https://doi.org/10.1017/S0954394521000028

Fridland, Valerie, Tyler Kendall, Betsy E. Evans & Alicia Beckford Wassink (eds.). 2016. *Speech in the Western States* [Publication of the American Dialect Society 101]. Duke University Press.

Fridland, Valerie, Tyler Kendall & Charlie Farrington. 2014. Durational and spectral differences in American English vowels: Dialect variation within and across regions. *Journal of the Acoustical Society of America* 136(1). 341–349. https://doi.org/10.1121/1.4883599

Gauchat, Louis. 1905. *L'unité phonétique dans le patois d'une commune*. In *Aus romanischen Sprachen und Literature: Festschrift für Heinrich Morf*, 175–232. Halle/S. Max Niemeyer.

Gordon, Elizabeth & Margaret Maclagan. 2001. "Capturing a sound change": A real time study over 15 years of the NEAR/SQUARE Diphthong Merger in New Zealand English. *Australian Journal of Linguistics* 21(2). 215–238. https://doi.org/10.1080/07268600120080578

Gordon, Matthew J. 2006. Tracking the low back merger in Missouri. In Thomas E. Murray & Beth Lee Simon (eds.), *Language variation and change in the American Midland: A new look at "Heartland" English*, 57–68. John Benjamins.

Gylfadottir, Duna. 2015. Shtreets of Philadelphia: An acoustic study of /str/-retraction in a naturalistic speech corpus. *University of Pennsylvania Working Papers in Linguistics* 21(2). Article 11. https://repository.upenn.edu/pwpl/vol21/iss2/11

Haddican, Bill, Cecilia Cutler, Michael Newman & Christina Tortora. 2022. Cross-speaker covariation across six vocalic changes in New York City English. *American Speech* 97(4). 512–542. https://doi.org/10.1215/00031283-9616153

Hall-Lew, Lauren. 2013. "Flip-flop" and mergers-in-progress. *English Language & Linguistics* 17(2). 359–390. https://doi.org/10.1017/S1360674313000063

Harrington, Jonathan, Felicitas Kleber & Ulrich Reubold. 2008. Compensation for coarticulation, /u/-fronting, and sound change in Standard Southern British: An acoustic and perceptual study. *Journal of the Acoustical Society of America* 123(5). 2825–2835. https://doi.org/10.1121/1.2897042

Hay, Jennifer, Paul Warren & Katie Drager. 2006. Factors influencing speech perception in the context of a merger-in-progress. *Journal of Phonetics* 34(4). 458–484. https://doi.org/10.1016/j.wocn.2005.10.001

Hermann, Eduard. 1929. *Lautveränderungen in den Individualsprachen einer Mundart: Charmey*. Nachrichten von der Gesellschaft der Wissenschaften zu Göttingen, Philologisch-Historische Klasse 3.

Herold, Ruth. 1990. *Mechanisms of merger: The implementation and distribution of the low back merger in eastern Pennsylvania*. PhD dissertation, University of Pennsylvania.

Hickey, Raymond. 1999. Dublin English: Current changes and their motivation. In Foulkes & Docherty, 265–281.

Hickey, Raymond. 2005. *Dublin English: Evolution and change*. John Benjamins.

303

Hinton, Leanne, Birch Moonwomon, Sue Bremner, Herb Luthin, Mary Van Clay, Jean Lerner & Hazel Corcoran. 1987. It's not just the Valley Girls: A study of California English. *Proceedings of the Thirteenth Annual Meeting of the Berkeley Linguistics Society*. 117–128. https://doi.org/10.3765/bls.v13i0.1811

Hoffman, Michol F. 2010. The role of social factors in the Canadian Vowel Shift: Evidence from Toronto. *American Speech* 85(2). 121–140. https://doi.org/10.1215/00031283-2010-007

Horvath, Barbara M. & Ronald J. Horvath. 2001. A multilocality study of a sound change in progress: The case of /l/ vocalization in New Zealand and Australian English. *Language Variation and Change* 13(1). 37–57. https://doi.org/10.1017/S0954394501131029

Irons, Terry Lynn. 2007. On the status of low back vowels in Kentucky English: More evidence of merger. *Language Variation and Change* 19(2). 137–180. https://doi.org/10.1017/S0954394507070056

Jacewicz, Ewa, Robert Allen Fox & Joseph Salmons. 2011a. Cross-generational vowel change in American English. *Language Variation and Change* 23(1). 45–86. https://doi.org/10.1017/S0954394510000219

Jacewicz, Ewa, Robert Allen Fox & Joseph Salmons. 2011b. Vowel change across three age groups of speakers in three regional varieties of American English. *Journal of Phonetics* 39(4). 683–693. https://doi.org/10.1016/j.wocn.2011.07.003

Johnson, Daniel Ezra. 2010. *Stability and change along a dialect boundary: The low vowels of southeastern New England* [Publication of the American Dialect Society 95]. Duke University Press.

Kendall, Tyler & Valerie Fridland. 2017. Regional relationships among the low vowels of US English: Evidence from production and perception. *Language Variation and Change* 29(2). 245–271. https://doi.org/10.1017/S0954394517000084

Kennedy, Robert & James Grama. 2012. Chain shifting and centralization in California vowels: An acoustic analysis. *American Speech* 87(1). 39–56. https://doi.org/10.1215/00031283-1599950

Kettig, Thomas & Bodo Winter. 2017. Producing and perceiving the Canadian Vowel Shift: Evidence from a Montreal community. *Language Variation and Change* 29(1). 79–100. https://doi.org/10.1017/S0954394517000023

Kurath, Hans, et al. 1939–1943. *Linguistic atlas of New England*. 3 vols. Brown University Press.

Labov, William. 1963. The social motivation of a sound change. *Word* 19(3). 273–309. https://doi.org/10.1080/00437956.1963.11659799

Labov, William. 1966. *The social stratification of English in New York City*. Center for Applied Linguistics.

Labov, William. 1972. *Sociolinguistic patterns*. University of Pennsylvania Press.

Labov, William. 1980. The social origins of sound change. In William Labov (ed.), *Locating language in time and space*, 251–265. Academic Press.

Labov, William. 1981. Resolving the Neogrammarian controversy. *Language* 57(2). 267–308. https://doi.org/10.2307/413692

Labov, William. 1990. The intersection of sex and social class in the course of linguistic change. *Language Variation and Change* 2(2). 205–254. https://doi.org/10.1017/S0954394500000338

Labov, William. 1991. The three dialects of English. In Penelope Eckert (ed.), *New ways of analyzing sound change*, 1–44. Academic Press.

Labov, William. 1994. *Principles of linguistic change*, vol. 1, *Internal factors*. Blackwell.

Labov, William. 2001. *Principles of linguistic change*, vol. 2, *Social factors*. Blackwell.

Labov, William. 2007. Transmission and diffusion. *Language* 83(2). 344–387. https://doi.org/10.1353/lan.2007.0082

Labov, William, Sharon Ash & Charles Boberg. 2006. *The atlas of North American English: Phonetics, phonology, and sound change: A multimedia reference tool*. De Gruyter.

Labov, William, Sabriya Fisher, Duna Gylfadottir, Anita Henderson & Betsy Sneller. 2016. Competing systems in Philadelphia phonology. *Language Variation and Change* 28(3). 273–305. https://doi.org/10.1017/S0954394516000132

Labov, William, Ingrid Rosenfelder & Josef Fruehwald. 2013. One hundred years of sound change in Philadelphia: Linear incrementation, reversal, and reanalysis. *Language* 89(1). 30–65. https://doi.org/10.1353/lan.2013.0015

Labov, William, Malcah Yaeger & Richard Steiner. 1972. *A quantitative study of sound change in progress*. US Regional Survey.

Luthin, Herbert W. 1987. The story of California (ow): The coming-of-age of English in California. In Keith M. Denning (ed.), *Variation in language: NWAV-XV at Stanford*, 312–324. Stanford University Department of Linguistics.

MacKenzie, Laurel & Gillian Sankoff. 2010. A quantitative analysis of diphthongization in Montreal French. *University of Pennsylvania Working Papers in Linguistics* 15(2). Article 11. https://repository.upenn.edu/pwpl/vol15/iss2/11

Majors, Tivoli. 2005. Low back vowel merger in Missouri speech: Acoustic description and explanation. *American Speech* 80(2). 165–179. https://doi.org/10.1215/00031283-80-2-165

Mather, Patrick-André. 2012. The social stratification of /r/ in New York City: Labov's department store study revisited. *Journal of English Linguistics* 40(4). 338–356. https://doi.org/10.1177/0075424211431265

McCarthy, Corrine. 2011. The Northern Cities Shift in Chicago. *Journal of English Linguistics* 39(2). 166–187. https://doi.org/10.1177/0075424210384226

McLarty, Jason, Tyler Kendall & Charlie Farrington. 2016. Investigating the development of the contemporary Oregonian English vowel system. In Fridland et al., 135–157.

Mesthrie, Rajend. 2010. Socio-phonetics and social change: Deracialisation of the GOOSE vowel in South African English. *Journal of Sociolinguistics* 14(1). 3–33. https://doi.org/10.1111/j.1467-9841.2009.00433.x

Mielke, Jeff, Christopher Carignan & Erik R. Thomas. 2017. The articulatory dynamics of pre-velar and pre-nasal /æ/-raising in English: An ultrasound study. *Journal of the Acoustical Society of America* 142(1). 332–349. https://doi.org/10.1121/1.4991348

Moonwomon, Birch. 1991. *Sound change in San Francisco English*. PhD dissertation, University of California, Berkeley.

Nagy, Naomi & Patricia Irwin. 2010. Boston (r): Neighbo(r)s nea(r) and fa(r). *Language Variation and Change* 22(2). 241–278. https://doi.org/10.1017/S0954394510000062

Nesbitt, Monica & James N. Stanford. 2021. Structure, chronology, and local social meaning of a supra-local vowel shift: Emergence of the Low-Back-Merger Shift in New England. *Language Variation and Change* 33(3). 269–295. https://doi.org/10.1017/S0954394521000168

Osthoff, Hermann & Karl Brugmann. 1878. *Morphologische Untersuchungen auf dem Gebiete der indogermanischen Sprachen*. S. Hirzel.

Peterson, Gordon E. & Harold L. Barney. 1952. Control methods used in a study of the vowels. *Journal of the Acoustical Society of America* 24. 175–184. https://doi.org/10.1121/1.1906875

Podesva, Robert J. 2011. The California vowel shift and gay identity. *American Speech* 86(1). 32–51. https://doi.org/10.1215/00031283-1277501

Podesva, Robert J., Annette D'Onofrio, Janneke Van Hofwegen & Seung Kyung Kim. 2015. Country ideology and the California vowel shift. *Language Variation and Change* 27(2). 157–186. https://doi.org/10.1017/S095439451500006X

Prichard, Hilary. 2010. Linguistic variation and change in Atlanta, Georgia. *University of Pennsylvania Working Papers in Linguistics* 16(2). Article 17. https://repository.upenn.edu/pwpl/vol16/iss2/17

Purnell, Thomas C. 2008. Prevelar raising and phonetic conditioning: Role of labial and anterior tongue gestures. *American Speech* 83(4). 373–402. https://doi.org/10.1215/00031283-2008-028

Roeder, Rebecca V. 2012. The Canadian Shift in two Ontario cities. *World Englishes* 31(4). 478–492. https://doi.org/10.1111/j.1467-971X.2012.01775.x

Roeder, Rebecca V. & Lidia-Gabriela Jarmasz. 2010. The Canadian Shift in Toronto. *Canadian Journal of Linguistics* 55(3). 387–404. https://doi.org/10.1017/S0008413100001614

Roeder, Rebecca V., Sky Onosson & Alexandra D'Arcy. 2018. Joining the western region: Sociophonetic shift in Victoria. *Journal of English Linguistics* 46(2). 87–112. https://doi.org/10.1177/0075424217753987

Rosen, Nicole & Crystal Skriver. 2015. Vowel patterning of Mormons in southern Alberta, Canada. *Language & Communication* 42. 104–115. https://doi.org/10.1016/j.langcom.2014.12.007

Sankoff, Gillian & Hélène Blondeau. 2007. Language change across the lifespan: /r/ in Montreal French. *Language* 83(3). 560–588. https://doi.org/10.1353/LAN.2007.0106

Saussure, Ferdinand de. 1916. *Cours de linguistique générale*. Payot.

Stanford, James N. 2019. *New England English: Large-scale acoustic sociophonetics and dialectology*. Oxford University Press.

Stanley, Joseph A. 2018. Changes in the timber industry as a catastrophic event: BAG-raising in Cowlitz County, Washington. *University of Pennsylvania Working Papers in Linguistics* 24(2). Article 16. https://repository.upenn.edu/pwpl/vol24/iss2/16

Stevens, Mary & Jonathan Harrington. 2016. The phonetic origins of /s/-retraction: Acoustic and perceptual evidence from Australian English. *Journal of Phonetics* 58. 118–134. https://doi.org/10.1016/j.wocn.2016.08.003

Strelluf, Christopher. 2018. *Speaking from the Heartland: The Midland vowel system of Kansas City* [Publication of the American Dialect Society 103]. Duke University Press.

Stuart-Smith, Jane, Gwilym Pryce, Claire Timmins & Barrie Gunter. 2013. Television can also be a factor in language change: Evidence from an urban dialect. *Language* 89(3). 501–536. https://doi.org/10.1353/lan.2013.0041

Stuart-Smith, Jane, Morgan Sonderegger, Rachel Macdonald, Jeff Mielke, Michael McAuliffe & Erik Thomas. 2019. Large-scale acoustic analysis of dialectal and social factors in English /s/-retraction. In Sasha Calhoun, Paola Escudero, Marija Tabain & Paul Warren (eds.), *Proceedings of the 19th International Congress of Phonetic Sciences, Melbourne, Australia 2019*, 1273–1277. Australasian Speech Science and Technology Association.

Swan, Julia Thomas. 2016. The effect of language ideologies on the Canadian Shift: Evidence from /æ/ in Vancouver, BC and Seattle, WA. *International Journal of Language and Linguistics* 3(6). 1–14.

Swan, Julia Thomas. 2020. *Bag* across the border: Sociocultural background, ideological stance and BAG-raising in Seattle and Vancouver. *American Speech* 95(1). 46–81. https://doi.org/10.1215/00031283-7587892

Sweet, Henry. 1888. *History of English sounds*. Clarendon Press.

Thiel, Anja & Aaron J. Dinkin. 2021. Escaping the TRAP: Losing the Northern Cities Shift in real time. *Language Variation and Change* 33(2). 373–398. https://doi.org/10.1017/S0954394520000137

Thomas, Erik R. 2001. *An acoustic analysis of vowel variation in New World English* [Publication of the American Dialect Society 85]. Duke University Press.

Thomas, Erik R. 2010. A longitudinal analysis of the durability of the Northern-Midland dialect boundary in Ohio. *American Speech* 85(4). 375–430. https://doi.org/10.1215/00031283-2010-022

Van de Velde, Hans, Marinel Gerritsen & Roeland van Hout. 1996. The devoicing of fricatives in Standard Dutch: A real-time study based on radio recordings. *Language Variation and Change* 8(2). 149–175. https://doi.org/10.1017/S0954394500001125

Wagner, Suzanne Evans, Alexander Mason, Monica Nesbitt, Erin Pevan & Matt Savage. 2016. Reversal and re-organization of the Northern Cities Shift in Michigan. *University of Pennsylvania Working Papers in Linguistics* 22(2). Article 19. https://repository.upenn.edu/pwpl/vol22/iss2/19

Wassink, Alicia Beckford. 2015. Sociolinguistic patterns in Seattle English. *Language Variation and Change* 27(1). 31–58. https://doi.org/10.1017/S0954394514000234

Watt, Dominic. 2002. "I don't speak with a Geordie accent, I speak, like, the Northern accent": Contact-induced levelling in the Tyneside vowel system. *Journal of Sociolinguistics* 6(1). 44–63. https://doi.org/10.1111/1467-9481.00176

Weinreich, Uriel, William Labov & Marvin Herzog. 1968. Empirical foundations for a theory of language change. In Winifred P. Lehmann & Yakov Malkiel (eds.), *Directions for historical linguistics: A symposium*, 95–195. University of Texas Press.

Wells, John C. 1982. *Accents of English*. 3 vols. Cambridge University Press.

Wilbanks, Eric. 2017. Social and structural constraints on a phonetically-motivated change in progress: (str) retraction in Raleigh, NC. *University of Pennsylvania Working Papers in Linguistics* 23(1). Article 33. https://repository.upenn.edu/pwpl/vol23/iss1/33

Williams, Ann & Paul Kerswill. 1999. Dialect levelling: Change and continuity in Milton Keynes, Reading and Hull. In Foulkes & Docherty, 141–162.

Wood, Jim. 2011. Short-a in northern New England. *Journal of English Linguistics* 39(2). 135–165. https://doi.org/10.1177/0075424210366961

Yaeger-Dror, Malcah. 1994. Phonetic evidence for sound change in Quebec French. In Patricia A. Keating (ed.), *Phonological structure and phonetic form: Papers in laboratory phonology III*, 267–293. Cambridge University Press.

Yaeger-Dror, Malcah. 1996. Phonetic evidence for the evolution of lexical classes: The case of a Montreal French vowel shift. In Gregory R. Guy, Crawford Feagin, Deborah Schiffrin & John Baugh (eds.), *Towards a social science of language*, vol. 1, *Variation and change in language and society*, 263–287. John Benjamins.

Zeller, Christine. 1997. The investigation of a sound change in progress: /ae/ to /e/ in Midwestern American English. *Journal of English Linguistics* 25(2). 142–155. https://doi.org/10.1177/007542429702500207

14

SOCIOPHONETICS AND IDENTITY

Erez Levon and Stamatina Katsiveli

Introduction

Research in sociolinguistics (and sociophonetics) has long relied on appeals to "identity" as a means of accounting for patterns of variation in language use (for reviews of this work, see Le Page 1997; Tabouret-Keller 1997; Llamas & Watt 2010; Levon forthcoming). At its core, an appeal to "identity" as an explanatory factor is based on the assertion that linguistic differences are not (or not only) determined by physiological differences among speakers or by automatic routines established during early language socialization. Instead, identity-based approaches treat linguistic variation as a fundamentally social phenomenon, related to an individual's positioning in society and/or their understanding and interpretation of that positioning.

Yet even within this more socially oriented body of work, "identity" remains a contentious term and academic disagreements about the utility of "identity" as an analytical concept are long-standing. Cameron & Kulick (2003), for example, famously argued that there exists an over-emphasis on the use of language as a way to claim membership in an identity category in language, gender, and sexuality scholarship to the exclusion of other ways in which language and gender/sexuality may interact (including, for example, as a means for rejecting category affiliation or via a more indirect, higher-order indexical relation between language and a given social label). In response to Cameron & Kulick's argument, Bucholtz & Hall (2004) countered that a nuanced examination of how people dynamically and relationally enact category membership is central to this line of enquiry (see also Bucholtz & Hall 2005; Cameron & Kulick 2005). Similarly, Trudgill (2008) proposed that "identity concerns" play no role in the formation of new dialects in language contact situations and that long-term automatic accommodation between speakers can account for the developmental patterns observed in the literature. This position that was explicitly rebutted by Coupland (2008) and Holmes & Kerswill (2008), among others, who, while acknowledging the problem with "simplistic purposive accounts of identity as motive" (Coupland 2008:268), nevertheless argued that accommodation is never wholly automatic, that accommodation occurs when people—not language varieties—come into contact, and that interpersonal and intersubjective factors always play a role (see also Labov 2012). Within phonetics, proposals like Ohala's (1983, 1994) Frequency Code and Gussenhoven's (2004) Effort and Production Codes seek to account for patterns of sociophonetic variation via recourse to universal biological rules that are

DOI: 10.4324/9781003034636-16

independent of social or identity-linked factors. In contrast, scholars such as Eckert (2017) have argued that, universal meaning potentials notwithstanding, agency and identity are crucial for sound symbolic meaning to be realized in interaction, such that we cannot divorce our analyses of sound symbolism from the specific social contexts in which it occurs.

Part of the reason why there is so much disagreement about the role of identity in linguistic variation is because the term "identity" is often used to refer to a number of very different things. This is due in large part to the fact that "identity" is what Giddens (1987) calls a "double hermeneutic," a concept that is used both as a technical term of analysis in scholarly work and as a popular term for organizing experience in wider society. According to Giddens, scholarly and popular understandings of such concepts influence one another, with popular conceptualizations conscripted into scholarly work and vice versa. While not necessarily a problem in and of itself, the danger of this kind of mutual influence is a proliferation of meanings of a given term, resulting in a lack of scholarly precision and a potential degradation in the perceived merit of academic enquiry. With respect to the term "identity," Brubaker & Cooper (2000:1) summarize the issue succinctly by stating "if identity is everywhere, identity is nowhere." In other words, if "identity" can mean different things to different people in different contexts (e.g., an overt category membership, an in-the-moment interpersonal relation, a deeply held sense of self), what sort of analytical purchase does the term have for scholars?

It is not our intention to provide a definitive answer to this question in the current chapter. Instead, our goal is to provide an overview of the different ways in which the issue of identity has been approached in sociophonetics. We begin in the next section with a brief introduction to Brubaker & Cooper's system for classifying different treatments of identity in social research into three broad categories: identity as category positioning (by self or other), identity as the expression of commonality or groupness, and identity as situated subjectivity. We use this system not as a prescriptive taxonomy, but as a way to organize our review of sociophonetic research on identity, demonstrating how examinations of variation in both speech perception and production have contributed to each of these areas. Through this review, we hope to demonstrate the relevance of identity-linked questions to sociophonetic investigation and to outline some of the different ways in which the topic can be approached.

Theorizing identity without "identity"

As Brubaker & Cooper (2000:2–4) describe, the term "identity" first gained currency in the social sciences in the middle of the twentieth century via its use in US-based research in social and developmental psychology (Allport 1954; Erikson 1968) and sociology (Goffman 1963; Berger & Luckmann 1967), where it replaced earlier psychoanalytic concepts including "identification" and "self" (see also Gleason 1983). For various reasons, the term began to resonate beyond its original academic origins and was actively taken up in popular and political discourse throughout the 1960s and 1970s, undergirding the generational "rebellions" of the late 1960s and providing a vocabulary for the continued coalescence of anti-racist and anti-sexist movements across the 1970s. As a result of this popular uptake of the term, "identity" shifted from a "category of analysis"— applied as a label by researchers to describe divisions in the social world—to a "category of practice"—something that people outside of academia began to use to mark their positioning in society (Brubaker & Cooper 2000:4). Through this shift, identity came to be reified and (strategically) essentialized (Spivak 1996), a simplification that, for political purposes, treated "identity" as something that is both "real" and that is shared across members of a given social group. According to Brubaker & Cooper, the emergence of cultural studies in the 1980s brought this more reified conceptualization of "identity" (back) into scholarly research, yielding the multiplicity of different meanings for the term that still exists today.

Brubaker & Cooper warn that, when faced with this multiplicity of meanings, it becomes easy to unintentionally reinforce and/or reproduce popular and essentialized understandings of identity. As they explain:

> The mere use of a term as a category of practice, to be sure, does not disqualify it as a category of analysis [...] What is problematic is not *that* a particular category is used, but *how* it is used. The problem, as Loïc Wacquant has argued with respect to "race," lies in the "uncontrolled conflation of social and sociological [... or] folk and analytic understandings" (Wacquant 1997:222). The problem is that "nation," "race," and "identity" are used analytically a good deal of the time more or less as they are used in practice, in an implicitly or explicitly reifying manner, in a manner that implies or asserts that "nations," "races," and "identities" *exist* and that people *have* a "nationality," a "race," an "identity."
>
> Brubaker & Cooper 2000:5–6, emphasis in the original

Brubaker & Cooper recognize that there have been concerted efforts within scholarly research to avoid reifying identity, to theorize it as something that is dynamic and contingent. In response, Brubaker & Cooper (2000:6) claim that for them "it is not clear why what is routinely characterized as multiple, fragmented, and fluid should be conceptualized as 'identity' at all."

Instead, Brubaker & Cooper introduce a series of terms to demarcate distinct social phenomena that, they argue, are conflated in the existing literature under the cover term "identity." Their goal in doing so is both to focus on the more processual aspects of the various phenomena in question, by side-stepping the essentializing connotations of "identity," and to allow for a higher level of analytical nuance and precision, by more clearly specifying the particular type of identity-linked process involved. The first term they introduce is "categorization," by which they mean the positioning of an individual (by self or other) as a member of a relevant social category or group, one that is widely recognized and features in the broader social landscape. Categorization of this kind is intrinsic to social life: in a variety of contexts, people identify themselves, characterize themselves, and locate themselves vis-à-vis known others, though without necessarily talking about "identity." Thus, to speak of categorization rather than identity allows us to highlight the "process" instead of the "condition" and to focus on the individual agency involved. At the same time, by acknowledging that categorization is equally something that others do to us, Brubaker & Cooper are able to capture the limits on agentive positioning and the intersubjective nature of categorization processes.

The second type of phenomenon that Brubaker & Cooper describe is what they term "commonality" or "groupness." Here, they refer to uses of "identity" to denote a sense of connection and/or affinity between individuals. This connection can be strongly felt and affectively loaded (groupness), such as a feeling of belonging to a distinct ethnic or political group, for example, or it can be somewhat looser and potentially fleeting (commonality). Through groupness and commonality, Brubaker & Cooper advance a more nuanced way of describing the relations that dynamically emerge among members of a collectivity but that are not necessarily based on fixed or identifiable categories. Rather, groupness and commonality refer to a sense of belonging that emerges from the relational ties between individuals. Finally, Brubaker & Cooper also describe "self-understanding" as the third type of identity phenomenon. They consider self-understanding as a dispositional term, one that designates an individual's situated subjectivity: that is, one's own understanding of who one is, of one's social location, and of how one is prepared to act in a variety of situations. Brubaker & Cooper (2000:17) relate self-understanding to Bourdieu's (1990) notion of *sens pratique*, "a practical sense—at once cognitive and emotional—that persons have of themselves and their social world." While this sense is potentially related to an individual's relevant category memberships and social networks, situated subjectivity focuses on an individual's interpretive understandings of these and how these understandings give rise to a phenomenal experience of self.

None of the three types of identity-linked phenomena that Brubaker & Cooper name is new to sociolinguistic theorizing. Bucholtz & Hall (2005), for example, describe identity as relational, positional, and emergent, echoing Brubaker & Cooper's division into categorization, groupness, and (situated) subjectivity. Similarly, a great deal of work on stylistic variation in sociolinguistics has argued that identity-linked linguistic practice is the result of individuals' negotiating between their category affiliations and their own understandings of self (e.g., Coupland 2007; Levon 2009). Yet, the similarity between Brubaker & Cooper's tripartite division of identity phenomena, on one hand, and prior claims about identity in the sociolinguistics literature, on the other, is precisely the point of Brubaker & Cooper's argument: they suggest that using the same term ("identity") to refer to what, in reality, are very different socio-psychological processes (people constructing an identity, experiencing an identity, or enacting an identity) is, at best, confusing and, at worst, detrimental to our analyses. If our goal is to understand how language participates in social life (Eckert 2019), it is useful to distinguish among the specific identity-linked phenomena language is involved in.

For this reason, our review in this chapter of how issues of identity have been approached within sociophonetics follows the taxonomy of phenomena that Brubaker & Cooper (2000) propose. We begin in the next section by considering work on categorization, before turning to commonality/groupness and, subsequently, situated subjectivity. In each of these sections, we review both classic and more recent studies in order to underscore that differences in theoretical approach are not purely chronological, but are instead linked to the types of social and linguistic phenomena under investigation.

Before doing this, it is useful to briefly sketch how the taxonomy that Brubaker & Cooper propose, and which we follow below, relates to another well-known taxonomy in sociolinguistics: Eckert's (2012) waves model for the study of variation. According to Eckert, the study of the social meaning of linguistic variation can be divided into three main approaches (or waves). In the first wave (surveys), the meanings of variation are linked to broad demographic categories (e.g., class, gender) to which speakers nominally belong. The second wave (local communities), in contrast, "delve[s] under the large social aggregates of the First Wave" (Eckert 2016:69) to consider how variation comes to be associated with more locally meaningful social divisions and configurations (e.g., whether you are a Jock or a Burnout; Eckert 2000). Finally, the third wave offers a radical departure from the previous waves, arguing that the meanings of variants are not based on their surface-level correlations with social groups (whether broad demographic categories or more locally meaningful ones) but instead emerge as a part of socially relevant styles that speakers actively and strategically deploy in interaction. While there are certain thematic overlaps between Eckert's (2012) wave model and Brubaker & Cooper's taxonomy, the two are nevertheless orthogonal. In essence, Eckert's waves offer a typology of the different ways in which variables accrue (and communicate) social meaning: through association with broad social categories, through locally meaningful divisions, or through specific stylistic composites. Brubaker & Cooper are instead focused on describing the different identity-linked goals that people can use language (or any other form of social practice) to achieve: to index group membership, to signal connection and belonging, or to express a situated understanding of self. In principle, any of the "waves" can be used to examine the different types of identity-linked processes that Brubaker & Cooper define (though, admittedly, certain waves are more amenable to the study of particular identity phenomena than others). Since our goal in this chapter is to review sociophonetic research on identity, we draw on Brubaker & Cooper's taxonomy to structure our discussion, though we fully recognize that the implementation of sociophonetic research on identity-linked issues necessarily also involves a close engagement with Eckert's claims.

The phonetics of categorization

Sociophonetic research on identity has traditionally focused primarily on the first type of identity-linked phenomenon that Brubaker & Cooper (2000) describe, namely categorization and the ways in which variation in both the production and perception of phonetic features is linked to the larger social categories that speakers are affiliated with (whether by themselves or by others). Research on this dimension began as early as Labov's (1966) classic study of English in New York City, where he demonstrated a systematic link between the production of a range of phonetic features—including the realization versus absence of post-vocalic /r/, the tensing of the mid-front DRESS vowel, and the tensing of the mid-back BOUGHT vowel—to a speaker's social class. Labov shows that not only do these features serve to distinguish individuals from different social class backgrounds in production, they also show systematic variation across different speech contexts, such that when engaged in talk that calls for more explicit attention to widespread norms of language use (such as a more formal reading task, for example), speakers vary their phonetic productions so as to orient to these global linguistic norms. The importance of the patterns that Labov describes is that they indicate both that there are characteristic speech patterns associated with social groups and that speakers are on some level aware of these associations and vary their productions across contexts in response to them. In this respect then, in his work over 50 years ago, Labov already demonstrated that speech can be used by others to categorize an individual and that speakers can also use variation in an attempt to actively and agentively categorize themselves.

As is well known, Labov's insights in this regard inspired a range of studies examining the connections between specific phonetic realizations and relevant social categories. Over the years, research has become increasingly sensitive to the fluid and dynamic nature that such categorization practices can take. Hoffman & Walker (2010), for example, examine how various features of English in Toronto are linked to speakers' ethnic categorizations. They consider two elements of the Canadian Vowel shift, the lowering and retraction of the DRESS vowel and the retraction of TRAP, in the speech of 80 participants during individual sociolinguistic interviews. While the analysis in Hoffman & Walker (2010) relies on a binary split between shifted and non-shifted vowels, a parallel analysis (Hoffman 2010) details that shifted realizations of DRESS (lowered and retracted) are characterized by a mean F1 value of 690 Hz (greater than the threshold of 660 Hz for shifted vowels in this class cited in Labov, Ash & Boberg 2006) and a mean F2 of 1738 Hz, whereas retracted realizations of TRAP have a mean F2 of 1588 Hz, lower than the threshold for TRAP backing of 1725 Hz in Labov, Ash and Boberg (2006) and the value previously reported by Boberg (2008) for Canadian English (1724 Hz).

Hoffman & Walker report that these speakers from different ethnic backgrounds do not all participate in these changes to the same extent. The shifting of DRESS and the retraction of TRAP is led by speakers of British/Irish heritage (n=20 in their sample) and of Italian heritage (n=27), whereas speakers of Chinese heritage (n=33) are not participating as readily. There exists, moreover, a significant difference in the extent of participation in this change as a function of Italian and Chinese speakers' ethnic orientations (i.e., the extent to which they categorize themselves as Italian or

Chinese). While all Italian-heritage speakers favor the change, those with a high orientation to their Italian heritage show greater rates of use of the shifted vowels. Among Chinese-heritage individuals, in contrast, it is those with a lower orientation to their Chinese heritage that are more frequent adopters of the shifts.

Hoffman & Walker relate these differences across ethnic categories and ethnic orientation levels to the relative degrees of integration within Toronto that Italian- versus Chinese-heritage individuals experience. Arguing that participation in the Canadian Vowel Shift is related to a sense of belonging to the category "Canadian," Hoffman & Walker describe the distinct migration histories and local practices of the Italian and Chinese communities, and relate these differences to the distinct linguistic patterns observed. Hoffman & Walker's (2010) analysis illustrates the ways in which external (i.e., etic; Pike 1967) categorization of speakers as belonging to a particular ethnic group interacts with individuals' own (i.e., emic) categorizations of self to constrain observed patterns of phonetic variation.

The relationship between self- and other-categorization is also central to Podesva & Von Hofwegen's (2016) analysis of variation in the acoustic realization of /s/ among lesbian and gay speakers in Redding, a rural town at the northern tip of California's Central Valley. Based on an acoustic analysis of over 60,000 tokens of /s/ that occurred in interviews with 51 speakers, Podesva & Van Hofwegen demonstrate that there exist significant differences in /s/ center of gravity (COG) values in their sample as a function of gender and sexuality: heterosexual men have the lowest COG values ($\bar{x}$ = 5250 Hz), heterosexual women the highest ($\bar{x}$ = 7450 Hz), and lesbians ($\bar{x}$ = 6300 Hz) and gay men ($\bar{x}$ = 6150 Hz) are in between (with gay men's values significantly higher than heterosexual men's, and lesbians' values significantly lower than heterosexual women's). Among heterosexual speakers, there also exists a significant difference across speakers with a more local, "country" orientation and those with a more urban, "town" orientation. For both heterosexual women and men, country-oriented speakers have lower COG levels than town-oriented speakers. Podesva & Van Hofwegen therefore describe two overlapping patterns of association between /s/-realization and social categorization. There is a broad gender difference between heterosexual women (higher COG) and men (lower COG), with nonheterosexual speakers positioned in a sort of gender nonnormative in-between. There is then also a category distinction among heterosexual speakers between "town" and "country" orientations, that is also relevant to how /s/ is realized.

To complicate things further, Podesva & Van Hofwegen also compare the realizations they observe in Redding to those in nearby (and urban) San Francisco. They find that gay men in Redding, for example, produce /s/ with significantly lower COG ($\bar{x}$ = 6150 Hz) than gay men in San Francisco do ($\bar{x}$ = 6550 Hz; see Zimman 2013). Thus, while there exists a perhaps predicted differentiation between gay men and heterosexual men in Redding in terms of /s/, there are also significant differences across gay men from Redding and San Francisco. Podesva & Van Hofwegen account for this latter difference between Redding and San Francisco in terms of the realities of gay life in the rural Redding area. Drawing on testimonials from local community members, Podesva & Van Hofwegen describe the constant threat of violence and harassment that lesbian and gay individuals in Redding face, and the need to conform to local gendered behavioral norms for their own safety. Podesva & Von Hofwegen argue that these local social constraints subsequently affect the ways in which lesbians and gays in Redding categorize themselves through language. While linguistically they are significantly differentiated from their local heterosexual counterparts, they are also significantly different from lesbian and gay speakers in San Francisco. Like Hoffman & Walker's (2010) study in Toronto, Podesva & Von Hofwegen (2016) thus demonstrate how phonetic variation can act as a resource for individuals to categorize themselves in relation to a broader taxonomy of categories that is locally socially available. In other words, speakers are not just mechanistically reproducing social structure. Rather, they are making active choices about how to use language to position themselves within relevant categories.

In addition to work on phonetic production, a great deal of research on categorization within sociophonetics has focused on perception, looking at the ways in which listeners use phonetic cues to assign speakers to categories and how such category assignments participate in phonetic processing more generally. Munson, McDonald, DeBoe & White (2006), for instance, investigated the specific phonetic cues that listeners may attend to when making judgments of a speaker's sexuality. In a first experiment, Munson and colleagues recorded 44 speakers, including lesbians, gay men and heterosexual women and men, from the St. Paul/Minneapolis metropolitan area in the Midwestern United States reading 32 individual CVC words of English. Acoustic analyses revealed significant differences in phonetic production across the speaker categories, particularly in the F1 frequencies of front vowels (significantly lower among lesbian/bisexual women as compared to their heterosexual counterparts and significantly higher among gay/bisexual men as compared to their heterosexual counterparts), the F2 frequencies of back vowels (significantly higher among lesbian/bisexual women than heterosexual women) and the spectral properties of /s/ (significantly more negatively skewed spectra for gay/bisexual men than heterosexual men) (see also Pierrehumbert et al. 2004). In a second experiment, Munson, McDonald, DeBoe & White (2006) showed that listeners are sensitive to these systematic differences in production when making category judgments in perception. Judgments of speaker sexuality were predicted by F1 frequency in front vowels, F2 frequency in back vowels, and /s/ spectral skewness. In other words, listeners appear to rely on precisely those features that differ in a production task when they are categorizing speakers in a perception task.

In a subsequent study, Munson, Jefferson & McDonald (2006) test the extent to which categorial sensitivity in perception affects the linguistic processing of acoustic input. Examining phonetic discrimination in a lexical decision task (e.g., Strand 1999), Munson, Jefferson & McDonald (2006) consider whether listeners are more likely to categorize a phonetically ambiguous token on a continuum between /s/ and /ʃ/ as one or the other depending on whether the speaker is identified as lesbian/gay or heterosexual. They found that perceived sexuality has a significant effect on phoneme identification for women speakers, though not for the men. Among the women, results demonstrate that listeners were more likely to perceive an ambiguous token (e.g., with a COG of 4546 Hz and a skewness of −2.15) as *sip* rather than *ship*, for instance, when the speaker was heard as sounding lesbian or bisexual. They take this finding as evidence that listeners have a stored representation of lesbian/bisexual women's speech as containing more backed articulations of fricatives. This then causes listeners to be more likely to categorize a token that is closer to the [ʃ] end of the spectrum as a realization of /s/ when listening to a lesbian/bisexual-sounding woman than when listening to a heterosexual-sounding woman. Munson, Jefferson & McDonald's (2006) study thus provides support for the idea that linguistic and social information are linked in cognitive storage (i.e., that speakers rely on a set of identity-linked assumptions and expectations when normalizing the speech stream in perception), and hence that perceived social categorizations (i.e., whether a speaker is heterosexual or not) can affect very low-level linguistic processing.

Studies have also shown that such categorization effects can emerge when no objective difference exists within an audio stimulus. For instance, Hay, Warren & Drager (2006) investigated the role of social category priming on listeners' classification of a merger-in-progress between the NEAR and SQUARE vowels in New Zealand English. The merger in question has been ongoing for the past three decades, such that in New Zealand today older speakers are more likely to keep the realization of NEAR and SQUARE distinct whereas younger speakers are more likely to show a merger to NEAR. Hay, Warren & Drager (2006) consider the extent to which this social conditioning of the change in production affects how listeners perceive tokens of NEAR and SQUARE in perception. To test this, a binary forced-choice identification task was designed in which listeners were auditorily presented with a word containing either a NEAR or SQUARE vowel (e.g., *dare*) and were asked to choose which word they had heard between two written options on a computer screen (e.g., *dare* or *deer*). The audio presented was always identical, and always produced by speakers who produce the distinction between the two vowel classes. What differed across trials, however, was the visual presentation of a photograph of either a younger speaker or an older speaker.

They found that visual priming for age influenced how listeners categorized the audio stimulus, even though the auditory input was held constant. Listeners were able to more accurately distinguish between auditory tokens of NEAR and SQUARE when they were presented with a photo of an older speaker than when they were presented with a younger speaker. When visually primed for younger speech, in contrast, listeners showed significantly higher error rates. Hay, Warren & Drager argue that this visual priming effect is due to an expectation that younger speakers will be merged in their production, thus making their acoustic realizations more difficult to classify. These results therefore show how social information can interfere with acoustic processing, such that how we categorize a speaker (e.g., as either young or old) affects our understanding of the speech signal (see also Warren this volume).

Finally, recent studies of these kinds of social priming effects in perception have examined more nuanced types of social categorizations, going beyond standard demographic categories such as age, gender, and sexuality to consider locally relevant personae. D'Onofrio (2018), for example, employs the same type of binary forced-choice identification task as in Hay, Warren & Drager (2006), though in D'Onofrio's (2018) case this is used to examine listeners' categorizations of ambiguous vowels on an acoustic continuum between TRAP and LOT in US English. Research on production has shown that two salient social personae in the United States—the "valley girl" and the "business professional"—are both associated with the backing of TRAP. D'Onofrio therefore sought to examine whether the activation of these personae in context could trigger the same kinds of social category effects on phoneme classification as had been found for more "traditional" social categories, like age.

To test the possible effects of priming for a valley girl or business professional, D'Onofrio asked listeners to classify ambiguous tokens on a nine-step acoustic continuum between TRAP and LOT, with continuum steps varying both F1 (ranging from a low of 964 Hz to a high of 1042 Hz) and F2 (ranging from 1289 Hz to 2098 Hz). When completing the forced-choice classification task, listeners ($N = 360$) were told that a given speaker was "often described as a valley girl/business professional." Even with this minimal amount of information, D'Onofrio (2018) demonstrates a clear social category effect on classification. Mixed-effects logistic regression models show that listeners were more likely to classify tokens as TRAP in the valley girl and business professional conditions than they were in a control condition (where no social information was provided). This finding shows that listeners associate TRAP backing with the persona categories named by the labels "valley girl" and "business professional" and rely on these category-level associations in making their judgments. D'Onofrio (2018:529) also found that the precise shape of the response curves across the nine-step continuum was different for the two target personae. This demonstrates that not only are listeners sensitive to the overall persona categories, they also associate distinct acoustic profiles with them. Taken together, D'Onofrio's (2018) results clearly illustrate the relevance of locally salient personae for speech perception and processing, and so demonstrate the malleability and evolving nature of listeners' categorial schemas.

As the brief survey above illustrates, research on categorization as an identity-linked practice has demonstrated the relevance of social categories when accounting for patterns of sociophonetic variation in both production and perception. Categories serve as landmarks that speakers and listeners orient to, providing speakers with a way to characterize themselves through talk and influencing how listeners process and interpret the speech stream. Research on categories and their phonetic manifestations has become increasingly more sophisticated over the past 50 years, moving from high-level associations with demographic categories to examine the ways language is recruited to signal more locally meaningful affiliations, roles, and orientations. In this process, research also began to consider how the sociophonetic enactment of category membership can vary across contexts and situations, as speakers use sociophonetic variation to achieve immediate interactional goals. In this respect, research on categorization led scholars to begin considering how individuals use language to variably construct groupness and commonality. We review some of the research in this area in the following section.

The phonetics of groupness

The roots of sociophonetic research on groupness and commonality as a more malleable and dynamic dimension of identity than categorization can be traced to Eckert's (1989a, 1989b, 2000) study of language change in a Detroit-area high school. In that work, Eckert showed that participation in an ongoing sound change (the Northern Cities Shift) was constrained not only by speakers' membership in broad demographic categories (e.g., gender and social class) but also by their more local affiliations and orientations. Eckert identified three groups of students in the school: the Jocks, who oriented to suburban life and school-based activities; the Burnouts, who oriented to urban life and rejected school as their locus on engagement; and the In-Betweens, who were not positioned in either of the other groups. Through detailed ethnographic and linguistic analyses, Eckert demonstrates how members of these three groups draw on the social connotations of sociolinguistic variants (their association with a more "urban" versus "suburban" style, for example) to position themselves within the social landscape of the school. Eckert's research on this topic did not itself go beyond an examination of identity as categorization, since the discussion focused on how local category membership as a Jock or a Burnout constrained observed practice (though Eckert did develop a more nuanced way of conceiving of categories as "communities of practice"; see Eckert & McConnell-Ginet 1992). Nevertheless, the insights that Eckert developed about language style and the ability of speakers to use sociophonetic variation for stylistic purposes laid the foundation for subsequent research on linguistic constructions of what we describe, following Brubaker & Cooper (2000), as commonality and groupness.

Unlike identity as categorization, identity as commonality and/or groupness refers to the interactional construction of affiliation and belonging—not the use of language to mark "I am a Burnout, a lesbian, a Torontonian," but rather to index an orientation to, and similarity with, others who share some immediately relevant characteristic. This characteristic can be categorical in nature (a shared ethnic affiliation, for example), but need not be (as in a shared emotional reaction to an event). Constructions of commonality and groupness are about the kinds of relational positioning and rapport-building that individuals do in the context of situated interaction, including but also exceeding the confines of named identity categories.

A useful example of what we mean can be found in Eckert's later work looking at the progress of the California Vowel Shift (CVS) among students at two primary schools in Northern California (e.g., Eckert 1996, 2008, 2011a, 2011b). In those studies, Eckert shows how participation in the ongoing shift is constrained both by group membership (i.e., categories) and by more immediate interactional concerns (i.e., constructing commonality). For example, Colette, one of the pre-adolescent girls in Eckert's (2011b) sample, uses significantly higher and backer articulations of the (merged) LOT/THOUGHT vowel when she is expressing negative affect, such as when complaining about the bad behavior of a boy (Josh) that Colette had a crush on. This type of raising and backing of LOT/THOUGHT is a salient component of the CVS, and positions these articulations as on the leading edge of current changes in the region. When she is not expressing negative affect, in contrast, Colette's LOT/THOUGHT vowels are lower and fronter, and so aligned with more traditional (i.e., nonshifted) California pronunciations. By coding the affect of Collette's utterances across dozens of recorded conversations over two years of ethnographic observations, Eckert is able to identify how Colette and her friends systematically associate the expression of negative affect with being more socially mature, that is, with liking boys and no longer being a "child." Based on this and the correlation between negative affect and shifted articulations of LOT/THOUGHT, Eckert argues that Colette uses this phonetic realization as a way of positioning herself as a mature social actor, interactionally creating a commonality or groupness with the older teenagers she wants to be associated with. In other words, Colette's variable practice is not grounded in a process of self-categorization as "old" or a "teenager," per se, but is instead better understood as an aspirational practice designed to highlight the similarity in socially meaningful traits between Colette and her older peers.

Levon (2009, 2010, 2011) also examined how speakers use sociophonetic features to dynamically construct groupness in his research on pitch variation in Israel. There, Levon argues, for example, that certain groups of gay men in Israel vary their mean spoken pitch when discussing topics explicitly related to sexuality as opposed to topics that are not. Moreover, Levon found that the direction of differentiation between "gay" and "nongay" topics depends on the type of speech activity involved. When speaking in a more private frame, the men produce significantly lower mean pitch levels on "gay" topics. Based on evidence from ethnographic observations and speakers' own metalinguistic commentary, Levon argues that this difference is linked to normative ideologies of gender and sexuality in Israel, such that what is considered appropriate and attractive for gay Israeli men is to behave in a normatively masculine way. When the men speak in a more public frame, in contrast, mean pitch levels are significantly higher on "gay" topics than on "nongay" topics. Levon suggests that the higher pitch levels in more public talk correspond to dominant homonationalist ideologies in Israel, whereby tolerance and inclusion of gendered and sexual nonnormativity have become central to contemporary Israeli nationalist discourse (cf. Milani & Levon 2016). In both types of speech activities, the men in question are therefore linguistically constructing gay presentations of self (i.e., categorizations). But the precise way in which they do this in more private versus more public talk is indicative of a more flexible process of constructing groupness, demonstrating an affiliation to (and commonality with) dominant gender norms in the private frame and dominant sexual ones in the public frame.

These types of more interactionally-specific presentations of self as a function of speech topic have also been shown in research in different contexts. Schilling (Schilling-Estes 2004), for instance, investigates shifting rates of post-vocalic /r/-lessness and PRICE-monophthongization in an interview between two speakers in Robeson County, North Carolina: Lou, a Lumbee-American man, and Alex, an African American man. These features are interesting because they are variably present in local varieties of Lumbee speech, African American speech, and white speech. Tracking the appearance of /r/-lessness and PRICE-monophthongization (both coded auditorily) across the interview thus allows Schilling to consider the way in which the two men forge temporary alliances with one another through talk, as well as how they indicate their divergence. Schilling shows, for example, that when the men discuss local race relations, they produce rates of

/r/-lessness and PRICE-monothphongization that highlight their ethnic difference, with Lou produc-ing very low levels of /r/-lessness and intermediate levels of PRICE-monophthongization and Alex producing high levels of both. In contrast, when they discuss local friendship groups and activ-ities, this linguistic differentiation fades and the men converge on similar patterns of variable use. Taken together, these systematic patterns of convergence and divergence as a function of speech topic illustrate the possibility of using phonetic variability as a tool for positioning themselves in relation to one another in the conversation, of creating what Du Bois (2007) terms interactional dis/alignment. While Lou and Alex as individuals do not change ethnic categorizations over the course of the conversation, they clearly manipulate the extent to which those categories are treated as sharing common experiences and perspectives. In this way, speaking of building temporary "commonality" between Lou and Alex provides greater analytical nuance than speaking of "iden-tity" would.

Another recent example of an analysis that considers groupness instead of (or in addition to) categories comes from Holliday (2021), where the author examines intonational variation among young men with one Black parent and one white parent. Working from the ToBI framework (see Beckman et al. 2005), Holliday investigates the variable occurrence of specific intonational features of African American Language (AAL), including the presence of L + H* pitch accents, especially in broad focus contexts (Holliday 2016; see also Pierrehumbert & Hirschberg 1990), and the length of time between the onset and the maximum f0 of a pitch-accented stressed vowel (i.e., peak delay). Holliday finds that, unlike when they engage in more metapragmatic discussions about race and their own experiences of being biracial, the men in her study make significantly less use of AAL intonational features when discussing the police. Holliday interprets this pattern as a strategic move on the part of the men to create a temporary commonality with whiteness (or at least a distance from Blackness) when interacting with specific (imagined) interlocutors. As in the discussion of Lou and Alex in Schilling-Estes (2004), what governs the phonetic variability that Holliday (2021) describes is thus not so much the categories that the biracial men in her study inhabit but the types of identity-linked alliances the men choose to build in specific interactional moments. Distinguishing linguistic constructions of commonality/groupness from the linguistic marking of category membership thus enables us to more finely pinpoint the specific social work that variation performs and to avoid overly essentialized treatments of "identity" as a motivating factor of language use.

The phonetics of subjectivity

In the previous section, we saw how distinguishing categorization phenomena from more tem-porary and relational constructions of groupness can lend greater explanatory power to analyses of sociophonetic variation. Building on this insight, research has also begun to consider how phon-etic variability may be related to speakers' own conceptualizations of self and the ways that such conceptualizations extend beyond single interactional encounters. In other words, rather than focusing on speakers in the aggregate (as categorization studies often do) or individual interactional moments (as studies of commonality and groupness often do), studies of language and subject-ivity have examined how single individuals vary their speech (or not) across speech contexts and what such patterns of variation can tell us about the role that subjective understandings of self play in motivating observed patterns. This type of work is greatly influenced by discussions of indi-vidual speaker styles and what Johnstone (1999, 2009) calls speakers' "lingual biographies." By this term, Johnstone means the unique constellation of meaningful linguistic practices that com-bine to form a distinctive individual style, one that reflects an individual's multiple experiences, affiliations, and orientations. While originally developed within studies of discourse and rhetoric, the notion of a lingual biography—and the corresponding idea of speaker repertoires—has become a useful perspective in sociophonetic studies of variation as well.

In his analysis of vowel variation in the speech of Regan, a gay man in San Francisco, Podesva (2011) describes how Regan alternates between more and less advanced forms of the California Vowel Shift across different speech contexts. While somewhat similar in focus to Eckert's (2011b) study of Collette, Podesva's analysis examines Regan's behavior across multiple situations in order to identify the different social personae that Regan enacts across contexts and so obtain a more holistic understanding of Regan's subjectivity. In a meeting with his work supervisor, for instance, Podesva finds that Regan produces the least advanced forms of CVS vowels, including backer realizations of GOOSE and GOAT and more centralized and overlapping realizations of TRAP in pre-oral (BAT) and pre-nasal (BAN) environments. When socializing with a group of gay male friends, a very different pattern emerges, whereby Regan produces fronted realizations of GOOSE and GOAT and a clear separation between BAT and BAN, consistent with more advanced realizations of the CVS. Podesva analyses these differences as indicative of the different types of personae that Regan seeks to project in the two contexts. When out with friends, Regan constructs a "partier" persona that draws on the connotations of being "fun" and "laid-back" that are stereotypically associated with California speech styles. With his supervisor, Regan is instead more invested in presenting an image of himself as a competent worker, one more associated with a General American style of speech.

For the purposes of our current discussion, what is important about Podesva's (2011) argument is that it crucially relies on a comparison of what Regan does in different contexts in order to unpack the specific meanings that CVS-like vowel forms may have. We can only interpret Regan's behavior with his friends as linked to the construction of a "partier" persona by contrasting that behavior with what he does in the meeting with his supervisor. And it is through this contrast of distinctive practices that we begin to get an understanding of who Regan is as a person—how partying, for example, is an important part of his own subjectivity, but one that is nevertheless kept distinct from his professional interactions. Had Podesva only examined Regan's practice in one social context (as Eckert 2011b did with Colette), he could potentially have made an argument about Regan's attempt to (self)categorize or construct a sense of groupness. But by considering the relationships between Regan's behavior in different contexts, Podesva is able to build a more comprehensive picture of the relationship between language and identity for Regan, one in which disparate moments of stylistic practice are stitched together into a subjective whole.

The analysis of style dominance in the speech of Indian-American media personality Fareed Zakaria by Sharma (2018) further underscores the importance of this type of cross-situational attention in analyses of language and subjectivity. Born in India and raised speaking Indian English, among other languages, Zakaria moved to the United States at age seventeen and has since established himself as a prominent political commentator there. In her analysis, Sharma investigates the ways in which Zakaria switches between two highly cohesive phonetic styles—an Indian English one and a US English one—when addressing Indian versus US audiences. These styles contain a range of distinctive features, including differing articulations of the GOAT, FACE, LOT, and BATH vowels, voiced and voiceless interdental fricatives, and coda laterals. Sharma (2018) demonstrates that while Zakaria is highly adept at switching between these styles as a function of audience, his phonetic productions sometimes "slip" when other cognitive demands in the immediate context are high, leading him to "default" to more Indian English-like productions. The other contexts include encountering doubt from his audience, thus leading him to devote more attention to constructing a counter argument, inserting a parenthetical aside, and dismissing skeptical responses. Sharma notes that in each of these types of contexts, Zakaria's increased use of Indian English forms dovetails with a small, yet consistent increase in speech rate (measured as syllables/sec per utterance unit). Building on prior research on speech rate and attention (e.g., Kendall 2009, this volume), Sharma takes this speech rate effect to indicate that Indian English is Zakaria's "dominant" style, one that is more integrated into his cognitive grammar and that he automatically switches into when his attention is directed elsewhere.

In addition, however, Sharma also argues that Zakaria occasionally makes strategic (i.e., nonautomatic) use of brief snippets of Indian English phonology in otherwise US English stretches of talk, even when competing cognitive demands are not an issue. These more strategic "micro-shifts" occur when Zakaria is concerned with sounding authentic, drawing on what Sharma calls a "real me" presentation of self (see Sharma 2021), and crucially do not co-occur with any changes in speech rate. For Sharma, then, the issue here is not one of dominant or default styles. Rather, she argues that Zakaria deploys these very brief instances of Indian English phonology as a way of signaling to his interlocutors that he is being frank and honest with them, that the person delivering the message is the person that he "really" is. This type of "biographical indexicality," as Sharma calls it, is only possible with reference to Zakaria's broader stylistic repertoire. In other words, only by knowing that Zakaria commands both Indian English and US English styles, and that Indian English phonology is more stylistically dominant, can a listener interpret the strategic meaning of "honesty" that these micro-shifts are meant to signal. While Sharma's study focuses on contrasts between dialects in the repertoire of a bidialectal speaker, the basic insight of biographical indexicality can apply to the contrasting varieties that all speakers maintain (between more formal and more informal styles). Indeed, in their study of how listeners evaluate the production of audible /t/-release bursts in the speech of six prominent US politicians, Podesva et al. (2015) demonstrate that listener reactions to /t/-release in the speech of Barack Obama, for example, depend on their beliefs about how often Obama produces released /t/ across a variety of contexts. These studies all demonstrate that there is a dimension of identity-linked speech that goes beyond isolated categories or interactions, and instead relates to the totality of an individual's subjectivity as reflected in their multifaceted linguistic repertoire.

Investigating how multiple subjective dimensions affect observed variation is also the focus of Levon (2016), who examined the prevalence of creaky voice in the speech of an Orthodox Jewish man in Israel, called Igal, who is married to a woman and lives an otherwise normative Orthodox Jewish life except for the fact that he also has sexual and romantic relationships with other men. Levon describes how, in addition to using creaky voice where it is phonetically predicted to occur (e.g., at the ends of intonation phrases, co-occurring with other glottal elements), Igal makes extensive use of creaky voice (as determined by auditory coding) as a stylistic device, particularly when discussing the subjective tension he experiences between his identification as an Orthodox Jew and his same-sex desire. Drawing on psychological theories of dialogical selfhood (e.g., Hermans 2001) and linguistic theories of stance (particularly McIntosh 2009), Levon suggests that Igal does not use creaky voice as a way to construct an identity as either "gay" or "Orthodox." Instead, Levon argues that Igal uses creaky voice as a way to manage these two conflicting dimensions of his subjectivity and to prioritize his affiliation with Orthodox Judaism over his attachment to same-sex practice. Creaky voice is a useful phonetic resource for this kind of subjective position management given its broader symbolic association with the expression of "tension under control" (Bolinger 1982). Igal's use of creaky voice is thus a tactic for subjective management, a form of identity-linked practices that is not about the enactment (or suppression) of any one specific category, but rather a means to negotiate the multiple categories that Igal's subjectivity contains.

CASE STUDY   The phonetics of Igal's creak

Levon's (2016) analysis of the distribution of creaky voice in Igal's interview reported impression-istic auditory coding of the presence or absence of creak. Yet we know that voice quality is a con-tinuous phenomenon, with multiple gradations possible between creaky and modal voice (Podesva 2013; Podesva & Callier 2015). We also know that speech that is auditorily perceived as creak can correspond to a variety of different vocal fold configurations, each associated with a distinct acoustic profile (Keating, Garellek & Kreiman 2015). Examining the phonetic detail of what Levon (2016) simply labeled "creak" could therefore provide further and complementary insight into the variable patterns that Igal deploys, and hence the specific social/interactional outcomes that Igal uses language to accomplish. In this section, we briefly outline one possible phonetic analysis of Igal's data, as a case study of how detailed attention to fine-grained phonetic variation can contribute to studies of language and identity.

Methods

For the purposes of illustration, we focus solely on utterances that Levon (2016) auditorily coded as creak, and examine possible variation in the specific type of creaky voice that is realized. We do this primarily for practical reasons. Ideally, we would consider all vowels in Igal's speech across the interview, allowing us to consider the full range of phonation types Igal employs. Yet given the lack of reliable automatic forced alignment for conversational Israeli Hebrew and the at times poor audio quality of the recording, we elect instead to focus on the more manageable 587 intonational phrases (IPs) in the interview that were previously coded as perceptually creaky. Using Praat, we manually segmented the vowels in these 587 IPs, to enable automated extraction of voice quality measurements. We removed vowel tokens that contain background noise or overlapping speech, which would render the measurement of acoustic features unreliable. This left 3696 vowel tokens, which had all been pre-viously auditorily coded as creaky, for analysis.

Acoustically, we examine variation in the formant-corrected amplitude difference between the first and second harmonics (H1*-H2*) as a measure of glottal constriction (Iseli, Shue & Alwan 2007; Keating, Garellek & Kreiman 2015). Prototypically, creaky voice is characterized by low rates of vocal fold vibration (indicated by low f0), irregular f0 (indicated by high noise in the signal), and high levels of glottal constriction (indicated by low H1*-H2* values). Yet Slifka (2006) notes that there exists an alternative form of creak that, while maintaining low and irregular f0, does not involve glottal constric-tion, but rather glottal spreading such that airflow through the glottis is increased. Callier & Podesva (2015) show that both constricted and non-constricted creak are used by speakers in California, and that the distribution of the two types of creak is both socially and phonologically conditioned. We therefore use H1*-H2* variation in Igal's speech to determine whether he alternates between more versus less constricted versions of creaky voice, and whether such variation correlates with the topical distributions identified in Levon (2016).

Using a Praat script, we extracted H1*-H2* measurements for all vowels at the midpoint, as well as F1 and F2 values, f0 values, vowel duration, vowel intensity and the position of the vowel in the IP (expressed as a percentage to the end of the IP, measured in msec from the vowel midpoint). We built linear mixed-effects regression models to test whether H1*-H2* measurements varied as a function

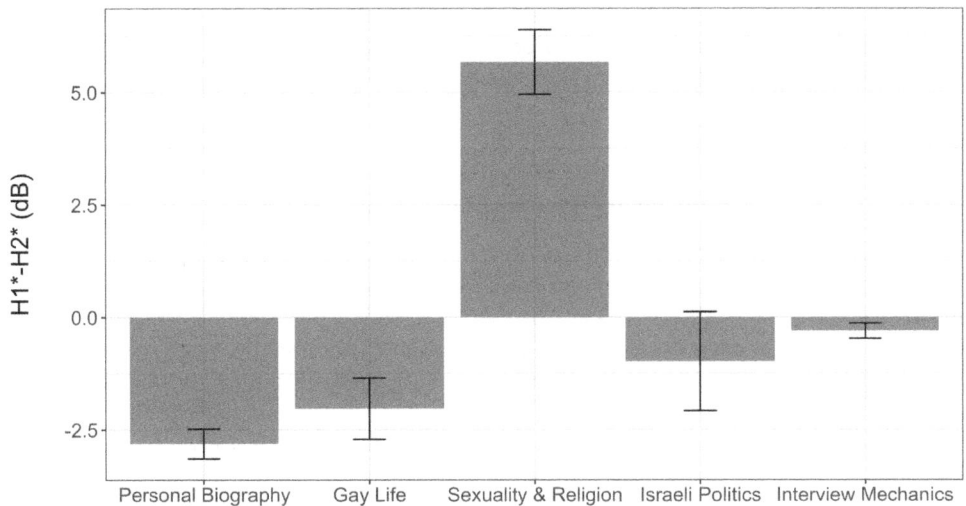

Figure 14.1   Mean values of H1*-H2* in Igal's speech across topic categories

of the five topic categories used in Levon (2016)—Personal Biography, Gay Life, Sexuality and Religion, Israeli Politics, Interview Mechanics—when the other linguistic factors (f0, F1, F2, duration, intensity, position) were included as co-variates (word and preceding and following sound were included as random intercepts). The goal of the model was therefore to test whether the level of glottal constriction in Igal's creaky voice varies as a function of topic when other linguistic constraints are controlled for.

Results

The results of variation across topic categories are presented in Figure 14.1.

We see in Figure 14.1 that there is a stark difference in the amount of glottal constriction in Igal's creaky voice when speaking on Sexuality and Religion as opposed to the other topic categories. This pattern is confirmed by the results of the regression model, which show that when position in IP, f0, and intensity are controlled for, talk on Sexuality and Religion topics is characterized by significantly higher H1*-H2* values ($F = 5.53$, $p = 0.019$) than talk on other topics.

Discussion

This result indicates that the creak that Igal uses on Sexuality and Religion topics is characterized by lower glottal constriction, increased airflow, and a certain breathiness to the voice quality, making it qualitatively very different to the more prototypical (i.e., constricted) creak he uses elsewhere. While further research would be required to understand the different meanings that these distinct forms of creaky voice carry (for example, whether the distinction between glottal constriction versus spreading is a symbolically meaningful one), the acoustic patterns support the general argument of Levon (2016) that Igal is doing something different and "stylistic" when speaking on Sexuality and Religion topics as opposed to all others. Phonetic detail thus provides further depth to the main sociolinguistic argument, and indicates a possible path for future research on how Igal materializes his subjectivity through language.

Advancing the sociophonetics of identity

The relationship between language and identity is a complex one. In this chapter, we have shown that this complexity can be productively explored by clearly specifying which particular dimension of identity a given analysis aims to tackle. The use of sociophonetic variation to engage in identity-linked practices is pervasive. As described above, speakers vary subtle aspects of the phonetic signal as a way of claiming (or rejecting) category membership, of forging shifting alliances with interlocutors, and of managing a more holistic maintenance and presentation of self in interaction. The studies outlined here only scratch the surface of research that has been conducted in this vibrant and increasingly popular area. Moreover, it bears noting that the studies described in this chapter focus primarily on (different varieties of) English and have been conducted by scholars located primarily in the United Kingdom and North America. While this is partially the fault of our own academic trajectories, and hence the research we are most familiar with, it is also an indication of the fact that the large majority of sociophonetic research on identity has been geographically quite limited (though see Matsuda et al. this volume). For this reason, we strongly encourage scholars from diverse cultural and linguistic backgrounds to engage in this type of research.

More generally, we hope to have demonstrated the benefit that detailed analyses of phonetic variation have for studies of identity and language, as well as the social richness that a nuanced understanding of identity can offer to sociophonetics. We encourage further research that uses sociophonetic methods and insights to explore identity-linked phenomena, and in particular those that go beyond treating identity as only referring to the construction or perception of categories to also include the ways in which sociophonetic variation can be used to create rapport and alignment between speakers, to indicate identity-linked emotional attachments and aspirations, and to organize complex and multidimensional subjectivities. As we describe here, "identity" encompasses a wide range of social and (inter)subjective phenomena, all of which are amenable to (and would further profit from) detailed sociophonetic enquiry.

References

Allport, Gordon. 1954. *The nature of prejudice*. Addison-Wesley.

Beckman, Mary E., Julia Hirschberg, Stefanie Shattuck-Hufnagel & Sun-Ah Jun. 2005. The original ToBi system and the evolution of the ToBi framework. In Sun-Ah Jun (ed.), *Prosodic typology: The phonology of intonation and phrasing*, 9–54. Oxford University Press. https://doi.org/10.1093/acprof:oso/978019 9249633.003.0002

Berger, Peter & Thomas Luckmann. 1967. *The social construction of reality*. Doubleday.

Boberg, Charles. 2008. Regional phonetic differentiation in Standard Canadian English. *Journal of English Linguistics* 36(2). 129–154. https://doi.org/10.1177/0075424208316648

Bolinger, Dwight. 1982. Intonation and its parts. *Language* 58(3). 505–533. https://doi.org/10.2307/413847

Bourdieu, Pierre. 1990. *The logic of practice*. Polity Press.

Brubaker, Rogers & Frederick Cooper. 2000. Beyond "identity." *Theory and Society* 29(1). 1–47. https://doi.org/10.1023/A:1007068714468

Bucholtz, Mary & Kira Hall. 2004. Theorizing identity in language and sexuality research. *Language in Society* 33(04). 469–515. https://doi.org/10.1017/S0047404504334020

Bucholtz, Mary & Kira Hall. 2005. Identity and interaction: A sociocultural linguistic approach. *Discourse Studies* 7(4–5). 585–614. https://doi.org/10.1177/1461445605054407

Callier, Patrick & Robert Podesva. 2015. Multiple realizations of creaky voice: Evidence for phonetic and sociolinguistic change in phonation. Paper presented at New Ways of Analyzing Variation 44 [NWAV44], Toronto, ON.

Cameron, Deborah & Don Kulick. 2003. *Language and sexuality.* Cambridge University Press.

Cameron, Deborah & Don Kulick. 2005. Identity crisis? *Language and Communication* 25(2). 107–125. https://doi.org/10.1016/j.langcom.2005.02.003

Coupland, Nikolas. 2007. *Style: Language variation and identity.* Cambridge University Press.

Coupland, Nikolas. 2008. The delicate constitution of identity in face-to-face accommodation: A response to Trudgill. *Language in Society* 37(2). 267–270. https://doi.org/10.1017/S0047404508080329

D'Onofrio, Annette. 2018. Personae and phonetic detail in sociolinguistic signs. *Language in Society* 47(4). 513–539. https://doi.org/10.1017/S0047404518000581

Du Bois, John W. 2007. The stance triangle. In Robert Englebretson (ed.), *Stancetaking in discourse*, 139–182. John Benjamins.

Eckert, Penelope. 1989a. *Jocks and Burnouts: Social categories and identity in the high school.* Teachers College Press.

Eckert, Penelope. 1989b. The whole woman: Sex and gender differences in variation. *Language Variation and Change* 1(03). 245–267. https://doi.org/10.1017/S095439450000017X

Eckert, Penelope. 1996. Vowels and nail polish: The emergence of linguistic style in the preadolescent heterosexual marketplace. In Natasha Warner, Jocelyn Ahlers, Laura Bilmes, Monica Oliver, Suzanne Wertheim & Melinda Chen (eds.), *Gender and belief systems*, 183–190. Berkeley Women and Language Group.

Eckert, Penelope. 2000. *Linguistic variation as social practice: The linguistic construction of identity in Belten High.* Blackwell.

Eckert, Penelope. 2008. Where do ethnolects stop? *International Journal of Bilingualism* 12(1–2). 25–42. https://doi.org/10.1177/13670069080120010301

Eckert, Penelope. 2011a. Language and power in the preadolescent heterosexual market. *American Speech* 86(1). 85–97. https://doi.org/10.1215/00031283-1277528

Eckert, Penelope. 2011b. Where does the social stop? In Frans Gregersen, Jeffrey Parrott & Pia Quist (eds.), *Language variation–European perspectives III: Selected papers from the 5th International Conference on Language Variation in Europe (ICLaVE 5), Copenhagen, June 2009*, 13–30. John Benjamins.

Eckert, Penelope. 2012. Three waves of variation study: The emergence of meaning in the study of sociolinguistic variation. *Annual Review of Anthropology* 41(1). 87–100. https://doi.org/10.1146/annurev-anthro-092611-145828

Eckert, Penelope. 2016. Variation, meaning and social change. In Nikolas Coupland (ed.), *Sociolinguistics: Theoretical debates*, 68–85. Cambridge University Press.

Eckert, Penelope. 2017. Comment: The most perfect of signs: Iconicity in variation. *Linguistics* 55(5). 1197–1207. https://doi.org/10.1515/ling-2017-0025

Eckert, Penelope. 2019. The limits of meaning: Social indexicality, variation, and the cline of interiority. *Language* 95(4). 751–776. https://doi.org/10.1353/lan.2019.0072

Eckert, Penelope & Sally McConnell-Ginet. 1992. Think practically and look locally: Language and gender as community-based practice. *Annual Review of Anthropology* 21(1). 461–490. https://doi.org/10.1146/annurev.an.21.100192.002333

Erikson, Erik. 1968. *Identity: Youth and crisis.* Norton.

Giddens, Anthony. 1987. *Social theory and modern sociology.* Stanford University Press.

Gleason, Philip. 1983. Identifying identity: A semantic history. *Journal of American History* 69(4). 910–931. https://doi.org/10.2307/1901196

Goffman, Erving. 1963. *Stigma: Notes on the management of a spoiled identity.* Prentice Hall.

Gussenhoven, Carlos. 2004. *The phonology of tone and intonation.* Cambridge University Press.

Hay, Jennifer, Paul Warren & Katie Drager. 2006. Factors influencing speech perception in the context of a merger-in-progress. *Journal of Phonetics* 34(4). 458–484. https://doi.org/10.1016/j.wocn.2005.10.001

Hermans, Hubert. 2001. The dialogical self: Toward a theory of personal and cultural positioning. *Culture & Psychology* 7. 243–281. https://doi.org/10.1177/1354067X0173001

Hoffman, Michol F. 2010. The role of social factors in the Canadian Vowel Shift: Evidence from Toronto. *American Speech* 85(2). 121–140. https://doi.org/10.1215/00031283-2010-007

Hoffman, Michol F. & James Walker. 2010. Ethnolects and the city: Ethnic orientation and linguistic variation in Toronto English. *Language Variation and Change* 22(1). 37–67. https://doi.org/10.1017/S0954394509990238

Holliday, Nicole. 2016. *Intonational variation, linguistic style and the Black/biracial experience*. PhD dissertation, New York University.

Holliday, Nicole. 2021. Intonation and referee design phenomena in the narrative speech of Black/Biracial men. *Journal of English Linguistics* 49(3). 283–304. https://doi.org/10.1177/00754242211024722

Holmes, Janet & Paul Kerswill. 2008. Contact is not enough: A response to Trudgill. *Language in Society* 37(2). 273–277. https://doi.org/10.1017/S0047404508080342

Iseli, Markus, Yen-Liang Shue & Abeer Alwan. 2007. Age, sex, and vowel dependencies of acoustic measures related to the voice source. *Journal of the Acoustical Society of America* 121(4). 2283–2295. https://doi.org/10.1121/1.2697522

Jaffe, Alexandra (ed.). 2009. *Stance: Sociolinguistic perspectives*. Oxford University Press.

Johnstone, Barbara. 1999. Lingual biography and linguistic variation. *Language Sciences* 21(3). 313–321. https://doi.org/10.1016/S0388-0001(98)00031-X

Johnstone, Barbara. 2009. Stance, style and the linguistic individual. In Jaffe, 29–52.

Keating, Patricia A., Marc Garellek & Jody Kreiman. 2015. Acoustic properties of different kinds of creaky voice. In The Scottish Consortium for ICPhS 2015 (ed.), *Proceedings of the 18th International Congress of Phonetic Sciences*, Paper 0821. University of Glasgow.

Kendall, Tyler. 2009. *Speech rate, pause, and linguistic variation: An examination through the Sociolinguistic Archive and Analysis Project*. PhD dissertation, Duke University.

Labov, William. 1966. *The social stratification of English in New York City*. Center for Applied Linguistics.

Labov, William. 2012. What is to be learned: The community as the focus of social cognition. *Review of Cognitive Linguistics* 10(2). 265–293. https://doi.org/10.1075/rcl.10.2.02lab

Labov, William, Sharon Ash & Charles Boberg. 2006. *The atlas of North American English: Phonetics, phonology, and sound change: A multimedia reference tool*. De Gruyter.

Le Page, Robert. 1997. The evolution of a sociolinguistic theory of language. In Florian Coulmas (ed.), *The handbook of sociolinguistics*, 15–32. Blackwell.

Levon, Erez. 2009. Dimensions of style: Context, politics and motivation in gay Israeli speech. *Journal of Sociolinguistics* 13(1). https://doi.org/10.1111/j.1467-9841.2008.00396.x

Levon, Erez. 2010. *Language and the politics of sexuality: Lesbians and gays in Israel*. Palgrave. https://doi.org/10.1057/9780230281318

Levon, Erez. 2011. Teasing apart to bring together: Gender and sexuality in variationist research. *American Speech* 86(1). https://doi.org/10.1215/00031283-1277519

Levon, Erez. 2016. Conflicted selves: Language, sexuality and religion in Israel. In Erez Levon & Ronald Beline Mendes (eds.), *Language, sexuality and power: Studies in intersectional sociolinguistics*, 215–239. Oxford University Press.

Levon, Erez. Forthcoming. Variation, differentiation and the emergence of social meaning. In Alexandra D'Arcy, Paul Kerswill & Yoshiyuki Asahi (eds.), *The Routledge handbook of variationist sociolinguistics*. Routledge.

Llamas, Carmen & Dominic Watt (eds.). 2010. *Language and identities*. Edinburgh University Press.

McIntosh, Janet. 2009. Stance and distance: Social boundaries, self-lamination and metalinguistic anxiety in White Kenyan narratives about the African occult. In Jaffe, 72–91.

Milani, T.M. & E. Levon. 2016. Sexing diversity: Linguistic landscapes of homonationalism. *Language and Communication* 51. https://doi.org/10.1016/j.langcom.2016.07.002

Munson, Benjamin, Sarah Jefferson & Elizabeth McDonald. 2006. The influence of perceived sexual orientation on fricative identification. *Journal of the Acoustical Society of America* 119(4). 2427–2437. https://doi.org/10.1121/1.2173521

Munson, Benjamin, Elizabeth McDonald, Nancy DeBoe & Aubrey White. 2006. The acoustic and perceptual bases of judgments of women and men's sexual orientation from read speech. *Journal of Phonetics* 34(2). 202–240. https://doi.org/10.1016/j.wocn.2005.05.003

Ohala, John J. 1983. Cross-language use of pitch: An ethological view. *Phonetica* 40(1). 1–18. https://doi.org/10.1159/000261678

Ohala, John J. 1994. The frequency code underlies the sound symbolic use of voice pitch. In Leanne Hinton, Johanna Nichols & John J. Ohala (eds.), *Sound symbolism*, 325–347. Cambridge University Press.

Pierrehumbert, Janet B., Tessa Bent, Benjamin Munson, Ann R. Bradlow & J. Michael Bailey. 2004. The influence of sexual orientation on vowel production. *Journal of the Acoustical Society of America* 116(4). 1905–1908. https://doi.org/10.1121/1.1788729

Pierrehumbert, Janet B. & Julia Hirschberg. 1990. The meaning of intonational contours in the interpretation of discourse. In Philip Cohen, Jerry Morgan & Martha Pollack (eds.), *Intentions in communication*, 271–311. MIT Press.

Pike, Kenneth. 1967. *Language in relation to a unified theory of structure of human behaviour*. Mouton.

Podesva, Robert J. 2011. The California vowel shift and gay identity. *American Speech* 86(1). 32–51. https://doi.org/10.1215/00031283-1277501

Podesva, Robert J. 2013. Gender and the social meaning of non-modal phonation types. *Proceedings of the Berkeley Linguistics Society* 37. 427–448. https://doi.org/10.3765/bls.v37i1.832

Podesva, Robert J. & Patrick Callier. 2015. Voice quality and identity. *Annual Review of Applied Linguistics* 35. 173–194. https://doi.org/10.1017/S0267190514000270

Podesva, Robert J., Jermay Reynolds, Patrick Callier & Jessica Baptiste. 2015. Constraints on the social meaning of released /t/: A production and perception study of US politicians. *Language Variation and Change* 27(1). 59–87. https://doi.org/10.1017/S0954394514000192

Podesva, Robert J. & Janneke Van Hofwegen. 2016. /s/exuality in small-town California: Gender normativity and the acoustic realization of /s/. In Erez Levon & Ronald Beline Mendes (eds.), *Language, sexuality and power: Studies in intersectional sociolinguistics*, 168–188. Oxford University Press.

Schilling-Estes, Natalie. 2004. Constructing ethnicity in interaction. *Journal of Sociolinguistics* 8(2). 163–195. https://doi.org/10.1111/j.1467-9841.2004.00257.x

Sharma, Devyani. 2018. Style dominance: Attention, audience, and the "real me." *Language in Society* 47(1). 1–31. https://doi.org/10.1017/S0047404517000835

Sharma, Devyani. 2021. Biographical indexicality: Personal history as a frame of reference for social meaning in variation. In Emma Moore, Lauren Hall-Lew & Robert Podesva (eds.), *Social meaning and linguistic variation: Theorizing the Third Wave*, 243–264. Cambridge University Press. https://doi.org/10.1017/9781108578684.011

Slifka, Janet. 2006. Some physiological correlates to regular and irregular phonation at the end of an utterance. *Journal of Voice* 20(2). 171–186. https://doi.org/10.1016/j.jvoice.2005.04.002

Spivak, Gayatri. 1996. Subaltern studies: Deconstructing historiography. In Donna Landry & Gerald MacLean (eds.), *The Spivak reader*, 203–237. Routledge.

Strand, Elizabeth A. 1999. Uncovering the role of gender stereotypes in speech perception. *Journal of Language and Social Psychology* 18(1). 86–99. https://doi.org/10.1177%2F0261927X99018001006

Tabouret-Keller, Andrée. 1997. Language and identity. In Florian Coulmas (ed.), *The handbook of sociolinguistics*, 315–326. Blackwell.

Trudgill, Peter. 2008. Colonial dialect contact in the history of European languages: On the irrelevance of identity to new-dialect formation. *Language in Society* 37(2). 241–254. https://doi.org/10.1017/S0047404508080287

Wacquant, Loïc. 1997. For an analytic of racial domination. *Political Power and Social Theory* 11. 221–234.

Zimman, Lal. 2013. Hegemonic masculinity and the variability of gay-sounding speech. *Journal of Language and Sexuality* 2. 1–39. https://doi.org/10.1075/jls.2.1.01zim

15

SOCIOPHONETICS AND PSYCHOLINGUISTICS

Paul Warren

Introduction

Although the discipline of sociophonetics is firmly rooted in phonetic description and in vari-ationist sociolinguistics, it is also deeply connected with theoretical and experimental work in psycholinguistics (see also Kendall & Fridland 2021). This relationship is two-way. One direction is the contribution of psycholinguistic theory and research to the development of sociophonetics as a true branch of cognitive science. This is seen in the types of theorizing that have developed in sociophonetics, such as considerations of abstract versus episodic memory representations for language, and in the increasing use of a diverse range of methodologies and statistical approaches found in psycholinguistic studies. A somewhat less obvious direction is the impact that sociophonetic research has had on psycholinguistics, discussion of which will form the focus of this chapter. That is, my aim is to explore some implications of findings in sociophonetics for discussion of speech processing, especially perception and spoken word recognition.

As a broad introduction to the area, consider the experience of travelers arriving in a country in which their native language is spoken, but with a different accent. For instance, many travelers to New Zealand from other English-speaking countries are at first a little bemused and then amused at the thought of an *online chicken*, or that the national airline has *fears to suit every traveler*. New Zealand English (NZE) has experienced a number of vowel changes, such as the raising of the short front vowels (resulting in a closer articulation for the DRESS vowel, which is more like Standard Southern British English (SSBE) KIT, so that NZE *check-in* sounds like SSBE *chicken*), and the merger of the NEAR and SQUARE diphthongs (so that *fear* and *fare* are homophones). These developments in the sound system of NZE have provided data for many sociophonetic studies, some of which will be mentioned later in this chapter. But any misunderstandings resulting from these differences, fleeting though they may be, are of interest to psycholinguistics because they highlight the fact that to avoid them listeners have to adapt their speech processing system to different patterns in the input. Any initial ambiguity experienced by new arrivals will be short-lived and moderated by contextual information, so that while *earbags* are apparently a thing, they are less likely to be mentioned as a feature of a car than *airbags*. Over the longer term, the level of perceived ambiguity will diminish as the perceptual system adjusts and becomes used to switching

DOI: 10.4324/9781003034636-17

between accents. Importantly, this will be guided by knowledge of who the speaker is, in terms of the social characteristics that are fundamental to the study of sociophonetics.

These experiences are not limited to new arrivals in a strange country, since we regularly encounter variability in speech, some of which can be linked to social characteristics of the speakers. For instance, there are features of NZE pronunciation that are representative of ongoing sound changes, the extent of which differs according to social characteristics such as age, gender, and class. This is reflected in letters to the editors of newspapers and magazines, which are very much in the complaint tradition and which raise the specter, for example, of young people becoming incomprehensible because of their pronunciation of *women* as though it were *woman* (another feature of NZE).

Languages and language users are fundamentally adaptive and evolving systems and therefore susceptible to variation and change at various linguistic levels, influenced by speaker-related factors such as age, sex, sexuality, ethnicity, educational, and social backgrounds, as well as by contextual factors such as the setting and nature of communicative acts. However, much of our psycholinguistic understanding of how we produce and understand language is based on an assumption of relative stability. That is, researchers have investigated the relevant linguistic phenomena as though they were static objects rather than moving targets. As stated in the introduction to a special issue of *Linguistics Vanguard*: "It is somewhat surprising […] that psycholinguistics, the field that seeks to understand how language is processed in and acquired by the human mind, ha[s] neglected variation phenomena" (Boland et al. 2016:1). The challenge to psycholinguistics is to consider how the perceptual system makes the appropriate accommodations to deal with variability in pronunciation. But just as our experience of the social distributions of variants allows us to associate them with speaker characteristics, so too our interpretation of the input speech signal is influenced by what we know or can assume of the social characteristics of the speaker.

Some implications of sociophonetic research findings for psycholinguistics

As implied above, psycholinguistics has for much of its history disregarded most types of variability in the speech signal and assumed a relatively homogeneous speech community. Most considerations of variation focused on linguistically predictable variation, such as how listeners might make use of allophonic variants and the results of connected speech processes. For instance, it has been observed that listeners are able to exploit allophonic variation in how stop bursts are realized when they make parsing decisions, for example, in distinguishing *play taught* from *plate ought* (Nakatani & Dukes 1977). Phonetic assimilations resulting from connected speech processes are also largely predictable, and psycholinguistic research has investigated the use of co-articulatory information in the determination of word identity. For instance, formant transitions at the end of a vowel give early cues to the identity of the following consonant, which has implications for spoken word recognition (for early work in this area, see Warren & Marslen-Wilson 1987). Other research has considered how listeners might compensate for such phenomena. For instance, the relative articulatory positions of /ʃ/ and /s/ result in changes in the pronunciation of adjacent /t/ and /k/ sounds. Listeners compensate for this, by expecting for instance a more retracted /t/ in a /ʃ/ context. This results in categorical perception experiments in shifts in the location of the perceptual boundary between /t/ and /k/, such that an identical ambiguous stimulus on a manipulated /t/-/k/ continuum is more likely to be heard as /t/ in the sequence *Christmas_apes* and as /k/ in the sequence *foolish_apes* (Elman & McClelland 1988).

Tellingly, Elman & McClelland (1988:150) commented that "it has been suggested that one of the essential functions of the apparatus used for the perception of speech is to factor out the contextual influences and recover the underlying phonetic code." This involves either the kinds of compensatory mechanisms discussed by those authors or alternatively seeking out "islands of reliability" (Diehl et al. 1987). However, while the overt focus of such psycholinguistic research was largely on linguistic contextual influences, it has generally been assumed that other contextual influences, such as those related to social aspects of the speech event and its participants, also need to be "factored out" for successful phoneme and word recognition. This is where sociophonetics comes into play. This discipline, new though it may be, has already amply demonstrated that the contextual influences related to social factors are not causes of "noise" to be factored out, but important sources of information about speakers and contexts of speaking.

Sociophonetic variation and psycholinguistics

A challenge for psycholinguistics is to be aware of such socially conditioned variation highlighted in sociophonetics research. If it is seen as a confounding factor and not of direct relevance to the research agenda, then it should be controlled for or built into the analysis.

Controlling for sociophonetic variation is difficult. For instance, those researchers who are interested in speech perception but consider sociophonetic variation to be a source of unwanted variability rather than an intrinsic research goal are unlikely to find homogeneous language communities from which they can draw participants with uniform patterns of phonetic variation. Likewise, it is unlikely that they will be able to match their participants' patterns of variation to those found in the stimuli that they plan to play to those participants. Given that most language users move fluidly between different speech communities, we can even challenge the ecological validity of controlling for variation; how representative of most listeners' experience is hearing spoken-language materials produced only by members of their own group as defined by a range of demographic features?

Indeed, even when researchers have had social variation as a target of their research, there are aspects of data collection that can be influenced by sociophonetic variation but which they might nevertheless have overlooked. For example, an accidental finding in research described in more detail below (Hay, Drager & Warren 2009) was that the accents of the experimenters who greeted the research participants had an impact on their performance in speaking and listening tasks. The implications of this finding are considerable, since it is likely that most psycholinguistic research has not considered the potential influence of the experimenter's voice on participants' performance.

Recent advances in data analysis have allowed researchers to control for sociophonetic variation in another way, by building it into the statistical modeling of their results. Developments involving the use of mixed-effects regression modeling have, for instance, permitted the inclusion of participants as random effects, so that variation between speakers or listeners can be allowed for (Baayen 2012; Winter 2020). These modeling techniques also allow the addition of multiple control variables, such as the social characteristics of participants. Compared to previous statistical techniques, they importantly also accommodate more readily the inclusion of social variables as experimental predictors of the outcome variable. This has opened up possibilities when it comes to the examination of the influence of sociophonetic variation on production and perception, although researchers should be wary of overcomplicating their statistical models, especially given concerns over statistical power and the large number of participants required to meet the demands of complex statistical models (Brysbaert & Stevens 2018; Brysbaert 2019).

A more exciting advance for psycholinguistics than controlling for sociophonetic variation is to acknowledge that such variation is worthy of psycholinguistic exploration in its own right, and to build it more deliberately into psycholinguistic investigation. The principal areas of psycholinguistic processing where this kind of variation is likely to have an impact involve speech sounds and spoken words, namely speech perception and spoken word recognition, along with speech production. While sociophonetics has looked mainly to the latter—that is, using data from speech recordings for evidence of socially influenced variation in pronunciation—it has rightly been pointed out that spoken output "does not fully specify what it means to *have* a dialect" (Sumner & Samuel 2009:487; emphasis in original), since this also involves perceptual issues. There has been a recent increase in the number of perceptual sociophonetic studies. In many early perceptual studies, researchers played recordings to listeners to elicit their judgments of speaker characteristics such as their regional dialects, ethnic backgrounds, socioeconomic status, or personality traits. More recent work has moved beyond these approaches to examine how the social characteristics assumed of speakers might affect the processes and outcomes of speech perception, some of which will be discussed below (see further Thomas 2002). Nevertheless, perceptual sociophonetics is still a relatively novel research area (see discussion in Kendall & Fridland 2021).

The processes involved in spoken word recognition are key to making sense of what we hear, since word recognition gives access to lexical information which in turn forms an important part of the processes of parsing and interpreting phrases and sentences. If word recognition is affected by sociophonetic variation, then there are consequences for these other aspects of processing. For example, imagine that sociophonetic variation results in ambiguity, such that a given phonetic token could potentially be a realization of either word A or word B. This ambiguity might impact further processing such as sentence parsing (which will particularly be the case if words A and B signal different parts of speech) or sentence interpretation, or both. Note, though, that even though the complaint tradition noted earlier indicates that the ambiguity is often noticed (especially by speakers who believe that they do not produce such ambiguities), the effects of lexical ambiguity on sentence processing are generally short-lived. It was demonstrated very early in psycholinguistic research that the language processing system copes very effectively with ambiguity, rapidly using contextual information to decide between alternatives (e.g., Swinney 1979; Marslen-Wilson & Tyler 1980). Another possibility is that sociophonetic variation results not in ambiguity but in a "less good" realization of a phoneme and potentially therefore of a word. In such cases, pre-lexical and lexical processing might become more effortful, but is unlikely to result in complete breakdown of communication (Kapnoula, Edwards & McMurray 2021). What is more intriguing, however, is evidence that suggests that listeners, in the process of recognizing words, are able to use information about speaker characteristics and their experience of the distribution of variants with respect to those characteristics—information that might prevent the ambiguity arising in the first place.

Sociophonetic variation and processing

Early research explored the role of dialectal variation in speech perception and word recognition. Niedzielski (1999) asked natives of Detroit to match synthesized vowel stimuli to tokens recorded by another native speaker of Detroit. Her interest was in how Detroiters would categorize variants of the MOUTH vowel, which typically has a raised first element in Canadian English. While it is frequently also raised in Detroit English, it is more stereotypically associated by Detroiters with Canadian English and not with their own variety. Niedzielski found that different tokens were chosen as matches for the MOUTH vowel depending on whether participants were told that the speaker was from Detroit or from Canada. In other words, the same phonetic signal was interpreted differently depending on the dialect background that participants assumed of the speaker. As summarized by Thomas (2002:124), Niedzielski's results show that "variationists can contribute a great deal to theories of speech perception: it is not just the other way around." In category identification experiments, Kraljic, Brennan & Samuel (2008) found that perceptual learning, namely learning that an /ʃ/-like variant could be a realization of /s/, only occurred if participants had been exposed to variation that was most readily interpreted as idiolectal, with /ʃ/-like pronunciations in a range of context in which an /s/ could occur. No perceptual learning resulted If /ʃ/-like pronunciations were restricted to /str/ contexts, which matched the distribution found in certain dialects. This suggests that listeners treat the same acoustic token differently depending on whether it is most readily interpreted as a dialectal or idiolectal feature.

Listeners' familiarity with dialects has also been shown to affect word recognition. Using a range of priming experiments (in which words related in various ways to a target are presented before that target), Sumner & Samuel (2009) found that experience with the relevant dialects strongly influenced listeners' recognition speed for /r/-full vs. /r/-less variants of words like *baker* ([beɪkɚ] vs. [beɪkə]). In other research, comprehension of sentences in noisy conditions has been shown to be influenced by listeners' familiarity with the accent of the speaker (Adank et al. 2009). Fridland & Kendall (2018) found that photo prompts indicating the likely dialect region of a speaker allowed listeners to align synthesized tokens with vowel categories in ways that reflected both their own experiences of different accents and their expectations concerning what those accents sound like.

An interesting further twist on the impact of perceived dialect on speech processing comes in a series of studies that has looked at the effects on perception of various types of information suggesting that the same stimuli might be either from a New Zealander or an Australian, culminating in the finding that merely the presence of a kiwi toy versus a koala or kangaroo toy in the experiment room can cause a shift in perceptual category boundaries for vowels towards those expected for a New Zealand or Australian accent (Hay & Drager 2010).

Further research has explored the effects in perception and word recognition of the "big four" social features that impact pronunciation: class, gender, age, and ethnicity. While there is growing evidence that phonetic variants can influence listeners' perceptions of a speaker's social identity, what is of increasing interest to psycholinguistics is how knowledge of the speaker's identity has in turn an impact on how listeners interpret the phonetic variants the speaker produces.

In a study of New Zealanders' perception of the merger of the NEAR and SQUARE vowels in their dialect, Hay, Warren & Drager (2006) utilized photographs of the same individuals wearing clothes that suggested differences in socioeconomic status. The effectiveness of the photographs in signaling middle versus working class were confirmed in a separate rating task. In the main listening task, participants were told that the photographs were of the speaker they would next hear, under the guise of a warning to participants of the sex of the next voice. They had to decide between minimal pair words with the NEAR and SQUARE vowels (e.g., *beer* and *bear*). The results showed an effect of social class as indicated by the photograph, but one that was also mediated by the overall strength of the NEAR-SQUARE distinction for the individual speakers being listened to. Critically, for the most distinct voices, listeners' ability to hear the difference between the vowels diminished with decreasing social class of the photo. This matches production data indicating that lower-status socioeconomic groups are more likely to show the merger and shows that there is an expected social distribution in the patterning of these vowels that can be primed by the differences in the photographs.

A series of pioneering studies by Strand and her colleagues (Johnson, Strand & D'Imperio 1999; Strand 1999) showed that the interpretation of a phonetic stimulus depends not just on the physical properties of the sound but also on gender information about the speaker. The studies used a version of the McGurk effect, a well-known phenomenon in psycholinguistics where a perceptual illusion can result from the cross-splicing of a video recording of a speaker saying one thing (e.g., the syllable [ga]) with the audio of a speaker saying another thing (e.g., [ba], the combination resulting in the percept [da]). Strand and colleagues found that phonetic boundaries, for example between the fricatives /s/ and /ʃ/ or between the vowels /ʊ/ and /ʌ/, were shifted depending on whether the video accompanying the audio showed a female or male speaker, and that this effect was even found when listeners saw no audio but were told to imagine a female or male speaker.

It is often claimed that the only constant is change, and this is certainly true of language. It is not surprising then that speaker age, whether perceived or actual, is also a key factor in the interpretation of the speech signal. With generational changes, age-related sociophonetic variation becomes particularly salient, with listeners experiencing exposure to multiple variants of the sounds in question. Acoustic analyses of the NEAR and SQUARE diphthongs in NZE have highlighted the significance of both social class and age, with younger working-class speakers more likely to merge the diphthongs (Warren, Hay & Thomas 2007). Longitudinal studies have confirmed that the merger is a change in progress (e.g., Gordon & Maclagan 2001). The consequences of age-grading for word identification were shown in the forced-choice identification task mentioned above (Hay, Warren & Drager 2006). Participants "switched off" their discrimination when they thought they were listening to a younger speaker, who was more likely to merge the vowels.

This shift in the interpretation of the same phonetic input has consequences for lexical processing, as demonstrated in a pair of lexical decision tasks involving semantic priming (Warren & Hay 2006; Warren, Hay & Thomas 2007). In semantic priming tasks, responses to one word (e.g., *nurse*) are faster when they follow a word related to it in meaning (e.g., *doctor*) than when they follow an unrelated word (e.g., *table*). In the tasks in question, participants were all young native speakers of NZE, likely to collapse the NEAR-SQUARE distinction in their own speech. They listened to a long sequence of stimuli made up of equal numbers of existing words of English and nonsense words. Nonsense words were words that had the phonetic structure of English words but happened not to be real words, such as *grunk*. The experimenters were only interested in responses to the real words of English. For each stimulus participants had to press one of two response buttons to indicate whether it was an existing word in English or not. The sequence included pairs of words that have a semantic relationship to one another, such as *cheer* [ʧiə] (the prime) followed by *shout* (the target), or *chair* [ʧeə] followed by *sit*. It also included crossed pairs such as *cheer* followed by *sit*, as well as unprimed control conditions (*bee* followed by *shout* or by *sit*). In the first experiment the speaker was from the same age group as the listeners and therefore likely to merge the vowels, although she actually kept them distinct. (As this is a change-in-progress, there is some variation in the extent of the merger, even amongst younger speakers.) The second experiment used an older speaker from an age group that is more likely to keep the vowels distinct. Listeners in the first experiment showed asymmetric priming that matches their experiences as listeners, given that they hear speakers who merge the two vowels on NEAR as well as speakers who keep them distinct. That is, [ʧiə] primed both *shout* and *sit* (i.e., both were recognized more quickly than when they followed the unrelated control prime), but [ʧeə] primed only *sit*. The second experiment did not show this asymmetry—[ʧiə] again primed *shout* and [ʧeə] primed *sit*, but [ʧiə] did not strongly prime *sit*. This suggests that listeners deduce information about the likely age of the speaker (in these experiments presumably from voice quality features) and generate expectations about whether or not this speaker will merge the diphthongs.

Reanalyzing auditory data from an earlier study by Holmes & Bell (1992), Warren (2006) suggested that the merger of NEAR and SQUARE is a consequence of listeners "forgetting" the co-articulatory grounds for a change in the pronunciation in SQUARE. The co-articulatory effect is that the tongue has a higher position at the beginning of the SQUARE vowel when it follows coronal consonants (e.g., /t, d, ʃ/) because the tongue needs to be high for such consonants. For mid-age speakers, SQUARE had a higher onset (therefore more like NEAR) only in contexts where it followed coronal consonants. For young speakers, the closer onset was found to have also spread to other contexts, suggesting that such speakers had reanalyzed the quality of the SQUARE vowels and categorized them as NEAR vowels. This idea that sound change might result from the misperception by younger speakers of co-articulatory effects (Ohala 1993) has also been presented as an explanation for the age-graded fronting of GOOSE and FOOT vowels in British English (Harrington et al. 2008).

While, as pointed out by Kendall & Fridland (2021:113) "psycholinguistic research […] is often silent on the ethnic identities of the research participants," there are studies that show effects of the (assumed) ethnic identity of the speaker on speech perception. Szakay, Babel & King (2012) demonstrated that Māori-English bilinguals in New Zealand showed greater priming of Māori translation equivalents by the corresponding English words if those English words were spoken in the ethnic dialect (Māori English) associated with ethnically Māori speakers than if they were spoken by European New Zealanders. Staum Casasanto (2010) found that listeners were more likely to ascribe final t/d deletion (*fas(t) car; ban(d) practice*), a feature that occurs more frequently in African American Vernacular English than in many other Englishes, to a potential speaker who was Black than to one who was white. Importantly, her second experiment showed that if listeners saw a picture of a Black speaker when hearing a fragment such as *The* [mæs] *probably lasted,* then they were faster in selecting a continuation compatible with a deleted /t/ (i.e., with the word *mast* in the fragment, rather than *mass*), than if they saw a white speaker. Expectations about intelligibility also appear to be affected by social expectations. For example, Babel & Russell (2015) found that the intelligibility of Chinese Canadian voices dropped if the speech was accompanied by photographs of the speakers, in line with expectations about clarity of diction in certain ethnic groups, while that of white Canadian voices did not.

In addition to the largely first-wave sociolinguistic parameters outlined above, research at the interface of sociophonetics and perception has embraced the consideration of emergent social meaning that is more typically associated with third-wave sociolinguistics (Eckert 2012). For example, Soukup (2013) shows that knowledge of how speakers deploy stylistic features is used by listeners during their retrieval of social meanings from linguistic cues, and D'Onofrio (2018) shows that the priming of social personae can influence the perceptual categorization of vowels. For example, D'Onofrio's participants were required to identify tokens on a phonetic continuum as TRAP or LOT vowels. When they were told that the speaker they were going to hear was a "Valley Girl" (a speaker of Californian English), then the point at which they divided the vowels into the two categories differed from when they were told the speaker was a fan of the Chicago Bears NFL football team. The categorization reflects differences between the dialect areas concerned.

We see that the social characteristics shown by sociophonetic research to have an impact on variation also influence processing, and that this can affect intelligibility, speech perception, word recognition, and sentence interpretation.

Evolving representations

It is well known that we adapt our behaviors in response to those of others around us, and there is plenty of evidence of convergence in language production, and how this is affected by the strength of interpersonal connection and rapport (Hove & Risen 2009; Babel 2010; Kim, Horton &

Bradlow 2011). It was noted earlier that experiments involving the NEAR-SQUARE merger in NZE showed some unexpected experimenter effects. Participants met by an American English (AmE) experimenter were better able to produce a distinction between NEAR and SQUARE than those met by the NZE experimenter. Since the vowels in question were not modeled by the experimenters, this appears to be a general accommodation to their accents, in this case in the absence of genuine interaction. However, the perceptual task showed a reversal of this pattern; participants met by the AmE experimenter were less well able to discriminate between the NZE vowels. The explanation offered for this outcome is that the NZE NEAR and SQUARE vowels being listened to in the experiment, although distinct in NZE terms, were nevertheless both better instances of AmE NEAR than of AmE SQUARE, making them more difficult to tell apart than in the context of the NZE experimenter, even though the same set of stimuli was presented to all participants.

Listener expectations can change dynamically over the short term. Van Berkum et al. (2008) measured participants' electrophysiological responses (measured on the scalp) as they listened to a sequence of sentences from a number of different speakers. They found evidence of rapid detection of mismatches between social characteristics indicated by the voice, such as sex, age, or social class, and the sentence content. This included obvious mismatches such as a male voice declaring "I recently had a check-up at the gynecologist in the hospital," but also more subtle ones such as a lower-class voice stating "My wife works as a judge in criminal law." This re-setting of perceptual expectations on the basis of short-term exposure to another speaker can lead to perceptual learning, as shown in the study cited earlier of /s/-retraction as an idiolectal versus dialectal feature by Kraljic, Brennan & Samuel (2008). Work such as that by Sumner & Samuel (2009), also cited earlier, shows how familiarity with a dialect can improve processing. Understandably, such experiential learning also proves to be dependent on the frequency with which listeners hear the range of possible tokens of a word or sound.

To return to earlier discussion of how variation is treated by the perceptual system, research in both acquisition (Maye, Werker & Gerken 2002; Rost & McMurray 2009) and adult speech perception (Bradlow & Bent 2008; Lev-Ari 2016) has shown that—rather being "noise" that has to somehow be filtered out—variability can actually enhance performance. For example, Rost & McMurray (2009) show that hearing tokens produced by multiple speakers with all their individual variation helps children learn phonological distinctions more effectively than if they hear the same contrasting items produced an equivalent number of times by just one speaker. Similarly, Lev-Ari (2016) reports that adults with broader social networks and who therefore interact with a wider range of other speakers proved to be better at understanding speech embedded in noise, even when the overall quantity of input is controlled for.

Sumner & Samuel (2009:488) raise a number of questions concerning how the perceptual system adjusts on exposure to sociophonetic variants. A key set of questions revolves around the issue of whether the system finds new ways of mapping from novel instances of a word or sound to existing representations or develops new representations for the novel experiences. This relates to psycholinguistic questions concerning abstract vs. episodic representations for language.

As signaled in the introduction, much early psycholinguistic research assumed that variation somehow had to be stripped away in order to find underlying representations. This was however challenged in subsequent work that suggested that the possibility of efficient processing of the speech input on the basis of rapidly changing phonetic features casts doubt over the psychological reality of certain abstract notions of underlying forms such as the phoneme (e.g., Marslen-Wilson & Warren 1994). Subsequently, episodic models of perception and mental representation have evolved, and the contribution of sociophonetic research to the development of such models should not be underestimated.

Exemplar theory, for instance, argues that our memories for the linguistic events that we have encountered are richly detailed and include information about the speaker, including social information (Johnson 1997; Pierrehumbert 2006). The speaker/listener's mental representations are built up over time to reflect statistical probabilities of how sounds are distributed, phonetically and socially. These distributions play a central role both in the selection of forms for production (which might be influenced for instance by information about the addressee or audience) and in the recognition of heard sounds and words. The exemplar approach is of general psycholinguistic interest because it can also deal quite neatly with phenomena such as frequency effects (more frequent words are produced and recognized more rapidly than less frequent words).

More recently, proponents of exemplar theory have sought to accommodate at least some abstract representations, to support for instance the fact that listeners are able to process words that they have not previously encountered, and for which they therefore have no exemplars. This has led to proposals of hybrid models with both abstract and richly detailed episodic representations (Pierrehumbert 2016). Nevertheless, the centrality of the notion of variation in exemplar theory means that this type of model is well suited to provide an account not only for how the perceptual system deals with variation in the input but indeed for how it exploits the indexical nature of the variation, as we have seen in many of the phenomena introduced above. For example, a suggested account for the different pattern of semantic priming by NEAR and SQUARE tokens in NZE in the context of younger vs. older speakers' voices (Warren & Hay 2006; Warren, Hay & Thomas 2007) is that sets of exemplars are triggered that are associated with innovative and conservative speakers respectively. It is additionally interesting that results show that NZE participants who claim not to distinguish specific pairs of NEAR and SQUARE words in their own speech are less accurate in distinguishing these specific words in the speech of others (Hay, Warren & Drager 2006). Since we tend to socialize with those who are similar to ourselves, such participants presumably have had less exposure to speakers who still distinguish the vowels.

CASE STUDY   **The influence of one sociophonetic variable on the interpretation of another**

Across a series of experiments run with Jen Hay and others, we have previously investigated the factors that contribute to the accuracy with which participants are able to identify stimuli from word pairs that are undergoing merger as a result of a sound change in New Zealand English (Holmes & Bell 1992; Gordon & Maclagan 2001). As noted above, the sound change is an ongoing merger by approximation (towards NEAR) of the NEAR and SQUARE vowels. Amongst the significant effects that these studies have revealed are participant factors such as the participants' age and sex and the extent to which they maintain the relevant distinction in their own speech, and item factors such as the lexical frequency of the stimulus item (and of its minimal pair competitor) and the extent to which individual word pairs are kept distinct in the speech of the community represented by the participants. Intriguingly, accuracy in identification is also influenced by both known and perceived characteristics of the speakers whose voices are being responded to. For example, participants are more accurate at distinguishing NEAR/SQUARE pairs when they think they are listening to an older speaker than a younger speaker (Hay, Warren & Drager 2006).

That perceived aspects of speaker identity can influence accuracy in a perception task raises questions about whether relevant information about speaker identity may be extracted from the signal itself. Our previous work on this topic manipulates perceived speaker characteristics with photos. However, variation within the linguistic signal itself carries a vast amount of information about the speaker. In previous research we have also examined whether social information carried by a segmental linguistic variable may affect the processing of a suprasegmental variable. Thus Warren (2017) resynthesized the SQUARE vowel in a word early in an utterance so that it was typical of a SQUARE or of a NEAR vowel for an NZE speaker who distinguishes these vowels. In addition, the alignment of an intonational rise on the final word of the utterance was manipulated so that it was characteristic either of a question rise (early in the accent unit) or of a statement rise (late in the accent unit, as is typical of uptalk rises in NZE—see, e.g., Warren & Fletcher 2016). The presence of a NEAR-like SQUARE vowel early in the utterance signaled a more innovative NZE speaker, who was also likely to use uptalk. This resulted in participants making a clearer choice compatible with early rises for questions and late rises for statements than was the case after more conservative SQUARE vowels. In the previously unpublished research summarized below we focused on the effect that sociophonetic segmental cues indicating the regional origin of a speaker might have on the interpretation of other segmental cues.

One of the most salient differences between NZE and Australian English (AusE) is the quality of the KIT vowel. This vowel is centralized in NZE and fronted and raised in AusE. This contrast stands as a shibboleth for distinguishing the two varieties. The contrast is at a general level of consciousness, with speakers either side of the Tasman Sea making fun of the others' KIT vowel. As AusE makes a reliable distinction between the NEAR/SQUARE vowels, we hypothesized that the phonetic quality of KIT vowels in "filler" words in a listening experiment would affect the discriminability of NEAR/SQUARE words produced by the same voice.

Methods

Two groups of NZE participants (total N=32) carried out a forced-choice identification task that included words with NEAR and SQUARE vowels, and also words containing the KIT vowel. The speaker who recorded the stimuli was a female native speaker of NZE who distinguished the NEAR and SQUARE diphthongs in her speech. The first target of her NEAR diphthongs in the recordings used in the experiment had mean F1 and F2 values of 350 Hz (SD 38 Hz) and 2658 Hz (SD 52 Hz). The corresponding values for SQUARE were 436 Hz (SD 16 Hz) and 2493 Hz (SD 55 Hz).

The stimuli heard by each group were identical, except that for one group the female speaker's KIT words were resynthesized using a custom-designed LPC resynthesis script in Praat (Boersma & Weenink 2021) with a centralized KIT vowel appropriate to NZE. For the other group the KIT words had a resynthesized vowel with the fronted and raised quality typical of AusE. All other vowels in filler words were compatible with both varieties. The NZE and AusE variants of the KIT vowel were produced by manipulating formant values (F1, F2, and F3), to achieve target values of 564 Hz, 2011 Hz, and 3056 Hz for the NZE version and 388 Hz, 2659 Hz, and 3313 Hz for the AusE version. These target values are based on analyses of KIT vowels from /hVd/ contexts produced by 10 young female speakers of each variety, taken from the New Zealand Spoken English Database (NZSED; see Warren 2002) and the Australian National Database of Spoken Language (ANDOSL; see Millar et al. 1990). In total the experiment included 38 KIT fillers, 12 NEAR and 12 SQUARE test words (each repeated twice), and 24 filler words with other vowels. With the inclusion of 9 practice items this provided a total of 119 items. Before they heard any NEAR or SQUARE words, participants heard 6 KIT items (along with other fillers), giving them repeated exposure to either an NZE or an AusE KIT before hearing any test items.

On each trial, participants saw two words, one on either side of the computer screen, and they then heard the audio file of a test or filler item, matching one of the words on the screen. In the case of the test items the displayed alternative was the NEAR/SQUARE minimal pair word (e.g., for the test item *beer*, the words appearing on the screen were BEER and BARE). On the repetition of a test item the position of the words on the screen was swapped. In the case of KIT items, the alternative word was one that differed not in the vowel but in one of the consonants; for example, for *fish* the words displayed on the screen were FISH and FIZZ. This choice of words was made to avoid drawing attention directly to the KIT vowel. The word choices for the KIT words and for the remaining fillers had equal numbers of contrasts in the onset (SKILL, STILL) and in the coda (FISH, FIZZ). Participants had to press a response button as quickly as possible to indicate which word they thought they had heard. Their response choice and times (RT) were recorded. Responses were categorized as accurate if the participant chose the word produced by the speaker. After the listening task, participants completed a naming task, in which they read aloud words that were presented on the computer screen. These included the NEAR and SQUARE words from the listening task, which were analyzed acoustically to provide a measure of how distinct these words were for each participant and also how distinct each word was across the participant. This measure was Bhattacharyya's Affinity (BA), a measure of the relative overlap of two distributions in two-dimensional space, the two dimensions here being the first and second formants of each vowel (see also Warren 2018 for further discussion of the use of this measure).

Analysis of the response data was by mixed-effects regression, using logistic models for response accuracy and linear models for response time. The experimental fixed effects included KIT Accent (NZE vs. AusE versions of the KIT vowel) and Diphthong (i.e., the test word that participants heard contained NEAR vs. SQUARE) and their interaction. The log lexical frequencies of the target word and of its competitor were also included as additional predictors, given the widely attested effects of lexical frequency on word recognition. Exploratory analysis of the data showed that responses were affected by the degree to which participants in the listening experiment maintained the distinction in their own speech (the BA measure introduced above). It also revealed differences between male and female respondents. The BA measure from participants' production data and participant sex were therefore included in initial models, as well as interactions between these and the experimental factors. The random effect structure included intercepts for participants and items and by-participant slopes for the sequential position of stimuli in the experiment. The final models reported below for accuracy and response times resulted from model comparisons.

Our main hypotheses were that i) participants in the AusE-KIT condition in our experiment would show a processing advantage over participants in the NZE-KIT context, since they would assess the NEAR and SQUARE words against their experience of the more separate vowels in AusE; ii) there would be a processing advantage for SQUARE words over NEAR words, because a consequence of the merger towards NEAR is that NEAR tokens are ambiguous, but SQUARE tokens are not (as reflected also in the asymmetric pattern of semantic priming reported by Warren & Hay 2006); and iii) that this effect should be stronger for the NZE-KIT context as a consequence of the strong association of this merger with NZE and not with AusE.

Results

The modeling of the accuracy data returned a random effects structure consisting of just the participant and item intercepts. The significant fixed effects were as follows.

First, we found strong support for the first two predictions. Error rates predicted by the logistic regression model for the AusE-KIT condition were significantly lower than those in the NZE-KIT condition (5.4% vs. 9.0%, $\chi^2(1) = 4.03$, $p < 0.05$). Error rates were significantly higher for words with NEAR than for words with SQUARE (9.5% vs. 5.1%, $\chi^2(1) = 4.20$, $p < 0.05$). The third prediction was not strongly supported, as the interaction between the two factors was not significant, although numerically the difference between NEAR and SQUARE errors was in the right direction, as it was larger in the NZE context (12.2% vs. 6.6%) than in the AusE context (7.4% vs. 3.9%). The analysis also returned a significant effect of participants' BA ($\chi^2(1) = 40.21$, $p < 0.001$) and a significant interaction of this with which diphthong was heard ($\chi^2(1) = 4.40$, $p < 0.05$). Participants with more merged NEAR and SQUARE in their own productions found it more difficult to distinguish the vowels in the listening task, and the difference in error rates for NEAR and SQUARE was larger for participants with less distinct productions. The effect of participant sex was also significant, with a higher error rate from male than from female listeners (9.5% vs. 5.1%, $\chi^2(1) = 6.61$, $p < 0.05$). There were no other significant effects.

The analysis of the forced-choice response times focused on the correct responses. Since the distribution of reaction times was right-skewed, they were logged prior to analysis. The random effects structure of the final model included both participant and item intercepts and by-participant slopes for stimulus position in the experiment. Although the first main prediction, that participants in the AusE group would find the task easier than those in the NZE group, was reflected in the accuracy scores reported above, it did not show in the response times; correct response times were almost identical for the two groups. Response times did however differ by diphthong; NEAR stimuli took longer to respond to than SQUARE stimuli (842 ms vs. 770 ms, $\chi^2(1) = 35.60$, $p < 0.001$). This effect did not interact with KITAccent, but it did interact with participant sex ($\chi^2(1) = 5.85$, $p < 0.05$); the Diphthong effect was stronger for females (887 ms vs. 787 ms) than for males (799 ms vs. 753 ms). In addition, participant sex interacted with KITAccent ($\chi^2(1) = 5.33$, $p < 0.05$); post hoc comparisons showed that female participants were faster in the NZE-KIT condition than in the AusE-KIT condition, whereas the pattern was reversed for the males. However, neither post hoc comparison was significant. There was also a significant effect of the lexical frequency of the competitor word ($\chi^2(1) = 10.92$, $p < 0.001$): the higher the frequency of the word not being heard, the faster the response times (for example, *share* and *hair* have very similar frequencies, but their competitor words in the task, *sheer* and *hear*, are quite different in terms of their frequency, and this difference was predictive of participants' response times to *share* and *hair*). There were no other significant effects, including for the BA measure that had shown such as strong effect in the accuracy analysis.

Discussion

Overall, the study showed that participants responded with greater accuracy and speed to SQUARE stimuli than to NEAR stimuli. This result is compatible with previous findings of asymmetric responses, reflecting the fact that the merger of these diphthongs is towards NEAR and that a NEAR stimulus is therefore ambiguous between NEAR and SQUARE words, whereas a SQUARE stimulus (which participants also hear from non-merging speakers around them) is less ambiguously SQUARE. In terms of response speeds (but not accuracy), this difference was stronger for female participants than for males. Given the evidence that female speakers are generally more advanced in sound changes, including the NZE NEAR-SQUARE merger (Gordon & Maclagan 2001; Warren 2019), they may be more regularly exposed to ambiguous NEAR tokens in their groups of acquaintances and may therefore respond to such tokens more cautiously in the forced-choice task.

The greater identification accuracy shown by participants with less merged NEAR and SQUARE vowels (as measured through BA), and the lower error rate for participants in the AusE-KIT condition are compatible with an approach to lexical identification that assumes that perception is determined to a large extent by our prior experiences of relevant tokens. Activating "Australian" variants of one vowel leads a listener to process other vowels produced by the same voice as Australian. Note that this is not a conscious maneuver; most New Zealanders are unaware that Australians produce NEAR and SQUARE forms as distinct.

While we have found this result in the realm of perceived speaker origin, it is compatible with findings for other social variables such as age, which also leads to different expectations concerning the likelihood of the NEAR-SQUARE merger (Warren, Hay & Thomas 2007). Such results underline the significance of sociophonetics for psycholinguistics, establishing the clearly intricate details of the interrelationship between the processing of social and linguistic information in the acoustic signal.

Conclusion

A quarter of a century ago, Applebaum (1996:1541) commented that speech perception research had spent "half a century of sustained effort" in trying to find, without any clear success, a solution to the problem of the lack of invariance—that is, to overcoming the intra- and inter-individual variation that complicates the retrieval of the underlying units of phonetic structure. She proposed that the central problem needed redefinition. Since then, and contributing to such a redefinition of the problem, considerable work in sociophonetics has considered the question of how variation in the speech signal is interpreted. Informed by insights from both sociophonetics and psycholinguistics, this research has embraced the notion of variation not as an intractable problem but as something to be explored in its own right, as a phenomenon that has social relevance and that can consequently be best understood in its social context.

Importantly, social contexts are neither permanent nor static. We interact with other speakers from a wide range of backgrounds, and these interactions contribute dynamically to our experience of the multiple patternings of language. Our linguistic repertoire is being continually updated by our experiences. Even potentially negative experiences such as mishearings or misunderstandings have the potential to alert us to the connections we need to forge between features of pronunciation and the characteristics of speakers. It is a natural consequence of our experience as listeners that we dynamically adapt to variation in speech features and exploit this variation to make sense of what and who we are listening to.

In this chapter I have focused on a sample of recent studies that have investigated the psycholinguistic interpretation of phonetic cues which vary in line with social factors. It is clear that listeners are sensitive to the social indexing carried by these phonetic cues. This is reflected in how the same tokens are categorized differently depending on social indexing that might be signaled by something as simple as the age of the purported speaker as shown in an accompanying photograph. It is apparent also in how recent experience of a voice—even the voice of the experimenter—can influence subsequent performance in both the perception and the production of contrasts. Clearly sociophonetics has benefited from consideration of the cognitive mechanisms underlying human language that have long been studied in psycholinguistics. Similarly, psycholinguistics can ill afford to ignore the progress made in sociophonetic research and the implications of such research for speech processing.

References

Adank, Patti, Bronwen G. Evans, Jane Stuart-Smith & Sophie K. Scott. 2009. Comprehension of familiar and unfamiliar native accents under adverse listening conditions. *Journal of Experimental Psychology: Human Perception and Performance* 35(2). 520–529. https://doi.org/10.1037/a0013552

Applebaum, Irene. 1996. The lack of invariance problem and the goal of speech perception. *ICSLP-1996.* 1541–1544.

Baayen, R. Harald. 2012. *Analyzing linguistic data: A practical introduction to statistics using R.* Cambridge University Press.

Babel, Molly. 2010. Dialect divergence and convergence in New Zealand English. *Language in Society* 39(4). 437–456. https://doi.org/10.1017/S0047404510000400

Babel, Molly & Jamie Russell. 2015. Expectations and speech intelligibility. *Journal of the Acoustical Society of America* 137(5). 2823–2833. https://doi.org/10.1121/1.4919317

Boersma, Paul & David Weenink. 2021. *Praat: Doing phonetics by computer* [Computer program], ver. 6.1.50. www.praat.org

Boland, Julie E., Edith Kaan, Jorge Valdés Kroff & Stefanie Wulff. 2016. Psycholinguistics and variation in language processing. *Linguistics Vanguard* 2(s1). https://doi.org/10.1515/lingvan-2016-0064

Bradlow, Ann R. & Tessa Bent. 2008. Perceptual adaptation to non-native speech. *Cognition* 106(2). 707–729. https://doi.org/10.1016/j.cognition.2007.04.005

Brysbaert, Marc. 2019. How many participants do we have to include in properly powered experiments? A tutorial of power analysis with reference tables. *Journal of Cognition* 2(1). 16. http://doi.org/10.5334/joc.72

Brysbaert, Marc & Michaël Stevens. 2018. Power analysis and effect size in Mixed Effects Models: A tutorial. *Journal of Cognition* 1(1). 9. http://doi.org/10.5334/joc.10

D'Onofrio, Annette. 2018. Personae and phonetic detail in sociolinguistic signs. *Language in Society* 47(4). 513–539. https://doi.org/10.1017/S0047404518000581

Diehl, Randy L., Keith R. Kluender, Donald J. Foss, Ellen M. Parker & Morton A. Gernsbacher. 1987. Vowels as islands of reliability. *Journal of Memory and Language* 26(5). 564–573. https://doi.org/10.1016/0749-596X(87)90143-4

Eckert, Penelope. 2012. Three waves of variation study: The emergence of meaning in the study of sociolinguistic variation. *Annual Review of Anthropology* 41(1). 87–100. https://doi.org/10.1146/annurev-anthro-092611-145828

Elman, Jeffrey L. & James L. McClelland. 1988. Cognitive penetration of the mechanisms of perception: compensation for coarticulation of lexically restored phonemes. *Journal of Memory and Language* 27(2). 143–165. https://doi.org/10.1016/0749-596X(88)90071-X

Fridland, Valerie & Tyler Kendall. 2018. Regional identity and listener perception. In Betsy E. Evans, Erica J. Benson & James N. Stanford (eds.), *Language regard: Methods, variation and change*, 132–150. Cambridge University Press.

Gordon, Elizabeth & Margaret Maclagan. 2001. Capturing a sound change: A real time study over 15 years of the NEAR/SQUARE Diphthong Merger in New Zealand English. *Australian Journal of Linguistics* 21(2). 215–238. https://doi.org/10.1080/07268600120080578

Harrington, Jonathan, Felicitas Kleber & Ulrich Reubold 2008. Compensation for coarticulation, /u/-fronting, and sound change in standard southern British: An acoustic and perceptual study. *Journal of the Acoustical Society of America* 123(5). 2825–2835. https://doi.org/10.1121/1.2897042

Hay, Jennifer & Katie Drager. 2010. Stuffed toys and speech perception. *Linguistics* 48(4). 865–892. https://doi.org/10.1515/ling.2010.027

Hay, Jennifer, Katie Drager & Paul Warren. 2009. Careful who you talk to: An effect of experimenter identity on the production of the NEAR/SQUARE merger in New Zealand English. *Australian Journal of Linguistics* 29(2). 269–285. https://doi.org/10.1080/07268600902823128

Hay, Jennifer, Paul Warren & Katie Drager. 2006. Factors influencing speech perception in the context of a merger-in-progress. *Journal of Phonetics* 34(4). 458–484. https://doi.org/10.1016/j.wocn.2005.10.001

Holmes, Janet & Allan Bell. 1992. On shear markets and sharing sheep: The merger of EAR and AIR diphthongs in New Zealand English. *Language Variation and Change* 4(3). 251–273. https://doi.org/10.1017/S0954394500000806

Hove, Michael J. & Jane L. Risen. 2009. It's all in the timing: Interpersonal synchrony increases affiliation. *Social Cognition* 27(6). 949–960. https://doi.org/10.1521/soco.2009.27.6.949

Johnson, Keith. 1997. Speech perception without speaker normalization: An exemplar model. In Keith Johnson & John W. Mullennix (eds.), *Talker variability in speech processing*, 145–165. Academic Press.

Johnson, Keith, Elizabeth A. Strand & Mariapaola D'Imperio. 1999. Auditory–visual integration of talker gender in vowel perception. *Journal of Phonetics* 27(4). 359–384. https://doi.org/10.1006/jpho.1999.0100

Kapnoula, Efthymia C., Jan Edwards & Bob McMurray. 2021. Gradient activation of speech categories facilitates listeners' recovery from lexical garden paths, but not perception of speech-in-noise. *Journal of Experimental Psychology: Human Perception & Performance* 47(4). 578–595. https://doi.org/10.1037/xhp0000900

Kendall, Tyler & Valerie Fridland. 2021. *Sociophonetics*. Cambridge University Press.

Kim, Midam, William S. Horton & Ann R. Bradlow. 2011. Phonetic convergence in spontaneous conversations as a function of interlocutor language distance. *Laboratory Phonology* 2(1). 125–156. https://doi.org/10.1515/labphon.2011.004

Kraljic, Tanya, Susan E. Brennan & Arthur G. Samuel. 2008. Accommodating variation: Dialects, idiolects, and speech processing. *Cognition* 107(1). 54–81. https://doi.org/10.1016/j.cognition.2007.07.013

Lev-Ari, Shiri. 2016. Studying individual differences in the social environment to better understand language learning and processing. *Linguistics Vanguard* 2(s1). 1–10. https://doi.org/10.1515/lingvan-2016-0015

Marslen-Wilson, William D. & Lorraine K. Tyler. 1980. The temporal structure of spoken language understanding. *Cognition* 8. 1–71. https://doi.org/10.1016/0010-0277(80)90015-3

Marslen-Wilson, William D. & Paul Warren. 1994. Levels of perceptual representation and process in lexical access: words, phonemes, and features. *Psychological Review* 101(4). 653–675. https://doi.org/10.1037/0033-295X.101.4.653

Maye, Jessica, Janet F. Werker & LouAnn Gerken. 2002. Infant sensitivity to distributional information can affect phonetic discrimination. *Cognition* 82(3). B101–111. https://doi.org/10.1016/s0010-0277(01)00157-3

Millar, John Bruce, Phillip Dermody, M. Harrington & Julie Vonwiller. 1990. A national database of spoken language: Concept, design, and implementation. *Proceedings of the First International Conference on Spoken Language Processing (ICSLP 1990)*. 1281–1284. https://doi.org/10.21437/ICSLP.1990-291

Nakatani, Lloyd H. & Kathleen D. Dukes. 1977. Locus of segmental cues for word juncture. *Journal of the Acoustical Society of America* 62(3). 714–719. https://doi.org/10.1121/1.381583

Niedzielski, Nancy. 1999. The effect of social information on the perception of sociolinguistic variables. *Journal of Language and Social Psychology* 18(1). 62–85. https://doi.org/10.1177/0261927X99018001005

Ohala, John J. 1993. Sound change as nature's speech perception experiment. *Speech Communication* 13(1–2). 155–161. https://doi.org/10.1016/0167-6393(93)90067-U

Pierrehumbert, Janet B. 2006. The next toolkit. *Journal of Phonetics* 34(4). 516–530. https://doi.org/10.1016/j.wocn.2006.06.003

Pierrehumbert, Janet B. 2016. Phonological representation: Beyond abstract versus episodic. *Annual Review of Linguistics* 2(1). 33–52. https://doi.org/10.1146/annurev-linguistics-030514-125050

Rost, Gwyneth C. & Bob McMurray. 2009. Speaker variability augments phonological processing in early word learning. *Developmental Science* 12(2). 339–349. https://doi.org/10.1111/j.1467-7687.2008.00786.x

Soukup, Barbara. 2013. Austrian dialect as a metonymic device: A cognitive sociolinguistic investigation of Speaker Design and its perceptual implications. *Journal of Pragmatics* 52. 72–82. https://doi.org/10.1016/j.pragma.2012.12.018

Staum Casasanto, Laura. 2010. What do listeners know about sociolinguistic variation? *University of Pennsylvania Working Papers in Linguistics* 15(2). Article 6. https://repository.upenn.edu/pwpl/vol15/iss2/6

Strand, Elizabeth A. 1999. Uncovering the role of gender stereotypes in speech perception. *Journal of Language and Social Psychology* 18(1). 86–100. https://doi.org/10.1177/0261927X99018001006

Sumner, Meghan & Arthur G. Samuel. 2009. The effect of experience on the perception and representation of dialect variants. *Journal of Memory and Language* 60(4). 487–501. https://doi.org/10.1016/j.jml.2009.01.001

Swinney, David A. 1979. Lexical access during sentence comprehension: (Re)consideration of context effects. *Journal of Verbal Learning and Verbal Behavior* 18(6). 645–659. https://doi.org/10.1016/S0022-5371(79)90355-4

Szakay, Anita, Molly Babel & Jeanette King. 2012. Sociophonetic markers facilitate translation priming: Maori English GOAT–a different kind of animal. *University of Pennsylvania Working Papers in Linguistics* 18(2). 138–146. https://repository.upenn.edu/pwpl/vol18/iss2/16

Thomas, Erik R. 2002. Sociophonetic applications of speech perception experiments. *American Speech* 77(2). 115–147. https://doi.org/10.1215/00031283-77-2-115

Van Berkum, Jos J., Danielle van den Brink, Cathelijne M. Tesink, Miriam Kos & Peter Hagoort. 2008. The neural integration of speaker and message. *Journal of Cognitive Neuroscience* 20(4). 580–591. https://doi.org/10.1162/jocn.2008.20054

Warren, Paul. 2002. NZSED: building and using a speech database for New Zealand English. *New Zealand English Journal* 16. 53–58.

Warren, Paul 2006. Word recognition and sound merger. In June Luchjenbroers (ed.), *Cognitive linguistics investigations: Across languages, fields and philosophical boundaries*, 169–186. John Benjamins.

Warren, Paul. 2017. The interpretation of prosodic variability in the context of accompanying sociophonetic cues. *Laboratory Phonology* 8(1). 11. https://doi.org/10.5334/labphon.92

Warren, Paul. 2018. Quality and quantity in New Zealand English vowel contrasts. *Journal of the International Phonetic Association* 48(3). 305–330. https://doi.org/10.1017/S0025100317000329

Warren, Paul. 2019. Non-linear analysis of a diphthong merger. In Sasha Calhoun, Paola Escudero, Marija Tabain & Paul Warren (eds.), *Proceedings of the International Congress of Phonetic Sciences, Melbourne, Australia*, 1883–1887. ASSTA.

Warren, Paul & Janet Fletcher. 2016. Phonetic differences between uptalk and question rises in two Antipodean English varieties. *Proceedings of Speech Prosody 2016*. 148–152. https://doi.org/10.21437/SpeechProsody.2016-31

Warren, Paul & Jennifer Hay. 2006. Using sound change to explore the mental lexicon. In Claire Fletcher-Flinn & Gus Haberman (eds.), *Cognition and language: Perspectives from New Zealand*, 105–125. Australian Academic Press.

Warren, Paul, Jennifer Hay & Brynmor Thomas. 2007. The loci of sound change effects in recognition and perception. In Jennifer Cole & José Ignacio Hualde (eds.), *Laboratory Phonology* 9. 87–112. Mouton de Gruyter.

Warren, Paul & William D. Marslen-Wilson. 1987. Continuous uptake of acoustic cues in spoken word recognition. *Perception & Psychophysics* 41(3). 262–275. https://doi.org/10.3758/BF03208224

Winter, Bodo. 2020. *Statistics for linguists: An introduction using R*. Routledge.

16

SOCIOPHONETICS AND LANGUAGE PREJUDICE

Accent matters: a socio-psychological perspective on sociophonetics

Marta Witkowska, Silvia Filippi, Magdalena Formanowicz, and Caterina Suitner

Introduction

Communication is usually associated with what people say—the specific content they convey to others. However, individuals also place a high value on how people speak, and the differences in the ways people articulate their message are immediately and easily detected (Giles & Johnson 1981, 1987; Kinzler, Shutts & Correll 2010; Giles & Watson 2013). Indeed, based on a range of vocal aspects, such as pitch, intonation, and speech rate, just a few words are enough to communicate substantial information about who is speaking, and listeners use this information to assess a speaker's background and generate impressions about their personal characteristics (Roessel, Schoel & Stahlberg 2018).

A key part of how we speak pertains to our accents. In this chapter, we will use "accent" to refer broadly to a distinctive way of pronouncing a language variety, including phonetic characteristics of segments, rhythm, intonation, and speech tempo. Through their accents, people communicate (among other things) their location of residency (e.g., a regional accent), ethnicity, and socio-economic group (Lippi-Green 1997).

Exposed to an overwhelming amount of incoming information about other people and the world, humans need to narrow this overload and automatically sort information into meaningful categories. Understanding this process of social categorization is a crucial contribution of social psychology to the study of accents, as it addresses processes relevant to self-presentation, the perception of others, and the social ordering of groups (hierarchy). An accent leads to complex interpersonal interactions and is an integral part of the way some individuals define and present themselves to others (Gasquet-Cyrus 2012; Freynet, Clément, & Sylvestre 2018). In turn, others can use linguistic cues to diagnose whether a speaker is a member of the ingroup. A further important function of accent pertains to its role in maintaining group hierarchies, since the evaluation or perception of accents mirrors the perception of groups that speak with a certain accent. Specifically, some accents are considered "normal" or "conventional" for a country and are typically linked to the high-status majority group (Roessel, Schoel & Stahlberg 2018). Through cultural

DOI: 10.4324/9781003034636-18

and intergroup processes, such specific varieties of accent are acculturated as the standard, and as such perceived as correct, acquiring a normative, referential function against which the other varieties are evaluated. Generally, this standard does not match the linguistic varieties offered by non-L1 speakers (the label "nonnative" speakers for this group is in line with the cited literature; however, we acknowledge that this label is increasingly recognized as problematic, especially in language teaching contexts) or by speakers who belong to a social minority. These accents are thought to "sound strange" because they depart from what is considered a standard, conventional way of speaking. Accordingly, they are often linked to a lower social status (Fuertes et al. 2012) and are evaluated more negatively compared to the accents of the dominant group. Thus, those who stray from standard pronunciation are sometimes referred to as "speaking with an accent." Of course, a fundamental tenet of linguistics is that all language varieties are equally valid and linguists have engaged in public outreach to challenge popular ideologies of the superiority of some varieties over others (e.g., Lippi-Green 1997; Bauer & Trudgill 1998; Rickford & Rickford 2000; Giles & Rakić 2014). From the social psychology perspective, however, what is considered a norm versus what is considered a norm violation in accents marks important group processes.

By offering a contribution embedded in the social psychological theoretical framework within this book on sociophonetics, we hope to encourage future research to adopt an interdisciplinary approach that integrates the two perspectives. We strongly believe that the dialogue between social psychology and sociophonetics may offer a unique contribution to understanding and combating language prejudice.

The present chapter begins by offering a summary of three theoretical accounts (evolutionary, social, and cognitive) that can explain accentism, namely the negative implications of sounding different from the "norm." We will then address and interpret instances of accentism by focusing on the cognitive processes that result from these three theoretical approaches. We will explore effects related to the difficulty of elaboration (fluency effects), the activation of social categories by vocal and other concomitant cues (social categorization effects), and the stereotypes and expectations that permeate social categories. We will see how different accents can prompt the distinction between groups of people, how accents can be a stronger cue denoting group member-ship than group member appearance (Rakić, Steffens & Mummendey 2011), and how this can lead to ingroup favoritism (i.e., preference for people like us; Kinzler, Dupoux & Spelke 2007; Kinzler et al. 2009). Differences in accents can also lead to differences in the perceived ingroup and out-group, thus enhancing people's negative evaluations of those with a nonnative accent (Paquette-Smith et al. 2019). We will therefore turn to the two major outcomes of sounding different from the norm: 1) prejudice and discriminatory behaviors, and 2) self-stereotyping and stigma for the speakers. Finally, we will address potential future directions for accentism research, including the development of interventions to mitigate the costs of vocal variety, highlighting the imperative for social psychologists and sociophonetics to work together to combat language prejudice.

Social psychology and accentism

Three theoretical models

At least three main theoretical approaches—evolutionary, social, and cognitive—can explain why sounding phonetically different from the norm leads to negative outcomes.

The evolutionary approach grounds the explanations of phenomena in their potential role for ancestors' survival and reproduction within their environment. Accentism is therefore interpreted as an adaptive mechanism functional to the natural selection in human evolution. From the evolutionary standpoint, an accent may denote outgroup membership, and such foreignness may be perceived as biologically or physically harmful. Accented speakers may originate from a different geographical location and, therefore, represent not only a competitor group for resources but also a risk of unfamiliar infection. Schaller and Neuberg (2012) connect this fear of outsiders to a fear of diseases they might bring and argue that a disease-avoidance mechanism induces an innate emotional response that can lead to xenophobic and ethnocentric attitudes toward those who speak differently from one's group.

Concerning physical protection, it has also been claimed that vocal cues serve as a reliable indicator of coalitions (unions of people with common characteristics and mutual benefits), as people prefer to create groups with others who are like themselves. This preference triumphs even over the preference for one's own race. (The term "race" is here used to label social categories that are arbitrarily defined by physical differences, so we refer to a social construct.) For example, white 5-year-olds were found to prefer to be friends with Black individuals who speak a standard accent rather than white individuals who speak with a foreign accent (Kinzler et al. 2009). Kinzler, Dupoux & Spelke (2007) argued that preference for vocal cues over visual cues is evolutionarily determined because, historically, neighboring tribes likely spoke with different accents or dialects but looked like one's own kinsfolk. Kinzler, Dupoux & Spelke (2007) found that 5- to 6-month-old infants preferred to look at people who spoke similarly to them, and that 10-month-old infants were more likely to accept toys from people who previously spoke in their native language. In sum, studies attesting to preference for native-accented people in early developmental stages may provide evidence for the evolutionary account.

The social psychology account also explains reactions toward different accents by focusing on the use of auditory cues to distinguish "us" and "them," albeit from a different perspective. At the core of this process lies the automatic categorization of external stimuli into social categories to simplify the complexity of the stimuli to which we are constantly exposed. From this theoretical point of view, humans tend to categorize people based on macro-level social categories like gender, age, and race, all of which are communicated by vocal signals (for a review, see Latinus & Belin 2011). Social categorization by means of accents can therefore be seen through the lens of traditional theoretical accounts of intergroup dynamics. One of the most influential theories within social psychology is the Social Identity Theory (SIT; Tajfel & Turner 1979), which explains that people tend to associate their own social group with positive features and look for positive distinctiveness from outgroups. Language is an important part of people's social identity (Gluszek & Dovidio 2010b) and carries significant information about social groups. In line with the SIT theoretical framework, the categorization prompted by vocal cues entails the need to envisage the ingroup as unique, positive, and different from the outgroup. The devaluation of the outgroup can be explained through a social identity approach, as individuals tend to increase differences between ingroup and outgroup, specifically when they have a strong ingroup identification (Gagnon & Bourhis 1996) or under conditions of competition for power or scarce resources (Brewer 1999). Social exclusion and discrimination can therefore be prompted or exacerbated by accents because an accent is strongly related to the speaker's identity, as manifested through a variety of characteristics, such as race, ethnicity, national origin, regional affiliation, or economic class (Lippi-Green 1997; Chakraborty 2017). An accent can also signal one's status, with native accents associated with a higher status than nonnative accents. Following this line of reasoning, people of higher status are more likely to show ingroup bias, as they are motivated to maintain their privilege in resource allocation (Scheepers, Ellemers & Sintemaartensdijk 2009; Scheepers 2017).

People with a strong foreign accent are not only categorized as an outgroup, and therefore devalued, but they are also more difficult to understand compared to native speakers. This leads to the third theoretical approach, which contends that the negative implications of sounding different from the norm stem from the fundamental cognitive mechanisms associated with information processing. Since nonstandard speech deviates from what the listener is used to hearing, the cognitive effort required to process the information is greater (Rönnberg et al. 2013; Engen & Peelle 2014). Lev-Ari & Keysar (2012) tested the effect of accents on listeners' perceptions in two experiments. In the first experiment, when exposed to brief stories spoken by a speaker with accent, American respondents tended to portray nonstandard ways of communicating as conveying messages of poorer quality and less importance than the stories of L1 American English speakers. The mismatch between what is expected (a "normal" accent) and what is experienced (a "strange" accent) could lead to a cognitive response, such as liking the speaker less (Engen & Peelle 2014). Indeed, this disruption is stressful, and the negative effect is transferred to a negative evaluation of the speaker (Munro & Derwing 1995; Schmid & Yeni-Komshian 1999; Bent & Bradlow 2003; Clarke & Garrett 2004; Dragojevic 2019). For example, Lev-Ari and Keysar (2010) provided evidence that nonnative speakers sound less credible than native speakers. In their experiment, participants were asked to listen to recorded trivial sentences, such as "Ants don't sleep," pronounced by speakers with different accents and to judge the credibility of the statement. The sentences were spoken and recorded by native English speakers, nonnative English speakers with mild accents, or nonnative English speakers with heavy accents (according to the evaluation of native English judges). Results showed that people judged statements as less true when spoken by a nonnative than by a native speaker.

It is worth noting that these results could be interpreted as being in line with the SIT framework, not only because nonstandard-accented utterances are harder to understand but also because the speakers could be categorized as an outgroup. The study of Hendriks, Meurs & Usmany (2021) partially disentangled the social and cognitive processes, moving a step forward in the theoretical discussion. They asked students (native English listeners, Dutch listeners, and international nonnative listeners) to evaluate the quality of lecturers' English teaching characterized by a moderate nonnative Dutch accent, a slightly nonnative Dutch accent, or a native accent. The authors contrasted not only the accent of the teacher but also the linguistic background of students who were evaluating it (i.e., students with different backgrounds vs. the same background, that is, Dutch). This paradigm provides an opportunity to disentangle the independent contributions of social and cognitive mechanisms. If processes related to the ingroup's versus outgroup's social categorization were the cause of the negative outcomes of having a foreign accent, then a listener sharing the same linguistic background as a speaker with a nonnative accent should be more indulgent in their evaluation, as the person is recognized as an ingroup member. However, the results showed exactly the opposite, since the most negative evaluations were those of the Dutch listeners when rating the teachers with moderate nonnative accents, with comprehensibility being a critical mediator. However, for the native English listeners, no effect in terms of accent was observed, and comprehensibility did not play a role. These results indicate that the fluency factor was critical in the evaluation of speakers, while ingroup membership was not. It should be noted, however, that in this study, all speakers were of high status (i.e., lecturers). Status is a key factor in intergroup relations, as members of high-status groups consistently derogate members of low-status outgroups. Belonging to a high status may represent a source of protection from derogations from outgroup members, who may even show favoritism toward exponents of groups recognized as high in status, as their position is the goal that people are trying to achieve through their social mobility (i.e., changing one's group membership; Guimond, Dif & Aupy 2002). Possibly in line with this account, a speaker's social status is a critical protective factor against negative stereotyping in terms of a nonnative accent. Indeed, high-status groups are frequently perceived as the linguistic point of reference (Bruckmüller, Hegarty & Abele 2012). Further studies in which the design offers a full comparison of speakers of different statuses and with different accents are needed to disentangle the contribution of social and cognitive mechanisms in accentism and the boundary conditions of their relative contribution.

Roessel, Schoel & Stahlberg (2018) provided one fruitful example of the integration of different theoretical stances into accentism. In three experiments, the authors demonstrated that accentism, rather than being linked to the respective accents' origins, is a general reaction arising in response to nonnative sounds. They overcame the traditional assumption that the perception of nonstandard accents is an epiphenomenon of the specific social membership activated by the accent and showed that recipients are biased against nonstandard speakers, not simply because their accents represent deteriorated social categories (e.g., minorities or migrants as in Giles & Billings 2004) but because nonstandard accents represent a self-standing meaningful source of social information. Specifically, Roessel, Schoel & Stahlberg (2018) addressed accentism as a more basic phenomenon and showed that the accent itself carries critical information pertaining to one's foreignness, unrelated to the specific social membership. By bridging the social and cognitive theoretical frameworks, Roessel, Schoel & Stahlberg (2018; see also Roessel et al. 2019) postulated that a "general nonnative accent category" is associated with perceived foreignness (social mechanic) and disfluency (cognitive mechanic).

Rather than contrasting the three accounts, it might be useful to have an integrated perspective since, taken together, these three perspectives stress different nuances of this issue and can help explain accentism as a common and dangerous social problem. In the following sections, we will present psychological processes that emerge in response to accents sounding different from the norm, usually rooted in more than one of the above-mentioned perspectives.

Disrupted fluency

As we noted while describing the cognitive theoretical perspective, understanding nonstandard-accented speech consumes more cognitive resources than standard-accented speech, and the subjective burden is even higher for this type of communication when judged by recipients who speak with a standard accent (see Roessel et al. 2019). Low-processing fluency, per se, is assumed to elicit a negative affect (Winkielman & Cacioppo 2001; Winkielman et al. 2003), and people can project it onto related social categories (Topolinski & Strack 2009). Therefore, the negative affect resulting from disrupted fluency might be the actual core of the aversive reaction triggered by nonnative accents.

To understand which factors facilitate accentism, it is crucial to thoroughly address the role of disrupted fluency in communication. Specifically, any impediment to speech processing should be particularly detrimental for nonstandard accents. This has been proven in cases of noise, where the frustration related to the elevated costs of communication with nonstandard-accented speakers is enhanced when the speech appears in a noisy background. The negative impact of a noisy background particularly affects the perception of nonstandard speakers, who are evaluated more negatively than when speaking in a quieter environment (Dragojevic & Giles 2016). It is worth noting that, under the same conditions, the effect of noise has not been observed for standard-accented speakers. Interestingly, in a study by Gittleman & Engen (2018), the detrimental effect of noise was not replicated for English speakers evaluating Mandarin speakers, who judged the speakers as less accented in noisy conditions than in silence. The reasons for this result are unclear and either point to an incidental finding or indicate a need for further studies applying a number of accents and boundary conditions to attest to the generalizability of the findings.

One such boundary condition has already been established. Noise influences native hearers' perceptions only when they are informed that their task is to comprehend as much as possible from the speech. One might speculate that a reason for the above-mentioned asymmetry is that, compared to standard speakers, nonstandard speakers are more suitable targets to blame for effortful communication. They are already expected to make comprehension more demanding and, therefore, when difficulties arise the hearer might dismiss background noise as an additional cause. Indeed, given that people prefer to attribute an event to one rather than multiple causes (Kelley 1973), listeners are likely to (mis)attribute all difficulties in communication to nonstandard-accented speakers, even if the actual source is situational.

Contrary to additional fluency impediments such as noise, factors facilitating the ease of communication should play in favor of nonstandard accents. One such factor is familiarity with phonetic diversity. Investigating a group of raters evaluating the strength of accents in speeches, Thompson (1991) observed that raters who were more exposed to foreign accents perceived them as less prominent. Along the same lines, the negative effects of nonstandard language failed to replicate in multilingual countries. For example, Eisenchlas & Tsurutani (2013) found that Australian university students held a very positive attitude toward instructors with a foreign accent. Along the same line, Stocker (2017) reported a lack of prejudice among Swiss respondents (French and Swiss-German L1) that evaluated the truthfulness of trivia statements spelled with French, Swiss-German, Italian, or English accents. One might argue that this lack of evidence for accentism is related to greater exposure to linguistic diversity. Indeed, some studies have shown that people can become accustomed to foreign speech patterns, which helps reduce the cost and increase the speed of speech processing (Clarke & Garrett 2004; Porretta, Tucker & Järvikivi 2016). Specifically, people learn to encode nonstandard-accented speech in the same way that they learn to encode native sounds—by storing numerous examples of each word in memory and comparing those newly encountered with the stored ones, and the more similar the sound, the faster it is stored (see Weil 2001). The repository of native speech patterns is obviously very extensive because we hear and store numerous examples of native utterances in memory. Even though every speaker (L1 or non-L1) has their own individual way of speaking, one can easily encode and decode L1 speech by finding similar tokens in their memory. By the same logic, extensive contact with nonstandard-accented samples should increase the speed of processing, reduce negative emotions related to disruption of fluency, and therefore inhibit accentism. Further research is needed to investigate how universal or stable in time such effects are (as discussed, e.g., by Floccia et al. 2006).

The above-mentioned studies provide interesting insights into how basic socio-cognitive processes of fluency and affect are involved in the reception of nonstandard accents. In the following section, we will switch our attention to further stages of evaluating speakers, such as social categorization.

Social categorization: The role of accent vs. appearance for the us/them distinction

To filter and simplify the information with which they come into contact, humans tend to sort it into pre-existing categories. Specifically, social categorization refers to the process of categorization "applied to people and/or as shaped by interactions with people" (McGarty 2018:2).

People's categorization into ingroup and outgroup occurs automatically and can be boosted by vocal signals, such as accent. If we imagine an interaction between two Caucasian women, one from Italy and another from Canada, we could not tell much about their ethnic and cultural backgrounds based solely on their physical appearance. The distinctions would become apparent only after we heard them talking. A study by Rakić, Steffens & Mummendey (2011) demonstrated that an accent is a crucial feature in the categorization process, finding that, when accent and appearance were pitted against each other (e.g., presenting an individual with a standard accent but a foreign appearance), the accent was more important in guiding social categorization (see also Kinzler et al. 2009).

Paladino & Mazzurega's (2020) real-time ingroup categorization study based on reaction times and participants' hand movements revealed more details of this process. In this study, Italian participants categorized individuals who were characterized by inconsistent cues (i.e., Black speakers with a native accent and white speakers with a nonnative accent) as ingroup members or outgroup members (importantly, white is the predominant race in Italy). The computerized categorization task was performed through the mouse clicks to determine whether the stimuli belong to the "Italian" or "Foreign" category, so that the cursor trajectory of participants was tracked. This allows to capture participants' readiness (how fast they moved the mouse toward the category) and certainty (how straight the trajectory was as they traced to reach the category) in the categorization task. The first phase of the study found that both ingroup and outgroup representations were activated simultaneously and in parallel, which means that both cues—accent and appearance— were equally processed. However, in the later phase, accent overruled appearance and was pivotal for the final categorization of whether the individual presented belonged to the ingroup.

Following a cognitive theoretical framework, the primacy of accent is consistent with findings in the field of developmental psychology showing that vocal cues, even without a visual reference, are more potent than facial cues in guiding infants' behavior (Vaish & Striano 2004). Indeed, vocal stimuli have several cognitive advantages, as they rely on simpler and faster neural circuits and provide wider information. Sound signals allow to monitor a space of 360 degrees around the person (Horowitz 2012), whereas visual system covers only 180 degrees (Westheimer 1954). Vocal cues emerged as superior in other socially relevant tasks; for example, signals of pain that rely on the auditory system are more evocative of empathic reactions than visual equivalents (Agahi & Wanic 2020). As such, accent, being a social cue that relies on the auditory system, is clearly a highly reliable and important source of information.

An evolutionary perspective may interpret the above result as the outcome of an adaptive development of selective attention to vocal cues, which are also available when visual cues are impeded (for example, by an obstacle blocking the sight or during the night). Therefore, the primacy of auditory signals, compared to visual ones, would offer a more efficient strategy for elaborating signals related to danger, such as enemy detection.

The primacy of vocal versus visual cues, however, has been challenged by the literature that focuses on the categorization of sexual orientation based on vocal cues. Some research comparing the effect of voice and physical characteristics (e.g., face) in predicting sexual orientation has found different results from research exploring the difference between native (vs. nonnative) accents. In fact, Kachel et al.'s (2020) study investigated the phenomenon of the "gaydar" ('skill of detecting others' sexual orientations' [Fasoli et al. 2018:59]) and found that this process might follow a different pattern than the one for nonnative accents, since sexual orientation is more accurately recognized from faces than voices when studied separately. Indeed, the accuracy of the gaydar based on vocal features is highly unreliable (Fasoli, Maass & Berghella 2023), which makes it understandable why it is overcome by other available features.

The Social Identity Theory (SIT) seems to be particularly relevant here. Since its early theorizations, the SIT stressed the flexibility of categorization processes, showing that even meaningless categories trigger social processes (see the minimal group paradigm; Tajfel & Turner 1979) if they are made relevant in the given context. For example, Leonardelli & Brewer (2001) randomly assigned their participants into two fictitious groups (the under-estimators and the over-estimators) after participants estimated the number of dots in an image. These two groups are minimal as they are created within the experiment and are not based on any given content or previous social membership. Participants were also told that their ingroup was either the biggest (majority group) or the smallest (minority). Within these minimal conditions, the salience of group belonging is experimentally manipulated by asking participants to reflect (or not) on the meaning of the social category they "belong" to ("I find myself over (under)estimating the amount of time I need to complete a task"). When the social category was made contextually salient, participants favored more their fictitious group, whereas when the social category was not relevant majority members did not exhibit ingroup favoritism. This flexibility of social cues can explain why the primacy of auditory cues is not always observed, as it may vary depending on the social context.

Therefore, one factor affecting group categorization based on accents is which of the many groups that people belong to is salient (cognitively activated) in a given moment. For example, referring to a broader social category (e.g., Europeans) reduces prejudice regarding its subcategories (e.g., Germans; see "common ingroup identity" as presented by Gaertner & Dovidio 2000 and "superordinate identity" in Wenzel, Mummendey & Waldzus 2008). Consistent with these results, the social costs of speaking a nonstandard accent are higher when the salient ingroup category is of a narrow scope and does not include nonstandard-accented speakers. For example, the American Southern English (ASE) accent indexes both a regional (e.g., Southerner) and national identity (e.g., American). From the American West Coast point of view, an ASE-accented speaker would therefore be an ingroup member if thinking in terms of the national identity, but an outgroup member if considering the regional one. As demonstrated by Dragojevic & Giles (2014), Californians who were presented with either an ASE- or Punjabi-accented English speaker evaluated the ASE speaker differently, depending on the context of the evaluation. When the point of reference was international rather than local, the Southern-accented speaker was perceived as more similar to the ingroup. Consistent with this result, Abrams & Hogg (1987) found that listeners from Dundee (Scotland) evaluated speakers with a Glasgow accent (local Scottish variety) less favorably when comparing them to the Dundee-accented speakers than when comparing them to speakers with standard British English accents. Altogether, research indicates that both prioritizing auditory versus visual cues and evaluating people based on the inferred category membership are highly contextual. Given that different categories may trigger different responses, it is important now to turn our attention to stereotypes.

The role of stereotypes in the reception of nonstandard-accented speakers

Stereotypes are mental schemas about the features that characterize members of social groups. They constitute cognitive heuristics used when navigating intergroup interactions. Broadly, they can all be labeled as heuristics—generalized, oversimplified proxies of what to think and what to do in respective situations. They contain beliefs about characteristics of members of social groups, socially shared and learned through upbringing, education, and media (e.g., Stangor 2000). As one of the most popular and classic topics in social psychology, research on stereotypes has notably evolved over the decades. Starting from research on isolated stereotypes of a specific group (e.g., creating extensive lists of stereotypical traits attributed to categories like Jewish or Black), attention has later shifted toward a more holistic approach ordering stereotypes along two main dimensions of social perception (Fiske et al. 2002). The first dimension, labeled as "warmth" (or "communion"), describes others' intentions and comprises such as traits as morality, trustworthiness, sincerity, kindness, and friendliness. The second is labeled as "competence" (in other nomenclatures, "agency") and pertains to others' abilities to pursue their intention. Therefore, it comprises traits such as efficacy, creativity, confidence, and intelligence. The dimensions have proven to be universal across cultures and contexts, underlying and differentiating all group stereotypes (see Abele & Wojciszke 2019).

Since accents serve as cues for an instant social categorization, once categorized, nonstandard-accented individuals have been attributed with traits prescribed by stereotypes of the social category they fall within. In a meta-analysis, Fuertes et al. (2012) explored the effects of accents on interpersonal evaluations in 20 studies, finding that people with nonstandard accents are rated less positively than people with standard accents in trustworthiness, attractivity, and benevolence, pertaining to the dimension of warmth, and dynamism and status, pertaining to the dimension of competence. The findings of Birney et al. (2020) add more nuance to the stereotypical perception of nonstandard-accented speakers. In their study, when information about speakers' nationalities was available, listening to speakers from high-status (compared to low-status) countries activated more stereotypes of threatening immigrants. This is in line with the understanding that a group's status represents the dimension of the group's competence—for instance, whether they are capable of pursuing their intentions (e.g., "taking our jobs"; see McLaren 2003). A nonnative accent combined with high status conveys two important pieces of information related to the speaker: foreign and powerful. This realization seems to make listeners more attentive to threats coming from the outside.

Many examples of the role of stereotypes for nonstandard speakers come from the growing body of literature on having a gay/lesbian- versus heterosexual-sounding voice. These studies build on gender-inversion theory, which posits that gay men are believed to be similar to heterosexual women, and lesbians are believed to be similar to heterosexual men (Kite & Deaux 1987). Fasoli, Maass & Sulpizio (2018) demonstrated that listeners attribute a likelihood of diseases to gay/lesbian and heterosexual men and women in line with stereotypes based solely on vocal information; that is, gay speakers were associated with gay and female diseases and lesbian speakers with male diseases. In another line of studies, Fasoli et al. (2017) found that heterosexual listeners exposed to single-sentence voice samples made gender-typical inferences about traits and preferences of heterosexual speakers but gender-inverse inferences about those of gay or lesbian speakers. Further measures showed that listeners considered lesbian and gay speakers less suitable for a leadership position due to their low evaluation on the dimension of competence. Finally, Fasoli & Maass (2020) showed that gay-sounding speakers were perceived as warmer and as having better parenting skills, which is in line with the stereotype of gays as having traits typical of females. This aligns with Clausell & Fiske's (2005) research on gay stereotypes that revealed a gay subgroup perceived as possessing feminine characteristics and therefore receiving relatively low competence but high warmth ratings.

Stereotypical perception of the group to which nonstandard speakers belong has proven to be crucial for how speakers are perceived. As summarized by Fuertes et al.'s (2012) meta-analysis, this perception is generally negative, according to the fact that nonstandard accents are usually spoken by minorities or foreigners—groups typically negatively stereotyped as strangers, in line with the social categorization perspective.

The role of expectations toward nonstandard accent speakers

Expectations are an essential part of human cognitive functioning, and social and social-cognitive psychology have addressed this topic in many contexts under the broader term of "heuristics" (see Bless & Fiedler 2014). To expect means to learn from the past in order to be better prepared for the future. However, it is not always possible to generalize past experiences to make valid predictions. This strategy is therefore necessarily accompanied by an essential risk of error. The burden of cognitive frustration related to the occurrence of errors might fall on those who have surprised us (i.e., did not meet our expectations) in the first place, and this role is often played by nonstandard-accented speakers, especially in initial encounters.

People draw conclusions about others based on the first available cues and expect the next cues to match their first impression. Therefore, they expect the person's appearance or name to match their accent. However, if cues mismatch and a person who at first seems local turns out to be a foreigner, the expectation system crashes. Therefore, the position of a nonstandard-accented speaker whose appearance or name makes recipients expect them to speak in the standard way is difficult; that is, they might be evaluated even worse than foreigners who are congruently perceived as foreign (see Burgoon 2015).

An expectancy violation can be discussed from the cognitive perspective, since the processing of incongruent social cues (e.g., a native-looking person speaking with a nonstandard accent) is more effortful on the neural level, as has been demonstrated in neuroimaging research (Hansen et al. 2017). As we elaborated in the subsection on fluency, effortful processing is accompanied by a negative affect at a very basic level. Furthermore, the negative evaluation of nonstandard-accented speakers under an expectancy violation also fits the social-evolutionary perspective. Specifically, being able to distinguish us from them is central, as it allows us to decide who to trust. Individuals who would make this distinction difficult endanger group safety and, therefore, pay the cost of social rejection—a cost higher than for an actual outgroup member (see Pinto et al. 2010). For instance, white job candidates who spoke nonstandard English were viewed more negatively than Black candidates who spoke the same dialect by US university students (Jussim, Coleman & Lerch 1987). In a similar vein, Purkiss et al. (2006) found that a nonstandard-accented speaker (Hispanic accent while speaking English) with a name typical for locals (e.g., "Michael Fredrickson") was evaluated as less competent than a person speaking with the same accent but a foreign name (Hispanic accent but having a foreign name, e.g., "Miguel Fernandez"). Similar results were obtained in the German context by Hansen, Rakić & Steffens (2014, 2018). When a job candidate looked native, but later spoke with a nonstandard accent (Turkish), his evaluations dropped, and he was evaluated lower than nonstandard speakers with an ethnic (Turkish) appearance. By the same token, Gowen & Britt (2006) demonstrated that the mismatch between homosexual linguistic variation and sexual orientation backfires on speakers. Specifically, listeners responded more positively to a homosexual speaker when he spoke with stereotypical gay speech than with standard speech. Furthermore, they responded more negatively to a heterosexual speaker when he spoke with stereotypical gay rather than standard speech.

Ironically, once nonstandard-accented speakers are recognized as such, they might actually benefit in terms of comprehensibility from lower expectations of their linguistic performance. For instance, in messages delivered with a nonstandard accent, linguistic mistakes are less cognitively notable, as demonstrated in studies using event-related potentials. Specifically, Dutch listeners were fairly blind to grammatical errors in the utterances of nonnatives, while they reacted to failed grammar if natives were speaking (Hanulíková et al. 2012). In that study, listeners reacted to semantic errors of both natives and nonnatives. However, other researchers found that even nonsensical sentences can be disregarded in a nonnative person's speech (Gibson et al. 2017; Fairchild & Papafragou 2018).

Finally, specific expectations toward individuals already recognized as nonstandard-accented speakers have been linked to broader belief systems. Specifically, what people expect from nonstandard-accented speakers is based on what they believe one can or should achieve.

Hansen (2020) demonstrated that people differ in terms of how they understand the nature of accent: whether it can be changed, how much it is controlled by the speaker, and how much can be inferred about a person from their accent. For instance, people who believed that a person's accent is a diagnostic of their other traits (i.e., agreeing with statements like "The strength of an accent in one's speech is a sign of their personality" or "It is possible to tell how someone will act by hearing their accent") evaluated a speaker with a strong nonstandard accent as less hirable. By the same token, people who believed in the controllability of accents (e.g., "People are capable of eliminating their accent"; "An accent is something that is learned, so one can change it if necessary") perceived a nonstandard-accented speaker as worse, especially in terms of the speaker's assimilation to the host society. Beliefs about accents were found to be linked to more general attitudes that were not related to the context of accents or language. Therefore, expectations toward nonstandard-accented speakers and the reaction to them should be perceived in a broader context of a recipient's world view.

Consequences of accentism

We have extensively shown how accents are fundamental to the process of inferring a speaker's social membership and expected characteristics. Now we turn to the consequences of this phenomenon for interpersonal and intergroup relations. In fact, social categorization based on accents has the potential to exacerbate intergroup conflict, causing prejudice and discrimination against those who sound different from the norm. Importantly, such processes can emerge even on an automatic level. For example, strong nonnative accents were found to trigger negative evaluations of Japanese (Cargile & Giles 1998) and Greek (Tsalikis, DeShields & LaTour 1991) speakers among American perceivers. Moreover, Romero-Rivas, Morgan & Collier (2022) demonstrated prejudice through the Implicit Association Test (IAT), a test that measures automatic associations based on the reaction times of respondents in sorting stimuli into associated categories (see Greenwald, McGhee & Schwartz 1998). Romero-Rivas, Morgan & Collier (2022) found that participants held implicit positive biases toward native speakers but negative ones toward foreign-accented speakers, since the participants were faster in sorting when the stimuli were associated with nonstandard accents and words with a negative valence rather than with nonstandard accents and words with a positive valence. The same pattern was then confirmed through a mock trial task in which L1 English-speaking participants had to listen to a statement made by an L1 English-speaking defendant (vs. Spanish-accented defendant) and then judge whether or not the defendant was guilty and how many years of prison he should serve. Here, the participants gave foreign-accented defendants heavier penalties than L1 English-speaking defendants, but only when the defendants' statements were free of noise (vs. mixed with background white noise). Differences in accents can therefore lead to negative evaluations from listeners, especially those belonging to the linguistically normative group (Calamai & Ardolino 2020), and provoke stereotypes of minorities (Schmaus & Kristen 2021). For example, in a study by Ryan, Carranza, & Moffie (1977), participants in the United States were asked to evaluate Spanish-English bilingual speakers based on an audio recording of an English text. The results revealed that the participants held more unfavorable opinions toward people with a stronger Spanish accent.

Having a foreign or nonstandard accent has also been shown to have negative repercussions in the workplace (e.g., Huang, Frideger & Pearce 2013; Kim et al. 2019). For example, Schmaus & Kristen (2021) explored the effect of foreign accents in the early hiring process through a field experiment and found that accented speakers were more likely to be told that the work position was already filled and were less frequently recommended for a promotion. Along the same line of research, Hosoda & Stone-Romero (2010) investigated the impact of foreign accents on employment-related outcomes. Results revealed that nonnative speakers were less likely to be hired for a job, especially if the position demanded a great deal of communication. Iheduru-Anderson (2020) explored the impact of Black African-accented nurses on the possibility of career advancement using individual interviews. The author found that all participants believed that their accent, paired with being Black, had some negative effects on how they were perceived by colleagues and on their nursing career progression. In a study conducted in Germany by Schmaus & Kristen (2021), job applicants with Turkish accents were less likely to be invited for an interview. The authors also observed that the applicant's accent was a better predictor of the negative outcome than their name.

An accent that deviates from the norm can also lead to negative consequences in the legal sphere. Cantone et al. (2019) explored how legal decision-makers are affected by what they hear in the sound of the defendant's voice. In this study, the authors randomly assigned participants into one of six conditions, whereby they experimentally manipulated the defendant's race (Black vs. Mexican American vs. white) and accent (with native vs. nonnative) using a between-subjects design (each participant was exposed to just one of the six combinations of race and accent). They were asked to read a brief description of a case in which the race of the defendant emerged with peculiar characteristics of his name (Alexander Holt vs. Jamaal Robinson/John Rodgers/Jose Rodriguez) and then listen to the defendant's testimony (accented or not). The results provided evidence that African American targets were judged as guiltier in legal processes than white American and Mexican American people, and that this prejudice was even stronger when the African American person spoke with a stereotyped accent. In this case, matching the expectations may have exacerbated the accessibility of the stereotype, which in the specific case of criminality is particularly negative towards African Americans. Another form of language-based discrimination in court relates to transcription of African American English which has been shown to have lower accuracy than standard American English (Jones et al. 2019). Potential repercussions of such cross-dialect miscomprehension might have severe legal consequences and jeopardize legal justice, especially since observed mistakes occurred even in regard to crucial facts, changing information of who, what, when, or where.

The effect of accent in the educational context is particularly relevant, given the increasing globalization and the rapid spread of English as a teaching language, even in countries where it is not widely spoken as an L1. In Hendriks, Meurs & Usmany's (2021) experiment, students (Dutch and international) rated professors who spoke foreign-accented Dutch more negatively than lecturers with light nonnative or native accents in terms of intelligibility, comprehensibility, and attitudinal impressions. These results are in line with the hypothesis that a nonnormative accent leads to more negative consequences, such as prejudice. Calamai & Ardolino (2020) found complementary results addressing the perception of students by professors in the context of Italian high schools. The authors studied the effect of spoken Italian by native Chinese speakers on attitudes using both implicit and explicit measures. Specifically, they assessed participants' implicit attitudes using an IAT and explicit attitudes using a self-report questionnaire. While the results showed no differences concerning explicit attitudes toward native Chinese speakers compared to native Italian speakers, professors held implicit negative attitudes toward Chinese-accented students. Negative attitudes towards children who speak differently have a longer tradition since it was one of the pronounced manifestations of racism in US school systems. Interestingly, in 1997 William Labov as a professor of linguistics, testified for the senate subcommittee regarding the role of "Ebonics" in education (Labov 1997). He pointed to the fact that African American children are denied the possibility to learn through their home language, that is, Ebonics, the use of which was prohibited in schools. Therefore, their access to education was not equal to the students speaking standard English who were not expected to learn another language or dialect at such an early stage of schooling.

Finally, in a series of experiments (Purnell, Idsardi & Baugh 1999) showed that people might be discriminated against based on their way of speaking in regard to housing. Using a matched-guise approach, one of the authors (John Baugh) called landlords in response to apartment rental advertisements. Baugh—who grew up speaking a range of Englishes associated with Black, Latino, and white speakers—affected different accents during calls to landlords, but otherwise used the same script to make his inquiries. His white-accented persona was more likely than his Black or Latino personae to secure appointments from landlords, and Baugh's non-white personae were in many cases told that an apartment was no longer available, only for his white persona to subsequently be offered an appointment by the same landlord. Therefore, based on accent, one might be deprived of chances to fulfill such a basic human need as housing. Subsequent experimentation revealed that listeners reliably identified the race indexed by Baugh's personae during his utterance of *hello*, the first word of his inquiry, revealing the immediacy of accent-based language discrimination in a conversational interaction.

Taken together, the literature shows that negative attitudes, discrimination, and prejudice toward nonnative-accented people start at an early age and spread, although not always explicitly, to key areas of life, including the housing, education, and work, as well as the judicial sphere.

Nonstandard-accented speakers' stigma

So far, we have mainly focused on the perceivers of accents and neglected the speakers. Yet, given the wide range of external social repercussions of speaking with a nonstandard accent, it comes as no surprise that there are also internal psychological consequences for nonstandard speakers once they become conscious of their disadvantages. Such effects are part of a well-known phenomenon that falls within a broader category of social stigma—the experience of being visibly marked with a characteristic perceived by others as inferior (e.g., Major & O'Brien 2005; Inzlicht & Good 2006). Much of the current knowledge about stigma-related stress draws from research on minority stress focusing on ethnicity or race (Meyer 2003). However, it also fits well into the context of accents. Stigma-related stressors take many forms and usually cumulate from isolated events (e.g., being fired, being victimized due to hate crimes), everyday discrimination (e.g., receiving poorer service in restaurants), stigma management (e.g., attempts to switch between patterns of speech), and, finally, the expectation of rejection and stigma internalization (i.e., self-devaluation; see Frost 2011).

Signs of stigma-related stress have also been specifically observed in the context of accents. Gluszek & Dovidio (2010a) demonstrated that nonstandard speakers actually expected to be stigmatized and to have problems communicating. The fact that they anticipated problems in communicating weakened the feeling of belonging to their country of residence (the United States) among nonnative-accented speakers (but not native-accented speakers who spoke a socially salient regional accent). In another study, Chinese Americans who spoke English with a nonstandard accent declared that others perceive them as perpetual foreigners—that is, inherently unassimilable ones (Kim et al. 2011). Eventually, those participants declared themselves targets of chronic daily discrimination or even discriminatory victimization experiences, which eventually increased the risk of the depressive symptoms they experienced.

One of the most pronounced social-psychological advancements in the study of the consequences of stigma is research on stereotype threat (Steele & Aronson 1995; Steele 1997). This phenomenon applies when one's awareness of the stigma attached to their identity overwhelms cognitive resources and, therefore, handicaps their performance. Such a threatening effect of stereotype awareness has been observed in the case of Black and Latino individuals across a variety of testing situations when tests are presented as diagnostics for intelligence (e.g., Osborne 2001). Similarly, women's performances in mathematics or political knowledge have been found to be inhibited once they are presented as diagnostics (e.g., Spencer, Steele & Quinn 1999). In the context of accents, it seems that contact with native standard-accented speakers, just as with test diagnosticity, might be a trigger for the appearance of stereotype threat. In this vein, Kim et al. (2019) found that, when working with native speakers, nonnative speakers experienced more negative emotions, especially fear of negative judgment. They declared fatigue from communicating, monitoring their own actions and those of native speakers, and the desire to limit interactions with native speakers. Ultimately, the experience of stereotype threat deteriorated nonnative speakers' perceptions of their own abilities and self-esteem. Interestingly, recent findings have documented the effect of accent-based stereotype threat in conflictual situations with native speakers, as well. Kim, Ramirez-Marin & Tasa (2021) found that, because nonstandard-accented individuals experienced stereotype threat, they used more passive conflict behaviors, such as yielding and avoiding, and were therefore less satisfied with conflict outcomes.

Kim et al. (2019:79) quote several interviewees who explicitly reported the effects of their accent, confirming these included awareness and the anxiety of being a target of stigma. For example, "I tried to explain to the best of my abilities my view on how things should be done, but it was met with skepticism and I think that it is due to the fact that I have an accent." Experiences of powerlessness and lack of efficacy in the work environment might have detrimental consequences for personal well-being as well as employee productivity. However, as noted by Rogan et al. (2006), for the multicultural populations in Western societies, it is inevitable to educate and support the professional growth of culturally and linguistically diverse experts. Due to the effect of social stigma, those who do not speak with a standard accent are at high risk of failure in university programs or internships. While some tools aiming to facilitate nonstandard-accented speakers' accommodation in clinical professions have been discussed (Rogan et al. 2006; San Miguel et al. 2006), it is still just a drop in the ocean of wasted potential.

CASE STUDY   Interventions to overcome accentism

Speaking nonstandard language has proven to have negative social consequences and, therefore, there is an urgent need to understand how these consequences can be prevented or overcome. The interventions proposed in this section attempt to adapt existing knowledge about prejudice reduction in the context of accentism. First, the perspective-taking paradigm (e.g., Vescio, Sechrist & Paolucci 2003) has been proposed as an inhibitor of negative evaluations of nonstandard speakers. It builds on the premise that we have limited knowledge about others' motives and feelings or the situational context of their actions. The human cognitive system is egocentric, and therefore, when communicating in a native language, our most accessible perspective is that it is easy to speak with the standard accent, while disregarding the difficulties related to acquiring it as a foreign language. In a study by Weyant (2007), participants were explicitly encouraged to take the perspective of nonstandard-accented speakers. This exercise positively influenced their later evaluation of nonnative speakers' audio recordings. Hansen, Rakić & Steffens (2014) replicated this result in a procedure less prone to social desirability effects. Specifically, half of the participants were asked to speak in a foreign language before evaluating a nonstandard speaker. When it came to the evaluation, participants who had the perspective-taking experience (i.e., speaking in a foreign language) did not discriminate against nonnative speakers, whereas other participants did (i.e., they evaluated accented speakers worse than native ones).

Another approach to fighting prejudice that was adapted to the context of accents builds on the normative social influence (Crandall, Eshleman & O'Brien 2002). This phenomenon means that, if the expression of prejudice towards certain groups is not accepted in one's social group, individuals self-correct their behavior in an attempt to conform to the perceived social rules of appropriateness. A successful attempt to implement the social norms-based approach to the context of accentism was reported by Roessel et al. (2019). In their study, participants were informed about the phenomenon of accent-based prejudice and asked not to base their evaluations on feelings or stereotypes evoked by the speaker's accent. Indeed, those participants' evaluations of speakers were not influenced by the speakers' accents. In a similar vein, Dragojevic & Giles (2016) found that, by making the speakers' ethnicity salient, they reduced the bias in the evaluation of speakers' status. As suggested by Roessel, Schoel &Stahlberg (2020), the media might and should play a crucial role in creating the norms of inclusion for nonstandard-accented speakers, actively contrasting the actual habit of not representing nonstandard-accented speakers (see Gluszek & Dovidio 2010b; Gluszek & Hansen 2016; Dragojevic et al. 2016). Interestingly, as noted by Roessel, Schoel & Stahlberg (2020), the normative influence seems to have already been observed in several studies, where the evaluation of nonstandard speakers was not downgraded or was even enhanced (i.e., overcorrected).

However, the status quo of knowledge about prejudice prescribes caution in interpreting these results, since prejudice-related declarations (explicit prejudice) are often inconsistent with the actual core of an attitude (see Imhoff & Banse 2009). Implicit attitudes are automatic and might influence behavior when the individual motivation to act in line with social norms is deteriorated or when one's auto monitoring system is overwhelmed (see Roessel, Schoel & Stahlberg 2020). However, on the optimistic side, Crandall, Eshleman & O'Brien (2002) argued that the motivation to conform to norms might be internalized if individuals value their group membership and are strongly identified (see also Devine et al. 2002). Similarly, the previously mentioned study by Calamai & Ardolino (2020) within Italian schools showed that the perception of the school climate and of professors' attitudes toward Chinese students was more in line with professors' self-reported positive explicit attitudes than with their negative implicit associations. In fact, students (both Chinese and Italian) claimed that Chinese-accented students were welcomed and not discriminated against. Possibly, the explicit values of inclusion were strong enough to overcome the risk of spillover effects from implicit associations to discriminant behaviors.

Scholars have also shown some positive outcomes from educational interventions against accentism. In research by Hansen (2020), sharing false convictions, such as "People are capable of eliminating their accent" or "An accent is something that is learned, one can change it if necessary," was related to negative evaluations of nonstandard speakers. Although such beliefs may be motivated by prejudice, they may also be caused by a mere lack of knowledge. In fact, the two sources of misconception are not mutually exclusive, but as formulated by Stephan & Stephan (2000), "if fear is the father of prejudice, ignorance is the grandfather." Gluszek & Dovidio (2010b), in their theoretical review, also noted that the key issue to be addressed in future interventions needs to be the expectation that nonnative speakers should lose their accents. Finally, in line with the intergroup contact hypothesis, which posits that contact with outgroup members reduces prejudice toward this outgroup (Allport 1954), it has been shown that an ethnically diverse upbringing and experiences such as living or working abroad are positively related to attitudes toward accented speech (Dewaele & McCloskey 2015). Therefore, creating multilingual and multiaccent spaces might be an intervention directed at both adults and children. Once again, the role of the media seems invaluable, as it could increase the visibility (and audibility) of nonstandard-accented speakers on a massive scale and, therefore, increase the familiarity of respective accents. The presence of nonstandard speakers in the media might work as a vicarious contact; that is, the observation of interactions between ingroup and outgroup members could provide a vicarious learning experience, as it is a well-established method of reducing prejudice (Mazziotta, Mummendey & Wright 2011; Stahi & Vezzali 2020). This and many other techniques could be adapted from what has already been found in the research on prejudice-reduction interventions in earlier established contexts, such as racism or interethnic attitudes.

Integrating social psychology and sociophonetics

The topic of nonstandard accents and their reception has recently received increasing attention. As summarized in this review, many fascinating findings have been reported, opening new doors for further and more in-depth investigation on the social meaning of this phenomenon.

We have highlighted possible future paths in the sections above. However, here we would like to point out a few which are, in our opinion, the most urgent directions. One of the most important paths for future research would be to address under-represented geographical and linguistic contexts to better understand to what extent the theories and the reported effects are universal. Some inconsistencies found in previous research should be further investigated involving more languages and accents to uncover patterns that might be typical of certain language families or accent types. In addition to the diversity of the studied targets, the field requires a greater diversity of scientific perspectives through more interdisciplinary collaboration. The phenomenon of nonstandard accents is interdisciplinary in nature. However, existing research is rather fragmented and still limited to narrow theoretical perspectives. To better understand its complexity, a more holistic approach should be applied to connect the findings from social, cognitive, linguistic, and other domains. In particular, here, we strongly encourage a tighter integration of the social psychological perspective with the sociophonetics approach. Sociophonetics addresses the interface of sociolinguistics and phonetics (Strelluf this volume) by specifically inspecting the sources and reasons for diversity in speech. Research focusing on differences in pronunciation between regions, socioeconomic classes, ethnicities, genders, and sexual orientations (e.g., Henton 1989) could enrich our understanding of intergoup psycho-social dynamics. Within this multidisciplinary approach, we call upon sociophonetics to identify the microscopic features that socially characterize a speaker, revealing social identity negotiations and affirmations. In many areas, the sociophonetics domain and the study of accents within social psychology show a large overlap as both fields aim to identify 1) the consequences of accented speech for the speakers, 2) how listeners expectations are shaped by the speakers accent (Niedzielski 1999; Campbell-Kibler 2013; Hay, Warren & Drager 2006), and 3) how they form attitudes towards accented speakers (Purnell, Idsardi & Baugh1999; Niedzielski & Preston 2010; Evans, Benson & Stanford 2018). Research investigating the consequences of accented speech for speakers and how listener expectations are shaped by the speaker's accent sits at the intersection between linguistics and social psychology (see also Warren in this volume). Along the same line, the study of how people form attitudes towards accented speakers mobilizes scholars of both socio-psychology and sociophonetics. Given these similarities between the two fields of research, an interdisciplinary effort would make a unique contribution to the study of issues by integrating sociophonetics and social psychology. Furthermore, while research on accents has already crossed with appearance, more research is needed to cover additional intersections, such as the content of communication or nonverbal behavior (Formanowicz & Suitner 2020). After all, communication is a multifaceted process in which a number of factors affect its outcomes. Finally, we certainly hope that, in the future, scientific knowledge about nonstandard accents can be used practically to afford nonstandard-accented speakers a more peaceful existence within society, allowing them to draw from their full potential.

Acknowledgments

Contribution of all authors to this chapter was equal. Authors' order was established randomly (see www.aeaweb.org/journals/policies/random-author-order/search?RandomAuthorsSearch%5Bsearch%5D=oTNZLkSxDW2Z).

References

Abele, Andrea E. & Bogdan Wojciszke (eds.). 2019. *Agency and communion in social psychology.* Routledge.

Abrams, Dominic & Michael A. Hogg. 1987. Language attitudes, frames of reference, and social identity: A Scottish dimension. *Journal of Language and Social Psychology* 6(3–4). 201–213. https://doi.org/10.1177/0261927X8763004

Agahi, Sepideh & Rebekah Wanic. 2020. Supremacy of auditory versus visual input in somatic empathy and perceived pain level. *Pain Management Nursing* 21(2). 201–206. https://doi.org/10.1016/j.pmn.2019.06.013

Allport, Gordon. 1954. *The nature of prejudice.* Addison-Wesley.

Bauer, Laurie & Peter Trudgill (eds.). 1998. *Language myths.* Penguin.

Bent, Tessa & Ann R. Bradlow. 2003. The interlanguage speech intelligibility benefit. *Journal of the Acoustical Society of America* 114(3). 1600–1610. https://doi.org/10.1121/1.1603234

Birney, Megan E., Anna Rabinovich, Thomas A. Morton, Hannah Heath & Sam Ashcroft. 2020. When speaking English is not enough: The consequences of language-based stigma for nonnative speakers. *Journal of Language and Social Psychology* 39. 67–86. https://doi.org/10.1177/0261927X19883906

Bless, Herbert & Klaus Fiedler. 2014. *Social cognition: How individuals construct social reality.* Psychology Press.

Brewer, Marilynn B. 1999. The psychology of prejudice: Ingroup love or outgroup hate? *Journal of Social Issues* 55(3). 429–444. https://doi.org/10.1111/0022-4537.00126

Bruckmüller, Susanne, Peter Hegarty & Andrea E. Abele. 2012. Framing gender differences: Linguistic normativity affects perceptions of power and gender stereotypes. *European Journal of Social Psychology* 42(2). 210–218. https://doi.org/10.1002/ejsp.858

Burgoon, Judee K. 2015. Expectancy violations theory. In Charles R. Berger, Michael E. Roloff, Steve R. Wilson, James Price Dillard, John Caughlin & Denise Solomon (eds.), *International encyclopedia of interpersonal communication.* https://doi.org/10.1002/9781118540190.wbeic102

Calamai, Silvia & Fabio Ardolino. 2020. Italian with an accent: The case of "Chinese Italian" in Tuscan high schools. *Journal of Language and Social Psychology* 39(1). e132–147. https://doi.org/10.1177/0261927X19883899

Campbell-Kibler, Kathryn. 2013. Connecting attitudes and language behavior via implicit sociolinguistic cognition. In Tore Kristiansen and Stefan Grondelaers (eds.), *Language (de)standardisation in late modern Europe: Experimental studies,* 307–330. Novus.

Cantone, Jason A., Leslie N. Martinez, Cynthia Willis-Esqueda & Taija Miller. 2019. Sounding guilty: How accent bias affects juror judgments of culpability. *Journal of Ethnicity in Criminal Justice* 17(3). 228–253. https://doi.org/10.1080/15377938.2019.1623963

Cargile, Aarin Castelan & Howard Giles. 1998. Language attitudes toward varieties of English: An American-Japanese context. *Journal of Applied Communication Research* 26(3). 338–356. https://doi.org/10.1080/00909889809365511

Chakraborty, Rahul. 2017. A short note on accent–bias, social identity and ethnocentrism. *Advances in Language and Literary Studies* 8(4). 57–64. https://doi.org/10.7575/aiac.alls.v.8n.4p.57

Clarke, Constance M. & Merrill F. Garrett. 2004. Rapid adaptation to foreign-accented English. *Journal of the Acoustical Society of America* 116. 3647–3658. https://doi.org/10.1121/1.1815131

Clausell, Eric & Susan T. Fiske. 2005. When do subgroup parts add up to the stereotypic whole? Mixed stereotype content for gay male subgroups explains overall ratings. *Social Cognition* 23(2). 161–181. https://doi.org/10.1521/soco.23.2.161.65626

Crandall, Cristian S., Amy Eshleman & Laurie O'Brien. 2002. Social norms and the expression and suppression of prejudice: The struggle for internalization. *Journal of Personality and Social Psychology* 82(3). 359–378. https://doi.org/10.1037/0022-3514.82.3.359

Devine, Patricia G., Ashby E. Plant, David M. Amodio, Eddie Harmon-Jones & Stephanie L. Vance. 2002. The regulation of explicit and implicit race bias: The role of motivations to respond without prejudice. *Journal of Personality and Social Psychology* 82(5). 835–848. https://doi.org/10.1037/0022-3514.82.5.835

Dewaele, Jean-Marc & James McCloskey. 2015. Attitudes towards foreign accents among adult multilingual language users. *Journal of Multilingual and Multicultural Development* 36(3). 221–238. https://doi.org/10.1080/01434632.2014.909445

Dragojevic, Marko. 2019. Extending the fluency principle: Factors that increase listeners' processing fluency positively bias their language attitudes. *Communication Monographs* 87(2). 158–178. https://doi.org/10.1080/03637751.2019.1663543

Dragojevic, Marko & Howard Giles. 2014. The reference frame effect: An intergroup perspective on language attitudes. *Human Communication Research.* 40(1). 91–111. https://doi.org/10.1111/hcre.12017

Dragojevic, Marko & Howard Giles. 2016. "I don't like you because you're hard to understand": The role of processing fluency in the language attitudes process. *Human Communication Research* 42(3). 396–420. https://doi.org/10.1111/hcre.12079

Dragojevic, Marko, Dana Mastro, Howard Giles & Alexander Sink. 2016. Silencing nonstandard speakers: A content analysis of accent portrayals on American primetime television. *Language in Society* 45(1). 59–85. https://doi.org/10.1017/S0047404515000743

Eisenchlas, Susana A., Andrea C. Schalley & Diana Guillemin. 2013. The importance of literacy in the home language: The view from Australia. *SAGE Open* 3(4). https://doi.org/10.1177/2158244013507270

Engen, Kristin J. van & Johnatan E. Peelle. 2014. Listening effort and accented speech. *Frontiers in Human Neuroscience* 8. Article 577. https://doi.org/10.3389/fnhum.2014.00577

Evans, Betsy E., Erica J. Benson & James N. Stanford (eds.). 2018. *Language regard: Methods, variation and change.* Cambridge. https://doi.org/10.1017/9781316678381

Fairchild, Sarah & Anna Papafragou. 2018. Sins of omission are more likely to be forgiven in non-native speakers. *Cognition* 181. 80–92. https://doi.org/10.1016/j.cognition.2018.08.010

Fasoli, Fabio, Peter Hegarty, Anne Maass & Antonio Raquel. 2018. Who wants to sound straight? Sexual majority and minority stereotypes, beliefs and desires about auditory gaydar. *Personality and Individual Differences* 130. 59–64. https://doi.org/10.1016/j.paid.2018.03.046

Fasoli, Fabio & Anne Maass. 2020. The social costs of sounding gay: Voice-based impressions of adoption applicants. *Journal of Language and Social Psychology* 39(1). 112–131. https://doi.org/10.1177/0261927X19883

Fasoli, Fabio, Anne Maass & Luna Berghella. 2023. Who has a better auditory gaydar? Sexual orientation categorization by heterosexual and lesbian, gay and bisexual people. *Journal of Homosexuality* 70(5). 876–899. https://doi.org/10.1080/00918369.2021.2004796

Fasoli, Fabio, Anne Maass, Maria P. Paladino & Simone Sulpizio. 2017. Gay- and lesbian-sounding auditory cues elicit stereotyping and discrimination. *Archives of Sexual Behavior* 46. 1261–1277. https://doi.org/10.1007/s1050801709620

Fasoli, Fabio, Anne Maass & Simone Sulpizio. 2018. Stereotypical disease inferences from gay/lesbian versus heterosexual voices. *Journal of Homosexuality* 65(8). 990–1014. https://doi.org/10.1080/00918369.2017.1364945

Fiske, Susan T., Amy J.C. Cuddy, Peter Glick & Jun Xu. 2002. A model of (often mixed) stereotype content: Competence and warmth respectively follow from perceived status and competition. *Social Cognition* 82(6). 171–222. https://doi.org/10.1037//0022-3514.82.6.878

Floccia, Caroline, Jeremy Goslin, Frédérique Girard & Gabrielle Konopczynski. 2006. Does a regional accent perturb speech processing? *Journal of Experimental Psychology*: *Human Perception and Performance* 32(5). 1276–1293. https://doi.org/10.1037/0096-1523.32.5.1276

Formanowicz, Magdalena & Caterina Suitner. 2020. Sounding strange(r): Origins, consequences, and boundary conditions of sociophonetic discrimination. *Journal of Language and Social Psychology* 39(1). 4–21. https://doi.org/10.1177/0261927X19884354

Freynet, Nathalie, Richard Clément & John Sylvestre. 2018. A qualitative investigation of the experience of accent stigmatization among native and non-native French speakers in Canada. *Journal of Language and Discrimination* 2(1). 5–31. https://doi.org/10.1558/jld.32226

Frost, David M. 2011. Social stigma and its consequences for the socially stigmatized. *Social and Personality Psychology Compass* 5(11). 824–839. https://doi.org/10.1111/j.1751-9004.2011.00394.x

Fuertes, Jairo N., William H. Gottdiener, Helena Martin, Tracey C. Gilbert & Howard Giles. 2012. A meta-analysis of the effects of speakers' accents on interpersonal evaluations. *European Journal of Social Psychology* 42(1). 120–133. https://doi.org/10.1002/ejsp.862

Gaertner, Samuel L. & John F. Dovidio. 2000. *Reducing intergroup bias: The common ingroup identity model.* Psychology Press.

Gagnon, André & Richard Y. Bourhis. 1996. Discrimination in the minimal group paradigm: Social identity or self-interest? *Personality and Social Psychology Bulletin* 22(12). 1289–1301. https://doi.org/10.1177/01461672962212009

Gasquet-Cyrus, Médéric. 2012. Hétérogénéité, catégorisation et description linguistique: de l'accent "du Midi" aux accents du sud de la France. In Martine Dreyfus & Jean-Marie Prieur (ed.), *Hétérogénéité et variation*, 50–65. Michel Houdiard Editeur.

Gibson, Edward, Caitlin Tan, Richard Futrell, Kyle Mahowald, Lars Konieczny, Barbara Hemforth & Evelina Fedorenko. 2017. Don't underestimate the benefits of being misunderstood. *Psychological Science* 28(6). 703–712. https://doi.org/10.1177/0956797617690277

Giles, Howard & Andrew C. Billings. 2004. Assessing language attitudes: Speaker evaluation studies. In Alan Davies & Catherine Elder (eds.), *The handbook of applied linguistics*, 187–209. Blackwell.

Giles, Howard & Pat Johnson. 1981. The role of language in ethnic group relations. In John C. Turner & Howard Giles (eds.), *Intergroup behavior*, 199–243. Blackwell.

Giles, Howard & Patricia Johnson. 1987. Ethnolinguistic identity theory: A social psychological approach to language maintenance. *International Journal of the Sociology of Language* 68. 69–100. https://doi.org/10.1515/ijsl.1987.68.69

Giles, Howard & Tamara Rakić. 2014. Language attitudes: Social determinants and consequences of language variation. In Thomas M. Holtgraves (ed.), *The Oxford handbook of language and social psychology,* 11–26. Oxford University Press.

Giles, Howard & Bernadette M. Watson (eds.). 2013. *The social meanings of language, dialect and accent: International perspectives on speech styles.* Peter Lang.

Gittleman, Sarah & Kristin van Engen. 2018. Effects of noise and talker intelligibility on judgments of accentedness. *Journal of the Acoustical Society of America* 143. 3138–3145. https://doi.org/10.1121/1.5038653

Gluszek, Agata & John F. Dovidio. 2010a. Speaking with a nonnative accent: Perceptions of bias, communication difficulties, and belonging in the United States. *Journal of Language and Social Psychology* 29(2). 224–234. https://doi.org/10.1177/0261927X09359590

Gluszek, Agata & John F. Dovidio. 2010b. The way they speak: A social psychological perspective on the stigma of nonnative accents in communication. *Personality and Social Psychology Review* 14(2). 214–237. https://doi.org/10.1177/1088868309359288

Gluszek, Agata & Karolina Hansen. 2016. What does speaking with a foreign accent mean? Content analysis of newspaper articles. Unpublished manuscript. https://doi.org/10.13140/RG.2.1.1912.3281

Gowen, Catherine W. & Thomas W. Britt. 2006. The interactive effects of homosexual speech and sexual orientation on the stigmatization of men: Evidence for expectancy violation theory. *Journal of Language and Social Psychology* 25(4). 437–456. https://doi.org/10.1177/0261927X062927

Greenwald, Anthony G., Debbie E. McGhee & Jordan L. Schwartz. 1998. Measuring individual differences in implicit cognition: The implicit association test. *Journal of Personality and Social Psychology* 74(6). 1464. https://doi.org/10.1037/0022-3514.74.6.1464

Guimond, Serge, Stephane Dif & Annabelle Aupy. 2002. Social identity, relative group status and intergroup attitudes: When favourable outcomes change intergroup relations … for the worse. *European Journal of Social Psychology* 32(6). 739–760. https://doi.org/10.1002/ejsp.118

Hansen, Karolina. 2020. Accent Beliefs Scale (ABS): Scale development and validation. *Journal of Language and Social Psychology* 39(1). 148–171. https://doi.org/10.1177/0261927X19883903

Hansen, Karolina, Tamara Rakić & Melanie C. Steffens. 2014. When actions speak louder than words: Preventing discrimination of nonstandard speakers. *Journal of Language and Social Psychology* 33(1). 68–77. https://doi.org/10.1177/0261927X13499761

Hansen, Karolina, Tamara Rakić & Melanie C. Steffens. 2018. Foreign-looking native-accented people: More competent when first seen rather than heard. *Social Psychological and Personality Science* 9(8). 1001–1009. https://doi.org/10.1177/1948550617732389

Hansen, Karolina, Melanie C. Steffens, Tamara Rakić & Holger Wiese. 2017. When appearance does not match accent: Neural correlates of ethnicity-related expectancy violations. *Social Cognitive and Affective Neuroscience* 12(3). 507–515. https://doi.org/10.1093/scan/nsw148

Hanulíková, Adriana, Petra M. van Alphen, Merel M. van Goch & Andrea Weber. 2012. When one person's mistake is another's standard usage: The effect of foreign accent on syntactic processing. *Journal of Cognitive Neuroscience* 24(4). 878–887. https://doi.org/10.1162/jocn_a_00103

Hay, Jennifer, Paul Warren & Katie Drager. 2006. Factors influencing speech perception in the context of a merger-in-progress. *Journal of Phonetics* 34(4). 458–484. https://doi.org/10.1016/j.wocn.2005.10.001

Hendriks, Berna, Frank van Meurs & Nina Usmany. 2021. The effects of lecturers' non-native accent strength in English on intelligibility and attitudinal evaluations by native and non-native English students. *Language Teaching Research.* https://doi.org/10.1177/1362168820983145

Henton, Caroline G. 1989. Sociophonetic aspects of creaky voice. *Journal of the Acoustical Society of America* 86(S1). S26–S26. https://doi.org/10.1121/1.2027434

Horowitz, Seth S. 2012. *The universal sense: How hearing shapes the mind.* Bloomsbury Publishing USA.

Hosoda, Megumi & Eugene Stone-Romero. 2010. The effects of foreign accents on employment-related decisions. *Journal of Managerial Psychology* 25(2). 113–132. https://doi.org/10.1108/02683941011019339

Huang, Laura, Marcia Frideger & Jone L. Pearce. 2013. Political skill: Explaining the effects of nonnative accent on managerial hiring and entrepreneurial investment decisions. *Journal of Applied Psychology* 98(6). 1005–1017. https://doi.org/10.1037/a0034125

Iheduru-Anderson, Kechi. 2020. Accent bias: A barrier to Black African-born nurses seeking managerial and faculty positions in the United States. *Nursing Inquiry* 27(4). e12355. https://doi.org/10.1111/nin.12355

Imhoff, Roland & Rainer Banse. 2009. Ongoing victim suffering increases prejudice: The case of secondary anti-Semitism. *Psychological Science* 20(12). 1443–1447. https://doi.org/10.1111/j.1467-9280.2009.02457.x

Inzlicht, Michael & Catherine Good. 2006. How environments can threaten academic performance, self-knowledge, and sense of belonging. In Shana Levin & Colette van Laar (eds.), *Stigma and group inequality: Social psychological perspectives*, 129–150. Lawrence Erlbaum.

Jones, Taylor, Jessica R. Kalbfeld, Ryan Hancock & Robin Clark. 2019. Testifying while black: An experimental study of court reporter accuracy in transcription of African American English. *Language* 95(2). e216–e252. https://doi.org/10.1353/lan.2019.0042

Jussim, Lee, Lerita M. Coleman & Lauren Lerch. 1987. The nature of stereotypes: A comparison and integration of three theories. *Journal of Personality and Social Psychology* 52(3). 536–546. https://doi.org/10.1037/0022-3514.52.3.536

Kachel, Sven, Melanie C. Steffens, Sabine Preuß & Adrian P. Simpson. 2020. Gender (conformity) matters: Cross-dimensional and cross-modal associations in sexual orientation perception. *Journal of Language and Social Psychology* 39(1). 40–66. https://doi.org/10.1177/0261927X19883902

Kelley, Howard H. 1973. The processes of causal attribution. *American Psychologist* 28(2). 107–128. https://doi.org/10.1037/h0034225

Kim, Regina, Jimena Y. Ramirez-Marin, & Kevin Tasa. 2021. Do you hear my accent? How nonnative English speakers experience conflictual conversations in the workplace. *International Journal of Conflict Management* 33(1). 155–178. https://doi.org/10.1108/IJCMA-10-2020-0177

Kim, Regina, Loriann Roberson, Marcello Russo & Paola Briganti. 2019. Language diversity, non-native accents and its consequences at workplace: Recommendations for individuals, teams, and organizations. *Journal of Applied Behavioral Science* 55(1). 73–95. https://doi.org/10.1177/00218863188009

Kim, Su Y., Yijie Wang, Shiying Deng, Rocio Alvarez & Jing Li. 2011. Accent, perpetual foreigner stereotype, and perceived discrimination as indirect links between English proficiency and depressive symptoms in Chinese American adolescents. *Developmental Psychology* 47(1). 289–301. https://doi.org/10.1037/a0020712

Kinzler, Katherine D., Emmanuel Dupoux & Elizabeth S. Spelke. 2007. The native language of social cognition. *Proceedings of the National Academy of Sciences of the USA* 104(30). 12577–12580. https://doi.org/10.1073/pnas.0705345104

Kinzler, Katherine D., Kristin Shutts & Joshua Correll. 2010. Priorities in social categories. *European Journal of Social Psychology* 40(4). 581–592. https://doi.org/10.1002/ejsp.739

Kinzler, Katherine D., Kristin Shutts, Jasmine DeJesus & Elisabeth S. Spelke. 2009. Accent trumps race in guiding children's social preferences. *Social Cognition* 27(4). 623–634. https://doi.org/10.1521/soco.2009.27.4.623

Kite, Mary E. & Kay Deaux. 1987. Gender belief systems: Homosexuality and the implicit inversion theory. *Psychology of Women Quarterly* 11(1). 83–96. https://doi.org/10.1111/j.1471-6402.1987.tb00776.x

Latinus, Marianne & Pascal Belin. 2011. Human voice perception. *Current Biology* 21(4). R143–R145. https://doi.org/10.1016/j.cub.2010.12.033

Labov, William. 1997. Testimony submitted by William Labov, Professor of Linguistics at the University of Pennsylvania, Past President of the Linguistic Society of America, member of the National Academy of Science. www.ling.upenn.edu/~wlabov/Papers/Ebonic%20testimony.pdf

Leonardelli, Geoffrey J. & Marilynn B. Brewer. 2001. Minority and majority discrimination: When and why. *Journal of Experimental Social Psychology* 37(6). 468–485. https://doi.org/10.1006/jesp.2001.1475

Lev-Ari, Shiri & Boaz Keysar. 2010. Why don't we believe non-native speakers? The influence of accent on credibility. *Journal of Experimental Social Psychology* 46(6). 1093–1096. https://doi.org/10.1016/j.jesp.2010.05.025

Lev-Ari, Shiri & Boaz Keysar. 2012. Less-detailed representation of non-native language: Why non-native speakers' stories seem more vague. *Discourse Processes* 49(7). 523–538. https://doi.org/10.1080/0163853X.2012.698493

Lippi-Green, Rosina. 1997. *English with an accent: Language, ideology, and discrimination in the United States*. Routledge.

Major, Brenda & Laurie O'Brien. 2005. The social psychology of stigma. *Annual Review of Psychology* 56. 393–421. https://doi.org/10.1146/annurev.psych.56.091103.070137

Mazziotta, Agostino, Amélie Mummendey & Stephen C. Wright. 2011. Vicarious intergroup contact effects: Applying social-cognitive theory to intergroup contact research. *Group Processes & Intergroup Relations* 14(2). 255–274. https://doi.org/10.1177/1368430210390533

McGarty, Craig. 2018. Social categorization. In Michael Hogg (ed.), *Oxford Research Encyclopedia of Psychology*. Oxford University Press. https://doi.org/10.1093/acrefore/9780190236557.013.308

McLaren, Lauren M. 2003. Anti-immigrant prejudice in Europe: Contact, threat perception, and preferences for the exclusion of migrants. *Social Forces* 81(3). 909–936. https://doi.org/10.1353/sof.2003.0038

Meyer, Ilan H. 2003. Prejudice, social stress, and mental health in lesbian, gay, and bisexual populations: Conceptual issues and research evidence. *Psychological Bulletin* 129(5). 674–697. https://doi.org/10.1037/0033-2909.129.5.674

Munro, Murray J. & Tracey M. Derwing. 1995. Foreign accent, comprehensibility, and intelligibility in the speech of second language learners. *Language Learning* 45(1). 73–97. https://doi.org/10.1111/j.1467-1770.1995.tb00963.x

Niedzielski, Nancy. 1999. The effect of social information on the perception of sociolinguistic variables. *Journal of Language and Social Psychology* 18(1). 62–85. https://doi.org/10.1177/0261927X99018001005

Niedzielski, Nancy A. & Dennis R. Preston. 2010. *Folk linguistics*. De Gruyter. https://doi.org/10.1515/9783110803389

Osborne, Jason W. 2001. Testing stereotype threat: Does anxiety explain race and sex differences in achievement? *Contemporary Educational Psychology* 26(3). 291–310. https://doi.org/10.1006/ceps.2000.1052

Paladino, Maria P. & Mara Mazzurega. 2020. One of us: On the role of accent and race in realtime in-group categorization. *Journal of Language and Social Psychology* 39(1). 22–39. https://doi.org/10.1177/0261927X19884090

Paquette-Smith, Melissa, Helen Buckler, Katherine S. White, Jiyoun Choi & Elizabeth K. Johnson. 2019. The effect of accent exposure on children's sociolinguistic evaluation of peers. *Developmental Psychology* 55(4). 809–822. https://doi.org/10.1037/dev0000659

Pinto, Isabel R., Jose M. Marques, John M. Levine & Dominic Abrams. 2010. Membership status and subjective group dynamics: Who triggers the black sheep effect? *Journal of Personality and Social Psychology* 99(1). 107–119. https://doi.org/10.1037/a0018187

Porretta, Vincent, Benjamin V. Tucker & Juhani Järvikivi. 2016. The influence of gradient foreign accentedness and listener experience on word recognition. *Journal of Phonetics* 58. 1–21. https://doi.org/10.1016/j.wocn.2016.05.006

Purkiss, Sharon L.S., Pamela L. Perrewé, Treena L. Gillespie, Bronston T. Mayes & Gerald R. Ferris. 2006. Implicit sources of bias in employment interview judgments and decisions. *Organizational Behavior and Human Decision Processes* 101(2). 152–167. https://doi.org/10.1016/j.obhdp.2006.06.005

Purnell, Thomas, William Idsardi & John Baugh. 1999. Perceptual and phonetic experiments on American English dialect identification. *Journal of Language and Social Psychology* 18(1). 10–30. https://doi.org/10.1177/0261927X99018001002

Rakić, Tamara, Melanie C. Steffens & Amélie Mummendey. 2011. Blinded by the accent! The minor role of looks in ethnic categorization. *Journal of Personality and Social Psychology* 100(1). 16–29. https://doi.org/10.1037/a0021522

Rickford, John Russell & Russell John Rickford. 2000. *Spoken soul: The story of Black English*. Wiley.

Roessel, Janin, Christiane Schoel & Dagmar Stahlberg. 2018. What's in an accent? General spontaneous biases against nonnative accents: An investigation with conceptual and auditory IATs. *European Journal of Social Psychology* 48(4). 535–550. https://doi.org/10.1002/ejsp.2339

Roessel, Janin, Christiane Schoel & Dagmar Stahlberg. 2020. Modern notions of accentism: Findings, conceptualizations, and implications for interventions and research on nonnative accents. *Journal of Language and Social Psychology* 39(1). 87–111. https://doi.org/10.1177/0261927X19884619

Roessel, Janin, Christiane Schoel, Renate Zimmermann & Dagmar Stahlberg. 2019. Shedding new light on the evaluation of accented speakers: Basic mechanisms behind nonnative listeners' evaluations of nonnative accented job candidates. *Journal of Language and Social Psychology*. 38(1). 3–32. https://doi.org/10.1177/0261927X17747904

Rogan, Fran, Caroline San Miguel, Di Brown & Kathleen Kilstoff. 2006. "You find yourself": Perceptions of nursing students from non-English speaking backgrounds of the effect of an intensive language support program on their oral clinical communication skills. *Contemporary Nurse* 23(1). 72–86. https://doi.org/10.5172/conu.2006.23.1.72

Romero-Rivas Carlos, Charlotte Morgan & Thomas Collier. 2022. Accentism on trial: Categorization/stereotyping and implicit biases predict harsher sentences for foreign-accented defendants. *Journal of Language and Social Psychology* 41(2). 191–208. https://doi.org/10.1177/0261927X211022785

Rönnberg, Jerker, Thomas Lunner, Adriana Zekveld, Patrik Sörqvist, Henrik Danielsson, Björn Lyxell, Örjan Dahlström, Carine Signoret, Stefan Stenfelt, Kathleen M. Pichora-Fuller, & Mary Rudner. 2013. The Ease of Language Understanding (ELU) model: Theoretical, empirical, and clinical advances. *Frontiers in Systems Neuroscience* 7. 1–17. https://doi.org/10.3389/fnsys.2013.00031

Ryan, Ellen Bouchard, Miguel A. Carranza & Robert W. Moffie. 1977. Reactions toward varying degrees of accentedness in the speech of Spanish-English bilinguals. *Language and Speech* 20(3). 267–273. https://doi.org/10.1177/002383097702000308

San Miguel, Caroline, Fran Rogan, Kathleen Kilstoff & Di Brown. 2006. Clinically speaking: A communication skills program for students from non-English speaking backgrounds. *Nurse Education in Practice* 6(5). 268–274. https://doi.org/10.1016/j.nepr.2006.02.004

Schaller, Mark & Steven L. Neuberg. 2012. Danger, disease, and the nature of prejudice(s). *Advances in Experimental Social Psychology* 46. 1–54. https://doi.org/10.1016/B978-0-12-394281-4.00001-5

Scheepers, Daan. 2017. Intergroup status differences as challenge or threat: The role of legitimacy. *Group Processes & Intergroup Relations* 20(1). 75–90. https://doi.org/10.1177/1368430215595108

Scheepers, Daan, Naomi Ellemers & Nieska Sintemaartensdijk. 2009. Suffering from the possibility of status loss: Physiological responses to social identity threat in high status groups. *European Journal of Social Psychology* 39(6). 1075–1092. https://doi.org/10.1002/ejsp.609

Schmaus, Miriam & Cornelia Kristen. 2021. Foreign accents in the early hiring process: A field experiment on accent-related ethnic discrimination in Germany. *International Migration Review* 56(2). 562–593. https://doi.org/10.1177/01979183211042004

Schmid, Peggy M. & Grace H. Yeni-Komshian. 1999. The effects of speaker accent and target predictability on perception of mispronunciations. *Journal of Speech, Language, and Hearing Research* 42(1). 56–64. https://doi.org/10.1044/jslhr.4201.56

Spencer, Steven J., Claude M. Steele & Diane M. Quinn. 1999. Stereotype threat and women's math performance. *Journal of Experimental Social Psychology* 35(1). 4–28. https://doi.org/10.1006/jesp.1998.1373

Stangor, Charles (ed.). 2000. *Stereotypes and prejudice: Essential readings.* Psychology Press.

Stathi, Sofia & Loris Vezzali. 2020. Vicarious intergroup contact and media vicarious contact: Theoretical, methodological, and practical distinctions. In Loris Vezzali & Sofia Stathi (eds.), *Using intergroup contact to fight prejudice and negative attitudes*, 35–54. London: Routledge.

Steele, Claude M. 1997. A threat in the air: How stereotypes shape intellectual identity and performance. *American Psychologist* 52(6). 613–629. https://doi.org/10.1037/0003-066X.52.6.613

Steele, Claude M. & Joshua Aronson. 1995. Stereotype threat and the intellectual test performance of African Americans. *Journal of Personality and Social Psychology* 69. 797–811. https://doi.org/10.1037/0022-3514.69.5.797

Stephan, Walter G. & Cookie White Stephan. 2000. An integrated threat theory of prejudice. In Stuart Oskamp (ed.), *Reducing prejudice and discrimination*, 23–45. Psychology Press.

Stocker, Ladina. 2017. The impact of foreign accent on credibility: An analysis of cognitive statement ratings in a Swiss context. *Journal of Psycholinguistic Research* 46. 617–628. https://doi.org/10.1007/s10936-016-9455-x

Tajfel, Henri & John C. Turner. 1979. An integrative theory of intergroup conflict. In William G. Austin & Stephen Worchel (eds.), *The social psychology of intergroup relations*, 33–47. Brooks-Cole.

Thompson, Irene. 1991. Foreign accents revisited: The English pronunciation of Russian immigrants. *Language Learning* 41(2). 177–204. https://doi.org/10.1111/j.1467-1770.1991.tb00683.x

Topolinski, Sascha & Fritz Strack. 2009. The analysis of intuition: Processing fluency and affect in judgements of semantic coherence. *Cognition and Emotion* 23(8). 1465–1504. https://doi.org/10.1080/02699930802420745

Tsalikis, John, Oscar W. DeShields, Jr. & Michael S. LaTour. 1991. The role of accent on the credibility and effectiveness of the salesperson. *Journal of Personal Selling & Sales Management* 11(1). 31–41. https://doi.org/10.1080/08853134.1991.10753857

Vaish, Amrisha & Tricia Striano. 2004. Is visual reference necessary? Contributions of facial versus vocal cues in 12-month-olds' social referencing behavior. *Developmental Science* 7(3). 261–269. https://doi.org/10.1111/j.1467-7687.2004.00344.x

Vescio, Theresa K., Gretchen B. Sechrist & Matthew P. Paolucci. 2003. Perspective taking and prejudice reduction: The mediational role of empathy arousal and situational attributions. *European Journal of Social Psychology* 33(4). 455–472. https://doi.org/10.1002/ejsp.163

Vezzali, Loris & Sofia Weil, Shawn. 2001. Foreign accented speech: Encoding and generalization. *Journal of the Acoustical Society of America* 109. 2473–2473. https://doi.org/10.1121/1.4744779

Wenzel, Michael, Amélie Mummendey & Sven Waldzus. 2008. Superordinate identities and intergroup conflict: The ingroup projection model. *European Review of Social Psychology* 18(1). 331–372. https://doi.org/10.1080/10463280701728302

Westheimer, Gerald. 1954. Eye movement responses to a horizontally moving visual stimulus. *AMA Archives of Ophthalmology* 52(6). 932–941. https://doi.org/10.1001/archopht.1954.00920050938013

Weyant, James M. 2007. Perspective taking as a means of reducing negative stereotyping of individuals who speak English as a second language. *Journal of Applied Social Psychology* 37(4). 703–716. https://doi.org/10.1111/j.1559-1816.2007.00181.x

Winkielman, Piotr & John T. Cacioppo. 2001. Mind at ease puts a smile on the face: Psychophysiological evidence that processing facilitation elicits positive affect. *Journal of Personality and Social Psychology* 81(6). 989–1000.

Winkielman, Piotr, Norbert Schwarz, Tedra A. Fazendeiro & Rolf Reber. 2003. The hedonic marking of processing fluency: Implications for evaluative judgement. In Jochen Musch & Karl C. Klauer (eds.) *The psychology of evaluation: Affective processes in cognition and emotion*, 195–223. Psychology Press.

17

SOCIOPHONETICS AND ORAL HISTORY

Silvia Calamai

Introduction: Oral documents as an El Dorado for sociophoneticians

Fieldwork by means of an audio or video recorder is not specific to any single discipline. On the contrary, it is a popular practice across many social sciences and humanities disciplines (e.g., sociology, anthropology, psychology, history, ethnography, and ethnomusicology). In the domain of contemporary history, the subdiscipline of oral history has grown to be an independent field of research, dealing with the systematic collection of living people's testimony about their experiences, and having its own academic journal and associations (Thompson 2000; Descamps 2001; Perks & Thomson 2015). From this respect, oral history appears to be one of the biggest producers of oral data, gathered in oral archives.

In simple terms, oral history collects memories, personal commentaries, and life stories of historical significance through interviews. During an oral history interview, the researcher questions an interviewee on the basis of a well-prepared canvas of questions. The interviews are audio or audiovisually recorded, and the recording is usually transcribed, summarized, indexed, and coded with metadata. Human exchange, dialogue, and mutual confidence between interviewer and interviewee are central to oral history, which in the strictest sense does not include random-sample taping (i.e., recording of casual speech, recording of public events).

Likewise, sociophonetics investigates the social life of voices. Therefore, both oral history and sociophonetics work with speakers in their oral dimension—although in principle an oral history and also a sociophonetics based solely on written documents is possible, albeit little practiced (e.g., Ginzburg 1976; Jaffe & Walton 2000).

Although oral history and sociophonetics work to some extent with different aims, different research questions, and different frameworks and scenarios, oral archives of the past, collected by oral historians, can answer new research questions raised by sociophoneticians. Likewise, there is certainly something in the acoustic signal stemming from a human voice that can be useful for the oral historian to better understand words and silence, emphasis, and hesitations. A voice is a marker of identity, and it is embodied in the physics of human beings. Variation in speech may contribute to expressing solidarity with, or distance from, an interlocutor. Phonetic cues can help in understanding the relationship between the interviewer and the interviewee, how they build the interaction, how the phonetic style evolves during an interview. Thus, spoken materials collected

DOI: 10.4324/9781003034636-19

by linguists can be of interest to nonlinguists, and historical narratives can be used for linguistic analysis. In this regard, oral archives are powerful artifacts, able to strengthen the collaboration between oral history, digital humanities, and sociophonetics.

This chapter investigates the relationships between sociophonetics and oral history. Differences and similarities with respect to fieldwork and data collection, the relationship between researchers and speakers, and the transcription of oral documents are discussed. FAIR principles and issues concerning data reuse are presented to introduce open science principles and challenges. Finally, the potential of a closer cooperation among oral historians, sociolinguistics and sociophonetics, speech technologists, and digital humanists is envisaged, especially in the light of a case study.

Preservation and access: A growing crisis for analog collections

In 2019 UNESCO, in cooperation with the International Association of Sound and Audiovisual Archives (IASA), launched the Magnetic Alert Project, aimed at alerting stakeholders and the general public to the imminent threat of losing access to analog audiovisual documents. It is no secret that a large proportion of the knowledge of linguistic and cultural diversity is based on magnetic tape recordings produced over the past 60 years. Given the rapid pace of technological change, magnetic audio (open reels, cassettes) and video tape formats and their replay equipment are subject to obsolescence and inoperability.

The Magnetic Alert Project survey (see www.iasa-web.org/magnetic-tape-alert-project) is the latest in a long line of surveys aimed at gathering knowledge about audiovisual collections scattered throughout the world. Some findings deserve consideration in order to give an idea of who the major collectors of data in the world are, what the main topics documented in the recordings are, and where the recordings are stored. Firstly, schools, colleges, and universities (34.4 percent of respondents) and libraries and archives (27.6 percent) account for the majority of the respondents, followed by individuals (13.8 percent). Secondly, the most commonly found content categories are "documentary, speeches, and events" (21.3 percent of content), "oral history" (16.9 percent), and "world, folk, and traditional music" (16.2 percent). Crucially, the lack of a preservation plan is a problem across all institution types, but represents a clear issue for individuals: 52 percent of the individual respondents had no preservation plan in place. They cannot access equipment and funding to digitize on-hand physical collections, and they cannot guarantee their safe storage. Collections containing thousands of interviews are unprocessed, analog, and inaccessible. Nobody can ask any research questions of them or offer insights on data previously collected by others. This situation is of course antithetical to the principles of the cross-disciplinary open science movement and scientific data reuse more broadly (Pasquetto, Borgman & Wofford 2019), and also places the vast stores of potential data in a tenuous existence.

The only way to preserve such huge amounts of speech, sounds, and images in the long term, and to keep them accessible for future generations, is their digitization and transfer to safe digital repositories. Once that is done, an El Dorado of data is waiting for sociophoneticians to work on with their research questions, their habitus of analysis, and their quantitative and qualitative tools.

Interviewing: More than a matter of labels

The voice, with its nuances and peculiarities, is central both in sociophonetics and in oral history, with the substantial difference being the role of the speakers and their interaction with the researcher. Considerable space in oral history and sociophonetics manuals is devoted to how potential interviewees should be identified and selected, as well as to the profile of the interviewer.

But as disciplines, oral history and sociophonetics value interviews and the people who take part in them in different ways.

In oral history the speaker is a witness, a "bearer of memory," a source of unconventional knowledge (especially if his/her narratives are compared to an official historical source); the speaker is speaking in the first person, often uttering personal and confidential information. Precisely for this reason, some oral historians use "more active designations like 'informant,' 'respondent,' 'oral author,' and 'narrator,'" instead of the label "interviewee," which instead connotes passiveness, reflecting the ethos that oral history is a collaborative work or (better) "a joint product, shaped by both parties" (Ritchie 2003:30).

In sociophonetics, the speaker is often a "subject" (or a "participant" in an experiment), and they are usually one amongst many other subjects. Moreover, what is uttered during a sociophonetic interview is often (much) less relevant than how it is uttered. For this reason, sociophoneticians tend to analyze short segments of speech devoid of biographical and historical context. The speech which is collected by a sociophonetician is put into a relationship with extra-linguistic parameters (e.g., macro-level social category labels such as age, ethnicity, space, sex, and gender) in order to verify—by means of an experimental design and a subsequent statistical analysis—a particular research hypothesis. Although macro-level categories like social class are sometimes contested in order to investigate variation at the most local level, even third-wave sociolinguistics sometimes seem to disregard stories narrated by the interviewees, focusing on how speakers construct personal and group identity by means of language (Eckert 2012).

Oral history approaches generate narratives collected in an interview format, which can be either life-story interviews (i.e., a number of in-depth interviews documenting the life of the narrator) or topical interviews (i.e., multiple interviews organized around a particular theme or event). From the oral historian's point of view, an interview is genuinely a dialogue between two people, one with a story to tell and another who wants to hear it. The focus of oral history research is therefore on subjective experiences, individual memories, and biographical meaning. Oral history can be used to build community and to foster community development, as well as in several research areas, such as family studies, ethnic history, civil rights, women's studies, labor studies, and contemporary war studies.

The classic approach to interviews in sociophonetics is the "sociolinguistic interview," which was developed by William Labov with the aim of collecting a sample of occurrences of a linguistic variable while controlling the amount of attention language users pay to their own linguistic productions. As described by Labov (1972), this goal is related to "Observer's Paradox," a well-known dilemma of social sciences fieldwork that arises between the desire to record the way people speak when they are not observed and recorded, and the need for the researcher's presence to collect that recording. Almost all sociolinguistic manuals devote space to fieldwork ethics, approaches to entering a speech community, and ways to conduct sociolinguistic interviews through the lens of mitigating the Observer's Paradox. Typical practices are that a sociolinguistic interview should begin with more general questions dealing with the community and progress to more personal questions relating to, for example, dreams, dating, and fear (recall Labov's famous "danger of death" question), followed by formal elicitation tasks such as reading passages and word lists. Because the traditional goal of a sociolinguistic interview was narrowly to sample a sufficient amount of speech in varying contextual styles while also capturing demographic data for speakers, Tagliamonte (2013:37) noted ironically that "a sociolinguistic interview should be anything but an 'interview.'"

While the primary goal of a sociolinguistic interview is to record a sufficient amount of speech along with demographic data for each speaker, an oral history interview aims at collecting memories and personal commentaries of historical significance. In an oral history, "what is said" is much more important than "how it is said." Thus, following the logic of the sociolinguistic interview's construction—that people will speak less "naturally" as they become more conscious of their own speech—oral histories are arguably better positioned than sociolinguistic interviews to reduce the Observer's Paradox. Denis (2016) draws comparisons between the genres, noting that oral history interviews "exhibit Labovian 'casual speech' and high-emotive topics, diminish the role of the interviewer, and [...] contain sociolinguistic variation." Moreover, because oral histories are often organized around a single topic, interviewees sometimes know each other, know of each other, or know the same people; and they frequently use the same jargon and/or share the same professional or local values and reference points. From a certain point of view, it might be useful to consider that the interviewees represent more narrowly defined social categories, such as the community of practice (Strelluf & Gordon forthcoming).

Recording and curating oral archives between past and future

The invention of the portable tape recorder represented a turning point in oral history, and the 1960s and 1970s were a very prolific time for data collection. At that time folklorists and ethnomusicologists, too, were collecting oral sources extensively. Artists, activists, community organizers, and other non-university-affiliated researchers also collected oral recordings to document cultures and perspectives. Among linguists, dialectologists and phoneticians were early to record voices—dialectologists with the aim of documenting disappearing vernacular speeches, and phoneticians with the goal of analyzing acoustic features of speech.

The oral archives that resulted from this initial explosion of recording speech are complex, often multimodal artifacts (as, of course, are collections that have been curated more recently). They usually are made up of analog or/and digital recordings, fieldnotes, personal information about the speakers, and records of informed consent and usage permissions. Ideally, verbatim transcriptions of oral data are also available, and collections might further include materials such as photographs of the interview settings, artifacts provided by the informant, notes on the presence of other people during the interview, and any other relevant elements.

Older archives are sometimes labeled "legacy data," being "recordings made at any time in the past [...] as opposed to new recordings made in the field or the laboratory in the course of a new study" (Bounds, Palosaari & Kretzschmar 2011:46). Those created in the early days of oral history and linguistics were produced under very different practical and legal frameworks from those of today. In many cases, recordings are devoid of contextual information (e.g., the time and the location of the recordings, biographical data about speakers), and ethical and regulatory standards for participant protections, data sharing, and copyright were very different from those of today. Moreover, legacy data were usually collected in analog formats and need to be digitized—not only to assure their long-term preservation but also for sociophoneticians to extract acoustic measurements.

The passage from analog to digital domain is far from being a mere technical affair, since it calls into question the concept of the document itself. The documents contained inside a physical unit (e.g., discs, tapes) often need to be reorganized during the cataloging and interpretation process. One must not forget that in speech recording, fieldworkers used to fully exploit carriers such as open reels, and compact cassettes by using any portion of them due to high costs of the carriers and the importance of the document's transcription and analysis over and above the recording itself. Consequently, a document (e.g., an interview or a biography) can be distributed over various carriers or portions of carriers, so that one and the same carrier may contain various unrelated documents, while more than one carrier can refer to one and the same document. While the "preservation copy"—the object that directly stems from the digitization process—is the equivalent of the diplomatic edition, often the object that is offered to public access is the result of an interpretative activity. The "documental unit" (or "intellectual unit," according to oral history literature; MacKey 2007:16) must be viewed as independent from the carrier(s), to be seen as a mere container (Calamai, Biliotti & Bertinetto 2014).

As recording media have differed across time and among disciplinary approaches, so does what counts as a "good" recording. This is not only a matter of technological improvements since the early days of field recording. Best practices for recording are different from best practices for preservation. While best practices for preservation are ideally independent of a single field of knowledge, best practices for recordings might be partially dependent on the aims of the research. Very high-quality speech is essential for sociophonetics analysis, which makes use of acoustic analysis and therefore needs a "clean" speech signal to capture accurate measurements. Phonetic analysis can be invalidated by poor sound quality, background noises, and nonprofessional recording techniques and equipment. Sociophoneticians will sometimes find the recording quality of the past less than optimal or even unusable, especially if they must deal with restored material. Sociophoneticians working with older oral history data will often need to be very selective about the measurements they collect (see Thomas 2017). On the other hand, sociophoneticians may be surprised to learn that recordings they have collected and consider to be high-quality may actually be too poor in quality for preservation. IASA guidelines (IASA-TC03) are unequivocal with respect to sampling rate (48 kHz for analog originals as a minimum) and amplitude resolution (24 bit), but many sociophoneticians have sampled at lower rates to limit sampling to frequencies and bit depths relevant to speech.

Today, the availability and accessibility of audio and video recording tools make it easier than it has been at any other time to collect oral archives that are technically and informationally usable across a range of scientific and humanistic disciplines. For those who are just approaching both sociophonetics and oral history, it is important to stress that doing the work to create high-quality field recordings undoubtedly represents an investment for the future, generating data that can be reused by others and remain suitable for different projects and collaborations.

Standardizing practices: Data FAIRification in oral archives

In sociolinguistics and sociophonetics literature there has been an extensive focus on fieldwork and interviewing strategies but very few concerns about data management and data's future accessibility (Kendall 2013, 2014). There are many manuals describing interview methods and theories (i.e., the "human" side of the relationship between two subjects), both on the side of sociophonetics and of oral history. Nevertheless, guidance on what happens after the interview has ended is missing. Processing, cataloging, rights management, preservation, and access are relevant tasks which deserve time, attention, and competence. It is no coincidence that oral archives are often neglected in libraries and archives. Both the collecting of new original archives and the preservation of past archives imply some choices: data need to be described, and metadata (i.e., data about data) may vary in scope and format. Consequently, important issues arise as to the correct formats to be used for such data, as well as to the types of metadata used to describe them and make them searchable (Good 2022).

The "FAIR" principles establish best practices to make oral data findable, accessible, interoperable, and reusable. They were first proposed by the Future of Research Communications and E-scholarship (FORCE11) group in 2015 (www.force11.org/group/fairgroup/fairprinciples).

The stated principles are applicable to all fields in the sciences and humanities, and they largely draw on previous initiatives and standards (see Wilkinson et al. 2016). In European contexts, the application of FAIR principles to the social sciences and humanities has coincided with several transnational research projects aimed at harmonizing and systematizing existing and partly overlapping practices in Social Sciences and Humanities Research Infrastructures and at developing the social sciences and humanities area of the European Open Science Cloud (EOSC) (e.g., Social Sciences & Humanities Open Cloud, SSHOC: https://sshopencloud.eu/project). Outside Europe, the Linguistic Data Consortium (LDC) is an open consortium of universities, libraries, corporations, and government research laboratories, founded in 1992 at the University of Pennsylvania to support language technology research and development (www.ldc.upenn. edu/about). The Research Data Alliance (RDA) has an internal section devoted to linguistics (https://rd-alliance.org/rda-disciplines/rda-and-linguistics), with the aim of increasing reproducible research in linguistics, trying also to make linguists more aware of the principles of data creation, curation methodology, and scientific accountability. Chapters collected in Berez-Kroeker et al. (2022) emphasize the value of consistency and a future-minded orientation in linguistic data management.

The FAIR principles provide a discipline-neutral set of 15 criteria that current practices can be mapped onto (see Table 17.1). (See Calamai & Frontini 2018 for a review of current practices in oral archives curation against the background of the FAIR principles, as well as some issues that might slow down their implementation.)

In order to facilitate the reuse of oral archives, it is fundamental to have a management system to track the following stages of curation: processing, cataloging, presence/absence of legal forms, and accessibility (i.e., legal consent forms, restrictions, intellectual property rights, permissions to use and reuse). Legal issues are crucial in this workflow and refer to a bundle of legal transactions: how to transfer the ownership of the interview, how to handle copyright issues

Table 17.1 FAIR principles

TO BE FINDABLE	F1. (Meta)Data are assigned a globally unique and eternally persistent identifier. F2. Data are described with rich metadata. F3. (Meta)Data are registered or indexed in a searchable resource. F4. Metadata specify the data identifier.
TO BE ACCESSIBLE	A1 (Meta)Data are retrievable by their identifier using a standardized communications protocol. A1.1 The protocol is open, free, and universally implementable. A1.2 The protocol allows for an authentication and authorization procedure, where necessary. A2 Metadata are accessible, even when the data are no longer available.
TO BE INTEROPERABLE	I1. (Meta)Data use a formal, accessible, shared, and broadly applicable language for knowledge representation. I2. (Meta)Data use vocabularies that follow FAIR principles. I3. (Meta)Data include qualified references to other (meta)data.
TO BE REUSABLE	R1. (Meta)Data have a plurality of accurate and relevant attributes. R1.1. (Meta)Data are released with a clear and accessible data usage license. R1.2. (Meta)Data are associated with their provenance. R1.3. (Meta)Data meet domain-relevant community standards.

(which are often country-specific), how to access the oral and written material, how to honor any restrictions attached to it, and finally how to manage use and future use (see, e.g., Perks & Robinson 2005; Collister 2022). This suggests a "life cycle" for constructing oral histories:

Phase I. Fieldwork preparation (legal issues) > data collection > metadata description > transcription > analysis

Phase II. Preservation and storage (legal issues)

Phase III. Reuse (legal issues)

This life cycle highlights that legal issues are cross-sectional and ubiquitous, and failing to account for them can jeopardize a dataset. Awareness of this fact allows sociophoneticians to assure future legal compliance as their work is investigated by oral historians, and for oral historians as their work is examined by sociophoneticians.

Transcription: Complexities of capturing what is said

Ostensibly, a transcript is a verbatim version of spoken data—the output of an interpretative process offering a written representation of the content of an audio file. "Verbatim" is not straightforward, though. The degree of detail to be included in a transcription depends on its scope, use, and audience. The relevance of theories and methods in transcription is paramount and cannot be addressed here, since different fields of knowledge address transcription procedures in very different ways. Sociophoneticians, for instance, may work between extremes in degree of detail: orthographic versus phonetic time-aligned transcription (Maclagan & Hay 2011). Similarly, oral historians are not unanimous in defining the role and scope of a transcription, which might be viewed as a record, translation, or adaptation. Dissemination practices also vary from project to project as to whether researchers make recordings available, and whether transcriptions are published or replaced (by detailed summaries or as datasets extracted from recordings).

What is especially relevant here is the role of transcription in oral archives. Initially both oral history and sociolinguistic practices favored transcription over recording. It was not infrequent for the researcher to preserve the transcription rather than a recording. The transcript, not the original recording, was considered the primary document, and carriers were very often discarded or erased and reused. Some had more confidence in the ear of the researcher than in the contraption. These are familiar themes from dialectology; as late as 1967, the Italian linguist Carlo Battisti felt compelled to challenge the predominant practice of dialectologists transcribing data by ear during field interviews, insisting that interviews should be "documented by tape recordings" to "verify an aural phonetic transcription" (Battisti 1967, my translation). Lee Pederson noted (1974:8) that the use of tape recorders in the Linguistic Atlas of the Gulf States triggered admonitions from some phoneticians even in the 1960s (Pederson 1974: 8).

This was not unlike in oral history. Although "it was from technology that oral history was born" (Boyd & Larson 2014b:2), the debate raised among oral history's first generation concerning the practice of destroying the tapes is worth mentioning because it testifies to the struggle and the tension between voice and text, which cross over all the disciplines dealing with the oral dimension of speech (from anthropology to folklore, from linguistics to oral history and sociology). It is no coincidence that oral historians, "custodians of real, living voices, have often been at pains to embalm them in print, to remove the oral from oral history" (Karpf 2014: 51). To a certain extent, favoring the transcription means abandoning a commitment to orality—and therefore the peculiarity of oral history itself.

MacKay (2007:50) summarized the pros and cons of transcription activities. A transcript can clarify unclear sections of the recordings, is easy to edit, provides the correct spelling of proper names, can be used as an index to the audio recording, is easy to handle, and efficient for a person to navigate and browse. On the other hand, a transcript can be misleading (i.e., irony, sarcasm, hesitancy, and insecurity are difficult to represent in the text) and it can discourage listening. Moreover, the transcriptionist might have taken part in the speech event as an interviewer or witness, or might act as a mere executor, and each of these positionalities affects their interpretative process of offering a written representation of the content of an audio file. Additionally, transcription remains time- and cost-intensive to produce on a mass scale.

The oral historian's transcripts really differ from those of the sociophonetician. In the first instance, there is a difference in the level of detail: an oral historian will often leave out hesitations, corrections, overlap, or false starts, or standardize some productions—all of which might be of interest to sociophoneticians (or linguists more generally). Also suprasegmental features (tone of voice, voice quality, speech rate and prosody/intonation) are missing. Nonverbal communication features (e.g., posture, gestures, movement and body position, kinesics, haptics, proxemics) can be present according to the aim of the transcription. On the other hand, sociophoneticians and oral historians deeply differ in their concept of "fidelity." In sociophonetics the speech is the primary source for analysis and it necessitates accurate and consistent transcription. Yet the highest accuracy in the transcription leads to an unsolvable paradox: the maximum level of fidelity to the oral dimension mirrors the minimum of intelligibility (that is, only trained phoneticians can appreciate a phonetic transcription).

Although both disciplines extensively use transcription, a notable difference can also be found in the role of the speaker (the "narrator," in oral history terms). In oral history interviews, the narrator is often in the position of reviewing the transcription, in order to make editorial changes, to clean up the text, and possibly to delete some parts, in case an informant says something defamatory or reveals sensitive information about other subjects. The possibility of sharing the transcription with the speaker has recently been taken into account in the realm of sociophonetics (see Maclagan & Hay 2011:38). In this case, "the transcription conventions used for 'sharing' with the speakers may differ radically from those appropriate for linguistic analysis," thus resulting in two rather diverse objects.

Misspellings in the writing of speech might be considered a sort of routine activity by linguists and folklorists in their efforts to represent nonstandard spellings and social and regional features of pronunciation without using phonetic symbols. Preston (1985) argued convincingly that academic respellings promote negative character evaluations of speakers by readers. In a similar vein, oral historian Alessandro Portelli railed against certain kinds of transcription:

If somebody coughs, because he is choking on a sip of water, you don't necessarily write down that this is the reason for coughing, you just write "cough" (provided you don't think that the cough has been caused by something significant, but then you are interpreting and not merely transcribing). [...] With regard to an interview transcript presented by an historian, it informed me to take notice of the "cough," but then I wondered, "What kind of cough is it?," in other words, what kind of information does the cough reveal? That he suffers from consumption or that he has choked on a sip of water? Or that it is an expression of irony? The only information in this case is that I am reading a transcript of an historian who is scrupulous enough to indicate someone's cough, but does not take the responsibility to tell me what kind of cough it is. This is a positivist approach to transcription, assuming that the transcript is the object, whereas it is only an interpretation, well, then, if you offer me an interpretation, then add a characterization of the cough, if it is merely a signal of choking with no relation to a mood or form of human expression, then leave the "cough" out. [...] There are those things in a dialect that can remain in the written form because the attempt to reproduce the sounds in a dialect is patronizing and always wrong. [...] I learned this from William Faulkner, who said: "If you are from the South you know how my characters speak, if you are not, I'm wasting my time."

Portelli 2008:117, 130, my translation

It seems that both the interviewers described by Alessandro Portelli and the nonlinguists investigated by Dennis Preston share the same set of values on the patronizing effect of some transcription styles. Nevertheless, some kind of transcription is useful in both directions: sociophoneticians working with oral history recordings may generate a new (or first) transcript that can be given back to an archive's holder. The sociophonetic transcripts then support preservation (by creating a written record of recordings) and access (by creating a text record that patrons might search). At the same time, oral historians' transcriptions might be useful for sociophoneticians in order to evaluate whether a certain type of speech merits auditory or acoustic analysis. Furthermore, one should not forget that if recordings have been lost, transcripts represent the only proof of the interviews and of data collection in general.

Using the past to explain the present

Oral archives' key strength is the opportunity for making a linguistic analysis according to a real-time paradigm. It is well known that sociolinguistic research usually investigates language change by comparing speakers of different ages at one point in time, according to the uniformitarian principle and apparent-time hypothesis (see Labov 1994 and in particular his introduction in "The use of the present to explain the past"; see also Boberg this volume). Such research perspectives assume that the degree of differences between older and younger speakers mirrors "the amount of change which has taken place in the dialect between the older speakers' and the younger speakers' dialect formation" (Di Paolo & Yaeger-Dror 2011b:16). The corollary of the apparent-time hypothesis is that an individual does not modify significantly their speech over the course of their lifetime.

While there is widespread agreement in sociolinguistics that sound changes observed in apparent time generally reflect changes that must have occurred in real time, there is also agreement that longitudinal or real-time panel studies provide a truer view (see Cukor-Avila & Bailey 2013 for discussion). However, longitudinal and panel studies are costly and difficult to pursue, since it is challenging to follow the same participants across long stretches of time, or to find among different speakers the very same social characteristics of the speakers recorded in the first fieldwork.

This is where legacy data come into play. Di Paolo & Yaeger-Dror (2011b:17) specifically mentioned archival broadcasting recordings and oral histories—the latter are labeled a "rich source for analysis of real-time data." One of the seminal works using archival broadcast recordings for acoustical analysis is the analysis of the vowel system of Queen Elizabeth II over 30 years of Christmas messages (Harrington, Palethorpe & Watson 2000; Harrington 2006). Broadcast archives have two considerable advantages. Firstly, they are usually of high quality (which is fundamental for acoustic analysis). Secondly, they often include recordings of the very same public speakers stretching over decades. However, broadcast archives also have unquestionable limits, with respect to the social profile of the speakers (very few segments of a population are involved with presenting a transmission), and speech style, which is likely to be limited to a single (probably highly self-monitored) style in any given recording.

Exactly for this reason, oral history offers a rich variety of social and cultural profiles and a huge amount of different topics that might be profitably reused by sociophoneticians. One must not forget that oral history was born in the 1960s and 1970s precisely to give voice to under-represented groups like women, migrants, and victims of racial and political persecutions. The profiles of the recorded speakers are multifaceted and thus very different from the stereotypical nonmobile, older, rural male (NORM) subjects of traditional dialectology that sought the speech patterns of the most conservative speakers. Therefore, although caution is called for (see, e.g., Di Paolo & Yaeger-Dror 2011b:18), the reuse of oral archives by sociophoneticians is worth the effort.

Conversely, the reuse of oral archives collected by oral historians calls into question authenticity, which appears to be a crucial issue in sociolinguistics (see, among others, Bucholtz 2003; Coupland 2014). Obviously, the goal of any sociolinguistic fieldwork is to collect "real," "authentic," "unscripted" speech in order to assess a research hypothesis concerning speakers and their community. At the same time, such unmonitored speech is not always obtainable. According to the Observer's Paradox, speakers might alter their speech in rather different and subtle ways when they know they are being recorded. In addition, speakers might accommodate their speech to that of the interviewer, as the social psychology of language and sociolinguistics has demonstrated. In this respect, oral history material can offer a different perspective on such issues. The collected speech materials were primarily elicited not for linguistic purposes (i.e., collecting personal narratives on a certain historical or social fact) and, crucially, were collected by scholars other than linguists, who were not interested in the speech itself. Oral archives might enhance, indirectly, the authenticity of speech.

Again, the speech materials gathered in legacy archives can be very different in quality and typology, ranging from individual interviews to group discussions, with massive conversational overlap and interruption. Therefore, in a sociophonetic work it is necessary to identify similar speech events and create a representative sample of speakers. Moreover, the unbalanced distribution of tokens is another tricky consequence of working with legacy data. The phenomena that capture our attention can be under-represented, or the lexical frequency can be constrained and skewed by the topic of the interview (see Roller 2015).

Sociophonetic findings from oral histories

In the last few years, there has been much evidence of dialogue between oral history and linguistics. "Oral history meets linguistics" was the title of a 2015 workshop organized at the Freiburg Institute for Advanced Studies. It aimed at answering the following questions:

> What can linguistic approaches to oral history data look like? What challenges and opportunities do such archived data present for linguistic research? In which ways can historians profit from close collaboration with linguists? Are there archived oral history materials currently unknown to linguists that could be useful for future research? Or, concomitantly, what about linguistic data that could be useful to oral historians?
>
> Kasten, Roller & Wilbur 2017:7

Linguists, historians, and anthropologists participated in the workshop, and language documentation research as well as discourse analysis and conversational analysis clearly benefited from such collaboration. On the other hand, sociophonetics as a field was not strongly represented, and few presentations explored the reuse of oral histories for sociophonetic research.

The discovery and reuse of legacy oral archives in the history of sociolinguistics and sociophonetics represents a kind of serendipitous epiphany. Below we give an overview to highlight the revolutionary significance of some rediscoveries (without in any way claiming to be exhaustive). It would be well to remember that i) under-investigated languages are often devoid of oral archives and corpora; and, in parallel, ii) languages with few resources are often endangered or less vital languages. From this respect, open-source technology and co-construction of oral archives with Indigenous communities are an excellent way for mapping, safeguarding, and protecting traditional knowledge. Needless to say, the lion's share of material is in English, inasmuch as audio recordings in English have been available since the first half of the twentieth century and thus complement the written data sources for the recent history of English, as shown in the volume edited by Hickey (2017). Guy Bailey's discovery of the mechanical recordings of interviews with former slaves born between 1844 and 1861 in the Library of Congress and the subsequent publication of the transcripts has made it possible to explore this crucial source of data for the study of African American Language and provide direct evidence on its earlier stages (Bailey, Maynor & Cukor-Avila 1991). In 1986, Elizabeth Gordon discovered the Radio New Zealand Mobility Unit Recordings containing oral histories collected between 1946 and 1948 from the voices of speakers born between 1851 and 1904 (Gordon et al. 2004); this discovery led to the design of a sociolinguistic project on the Origins of New Zealand English (ONZE). The sociophonetic analysis of /t/ and /d/ in the ONZE corpus gave rise to seminal research on the interaction between word frequency, repetition, conversation topic, and speaker age according to exemplar theory (Hay & Foulkes 2016).

It is precisely in oral narratives that it is possible to verify whether frequent words can be exploited by speakers as "loci of style," conveying social meaning and social positioning. The pilot work carried out by Nodari & Calamai (2021) on the degemination of –rr– and –ff– at Elba Island (Tuscany) starting from the analysis of oral narratives among former miners and collected in the 1980s by the oral historian Tiziana Noce showed how degemination was partially correlated to the lexical frequency and social roles of the speakers.

There is also a branch of studies investigating the link between narratives and identity construction in the realm of discourse studies (e.g., Van de Mieroop 2009) where sociophonetics can also offer its own contribution. Life stories and personal narratives elicited by oral historians are rooted in the past but at the same time are performed in the present, during the space of an interview where two subjects meet and speak to each other (De Fina 2000). The friction between past and present and their nonlinear relationships may very well produce interesting effects on the phonetic domain.

Where technology, oral history, and sociophonetics meet

Oral archives represent a digital virtual space in which humanities scholars and ICT researchers can meet and collaborate from different perspectives. On the other hand, automatic speech recognition (ASR) systems are increasingly powerful and they can speed up a process usually considered expensive and labor-intensive such as transcription. There is also an increasing desire to have a transcriptions time-aligned with the audio signal, in order to automatically listen to the audio file while reading the transcription. ASR can relieve scholars from the burden of manually transcribing their oral data. Moreover, ASR together with spoken document retrieval (SDR) and linked data can increase the efficiency of discovery in large collections of speech. At the same time, oral history communities look at ASR systems with suspicion, particularly when use of these technologies requires entrusting speakers' identities and data to commercial services. Researchers have a challenging task in navigating the rapidly changing landscape of ASR technologies. Whisper (OpenAI 2022), for instance, is a multilingual system trained on 99 languages from 680,000 hours of annotated recordings (Radford et al. 2022). Google is working on a competing universal language recognition model (https://sites.research.google/usm/). Outside big tech industries, the LINDAT/CLARIAH-CZ research team is developing speech recognition and other natural language processing technologies specifically for oral history archives (Lehečka et al. 2023; see https://www.clarin.eu/impact-stories/state-art-speech-recognition-understanding-oral-histories).

It was exactly with the aim of bridging the gap between speech technologies and the ethical commitments of scientists working with spoken data that a web portal entitled "Speech data and technology" has grown recently from the CLARIN ERIC research infrastructure through an international collaboration among oral historians, computational linguists, sociolinguists, phoneticians, and phonologists (https://speechandtech.eu/). Several workshops have been organized since 2016. These experts first designed a transcription chain (see Figure 17.1) which was then implemented in the Bavarian Archive for Speech Signals, in order to offer the so-called "Oral History portal" (https://speechandtech.eu/oh-portal).

This transcription portal is meant to facilitate scholars with their audio transcriptions. After logging in, scholars can upload their audio files to the CLARIN Centre BAS, select the spoken language and, if desired, a language model, and then process the files. The results of the processing can be downloaded and further processed. On the website, much information concerning technologies and tools for speech data can also be found. In addition, more software solutions for the work that often occurs after using ASR can be downloaded.

Since sociophoneticians' work is also made of (acoustic, articulatory, perceptual) measurements and not only of (orthographic and phonetic) transcriptions, the application of new computational techniques to legacy data can significantly increase the size of corpora that sociophoneticians can work with. Several software packages (e.g., FAVE, Rosenfelder et al. 2014) automate the process of measuring vowel formants, and they can also be profitably applied to old sound recordings, although the issues related to the problematic nature of vowel formant estimation must be kept separate from technical issues like recording quality and equipment. In this respect, a significant finding is that automated measurement systems that make assumptions about the segments they are measuring can introduce bad measurements if the phonemic inventories in old recordings are different from modern phonemic inventories (Strelluf 2019).

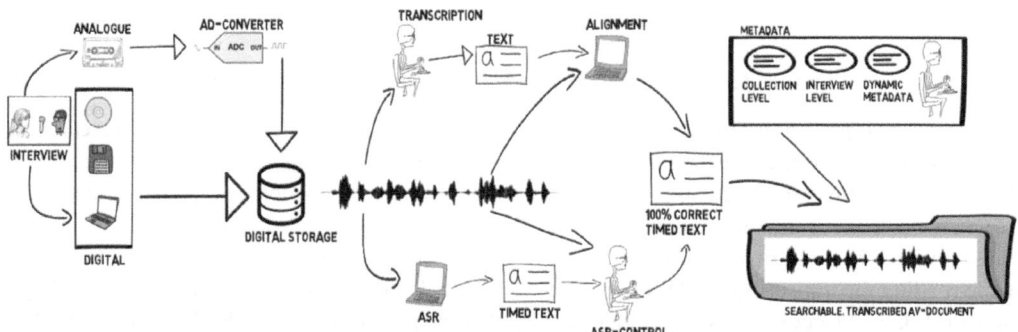

Figure 17.1 The transcription chain

Source: Draxler et al. 2020:3354

CASE STUDY   Vulnerable voices in an asylum

Oral archives have given voices to under-represented samples of people, usually outside the lens of a sociolinguistic investigation. The discovery of Anna Maria Bruzzone's oral archive in Italy is emblematic, since it offered the opportunity to listen to (and also investigate) the voices of people recorded inside a psychiatric hospital, during Franco Basaglia's movement which led to the closure of the asylums. To our knowledge, it is the only oral archive collected inside a psychiatric hospital. It contains the testimonies of 41 patients of the Arezzo psychiatric hospital collected in 1977, and provided the basis for Bruzzone (1979[2021]). The author—an independent researcher, working outside academia—wrote it after a two-month stay in Arezzo, when she spent almost every day in the hospital, attending the general meetings and participating in the lives of the inpatients, in a continuous dialogue of which only a part is collected in the published interviews. The oral recordings on which the book is based were believed to be lost forever. After a long and strenuous search, the original tapes were located in a private home in Turin. These were donated to the University of Siena, together with written transcriptions of the interviews at different stages, showing all the work of editing done by Bruzzone so that the interviews could be prepared for publication (see Figures 17.2–17.3).

Reading a testimony and listening to it from the voice of the interviewee are not the same thing, and Bruzzone herself was well aware of this (Bruzzone 1979:22). Furthermore, the published texts are not the exact transcriptions of the original testimonies; after producing the first, complete transcriptions, Bruzzone had to edit them to make them suitable for publishing. In addition to editing out the speeches so that the interviewees' voices could flow without interruptions, she had to make other cuts and adjustments to make the text clearer or more readable, and she even had to give up on publishing

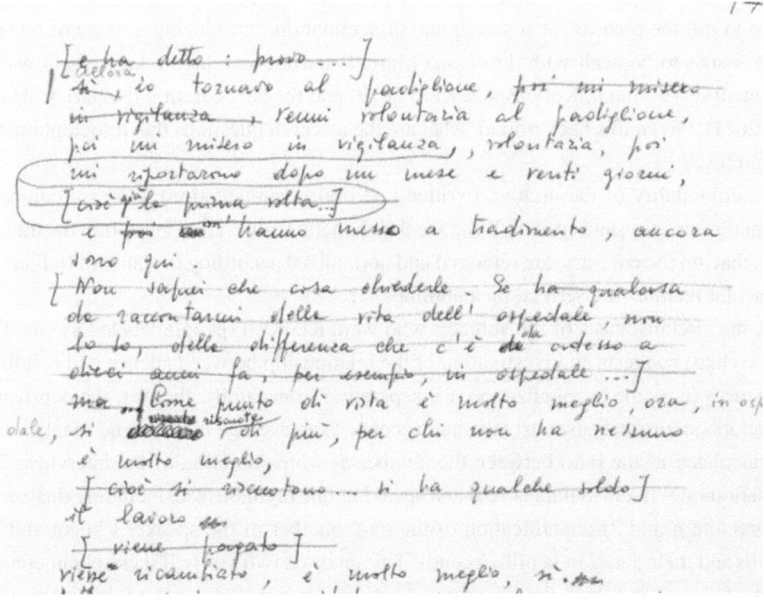

Figure 17.2   Handwritten transcription of an interview conducted by Anna Maria Bruzzone

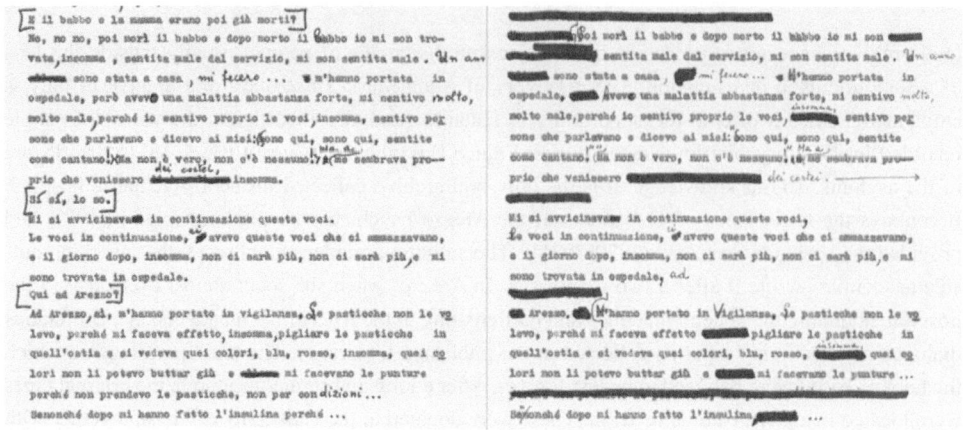

Figure 17.3   Two versions of a typewritten transcription of an interview conducted by Bruzzone

some of the testimonies, because otherwise the book would have been too long. Therefore, having the original tapes at our disposal is of fundamental importance, as it allows us to reconnect the published testimonies to the original ones.

Obtaining and reusing collections of written or spoken data involving vulnerable people (i.e., subjects with mental disorders, or people who have experienced traumatic events) is not easy. Considerable effort (and serendipity) is required, but that is only the first hurdle. Corpora and datasets of pathological and trauma speech are hard to get mainly because they are hard to share. Permission must be obtained to use the records for research and dissemination, introducing a range of technical, ethical, and legal issues to be dealt with. For Anna Maria Bruzzone's archive a legal chain was thus envisaged for reanalysis (Calamai, Kolletzek & Kelli 2019) and for data curation (Nodari, Calamai & van den Heuvel 2021). Given this background, what are the research questions that a sociophonetician can ask of such archive?

Firstly, the multimodality of the archive (written and oral documentation) allows a comparison between verbatim transcription and speech. What are the phonetic features that leach into the transcription and the ones that, on the contrary, are removed and normalized according to standard Italian? How are certain vernacular features transcribed by a nonlinguist?

Furthermore, the circumstances of the subjects who were recorded (people labeled as "mad" and living inside an asylum) suggests an investigation of the relationship between silence and recalling of traumatic experiences (e.g., the hospitalization, the separation from family, the war, the deprivation). To that end, a sociophonetic analysis must take into account 1) an average index of the speaker's "lexical richness," calculated as the ratio between the number of words/duration of the interview; 2) the speaker's articulation rate (fluent syllables/sec) and speaking rate (syllable/sec, including disfluencies, pauses, false starts, etc.); and 3) quantification of the total number of the speaker's silent and filled pauses and breaths and their duration in milliseconds. This analysis will verify if these parameters vary in certain strings of speech in which the traumatic experience is expressly evoked, in comparison to more "neutral" speech excerpts (Calamai & Nodari forthcoming).

Conclusion

Both oral history and sociophonetics face challenges in the twenty-first century. Among them is making the best use of human resources, according to the 2030 Agenda for Sustainable Development. There is an urgent need for standards and best practices, and for the preservation of oral archives as part of our intangible cultural heritage.

While digital technologies are in the position to solve most preservation issues and theoretically there is space to preserve high-quality copies of oral history analog archives, at the same time other dangers have arisen, such as hardware, software, and infrastructure obsolescence, as well as legal and ethical issues. For the former, there are issues on both sides of digitization: loss of equipment needed to access original materials (and degradation of those materials), and future access (e.g., while hard drives seem to be safe now, 20 years ago we would have thought the same about media like CD-ROMs and DVDs). Thus any proprietary digital standard could become obsolete. Moreover, web distribution is totally different from earlier forms of distributions (papers in academic journals, published books), and placing an oral history on the web may have personal, political, and legal implications, allowing unintended and uncontrolled uses by others (Berger Gluck 2014). Indeed, one's voice is considered biometric data (Jain, Ross & Prabhakar 2004; González-Rodríguez, Torre Toledano & Ortega-García 2008), and each initiative must take into consideration privacy issues according to the different national legal requirements for further dissemination of the data. Ethical issues are also potentially raised when interviews are revisited with different purposes than the ones they were collected under (see Bornat 2003; Braber & Davies 2016).

This chapter has demonstrated that a dialogue between oral history and sociophonetics is not only possible but also desirable. The similarities between fields are much more than the differences and, crucially, one of the research achievements they both produce—oral archives—is fundamentally the same. Oral archives represent a training ground for future generations of sociophoneticians, since they offer a pure concentration of challenges dealing with the nature of speech data, their curation, representation, and interpretation, and also with research activity per se (data reuse, ethical and legal issues, sustainability, and accountability of research projects). There is a growing sense that oral archives ought to be more "public" and more accessible than they have been in the past. Achieving this is not only a matter of infrastructure or resources, but also represents a change of mindset. Research on legacy data will definitely raise as many challenging questions as it answers, proving that their digitization and curation is worth the effort for new generations of scholars coming from any field of knowledge.

Acknowledgments

This paper strives to summarize almost 25 years of study and research in the field of oral archives, on which the author worked first as a PhD student and then as a researcher in charge of several research projects dealing with oral archives. The author wishes to express her gratitude to Alessandro Casellato and the Italian Oral History Association, and to her research group (Rosalba Nodari, Duccio Piccardi, Fabio Ardolino, Cecilia Valentini) who in recent years has started working by her side in this field. She would also like to thank the Speech Data and Technology research group inside the CLARIN infrastructure—Christopher Draxler, Arjan van Hessen, Henk van den Heuvel, and Stef Scagliola—for their invaluable discussion on the fascinating world of voices and narratives.

References

Bailey, Guy, Natalie Maynor & Patricia Cukor-Avila (eds.). 1991. *The emergence of Black English: Text and commentary*. John Benjamins.

Battisti, Carlo. 1967. Nuovi indirizzi collettivi della dialettologia italiana. *Bollettino della Carta dei Dialetti Italiani* 2. 55–71.

Berez-Kroeker, Andrea, L. Bradley McDonnell, Eve Koller & Lauren B. Collister (eds.). 2022. *The open handbook of linguistic data management*. MIT Press. https://doi.org/10.7551/mitpress/12200.001.0001

Berger Gluck, Sherna. 2014. Why do we call it oral history? Refocusing on orality/aurality in the digital age. In Boyd & Larson 2014a, 35–52.

Bornat, Joanna. 2003. A second take: Revisiting interviews with a different purpose. *Oral History* 31(1). 47–53.

Bounds, Paulina, Naomi Palosaari & William A. Kretzschmar, Jr. 2011. Issues in using legacy data. In Di Paolo & Yaeger-Dror 2011a, 46–57.

Boyd, Douglas A. & Mary A. Larson (eds.). 2014a. *Oral history and digital humanities: Voice, access, and engagement*. Palgrave.

Boyd, Douglas A. & Mary A. Larson. 2014b. Introduction. In Boyd & Larson 2014a, 1–16.

Braber, Natalie & Diane Davies. 2016. Using and creating oral history in dialect research. *Oral History* 44(1). 98–107.

Bruzzone, Anna Maria. 1979[2021]. *Ci chiamavano matti. Voci dal manicomio (1968–1977)*. Marica Setaro & Silvia Calamai (eds.). Il Saggiatore.

Bucholtz, Mary. 2003. Sociolinguistic nostalgia and the authentication of identity. *Journal of Sociolinguistics* 7(3). 398–416. https://doi.org/10.1111/1467-9481.00232

Calamai, Silvia & Francesca Frontini. 2018. FAIR data principles and their application to speech and oral archives. *Journal of New Music Research* 47(4). 339–354. https://doi.org/10.1080/09298 215.2018.1473449

Calamai, Silvia, Francesca Biliotti & Bertinetto Pier Marco. 2014. Fuzzy archives: What kind of an object is the documental unit of oral archives? In Marinos Ioannides et al. (eds.), *Digital heritage. Progress in cultural heritage: Documentation, preservation, and protection*, 777–785. Springer.

Calamai, Silvia, Chiara Kolletzek & Aleksei Kelli. 2019. Towards a protocol for the curation and dissemination of vulnerable people archives. In Inguna Skadina & Maria Eskevich (eds.), *Selected papers from the CLARIN Annual Conference 2018*, 28–38. Linköping University Electronic Press.

Calamai, Silvia & Rosalba Nodari. Forthcoming. Misurare il silenzio nel parlato dei pazienti psichiatrici. In Francesca M. Dovetto (ed.), *Medici e linguisti IV–Parole dentro, parole fuori*. Aracne.

Collister, Lauren B. 2022. Copyright and sharing linguistic data. In Berez-Kroeker et al. https://doi.org/ 10.7551/mitpress/12200.003.0013

Coupland, Nikolas. 2014. Language, society and authenticity: Themes and perspectives. In Véronique Lacoste, Jakob Leimgruber & Thiemo Breyer (eds.), *Indexing authenticity*, 14–40. De Gruyter.

Cukor-Avila, Patricia & Guy Bailey. 2013. Real time and apparent time. In J.K. Chambers & Natalie Schilling (eds.), *The handbook of language variation and change*, 237–262. Wiley.

De Fina, Anna. 2000. Orientation in immigrant narratives: The role of ethnicity in the identification of characters. *Discourse Studies* 2(2). 131–157. https://doi.org/10.1177/1461445600002002001

Denis, Derek. 2016. Oral histories as a window to sociolinguistic history and language history: Exploring earlier Ontario English with the Farm Work and Farm Life Since 1890 oral history collection. *American Speech* 91(4). 513–516. https://doi.org/10.1215/00031283-4153153

Descamps, Florence. 2001. *L'historien, l'archiviste et le magnétophone: De la constitution de la source orale à son exploitation*. Comité pour l'histoire économique et financière de la France.

Di Paolo, Marianna & Malcah Yaeger-Dror (eds.). 2011a. *Sociophonetics: A student's guide*. Routledge.

Di Paolo, Marianna & Malcah Yaeger-Dror. 2011b. Field methods: Gathering data, creating a corpus, and reporting your work. In Di Paolo & Yaeger-Dror 2011a, 7–23.

Draxler, Christoph, Henk Van den Heuvel, Arjan Van Hessen, Silvia Calamai, Louise Corti & Stef Scagliola. 2020. A CLARIN Transcription Portal for Interview Data. In Nicoletta Calzolari et al. (eds.), *Proceedings of the 12th International Conference on Language Resources and Evaluation* [LREC2020], 3346–3352. European Language Resources Association.

Eckert, Penelope. 2012. Three waves of variation study: The emergence of meaning in the study of sociolinguistic variation. *Annual Review of Anthropology* 41. 87–100. https://doi.org/10.1146/annurev-anthro-092 611-145828

Ginzburg, Carlo. 1976. *Il formaggio e i vermi* [The cheese and the worms: The cosmos of a sixteenth-century miller]. Johns Hopkins University Press.

González-Rodríguez, Joaquín, Doroteo Torre Toledano & Javier Ortega-García. 2008. Voice biometrics. In Anil K. Jain, Patrick Flynn & Arun A. Ross (eds.), *Handbook of biometrics*, 151–170. Springer.

Good, Jeff. 2022. The scope of linguistic data. In Berez-Kroeker et al. https://doi.org/10.7551/mitpress/12200.003.0007

Gordon, Elizabeth, Lyle Campbell, Jennifer Hay, Margaret Maclagan, Andrea Sudbury & Peter Trudgill. 2004. *New Zealand English: Its history and evolution*. Cambridge University Press.

Harrington, Jonathan. 2006. An acoustic analysis of "HAPPY-tensing" in the Queen's Christmas broadcasts. *Journal of Phonetics* 34(4). 439–457. https://doi.org/10.1016/j.wocn.2005.08.001

Harrington, Jonathan, Sallyanne Palethorpe & Catherine Watson. 2000. Monophthongal vowel changes in Received Pronunciation: An acoustic analysis of the Queen's Christmas broadcasts. *Journal of the International Phonetic Association* 30(1/2). 63–78. https://doi.org/10.1017/S0025100300006666

Hay, Jennifer & Paul Foulkes. 2016. The evolution of medial /t/ over real and remembered time. *Language* 92(2). 298–330. https://doi.org/10.1353/lan.2016.0036

Hickey, Raymond (ed.). 2017. *Listening to the past: Audio records of accents of English*. Cambridge University Press.

Jaffe, Alexandra & Shana Walton. 2000. The voices people read: Orthography and the representation of non-standard speech. *Journal of Sociolinguistics* 4(4). 561–587. https://doi.org/10.1111/1467-9481.00130

Jain, Anil K., Arun Ross & Salil Prabhakar 2004. An Introduction to Biometric Recognition. *IEEE Transactions on Circuits and Systems for Video Technology* 14(1). 4–20.

Karpf, Anne 2014. The human voice and the texture of experience. *Oral History* 42(2). 50–55.

Kasten, Erich, Katja Roller & Joshua Wilbur. 2017. Introduction. In Erich Kasten, Katja Roller & Joshua Wilbur (eds.), *Oral history meets linguistics*, 7–11. Verlag der Kulturstiftung Sibirien.

Kendall, Tyler. 2013. *Speech rate, pause and sociolinguistic variation: Studies in corpus sociophonetics*. Palgrave.

Kendall, Tyler. 2014. Archiving and managing sociolinguistic data: The problems of portability, access and security, and discoverability and relevance. *Language and Linguistics Compass* 8(11). 495–504. https://doi.org/10.1111/lnc3.12108

Labov, William. 1972. *Sociolinguistic patterns*. University of Pennsylvania Press.

Labov, William. 1994. *Principles of linguistic change*, vol. 1, *Internal factors*. Blackwell.

Lehečka Jan, Jan Švec, Josef V. Psutka & Pavel Ircing. 2023. Transformer-based speech recognition models for oral history archives in English, German, and Czech. *Proceedings of Interspeech 2023*. 201–205. https://doi.org/10.21437/Interspeech.2023-872

MacKay, Nancy. 2007. *Curating oral histories: From interview to archive*. Left Coast Press.

Maclagan, Margaret & Jennifer Hay. 2011. Transcription. In Di Paolo & Yaeger-Dror 2011a, 36–45.

Nodari, Rosalba & Silvia Calamai. 2021. Degemination in marginal Tuscan speech: Temporal analysis in legacy speech data. In Daniel Recasens & Fernando Sánchez-Miret (eds.), *Production and perception mechanisms of sound change*, 67–85. Lincom Europa.

Nodari, Rosalba, Silvia Calamai & Henk van den Heuvel. 2021. Less is more when FAIR: The minimum level of description in pathological oral and written data. In Monica Monachini & Maria Eskevich (eds.), *CLARIN Annual Conference Proceedings, 2021*, 166–171.

OpenAI. 2022. Whisper: Robust speech recognition via large-scale weak supervision. https://openai.com/research/whisper

Pasquetto, Irene V., Christine L. Borgman & Morgan F. Wofford. 2019. Uses and reuses of scientific data: The data creators' advantage. *Harvard Data Science Review* 1(2). https://doi.org/10.1162/99608f92.fc14bf2d

Pederson, Lee. 1974. Tape/text and analogues. *American Speech* 49(1/2). 5–23. https://doi.org/10.2307/3087915

Perks, Robert & Jonnie Robinson. 2005. "The way we speak": Web-based representations of changing communities in England. *Oral History* 33(2). 79–90.

Perks, Robert & Alistair Thomson (eds.). 2015. *The oral history reader*. Routledge.

Portelli, Alessandro. 2008. Materiali orali e loro aspetto narrativo. In Cesare Bermani & Antonella De Palma (eds.), *Fonti orali istruzioni per l'uso*, 107–136. Società Mutuo Soccorso Ernesto de Martino.

Preston, Dennis R. 1985. The Li'l Abner syndrome: Written representations of speech. *American Speech* 60(4). 328–336. https://doi.org/10.2307/454910

Radford, Alec, Kim Jong Wook, Tao Xu, Greg Brockman, Christine McLeavey & Ilya Sutskever. 2022. Robust speech recognition via large-scale weak supervision. *arXiv:2212.04356*. https://doi.org/10.48550/arXiv.2212.04356

Ritchie, Donald A. 2003. *Doing oral history. A practical guide*. Oxford University Press.

Roller, Katja. 2015. Towards the "oral" in oral history: Using historical narratives in linguistics. *Oral History* 43(1). 73–84.

Rosenfelder, Ingrid, Josef Fruehwald, Keelan Evanini, Scott Seyfarth, Kyle Gorman, Hilary Prichard & Jiahong Yuan. 2014. *FAVE: Forced Alignment and Vowel Extraction* [computer program], ver. 1.2.2. https://doi.org/10.5281/zenodo.22281

Strelluf, Christopher. 2019. Machine-automated vowel measurement, old sound recordings, and error-correction procedures. Paper presented at the First Annual Meeting of the North American Research Network in Historical Sociolinguistics, New York.

Strelluf, Christopher & Matthew J. Gordon. Forthcoming. *The origins of Missouri English: A historical sociophonetic analysis*. Lexington.

Tagliamonte, Sali A. 2013. *Variationist sociolinguistics: Change, observation, interpretation*. Wiley-Blackwell.

Thomas, Erik R. 2017. Analysis of the Ex-Slave Recordings. In Hickey, 350–374. https://doi.org/10.1017/9781107279865.015

Thompson, Paul 2000. *The voice of the past: Oral history*. Oxford University Press.

Van de Mieroop, Dorien. 2009. A rehearsed self in repeated narratives? The case of two interviews with a former hooligan. *Discourse Studies* 11(6). 721–740. https://doi.org/10.1177/14614456093472

Wilkinson, Mark D. et al. 2016. The FAIR guiding principles for scientific data management and stewardship. *Scientific Data* 3. 160018. https://doi.org/10.1038/sdata.2016.18

18

SOCIOPHONETICS AND LANGUAGE DOCUMENTATION AND REVITALIZATION

Marianna Di Paolo

Introduction

As linguists we are well aware that most of the languages of the world are endangered and most of them are also under-documented. The two often go hand in hand. Now at the beginning of UNESCO's International Decade of Indigenous Languages (https://en.unesco.org/idil2022-2032), it is important for us to consider how each subfield of linguistics can substantially contribute to the conservation of the world's languages and provide expert assistance to communities in their plans for revitalization. One of the primary goals of this brief introduction and the following case study is to encourage more sociophoneticians to take part in language documentation and revitalization.

Researchers in sociophonetics may wonder whether our field has anything to contribute to this effort. Stanford & Preston (2009) demonstrate in their 13 chapters on variation in the phonetics and phonology of small, indigenous languages that sociophonetic work on under-documented languages is not only possible but also advances our field of study. Fitzgerald (2021), in her inaugural statement as editor of a new section of the journal *Language*, "Language revitalization and documentation," welcomes papers in language documentation from a sociophonetics perspective. The definition of language documentation she offers is from Himmelmann (1998:166), who states that "language documentation [...] aims at the record of the linguistic practices and traditions of a speech community [... and] may include a description of the language system." Included within this definition are sociological and anthropological approaches such as variationist linguistics and sociolinguistics.

We sociophoneticians may need to be proactive in communicating what we can add to documentation and revitalization. Childs, Good & Mitchell (2014) report that many of the participants in a workshop on sociolinguistic documentation in Sub-Saharan Africa questioned whether a variationist approach (which is, of course, taken in sociophonetics) is of use in the study of their under-documented languages. At the same time, they expressed an interest in the study of registers of their languages. Such a misunderstanding suggests that sociophoneticians working on documentation projects may need to explain how sociophonetic variation may be a vital part of any style/register, especially at the most crucial, unconscious level. (Contrary to the opinion of the workshop participants, the authors of the report, Childs, Good & Mitchell 2014, recognized that variationist sociolinguistics has a part to play in documentation.)

DOI: 10.4324/9781003034636-20

Language documentarians and sociophoneticians share a number of common interests that I have come to appreciate in my work over the last two decades while assisting the Goshute, Shoshone, and other Numic-speaking communities and languages in their revitalization efforts. (The spellings *Shoshone* and *Goshute* refer to cultural groups and *Shoshoni* refers to their ancestral language. The ISO code for the language is shh [https://iso639-3.sil.org]. Numic is the branch of Uto-Aztecan languages which includes Shoshoni.) The Shoshoni Language Project website https://shoshoniproject.utah.edu/ provides information about the scope of work. In the discussion on these shared methods and goals, I will also draw from my collaboration with Adrian V. Bell and Lisa M. Johnson on a project documenting variation in homeland and post-migration Tongan (ISO ton) and our Tongan Ethnolinguistic Corpus.

Currently, data collection methods are very similar in documentary linguistics and sociophonetics, as the methods for both subfields originated in early twentieth-century cultural and linguistic anthropology field methods, and today take advantage of similar technological innovations. Because of the overlap in data collection and corpus creation and management, the corpora of data collected by language documentarians is usually conducive to sociophonetic analysis. Today both documentary linguists and sociophoneticians are engaged in collecting and building digital language corpora of authentic speech from particular speech communities with metadata regarding demographic and ethnographic information about the speakers and their speech community. Documentary field workers, like sociophoneticians, usually capture different styles/registers of language from a variety of speakers. Both also face the challenges and joys of recording in the field, as opposed to a pristine lab setting. To facilitate the creation and use of the language corpora and to automate processes whenever possible—including audio capture, annotation, and analysis—the norm in both of these subfields of linguistics is to produce digital recordings and employ digital tools such as ELAN and Praat.

Although documentary linguists study many moribund languages which may have only a handful of speakers to work with, the usual aim currently is to record as many speakers as possible. For example, at least a dozen speakers participated in recent dictionary projects in each of two Numic communities, regardless of the fact that the speaker base for these language varieties now numbers in the dozens and almost all of the speakers are over 60 years of age. It is also important to keep in mind that there are many under-documented languages that have large speaker bases and are not endangered. Tongan is such a language. Our Tongan project already includes dozens of speakers from communities throughout the Kingdom of Tonga and in the Salt Lake Valley of Utah.

As an example of a documentary corpus, the Wick R. Miller Collection contains about 80 hours of speech recorded from 1967–1972 from over 60 speakers of Shoshoni representing the wide range of communities where the language was and is spoken today. (There are currently over a dozen Federally recognized Shoshoni-speaking tribes.) Miller made very good recordings using a portable reel-to-reel recorder and microphone. (All of the recordings were transferred to high-quality digital format in 2004–2005 with funding from NSF#0418351, PI M.J. Mixco, Co-PI M. Di Paolo.) While most of the recorded speech is of traditional stories, Miller also recorded other styles: elicited word lists and short sentences, as well as unscripted conversations and ethnographic narratives. (For the history of documentary linguists' reliance on recording oral texts based on Boazian practices, see Epps, Webster & Woodbury 2017.) Quite often the recordings were made in the speaker's own home, with family and friends serving as the audience. The collection includes biographical information for each speaker and usually for their family members, as well as notes about the recording environment. Some of the speakers were monolingual or nearly monolingual in Shoshoni and others were bilingual in Shoshoni and English.

Another connection between current practices in sociophonetics and in language documentation is an interest in speech in its ethnographic context. Sociophoneticians seek an understanding of the relationship between variation and change in the sound system of the language variety and the language ideology of the speech community. The focus is unmonitored speech, although other styles are often included. While the aims of language documentation are varied, a successful documentation project has long required building an effective collaboration with the speakers and their community, which depends on understanding the language ideology of the community, including the community's aims in the documentation process. Even in the early days of language documentation, the aim—especially in communities whose language was slipping away—rarely (if ever) was to capture a first-world type of "standard" language, because that concept is unlikely to be a part of the language ideology of most such communities. Likewise, the first goal of a language documentarian of an under-documented language is unlikely to be language standardization. Even if standardization is the primary aim of the community, to achieve that goal various styles of the varieties by various speakers must first be documented.

In fact, in contrast to first-world language standardization as a suppression of variation, the members of Numic-speaking communities I have worked with have as a primary goal to keep the language varieties spoken in their own communities alive. Typically, a young second-language speaker of Shoshoni voices this element of their language ideology by saying that they want to "speak like my grandmother," as opposed to learning a different variety of the language. To assist in meeting this important community goal, the documentation and revitalization work carried on by the Shoshoni Language Project honors all dialects of the language, and has found ways to allow for variation in language teaching materials and teacher training.

In addition, every grammar of Shoshoni I have used, all written by documentary academic linguists usually in collaboration with a native speaker linguist, provides an analysis of the primary patterns of the linguistic structures of the language, including the phonetics and phonology of the language, and lists exceptions, noting possible social or linguistic conditioning when such factors could be determined. Sociophoneticians who wish to work on an under-documented language can develop a variable to study by paying attention to the variation noted in documentary sources. For example, the first variable we will be working on from the Tongan Ethnolinguistic Corpus is /l/, which according to published works has [l] and [r] as variants (Churchward 1953; Feldman 1978; Shumway 2009). Because Polynesian languages are usually reported to have either /l/ or /r/, but not both, depending on migration history, our study may shed light on both language variation and change as well as the settlement history of Polynesia.

Because revitalization needs to be at the behest of and in collaboration with a speech community's desires for its own language, anyone engaged in language revitalization needs to understand the community and its language ideology, and how they are reflected in varieties of language to be revitalized. This is necessary in order to assist with central tasks such as materials development, reintroduction of the language in domains desired by the community, and the choice of formal or informal teaching of the language. To come to understand such a community requires the same sort of ethnographic field work that is required at the start of any sociophonetic study in any community.

While much of the work in documentary linguistics is focused on the language per se, the scholarly impetus for work on an under-documented language may vary. For example, the Tongan Ethnolinguistic Corpus project is an integral part of A.V. Bell's research on Tongan migration and the development of ethnic markers in post-migration communities. Bell invited me to work on his project because of my expertise in sociophonetics, which will facilitate the exploration of possible linguistic ethnic markers.

Sociophonetics as well as documentary linguistics also share a fundamental interest in language change. Among the founding works of sociophonetics is Weinreich, Labov & Herzog (1968). Similarly, the early twentieth-century impetus for the documentation of indigenous languages of the United States is rooted not only in preserving a record of the indigenous languages of the Americas before they disappeared, but also in using the resulting data to classify the hundreds of languages of the Americas into language families via Neogrammarian methods. The use of these (then) cutting-edge diachronic methods on non-Indo-European languages was first shown to be feasible by Sapir (1913, 1914–1919).

Sociophonetics has developed during an era of increasingly available ways to carry on instrumental phonetic studies. Likewise, documentary linguists have taken advantage of instrumental phonetic methods to study the sound system of under-documented languages. In fact, as pointed out in Gordon (2017), instrumental phonetic studies of indigenous languages of the Americas began in the early twentieth century and continue to this day.

With so many commonalities shared between language documentation and sociophonetics it would be expected that many researchers would be working on projects involving both subfields. But that is not the case. What may be preventing such crossover work? In part, it may be that practitioners in the two subfields of linguistics are not familiar enough with each other's work to know that there are commonalities. Without that, interesting problems that developed in language documentation (such as the one posed in the case study below) and which could possibly be the focus of a sociophonetic study will never come to the attention of the sociophonetician (and vice versa).

Another barrier may be that since the current rise of awareness that most of the languages of the world are endangered, sociophoneticians have been increasingly focusing on technological and analytical innovations, leaving little time to expand our sights into lesser-known languages embedded in unfamiliar social settings. In addition, most major advances in sociophonetics have been based on the study of just a few sets of variables in large languages in urbanized, first-world settings. Amassing the kind of dataset needed for sociophonetic work, even from a well-documented large language, and learning the technical skills to do that work takes a very long time. Most young researchers can't afford to do such work without jeopardizing their careers. Practically speaking, a language like English, French, or Spanish is a wiser choice at the beginning of an academic career. The problem that junior sociophoneticians face in developing a corpus to work on and publishing high-quality work quickly enough to meet the demands of academia is analogous to the problem that young documentary linguists face. While the problem for young documentary linguists has been a topic of conversation in academic societies such as the Linguistic Society of America (LSA) and the Society for the Study of the Indigenous Languages of the Americas (SSILA), it may not be as widely recognized for junior sociolinguists.

In addition, those sociophoneticians who have had experience in working with minoritized communities may be more aware than other linguists of the need to give back to the community that provided the data for our sociophonetic work. Assisting communities in language revitalization is a meaningful way to give back to language communities. Working with communities is rewarding to the researcher, but may add another roadblock to the development of a career in academia.

My speculations on the reasons for sociophoneticians to have little involvement in language documentation is not meant to be exculpatory. Rather, I believe that all of us linguists have a professional obligation to act in a meaningful way regarding the loss of the world's languages. While junior faculty may be greatly constrained in what they can do, we as senior sociophoneticians need to be encouraged to use sociophonetic methods and theory to explore a fuller range of languages and speech communities. Possible ways to start include building collaborations with documentary linguists, or supporting their efforts in other ways—minimally by learning about what language documentation and revitalization actually involves. Pushing out of our safe zones of large, first-world languages may allow us to test the universality of our practices and theories about phonetic variation and change outside of the more restricted conditions in which they were developed.

Because this chapter is modeling a novel approach for sociophonetics and for language documentation and revitalization, there is not a large body of literature to cite for precedent. Instead, the chapter is structured as a long case study that will provide necessary background on the language varieties under consideration and the theoretical models being used to interpret the data.

The case study that follows (which is based especially on Di Paolo 2015) is one of the serendipitous outcomes of my involvement in the revitalization of Shoshoni. In developing materials for our Shoshoni revitalization projects, we were forced to make decisions requiring an understanding of the phonetic and phonological variation of the fluent speakers' varieties of Shoshoni. Because none of the documentation of Shoshoni at that time provided clear answers to our questions, we began a series of sociophonetic studies. Unexpectedly, we discovered that the results of those studies added significantly to the diachronic study of the Uto-Aztecan language family and to a general theory of vowel shifts. The case study, an example of language documentation and sociophonetics, reports on that line of research.

By making use of evidence from Present-Day Shoshoni (henceforth, Shoshoni) to support a historical sound change in earlier Uto-Aztecan languages, this chapter is an exercise of the Uniformitarian Principle, the use of the present to explain the past, invoked in the foundational sociolinguistic work of Weinreich, Labov & Herzog (1968).

More specifically, principles of vowel shifts from Labov (1994:113–291; henceforth, PLC) will be shown to elucidate the diachronic development of the vowel system of Proto-Uto-Aztecan (PUA) into the southernmost subfamilies of UA as set out in Langacker (1970) and Campbell & Langacker (1978). These two diachronic studies crucially regarded the northernmost Numic subfamily as having a conservative vowel system much like PUA. The present study then turns to synchronic variation in the modern vowel system of Shoshoni, the northernmost UA language of the Numic subfamily, still spoken in the American West. Both acoustic evidence as well as evidence from dialect dictionaries shows that the vowel shift in Present-Day Shoshoni is remarkably similar to the historical vowel shift reported in Langacker (1970) and Campbell & Langacker (1978). By showing that the modern-day Shoshoni vowel shift mirrors the ancient developments, this study also supports Labov (1989) and Joseph (2006), reconceptualizing drift as stable variation or parallel developments—essentially variation persisting over time.

CASE STUDY   Present-day evidence from Numic for a historical Uto-Aztecan vowel shift

Background

A brief introduction to the Uto-Aztecan language family

Uto-Aztecan (UA) is one of the largest and most geographically dispersed language families of the Americas. It has over 30 languages, now spread over about 4000 miles from north to south, ranging from the northernmost Shoshoni (found today in a range similar to that of pre-contact times in tribal communities in California, Oregon, Nevada, Utah, Idaho, and Wyoming) to Pipil in Central America

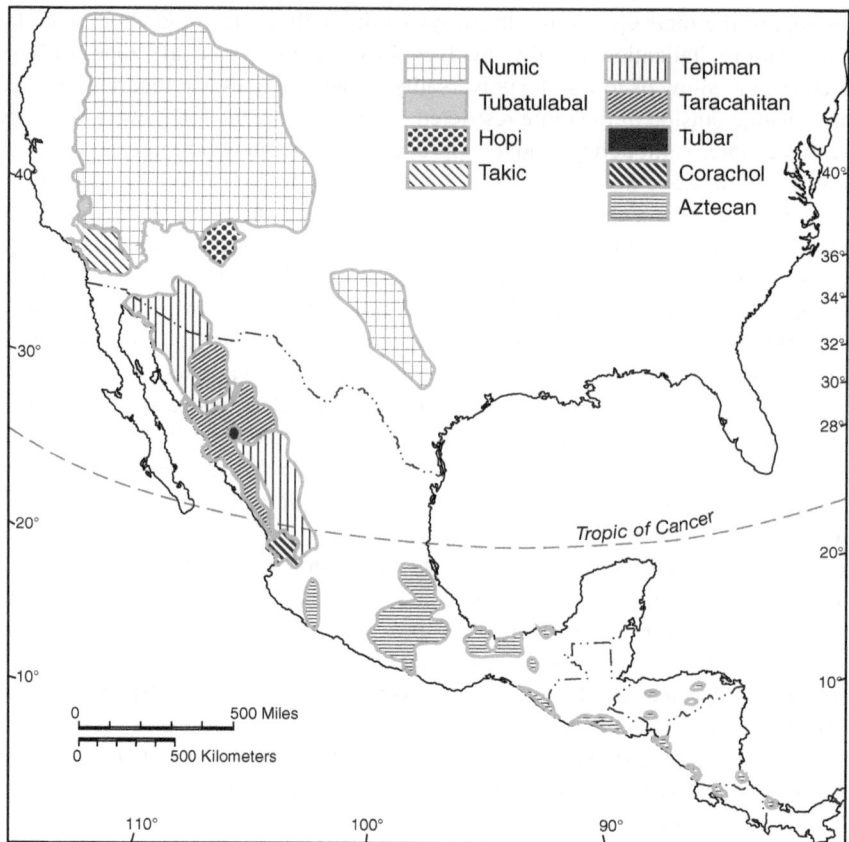

Figure 18.1 Map of Uto-Aztecan languages

Source: "The genetic unity of Southern Uto-Aztecan," by William L. Merrill, in *Language Dynamics and Change* 3(1), 2013. Used with permission of Brill; permission conveyed through Copyright Clearance Center, Inc.

(see Figure 18.1). While most UA languages today are small languages, rapidly losing speakers, Nahuatl is still a robust language of well over a million speakers.

The study of UA languages is foundational to the development of twentieth-century linguistic theory because of Edward Sapir's carefully detailed data collection on key UA languages and his theoretical insights. For example, Sapir's (1933) paper on the psychological reality of the phoneme was based on data from the Southern Paiute consonant system, a Numic UA language closely related to Shoshoni. (See also the original English version, which first appeared in Mandelbaum 1949.) This publication laid the groundwork for the modern study of phonology and, therefore, for sociophonetics. In addition, Sapir (1913, 1914–1919) confirmed the UA language family and showed that the comparative method (innovative at the time) could be successfully applied to phonological correspondences of non-Indo-European languages. (See more on the importance of Sapir's work on UA in Bright 1990.)

Synchronic and diachronic work on individual UA languages as well as on Proto-Uto-Aztecan (PUA) and its branches continue to this day. Relatively recently, linguists have provided evidence that

PUA had two daughters, Northern Uto-Aztecan (Manaster-Ramer 1992) and Southern Uto-Aztecan (Merrill 2013), from which all of the branches of the proto-language developed.

The present study focuses on another milestone in the study of UA, when Langacker (1970) and Campbell & Langacker (1978a, 1978b) addressed an unresolved problem in the vowel system of Proto-Uto-Aztecan (PUA). While there had been general agreement that PUA had five vowels in its short vowel system and that four of the vowels—**i, **u, **o, and **a —were uncontroversial, the quality of the fifth vowel was in dispute. As will be discussed below, Langacker and Campbell & Langacker argued persuasively for ***i as the fifth vowel.

Following Langacker (1970), the vowels in the long vowel series will be omitted from discussion unless their history is particularly noteworthy. This approach allows the complexities of the development of the UA vowel systems to be reviewed within the confines of the present chapter. (Langacker & Campbell's original data-rich articles should be consulted for further study.)

The classification found in Table 18.1 (Merrill 2013) represents a recent classification, reflecting the advances in the understanding of the language family. (For a review of the time-depth for the breakup of PUA into NUA and SUA, see Merrill et al. 2009, in which they argue for the breakup of this speech community at 6900 cal. BC, as opposed to the Bellwood-Hill hypothesis with the much more recent date of ~3500 BC.)

Before moving on to the PUA vowel system and its historical development into the daughter languages and present-day variation in Shoshoni, a brief summary of vowel shift theory is in order.

Table 18.1 The Uto-Aztecan language family (Based on Table 1 of Merrill 2013: 70–71)

Northern Uto-Aztecan

- Numic
  - Western Numic
    - Northern Paiute
    - Mono
  - Central Numic
    - Timbisha Shoshone
    - Shoshone (Sh)
    - Comanche (Cm)
  - Southern Numic
    - Kawaiisu
    - Colorado River Numic (Southern Paiute, Chemehuevi, Ute)
- Tubatulabal
- Hopi
- Takic
  - Cupan
    - Cahuilla (Ca)
    - Cupeño (Cu)
    - Luiseño (Lu)
  - Gabrielino-Fernandeño
  - Serran
    - Kitanemuk
    - Serrano

(Continued)

Table 18.1 (Continued)

Southern Uto-Aztecan

- Tepiman
  - ◦ Upper Pima (Tohono O'odham and other variants)
  - ◦ Lower Pima (Névome, Yepachi Pima, and other variants)
  - ◦ Northern Tepehuan
  - ◦ Southern Tepehuan
- Taracahitan
  - ◦ Cahitan
    - Yaqui-Mayo
  - ◦ Ópatan
    - Eudeve
    - Ópata
  - ◦ Tarahumaran
    - Rarámuri
    - Warihó
- Tubar
- Corachol
  - ◦ Cora
  - ◦ Huichol
- Aztecan
  - ◦ Pochutec
  - ◦ General Aztecan
    - Nahuatl
    - Pipil

Systematic nature of vowel shifts

Based on extensive acoustic evidence from a wide range of languages, PLC (Labov 1994:113–291) proposed a set of empirically verified General Principles of Vowel Shifting (GPVS). (See also Boberg this volume; Cox & Docherty this volume). Here they will be simplified as follows:

I) In chain shifts, tense nuclei rise along the peripheral track.
II) In chain shifts, lax nuclei fall along the nonperipheral track.
II) In chain shifts, back vowels move to the front.

The peripheral/nonperipheral distinction in Germanic languages such as English usually corresponds well to the tense/lax distinction. However, with special consideration of how peripherality would play out in a language family such as Romance without a tense/lax distinction, the large body of evidence examined by PLC suggests that peripherality is best defined relative to the vowel system as a whole for a particular language or language family. The findings also suggest that vowels shift along predictable paths governed by the GPVS, and that within the same language family, the same paths are taken (and may be taken repeatedly) over time. While Labov is reluctant to call the principles he proposes "universal," it is clear that the ultimate aim is a theory of vowel shifts accounting for variation and change across the languages of the world.

The question in this present study is whether the GPVS is applicable to the UA language family, which was not included in PLC's dataset. The results show that the GPVS provides insight into the historical developments in PUA by providing a relative chronology for the elements of the vowel shift, supporting **ɨ as the fifth vowel in PUA, and establishing a UA vowel shift path. In addition, the study shows that variation in one daughter language of the Numic branch, Shoshoni, provides present-day support for the historical UA vowel shift.

In the case of UA languages, some of which have a short-long distinction as well, the focus here will be on the PUA historical vowel shift and present-day variation in Shoshoni in the five-vowel PUA short system, **i, **ɨ, **u, **o, and **a. The evidence that will be presented suggests that **ɨ, **u, **o, and **a have been involved in a UA vowel shift for well over a millennium (but **i has been remarkably stable). The inception of the UA shift begins with **ɨ, which behaves as the only PUA nonperipheral vowel. Following Principle II, **ɨ falls to mid central position. After this first stage and depending on the subfamily, the four active vowels or their reflexes are subject to Principle III shifting and/or Principle I shifting.

The Proto-Uto-Aztecan vowel shift

In light of the GPVS, this section begins with a review of Langacker and Campbell's studies, which crucially posit a remarkably similar vowel shift in different branches of UA. Their studies argue for innovative vowel systems for Proto-Takic Cupan (PTC) and Proto-Aztecan (PA), while assuming that Numic, which is assumed to have retained **ɨ, serves as a conservative counterpoint. In the next section, the notion that Numic retains a conservative vowel system is challenged by results of acoustic studies of present-day Shoshoni and Comanche, which indicate that the UA vowel shift characterizes synchronic variation of Numic languages today.

The two likely contenders for the fifth vowel of PUA were **ɨ and **e. While a roughly equal number of the daughter languages had either **ɨ or **e, the high central vowel was disfavored for two reasons. First, it is highly marked, while /e/ is universally unmarked. (Marked phonemes have a much lower probability of occurrence in languages of the world than unmarked ones. Studies of language universals have shown that /i e a o u/ are the most likely vowels to occur in languages, and thus they are unmarked. Unmarked linguistic elements tend to be favored in historical change and child language.) Second, a five-vowel system with **ɨ rather than **e was oddly shaped, with an unusual ratio of central and back vowels to front vowels (see Figure 18.2). Nevertheless, Langacker (1970) argued convincingly that **ɨ led to a more plausible vowel shift, which was necessary to produce the daughter-language reflexes of the fifth vowel for Takic Cupan (TC) languages in particular. (In the earlier Langacker and Campbell studies cited here, *Takic* refers only to Cahuilla, Cupeño, and Luiseño, the languages that Table 18.1 now shows to be the Cupan branch of Takic. For purposes of clarity to a

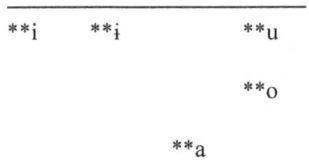

Figure 18.2 The PUA short vowel system posited in Langacker (1970)

1) Stages 1 and 2: Proto-Takic Cupan vowel shift to Cahuilla, Cupeño, and Luiseño
The two elements of the shift in Stage 2 are unordered with respect to one another, but both must precede Stage 3 because for Ca Stage 2a bleeds Stage 3, and for Lu Stage 2b feeds Stage 3:

Stage 1: Ca, Cu, Lu **o > *ə > *ŏ > e
Principle III. In chain shifts, back vowels move to the front.

Stage 2a: Ca, Cu e > i
Principle I. In chain shifts, tense nuclei rise along the peripheral track.
Stage 2b: Ca, Cu, Lu **ɨ > ə
Principle II. In chain shifts, lax nuclei fall along the nonperipheral track.

2) **Stage 3a: Lu ə > o**
Possibly explained by
Principle III′. In chain shifts, tense vowels move to the front along peripheral paths, and lax vowels move to the back along nonperipheral paths.

Stage 3b: Ca ə > *ŏ > e
Not obviously predicted by PLC's principles, but may be
Principle III. In chain shifts, back vowels move to the front.

**ɨ	**ɨ	**u
2b Ca, Cu i (<**o)	↓2a Ca, Cu, Lu	
1 Lu e (<**o) ←1 *ŏ	←1 *ə	←1 Ca, Cu, Lu **o
↑2b Ca, Cu *e		
	2a Cu ə (<**ɨ)	
3 Ca e (< *ə <**ɨ) ←←←3 Ca *ŏ	←3 Ca *ə—3 Lu *ə→ 3 Lu→→→	3 Lu o (<*ə <**ɨ)
	**a	

Figure 18.3 Temporal order of the Takic Cupan shift

wide range of readers, these three languages will be referred to in the present work as "Takic Cupan" or TC.)

Beginning with the findings from Langacker (1970), three ordered stages can be established for the vowel shift that led from PUA to the Takic Cupan languages, described below and shown in Figure 18.3. This temporal ordering is built on evidence from Langacker (1970) and evidence of bleeding or feeding relationships found in that data, as well as from the theoretical framework provided by the GPVS and the principle that two vowels cannot occupy the same space in the vowel system without merging irreversibly. Given these criteria, the stages are assigned the lowest possible number. For the sake of brevity, long vowels are excluded from the exposition unless their behavior differs from the corresponding short vowels. Additionally, minor patterns are excluded unless Langacker and Campbell & Langacker found clear phonological conditioning.

Langacker actually posited **ɨ > *ŏ > e rather than **ɨ >*ə > e, probably on the basis of Hopi, which does have /ŏ/ as the reflex of **ɨ. Campbell & Langacker (1978a) recognized that /ə/ is more likely as the intermediate stage in order to account for Cahuilla /e/ and Luiseño /o/, as well as the more conservative Cupeño /ə/. In addition, the GPVS also support *ə. Here, *ö and the more likely *ə are both included to indicate that the shift in the various UA branches and languages usually follow a similar path and that vowel shifts tend to occur gradually in the F1 or F2 dimensions.

The by-product of positing these separate, ordered elements to the changes in the Takic Cupan vowels is that the framework not only accounts for the Takic Cupan vowel system but also for the Hopi /ö/. In addition, it also suggests that the basic principle of the UA vowel shifts is that nonperipheral vowels become peripheral by following the GPVS. In UA, they do so most commonly by fronting.

However, because Hopi o < **u resulted from a tense vowel that lowered, it is problematic for the GPVS and for the UA vowel shift framework that is beginning to emerge from Figure 18.3. In contrast, for a relatively post hoc, general, unprincipled theory of sound change in which vowel shifts are unpredictable, o < **u is not problematic.

The framework continues to fare well as we move on to Campbell and Langacker (1978a, 1978b), which show that positing **i along with a subsequent vowel shift paralleling that of Takic Cupan also accounts for the vowel system of Southern Uto-Aztecan (SUA) languages. In particular, they focus on Proto-Aztecan (PA) and one of its daughters, Pochutec (Po), a now extinct language known primarily from the data collected by Franz Boas from the last speakers in 1912. (While no method for the determination of a time-depth for Proto-Aztecan and its splitting into General Aztecan and its coordinate, Pochutec, is without problems, these splits may have taken place from about 500–800 AD; Campbell & Langacker 1978a:fn. 4.) Before Campbell & Langacker's work, the Pochutec vowel system had posed a problem for the reconstruction of the proto-language.

Considering Campbell & Langacker's results for only Classical Nahuatl and Pipil (to keep the discussion here manageable) and the theoretical framework, there were two stages in the vowel shift from PUA to PA, resulting in a skewed vowel system with two central vowels PA **i and **ə, as shown in Table 18.2. The PA to General Aztecan (GA) changes must have also taken place in two ordered stages because PUA > PA > GA Stage 2 must be in a bleeding relationship with PUA > PA > GA > Pi Stage 3 (Figure 18.4).

The GPVS is a very good predictor of the stages of the PA vowel shift to its GA daughter languages. Notably, Principle II predicts Stage 2 from PUA > PA > GA, which is the high vowel equivalent of the Takic Cupan Stage 1 mid vowel change **o > *ə > *ö > e. However, what the GPVS does not predict is that the lowering path taken in Stage 1 by ***i (the same path as Stage 2a+3 of the development from Takic Cupan to Cahuilla) differs from the fronting path taken in Stage 2 by **i. The evidence suggests that the path taken is i > ə if there is no /ə/, and otherwise i > i. The question then is why mergers to /ə/

Table 18.2 Proto-Uto-Aztecan to Proto-Aztecan, and to General Aztecan and Pipil

PUA > PA > GA > Pi	*PUA >*	*PA >*	*GA*	*> CN*	*> Pi*
	***i	**i	i	i	i
	***a	**a	a	a	a
Stage 1 (PUA > PA)	***i >	**ə >	e	e	e
Stage 2 (PUA > PA)	***u >	**i >	i	i	i
Stage 3 (PUA > PA > GA > Pi)	***o >	**o	*o	o	> u

PUA > PA > GA
Stage 1: ***ɨ > **ə
 Principle II. In chain shifts, lax nuclei fall along the nonperipheral track.
  **ə > e is not obviously predicted by PLC's principles, but may be:
   Principle III. In chain shifts, back vowels move to the front.

Stage 2: ***u > **ɨ > i
Principle III. In chain shifts, back vowels move to the front.

GA > Pi
Stage 3: *o > u
Principle I. In chain shifts, tense nuclei rise along the peripheral track.

***ɨ		↓1 PA ***ɨ		
2 GA i (<**u)	←2 PA	2 PA **ɨ	←	← 2 PA ***u
				3 Pi u (< ***o
1 GA e (<***ɨ)	←1 GA *ö	1 PA **ə (< **ɨ)		↑3 GA ***o
			**a	

Figure 18.4 Temporal order of the General Aztecan shift

are avoided. Perhaps mergers to nonperipheral vowels are disfavored in UA, a prohibition not found in a language such as English. An alternative possibility is that the vowel system just before Stage 1 differs in some crucial way from the system that is in place when Stage 2 begins. Although phonetic data from the proto-languages are obviously not available to help us untangle this mystery, the hope is that our present-day work on existing languages from the UA family or from other language families can help us to solve it.

   Next we turn to the more complex set of changes that led from PA > Pochutec, but which for the most part are remarkably similar to the elements of the UA shifts already discussed. As is shown in Table 18.3, almost every one of the elements of the Pochutec shift is phonologically conditioned, as opposed to the other elements of UA language shifts described above. In this ordering, the same two stages for GA also apply to Pochutec, but the subsequent Pochutec changes are more complex. Stage 5 begins the process again, to right the unstable new ɨ.

   Although Campbell & Langacker state that the reflex of PA **ɨ (< PUA ***u) and the original PA *ə merged, merger cannot explain why just the reflexes of PA *ə (< PUA ***ɨ) were subject to the phonological conditioning in the evidence they presented. The ordering of the elements of the shift shown here indicates that the two original word classes remained distinct in the first stages of the development of Pochutec.

   While there are more changes from PA > Pochutec than from PA > GA, they are largely similar to those from PUA > PA. Both Pochutec and Pipil had PA **o > *u, Pipil as Stage 3 and Pochutec as Stage 1. The elements of the shift that led to the Pochutec vowel system are also similar to those within Takic Cupan. The notable exception is that PA **ə split, resulting in a Pochutec /o/ reflex (as in Luiseño) and a Pochutec /e/ reflex (as in Cahuilla), as well as loss of the segment under other phonological conditions.

Table 18.3 Proto-Uto-Aztecan to Proto-Aztecan, and to Pochutec

	PUA	PA >	Po	Phonological conditioning, if any	Applicable principle
	***i	**i	i		
Stage 1a	***i >	**ə			Principle II
Stage 1b	***a	**a >	e	Except before saltillo	Principle I
Stage 2a	***u >	**ɨ	—		Principle III
Stage 2b	***aa	**aa >	a	—	—
Stage 3a	***o	**o >	u	Usually only raises if *ow or if *o adjacent to saltillo	Principle I
Stage 3b	***oo	**oo >	u	Perhaps inhibited by adjacent /m/	Principle I
Stage 4a	(***i)	**ə >	o	Stressed	Principle III'
Stage 4b	(***i)	**ə >	Ø	Unstressed	—
Stage 4c	(***i)	**ə >	e	Word-initial and before saltillo	Principle III
Stage 5	(***u)	**ɨ >	*ə > o	—	Principle II + Principle III'

Source: Campbell & Langacker 1978a:97

Table 18.4 Proto-Uto-Aztecan to Proto-Corachol

PUA > PC	PUA >	PC	Applicable principle
	***i	i	
	***a	a	
Stage 1	***i >	(*ə >) e	Principle II +?Principle III
Stage 2	***u >	ɨ	Principle III
Stage 3	***o >	u	Principle I

Source: adapted from Campbell & Langacker 1978a:102

Interestingly, as shown in Table 18.4, Campbell & Langacker's work shows that the PUA > Proto-Corachol (PC) Vowel Shift makes use of the same paths for the same PUA vowels; most noteworthy is the lowering and fronting of ***i. Again, Stage 1 of PUA > PC is the same as Stage 1 of PUA > PA > GA.

The same exact path accounts for the Taracahitan vowel system, perhaps the most conservative of the SUA subfamilies. It is represented by Yaqui in Langacker (1970), shown in Table 18.5.

As suggested in Campbell & Langacker, ***i > **ə is the core element of the UA shift. It appears in the development of the vowel systems of the Takic branch of NUA, as well as the SUA branches Aztecan, Corachol, and Taracahitan. (The historical development of Tepiman's vowel system is not at issue; according to the data in Langacker, it is identical to that posited for PUA. Tubar is not included in his study.) Because both NUA and SUA are involved, this core element may be quite old. In addition, the i > ə element may reapply within the subfamily, as in PA > Pochutec Stage 5. While ***i > **ə resolves the problem of the highly marked, nonperipheral ***i, it produces another problem of having **ə in a four- to five-vowel system. The resolution is either fronting to /e/ (the most common path) or backing to /o/; either path results in a peripheral vowel and produces a symmetrical vowel system. The pervasiveness of the i > ə > e path indicates one relatively unified

Table 18.5 Proto-Uto-Aztecan to Yaqui

PUA > PT	PUA >	PT (Yaqui)	Applicable principle
	***ɨ	i	
	***u	u	
	***o	o	
	***a	a	
Stage 1	***ɨ >	(*ə >) e	Principle II +?Principle III

Source: adapted from Langacker 1978

UA vowel shift played out over the course of centuries. It not only presents strong evidence for /ɨ/ as the fifth vowel, but also points to /ɨ/ as the source of the instability in the relatively small UA vowel system. The instability associated with /ɨ/ is predictable if it is theorized to be a nonperipheral vowel in UA, taking into account the discussion on the peripherality of /ɨ/ in PLC (Labov 1994:177, 231) and the GPVS.

The Langacker and Campbell studies relied on the diachronic methods of comparative reconstruction along with theoretically plausible sound changes. We now turn to synchronic sociophonetic evidence from variation found in Shoshoni, a Numic language. The Numic languages were represented by Comanche in Langacker (1970) and Campbell & Langacker (1978). The data they used suggested that Comanche (and by extension the other Numic languages) had /ɨ/ as the reflex of the fifth vowel, and were therefore conservative representatives of the original PUA system. In contradiction, acoustic evidence from Shoshoni indicates that the UA vowel shift is variably expressed in its synchronic vowel system.

Shoshoni

Shoshoni is the northernmost language of Numic, the northernmost subfamily of UA. It is closely related to Timbisha (aka Tümpisa or, previously, Panamint) and Comanche. Shoshoni today is still spoken by about 2500 speakers from tribal communities in California, Nevada, Utah, Idaho, and Wyoming. For an American Indian language, it is fairly well documented. (See https://shoshoniproj ect.utah.edu/ for more on the documentation.) Variation in Shoshoni has been documented in its various dialect dictionaries, in its grammars (usually dialect-specific), and in the extensive audio recordings found in Wick R. Miller Collection collected in the 1960s and 1970s. Miller (1970) reported that various regional dialects were spoken in the same community, in part, due to traditional marriage patterns. In addition, the post-contact displacement from loss of foraging and hunting ranges led to migration across dialect boundaries along with the subsequent forced reservation system. As is the case for other indigenous people of North America, the boarding schools wreaked havoc on the Shoshoni language. The result today is widespread dialect contact, loss of domains, and a diminishing speaker base.

Present-day variation in the Shoshoni vowel system

Shoshoni has a six-vowel short vowel system: i < ***i, ɨ < ***ɨ, u < ***u, o < ***o, a < ***a, and /eɪ/. As to the latter vowel, the reconstructions of Proto-Central Numic provided by Miller, Elzinga &

McLaughlin (2005), the review presented in Mitchell (2012), and our acoustic studies suggest that *a > ai > eɪ, with [ai] still in variation with [eɪ] although the phonological and social conditioning factors are unknown (Di Paolo 2006, 2007, 2013, 2015; Di Paolo, Sykes & Mitchell 2008; Di Paolo & Sykes 2010). What is important for the present study is that Shoshoni (and Comanche) /e/ is not a reflex of PUA ***i̵ or of Proto-Numic (PN) **i̵. Interestingly, the path *a > ai > eɪ is similar to PA > Pochutec Stage 1b.

In addition to these short vowels, all the grammars of Shoshoni report a long vowel series as well. However, the phonological contrast between the short and long vowels is not robust. (See Mitchell 2012 for a discussion of some of the issues.) Furthermore, vowel length is made opaque by the phonological lengthening of short vowels in stressed syllables, which results in variable spelling by speakers and linguists. Here, only the short vowels systematically documented as short will be under consideration.

Next we turn to acoustic evidence for a Shoshoni vowel shift that parallels the UA vowel shifts in the southernmost subfamilies reviewed above. Following that, we present corroborating evidence from entries in a pan-dialect database comprised of lexicons from a wide range of Shoshoni varieties, some compiled by speakers themselves.

Methods

One of the issues that comes with working on variation in a language that has not been standardized is how to ensure accountability to the data. While the question is rarely discussed in sociophonetic studies of English (though see also Methrie et al. this volume), establishing word class membership in an under-documented language is no trivial matter. What do we do to establish word classes in a language that has not had a long written tradition and has not undergone standardization? In our work, we have decided to use the largest and possibly best-edited published dictionary of Shoshoni: that of Crum, Crum & Dayley (2001; CCD), produced by native speakers, Beverly and Earl Crum, and Jon Dayley, a linguist with deep knowledge of Numic languages. (To access this and other Shoshoni dictionaries and lexicons online, see https://shoshoniproject.utah.edu/language-materials/shoshoni-dictionary/.) In so doing, we are in some way treating the varieties from the Duck Valley Reservation from the latter half of the twentieth century that this dictionary is based on as the touchstone. However, the reader is cautioned that we are by no means claiming or even considering that other varieties of Shoshoni descended from those found in Duck Valley. It merely serves as a stable reference point. As such, when CCD showed variation in the pronunciation of a stem morpheme in a word under consideration, the word was omitted from our dataset. Otherwise, the vowel that appears in CCD was used to code the word. When the stem morpheme was not found in CCD, it was checked against entries from similar dialects found in our electronic dictionary of 30,000+ words.

Another methodological issue needing consideration in working with under-documented languages is that of dataset size. In recent years, the datasets for sociophonetic studies have grown exponentially, facilitated by improvements in data capture, transcription, automated processing of acoustic features, and sophisticated statistical analysis. Such advancements have been mostly available to researchers working on large, already well-documented languages. In the case of under-documented languages, there are often certain limitations: many fewer speakers, often elderly, and fewer funding resources for research beyond basic grammars or language revitalization materials. However, none of these should deter sociophoneticians from doing what is possible to contribute to a deeper understanding of variation in all languages, including Native American languages.

The first set of data used in the acoustic study comes from legacy recordings of oral histories and traditional stories from the Wick R. Miller Collection (WRMC). (See https://shoshoniproject.utah.edu/language-materials/wick-r-miller-collection.php for more details.) The narrators included in this study were early childhood monolinguals in Shoshoni, who acquired English in later childhood (if at all). They were chosen to represent the speech of four neighboring dialects of the language. The choice of speakers for the study covers much of the Central Numic portion of the Numic fan, which reflects the migration of the people some 1500 years ago from the southern apex to the northwest and northeast (see Figure 18.5). To control for gender, only females were included. All four women were born within a few years of one another, at a time when many Shoshone and Goshute people were monolingual and the language was still used in the home. All four married men from their own dialect area. Table 18.6 summarizes demographic information about the speakers and the following map shows their home communities.

The norm for choosing tokens for studies of English vowels is to only measure monosyllabic words (Di Paolo & Yaeger-Dror 2011). However, that would be too limiting for Shoshoni, an agglutinative language with few monosyllabic words. Instead, the tokens were taken from stressed, voiced syllables in which the adjacent consonants were not nasals, /ʔ/, or /h/. (Shoshoni does not have liquids. Vowels may be phonologically voiceless.) Demonstrative pronouns such as *suten*, *suttu*, and *sukkuh*, which are very common in narratives, were limited to one token per speaker. Table 18.7 lists all of the vowels included. They comprise all of the short monophthongs and /e/, which ranges from [aɪ]-[ɛɪ]~[eɪ] but functions phonologically as a short vowel.

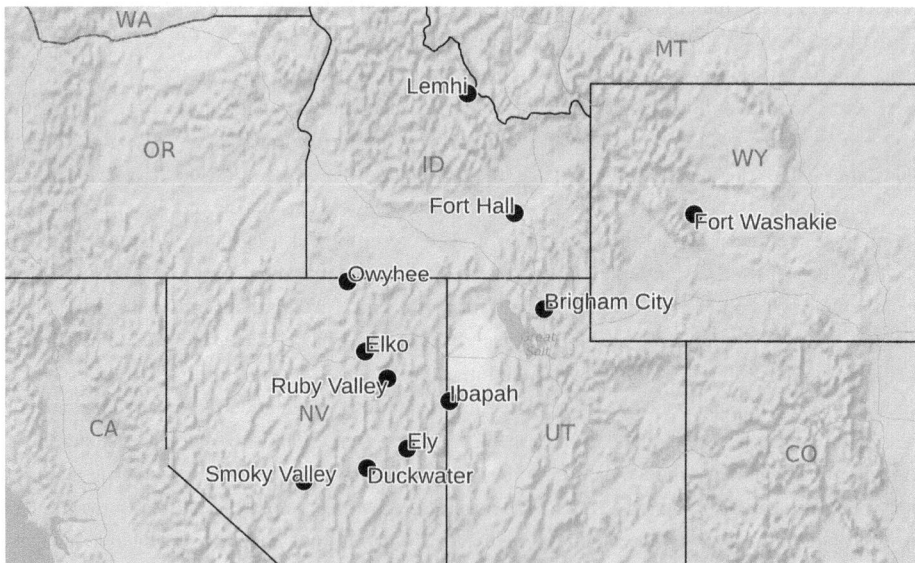

Figure 18.5 Home communities of the Shoshoni speakers

Table 18.6 Speakers and segments: Legacy speakers from the Wick R. Miller Collection

Speaker	Access # of audio	Length (min:sec)	Title
Martha Hooper Duck Valley Shoshone-Paiute Reservation Western Shoshoni b. 1906, Owyhee, NV	WRMC_073_01 WRMC_073_02	10:41 3:10	Traditional story: Coyote marries his daughter Traditional story: Tso'apittseh
Molly McCurdy Confederated Tribes of the Goshute Reservation Goshute dialect of Shoshoni b. 1908, Ibapah, UT	WRMC_160_01	12:39	Oral history: Upper reservation, the soldier's camp
Florence Garcia Northwestern Band of the Shoshone Northwestern Shoshoni b. 1912, Brigham City, UT	WRMC_051_01 WRMC_052_01	5:28 18:30	Oral history: parade in Washakie Elicitation session
Sadie Ariwite Ft. Hall Shoshone-Bannock Reservation Lemhi (Northern) Shoshoni b. 1912, near Blackfoot, ID	WRMC_113_02 WRMC_114_04	4:32 20:06	Traditional story: Coyote and Mountain Goat Traditional story: Otter, Weasel, and nenemmusi

Note. Western Shoshoni is probably the most common dialect spoken in Duck Valley, with many of the original settlers coming from Ruby Valley. Western Shoshoni was and is the dialect of most of Eastern Nevada, adjacent to the Gosiute dialect.

For each token of the targeted vowels, F1 and F2 measurements were automatically taken at 20 percent, 50 percent, and 80 percent using a Praat (Boersma & Weenink 2022) script developed by Tyler Kendall and modified by Robert Sykes. Here only the results of the normalized midpoints and plots made using NORM vowel normalization and plotting suite (Thomas & Kendall 2007) will be reported.

Results

Vowel system of the legacy speakers

Table 18.7 presents the normalized F1 and F2 means of all tokens extracted from the recordings for each speaker for this study. At the time we conducted this study, the counts for each speaker for almost all vowels were fairly high, especially for a dataset from an under-documented language. Each speaker's distribution of tokens of vowels is plotted in Figure 18.6.

Table 18.7 Midpoint normalized means per vowel of WRMC legacy speakers

Vowel	Molly McCurdy			Martha Hooper			Florence Garcia			Sadie Ariwite		
	n	*F1*	*F2*	*N*	*F1*	*F2*	*n*	*F1*	*F2*	*n*	*F1*	*F2*
i	8	376.7	1790.6	26	323.5	1809.6	24	338.7	2152.6	24	329.7	1987.0
e	23	455.3	1823.0	40	373.8	1677.6	3	383.5	1977.0	66	398.1	1748.4
ɨ	11	443.2	1500.0	50	416.1	1532.6	42	398.2	1578.2	59	370.2	1635.3
a	12	537.6	1424.0	73	526.6	1380.7	36	627.8	1462.4	89	485.5	1418.6
u	30	419.8	1117.2	10	371.3	1148.9	68	362.7	1390.8	38	363.3	1337.9
o	20	516.7	1117.9	26	452.0	1125.8	14	445.3	1184.8	11	413.2	1151.2

The discussion will begin with the vowel system of Molly McCurdy (Figure 18.6a), the speaker with the most conservative vowel system of the four legacy speakers, most like what is commonly reported in grammars of the language. While her vowel system has clear front, central, and back vowel spaces, even she has /ɨ/ as a mid-central vowel, with an F1 similar to that of /e/. Her /ɨ/ has an F2 mean somewhat front of /a/ but 323.1 Hz less than that of /e/. The position of her /ɨ/ lends support to the core element of the UA shift, ***i > **ə. On the other hand, her /u/ and /o/ show a conservative F2, with both being well back of /a/. In addition, her /o/ has the highest F1 mean of any of the four legacy speakers, substantially overlapping in F1 space with /a/.

Martha Hooper's vowel distribution (Figure 18.6b) shows a slight overlap between /ɨ/ and /e/, although the differences in both F1 and F2 are likely large enough to differentiate them acoustically. Her /ɨ/ is clearly a mid vowel, but more fronted than Molly McCurdy's /ɨ/, as evidenced by the F2 difference between /ɨ/ and /a/. Her more fronted /ɨ/ lends support for the ***i > ə > (ö >) e path of the UA shift. Both /o/ and /u/ are located back of /a/. While /o/ overlaps in F1 space with /a/, it is more clearly in mid vowel range than Mrs. McCurdy's.

Although Florence Garcia's (Figure 18.6c) /ɨ/ is not as fronted as Mrs. Hooper's, it is also a mid-central vowel with an F1 differing by only 15 Hz from her /e/. (However, we were able to find only three tokens of /e/ in her narratives.) What makes Mrs. Garcia's vowel system more innovative is that her /u/ is well front of /o/. With the /u/ vowel space overlapping that of /a/ in F2, her /u/ is in the central vowel range, where a canonical /ɨ/ might be expected. (Consistent lip rounding may still characterize the /u/ tokens, but it was not assessed.) In addition, her /o/ is raised. Her overall vowel space is characterized by /ɨ/, /e/, /ɨ/, and /u/ clustering in the high-mid to high space.

The speaker of the northernmost dialect, Sadie Ariwite (Figure 18.6d), has a vowel system suggesting a much more advanced participation in the UA shift. Her /ɨ/ is much more fronted, overlapping substantially with /e/ in both F1 and F2. Like Mrs. Garcia's, her /u/ is centralized and overlaps /a/ in F2. Her overall short vowel distribution for the historical word classes of PUA is quite similar to the ***i > ə > (ö >) e path of the UA shift. In addition, /u/ is in the F2 territory of what may be ***i.

To sum up, the relative positioning of /ɨ/, /u/, /o/, and /a/ is an indicator for how innovative speakers are. All four have /ɨ/ in mid position, relative to their /e/ and /u/, as in Stage 1 of the UA shift. While Mrs. McCurdy has a very low /o/, the others have mid or higher /o/, the possible beginnings of Stage 3 of PUA > PC, PA > Pochutec, and GA > Pipil. Finally, only Mrs. Garcia and Mrs. Ariwite, the

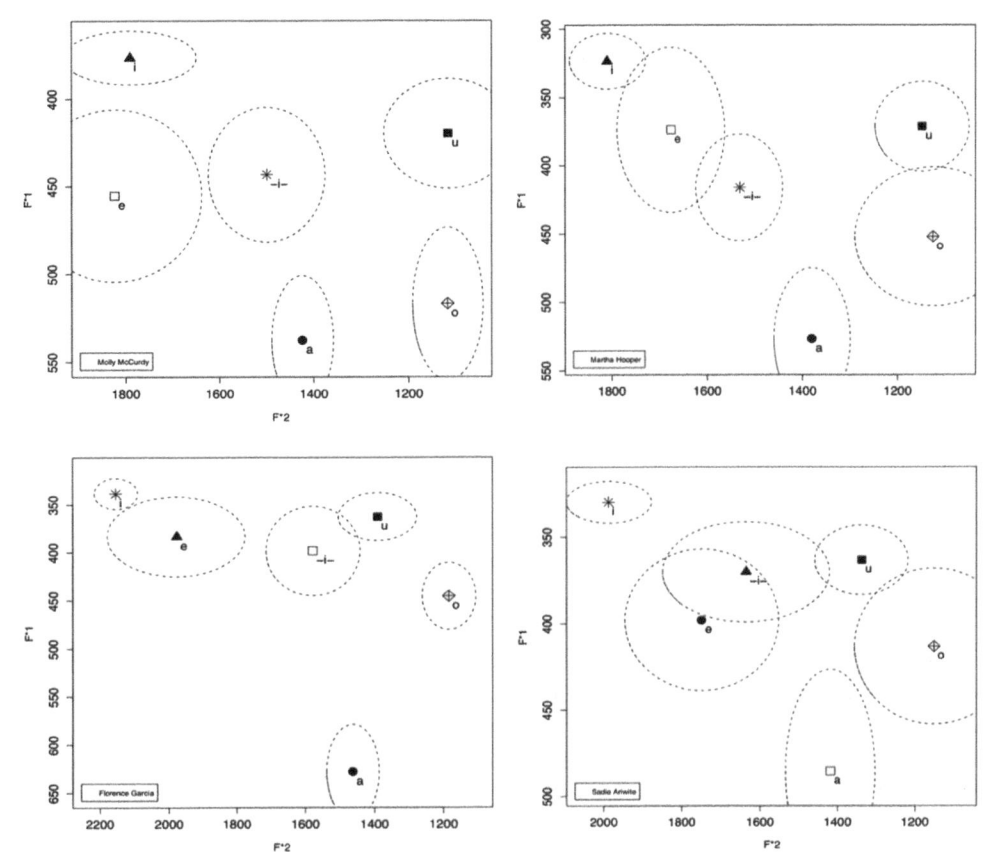

Figure 18.6 Vowel plots of legacy speakers
Figure 18.6a (top left) Molly McCurdy (Goshute)
Figure 18.6b (top right) Martha Hooper (Western Shoshoni)
Figure 18.6c (bottom left) Florence Garcia (Northwestern Shoshoni)
Figure 18.6d (bottom right) Sadie Ariwite (Lemhi (Northern) Shoshoni)

northern- and eastern-most speakers, have /u/ substantially overlapping with F2 of /a/, suggesting a more advanced stage of the UA vowel shift, much like that found for PA Stage 2 and Pochutec Stage 2a.

Acoustic study of recent speakers

The second dataset, consisting of word list data from two current speakers, was collected by Jennifer Mitchell (Mitchell 2012). The recorded word list data collection served as the basis for an acoustic study of the reflexes of PN *aCi or PN *a > Shoshoni e. Of the 160 words on the list, nine words represented these word classes and the remainder were filler words containing other Shoshoni vowels. The speakers were given the words written in Shoshoni with an accompanying English gloss for each word. This method was necessary because very few people can read Shoshoni fluently. Words that were not recognized by the speakers were omitted from the analysis. The word list was read three times for a total of about 480 tokens for each speaker. F1/F2 and duration were measured with a Praat script. For the present study, the mean F1/F2 measurements for all usable recorded tokens were used to produce the vowel plots shown in Figure 18.7.

Two speakers volunteered to read the words. Boyd Graham (b. 1934) spoke the Smoky Valley dialect and resided on the Duckwater Shoshone Reservation. Of all the dialect areas included in the present study, his is the southernmost and westernmost. Ruby Ridesatthedoor (b. 1942), a speaker of Goshute, was raised on the Confederated Tribes of the Goshute Reservation when the language was still spoken by other children. She (as her mother before her) is a member of the Ute Indian Tribe of the Uintah and Ouray Reservation. Both speakers were fully fluent speakers and both taught the language in informal and formal school settings.

Mr. Graham's vowel plot (Figure 18.7a) shows him to be the most conservative speaker in the present study. His /ɨ/ is a high central vowel, overlapping in F1 with both /i/ and /u/, but front of /a/. Both /o/ and /u/ are raised relative to /i/ but still remain back of /a/. The high F1 for /e/ and the large distribution suggests that many tokens were likely to be [ai] rather than [ei] but that he also produced [ei] tokens, again suggesting a conservative vowel system.

The plot of Mrs. Ridesatthedoor's /ɨ/ in Figure 18.7b suggests that it is a mid vowel, lower than her /i/, but overlapping /e/ and /o/ in F1, and /u/ to some extent. Her /u/ is somewhat fronted, overlapping /a/ in F2. While /o/ is raised, it remains a mid vowel.

Mr. Graham's vowel system completes the picture of the vowel shift in Shoshoni, showing the most conservative vowel system in that it is the one of all six speakers that is most consistent with the descriptions in Shoshoni grammars. Also noteworthy for the purposes of validation of the results, Mrs. Ridesatthedoor's system is consistent with that of Mrs. McCurdy, born about two generations earlier in the same community. They both have lowered /ɨ/ overlapping with /e/. However, Mrs. Ridesatthedoor

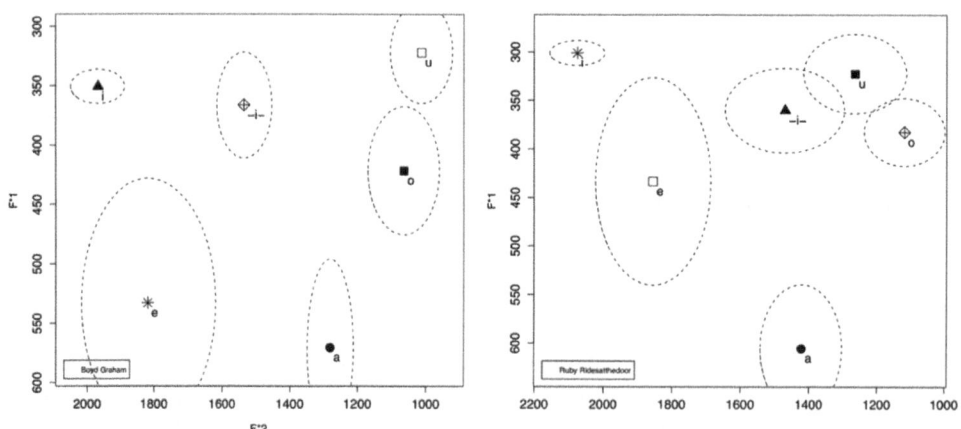

Figure 18.7   Vowel plots of recent speakers
Figure 18.7a (left)   Boyd Graham (Smoky Valley dialect, Duckwater Reservation, NV)
Figure 18.7b (right)   Ruby Ridesatthedoor (Goshute dialect, born and raised Confederated Tribes of the Goshute Reservation)

has a more innovative back vowel system. These findings suggest that the vowel shift was progressing in the early twentieth century, at the end of the time when the language was still used as the primary language of the home and for other everyday interactions. They also indicate that Shoshoni Stage 1 was the lowering of /i/, followed by the fronting of /u/ and the raising of /o/. Furthermore, the results from all six speakers suggest that the vowel system may be more conservative in the more southern and western Shoshoni dialects and more innovative in the north and east.

The discussion now turns to Comanche, which represented Numic in Langacker (1970). Langacker's cognate sets indicated that the PUA fifth vowel in Comanche is /i/. Although linguists classify Shoshoni and Comanche as separate languages, speakers of Comanche and speakers of Shoshoni have told me that these two varieties of Central Numic are mutually intelligible. The Comanche left the Great Basin several hundred years ago, splitting off from Eastern Shoshoni (now spoken on the Wind River Reservation; see Ft. Washakie on the map). Are the elements of the UA vowel shift evident in the Shoshoni data also found in Comanche?

Phonetic evidence for Comanche is from Herrick's (2009, 2011) report on a preliminary acoustic study of the long and short vowels of six speakers of Comanche from legacy recordings. Because his methodology for taking F1/F2 measurements and for producing vowel plots was quite different than that of our studies and his F1/F2 measurements were not normalized, a direct comparison with the results of our studies is not possible. Nevertheless, his primary finding is that the reflex of the PUA fifth vowel in present-day Comanche is a mid-central vowel. Herrick (2011:392–393) also notes reports of variation in the height of both the back and the front mid and high vowels. All of these findings suggest a similar scenario to that of our Shoshoni results (contrary to what Herrick 2011 reports of our results).

Herrick (2011) suggests that the fronting of /u/ by the Comanche speakers is due to the influence of fronted /u/ in the surrounding varieties of Oklahoma English. Although the English of the Great Basin has /u/ fronting (Bowie 2017; Fridland et al. 2017), English influence on the Shoshoni /u/ fronting in our datasets is unlikely. First, the four women in the WRMC legacy sample were speakers of Shoshoni before English, and they married Shoshone/Goshute men, making it likely that Shoshoni was their primary language for most of their lives. It is also likely that Mr. Graham and Mrs. Ridesatthedoor, having grown up on relatively isolated reservations, had Shoshoni as their first language and may have only been introduced to English when they started school.

Discussion

While grammars and cognate sets report that Shoshoni and its close sister language, Comanche, have /i/ as the fifth vowel, acoustic evidence from present-day speakers suggests that these Central Numic varieties have been involved in the first stages of the UA vowel shift ***i > ə (> ö > e) and that the back vowels may have been in a state of change as well. In addition, although we have no evidence for the temporal ordering of the Shoshoni path *a > ai > eɪ, its similarity to PA > Pochutec Stage 1b is noteworthy.

Are the results of the sociophonetic study presented above valid? How can it be that Shoshoni, a relatively well-studied American Indian language, was never reported to have a vowel shift? First, some linguists did in fact notice that there was variation in Shoshoni vowels. For example, Miller (1972:16) reported some of these same alternations as those evident in the results of the sociophonetic study, but did not provide any explanation. Second, the results reported above are corroborated by a preliminary study using a hybrid methodology from comparative dialectology and sociophonetics. We will now turn to it.

Other sources of evidence

A preliminary study of data from two Shoshoni dictionary databases supports the findings of the acoustic studies. (Please see the Appendix.) The first of these is a pan-dialect database (ShPDD) compiled from lexicons or dictionaries from a wide range of Shoshonean varieties, some produced by speakers themselves, most of which can be accessed at https://shoshoniproj ect.utah.edu/language-materials/shoshoni-dictionary/index.php. (Only entries from lexicons compiled by native speakers or by linguists working closely with known native speakers were used in the work reported here.) A few of the entries come from the WRMC narratives or our work related to the transcription of the narratives. Because the orthographies used for the most recent of these lexicons spell vowels out at a phonemic level, those dialect lexicons are a valuable source for a comparative dialectology approach to studying vowel shifting. The second is our Shoshoni Talking Dictionary (ShTD), a database consisting of recently recorded word lists from speakers representing dialects spoken from southern Nevada to southern Idaho (https://shos honiproject.utah.edu/language-materials/shoshoni-dictionary/index.php). The ShTD entries were transcribed using IPA. (Two speakers may have an outsized influence of the data examined for this chapter: Boyd Graham's and Ruby Ridesatthedoor's speech appear in both the acoustic analysis and in the Appendix.)

The ShPDD and the ShTD were searched for glosses of 63 common words, taken from the 200-word Swadesh list and supplemented by culturally salient items such as 'antelope surround,' 'pudding,' 'bow and arrow,' and 'jackrabbit.' This provided an objective method for choosing lexical items, making it more likely that the results of the search are generalizable, and for ensuring that there were entries for the words to be compared in many of the dialect dictionaries.

The results were that 46 of the 63 words showed variation in vowels. The entries in the Appendix represent the kind of variation found in the two databases; no other vowel variant correspondences were found. The variation is systematic and consistent with that of the vowel shift necessary for accounting for the subfamilies and languages discussed in Langacker and Campbell, and also with the results of the acoustic analysis from present-day speakers of Shoshoni.

On a final note, notice that neither i ~ ə nor i ~ e are found in this lexical dataset. All of orthographies used in the lexicons included in the search represent i, but none distinguish it from ə. Although this is an important point, an exploration of why this is the case is beyond the scope of this chapter but perhaps may be found by an examination of sources such as Wick Miller's notebooks.

The lack of the i ~ e alternation in the dataset may be more problematic because every systematic orthography distinguishes [i] from [e]. However, there are indications that the lowering and then fronting of the reflex of ***i in Shoshoni does not result in [e], but instead in a rhoticized [ö] at least for some speakers in some phonological environments. (The distinction between rhoticized [ö] and [e] may be hard to capture in F1/F2 midpoint data, but may correlate with visible formant pinch in spectrograms.) This rhoticized [ö] sounds similar to the reflex of ***o in Ute Mountain Ute spoken

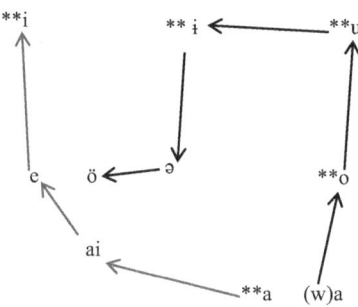

Figure 18.8   Shoshoni Vowel Shift

currently in southwestern Colorado. (Likewise, rhoticized [ö] may be similar to the reflex of ***o in Hopi.) A preliminary study of the Shoshoni variant based on auditory coding of data from my own fieldwork and from the ShTD shows the retroflexed [ö] to be common in /–ti/, the habitual aspect suffix, in words such as *yahnaisuante* 'smile,' *tuhusuante* 'be angry,' *yewekante* 'be alive.' It seems to be found among speakers from the Goshute area to the south, but not found in speakers to the east and north of that area. This front-of-center vowel may be taking on the retroflexed feature of /t/, usually articulated as a flap in this environment.

To sum up, there are two sets of correspondences evident in the dataset from the dictionaries and WRMC narratives: ɨ ~ u ~ o ~ (w)a and a ~ ai ~ e ~ i. It is not possible to easily establish temporal ordering of the elements of the chain shifts from these correspondences, nor is it possible because of the post-contact disruption of the social structures of the Shoshoni communities to easily establish social factors which may underlie the variation. However, these correspondences lend further support to the elements and paths based on the diachronic UA findings from Langacker and Campbell, and with the acoustic evidence.

Variation in the acoustic study, the lexical study, and ongoing study of the reflexes of ɨ suggests a chain shift involving all the Shoshoni vowels, as shown in Figure 18.8.

Towards a sociophonetics of language documentation and revitalization

This chapter has shown how sociophonetic theory and methodology can be a valuable addition to the documentation of an endangered language and to the tool chest employed in diachronic linguistics. In particular, this study of synchronic variation of the Shoshoni vowel system shows the early signs of a vowel shift similar to that theorized in Langacker (1970) and Campbell & Langacker (1978a), and thus supports their diachronic analysis that the fifth vowel of Proto-Uto-Aztecan was /ɨ/. Furthermore, variation and change in the northernmost to the southernmost branches of UA are shown to be one systematic vowel shift being played out over the course of millennia.

These long-term vowel shift paths could be referred to as drift and set aside with no further explanation. However, Labov's (1989) stable variation, as the long-term persistence of language variation, or Joseph's (2006) notion of parallel development as "independent developments in related languages" that are remarkably similar to one another, both provide a more satisfying explanation based on long-term variation with the potential to destabilize and come to completion. Joseph argues that if linguistic variation is a synchronic phenomenon, inherent variation must have also been a design feature of languages in the past that could be passed down to daughter languages. The UA case provides evidence for theories of inheritable, long-term variation.

This chapter also shows how studies of under-documented languages can help us to fine-tune sociophonetic theoretical constructs such as the principles of vowel shifts. Here we see that the instability of Uto-Aztecan /ɨ/ and the type of shift it has led repeatedly over time in almost every branch of UA is predictable if we assume that in UA /ɨ/ behaves as a nonperipheral vowel. In contrast, while markedness theory explains that /ɨ/ is subject to change, it does not predict what kind of change it is likely to undergo. For example, markedness cannot explain why there is no evidence in UA that ɨ > u, which would also lead to an unmarked outcome for /ɨ/. The fact that the UA path is ɨ > ə (> e/o) finds an explanation in Labov's GPVS.

In addition, the UA vowel shift pushes us in sociophonetics to be more thoughtful of our explanations for ongoing changes. We readily attribute the instability in a vowel system such as English with around a dozen vowel phonemes to competition for articulatory and acoustic space. But that does not help us at all at explaining why the small UA system of only five vowels is so unstable, while the language-specific peripheral-nonperipheral distinction in vowel systems does.

In the near future, we hope that the time-aligned corpus of Shoshoni that the Shoshoni Language Project is building by using the Montreal Forced Aligner (McAuliffe et al. 2017) (funded by NSF #1911603) will spur more sociophonetic work on this language. The MFA corpus contains word list data, short elicited sentences, and traditional stories and oral histories from present-day as well as legacy speakers from the WRMC. It will include about 20 speakers, from Reese River, Nevada to Wind River, Wyoming. Some of the speakers are from different generations from the same communities.

This project on Shoshoni vowels developed from the Shoshoni Language Project's revitalization work with Shoshone and Goshute communities in the Great Basin. Because the work was not funded by any specific tribal community and because it was apparent from early on that people valued their own family's varieties above all others, we honored and promoted all ways of speaking the language. We also saw this pan-dialect approach as necessary to keep a language alive that was rapidly losing fluent speakers. Our stance led us to compile what may have been the first pan-dialect dictionary of Shoshoni and to include speakers from any community in all of the events we offered whenever possible. As we recorded speakers for various revitalization projects, most importantly our Shoshoni Talking Dictionary, we began to notice systematic variation that had not been previously reported as patterned. To spell out the entries in the dictionary, we had to delve into various sociophonetic issues; first among these was whether graphemic <ai> represented the same sound as <u̲a̲i̲> (Di Paolo 2006, 2007; Di Paolo, Sykes & Mitchell 2008). These acoustic studies of the vowel system led us to notice the Present-Day Shoshoni shift reported on in this present study (Di Paolo & Sykes 2010; Di Paolo 2013, 2015).

We hope that our work will continue to be valuable to the Shoshoni-speaking communities and that it may serve as a useful model on how to bring theoretical concerns in language variation and change together with assisting communities in language documentation and revitalization.

Acknowledgments

I would like to thank Rob Sykes and Jennifer Mitchell for their support in numerous ways over many years. I also thank Beverly and Earl Crum, Boyd Graham, Ruby Ridesatthedoor, Elwood Mose, Drusilla Gould, Mauricio Mixco, Dirk Elzinga, Sarah Arnoff, and Lyle Campbell. Without

Lisa M. Johnson and Adrian V. Bell I would have never had the opportunity to expand my horizons to Polynesia. And for mentoring me in pushing back the frontiers of science, Wick Miller.

The Shoshoni databases and the studies referred to in this work were funded by the following:

NSF #0418351 Preserving and Enhancing Accessibility of Gosiute/Shoshoni Materials in the Wick R. Miller Collection. 2004–07. PI: Mauricio Mixco, co-PI Marianna Di Paolo.

ANA grant to the Ely Shoshone Tribe. 2009. Subcontract.

Barrick Gold Corporation 2007–2012 grants: The Wick R. Miller Collection: Returning to the Community. PI: Marianna Di Paolo.

DEL/NSF #1911603. Integrating, Disseminating, and Archiving Components of the Shoshoni (shh) Language Project. 2019–2023. PI: Marianna Di Paolo.

References

Boersma, Paul & David Weenink. 2022. *Praat: Doing phonetics by computer* [Computer program], ver. 6.2.19. www.praat.org/

Bowie, David. 2017. Early development of the Western Vowel System in Utah. In Fridland et al., 83–105. https://doi.org/10.1215/00031283-4295211

Bright, William (ed.). 1990. *The collected works of Edward Sapir*, vol. 5, *American Indian languages.* Mouton de Gruyter.

Campbell, Lyle & Ronald W. Langacker. 1978a. Proto-Aztecan vowels: Part I. *International Journal of American Linguistics* 44(2). 85–102. https://doi.org/10.1086/465526

Campbell, Lyle & Ronald W. Langacker. 1978b. Proto Aztecan vowels: Part II. *International Journal of American Linguistics* 44(3). 197–210. https://doi.org/10.1086/465545

Childs, Tucker, Jeff Good & Alice Mitchell. 2014. Beyond the ancestral code: Towards a model for sociolinguistic language documentation. *Language Documentation & Conservation* 8.168–191. http://hdl.handle.net/10125/24601

Churchward, C. Maxwell. 1953. *Tongan grammar*. Oxford University Press.

Crapo, Richley H. 1976. *Big Smokey Valley Shoshoni*. Desert Research Institute.

Crum, Beverly, Earl Crum & Jon P. Dayley. 2001. *Newe Hupia: Shoshoni poetry songs*. Utah State University Press.

Di Paolo, Marianna. 2006. Variation in Shoshoni (ai). Paper presented at the Friends of Uto-Aztecan Conference, University of Utah.

Di Paolo, Marianna. 2007. Applying sociophonetic methods to Shoshoni vowels. Paper presented at the Linguistic Society of America Annual Meeting, Anaheim, CA.

Di Paolo, Marianna. 2013. A reconsideration of the Uto-Aztecan vowel shift from a sociophonetic perspective. Plenary presentation at Phonology Festa (Joint meeting of the Tokyo Circle of Phonologists [TCP] and the Phonology Association in Kansai [PAIK]), Ogota Onsen, Japan.

Di Paolo, Marianna. 2015. A Uto-Aztecan vowel shift: Evidence from Takic, Southern Uto-Aztecan, and Numic. Paper presented at the Uto-Aztecan Historical Linguistics at the Centennial Symposium, Portland, OR.

Di Paolo, Marianna & Robert D. Sykes. 2010. Acoustic evidence for a vowel shift in Shoshoni. Paper presented at Society for the Study of Indigenous Languages Annual Meeting, Baltimore, MD.

Di Paolo, Marianna, Robert D. Sykes & Jennifer Mitchell. 2008. Variation in Shoshoni/Gosiute vowels. Invited Session: Variation in less commonly studied minority languages. Paper presented at New Ways of Analyzing Variation [NWAV] 37, Houston, TX.

Di Paolo, Marianna & Malcah Yaeger-Dror (eds.). 2011. *Sociophonetics: A student's guide*. Routledge.

Epps, Patience L., Anthony K. Webster & Anthony C. Woodbury 2017. A holistic humanities of speaking: Franz Boas and the continuing centrality of texts. *International Journal of American Linguistics* 81(1). 41–78. https://doi.org/10.1086/689547

Feldman, Harry. 1978. Some notes on Tongan phonology. *Oceanic Linguistics* 17(2). 133–139.

Fitzgerald, Colleen M. 2021. A framework for language revitalization and documentation. *Language* 97(1). e1–e11. https://doi.org/10.1353/lan.2021.0006.

Fridland, Valerie, Alicia Beckford Wassink, Tyler Kendall & Betsy E. Evans (eds.). 2017. *Speech in the western states*, vol. 2, *The mountain West* [Publication of the American Dialect Society 102]. Duke University Press.

Gordon, Matthew K. 2017. Phonetic and phonological research on Native American Languages: Past, present, and future. *International Journal of American Linguistics* 81(1). 79–110. https://doi.org/10.1086/689303

Herrick, Dylan. 2009. A six-speaker analysis of Comanche's high central vowel. Paper presented at the 2009 Conference on Endangered Languages and Cultures of Native America, University of Utah.

Herrick, Dylan. 2011. On Comanche's central mid vowel. *International Journal of American Linguistics* 77(3). 373–396. https://doi.org/10.1086/660973

Himmelmann, Nikolaus P. 1998. Documentary and descriptive linguistics. *Linguistics*, 36(1), 161–196. https://doi.org/10.1515/ling.1998.36.1.161

Joseph, Brian D. 2006. On projecting variation back into a Proto-Language, with particular attention to Germanic evidence. In Thomas D. Cravens (ed.), *Variation and reconstruction*, 103–118. John Benjamins. https://doi.org/10.1075/cilt.268.06jos

Labov, William. 1989. The child as linguistic historian. *Language Variation and Change* 1(1). 85–97. https://doi.org/10.1017/S0954394500000120

Labov, William. 1994. *Principles of linguistic change*, vol. 1, *Internal factors*. Blackwell.

Langacker, Ronald W. 1970. The vowels of Proto-Uto-Aztecan. *International Journal of American Linguistics* 36(3). 169–180. https://doi.org/10.1086/465108

Manaster Ramer, Alex. 1992. A Northern Uto-Aztecan sound law: *-c⟶ -y-. *International Journal of American Linguistics* 58(3). 251–268. https://doi.org/10.1086/ijal.58.3.3519784

Mandelbaum, David C. (ed.). 1949. *Selected writings of Edward Sapir in language, culture, and personality*. University of California Press. https://doi.org/10.1525/9780520324077

McAuliffe, Michael, Michaela Socolof, Sarah Mihuc, Michael Wagner & Morgan Sonderegger. 2017. Montreal Forced Aligner: Trainable text-speech alignment using Kaldi. *Proceedings of Interspeech 2017*. 498–502. https://doi.org/10.21437/Interspeech.2017-1386

Merrill, William L. 2013. The genetic unity of Southern Uto-Aztecan. *Language Dynamics and Change* 3(1). 68–104. https://doi.org/10.1163/22105832-13030102

Merrill, William L., Robert J. Hard, Jonathan B. Mabry, Gayle J. Fritz, Karen R. Adams, John R. Roney & A.C. MacWilliams. 2009. The diffusion of maize to the southwestern United States and its impact. *Proceedings of the National Academy of Sciences* 106(50). 21019–21026. https://doi.org/10.1073/pnas.090607510

Miller, Wick R. 1970. Western Shoshoni dialects. In Earl H. Swanson, Jr. (ed.), *Languages and cultures of western North America*, 17–36. Idaho State University Press.

Miller, Wick R. 1972. *Newe Natekwinappeh: Shoshonoi Stories and Dictionary* [University of Utah Anthropological Papers 94]. University of Utah Press.

Miller, Wick R., Dirk Elzinga & John E. McLaughlin. 2005. *International Journal of American Linguistics* 71(4). 413–444. https://doi.org/10.1086/501246

Mitchell, Jennifer L. 2012. *Shoshoni (a'i): A historical perspective*. MA thesis, University of Utah.

Sapir, Edward. 1913. Southern Paiute and Nahuatl: A study in Uto-Aztekan. In Bright, 351–397.

Sapir, Edward. 1914–1919. Southern Paiute and Nahuatl: A study in Uto-Aztekan, part 2. In Bright, 398–443.

Sapir, Edward. 1933. The psychological reality of phonemes. In Mandelbaum, 46–60.

Shumway, Eric B. 2009. *Intensive course in Tongan*, revised edn. The Jonathan Napela Center for Hawaiian and Pacific Islands Studies, Brigham Young University-Hawaii.

Stanford, James N. & Dennis R. Preston (eds.) 2009. *Variation in indigenous minority languages*. John Benjamins.

Thomas, Erik R. & Tyler Kendall. 2007. *NORM: The vowel normalization and plotting suite*. http://lingtools.uoregon.edu/norm/

Weinreich, Uriel, William Labov & Marvin Herzog. 1968. Empirical foundations for a theory of language change. In Winifred P. Lehmann & Yakov Malkiel (eds.), *Directions for historical linguistics: A symposium*, 95–195. University of Texas Press.

Appendix

Appendix 18.1 Shoshoni Dialect Correspondences Providing Evidence for Shoshoni Vowel Shift

i ~ u ~ o ~ (w)a				
i ~ u ~ a	-nke CD	-nku EM, AS WRMC_043_03	-nka CD	applicative suffix
wi ~ u ~ wa	magwindubi Harbin 'wrap up'	wekkuntupi, makuntupi EST 'roll up with hands'	kwantupi AS; wekkwantupi CCD 'wrap up in a bundle, roll up'	roll up
i ~ u ~ o	kamme CCD —————— kammi ShTD:RJ:DuckValley	kammu CCD: ShTD:RR:Goshute, ga'mmu(-i) G&L; kammuwiya 'rabbit blanket' ShTD:BG:SmokyValley	kammo ShTD:BG:SmokyValley, ShTD:EM:Te-Moke, ShTD:RR: Goshute, ShTD:DrG:Ft.Hall	jackrabbit
i ~ u ~ o	awe CCD, Miller, Graham; awy Crapo; awi Harbin	awu 'u Florence Garcia 050_02	awo CCD, Ft. Hall; awogozhol[']hai G&L 'to wash dishes'	cup, dish
i ~ u	hakatte'e ToWhere_027_08_EMNT_BG.wav	hakattu'u ToWhere_028_08_EMNT_DG.wav		to where?
i ~ u	kwettih CCD, Miller; kweti Tidzump; aiti-ma makwyttih; Crapo; dokgwing Harbin	kuttih CCD, EM, AS WRMC_043_03; guuti Harbin; gutiH Shaul (ESh)		shoot
u ~ o ~ a	tu'i Graham, CCD	to'i CCD; to'ai RY WRMC_093_01	ta'i MixcoNWSh	future realis suffix
u ~ o ~ a	masitu EST, Harbin; situn, sittun Crapo	masito Miller; masitoo CCD; masidowaq Tidzump	masita EST	fingernail, claw
u ~ o ~ wa	kuttsaappeh CCD; guzaape Graham; kutsa:pʰi ShTD:BG:SmokyValley, ShTD:AK:Te-Moke	kottsaappeh CCD; kotsa:pʰi ShTD:DrG:Ft.Hall, ShTD:DelG:Ft.Hall	kwattsaappeh CCD; gwazaape Graham; kwatsa:pʰi ShTD:BG:SmokyValley; kwatsa:pʰi ShTD:EM:Te-Moke, ShTD:BL:Te-Moke	pudding (boiling seeds, including pine nuts, in water was a traditional food preparation)
u ~ o ~ wa	nakuitsoih CCD 'to wash oneself'	koitsoiH Miller; nakoicoih Crapo 'to wash oneself'; awogozhol[']hai G&L 'to wash dishes'	kwaïtsoiH Miller; nakwaicoih Crapo 'to wash oneself'	to wash
u ~ o ~ wa	aiku Tidzump; e:ɣu ShTD:RR:Goshute	aikon Miller; aikon, ekon Crapo; aiko(n) CCD; e:ko ShTD:AK:Te- Moke, ShTD:RJ: DuckValley, ShTD:DrG:Ft.Hall	egwa Harbin; aigwa Graham; e:ɣwa ShTD:BG:SmokyValley	tongue

(Continued)

Appendix 18.1 (Continued)

i ~ u ~ o ~ (w)a

u ~ wa	kun CD	-kwan CD		past, momentaneous completive (final suffix)
u ~ wa	kun CD	-kwan CD		movement away from speaker (prefinal suffix)
o ~ a	koonta EM; goonda'a Harbin, Graham; koontex Miller	koanta CCD		sandhill crane
o ~ wa	ko'i RY WRMC_093_01	kwa'i CCD		focus; emphatic particle

a ~ ai ~ e ~ i

ai ~ e ~ i	wetsonai Miller	wesunaih CCD	wesoni EST	comb, vt.
a ~ ai ~ e	kwasi CCD, EST	kwaisi EM, Miller, Crapo, Tidzump	gweshi Harbin	tail
a ~ ai ~ e	nankih CCD	nainkih Crapo: nainyi ShTD:BG:SmokyValley	nainkih CCD; nenkih Crapo; nenke ShTD:IS:Goshute; nenkʰi ShTD:RS:Goshute; nenkʰi ShTD:MB:Goshute; neinyi ShTD:DrG:Ft.Hall	ear (neinyi may indicate the beginning of raising to [i])

a ~ ai ~ e ~ i

ai ~ e	aigwa Graham; aikon Crapo; aiku Tidzump	egwa Harbin; aikon Miller; ekon Crapo: aiko(n) CCD; e:ɣu ShTD:RR:Goshute; e:ko ShTD:AK:Te-Moke, ShTD:RJ:DuckValley, ShTD:DrG:Ft.Hall; e:ɣwa ShTD:BG:SmokyValley	tongue
e ~ i	to'ai RY WRMC_093_01	to'i CCD	future realis suffix
e ~ i	kai himpai 'never' CCD; kaitsaan(ten) CCD, gaiza'a Graham 'not good'	gizhaa 'not good' G&L	negative combining form
e ~ i	ke himbe ~ ke maqah ShTD:BG:SmokyValley; ke himbiɣa ShTD:LG:DuckValley	ki sakuh ShTD:EM:Te-Moke; ki himbeʔ ShTD:NC:DuckValley	never

19

SOCIOPHONETICS AND MULTILINGUALISM

Bronwen G. Evans and Gisela Tomé Lourido

Scope and definitions

Sociophonetics is concerned with the everyday talk of everyday people. Sociophonetic projects have shown that speakers of the same language use fine-grained phonetic detail in order to mark identity and establish and contest group boundaries (e.g., Foulkes & Docherty 2006; Eckert 2008; Moore & Montgomery 2018). This work has focused largely on variation in monolingual communities, working with participants who are raised speaking a single language from birth and where this language continues to form the majority of their linguistic experience. That is, although they may learn other languages, for example in school or for work, and potentially speak these to a high level, they live in a community where the language they have learned from birth is the dominant language and where this is the language they use most frequently, perhaps exclusively. Studies in these communities have shown that relatively small, subtle differences in talk can have far-reaching social consequences. They can, for example, form the basis of distinct styles associated with different peer groups in a high school (Bucholtz 1999; Eckert 2000) and might affect whether or not someone is perceived to be capable of doing a particular job (Levon et al. 2021).

However, more than half the world's population use two or more languages in everyday life—that is, they are multilingual (Grosjean 2021). It is difficult to be more exact than this because, as Grosjean (2021) points out, estimating the number of multilingual speakers is challenging. He argues that this is for two reasons. First, national censuses or surveys rarely include questions that directly address whether or not someone speaks two or more languages. Instead, those surveys typically ask questions about which languages respondents "know." Second, the questions themselves also tend to reflect a very restrictive view of multilingualism. Questions typically assume that speakers have a main language, and often explicitly state that if they have others, they must know them very well. These questions reflect a long-held view that to be multilingual means that a speaker must be equally and fully fluent in all of their languages, that is, indistinguishable from monolinguals in all their languages (see Kachru 1980 for a summary of different historic definitions of multilingualism). Yet, as Grosjean (2021:6–7) points out, if we only counted those who passed as monolinguals in all of their languages as multilingual, we would have no way of describing the vast majority of people who use two or more languages regularly but who do not have native-like proficiency in them all.

DOI: 10.4324/9781003034636-21

Still another issue is that recent discourse can often give the impression that multilingualism is a recent phenomenon. One of the most widely cited articles on diversity in the United Kingdom talks about the "growth of multilingualism" (Vertovec 2007:1032). But being multilingual is not new. Historically, countries which are often thought of as monolingual, such as the United Kingdom and United States, were linguistically diverse. As Vertovec himself points out, the UK has a long history of immigration (see, e.g., Ackroyd 2000 for a discussion of immigration in the UK from Roman times to the present day), and contact between these different communities as a result of immigration, trade, and business will have meant learning other languages or, at the very least, acquiring a common language of communication (Grosjean 2021). Likewise, the United States was home to numerous indigenous languages, the languages of enslaved African peoples, colonial English, French, Spanish, and other European and Asian languages spoken by immigrants. States such as Alabama were fought over by three European powers (English, French, Spanish) who were in constant interaction with each other as well as with indigenous peoples and with peoples of African descent (Picone 2008). As Picone notes "this sociopolitical and ethnic diversity was accompanied by an enormous amount of language diversity, but the story of that linguistic diversity is not well known and is rarely told" (Picone 2008:34).

Arguably, sociophoneticians have been just as guilty of trying to contain linguistic diversity. Experimental studies in particular, have often steered away from studying multilingual populations, perhaps because researchers have tended to work with the communities they are from and/or with whom they are most familiar, or out of a desire to avoid complexity by controlling for variables such as language background. But in multilingual communities, where the use of one language may serve to mark not just community membership but also political affiliation, issues of language and identity are likely central. In these communities, speakers may use both within- and between-language variation to do work in talk. They may use features from different varieties of the same language, incorporate features from another language, or use another language altogether to show identification with a particular group. We might think of these multilingual speakers as having access to a wider "feature pool" (Cheshire et al. 2011), an expanded "variation toolkit," in comparison to monolinguals. For example, children growing up in London acquiring both English and Punjabi from an early age, and whose parents are native (L1) speakers of Punjabi, will be exposed to retroflex /t/ (Punjabi) along with alveolar and glottal variants (English; e.g., Hirson & Sohail 2007; Sharma & Sankaran 2011). This in turn, means that all people in these communities, both monolingual and multilingual, will come into contact not just with speakers of different regional sound systems, but also different languages (e.g., Cheshire et al. 2011). In large urban centers like this, contact between these different communities has led to the emergence of new, multiethnic vernaculars—for example, Multicultural London English (MLE; e.g., Kerswill 2013), Kiezdeutsch in Berlin (Weise 2009, 2020), youth language in Copenhagen (Quist 2008), and Multicultural Parisian French (Cheshire & Gardner-Chloros 2018). However, exactly what is available for use is likely dependent on how these multilinguals acquired their languages. For example, speakers in the multilingual community of Galicia, Spain, who are raised speaking Spanish but who learn Galician later in life may be able to use some but not all phonetic features to do social work, even after switching to using Galician as their everyday language (Tomé Lourido & Evans 2019; see also Mayr et al. 2017 for Welsh). Studying multilingual populations is therefore central to a full understanding of variation and change.

The study of multilingualism can take many different perspectives, from language policy and planning to psycholinguistic studies investigating the effects of language dominance on speech processing. Many of these subfields differ in how they define the term multilingualism and who they consider to be multilingual. In this chapter, we take a broad definition of multilingualism, using this term to refer to speakers who regularly use two or more languages in their everyday life (cf. Grosjean 2021). We will explore work that has investigated phonetic variation in multi-lingual communities where speakers have learned two or more languages simultaneously from birth (simultaneous multilinguals), or one language after another (sequential multilinguals), and in language revitalization contexts, where speakers have learned a minoritized language through immersion education or adult education classes (e.g., O'Rourke & Pujolar 2013; O'Rourke & Ramallo 2013; O'Rourke, Pujolar & Ramallo 2015). We will review work that has investigated how fine-grained phonetic variation is used by speakers in these communities to mark identities and navigate their social worlds, before presenting data from a case study that investigates whether growing up mono- or multilingually affects how children develop the ability to extract and use phonetic variation in speech processing.

Phonetic variation in multilingual communities

Central to the study of phonetic variation in multilingual communities is the complex relationship between cognitive and social factors. That is, how much variation is accounted for by cognitive factors such as age of acquisition and the relationship between the sound systems of the different languages being learned (cf. Best 1994; Flege 1995; Iverson et al. 2003; Best & Tyler 2007; Flege & Bohn 2021), and how much is accounted for by environmental and social factors such as quality and amount of input (Mora & Nadeu 2012; Mayr et al. 2019), motivation to learn (e.g., Dewaele 2019; Tomé Lourido & Evans 2019), and the desire to mark identity (e.g., Sharma & Sankaran 2011; Drummond 2013; Tomé Lourido & Evans 2021)?

As noted above, studies of multilingual speakers typically make a distinction between, on the one hand, simultaneous learners who acquire their languages from birth (often one language from each parent; Grosjean 1998) and sequential learners who acquire their languages one after the other, with the first language (L1) typically being their home language and the second (L2) or other languages acquired through the community or education (e.g., Kohnert 2008; Darcy & Krüger 2012; McCarthy et al. 2014). In terms of phonetic and phonological development, simultaneous learners are thought to acquire the full phonology of all of their languages. The expectation is that although there may be fine-grained differences in phonetic details, simultaneous learners estab-lish native-like sound systems which are the same as or closely resemble those of monolinguals (e.g., Sundara et al. 2008). On the other hand, sequential learners, defined as those who acquire their other language(s) after the age of 3 years, are typically thought to be less likely to establish monolingual-like sound systems (Tsukada et al. 2005; Darcy & Krüger 2012; McCarthy et al. 2014). This implies a dichotomy between simultaneous and sequential learners, with sequential learners considered to be more like early L2 learners.

However, defining what is "native-like" for a multilingual is not straightforward. Multilingual sound systems are dynamic, and phonetic category representations may change over the lifespan depending on experience. For example, sequential bilinguals who acquire their L1 at home and L2 in school, but then become more dominant in their L2, experience attrition in their L1 (e.g., de Leeuw, Mennen & Scobbie 2012; Mayr et al. 2012). This then means that these multilinguals would not have a "native-like system" in their L1, or possibly in either language. Further, not only is it likely that multilinguals receive different input from monolingual speakers of their different languages, but social identity and group affiliation are also likely to differ. Khattab (1999) combines the study of multilingualism, phonology, and sociophonetics to investigate speech production in two Lebanese boys, aged 6 and 9 years, growing up bilingually in English and Arabic in Leeds. Analysis of their use of the glottal stop [ʔ] and key vocalic variables showed that the boys had developed separate phonological and articulatory systems for their languages and were aware of the social and linguistic factors affecting usage of the different variants in English. However, they had a tendency to use more standard-like variants. For example, in English, they used [t] and [ʔ] in appropriate phonological environments and with the same relative frequency as monolinguals—they used a higher proportion of [ʔ] in syllable-final and pre-consonantal position (e.g., *lot*, *put down*, *bats*) than in pre-vocalic and pre-lateral position (e.g., *sit on*, *water*, *bottle*)—but they used far fewer glottal stops than would be expected in English children of the same age. Khattab argues that this is likely due to a complex interplay of factors, including both the amount of exposure to standard versus local features and attitudinal factors related to the family and school. Studies of monolingual children suggest an important role for parents in the transmission of local accent features and many of the features found in these bilingual children's speech reflect the near-RP variants that their parents learned in language courses. The children in this study were also being raised in a monolingual rather than bilingual community, with parents who had learned English as an L2 later in life. Khattab suggests that their avoidance of local variables may be because, having no frequent association with other similar bilinguals, they felt "different" from other children their age in terms of their ethnic minority background.

Differences in the production of sociophonetic variables can also be found in larger, more established multilingual communities. In their recent study of production of laterals by second-generation Sylheti-English bilingual children in London, Kirkham & McCarthy (2020) show that these bilinguals behave like monolinguals in Sylheti, but that there are subtle differences in how they produce /l/ in English compared to monolingual English speakers. Laterals are typically described as "clear" or "dark"/velarized; clear /l/ has a raised and fronted tongue body, whilst dark or velarized /l/ has a lower and retracted tongue dorsum. In English spoken in London, clear /l/ is found syllable-initially whilst dark /l/ is found syllable-finally, but in Sylheti /l/ is always clear. Sylheti-English bilingual children do show evidence of initial ~ final contrast in English laterals, but they have much less of a contrast than English monolinguals: bilinguals produce much clearer (higher F2−F1) /l/ in both positions than do monolinguals.

Variation in production may reflect the fact that monolingual and multilingual speakers construct their different identities differently through talk. Indeed, studies of language use conducted within a sociolinguistic framework have demonstrated that social identity, as defined by factors such as ethnicity (e.g., Harris 2006; Fox 2015), religious belief (Alam 2015), and sociopolitical affiliation (O'Rourke & Ramallo 2013; Tomé Lourido & Evans 2019), is central to explaining patterns of variation in multilingual communities. In the UK, much of this work has focused on the British Asian community, showing that there are fine-grained differences in phonetic variation, perhaps attributable to language contact (e.g., Kerswill, Torgersen & Fox 2008; Kirkham & Wormald 2015) and cross-linguistic effects (e.g., Kirkham & McCarthy 2020), but which are also used to establish complex identities. Some of the most well-known work in this area has focused on the emergence of Multicultural London English (MLE), a multiracial variety initially found in multiethnic and multilingual communities in inner London, in particular the traditional East End (e.g., Fox 2015). Studies of variation in London English among adolescents have shown that minority ethnic speakers in the East End of London have diverged from Cockney, the variety traditionally associated with the East End (Fox 2015; Cole & Evans 2020), and leveled varieties, such as Estuary English, to use innovative variants with much of the variation carried in the vowel system (Cheshire et al. 2011; Kerswill & Williams 2000, 2005; Kerswill, Torgersen & Fox 2008). The monophthong TRAP is produced using a more centralized, open variant, [ɐ]; STRUT is backing and is less open; and FOOT is produced with a back rather than front realization (Fox 2015). In the diphthong system, the MOUTH and PRICE vowels, which typically have shorter or absent trajectories in Cockney, are both lowering and centralizing. GOAT also has shorter trajectories and is realized as either a fronted variant ([əʊ]) or back variant ([oː] or [ɔʊ]) (Kerswill, Torgersen & Fox 2008). These changes have been shown to be led by minority ethnic groups, in particular the Bangladeshi community in Tower Hamlets (Fox 2015), where many speakers are sequential multilinguals who learn their community language (Sylheti, Bengali) at home before acquiring English when starting preschool/school (McCarthy et al. 2014). Interestingly, these changes have also spread to the dominant white Anglo group, indicating that they are used by both monolingual and multilingual speakers to index heritage, ethnicity, and friendship network (Kerswill, Torgersen & Fox 2008).

The same variants that are used to signal belonging to a local community, can also be used to signal identification with a global diaspora. In the Blackhill community in London, Harris (2006) shows that the use of local London English variants (e.g., t-glottalling) is interwoven with other linguistic markers of identity and affiliation that are separated into what she labels the "traditional" and the "emergent contemporary." The traditional are residual linguistic markers connected with community languages (e.g., Punjabi, Gujarati, Hindi), whilst the emergent contemporary markers are acquired either through contact with other local ethnic communities (e.g., Jamaican) or are encountered through global, popular culture (e.g., African American Language). Harris (2006) proposes the term "Brasian" to capture this hybrid culture, a term that embodies the fact that elements of British and Asian identity are always co-present or blended.

Similar findings have emerged from studies of other multiethnic, urban communities, with speakers using fine-grained phonetic variation to simultaneously signal ethnic identity alongside wider local, regional, national, and international identities. For example, Khan (2006) found that Pakistani and Caribbean heritage speakers in Birmingham, England use innovative variants for PRICE and GOAT, similar to those found in London, as markers of ethnic orientation. Alam (2015) used an ethnographic approach to investigate variation in multilingual adolescent girls aged 16–18 years from a Pakistani-Muslim background in Glasgow, Scotland. Through investigation of a number of consonantal and vocalic variables, she found that fine-grained differences in realization reflected distinct communities of practice (CofPs), and that these groupings symbolized affiliation to a range of social practices (cf. Kirkham 2015 for Sheffield). The girls used a system of accent variation to simultaneously index ethnicity, personal, regional, and social identity, which she describes as embodied in the concept of "Glaswasian" (see also Lambert, Alam & Stuart-Smith 2007; Alam & Stuart-Smith 2015). For example, word-initial /t/ in Glaswasian tends to be produced as a retracted, postalveolar stop in contrast to the fronted, dentialveolar, or dental allophones used in Glasgow English. Spectral moment analysis of /t/ (see Chodroff & Foulkes this volume) showed a consistent effect of CofP: those who identified as "Messabout" used variants that were heard as laminal dental stops, whilst those who identified as "Conservative" used variants that were closer to apico-postalveolars. Likewise, Sharma & Sankaran (2011) find that in the multiethnic community in Southall, London, speakers develop complex multidimensional repertoires that reflect their age and the sociohistorical context, in particular community relations, and shift among these to dial up or down different aspects of their identity.

Issues of ideology are also central for multilingual speakers of minoritized languages. In some of these communities, there are a particular group of speakers known as "new speakers," who typically acquire the minoritized language through immersion educational programs or as adult learners (O'Rourke, Pujolar & Ramallo 2015) or as early bilinguals (Tomé Lourido & Evans 2019). These speakers may become dominant in this "new" language; that is, they may use the new language significantly more than their first-learned language, and this "new" language may even displace their first language altogether. In the bilingual Spanish-Galician community in northwest Spain, there are three main groups of bilingual speakers: Galician-dominant speakers who acquire Galician at home and Spanish through the community and school; Spanish-dominant speakers who have learned Spanish at home and who acquire Galician through the community and/or school (e.g., grandparents and the wider community; Ramallo & O'Rourke 2014); and *neofalantes* 'new speakers.' *Neofalantes* are speakers who are initially Spanish-dominant, but who at some stage in their lives, usually adolescence or early adulthood, choose to use their non-dominant language predominantly or regularly for ideological or cultural reasons (O'Rourke & Ramallo 2011, 2015; Tomé Lourido & Evans 2019, 2021). This means that they switch from using mostly or always Spanish to using mostly or always Galician. Previous research has investigated the consequences of the switch in language dominance on their speech production and found that *neofalantes* develop a hybrid variety. They pattern with Galician-dominant speakers in the production of unstressed word-final vowels, a highly salient feature of Galician, but with Spanish-dominant speakers in the production of mid vowel and fricative contrasts (Tomé Lourido & Evans 2019; Regueira & Fernández Rei 2020). This hybrid variety of Galician may reflect a desire to fit in with a group of speakers, Galician-dominants, constrained by the influence of the speakers' language experience (Tomé Lourido & Evans 2019, 2021).

Nance (2015) found similar evidence of an emerging variety among new speakers of Gaelic in Scotland. Nance investigated Gaelic speakers' productions of three phonetic variables: the high back vowel /u/, the lateral system, and intonation. Young adults attending Gaelic-medium secondary schools in Glasgow, an area with a low number of Gaelic speakers, differed in all three variables from both younger and older speakers in Lewis, the area with the densest concentration of Gaelic speakers. This suggests that the new speakers' variety is different from that of previous generations. However, in a comparison of the production of word-final rhotics by highly proficient urban adult new speakers and traditional speakers, Nance et al. (2016) found that although some new speakers distinguished traditional Gaelic rhotic categories, others did not. Likewise, Mayr et al. (2017) found few differences in the production of monophthongal vowels in a sample of adolescent Welsh speakers, some of whom had a Welsh-speaking home background and some of whom had an English-speaking one—that is, had learned Welsh in an immersion setting. Overall, these findings suggest a need for careful interpretation of the data at a local level. On the one hand, there may be similarities between traditional and new speakers, but there is often also evidence for rapid change, with new speakers using the language differently from previous generations, in terms of both linguistic and social practice (Nance 2015).

An interesting question that arises from this work is, if a new speaker variety emerges, when and in what way is it recognized by listeners? That is, at what point does the variety become enregistered (Agha 2003; Silverstein 2003; Johnstone, Andrus & Danielson 2006)? In an accent identification task, Tomé Lourido & Evans (2021) investigated whether listeners from the three language backgrounds in Galicia described above (Spanish-dominant, Galician-dominant, and *neofalantes*) could categorize talkers based on their language background. Listeners were able to identify Galician-dominant better than Spanish-dominant bilinguals but could not identify *neofalantes*. Instead, *neofalantes* were categorized as both Spanish- and Galician-dominant, supporting the idea that *neofalantes* have a hybrid variety (Tomé Lourido & Evans 2021). One explanation for these findings is that listeners have a gradient representation of variation, and that in this community Galician-like and Spanish-like accents function as anchors with the *neofalantes*' accent situated somewhere in the middle. However, although overall identification accuracy was similar for listeners from all language backgrounds, there were some differences in the patterns of identification. This suggests that representations of accent variation may vary according to language background and provides further evidence that the evaluation as well as the usage of phonetic features not only varies as a function of context but also depends on the social and language experience of the individual (Tomé Lourido & Evans 2021).

In the following case study, we present work that investigates how the ability to extract and use fine-grained patterns of phonetic variation to categorize talkers develops in childhood, and how this might be affected by the linguistic environment—that is, whether a child is growing up monolingually or multilingually in a monolingual or multilingual community.

CASE STUDY   The development of sociolinguistic awareness in a multilingual context

In a previous study, we showed that growing up multilingually affected children's ability to use variation in an explicit categorization task (Evans & Tomé Lourido 2019). Sixty children (30 monolingual, 30 bilingual) aged 5–7 years, were tested on their ability to comprehend and categorize talkers in two out of three accents: a home (Popular London English; Wells 1982), unfamiliar regional (Yorkshire), or unfamiliar foreign-accented (Singaporean) variety. All children demonstrated high, above-chance performance in the comprehension task, but language background significantly affected the children's ability to categorize talkers. Multilingual but not monolingual children were able to categorize talkers in three accent pairings, but monolingual children were only able to categorize talkers in the home-foreign condition where the differences between the accents were maximized.

These results support the idea that children's representations are likely initially influenced primarily by their core set of experiences with their home dialect(s) (cf. Wagner, Clopper & Pate 2014), but they also suggest an important role for social context. The fact that our bilinguals, who were exposed to greater amounts of variation than our monolinguals, were highly successful at this task indicates that although all children likely have the capacity to perceive differences between talkers early in development, the ability to do this might present differently and at a different stage in development, depending on the child's linguistic environment. For bilinguals growing up in a diverse environment, an understanding of the social significance of variation may begin to emerge earlier.

But not all multilingual children grow up in this kind of environment. Others grow up in communities where they are exposed to a single, dominant variety of the host country language in their community and may only speak their other language at home with a caregiver or other close family members (cf. Grosjean 1998). This means that they may not develop awareness of variation as early in development (cf. Khattab 1999, 2002). Likewise, monolinguals growing up in a community like this may not perform as well as their monolingual peers growing up (monolingually) in a multilingual community. In this case study, we want to use a similar experimental design to test these hypotheses. Specifically, we want to investigate whether children growing up mono- and multilingually in a suburban community develop an understanding of the social significance of variation at a similar stage of language development to their peers growing up in more diverse environments.

We also want to address some methodological questions. Working with young children presents some challenges: children have a shorter attention span than adults, which means that they cannot complete the same number of experimental trials and, in order to ensure reliability of data, tasks need to be designed to be both engaging and appropriate for their developmental stage. Our initial study, based on Wagner, Clopper & Pate (2014), included only a small number of trials. Children completed four training trials (two per accent) and six test trials (three per accent) with two reminder trials (one per accent). In the test phase, children were tested with one familiar and two new talkers, but they only heard each talker once. Whilst this meant that the task took only a short amount of time and we were able to test generalization to two new talkers, it is possible that children were able to do the task by learning to associate a given accent with a given talker. In this study, we again tested categorization with three talkers (one familiar, two unfamiliar) but doubled the number of trials to twelve (six per accent) so that children heard each talker twice.

We also made some changes to the accents selected. Singaporean English is an established World English and so this was replaced with a foreign-accent, Spanish-accented English, produced by L2 speakers of English. Yorkshire English was replaced with speakers of another northern variety, recorded in Ashby-de-la-Zouch, Leicestershire, where the local variety is similar to Derby English (e.g., Evans & Iverson 2004). For practical reasons, our Yorkshire speakers were recorded in London where they had been living for 3–15 years. Although they had key features of Yorkshire English (BATH produced with a short [æ], STRUT produced with either [ʊ] or [ə]), they also used some more standard rather than regionally specific variants. For example, they all produced FACE with a diphthong [eɪ], rather than a monophthong [eː], and GOAT as [ɵʊ] (raised onset) or [əʊ], rather than as a monophthong [oː]. For this study, we recorded speakers who had been born and raised and were living in Ashby-de-la Zouch and who maintained key local features. They all produced BATH as [æ] and STRUT with [ʊ]. They also had other features typical of Derby English (e.g., Foulkes & Docherty 1999), including [aː] for MOUTH and glottal stops in clusters where epenthetic [t] might be expected, for example *else* [el?s].

Methods

Participants

Fifty-three children were recruited from a primary school in the London borough of Richmond-upon-Thames, close to the Greater London/Surrey border. None of the children who participated had any reported speech, hearing, or language impairments. Prior to testing, all children obtained age-appropriate scores on the British Picture Vocabulary Scale 3 (Dunn & Dunn 2009).

Ethical approval for the study was granted by the UCL Ethics committee (1719/006), and all children completed the study on an opt-in basis. Parents of all children in the target age group received a letter and information sheet informing them about the study and asking them if they would like their child to take part. Only those who returned the completed questionnaire and consent form to school and met the criteria took part. The questionnaire asked for basic details of the child's language background and exposure to other foreign languages or accents.

Two children were excluded from the final sample because of failure to complete. This gave a final group of 51 children (38 monolingual, 13 bilingual) with an age range of 4;6–6;5 years. Bilingual children were from a range of language backgrounds, but none were bilingual in Spanish. The majority (*n*= 11) were simultaneous bilinguals who had learned both English and their other language from birth. They spoke English at school and with one parent, and used their other language with their other parent and family members. The remainder were sequential bilinguals (*n*=2) who had learned their home language first, before receiving consistent exposure to English when attending nursery or preschool. The majority of children had been born and raised within the area of southwest London in which they were tested. A small number of children (monolingual and bilingual) had either been born or spent some time living outside the UK, but had moved or returned to the UK to attend nursery school at the age of 3 years, where they had lived ever since.

Information from the parental questionnaire was also used to inform the assignment of children to the different experimental conditions. For example, if a child fit the criteria for selection but had regular exposure to a variety of northern English, then they were placed in the home-foreign condition. As in Evans & Tomé Lourido (2019), regular exposure was defined as a child having a close or near-relative (e.g., a parent, aunt/uncle, grandparent) or caregiver with whom the child had regular contact (e.g., a childminder). This ensured that, as far as possible, all children across all conditions were equally unfamiliar with both the regional and foreign accent.

Stimuli

Stimuli were recorded by 12 speakers (4 talkers per accent; 2 male, 2 female; age 20–49 years). They were encouraged to read in an engaging, child-friendly style, and were judged to have a representative accent. Home- and foreign-accented talkers were recorded in a sound-attenuated booth at Chandler House at University College London (UCL), whilst those in Ashby were recorded in a quiet room. All recordings were made at a sampling rate of 44.1 kHz, 16-bit resolution, using a Rode NT-1A condenser microphone connected to a PC (UCL) or MacBook (Ashby) via an RME Fireface UC (UCL) or Focusrite (Ashby) processor. Recordings were made in stereo and later converted to mono. Sentence stimuli were manually extracted and saved to individual .wav files with boundaries placed as close as possible to the onset and offset of each sentence. Stimuli were then band-pass filtered from 60 Hz to 20 kHz and equalized for intensity at 70 dB, and a buffer of 100 ms was added to the beginning and end of each file. All processing was completed in Praat (Boersma & Weenink 2017).

The home-accented speakers were the same as those used in Evans and Tomé Lourido (2019). They were all monolingual speakers, who had been born and raised in London and spoke Popular London English. This variety is characterized by the use of glottal stops word-medially, TH-fronting, vocalized /l/, labialized /ɹ/, and differences in the realization of some vowels, for example PRICE and MOUTH. We chose this accent rather than Standard Southern British English (SSBE) because, although SSBE is also commonly used in this community alongside Popular London, SSBE has been shown to be particularly highly intelligible (Pinet et al. 2015). The regional-accented speakers were from Ashby. They were all monolingual English speakers. Three speakers had been born and raised in Ashby and had not lived outside the local area. One speaker was born in Ireland but his mother was from Ashby and he moved to Ashby aged 9 years, where he had lived ever since. The foreign-accented speakers were native monolingual Spanish speakers. They had started learning English at school aged 11 years and were studying at UCL at the time of recording.

All stimuli were designed to include key phonetic differences between the accents but were not intended to be highly confusable. The Spanish accent differed in many ways from both the London and Ashby accents. London and Ashby sentences were designed to include salient differences between London and Ashby English, that is, a BATH or STRUT vowel. The sentences for the comprehension task were the same as those used in Evans & Tomé Lourido (2019). These consisted of six one- to two-sentence phrases, four of which were themed to include characters from *The Gruffalo's Child* (Donaldson & Scheffler 2004), a popular children's book which was familiar to all children. These characters were used in the categorization task. The sentences for the categorization task consisted of

18 short clips of one to two sentences. Twelve of these were taken from the children's books *Mrs Plug the Plumber* (Ahlberg & Wright 1980) and *Paddington: Please look after this Bear* (Bond 1958) and six were original. Vocabulary was selected to be age-appropriate.

Procedure

All testing took place in a quiet area in the school. During the experiment, the child and the experimenter were seated next to each other. Stimuli were presented at a comfortable listening level via a laptop PC/MacBook over headphones, worn by both the experimenter and child, using the Experiment MFC interface in Praat. The child was seated so that they could not see the computer screen and gave their responses using picture response cards (comprehension task) or by pointing to a soft toy (categorization task). Responses were logged by the experimenter via the Experiment MFC interface. Children completed the comprehension task and then the categorization task in a single testing session lasting 10–15 minutes.

Comprehension task

The task was a four-alternative forced-choice (4AFC) task. Children heard a sentence and then selected the picture which they thought best matched the sentence they had heard. Adults are able to quickly tune into an unfamiliar accent (e.g., Clarke & Garrett 2004) and so the purpose of this task was both to familiarize children with the accents as well as to test that they were able to understand them. This meant that any differences in performance in the categorization task were not due to difficulties in intelligibility. Children completed six trials in each accent, produced by two talkers (one per accent: one male, one female), in a fixed order. The experimenter explained to the child that they would hear someone speaking and that it was their job to listen carefully and point to the picture that the speaker had asked for or described. To keep the child "on task," the first, third, and fifth trials were preceded by appropriate attention-grabbing audio clips. For example, trial 5 was "His favorite food is a glass of mouse milkshake," which was preceded by the sound of liquid being sucked through a straw. Clips were downloaded from the Internet and converted to mono .wav files in Praat. The experimenter controlled the pace of experiment and praised the children uniformly throughout.

Categorization task

This had two parts: training and categorization. Children completed four training trials, followed by a test phase in which they completed twelve categorization trials, interspersed with two reminder trials which followed the fourth categorization trial. Otherwise, the procedure was the same as that described in Evans & Tomé Lourido (2019).

Children were introduced to soft toys of two characters from *The Gruffalo's Child*, the Gruffalo's Child and the Mouse. As well as being a well-known story which we knew would be familiar to all children, we also chose to use *The Gruffalo's Child* because in the animated short film the different characters are voiced by actors with different UK regional accents. As such, each toy was represented with one of the three stimulus accents to create three conditions (home-foreign, home-regional, regional-foreign) with the assignment of character to accent counterbalanced across participants. Children were told that the characters' families had got lost in the deep, dark wood (the setting for the story) and that their job was to help each of them find the correct family (Mouse or Gruffalo's

Child). However, because the wood was dark, they wouldn't be able to see them and would have to listen carefully to their voices instead. The children were then introduced to how the Mouse and the Gruffalo's Child's families talked (training trials). At the beginning of each of the four training trials the experimenter held up the appropriate soft toy and said "This is what the Mouse/Gruffalo's Child sounds like!" and then played the sound file. Before starting the test phase, children were reminded that they would hear a character speaking and that their job was to say which family they belonged to by pointing to the appropriate picture. There were twelve test trials (six per accent). In total, children heard six talkers (three per accent), three male and three female, with at least one female and one male speaker per accent. For each accent, the speakers were one familiar talker from the comprehension and training task and two novel talkers, with two trials per talker. The order of presentation was pseudo-randomized, but to give children confidence in doing the task, one of the first two trials was a familiar talker. To further reduce cognitive load, there were two reminder trials (one per accent) after the first four categorization trials. These were familiar talkers from the training. As in the comprehension task, the experimenter controlled the speed of presentation, logged responses, and uniformly praised children throughout.

Results

Comprehension

Table 19.1 shows performance (proportion correct) for each accent condition tested in the comprehension task (Home, Regional, Foreign) for monolingual and bilingual children. All children performed very well in this task, although monolingual children appeared to perform slightly better overall than bilinguals (monolingual average = 0.84; bilingual average = 0.76). Monolingual children performed best with in the Home and Regional conditions, whilst bilingual children performed best in the Foreign condition.

These observations were tested in a series of analyses. First, a series of one-sample t-tests confirmed that all children performed above chance in all conditions: Home accent, monolinguals, $t(27) = 11.05$, $p < 0.001$, bilinguals, $t(8) = 6.01$, $p < 0.001$; Regional accent, monolinguals, $t(22)= 17.59$, $p < 0.001$, bilinguals, $t(8) = 9.02$, $p < 0.001$; Foreign accent, monolinguals, $t(24) = 8.64$, $p < 0.001$, bilinguals, $t(8) = 3.38$, $p = 0.001$. Second, a univariate ANOVA, with proportion correct as the dependent variable and accent condition (Home, Regional, Foreign) and language background (monolingual, bilingual) as independent variables, demonstrated that there were no main effects or interactions of accent or language background ($p < 0.05$). This confirms that although there were small differences in performance between monolinguals and bilinguals, all children performed similarly with all accents.

Table 19.1 Mean proportion correct (standard deviation in parentheses) for each accent in the comprehension task, by language background

Language background	Home	Foreign	Regional
Monolingual	0.88 (0.16)	0.75 (0.24)	0.90 (0.16)
Bilingual	0.69 (0.29)	0.74 (0.36)	0.85 (0.18)

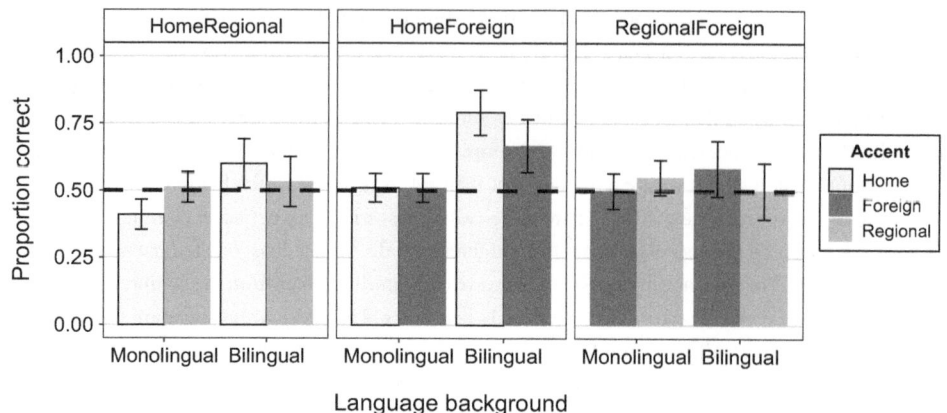

Figure 19.1 Mean categorization score for monolingual and bilingual children in each condition split by accent

Categorization

Figure 19.1 displays the mean proportion correct for each accent condition (Home, Regional, Foreign) in each condition (Home-Regional, Home-Foreign, Regional-Foreign) split by language background (monolingual, bilingual). Responses were coded as correct when children selected the appropriate soft toy for the accent they had been trained to associate with that character. Children found the task difficult; all children, monolingual and bilingual, performed at chance-level in the home-regional and regional-foreign condition. Monolingual children additionally performed at chance in the home-foreign condition. However, bilingual children performed better. They appeared to be able to categorize talkers in this condition at above-chance levels.

To assess children's overall performance, an overall categorization score (i.e., the mean categorization score across both dialects in the pair) was calculated for each child in each group (monolingual, bilingual) for each condition (home-regional, home-foreign, regional-foreign) and compared to chance. Bilinguals but not monolinguals performed above chance in the Home-Foreign condition [Bonferroni-corrected for multiple comparisons, $t(3) = 7.25$, $p < 0.01$]. Neither bilinguals nor monolinguals performed above chance in any other condition ($p < 0.05$).

Following Evans & Tomé Lourido (2019), a mixed-effects logistic regression model was built with the binomial response (correct/incorrect) as the dependent variable, condition (Home-Regional, Home-Foreign, Regional-Foreign) and language background (monolingual, bilingual) as fixed factors, and participant and speaker as crossed random effects. Treatment coding was used for both factors, with Home-Foreign as the reference level for condition and monolingual as the reference level for language background.

As displayed in Table 19.2, the model revealed no significant contrasts between the Home-Foreign, Home-Regional, or Regional-Foreign conditions, and no interaction of condition and language background. However, there was a significant effect of language background. To further investigate this, pairwise post hoc tests were calculated using the lsmeans package (Lenth 2016) in R (R Core Team 2022), adjusting for multiple comparisons using the Tukey method. These indicated that bilinguals

Table 19.2 Summary of the results of the regression model for accent categorization

	β	SE	z-value	p-value
Intercept	0.047	0.183	0.259	0.796
Condition (H-R)	−0.208	0.269	−0.773	0.44
Condition (R-F)	0.057	0.289	0.198	0.843
Language background (B)	0.977	0.426	2.292	0.022*
Condition (H-R): Language background (B)	−0.539	0.567	−0.951	0.341
Condition (R-F): Language background (B)	−0.909	0.598	−1.521	0.128

Note. H-R = home-regional; R-F = regional-foreign; B = bilingual. Baselines for predictor variables: home-foreign condition. Baselines for predictor variables: home-foreign for condition; monolingual for language background.

outperformed monolinguals in the Home-Foreign condition, but not the Home-Regional or Regional-Foreign condition (Home-Foreign: $\beta = -1.0011$, SE $= 0.494$, $z = -2.027$, $p < 0.05$).

Measures of correct responses could be confounded by effects of response bias, that is, the possibility that children might over- or under-estimate the number of unfamiliar/untrained accented sentences in the categorization task (Floccia et al. 2009). To assess whether or not children were able to detect the unfamiliar/untrained accent using a bias-free measure, separate measures of sensitivity (A') and bias (B''_D) were calculated using signal detection analysis (see Girard, Floccia & Goslin 2008; Floccia et al. 2009). Signal detection analysis is a widely used tool in experimental psychology because it allows us to analyze how well someone can detect, discriminate, or classify stimuli. Sensitivity (A') measures how hard or easy it is to detect a given stimulus. The measure varies between 0 and 1 with a score of 1 representing a 100 percent correct hit-rate (i.e., no false alarms) and a value of 0.5 indicating chance performance. Here, a hit was defined as correct categorization of the home accent in the Home-Foreign and Home-Regional conditions, and of the regional accent in the Regional-Foreign condition. A false alarm occurred when the regional (Home-Regional condition) or foreign accent (Home-Foreign and Regional-Foreign condition) was mistakenly identified as the home or regional accent respectively. B''_D refers to the extent to which one response is more probable than other, that is, if a participant is more likely to respond that a stimulus is present or not. It is independent from sensitivity and ranges from −1 to 1. Negative values indicate a liberal response bias, and positive values indicate a conservative bias (Donaldson 1992).

Average sensitivity (A') and bias (B''_D) scores for monolingual and bilingual children in each condition (Home-Regional, Home-Foreign, Regional-Foreign) are displayed in Table 19.3. The pattern of results for sensitivity is similar to those for overall categorization. In the Home-Foreign condition, bilinguals had above-chance levels of sensitivity ($A' = 0.82$) and had greater sensitivity than monolinguals, who were at chance. In the Home-Regional condition, sensitivity was low overall but bilinguals had higher sensitivity than monolinguals. Bilinguals also appeared to have a more liberal response bias than monolinguals in these conditions (Home-Regional and Home-Foreign), indicating that although they were able to do the task with some success in the Home-Foreign condition they were still more likely to categorize the talker as "Home." In the Regional-Foreign condition, all children performed similarly with sensitivity at around chance-level.

Due to the small number of bilinguals in each condition, data were pooled across conditions and potential differences in overall sensitivity and bias in monolingual and bilingual children were tested

Table 19.3 Mean measures of sensitivity (A') and bias (B''_D) for monolingual and bilingual children calculated for each condition

	Home-Regional		Home-Foreign		Regional-Foreign	
	A'	B''_D	A'	B''_D	A'	B''_D
Monolingual	0.42	0.22	0.52	0.02	0.55	−0.03
Bilingual	0.62	−0.12	0.82	−0.34	0.58	0.15

using separate independent samples *t*-tests. For sensitivity, there was a near-significant effect of language background, $t(48) = -1.93$, $p = 0.06$, indicating that bilinguals had a tendency to perform better in this task. This was likely driven by the above-chance sensitivity levels in the home-foreign condition but failed to reach significance because of the small number of bilinguals ($n=4$). Although there were small observed differences in bias, there was no significant difference between monolinguals and bilinguals on this measure ($p > 0.05$).

Discussion

In a previous study (Evans & Tomé Lourido 2019), we investigated whether monolingual and bilingual children growing up in a diverse, multilingual community (inner London) would be better able to categorize talkers according to accent. Previous research with monolingual children growing up in more homogenous speech communities had shown that the ability to explicitly categorize talkers emerges at around 5 years but that initially they can only successfully categorize talkers when the acoustic-phonetic differences between the accents are maximized, that is, in the Home-Foreign condition (Girard, Floccia & Goslin 2008; Floccia et al. 2009; Wagner, Clopper & Pate 2014). This led researchers to hypothesize that children have gradient representations of accent variation, with their Home accent, the one that is experienced the most, forming the core set of experiences and other varieties identified relative to this (Wagner, Clopper & Pate 2014). Children thus perform poorly in categorizing talkers from their home versus an unfamiliar regional accent community because, even though these accents might be phonetically quite different, they are interpreted by the children as being similar enough that they cannot be well differentiated. In contrast, foreign accents are hypothesized to go well beyond what children will accept as similar, and so they are able to categorize these as separate from their own native accent (Wagner, Clopper & Pate 2014).

This work led us to hypothesize that the children in our 2019 study, growing up in inner London where they are frequently exposed to regional and foreign-accented speech, would perform well in an accent categorization task, and that our bilingual children, exposed to the greatest amount of variability, would perform best. This prediction was supported. Bilingual children in inner London were able to categorize talkers successfully in all three conditions (Home-Regional, Home-Foreign, Regional-Foreign). However, our monolingual children were only able to categorize talkers with above-chance accuracy in the Home-Foreign condition, replicating findings from these previous studies. We interpreted these results as consistent with a gradient representation approach, but as also suggesting an important role for social context, with the ability to extract and use patterns of variation to categorize talkers differing according to a child's linguistic environment. However, the experience of bilingualism varies greatly between individuals. Thus, it could be the environment rather than bilingualism per se that led to bilinguals in inner London performing better. That is, bilinguals who grow up in a more homogenous community might behave more like monolinguals.

In this study, we sought to further investigate the effect of linguistic environment on accent awareness by testing a group of monolingual and bilingual children of the same age, but living in an area of Greater London where they are exposed to lower levels of accent variation. We also wanted to make some methodological changes—in particular, increasing the number of trials and talkers. Based on previous studies, our hypothesis was that all children would be able to categorize talkers in the Home-Foreign condition where the differences were maximized. Of interest was whether or not our bilingual children, growing up in a more homogenous area, would perform better overall. Our results were somewhat surprising. Although all children were able to understand the different accents, only bilingual children were able to categorize talkers with above-chance accuracy in the Home-Foreign condition.

Why did children, in particular monolinguals, perform poorly in the categorization task? One possibility is that we made the task too difficult by increasing the number of test trials from six to twelve (six per accent) and the number of talkers from three to six. At this age, children might not have the cognitive resources to complete a task this complex. Successful completion of the task relies on learning to associate a given accent with a given toy and then remembering this for use as comparison in subsequent test trials. Although we included reminder trials at a similar point in the task as before, children may have been unable to reliably retain the link between the toy and accent for the duration of the experiment given the increased number of trials.

Another possibility is that the choice of accents contributed towards making the task more difficult. In exemplar-theoretic models, adults have been hypothesized to identify talkers according to their regional accent by mapping to stored memories of similar talkers (e.g., Johnson 1997). In many parts of London, Popular London exists on a continuum with SSBE. Different speakers, communities, and areas move along this continuum, but it is often the case that one variety (Popular London or SSBE) is more commonly used than the other. Usage is often closely linked to socioeconomic factors, and the community in which our study took place is in an area of Greater London where an accent more similar to SSBE would likely have formed children's core accent experience (Wagner, Clopper & Pate 2014; Evans & Tomé Lourido 2019). This means that children may not have had enough experience with Popular London, and these sparse representations may have meant that they were unable to reliably separate the Home in the different conditions. Likewise, the choice of regional accent may also have made it difficult for children to separate the home- and regional-accented talkers reliably. Although the accent spoken in Ashby is a northern variety, it has greater phonetic overlap with southern varieties of English than does Yorkshire English, the accent used in our 2019 study. That is not to say that children heard the regional- and home-accented talkers as equivalent, but that the regional accent may have been within children's "noise" tolerance for the Home accent.

Bilingual children, on the other hand, behaved like the monolinguals in inner London: they were able to successfully categorize talkers in the Home-Foreign condition, but not the Home-Regional or Regional-Foreign condition. One possibility is that our bilinguals had had more exposure to variation than our monolinguals, similar to that of our monolinguals in inner London but less than that of bilinguals in inner London (Evans & Tomé Lourido 2019). In our previous study, we argued that successful categorization of talkers according to accent involves not only development of the ability to track acoustic-phonetic differences between talkers, consistent with the gradient representation hypothesis, but also development of an understanding of how patterns of variation are used meaningfully within a community. In turn, this enables children to associate patterns of variation with a given attribute. In our previous study, the bilingual children were growing up in dense immigrant communities, where they had increased exposure to both different native-speaker varieties of English (e.g., through their monolingual peers and/or teachers) and also to foreign-accented varieties (McCarthy et al. 2013). Increased exposure to variation in a community where such variation serves to differentiate talkers as belonging to different sections of that community may thus promote sensitivity to talker variation, such that children growing up bilingually in a diverse, multilingual community develop the ability to extract, store, and use talker variation in speech processing in a more fine-grained way earlier in development. Based on this, we hypothesized that bilinguals, exposed to less variation, would perform more like monolinguals, with the ability to categorize talkers according to spoken accent emerging later in development.

The results here support this hypothesis. The bilinguals in the current study were predominantly exposed to a single variety in the community and used their other language at home with only a small number of family members, with only limited experience of it outside of this setting (cf. Grosjean 1998). This suggests an important role for social context, such that the development of the ability to extract and use patterns of variation to categorize talkers may differ according to a child's linguistic environment. Knowledge of phonetic and social variation is thus likely emergent, with any abstract categories formed in part at least, from social and phonetic knowledge gained and filtered through experience (cf. Evans & Tomé Lourido 2019).

Conclusion

Multilingual communities can take many different forms. They encompass different types of multilinguals (e.g., simultaneous, sequential, new speakers) living in a wide variety of communities, where the linguistic environment can be very different. Some speakers may hear and use all of their languages regularly both in the home and the wider community, whilst others use one language in the home and another in the wider community. Still others may use a different language outside the home in a specific setting (e.g., school) or change the language they choose to use for ideological reasons, but may continue to hear and interact with speakers of their other language(s) in their daily life. Studies of phonetic variation have shown that speakers in these communities, monolingual and multilingual, draw on a rich, dynamic repertoire to establish, maintain, and contest complex identities, and that listeners use this information in speech processing to both understand speech and navigate their social worlds.

Acknowledgments

This first author would like to dedicate this chapter to four wonderful women who inspired her in her multilingual journey: Sian Dyer, Mary Beadman, and Moira Tipping who sent me on my way, and the late Professor Vivian Law, a constant source of wonder and inspiration. This chapter was written during the 2020 COVID-19 pandemic whilst juggling work with home-schooling my young son: I hope to have inspired him on his multilingual journey.

Both authors gratefully acknowledge the help and support of those who made our work possible: Xosé Luís Regueira and Elisa Fernández Rei for studies in Galicia, Courtney Kaleta and

Josiane Riverin-Coutlée for support with the study in London, UK, and the parents, children, and their school, who generously gave of their time to take part.

References

Ackroyd, Peter. 2000. *London: The biography*. Vintage.

Agha, Asif. 2003. The social life of cultural value. *Language and Communication* 23(3–4). 231–273. https://doi.org/10.1016/S0271-5309(03)00012-0

Ahlberg, Alan & Janet Wright. 1980. *Mrs Plug the Plumber*. Puffin.

Alam, Farhana. 2015. *'Glaswasian'? A sociophonetic analysis of Glasgow-Asian accent and identity*. PhD thesis, University of Glasgow.

Alam, Farhana & Jane Stuart-Smith. 2011. Identity and ethnicity in /t/ in Glasgow-Pakistani high-school girls. In Wai Sum Lee & Eric Zee (eds.), *Proceedings of the 17th International Congress of Phonetic Sciences (ICPhS XVII): August 17–21, 2011*. City University of Hong Kong.

Best, Catherine T. 1994. The emergence of native-language phonological influences in infants: a perceptual assimilation model. In Judith C. Goodman & Howard C. Nusbaum (eds.), *The development of speech perception: The transition from speech sounds to spoken words*, 167–224. MIT Press.

Best, Catherine T. & Michael D. Tyler. 2007. Nonnative and second-language speech perception: Commonalities and complementarities. In Ocke-Schwen Bohn & Murray J. Munro (eds.), *Second language speech learning: The role of language experience in speech perception and production*, 13–34. John Benjamins. https://doi.org/10.1075/lllt.17

Boersma, Paul & David Weenink. 2017. *Praat: Doing phonetics by computer* [Computer program]. www.praat.org/

Bond, Michael. 1958. *Please look after this Bear*. Puffin.

Braber, Natalie & Jonnie Robinson. 2018. *East Midlands English*. De Gruyter Mouton. https://doi.org/10.1515/9781501502354

Bucholtz, Mary. 1999. "Why be normal?": Language and identity practices in a community of nerd girls. *Language in Society* 28(2). 203–223. https://doi.org/10.1017/S0047404599002043

Cheshire, Jenny & Penelope Gardner-Chloros. 2018. Introduction: Multicultural youth vernaculars in Paris and urban France. *Journal of French Language Studies* 28(2). 161–164. https://doi.org/10.1017/S0959269518000182

Cheshire, Jenny, Paul Kerswill, Susan Fox & Eivind Torgersen. 2011. Contact, the feature pool and the speech community: The emergence of Multicultural London English. *Journal of Sociolinguistics* 15(2). 151–196. https://doi.org/10.1111/j.1467-9841.2011.00478.x

Clarke, Constance M. & Merrill F. Garrett. 2004. Rapid adaptation to foreign-accented English. *Journal of the Acoustical Society of America* 116. 3647–3658. https://doi.org/10.1121/1.1815131

Cole, Amanda & Bronwen G. Evans. 2020. Phonetic variation and change in the Cockney Diaspora: The role of place, gender, and identity. *Language in Society* 50(5). https://doi.org/10.1017/S0047404520000640

Darcy, Isabelle & Franziska Krüger. 2012. Vowel production and perception in Turkish children acquiring L2 German. *Journal of Phonetics* 40(4). 568–581. https://doi.org/10.1016/j.wocn.2012.05.001

Dewaele, Jean-Marc. 2019. The effect of classroom emotions, attitudes toward English, and teacher behavior on willingness to communicate among English foreign language learners. *Journal of Language and Social Psychology* 38(4). 523–535. https://doi.org/10.1177/0261927X19864996

Donaldson, Wayne. 1992. Measuring recognition memory. *Journal of Experimental Psychology: General* 121(3). 275–277. https://doi.org/10.1037/0096-3445.121.3.275

Donaldson, Julia & Axel Scheffler. 2004. *The Gruffalo's child*. Macmillan.

Drummond, Robert. 2013. The Manchester Polish STRUT: Dialect acquisition in a second language. *Journal of English Linguistics* 41(1). 65–93. https://doi.org/10.1177/0075424212449172

Dunn, Douglas M. & Lloyd M. Dunn. 2009. *The British picture vocabulary scale*. GL Assessment.

Eckert, Penelope. 2000. *Linguistic variation as social practice: The linguistic construction of identity in Belten High*. Blackwell.

Eckert, Penelope. 2008. Variation and the indexical field. *Journal of Sociolinguistics* 12(4). 453–476. https://doi.org/10.1111/j.1467-9841.2008.00374.x

Evans, Bronwen G. & Paul Iverson. 2004. Vowel normalization for accent: An investigation of best exemplar locations in northern and southern British English sentences. *Journal of the Acoustical Society of America* 115(1). 352–361. https://doi.org/10.1121/1.1635413

Evans, Bronwen G. & Gisela Tomé Lourido. 2019. Effects of language background on the development of sociolinguistic awareness: The perception of accent variation in monolingual and multilingual 5–7 year old children. *Phonetica* 76(2–3). https://doi.org/10.1159/000493983

Flege, James E. 1995. Second language speech learning: Theory, findings, and problems. In Winifred Strange (ed.), *Speech perception and linguistic experience: Issues in cross-language research*, 233–277. York Press.

Flege, James E. & Ocke-Schwen Bohn. 2021. The revised speech learning model (SLM-r). In R. Wayland (ed.), *Second language speech learning: Theoretical and empirical progress*, 3–83. Cambridge University Press. https://doi.org/10.1017/9781108886901

Floccia, Caroline, Joseph Butler, Frédérique Girard & Jeremy Goslin. 2009. Categorization of regional and foreign accent in 5- to 7-year-old British children. *International Journal of Behavioral Development* 33(4). 366–375. https://doi.org/10.1177/0165025409103871

Foulkes, Paul & Gerard J. Docherty. 1999. Derby and Newcastle: Instrumental phonetics and variationist studies. In Paul Foulkes & Gerard J. Docherty (eds.), *Urban voices: Accent studies in the British Isles*, 47–71. Arnold.

Foulkes, Paul & Gerard J. Docherty. 2006. The social life of phonetics and phonology. *Journal of Phonetics* 34(4). 409–438. https://doi.org/10.1016/j.wocn.2005.08.002

Fox, Susan. 2015. *The new Cockney. New ethnicities and adolescent speech in the traditional East End of London*. Palgrave.

Girard, Frédérique, Caroline Floccia & Jeremy Goslin. 2008. Perception and awareness of accents in young children. *British Journal of Developmental Psychology* 26(3). 409–433. https://doi.org/10.1348/02615 1007X251712

Grosjean, Francois. 1998. Studying bilinguals: Methodological and conceptual issues. *Bilingualism: Language and Cognition* 1(2). 131–149. https://doi.org/10.1017/S136672899800025X

Grosjean, Francois. 2021. *Life as a bilingual*. Cambridge University Press. https://doi.org/10.1017/978110 8975490

Harris, Roxy. 2006. *New ethnicities and language use*. Palgrave.

Hirson, Allen & Nabiah Sohail. 2007. Variability of rhotics in Punjabi-English bilinguals. In Trouvain & Barry, 1501–1504.

Iverson, Paul, Patricia K. Kuhl, Reiko Akahane-Yamada, Eugen Diesch, Yoh'ich Tohkura, Andreas Kettermann & Claudia Siebert. 2003. A perceptual interference account of acquisition difficulties for non-native phonemes. *Cognition* 87(1). 47–57. https://doi.org/10.1016/s0010-0277(02)00198-1

Johnson, Keith. 1997. Speech perception without speaker normalization: An exemplar model. In Keith Johnson & John W. Mullennix (eds.), *Talker variability in speech processing*, 145–165. Academic Press.

Johnstone, Barbara, Jennifer Andrus & Andrew E. Danielson, 2006. Mobility, indexicality, and the enregisterment of "Pittsburghese." *Journal of English Linguistics* 34(2). 77–104. https://doi.org/10.1177/0075424206290692

Kachru, Braj. 1980. Bilingualism. *Annual Review of Applied Linguistics* 1. 2–18. https://doi.org/10.1017/S0267190500000441

Kerswill, Paul. 2013. Identity, ethnicity and place: The construction of youth language in London. In Peter Auer, Martin Hilpert, Anja Stukenbrock & Benedikt Szmrecsanyi (eds.), *Space in language and linguistics: Geographical, interactional, and cognitive perspectives*, 128–164. Walter De Gruyter. https://doi.org/10.1515/9783110312027

Kerswill, Paul, Eivind Torgersen & Susan Fox. 2008. Reversing "drift": Innovation and diffusion in the London diphthong system. *Language Variation and Change* 20(3). 451–491. https://doi.org/10.1017/S0954394508000148

Kerswill, Paul & Ann Williams. 2000. Creating a new town koine: Children and language change in Milton Keynes. *Language in Society* 29(1). 65–115. https://doi.org/10.1017/S0047404500001020

Kerswill, Paul & Ann Williams. 2005. New towns and koineization: Linguistic and social correlates. *Linguistics* 43(5). 1023–1048. https://doi.org/10.1515/ling.2005.43.5.1023

Khan, Arfaan. 2006. *A sociolinguistic study of Birmingham English: Language variation and change in a multi-ethnic British community*. PhD thesis, Lancaster University.

Khattab, Ghada. 1999. A socio-phonetic study of English-Arabic bilingual children. *Leeds Working Papers in Linguistics & Phonetics* 7(1). 79–94.

Khattab, Ghada. 2002. /r/ production in English and Arabic bilingual and monolingual speakers. *Leeds Working Papers in Linguistics & Phonetics* 9(1). 91–129.

Kirkham, Sam. 2015. Intersectionality and the social meanings of variation: Class, ethnicity, and social practice. *Language in Society* 44(5). 629–652. https://doi.org/10.1017/S0047404515000585

Kirkham, Sam & Kathleen M. McCarthy. 2020. Acquiring allophonic structure and phonetic detail in a bilingual community: The production of laterals by Sylheti-English bilingual children. *International Journal of Bilingualism* 25(3). https://doi.org/10.1177/1367006920947180

Kirkham, Sam & Jessica Wormald. 2015. Acoustic and articulatory variation in British Asian English liquids. In Scottish Consortium for ICPhS 2015, Paper 640.

Kohnert, Kathryn. 2008. Second language acquisition: Success factors in sequential bilingualism. *ASHA Leader* 13(2). 10–13. https://doi.org/10.1044/leader.FTR1.13022008.10

Lambert, Kirsten, Farhana Alam & Jane Stuart-Smith. 2007. Investigating British Asian accents: Studies from Glasgow. In Trouvain & Barry, 1509–1512.

Leeuw Esther de, Ineke Mennen & James M. Scobbie. 2012. Singing a different tune in your native language: First language attrition of prosody. *International Journal of Bilingualism* 16(1). 101–116. https://doi.org/10.1177/1367006911405576

Lenth, Russell V. 2016. Least-squares means: The R package lsmeans. *Journal of Statistical Software* 69(1). 1–33. https://doi.org/10.18637/jss.v069.i01

Levon, Erez, Devyani Sharma, Dominic Watt, Amanda Cardoso & Ye Yang. 2021. Accent bias and perceptions of professional competence in England. *Journal of English Linguistics* 49(4). 355–388. https://doi.org/10.1177/00754242211046316

Mayr, Robert, Sacha Price & Ineke Mennen. 2012. First language attrition in the speech of Dutch-English bilinguals: The case of monozygotic twin sisters. *Bilingualism: Language and Cognition* 15(4). 687–700. https://doi.org/10.1017/S136672891100071X

Mayr, Robert, Jonathan Morris, Ineke Mennen & Daniel Williams. 2017. Disentangling the effects of long-term language contact and individual bilingualism: The case of monophthongs in Welsh and English. *International Journal of Bilingualism* 21(3). 245–267. https://doi.org/10.1177/1367006915614921

Mayr, Robert, Laura López-Bueno, Martín Vázquez Fernández & Gisela Tomé Lourido. 2019. The role of early experience and continued language use in bilingual speech production: A study of Galician and Spanish mid vowels by Galician-Spanish bilinguals. *Journal of Phonetics* 72. 1–16. https://doi.org/10.1016/j.wocn.2018.10.007

McCarthy, Kathleen M., Bronwen G. Evans & Merle Mahon. 2013. Acquiring a second language in an immigrant community: The production of Sylheti and English stops and vowels by London-Bengali speakers. *Journal of Phonetics* 41(5). 344–358. https://doi.org/10.1016/j.wocn.2013.03.006

McCarthy, Kathleen M., Merle Mahon, Stuart Rosen & Bronwen G. Evans, 2014. Speech perception and production by sequential bilingual children: A longitudinal study of voice onset time acquisition. *Child Development* 85(5). 1965–1980. https://doi.org/10.1111/cdev.12275

Moore, Emma F. & Chris Montgomery. 2018. Evaluating S(c)illy voices: The effects of salience, stereotypes, and co-present language variables on real-time reactions to regional speech. *Language* 94(3). 629–661. https://doi.org/10.1353/lan.2018.0038

Mora, Joan C. & Marianna Nadeu. 2012. L2 effects on the perception and production of a native vowel contrast in early bilinguals. *International Journal of Bilingualism* 16(4). 484–500. https://doi.org/10.1177/1367006911429518

Nance, Claire. 2015. "New" Scottish Gaelic speakers in Glasgow: A phonetic study of language revitalisation. *Language in Society* 44(4). 553–579. https://doi.org/10.1017/S0047404515000408

Nance, Claire, Wilson McLeod, Bernadette O'Rourke & Stuart Dunmore. 2016. Identity, accent aim, and motivation in second language users: New Scottish Gaelic speakers' use of phonetic variation. *Journal of Sociolinguistics* 20(2). 164–191. https://doi.org/10.1111/josl.12173

O'Rourke, Bernadette & Joan Pujolar. 2013. From native speakers to "new speakers"—Problematizing nativeness in language revitalization contexts. *Histoire Épistémologie Langage* 35(2). 47–67.

O'Rourke, Bernadette & Fernando F. Ramallo. 2011. The native-non-native dichotomy in minority language contexts: Comparisons between Irish and Galician. *Language Problems and Language Planning* 35(2). 139–159. https://doi.org/10.1075/lplp.35.2.03oro

O'Rourke, Bernadette & Fernando Ramallo. 2013. Competing ideologies of linguistic authority amongst new speakers in contemporary Galicia. *Language in Society* 42(3). 287–305. https://doi.org/10.1017/S00474 04513000249

O'Rourke, Bernadette & Fernando Ramallo. 2015. *Neofalantes* as an active minority: Understanding language practices and motivations for change amongst new speakers of Galician. *International Journal of the Sociology of Language* 231. 147–165. https://doi.org/10.1515/ijsl-2014-0036

O'Rourke, Bernadette, Joan Pujolar & Fernando Ramallo. 2015. New speakers of minority languages: The challenging opportunity–Foreword. *International Journal of the Sociology of Language* 231. 1–20. https://doi.org/10.1515/ijsl-2014-0029

Picone, Michael D. 2008. Multilingual Alabama. *Tributaries* 10. 32–71.

Pinet, Melanie, Yuanlin Gan, Bronwen G. Evans & Paul Iverson. 2015. Intelligibility of British English accents in noise for second-language learners. In Scottish Consortium for ICPhS 2015, Paper 433.

Quist, Pia (2008). Sociolinguistic approaches to multiethnolect: Language variety and stylistic practice. *International Journal of Bilingualism* 12(1–2). 43–61. https://doi.org/10.1177/13670069080120010401

R Core Team. 2022. *R: A language and environment for statistical computing*. R Foundation for Statistical Computing. www.R-project.org

Ramallo, Fernando & Bernadette O'Rourke. 2014. Perfiles de neohablantes de gallego. *Digithum* 16. 98–105.

Regueira, Xosé Luis & Elisa Fernández Rei. 2020. The Spanish sound system and intonation in contact with Galician. In Rajiv Rao (ed.), *Spanish phonetics and phonology in contact: Studies from Africa, the Americas, and Spain*, 325–362. John Benjamins. https://doi.org/10.1075/ihll.28

The Scottish Consortium for ICPhS 2015 (ed.). 2015. *Proceedings of the 18th International Congress of Phonetic Sciences*. University of Glasgow.

Sharma, Devyani & Lavanya Sankaran. 2011. Cognitive and social forces in dialect shift: Gradual change in British Asian speech. *Language Variation and Change* 23(3). 399–428. https://doi.org/10.1017/S09543 94511000159

Silverstein, Michael. 2003. Indexical order and the dialectics of sociolinguistic life. *Language and Communication* 23 (3–4). 193–229. https://doi.org/10.1016/S0271-5309(03)00013-2

Sundara, Meghan & Adrienne Scuttellaro. 2011. Rhythmic difference between languages affects the development of speech perception in bilingual infants. *Journal of Phonetics* 39(4). 505–513. https://doi.org/10.1016/j.wocn.2010.08.006

Tomé Lourido, Gisela & Bronwen G. Evans. 2019. The effects of language dominance switch in bilinguals: Galician new speakers' speech production and perception. *Bilingualism: Language and Cognition* 22(3). 637–654. https://doi.org/10.1017/S1366728918000603

Tomé Lourido, Gisela & Bronwen G. Evans. 2021. Sociolinguistic awareness in Galician bilinguals: Evidence from an accent identification task. *Languages* 6(1). 53. https://doi.org/10.3390/languages6010053

Trouvain, Jürgen & William J. Barry (eds.). 2007. *Proceedings of the 16th International Congress of Phonetic Sciences: ICPhS XVI, Saarbrücken, Germany*. Universität des Saarlandes.

Tsukada, Kimiko, David Birdsong, Ellen Bialystok, Molly Mack, Hyekyung Sung & James E. Flege. 2005. A developmental study of English vowel production and perception by native Korean adults and children. *Journal of Phonetics* 33(3). 263–290. https://doi.org/10.1016/j.wocn.2004.10.002

Vertovec, Steven. 2007. Super-diversity and its implications. *Ethnic and Racial Studies* 30(6). 1024–1054. https://doi.org/10.1080/01419870701599465

Wagner, Laura, Cynthia G. Clopper & John K. Pate. 2014. Children's perception of dialect variation. *Journal of Child Language* 41(5). 1062–1084. https://doi.org/10.1017/S0305000913000330

Wiese, Heike. 2009. Grammatical innovation in multiethnic urban Europe: New linguistic practices among adolescents. *Lingua* 119(5). 782–806. https://doi.org/10.1016/j.lingua.2008.11.002

Weise, Heike. 2020. Contact in the city. In Raymond Hickey (ed.), *Handbook of language contact*, 2nd edn., 261–280. Wiley.

Wells, J. C. 1982. *Accents of English*, vol. 2, *The British Isles*. Cambridge University Press.

20

SOCIOPHONETICS AND SECOND LANGUAGE ACQUISITION

Ksenia Gnevsheva

Introduction

Most of the research in sociophonetics has traditionally focused on monolingual, first language (L1) speakers. Despite a substantial number of sociophonetic studies involving second language (L2) speakers appearing in recent years, the fields of sociophonetics and second language acquisition (SLA) remain to a large extent divided, with sociophonetics exhibiting a monolingual research bias and SLA largely ignoring sociolinguistic variability. However, the subfield of L2 sociophonetics has a lot to offer to both; sociophonetic variation in L2 speakers can help shed light on some universal sociophonetic processes on the one hand and, on the other, add to the understanding of an important part of L2 speakers' language acquisition and linguistic behavior. This chapter aims to showcase the strengths and contributions of L2 sociophonetics. It will review existing L2 sociophonetic studies in both speech production and perception, present a case study illustrating this branch of research, and discuss the field's future directions.

SLA, phonetics, and sociolinguistic variation

The field of SLA concerns itself with the acquisition of second and additional languages. L1 is generally understood as the first language that a speaker acquires in childhood, and L2 as an additional language, usually acquired in adulthood (references to L1 and L2 have largely replaced other related terms such as "mother tongue" and "native speaker"). Some of the key questions driving SLA research revolve around the predictors of successful L2 acquisition, the neuropsychological and sociocultural aspects of language learning, and the pedagogical methods for effective L2 teaching in the classroom context.

The fields of phonetics and SLA come in contact most readily in the study of L2 pronunciation pedagogy. Over the history of the field, L2 teaching methods ranged from ignoring pronunciation teaching to focusing on it as a base for other language skills. Because of its applied angle, L2 pronunciation pedagogy has often been prescriptive in nature. Two contradicting principles have guided pronunciation teaching (Levis 2005). The "nativeness principle" took an abstract native speaker as an ideal or benchmark in early pronunciation instruction, making any deviation from the native speaker model undesirable and a potential focus for intervention. With promotion of the

DOI: 10.4324/9781003034636-22

view that nativelikeness is an unachievable goal for the vast majority of L2 learners, the nativeness principle was largely (but not totally) replaced by the "intelligibility principle," which focuses on listener understanding instead. This shift in perspective meant that only L2 features which hindered intelligibility were addressed in teaching.

Related to these principles are the constructs of accentedness, comprehensibility, and intelligibility as applied to L2 speech (Munro & Derwing 1995), which have been used widely in pronunciation teaching and research. Here accentedness means the degree of phonetic deviation of an L2 speaker from an L1 ideal; comprehensibility is conceptualized as the ease of understanding, and intelligibility stands for the extent to which the speaker is actually understood. These concepts are related but not identical, so that a strongly accented speaker may still be quite intelligible. Many studies found a strong relationship between these perceptual measures of speaking ability and acoustic measures of segmental and suprasegmental features (e.g., Kang 2010; Isaacs & Trofimovich 2012).

Historically, SLA has focused on ultimate attainment and did not concern itself with variation in phonetics and at other linguistic levels. Where variation was considered, it was not regarded to be sociolinguistic but rather acquisitionist in nature; that is, the focus was on diachronic variation in proficiency as a speaker acquires the language rather than on synchronic variation conditioned by social factors. Young (1988) acknowledges this dichotomy and makes a distinction between two types of variation. As such, early SLA work investigated the predictors of variation on the acquisition continuum—"Type 1" or "vertical" variation ("vertical" in this sense refers to progressive development of language skills along a proficiency continuum over time; Young 1988; Mougeon, Rehner & Nadasdi 2004). Such research found that age of acquisition is a strong predictor of target-like performance, especially in pronunciation (e.g., Flege, Yeni-Komshian & Liu 1999); other participant-related characteristics that have been shown to affect variation on the vertical continuum are length of residence in the L2 country (e.g., Derwing & Munro 2013) and affiliation/orientation (e.g., Gatbonton, Trofimovich & Segalowitz 2011), among many others. Although this line of research examines the relationship between some participant social categories and interspeaker linguistic variation in pronunciation, variability in the target language is ignored and the focus is on the attainment of an idealized, invariant model. With the expansion of the field of sociolinguistics, and sociophonetics specifically, SLA researchers also began considering the acquisition of the sociolinguistic constraints on variation by L2 speakers—"Type 2" or "horizontal" variation ("horizontal" refers to synchronic, sociolinguistic variation; Young 1988; Mougeon, Rehner & Nadasdi 2004).

Sociophonetic variation in L2 speech production

One of the earliest studies that applied sociophonetics questions and methods to L2 speech was Adamson & Regan (1991), which investigated the acquisition of (ING) by Vietnamese and Cambodian immigrants in the United States and asked whether L2 speakers would replicate the L1 linguistic and social constraints on variation. The participants were audio-recorded in a sociolinguistic interview, a common data collection method in sociolinguistics in general and sociophonetics in particular. The L2 speakers demonstrated acquisition of some of the L1 variable rules: following velar stops favored [ŋ], progressive verbs favored [n], males produced [n] more than females, and females produced more [ŋ] in monitored than unmonitored speech. At the same time, there were some differences in the effect of the following phonological environment and grammatical category, but the biggest difference was in the effect of style, with L2 males producing more [n] in monitored than unmonitored speech. Since this early research a number of studies have found evidence for L2 acquisition of sociophonetic variation with certain deviations in social and linguistic constraints from L1 speakers. Such patterns have been identified in naturalistic environments (Schleef, Meyerhoff & Clark 2011; Drummond 2012), in study-abroad contexts (Regan, Howard & Lemée 2009), and in immersion settings (Mougeon, Rehner & Nadasdi 2004 and references therein; Uritescu et al. 2004).

In addition to the differences in sociolinguistic constraints on variation, L2 speakers have been found to be less variable in absolute terms and to prefer the standard form. For example, lower rates of use of the vernacular variant by L2 speakers have been found for (ING) (Adamson & Regan 1991) and t-glottalling (Drummond 2011) in English. It has been argued that speaker-related factors such as proficiency and length of residence predict rates of use of the vernacular variant. For example, Polish migrants who had spent more time in Manchester and those with higher proficiency had a higher level of t-glottalization (Drummond 2011). Studies that investigated the acquisition of sociophonetic variation in a classroom context found even lower rates of acquisition. Howard, Lemée & Regan (2006), for instance, compared the acquisition of /l/ deletion by Irish learners of French in a classroom and study-abroad setting. They found that participants who had never visited France deleted /l/ less than those who had (6 percent vs. 33 percent). In contrast, Solon, Linford & Geeslin (2018), who studied intervocalic /d/ reduction in L1 and L2 speakers of Spanish, found comparable rates of /d/ reduction in the two groups, though with differences in the rates of type of reduction (spirantization and deletion) and factors predicting it. These findings show that, overall, more exposure to the L1 community (and, consequently, the vernacular) results in a higher usage of vernacular variants. Importantly, some of these results suggest that L2 proficiency does not equal level of education in the L1 sociolinguistic literature, as higher proficiency is often associated with a higher usage of vernacular variants. That is, more proficient L2 speakers are more proficient in the sociolinguistic sense as well.

Theoretical accounts of variation that had been developed for L1 speech were demonstrated to largely hold when applied to L2 speech as well. The principles of Labov's (1972) attention-to-speech model, for instance, were found to predict variation among Thai learners of English by Beebe (1980). Beebe showed that learners produced more target-like /ɹ/ in a higher attention-to-speech task (list reading) than in a lower attention-to-speech task (interview), and that they reversed this pattern for word-initial /ɹ/. Beebe (1980) concluded that self-monitoring increased in more formal situations and resulted in influences from L1 or L2 depending on the sociolinguistic status of the variable in the two languages (see also Major 2001). Accommodation theory (e.g., Giles & Powesland 1975) was applied by Beebe & Zuengler (1983) in the context of L2 speech, revealing that bilingual speakers converged to their interlocutors in pronunciation and syntax. Finally, identity-focused approaches (e.g., Eckert 2000) were explored by Dolgova Jacobsen (2008), who found that participants varied in their pronunciation of the KIT vowel depending on topic of the interview, and that those who identified as "Russian-American" rather than "American" produced a tenser (more accented) vowel.

Some researchers have argued that L2 speakers are not limited to Type 1 and Type 2 variation and have proposed a Type 3 variation—that is, synchronic variation between more L1-like and L2-like variants (e.g., Nance et al. 2016). In this approach, alternation between L1 and L2 variants is not always considered developmental (as in Type 1 variation) and is not derived from the target language (as in Type 2 variation). Instead, it is considered synchronic and is used for sociolinguistic positioning on the L1–L2 continuum. For example, Gnevsheva (2015) collected interviews and self-recordings of L2 speakers of English in several different settings. The participants were found to style-shift by producing more L1-like vowels when speaking about their family than when speaking on other topics, arguably because this topic was conducive to activating L1-like exemplars. Similar variation on the L1–L2 continuum associated with changes in interlocutor, topic, and/or setting was found in Beebe (1980), Sancier & Fowler (1997), Major (2004), Dolgova Jacobsen (2008), Rampton (2011), Sharma (2011), and Hwang, Brennan & Huffman (2015).

A related branch of research focuses on such variation between L1 and L2 features and compares speech production by L2 speakers to that of L1 speakers of the same ethnic background in an attempt to identify ethnolectal features and predictors of their usage. For instance, Gnevsheva (2020) compared the realization of two vowels by L2 speakers of English of Russian-speaking background, L1 speakers of English of Russian-speaking background, and Anglo L1 speakers of English across three different styles (conversation, interview, and reading). The analysis revealed that Anglo participants did not style-shift in their production of the vowels, meaning that any variation in the bilinguals would not be a Type 2 variation. The L1 and L2 speakers of English of Russian-speaking background exhibited variation across styles, but it was not identical in the two groups (they style-shifted similarly in their production of the TRAP vowel, but L2 speakers did not style-shift in their production of GOOSE), which was used to argue that ethnolectal features may be derived from the minority language but used differently by L1 speakers of the majority language.

With the goal of explicating interspeaker difference in style-shifting, Sharma (2017) used the diversity of participants' social networks to explain between-speaker variation in "accent range" (i.e., the variation in percentage of ethnic variant use between styles) and found that participants' linguistic variability increased with increased diversity of their social networks. Other similar comparisons have resulted in contradictory findings: sometimes L1 speakers of minority ethnicity are shown to be more similar to L2 speakers of minority ethnicity and, at other times, to L1 speakers of majority ethnicity (Hoffman & Walker 2010; Sharma & Sankaran 2011), making it a focal point for current research.

Methodologically, most of the production studies utilize acoustic or auditory analysis performed by the researcher. Auditory coding is usually done for categorical variables (e.g., velar vs. alveolar nasals in Adamson & Regan 1991), and acoustic analysis is better suited for when the variable is treated as continuous (e.g., vowel formants in Gnevsheva 2020). These are not incompatible approaches, with Solon, Linford & Geeslin (2018) supplementing visual spectrographic coding of Spanish /d/ reduction with acoustic measurement.

In short—though comparatively much less common—sociophonetic studies of L2 speech are creating a space for the study of variation in SLA and are helping to shift the focus from an ideal, invariant L1 speaker model to variation as the norm and part of a proficient L2 speaker's competence. Moreover, such an approach to variation in the L2 positions L2 speakers as active agents with ownership of their language use as opposed to them being language borrowers constrained by their L2. At the same time L2 speakers offer fertile ground for testing sociolinguistic and sociophonetic theories because of a different relationship with the L2 and storage of linguistic representations.

Sociophonetic variation in L2 speech perception

Perception work in sociophonetics expands into the field of SLA by employing L2-speaking listeners or speakers (for a recent review of perception of L2 speech, see Baese-Berk, McLaughlin & McGowan 2020). Traditional SLA research concerns itself with the development of L2 learners' listening skills (e.g., Vandergrift & Goh 2012). Additionally, it focuses on L1 listeners' evaluations of L2 speakers (e.g., in terms of accentedness, comprehensibility, and intelligibility in Munro & Derwing 1995), relying on and establishing L1 listeners as judges and models. The social aspect of L2 perception (both as speakers and listeners) remains largely unexplored.

L2 sociophonetics work in perception can be divided into studies that investigate how speakers' assumed social attributes vary depending on their linguistic production and studies that investigate how speakers' differing social characteristics result in variation in perception of linguistic information. The former, which are sometimes designated as studies of linguistic stereotyping (e.g., Kang & Rubin 2009), often focus on how speakers with foreign accents are evaluated compared to L1 speakers (Nesdale & Rooney 1996; Watanabe 2008; Bauman 2013; Nelson, Signorella & Botti 2016) and have important social implications. In general L2 accents are often found to be downgraded in comparison to L1 ones. For example, in Gallois & Callan (1981), 80 Australian listeners reacted to speakers from different L1 and L2 English backgrounds by rating them on 16 semantic differential scales (e.g., beautiful–ugly, educated–uneducated). They found that L1 accents were generally evaluated more positively. However, the picture is more complex with an interaction with speaker sex. Italian males, for example, were rated most negatively and Italian females more positively in comparison. It is then not surprising that such negative evaluations, especially in regards to competence, often lead to foreign-accented speakers' lower assessment in employment and other contexts, leading to powerful social implications such as linguistic discrimination (e.g., Seggie, Smith & Hodgins 1986; Cargile 2000; Carlson & McHenry 2006; Hosoda, Nguyen & Stone-Romero 2012; Witkowska et al. this volume).

Another set of studies investigates how well listeners, L1–or L2-speaking, can estimate L2 speakers' objective social characteristics such as age (Gnevsheva & Bürkle 2020; Jiao et al. 2020), region/country of origin, and first language (e.g., Watanabe 2008; Clopper & Bradlow 2009; Clark & Schleef 2010; McKenzie 2015; Gnevsheva 2017, 2018b; McKenzie et al. 2019). For example, in McKenzie (2015) L1-speaking listeners performed a speaker origin identification task with speech samples from L1 and L2 speakers of English and showed higher identification accuracy with L1 than L2 speakers, suggesting an important distinction that listeners make between L1 and L2 speakers. Using a similar methodology Gnevsheva (2017) additionally found that lower proficiency L2 speakers were better identified than higher proficiency participants—perhaps because of more readily available and consistent linguistic cues as L1 phonology rules have a comparatively stronger influence. A similar distribution of identification accuracies between L1 and L2 speakers was also found for L2 listeners, suggesting a parallelism in the underlying processes in L1 and L2 listeners (McKenzie et al. 2019), though their evaluative judgments were found to differ (Alford & Strother 1990).

If the direction of effect is reversed, we find studies that investigate the effect of social information on the perception of linguistic information (e.g., McGowan & Babel 2020). A substantial branch of this type of research considers the effect of ethnicity on perception of speaking proficiency in L2 speakers (Yi et al. 2013; McGowan 2015; Zheng & Samuel 2017; Gnevsheva 2018a; Hanulíková 2018). For instance, Yi et al. (2013) investigated the effect of visual information (a video recording) on perception of L1 (Caucasian) and L2 (Asian) English speakers by L1-speaking listeners. Both groups of speakers were found to be more intelligible in the audiovisual condition (when listeners could see and hear them) compared to the audio condition (when listeners could only hear them), but the improvement was larger for the L1 speakers. Additionally, L2 speakers were perceived to be more accented in the audiovisual condition than in the audio condition, which the authors attribute to negative bias against Asian speakers, similarly to some L1 speaker research (Kang & Rubin 2009). McGowan (2015), however, argued against the negative bias hypothesis having found that Chinese-accented speech was more intelligible to listeners when presented with a picture of an Asian person. He explained this finding through usage-based models of speech perception instead, arguing that a match between visual and linguistic information facilitated activation of relevant representations. The mismatch account was also used in the explanation of the Gnevsheva (2018a) result; there was no difference in perceived accentedness for Asian L2 speakers in audio, video, and audiovisual conditions, but Caucasian L2 speakers were rated more accented in the audiovisual and less accented in the video condition than the audio one, presumably due to the listeners' expectation to hear standard-accented speech from a Caucasian person.

Such integration of social and linguistic information in perception is neither universal nor uniform (e.g., Kang & Rubin 2009). Between-listener variation has been attested in many L1 studies (Niedzielski 1999; Hay, Nolan & Drager 2006; Hay & Drager 2010). For example, in Walker (2014) American participants exhibited a priming advantage in a cross-dialect intelligibility task, with no such effect for British participants. One recent study that considered variable reliance on social cues in L2 speech perception is Gnevsheva (2021). In the English data part of the experiment, first- and second-generation migrants to Australia who were bilingual in Russian and English rated the degree of foreign accent in a group of monolingual and bilingual speakers of English. The stimuli included three audio recordings per speaker that differed in topic: bears (associated with Russia), kangaroos (associated with Australia), and unidentified animals (neutral). The findings revealed that first-generation listeners used the topic as a cue in their judgment by rating speakers as more accented when the topic was Russia-related. This between-group difference was explained through first-generation participants' L2 speaker status and increased reliance on social cues as a compensatory strategy in a situation with a lack of confidence in evaluation of linguistic cues.

As can be seen from this brief overview, though the trident division of variation in L2 production into Types 1, 2, and 3 is quite well-established (with Type 3 being a more recent addition), this typological trinity has not been applied to L2 perception. To mirror the L2 variation in production types, one could think of Type 1 variation in perception by L2 listeners as developmental, of Type 2 as reflective of variation in perception by L1 listeners, and of Type 3 as synchronic and specific to L2 listeners only. As in the case of L2 speech production, research on Type 1 variation in L2 perception lies mostly within the SLA tradition and shows improvement in listening skills with increased language proficiency (e.g., Vandergrift & Goh 2012). Type 2 studies often compare how L2 listeners differ from L1 listeners in the perception of existing variation in production associated with speaker origin (e.g., Clopper & Bradlow 2009; McKenzie 2015; McKenzie et al. 2019); in intelligibility, comprehensibility, and accentedness (e.g., Bent & Bradlow 2003; Munro, Derwing & Morton 2006); or by phonetic variation (Schmidt 2011). Similarly to research on production, these studies often find that L2 listeners demonstrate incomplete acquisition of variation in perception. For example, L1 and L2 listeners in Clopper & Bradlow (2009) were instructed to group together L1 speakers of American English from different dialectal regions. L2 listeners were found to use similar classification strategies, but they were less accurate compared to L1 listeners.

Type 3 studies are very rare and aim to explain sociophonetic variation found in L2 but not L1 listeners (e.g., Gnevsheva 2021). In fact, Types 2 and 3 variation studies in L2 perception are practically non-existent, mostly because the field of SLA has largely ignored non-developmental variation in perception. In the majority of cases L2 sociophonetics research in perception is conducted by sociophoneticians who are more sociophonetics-focused and are interested in testing existing sociophonetics theories on a broader population. As such this work is often limited in its engagement with SLA theories.

Looking toward production + perception

Some studies combine the production and perception methodologies in an attempt to link them. These are very rare, and the majority are of the Type 1, developmental class. For example, a number of studies have worked to link acoustic measurements and their perceptual correlates of accentedness, comprehensibility, and intelligibility. For example, Kang, Rubin & Pickering (2010) analyzed 29 different suprasegmental measures in their relationship with comprehensibility and found suprasegmental fluency, high-rising tones, mid-rising tones, boundary markers, word stress, and pitch height to be significant predictors. Such studies are acquisitionist in nature and lack a true socio aspect.

An obvious way to connect production and perception—for Types 2 and 3 variation studies—is to expand speech production work with perception experiments. On the one hand, speech production research can be supplemented with perception experiments where different types of perceptual coding or rating are completed by a separate group of participants. This permits the researcher to ascertain whether any variation found in production is also noticeable in perception. In an L1 example of such integration, New Zealand and American English speakers participated in a shadowing task in order to test their convergence to different English varieties. Their speech was both analyzed acoustically and used as stimuli in an AXB task (Walker & Campbell-Kibler 2015). This work can be replicated with L2 speakers to explore their degree of assimilation (see Gnevsheva, Szakay & Jansen 2021 for an example using acoustic analysis only).

On the other hand, studies that test the same L2-speaking participants on dimensions of both production and perception would provide a direct view of relationships between individuals' production and perception. Such studies could take the form of investigating L2 speakers' variation in production in regard to a variable, and then also testing whether these same participants can recognize and evaluate productions of the variable. The following case study illustrates this approach.

CASE STUDY   L2 speaker sociophonetic variability in production and perception

Several speech production studies have investigated Type 3 variation (synchronic variation on the L1–L2/ethnic–mainstream continuum) in bilingual and/or L2 speakers. L2 speakers have been shown to style-shift according to different situational characteristics, such as interlocutor and/or topic (Major 2004; Dolgova Jacobsen 2008; Rampton 2011; Gnevsheva 2015). It has also been suggested that such style-shifting is not uniform and that some speakers may be more variable than others (e.g., Sharma 2011). Participant characteristics may be able to explain and predict speaker variability in style-shifting (e.g., proficiency and length of residence in Drummond 2011, and ethnic orientation in Hoffman & Walker 2010). With a lack of research into the predictors of L2 speaker variability in style-shifting, the first research question that I set out to address here is: What is the relationship between L2 speaker variability in Type 3 style-shifting and such participant characteristics as L2 proficiency, length of residence in the L2 country, and ethnic orientation?

A similar question about predictors of subject variability in displaying sociophonetic variation can be asked about L2 perception. As has been shown in this chapter and others in this handbook (see, e.g., Warren this volume), social information can affect the perception of linguistic information. Despite such seeming universality in the influence of social information on linguistic perception, a number of studies found variation in listener reliance on social cues in speech perception tasks (e.g., Gnevsheva 2021). Thus, the second research question that I ask in this case study is: What is the relationship between L2 listener sociophonetic variability in perception and such participant characteristics as L2 proficiency, length of residence, and ethnic orientation?

Finally, a number of recent L1 studies investigated between-speaker co-occurrence of linguistic features, with many finding weak correlations (e.g., Becker 2016). While few sociophonetic studies

---

consider variation in production and perception concurrently, this is a worthwhile question to ask if our goal is a united model of speech production and perception. As the data that will be used to ask the above-mentioned research questions about production and perception stem from the same population, this dataset allows us to ask: What is the relationship between an L2 speaker's sociophonetic variability in production and in perception?

Methods

The data in the study come from production (Gnevsheva 2020) and perception (Gnevsheva 2021) experiments (see these publications for methodological detail). The subset of participants discussed in this chapter are 10 Russian L1 adult migrants to Australia, split evenly by sex (Table 20.1). They were 32 years old on average (SD 5.9) at the time of data collection and had completed at least a bachelor's degree. Their length of residence in Australia was an average of four years. The participants had a relatively high level of English, evidenced by their work and/or formal study experience in Australia and, although a formal assessment of their proficiency was not performed, on average they rated themselves to have an English speaking ability of 3.55 (range 2–5) on a five-point Likert scale, with 5 being native-like (Bongaerts, Mennen & Slik 2000). They also completed an ethnic orientation questionnaire, where each question could get a score between 1 (least involvement with Russian) and 3 (most involvement with Russian), following Hoffman & Walker (2010). These were averaged for each participant, resulting in a group mean of 2.3.

In the production part of the study, the participants were audio-recorded with an Hn5 Zoom audio-recorder and a Samson SE10 head-mounted microphone in three different styles: a self-recorded conversation, a sociolinguistic interview, and a standardized reading passage. The recordings were orthographically transcribed and segmented at the level of utterance manually and then automatically time-aligned at the phone level using LaBB-CAT (Fromont & Hay 2012) with CELEX as its dictionary (Baayen, Piepenbrock & Gulikers 1995). F1 and F2 were automatically extracted at 50% for all lexically stressed monophthongs using Praat (Boersma & Weenink 2019). Outliers were regulated by excluding physiologically improbable realizations and tokens with formant measurements outside

Table 20.1 Participant demographic information

Participant code	Sex	Age	Self-rated English speaking ability	Length of residence in Australia (years)	Ethnic orientation index
RF01	F	31	3.5	6.5	2.07
RF02	F	25	4	1.5	2.07
RF03	F	31	3	1	2.35
RF04	F	40	3	2.5	1.94
RF05	F	28	2	3	2.47
RM01	M	28	5	3.5	2.41
RM02	M	41	5	8.5	2.21
RM03	M	39	4	10	2.32
RM04	M	31	3	3	2.17
RM05	M	24	3	0.25	2.61

two standard deviations from the mean for each participant, style, and vowel. The remaining data were normalized using the transformation described in Lobanov (1971).

As described in the previous section (and in Gnevsheva 2021), in the perception part of the study, the same participants listened to audio-recordings of 12 bilingual (split between first- and second-generation migrants) and 6 monolingual speakers of English, and rated each speaker's degree of foreign accentedness on a five-point Likert scale. Each listener heard each speaker three times, reading short extracts about bears (priming Russia), kangaroos (priming Australia), and on a neutral topic.

Quantification of participants' sociophonetic variability necessitated a methodological innovation. Sharma (2017)'s "accent range" may work well for discrete variables and in production, but it is not easily applied to continuous variables and in perception. Here I developed a novel index of by-style variability in production and by-topic variability in perception that can be used for continuous variables. To explicate it I will use the perception data as an example.

To quantify the size of the topic effect for individual L2-speaking listeners, I decided to focus on random slope values for topic in linear mixed effects models (Baayen, Davidson & Bates 2008). Random intercept values for individual participants have been used successfully in the past to demonstrate within-group variation and individual participants' deviation from model predictions (e.g., Drager & Hay 2012). In this perception study the random intercept for listener would indicate how likely a given participant is to give a higher or lower accentedness score in general. Following a similar principle, random slope values for topic levels for a given participant would allow us to estimate the listener's deviation from model prediction for each topic level. To quantify this deviation, I refit the model from the original analysis in Gnevsheva (2021) with some changes: topic was taken out as a fixed effect (otherwise, the slope will only show us deviation from model prediction for the fixed effect) and kept as the only random slope for listener to get by-listener estimates of slope with no random intercept values (formula = lmer(Score~Listener.group*Speaker.group+(1|speaker) + (−1+ Stimulus.topic|listener)), using the lmerTest package (Kuznetsova, Brockhoff & Christensen 2017) in R (R Core Team 2022). This random effects structure results in a by-listener offset estimate for each of the three topics.

To calculate variability in the size of these offsets, the following were computed for each listener in turn: 1) an average of offsets for the three topics, 2) an absolute difference between the average and offset for each topic, and 3) a sum of absolute difference values for the three topics. The resulting sum of absolute difference values, or by-topic variability index, reflects listener variability in the size of the topic effect such that a larger value means bigger differences between topics and a smaller value means smaller differences. For example (Figure 20.1), participant RM01's offset estimate for the Bears topic was 0.539, for Kangaroos 0.382, and for Neutral 0.353, resulting in the average offset of 0.425 across the three topics. Thus, the absolute difference values between the topic offsets and the mean were 0.114, 0.043, and 0.072 respectively, with a total sum of 0.229. For a different participant, RM02, the offset estimates for Bears, Kangaroos, and Neutral were −0.159, −0.112, and −0.104, respectively, with an average of −0.125 across the three topics. The respective absolute differences were 0.034, 0.013, and 0.021, with a total sum of 0.068. By comparing the total sum of differences between RM01 (0.229) and RM02 (0.068), we can observe that the value for RM01 is greater than that for RM02 indicating higher by-topic variability for RM01 in comparison to RM02. As such, these values can be used as a quantitative representation of individual participants' by-topic variability and can be used in further statistical analyses.

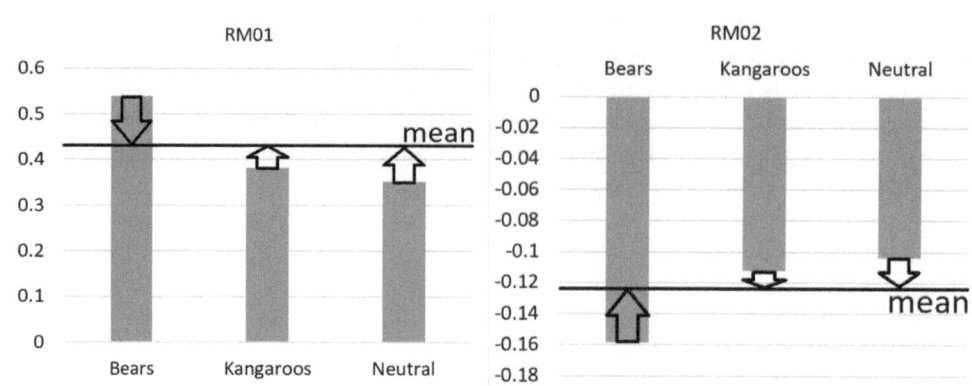

Figure 20.1 Procedure for calculating by-listener variability by topic: Offset estimates by topic for participants RM01 (left panel) and RM02 (right panel)

Following the same protocol, I calculated a by-style variability index for the same participants in production. The original models for GOOSE F2 and TRAP F1 from Gnevsheva (2020) were refitted with some changes: style was taken out of the fixed effects structure and only kept as a random slope for speaker (GOOSE F2 formula: lmer(F2~Duration*Speaker.group+Following.environment*Speaker.group+Preceding.environment*Speaker.group+(1|word)+(−1+style|speaker)); TRAP F1 formula: lmer(F1~Duration*Speaker.group+Following.environment*Speaker.group+(1|word)+(−1+style|speaker)). The by-style random slope values for speaker were averaged to first calculate an absolute difference between the mean and slope values for each style and then to obtain a sum of these differences as a by-style variability index for each participant.

Results

For the perception data, I calculated Pearson product-moment correlations between the participants' by-topic variability index and their self-assessed English proficiency, length of residence in Australia, and ethnic orientation score. The first two analyses revealed no to weak correlations of $r = 0.000$ ($p > 0.05$) and $r = −0.203$ ($p > 0.05$) respectively. The third one, however, resulted in a moderate negative correlation of $r = −0.549$ ($p = 0.01$), suggesting that with increased ethnic orientation the participants' by-topic variability decreased (Figure 20.2). This means that the participants who were more engaged with the culture of Russian-speaking communities were less affected by the topic in their accentedness rating behavior. It is possible that stronger engagement provided them with more exposure to linguistic cues, resulting in less reliance on social information (similarly to the original argument in Gnevsheva 2021).

Similarly, for the production data, I calculated Pearson correlations between the participants' by-style variability index for the two vowels of interest (GOOSE F2 and TRAP F1) and their self-assessed English proficiency, length of residence in Australia, and ethnic orientation index. Weak correlations were found for GOOSE F2: $r = 0.212$ ($p > 0.05$), 0.349 ($p > 0.05$), and −0.256 ($p > 0.05$) respectively. Very weak ($r = 0.194$; $p > 0.05$), strong ($r = 0.686$; $p = 0.03$), and weak ($r = −0.253$; $p > 0.05$) correlations were found for TRAP F1. The strong positive correlation between participants' by-style

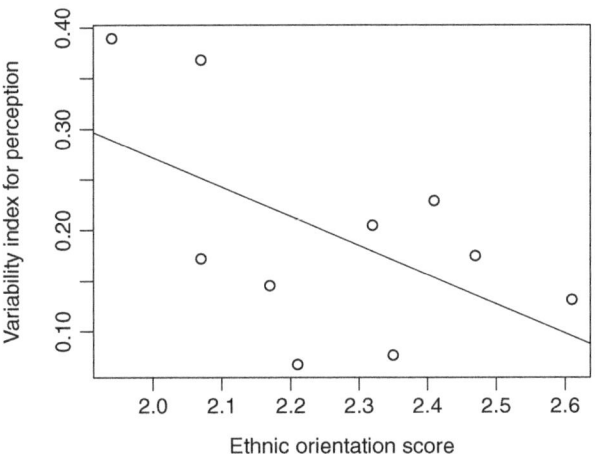

Figure 20.2   Relationship between participants' ethnic orientation score and by-topic variability index

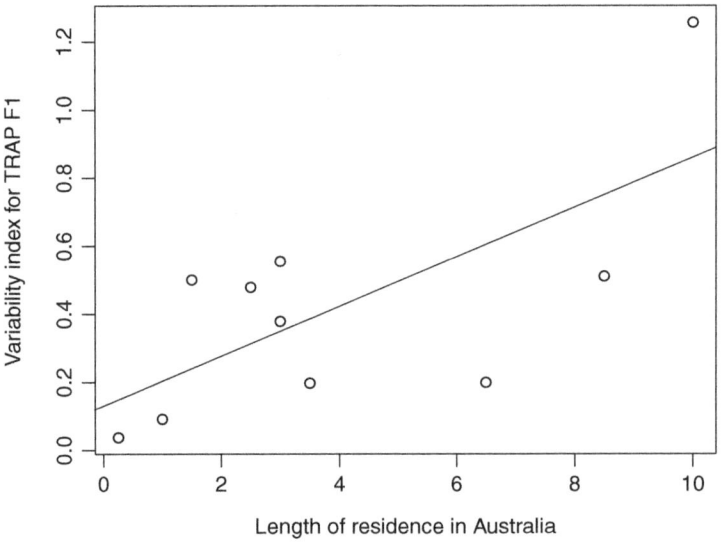

Figure 20.3   Relationship between participants' length of residence in Australia and by-style production variability index for TRAP F1

variability index for TRAP F1 and length of residence in Australia (Figure 20.3) suggests that the longer
they have lived in Australia, the more style-shifting they demonstrated, which is similar to previous
arguments on Type 2 variation acquisition by L2 speakers (e.g., Drummond 2011). The difference
between the two vowels can be explained by the fact that no significant group-wide variation by style
was found for GOOSE F2, which was attributed to different pathways of acquisition (phonetic change
vs. creation of a new phonological category) in Gnevsheva (2020).

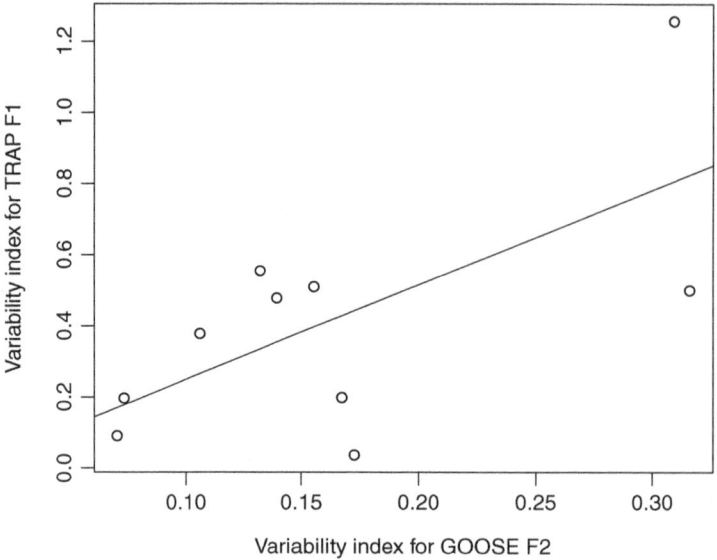

Figure 20.4   Relationship between participants' by-style production variability indices for GOOSE F2 and TRAP F1

Additionally, despite this difference in the status of the two vowels for L2 speakers, when their by-style production variability indices were compared, a strong positive correlation of $r = 0.656$ ($p = 0.04$) was found (Figure 20.4). This suggests that while the scale of sociophonetic variation for different variables may be different, the same speaker is likely to be more or less variable on multiple variables (cf. Becker 2016).

Finally, when production and perception were compared, a weak positive correlation of $r = 0.225$ ($p > 0.05$) and a moderate positive correlation of 0.407 ($p > 0.05$) were found between the by-topic perception variability index and the by-style production variability indices for TRAP F1 and GOOSE F2 respectively. Similarly to Figure 20.4, this means that the same participants were likely to be more or less variable in both production and perception, on top of co-variation in production variables. This indicates that the strength of links between social and linguistic information or ability to use them is similar between production and perception suggesting a similar underlying cognitive mechanism.

Discussion

To return to the research questions, L2 speakers demonstrated a significant negative correlation between by-topic variability in perception and ethnic orientation, a positive correlation between by-style variability in TRAP F1 and length of residence in Australia, as well as a positive correlation between GOOSE F2 and TRAP F1 variability indices. These suggest that L2 speaker sociophonetic variability in production and perception may be affected by their social characteristics, particularly exposure to and familiarity with the respective linguistic varieties and their sociophonetic variables. And while a relationship was found between the variability on the two production variables, the correlations between perception and production variables did not reach significance.

As is obvious from the above visualizations, much of the effect is driven by a few outliers, and a much larger dataset as well as more robust statistical analyses are needed to test these observations more thoroughly. Yet, this case study serves as a proof-of-concept for studies linking sociophonetic variability in production, perception, and multiple variables by using random slopes for computing a variability index for each participant.

Future directions for L2 sociophonetics

As can be seen from the overview presented in this chapter, there has been an expansion of production studies in L2 sociophonetics in the last few years. Yet, there is still a lot to be done in this area. There is a clear need for more sociophonetic studies investigating variation in the production of different and multiple variables by speakers from different language backgrounds and in different contexts. In particular, research into the teaching and classroom acquisition of sociophonetic variation seems a fruitful direction.

Most of the existing work on perception of sociophonetic variation by L2 listeners asks whether they acquire L1 speaker-like associations and evaluations. While it has been shown that L2 listeners generally have weaker ties between social and linguistic information and exhibit lower accuracy in, for example, speaker origin identification, there is a dearth of L2 sociophonetics research and there have been very few replication studies with L2 listeners in some of the research directions. For example, there have been very few, if any, studies of acquisition of sociolinguistic variation in perception beyond dialectal variation, so we do not know whether L2 participants acquire class, age, and sex-related representations of L1 patterns of usage (in the manner of, e.g., Hay, Warren & Drager 2006).

Most of the existing studies in L1 and L2 sociophonetics address speech production and perception separately. More research linking production and perception is needed. To continue with the L2 pedagogy example, there is need for research into learners' acquisition of sociophonetic variation in both production and perception, and also into how these are related and may support each other.

In this sense the subfield of L2 sociophonetics has a lot of replication and validation work to do to establish similarities and differences in L1 and L2 behavior and processing. But this work would not only be of interest to SLA researchers, as L1 and L2 participants' differing relationship with the target language would allow researchers to test their theories of speech production and perception by isolating certain variables—which is impossible within the L1 participant group by itself.

Acknowledgments

Many thanks to Solène Inceoglu for valuable feedback on earlier drafts of this chapter and the ANU Statistical Consulting Unit for discussion of the statistical analysis techniques. I am also grateful to the case study participants, Ben Volchok for help in data collection, and the ARC CoEDL TIG662017 for supporting it financially.

References

Adamson, H.D. & Vera M. Regan. 1991. The acquisition of community speech norms by Asian immigrants learning English as a second language: A preliminary study. *Studies in Second Language Acquisition* 13(1). 1–22. https://doi.org/10.1017/S0272263100009694

Alford, Randall L. & Judith B. Strother. 1990. Attitudes of native and nonnative speakers toward selected regional accents of US English. *TESOL Quarterly* 24(3). 479–496. https://doi.org/10.2307/3587231

Baayen, R. Harald, D.J. Davidson & D.M. Bates. 2008. Mixed-effects modeling with crossed random effects for subjects and items. *Journal of Memory and Language* 59(4). 390–412. https://doi.org/10.1016/j.jml.2007.12.005

Baayen, R. Harald, R. Piepenbrock & L. Gulikers. 1995. *The CELEX Lexical Database* (CD-ROM). Linguistic Data Consortium.

Baese-Berk, Melissa M., Drew J. McLaughlin & Kevin B. McGowan. 2020. Perception of non-native speech. *Language and Linguistics Compass* 14(7). https://doi.org/10.1111/lnc3.12375

Bauman, Carina. 2013. Social evaluation of Asian accented English. *University of Pennsylvania Working Papers in Linguistics* 19(2). Article 3. https://repository.upenn.edu/pwpl/vol19/iss2/3

Becker, Kara. 2016. Linking community coherence, individual coherence, and bricolage: The co-occurrence of (r), raised BOUGHT and raised BAD in New York City English? *Lingua* 172. 87–99. https://doi.org/10.1016/j.lingua.2015.10.017

Beebe, Leslie M. 1980. Sociolinguistic variation and style shifting in second language acquisition. *Language Learning* 30(2). 433–445. https://doi.org/10.1111/j.1467-1770.1980.tb00327.x

Beebe, Leslie M. & Jane Zuengle. 1983. Accommodation theory: An explanation for style shifting in second language dialects. In Nessa Wolfson & Elliot Judd (eds.), *Sociolinguistics and Language Acquisition*, 195–213. Newbury House.

Bent, Tessa & Ann R. Bradlow. 2003. The interlanguage speech intelligibility benefit. *Journal of the Acoustical Society of America* 114(3). 1600–1610. https://doi.org/10.1121/1.1603234

Boersma, Paul & David Weenink. 2019. *Praat: Doing phonetics by computer* [Computer program], ver. 6.0.19. www.praat.org/

Bongaerts, Theo, Susan Mennen & Frans van der Slik. 2000. Authenticity of pronunciation in naturalistic second language acquisition: The case of very advanced late learners of Dutch as a second language. *Studia Linguistica* 54(2). 298–308. https://doi.org/10.1111/1467-9582.00069

Cargile, Aaron Castelan. 2000. Evaluations of employment suitability: Does accent always matter? *Journal of Employment Counseling* 37(3). 165–177. https://doi.org/10.1002/j.2161-1920.2000.tb00483.x

Carlson, Holly K. & Monica A. McHenry. 2006. Effect of accent and dialect on employability. *Journal of Employment Counseling* 43(2). 70–83. https://doi.org/10.1002/j.2161-1920.2006.tb00008.x

Clark, Lynn & Erik Schleef. 2010. The acquisition of sociolinguistic evaluations among Polish-born adolescents learning English: Evidence from perception. *Language Awareness* 19(4). 299–322. https://doi.org/10.1080/09658416.2010.524301

Clopper, Cynthia G. & Ann R. Bradlow. 2009. Free classification of American English dialects by native and non-native listeners. *Journal of Phonetics* 37(4). 436–451. https://doi.org/10.1016/j.wocn.2009.07.004

Derwing, Tracey M. & Murray J. Munro. 2013. The development of L2 oral language skills in two L1 groups: A 7-year study. *Language Learning* 63(2). 163–185. https://doi.org/10.1111/lang.12000

Dolgova Jacobsen, Natalia. 2008. "Identity [iz] a [djifikəlt] question": A variationist analysis of the relationship between L1 features and ethnic identity in the speech of Russian learners of English. *Georgetown Working Papers in Language, Discourse, & Society* 2. 1–28.

Drager, Katie & Jennifer Hay. 2012. Exploiting random intercepts: Two case studies in sociophonetics. *Language Variation and Change* 24(1). 59–78. https://doi.org/10.1017/S0954394512000014

Drummond, Rob. 2011. Glottal variation in /t/ in non-native English speech. Patterns of acquisition. *English World-Wide* 32(3). 280–308. https://doi.org/10.1075/eww.32.3.02dru

Drummond, Rob. 2012. Aspects of identity in a second language: ING variation in the speech of Polish migrants living in Manchester, UK. *Language Variation and Change* 24(1). 107–133. https://doi.org/10.1017/S0954394512000026

Eckert, Penelope. 2000. *Linguistic variation as social practice: The linguistic construction of identity in Belten High.* Blackwell.

Flege, James E., Grace H. Yeni-Komshian & Serena Liu. 1999. Age constraints on second-language acquisition. *Journal of Memory and Language* 41(1). 78–104. https://doi.org/10.1006/jmla.1999.2638

Fromont, Robert & Jennifer Hay. 2012. LaBB-CAT: An annotation store. In Paul Cook & Scott Nowson (eds.), *Proceedings of Australasian Language Technology Association Workshop*, 113–117.

Gallois, Cynthia & Victor J. Callan. 1981. Personality impressions elicited by accented English speech. *Journal of Cross-Cultural Psychology* 12(3). 347–359. https://doi.org/10.1177/0022022181123006

Gatbonton, Elizabeth, Pavel Trofimovich & Norman Segalowitz. 2011. Ethnic group affiliation and patterns of development of a phonological variable. *Modern Language Journal* 95(2). 188–204. https://doi.org/10.1111/j.1540-4781.2011.01177.x

Giles, Howard & Peter F. Powesland. 1975. *Speech style and social evaluation*. Academic Press.

Gnevsheva, Ksenia. 2015. Style-shifting and intra-speaker variation in the vowel production of non-native speakers of New Zealand English. *Journal of Second Language Pronunciation* 1(2). 135–156. https://doi.org/10.1075/jslp.1.2.01gne

Gnevsheva, Ksenia. 2017. Within-speaker variation in passing for a native speaker. *International Journal of Bilingualism* 21(2). 213–227. https://doi.org/10.1177/1367006915616197

Gnevsheva, Ksenia. 2018a. The expectation mismatch effect in accentedness perception of Asian and Caucasian non-native speakers of English. *Linguistics* 56(3). 581–598. https://doi.org/10.1515/ling-2018-0006

Gnevsheva, Ksenia. 2018b. Variation in foreign accent identification. *Journal of Multilingual and Multicultural Development* 39(8). 688–702. https://doi.org/10.1080/01434632.2018.1427756

Gnevsheva, Ksenia. 2020. The role of style in the ethnolect: Style-shifting in the use of ethnolectal features in first- and second-generation speakers. *International Journal of Bilingualism* 24(4). 861–880. https://doi.org/10.1177/1367006920902520

Gnevsheva, Ksenia. 2021. Topic affects perception of degree of foreign accent in a non-dominant language. *Linguistics* 59(1). 101–121. https://doi.org/10.1515/ling-2020-0263

Gnevsheva, Ksenia & Daniel Bürkle. 2020. Age estimation in foreign-accented speech by native and non-native speakers. *Language and Speech* 63(1). 166–183. https://doi.org/10.1177/0023830919827621

Gnevsheva, Ksenia, Anita Szakay & Sandra Jansen. 2021. Phonetic convergence across dialect boundaries in first and second language speakers. *Journal of Phonetics* 89. https://doi.org/10.1016/j.wocn.2021.101110

Hanulíková, Adriana. 2018. The effect of perceived ethnicity on text comprehension under clear and adverse listening conditions. *Linguistics Vanguard* 4(1). https://doi.org/10.1515/lingvan-2017-0029

Hay, Jennifer & Katie Drager. 2010. Stuffed toys and speech perception. *Linguistics* 48(4). 865–892. https://doi.org/10.1515/ling.2010.027

Hay, Jennifer, Aaron Nolan & Katie Drager. 2006. From fush to feesh: Exemplar priming in speech perception. *Linguistic Review* 23(3). https://doi.org/10.1515/TLR.2006.014

Hay, Jennifer, Paul Warren & Katie Drager. 2006. Factors influencing speech perception in the context of a merger-in-progress. *Journal of Phonetics* 34(4). 458–484. https://doi.org/10.1016/j.wocn.2005.10.001

Hoffman, Michol F. & James A. Walker. 2010. Ethnolects and the city: Ethnic orientation and linguistic variation in Toronto English. *Language Variation and Change* 22(1). 37–67. https://doi.org/10.1017/S0954394509990238

Hosoda, Megumi, Lam T. Nguyen & Eugene F. Stone-Romero. 2012. The effect of Hispanic accents on employment decisions. *Journal of Managerial Psychology* 27(4). 347–364. https://doi.org/10.1108/02683941211220162

Howard, Martin, Isabelle Lemée & Vera Regan. 2006. The L2 acquisition of a phonological variable: The case of /l/ deletion in French. *Journal of French Language Studies* 16(1). 1–24. https://doi.org/10.1017/S0959269506002298

Hwang, Jiwon, Susan E. Brennan & Marie Huffman. 2015. Phonetic adaptation in non-native spoken dialogue: Effects of priming and audience design. *Journal of Memory and Language* 81. 72–90. https://doi.org/10.1016/j.jml.2015.01.001

Isaacs, Talia & Pavel Trofimovich. 2012. Deconstructing comprehensibility: Identifying the linguistic influences on listeners' L2 comprehensibility ratings. *Studies in Second Language Acquisition* 34(3). 475–505. https://doi.org/10.1017/S0272263112000150

Jiao, Dan, Vicky Watson, Sidney Gig-Jan Wong, Ksenia Gnevsheva & Jessie S. Nixon. 2019. Age estimation in foreign-accented speech by non-native speakers of English. *Speech Communication* 106. 118–126. https://doi.org/10.1016/j.specom.2018.12.005

Kang, Okim. 2010. Relative salience of suprasegmental features on judgments of L2 comprehensibility and accentedness. *System* 38(2). 301–315. https://doi.org/10.1016/j.system.2010.01.005

Kang, Okim & Donald L. Rubin. 2009. Reverse linguistic stereotyping: Measuring the effect of listener expectations on speech evaluation. *Journal of Language and Social Psychology* 28(4). 441–456. https://doi.org/10.1177/0261927X09341950

Kang, Okim, Donald L. Rubin & Lucy Pickering. 2010. Suprasegmental measures of accentedness and judgments of language learner proficiency in oral English. *Modern Language Journal* 94(4). 554–566. https://doi.org/10.1111/j.1540-4781.2010.01091.x

Kuznetsova, Alexandra, Per B. Brockhoff & Rune H. Christensen. 2017. lmerTest package: tests in linear mixed effects models. *Journal of Statistical Software* 82(13). 1–26. https://doi.org/10.18637/jss.v082.i13

Labov, William. 1972. *Sociolinguistic patterns*. University of Pennsylvania Press.

Levis, John M. 2005. Changing contexts and shifting paradigms in pronunciation teaching. *TESOL Quarterly* 39(3). 369–377. https://doi.org/10.2307/3588485

Lobanov, Boris M. 1971. Classification of Russian vowels spoken by different speakers. *Journal of the Acoustical Society of America* 49. 606–608. https://doi.org/10.1121/1.1912396

Major, Roy C. 2001. *Foreign accent: The ontogeny and phylogeny of second language phonology*. Erlbaum.

Major, Roy C. 2004. Gender and stylistic variation in second language phonology. *Language Variation and Change* 16(3). 169–188. https://doi.org/10.1017/S0954394504163059

McGowan, Kevin B. 2015. Social expectation improves speech perception in noise. *Language and Speech* 58(4). 502–521. https://doi.org/10.1177/0023830914565191

McGowan, Kevin B. & Anna M. Babel. 2020. Perceiving isn't believing: Divergence in levels of sociolinguistic awareness. *Language in Society* 49(2). 231–256. https://doi.org/10.1017/S0047404519000782

McKenzie, Robert M. 2015. The sociolinguistics of variety identification and categorisation: Free classification of varieties of spoken English amongst non-linguist listeners. *Language Awareness* 24(2). 150–168. https://doi.org/10.1080/09658416.2014.998232

McKenzie, Robert M., Mimi Huang, Theng Theng Ong & Navaport Snodin. 2019. Socio-psychological salience and categorisation accuracy of speaker place of origin. *Lingua* 228. https://doi.org/10.1016/j.lingua.2019.06.006

Mougeon, Raymond, Katherine Rehner & Terry Nadasdi. 2004. The learning of spoken French variation by immersion students from Toronto, Canada. *Journal of Sociolinguistics* 8(3). 408–432. https://doi.org/10.1111/j.1467-9841.2004.00267.x

Munro, Murray J. & Tracey M. Derwing. 1995. Foreign accent, comprehensibility, and intelligibility in the speech of second language learners. *Language Learning* 45(1). 73–97. https://doi.org/10.1111/j.1467-1770.1995.tb00963.x

Munro, Murray J., Tracey M. Derwing & Susan L. Morton. 2006. The mutual intelligibility of L2 speech. *Studies in Second Language Acquisition* 28(1). 111–131. https://doi.org/10.1017/S0272263106060049

Nance, Claire, Wilson McLeod, Bernadette O'Rourke & Stuart Dunmore. 2016. Identity, accent aim, and motivation in second language users: New Scottish Gaelic speakers' use of phonetic variation. *Journal of Sociolinguistics* 20(2). 164–191. https://doi.org/10.1111/josl.12173

Nelson Jr., Larry R., Margaret L. Signorella & Karin G. Botti. 2016. Accent, gender, and perceived competence. *Hispanic Journal of Behavioral Sciences* 38(2). 166–185. https://doi.org/10.1177/0739986316632319

Nesdale, Drew & Rosanna Rooney. 1996. Evaluations and stereotyping of accented speakers by preadolescent children. *Journal of Language and Social Psychology* 15(2). 133–154. https://doi.org/10.1177/0261927X960152002

Niedzielski, Nancy. 1999. The effect of social information on the perception of sociolinguistic variables. *Journal of Language and Social Psychology* 18(1). 62–85. https://doi.org/10.1177/0261927X99018001005

R Core Team. 2022. *R: A language and environment for statistical computing*. R Foundation for Statistical Computing. www.R-project.org

Rampton, Ben. 2011. Style in a second language. *King's College London Working Papers in Urban Language and Literacies* 65. 1–40.

Regan, Vera, Martin Howard & Isabelle Lemée. 2009. *The acquisition of sociolinguistic competence in a study abroad context*. Multilingual Matters. https://doi.org/10.21832/9781847691583

Sancier, Michele L. & Carol A. Fowler. 1997. Gestural drift in a bilingual speaker of Brazilian Portuguese and English. *Journal of Phonetics* 25(4). 421–436. https://doi.org/10.1006/jpho.1997.0051

Schleef, Erik, Miriam Meyerhoff & Lynn Clark. 2011. Teenagers' acquisition of variation: A comparison of locally-born and migrant teens' realisation of English (ing) in Edinburgh and London. *English World-Wide* 32(2). 206–236. https://doi.org/10.1075/eww.32.2.04sch

Schmidt, Lauren B. 2011. *Acquisition of dialectal variation in a second language: L2 perception of aspiration of Spanish /s/*. PhD dissertation, Indiana University.

Seggie, Ian, Nancy Smith & Patricia Hodgins. 1986. Evaluations of employment suitability based on accent alone: An Australian case study. *Language Sciences* 8(2). 129–140. https://doi.org/10.1016/S0388-0001(86)80011-0

Sharma, Devyani. 2011. Style repertoire and social change in British Asian English. *Journal of Sociolinguistics* 15(4). 464–492. https://doi.org/10.1111/j.1467-9841.2011.00503.x

Sharma, Devyani. 2017. Scalar effects of social networks on language variation. *Language Variation and Change* 29(3). 393–418. https://doi.org/10.1017/S0954394517000205

Sharma, Devyani & Lavanya Sankaran. 2011. Cognitive and social forces in dialect shift: Gradual change in London Asian speech. *Language Variation and Change* 23(3). 399–428. https://doi.org/10.1017/S0954394511000159

Solon, Megan, Bret Linford & Kimberly L. Geeslin. 2018. Acquisition of sociophonetic variation: Intervocalic /d/ reduction in native and non-native Spanish. *Revista Española de Lingüística Aplicada/Spanish Journal of Applied Linguistics* 31(1). 309–344. https://doi.org/10.1075/resla.16028.sol

Uritescu, Dorin, Raymond Mougeon, Katherine Rehner & Terry Nadasdi. 2004. Acquisition of the internal and external constraints of variable schwa deletion by French immersion students. *International Review of Applied Linguistics in Language Teaching* 42(4). 349–364. https://doi.org/10.1515/iral.2004.42.4.349

Vandergrift, L. & C.C.M. Goh. 2012. Teaching and learning second language listening: Metacognition in action. *Applied Linguistics* 35(2). 224–226. https://doi.org/10.1093/applin/amu002

Walker, Abby. 2014. *Crossing oceans with voices and ears: Second dialect acquisition and topic-based shifting in production and perception*. PhD dissertation, The Ohio State University.

Walker, Abby & Kathryn Campbell-Kibler. 2015. Repeat what after whom? Exploring variable selectivity in a cross-dialectal shadowing task. *Frontiers in Psychology* 6. 1–18. https://doi.org/10.3389/fpsyg.2015.00546

Watanabe, Yutai. 2008. New Zealand attitudes towards foreign-accented English. *Te Reo* 51. 99–127.

Yi, Han-Gyol, Jasmine E.B. Phelps, Rajka Smiljanic & Bharath Chandrasekaran. 2013. Reduced efficiency of audiovisual integration for nonnative speech. *Journal of the Acoustical Society of America* 134(5). EL387–EL393. https://doi.org/10.1121/1.4822320

Young, Richard. 1988. Variation and the interlanguage hypothesis. *Studies in Second Language Acquisition* 10(3). 281–302. https://doi.org/10.1017/S0272263100007464

Zheng, Yi & Arthur G. Samuel. 2017. Does seeing an Asian face make speech sound more accented? *Attention, Perception, & Psychophysics* 79(6). 1841–1859. https://doi.org/10.3758/s13414-017-1329-2

21

SOCIOPHONETICS AND SPEECH-LANGUAGE PATHOLOGY

Toby Macrae and Margaret Maclagan

Introduction

"The term *sociophonetics* refers to the study of those aspects of phonetic realization that vary as a function of a range of social factors, such as age, gender, ethnicity, class, style, and individual identity" (Docherty & Khattab 2008:603). Since speech-language pathologists (SLPs) work with clients of different ages, sexes, genders, ethnicities, and social classes, all with their own individual styles and identities, sociophonetics has much to potentially offer the SLP.

However, the relatively small number of SLPs and the scarcity of funding in most countries mean that SLPs can only treat the most serious of potential clients. Sociophonetic variation must usually take second place to the needs of basic communication for a frustrated 3-year-old whose speech is unintelligible and who cannot get their message across, or the teenager whose dysfluency (stuttering) is so bad that they have almost stopped trying to talk with peers, or the anxious singer who has developed vocal nodules, or the thoroughly frustrated 80-year-old whose only language post-stroke is the swear words they would never have used earlier in life.

Any language-based therapy must equally take second place behind life-saving swallowing therapy for some patients post-stroke. Some practitioners' work goes beyond traditional linguistic concerns and into the more medical realms of cleft palate and swallowing. Other SLPs work with voice issues for transgender people who are transitioning. While SLPs do not diagnose hearing loss, they regularly refer clients to audiologists for diagnosis and can work with Deaf people and with people who have cochlear implants.

As the previous paragraphs illustrate, the scope of practice for SLPs is very wide. In this chapter we will emphasize the areas of practice where sociophonetic information plays an important role in the assessment and treatment of clients who come to SLPs with speech and language problems. As we emphasize sociophonetic issues, we will also indicate where sociolinguistic concerns impinge on the work of SLPs.

In this chapter we use the terminology "speech-language pathologist." Such practitioners are also known as "speech-language therapists" or "logopaedists." We first cover the profession of SLP, including its scope of practice, training, and the principles guiding both training and practice. We then cover the areas of SLP practice where sociophonetic insights are relevant, including dialectal variation, speech sound disorders in children, and, perhaps the most important of these

DOI: 10.4324/9781003034636-23

areas, differentiating speech differences from speech sound disorders, with a particular focus on African American English. We then consider the functional impact of speech sound errors on the people who make them, accent services, and issues concerned with hearing. Finally we offer a case study that describes a therapeutic encounter during the first author's clinical work in the United States, in which he was required to become familiar with the phonological characteristics of Spanish-Influenced English in order to differentiate speech sound difference from speech sound disorder in a young child.

Speech-language pathology contexts and conditions

Scope of practice

SLPs, regardless of geography, typically have a very wide scope of practice. SLPs work with clients who have difficulties with all areas of speech, language, and swallowing. An important distinction is between those who work in an educational environment (e.g., in school classrooms or in specialized classrooms) and those who work in a medical environment, within general hospitals or in specialized clinics. Perhaps the broadest distinction among clients relates to age. SLPs tend to serve either predominantly child clients or predominantly adult clients. Children typically present with developmental communication or swallowing concerns, whereas adults typically present with acquired concerns such as language difficulties following a stroke, although there are exceptions. For example, children may acquire a communication impairment following a brain injury, for example through a contact sport, or, more rarely, they may suffer a stroke. Conversely, SLPs may work with adults who have had a communication impairment since childhood such as a stutter. Some areas of communication and swallowing are impaired in children more often than adults, while others are impaired more often in adults than in children. For example, speech concerns resulting from a cleft palate are found in children much more often than in adults. Most of the therapy for these children takes place between the ages of 3 and 5 years, and most children with cleft palate eventually attain normal speech (Kummer 2014). Conversely, voice disorders are most often experienced by adults (Hoffman, Ming & Losonczy 2014; Black, Vahratian & Hoffman 2015).

Professional associations in different countries delineate areas of professional practice for their members. In the United States, the American Speech-Language-Hearing Association (ASHA) represents more than 200,000 members and categorizes their work according to the "Big Nine" areas of practice (www.asha.org/events/slp-summit-glossary/). Professional associations in other countries, including the Royal College of Speech & Language Therapists in the United Kingdom, Speech Pathology Australia, and the New Zealand Speech-language Therapists' Association, include similar areas of practice. Those areas of practice where sociophonetic insights are particularly relevant include any that involve speech production, language expression and comprehension, hearing, and social aspects of communication in both children and adults.

Training

SLP training typically takes place in universities, either at undergraduate or postgraduate level. In the United States, the qualification required to work as an SLP in most states is a master's degree. In most cases, students complete a four-year undergraduate degree in SLP before applying to a master's program. The undergraduate degree typically consists of two years of general coursework and two years of courses in the SLP major that teach foundational knowledge, for example speech acoustics and typical speech and language development in children. Master's programs typically focus more on disorders of communication and swallowing as well as clinical training, and include courses such as speech disorders in children and aphasia (acquired language disorder following a stroke or a brain injury).

In the United Kingdom, Australia, and New Zealand, professional entry qualifications include both undergraduate and postgraduate degrees. Postgraduate degrees are like those in the United States and take two years to complete. Undergraduate degrees typically take four years and tend to teach foundational knowledge early on. This means that, wherever they are taught, university programs must cover all areas of SLP practice and train students to be able to competently assess and treat all manner of communication and swallowing disorders in both children and adults within two to four years. Theory is mostly covered in academic coursework and application is mostly covered in clinical coursework. However, good academic courses will help students apply theory to practice, for example through case-based learning, and good clinical courses will have strong theoretical foundations.

Phonetics training needs to cover both articulatory and acoustic areas of speech. Acoustic analysis allows trainee SLPs to visualize the characteristics of consonants and vowels and to understand more clearly the interactions between neighboring sounds. Laboratory sessions also allow them to manipulate the speech signal. Progressive low-pass filtering, for example, allows students to experience the effects of high frequency hearing loss, and progressively adding more noise to the speech signal simulates the effects of increasing background noise on speech intelligibility.

Within the articulatory component of SLP training, practice at transcribing spoken speech is essential. Practice with running speech demonstrates clearly the assimilations and elisions that are part of normal, fluent speech. Dictation of nonsense words teaches students to focus on what their ears are hearing rather than using their knowledge of the language to fill in what they think they heard. Students must also learn sounds that do not occur in their own language but that are common in the speech of people with articulation problems. For example, SLPs must know the implosives [ɓ], [ɗ], and [ɠ] because their greater articulatory feedback means they are sometimes used by Deaf children. Similarly, the laterals [ɬ] and [ꞎ] are essential for SLPs working with speakers of English because without treatment these speech errors can persist into adulthood.

SLPs must have a comprehensive understanding of typical speech sound development in children. Trainees will typically take an entire course in speech sound development and disorders in children. Courses in speech sound disorders (SSDs) will usually cover the typical course of speech sound acquisition, with a focus on consonants. This is because most children master vowels well before they master consonants, with most children mastering vowels before the age of 3 years (Donegan 2013). Most children who have SSDs have difficulties with consonants rather than vowels (McLeod & Baker 2017), and the vast majority of work that SLPs do with children who have SSDs focuses on the accurate production of consonants. This is particularly important because consonants carry more speech information than vowels, which carry the intonation patterns.

Principles affecting training and practice

There are a number of guiding principles that influence how SLPs are trained and how they work. One key principle is clinical importance or functional impact. The Word Health Organization's (WHO) International Classification of Functioning, Disability, and Health (ICF) (WHO 2001:3) provides a "framework for the description of health and health-related states." The ICF focuses on an individual's health and functioning in society, rather than simply on the individual's disability.

SLPs are required to consider the impact of an individual's disability on their ability to function in everyday life. Academic and clinical educators in SLP programs must therefore maintain this perspective when designing their courses. What must students know in order to be able to assess the functional impact of a communication or swallowing disorder and improve the client's ability to function in society? This inevitably impacts upon how much sociophonetic content is covered in an SLP curriculum. Sociophonetic features of a client's communication disorder must be considered in the context of their impact on the client's ability to function in society.

Another key principle influencing training and practice is caseload size. In most countries, SLPs are in short supply and high demand. In 2019, one in eleven people in the world was over the age of 65. This is projected to increase to one in six people by 2050 (United Nations 2019). This aging global population will increasingly require the assistance of health professionals such as SLPs. This will lead to growing caseloads for SLPs who work with adults. Large caseloads are also a reality for SLPs who work with children. For example, in 2016 the median caseload for school-based SLPs was 48 across all states in the United States and as high as 64 (Florida) (ASHA 2016). Large caseloads mean funding agencies and SLPs must prioritize some clients over others. For example, a school district might allocate a limited amount of funding for SLP services for students. Eligibility criteria usually will be established that ultimately restrict services to those students with the most severe communication and swallowing impairments. In many cases, school-aged children with mild or even moderate speech and/or language disorders will not qualify for services. Large caseloads also dictate that SLPs must prioritize communication and swallowing goals for each client. This means that many areas where sociophonetic insights would be relevant may not be addressed if they do not impact upon a client's ability to function in everyday life.

These guiding principles ultimately have a top-down influence on what is taught in SLP programs as they must match how SLPs practice in the workplace. SLP programs are, after all, professional degree programs. That is, the degree is an entry-level qualification that allows graduates to work in the field. Programs must train their graduates to a high level of competency in all areas of practice. Accreditation bodies, which are usually a part of each country's professional association, are tasked with ensuring accredited SLP programs meet a variety of standards that relate to the professional preparation of their graduates.

Sociophonetic insights and applications

Dialectal variation

Dialectal variation is a topic that is familiar to both linguists and phoneticians, with phoneticians often focusing on dialectal sociophonetic differences. SLPs need to have an understanding of dialectal variation, particularly related to dialects spoken in their language communities. Training programs may include a dedicated course in linguistic (and possibly cultural) diversity, or this content may be included in other courses, such as clinical phonetics, speech sound disorders in children, or typical language development in children. Knowing the characteristics of the dialects spoken in one's language community allows SLPs to differentiate between speech sound difference and speech sound disorder. For example, parts of England and most of the United States are rhotic, as are most parts of Scotland and Ireland (see Sebregts, van Hout & Van de Velde this volume). They pronounce /ɹ/ in words like *car* or *park* or *another*. Australia and New Zealand and most of England are non-rhotic. They pronounce /ɹ/ before a vowel, as in *marry*, but not before a consonant or pause. Rhotic speakers use schwar [ɚ] in words like *teacher* that end in <er> where non-rhotic speakers use schwa [ə]. An awareness of the sociolinguistic norms of the community will help the

SLP determine whether a child who does not produce word-final /ɹ/ has difficulty with the sound and requires intervention or is simply demonstrating the features of his or her dialect. Time restrictions usually mean that SLPs cannot focus on sociophonetic details of their clients' speech, including, for example, details of ways in which linking and intrusive /r/ are used in the community in question.

Speech sound disorders in children

Speech sound disorders are the most common disorder type among children served by pediatric SLPs (Broomfield & Dodd 2004; Mullen & Schooling 2010; ASHA 2011a, 2014). An SSD occurs when a child fails to fully master the phonetic and/or phonological features of his or her language within a typical developmental timeframe. "Mastery" of a speech sound implies the phonetic ability to articulate it correctly as well as the phonological ability to use it contrastively. Most phonemes are mastered by approximately age 6. The sociophonetic ability to articulate allophones of the phoneme as used in the child's speech community usually also develops by this age.

There are many different types of SSD, with those that reflect phonological deficits being more common than those that reflect phonetic/articulatory deficits in preschool- and early school-age children (Broomfield & Dodd 2005; Shriberg 2010). SLPs are just as concerned with whether or not a child can use a particular phoneme contrastively in words as whether or not the child can produce the phone accurately in isolation. Children with phonological deficits have difficulties using phonemes contrastively in words rather than difficulties with articulatory requirements. Parents can become frustrated when their child produces a clear /s/, for example, in isolation and can hiss like a snake "sssssssss," but reverts to their habitual /t/ or /d/ substitution as soon as the sound is placed within a meaningful word so that *sun* is pronounced [tʌn] or *toes* becomes [toʊd].

A loss of contrastivity results in widespread homonymy and a resultant loss of intelligibility. For example, a common childhood speech error reflects an absence of a contrast between back phonemes produced at the velum and coronal ones produced at the alveolar ridge. This results in /k g ŋ/ being realized as [t d n], so that the child produces *key*, *gun*, and *sing* as [ti], [dʌn], and [sɪn], which represent different words in English. This speech error, commonly referred to as "velar fronting" or simply "fronting," is characteristic of typical phonological development in children younger than approximately 4 years (see McLeod & Baker 2017). Studies of ages of English consonant acquisition in children almost always assess production in words rather than in isolation. In the field of speech-language pathology, whether a particular phonetic realization of a word represents typical phonological development or an SSD depends on the age of the child. It also depends on the phonetic realization. Persistence of fronting beyond age 4 is therefore associated with an SSD.

Another childhood speech error reflects an absence of this same phoneme contrast, except in reverse. "Backing" results in /t, d, n/ being realized as [k, g, ŋ] so that *dot* is pronounced [gɒk] (Dunn & Davis 1983; Dodd & Lacano 1989; Preston 2008). This speech error is not characteristic of typical phonological development and occurs infrequently in children's speech. Its presence at any age is associated with an SSD. The examples we have cited come from English, but many early speech sound substitutions follow Stampe's "natural phonological processes," the applications of which are not restricted to English (Donegan & Stampe 2009).

While most children with SSD have intact speech perception, perceptual deficits in some children with SSD are well attested (see Hearnshaw, Baker & Munro 2019). SLPs often differentiate between perceptual phonemic knowledge and productive phonemic knowledge. A child who can distinguish perceptually between *white* and *right*, for example, even though they are unable to produce an adult-like version of /ɹ/ and they produce both as *white*, would be considered to have perceptual but not productive phonemic knowledge. SLPs are mostly concerned with a child's productive knowledge/capabilities.

Differentiating dialectal variation from speech sound disorder

One area of speech-language pathology to which sociophonetics is particularly relevant is differential diagnosis of SSDs in children. Differential diagnosis is mainly concerned with separating genuine SSDs from "errors" that are part of normal sound development. An important role of an SLP is diagnosing an SSD and ruling out a speech sound difference associated with a nonstandard dialect of English. What counts as an error in one language community may be normal in another.

For example, deleting word-final consonants (e.g., so that *smooth* would be produced as [smu]) beyond approximately 4 years of age is considered indicative of an SSD in Mainstream American English (MAE) (McLeod & Baker 2017). However, this is a normal feature of African American English (AAE; Craig et al. 2003). Children who speak AAE, therefore, may delete many word-final consonants without this being an error in their variety of English (we will discuss this further in the section on AAE below).

What is counted as an error can also change over time. Within New Zealand, for example, SLPs used to treat children who were using [f] where older speakers used [θ] for the phoneme /θ/. Over time, more and more children used [f] instead of [θ] to the extent that therapists have not treated it for some years. If it is important to the child's parents that the child can produce /θ/ as a dental fricative, then registered speech teachers may provide appropriate help. SLPs in New Zealand have noticed that some parents who realize /θ/ as [f] nevertheless want their child to pronounce /θ/ "correctly." However, if almost all examples of /θ/ are realized as [f], the phonemes /θ/ and /f/ may be in the process of merging. If this is the case, then SLPs may profitably talk to parents about sound mergers, giving other appropriate examples. In New Zealand another example of a sound merger would be the merger of NEAR and SQUARE (Gordon & Maclagan 2001); in parts of North America the merger between LOT and THOUGHT or the *pin-pen* merger could be appropriate examples (e.g., Labov, Ash & Boberg 2006).

Differentiating between a speech sound difference and a disorder is important for adults as well as children. While a dental [s̪] or lateral [ɬ] lisp might be targeted for treatment in a child, the well-documented acoustic differences in /s/ and vowel productions by gay, lesbian, and bisexual speakers (Pierrehumbert et al. 2004; Munson et al. 2006; Munson 2007) are not considered speech errors that require remediation (Mack & Munson 2012).

Nonstandard varieties of English

SLPs must become familiar with the nonstandard varieties of language spoken in the communities in which they work. There are countless other examples of dialects that have phonetic and phonological characteristics that differ from mainstream dialects.

In the United States, for example, Spanish-Influenced English (SIE) is widely spoken, particularly in the American Southwest. In 2019, 13.5 percent of the US population (approximately 42 million people) spoke Spanish and more than 40 percent of all Spanish speakers lived in California and Texas (US Census Bureau 2019). "Interference" occurs when phonemes and phonological rules of a speaker's first language, in this case Spanish, interfere with their learning of another language, in this case English. SIE features include /v/ being realized as [b], since Spanish does not include /v/, as well as word-final consonant clusters being reduced to a single consonant, since Spanish does not include word-final clusters. SLPs working in communities that include

SIE speakers must be aware of these features of SIE that contrast with MAE (contrastive features) and focus only on those features that are shared by both varieties (noncontrastive features) when evaluating and treating speech and language disorders in these speakers. While working as an SLP in the US state of Nevada, the first author worked with children who spoke SIE and accordingly he took a different approach to these speech sound differences, depending on the client. Accurate /v/ production was an intervention target for 5-year-old children who spoke MAE but not those who spoke SIE, since this phoneme is not part of the dialect.

As another example, te reo Māori is the indigenous language of New Zealand and one of three official languages together with English and NZ Sign Language. It was spoken fluently by 4 percent of the general New Zealand population in 2018 (Statistics New Zealand 2018). Māori English is a dialect spoken by Māori and non-Māori and includes phonological, lexical, pragmatic, and rhythmic features that, while also present in general New Zealand English (NZE), occur less frequently in that variety (Maclagan, King & Gillon 2008). Historically the features of Māori English probably came about from interference between te reo Māori and NZE. However, they are "most probably now being passed on intergenerationally in the absence of the language which gave rise to the features" (Maclagan, King & Gillon 2008:662). One phonological feature of Māori English is the realization of the interdental fricatives /θ/ and /ð/ as [t] and [d], [tθ] and [dð], or [f] and [v] (Maclagan, King & Gillon 2008). SLPs in New Zealand who work with children who speak Māori English would avoid targeting these phoneme changes in treatment.

Our examples are all from English because this is the language with which we are familiar. Similar issues will occur in other languages, such as the different pronunciations of /s/ in Castilian and Mexican Spanish, and a knowledge of the sociophonetic characteristics of different varieties of the "same" language can help SLPs to be aware of these differences (see Collins Dictionary 2021).

African American English

Historically, children in the United States who spoke AAE were often misdiagnosed with SSDs (Seymour, Bland-Stewart & Green, 1998; Seymour 2004a; Stockman 2006). In some cases, over-diagnosis may have occurred because the phonological features of AAE that contrast it with MAE are often associated with an SSD in MAE—for instance, the example of word-final consonant deletion given above. But over-diagnosis also likely arose because of a historical view of AAE as a substandard form of English (Seymour & Seymour 1981; Seymour, Bland-Stewart & Green 1998). Linguists, of course, have challenged these racist language ideologies by demonstrating that AAE is a legitimate and rule-governed dialect of English (Labov 1969, 1972; Seymour & Seymour 1977; Green 2002; Blake & Cutler 2003; Seymour 2004a). However, implicit and explicit bias may still affect listeners' attitudes, beliefs, and perceptions of AAE (Jackson & Pearson 2008; Pearson, Connor & Jackson 2013) and other regional, social, or ethnic varieties of various languages.

In the United States, ASHA requires in its scope of practice that SLPs utilize culturally and linguistically appropriate methods when assessing children for SSDs, including taking into account the unique features of non-mainstream varieties of American English. This requires SLPs to understand the features of English dialects other than their own, especially those dialects spoken by children in the communities SLPs serve, and to account for dialectal differences when scoring standardized tests of speech production. Unfortunately, too few SLPs interpret test scores differently for students who speak AAE (Hendricks & Diehm 2020). First-grade children who speak AAE and who had no history of speech-language therapy were more likely to be incorrectly diagnosed with an SSD using these tests if those features that are associated with AAE were scored as errors rather than treated as acceptable (Cole & Taylor 1990). Therefore, SLP training programs must increase students' awareness of cultural and linguistic diversity and this should take place "within current coursework, as stand-alone courses dedicated to the topic, and through opportunities for clinical placements which provide practical experience to work with students from culturally and linguistically diverse backgrounds" (Hendricks & Diehm 2020:11). Furthermore, SLP programs must seek to increase ethnic and linguistic diversity among students and professionals (see Grover, Namasivayam & Mahendra 2021). Approximately 38 percent of the US population was racially or ethnically diverse in 2020 (US Census Bureau 2021a), compared with only 8.5 percent of ASHA's membership (ASHA 2021). Approximately 22 percent of the US population spoke a language other than English in 2018 (US Census Bureau 2018), whereas only 8 percent of ASHA's membership reported providing services in a language other than English (ASHA 2021).

There has been a concerted effort by researchers to elucidate the features of AAE and determine the most culturally and linguistically sensitive approaches to assessment of SSDs in children who speak AAE. Some of the most important research has come from the University of Massachusetts, Amherst National Institutes of Health (NIH) Working Groups on AAE. These researchers, as well as others, recommend that SLPs focus on those features of AAE that are shared with MAE (Seymour & Seymour 1977; Seymour, Bland-Stewart & Green 1998; Seymour 2004a, 2004b; Pearson et al. 2009; Pearson, Connor & Jackson 2013; Hendricks & Diehm 2020). For the most part, contrastive features are ambiguous in that they may be characteristic of either AAE or an SSD in a child who speaks either MAE or AAE. Noncontrastive features are unambiguous in that they are used by speakers of both dialects. If they are absent at an age beyond when they are typically acquired by speakers of both dialects, this would most likely reflect an SSD.

A clinical tool that has been developed by this group includes a focus on the noncontrastive features of the dialect. The Diagnostic Evaluation of Language Variation (DELV; Seymour et al. 2003) was designed to evaluate speech and language disorders in English-speaking children from different cultural and linguistic backgrounds. Pearson et al. (2009) examined data obtained during field-testing of the DELV. As part of this field-testing, 854 children aged 4 through 12 years with typical speech and language development, of whom 537 were identified as speaking AAE and 317 were identified as speaking MAE, were asked to repeat sentences. The sentences contained words that sampled most consonant singletons and those consonants clusters that were considered the most and least contrastive between AAE and MAE. The children's productions of these singletons and clusters were analyzed for similarities and differences across the two dialects.

One of the most striking findings was that of a word position effect. When it came to ages of acquisition, Pearson et al. (2009) found that both groups of children acquired the vast majority of word-initial singletons at similar ages, with the exception of /ð/. In this study, the MAE speakers acquired this consonant by age 8, while AAE speakers had not acquired it by age 12. While some word-initial clusters were acquired earlier by MAE speakers, twice as many were acquired earlier by AAE speakers. However, the vast majority of word-final singletons and clusters were acquired earlier by MAE speakers. When it came to the degree of match between children's productions and the MAE targets, there were no significant differences between MAE and AAE speakers for word-initial singletons (when /ð/ was excluded) and clusters. However, there was a significant difference between MAE and AAE speakers for word-final singletons and clusters combined. Furthermore, there was a highly significant difference and a large effect size between word-initial and word-final positions for the AAE speakers but not for the MAE speakers. This study provided concrete evidence of the extent to which AAE and MAE speakers differed in rates of word-final consonant deletion.

The implications of the findings from Pearson et al.'s (2009) study were wide-ranging. The study received the Editor's Award for the most meritorious single article published in *Language,*

Speech, and Hearing Services in Schools, an ASHA publication, in 2009. The authors used the results of their study to strengthen their argument for focusing on noncontrastive features of AAE when differentiating between speech sound difference and SSD. Quite simply, practitioners were encouraged to ignore word-final consonants and focus instead on word-initial singletons and clusters. Since MAE and AAE speakers acquire these at similar ages and produce them with similar degrees of match to the MAE form, any difficulties can reasonably be assumed to be indicative of a disorder and not a dialectal difference. Pearson et al.'s (2009) findings also helped inform the development of the DELV, which has become the gold standard in the field for evaluating speech and language disorders in AAE-speaking children.

This research demonstrates the practical value of sociophonetic approaches within the field of SLP. Use of the DELV test has ensured that many young AAE children whose speech is totally appropriate for their own variety of English are not subjected to unnecessary "treatment." This saves them from the potential harm that can result when an "expert" implies that a child's or adult's speech or language is somehow inadequate, even though it seems perfectly appropriate to the potential client. It also saves parents from the cost and inconvenience of unnecessary treatment.

Functional impact of speech sound errors

Another issue in SLP where sociophonetics is relevant, and which in some ways relates to the identification of SSDs in children who speak non-mainstream varieties of English, relates to the functional impact of atypical speech sound productions in the context of the WHO's International Classification of Functioning, Disability, and Health described earlier. The ICF focuses on an individual's functioning in society. SLPs are required to consider the impact of an individual's disability on their ability to function in everyday life. Not all children who have difficulties producing speech sounds accurately will experience the same impact on functioning. For example, preschool children who have SSDs that are characterized by phonological, rather than articulatory, deficits are at increased risk for reading and/or spelling difficulties at school (Bird, Bishop & Freeman 1995; Larrivee & Catts 1999; Lewis, Freebairn & Taylor 2000; Gillon 2002). These children should be prioritized for intervention.

In contrast, older children (age 9+) who speak MAE and who have common clinical distortions of sibilants and/or rhotics, for example dentalized or lateralized /s/ ([s̪] or [ɬ]) or derhoticized /ɹ/ or rhotic vowels /ɝ, ɚ/ ([ɜ], [ə]), may not require intervention at all with respect to their ability to function in society. These phonemes are articulatorily complex (Kent 1992) and among the last to be mastered by children (Smit et al. 1990; Shriberg 1993). Kent (1992) found that earlier-acquired phonemes require more basic regulation of the velopharynx (which separates the oral and nasal cavities and is used to differentiate between oral and nasal phonemes), voicing distinctions, and rate of lingual movement. Later-acquired phonemes—for example, sibilants and rhotics—require more refined adjustments of lingual position and fine force control of the articulators. Some children present with distortions of these sounds until the later school years and beyond. In fact, these are the most common speech sound distortions in adult speakers of MAE (Shriberg 1994).

Children with these distortions form a large subgroup of children with SSDs. Approximately 5 percent of the general population of older children present with these sound distortions (Shriberg 1994). However, their difficulties are most often limited to these distortions and do not typically include other language concerns (Shriberg 1994), so their functional impact is less than might initially be expected. Functional impact does not only concern other areas of language and academic success. There are also social consequences to consider. For example, the therapist must consider how a child's SSD may impact on his or her ability to establish and maintain friendships. The first author once worked with a 10-year-old child in New Zealand with weak articulation for word-initial /ɹ/ (often referred to as "derhoticized" /ɹ/ by SLPs). After several weeks of limited success, the boy began to question why he was in therapy. He reported that he was happy with his speech and his mild distortion had no impact on his friendships. After discussions with his teacher and parents, it was decided that therapy would be ceased. This is an example of the need for SLPs to consider the wishes and priorities of clients and their families and teachers in determining whether or not to treat a mild speech distortion.

Accent services

SLPs do not only treat people who have communication disorders. A complex and controversial area of practice is accent services, also known as "accent reduction" or "accent modification" (see ASHA n.d.). Some speakers may wish to learn a new accent, for example, actors in films and plays. People who have learned English as a second or later language may seek services to improve intelligibility of their speech. Others may be perfectly intelligible but seek services to sound less "foreign" and more like the mainstream dialect of their language community.

What makes this a controversial area of practice is that, for many speakers, their accent is "a source of pride and ethnic or regional identity and comes bundled with rich linguistic and cultural experience" (Grover, Namasivayam & Mahendra 2021:2). The very existence of accent services within the practice of SLP risks pathologizing accents (Ennser-Kananen, Halonen & Saarinen 2021) and this can cause speakers psychological harm (ASHA 2011b). Many US universities provide accent services for international students. However, a review of the text used on their websites suggests that, rather than being a linguistic issue, many seem to present these services from an ideological perspective, "drawing on the students' ethnic or geographical origins and consequently racializing the question of language skills" (Ennser-Kananen, Halonen & Saarinen 2021:336). After all, the perception of accent involves more than just linguistic variables. Rubin (1992) found that, when a speech sample from a speaker with a MAE accent was paired with a photo of an Asian instructor and presented to listeners, the listeners perceived the accent as significantly more foreign and less standard than when the same sample of speech was paired with a photo of a Caucasian instructor.

While the scope of practice for SLPs continues to include accent services, there has been a recent call to adopt an "equity-minded, culturally sustaining stance and to advocate for affirmative, inclusive terms when working with accented speakers" (Grover, Namasivayam & Mahendra 2021:3). These authors suggest using the term "accent expansion," which is more positive and additive, rather than the terms accent reduction or accent modification, which imply the need to "temper or dilute" a speaker's accent (2021:2). In this sense, the speaker may retain features of their accent, "while acquiring an additional accent for functional communication, as needed" (2021:3). In their scoping review of research in the field of accent services since 1985, Grover, Namasivayam & Mahendra identified a shift from decreasing accentedness to increasing intelligibility. SLPs should only offer services when volitionally chosen by speakers. Moreover, even when speakers seek these services of their own volition, there is a need to acknowledge that many do so because of experiences of discrimination (Silman 2021).

Hearing issues

One of the most important issues in the area of hearing is the availability of appropriate hearing tests. However, SLPs are rarely directly involved in the development of such tests. This means that hearing tests rarely take account of phonetic differences among varieties of the same language. In order to obtain an accurate hearing threshold, the stimulus sounds, either pure tones or single words, are played at progressively lower intensities until the person being tested can no longer hear them.

Trying to work out whether or not you heard a word, let alone what word it was, is stressful, even when the words are spoken in your own variety of English. Since many people whose hearing is being tested are elderly, this mismatch between varieties of English can add an additional layer of difficulty. Members of the audiology department at the University of Canterbury, New Zealand, have recently developed several hearing tests that are specific to NZE. The New Zealand Hearing Test developed by Gregory O'Beirne and Robert Fromont, for example, is available online (https://nzhst.canterbury.ac.nz/). O'Beirne has also developed NZE versions of the matrix test, a diagnostic speech-in-noise test. These include an adult version (O'Beirne et al. 2015) and also a version suitable for children and older adults whose attention span has lessened (O'Beirne et al. 2019). When sociophonetic features of the local variety of English are taken into consideration, the person being tested does not have the stress of a different variety of English added to the general stress of a hearing test.

Although SLPs do not diagnose hearing problems, they often work directly or indirectly with adults and/or children who have hearing problems. If hearing loss is not recognized early there is a real risk that the child will experience language deprivation. This could mean severe functional effects on the child's language as well as on other areas of development that are interdependent with language, for example social emotional skills or executive functioning (Peterson 2018).

However, if children grow up in a household where the adults are fluent in sign language they will become native users of a sign language and their language development will be function-ally normal. Nevertheless, in spite of normal sign language development and even though their speech is "intelligible," the speech of Deaf children can contain differences in articulation such as "misarticulation of affricates and fricatives, mild-moderate hoarseness, mild resonance problems" (Elfenbein, Hardin-Jones & Davis 1994:216). Sign languages vary across different regions, and people working with the Deaf need to be aware of regional and local differences (see Becker et al. this volume). NZ sign language (NZSL), for example, is closely related to British Sign Language (BSL) and Australian Sign Language (Auslan), but less closely related to American Sign Language (McKee 2021). Some signs can differ depending on the age of the signer (McKee 2021). Differences between the various sign languages fall into the area of sociolinguistics because they concern distinctions at the level of vocabulary with different signs for the same word or different placement or syntax because of the varying ordering of signs. Differences between individual signers fall within the scope of sociophonetics because these concern individual preferences for ways of making individual signs.

A major issue for parents of babies who are diagnosed with hearing loss at birth is whether or not to allow the child to have a cochlear implant. If Deaf parents strongly identify culturally with the Deaf community they may not see deafness as a disability (Hall et al. 2018) and may choose not to implant their young Deaf children, but allow the children to make their own decision later. Here the parent's choice seems to fall within sociolinguistics, in that cochlear implants are not an inevitable part of their community's sociolinguistic identity. However for the children, such a choice becomes a matter of the sociophonetic variation within their community. As they grow older they will become aware that some children have cochlear implants and potentially different sounding speech and some don't. This is similar to children in other communities becoming aware of different ways of pronouncing words. Because cochlear implants are visible, this sociophonetic difference is potentially easier for children to notice than some of the less obvious differences discussed above.

CASE STUDY   Five-year-old boy speaking Spanish-Influenced English with a speech sound disorder

Sociophonetics played an important role in the first author's work as a private practitioner in Nevada in the United States. In Nevada, 29.2 percent of the population identifies as Hispanic or Latino, much higher than that of the nation's population (18.5 percent) (US Census Bureau 2021b). SLPs, therefore, are more likely to encounter Spanish-Influenced English-speaking children in that state than in many other parts of the country. SIE is a dialect of English spoken by individuals who speak Spanish as their first language that shares some of its features with Spanish. It is incumbent upon Nevada-based SLPs to familiarize themselves with the dialects spoken in their language community, which include SIE.

During the ten months the first author worked in a private SLP clinic in the state, he encountered several children who spoke Spanish as their first language. Their parents or caregivers sought speech-language services for their children for various reported concerns, including both speech and language difficulties. The first author had not previously worked clinically in Nevada and had limited knowledge of SIE, including its phonological features.

The first child, a 5-year-old boy who was referred by his parents and who spoke Spanish as his first language, had reported difficulties with speech sound production. One characteristic of his speech was a [b] for /v/ substitution, in which words such as *very* and *vacuum* were produced as [bɛri] and [bækjum], respectively. The child's parents first pointed out the child's substitution when the SLP took a case history. They reported that they had noticed it in their child's speech at home and his teacher had also noticed it at school. The parents noted that they did not see this same feature in their son's friends' speech. They were concerned about the effect that this feature would have on his ability to be understood and form relationships with his peers.

In English-speaking children, /v/ is typically mastered by age 4 (McLeod & Crowe 2018). However, Spanish does not include /v/ in its phonological system and so some speakers of SIE do not produce this sound when speaking English, instead producing [b] (Goldstein & Washington 2001; Goldstein, Fabiano & Washington 2005). It wasn't until the first author encountered other children who spoke Spanish as their first language who showed the same speech characteristic that he suspected it might be reflective of a dialectal difference rather than an underlying SSD. He then began to research the dialects that were spoken in Nevada and came across a number of sources that described the characteristics of SIE, one of which was the production of [b] where MAE speakers produce /v/ (e.g., Goldstein & Washington 2001; Goldstein, Fabiano & Washington 2005; Goldstein & Iglesias 2017).

The SLP counseled the parents as to the nature of this feature of their child's speech. He informed them that it is indicative of his particular dialect, one that is common in Nevada, and not of an SSD. It was agreed that the feature would not be targeted in treatment.

In contrast, the same child had difficulty with another consonant when speaking English: /f/. The child produced /f/ as [w], so that *fish* and *fun* were produced as [wɪʃ] and [wʌn]. In English-speaking children, /f/ is typically mastered by age 3 (McLeod & Crowe 2018) and word-initial /f/ produced as [w] is not a typical substitution (Preston 2008).

459

Again, the first author researched the characteristics of Spanish and SIE and discovered that /f/ is indeed part of the phonological system of Spanish and does not typically present difficulties for individuals who speak SIE (Goldstein & Washington 2001; Goldstein, Fabiano & Washington 2005). In contrast to the child's realization of /v/, it was decided that his production of /f/ as [w] would be targeted in speech treatment. In this way, sociophonetic information played a vital role in shaping this child's treatment plan by allowing the SLP to differentiate between those features of the child's speech that were indicative of dialectal difference and those that were indicative of an SSD.

Conclusion

Sociophonetics has particular relevance to the field of speech-language pathology, a field that deals with spoken communication, among other things. The wide scope of practice for SLPs includes several areas that benefit from an understanding of sociophonetics. SLPs work with people, all of whom vary with regards to age, sex, gender, ethnicity, cultural background, geography, social class, sexuality, language, and dialect. SLPs must understand how the different aspects of a person's identity can influence the way they speak. The dialect of English spoken by a young client will determine whether the features of their speech reflect their dialect or an underlying SSD. An older child who does present with a mild difficulty realizing /ɹ/ may experience no negative social or academic consequences and therefore be perfectly happy with how he or she sounds to others. Certain realizations of phonemes (e.g., [f] for /θ/ in NZE) used to be treated by SLPs but are now considered acceptable variants. A person's sexuality may influence whether their realization of /s/ requires remediation. Some people who have learned English as a second language may seek accent services from SLPs in an attempt to increase the intelligibility of their speech or even sound less "foreign." Whatever the reason an individual seeks services, a competent SLP understands the role sociophonetics plays in assessing and treating—and indeed whether or not to treat—the person's speech.

Acknowledgments

We gratefully acknowledge the input from Rosie Lamb, an SLP who has specialized in working with D/deaf and Hard of Hearing children, in the Hearing Issues section.

References

American Speech-Language-Hearing Association. n.d. *Accent modification.* www.asha.org/practice-portal/professional-issues/accent-modification/

American Speech-Language-Hearing Association. 2011a. *National Outcomes Measurement System: Pre-Kindergarten national data report 2011.* www.asha.org/content.aspx?id=8589940108&LangType=1033

American Speech-Language-Hearing Association. 2011b. *The clinical education of students with accents* [Professional issues statement]. www.asha.org/policy/PI2011-00324/

American Speech-Language-Hearing Association. 2014. *2014 schools survey report: SLP caseload characteristics.* www.asha.org/research/memberdata/schoolssurvey/

American Speech-Language-Hearing Association. 2016. *2016 Schools Survey report: SLP caseload characteristics.*

American Speech-Language-Hearing Association. 2021. *Demographic profile of ASHA members providing bilingual services, year-end 2020.*

Bird, Judith, Dorothy V.M. Bishop & Norman H. Freeman. 1995. Phonological awareness and literacy development in children with expressive phonological impairments. *Journal of Speech and Hearing Research* 38(2). 446–462. https://doi.org/10.1044/jshr.3802.446

Black, Lindsey I., Anjel Vahratian & Howard J. Hoffman. 2015. Communication disorders and use of intervention services among children aged 3–17 years: United States, 2012. *NCHS Data Brief, No. 205.* National Center for Health Statistics.

Blake, Renée & Celia Cutler. 2003. AAE and variation in teachers' attitudes: A question of school philosophy? *Linguistics and Education* 14(2). 163–194. https://doi.org/10.1016/S0898-5898(03)00034-2

Broomfield, Jan & Barbara Dodd. 2004. Children with speech and language disability: Caseload characteristics. *International Journal of Language and Communication Disorders* 39(3). 303–324. https://doi.org/10.1080/13682820310001625589

Broomfield, Jan & Barbara Dodd. 2005. Epidemiology of speech disorders. In Barbara Dodd (ed.), *Differential diagnosis and treatment of children with speech disorder*, 2nd edn., 83–99. Whurr.

Cole, Patricia A. & Orlando L. Taylor. 1990. Performance of working-class African-American children on three tests of articulation. *Language, Speech, and Hearing Services in Schools* 21(3). 171–176. https://doi.org/10.1044/0161-1461.2103.171

Collins Dictionary. 2021. IPA pronunciation guide: Spanish. https://blog.collinsdictionary.com/ipa-pronunciation-guide-spanish/ (27 December 2021).

Craig, Holly K., Connie A. Thompson, Julie A. Washington & Stephanie L. Potter. 2003. Phonological features of child African American English. *Journal of Speech, Language, and Hearing Research* 46(3). 623–635. https://doi.org/10.1044/1092-4388(2003/049)

Docherty, Gerrard & Ghada Khattab. 2008. Sociophonetics and clinical linguistics. In Martin J. Ball, Michael R. Perkins, Nicole Müller & Sara Howard (eds.), *The handbook of clinical linguistics,* 603–625. Blackwell.

Dodd, Barbara & Teresa Lacano. 1989. Phonological disorders in children: Changes in phonological process use during treatment. *International Journal of Language & Communication Disorders* 24(3). 333–352. https://doi.org/10.3109/13682828909019894

Donegan, Patricia & David Stampe. 2009. Hypotheses of natural phonology. *Poznań Studies in Contemporary Linguistics* 45(1). 1–31. https://doi.org/10.2478/v10010-009-0002-x

Donegan, Patricia. 2013. Normal vowel development. In Karen Pollock & Fiona E. Gibbon (eds.), *Handbook of vowels and vowel disorders,* 63–129. Taylor & Francis.

Dunn, Carla & Barbara L. Davis. 1983. Phonological process occurrence in phonologically disordered children. *Applied Psycholinguistics* 4(3). 187–207. https://doi.org/10.1017/S0142716400004574

Elfenbein, Jill L., Mary A. Hardin-Jones & Julia M. Davis. 1994. Oral communication skills of children who are hard of hearing. *Journal of Speech, Language, and Hearing Research* 37(1). 216–226. https://doi.org/10.1044/jshr.3701.216

Ennser-Kananen, Johanna, Mia Halonen & Taina Saarinen. 2021. "Come join us, and lose your accent!": Accent modification courses as hierarchization of international students. *Journal of International Students* 11(2). 322–340. https://doi.org/10.32674/jis.v11i2.1640

Gillon, Gail. 2002. Follow-up study investigating benefits of phonological awareness intervention for children with spoken language impairment. *International Journal of Language and Communication Disorders* 37(4). 381–400. https://doi.org/10.1080/1368282021000007776

Goldstein, Brian A., Leah Fabiano & Patricia S. Washington. 2005. Phonological skills in predominantly English-speaking, predominantly Spanish-speaking, and Spanish–English bilingual children. *Language, Speech, and Hearing Services in Schools* 36(3). 201–218. https://doi.org/10.1044/0161-1461(2005/021)

Goldstein, Brian A. & Aquiles Iglesias. 2017. Language and dialectal variations. In John E. Bernthal, Nicholas W. Bankson & Peter Flipsen, Jr. (eds.), *Articulation and phonological disorders: Speech sound disorders in children*, 8th edn., 277–301.

Goldstein, Brian & Patricia S. Washington. 2001. An initial investigation of phonological patterns in typically developing 4-year-old Spanish-English bilingual children. *Language, Speech, and Hearing Services in Schools* 32(3). 153–164. https://doi.org/10.1044/0161-1461(2001/014)

Gordon, Elizabeth & Margaret Maclagan. 2001. "Capturing a sound change": A real time study over 15 years of the NEAR/SQUARE Diphthong Merger in New Zealand English. *Australian Journal of Linguistics* 21(2). 215–238. https://doi.org/10.1080/07268600120080578

Green, Lisa J. 2002. A descriptive study of African American English: Research in linguistics and education. *Qualitative Studies in Education* 15(6). 673–690. https://doi.org/10.1080/0951839022000014376

Grover, Vikas, Aravind Namasivayam & Nidhi Mahendra. 2021. A viewpoint on accent services: Framing and terminology matter. *American Journal of Speech-Language Pathology.* https://doi.org/10.1044/2021_AJSLP-20-00376

Hall, Matthew L., Inge-Marie Eigsti, Heather Bortfield & Diane Lillo-Martin. 2018. Executive function in Deaf children: Auditory access and language access. *Journal of Speech, Language and Hearing Research* 61(8). 1970–1988. https://doi.org/10.1044/2018_JSLHR-L-17-0281

Hearnshaw, Stephanie, Elise Baker & Natalie Munro. 2019. Speech perception skills of children with speech sound disorders: A systematic review and meta-analysis. *Journal of Speech, Language, and Hearing Research* 62(10). 3771–3789. https://doi.org/10.1044/2019_JSLHR-S-18-0519

Hendricks, Alison E. & Emily A. Diehm. 2020. Survey of assessment and intervention practices for students who speak African American English. *Journal of Communication Disorders* 83. 105967. https://doi.org/10.1016/j.jcomdis.2019.105967

Hoffman, Howard J., Chuan-Ming Li, Katalin M. Losonczy, May S. Chiu, Jacqueline B. Lucas & Kenneth O. St. Louis. 2014. *Voice, speech, and language disorders in the US population: The 2012 National Health Interview Survey (NHIS). Abstracts of the 47th Annual Meeting of the Society for Epidemiologic Research, Seattle, WA. 156.*

Jackson, Janice E. & Barbara Z. Pearson. 2008. Non-mainstream dialect and the identification of risk for language impairment. Paper presented at the American Speech-Language-Hearing Association Annual Meeting, Chicago, IL, United States.

Kent, Ray D. 1992. The biology of phonological development. In Charles A. Ferguson, Lise Menn & Carol Stoel-Gammon (eds.), *Phonological development: Models, research, implications,* 65–90. York Press.

Kummer, A.W. (2014). *Cleft palate and craniofacial anomalies: Effects on speech and resonance,* 3rd edn. Delmar.

Labov, William. 1969. Contraction, deletion, and inherent variability of the English copula. *Language* 45(4). 715–762. www.jstor.org/stable/412333

Labov, William. 1972. *Language in the inner city: Studies in the black English vernacular.* University of Pennsylvania Press.

Labov, William, Sharon Ash & Charles Boberg. 2006. *The atlas of North American English: Phonetics, phonology, and sound change: A multimedia reference tool.* De Gruyter.

Larrivee, Linda S., & Hugh W. Catts. 1999. Early reading achievement in children with expressive phonological disorders. *American Journal of Speech-Language Pathology* 8(2). 137–148. https://doi.org/10.1044/1058-0360.0802.118

Lewis, Barbara A., Lisa A. Freebairn & Hudson G. Taylor. 2000. Follow-up of children with early expressive phonology disorders. *Journal of Learning Disabilities* 33(5). 433–444. https://doi.org/10.1177/002221940003300504

Mack, Sara & Benjamin Munson. 2012. The influence of /s/ quality on ratings of men's sexual orientation: Explicit and implicit measures of the 'gay lisp' stereotype. *Journal of Phonetics* 40(1). 198–212. https://doi.org/10.1016/j.wocn.2011.10.002

Maclagan, Margaret, Jeanette King & Gail Gillon. 2008. Maori English. *Clinical Linguistics & Phonetics* 22(8). 658–670. https://doi.org/10.1080/02699200802222271

McKee, Rachel. 2021. New Zealand Sign Language. *Te Ara–the Encyclopedia of New Zealand.* www.TeAra.govt.nz/en/new-zealand-sign-language (12 March 2021)

McLeod, Sharynne & Elise Baker. 2017. *Children's speech: An evidence-based approach to assessment and intervention.* Pearson.

McLeod, Sharynne & Kathryn Crowe. 2018. Children's consonant acquisition in 27 languages: A cross-linguistic review. *American Journal of Speech-Language Pathology* 27(4). 1546–1571. https://doi.org/10.1044/2018_AJSLP-17-0100

Mullen, Robert & Tracy Schooling. 2010. The national outcomes measurement system for pediatric speech-language pathology. *Language, Speech, and Hearing Services in Schools* 41(1). 44–60. https://doi.org/10.1044/0161-1461(2009/08-0051)

Munson, Benjamin. 2007. The acoustic correlates of perceived masculinity, perceived femininity, and perceived sexual orientation. *Language and Speech* 50(1). 125–142. https://doi.org/10.1177/00238309070500010601

Munson, Benjamin, Elizabeth C. McDonald, Nancy L. DeBoe & Aubrey R. White. 2006. The acoustic and perceptual bases of judgments of women and men's sexual orientation from read speech. *Journal of Phonetics* 34(2). 202–240. https://doi.org/10.1016/j.wocn.2005.05.003

O'Beirne, Greg A., Pace Jenkins-Foreman, Marie Lay & Rebecca J. Kelly-Campbell. 2019. Development of a paediatric version of the University of Canterbury Auditory-Visual Matrix Sentence Test. Poster presented at the 14th European Federation of Audiological Societies Congress, Lisbon.

O'Beirne, Greg A., R.H. Trounson, A.D. McClelland, S. Jamaluddin & Margaret A. Maclagan. 2015. Development of an auditory-visual matrix sentence test in New Zealand English. Paper presented at the 12th European Federation of Audiological Societies Congress, Istanbul.

Pearson, Barbara Z., Tracy Connor & Janice E. Jackson. 2013. Removing obstacles for African American English-speaking children through greater understanding of language difference. *Developmental Psychology* 49(1). 31–44. https://doi.org/10.1037/a0028248

Pearson, Barbara Z., Shelley L. Velleman, Timothy J. Bryant & Tiffany Charko. 2009. Phonological milestones for African American English-speaking children learning mainstream American English as a second dialect. *Language, Speech, and Hearing Services in Schools* 40(3). 229–244. https://doi.org/10.1044/0161-1461(2008/08-0064)

Peterson, Candida C. 2018. Development of social-cognitive and communication skills in children born deaf. *Scandinavian Journal of Psychology* 50(5). 475–483. https://doi.org/10.1111/j.1467-9450.2009.00750.x

Pierrehumbert, Janet B., Tessa Bent, Benjamin Munson, Ann R. Bradlow & J. Michael Bailey. 2004. The influence of sexual orientation on vowel production. *Journal of the Acoustical Society of America* 116(4). 1905–1908. https://doi.org/10.1121/1.1788729

Preston, Jonathan. 2008. *Phonological processing and speech production in preschoolers with speech sound disorders*. PhD dissertation, Syracuse University.

Rubin, Donald L. 1992. Nonlanguage factors affecting undergraduates' judgments of nonnative English-speaking teaching assistants. *Research in Higher Education* 33(4). 511–531.

Seymour, Harry N. 2004a. The challenge of language assessment for African American English-speaking children: A historical perspective. *Seminars in Speech and Language* 25(1). 3–12. https://doi.org/10.1055/S-2004-824821

Seymour, Harry N. 2004b. A noncontrastive model for assessment of phonology. *Seminars in Speech and Language* 25(1). 91–99. https://doi.org/10.1055/s-2004-824828

Seymour, Harry N., Linda Bland-Stewart & Lisa J. Green. 1998. Difference versus deficit in child African American English. *Language, Speech, and Hearing Services in Schools* 29(2). 96–108. https://doi.org/10.1044/0161-1461.2902.96

Seymour, Harry N., Thomas W. Roeper, Jill de Villiers & Peter A. de Villiers. 2003. *Diagnostic Evaluation of Language Variation*. Pearson.

Seymour, Harry N. & Charlena M. Seymour. 1977. A therapeutic model for communicative disorders among children who speak Black English Vernacular. *Journal of Speech and Hearing Disorders* 42(2). 247–256. https://doi.org/10.1044/jshd.4202.247

Seymour, Harry N. & Charlena M. Seymour. 1981. Black English and Standard American English contrasts in consonant development of four and five-year old children. *Journal of Speech and Hearing Disorders* 46(3). 274–280. https://doi.org/10.1044/jshd.4603.274

Shriberg, Lawrence D. 1993. Four new speech and prosody-voice measures for genetics research and other studies in developmental phonological disorders. *Journal of Speech and Hearing Research* 36(1). 105–140. https://doi.org/10.1044/jshr.3601.105

Shriberg, Lawrence D. 1994. Five subtypes of developmental phonological disorders. *Clinics in Communication Disorders* 4(1). 38–53.

Shriberg, Lawrence D. 2010. Childhood speech sound disorders: From postbehaviorism to the postgenomic era. In Rhea Paul & Peter Flipsen, Jr. (eds.), *Speech sound disorders in children*, 1–33. Plural.

Silman, John. 2021. *Accent modification: A shifting tide*. California Speech Language Hearing Association. www.csha.org/accent-modification/

Smit, Ann B., Linda Hand, Joseph J. Freilinger, John E. Bernthal & Ann Bird. 1990. The Iowa articulation norms project and its Nebraska replication. *Journal of Speech and Hearing Disorders* 55(4). 779–798. https://doi.org/10.1044/jshd.5504.779

Statistics New Zealand. 2018. New Zealand's 34th census of population and dwellings. www.stats.govt.nz/information-releases/2018-census-totals-by-topic-national-highlights-updated (3 March 2021)

Stockman, Ida J. 2006. Evidence for a minimal competence core of consonant sounds in the speech of African American children: A preliminary study. *Clinical Linguistics & Phonetics* 20(10). 723–749. https://doi.org/10.1080/02699200500322803

United Nations, Department of Economic and Social Affairs, Population Division. 2019. World Population Ageing 2019: Highlights (ST/ESA/SER.A/430).

US Census Bureau. 2018. 2018 American Community Survey 1-year estimates. https://data.census. gov/cedsci/table?t=Language%20Spoken%20at%20Home&y=2018&tid=ACSST1Y2018.S1601 (19 December 2021)

US Census Bureau. 2019. 2019 American Community Survey 1-year estimates. https://data.census.gov/ced sci/table?q=spanish%20speakers&tid=ACSST1Y2019.S1601&hidePreview=true (27 March 2021)

US Census Bureau. 2021a. 2020 Census illuminates racial and ethnic composition of the country. www. census.gov/library/stories/2021/08/improved-race-ethnicity-measures-reveal-united-states-population-much-more-multiracial.html

US Census Bureau. 2021b. Nevada QuickFacts from the US Census Bureau. www.census.gov/quickfacts/ fact/table/NV,US/RHI725219#qf-headnote-b

World Health Organization. 2001. International classification of functioning, disability and health: ICF. https://apps.who.int/iris/handle/10665/42407 (3 March 2021)

SECTION 3

Sociophonetics around the world

22

SOCIOPHONETICS AND SIGNED LANGUAGES

Amelia A. Becker, Julie A. Hochgesang,
Meredith Tamminga, and Jami N. Fisher

Introduction

Signed languages use components of the body, including the hands, arms, torso, head, and face, to implement physical manifestations of abstract representations—organized as handshape, movement, and location—in their mental grammar, just as spoken languages do. In other words, signed languages have phonetics. The introduction of this reality to academic linguists is attributed to the work of William Stokoe (1960) and Stokoe, Casterline & Croneberg (1965). Because signed languages are also used within social contexts where signers express not just lexical and grammatical meanings but also social meanings, identities, and stances, these types of meaning can become variables that correlate with phonetic realizations. Thus, as signed language phonetics and phonology have become fields of study, so has signed language sociophonetics. This chapter provides an overview of the sociophonetics of signed languages for those unfamiliar with signed language linguistics generally or for those who have studied other aspects of signed languages and wish to learn about the methods and findings of this particular subfield.

Because the authors study American Sign Language (ASL), as used in North America, and because findings from ASL are disproportionately represented in the field, this imbalance is reflected throughout this chapter. But we stress that signed languages are not a monolith. Glottolog (Hammarström et al. 2021) names 197–202 known signed languages throughout the world (depending on inclusion of auxiliary sign systems and International Sign Language). These languages, and doubtless the many other undocumented signed languages, differ from one another in myriad ways. Some of these differences have analogues in spoken language typology, such as phonological inventory distinctions. For example, Brentari & Eccarius (2010) conducted a cross-linguistic study of three-finger handshapes in ASL, Hong Kong Sign Language, and Swiss German Sign Language. They found four, five, and six three-finger handshapes in these languages, respectively. For categories which may be considered shared by multiple languages, their phonetic implementation will differ between languages, though investigation of these phonetic differences between signed languages is lacking.

Other concerns in signed language typology are less clearly analogous to questions in spoken language studies, such as the role of mouthing spoken language words or the degree to which fingerspelling systems (manual representations of the orthography used to write the surrounding

DOI: 10.4324/9781003034636-25

spoken language) are integrated into the broader linguistic system (Zeshan & Palfreyman 2017). Signing Deaf communities also differ from one another socioculturally in ways that will surely impact how they use language to index identities and stances. For example, some Deaf communities may be more or less integrated with the surrounding hearing communities, or with other Deaf communities around the world. In some parts of the world, Deaf education consists of dedicated schools in which everyone signs, whereas Deaf children in other places may attend hearing schools or be forbidden to sign in school. Understanding the breadth of the human capacity for employing sociolinguistic variation will require study of signed language use in all of these diverse contexts. It is important when presenting results from signed language studies to carefully note whether, why, and how results might or might not be expected to generalize to other signed languages. This allows us to generate testable hypotheses and avoid reinforcing the misconception that signed languages are less diverse than spoken languages.

The following sections will introduce some of the important questions, findings, and research tools in the field of signed language sociophonetics. As noted above, some of these topics will look familiar to those who have studied spoken language sociophonetics, and others will highlight differences from spoken language data. Methodological considerations are discussed first (data collection and textual representation) followed by theoretical topics (sociolinguistic variables, the phonetics–phonology interface, and connections between synchronic variation and diachronic change). The final section presents a brief case study of a phenomenon known as dominance reversal as observed among several signers of a variety of American Sign Language (ASL) signed in the Philadelphia, Pennsylvania area. Our conclusion will pose some questions that arise from this preliminary observation of data as well as some of the many other areas yet left unexplored within signed language sociophonetics.

Literature review

Sociolinguistic data collection in Deaf communities

The methods we use for signed language data collection and analysis depend on the theoretical questions at hand. While it is possible to use qualitative methods like introspection and self-analysis of linguistic production (Mittelberg 2007) to understand reasons for variation, much of the focus of current research centers on qualitative and quantitative analysis of free or semi-structured conversations (McCaskill et al. 2011) and elicitation tasks (Volterra et al. 1984), and mining corpora for specific linguistic tokens (see Fenlon et al. 2015; Börstell 2016; McKee, Safar & Alexander 2021 for examples). All of these methods require video-recording signers, which complicates data collection. High-quality cameras are likely more obtrusive than audio recording devices for spoken languages and may therefore be more likely to affect the perceived formality of the setting, thus reducing naturalistic conversational styles. To minimize this effect, researchers may adopt several different strategies: recording in a comfortable setting that is familiar to the participant, minimizing equipment use, and eliminating the first few minutes of recording from analysis (Van Herreweghe & Vermeerbergen 2012; Lucas 2013). In signing communities, it is also especially important to consider shared or differing cultural affiliations between the participant and any interviewer or bystanders. It is often suggested that including only interlocutors of the same audiological status (that is, Deaf, hard of hearing, or hearing; Lucas & Valli 1992), ethnicity (Lucas & Valli 1992; McCaskill et al. 2011; Hill et al. 2015; Hill 2017), and even regional background (Fisher, Hochgesang & Tamminga 2021) can put the participant at ease and thus facilitate authentic, naturalistic conversation. Lucas & Valli (1992) found that some signers may employ more English influence on their signing when interacting with hearing signers, while others may do so when signing with an interlocutor they don't know well.

Participant selection for sociolinguistic studies requires familiarity with local Deaf social contexts and, again, careful consideration of the research questions at hand. Effects of age, region, and language background as independent variables manifest differently in Deaf communities than in hearing communities (Lucas 2013). School affiliation has a significant impact on language variation in Deaf communities due to the prevalence of horizontal (peer-to-peer) language transmission over vertical (parent-to-child) transmission. This may be especially true for children attending Deaf residential schools. Participant age may correlate with educational language policy and therefore affect acquisition profiles in ways that are difficult to disentangle from other forces driving change. For example, in the United States (and probably elsewhere), older Deaf people and their signing tend to be affected by policies of strict oralism (no signing permitted in instruction) while the prevalence among younger Deaf children of education in the mainstream limits their exposure to native sign models and other Deaf peers (Johnson, Liddell & Erting 1989; Baynton 1996; Burch 2002). Van Herreweghe & Vermeerbergen (2012) suggest early onset of signed language acquisition, education in a school for the deaf, daily use of the signed language in question, and prolonged membership of the respective Deaf community as possible (though not exhaustive) criteria for selection. That said, these criteria could lead to disproportionate representation of elite or privileged Deaf community members (see Fisher, Hochgesang, Tamminga & Miller 2021), excluding significant populations of signers within a particular community. Costello, Fernández & Landa (2008) present the case of the Deaf community in Basque Country in Spain, where there is an extremely small number of deaf signers acquiring language from deaf language models. These authors point out that this situation necessitates special methodological considerations.

Thus signed language research is typical in that selection criteria must be determined by the research question at hand, but relevant selection criteria among Deaf communities are in fact unique. In addition to the previously studied factors just mentioned, we propose that being born to hearing signing or hearing non-signing families may be a source of variation among Deaf signers. Complementary research elucidating the historical context and social makeup of each community serve to support quantitative analysis of variation within a particular signing community (see Fisher, Tamminga & Hochgesang 2018; Fisher, Hochgesang, Tamminga & Miller 2021 for examples).

As Deaf signed language users have historically been oppressed and their language suppressed by hearing people, entry into signing communities is often limited to trusted points of contact referred to by Milroy (1987:70) as "brokers." Such brokers often have meaningful connections to the community members as well as the researchers, thereby implicitly and explicitly building trust for research participation (see McCaskill et al. 2011; Lucas 2013 for examples). Building on this model of trust is the researcher-participant model wherein early participants in research are trained to take part in data collection and other research activities (see the Philadelphia Signs Project; Fisher, Hochgesang & Tamminga 2021). This model extends beyond sociolinguistics research (see Singleton, Martin & Morgan 2015) and is good practice for research in and with Deaf communities as it advocates for a community-driven agenda and research with mutual benefit and reciprocity.

The need for video-recorded data poses an additional complication for signed language studies: it precludes the possibility of maintaining participant anonymity. Since both manual and nonmanual linguistic features are produced on and around the face, obscuring participants' faces to mask their identity is not a viable workaround. We must be clear about this in informed consent and protective of the participants in the ways in which we use these data in public forums (for example, restricting use of data by other sources, redacting any incriminating information, etc.). Crasborn (2010) describes a number of ways in which the publication of video data from signed languages raises ethical concerns that researchers need to take into consideration. For example, participants' varying degrees of literacy in the written form of the surrounding spoken language may impact the accessibility of written informed consent documents. Crasborn discusses several best practices for eliciting informed consent in this context. However, he also points out that the possibility for unforeseen future technological advancements means that it is very hard for anyone to understand what they might be consenting to when they agree to have videos of themselves publicly shared on the internet, even given the best possible consent procedure. These ethical considerations are especially acute for researchers building publicly accessible corpora. An example of a project that is adopting new technological approaches to help manage different tiers of availability for video data is the Motivated Look at Indicating Verbs in ASL (MoLo) project (Dudis et al. 2020). By adding watermarks indicating access levels (open, researcher only, MoLo team only) to their videos, they put data privacy considerations visually front and center.

While academics typically publish their results in academic journals, awareness of the history of marginalization of Deaf communities leads many signed language researchers to adopt an ethos that they must ensure global accessibility of findings for Deaf communities in order to avoid further exploitation. Thus, considerations based on register, language accessibility, and technology must be made in information dissemination efforts. For example, in presentation and publication, Wolfram (2013) cautions against the use of academic jargon, while Lucas (2013) suggests linguistic and visual accommodations to ensure accessibility to community members. In addition, it is imperative that researchers create materials that are both technically accessible and useful to the participants and other community members. For example, Lucas, Bayley & Valli's (2001) book caters to Deaf community members' interest in lexical variation, while the Philadelphia Signs Project website (https://pennds.org/phillysigns/) was created to highlight lexical variation and stories of and by Deaf people from the Philadelphia region.

Issues in textual representation

The question of how to textually represent data is important for any sociophonetician. This question is more complex for researchers studying signed languages for several reasons, however. There is no widely used written form of signed languages nor any standardized notation system equivalent to the International Phonetic Alphabet, so there is no obvious choice for representing lexical items, regardless of whether the goal is to be informative about phonetic form or not. This section overviews approaches and challenges to textual representation.

Researchers documenting signed language may distinguish between "annotation," referring to any form of textual representation of language data, and "notation," a form of textual representation that gives information about the linguistic form (Hochgesang 2014). Common forms of signed language annotation include glossing and ID glossing (e.g., Johnston 2010; Hodge & Crasborn 2022). Glossing uses writing, generally in small caps, to represent words from the surrounding spoken language that roughly correspond in meaning to a sign. For example, a researcher may use the gloss BIRTHDAY to represent an ASL sign on paper that has the meaning 'birthday.' The problem with this approach is that, without an accompanying photo or, better still, video, the form of this sign remains unknown to the reader (Hochgesang 2022). The concept 'birthday' in particular is known to be represented by many different signs depending on a signer's region. One solution to this problem is the use of ID glossing, in which each sign that is perceived as a distinct lexical item receives a unique textual label. These labels are then housed in a database of videos so that the precise form of each sign can be accessed. An example of such a database is ASL Signbank (Hochgesang, Crasborn & Lillo-Martin 2017–2021).

ID glossing greatly improves data accessibility over traditional glossing, especially by providing machine-readability. By linking to relevant entries in signbanks (through an External Controlled Vocabulary or ECV link in ELAN [Crasborn & Sloetjes 2008]), researchers can maintain the connection between textual representations and video and photo of the represented sign. Since this linking also connects ID glosses to additional information about a sign in its signbank entry (phonological and morphosyntactic properties), it allows for a certain amount of semi-automatic annotation in the linked transcripts. However, this approach is still insufficient for sociophonetic research. At the level of lemmatization, decisions must be made about what differences in form should justify a difference in labels. For example, there may be a sign that can occur as either a one- or two-handed sign. In some signers' lexicons, perhaps only the one-handed version exists. For other signers, the two-handed sign may be the citation form with the one-handed version surfacing in specific contexts. Database creators must make a systematic decision about whether only a single textual label should be used for both the one- and two-handed versions or whether two separate labels are warranted. If only one label is used, the information about handedness in a given production is lost in the textual representation. For less categorical distinctions than handedness, such as location or articulator velocity, the problem is even greater.

When textual representation needs to provide information about the form of a sign (or of a given production of a sign), a notation system must be used. Since the inception of signed language linguistics, multiple systems have been developed. The first, presented in Stokoe (1960), consisted of symbols for handshapes, movements, and locations, with diacritics representing palm orientation. For the most part, only phonemic contrasts were represented by Stokoe Notation; allophonic differences were generally obscured. For example, the same symbol was used to represent both of the handshapes in Figure 22.1 below, because this difference alone is not enough to produce a difference in meaning in conventionalized ASL signs (although it signals distinct letters in the ASL manual alphabet and could create distinct meaning within the classifier system).

This overlap in representation of distinct allophones makes Stokoe Notation ill-suited to phonetic and sociophonetic documentation. And since Stokoe's innovation, we have learned that signed language phonological structure can be described not just as an inventory of holistic handshapes, locations, movements, and orientations, but rather as features combining to produce these larger units. These features specify things like which fingers are involved in a sign's production and how flexed or extended the joints of those fingers are. Some notation systems that have grown out of Stokoe Notation still follow the same basic principle of holistic labels for handshapes, locations, movements, and orientations but with the ability to capture allophonic differences or errors in

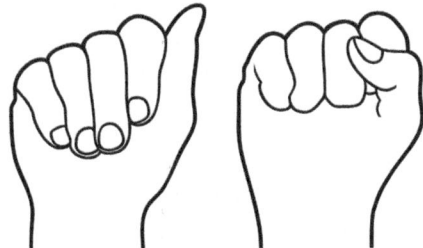

Figure 22.1   A handshape (left) and S handshape (right)

production. For example, the Hamburg Notation System for Sign Languages (HamNoSys; Hanke 2004) provides symbols to describe the handshape, orientation, and location at the beginning of a sign, and, where applicable, any changes in those categories that occur throughout the sign. HamNoSys also allows annotators to describe nonmanual (facial) gestures important to the sign production.

Even though our understanding of the mental organization of sign components has deepened, researchers still disagree about the precise inventory of smaller units that make up the phonological categories of handshapes, movements, and locations and how these units are organized with respect to one another in the phonology. Proposed notation systems vary in the degree to which they are designed to represent more abstract phonological categories or more phonetic detail (Hochgesang 2014), and because most correspond to a specific theory of the phonological organization of signs, this disagreement poses an obstacle to developing a single, widely used notation system.

Eccarius & Brentari (2008) provide a notation system for handshapes observed in ten different signed languages. This system is based on the Prosodic Model (Brentari 1998), which draws upon work from spoken language phonology such as autosegmental phonology, feature geometry, and Optimality Theory (Prince & Smolensky 2004) to propose a structure for the mental organization of the units of signed language phonology. In another model put forth by Liddell & Johnson (1989, 2019) and Johnson & Liddell (2011a, 2011b, 2011c, 2012), signs are composed of sequentially organized segments. Each segment contains values for the phonetic details involved in producing that portion of the sign, such as the flexion/extension of each finger joint and location of the hand(s) in space or on the signer's body. In other models, such as the Prosodic Model developed by Brentari (1998), the hierarchical organization of units in the phonology is reversed, where units that specify the timing relationship between different features (i.e., the segments) are isomorphic with the level of the morpheme, so that any change in handshape or location that occurs throughout the sign is specified only once as a property of the whole morpheme, rather than resulting from features that are specified independently at each temporally sequential portion of that morpheme. The reason for proposing this type of structure, rather than what is proposed by Johnson & Liddell, comes from evidence like the fact that handshapes tend to change in constrained ways throughout a sign: the handshapes at the beginning and end of a sign typically involve the same fingers and can only differ in joint configuration. Thus a single feature indicating the "important" fingers and another specifying opening or closing of those fingers can be used, rather than indicating the fingers and their configuration at the beginning, middle, and end of the sign.

Ultimately, the research question at hand determines which notation system is most appropriate to represent data for a given study. Even when expanded to allow for narrower transcription, Stokoe-based notation systems are still aimed more toward describing categories that distinguish signs within the lexicon, rather than representing distinctions in phonetic production. For example, Eccarius & Brentari's (2008) handshape coding system provides separate joint configuration symbols for the base finger joints, the base thumb joint, and the remaining finger joints. While this provides more information than a single label for an entire handshape, it still treats the second and third finger joints as a single category and so would not be useful for examining this level of phonetic detail. An alternative type of notation system can be found in Liddell & Johnson (1989, 2019) and Johnson & Liddell (2011a, 2011b, 2011c, 2012). This system treats signs as a series of static and dynamic segments (similar to consonants and vowels in articulatory manner). Within each static segment, the configuration of each individual joint, the location, and the palm orientation are identified. Within dynamic segments, these properties are identified as either changing or not. This type of system allows us to capture differences that do not result in a change in category (either phonemic or allophonic) but that may nonetheless be systematic and predictable based on linguistic and/or sociolinguistic variables.

The issues raised in this section ultimately reflect the fact that the conundrum of disentangling phonetics from phonology is not new; signed language sociophoneticians are like all phoneticians and phonologists in needing to grapple with this question. We continue to highlight these issues in the following subsections, as we turn to a survey of existing empirical research on sociophonetic variation and change in signed languages.

Social influences on signed language variation

The first published observations on social factors influencing ASL come in Croneberg's two appendices (C and D) to the 1965 *Dictionary of American Sign Language* (Stokoe, Casterline & Croneberg 1965). Here, he describes the extensive, cross-country network of deaf people and the various social and economic factors that contribute to community development and maintenance and their impact on signed language variation and change. This work is considered foundational to understanding the role of social factors in signed language variation and change. Early research on sociolinguistic variation, including lexical and grammatical variation, highlighted unique aspects of the social forces at play in Deaf communities. For example, Woodward's (1973) study of ASL verb reduplication examined whether variation in reduplication could be attributed to the participant's hearing status (deaf or hearing), whether they had deaf parents (to represent variety in modes of transmission), whether they learned sign before age 6 (examining the role of earlier language exposure and transmission), and whether or not they attended college (to examine the role of education in preserving cultural values and maintaining more formal registers in the language). He found that the most important factor was deafness and the second most important was having deaf parents, reflecting the fact that signed language transmission was, at the time, typically from peer to peer in residential settings rather than from parent to child, as is usually observed with spoken languages.

Much subsequent research on the social factors influencing phonetic and phonological variation in signed languages has developed in the variationist tradition, especially following from Lucas, Bayley & Valli (2001). Lucas and colleagues video-recorded sociolinguistic interviews with 207 Deaf native or near-native ASL signers in seven locations across the United States with large and active Deaf communities (Staunton, Virginia; Frederick, Maryland; Boston, Massachusetts; Olathe, Kansas; New Orleans, Louisiana; Fremont, California; and Bellingham, Washington). Other quantitative studies of the factors conditioning the use of sociolinguistic variables in the phonetics, phonology, and lexicon of ASL include Bayley, Lucas & Rose (2000, 2002); Lucas, Bayley, Reed & Wulf (2001); Lucas et al. (2002); Wulf et al. (2002); and Lucas & Bayley (2005). In comparing this conditioning to what we know about variation and change in spoken languages, Lucas, Bayley & Valli (2001) primarily emphasize the empirical similarities in sociolinguistic variation between signed languages and spoken languages. They find that, like in spoken languages, phonological variation in ASL is systematically conditioned by both linguistic factors, such as phonological context and grammatical function, and also social factors, like region, ethnicity, age, and gender. However, they also highlight that the typical mode of language transmission (via deaf peers at residential schools) and education policy affecting deaf children have critical impacts on—and thus must be at the forefront of analyzing—ASL variation and change.

These studies of ASL provided a foundational model for documenting and analyzing variation in other signed languages, including British Sign Language (BSL; Fenlon et al. 2013; Fenlon,

Schembri & Cormier 2018), Australian Sign Language (Auslan; Schembri et al. 2009), Brazilian Sign Language (Libras; Schmitt 2020), and Italian Sign Language (LIS; Geraci et al. 2011). These studies not only diversify the literature in which ASL is over-represented but also contribute novel findings about factors that predict phonetic variation that were not included in the ASL studies. For example, both Schembri et al. (2009) and Fenlon et al. (2013) found an effect of lexical frequency. Fenlon et al. in fact found only one significant social factor (region) in variation of the 1 handshape, and they attribute this difference from ASL findings to the fact that they only included up to three instances of any single lexical item from a given signer and included lexical item as a factor in their mixed-effects regression. They suggest that results attributed in Bayley, Lucas & Rose (2002) to complex interactions with social factors may have in fact been due to an over-representation of pronoun signs.

The project by Lucas, Bayley & Valli (2001) also provided a framework for an overlapping group of ASL researchers when they set out to document and analyze Black ASL as it is used in the American South. Research on the variety of ASL used by Black American signers in the United States goes back at least to Woodward & Erting's (1974, 1975) observations that some Black southern signing did not exhibit all of the phonological changes noted by Frishberg's (1975) study of historical change in ASL. Woodward (1976) subsequently reports on lexical items, phonological variation, and language attitudes among Black southern signers and compares these to white and northern signers. Building on these studies as well as drawing from anecdotal observation in southern Black Deaf communities and from research on African American English (AAE), McCaskill et al. (2011) filmed free conversation, interviews, and word-elicitation tasks at seven sites with 96 Black ASL users who attended segregated (signers age 55 and older) and desegregated (signers age 35 and younger) schools. One generalization that can be taken from the detailed findings published in McCaskill et al. (2011) and related publications (for example, Hill 2017) is that Black ASL is more linguistically conservative than mainstream ASL in a number of respects. The existence of a distinct variety of ASL among Black Deaf Americans has been argued to result from racial segregation: during the late 1800s and well into the twentieth century, the oralist approach was seen to be more advanced and thus more fitting for white signers. Black signers were not given access to oralist pedagogy and thus maintained their ASL use where white signers did not (Woodward 1976; McCaskill et al. 2011). A review by Toliver-Smith & Gentry (2017) suggests that while Black ASL is acknowledged as a distinct entity, systematic study of this variety is still scarce.

Recently, there has been a deliberate effort to understand how intersectional identities within Deaf communities impact variation and change in signed languages. For example, Blau (2017) looks at sociophonetic variation in Deaf gay men, finding that they articulate signs more distally (with joints farther away from the torso, closer to the hand) than the citation form as compared to participants who did not identify as part of that community. Though the study was small, it suggests that alternation in articulated joints may have more meaning than previously thought, giving rise to the possibility that this type of variation could be a distinctive marker of a particular social group. Palfreyman (2020) analyzes four variables in an Indonesian Sign Language (BISINDO) corpus and argues that variation reflects social meaning in that community in four ways: as a reinforcement of regional identity; as commentary on ASL influence on the language and people; as distinction between deaf and hearing roles in society; and as an indicator of Javanese identity. In this case, ASL plays a similarly imperialist role in the Indonesian Deaf community as English does in formerly colonized communities; it is a symbol of contact with outside communities and educational attainment while also evidence of how BISINDO has been supplanted by an outside influence with outsized power. The hearing–deaf dynamics are similarly fraught, in that hearing community members tend to have more power and decision-making abilities than do Deaf community members, and this plays out in the language in that it reflects identity and other affiliations. These dimensions point to the interface of complex intersectional experiences that must be considered in variationist research within Deaf communities. Lastly, Mirus, Fisher & Napoli (2019) look at lexical and sublexical changes in iconic signs in American Sign Language. Some of these changes are in response to inevitable misalignment of form and meaning due to environmental changes. For example, with technology updates, the sign for "using a credit card" now resembles the swiping movement of credit card use rather than the old form which imitates the manual carbon copying of a credit card by a merchant. Other changes reflect cultural and social realignment with the values and experiences of various Deaf social groups: the sign meaning 'lesbian' has changed contact location from the webbing between the thumb and index finger to the tip of the index finger in an L-handshape, thus moving away from an iconic sign suggestive of sexual acts to a more arbitrary sign to indicate a community of people. Ultimately, the authors suggest that language change must take into account the idea of correction prompted by sensitive topics within the community, as they are external forces that invariably influence the production of language itself.

Approaches to signed language variation at the phonetics–phonology interface

The variationist research discussed in the previous subsection has typically used logistic regression, implemented in programs such as Varbrul (Rousseau & Sankoff 1978), as its key statistical tool. Logistic (or relatedly, multinomial) regression requires the dependent variable to be discrete—that is, involving choices between a small class of qualitatively distinct options. Modeling the factors that make one choice or the other more likely is a natural fit for variable phonological phenomena, which arguably manipulate abstract symbolic units. For example, in Bayley, Lucas & Rose's (2002) study of variation in the 1-handshape variable, non-citation variants such as the L-handshape or the open hand are modeled as distinct options that a signer might choose. Similarly, treating the variation between ear-to-chin and chin-to-ear forms of the sign DEAF as involving discrete variants, as Bayley, Lucas & Rose (2000) do, is consistent with Liddell & Johnson's (1989:244–245) analysis of these forms as involving phonological metathesis.

In some cases the statistical tools of the variationist framework have led researchers into a more arbitrary discretization of a seemingly continuous dimension. For example, Lucas et al. (2002) coded a lexical class of one-handed signs canonically produced at the temple, the ASL "know" sign class, as being either citation form (above the eyebrow ridge) or lowered (below the eyebrow ridge). They found that grammatical category and phonological context significantly influenced the probability of lowering. Tamminga, Fisher & Hochgesang (2020) similarly bin weak-hand production variation into a small number of discrete categories even though the phenomena in their study—weak-hand lowering in canonically two-handed signs and weak-hand involvement in canonically one-handed signs—almost certainly exist on a continuous dimension. These weak-hand variable phenomena highlight two additional complications for research on signed language sociophonetics. First, it seems likely that there are multiple variable processes at play simultaneously: a two-handed sign could exhibit either gradient lowering or wholesale omission of the weak hand (the latter sometimes being called "weak hand drop"). Second, there is not agreement on what form is in fact "canonical" for any given sign, and the possibility space is quite complicated: different signers may have different or multiple lexical representations for different signs. Both of these issues, of course, have parallels in the study of intra- and inter-speaker variation in spoken languages. We see them as interesting areas of theoretical investigation rather than obstacles.

A recent development that may prove crucial in understanding these questions is a stream of research applying technological tools to measure variation along phonetically gradient dimensions (Tyrone & Mauk 2010; Tyrone 2015). The use of instrumental techniques to study the articulation of signed languages is comparable to the use of technology like ultrasound or electromagnetic articulography to track the speech articulators in spoken languages. The new technologies being used to automatically capture properties of sign articulation include motion capture systems and electronic data glove systems. Motion capture systems involve placing markers on the body and then recording motion at a high sampling rate in three-dimensional space. Optical motion capture systems such as Optotrak and Vicon use infrared light to track motion, although there are other options. Data glove systems, or cybergloves, involve gloves that the signer wears to capture the physical movement of the hands using strain gauges. Another technological development is the application of motion detection algorithms to normal video. Tyrone (2015) provides a thorough review of these instrumental options and their pros and cons. While researchers are exploring how these technologies may be further developed to facilitate automated processing of signed language, at the moment such technologies are limited and not in wide use by linguists.

Many of the instrumental studies that have been done so far in signed language phonetics have investigated location variation under experimentally controlled conditions. Results of these studies have shown that signing speed, characteristics of surrounding signs, and where a sign appears in an utterance can all affect sign location. For example, Tyrone & Mauk (2010) investigated the location of the ASL sign WONDER, which is specified for forehead location. In contrast to the variationist literature reviewed above, lowering here was not operationalized as a categorical variable. The location of each token of WONDER was measured using the optoelectronic system, Optotrak. Small infrared light emitting devices were fixed to each signer's index finger and their location was tracked by infrared cameras. Location was measured as millimeters above or below a device fixed to the signer's head. This approach allowed sign lowering to be treated as a gradient phonetic process and showed that the location of WONDER became lower as signing rate increased for five of their six participants. Signing rate also interacted with phonetic context (the location of preceding and following signs) and utterance position (initial or final) to affect lowering. Parameters other than location deserve treatment as gradient phonetic phenomena as well. Cheek (2001) found that handshape also varies in accordance with the phonetic impact of surrounding signs and signing rate. Such studies on handshape are scarce, however, and even fewer have addressed movement. Tyrone (2012) suggests this imbalance comes from the relative ease of measuring location and of comparing location data to spoken language phonetic data.

Even with the availability of new instrumental technologies, signed language phoneticians face several unique obstacles. One is the issue of data normalization. Spoken language phoneticians follow well-established and tested methods of transforming measurements such as formant values to account for the fact that speakers have vocal tracts of different shapes and sizes (see, e.g., Adank, Smits & van Hout 2004; Cox & Docherty this volume; Watt, Renwick & Stanley this volume). In contrast, we have no established way to account for the fact that signers' articulators also differ in size and shape. Furthermore, phonetic implementation of a feature like location may involve not only raising and lowering of the hand/arm. Mauk & Tyrone (2012) found that signers may move their head toward their hand rather than simply moving their hand toward their head to achieve a forehead location. Thus describing phonetic implementation requires attention even to movement of articulators which are typically considered passive. This level of description is typically not provided in the sociophonetic literature, however.

Yet another reason we know so little about signed language phonetics, and a partial explanation for the lack of precise articulatory description of data, stems from an assumption that has seemed to pervade thinking about the visual modality: that, because the articulators are visually accessible, there is no consequential mediation between perception and processing. That is, researchers have treated the phonetics–phonology interface as unimportant for signed languages because we have characterized the articulators as directly accessible because they are visible. For example, Crasborn (2012:7) suggests the lack of phonetic description of signed languages may proceed from "the impression that we can see the articulators in sign languages [which] has made it self-evident what the phonological form looks like, and in that way reduced the need for an accurate phonetic description." Similarly, Brentari (2019:47), describing signal differences between the spoken and signed modalities, writes, "the articulators in sign languages are directly visible, while the articulators in speech have to be inferred indirectly. For example, when the hands assume a particular shape we can see all moments of the articulatory process, while when the tongue assumes a particular shape we cannot." It is not clear, however, why visual perception should be considered any more direct than auditory perception. Tyrone (2012) argues that this assumption has been an obstacle to our understanding of signed language phonetics. We contend that the issue is perhaps a lack of integration of knowledge from the field of visual perception that has prevented signed language linguists from describing phonetics in terms of the visual signal, rather than that the bridge from phonetic signal to phonological form is trivial. The issues raised above in the study of weak-hand variation—where multiple analyses are available for any given surface form—highlight the problem with this assumption: even when the variable in question is as seemingly categorical as involvement of the weak hand, visual access to production does not provide automatic access to underlying representations or preclude mediating perceptual processes. Description of form is therefore, we argue, no less crucial to signed language research than to studies of spoken language.

Connections to diachronic change

While studies of synchronic variation have made progress highlighting the linguistic and social conditioning of variation in signed languages, the use of similar data to study signed language change-in-progress is somewhat less common. Of particular relevance to this chapter, the study of what in spoken languages is often called "sound change"—that is, change in the phonetics and phonology of a language (Boberg this volume)—is not a deeply developed area in the visual-manual modality. It has even been claimed that signed languages do not undergo this type of change at the phonological level (Moser 1990). Napoli & Sanders (in progress) propose iconicity as the force that rules out this type of change. We suggest that the rarity of uninterrupted generational transmission (i.e., Deaf parents to Deaf children) of signed languages may also play a role in why this type of change has not been observed. Investigation of change over time in a signed language of a relatively isolated Deaf community might shed light on this hypothesis. Despite our lack of understanding of regular change, or lack thereof, in signed languages, a handful of influential studies have laid the groundwork for future research activity in this area by connecting potential pressures from conversational signing to observations about historical outcomes.

A touchstone in the study of signed language change is Frishberg (1975), which lays out a number of dimensions of historical change that, she argues, all involve an overall tendency away from iconicity in favor of arbitrariness. Her discussion of the motivations for these trajectories draws a clear line between the pressures of conversational signing and the diachronic outcomes. For example, one dimension is an increase in both handshape and movement symmetry, which she attributes to the articulatory ease of programming both hands simultaneously and the perceptual benefits of redundancy. An opposing tendency she identifies, which she terms "head displacement" (1975:703), is for two-handed signs to become one-handed when they are near the face, where visual perception may be more easily able to detect smaller or subtler movements and therefore doesn't require as much redundant input. Frishberg's subsequent dissertation further develops the case that ASL "has evolved through regular linguistic change from a more pantomimic or iconic origin to its present day more arbitrary or symbolic state" (Frishberg 1976:2).

Frishberg's work is based on her observations of how the contemporaneous forms of signs as documented in Stokoe, Casterline & Croneberg (1965) compare to scholars' descriptions of nineteenth-century Old French Sign Language (from which ASL is generally argued to be descended) and, as an intermediate reference point, Long (1918). While groundbreaking, the generalizations she puts forward are probably best interpreted as hypotheses that could be supported or falsified through quantitative analysis. An example of such a study is Woodward & DeSantis's (1977) study of head displacement. Woodward & DeSantis (1977) elicit eight two-handed ASL signs canonically articulated on the face from 75 ASL signers (40 white and 35 Black) and French Sign Language (LSF) cognates from 60 LSF signers, and find an implicational relationship such that signers who have the one-handed form also have the two-handed form (but not necessarily vice versa). This suggests that the one-handed form is a later development. They also find that older signers retain more two-handed sign forms than younger signers among both their American and French participants, which could be an apparent-time reflection of change-in-progress.

Woodward & DeSantis (1977:334) also find quantitative support for the kinds of perceptual mechanisms Frishberg proposed, such as evidence that deletion of the second hand is "allowed first in those areas that are more salient to vision." On the other hand, Tamminga, Fisher & Hochgesang (2020) fail to find conversational signing evidence to support the related prediction that weak-hand lowering, construed as a gradient lenition process providing a pathway to weak-hand deletion, should occur more frequently around the face than around the torso.

Rimor et al. (1984) test the relationship between synchronic pressures and change with experimental evidence from a speeded serial transmission task (where a message is passed between signers in a chain) and a style-shifting task (eliciting isolated citation forms compared to conversational forms). They argue that their results support the proposal that both synchronic and diachronic reductions are attributable to the pressures of articulatory and perceptual ease. The treatment of ease of articulation and perception in the signed language literature has become more complex in recent years. Napoli, Sanders & Wright (2014) give an in-depth discussion of what articulatory ease means for both nonmanual and manual aspects of signed languages. For a sample of ASL lexical items, they advocate for the functional importance of ease of articulation by comparing elicited forms that signers would use in casual connected signing and a reference citation form for each sign. Sanders & Napoli (2016) introduce "reactive effort"—the effort required to hold the rest of the body still while the active articulators work—as a force shaping movement distributions in signed language lexicons. Finally, phonetic reduction processes have been identified as part of the grammaticalization pathways by which open-class lexical items can come to take on closed-class grammatical functions over time, in signed languages just as in spoken languages (Pfau & Steinbach 2006; Johnston et al. 2015).

CASE STUDY   Convergence in Philadelphia ASL dominance reversal

In addition to presenting methodologies and considerations particular to the sociophonetic study of signed languages, the previous sections have touched upon several sources of variation that can be fruitfully investigated from a sociophonetic perspective. In this section, we focus upon one in particular to provide a more in-depth demonstration of an area of investigation currently being pursued in the field: dominance reversal in ASL.

ASL and other signed languages make use of both hands as articulators, but the two hands can play independent roles in sign formation. Very broadly, signs may be one-handed, symmetrical two-handed, or asymmetrical two-handed. For one-handed signs, signers typically use their preferred hand to articulate the sign. A signer's preferred hand is determined by their handedness behavior across everyday tasks, whereas the concept of a dominant hand refers to abstract generalizations about how signs are formed. In asymmetrical two-handed signs, one hand plays the dominant role as an active articulator that has a fuller range of handshape possibilities. Meanwhile, the hand playing the non-dominant role serves as the passive articulator and can have only one of a small set of handshapes.

The notion of dominance here is a phonotactic one, characterizing abstract constraints on statistically more probable and improbable sign forms (Battison 1974). No signed language studied to date has a contrastive role for left-hand versus right-hand dominance (Crasborn 2011). While the default is often for signers to realize dominant hand forms with their preferred hand, they are free to switch which hand plays the dominant role during the production of conversational signing. This phenomenon, called "dominance reversal" (Frishberg 1985), tends to be attributed to cases where the preferred hand is otherwise occupied, such as if the signer is carrying a coffee cup. However, it is possible for dominance reversal to occur in conversational signing without obvious nonlinguistic motivation. Dominance reversal has been attested not only in ASL but also in a number of other signed languages (Nilsson 2007; Hendriks 2008; Crasborn & Sáfár 2016). We take dominance reversal to be phonetic in that it involves form variation that does not seem to be encoded in the phonology. Because dominance reversal is inherently categorical, however, it is not subject to the same obstacles of measurement described earlier in the chapter for more gradient phenomena.

Dominance reversal, and handedness more generally, is reported to be of low social or perceptual salience, at least for fluent signers. Crasborn (2011), for example, notes that signers do not report remembering the hand preference of their recent interlocutors. Nonetheless, it has been argued that reversal can be used "for the purpose of creating semantic connections or contrasts between elements within the narrative" (Frishberg 1985:83). There is also some preliminary evidence that dominance reversal in ASL can be sensitive to social factors (Frishberg 1985) and stylistic factors (Zimmer 1989), but most of the focus has been on the discourse-pragmatic uses of dominance reversal. Here we report a small case study suggesting convergence between interlocutors in dominance reversal in Philadelphia ASL.

Methods

The case study uses data from two participants in the Philadelphia Signs Project (PSP), a corpus of sociolinguistic interviews in ASL with Deaf Philadelphians. The interviews are modeled after Labov's (1984) interview methodology and previous sociolinguistic work in ASL (Lucas, Bayley & Valli 2001).

Our coding for dominance reversal relied on a simple categorization of whether the hand playing the dominant role was or was not reversed during continuous signing. Following Crasborn & Safar (2016:239), signs or stretches of signing were designated as reversed when the participant used their apparent non-preferred hand to play the dominant role in an asymmetrical two-handed sign or to articulate a one-handed sign. In our coding, the beginnings and endings of utterances were identified as soon as hand movement began or ended. The coding was done in ELAN on a tier separate from the other levels of annotation being used in the corpus. We coded two-handed symmetrical signs according to the hand dominance of the previously articulated signs, even though dominance is technically not a factor in these types of signs. In other words, we began coding a sequence of signs as reversed when there was first evidence for reversal, and continued this classification in the sequence until there was positive evidence that dominance was no longer reversed. When a two-handed sign began the utterance, we followed the hand dominance of the last sign in the previous utterance.

"Buoys" are a manual way of keeping track of referents in signed language discourse. They typically make use of the non-dominant hand as a persistent representation of the referent while the dominant hand continues to add new and meaningful content (see Quer et al. 2017:86). Following Hendriks (2008), we categorized buoys as simultaneous constructions and thus did not code them as reversed. We did include one-word responses such as RIGHT, NOT, or YES in dominance reversal coding, whereas Crasborn & Safar (2016) do not.

The dependent variable in our analyses in this section is the number of minutes during which a signer exhibited dominance reversal, reported as a percentage of the overall time during which that signer was signing during the interview. Many more fine-grained measures of dominance reversal could be adopted, but this approach provides a reasonable first-pass estimation of how prevalent dominance reversal is overall within an individual's signing behavior during a conversation.

While previous research has made clear that dominance reversal can be used for discourse-pragmatic purposes, it is equally clear that dominance reversal is never obligatory even when the discourse context would motivate its use. This means that there is more to be said about when and why signers use dominance reversal: What kinds of social and stylistic factors might additionally influence a signer's choice to reverse dominance? Here we take a preliminary look at the possible influence of social interaction between interlocutors on the rate at which those interlocutors use dominance reversal. We do this by looking at a case where we have data from the same signer across more than one interview event.

We focus on a series of three recorded interviews involving Domonic, a Black Deaf man in his late twenties at the time of the recordings. Domonic is now one of our project interviewers, but was himself interviewed as a participant before he joined the interviewer team. His initial interview was conducted by a Black Deaf woman in her late thirties named Janessa. We compare his use of dominance reversal in that interview to two interviews that he conducted with Danisha, a Black Deaf woman in her thirties. Danisha was interviewed twice because she felt her first interview used a less natural register than she would typically use in conversation and requested to redo it.

Results

Figure 22.2 presents Domonic's dominance reversal rate, alongside the dominance reversal behavior of his interlocutor in each interview. Figure 22.2 shows that Domonic's tendency to use dominance reversal varied across the three interviews he participated in. In his original participant interview,

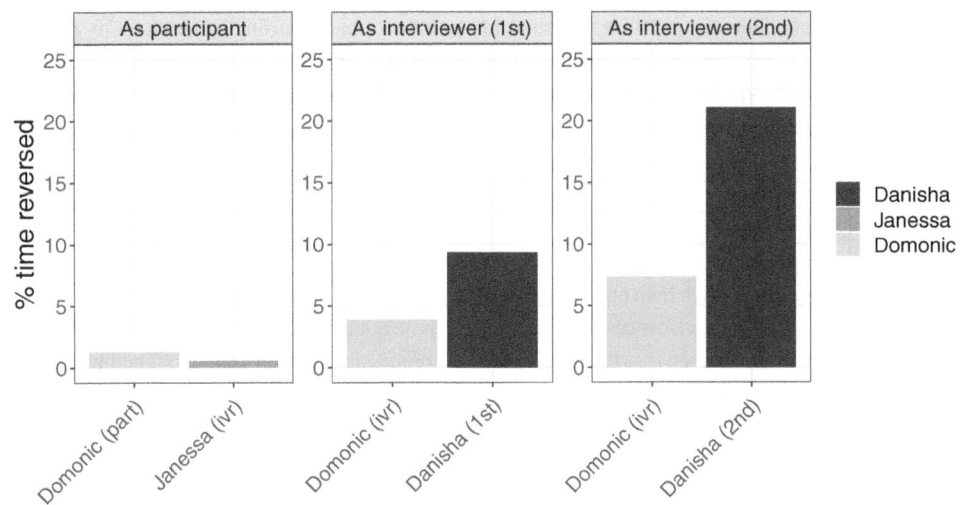

Figure 22.2 Dominance reversal rates in Domonic's signing across three interviews, compared to his interlocutor's reversal rate in each interview

shown in the first panel of Figure 22.2, he used a low rate of dominance reversal, around 1 percent. His interlocutor, Janessa, also used a minimal amount of less than 1 percent dominance reversal in that conversation. In the interviews that he conducted with Danisha, who uses reversal frequently, Domonic also uses a higher rate of dominance reversal, although not as high as Danisha herself. The second panel shows that he used reversal in 4 percent of his continuous signing time in the first interview with Danisha, where her reversal rate was 9 percent. Finally, the third panel shows that when Domonic interviewed Danisha for the second time, both signers used even more dominance reversal: 7 percent for Domonic, and 21 percent for Danisha. The basic generalization across the three panels of Figure 22.2 is that Domonic uses more dominance reversal in conversational interactions where his conversational partner also uses more dominance reversal.

One possibility to consider when we see within-signer variation mirroring the interlocutor's behavior in this way is that the pattern reflects socially motivated accommodation (also called convergence) between interlocutors, as in Communication Accommodation Theory (CAT; Giles, Coupland & Coupland 1991). CAT is closely related to Bell's (1984) Audience Design model of style-shifting, in which variation within the language use of individuals is derived from and motivated by the variation that is present in the larger community. On an accommodation analysis of Figure 22.2, we might think that Domonic is dynamically converging with his interlocutor, and likely they with him at the same time, in each of these situations. An account leaning on accommodation and style-shifting might eventually be able to help us make sense of the reversal frequency differences between the two conversations involving both Danisha and Domonic. Danisha characterized her first interview as conforming to certain prestige norms (which may be a reference to the hegemony of signing styles used more frequently by white signers), whereas in her second interview she explicitly articulated an intention to set aside such conformity in favor of using a style she called "Ebonics," which suggests the variety linguists call Black ASL (McCaskill et al. 2011; Hill et al. 2015). Since Danisha explicitly set up the second interview as reflective of her Black identity and linguistic style, which Domonic was aware of, their shared identity as Black signers could be a factor in supporting either mutually reinforcing convergence or Domonic's accommodation to Danisha's deliberately undertaken style-shifting.

Another possible explanation to consider for the pattern in Figure 22.2 is that a more mechanistic process such as priming may be involved. In psycholinguistics, priming is the phenomenon where a language user, having recently processed a stimulus (such as a single sign or a grammatical construction), can recognize or retrieve the same or a related stimulus more easily. Under this analysis, instances where one signer switches their dominance could prime their interlocutor to also reverse dominance soon afterward. If Domonic interacts with a high-reversal signer, priming alone could lead to him using dominance reversal more often than he would in interactions with signers using less reversal. While the bulk of the psycholinguistic evidence for priming is in spoken languages (Warren this volume), there is ample experimental evidence that it is also a relevant processing phenomenon in signed languages (Emmorey 1991; Corina & Grosvald 2012; Hall, Ferreira & Mayberry 2015). Although we are not aware of previous demonstrations that priming can influence variation in conversational signing, the spoken language sociolinguistic literature provides extensive support for the idea that priming shapes which variants language users choose in particular moments of conversational speech. Therefore, it is reasonable to propose that dominance may also respond to priming in conversational signing.

When language users repeat the features of each other's linguistic behavior in short-term interactions, it is notoriously difficult to disentangle the various cognitive and sociostylistic mechanisms that may be at play (Szmrecsanyi 2008; Clark 2018; Tamminga 2019). Furthermore, both of these possibilities rely on there being cross-signer variation in dominance reversal rates in the first place; neither accommodation nor priming can fully explain the different rates of reversal that we see in Figure 22.2. Nor are we in a position to assess who is accommodating to whom or who is priming whom. We are grateful to an editor for the suggestion that the increase in reversal amounts across subsequent interviews might reflect a lessening impact of the Observer's Paradox. As signers become more familiar with their interlocutors, they are likely to converse more with them as they would with others in their daily lives. However, we think it is an important first step to observe that dominance reversal is exhibiting not only differences between signers but also intra-signer fluctuations and patterns of alignment between signers in conversation. These observations motivate further investigation of dominance reversal as a phenomenon that is shaped by social and stylistic factors in addition to the pragmatic demands of the discourse context.

Discussion

This case study leads us to many follow-up research questions: Is dominance reversal subject to psycholinguistic priming? Is it used to index Black and/or other social identities or registers? Within a given conversation, what other variables are likely to co-occur with dominance reversal? With regard to the data presented above, evidence of priming might consist of close proximity between instances of dominance reversal for the two signers. Evidence that the signers are using dominance reversal to index Black identity or other identities might be found if the interviews were coded for topic or stance and dominance reversal were found to co-occur with certain identity-related topics or when the signer is expressing a certain stance toward places or people. Follow-up interviews with more signers would also be important for pursuing this question. These data can also be investigated further using a more precise measurement of dominance reversal, such as sign count, rather than time.

Future directions

We have cited work that examines correlations between certain sociophonetic variants and membership in particular demographic groups. However, the broader field now recognizes speaker agency through the concept of indexicality. Eckert (2008) argues that sociolinguistic variation is not simply a matter of constraints on which variants a person has access to based on aspects of identity like social class. Rather, variants constitute a set of variables from which a speaker constructs a style. The association of variants with types is locally constructed. That is, the same variant can be associated with different identities or stances in different contexts. We would not expect this process to be unique to any specific modality. The question of how signers use linguistic variants to index various types, addressed in preliminary works cited above by Blau (2017) and Palfreyman (2020), should therefore be taken up by more researchers. The relationship between Deaf and hearing identities and communities, and between signed and spoken languages, may also result in interesting patterns of indexical use of language by signers. The uniqueness of these dynamics represent an opportunity to learn about identity and language use in new ways, and are likely a promising area of future research.

Another much-needed area of development in signed language sociophonetics is the development of financially accessible and easy-to-learn tools for measuring aspects of production. The lack of affordable tools not only presents methodological limitations but also constitutes an ethical problem, as this bars students, community researchers, and linguists in less well-funded departments from full participation in the field. Once technology becomes more readily available, the field will need to develop methods for normalizing phonetic measurements across signers. Finally, as discussed, and as with all areas of signed language linguistics, data from more languages are needed in order to confirm, challenge, and deepen understandings that have been thus far based upon research of a limited number of languages. Investigation of the protactile modality (e.g., Edwards & Brentari 2020) and its sociophonetics is also needed. These advancements will serve to bring the phonetic and sociophonetic study of signed languages on a par with spoken language inquiries. This parity is necessary if we are to learn the scope of the human capacity for employing gradient linguistic phenomena for social expression.

Acknowledgments

While it may be unusual to include our short bios in the acknowledgments section, we wanted to include our connection to the signing communities, specifically the American Sign Language (ASL) communities in North America, because signing experience and identity is essential to connecting and working with signed language communities. Amelia is a white hearing American woman, fluent in English and a second language signer of ASL. Jami is a white hearing woman and L1 ASL/English user. Julie is a white Deaf American woman fluent in ASL and English. Meredith is a white hearing American woman fluent in English and learning ASL.

References

Adank, Patti, Roel Smits & Roeland van Hout. 2004. A comparison of vowel normalization procedures for language variation research. *Journal of the Acoustical Society of America* 116(5). 3099–3107. https://doi.org/10.1121/1.1795335

Battison, Robbin. 1974. Phonological deletion in American Sign Language. *Sign Language Studies* 5(1). 1–19. https://doi.org/10.1353/sls.1974.0005

Bayley, Robert, Ceil Lucas, & Mary Rose. 2000. Variation in American Sign Language: The case of DEAF. *Journal of Sociolinguistics* 4(1). 81–107. https://doi.org/10.1111/1467-9481.00104

Bayley, Robert, Ceil Lucas, & Mary Rose. 2002. Phonological variation in American Sign Language: The case of 1 handshape. *Language Variation and Change* 14(1). 19–53. https://doi.org/10.1017/S095439450 2141020

Baynton, Douglas. 1996. *Forbidden signs: American culture and the campaign against sign language*. University of Chicago Press.

Bell, Allan. 1984. Language style as audience design. *Language in Society* 13(2). 145–204. https://doi.org/ 10.1017/S004740450001037X

Blau, Shane. 2017. Indexing gay identities in American Sign Language. *Sign Language Studies* 18(1). 5–40. https://doi.org/10.1353/sls.2017.0019

Börstell, Carl, & Robert Östling. 2016. Visualizing lects in a sign language corpus: Mining lexical variation data in lects of Swedish Sign Language. In Nicoletta Calzolari et al. (eds.), *Proceedings of the Tenth International Conference on Language Resources and Evaluation (LREC 2016)*, 13–18. European Language Resources Association.

Brentari, Diane. 1998. *A prosodic model of sign language phonology*. MIT Press.

Brentari, Diane. 2019. *Sign language phonology*. Cambridge University Press.

Brentari, Diane & Petra Eccarius. 2010. Handshape contrasts in sign language phonology. In Diane Brentari (ed.), *Sign languages*, 284–311. Cambridge University Press.

Burch, Susan. 2002. *Signs of resistance*. New York University Press.

Cheek, Davina Adrianne. 2001. *The phonetics and phonology of handshape in American Sign Language*. PhD dissertation, University of Texas at Austin.

Clark, Lynn. 2018. Priming as a motivating factor in sociophonetic variation and change. *Topics in Cognitive Science* 10(4). 729–744. https://doi.org/10.1111/tops.12338

Corina, David P., & Michael Grosvald. 2012. Exploring perceptual processing of ASL and human actions: Effects of inversion and repetition priming. *Cognition* 122(3). 330–345. https://doi.org/10.1016/ j.cognition.2011.10.011

Costello, Brendan, Javier Fernández & Alazne Landa. 2008. The non-(existent) native signer: Sign language research in a small deaf population. In Ronice M. de Quadros (ed.), *Sign languages: Spinning and unraveling the past, present and future*, 77–94. Editora Arara Azul.

Crasborn, Onno. 2010. What does "informed consent" mean in the internet age? Publishing sign language corpora as open content. *Sign Language Studies* 10(2). 276–290. https://doi.org/10.1353/sls.0.0044

Crasborn, Onno. 2011. The other hand in sign language phonology. In Marc van Oostendorp, Colin J. Ewen, Elizabeth Hume & Keren Rice (eds.), *The Blackwell companion to phonology,* 223–240. Wiley.

Crasborn, Onno. 2012. Phonetics. In Roland Pfau, Markus Steinbach & Bencie Wol (eds.), *Sign Language: An international handbook*, 4–20. De Gruyter.

Crasborn, Onno & Anna Sáfár. 2016. An annotation scheme to investigate the form and function of hand dominance in the Corpus NGT. In Roland Pfau, Markus Steinbach & Annika Herrmann (eds.), *A matter of complexity*, 231–251. De Gruyter Mouton. https://doi.org/10.1515/9781501503238-010

Crasborn, Onno & Han Sloetjes. 2008. Enhanced ELAN functionality for sign language corpora. In Onno Crasborn, Eleni Efthimiou, Thomas Hanke, Ernst D. Thoutenhoofd & Inge Zwitserlood (eds.), *Proceedings of the LREC2008 3rd Workshop on the Representation and Processing of Sign Languages*, 39–43.

Dudis, Paul G., Julie A. Hochgesang, Emily Shaw, and Miako Villanueva. 2020. Introduction to 'Motivated Look at Indicating Verbs in ASL (MoLo)' Project. Poster presented at the HDLS14, Virtual Conference, November. https://doi.org/10.17605/OSF.IO/H8GK4

Eccarius, Petra & Diane Brentari. 2008. Handshape coding made easier: A theoretically based notation for phonological transcription. *Sign Language & Linguistics* 11(1). 69–101. https://doi.org/10.1075/ sl&l.11.1.11ecc

Eckert, Penelope. 2008. Variation and the indexical field. *Journal of Sociolinguistics* 12(4). 453–476. https:// doi.org/10.1111/j.1467-9841.2008.00374.x

Edwards, Terra & Diane Brentari. 2020. Feeling phonology: The conventionalization of phonology in protactile communities in the United States. *Language* 96(4). 819–840. https://doi.org/10.1353/lan.2020.0063

Emmorey, Karen. 1991. Repetition priming with aspect and agreement morphology in American Sign Language. *Journal of Psycholinguistic Research* 20(5). 365–388. https://doi.org/10.1007/BF0 1067970

Fenlon, Jordan, Adam Schembri, & Kearsy Cormier. 2018. Modification of indicating verbs in British Sign Language: A corpus-based study. *Language* 94(1). 84–118. https://doi.org/10.1353/lan.2018.0002

Fenlon, Jordan, Adam Schembri, Trevor Johnston & Kearsy Cormier. 2015. Documentary and corpus approaches to sign language research. In Eleni Orfanidou, Bencie Woll & Gary Morgan (eds.), *Research methods in sign language studies: A practical guide*, 156–173. Wiley. https://doi.org/10.1002/978111 8346013

Fenlon, Jordan, Adam Schembri, Ramas Rentelis, and Kearsy Cormier. 2013. Variation in handshape and orientation in British Sign Language: The case of the '1' hand configuration. *Language & Communication* 33(1). 69–91. https://doi.org/10.1016/j.langcom.2012.09.001

Fisher, Jami N., Julie A. Hochgesang & Meredith Tamminga. 2021. *Philadelphia Signs Project*. https://pen nds.org/phillysigns/

Fisher, Jami N., Julie A. Hochgesang, Meredith Tamminga & Robyn Miller. 2021. Uncovering the lived experiences of elderly Deaf Philadelphians. In *Our lives–our stories: Life experiences of elderly deaf people*, 277–322. De Gruyter Mouton. https://doi.org/10.1515/9783110701906-011

Fisher, Jami N., Meredith Tamminga & Julie A. Hochgesang. 2018. The historical and social context of the Philadelphia ASL community. *Sign Language Studies* 18(3). 429–460. https://doi.org/10.1353/sls.2018.0010

Frishberg, Nancy J. 1975. Arbitrariness and iconicity: Historical change in American Sign Language. *Language* 51(3). 696–719. https://doi.org/10.2307/412894

Frishberg, Nancy J. 1976. *Some aspects of the historical development of signs in American Sign Language.* PhD dissertation, University of California, San Diego.

Frishberg, Nancy J. 1985. Dominance relations and discourse structures. In William Stokoe & Virginia Volterra (eds.), *SLR'83. Proceedings of the 3rd International Symposium on Sign Language Research*, 79–90. CNR.

Geraci, Carlo, Katia Battaglia, Anna Cardinaletti, Carlo Cecchetto, Caterina Donati, Serena Giudice & Emiliano Mereghetti. 2011. The LIS corpus project: A discussion of sociolinguistic variation in the lexicon. *Sign Language Studies* 11(4). 528–574. https://doi.org/10.1353/sls.2011.0011

Giles, Howard, Nikolas Coupland & Justine Coupland. 1991. Accommodation theory: Communication, context, and consequence. In Howard Giles, Nikolas Coupland & Justine Coupland (eds.), *Contexts of accommodation: Developments in applied sociolinguistics*, 1–68. Cambridge University Press.

Hall, Matthew L., Victor S. Ferreira & Rachel Mayberry. 2015. Syntactic priming in American Sign Language. *PLoS ONE* 10(3). https://doi.org/10.1371/journal.pone.0119611

Hammarström, Harald, Robert Forkel, Martin Haspelmath & Sebastian Bank. 2021. *Glottolog 4.4.* Max Planck Institute for Evolutionary Anthropology. https://doi.org/10.5281/zenodo.4761960

Hanke, Tomas. 2004. HamNoSys – Representing sign language data in language resources and language processing contexts. In Maria Teresa Lino et al. (eds.), *The Fourth International Conference on Language Resources and Evaluation, LREC 2004*. European Language Resources Association.

Hendricks, Bernadet. 2008. *Jordanian Sign Language: Aspects of grammar from a cross-linguistic perspective*. PhD dissertation, University of Amsterdam.

Hill, Joseph C. 2017. The Importance of the sociohistorical context in sociolinguistics: The case of Black ASL. *Sign Language Studies* 18(1). 41–57. https://doi.org/10.1353/sls.2017.0020

Hill, Joseph, Carolyn McCaskill, Robert Bayley & Ceil Lucas. 2015. The Black ASL (American Sign Language) Project: An overview. In Jennifer Bloomquist, Lisa J. Green & Sonja J. Lanehart (eds.), *The Oxford handbook of African American language*, 316–337. Oxford University Press.

Hochgesang, Julie A. 2014. Using design principles to consider representation of the hand in some notation systems. *Sign Language Studies* 14(4). 488–542. https://doi.org/10.1353/sls.2014.0017

Hochgesang, Julie A., Onno Crasborn & Diane Lillo-Martin. 2017–2021. *ASL Signbank*. Haskins Lab, Yale University. https://aslsignbank.haskins.yale.edu/

Hochgesang, Julie A. 2022. Managing sign language acquisition video data: A personal journey in the organization and representation of signed data. In Andrea L. Berez-Kroeker, Bradley McDonnell, Eve Koller & Lauren B. Collister (eds.), *The Open handbook of linguistic data management*. MIT Press Open. https://mitp-web.mit.edu/books/open-handbook-linguistic-data management-and-archiving

Hodge, Gabrielle & Onno Crasborn. 2022. Good practices in annotation. In Jordan Fenlon & Julie A. Hochgesang (eds.), *Signed language corpora*, 46–89. Gallaudet University Press.

Johnson, Robert E. & Scott K. Liddell. 2011a. Toward a phonetic representation of signs: Sequentiality and contrast. *Sign Language Studies* 11(2). 241–274. https://doi.org/10.1353/sls.2010.0008

Johnson, Robert E. & Scott K. Liddell. 2011b. A segmental framework for representing signs phonetically. *Sign Language Studies* 11(3). 408–463. https://doi.org/10.1353/sls.2011.0002

Johnson, Robert E. & Scott K. Liddell. 2011c. Toward a phonetic representation of hand configuration: The fingers. *Sign Language Studies* 12(1). 5–45. https://doi.org/10.1353/sls.2011.0013

Johnson, Robert E. & Scott K. Liddell. 2012. Toward a phonetic representation of hand configuration: The thumb. *Sign Language Studies* 12(2). 316–333. https://doi.org/10.1353/sls.2011.0020

Johnson, Robert E., Scott Liddell & Carol Erting. 1989. Unlocking the Curriculum: Principles for achieving access in Deaf education. Working Paper 89-3.

Johnston, Trevor. 2010. From archive to corpus: Transcription and annotation in the creation of a signed language corpus. *International Journal of Corpus Linguistics* 15(1). 106–131. https://doi.org/10.1075/ijcl.15.1.05joh

Johnston, Trevor, Donovan Cresdee, Adam Schembri & Bencie Woll. 2015. FINISH variation and grammaticalization in a signed language: How far down this well-trodden pathway is Auslan (Australian Sign Language)? *Language Variation and Change* 27(1). 117–155. https://doi.org/10.1017/S0954394514000209

Labov, William. 1984. Field methods of the project on linguistic change and variation. In John Baugh & Joel Sherzer (eds.), *Language in use: Readings in sociolinguistics*, 28–53. Pearson.

Liddell, Scott K. & Robert E. Johnson. 1989. American Sign Language: The phonological base. *Sign Language Studies* 64(1). 195–277. www.jstor.org/stable/26204052

Liddell, Scott K. & Robert E. Johnson. 2019. Sign language articulators on phonetic bearings. *Sign Language Studies* 20(1). 132–172. https://doi.org/10.1353/sls.2019.0016

Long, J. Schuyler. 1918. The Sign Language. A manual of signs. *American Annals of the Deaf*. 230–249.

Lucas, Ceil. 2013. Methodological issues in studying sign language variation. In Laurence Meurant, Aurélie Sinte, Mieke Van Herreweghe & Myriam Vermeerbergen (eds.), *Sign language research, uses and practices*, 258–308. De Gruyter Mouton.

Lucas, Ceil & Robert Bayley. 2005. Variation in ASL: The role of grammatical function. *Sign Language Studies* 6(1). 38–75. https://doi.org/10.1353/sls.2006.0005

Lucas, Ceil, Robert Bayley, Ruth Reed & Alyssa Wulf. 2001. Lexical variation in African American and white signing. *American Speech* 76(4). 339–360. https://doi.org/10.1215/00031283-76-4-339

Lucas, Ceil, Robert Bayley, Mary Rose & Alyssa Wulf. 2002. Location variation in American Sign Language. *Sign Language Studies* 2(4). 407–440. https://doi.org/10.1353/sls.2002.0020

Lucas, Ceil, Robert Bayley & Clayton Valli. 2001. *Sociolinguistic variation in American Sign Language*. Gallaudet University Press.

Lucas, Ceil & Clayton Valli. 1992. *Language contact in the American Deaf community*. Academic Press.

Mauk, Claude E. & Martha E. Tyrone. 2012. Location in ASL: Insights from phonetic variation. *Sign Language & Linguistics* 15(1). 128–146.

McCaskill, Carolyn, Ceil Lucas, Robert Bayley & Joseph Hill. 2011. *The hidden treasure of Black ASL: Its history and structure*. Gallaudet University Press.

McKee, Rachel, Josefina Safar & Sara Pivac Alexander. 2021. Form, frequency and sociolinguistic variation in depicting signs in New Zealand Sign Language. *Language & Communication* 79. 95–117. https://doi.org/10.1016/j.langcom.2021.04.003

Milroy, Lesley. 1987. *Observing and analyzing natural language*. Blackwell.

Mirus, Gene, Jami N. Fisher & Donna Jo Napoli. 2019. (Sub)lexical changes in iconic signs to realign with community sensibilities and experiences. *Language in Society* 49(2). 283–309. https://doi.org/10.1017/S0047404519000745

Mittelberg, Irene. 2007. Methodology for multimodality: One way of working with speech and gesture data. In Monica Gonzalez-Marquez, Irene Mittelberg, Seana Coulson & Michael J. Spivey (eds.), *Methods in cognitive linguistics*. 225–248. https://doi.org/10.1075/hcp.18.16mit

Moser, Margaret G. 1990. The regularity hypothesis applied to ASL. In Ciel Lucas (ed.), *Sign language research: Theoretical issues*, 50–56. Gallaudet University Press.

Napoli, Donna Jo & Nathan Sanders. In progress. Iconicity and biomechanics in the historical reconstruction of sign languages: A case study of the movement parameter in the Old LSF family.

Napoli, Donna Jo, Nathan Sanders & Rebecca Wright. 2014. On the linguistic effects of articulatory ease, with a focus on sign languages. *Language* 90(2). 424–456. https://doi.org/10.1353/LAN.2014.0026

Nilson, Anna-Lena. 2007. The non-dominant hand in a Swedish Sign Language discourse. In Lorraine Leeson, Myriam Vermeerbergen & Onno Alex Crasborn (eds.), *Simultaneity in signed languages: Form and function*, 163–185. John Benjamins. https://doi.org/10.1075/cilt.281.08nil

Palfreyman, Nick. 2020. Social meanings of linguistic variation in BISINDO (Indonesian Sign Language). *Asia-Pacific Language Variation* 6(1). 89–118. https://doi.org/10.1075/aplv.00008.pal

Pfau, Roland & Markus Steinbach. 2006. *Modality-independent and modality-specific aspects of grammaticalization in sign languages*. Universitätsverlag Potsdam.

Pfau, Roland, Markus Steinbach & Bencie Woll (eds.). 2012. *Sign language: An international handbook*. De Gruyter Mouton

Prince, Alan & Paul Smolensky. 2004. *Optimality theory: Constraint interaction in generative grammar*. Wiley.

Quer, Josep, Carlo Cecchetto, Caterina Donati, Carlo Geraci, Meltem Kelepir, Roland Pfau & Markus Steinbach (eds.) with collaboration of Brendan Costello & Rannveig Sverrisdóttir. 2017. *SignGram blueprint: A guide to sign language grammar writing*. De Gruyter Mouton. https://library.oapen.org/bitstream/handle/20.500.12657/27399/9781501511806.pdf

Rimor, Mordechai, Judy Kegl, Harlan Lane & Trude Schermer. 1984. Natural phonetic processes underlie historical change & register variation in American Sign Language. *Sign Language Studies* 43. 97–119.

Rousseau, Pascale & David Sankoff. 1978. Advances in variable rule methodology. In David Sankoff (ed.), *Linguistic variation: Models and methods*, 57–69. Academic Press.

Sanders, Nathan & Donna Jo Napoli. 2016. Reactive effort as a factor that shapes sign language lexicons. *Language* 92(2). 275–297. https://doi.org/10.1353/LAN.2016.0032

Schembri, Adam, David McKee, Rachel McKee, Sara Pivac, Trevor Johnston & Della Goswell. 2009. Phonological variation and change in Australian and New Zealand Sign Languages: The location variable. *Language Variation and Change* 21(2). 193–231. https://doi.org/10.1017/S0954394509990081

Schmitt, Deonísio. 2020. The history of sign language: Diachronic Libras variation in Santa Catarina. In Deonísio Schmitt (ed.), *Brazilian Sign Language Studies*, 201–226. De Gruyter Mouton.

Singleton, Jenny L., Amber Martin & Gary Morgan. 2015. Ethics, deaf-friendly research, and good practice when studying sign languages. In Eleni Orfanidou, Bencie Woll & Gary Morgan (eds.), *Research methods in sign language studies: A practical guide*, 7–20. Wiley.

Stokoe, William C. 1960. *Sign language structure. An outline of the visual communication systems of the American Deaf*. Linstok Press.

Stokoe, William C., Dorothy Casterline & Carl Croneberg. 1965. *A dictionary of American Sign Language on linguistic principles*. Gallaudet College.

Szmrecsanyi, Benedikt. 2008. *Morphosyntactic persistence in spoken English*. De Gruyter Mouton.

Tamminga, Meredith. 2019. Sources of microtemporal clustering in sociolinguistic sequences. *Frontiers in Artificial Intelligence* 2(10). https://doi.org/10.3389/frai.2019.00010

Tamminga, Meredith, Jami N. Fisher & Julie A. Hochgesang. 2020. Weak hand variation in Philadelphia ASL: A pilot study. *University of Pennsylvania Working Papers in Linguistics* 25(2). Article 15. https://repository.upenn.edu/pwpl/vol25/iss2/15

Toliver-Smith, Andrea & Betholyn Gentry. 2017. Investigating Black ASL: A systematic review. *American Annals of the Deaf* 161(5). 560–570. https://doi.org/10.1353/aad.2017.0006

Tyrone, Martha E. 2012. Phonetics of sign location in ASL: Comments on papers by Russell, Wilkinson, & Janzen and by Grosvald & Corina. *Laboratory Phonology* 3(1). 61–70. https://doi.org/10.1515/lp-2012-0005

Tyrone, Martha E. 2015. Instrumented measures of sign production and perception: Motion capture, movement analysis, eye-tracking, and reaction times. In Eleni Orfanidou, Bencie Woll & Gary Morgan (eds.), *Research methods in sign language studies: A practical guide*, 89–104. Wiley. https://doi.org/10.1002/9781118346013.ch6

Tyrone, Martha E. & Claude E. Mauk. 2010. Sign lowering and phonetic reduction in American Sign Language. *Journal of Phonetics* 38(2). 317–328. https://doi.org/10.1016/j.wocn.2010.02.003

Tyrone, Martha E. & Claude E. Mauk. 2012. Phonetic reduction and variation in American Sign Language: A quantitative study of sign lowering. *Laboratory Phonology* 3(2). 425–453. https://doi.org/10.1515/lp-2012-0019

Van Herreweghe, Mieke & Myriam Vermeerbergen. 2012. Data collection. In Pfau, Steinbach & Woll, 1023–1044.

Volterra, Virginia, Alessandro Laudanna, Serena Corazza, Elena Radutzky & Francesco Natale. 1984. Italian Sign Language: The order of elements in the declarative sentence. In Filip Loncke, Penny Boyes Braem & Yvan Lebrun (eds.), *Recent research on European sign languages*, 19–48. Swets and Zeitlinger.

Wolfram, Walt. 2013. Language awareness in community perspective: Obligation and opportunity. In Robert Bayley, Richard Cameron & Ceil Lucas (eds.), *The Oxford handbook of sociolinguistics,* 754–772. Oxford University Press.

Woodward, James C. 1973. Some observations on sociolinguistic variation and American Sign Language. *Kansas Journal of Sociology* 9(2). 191–200.

Woodward, James C. 1976. Black southern signing. *Language in Society* 5(2). 211–218. https://doi.org/10.1017/S004740450000703x

Woodward, James C. & Carol Erting. 1974. Synchronic variation and historical change in American Sign Language. Paper presented at the summer meeting of the LSA, Amherst.

Woodward, James C. & Carol Erting. 1975. Synchronic variation and historical change in ASL. *Language Sciences* 37. 9–12.

Woodward, James C. & Susan De Santis. 1977. Two to one it happens: Dynamic phonology in two sign languages. *Sign Language Studies* 17. 329–346. https://doi.org/10.1353/sls.1977.0013

Wulf, Alyssa, Paul Dudis, Robert Bayley & Ceil Lucas. 2002. Variable subject presence in ASL narratives. *Sign Language Studies* 3(1). 54–76. https://doi.org/10.1353/sls.2002.0027

Zeshan, Ulrike & Nick Palfreyman. 2017. Sign language typology. In Alexandra Y. Aikhenvald & R.M.W. Dixon (eds.), *The Cambridge handbook of linguistic typology*, 178–216. Cambridge University Press. https://doi.org/10.1017/9781316135716.007

Zimmer, June. 1989. Toward a description of register variation in American Sign Language. In Ceil Lucas (ed.), *The sociolinguistics of the Deaf community*, 253–272. Academic Press. https://doi.org/10.1016/B978-0-12-458045-9.50018-5

Appendix

NOT – https://aslsignbank.haskins.yale.edu/dictionary/gloss/515.html

RIGHT – https://aslsignbank.haskins.yale.edu/dictionary/gloss/533.html

WONDER – https://aslsignbank.haskins.yale.edu/dictionary/gloss/853.html

YES – https://aslsignbank.haskins.yale.edu/dictionary/gloss/1472.html

23

SOCIOPHONETICS AND SOUTH AFRICAN STUDIES

Focus on ethnicity

Rajend Mesthrie, Alida Chevalier, Yolandi Ribbens-Klein,
Tracey Toefy, and Bruce Wileman

Introduction

This chapter discusses ways in which the concept of ethnicity in South Africa has been illuminated via the subtle lens of sociophonetics. Race—or more properly ethnicity—has continued to be a salient feature of the social fabric of South African life, long after a desired post-racial society came into being with the collapse of apartheid in the early 1990s. Despite the apartheid insistence on dividing society into "Whites," "Blacks," "Coloureds" (i.e., multiracial ethnic communities), and "Asiatics" (i.e., mainly Indian and Chinese), it has always been clear that South African society does not neatly follow such fault lines (Posel 2001). In particular, the Coloured category showed the development of culture that straddled alleged racial divides and hierarchies (Erasmus 2001; Reddy 2001). Thus, South Africa proves something of a sociolinguistic laboratory for the way relations between groups were once rigidly controlled and subsequently loosened. The complexities of the terms "race" and "ethnicity" in sociology and their overlaps are too great to unpack here; the reader is referred to a comprehensive account in Mesthrie (forthcoming). Suffice it to say, while race is a social construct that foregrounds phenotypical differences between groups of people, socialization in the modern world has made the neat categorization of former eras close to impossible. Ethnicity frequently involves different claims to ancestry (and possibly race), but may be modified by contemporary social groupings within crisscrossing social networks that may even include a sense of place.

Questions, methods, and approaches

Language variation and change in post-apartheid South Africa

Older preconceptions and senses of ethnicity have changed in South Africa, especially among the younger generations who have experienced a less constrained racial order in terms of schooling and social networks after the official end of apartheid in 1994. In this story of change, a prominent theme has been middle-class formation among Black people who have been able to access the economic and educational benefits of desegregation. (On the other hand, many critics charge that racial apartheid has been replaced by "economic apartheid.") A central concern of our research since 2008 has been the extent to which language has been responsive to the new deracializing social networks of young people. A corollary to this has been the extent to which traditional L2 varieties, like Black South African English (henceforth BSAE), are being maintained, and in what contexts and by whom. While studies of language attitudes and linguistic ideologies in South Africa have often focused on multilingualism (e.g., Bangeni & Kapp 2007; McKinney 2007), close acoustic sociophonetic work has tended to focus on English across social groups (with Ribbens-Klein 2016, on Afrikaans variation being an honorable exception).

The framework of studies undertaken by the present research group is that of language variation and change, using as much as possible the techniques of modern acoustic sociophonetics. The framework includes work on variation arising out of language contact, a theme that demands close attention to sociohistorical contexts of multilingualism in South Africa. Thus, while the focus falls on English variation, this is meant as a first step in relation to the more complex repertoires of plurilingual individuals and multilingual groups. Mesthrie (2012) argues that the palimpsest of Afrikaans cannot be ignored in a regional dialectology of English in South Africa. Equally, the social history of L1 English in the country (Lanham & Macdonald 1979; Lass & Wright 1986; Bekker 2009) remains of crucial significance, even when studying L2 Englishes in multilingual repertoires.

Ethnicity, place, and context

Tipping the balance towards ethnolectal variation in South Africa runs the risk of missing patterns of variation that show the intersection between ethnicities and place. For instance, with Coloured South Africa English (CSAE), existing descriptions of the vowel system have largely focused on speakers from the Western Cape Province (specifically Cape Town; see Wood 1987; Finn 2004; Toefy 2014). Since the 2000s, Mesthrie focused on five cities across five provinces as hubs for investigating not only ethnic variation in South African English (SAE), but also for exploring how finer-grained distinctions within the four main SAE ethnolects are discernible according to different senses of place and belonging. In collaboration with students, Mesthrie collected a main corpus of over 200 sociolinguistic interviews that forms the foundation of both completed and ongoing work toward a regional and social dialectology of SAE (see, inter alia, Mesthrie 2010, 2012; Mesthrie, Chevalier & Dunne 2015; Mesthrie & Wills 2019). Speakers in each of the five cities were selected through a combination of judgment, convenience, and snowball sampling, and the interviews were conducted in a range of settings, mainly speakers' homes and places of work or study. In the majority of these interviews, participants also read out a word list with minor adaptations of Wells's (1982) lexical sets. Reading passages were avoided, as initial experience showed that some interviewees struggled with this task and produced halting spelling pronunciations related to neither standard nor vernacular.

The COVID-19 pandemic placed constraints on further data collection, with many interactions restricted to online communication. Mesthrie & Ribbens-Klein (2022) investigated variation and change in the use of the TRAP vowel in BSAE by using a hybrid sample consisting of previously recorded in-person interviews and YouTube videos of speeches given by prominent South African politicians.

Developing tools for acoustic analysis

All the interviews in the SAE corpus were initially transcribed in Microsoft Word, and before the advent of automatic forced alignment, manual alignment and segmental coding was undertaken in Praat (Boersma & Weenink 2021) as required for the acoustic analyses of the specific variables under investigation. With the rise of forced alignment applications, Mesthrie and his students began to re-transcribe the interviews in ELAN (2021), capitalizing on the annotation and transcription features of this software, which provide interview transcripts that can be exported as Praat TextGrids, while also maintaining the transcript as a textual document. The remainder of this subsection focuses on the application of automatic forced alignment to SAE varieties.

Forced alignment is a process whereby orthographic transcriptions of sociolinguistic interviews are segmented at a phonetic level and time-aligned with audio recordings of the interviews (Meer 2020). Forced aligners are typically pre-trained on manually segmented speech data and rely on a pronunciation dictionary/lexicon of standard pronunciations transcribed in ARPABET, a machine-readable phonetic alphabet of General American English [GenAmE]. Various forced alignment tools are available which allow for large quantities of data to be processed. Comparability, reproducibility, and labor intensity are typical challenges associated with manual alignment and measurement; these are significantly reduced or eliminated using automatic alignment techniques.

For the bulk of the previous SAE research, the tool FAVE-align of the Forced Alignment and Vowel Extraction (FAVE) program suite (Rosenfelder et al. 2014) was used to conduct the forced alignment. The aligner uses a pre-trained acoustic model of GenAmE speech from a corpus of recordings from the United States Supreme Court (SCOPUS). The output is a Praat TextGrid file with two tiers per speaker—one orthographic, the other phonemic (based on the ARPABET notation in the pronunciation dictionary; Labov, Rosenfelder & Fruehwald 2013). We explore ARPABET further in our case study. The TextGrid file is submitted to the second component of the FAVE program, FAVE-extract. Based on Python programming, FAVE-extract automatically measures formant frequencies using settings stipulated in Labov, Rosenfelder & Fruehwald (2013).

With our SAE data, we faced two main challenges when using FAVE and other forced aligners such as Prosodylab-Aligner (Gorman, Howell & Wagner 2011). The first relates to the required operating systems for installation and use, together with the installation of a range of third-party toolkits such as the Hidden Markov Model Toolkit (HTK). The installation and use of FAVE, Prosodylab-Aligner, and HTK are not designed for Windows support, being primarily based on Macintosh Operating Systems. This makes it challenging for research done on Windows PCs. (Overall, the technological resources and critical mass of allied expertise in sub-Saharan Africa are a general challenge.) Secondly, as stated, FAVE's acoustic model is pre-trained on GenAmE, and our experience was that there was frequent derailment when we aligned the speech of the L2 varieties of SAE. This derailment necessitated an extra step of checking the aligned TextGrids in Praat to adjust segment boundaries. This problem is not limited to South Africa, and has to be faced by nonstandard varieties whose norms don't coincide with those of the ARPABET (see, e.g., Strelluf 2018, for the Midlands system of Kansas City).

Our more recent research projects (e.g., Mesthrie & Ribbens-Klein 2022) also utilized the Montreal Forced Aligner (MFA; McAuliffe et al. 2017a, 2017b), which is an update of the Prosodylab-Aligner. Like FAVE, MFA time-aligns a TextGrid containing the transcript to its corresponding audio file at the word and phonemic levels. Unlike FAVE, MFA uses the Kaldi ASR Toolkit (Povey et al. 2011) rather than HTK to create statistical models. Apart from being a stand-alone application that is more Windows-friendly, MFA's English acoustic model used for alignment is based on the LibriSpeech corpus of 2484 speakers and 982.3 audio hours (compared to FAVE's SCOPUS with a limited 25 hours of audio). The developers of LibriSpeech state that "acoustic models trained on LibriSpeech give lower error rates" (Panayotov et al. 2015).

For the recent research we conducted on TRAP variation in BSAE, we used the Dartmouth Linguistic Automation suite (DARLA; Reddy & Stanford 2015). DARLA is a web-based application that uses speech recognition technology and Prosodylab-Aligner to create aligned TextGrids and to provide automated vowel formant extraction. We used DARLA because one does not need to use transcripts annotated at the utterance level. The public speeches made by political leaders were available on YouTube, together with transcripts of these speeches (as found on the website of the South African Government, at www.gov.za/speeches). The availability of the transcripts saved us some time; however, since these speeches were live performances, the politicians made frequent strategic deviations off-script, necessitating extensive listening and editing of the transcripts on our part. We also had to edit the sound clips (using Audacity) to remove noise, applause, and stretches of speech where the politicians spoke in languages other than English. Two drawbacks with using DARLA are that it can only handle one speaker at a time, and unknown words in the transcript can cause problems since DARLA does not allow the user to customize the pronunciation dictionary. To alleviate the latter problem, we transcribed some words into English-like alternatives; for example, abbreviations like SASSA (South African Social Security Agency) or ESKOM (Electricity Supply Commission) were transcribed as "sa sa" and "es com." Words that were altered were not included as tokens.

Along with forced alignment, DARLA also supplies a spreadsheet with both unnormalized and Lobanov-normalized formant measurements of all the vowels. In general, after vowel extraction, decisions are made about which normalization method to use. NORM (Thomas & Kendall 2007), a web-based interface to the vowels package (Kendall & Thomas 2018) for R (R Core Team 2022), is a useful resource that allows us to compare different normalization techniques to decide which is ultimately the most applicable to our specific datasets.

Depending on the linguistic variable under investigation, the main statistical methods we use are mixed-effects linear or logistic regression, generalized random forests, and conditional inference, all via the open-source statistical program R. For vowel plots and other graphics, we use the ggplot2 package (Wickham 2016) in R.

Major findings

Segmental phonology

Crossovers and the related perception test

Whereas the label BSAE was a viable label for the relatively uniform variety spoken by Black people up to the 1990s (Van Rooy 2004), matters are more complex now. It is no longer the case that all Black people speak in a relatively uniform way. In particular, the practices since the 1990s of young Black children who studied at multiracial schools once specifically reserved for Whites, or Coloureds, or Indians, have become more diffuse. Mesthrie (2010, 2017) studied students who graduated from either the most prestigious private or the (nonprivate) model-C high schools, arguing that what they spoke was a crossover variety essentially the same as upper-middle-class English of Whites. ("Model-C" is now often used as a general label for these two types of schools, which were once reserved for "Whites Only.") Since this subvariety could no longer be identified with one ethnic group, it was essentially being deracialized. Both class and gender effects were discernible among young Black people implicated in this process. Social class bifurcation by type of schooling is salient enough in South Africa to have spawned the term *coconut*, which raises debates about the authenticity of those who have crossed over into the new accent space. They

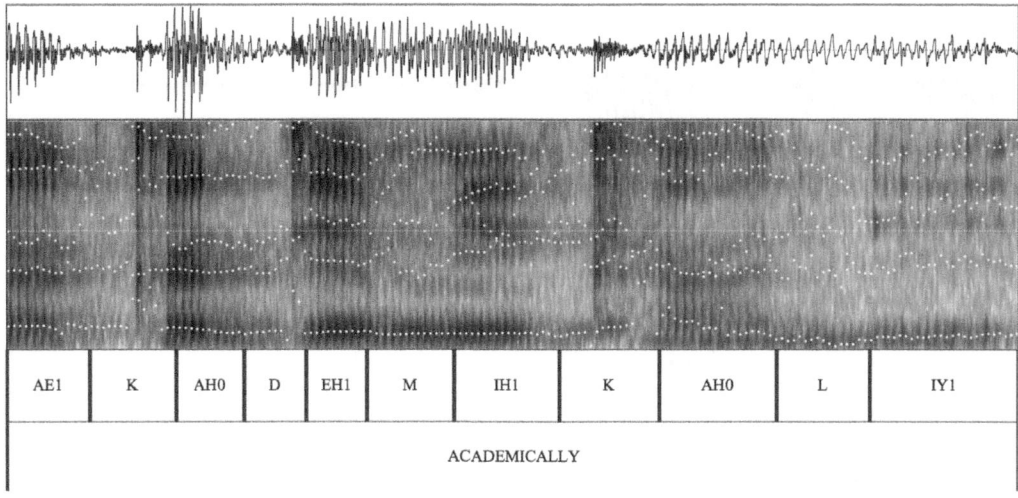

Figure 23.1 TextGrid showing forced alignment of the word *academically*, and penultimate schwa (AH0) as the longest vowel (0.123sec.), spoken by traditional BSAE male speaker in casual style

are alleged to be "dark on the outside, white on the inside." This is not a matter of accent alone, but of a shift in dominance to English as L1 and a shift in culture that is strongly influenced by western, metropolitan, and global trends. Thus, other mock-serious terms like *salads* and *cheese-boy/ cheese-girl* refer stereotypically to the nontraditional foods favored by the new young elites.

In terms of production, Mesthrie (2017) used the variable schwa to demonstrate acoustically the difference between traditional BSAE and crossover usage. At the same time, the variable showed the crisscrossing effects of gender and class within the English of Black South Africans. As with most sub-Saharan varieties of L2 English, BSAE tends to avoid schwa, turning it into a full vowel which may be realized as [a], [e], [i], [o], or [u] (Simo Bobda 2000; Mesthrie 2005). Figure 23.1 gives the spectrogram from an interview with a young male traditional BSAE speaker for the word *academically*, where the penultimate vowel (labeled AH0) is realized as [a:]. In most L1 varieties, including the crossover variety under scrutiny here, this penultimate vowel is reduced to [ə] or (more usually) elided altogether, as illustrated in Figure 23.2. Schwa thus proves a complex but rewarding variable in showing differences between four subgroups delineated in Mesthrie (2017) by sex (i.e., binary gender) and type of high school attended (as a proxy for social class or incipient social class for younger people).

Mesthrie (2017) reports on 18 statistical tests on schwa in different phonetic environments according to the four social groups. It is necessary to differentiate initial, medial, and final schwa further by relevant environments and to break medial schwa up into five types labeled "a-schwa," "e-schwa," "i-schwa," "o-schwa," and "u-schwa." The two AH0 tokens in the example of *academically* [akademIka:li·] in Figure 23.1, for example, falls under "a-schwa." Of these environments, four show no statistical differences between the groups (vowel height for initial and final schwa, and medial position for "o-schwa" and "u-schwa," respectively). The remaining 14 tests showed strong patterns regarding the interaction of class and gender with ethnicity:

1) The biggest differences occur between females of model-C background, for whom schwa is essentially a mid-central unstressed vowel, and males of township schooling, who show full

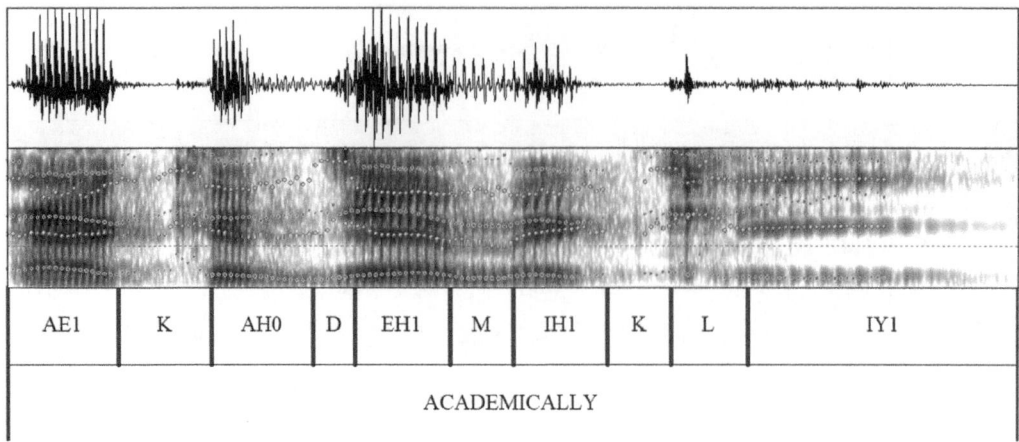

AE1	K	AH0	D	EH1	M	IH1	K	L	IY1

ACADEMICALLY

Figure 23.2   TextGrid showing forced alignment of the word *academically*, and absence of penultimate schwa by WSAE male speaker

realizations of all five types in medial position as well as occasional unstressed [ə]. Statistical differences occur between these two "exterior groups" in all 14 of the relevant environments.

2) Concerning males from model-C schools, in nine of the statistical tests model-C males cluster with model-C females. Here, class overrides gender. However, in three of the tests they side with males from township schools. This time gender overrides class.

3) Concerning females from township schools, in five of the 14 tests they side with model-C females, showing gender overriding class. However, in another five of these 14 cases they side with males from township schools, showing class overriding gender.

The most socially salient phonetic environment of these 14 in terms of societal awareness (as in playful presentations in advertisements) is final schwa. It is in this environment that the social hierarchy shows up most strongly. While backness does not prove socially diagnostic, the results for height show increases in Hz from [ə] values to [a] values as follows: All females (median F2 = 630 Hz) > model-C males (median F2 = 668 Hz) > Non-model-C males (median F2 = 761 Hz). These results are highly statistically significant ($p < 0.001$). The study overall thus supports claims of a crossover, with middle-class females using a different linguistic system for schwa from males who attended a township school. Middle-class males side largely with the females of their social class, but strategically retain some affinities with their township counterparts. Females who attended township schools show similarities with males of their class, but compared to them show a greater degree of aspiration towards middle-class norms.

Mesthrie, Chevalier & McLachlan (2015) devised a test to ascertain whether the findings for gender were matched by the way accents were perceived in the wider society. The main hypotheses were that accents of middle-class Black and White students were no longer easy to tell apart and that this applied more to females than males. The authors selected brief clips (of just under 12 seconds each) from interviews with young South Africans undertaken at the University of Cape Town, grouped as follows: a) the main group of eight Black females and five Black males who had been to model-C schools; b) two White females and two White males as "distractors"; c) one Black female and one Black male from "township" schools speaking a traditional L2 BSAE; and d) one Black female chosen as distractor as her accent could easily be identified for ethnic background but not gender. The respondents were 151 first-year linguistics students at the university who were at that stage untrained in accent variation within SAE. (Of these, 24 were excluded from the analysis as they had not been brought up in South Africa, or were screened out as explained below.) Respondents were asked as part of their weekly tutorials of nine separate small groups to listen to each clip and indicate whether the speaker was male or female, under or over 30, and Black or White (with an option for "not sure" as well). We report here on the responses to the perceived ethnicity of the 13 Black speakers by just the Black and White respondents, leaving out the Coloured and Indian South African students and foreign students. (The four White speakers were almost invariably perceived as White: mean = 92.6%, median = 94.9%; *N* = 444 responses.) Guttman (implicational) scales showed a consistency of responses among the 127 respondents, with no one giving judgments that placed them as outliers. The overall level of consistency across cells or scalability varied from 85.8% (for Black students' judgments of the eight Black female speakers) to 96.5% (for White students' judgments of the five Black male speakers). Figure 23.3 gives the percentage of correct responses to the ethnicity of each speaker, with a dark section of each bar recording a correct judgment as "Black," the white section an incorrect judgment as "White," and the grey section as "not sure." The results for the male and female speakers are given separately.

Figure 23.3 shows a clear differentiation of results for the female speakers compared to the males. Whereas 38.8 percent of responses (*n* = 1016) took the female subjects to be "White," the corresponding percentage for male subjects was only 4.6 percent (*n* = 604). A statistical test is still necessary to show that the judgments were consistently different across individual respondents and not random. The *Z*-statistic for a Wilcoxon signed rank test showed overwhelming evidence that the proportions of males exceeded the proportions of females identified correctly. For Black respondents, this statistic was *Z* = −3.97, and for White respondents *Z* = −6.74. In fact, only two respondents of the 127 identified a greater proportion of females than males correctly.

This perception test thus strongly supports the proposal that young women are in the lead over males in being perceived to cross over from the traditional BSAE accent space into the space

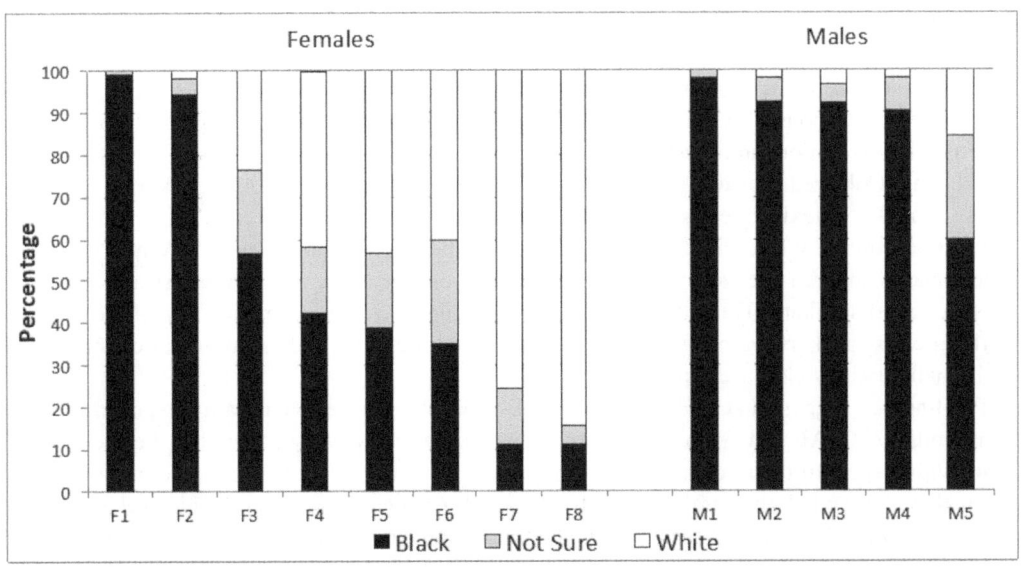

Figure 23.3 Judgments of 127 respondents regarding ethnicity of each of 13 Black speakers, by gender

once associated with White South African English (WSAE) alone. As far as English accents are concerned, ethnicity has significant intersections with class and gender. In fact, for young Black females ethnicity is trumped by social class. One unexpected finding was that Black respondents performed better at the test than White respondents (Pearson ρ = 0.72). Mesthrie, Chevalier & McLachlan (2015) raised the possibility that Black students were more responsive to the subtle effects of phonation and articulatory setting.

Coloured ethnicity and class

Coloured people have a unique identity within the South African social milieu. Erasmus (2001) noted that this identity is rooted historically in the group's origins as a result of race-based seg-regation from the colonial period through to the apartheid period. Post-apartheid desegrega-tion of education institutions led to unprecedented social mixing of children of different races/ethnicities at schools. Toefy (2014) set out to explore the extent to which young Coloured South African English (CSAE) speakers in Cape Town had adopted the WSAE variety that their peers were using in cases of significant social contact with White speakers. This contact had occurred in schools where Coloured children began filtering into schools previously designated for only White pupils. A class differentiation in the variety of CSAE in Cape Town was strengthened in this process. Through a detailed acoustic description of the vowel system of CSAE amongst both middle- and working-class speakers, the most salient changes to the variety amongst middle-class speakers were identified, as compared with earlier reports of the variety by Wood (1987) and Finn (2004).

A sample of 40 Coloured speakers (split equally by gender; also split by class) were interviewed for Toefy (2014). All speakers were young adults at the time of the interview, born between 1983 and 1993. They were raised and schooled during South Africa's transition from apartheid to dem-ocracy. The middle-class speakers had significant contact with White peers and teachers at the schools they attended for some or all of their education. The home and educational environments in which the working-class speakers interacted exposed them almost exclusively to Coloured peers and educators.

Acoustic data were processed using—to our knowledge for the first time in South African research—methods of forced alignment and automatic formant extraction described above. The findings provided acoustic confirmation of the aural analyses of previous accounts of CSAE, with some notable exceptions amongst middle-class speakers. The differences in the variety used by middle-class Coloured speakers approximated trends consistent with WSAE speakers. The TRAP, GOOSE, and FOOT lexical sets showed the most change: TRAP has lowered, while GOOSE and FOOT have fronted. While the changes approximate the vowel quality used by White speakers, middle-class Coloured speakers use an intermediate value between White speakers and working-class Coloured speakers. Thus, they have not fully adopted White norms for any of the vowels. Working-class speakers were found to have maintained the monophthongal vowel configuration traditionally used by Coloured speakers.

The findings suggest that middle-class CSAE speakers, whose lived reality exposed them to both traditional CSAE and WSAE varieties, occupy an intermediate space within the social spec-trum. With respect to their social identity, they feel connected to the Coloured community from which they descended ancestrally, and also to an emerging, deracialized, middle-class "South African" identity. This in-between identity is reflected quite neatly in the acoustic account of their vowel system. Acoustic sociophonetics in fact points to a double interiority for this subgroup. In apartheid times, Coloured people were sometimes considered to be "between Black and White."

The middle-class youngsters in this post-apartheid study may be now said to be sociolinguistically "between Coloured and White."

Elite flight? The Reverse Front Vowel Shift and globalization

Acoustic sociophonetic methods have proved especially fruitful in studying the undoing of an old vowel shift in SAE in favor of a newer, more globally responsive one. Lass & Wright (1986) documented the raising of the short front vowels in L1 SAE dateable to the nineteenth century. These involved the raising of /æ/ towards [ɛ] and raising of original /ɛ/ to [e], both of which led most of original /ɪ/ to centralize. The qualification "most of" is necessary, since /ɪ/ shows a split between a front [ɪ] allophone in (mainly) velar contexts and a central [ï] allophone in most other contexts. This is the famous South African KIT-split (a term coined by Wells 1982, but known in South African research before then; e.g., Lanham & Macdonald 1979). These historical changes are diagramed in broken lines in Figure 23.4 (adapted from Chevalier 2016). This was once a salient chain shift, which South Africa shared with the other Southern hemisphere varieties of Australia and New Zealand, as well as Cockney and southeastern dialects in England.

Chevalier (2016, 2020) revisited these patterns—with a toolkit of automated formant extraction and statistical analysis—and showed that not only were these changes being undone from about 2000 onwards, but that a new chain shift in the reverse direction was under way among younger speakers. Prototypical values of TRAP were moving from [ɛ] to [ä] (well beyond the older hypothetical starting point [æ]); DRESS from [e] (or even [ẹ]) to [ɛ̈] or [ɛ̈]; and of KIT from [ɪ] and [ï] to [e] and [ə] respectively—thus maintaining the KIT-split but at a "lower" level (half-close rather than close). Older speakers' anecdotes report misunderstandings of younger peoples' speech with *shatter-proof* being misheard as *shutter-proof* and *batter* as *butter*—both examples show the change of the expected [æ] in TRAP to [ä].

The newer or "reverse" front vowel shift is associated more with the middle classes, originating with White speakers. There is some differentiation by gender, with young women showing greater degrees of TRAP and KIT retraction. The opposite holds for DRESS lowering; young women lower the DRESS vowel, but not quite as much as young men. This indicates that there are two variants of lowered DRESS: a "female-oriented" [ẹ] variant and a "male-oriented" [ɛ̈] variant. Women appear to treat the former raised variant as prestigious, and so are more reticent in lowering it than

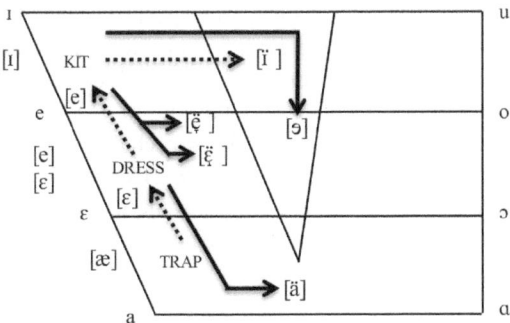

Figure 23.4   The older short front vowel shift (in broken arrows) and the newer reverse shift (solid arrows) in WSAE

Source: Chevalier 2016

men. Finally, two related earlier—but ongoing—changes that might prove of relevance are FOOT-fronting and STRUT-fronting.

The reversal of the older chain shift raises intriguing questions about its social motivations and sources. Here the jury is still out. Bekker (2009:206) noted that TRAP lowering was prestige-driven and structurally motivated, bringing WSAE in line with the Southeast Chain Shift in Britain (Torgersen & Kerswill 2004). Mesthrie (2012:209) noted the importance of the "gap year" between high school and university, during which young South African students voluntarily went to the United Kingdom to earn an income and travel. As this was very much a new-millennium phenomenon, the timing of the changes would fit in well. However, going against this hypothesis is the fact that similar changes have been reported in Australia, with Maclagan & Hay (2007:40) positing potential hyper-correction for the lowering of TRAP (in relation to previous raising). Mesthrie (2012) and Chevalier (2020), however, link the South African changes to global trends involving the Low-Back-Merger Shift (see Becker 2019), and similar changes in Dublin (see Hickey 2016 on short vowel lowering) and elsewhere. Even more intriguing is the noticeable lowering of these vowels in RP (Upton 2004), given the prestige of the latter historically. Chevalier provides evidence of the ongoing influence of American English on South African television, in young people's musical preferences, sitcoms, movies, and so forth. The reverse front vowel shift may be part of a package highly attractive to the globalizing middle classes that includes quotative BE LIKE, incipient rhoticity in "expressive" styles, and acceptance of American rather than British lexical innovation (*cellphones* and *GPS* over *mobile phones* and *satnav*). One objection that may be raised to this is that the influence primarily by television and social media is often discounted as a source of vernacular innovation and change (Chambers 1998). Stuart-Smith (2011) and Stuart-Smith et al. (2013) provide a counter voice to this assertion. Chevalier (2020) notes that children at the middle-class primary schools she observed sing and play in quasi-American accents; the children were very comfortable with American English features, while their teachers were not.

Peter Trudgill (p.c. June 2021) discounts the possibility of American influence in SAE, and cautions that the changes involved in the reverse shift are slightly disparate in the different continents. It is not our claim that the entire Low-Back-Merger shift has been imported as an effect of globalization. Rather its prestige triggers new variants that interact with South African particularities like the KIT-split. More importantly, skeptics would have to explain why these changes which "conspire" to induce vowel lowering-with-backing began to be noticed at roughly the same time (the decades either side of 2000 CE) in various continents and mostly by young middle-class users. The trenchant effects of globalization on youth culture would coincide very well with this periodization, and the dynamics between the local and the global orientations in respect of social class.

Prior to the influence of the reverse shift, teachers and broadcasters had provided a model that had [ɪ]/ [ï], [e], and [æ] as the standard variants for KIT, DRESS, and TRAP respectively, and this is largely what occurs with Black, Coloured, and Indian students integrated into model-C schools. On the other hand, the reverse shift has moved each vowel by one grid level each as the new prestige forms for especially young White middle-class speakers. Chevalier (2016) shows that Black students in Cape Town do not participate as strongly in the shift. This raises the intriguing possibility of the latter serving unconsciously as an instance of "elite flight" (Fisher 1958), which in the South African context is largely—but not entirely—a kind of symbolic "White flight."

BSAE resilience as L2: New variation in the TRAP vowel

Simo Bobda (2000, 2001) provides a framework for characterizing the largely five-vowel systems in the major L2 varieties of English in Africa. Apart from a five-vowel system, these

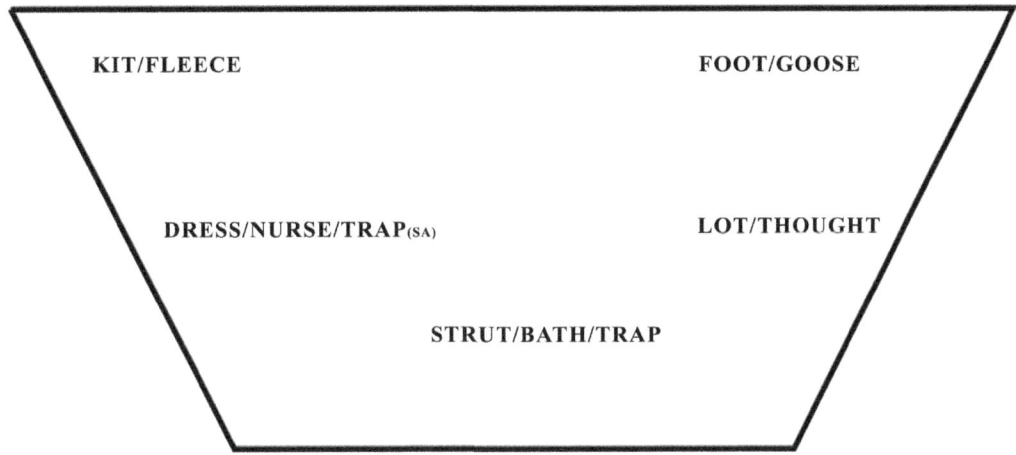

Figure 23.5 Five-vowel L2 system in Southern Africa
Source: based on Simo Bobda 2000

varieties—described by Simo Bobda as Southern African, East African, West African, and Cameroonian—often eschew phonological vowel length and schwa. Simo Bobda noted that while the Southern African region had STRUT, BATH, and TRAP as a low central vowel [a], South Africans differed in having TRAP as a mid-front vowel together with DRESS and NURSE (see Figure 23.5).

However, Mesthrie (2005, 2017) noted that in BSAE there was, in fact, a TRAP-split between [e] and [a], which he labeled TRAP$_1$ and TRAP$_2$ respectively. TRAP$_1$ is the variant that Simo Bobda took as the main exemplar, with a characteristically South African realization as [e] or [ɛ], not [a]. Salient pronunciations like [heˑv], [heˑd], and [beˑk] in *have, had,* and *back* perhaps reflect the historical influence of broader varieties of WSAE on BSAE, especially in terms of the South African Chain Shift described above. On the other hand, Mesthrie (2005) noted that there are nonraised [a] variants in forms like *standard, adamant,* and *manage.* Figure 23.6 shows Mesthrie's revision of the Bobdian vowel chart for BSAE.

Mesthrie & Ribbens-Klein (2022) investigate further variation of the TRAP vowel in BSAE, based on the hypothesis that, for some speakers, TRAP$_2$ is increasing at the expense of TRAP$_1$, since TRAP$_2$ can index pan-African connections and orientations in post-apartheid times. Acoustic analyses of two datasets of BSAE speakers were conducted: a) young Black university students, and b) speeches by South African political leaders concerning the COVID-19 crisis. Figure 23.7 shows a partitioning into TRAP$_1$ and TRAP$_2$ for MM, an undergraduate student in his early twenties at the time of interview in 2008. The graph illustrates a fairly typical TRAP-split as traditionally described in the literature. It also provides further indications for subdivisions into [e] and [ɛ] for TRAP$_1$ and [æ] and [a] for TRAP$_2$.

These subdivisions into four quadrants and a further curvilinear partitioning were done purely based on inspection—by listening to a subset of the tokens in Praat, and deciding whether to code the productions as TRAP$_1$ or TRAP$_2$ (and thus ultimately deciding where the curvilinear borderlines of TRAP$_1$ and TRAP$_2$ lie for each speaker). The four quadrants are labeled from 1 to 4 (starting top-left) in a clockwise direction as per basic trigonometry. (Partitioning was required, since we have not yet subjected the remaining BSAE vowels to close acoustic analysis that would have permitted normalization.) Any assignment into discrete labels is not without difficulties,

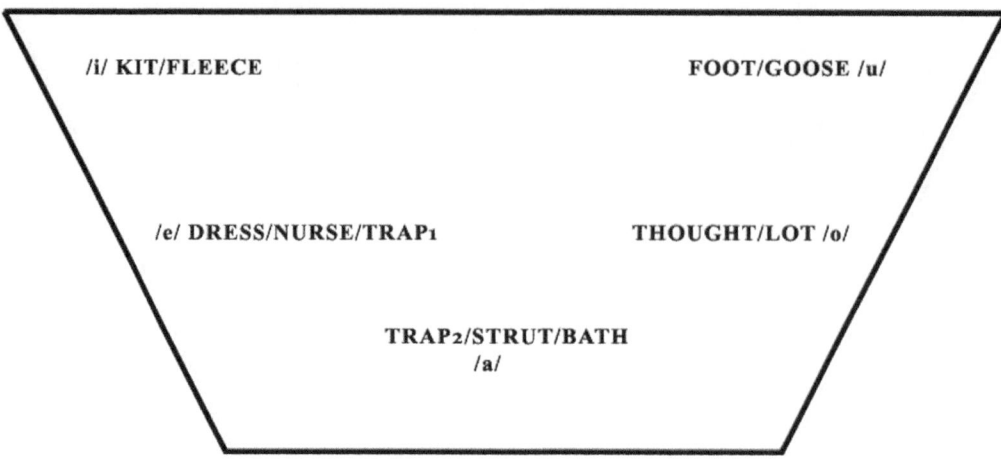

Figure 23.6   Older BSAE monophthongs

Source: based on Mesthrie 2017

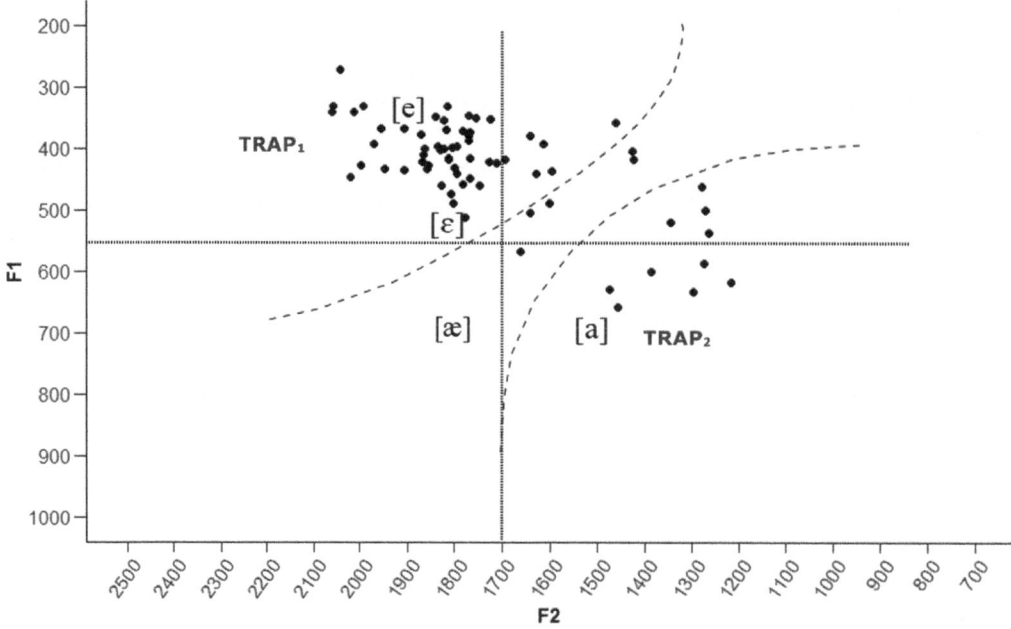

Figure 23.7   TRAP vowel formants for MM, partitioned into quadrants and TRAP₁ vs. TRAP₂

since the acoustic space is a continuum, making any segmentation to be of a somewhat arbitrary nature. However, Mesthrie & Ribbens-Klein (2022) found that the acoustic plots for all eight younger speakers were consistent in suggesting archetypal values, with only a few ambiguities between a low [ɛ] and a high [æ]. Figure 23.8 shows the partitioning of TRAP₁ and TRAP₂ for President Cyril Ramaphosa.

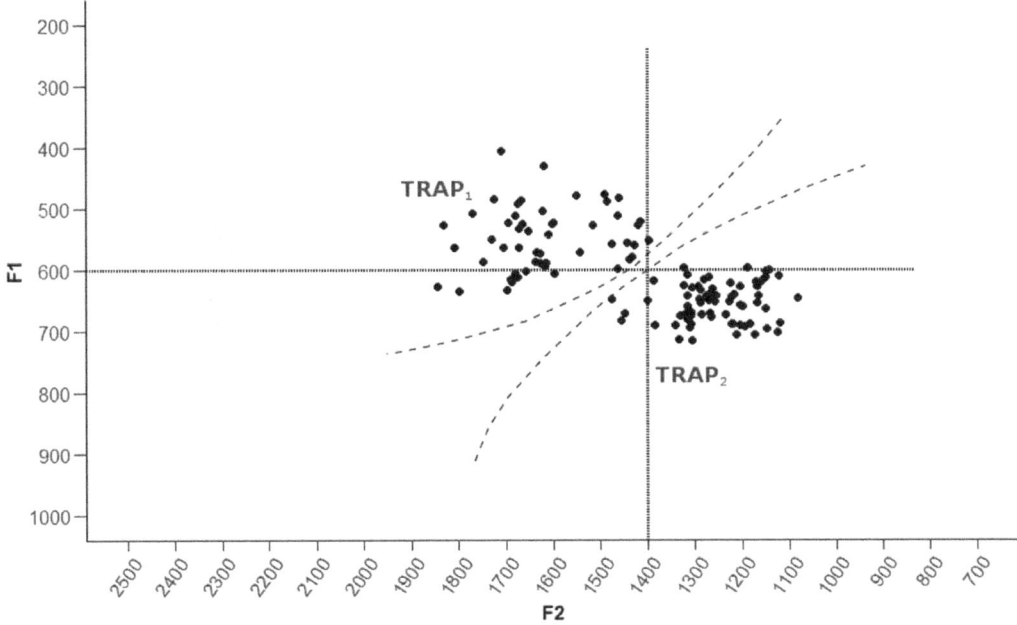

Figure 23.8 TRAP vowel formants for CR, partitioned into quadrants and TRAP₁ vs. TRAP₂

None of the descriptions in the literature on BSAE prepares us for the high ratios of TRAP₂ over TRAP₁ among the older politicians—especially the fact that TRAP₂ tends to be realized in the region of [a] rather than [æ]. We hypothesize that this is a feature of older speakers belonging to a new (post-apartheid) political community of practice with networks that include other parts of sub-Saharan Africa. In particular, South Africa has been prominent in the African Union since around 2000 CE. Having both TRAP₁ and TRAP₂ as variants opens up the variable as a resource for swaying from a South African identity (TRAP₁) to a pan-African one (TRAP₂). However, the change does not work entirely to the demise of TRAP₁ even in this community of practice, and remains a presence on more purely phonological grounds.

Afrikaans-based sociophonetics of ethnicity and place

As mentioned above, Afrikaans phonetics proves highly relevant in a historical dialectology of South African English. Ribbens-Klein (2016) studied Afrikaans /r/ as linguistic variable, with alveolar /r/ and uvular /r/ realizations as variants. Alveolar /r/ included trilled [r] and tapped [ɾ] realizations. Uvular /r/ realizations include uvular trill [ʀ] and uvular fricative [ʁ]. (See Ribbens-Klein 2019 for further qualitative analysis of variants of Afrikaans /r/ in the South Cape.) Uvular /r/ realizations showed strong associations with regional and rural use, which adds to Mesthrie's (2012) findings on the interaction between race and place. The majority of the L1 Afrikaans-speaking population are Coloured South Africans, especially in the Western Cape Province. However, similar to CSAE, when it comes to Coloured speakers of Afrikaans, previous sociolinguistic research predominantly focuses on the variety/dialect of Afrikaans spoken in Cape Town and its surrounds (sometimes referred to as *Kaaps*). In her study of rhotic variation in Afrikaans, Ribbens-Klein (2016) aimed to offer a glimpse into variation and change in a peri-urban, Afrikaans-dominant town in the Southern

Cape region. This was historically, a pre-colonial Khoekhoe settlement, a mission station during European colonization, and racially demarcated as a "Coloured" residential area during apartheid.

Previous studies claimed that in Afrikaans alveolar /r/ (the standard variant) historically replaced uvular /r/, with the latter confined to rural regions spread throughout the Western Cape Province of South Africa. In the fieldwork site, both alveolar /r/ and uvular /r/ were used. The participants showed varying degrees of awareness of the uvular /r/ as locally and socially meaningful. Based on the participants' metalinguistic comments, Ribbens-Klein found that local attitudes, styles, and the adoption of certain personae contributed to the complex social meanings of uvular /r/ in the town. The metalinguistic comments suggest that the different /r/ variants do not directly index macro-social categories. Comments made by participants younger than 30 years old show that they were more aware of uvular /r/ as a resource to index multiple social meanings, ranging from local group identities to individual personae. For instance, Lionel (aged 18) associated uvular /r/ with a "never-minded" (i.e., carefree or nonchalant) attitude of younger residents (see also Ribbens-Klein 2017). Age is thus metapragmatically salient. The younger speakers were also more aware that uvular /r/ is used particularly in their locality. They recognized uvular /r/ as a feature of their own way of speaking, and have had experiences of comments from other people on their use of uvular /r/, especially on visits to family or friends in Cape Town. Thus, uvular /r/ became visible to them because of their mobility, and thus indexically linked to place.

Furthermore, by combining binary gender and age, distribution patterns emerge that were potentially meaningful (see Figure 23.9).

Figure 23.9 Mean percentage use of uvular /r/ according to age and binary gender in a Southern Cape town
Source: Ribbens-Klein 2016

The distribution of /r/ use in Figure 23.9 allows one to compare smaller gender-by-age subgroups within the sample group and to identify patterns of similarities and differences. Within the overall finding that the youngest cohort had significantly higher use of uvular /r/ ($p = 0.011$), a cross-tabulation of gender and age indicates a sharp distinction between younger and older women. The young women showed a mean percentage of 52.2 percent for uvular /r/ use, compared to the other two age cohorts of women, who had less than 15 percent use. Both /r/ variants were found with men older than 30, and uvular /r/ occurred approximately 25 percent more compared to women older than 30. The participants younger than 30, from both genders, have high frequency use of uvular /r/, which indicates that the variant has local prestige and supports the notion of a possible change-in-progress. A relevant factor involving age, in particular, is post-apartheid racial desegregation in schools, which could have affected speakers younger than 30. Hence, increase in the use of uvular /r/ is found with participants under 30 from both genders. As argued above, changes in social networks and social contact can contribute to changes in the social meanings of linguistic forms. Through their contact with alveolar /r/ speakers, younger participants became more aware of uvular /r/ indexing place and belonging.

Voice quality and phonation

Suprasegmental variation has received relatively little attention compared with segmental variation (see, e.g., Zerbian 2012 on intonation). Voice quality in SAE has until recently been almost entirely ignored.

Two earlier sociophonetic studies of vowel quality variation in SAE, namely Bekker (2009) and Morreira (2012), explicitly mention voice quality phenomena. Bekker (2009) makes the impressionistic observation that creak is used towards the latter parts of vowel production and could potentially function as a prestige feature in General SAE. He also observes the phenomenon of word-final "pre-aspiration" before occlusion, proposing that this pre-aspiration phenomenon could play an indexical role in SAE. While the prestige variety of General SAE is in theory not limited to any particular population group, for methodological reasons Bekker's (2009) sample was restricted to young White female SAE speakers drawn from the higher socioeconomic strata of major urban centers. Thus, no conclusions could explicitly be made regarding the possibility that such features may play a role in indexing ethnolinguistic background. Bekker's (2009) observations do nevertheless allow for the possibility that creak and pre-aspiration phenomena could potentially play a role in expressing "White" racial identity, or perhaps that these phenomena could be associated with higher deracinated socioeconomic status more broadly.

Morreira (2012) however, explicitly mentions the possibility that voice quality features may play a role in the signaling of racial identity. Morreira (2012) makes the impressionistic observation that, at least for one variety of SAE, there is a particular voice quality which may act as an indicator of the race of her informants. Although the voice quality Morreira (2012) observes is reportedly more apparent for some speakers than for others, she claims that the presence or absence of this voice quality may indicate the race of a given speaker even if the speaker in question were identical to their White counterparts in terms of segmental pronunciation. Morreira (2012:126) also states that this observed difference in voice quality could potentially function "as an identifying feature" in the absence of other phonetic cues to signal ethnicity. This appears to be the first claim of its kind regarding SAE voice quality in the field of sociophonetics.

Because both Bekker's (2009) and Morreira's (2012) studies were primarily designed to investigate vowel quality variation in SAE, they unfortunately do not provide the data, either in quantity or in kind, necessary to put forward more specific hypotheses regarding the role played by voice quality features in SAE. Sociophonetic studies combining the use of acoustic measures as well as perceptual methods, which would be necessary in supporting such observations, were at this time still lacking, as was any account of voice quality variation in SAE based on appropriate articulatory data. Likewise, the role of voice quality in affective signaling, stance-taking, and other interaction-specific functions in this variety of English have yet to be examined; little can be offered by way of an account of linguistic change for voice quality features over time for SAE.

By using a set of relevant phonetic measures Wileman's (2018) investigation of ethnolinguistic differences in voice quality represented the first attempt to provide acoustic evidence of the kind of differences observed by Morreira (2012). By providing a replicable set of baseline measurements, Wileman laid the groundwork for the development and evaluation of further hypotheses regarding the use of voice quality as an important and hitherto largely ignored aspect of sociophonetic variation in SAE. Specifically, this work investigates, describes, and evaluates the acoustic evidence for differences in voice quality in General SAE linked to ethnolinguistic background. Wileman aimed to identify which specific set of acoustic features may characterize any voice quality differences observed between the two ethnolinguistic groups (thus potentially acting as a voice quality marker or indicator of ethnolinguistic identity). Using recent theories of voice, the latest findings pertaining to the available acoustic measures, and a preliminary auditory assessment, Wileman (2018) provides hypotheses regarding the articulation of these observed features.

The sample on which the study was based comprised 18 monolingual White English speakers and 18 Black speakers of an isiXhosa language background, recorded in a soundproofed studio. In Wileman's (2018) study, the effect of ethnolinguistic identity was found to be significant for several of the acoustic measures, including measures of spectral tilt (2K*-5K, H4*-2K*, H1*-H2* and H1*-A1*), as well as for cepstral peak prominence. 2K*-5K refers to the amplitude of the strongest harmonic at 2000 Hz minus the amplitude of the strongest harmonic at 5000 Hz; H4*-2K* refers to the fourth harmonic amplitude minus the amplitude of the strongest harmonic at 2000 Hz; H1*-H2* refers to the first harmonic amplitude minus the second harmonic amplitude; H1*-A1* refers to the first harmonic amplitude minus the amplitude of the strongest harmonic in the F1 region. For a definition of cepstral peak prominence, see Hillenbrand, Cleveland & Erickson (1994).

Higher values for spectral tilt measures in combination with lower values for cepstral peak prominence are generally associated with breathy voicing. For most spectral tilt measures, Black speakers (of an isiXhosa language background) exhibited consistently higher values, while on average higher values for fundamental frequency and cepstral peak prominence were observed for White speakers. Wileman (2018) suggests that one reasonable interpretation of these findings is that the voice quality of the Black speakers is characterized by greater breathiness and lesser glottal stricture in comparison to the voice quality of the White speakers, which is characterized by greater constriction of the vocal folds, less breathiness, and greater vocal fold tension. According to this hypothesis, Black female speakers tend towards the habitual use of a voice quality characterized by greater breathiness with the possible attendant use of "lax" or "slack" voice, while White female speakers habitually use a voice quality characterized by pressed voice (which in many instances may result in the habitual production of creak), accompanied by greater tension, stiffness, and constriction of the vocal folds.

In order to further explore this hypothesis, follow-up work in the form of a perceptual assessment was carried out by John Esling, using the audio recordings collected by Wileman (2018). The results of this assessment showed a high level of agreement with the findings for the acoustic measures in the original study, although they would suggest that what was originally coded as "breathy voice" quality could instead be more accurately described as "harsh voice quality." (These voice qualities may resemble one another with regards to the patterning of the acoustic measures, particularly for acoustic measures of noise.) The pattern observed for spectral tilt relates to a perceptual difference between the predominant use of creak on the one hand for White speakers, and "harsh" voice quality for Black speakers. This difference is, at least for individuals at the more extreme ends of the averages for spectral tilt measures, auditorily apparent and identifiable.

While not specifically investigating BSAE in particular, Wileman's (2018) work on voice quality is potentially relevant both for the study of BSAE, as well as middle-class SAE. The research is indirectly relevant for BSAE in that the hypotheses generated by the research findings regarding the origins of the voice quality variation observed should encourage more research on voice quality variation in BSAE. For example, some of Wileman's (2018) findings suggest intriguing possibilities regarding possible background language transfer effects and that such a scenario may be implicated as one of the potential origins of some of the observed variation in voice quality in SAE. Wileman (2018) notes that the "intrinsic voice quality pattern" observed for isiXhosa by Jessen & Roux (2002), as well as some of the more specifically consonant-linked effects may have been transferred to the English spoken by Black South Africans of an isiXhosa language background and that this would be consistent with and could partly account for the observed acoustic patterning. However, Wileman (2018) points out that this explanation remains speculative, citing not only a lack of the kinds of studies which would be needed to establish the link between the observed patterns and language transfer, but also the fact that, as noted by Giles (1979), such differences can also be adopted deliberately as ethnic speech markers for the purpose of asserting a distinct linguistic identity.

Wileman's (2018) findings and subsequent work provide some early indications that such a development may in fact have already started taking place. Follow-up work involving perceptual evaluations of the voice qualities identified in Wileman (2018) provided by Esling, and synthe-sizing this analysis with the analysis of the acoustic patterns, suggests that for those speakers towards the lower end of the spectral tilt scale—where White speakers predominate—creak is most prevalent. A combination of creak and modal voice predominate towards the middle of the scale, represented by a mix of both White speakers and those Black speakers who sound most similar to White speakers (in terms of our overall impression). However, at the extreme high end for spectral tilt, where Black speakers are predominantly represented, so-called "harsh" voice quality is used to a greater degree.

Were future studies to confirm this pattern, it may suggest that part of "sounding White" could entail the adoption of this form of "clear" unencumbered creak. This feature would be accom-panied by the perhaps paralinguistically or pragmatically determined norms for its use within phrases, while simultaneously avoiding the use of "harsh" voice quality. Conversely, in order to signal an isiXhosa-English ethnolinguistic identity one would need to produce sufficiently prom-inent "harsh" voice quality and potentially avoid the hypothetical norms for producing unen-cumbered creak seemingly followed by White speakers. Since the prevalence of this pattern beyond this one narrowly delineated ethnolinguistic group is not yet known, this research opens up avenues for explorations of "sounding Xhosa" versus "sounding Black." In any case, the research suggests an important role for voice quality variation, hitherto mostly unacknowledged, in middle-class SAE.

The question of whether the hypothesized differences are perceptible to South African listeners is ultimately a question which will, we hope, be answered using appropriate perception studies. Mesthrie, Chevalier & McLachlan (2015) showed that young South Africans could not tell Black and White females apart from short audio clips. However, a follow-up study focusing specifically on creak and "harsh voice" (and possibly also distinguishing "harsh voice" from breathy voice acoustically) in a more controlled experiment would be interesting to monitor.

CASE STUDY   Adapting the ARPABET to South African Englishes

The FAVE process relies on an internal dictionary, comprised of words and their phonemic transcriptions. FAVE's default dictionary is the Carnegie Mellon University (CMU) dictionary, based on North American English varieties. The transcription system used is called the ARPABET, devised in the 1970s by ARPA, the Advanced Research Projects Agency. It represents the phonemes of North American English using ASCII characters. Of two different options in the original, the one favored by linguists uses capital letters in sequences of one or two for the different phonemes. Consonants are marked in caps by alphabetic symbols which are by and large suggestive of phonemic values—for example, P T K B D G for /p,t,k,b,d,g/. Combinations like TH, DH, SH, and ZH are used for /θ/, /ð/, /ʃ/, and /ʒ/. The full system used for vowels and consonants is given in Table 23.1.

Table 23.1 ARPABET symbols of transcription for GenAmE with corresponding lexical sets

Vowels			*Consonants*		
Phoneme	*Example*	*Transcription*	*Phoneme*	*Example*	*Transcription*
AA	*bath*	B AA TH	B	*be*	B IY
AA	*lot*	L AA T	CH	*cheese*	CH IY Z
AE	*cat*	K AE T	D	*day*	D EY
AH	*strut*	S T AH T	DH	*they*	DH EY
	about	AH B AW T			
AO	*thought*	TH AO T	F	*fee*	F IY
AW	*mouth*	M AW TH	G	*go*	G OW
AY	*price*	P R AY S	HH	*he*	HH IY
EH	*dress*	D R EH S	JH	*just*	JH AH S T
ER	*nurse*	N ER S	K	*key*	K IY
EY	*face*	F EY S	L	*late*	L EY T
IH	*kit*	K IH T	M	*me*	M IY
IY	*fleece*	F L IY S	N	*knee*	N IY
OW	*goat*	G OW T	NG	*sing*	S IH NG
OY	*choice*	CH OY S	P	*pay*	P EY
UH	*foot*	F UH T	R	*read*	R IY D
UW	*goose*	G UW S	S	*sea*	S IY
			SH	*she*	SH IY
			T	*tea*	T IY
			TH	*thanks*	TH AE NG K S
			V	*vein*	V EY N
			W	*we*	W IY
			Y	*yes*	Y EH S
			Z	*zoo*	Z UW
			ZH	*pleasure*	P L EH ZH ER

Source: http://fave.ling.upenn.edu/usingFAAValign.html

The ARPABET has been widely used in the context of recent variation studies. This pronunciation dictionary or lexicon is a crucial component in forced alignment (FAVE-align), since it assists in the matching of segments of the continuous wave forms with the ARPABET-based transcript. For subsequent analytic purposes (using FAVE-extract), identification of the vowels with ARPABET notation is more accurate by far than a transcript based on the vagaries of ordinary English spelling or the IPA symbols, which are not as easily machine-readable. The ARPABET system includes stress marking on the vowels, using 0 for lack of stress, 1 for primary stress, and 2 for secondary stress.

One problem for researchers outside North America is that the vowel systems they study are not entirely compatible with those of North American English. Among the major differences to be addressed are the lack of rhoticity (or its marginal presence) in varieties like RP and SAE. There are also individual rather than systemic differences in the pronunciation of words like *vase*, *fertile*, *route*, etc. For this reason the British English Example Pronouncing (BEEP) dictionary was devised (Robinson 1994) as an adaptation of the ARPABET. BEEP has been proven the more useful for South African studies (Chevalier 2016).

For South Africa a broad division along the lines of L1 versus L2 English is desirable (and no longer by ethnicity per se, as we have shown above). The adaptations to the ARPABET are of two types: a) new lexical items from within South Africa, and b) specific pronunciations within a word class which do not accord with ARPABET or even BEEP norms. These are handled respectively by adding new entries to the ARPABET and/or adding alternate entries for items already in it, reflecting the South African pronunciation. Customizing the pronunciation dictionaries by insertion of items is fairly straightforward. To take the example of *lekker*, a ubiquitous South Africanism for 'nice, pleasing, tasty,' an entry like LEKKER (L EH1 K EH0) can be created. Less straightforward are cases where tweaks are needed to reflect common pronunciation variants. Mesthrie (2017) notes schwa (AH0) in South African English (rather than IH0 (IPA [ɪ]) in unstressed syllables as in *roses*, *wanted*, and *exactly*, as well as [ɒ] as a co-variant of schwa in initial prefixes like *com-*, *con-*, *col-* (e.g., *computers*, *concern*, *collect*). A specific problem encountered is with the LOT vowel: in the pronunciation dictionaries, LOT and BATH are both transcribed as AA1 (see row 2 of Table 23.1). In SAE, these are two different vowels, and the OH1 is the code introduced to refer to LOT as separate from AA1 for BATH. Furthermore BATH in SAE does not have the American English split between AE1 (e.g., in ARPABET, *class*, *fast*, *bath*) and AA1 (e.g., *father*, *calm*, *taco*). As explained by Chevalier (2016:79, 90), "given the complexity (or impossibility) of adding this OH phoneme to the FAVE Toolkit, the LOT tokens for SAE need to be manually changed from AA1 to OH1." A desideratum for future work in this field would require an easy way of allowing such a reprogramming of the two vowel phonemes.

L2 varieties like traditional Black South African English bring further challenges to the use of the ARPABET. One major systemic difference between BSAE and other South African varieties is the neutralization of vowel length (although this feature is not as prominent as it was a generation ago). Thus the KIT and FLEECE sets both have /i/; FOOT and GOOSE have /u/, LOT and THOUGHT have /o/, STRUT and BATH have /a/, while DRESS and NURSE have /e/ (Van Rooy 2004). As noted above, TRAP is split between TRAP₁ (siding with DRESS) and TRAP₂ (siding with BATH)—a complexity which we needn't dwell on here. On the other hand, all vowels are lengthened under conditions that include penultimate placement in an utterance as well as certain pragmatic considerations. How should these neutralizations (and the one split) be reflected in the ARPABET? The strategy used by Mesthrie (2017) was to keep the standard values, allowing for a subsequent joint analysis at FAVE-extract stage of each set or a comparison of their component parts (e.g., of all FOOT tokens versus all GOOSE tokens). What this emphasizes is that the ARPABET is a functional tool, not a ready reflection of actual dialect realities. If length is under-differentiated in traditional BSAE, schwa is over-differentiated with its six common realizations [a,e,i,o,u,ə]. In the ARPABET these are all designated AH0, the code for an unstressed vowel. The actual differentiation had to be studied by other means—largely by separation via phonological environments (see Mesthrie 2017:324–327). For all these reasons FAVE alignment was less effective in the study of traditional BSAE than for L1 varieties of South African English.

Conclusion

Varieties of South African English have proven of great interest for their historical connections not only with the United Kingdom but with Southern hemisphere varieties generally. At the same time, internal differentiation in a multiethnic and multilingual country continues to show important lines of differentiation as well as overlaps, depending mostly on networks pertaining to social class. As we have stressed in this chapter, the tools of acoustic sociophonetics have been crucial in dissecting and revealing new and ongoing variation and change not always obvious to the speakers themselves. At the same time, they have opened up a field of enquiry that we trust will remain available to, and attract, a range of scholarship from across the language spectrum of South Africa.

Acknowledgments

We are grateful to the National Research Foundation for funding for this research (SARChI grant no. 64805). We thank everyone who participated in the interviews and Alida Chevalier for managing the original database. For current research assistance, a special mention of Fatima Sadan is due. We are immensely grateful to a number of international scholars who have assisted us generously over the last two decades in coming to grips with acoustic phonetics and R statistics virtually from scratch: William Labov, Sherry Ash, Erik Thomas, Tyler Kendall, Christopher Strelluf, Matt Gordon, Paul Foulkes, Gerry Docherty, Thomas Hoffman, John Esling, Joe Fruehwald, Marianna Di Paolo, Keelan Evanini, Jane Stuart-Smith, and Paul Boersma. For matters statistical we acknowledge the collegial contributions of the late Tim Dunne.

References

Bangeni, Bongi & Rochelle Kapp. 2007. Shifting language attitudes in a linguistically diverse learning environment in South Africa. *Journal of Multilingual and Multicultural Development* 28(5). 253–269. https://doi.org/10.2167/jmmd495.0

Becker, Kara. (ed.) 2019. *The Low-Back-Merger Shift: Uniting the Canadian Vowel Shift, the California Vowel Shift, and Short Front Vowel Shifts across North America.* Duke University Press

Bekker, Ian. 2009. *The vowels of South African English.* PhD thesis, North-West University.

Boersma, Paul & David Weenink. 2021. *Praat: Doing phonetics by computer* [Computer program], ver. 6.1.39. www.praat.org/

Chambers, J.K. 1998. TV makes people sound the same. In Laurie Bauer & Peter Trudgill (eds.), *Language myths,* 123–131. Penguin.

Chevalier, Alida. 2016. *Globalisation versus internal development: The reverse short front vowel shift in South African English.* PhD thesis, University of Cape Town.

Chevalier, Alida. 2020. Internal push, external pull: The reverse short front vowel shift in South African English. In Raymond Hickey (ed.), *English in multilingual South Africa: The linguistics of contact and change*, 151–175. Cambridge University Press.

ELAN [Computer software], ver. 6.2. 2021. Max Planck Institute for Psycholinguistics. https://archive.mpi.nl/tla/elan

Erasmus, Zimitri (ed.) 2001. *Coloured by history, shaped by place: New perspectives on Coloured identities in Cape Town.* Kwela.

Finn, Peter. 2004. Cape Flats English: Phonology. In Kortmann et al., 964–984.

Fisher, John. 1958. Social influences on the choice of a linguistic variant. *Word* 14. 47–56. https://doi.org/10.1080/00437956.1958.11659655

Giles, Howard. 1979. Ethnicity markers in speech. In Klaus R. Scherer & Howard Giles (eds.), *Social markers in speech*, 251–289. Cambridge University Press.

Gorman, Kyle, Jonathan Howell & Michael Wagner. 2011. Prosodylab-Aligner: A tool for forced alignment of laboratory speech. *Canadian Acoustics* 39(3). 192–193.

Hickey, Raymond. 2016. English in Ireland: Development and varieties. In Raymond Hickey (ed.), *Sociolinguistics in Ireland*, 3–40. Palgrave Macmillan.

Hillenbrand, James, Ronald A. Cleveland & Robert L. Erickson. 1994. Acoustic correlates of breathy vocal quality. *Journal of Speech, Language, and Hearing Research* 37(4). 769–778. https://doi.org/10.1044/jshr.3704.769

Jessen, Michael & Justus C. Roux. 2002. Voice quality differences associated with stops and clicks in Xhosa. *Journal of Phonetics* 30(1). 1–52. https://doi.org/10.1006/jpho.2001.0150

Kendall, Tyler & Erik R. Thomas. 2018. *vowels: Vowel manipulation, normalization, and plotting in R*. R package ver. 1.2-2. https://cran.Rproject.org/package=vowels

Kortmann, Bernd & Edgar Schneider (eds.) in collaboration with Kate Burridge, Rajend Mesthrie & Clive Upton. 2004. *A handbook of varieties of English*. 2 vols. Mouton de Gruyter.

Labov, William, Ingrid Rosenfelder, & Josef Fruehwald. 2013. One hundred years of sound change in Philadelphia: Linear incrementation, reversal, and reanalysis. *Language* 89(1). 30–65. https://doi.org/10.1353/lan.2013.0015

Lanham, Len W. & C.A. Macdonald. 1979. *The standard in South African English and its social history*. Julius Groos Verlag.

Lass, Roger & Susan Wright. 1986. Endogeny vs. contact: "Afrikaans influence" on South African English. *English World-Wide* 7(2). 201–224. https://doi.org/10.1075/eww.7.2.03las

Maclagan, Margaret & Jennifer Hay. 2007. Getting *fed* up with our *feet*: Contrast maintenance and the New Zealand English "short" front vowel shift. *Language Variation and Change* 19(1). 1–25. https://doi.org/10.1017/S0954394507070020

McAuliffe, Michael, Michaela Socolof, Sarah Mihuc, Michael Wagner & Morgan Sonderegger. 2017a. *Montreal Forced Aligner* [Computer program], ver. 0.9.0. http://montrealcorpustools.github.io/Montreal-Forced-Aligner/

McAuliffe, Michael, Michaela Socolof, Sarah Mihuc, Michael Wagner & Morgan Sonderegger. 2017b. Montreal Forced Aligner: Trainable text-speech alignment using Kaldi. *Proceedings of Interspeech 2017*. 498–502. https://doi.org/10.21437/Interspeech.2017-1386

McKinney, Carolyn. 2007. "If I speak English, does it make me less Black anyway?": "Race" and English in South African desegregated schools. *English Academy Review* 24(2). 6–24. https://doi.org/10.1080/10131750701452253

Meer, Philipp. 2020. Automatic alignment for New Englishes: Applying state-of-the-art aligners to Trinidadian English. *Journal of the Acoustical Society of America* 147. 2283. https://doi.org/10.1121/10.0001069

Mesthrie, Rajend. 2005. Putting back the horse before the cart: The "spelling form" fallacy in second language acquisition studies, with special reference to the treatment of unstressed vowels in Black South African English. *English World-Wide* 26(2). 127–152. https://doi.org/10.1075/eww.26.2.02mes

Mesthrie, Rajend. 2010. Socio-phonetics and social change: Deracialisation of the GOOSE vowel in South African English. *Journal of Sociolinguistics* 14(1). 3–33. https://doi.org/10.1111/j.1467-9841.2009.00433.x

Mesthrie, Rajend. 2012. Ethnicity, substrate and place: The dynamics of Coloured and Indian English in five South African cities in relation to the variable (t). *Language Variation and Change* 24(3). 371–395. https://doi.org/10.1017/S0954394512000178

Mesthrie, Rajend. 2017. Class, gender, and substrate erasure in sociolinguistic change: A sociophonetic study of schwa in deracializing South African English. *Language* 93(2). 314–346. https://doi.org/10.1353/lan.2017.0016

Mesthrie, Rajend. Forthcoming. Studying ethnicity and its sociolinguistic fluidities: variationist perspectives from South Africa. In Christopher Cieri, Katie Drager & Malcah Yaeger-Dror (eds.), *Dimensions of linguistic variation*. Oxford University Press.

Mesthrie, Rajend, Alida Chevalier & Timothy Dunne. 2015. A regional and social dialectology of the BATH vowel in South African English. *Language Variation and Change* 27(1). 1–30. https://doi.org/10.1017/S0954394514000222

Mesthrie, Rajend, Alida Chevalier & Kate McLachlan. 2015. A perception test for the deracialisation of middle class South African English. *Southern African Linguistics and Applied Language Studies* 33(4). 391–409. https://doi.org/10.2989/16073614.2015.1061895

Mesthrie, Rajend & Yolandi Ribbens-Klein. 2022. Investigating possible changes to the trap vowel in Black South African English: A (post)Bobdian analysis. In Aloysius Ngefac, Hans-Georg Wolf & Thomas Hoffmann (eds.), *World Englishes and creole languages today*, vol. 2, *The Bobdian thinking and beyond*, 25–40. Lincom.

Mesthrie, Rajend & Simone Wills. 2019. The GOOSE vowel in South African English with special reference to Coloured communities in 5 cities. In Sandra Jansen & Lucia Siebers (eds.), *Processes of change: Studies in late modern and present-day English*, 227–246. John Benjamins.

Morreira, Kirsten. 2012. *Black South African English: A sociophonetic study*. PhD thesis, University of Cape Town.

Panayotov, Vassil, Guoguo Chen, Daniel Povey & Sanjeev Khudanpur. 2015. LibriSpeech: An ASR corpus based on public domain audio books. *2015 IEEE International Conference on Acoustics, Speech and Signal Processing (ICASSP)*. 5206–5210. https://doi.org/10.1109/ICASSP.2015.7178964

Posel, Deborah. 2001. What's in a name?: Racial categorisations under apartheid and their afterlife. *Transformation* 47. 50–74.

Povey, Daniel, Arnab Ghoshal, Giles Boulianne, Lukas Burget, Ondrej Glembek, Nagendra Goel, Mirko Hannemann, Petr Motlicek, Yanmin Qian, Petr Schwarz, Jan Silovsky, Georg Stemmer & Karel Vesely. 2011. The Kaldi Speech Recognition Toolkit. In *IEEE 2011 Workshop on Automatic Speech Recognition and Understanding*. IEEE Signal Processing Society.

R Core Team. 2022. *R: A language and environment for statistical computing*. R Foundation for Statistical Computing. www.R-project.org

Reddy, Thiven. 2001. The politics of naming: The constitution of Coloured subjects in South Africa. In Erasmus, 64–78.

Reddy, Sravana & James N. Stanford. 2015. Toward completely automated vowel extraction: Introducing DARLA. *Linguistics Vanguard* 1(1). 15–28. https://doi.org/10.1515/lingvan-2015-0002

Ribbens-Klein, Yolandi. 2016. *To bry or not to bry: The social meanings of Afrikaans rhotic variation in the South Cape*. PhD thesis, University of Cape Town.

Ribbens-Klein, Yolandi. 2017. Locality, belonging and the social meanings of Afrikaans rhotic variation in the South Cape: From patterns of frequency towards moments of meaning. *Multilingual Margins* 4(1). 7–26. https://doi.org/10.14426/mm.v4i1.50

Ribbens-Klein, Yolandi. 2019. A sociophonetic exploration of Afrikaans /r/ in the South Cape. Paper presented at 'R-atics 6 Colloquium, Paris.

Robinson, Anthony. 1994. *The British English example pronunciation dictionary*. Cambridge University Press.

Rosenfelder, Ingrid, Josef Fruehwald, Keelan Evanini, Scott Seyfarth, Kyle Gorman, Hilary Prichard & Jiahong Yuan. 2014. *FAVE: Forced Alignment and Vowel Extraction* [computer program], ver. 1.2.2. https://doi.org/10.5281/zenodo.22281

Simo Bobda, Augustin. 2000. Research on New Englishes: A critical review of some findings with a focus on Cameroon. *Arbeiten aus Anglistik und Amerikanistik* 25. 53–70.

Simo Bobda, Augustin. 2001. East and southern African English accents. *World Englishes* 20(3). 269–284. https://doi.org/10.1111/1467-971X.00215

Strelluf, Christopher. 2018. *Speaking from the Heartland: The Midland vowel system of Kansas City* [Publication of the American Dialect Society 103]. Duke University Press.

Stuart-Smith, Jane. 2011. The view from the couch: Changing perspectives on the role of the television in changing language ideologies and use. In Tore Kristiansen & Nikolas Coupland (eds.), *Standard languages and language standards in a changing Europe*, 223–239. Novus Press.

510

Stuart-Smith, Jane, Gwilym Price, Claire Timmins & Barrie Gunter. 2013. Television can also be a factor in language change: Evidence from an urban dialect. *Language* 89(3). 501–536. https://doi.org/10.1353/lan.2013.0041

Thomas, Erik R. & Tyler Kendall. 2007. *NORM: The vowel normalization and plotting suite.* http://lingtools.uoregon.edu/norm/.

Toefy, Tracey. 2014. *Sociophonetics and class differentiation: A study of working-and middle-class English in Cape Town's Coloured community.* PhD thesis, University of Cape Town.

Torgersen, Eivind & Paul Kerswill. 2004. Internal and external motivation in phonetic change: Dialect levelling outcomes for an English vowel shift. *Journal of Sociolinguistics* 8(1). 23–53. https://doi.org/10.1111/j.1467-9841.2004.00250.x

Upton, Clive. 2004. Received Pronunciation. In Kortmann et al., 217–230.

van Rooy, Bertus. 2004. Black South African English: Phonology. In Kortmann et al., 943–952.

Wells, John C. 1982. *Accents of English.* 3 vols. Cambridge University Press.

Wickham, Hadley. 2016. *ggplot2: Elegant graphics for data analysis.* Springer-Verlag New York. https://ggplot2.tidyverse.org.

Wileman, Bruce R. 2018. *A sociophonetic investigation of ethnolinguistic differences in voice quality among young, South African English speakers.* PhD thesis, University of Cape Town.

Wood, Tahir. 1987. *Perceptions of, and attitudes towards varieties of English in the Cape peninsula, with particular reference to the 'Coloured community.'* MA thesis, Rhodes University.

Zerbian, Sabine. 2012. Markedness in the prosody of contact varieties of South African English. In Qiuwu Ma, Hongwei Ding & Daniel Hirst (eds.), *Proceedings of the 6th International Conference on Speech Prosody 2012*, 446–449. Tongji University Press.

24

SOCIOPHONETICS AND JAPANESE

Kenjirō Matsuda, Shoji Takano, Yoshiyuki Asahi, and Ichiro Ota

Introduction

Studies in sociophonetics that focus on the languages spoken in various parts of the world necessarily reflect the characteristics of those languages, and the Japanese language is no exception to this rule. With a stable five-vowel system (in most dialects) where sound production does not show obvious signs of movement, a distinctive pitch-accent system, and extremely rich dialectal differences, there have been numerous studies on accentual variation, intonation patterns, and vowel devoicing across regional dialects, social groups, and styles.

To review the broad area of Japanese sociophonetics as efficiently as possible, we follow the structure below. We first trace the historical developments of Japanese sociophonetics, dividing it into three periods: the first period from the 1940s to 1970s, the second from the 1980s to early 1990s, and the third from the late 1990s to the present. The very first sociophonetic research on the language appeared in the first period and contrasted with earlier studies on sound change and variation on historical principles. The second period is marked by the emergence of instrumental studies, characterized by two large-scale projects sponsored by the Ministry of Education (Kakenhi, or Grant-in-Aid for Scientific Research): one by Fumio Inoue and the other by Miyoko Sugitō. The third period has seen further flourishing of sociophonetic studies, aided by the rapid development of devices and techniques related to the acoustic analysis of speech sounds. After tracing these historical developments, we focus on important works on the three major topics in Japanese sociophonetics, discussing their data and methods and contributions to the field. We close by discussing the future direction of Japanese sociophonetics.

Historical overview

The first attempt to put phonetic variation in the social context in Japanese linguistics is probably Haruhiko Kindaichi's (1942) study on the velar nasal /ŋ/ in Tōkyō Japanese. He used a word list to elicit pronunciations of the segment from 70 native speakers. Kindaichi identified several tendencies of the denasalization process of the segments. First, geographically western residents of the city tended to use the denasalized variant more than eastern residents. Second, lexically those

DOI: 10.4324/9781003034636-27

segments included in Chinese-origin words (kango) tended to be denasalized more than those in native Japanese words (wago). Third, phonologically following /i/ and /u/ tended to co-occur with /g/. Published at a time when phonological studies of the language were mostly occupied by historical research, Kindaichi's study was revolutionary and should be marked as one of the precursors of Japanese sociophonetics.

It was not until 1951 that such a socially informed study of phonetic variation surfaced again in Japanese linguistics. The National Institute for Japanese Language and Linguistics (NINJAL), a new national organization initially established to study various language problems of the country, released their first reports on what would become one of the pillars of the research body: a large-scale study on the standardization of the local dialects. Their approach was a precursor to the variation studies in western countries in the 1960s and 1970s: questionnaire-based interviews with hundreds of local speakers selected through random sampling. Starting with Shirakawa city (see Figure 24.1), they embarked on a series of standardization surveys in the cities Tsuruoka, Furano,

Figure 24.1   Dialectal map of Japan with city names in italics

Source: adapted from Hirayama 1968:74

and Sapporo (NINJAL 1953, 1965). Their research plan was later expanded to add panel samples as well as trend studies (NINJAL 1953, 1965, 1974, 1997, 2007; see https://mmsrv.ninjal.ac.jp/tsuruoka/ and https://mmsrv.ninjal.ac.jp/hokkaido/ to access data from Tsuruoka and Hokkaidō, respectively), which makes the surveys one of the earliest examples of panel studies of sociolinguistic variation. It is worth mentioning that although recordings were made in later surveys, the phonetic judgments have been made auditorily. The birth of Japanese sociophonetics is considered to be the era covering Kindaichi's work and the launch of NINJAL's standardization surveys.

In the 1980s, the second wave of sociophonetic studies emerged, involving instrumental measurements. Two major factors contribute to the rise of such studies. One factor was the rapid development in both hardware and software computer technology, which made UNIX workstations, personal computers, and associated programs easily accessible to researchers (Miwa 1995; Maekawa 2006). The second factor was the large-scale Kakenhi projects sponsored by MEXT and the Japan Society for the Promotion of Science (JSPS). With their enormous financial scale, Kakenhi projects are one of the most important resources for Japanese academic research, and the fact that two of the highest-level grants were awarded to linguistic projects gave a significant impetus to the acoustic analysis of dialectal speech. An enormous amount of dialectal speech was systematically collected and acoustically analyzed. Researchers obtained digital recordings of dialectal speech in 105 sites and 13 cities across the country and released them on CD-ROM.

Moreover, technological advances in digital signal processing, coupled with a surge of theoretical inquiries into intonational phenomena in the United States (e.g., Liberman 1975; Pierrehumbert 1980; Pierrehumbert & Beckman 1988; see also O'Rourke & Baltazani this volume), gave rise to a new strand of linguistic research on intonation. Thus, the three streams of computational development, the Kakenhi projects on dialectal speech, and the interest in intonation in the Japanese language led to a series of acoustic studies of various Japanese dialects.

Additionally, following developments in sociolinguistic methodologies in the US, variationist sociolinguistics introduced another stream of influence on Japanese sociophonetics. Most notably, Hibiya (1988, 1995) conducted the first variationist study on Japanese phonetics/phonology, albeit in an auditory fashion. Hibiya looked at the denasalization of the velar nasal /ŋ/ to /g/ in Tōkyō Japanese by analyzing speech from sociolinguistic interviews, reading passages, word list readings, and from group conversations. Her multivariate analysis revealed that the denasalization process correlates nicely with speaker age, and is also affected by such social factors as the biological sex of the speaker and residential area within the city (*shitamachi* [downtown] and *yamanote* [uptown]). She was also careful to note the internal constraint on the process, namely the three lexical strata in the Japanese language of wago, kango, and the loanwords from non-Chinese sources (gairaigo), with wago being the most susceptible to the process, mostly vindicating Kindaichi's (1942) findings.

The third era, the period from the 1990s to the present, is an epoch of full-fledged sociophonetic studies, integrating acoustic analysis and sociolinguistic theory. This period also stands out in the international nature of the researchers. In contrast to the previous stages, where most of the research was conducted by Japanese linguists, important contributions emerged from researchers overseas, such as Morris (2010), Kajino (2014), and Starr (2015).

The arrival of the third wave variationist sociolinguistics (Eckert 2012) was further influential in Japanese sociophonetics. This line of work is exemplified by Kajino (2014), where style is no longer regarded as a static variable but plays a dynamic role as a representation of the speaker's regional gender identity constructed in linguistic practices by using phonetic features together with other gender-marking elements, such as the Japanese woman's language and nonlinguistic practices.

The third period also saw an expansion of linguistic phenomena examined in Japanese sociophonetics. Voice quality has been a notoriously elusive notion, and much effort has been expounded to capture its acoustic correlates (Davidson this volume). Starr (2015) took a pioneering step into this area by examining the "sweet" voices of Japanese females. She showed that the voice with a light, gentle timbre produced by professional voice actors played a crucial role in creating an authentic feminine style, both in its acoustic property and in perceptions by their fans.

We have observed that the history of Japanese sociophonetics can be divided into three eras. With this historical background in mind, let us now turn to major topics in Japanese sociophonetics and investigate the contributions made on this topic thus far.

Major findings

Vowel devoicing

Vowel devoicing refers to a phonetic process in Japanese whereby the high vowels /i/ and /u/ in certain phonological conditions are weakened or deleted. It is one of the most well-studied topics in Japanese phonetics (Han 1962; Sugitō 1969; Yoshioka 1981; Vance 1987; Imai 2004, 2010; Fujimoto 2015; Amino et al. 2018), and similar phenomena have been observed in other languages including Korean, French, Greek, and German (Jun & Beckman 1994; Kondo 2005). In the 1960s, Japanese linguists conducted an auditory analysis of speech data collected from various parts of the country (Akinaga 1966; Hirayama 1966). Hirayama (1966) observed that devoicing decreased in the younger generation in Tōkyō Japanese, and Akinaga (1966) identified an increase in devoicing on accented vowels in the younger generation.

Dialectal distribution and change in vowel devoicing

The pioneering cross-dialect phonetic studies on vowel devoicing were steered by a series of studies by Miyoko Sugitō. Sugitō (1969) instrumentally analyzed variability in vowel devoicing from the viewpoint of dialect contact by examining the devoicing of /u/ between voiceless consonants in read-aloud speech of 124 controlled words. Her subjects were composed of three sociolinguistically distinct groups: three native speakers of Tōkyō Japanese, three native speakers of Ōsaka Japanese, and three speakers who were more mobile (e.g., born in Tōkyō but moved to Ōsaka during childhood) and linguistically more heterogeneous with regular daily contact with other dialects (e.g., born and raised in Ōsaka with mothers who speak the Tōkyō dialect) (coded as "bidialectal"). She demonstrated that Japanese vowel devoicing was a gradient phenomenon systematically linked to speakers' native dialects and related linguistic experiences. The rates of devoicing were 86.5% for Tōkyō Japanese, 51.1% for bidialectal, and 29.6% for Ōsaka Japanese.

Sugitō (1988a) then expanded her target to the whole nation by analyzing the read-aloud speech of an identical passage by ten native speakers from eight cities in Japan (Sendai, Tōkyō, Nagoya, Ōsaka, Okayama, Kōchi, Kumamoto, Naha). Previous auditory studies had illustrated that devoicing of high vowels was a characteristic of the dialects spoken in the first three of these cities. Focusing on /u/ and /i/ in three phonetic environments (immediately followed by pause, between voiceless consonants, and immediately followed by voiced consonants), Sugitō demonstrated that vowel devoicing was strongly favored by an utterance-final pause and between voiceless consonants. In western regions of Japan, except Naha and Kumamoto, devoicing was strongly disfavored in the order of Kōchi > Okayama > Ōsaka, with Nagoya as a notable exception, showing the most frequent vowel devoicing (even outdoing Tōkyō). These findings encouraged re-examination of a then-prevalent generalization that devoicing was primarily associated with Tōkyō (NHK 1985).

Byun (2007, 2010) also reported two large-scale nationwide surveys of vowel devoicing to examine regional, generational, and age differences. Her first survey targeted 608 respondents (two generations: old and young) in 41 prefectures in Japan. Data were collected from 1986 to 1989 with a list of 515 words and phrases, 51 short sentences, and 32 words. Her acoustic analysis revealed that while regional differences remained as before, the younger generation demonstrated a higher rate of devoicing than the older generation. However, in the Kantō region (of which Tōkyō is a prefecture), devoicing failed to show any generational differences. Note that this contradicts Hirayama's (1966) aforementioned findings, since the rate of devoicing in the Kantō region was high even in the older generation. Byun (2010) then conducted a real-time study to examine devoicing in five regions with 306 respondents for 120 words in 2006–2007. Through acoustic analyses, she showed that it was between the 1950s and the 1970s that the devoicing rate saw a significant increase.

Imai's (2004, 2010) meticulous work uncovered additional sociolinguistic dynamics of vowel devoicing. She investigated the social factors controlling vowel devoicing in Tōkyō Japanese. A total of 42 speakers from three age groups (young, middle-aged, and old) were interviewed, with each group containing males and females. Her multivariate analysis demonstrated a clear difference by style, with vowel devoicing more prevalent in a casual/informal style than in formal styles. However, what is most striking in her findings is the intersection between age and gender: young male speakers showed the highest frequency of vowel devoicing, while young female speakers showed the least. This trend was observed in both /i/ and /u/, but the gender difference was larger in /u/ than in /i/. Thus, it points to the fact that the age or generation differentiation claimed by Byun (2007, 2010) is not so simple—age and gender variables interact. The gender difference was also studied by Varden (2010) with ten speakers (six males and four females, ages 18 to 23). Through his analyses of the high vowels, he found that male speakers used more devoicing than female speakers.

Vowel devoicing in language acquisition

Vowel devoicing also displays interesting sociolinguistic patterns in language acquisition. Imaizumi, Fuwa & Hosoi (1999) focused on two regions in Japan (Tōkyō and Ōsaka) and collected data from 72 children, aged 4 to 5 (25 four-year-olds and 18 five-year-olds from Ōsaka and 15 four-year-olds and 14 five-year-olds from Tōkyō), and 37 adults (19 from Ōsaka and 18 from Tōkyō) as a control group. During the interviews, the child was asked to pronounce the names of four pictures in a natural way. It was found that the overall devoicing rates in adults and five-year-olds were significantly higher than that in the four-year-olds in Tōkyō, whereas no such difference was observed in Ōsaka. This result shows that the acquisition of vowel devoicing reaches the adult level by four to five years old.

Fais et al. (2010) targeted 10 monolingual Japanese-speaking mothers accompanied by 12-month-old infants. They collected data through 1) recording spontaneous speech between the mothers and infants who were communicating using picture books, 2) sentence-reading experiments by mothers, and 3) elicited tests to obtain spontaneous adult-directed speech. They found that mothers did not accommodate infants by changing the rate of vowel devoicing in their infant-directed speech. The mothers retained their usual vowel devoicing variability in both infant-directed and adult-directed speech.

Corpus studies of vowel devoicing

Speech corpora have been actively mobilized in sociophonetics-style vowel devoicing studies. Using the Corpus of Spontaneous Japanese (CSJ) developed and distributed by NINJAL containing 7.5 million words (about 660 hours of speech), Maekawa & Kikuchi (2005) computed the frequency of the devoicing of both high and non-high vowels and estimated the effects of the linguistic environments in both preceding and following consonants. In addition, they examined extralinguistic factors, such as speaking rate and laughter, claiming that laughter was an indicator that the casual style increased the devoicing rate. They also showed that simulated public speaking presented a significantly higher rate of devoicing than academic presentation speech.

Amino et al. (2018) utilized both academic presentation speech and simulated public speaking in the CSJ to examine the effect of speakers and their parents on vowel devoicing. Randomly choosing 226 speakers (163 males and 63 females) from the corpus, they first classified the speakers according to their exposure to frequently-devoicing dialects and infrequently-devoicing dialects based on the prefecture they lived in during childhood and on their mobility. Amino et al. (2018) found that speakers who devoice frequently tend to devoice consistently and that higher speech rate promotes devoicing. However, they failed to establish any effects of age, gender, or speakers' parents' dialectal background.

Perceptual studies

Relatively little is known about the perceptual attributes of vowel devoicing. To date, Morris (2010) has made the only attempt to fill this gap.

Using a recorded word list with devoiced and non-devoiced high vowels embedded in words with similar accentual patterns so that voicing could be the only key for disambiguation, Morris (2010) examined how speakers of Tōkyō and Kinki dialects use devoicing variation to make judgments of a speaker's region. She first established that a close examination of the previous studies (Sugitō 1969, 1988a; Yoshioka 1981; Tahara 1998; Fujimoto 2004) on vowel devoicing in Kinki area shows that, contrary to widespread belief, the region's vowel devoicing rate is not very different from that in Tōkyō, at least in the environments where devoicing is most frequent (Morris 2010:193). The result of the experiment shows, however, that respondents' strategy in identifying dialects principally comes from stereotypes that vowel devoicing is a feature of the Tōkyō dialect. The age distribution shows a mild age-grading, with the youngest and the oldest less associated with the expected judgments (i.e., Tōkyō respondents judging devoiced tokens as being from the same region, and Kinki respondents judging voiced tokens as being from the same region) than with the middle-aged respondents. In terms of gender, female respondents are more associated with the expected response, suggesting that they are more sensitive to voicing status. Morris convincingly demonstrated that these two social differentiations point to the standardness of vowel devoicing.

Lexical pitch accents, intonation, and other prosodic variables

Japanese is a tone language that exploits a dichotomous pitch accent (high and low) associated to each mora in a word for semantic distinction. In one type of the dialect, the accented dialect, the accentual pattern of the whole word is determined by the location of the nucleus, the previous mora before the pitch fall. Thus, in standard Japanese (SJ), where the first and second mora have a different pitch level, once the pitch drops, all the remaining morae are low pitched. For example, the accentual pattern of the word *atama* 'head' (LHL) is predictable given the knowledge that the nucleus is at the mora *ta*. In words with no nucleus (unaccented), the first mora is low, followed by high morae. The nucleus location and the rules governing the accentual pattern show a large dialectal difference. In another type of the dialect, the accentless dialect, the word does not have any fixed accentual pattern, and the actual accentual pattern is determined by the context. Interactions of such an intricate system with the sentential pitch pattern (intonation) exhibit rich and diverse prosodic variation by dialect, speech style, sex, and the age of the speaker. As such, prosody is one of the central topics in Japanese phonetic/phonological research.

Researchers began working on instrumental studies of the physical properties of Japanese speech sounds in the early to mid-twentieth century (see Sugitō 1982:26–30 for a review). In the 1970s, a series of pitch accent studies of Japanese dialects (e.g., Ōsaka Japanese) were conducted by several pioneering researchers who fully adopted acoustic measurements (Fujisaki & Sudō 1971; Fujisaki, Mitsui & Sugitō 1974). These studies not only analyzed speech production data but also used speech synthesis techniques to investigate native speakers' perceptions of pitch variability along with duration and intensity as variables.

Such a tradition was carried over to Japanese sociophonetics, where—in contrast to sociophonetic traditions in other languages—prosody has been an extremely popular topic. As is usual with such a popular theme, the literature in this area diverged into numerous strands. We divide this work into six strands: (in)stability of prosodic variables within and over individuals, changes in the prosodic systems, speech style, interaction between accent and intonation, paralinguistic aspects of prosody, and pragmatics/politeness.

(In)stability of prosodic variables within and over individuals

Earlier Japanese sociophonetic research shed light on intraspeaker variability in both the production and perception of lexical accents as differentially influenced by acoustic properties of speakers' native dialects. Sugitō's series of investigations (Sugitō, Nakatsuka & Takahashi 1974; Sugitō 1978, 1982) demonstrated that speakers of the Nagasaki dialect, which has relatively leveled realizations of pitch rises and falls across accented/unaccented morae, were more likely to be unstable both in their production and perceptions of pitch accents than speech in the Ōsaka dialect, which has more distinctive pitch movements.

Instrumental analyses of (in)stability in pitch accents have led to an intriguing typology of regional dialects in Japan in conjunction with style and linguistic change. By integrating the preceding findings on dialect-linked (in)stability in Japanese pitch accent phenomena, Sugitō (1988b) provided a more generalized typology based on seven regional dialects nationwide through her analysis of data from ten speakers each from Sendai, Tōkyō, Nagoya, Ōsaka, Kōchi, Okayama, and Kumamoto. Her typology divided these varieties into three major regional types of pitch accents: Tōkyō, Nagoya, and Okayama belong to the Tōkyō-accent type; Sendai and Kumamoto to the "accentless" type; and Ōsaka and Kōchi to the Kinki-region accent type. Based on read-aloud materials beyond the isolated word level (i.e., a weather forecast with 70 accentual phrases [AP]), she measured "linguistic distance from Tōkyō Japanese" (i.e., total points of pitch accent similarity with Tōkyō Japanese) and "stability in production of pitch accents" (derived from subjects' repeated reading of a passage; Sugitō 1988b:144). The results illustrated that the subjects' pitch accent patterns were found to be increasingly similar to those of Tōkyō Japanese (average of 68.6 pts out of 70) in the ascending order of Ōsaka (8.9), Kōchi (22.2), Sendai (36.8), Kumamoto (37.9), Okayama (57.0), and Nagoya (63.9). Thus, the aforementioned accent-type typology is further substantiated by her instrumental analyses but can be modified with discrete regional gradiences within each accent type. As for pitch accent stability, the subjects of the accentless type (i.e., Sendai and Kumamoto) were found to be the most unstable, whereas those of Tōkyō, Nagoya, and Okayama were highly stable, and those of Ōsaka were also found to be relatively stable despite its low scores of distance from Tōkyō Japanese. The subjects from Kōchi, in contrast, were found to be intermediately stable involving younger female speakers in particular leading the standardization of pitch accents to the Tōkyō type.

The significance of these findings is twofold. First, they point to a sociophonetic fact that speakers who have not acquired distinctive regional types of pitch accents are likely to have difficulty reproducing identical pitch accents in relatively formal style of speech—namely, they may "sound different" when engaging in a reading task, even in their native dialect. Furthermore, at least in this particular style, regionally differentiated degrees of pitch accent "distinctiveness" (and related productive [in]stability) could be a sociophonetic factor that differentially determines the course of linguistic change. That is, speakers of more distinct pitch accents with productive stability are likely to maintain their native dialect patterns, whereas those of less distinct ones with productive instability are likely to shift to a change-in-progress (e.g., the Tōkyō-accent type).

Changes in the prosodic systems

It has been pointed out that prosody is deeply engraved in one's competence from the earlier stages of first-language acquisition and is thus impervious to change (Chambers 2003). While regional dialects in Japan have been subjected to nationwide standardization over the past half-century, it has also been found that changes in prosodic features (including lexical accents) tend to be preserved (NINJAL & the Institute of Statistical Mathematics 2013; Takano 2021). The stubbornness of the prosodic system against language change may be related to the fact that the prosodic system is closely intertwined with such other subsystems as phonetics, phonology, morphology, and syntax. This might prevent the prosodic system from making any swift change, perhaps except for a minor change of accentual pattern of specific words.

Despite its stubbornness against change, there are empirical studies documenting changes in the prosodic systems in the Japanese language. Thus, to identify prosodic properties that contribute to "sounding local," Kōri (2004a, 2004b, 2005) examined the read-aloud speech of an experimentally designed sentence (*Kyo'nen Na'ra-no mo'miji-o Yu'mi-to mi'ta* '[I] saw maples in Nara with Yumi last year') elicited from younger speakers from seven cities throughout Japan (i.e., five to eight speakers each from Tōkyō, Akita [Tōhoku region], Nagoya, Ōsaka, Kōchi [Shikoku region], Hiroshima [Chūgoku region], and Fukuoka [Kyūshū region]). Exploiting the multidimensional scaling of f0 and duration, Kōri found that: 1) the range of f0 (particularly in *Nara-no momiji* 'maples in Nara') was widest in Tōkyō Japanese; 2) pitch accents (given to *momiji* and *mita* 'saw') were unlikely to be weakened in Ōsaka and Kōchi Japanese; 3) the f0 peak (of *Nara-no*) came earlier (thus, fell earlier) in Ōsaka Japanese; 4) the utterance duration tended to be longer in Hiroshima, Kōchi, and Akita Japanese; and 5) VOT of [k] (in *kyonen* 'last year') was longer in Akita and shorter in Kōchi Japanese. He then devised a four-way grouping of the dialects examined: 1) Tōkyō, 2) Ōsaka, 3) Hiroshima, Kōch, Akita, and 4) Nagoya and Fukuoka.

Inoue (1997) and Heffernan (2006) represent an approach to changes in prosodic systems that take into account social meanings of particular variables under investigation. Focusing on a phrase-final rising intonation in narratives, which conveys such social meanings as "insincere," "overdependent," and "immature," Inoue (1997) characterized acoustic traits as stemming from the violation of the listener's expectation of a natural pitch declination. Inoue also proposed various discourse-pragmatic functions that could be cross-linguistically shared with similar phenomena in other languages (e.g., high rising terminal contour in Australian English or uptalk in American English).

Heffernan (2006) attempts to shed light on lexical accent changes under the influence of standardization in those exceptional circumstances of language shift involving obsolescent Okinawan and incoming Japanese in the Yaeyama area of Okinawa prefecture. His multivariate analyses of 14 words read aloud by 92 Okinawan subjects and their demographic background displays the intriguing interplay between the acquisition of pitch contours of SJ and speakers' identity work. Overall, the results indicated that younger, more educated, female Okinawans tended to produce more SJ patterns of pitch accents. However, there were notable gender-related discrepancies in systematic correlations between the types of pitch contours and speakers' social/demographic attributes. While the SJ rising contour was typically adopted by the youngest age group and by the "tourism/commerce occupational group," the falling non-SJ contour characteristic of older Okinawans' Japanese was harnessed ("recycled") especially by younger men as linguistic displays of revitalized Okinawan cultural identity.

Linguistic changes in prosody are not limited to standardization. Based on two dialects that hold mutually discrepant accentual systems (Hokkaidō and Kagoshima), Takano & Ota (2017) empirically confirmed Sibata's (1978) introspective comment on a prosodic change-in-progress: flattening of sentential pitch (i.e., smaller degrees of ups and downs of f0 over successive accentual phrases) in the speech of younger generations. Analyzing two styles of speech (participants reading sentences out of context and participants describing a short story composed of six-framed pictures), they revealed that the younger generation from Hokkaidō and Kagoshima spoke uniformly in phonetically flattened realizations of pitch (demarcated by the intonation phrase) (Venditti 1995) accompanied by consistent, steeper declination due to less dynamic f0 movement than their older control groups. Furthermore, as illustrated in Figure 24.2, younger speakers' naturalistic speech, elicited spontaneously from a picture story description, involved more frequent occurrences of mergers (dephrasing) of successive unaccented accentual phrases, regardless of their native dialects. In Figure 24.2, an inherently unaccented accentual phrase /hangaku de/ 'at half price,' which would be generally realized as an independent accentual phrase in read-aloud materials, intonationally does not constitute an independent accentual phrase (indicated by Break Index 2-) but merges with its immediately following accented accentual phrase /uraretei'ru no o/ 'that (the clothes) were being sold' as a single accentual phrase.

The social meanings of flattened sentential pitch were also explored using a matched-guise experiment with 156 college students (77 from Sapporo and 70 from Kagoshima). The results demonstrated that identical speakers with synthesized flattened pitch contours tended to be judged as sounding younger than their original voices (Ota & Takano 2007, 2014).

Speech style and register

While most early Japanese sociophonetic literature was concerned with regional variability in lexically assigned pitch accents and was thus obliged to focus on controlled speech materials (e.g., read-aloud speech), there have also been rigorous attempts to approximate natural speech production as much as possible (e.g., Umeda 1982). Sugitō (1982), for example, examined stylistic variability in the production of Ōsaka Japanese-specific patterns of lexical accents and demonstrated that the use of pictures rather than reading target words in isolation yielded the speakers' clearer distinctions of the accentual patterns. Sugitō (1983) also highlighted the artificial effects of production tasks on phonetic variability, in that the researcher's overt instructions heavily affected how words were accented.

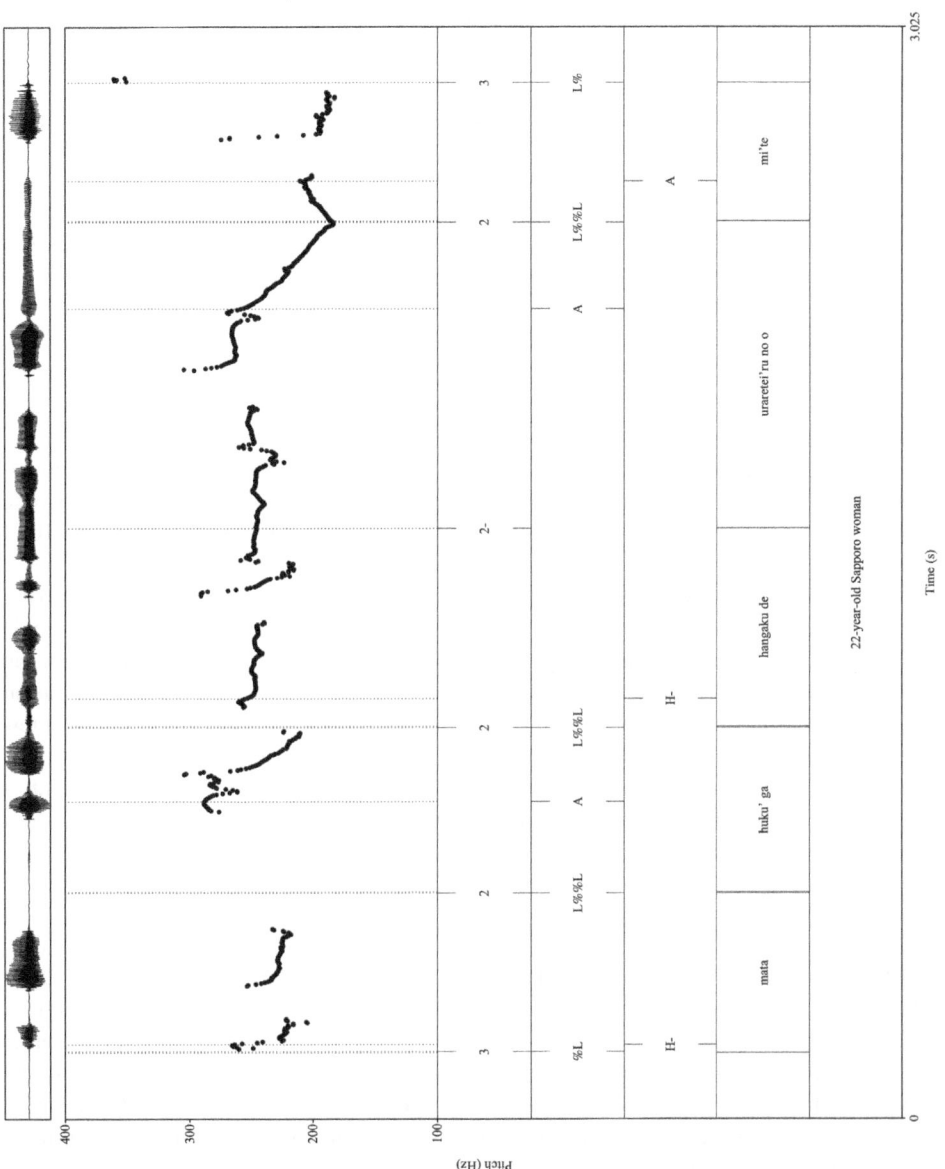

Figure 24.2 Dephrasing by a 22-year-old female Sapporo subject in the picture story-telling task: /mata/ /huku' ga/ /hangaku de/ /uraretei'ru no o/ /mi'te/ ˊAlso, (she) noticed the clothes were being sold at half price'

Source: adapted from Takano & Ota 2017:24

Some Japanese sociophonetics researchers are also concerned with pitch/intonational variability specific to some registers. Thus, Shirota (1999) investigated the acoustic characteristics of "comprehensibility" (i.e., listeners' subjective judgment on the degree of ease in processing information delivered) in news reading through perception experiments involving 36 college students from the Tōkyō and Ōsaka regions. Her results showed that dynamic f0 movement and the appropriate placement and length of pause at syntactic boundaries are the keys to enhancing listeners' perceptions of comprehensibility.

Kōri (2005) discussed diachronic changes in the prosodic characteristics of news reading in Japanese society. His instrumental analyses of actual broadcast news recordings made during the past approximately 70 years show that news reading on the radio up to the 1940s characteristically involved rapid enunciation and consistently high f0 (around 200 Hz for male speech) with relatively smaller degrees of f0 rises and falls. However, news reading (broadcast primarily on television since the 1950s) is produced at a slower pace and gains a relatively lower average of f0 involving more dynamic shifting movement. He pointed out that news reading today has become faster in pace with dynamic f0 movement.

A Japanese sociophonetic study of the speech style/register that strictly adopts the variationist framework of analysis is found in Takano (2002, 2008). Using naturally occurring interactions from three registers (telephone conversations, televised debates, and broadcast news), he demonstrated systematicity in variable prosodic focus on the Japanese negative *nai* (i.e., *nai* as a negative adjective, as in Figure 24.3, and -*nai* as a verbal suffix—e.g., *kamawanai* 'don't mind'). Figure 24.3 presents an example of the negative adjective in which prosodic focus was identified in terms of pitch reset given to *nai* (e.g., *anma NA'I jan*) based on the ToBI coding scheme.

Takano's results demonstrated that apparent prosodic variability observed in naturally occurring interactions was constrained in an orderly way by a number of intersecting factors. These include the type of negative—for example, the verbal suffix, which is perceptually less salient than the negative adjective, is more likely to be given prosodic focus as communicative compensation in political debates and news readings than in telephone conversations. They also include interactional allowance of "disagreeing with someone" that hierarchically differs among these social situations (debates > news > telephone conversations in descending order) and the types of interactive footing implicated by the negative (e.g., informative, supportive to the addressee, humorous, agreeable, etc.; cf. Yaeger-Dror 1996).

Interaction between accent and intonation

Kikuo Maekawa, who conducted a sociophonetic-style study in the 1980s by proposing a novel statistical test to check vowel mergers using the geometrical relations between the two vowels from dialectal speech in three styles (reading syllabic letters, reading sentences, and natural discourse) (Maekawa 1989), joined Kakenhi projects in the 1990s. He then set out to analyze intonational patterns in various dialects in a phonological framework (Pierrehumbert & Beckman 1988), which was state-of-the-art at that time (Maekawa 1990, 1994). He compared the intonational patterns of two accentless dialects (Fukui and Kumamoto). Although the accent of a word is the main determinant of intonation in accented dialects, accentless dialects lack a lexically specified tone; hence, phrasal, sentential, and discourse factors determine the intonation in those dialects. A critical point is that while previous studies on those accentless dialects were restricted to the lexical level, he departed from tradition and focused analyses on syntactic and discourse levels. The departure

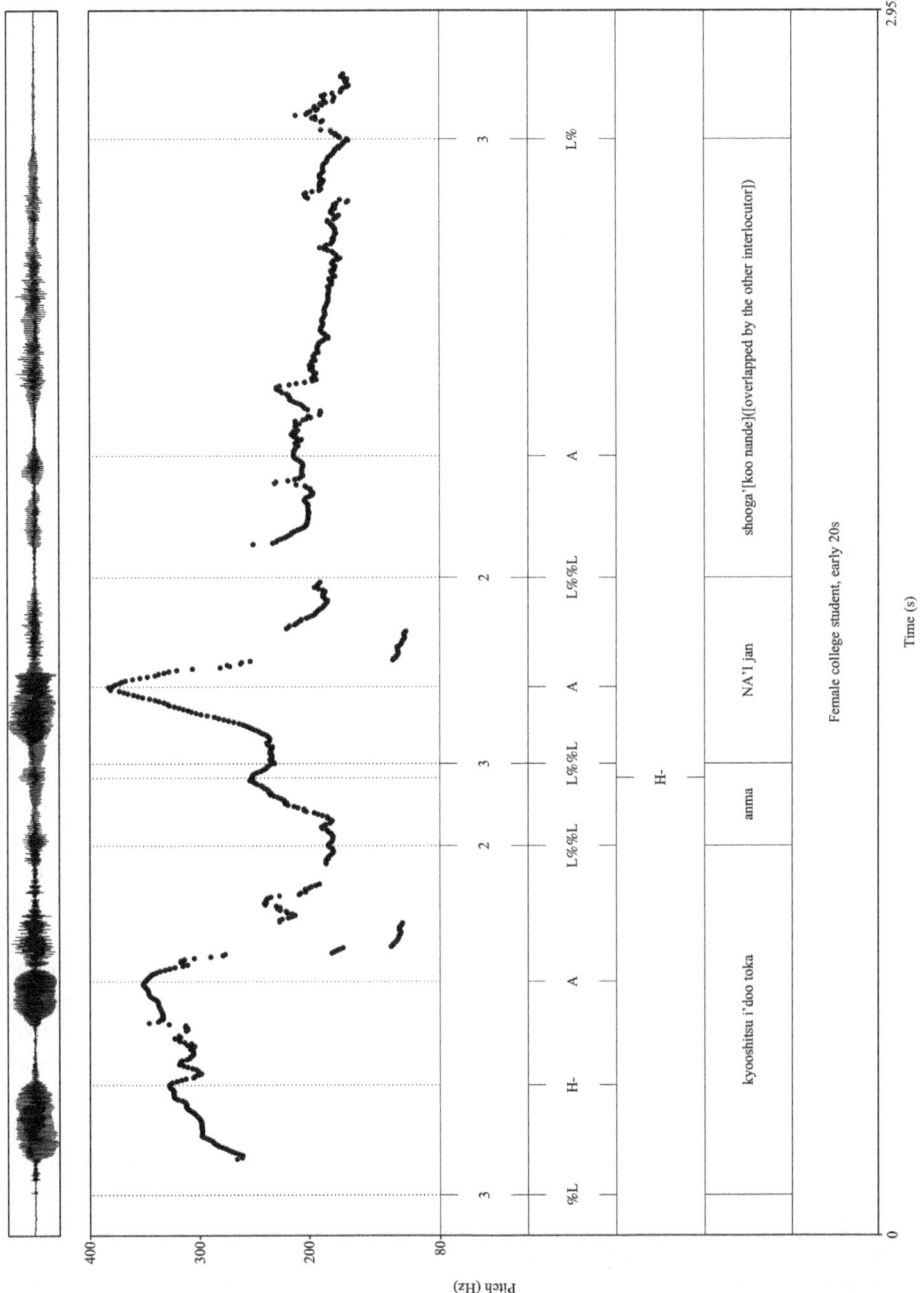

Figure 24.3 Prosodic focus on Japanese negative adjective *nai* in a telephone conversation: /kyooshitsu i'doo toka//anma/NA'I jan//shooga'koo nande/ 'There are NOT so many classroom changes because (it's) an elementary school, right?'

Source: adapted from Takano 2008:298

from data from reading experiments enabled him to demonstrate that although the dialects of Fukui, Kumamoto, and Tōkyō are geographically far apart, the three dialects behave similarly in reflecting syntactic and discourse information in intonational patterns.

More recently, Kōri's (2007) analysis of spontaneous conversational data in Tōkyō Japanese revealed that the weakening of lexical accents due to phonological downstep (Pierrehumbert & Beckman 1988; Kubozono 1989) could be a phenomenon specific to a particular style, such as read-aloud speech. Similarly to Umeda (1982), Kōri argued that the accentual weakening should rather be interpreted as a "marked" phenomenon in natural everyday speech production. As mentioned earlier, f0 declination also seems to involve age-related as well as stylistic dimensions of variability (Takano & Ota 2017).

Paralinguistic aspects of prosody

The third era of Japanese sociophonetics research expanded its scope of inquiry to the pragmatic and paralinguistic dimensions of language use. Miyatake & Sagisaka (1990) conducted perhaps the first Japanese sociophonetics study of affect and prosody correlates. Their analysis of narrative reproductions of a conversational script in diverse manners of communication (e.g., hasty, angry, polite, hesitant, etc.) proved that polite speech lasted longer, typically with a high f0 rise at the end of questioning, whereas angry speech maintained f0 with little declination to the end of sentences and incorporated a sudden high f0 leap immediately after plosives. As expected, hasty speech involved a shorter duration with relatively smaller degrees of declination. In general, f0 varied meaningfully in response to diverse ways of talking in Japanese.

Similarly, Sugitō (1992) discussed the paralinguistic functions of intonational contours given to identical utterances with various affects, such as blame, kindness, sympathy, and exclamation. In general, the timing of pitch changes, the temporal assignment of rise or fall to specific segments of speech, and their shifting degrees were all responsible for evoking different affective meanings. Kōri (2005) further confirmed the systematic correlations between the speaker's affect and the acoustic properties of speech. His perception experiment of a news passage read aloud in eight different vocal tones: 1) calm, 2) frantic, 3) tense, 4) very joyous, 5) grievous, 6) polite, 7) rude, and 8) ordinary revealed that native Japanese listeners tended to identify those tones of voice relying primarily on average f0 and its movement, pace/duration, and pause, which interacted with one another differentially depending on those different tones of voice.

Mori, Maekawa & Kasuya (2014) conducted a thorough analysis of paralinguistic information conveyed in Japanese speech from multiple perspectives. They claimed that a variety of acoustic variables (duration, pitch range, phrase-initial high tone, f0 falls, phrase-final pitch contours, vowel formants, and phonation) simultaneously and differentially contributed to the transmission of specific paralinguistic information in Japanese speech production. Six diverse types of paralinguistic information—doubt, admiration, disappointment, emphasis, indifference, and neutrality—were closely examined. Their results revealed that paralinguistic information, such as "admiration," "disappointment," and "doubt," tended to be transmitted to native listeners more successfully than to others and that various types (e.g., admiration, disappointment) resorted to different sets of variables in systematic ways (e.g., extremely long duration with breathy phonation). A question awaiting examination is how Sugitō's and Mori, Maekawa & Kasuya's findings relate to similar phenomena in other languages.

Pragmatics/politeness

The sentence-final position in Japanese language carries modal information as a head-final language, where the verbal part is situated sentence-finally. Kōri (1997) proposed four types of interplay between intonational contours and modality based on the pragmatic aspects of utterance-final intonational contours in naturalistic conversation: 1) rising contours evoke the speaker's requestive intent to receive responses, 2) emphatic rising contours evoke the speaker's persistent insistence, 3) rapid falling contours evoke the speaker's sense of unpredictability, and 4) rising-falling contours evoke the speaker's intent to urge certain actions. Such pragmatic meanings of intonation and its acoustic correlates have been perceptually confirmed by follow-up studies that examined how native speakers perceive differentially synthesized pitch contours on the sentence-final particle (SFP) *-ne* (Inukai 2001; Moriyama 2001; Sugitō 2001).

As a conveyor of pragmatic meaning, the SFP shows interesting interactions with prosody. Analyzing the Kumamoto dialect, which is a typical accentless dialect with a rich repertoire of SFPs as the marker of politeness (e.g., *-na*, *-to*, and *-ya*), Maekawa, Maki & Yoshioka (1999) examined the interdependence of intonational variability and SFPs. They also looked at generational changes in the relative weights of the two variables in the recognition of polite speech by four age groups of Kumamoto dialect speakers (older, middle-aged, college, and junior high students). They revealed that intonational patterns and SFPs contributed independently to their recognition of politeness. Rising pitch generally enhanced native listeners' perceptions of politeness more strongly than falling pitch did, but in the order of early rising with greater magnitude of prominence than late rising with smaller magnitude of prominence. Meanwhile, only older listeners tended to judge different degrees of politeness, primarily resorting to the types of SFPs. In contrast, younger listeners tended to take advantage of pitch prominence as perceptual cues to evaluate polite speech, neutralizing such distinctions encoded by SFPs. Thus, they managed to capture a rare case of clear generational changes in progress concerning prosody and pragmatics.

Among the topics in pragmatics, politeness is one of the most studied areas in Japanese sociophonetics. Based on previous findings on correlations between politeness and its acoustic properties in speech, Kawano (1995) specifically investigated whether either f0 or duration (or both) contributed to polite speech and, if so, their relative significance. His analyses of production data elicited from speakers of three regional dialects (Tōkyō, Ōsaka, and Nagoya), who produced short phrases in three styles (polite, rude, and ordinary), indicated that polite speech tended to involve a longer duration with a high maximum f0 peak, but there were some dialectal differences in the relative significance of the variables. His analyses of native speakers' perceptions of synthesized speech with varied duration and f0 peaks also demonstrated that longer duration and higher f0 peaks both contributed to their perceptions of politeness, although the former favored it more strongly. There were, however, some dialect-associated dimensions of people's perceptions of politeness. While the ratings by Tōkyō dialect listeners were affected more strongly by duration, those by Ōsaka and Nagoya dialect listeners were affected more strongly by maximum f0 peaks.

Voice quality

Voice quality (VQ) is the long-term characteristic of a person's voice resulting from the configuration of the vocal apparatus (Podesva 2007; Esling et al. 2019; Davidson this volume). In this domain of research, both linguists and researchers in speech information processing have made notable contributions. Regarding linguistics, Maekawa & Nishikawa (2019) claimed that VQ is a phonetic feature inherent to the speaker, which is stably observed in individuals in particular linguistic communities, although it also offers a broad range of research issues related to voice, such as dysphonia, emotion, and politeness. Phonation is constrained by the physiological conditions arising from the physical characteristics of a speaker. However, some VQ features, such as pitch range or breathiness, are manipulable to some extent by speakers (Podesva & Kajino 2014) for some purposes, for example, to construct gender identities. The acoustic characteristics of VQ are generally observed in three phonetic domains, frequency, energy, and spectral slope, by measuring values of parameters, such as f0, loudness, Harmonic to Noise Ratio (HNR), H1-H2, H1-A3, Cepstral Peak Prominence (CPP), and Hammarberg index (e.g., Keating 2014; Eyben et al. 2015).

Among a large number of contributions to VQ (e.g., Teshigawara 2003; Takano, Takezawa & Takeuchi 2014; Kawahara 2016; Utsugi et al. 2019; Wang 2019), Starr (2015) and Kajino (2014) made impressive discoveries from the variationist perspective. These studies examined how female speakers construct, maintain, or reinvent gender identities, in either real or fictional worlds, by controlling acoustic characteristics.

Starr (2015) discusses the socio-pragmatic functions of "Sweet Voice," a distinctive vocal style recognized in anime or public announcement, which works as "a marker of authenticity in the construction of linguistic style" (2015:1). To examine the acoustic properties produced by ten voice actors, she took the vowel /a/ and measured the values of acoustic parameters, such as H1-H2, 2k-4k, CPP, and HNR, for breathiness and f0 for pitch. The results of the inter- and intra-speaker comparisons between sweet and non-sweet voices indicate that a breathy, resonant, and tense voice sounds sweet, although unexpectedly accompanied by a relatively low pitch. Starr reminds that it provides "authenticity to feminine gender performance" (2015:20) when it is used together with other linguistic forms, such as "Japanese woman's language," a cultural category characterized by a set of linguistic features, which works as a prescribed norm for indexing traditional femininity, for example, "soft," "nonassertive," and "gentle" (Sunaoshi 2004; Inoue 2006).

Ryōsai kembo, "good wife, wise mother," is a widely established femininity in Japanese society under a hegemonic gender ideology, but the gender identity of Japanese women is not monolithic. Demonstrating that 47 young females from three metropolitan regions (Tōkyō, Kyōto, and Ōsaka) show striking differences in using phonetic features, Kajino (2014:254) argued that her speakers "produce gendered figures that typify particular geographic regions while negotiating the regional stereotypes." A close examination of the cross-regional and intra-regional patterns of phonetic feature use showed how young women adopt specific linguistic styles in social practices to display themselves as the gendered figures that they wish to portray.

Breathiness is also one of the key features for Kajino's discussion. Her speakers from Kyōto were more likely to use breathy voices with low intensity and high pitch than Tōkyō and Ōsaka speakers, so that they could represent a "soft," "feminine," and "classy" image of the Kyōto variety. Furthermore, she explored individual stylistic practices of her speakers and revealed how they control breathiness to construct femininities that they want to realize, in combination with other phonetic features (f0, pitch range, speech rate, and final lengthening of intonation phrase). Breathiness connotes an image of mature femininity, such as a motherly or gentle adult. However, the image would be significantly different depending on the value of f0. For instance, a breathy voice with higher f0 indexes a traditionally ideal woman (*ryōsai kembo*). However, when used together with a lower f0, it can emphasize being bold or strong rather than soft or sensitive (Kajino 2014:229–230; see also Ohara 1997). In addition, the combination of a less breathy voice and higher f0 with wide pitch range indexically indicates a childish or immature femininity like cute anime characters.

Starr's and Kajino's projects provide evidence that not only professional voice actors but ordinary people are aware of the social meaning of VQ and develop their linguistic styles against sociocultural backdrops of gender ideology. For example, previous studies, such as Ohara (1992, 1997, 2004) and Yuasa (2008), have reported that Japanese females' pitch behavior (e.g., using higher pitch or wider pitch range than males) conforms to social expectations of gender image. VQ can be indexical, even if changes occur in ideologies concerning language, gender, or other social conditions. Repeated use of certain types of vocal styles in socially meaningful contexts, whether in media or in real life, establishes the authenticity of voice associated with a particular character or figure, even if male roles are performed by female professional voice actor (*seiyūs*) (cf. Redmond 2016).

CASE STUDY   The voice of anime as a representation of cuteness in voice quality

Anime is one of the most well-known genres of Japanese popular culture. The voice of anime, dubbed by a *seiyū*, is generally recognized as *anime-goe* ('anime voice') with a distinctive auditory image evoked by particularity of phonetic features—for example, in f0, pitch range, intonation, speech rate, and timbre of voice (Ishii & Itō 2019). There are several types of voices whose acoustic characteristics fit personal images of characters, such as hero, villain, mother, and old man. Among them is the voice of a *kawaii* ('cute') girl.

However, previous studies of the anime voice with (socio)linguistic interests, such as those by Teshigahara (2003) and Starr (2015), did not concern the kawaii voice. Kawahara (2016), by contrast, examined *moe* voice, an attribute of kawaii characters connected with childish cuteness, but only in terms of intonation and intensity.

Here, we shed light on the voice quality of cute or kawaii girls in anime and provide tips to consider anime voice in broader cultural contexts. As Starr (2015) did, we investigate VQ of the vowel /a/ which is often preferred in the study of phonation and ascertain what acoustic characteristics the cute voice has in voice acting performance (Iseli, Shue & Alwan 2007). Results of acoustic analyses shown in the following sections were first reported in Ota, Utsugi & Ota (2021). We present some additional results on formant data and explore how cute voice is phonetically represented.

Methods

The data for the analyses are digitally recorded speech of female characters performed by 11 female students in their early 20s. The speakers were students of a voice actor course at a music college in Tōkyō Metropolitan Area. Many of them had professional experience dubbing anime. At the data collection, they played four different types of characters: a gentle adult woman or older sister (coded as "ordinary"), a strong, bold type like a woman warrior ("brave"), a sexually neutral or immature girl ("boyish"), and a kawaii girl ("cute"). When acting out characters, the speakers were asked to perform different tasks (sentence reading, passage reading, and dubbing) and 15-minute informal interviews were conducted to collect tokens in a natural setting.

Of the collected speech data, 4942 tokens of the vowel /a/ from passage reading and dubbing were analyzed using openSMILE, a program for VQ analysis, in which 18 acoustic parameters composing the Geneva Minimalistic Acoustic Parameter Set (GeMAPS) are measured (Eyben et al. 2015).

Analysis here focuses on acoustic parameters concerning formants (frequency and relative energy) and spectral slope, both of which would be involved in constructing the gender identity of characters.

Results

Representations of kawaii characters in formants

Figure 24.4 is a scatter plot of the trimmed mean values of the F1 and F2 frequencies for each character performed by the speakers. This figure indicates that there are trends in their performances to indicate differences among the characters via formant frequencies. The cute character appears in the higher frequency area. The brave appears in the lower area, and the ordinary and the boyish are placed in the middle. Given that similar trends for each character are observed across the actors, we could argue that manipulations of the first two formants are a shared Japanese social resource for actors to draw upon as they characterize stereotypical persons.

On the other hand, as shown in Figure 24.5, it is more difficult to discern the trends of F3 frequencies. However, it has been argued in previous studies that F3 could be an effective indicator for identifying individual speakers (Xu et al. 2013) or differentiating genders (Kasuya, Suzuki & Kido 1968). Therefore, it is quite possible that the speakers make use of some acoustic feature of this formant in their vocal performances—but perhaps do so in idiosyncratic ways. In Figure 24.6, the relative energies of formants of their performances are plotted in three dimensions. This clearly shows that the kawaii voice is the strongest in all the dimensions. Seiyūs have to distinguish characters through

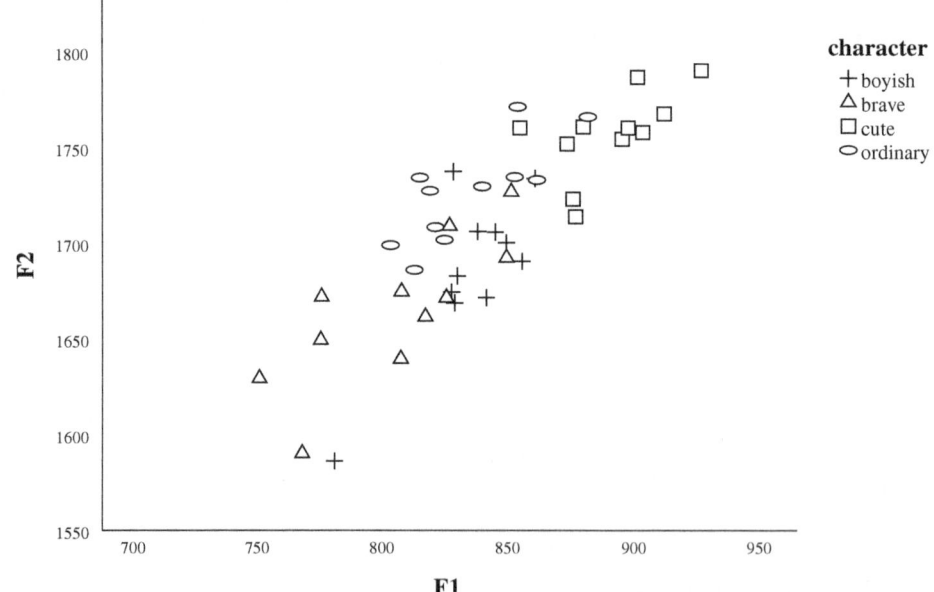

Figure 24.4 F1 and F2 frequencies for characters

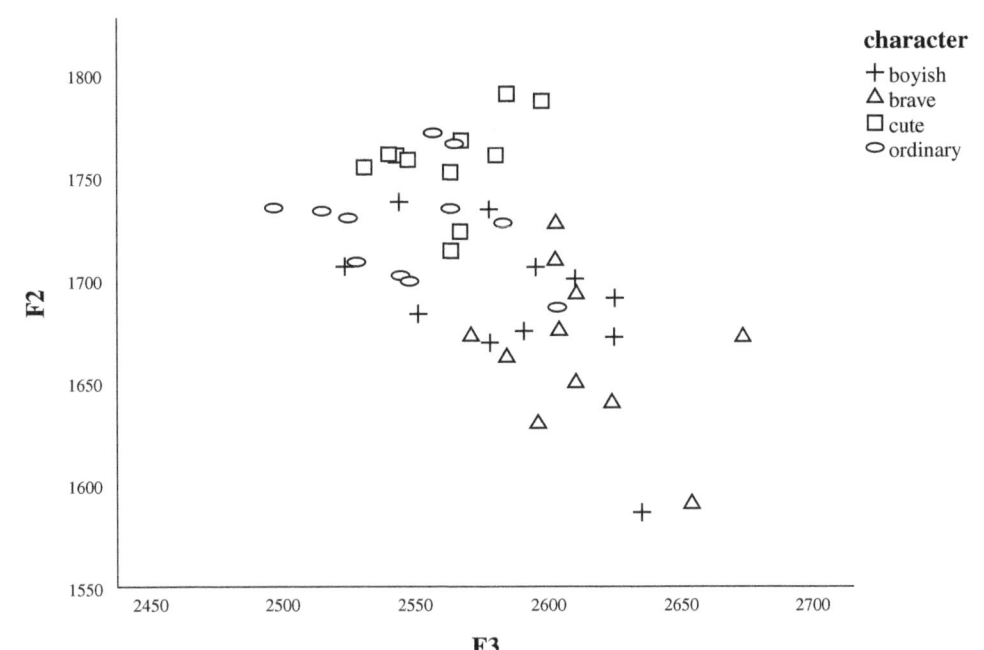

Figure 24.5　F2 and F3 frequencies for characters

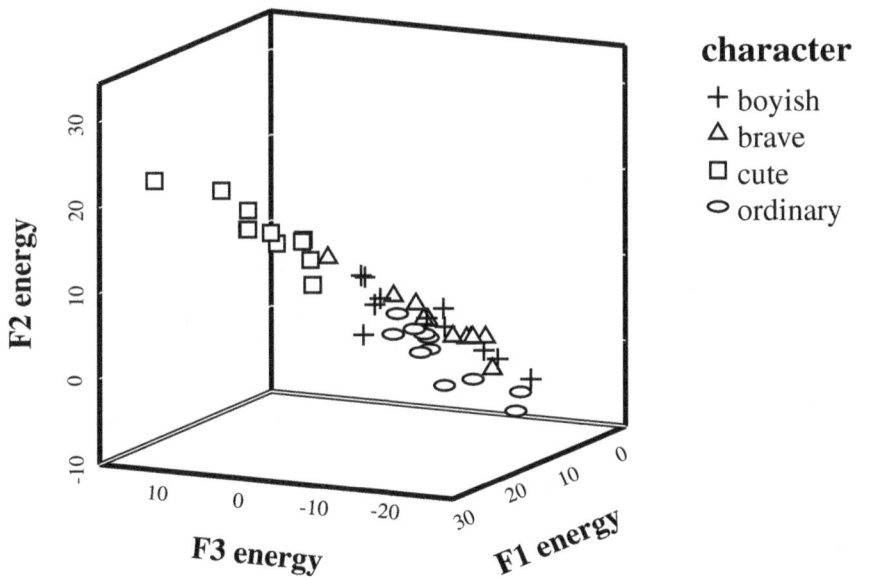

Figure 24.6　Formant energies for characters

auditory salience in acoustic features, although they can hardly change their physiological traits. This result indicates that, compared to the other three voices, the kawaii voice is articulated most distinctively with respect to the formant intensity. From these results, we can claim that cuteness of voice is characterized by higher F1 and F2 frequencies and stronger formant energy.

Representation of kawaii character in spectral slope

Next, we look at the characteristics of kawaii voice based on the measurements of spectral slope-related features. Table 24.1 presents the results of linear mixed regressions using Rbrul (Johnson 2009), with the values of each acoustic parameter as the dependent variable and "f0," "style" (dubbing and reading), and "character" (boyish, brave, cute, and ordinary) as independent variables. Since high

Table 24.1 Results of linear mixed regression

HNR (p = .29)			H1-H2 (p = .00503)		
character	mean	coef	character	mean	coef
cute	7.049	0.218	brave	2.035	1.582
ordinary	7.046	0.002	ordinary	1.351	0.354
boyish	7.067	-0.052	cute	0.688	-0.259
brave	6.703	-0.168	boyish	-0.128	-1.676
total.n df	intercept	grand.mean	total.n df	intercept	grand.mean
4942 8	3.593	6.946	4942 8	-15.014	1.059
Log likelihood: -15177.79		AIC: 30375.58	Log likelihood: -22560.47		AIC: 45140.94

H1-A3 (p < .0001)			alphaRatio (p < .0001)		
character	mean	coef	character	mean	coef
brave	13.278	3.919	cute	-0.086	1.808
boyish	13.781	1.257	boyish	-3.948	0.405
ordinary	11.926	-0.163	brave	-5.074	-1.077
cute	4.555	-5.013	ordinary	-6.566	-1.135
total.n df	intercept	grand.mean	total.n df	intercept	grand.mean
4941 8	-25.777	10.76	4942 8	-12.981	-3.777
Log likelihood: -20795.67		AIC: 41611.35	Log likelihood: -15439.49		AIC: 30898.97

Hammarberg Index (p < .0001)			F0 (semitone) (p < .0001)		
character	mean	coef	character	mean	coef
boyish	21.884	1.996	cute	41.09	1.171
brave	20.713	1.169	boyish	38.958	0.669
ordinary	19.456	-1.46	ordinary	37.391	-0.643
cute	15.624	-1.705	brave	36.92	-1.197
total.n df	intercept	grand.mean	total.n df	intercept	grand.mean
4942 8	26.947	19.343	4942 7	38.672	38.641
Log likelihood: -16513.77		AIC: 33047.54	Log likelihood: -16999.12		AIC: 34016.25

pitch is considered to be an attribute of a kawaii voice, f0 was analyzed as a dependent variable as well. In addition, the variable "speaker" was added as a random factor.

It has been argued that breathiness is closely related to gender representation (Podesva & Callier 2015). Previous studies, such as Ohara (2004) and Van Borsel·et al. (2009), associated a breathy voice with femininity and additional meanings, such as "traditional," "upper-class," "mature," and "sexual arousal" (cf. Kajino 2014). Therefore, it is possible that seiyūs will make use of a breathy voice to construct characters' gender identities.

The parameters related to breathiness here are HNR, H1-H2, and H1-A3. HNR is the measurement of the ratio between periodic and nonperiodic components of a speech sound (Fernandesa et al. 2018). The higher the value of this parameter, the smaller the amount of aperiodic noise—that is, less breathy. Despite the regression failing to reach statistical significance ($p = 0.29$), the result indicates that the cute voice is least breathy. As for H1-H2, the difference in the amplitude between the first and second harmonics, greater differences indicate greater breathiness. Here, H1-H2 is significantly predicted by character ($p = 0.005$). Cute has the second-lowest H1-H2 and a coefficient, indicating cute sounds less breathy than the brave and ordinary characters.

H1-A3 is the difference between the amplitudes of the first harmonic and F3. This acoustic measure correlates with the spectral tilt: the higher the parametric value, the steeper the spectral tilt. Breathier voice results in steeper spectral slope because the upper harmonics lose amplitude more quickly (Starr 2015:7). As shown in Table 24.1, the cute has the smallest mean H1-A3 and a negative coefficient. These results indicate that it is the breathiness that differentiates the cute girl from other types of femininity represented in, for example, Sweet Voice characters (Starr 2015) or *yamato nadeshiko*, a traditionally ideal type of Japanese woman (Sugihara & Katsurada 1999).

The other parameters related to the spectral slope are alpha ratio and Hammarberg index. Both are indicators of ratios with respect to energy. The alpha ratio is the ratio of the summed energy from 50–1000 Hz and 1–5 kHz, and the Hammarberg index is the ratio of the energy peak of 0–2 kHz to that of 2–5 kHz (Eyben et al. 2015). Higher values for alpha ratio and lower values for Hammarberg index are consistent with stronger energy in the upper frequency area. From the statistical results in Table 24.1, the highest alpha ratio and the lowest Hammarberg index are observed for the cute character. This suggests that the cute voice has an acoustic quality making the voice more ringing or resonant, like the so-called "Actor's Formant," which consists of a spectral peak in 3kHz region (Leino, Laukkanen & Radolf 2011; Schloneger 2014).

The final feature to be considered is the fundamental frequency, f0. Cute obtained the highest mean and coefficient among the four characters. This confirms the public awareness that high pitch is an attribute of cuteness (cf. Ohara 2019).

As Burdelski & Mitsuhashi (2010:66) state, *kawaii* is the word for people or things whose attributes can be described as being small, delicate, and immature. Moreover, Starr (2015:26) points out that what cuteness represents is a femininity of being "naïve and virtually asexual, rejecting the responsibilities of adulthood." Both are the social meanings of "kawaii," but the former corresponds to "(permanent) qualities" of cuteness, while the latter to the "stance" which a kawaii girl can take in real and/or media contexts. These are directly associated with linguistic forms, or in our case acoustic features, and work as a bridge toward identity construction (Nakamura 2020). We found that the voice quality of /a/ for a kawaii girl in seiyūs' performance consists of the following acoustic characteristics: higher frequency and stronger energy for formants, weak breathiness, ringing or resonant quality in the upper frequency region, and a high pitch. These acoustic features can be associated with the image of a person with kawaii attributes which are explicitly or implicitly presented in an indexical field (Eckert 2008). Seiyūs strategically manipulate acoustic features to construct a character's gender identity, just as people do in daily interaction.

Discussion

By exploring the acoustic quality of the vowel /a/, we have seen how a kawaii voice in anime can be constructed by manipulating acoustic parameters. Voice quality functions as an indexical of various types of individuality, including femininity. It should be noted that the social meanings of femininities constructed by VQ need to be interpreted with reference to gender ideologies. The relationship between femininity and VQ has often been discussed with reference to traditional stereotypes of gendered figures, such as *yamato nadeshiko* or *ryōsai kembo* (Sugihara & Katsurada 1999; Kajino 2014). These are still influential gender ideologies even in present-day Japanese society and have been repeatedly referenced in media texts, such as anime, manga, video games, and TV drama.

However, since the early 2000s, a gradual change in the meaning of femininity in media contents has emerged. Sugawa (2013:259) points out that the femininity of magical girls in the anime series *Pretty Cure* (or *PreCure*), which has been broadcast since 2004, has changed from the traditional princess type to "a true 'princess' with responsibility, determination and strength (as a representation of confidence)." The kawaii magical girls are changing their femininity toward heroic women not by the magical power gained through transformation but by the confidence they gain through battles, just as male hero characters in narratives do. This instance indicates that modern femininities in recent anime are represented as something that girls can achieve by negotiating with hegemonic ideologies of society.

Anime actors deploy VQ to index certain social meanings in the indexical field of the fictional world, and the constant association of voice quality with characters' identity construction in changing sociocultural situations would lead to newly establishing or reinventing sociolinguistic authenticity. This could in turn influence social/language practices of young female audiences in the real world. The media provide occasions for girls, or everyone, to face various problems around us and become more reflexive to overcome them. Therefore, sociohistorical perspectives of culture are indispensable when considering the indexical meaning of VQ in media contents. Corroborative works with related fields, such as media studies or popular culture studies, would bring about a promising change in methodology (cf. Ota, Utsugi & Ota 2021).

Conclusion: New horizons

We turn our attention to the future to look for a new horizon in Japanese sociophonetic research. It would certainly be a daunting and bold task to make predictions. Instead, we make an attempt to explore some possibilities relying on hints that emerge from the contributions reviewed above.

The first hint is the use of the speech corpora. Although speech corpora have rapidly grown from the late 1980s (originally due to their demand from the speech processing sectors; Hirst 2013), they offer a treasure trove for researchers in sociophonetics: a large volume of data with high-quality recordings transcribed, parsed, and made searchable. If they come with such detailed sociolinguistic information as speakers' age, sex/gender, and social class, they would provide an ideal tool for sociophoneticians.

As described above, the Corpus of Spontaneous Japanese is one such ideal resource for sociophoneticians in Japanese. With its sheer volume and detailed annotations, the CSJ has inspired a number of sociophonetic papers (Maekawa, Maki & Yoshioka 1999; Okada 2004; Jeon 2014, to mention a few). However, although it was annotated with speaker's dialectal backgrounds, the information was insufficient for detailed dialectal research. In 2020, NINJAL released a dialectal corpus, the Corpus of Japanese Dialects (COJADS; searchable through NINJAL's interface *Chūnagon* at https://chunagon.ninjal.ac.jp), which has collected 4000 hours of discourse in local speeches covering 200 sites all over the country, with every utterance morphologically parsed. Although it has been used mainly for grammatical studies thus far, its large amount of high-quality recording data presents a tremendous opportunity for sociophonetic research.

The second hint is offered by the innovations taking place in variationist sociolinguistics around the world. The variationist research paradigm first reached Japan with Hibiya (1988), and it has brought a number of innovations in sociophonetic research in the country since then. The use of naturally occurring speech and the introduction of logistic regression analyses are just a few examples of the innovations that were not the usual practice of researchers in the field before Hibiya's work. The variationist paradigm and its innovations will continue to affect Japanese sociophonetics in the future, especially through groundbreaking research by scholars of Japanese in North American universities (e.g., Kajino 2014). The field of VQ that Kajino (2014) and Starr (2015) ventured into is a new, exciting arena of inquiry. The exploration will continue to deepen our understanding of the nature of the sociolinguistics of speech in the Japanese setting.

Kajino (2014) and Starr (2015) are all works from the so-called third wave of sociolinguistics. The third wave of sociolinguistics, which arose around the 2010s, puts emphasis on the agency of the language users and the social meaning of the variation (Eckert 2012). The movement also brought about the widening of the scope of variation studies—a fact reflected in examinations of suprasegmental features like voice quality. The VQ literature in Japanese is currently limited to sweet voice, Japanese women's language, and anime voice. Potential topics concerning VQ in contemporary Japanese sociocultural settings are much more wide-ranging. The VQ of lesbian, gay, bisexual, transgender, and queer/questioning speakers would be one such promising research direction (Redmond 2018). The program suggested in Sadanobu's (2015, 2021) line of research on the characters people play in everyday life and their linguistic manifestations is also appealing. Widening the scope of the study is not only a desideratum to the area, but it would combine the third-wave sociolinguistics and VQ research into a more fruitful integration.

Another obvious hint is prosody, which has been one of the central themes of Japanese sociophonetics. Given the rich variation in the prosodic system and the considerable literature, one can easily expect that it will remain a focus in the future. However, there is another reason why one would expect its future status: its resistance to linguistic changes. There is no room for doubt that the regional features of Japanese language have been exposed to standardization for more than half a century, and some features are leveled out in favor of the standard form. Nevertheless, prosodic features stubbornly exhibit regional differences. Moreover, regional dialects sometimes show inherent changes that are independent of the standardization process (Takano & Ota 2017). These facts strongly suggest that prosodic change will remain one of the main topics of Japanese sociophonetics.

In the final hint, we should not omit mentioning the discoveries that might be achieved through real-time studies in Japanese sociophonetics. We have already mentioned in our short review of the history of Japanese sociophonetics that NINJAL's standardization surveys have been expanded to include panel samples. Analysis of the panel data of the phonetic variation has been reported (NINJAL 1965, 1974, 1997, 2007; NINJAL & the Institute of Statistical Mathematics 2013), but, certainly, this will not be a sole contribution to the real-time studies. All the accumulated past sociophonetic datasets await re-studies to test hypotheses emerging from the real-time studies that became popular over the past 20 years (Sankoff 2013; Wagner & Buchstaller 2019). With a long history of research, this is definitely one of the contributions that Japanese sociophonetics could make.

One would envision that future Japanese sociophonetic study of prosody will not be a monotonic extension of the present. Rather, what would be expected is a fertile exchange of ideas or synergetic progress across different approaches. Corpus-based approaches to sociophonetic variation of prosody would be just one such example. The connection between prosodic change and pragmatics is already evident in Maekawa, Maki & Yoshioka's study (1999), and this is just one area where corpus-based studies could provide crucial data. Or what if such an approach was extended to real-time studies? These kinds of intersections of different approaches are a part of the Japanese sociophonetics landscape that one foresees over the hazy horizon above the past contributions we reviewed here.

Acknowledgments

We benefited from a discussion with Kikuo Maekawa on various parts of this article. All remaining errors are the authors'. We also acknowledge the financial aid from JSPS KAKENHI Grant Number 17K18485, 19H00531, 21K18116, 22K00557, and 22H00655. The authors also thank Akira Utsugi, Han Wang, Yoshitaka Ota, and Kōta Kanno for allowing us to present the results of the corroborative work with Ichiro Ota as the case study, which was first reported in 2021 at the 16th International Conference of the European Association for Japanese Studies. And we are very grateful to KADOKAWA, Konosuba Partners, the voice actor agencies Music Ray'n, Office Osawa, and 81 Produce, and Senzoku Gakuen College of Music for facilitating the research.

References

Akinaga, Kazue. 1966. Kyōtsūgo-no akusento. In Nihon Hōsō Kyōkai (ed.), *Nihongo hatsuon akusento jiten. Kaitei shinpan*, 174–231. Nihon Hōsō Shuppan Kyōkai.

Amino, Kanae, Hisanori Makinae, Toshiaki Kamada & Takashi Osanai. 2018. Reference data on Japanese vowel devoicing: Effects of speakers' and parents' places of origin and within-speaker reproducibility. *Acoustical Science and Technology* 39(3). 207–214. https://doi.org/10.1250/ast.39.207

Burdelski, Matthew & Kōji Mitsuhashi. 2010. "She thinks you're *kawaii*": Socializing affect, gender and relationships in a Japanese preschool. *Language in Society* 39(1). 65–93. https://doi.org/10.1017/S00474 04509990650

Byun, Hi-Gyung. 2007. Semaboin-no museika-no zenkokuteki chīkisa-to sedaisa. *Nihongo-no kenkyū* 3(1). 33–48. https://doi.org/10.20666/nihongonokenkyu.3.1_33

Byun, Hi-Gyung. 2010. Go chīki-ni miru museika seikiritsu-no nenreiteki henka. *Nihongo-no kenkyū* 6(4). 79–94. https://doi.org/10.20666/nihongonokenkyu.6.4_79

Chambers, J.K. 2003. *Sociolinguistic theory*, 2nd edn. Blackwell.

Eckert, Penelope. 2008. Variation and the indexical field. *Journal of Sociolinguistics* 12(4). 453–476. https://doi.org/10.1111/j.1467-9841.2008.00374.x

Eckert, Penelope. 2012. Three waves of variation study: The emergence of meaning in the study of variation. *Annual Review of Anthropology* 41. 87–100. https://doi.org/10.1146/annurev-anthro-092611-145828

Esling, John H., Scott R. Moisik, Allison Benner & Lise Crevier-Buchman. 2019. *Voice quality: The laryngeal articulator model*. Cambridge University Press. https://doi.org/10.1017/9781108696555

Eyben, Florian, Klaus R. Scherer, Björn W. Schuller, Johan Sundberg, Elisabeth André, Carlos Busso, Laurence Y. Devillers, Julien Epps, Petri Laukka, Shrikanth S. Narayanan & Khiet P. Truong. 2015. The Geneva minimalistic acoustic parameter set (GeMAPS) for voice research and affective computing. *IEEE Transactions on Affective Computing* 7(2). 190–202. https://doi.org/10.1109/TAFFC.2015.2457417

Fais, Laurel, Sachiyo Kajikawa, Shigeaki Amano & Janet F. Werker. 2010. Now you hear it, now you don't: Vowel devoicing in Japanese infant-directed speech. *Journal of Child Language* 37(2). 319–340. https://doi.org/10.1017/S0305000909009556

Fernandesa, Joana, Felipe Teixeira, Vitor Guedes, Arnaldo Junior, João Paulo Teixeira. 2018. Harmonic to Noise Ratio Measurement: Selection of window and length. *Procedia Computer Science* 138. 280–285. https://doi.org/10.1016/j.procs.2018.10.040

Fujimoto, Masako. 2004. Boinchō-to boin-no museika-no kankei: Tōkyō hōgen washa-to Ōsaka hōgen washa-no hikaku. *Kokugogaku* 55(1). 2–15.

Fujimoto, Masako. 2015. Vowel devoicing. In Haruo Kuzobono (ed.), *Handbook of Japanese phonetics and phonology*, 167–214. Mouton de Gruyter. https://doi.org/10.1515/9781614511984.167

Fujisaki, Hiroya & Hiroshi Sudō. 1971. Nihongo tango akusento-no kihonshūhasū patān-to sono seisei kikō-no moderu. *Nihon Okyō Gakkaishi* 27(9). 445–452.

Fujisaki, Hiroya, Yasuyoshi Mitsui & Miyoko Sugitō. 1974. Tōkyō oyobi Kinki hōgen-no nihaku tango akusento-no bunseki, gōsei oyobi chikaku. In Nihon onkyō gakkai onsei kenkyū īnkai (ed.), *Nihon onkyō gakkai onsei kenkyū īnkai shiryō*, S73–51.

Han, Mieko Shimizu. 1962. Unvoicing of vowels in Japanese. *Onsei-no Kenkyū* 10. 81–100.

Heffernan, Kevin. 2006. Prosodic leveling during language shift: Okinawan approximations of Japanese pitch-accent. *Journal of Sociolinguistics* 10(5). 641–666. https://doi.org/10.1111/j.1467-9841.2006.00299.x

Hibiya, Junko. 1988. *A quantitative study of Tokyo Japanese.* PhD dissertation, University of Pennsylvania.

Hibiya, Junko. 1995. The velar nasal in Tokyo Japanese: A case of diffusion from above. *Language Variation and Change* 7(2). 139–152. https://doi.org/10.1017/S0954394500000958

Hirayama, Teruo. 1966. Zen'nippon-no hatsuon-to akusento. In Nihon Hōsō Kyōkai (ed.), *Nihongo hatsuon akusento jiten. Kaitei shinpan.* 123–173. Nihon Hōsō Shuppan Kyōkai.

Hirayama, Teruo. 1968. *Nihon-no hōgen.* Kōdansha.

Hirst, Graeme. 2013. Computational linguistics. In Keith Allan (ed.), *The Oxford handbook of the history of linguistics*, 707–726. Oxford University Press. https://doi.org/10.1093/oxfordhb/9780199585847.013.0033

Imai, Terumi. 2004. *Vowel devoicing in Tokyo Japanese: A variationist approach.* PhD dissertation, Michigan State University.

Imai, Terumi. 2010. An emerging gender difference in Japanese vowel devoicing. In Dennis Preston & Nancy Niedzielski (eds.), *A reader in sociophonetics*, 177–187. Mouton de Gruyter. https://doi.org/10.1515/9781934078068.1.177

Imaizumi, Satoshi, Kiyoko Fuwa & Hiroshi Hosoi. 1999. Development of adaptive phonetic gestures in children: Evidence from vowel devoicing in two different dialects of Japanese. *Journal of the Acoustical Society of America* 106(2). 1033–1044. https://doi.org/10.1121/1.427113

Inoue, Fumio. 1997. Intonēshon-no shakaisei. In Miyoko Sugitō, Tetsuya Kunihiro, Hajime Hirose & Morio Kawano (eds.), *Nihongo onsei*, vol. 2, 143–168. Sanseidō.

Inoue, Miyako 2006. *Vicarious language: Gender and linguistic modernity in Japan.* University of California Press. https://doi.org/10.1525/9780520939066

Inukai, Takashi. 2001. Hikuku mijikaku tsuku shūjoshi "ne." In Onsei bunpō kenkyūkai (ed.), *Bunpō-to onsei*, 17–29. Kurosio Shuppan.

Iseli, Markus, Yen-Liang Shue & Abeer Alwan. 2007. Age, sex, and vowel dependencies of acoustic measures related to the voice source. *Journal of the Acoustical Society of America* 121(4). 2283–2295. https://doi.org/10.1121/1.2697522

Ishii, Saki & Katsunobu Itō. 2019. Taiwa onsei-ni okeru inritsu-to seishitsu-no tokuchō-o riyō shita paragengo jōhō-no chūshutsu-no kentō. Paper presented at the 81st conference of Information processing society of Japan.

Jeon, Miju. 2014. Nihongo Hanashikotoba Kōpasu-o mochīta dephrasing seiki kankyō-no bunseki: Shūshoku kankei oyobi mōrasū-no kōka. *Onsei kenkyū* 18(3). 1–13. https://doi.org/10.24467/onseikenkyu.18.3_1

Johnson, Daniel Ezra. 2009. Getting off the GoldVarb standard: Introducing Rbrul for mixed-effects variable rule analysis. *Language and Linguistics Compass* 3(1). 359–383. https://doi.org/10.1111/j.1749-818X.2008.00108.x

Jun, Sun-Ah & Mary Beckman 1994. Distribution of devoiced high vowels in Korean. In *Proceedings of the 1994 International Conference of Spoken Language Processing*, vol. 2, 479–482.

Kajino, Sakiko. 2014. *Sociophonetic variation at the intersection of gender, region and style in Japanese female speech*. PhD dissertation, Georgetown University.

Kasuya, Hideki, Hisayoshi Suzuki & Ken'ichi Kido. 1968. Nenrei, seibetsu-ni yoru nihongo 5 boin-no pitchi shūhasū-to horumanto shūhasū-no henka. *Journal of the Acoustical Society of Japan* 24(6). 355–364.

Kawahara, Shigeto. 2016. Moe goe-to tsun goe-no inritsuteki tokuchō. *Journal of the Phonetic Society of Japan* 20(2). 102–110. https://doi.org/10.24467/onseikenkyu.20.2_102

Kawano, Toshiyuki. 1995. Purosodī-to teinei hyōgen. *Onsei gakkai kaihō* 208. 9–17.

Keating, Patricia A. 2014. Acoustic measures of falsetto voice. Paper presented at the annual meeting of the Acoustical Society of America, Providence, RI. https://doi.org/10.1121/1.4877544

Kindaichi, Haruhiko. 1942. Ga-gyō bion-ron. In Kokugogaku Shinkōkai (ed.), *Gendai nihongo-no kenkyū*, 197–247. Hakusuisha.

Kondo, Mariko. 2005. Syllable structure and its acoustic effects on vowels in devoicing environments. In Jeroen Weijer, Kensuke Nanjo & Tetsuo Nishihara (eds.), *Voicing in Japanese*, 229–246. Walter De Gruyter. https://doi.org/10.1515/9783110197686.2.229

Kōri, Shirō. 1997. Nihongo-no intonēshon. In Miyoko Sugitō, Tetsuya Kunihiro, Hajime Hirose & Morio Kawano (eds.), *Nihongo onsei, vol. 2*, 169–202. Sanseidō.

Kōri, Shirō. 2004a. Tōkyō-ppoi hatsuon-to Ōsaka-ppoi hatsuon-no onsei-teki tokuchō: Tōkyō Ōsaka hōgen-tomo atamadaka akusento-no go-dake-kara naru bun-o sozai-to shite. *Onsei kenkyū* 8(3). 41–56. https://doi.org/10.24467/onseikenkyu.8.3_41

Kōri, Shirō. 2004b. Zenkoku 7-chiten-no jakunensō washa-no inritsuteki tokuchō. *Proceedings of Nihongo Gakkai 2004-nen shunki taikai.* 123–130.

Kōri, Shirō. 2005. Inritsu-no sutairuteki tayōsei-to chīkiteki tayōsei. In Keikichi Hirose (ed.), *Inritsu-no tayōsei-to sono teiryōteki hyōgen* (MEXT Kaken Report), 1–8.

Kōri, Shirō. 2007. Tōkyō hōgen-no shizen kaiwa-ni mirareru akusento jakka-no jittai. Paper presented at the 21st conference of the Phonetics Society of Japan.

Kubozono, Haruo. 1989. Syntactic and rhythmic effects on downstep in Japanese. *Phonology* 6(1). 39–67. https://doi.org/10.1017/S0952675700000944

Leino, Timo, Anne-Maria Laukkanen & Vojtěch Radolf. 2011. Formation of the actor's/speaker's formant: A study applying spectrum analysis and computer modeling. *Journal of Voice* 25(2). 150–158. https://doi.org/10.1016/j.jvoice.2009.10.002

Liberman, Mark Y. 1975. *The intonational system of English*. PhD dissertation, MIT.

Maekawa, Kikuo. 1989. Statistical tests for the study of vowel merger. *Quantitative Linguistics* 39. 200–219.

Maekawa, Kikuo. 1990. Muakusento hōgen-no intonēshon (shiron). *Onsei Gengo* IV. 87–110.

Maekawa, Kikuo. 1994. Is there "dephrasing" of the accentual phrase in Japanese? *OSU Working Papers in Linguistics* 44 . 146–165.

Maekawa, Kikuo. 2006. Intonēsyon kenkyū hatten-no yōin. *Onsei kenkyū* 10(3). 7–17. https://doi.org/10.24467/onseikenkyu.10.3_7

Maekawa, Kikuo & Hideaki Kikuchi. 2005. Corpus-based analysis of vowel devoicing in spontaneous Japanese: An interim report. In Jeroen Maarten van de Weijer, Kensuke Nanjo & Tetsuo Nishihara (eds.), *Voicing in Japanese*, 205–228. Mouton de Gruyter. https://doi.org/10.1515/9783110197686.2.205

Maekawa, Kikuo, Yōichi Maki & Yasuo Yoshioka. 1999. Hatsuwa-no teineisa-no chikaku-ni oyobosu goiteki yōin-to inritsuteki yōin-no kankei-to sono shakaisa. *Denshi jōhō tsūshin gakkai gijutsu kenkyū hōkoku* 99(353). 9–16.

Maekawa, Kikuo & Ken'ya Nishikawa. 2019. Nihongo hanashi kotoba kōpasu-e-no seishitsu jōhōfuka-to yobiteki bunseki. *Proceedings of the Language Resources Workshop* 4. 205–221.

Miwa, Jōji. 1995. Gendai nihongo hōgen onsei-no onkyō bunseki. *Nihon onkyō gakkaishi* 51(11). 893–898.

Miyatake, Masanori & Yoshinori Sagisaka. 1990. Shushu-no hatsuwa yōshiki-ni mirareru inritsu tokuchō-to sono seigyo. *Denshi jōhō tsūshin gakkai ronbunshi* D–II, vol. J73–D, II(12), 1929–1935.

Mori, Hiroki, Kikuo Maekawa & Hideki Kasuya. 2014. *Onsei-wa nani-o tsutaeteiru-ka*. Koronasha.

Moriyama, Takuro. 2001. Shūjoshi 'ne'-no intonēshon. In Onsei bunpō kenkyūkai (ed.), *Bunpō-to onsei*, 31–54. Kurosio Shuppan.

Morris, Midori Yonekawa. 2010. Regional stereotypes and the perception of Japanese vowel devoicing. In Dennis Preston & Nancy Niedzielski (eds.), *A reader in sociophonetics*, 191–202. Walter de Gruyter. https://doi.org/10.1515/9781934078068.2.191

Nakamura, Momoko. 2020. *Shin keigo maji yabai-ssu!: Shakaigengogaku-no shiten kara.* Hakuteisha.

National Institute for Japanese Language and Linguistics. 1953. *Chīki shakai-no gengo Seikatsu: Tsuruokashi-ni okeru jittai chōsa.* Shūei Shuppan.

National Institute for Japanese Language and Linguistics. 1965. *Kyōtsūgoka-no katei: Hokkaidō-ni okeru oyako sandai-no kotoba.* National Institute for Japanese Language and Linguistics.

National Institute for Japanese Language and Linguistics. 1974. *Chīki shakai-no gengo Seikatsu: Tsuruoka-shi-ni okeru 20-nen-mae-tono hikaku.* Shūei Shuppan.

National Institute for Japanese Language and Linguistics. 1997. *Hokkaidō-ni okeru kyōtsūgoka-to gengo Seikatsu-no jittai. Chūkan hōkoku.* National Institute for Japanese Language and Linguistics.

National Institute for Japanese Language and Linguistics. 2007. *Chīki shakai-no gengo Seikatsu: Tsuruoka-ni okeru 20-nen kankaku 3-kai no keizoku chōsa.* National Institute for Japanese Language and Linguistics.

National Institute for Japanese Language and Linguistics & the Institute of the Statistical Mathematics. 2013. *Dai 4-kai tsuruokashi-ni okeru gengo chōsa, Kekka-no gaiyō.* Institute of Statistical Mathematics.

NHK. 1985. *Nihongo hatsuon akusento jiten.* Nihon Hōsō Shuppan Kyōkai.

Ohara, Yumiko. 1992. Gender-dependent pitch levels: A comparative study in Japanese and English. In Kira Hall, Mary Bucholtz & Birch Moonwoman (eds.), *Locating power: Proceedings of the Second Berkeley Women and Language Conference*, 469–477. Berkeley Women and Language Group.

Ohara, Yumiko. 1997. Shakai onseigaku-no kanten kara mita nihonjin-no koe-no kōtei. In Sachiko Ide (ed.), *Joseigo no sekai*, 42–59. Meiji Shoin.

Ohara, Yumiko. 2004. Prosody and gender in workplace interaction. In Shigeko Okamoto & Janet Shibamoto Smith (eds.), *Japanese language, gender, and ideology: Cultural models and real people*, 222–240. Oxford University Press.

Ohara, Yumiko. 2019. Gendered speech. In Patrick Heinrich & Yumiko Ohara (eds.). *The Routledge handbook of Japanese sociolinguistics*, 279–295. Routledge.

Okada, Shōhei. 2004. Nihongo Hanasi Kotoba Kōpasu-ni kansatsu-sareru boin renzoku/ei/-no bariēshon: Gairaigo-no bāi. *Denshi jōhō tsūshin gakkai gijutsu kenkyū hōkoku* SP2004-25. 35–40.

Ota, Ichiro, Akira Utsugi & Yoshitaka Ota. 2021. The voice quality of anime as a sociocultural register. Paper presented at 16th International Conference of the European Association for Japanese Studies.

Ota, Ichiro & Shoji Takano. 2007. Shakai onsēgakuteki hen'i-o toraeru tameno onsē chōshu jikken-ni kansuru kōsatsu. *Cultural Science Reports* 66. 23–42.

Ota, Ichiro & Shoji Takano. 2014. The media influence on language change in Japanese sociolinguistic contexts. In Jannis Androutsopoulos (ed.), *Mediatisation and sociolinguistic change*, 171–203. De Gruyter. https://doi.org/10.1515/9783110346831.171

Pierrehumbert, Janet B. 1980. *The phonology and phonetics of English intonation.* PhD dissertation, MIT.

Pierrehumbert, Janet B. & Mary E. Beckman. 1988. *Japanese tone structure.* MIT Press.

Podesva, Robert J. 2007. Phonation type as a stylistic variable: The use of falsetto in constructing a persona. *Journal of Sociolinguistics* 11(4). 478–504. https://doi.org/10.1111/j.1467-9841.2007.00334.x

Podesva, Robert J. & Patrick Callier. 2015. Voice quality and identity. *Annual Review of Applied Linguistics* 35. 173–194. https://doi.org/10.1017/S0267190514000270

Podesva, Robert J. & Sakiko Kajino. 2014. Sociophonetics, gender, and sexuality. In Susan Ehrlich, Miriam Meyerhoff & Janet Holmes (eds.), *The handbook of language, gender, and sexuality*, 103–122. Wiley-Blackwell. https://doi.org/10.1002/9781118584248.ch5

Redmond, Ryan C. 2016. Constructing boyishness: A sociophonetic analysis of Japanese anime voice actresses performing male roles. *Journal of the Acoustical Society of America* 140. 3402. https://doi.org/10.1121/1.4970920

Redmond, Ryan C. 2018. Imitation[s] or hyperarticulation[s]?: The role of the voiceless alveolar fricative in Japanese queer identity performance. Paper presented at Lavender Languages & Linguistics Conference 25, Providence, RI.

Sadanobu, Toshiyuki. 2015. "Characters" in Japanese communication and language: An overview. *Acta linguistica Asiatica* 5(2). 9–28. https://doi.org/10.4312/ala.5.2.9-28

Sadanobu, Toshiyuki. 2021. Kyara-towa nani-ka. *Nihongogaku* 40(1). 14–25.

Sankoff, Gillian. 2013. Longitudinal studies. In Robert Bayley, Richard Cameron & Ceil Lucas (eds.), *The Oxford handbook of sociolinguistics*, 261–279. Oxford University Press. https://doi.org/10.1093/oxfordhb/9780199744084.013.0013

Schloneger, Matthew J. 2014. *Assessments of voice use, voice quality, and perceived singing voice function among college/university singing students ages 18–24 through simultaneous ambulatory monitoring with accelerometer and acoustic transducers.* PhD dissertation, University of Kansas.

Shirota, Chieko. 1999. Nyūsubun-no kikitori-to inritsu. *Ōsaka university nihon gakuhō* 18. 117–133.

Sibata, Takesi. 1978. *Shakai gengogaku-no kadai.* Sanseidō.

Starr, Rebecca L. 2015. Sweet voice: The role of voice quality in a Japanese feminine style. *Language in Society* 44(1). 1–34. https://doi.org/10.1017/S0047404514000724

Sugawa, Akiko. 2013. *Shōjo-to mahō: Gāru hīrō-wa ikani juyō sareta-ka.* NTT Shuppan.

Sugihara, Yoko & Emiko Katsurada 1999. Masculinity and femininity in Japanese culture: A pilot study. *Sex roles* 40(7–8). 635–646.

Sugitō, Miyoko. 1969. Tōkyō Ōsaka-ni okeru musei boin-ni tsuite. *Onsei-no kenkyū* 14 . 249–264.

Sugitō, Miyoko. 1978. Tango akusento-no hatsuwa-to chikaku-ni okeru kojinsa oyobi hōgensa-no teiryōteki kenkyū. *Gengo kenkyū* 74. 57–82.

Sugitō, Miyoko. 1982. *Nihongo akusento-no kenkyū.* Sanseidō.

Sugitō, Miyoko. 1983. Akusento-no "yure." *Nihongogaku* 8(3). 15–26.

Sugitō, Miyoko. 1988a. Nihon-no hachi toshi-ni okeru boin-no museika. *Ōsaka shōin joshi daigaku ronshū* 25. 1–10.

Sugitō, Miyoko. 1988b. Rōdoku onsei-ni okeru akusento-no chīki, nenrei. seibetsu-ni yoru sai. *Kokugogaku* 154. 132–144.

Sugitō, Miyoko. 1992. Intonēshon-no kigōron. In Bunka gengogaku henshū īnkai (ed.), *Bunka gengogaku,* 1055–1068. Sanseidō.

Sugitō, Miyoko. 2001. Shūjoshi 'ne'-no imi, kinō-to intonēshon. In Onsei bunpō kenkyūkai (ed.), *Bunpō-to onsei,* 3–16. Kurosio Shuppan.

Sugitō, Miyoko, Yūko Nakatsuka & Mie Takahashi. 1974. Akusentogata-no kikoe-no yure-to hatsuwa-no yure (Sono 2): Nagasaki akusento-to Ōsaka akusento. *Shōin kokubungaku* 12. 40–55.

Sunaoshi, Yasuko. 2004. Farm women's professional discourse in Ibaraki. In Shigeko Okamoto & Janet S. Shibamoto Smith (eds.), *Japanese language, gender and ideology: Cultural models and real people,* 187–204. Oxford University Press.

Tahara, Hiroshi. 1998. Nihon shuyō toshi hōgen onsei dētabēsu (JCMD). "Hōgen onsei dētabēsu-no sakusei-to riyō–ni kansuru kenkyū." Kenkyū seika hōkokusho.

Takano, Shoji. 2002. Hokkaidō hōgen washa-no nichijōkaiwa-ni okeru inritsu kyōchō-no bariēshon kenkyū: Hiteiji *nai*-no bāi." *Onsei kenkyū* 6(3). 25–47. https://doi.org/10.24467/onseikenkyu.6.3_25

Takano, Shoji. 2008. Variation in Japanese prosodic focus: Issues of language specificity, interactive style and register. In Kimberly Jones & Tsuyoshi Ono (eds.), *Style shifting in Japanese,* 285–327. John Benjamins. https://doi.org/10.1075/pbns.180.00var

Takano, Shoji. 2021. Lifespan "changes from above" in the standardization of Japanese regional dialects: Levels of grammar, lexical properties and community characteristics. *Language Variation and Change* 33(3). 297–329. https://doi.org/10.1017/S0954394521000211

Takano, Shoji & Ichiro Ota. 2017. A sociophonetic approach to variation in Japanese pitch realizations: Region, age, gender and stylistic parameters. *Asia-Pacific Language Variation* 3(1). 5–40. https://doi.org/10.1075/aplv.3.1.02tak

Takano, Sayoko, Yuki Takezawa & Junki Takeuchi. 2014. Moe goe shinriteki hyōka, onkyō bunseki oyobi STRAIGHT-o mochīta gōsei onsei hyōka. *Reports of the 2014 Meeting of the Acoustical Society of Japan.* 503–506.

Teshigawara, Mihoko. 2003. *Voices in Japanese animation: A phonetic study of vocal stereotypes of heroes and villains in Japanese culture.* PhD dissertation, University of Victoria.

Umeda, Noriko. 1982. 'F0 declination' is situation dependent. *Journal of Phonetics* 10(3). 279–290. https://doi.org/10.1016/S0095-4470(19)30989-1

Utsugi, Akira, Han Wang & Ichiro Ota. 2019. A voice quality analysis of Japanese anime. In Sasha Calhoun, Paola Escudero, Marija Tabain & Paul Warren (eds.), *Proceedings of the 19th International Congress of Phonetic Sciences, Melbourne, Australia 2019,* 1853–1857. Australasian Speech Science and Technology Association Inc.

Van Borsel, John, Joke Janssens & Marc De Bodt. 2009. Breathiness as a feminine voice characteristic: A perceptual approach. *Journal of Voice* 23(3). 291–294. https://doi.org/10.1016/j.jvoice.2007.08.002

Vance, Timothy. 1987. *An introduction to Japanese linguistics.* Blackwell.

Varden, John Kevin. 2010. On vowel devoicing in Japanese. *Karuchūru* 4(1). 223–235.

Venditti, Jennifer. 1995. The J_ToBI labeling guidelines. *OSU Working Papers in Linguistics* 50. 127–162.

Wagner, Suzanne Evans & Isabelle Buchstaller. 2019. *Panel studies of variation and change.* Routledge.

Wang, Han. 2019. *Nihongo kanjō onsei-no sanshutsu-ni okeru seishitsu-no tokuchō.* MA thesis, Nagoya University.

Xu, Mingd, Fumitaka Homae, Ryu-ichiro Hashimoto & Hiroko Hagiwara. 2013. Acoustic cues for the recognition of self-voice and other-voice. *Frontiers in Psychology* 4. Article 735. https://doi.org/10.3389/fpsyg.2013.00735

Yaeger-Dror, Malcah. 1996. Register as a variable in prosodic analysis: The case of the English negative. *Speech Communication* 19(1). 39–60. https://doi.org/10.1016/0167-6393(96)00013-1

Yoshioka, Hirohide. 1981. Laryngeal adjustments in the production of the fricative consonants and devoiced vowels in Japanese. *Phonetica* 38(4). 236–251. https://doi.org/10.1159/000260027

Yuasa, Ikuko Patricia. 2008. *Culture and gender of voice pitch: A sociophonetic comparison of the Japanese and Americans.* Equinox.

25

SOCIOPHONETICS AND FRENCH

Aurélie Nardy and Maria Candea

Introduction

Although occasional references were made to the sociophonetics of French in the 1970s and 1980s, it is only recently that research in this area has started to use this label. The trend is now sufficiently robust to be described as an emerging field of research in its own right, beginning to take on a structure and to become both visible and legible. In this chapter, however, we discuss the sociophonetics of French in its broadest sense, understood as encompassing all studies focusing on "an aspect of pronunciation or its perception in connection with all other forms of human behavior or all social affiliations of individuals" (Candea & Trimaille 2015:8), even when the authors themselves make no explicit claim to this categorization.

Consequently, the field we cover is vast in scope. We have chosen to reflect its wealth and diversity by giving equal attention, on the one hand, to long-standing, well-documented issues that have given rise to many publications and that remain essential and, on the other hand, to more recent emerging questions.

Central research questions in French sociophonetics

The first questions addressed in this field arose directly from dialectology and focused on regional pronunciation variants in different French-speaking countries as well as, at a more fine-grained level, between one region and another within the same country. In France, this scientific interest in diatopic variation in sociophonetics stretches back to the pioneering study by Gauchat (1905) on a town in Eastern France and became more firmly established after Martinet's (1945) study on regional variation. The questions addressed related to regional dialects in French but also to sound changes in micro-diachrony, examined through quantitative questionnaire-based surveys with people from different generations.

The most recent iteration of this tradition is the project entitled *Phonologie du Français Contemporain* ('Phonology of Contemporary French' [PFC], available at www.projet-pfc.net/; Carton et al. 1983), which is a vast research program offering a database of contemporary spoken French from across all French-speaking countries in the 2010s. It describes the heterogeneous

DOI: 10.4324/9781003034636-28

pronunciation of French in terms of regularities and trends according to region and age of speakers, with a particular focus on micro-diachrony.

It took some time for an interest in broader social questions to become established in phonetics. Between the 1950s (Straka 1952; Fouché 1959) and the 1990s, most studies focusing on the phonetics of French gave more or less attention to stylistic and situational variation, sometimes imbricated with diastratic variation and the study of sociolects (Fónagy 1983; Léon 1973, 1993; Peretz 1977). However, during this period there was little theorization of how stylistic variation and social variation were imbricated. Questions about gender emerged progressively, initially driven by the sociolinguistic tradition of studying women's pronunciation for bourgeois speech (Mettas 1979) and men's pronunciation for working-class speech (Laks 1983).

Currently, the central questions explored in this area focus on the dynamics of regional and social accents, with heightened consideration given to the social meaning of phonetic variants and to discrimination in terms of the privilege or prejudice associated with certain dialectal pronunciations (Gasquet-Cyrus 2012). In order to address these issues, research has increasingly begun to focus explicitly and systematically on the perception of pronunciation (sometimes convergent, sometimes socially stratified) rather than simply on the production of speech (Candea & Trimaille 2015). Under the influence of linguistic anthropology, it has become more common to include a reflexive dimension in research involving interactions, notably by analyzing the influence of the researcher's own profile on the data collected (Fagyal et al. 2010; Lehka-Lemarchand 2015).

The sociophonetics of language acquisition (in children or among those learning French as a second or foreign language) also took time to become established. The first sociophonetic study of L1 acquisition in France was Chevrot's (1991) PhD thesis. In child language acquisition, research initially focused essentially on determining at what age patterns of sociophonetic variation become established in production and perception. Questions then turned to the developmental dynamics at play in the acquisition of sociophonetic variation, and theoretical propositions were advanced to explain patterns of variation. Such studies aim, in particular, to move towards a conception of language development that would explain how children and learners construct linguistic knowledge in a language environment that is variable but organized according to contextual and social dimensions. They also aim to understand how relationships are built between linguistic knowledge (phonetic, in this instance) and social knowledge (Nardy, Chevrot & Barbu 2013, 2015).

More recent (but less numerous) investigations, especially in France, have begun to look at the cognitive representation of different sociophonetic variants. These studies fall within the field of sociolinguistic cognition, which uses methods drawn from experimental psychology to explore the cognitive mechanisms underpinning the production of sociophonetic variants, their memorization, and their processing in language perception. For example, Buson et al. (2018) have sought to understand how, in reception, individuals manage to devise a homogeneous cognitive representation of utterances composed of a heterogeneous set of linguistic, and particularly sociophonetic, features.

The studies listed in this chapter, focusing on these different issues, fall within the scope of different theoretical frameworks (variationism, theories of indexicality, agency, stylistics, usage-based models, and so on) and concern different sociophonetic features of the French language. Our review focuses particularly on studies in France, but we also note findings and possibilities for future exploration of French as a global language spoken across Europe, the Americas, Africa, and Oceania.

Units of analysis

As in all languages, the different areas of French phonetics are not uniformly exposed to variation. Some give rise to greater social indexing than others for reasons linked to the history of the language, its phonology, and the logics underpinning its dynamics of change. Variable liaison and schwa, in particular, have been the focus of a considerable number of studies in the sociophonetics of French. As an example, the *Phonologie du Français Contemporain* project (Durand, Laks & Lyche 2009) chose these two features as cross-cutting research topics through which to describe all regional varieties of French throughout all French-speaking countries. In this section, we review work on variable liaison and schwa, as well as the sociophonetic phenomena that affect the vowels, consonants, and prosody of French.

Variable liaison

Liaison in French is a sandhi phenomenon resulting from the diachronic evolution of pronunciation (Langlard 1928). It is characterized by the realization of a consonant (/z/, /t/, or /n/ in 99.8 percent of cases; Boë & Tubach 1992) between two words—word1 and word2—in certain lexical and syntactical contexts. In order for the liaison consonant to appear, word2 must begin with a vowel when produced alone. The phonetic nature of the liaison consonant depends on the final graphic consonant of word1: word1s such as *un* or *aucun* result in a /n/ liaison, word1s such as *petit* or *grand* result in a /t/ liaison, and word1s such as *gros*, *très*, or *deux* result in a /z/ liaison. Finally, the liaison consonant is never realized at the end of word1 when it is at the end of an utterance. The sequence *deux amis* is therefore pronounced [døzami] but when the two words are uttered separately, *deux* is pronounced [dø] and *amis* is pronounced [ami]. Two types of liaison exist in usage: obligatory liaisons, realized by 100 percent of speakers whatever the context or their sociodemographic characteristics (Booij & De Jong 1987; Durand & Lyche 2008), and variable liaisons, where the frequency of realization depends on internal and external factors such as social background, sex/gender, age, and context (Malécot 1975; Ashby 1981; De Jong 1994; Moisset 2000; Armstrong 2001). Furthermore, the phenomenon is extremely frequent, since a liaison context occurs every 16 words in adult speech (Boë & Tubach 1992). The complex, heterogeneous, and variable nature of this phonological alternation has made it into a central object of study for over half a century now, with research focusing on its linguistic, phonological, psycholinguistic, and sociolinguistic aspects (Soum-Favaro, Coquillon & Chevrot 2014).

Schwa

In French, where vowels are concerned, the variable phenomenon that has given rise to the most studies and references is schwa (Hambye 2005; Durand 2014; Racine, Durand & Andreassen 2016), which is acoustically positioned in the center of the French vowel system and can be either realized or not. Its pronunciation varies considerably according to different factors. These can be intrinsic (paratactic constraints, position rules), morphosyntactic, stylistic, or regional. As with variable liaison, its description poses considerable challenges to both phonology and sociophonetics. Analysis of large parallel spoken language corpora has shed new light on the stability of paratactic constraint (realization of schwa to avoid consonant clusters that are too complex, earning it the description of "phonetic lubricant") (Hutin et al. 2020). Sociophonetics focuses on certain positions in particular and notably absolute final position of polysyllabic words, which is very sensitive to dialectal variation and retains the capacity to index a more formal style

(Hutin et al. 2020). In monosyllabic words or in the first syllable of polysyllabic words, schwa is said to vary with speed of delivery and degree of formality, but its capacity to index formal speech seems to weaken in micro-diachrony. In a reading-aloud task, Hansen (2000) shows that it is more often realized by speakers with a low level of education who are more linguistically insecure and use it as an overt prestige marker, whereas it is no longer used in that way by more educated speakers. From the end of the 1980s, this variable vowel extended its domain in the northern half of France and French-speaking Belgium to unexpected contexts, referred to as epenthetic or pre-pausal (adding a word-final schwa in positions not expected by phonology, first after a consonant and then in all pre-pausal contexts). These types of usage have been described, in particular, by Carton (1999) and Hansen & Hansen (2003) and have been associated with pronunciation that was initially perceived as affected and precious and then (probably under the influence of successful parodies by comedians such as *Les Inconnus*; see, e.g., the sketch "Les Pétasses" 'Bimbos', available on YouTube) as exaggerated and vulgar, and has sometimes been parodied as feminine or effeminate (Trimaille 2007).

Vowels

Aside from schwa, sociophonetic studies have explored different characteristics linked to the variable production of vowels in French. For example, in positions where standard French uses nasal vowels, speakers of Southern French pronounce oral vowels followed by a nasal consonant segment (Clairet 2008). In Canadian French, the trend towards the denasalization of vowels has also been described (Léon 1983), as well as the diphthongization of open vowels (e.g., *neige* 'snow' pronounced [nɛ͡ʒ] in France and [naɛ͡ʒ] in Quebec) and the laxing of closed vowels /i, y, u/ (see Remysen 2014 particularly about Quebec). Finally, in both France and Quebec, it has been demonstrated that, depending on context and time period, the backing of vowels can index either a rural style or a snobbish and affected one (see, for example, Mettas 1979 for France and Remysen 2016b for Quebec).

Consonants

(R) is probably the consonant that has been most studied in the sociophonetics of French, and it provides a good example of phonological conditioning. This vibrant phoneme can be realized phonetically in many different ways: voiced, voiceless, by vibrations of the apex of the tongue or of the soft palate, as a velar or uvular fricative, or even as a semi-consonant [w]. Its realizations have varied throughout the history of the language, both in France (where it was apical until at least the seventeenth century) and across French-speaking countries, and they continue to vary according to region and language contact. This has favored its indexing of social values and it enjoys considerable perceptual salience. According to Akpossan (2015), it is an emblematic marker of social stratification in Guadeloupe (an island in the West Indies), where its prestige realizations, in French, are close to the voiceless velar fricative, while its basilectal realizations are close to the semi-consonant [w] that is part of the phonetic repertoire of Guadeloupian Creole.

Word-final post-consonant liquid deletion of /ʀ/ and /l/ is also an area of interest in French sociophonetics. This variation phenomenon has been present in usage for several centuries (since the seventeenth century for /ʀ/ and the sixteenth for /l/), and social judgment markers are attested from the same period (Bourciez & Bourciez 2006). Speakers can either conserve or delete the liquid consonant (*quatre* 'four' can be realized as [katʁ] or as [kat], *table* can be realized as [tabl] or as [tab]). The usage frequency of variants is known to be subject to diastratic variation (Laks

1977; Boughton 2015), diaphasic variation (Armstrong 2001), and diatopic variation (Pustka 2011; Myers & Ranson 2014).

The palatalization and affrication of the stops /k, g, t, d/ offers a good example of phonotactic conditioning favored by the absence of this feature in the system of distinctive oppositions in French phonology. The palatalized pronunciation (or more specifically the spirantized pronunciation [tsi, tsy, dzi, dzy]) is a stereotypical marker of the pronunciation of Quebec French, whereas in France the hushing sibilant palatalization with or without affrication [tʃi, tʃy, dʒi, dʒy] has been mentioned as a possible social marker or ongoing change.

Finally, more recently, sociophoneticians of French have identified a new linguistic unit of study: the fricative lengthened coda (for example, *oui,* 'yes,' [wi] pronounced [wiç::::], or *unanimité* 'unanimity' pronounced [ynanimiteç:::]), produced by speakers in socially dominant positions (Candea, Adda-Decker & Lamel 2013; Candea et al. 2020). This variant in pronunciation was identified earlier by Fónagy (1989), who initially described it as a simple devoicing of the final vowel in an intonational group.

Prosody

The sociophonetics of French has also focused considerably on prosody, owing to the perceptual salience of certain contours and certain stress regularities. Among the most studied parameters is the position of lexical stress, and whether it is placed on the final or penultimate syllable (Fagyal 2010) or on the first syllable (Duez 1991; Ko 1996) of an intonational group. Also extensively research is the ratio of duration between the final and penultimate syllable, with lengthening of the penultimate syllable cited as a feature of regional accents in different areas of French-speaking countries or as a feature of working-class accents in France's large cities (Lehka-Lemarchand 2007; Fagyal 2010; Simon et al. 2012). Lehka-Lemarchand (2015) has also studied the perceptual salience of a particular contour of the final syllable (very fast rise-fall) which has been used as a stylistic marker of the "*banlieue*" accent. The *banlieue* accent is made up of a set of features that, since the 1990s, have been associated with the pronunciation of the urban working-class youth of France's multiethnic cities. Although it seems to be more a situational phonostyle than a stable accent (Candea 2017), its perceptual salience and prevalence in epilinguistic discourse has led many researchers in France to devote studies to prosody in connection with social issues. By studying prosody, it is possible to examine how identities (particularly regional, social, and gender identities) are negotiated in interaction and how phonostyle is used as a resource to construct an ethos—something that has been studied in particular among journalists (Ko 1996; Boula De Mareüil, Rilliard & Allauzen 2012) and political leaders (Duez 1991).

Finally, the most recent approaches include analysis of voice quality in sociophonetics, in particular with a view to understanding the performance of gender through voice, both in terms of production and perception (Arnold 2015a; Candea & Brown 2022).

Prominent methods and approaches

Studies in French sociophonetics draw their methods and tools primarily from perceptual and articulatory acoustic phonetics, sociolinguistics (especially variationism), and the linguistics of language contact. However, research in the area of sociophonetics as defined in our introduction also borrows tools and methods from social psychology, ethology, interaction analysis, gender theory, and cognitive science in its broadest sense.

Speech production

The methods used to collect linguistic productions in French sociophonetics are those traditionally used in the wider field of sociolinguistics. These can be divided into two broad categories: studies drawing on elicited speech and studies drawing on "ecological" nonelicited speech.

For elicited speech, research uses recordings of interviews or conversations with the investigator (Laks 1980; Durand, Laks & Lyche 2002) or reading tasks (prose or word lists) given to respondents (Lucci 1983; Moisset 2000). Researchers often use these two methods to collect more formal French. Moreover, as well as eliciting a particular type of spoken language, reading tasks enable different intralinguistic factors to be controlled, such as the position of the variable in the word, the phonological context, or the frequency of the word. More recently, more experimental tasks inspired by psycholinguistic methods have been adapted to investigation of the different sociophonetic varieties of French, for example picture naming (Chevrot, Nardy & Barbu 2011) and utterance repetition (Buson et al. 2018).

Some collections of nonelicited speech use recordings of spontaneous conversation among peers, with or without the researcher's presence (Armstrong 2001). Thanks to recent technological progress, it is now possible to equip individuals with compact portable recording devices, allowing all verbal interactions to be recorded over very long periods (Nardy et al. 2021). This enables individuals' linguistic productions to be collected in an ecological context, thus offering access to both more informal and more formal French depending on the situations and interlocutors encountered by the participants. Other studies analyze speech produced in political debates (Encrevé 1988; Duez 1991; Milne 2013) or in corpora from radio programs (Ågren 1973; Ahmad 1993) with a view to examining usage that is expected to be more formal.

Studies conducted in the sociophonetics of French often combine these different methods for collecting spoken language (both elicited and nonelicited) with a view to examining the stylistic variation of variables (Laks 1980; Lucci 1983; Mettas 1979; Durand, Laks & Lyche 2002).

Thanks to online databases of French speech corpora (a number of them can be found on the ORTOLANG platform: www.ortolang.fr/market/corpora/cluster/speech_corpora), researchers in sociophonetics can also carry out semi-automated searches in aligned databases of speech/phonetic transcriptions for synchronic or diachronic analysis of certain variants (e.g., Adda-Decker et al. 2012; Candea, Adda-Decker & Lamel 2013).

Similarly, widespread use of the Internet now allows large online surveys to be conducted, collating declared phonic usage from vast samples of respondents, with a view to studying regional variation as in the example of the "*français de nos régions*" surveys (Avanzi 2019). In these cases, Internet users either hear a sentence with blanks and two ways of pronouncing the missing word and are asked to choose which variant they would produce, or they are given two pairs of words to listen to and are asked whether they would pronounce them in the same way or differently.

Finally, it should be noted that while more ethnographic approaches are less frequent, they have also been used to study pronunciation via on-the-fly notation (Gasquet-Cyrus 2015).

Speech perception

Systematic work on speech perception in French was late off the mark, despite a few pioneering studies including Lambert, Frankle & Tucker (1966) on the perception of bilingual speakers in Montréal depending on whether the language heard was French or English (a technique known as "matched guise"), by Léon (1968) on regional accents, and, in part, by Mettas (1979) on the phonostyle of the Parisian bourgeoisie. These types of study essentially set up experimental approaches in which a sample of listeners is asked, either face to face or via an online interface, to listen to short excerpts of speech and to answer questions. Two broad categories of investigations can be identified: those aimed at understanding representations of the speakers heard in a short sound sample, and those aimed at defining representations of the pronunciations heard, and thus of different ways of pronouncing things.

The first group comprises studies that focus most often on identifying speakers' regional origin (Boughton 2005; Boula De Mareüil et al. 2008; Simon et al. 2012; Remysen 2016a). Sometimes respondents are asked to identify speakers' social profiles, either with open-ended questions or, more often, with closed questions: middle class, rural, working class, etc. (Boughton 2005, 2006). Certain tests aim to explore the indexing of specific markers through questions drawing on stereotypes, such as the speakers' employability as journalists or teachers (Castellotti & Robillard 2003; Trimaille, Candea & Lehka-Lemarchand 2012) or questions asking respondents to express a preference (e.g., subjective reaction tests that ask whether the speaker seems nice/unpleasant, competent/incompetent, based on pairs of utterances— see Viana Dos Santos 2021). Paternostro (2014), for example, has tested the ability to iden-tify a *banlieue* youth—understood as a stereotypical category corresponding to a young working-class profile from the *banlieue*, with a post-colonial immigrant background—based on the presence/absence of a prosodic contour. Other tests complement these approaches by drawing on social psychology methods to show the importance of stereotypes (and particu-larly socially constructed expectations) in speech perception, using "priming." This technique allows researchers to study the influence of gendered, racial, and ethnic stereotypes (Arnold & Candea 2015; Prikhodkine 2019), in particular, on speech perception, by indicating from the outset categories to which speakers belong, and studying the precise effects produced by this priming alone.

The second group comprises studies asking whether the person heard is speaking with a par-ticular accent or not, whether the person is speaking informally or not (Viana Dos Santos 2021), or whether the person's voice is more feminine or more masculine (Candea & Brown 2022).

Finally, another approach to studying the perception of pronunciation, which has been less often explored, consists in analyzing epilinguistic discourse on accents through interviews or open-ended questions particularly to reveal explicit discrimination in daily life or in the field of audiovisual creation (Gasquet-Cyrus 2012; Gasquet-Cyrus & Planchenault 2019).

Major findings

In this section, we have chosen to focus on five topics that we consider representative of the work carried out in the sociophonetics of French: micro-diachronic sound change, regional dialects and more recent investigations on language prejudice, identity issues linked to sociophonetic usage and representations, child language learning, and second language acquisition.

Sound change

The major changes in French pronunciation took place before Middle French, but various changes can still be identified in contemporary French.

At the level of prosody, an evolution in journalistic style has been identified between the 1940s and the end of the 1990s. News announcers' mean pitch, pitch rise associated with initial stress, and vowel duration have decreased, while the onsets of stressed initial syllables have lengthened (Boula De Mareüil, Rilliard & Allauzen 2012).

At the level of phonetics, changes in micro-diachrony have been identified for variables of general and regional French. For example, based on a panel study of seven speakers from the town of Orléans, who were recorded in semi-structured interviews in the 1970s and then again in 2010, Dugua & Baude (2017) identified a decrease in the frequency with which variable liaison was realized among half the participants, which could be a sign of an ongoing change as previously suggested by Léon (2007). Other studies have shown a trend towards the backing of nasal vowels in French (Walter 1994; Hansen 2001). A general trend has also been noted towards the progressive weakening of regional phonetic variants in favor of variants from more general French. For example, drawing on synchronic analysis of speakers from Southern France from three successive generations of the same family, Thomas (2006) noted that rates of schwa maintenance and of nasal vowels with a homorganic consonant (characteristic variants of Southern French speech) decreased significantly from one generation to the next, even disappearing completely in some cases. The same observation has been made in Quebec French for the loss of the apical variant of [r] replaced with the dorsal variant [ʁ] which is becoming widespread (Léon 1993; Sankoff & Blondeau 2007). Finally, in contemporary French, we are seeing a diffusion of new variants such as the palatalized/affricated dental consonants which were first identified in the speech of young people from neighborhoods considered to be "working class" (Jamin 2005; Candea 2016) and are now attested (albeit to a lesser degree) in the speech of government ministers (Trimaille 2010).

Regional dialects and language prejudice

Studies all converge when it comes to regional variation and perceptual dialectology. First, French is a language in which the myth of the "standard" remains strong and broadly shared across French-speaking countries. Speakers tend to use the expression "accentless" to refer to a variety of pronunciation supposedly perceived as internationally neutral. While the variety of pronunciation perceived as "accentless" varies according to region, the idea that such a thing exists is always posited. This myth has contributed to a widespread dynamic of leveling across all French-speaking zones; despite regionally rooted dialectal specificities, pronunciation is tending to converge and to become homogeneous. This has been demonstrated both by studies in micro-diachrony, comparing different generations, and by perceptual studies that, overall, testify to French speakers' poor ability to identify regional origin just by listening to speech without any other indicators. If we try to summarize the results, it seems that, perceptually, French speakers are generally capable of distinguishing the main French-speaking areas: French-speaking Canada, French-speaking Africa, Southern France, Northern France, and Belgium, which is sometimes confused with Eastern France or Switzerland (Woehrling 2009; Boula De Mareüil & Boutin 2011; Racine et al. 2013; Bardiaux 2014; Remysen 2016a; Avanzi & Boula De Mareüil 2019), but they are unable to make more fine-grained distinctions. Studies show that, perceptually, people often confuse the accent of their own region with that of another region (Avanzi & Boula De Mareüil 2019). However, French speakers are generally capable of distinguishing more robustly whether speakers are from the working class/*banlieue* or the middle class, or whether they are rural or urban (Boughton 2006). These poles remain perceptually operational.

In this field, another consensus seems to be emerging regarding the persistence of strongly prevalent glottophobia throughout the French-speaking world (Blanchet 2016). Glottophobia functions like a form of racism based on accents and is directed in particular against people perceived as having minority accents from regions where pronunciation is considered to be distant from that of standard French, including certain foreign accents. This phenomenon is relatively well accepted in societies where French is the official language, including by the people against whom it is directed. One consequence is that it excludes many from certain professions (especially in the media, in theater and cinema, and in certain national political roles); it also guides the choice of pronunciation variants that are emphasized in the teaching of French as a foreign language, thus ensuring the persistence of the myth of accentless French speech. This issue has recently gained traction in the French media, leading to a bill being drafted to add accent to the list of officially prohibited grounds for discrimination. In November 2020, the bill was passed in the Assemblée Nationale (France's lower chamber) but at the time of writing has not yet been examined by the Senate (the country's upper chamber).

Identity

For the moment, research on indexicality and on performing identity through voice or pronunciation has focused in particular on the perception of speech and the categorization of speakers. Beyond the performance of regionally rooted identities, discussed in the previous section, the sociophonetics of French has also revealed the means through which speakers perform and make perceptible their affiliations in terms of social group, gender, and ethnicity.

The sociophonetics of French has benefited from its foundations in phonostylistics (notably the emblematic work by Léon 1993) as well as from the original attempts made by Fónagy (1983) to link the study of phonation with deeper psychoanalytical symbolism. These pioneering studies drew attention to how important modes of pronunciation (opening of vowels, backing, nasalization, palatalization, voice quality, melodic patterns) are when it comes to producing social and professional identities through stylization. These studies have also allowed a linguistic imaginary to be created around the long-standing notion of style, which is highly valued in the teaching of language and literature across all French-speaking countries and linked to prestigious pronunciation, and therefore to any socially valued pronunciation technique. It is now clear, however, that these studies focused mainly on the French language situated close to the "accentless" end of the linguistic continuum and therefore that phonostylistics was in fact the opposite of the study of accents. Accents in French are always positioned close to the minority end of the social spectrum, supposedly regulated by social or ethnic determinism. By calling into question this traditional division (style and awareness on the one hand, accent and lack of awareness on the other), current research in the sociophonetics of French has made it possible better to take into account speakers' agency when it comes to pronunciation practices, blurring the boundaries between all the main categories. Thus, for example, research focusing on the *banlieue* accent has shown that it is just as much about conscious style as it is about unconscious imitation (Lehka-Lemarchand 2015; Candea 2017). In spontaneous descriptions of the *banlieue* accent, there is no trace of agency, whereas in reality agency is key to understanding the dynamics at play, especially among groups of teenagers (Fagyal 2010). Research has also shown that this accent is part of a continuum with working-class style and emphatic prosody (Paternostro 2016).

Studies on identity all increasingly distinguish the categorization of pronunciation from the categorization of speakers. Hypotheses foregrounding agency, pluristylistic speakers, and accommodation are explored in terms of all identity affiliations, not simply social class, and result in the same blurring of boundaries. Examples include the negotiated role of vocal practices in gender transitioning described by Arnold (2015b), the fluidification of gender categories upheld by nonbinary people described by Candea & Brown (2022), and also the racialization processes claimed or rejected thanks to the concept of "whitisation" (a neologism which refers to the act of speaking French like a white person without a local accent) described by Telep (2018) in Cameroon.

In this respect, there is what could be described as a large-scale endeavor to deconstruct the rigid categories inherited from twentieth-century social psychology. This endeavor involves studies devoted both to production and perception, particularly regarding gender and racial categories, which are sensitive to priming and so to stereotypes. Investigations demonstrating that perception of gendered or ethnicized speech depends just as much upon pronunciation features as upon listeners' expectations (Arnold 2015b; Arnold & Candea 2015; Prikhodkine 2019) also contribute to challenging category boundaries and to creating new dynamics that allow analysis at the level of communities of practice (Eckert 2000) rather than at the level of large-scale traditional categories of gender, class, and race.

Child language learning

Developmental studies conducted on the sociophonetics of French follow on from variationist studies and focus on identifying developmental milestones, identifying at what age and in what order the main factors of variation appear. All the studies that have tested the impact of social background show that the higher the family's position on the social scale, the more children produce standard variants. This effect is robust and early because it first appears for the production of variable liaisons at the age of 3 (Chabanal 2003) and differences seem to increase as development progresses (Nardy 2008; Chevrot, Nardy & Barbu 2011). Where patterns of variation according to sex/gender are concerned, the results are less clear-cut. Whereas at age 6, certain studies have found no effect on the production of liquid consonants (Chabanal 2001), others have identified an effect that does not arise independently but rather in interaction with other factors, namely social background and situation (Chevrot 1991; Armstrong 2001). Children's usage of sociophonetic variants according to context follows similar patterns as in adults, as they produce more standard variants in the most formal contexts (Chevrot 1991; Armstrong 1996, 2001; Chevrot, Beaud & Varga 2000). This is an early skill because it is also seen in preschool children who produce more variable liaisons in activities involving a particular language stance, such as playing teacher or pretending to read (Martin 2005).

Comparisons between production and evaluation have produced disparate results. In a study by Chevrot, Beaud & Varga (2000) with children aged 10–12 years, the capacity to adapt speech according to the situation appeared to be independent of the capacity to produce acceptability judgments valuing standard variants. However, in younger children, a study conducted with 185 children aged between 2 and 6 looking at the production and evaluation of variable liaisons seems to contradict this observation. From as early as age 4–5, Barbu et al. (2013) found a positive correlation between production and evaluation. The children who give the most positive evaluations of standard variants also produce the most standard variants (the production task consisted in a picture-naming activity). Moreover, these authors identified a significant effect of social background on children's production and judgment. Familiarity with certain variants— more or less standard, depending on background—may therefore guide both skills. It would then follow that the normative prescriptive language of the school context instills in all children a system of common rules valuing standard variants (Lafontaine 1986) and evaluation becomes grounded in a more general conception of the norm, which is less dependent upon familiarity with variants. Indeed, from age 6–7 onwards, the age at which children begin primary school in France, Chevrot, Beaud & Varga (2000) note socially uniform evaluations similar to those observed in adults.

549

Second language acquisition

Sociophonetic studies on L2 acquisition, like those on L1 acquisition, are strongly marked by the variationist approach. They examine acquisition of sociophonetic competence by L2 learners, looking at how the latter draw closer to the patterns of L1 speakers during the acquisition process and checking whether they use all the variants present among L1 speakers or whether they use their own variants (Mougeon & Dewaele 2002).

In a study conducted with 35 American students learning French as a Foreign Language (FFL), Sax (2003) observed a pattern of variation in /l/ deletion that is well known among native speakers: learners produce higher rates of nonstandard variants in more informal settings and higher rates of standard variants in more formal settings. However, in comparison with native speakers, their usage is less differentiated according to this factor. Moreover, in similar communication situations, learners demonstrate a higher rate of use of formal variants than native speakers (Sax 2003; Howard, Lemée & Regan 2006; Mougeon, Nadasdi & Rehner 2010). This over-representation of standard variants, which are characteristic of the formal style of the language classroom (Bayley 2005), in comparison with native speakers, has also been observed for other sociophonetic variables such as variable liaison (Howard 2006, 2013; Gautier & Chevrot 2015, 2021) and schwa (Thomas 2004; Uritescu et al. 2004; Mougeon, Nadasdi & Rehner 2010). Of course, the development of sociophonetic competence also depends on the context in which the L2 is acquired. For example, Thomas (2004) compared uses of schwa and variable liaison in FFL learners, among whom 48 spent a year in France on a study abroad program and 39 stayed in Ontario, and found a clear difference in the productions of the two groups. Use of the standard form decreased among those who went on the study abroad program and increased among those who remained in their home country. Duration of the stay abroad and of contact with native speakers also has an impact on production. Those who have spent a longer time abroad (Sax 2003) and those who have had more contacts with native speakers (Blondeau et al. 2002) tend to produce higher rates of /l/ elision.

More recently, Viana dos Santos, Buson & Chevrot (2018) examined the cognitive organization of sociophonetic variants among 66 FFL learners in a study abroad program in France. In order to do so, they used the experimental sociolinguistic repetition task developed by Buson et al. (2018) consisting in participants listening to, and then repeating, stylistically homogeneous and nonhomogeneous utterances, some of which imply a variable liaison and the optional deletion of /l/ in the clitic *il* 'he'. When the input utterance that listeners here is "homogeneous," lexicon, syntactic structure, and sociophonetic variant are all coherent. For example, in the sentence, *C'est_un* [variable liaison realized] *pays accueillant où il ferait certes bon vivre* 'It is a welcoming country where one could certainly live the good life', the topic and register are consistent with the formal variant. When the input utterance is "nonhomogeneous," lexicon and structure are coherent, but the sociophonetic variable is not. For example, in the sentence, *Certes les débordements dans l'hémicycle étaient_inévitables* [without realization of the variable liaison] 'Clearly, outbursts from the benches were inevitable', the topic and register are not consistent with the informal variant. Viana dos Santos, Buson & Chevrot (2018) note that L2 learners (like the native speakers examined by Buson et al. 2018) tend to make the utterance homogeneous when they repeat it by changing the inconsistent variant. This has revealed the existence, at a cognitive level, of coherent sociophonetic schemata according to indexical value.

CASE STUDY   Ongoing debates about the palatalization of /t/ and /d/ before /i/ and /y/

In this section, we outline the ongoing debates about the palatalization and even affrication of /t/ and /d/ before /i,j/ and /y,ɥ/, a sociophonetic variable of French that, for several years now, has been the subject of numerous studies both in France and in other French-speaking countries.

Changes in the articulation of dental stops in French—first before the glides /j, ɥ/ (as in *tiens, média, actuel, conduire*) and then before the closed vowels /i/ and /y/ (as in *petit, tu, dire, dur*)—have been described at different times with different hypotheses. These changes may also concern the shape of the tongue and its position (when it is retracted, the consonant is palatalized or velarized if the contact point is on the velum), as well as the extension of contact between the tongue and the hard palate (when the tongue produces a friction noise, we talk about affrication). The phenomenon has affected all stops in French—for example, velarized pronunciation of [dʲ] as a [gʲ] (*Dieu* 'God' as *Guieu*) has been described as archaic since the early twentieth century (Trimaille & Candea 2021). In contemporary French, the pronunciation of /t/ and /d/ in these contexts has stabilized in Quebec French with spirantized variants [ts, dz] perceived as emblematic of this French-speaking area. This seems to be becoming dissociated from any correlation with specific social affiliations (Bento 1998). This stabilization in Quebec French was possible for systemic reasons; there is no phonological opposition in French between palatalized, aspirated, or clear stops, which leaves room for regional, social, or stylistic variations. The same hypothesis has been advanced since Fónagy (1989) concerning the palatalized/affricated pronunciation of /t, d/ in French in France. This could be a rising trend that is being subconsciously diffused from below. This hypothesis has also been defended by Romano (2003) and Armstrong & Pooley (2010), who even consider it to be the only "candidate" for a consonantal phonetic change occurring in European French.

In production, for example, Romano (2003) highlights a large distribution of palatalized/affricated variants, including among students recorded reading out loud in a laboratory setting, while Trimaille (2010) has shown that palatalized/affricated pronunciation of these consonants can be identified even in the public speech of certain government ministers.

Of course, rates of realization of palatalized/affricated variants differ from one group to the next and from one speaker to the next (they varied from 4 percent to 80 percent in a group of teenagers observed by Vernet & Trimaille 2007 in Grenoble). Nevertheless, the trend seems to be towards a rise, particularly for the palatalized/affricated pronunciation of /t/, even in more formal registers and among the speakers who are most subject to normative pressure, such as journalists working for national radio stations. Thus, even in this conservative group, according to a study by Candea, Adda-Decker & Lamel (2013) based on large parallel corpora, the rate of realization with affrication—detected automatically thanks to the friction noise produced when consonants are affricated as [tçi] or [tʃĩ]—increased from 4 percent in 1997 to 8 percent in 2010.

The results of studies on perception corroborate this hypothesis of an ongoing phonetic change. Different studies show that palatalized/affricated pronunciation is largely not perceived in experimental situations. It may well lack salience, especially for subjects under the age of 25 and more so for /t/ than for /d/ (for an overview, see Trimaille, Candea & Lehka-Lemarchand 2012; Trimaille & Candea 2021).

The hypothesis of an ongoing phonetic change is supported by several converging indicators, both in production and perception. One indicator, however, is not consistent with lack of salience. Certain French caricaturists and comedians seem to want to provoke hilarity by using phonography based on these variants. The researchers cited above identified a poster for a show, staging a North African woman, in which the word *humoristique* was written with the phonography *humoristchiques* suggesting palatalization. They also identified several comic strip panels in which certain words in the speech bubbles were attributed to young characters from the *banlieue* and phonography (improvised writing system that denotes pronunciation) was used to suggest palatal pronunciation with affrication of /t/, for example *petchites* and *tu neu tchues pas* in place of the standard forms *petites* 'small' and *tu ne tues pas* 'you don't kill.' This suggests that the authors assume the public will be capable of identifying the variants suggested by this phonography as markers of the stereotype of "*banlieue* youths." However, while the audience targeted is very large, this type of humoristic production remains infrequent.

The hypothesis of an ongoing change remains valid at the time of writing, but at any point this process could slow down or be inhibited should the palatalized and affricated variant become a stereotype and thus acquire perceptual salience. This is an interesting case because it allows two hypotheses to be confronted based on a variant with dual contradictory potential. Its structurally conditioned potential (displacement of the point of articulation without risking lack of intelligibility owing to the phonological structure of the language) could lead to a phonetic change and show converging tendencies throughout the French-speaking world. At the same time, its socially constructed potential (attribution of indexical value to a variant) could lead to the emergence and stabilization of a stereotype which would in turn encourage preferential or dispreferential production of the variant in question. This dynamic warrants continued observation.

Conclusion

In this general overview, we have tried to identify the main topics addressed by the sociophonetics of French. These included both long-standing areas of inquiry, inherited from dialectology (first on production then on perception) as well as more recent topics still under investigation. It was not, however, possible to go into all the subfields that could have been included, such as French in contact with other languages: languages of immigration, Creoles, and other national languages that stand alongside French in certain French-speaking countries (Vieru-Dimulescu 2008; Lyche & Skattum 2012).

In France, sociophonetics remains an emerging field, still in the process of being structured, that incorporates other disciplinary fields with an interest in social issues linked to pronunciation. For example, the current progress in cognitive science, especially in relation to modeling socially structured intergroup variability, will no doubt open up new horizons for the sociophonetics of French and other languages. Certain areas have not yet attracted extensive research in the French-speaking context but are beginning to prompt interest. These include taking advantage of the sociophonetic insights to be gained by revisiting articulatory phonetics and the classical hypothesis about the principle of least effort being the source of social variation, as well as sociophonetic studies conducted in ecological situations based on unsupervised investigative methods, for example the DyLNet project (Nardy et al. 2016; Nardy et al. 2021).

References

Adda-Decker, Martine, Elisabeth Delais-Roussarie, Cécile Fougeron, Cédric Gendrot & Lori Lamel. 2012. La liaison dans la parole spontanée familière: Explorations semi-automatiques de grands corpus. *Journées d'Études sur la Parole (JEP-TALN-RECITAL 2012)*. 545–552.

Ågren, John. 1973. *Étude sur quelques liaisons facultatives dans le français de conversation radiophonique*. Uppsala University Press.

Ahmad, Mohammad. 1993. *Vingt heures de français parlé: Aspects phonétiques de la liaison*. PhD thesis, Université Stendhal.

Akpossan, Johanne. 2015. *La consonne /R/ comme indice de la variation lectale: Cas du français en contact avec le créole guadeloupéen*. PhD thesis, Sorbonne Nouvelle Université.

Armstrong, Nigel. 1996. Variable deletion of French /l/: Linguistic, social and stylistic factors. *Journal of French Language Studies* 6(1). 1–21. https://doi.org/10.1017/S0959269500004956

Armstrong, Nigel. 2001. *Social and stylistic variation in spoken French: A comparative approach*. John Benjamins. https://doi.org/10.1075/impact.8

Armstrong, Nigel & Timothy Pooley. 2010. *Social and linguistic change in European French*. Palgrave Macmillan. https://doi.org/10.1057/9780230281714

Arnold, Aron. 2015a. *La voix genrée, entre idéologies et pratiques: Une étude sociophonétique*. PhD thesis, Université Sorbonne Nouvelle.

Arnold, Aron. 2015b. Voix et transidentité: Changer de voix pour changer de genre? *Langage et Société* 151(1). 87–105. https://doi.org/10.3917/ls.151.0087

Arnold, Aron & Maria Candea. 2015. Comment étudier l'influence des stéréotypes de genre et de race sur la perception de la parole? *Langage et Société* 152(2). 75–96. https://doi.org/10.3917/ls.152.0075

Ashby, William. 1981. French liaison as a sociolinguistic phenomenon. In William Cressey & Diana Napoli (eds.), *Linguistics Symposium on Romance Languages 9*, 46–57. Georgetown University Press.

Avanzi, Mathieu. 2019. Cartographier les régionalismes de Suisse romande et de France voisine à l'ère des sciences participatives. *Cahiers Internationaux de Sociolinguistique* 14(2). 43–104. https://doi.org/10.3917/cisl.1802.0043

Avanzi, Mathieu & Philippe Boula De Mareüil. 2019. Peut-on identifier perceptivement huit accents régionaux en français? La réponse des sciences participatives. *Glottopol* 31. 53–73.

Barbu, Stéphanie, Aurélie Nardy, Jean-Pierre Chevrot & Jacques Juhel. 2013. Language evaluation and use during early childhood: Adhesion to social norms or integration of environmental regularities? *Linguistics* 51(2). 381–411. https://doi.org/10.1515/ling-2013-0015

Bardiaux, Alice. 2014. *La prosodie de quelques variétés de français en Belgique: Analyse perceptive et acoustique*. PhD thesis, Université Catholique de Louvain.

Bayley, Robert. 2005. Second language acquisition and sociolinguistic variation. *Intercultural Communication Studies* 14(2). 1–15.

Bento, Margaret. 1998. Une étude sociophonétique des affriquées désonorisées en franco-québécois. *Revue Québécoise de Linguistique* 26(1). 13–26. https://doi.org/10.7202/603142ar

Blanchet, Philippe. 2016. *Discriminations: Combattre la glottophobie*. Textuel.

Blondeau, Hélène, Naomi Nagy, Gillian Sankoff & Pierrette Thibault. 2002. La couleur locale du français L2 des anglo-montréalais. *Acquisition et Interaction en Langue Étrangère* 17. 73–100. https://doi.org/10.4000/aile.1046

Boë, Louis-Jean & Jean-Pierre Tubach. 1992. *"De A à Zut": Dictionnaire phonétique du français parlé*. Ellug.

Booij, Geert & Daan De Jong. 1987. The domain of liaison: Theories and data. *Linguistics* 25(5). 1005–1025. https://doi.org/10.1515/ling.1987.25.5.1005

Boughton, Zoë. 2005. Accent levelling and accent localisation in northern French: Comparing Nancy and Rennes. *Journal of French Language Studies* 15(3). 235–256. https://doi.org/10.1017/S0959269505002140

Boughton, Zoë. 2006. When perception isn't reality: Accent identification and perceptual dialectology in French. *Journal of French Language Studies* 16(3). 277–304. https://doi.org/10.1017/S0959269506002535

Boughton, Zoë. 2015. Social class, cluster simplification and following context: Sociolinguistic variation in word-final post-obstruent liquid deletion in French. *Journal of French Language Studies* 25(1). 1–21. https://doi.org/10.1017/S0959269513000446

Boula De Mareüil, Philippe & Béatrice Akissi Boutin. 2011. Évaluation et identification perceptives d'accents ouest-africains en français. *Journal of French Language Studies* 21(3). 361–379. https://doi.org/10.1017/S0959269510000621

Boula De Mareüil, Philippe, Albert Rilliard & Alexandre Allauzen. 2012. Variation diachronique dans la prosodie du style journalistique: Le cas de l'accent initial. *Revue Française de Linguistique Appliquée* 17(1). 97–111. https://doi.org/10.3917/rfla.171.0097

Boula De Mareüil, Philippe, Bianca Vieru-Dimulescu, Cécile Woehrling & Martine Adda-Decker. 2008. Accents étrangers et régionaux en français: Caractérisation et identification. *Traitement Automatique des Langues* 49(3). 135–162.

Bourciez, Édouard & Jean Bourciez. 2006. *Phonétique française: Étude historique*. Klincksieck.

Buson, Laurence, Aurélie Nardy, Dominique Muller & Jean-Pierre Chevrot. 2018. The sociolinguistic repetition task: A new paradigm for exploring the cognitive coherence of language varieties. *Topics in Cognitive Science* 10(4). 803–817. https://doi.org/10.1111/tops.12380

Candea, Maria. 2016. L'accent dit "de banlieue", une mode? Étude auprès de lycéens en ZEP inscrits dans une dynamique de réussite scolaire. In Gilles Siouffi (ed.), *Modes langagières dans l'histoire*, 323–338. Honoré Champion.

Candea, Maria. 2017. La notion d'"accent de banlieue" à l'épreuve du terrain. *Glottopol* 29. 13–26.

Candea, Maria, Martine Adda-Decker & Lori Lamel. 2013. Recent evolution of non-standard consonantal variants in French broadcast news. *Proceedings of Interspeech 2013*. 412–416. https://doi.org/10.21437/Interspeech.2013-125

Candea, Maria & Leann Brown. 2022. Variation interculturelle de la perception du spectre masculin-féminin: Indexation de la voix genrée en France et aux Etats-Unis. In Vinay Swamy & Louisa Mackenzie (eds.), *Devenir non-binaire en français*, 127–153. Le Manuscrit.

Candea, Maria & Cyril Trimaille. 2015. Introduction. Phonétique, sociolinguistique, sociophonétique: Histoires parallèles et croisements. *Langage et Société* 151(1). 7–25. https://doi.org/10.3917/ls.151.0007

Candea, Maria, Jane Wottawa, Martine Adda-Decker & Lori Lamel. 2020. Merci·chh, entendu·chh: Variation phonétique ancienne ou émergence d'une proto-particule en voie de stabilisation? In Federica Diemoz, Gaetane Dostie & Florence Lefeuvre (eds.), *Le français innovant*, 291–308. Peter Lang.

Carton, Fernand. 1999. L'épithèse vocalique et son développement en français parlé. *Faits de Langues* 13. 35–45.

Carton, Fernand, Mario Rossi, Denis Autesserre & Pierre Léon. 1983. *Les accents des Français*. Hachette.

Castellotti, Véronique & Didier De Robillard. 2003. Des Français devant la variation: Quelques hypothèses. *Cahiers de l'Institut Linguistique de Louvain* 29. 223–240.

Chabanal, Damien. 2001. L'acquisition de phonèmes variables: Influences orthographique et sociolectale. *Travaux de Didactique de FLE* 45. 87–96.

Chabanal, Damien. 2003. *Un aspect de l'acquisition du français oral: La variation socio-phonétique chez l'enfant francophone*. PhD thesis, Université Paul Valéry.

Chevrot, Jean-Pierre. 1991. *La variation phonétique chez des enfants de 6 à 12 ans: Aspects développementaux et incidence des apprentissages alphabétiques*. PhD thesis, Université Stendhal.

Chevrot, Jean-Pierre, Laurence Beaud & Renata Varga. 2000. Developmental data on a French sociolinguistic variable: The word-final post-consonantal /R/. *Language Variation and Change* 12(3). 295–319. https://doi.org/10.1017/S095439450012304X

Chevrot, Jean-Pierre, Aurélie Nardy & Stéphanie Barbu. 2011. Developmental dynamics of SES-related differences in children's production of obligatory and variable phonological alternations. *Language Sciences* 33(1). 180–191. https://doi.org/10.1016/j.langsci.2010.08.007

Clairet, Sandrine. 2008. Une étude aérodynamique de la nasalité vocalique en français méridional. *Journées d'Etudes sur la Parole [JEP 2008]*.

De Jong, Daan. 1994. La sociophonologie de la liaison orléanaise. In Chantal Lyche (ed.), *French generative phonology: Retrospective and perspectives*, 95–130. Association for French Language Studies in association with the European Studies Research Institute.

Duez, Danielle. 1991. *La pause dans la parole de l'homme politique*. Éditions du CNRS.

Dugua, Céline & Olivier Baude. 2017. La liaison à Orléans, corpus et changement linguistique: Une première étude exploratoire. *Journal of French Language Studies* 27(1). 41–54. https://doi.org/10.1017/S0959269516000399

Durand, Jacques. 2014. À la recherche du schwa: Données, méthodes et théories. *SHS Web of Conferences* 8. 23–43. https://doi.org/10.1051/shsconf/20140801396

Durand, Jacques, Bernard Laks & Chantal Lyche. 2002. La phonologie du français contemporain: Usages, variétés et structure. In Claus D. Pusch & Wolfgang Raible (eds.), *Romanistische Korpuslinguistik–Korpora und gesprochene Sprache/Romance corpus linguistics–corpora and spoken language*, 93–106. Gunter Narr Verlag.

Durand, Jacques, Bernard Laks & Chantal Lyche. 2009. *Phonologie, variation et accents du français*. Hermès.

Durand, Jacques & Chantal Lyche. 2008. French liaison in the light of corpus data. *Journal of French Language Studies* 18(1). 33–66. https://doi.org/10.1017/S0959269507003158

Eckert, Penelope. 2000. *Linguistic variation as social practice: The linguistic construction of identity in Belten High.* Blackwell.

Encrevé, Pierre. 1988. *La liaison avec et sans enchaînement.* Édition du Seuil.

Fagyal, Zsuzsanna. 2010. *Accents de banlieue: Aspects prosodiques du français populaire en contact avec les langues de l'immigration.* L'Harmattan.

Fagyal, Zsuzsanna, Samarth Swarup, Anna María Escobar, Les Gasser & Kiran Lakkaraju. 2010. Centers and peripheries: Network roles in language change. *Lingua* 120(8). 2061–2079. https://doi.org/10.1016/j.lingua.2010.02.001

Fónagy, Iván. 1983. *La vive voix: Essais de psycho-phonétique.* Payot.

Fónagy, Iván. 1989. Le français change de visage? *Revue Romane* 24. 225–254.

Fouché, Pierre. 1959. *Traité de prononciation française.* Klincksieck.

Gasquet-Cyrus, Médéric. 2012. La discrimination à l'accent en France: Idéologies, discours et pratiques. *Carnets d'Atelier de Sociolinguistique* 6. 227–245.

Gasquet-Cyrus, Médéric. 2015. "Je vais et je viens entre terrains": Réflexions sur le terrain dans la théorisation sociolinguistique. *Langage et Société* 154(4). 17–32. https://doi.org/10.3917/ls.154.0017

Gasquet-Cyrus, Médéric & Gaëlle Planchenault. 2019. Jouer (de) l'accent marseillais à la télévision, ou l'art de mettre l'accent en boite. *Glottopol* 31. 113–132.

Gauchat, Louis. 1905. *L'unité phonétique dans le patois d'une commune.* Map Niemeyer.

Gautier, Rozenn & Jean-Pierre Chevrot. 2015. Social network and acquisition of sociolinguistic variation in a study abroad context: A preliminary study. In Rosamond Mitchell, Nicole Tracy-Ventura & Kevin McManus (eds.), *Social interaction, identity and language learning during residence abroad*, 169–184. Eurosla Monograph Series 4. https://eprints.soton.ac.uk/381255/1/EM04tot.pdf

Gautier, Rozenn & Jean-Pierre Chevrot. 2021. Usage, evaluation and awareness of French sociolinguistic variables by second-language learners during a stay abroad: The case of negative ne and optional liaison. In Anna Ghimenton, Aurélie Nardy & Jean-Pierre Chevrot (eds.), *Sociolinguistic variation and language acquisition across the lifespan*, 228–250. John Benjamins.

Hambye, Philippe. 2005. *La prononciation du français contemporain en Belgique: Variations, normes et identités.* PhD thesis, Université Catholique de Louvain.

Hansen, Anita Berit. 2000. Le E caduc interconsonantique en tant que variable sociolinguistique. *Linx* 42. 45–58. https://doi.org/10.4000/linx.777

Hansen, Anita Berit 2001. Les changements actuels des voyelles nasales du français parisien: Confusions ou changement en chaine? *La Linguistique* 37(2). 33–48. https://doi.org/10.3917/ling.372.0033

Hansen, Anita Berit & Maj-Britt Mosegaard Hansen. 2003. Le [E] prépausal et l'interaction. *Études Romanes* 54. 89–109.

Howard, Martin. 2006. Variation in advanced French interlanguage: A comparison of three (socio)linguistic variables. *Canadian Modern Language Review* 62(3). 379–400. https://doi.org/10.3138/cmlr.62.3.379

Howard, Martin. 2013. La liaison en français langue seconde: Une étude longitudinale préliminaire. *Language, Interaction and Acquisition* 4(2). 190–231. https://doi.org/10.1075/lia.4.2.04how

Howard, Martin, Isabelle Lemée & Vera Regan. 2006. The L2 acquisition of a phonological variable: The case of /l/ deletion in French. *Journal of French Language Studies* 16(1). 1–24. https://doi.org/10.1017/S0959269506002298

Hutin, Mathilde, Adèle Jatteau, Ioana Vasilescu, Lori Lamel & Martine Adda-Decker. 2020. Le schwa final en français standard est-il un "lubrifiant phonétique"? *SHS Web of Conferences* 78. Article 09004. https://doi.org/10.1051/shsconf/20207809004

Jamin, Mikael Jan. 2005. *Sociolinguistic variation in the Paris suburbs.* PhD thesis, University of Kent.

Ko, Young-Lim. 1996. *Étude prosodique du discours oral en français: Variables temporelles et variables mélodiques dans l'interview radiophonique.* PhD thesis, Université de Strasbourg.

Lafontaine, Dominique. 1986. *Le parti pris des mots.* Mardaga.

Laks, Bernard. 1977. Contribution empirique à l'analyse socio-différentielle de la chute de /r/ dans les groupes consonantiques finals. *Langue Française* 34. 109–125.

Laks, Bernard. 1980. *Différenciation linguistique et différenciation sociale: Quelques problèmes de sociolinguistique française.* PhD thesis, Université de Paris VIII–Vincennes.

Laks, Bernard. 1983. Langage et pratiques sociales. "*L'usage de la parole.*" *Actes de la Recherche en Sciences Sociales* 46 . 73–97.

Lambert, Wallace E., Hannah Frankle & G. Richard Tucker. 1966. Judging personality through speech: A French-Canadian example. *Journal of Communication* 16(4). 305–321. https://doi.org/10.1111/j.1460-2466.1966.tb00044.x

Langlard, H. 1928. *La liaison dans le français*. Librairie Ancienne Édouard Champion.

Lehka-Lemarchand, Iryna. 2007. *Accent de banlieue: Approche phonétique et sociolinguistique de la prosodie des jeunes d'une banlieue rouennaise*. PhD thesis, Université de Rouen.

Lehka-Lemarchand, Iryna. 2015. Questionner la signification sociale d'un indice prosodique de l'accent dit de banlieue en France. *Langage et Société* 151(1). 67–86. https://doi.org/10.3917/ls.151.0067

Léon, Pierre. 1968. L'accent méridional: Problème d'idiomatologie. *Studia Linguistica* 22(1). 33–50.

Léon, Pierre. 1973. Modèle standard et système vocalique du français populaire de jeunes Parisiens. In Guy Rondeau (ed.), *Contributions canadiennes à la linguistique appliquée*, 55–79. CEC.

Léon, Pierre. 1983. Les voyelles nasales et leurs réalisations dans les parlers français du Canada. *Langue Française* 60(1). 48–64.

Léon, Pierre. 1993. *Précis de phonostylistique: Parole et expressivité*. Nathan.

Léon, Pierre. 2007. *Phonétisme et prononciations du français*. Armand Colin.

Lucci, Vincent. 1983. *Étude phonétique du français contemporain à travers la variation situationnelle*. Publications de l'Université des Langues et Lettres de Grenoble.

Lyche, Chantal & Ingse Skattum. 2012. The phonological characteristics of French in Bamako, Mali. In Randall Gess, Chantal Lyche & Trudel Meisenburg (eds.), *Phonological variation in French: Illustrations from three continents*, 73–101. John Benjamins.

Malécot, André. 1975. French liaison as a function of grammatical, phonetic and paralinguistic variables. *Phonetica* 32. 161–179. https://doi.org/10.1159/000259697

Martin, Nathaël. 2005. *Réseaux sociaux et variations phonétiques*. PhD thesis, Université Stendhal.

Martinet, André. 1945. *La prononciation du français contemporain*. Droz.

Mettas, Odette. 1979. *La prononciation parisienne: Aspects phoniques d'un sociolecte parisien (du faubourg Saint-Germain à La Muette)*. SELAF.

Milne, Peter M. 2013. The relationship between schwa insertion and consonant cluster simplification in French: An analysis of covariance. *University of Pennsylvania Working Papers in Linguistics* 19(1). 123–128.

Moisset, Christine. 2000. *Variable liaison in Parisian French*. PhD dissertation, University of Pennsylvania.

Mougeon, Raymond & Jean-Marc Dewaele. 2002. Préface: L'acquisition de la variation par les apprenants du français langue seconde. *Acquisition et Interaction en Langue Étrangère* 17. 3–5. https://doi.org/10.4000/aile.1053

Mougeon, Raymond, Terry Nadasdi & Katherine Rehner. 2010. *The sociolinguistic competence of immersion students*. Multilingual Matters.

Myers, Emily L. & Diana L. Ranson. 2014. L'élision variable des /R/ et /l/ postconsonantiques finals en français méridional et septentrional: L'effet de l'âge, du lieu d'origine et des facteurs linguistiques. *SHS Web of Conferences* 8. 1345–1364. https://doi.org/10.1051/shsconf/20140801380

Nardy, Aurélie. 2008. *Acquisition des variables sociolinguistiques entre 2 et 6 ans: Facteurs sociologiques et influences des interactions au sein du réseau social*. PhD thesis, Université Stendhal.

Nardy, Aurélie, Hélène Bouchet, Isabelle Rousset, Loïc Liégeois, Laurence Buson, Céline Dugua & Jean-Pierre Chevrot. 2021. Variation sociolinguistique et réseau social: Constitution et traitement d'un corpus de données orales massives. *Corpus* 22. https://doi.org/10.4000/corpus.5561

Nardy, Aurélie, Jean-Pierre Chevrot & Stéphanie Barbu. 2013. The acquisition of sociolinguistic variation: Looking back and thinking ahead. *Linguistics* 51(2). 255–284. https://doi.org/10.1515/ling-2013-0011

Nardy, Aurélie, Jean-Pierre Chevrot & Stéphanie Barbu. 2015. Variation phonétique et acquisition du langage: Repères, débats, perspectives. *Langage et Société* 151(1). 27–44. https://doi.org/10.3917/ls.151.0027

Nardy, Aurélie, Éric Fleury, Jean-Pierre Chevrot, Márton Karsai, Laurence Buson, Maryse Bianco, Isabelle Rousset, Céline Dugua, Loïc Liégeois, Stéphanie Barbu, Christophe Crespelle, Anthony Busson, Yannick Léo, Hélène Bouchet & Sicheng Dai. 2016. DyLNet – Language dynamics, linguistic learning, and sociability at preschool: Benefits of wireless proximity sensors in collecting big data. https://dylnet.univ-grenoble-alpes.fr/

Paternostro, Roberto. 2014. *L'intonation des jeunes en région parisienne: Aspects phonétiques et sociolinguistiques, implications didactiques*. PhD thesis, Université Paris Ouest Nanterre La Défense.

Paternostro, Roberto. 2016. *Diversité des accents et enseignement du français. Les parlers jeunes en région parisienne.* L'Harmattan.

Peretz, Caroline. 1977. Aspects sociolinguistiques du parler parisien contemporain. *Studia Phonetica* 13. 65–78.

Prikhodkine, Alexei. 2019. Accents régionaux du français: Interroger des évidences. *Glottopol* 31. 10–26.

Pustka, Elissa. 2011. Le conditionnement lexical de l'élision des liquides en contexte post-consonantique final. *Langue Française* 169(1). 19–38. https://doi.org/10.3917/lf.169.0019

Racine, Isabelle, Jacques Durand & Helene N. Andreassen. 2016. PFC, codages et représentations: La question du schwa. *Corpus* 15. https://doi.org/10.4000/corpus.3014

Racine, Isabelle, Sandra Schwab & Sylvain Detey. 2013. Accent(s) suisse(s) ou standard(s) suisse(s)? Approche perceptive dans quatre régions de Suisse romande. In Anika Falkert (ed.), *La perception des accents du français hors de France*, 41–59. CIPA.

Remysen, Wim. 2014. Les Québécois perçoivent-ils le français montréalais comme une variété topolectale distincte? Résultats d'une analyse perceptuelle exploratoire. *Revue Canadienne de Linguistique* 1(59). 109–135. https://doi.org/10.1017/S0008413100000177

Remysen, Wim. 2016a. Langue et espace au Québec: Les Québécois perçoivent-ils des accents régionaux? In Dino Gavinelli & Chiara Molinari (eds.), *Espaces réels et imaginaires au Québec et en Acadie: Enjeux culturels, linguistiques et géographiques*, 31–57. LED.

Remysen, Wim. 2016b. Le "vent" dans les voiles à Montréal, ou la diffusion sociale et géographique de la réalisation postérieure de la voyelle nasale ouverte /ɑ̃/ en français québécois. *Cahiers Internationaux de Sociolinguistique* 10(2).135–158. https://doi.org/10.3917/cisl.1602.0135

Romano, Antonio. 2003. Étude phonétique de quelques éléments des pratiques langagières intra-groupales de jeunes grenoblois. In Jacqueline Billiez (ed.), *Pratiques et représentation langagières de groupes de pairs en milieu urbain [rapport de recherche pour l'Observatoire des pratiques linguistiques]*, 44–49 + IX–XII (ANNEXE IV). Laboratoire Lidilem.

Sankoff, Gillian & Hélène Blondeau. 2007. Language change across the lifespan: /r/ in Montreal French. *Language* 83(3). 560–588. https://doi.org/10.1353/lan.2007.0106

Sax, Kelly J. 2003. *Acquisition of stylistic variation in American learners of French.* PhD dissertation, Indiana University.

Simon, Anne-Catherine, Philippe Hambye, Alice Bardiaux & Philippe Boula de Mareüil. 2012. Caractéristiques des accents régionaux en français: Que nous apprennent les approches perceptives? In Anne Catherine Simon (ed.), *La variation prosodique régionale en français*, 27–40. De Boeck supérieur.

Soum-Favaro, Christiane, Annelise Coquillon & Jean-Pierre Chevrot. 2014. *La liaison: Approches contemporaines.* Peter Lang.

Straka, Georges. 1952. La prononciation parisienne, ses divers aspects et ses traits généraux. *Bulletin de la Faculté des Lettres de Strasbourg* 30(5–6). 212–253.

Telep, Suzie. 2018. "Moi je whitise jamais." Accent, subjectivité et processus d'accommodation langagière en contexte migratoire et postcolonial. *Langage et Societé* 165(3). 31–49. https://doi.org/10.3917/ls.165.0031

Thomas, Alain. 2004. Phonetic norm versus usage in advanced French as a second language. *International Review of Applied Linguistics in Language Teaching* 42(4). 365–382. https://doi.org/10.1515/iral.2004.42.4.365

Thomas, Alain. 2006. L'évolution des variantes phonétiques méridionales dans le sud-est de la France. *La Linguistique* 42(1). 53–72. https://doi.org/10.3917/ling.421.0053

Trimaille, Cyril. 2007. Stylisation vocale et autres procédés dialogiques dans la socialisation langagière adolescente. *Cahiers de Praxématique* 49. 183–206. https://doi.org/10.4000/praxematique.2056

Trimaille, Cyril. 2010. Consonnes dentales palatalisées/affriquées en français contemporain: Indicateurs, marqueurs et/ou variantes en développement? In Michaël Abecassis & Gudrun Ledegen (eds.), *Les voix du français: Usages et représentations*, 89–100. Peter Lang.

Trimaille, Cyril & Maria Candea. 2021. Urban youth accents in France: Can a slight palatalization of /t/ and /d/ challenge French sociophonetics? In Gaëlle Planchenault & Livia Poljak (eds.), *Pragmatics of accents*, 41–62. John Benjamins.

Trimaille, Cyril, Maria Candea & Iryna Lehka-Lemarchand. 2012. Existe-t-il une signification sociale stable et univoque de la palatalisation/affrication en français? Étude sur la perception de variantes non standard. *SHS Web of Conferences* 1. 2249–2262. https://doi.org/10.1051/shsconf/20120100122

Uritescu, Dorin, Raymond Mougeon, Katherine Rehner & Terry Nadasdi. 2004. Acquisition of the internal and external constraints of variable schwa deletion by French immersion students. *International Review of Applied Linguistics* 42(4). 349–364. https://doi.org/10.1515/iral.2004.42.4.349

Vernet, Marie & Cyril Trimaille. 2007. Contribution à l'analyse de la palatalisation en français parlé contemporain. *Nottingham French Studies* 46(2). 82–99.

Viana dos Santos, Gabriela. 2021. *Représentations et schémas sociolinguistiques en langue étrangère: L'exemple d'apprenants sinophones et anglophones du FLE*. PhD thesis, Université Grenoble Alpes.

Viana dos Santos, Gabriela, Laurence Buson & Jean-Pierre Chevrot. 2018. Acquisition et structure des schémas sociolinguistiques en langue étrangère. *SHS Web of Conferences* 1. 9–13. https://doi.org/10.1051/shsconf/20184610007

Vieru-Dimulescu, Bianca. 2008. *Caractérisation et identification d'accents étrangers en français*. PhD thesis, Université Paris-Sud 11.

Walter, Henriette. 1994. Variétés actuelles des voyelles nasales du français. *Communication and Cognition* 27(1–2). 223–235.

Woehrling, Cécile. 2009. *Accents régionaux en français: Perception, analyse et modélisation à partir de grands corpus*. PhD thesis, Université Paris-Sud 11.

26

SOCIOPHONETICS AND ARABIC

Ghada Khattab and Paul Foulkes

Introduction

In this chapter we review sociophonetic research from the perspective of Arabic. In doing so we serve two main aims. First, we provide a guide for researchers of Arabic who are interested in sociophonetics, considering data collection, data analysis, and a range of theoretical and applied issues informed by such work. Second, we highlight issues where Arabic presents particular challenges for those methodologies and theoretical developments that have largely been developed in the United States and Europe, and via a dominant focus on mainstream European languages. The review thus contributes to the small but growing body of work focusing on sociophonetic variation in diverse languages and communities (cf. Stanford & Preston 2009), and seeks to encourage expansion of the still small body of sociophonetic work dedicated to Arabic.

We begin with a justification for our focus on Arabic sociophonetics. We then address some methodological issues in sociophonetics relating to sampling the community and sampling the language. This is followed by a survey of theoretical issues where Arabic presents certain difficulties but also offers particular insights. We finish with a brief agenda for future work in Arabic sociophonetics.

Motivation for the spotlight on Arabic

Sociophonetic research, like much of linguistics in general, has traditionally been WEIRD: strongly concentrated on Western, Educated, Industrialized, Rich, and Democratic communities. The empirical basis for sociophonetics is dominated by monolingual speakers of English and other mainstream languages in Western urban centers, characterized by particular types of housing, education, work, leisure activities, social networks, and social mobility. Our understanding of sociophonetic variation is thus rather skewed and perhaps unrepresentative of all languages and communities. A more diverse empirical base allows us to challenge widely held claims and assumptions.

For example, scholars of language variation and change often take various principles as axiomatic, such as the following: language varies as a function of gender (usually in fact addressed via the binary biological categories of male versus female); women use more standard variants than men; standard varieties confer prestige on the speaker; changes are generally led by younger

DOI: 10.4324/9781003034636-29

women in the middle of the social hierarchy; and change is promoted through geographical mobility and open social networks (see, e.g., Chambers 2003).

Putting the spotlight on people in the Arab World and on the Arabic language, as we do here, is an excellent way to test and challenge such widely held assumptions and to further our understanding of sociophonetic variation.

Self-consciously "sociophonetic" research on Arabic is a relatively small but growing body of research—although it is much wider if we include studies in dialectology, sociolinguistics, and language variation and change (many of which are reviewed below; see also Bassiouney 2009; Al-Wer & Horesh 2019; Al-Wer et al. 2022). Dialectology has a long history and furnishes a wealth of important descriptive detail in terms of social as well as regional variation (e.g., Christie 1901; Bauer 1910; Bergsträßer 1915; Grant 1921; Johnstone 1967; Versteegh 2014; Cotter & de Jong 2019).

The Arabic language also differs typologically, structurally, and culturally from languages such as English, and is complicated via the presence of diglossia (Ferguson 1959; Kaye 1994; Albirini 2016). It is important to emphasize that we do not assume that Arabic research will necessarily reveal differences compared with, for example, work on English. Finding comparable patterns across diverse languages and communities serves only to strengthen theoretical models of sociolinguistic variation or of language more generally. We should also bear in mind that there is enormous social and linguistic diversity in the Arab World, unsurprisingly given its geographical spread and estimated population of over 420 million L1 speakers (UNESCO 2012). It is important in any discussion of variation in Arabic that we therefore do not overgeneralize, and that we do not portray a simplistic orientalist comparison between the Arab World and "the West."

We turn now to consider the main stages of sociophonetic research, from data collection to analysis. Two key sets of methodological decisions need to be made by any researcher in empirical linguistics: sampling the community and sampling the language (Milroy & Gordon 2003; Tagliamonte 2006). We address these two topics below, highlighting ways in which study of Arabic might differ from that of languages like English.

Methodological challenges and innovations: Sampling the community

The first issue in sociophonetic studies is to decide whose language to study. In sociolinguistics in general it is accepted that we need a representative sample of a community. Defining the speech community, however, is far from simple (Patrick 2002; Buchstaller & Khattab 2014). Pragmatic decisions are therefore usually based on regional and broad demographic divisions. It is also usual practice to seek data from both men and women, and from different ages and social backgrounds. In sociolinguistics the latter are usually sampled along axes of biological/chronological age and socioeconomic class. None of these demographic categories is unproblematic in any community (see, e.g., Ash 2002; Cheshire 2002), and in the Arab World, defining the community and identifying relevant demographic categories may all present particular challenges.

Delimiting the community

Delimiting the community can be extremely complex. Whereas sociolinguists in North America and Europe have traditionally worked primarily on stable communities in cities and rural areas, or self-defined communities of practice, in parts of the Arab World it might be necessary to take into account issues of major social change such as waves of migration or displacement, and ethnicities linked to religion and/or historical tribal or clan affiliation (Owens 2001). These factors mean that physical communities can change rapidly in terms of the numbers and composition of inhabitants. Long-term and widespread mobility may yield dramatic language change, including the development of new dialects (see, e.g., Kerswill & Williams 2000 and Trudgill 2004 for examples of mobility and dialect contact in English-speaking communities). Al-Wer (2007, 2020) offers a detailed discussion of new dialect formation in Amman, Jordan, with a particular focus on Palestinian migrants. Palestine itself provides a particularly revealing example of dramatic social change and its effects on linguistic variation, after repeated population movements— most of them forced—and subsequent constraints in terms of networks and mobility in day-to-day life (Al-Shareef 2002; Cotter & Horesh 2015; Cotter 2022). Kuwait is another example, as the country's population underwent large-scale migration following the discovery of oil in the 1970s. Present-day Kuwait has more than twice as many non-nationals living and working in the country than nationals, with pronounced repercussions for language and dialect contact (Hassan 2009; Taqi 2010).

Ethnicity, religious, and sectarian affiliation

Studies within Arabic sociolinguistics have looked at dialect variation that correlates with ethnicity relating to both religious and sectarian affiliation (Germanos & Miller 2015; Holes 2019). Religious-based dialect descriptions include those of speakers of Arabic who are not only Muslim but also Jewish (e.g., Blanc 1964; Heath 2002), Druze (Blanc 1953; Salonen 1979; Al-Khatib & Alzoubi 2009), or Christian (Abu-Haidar 1990; Habib 2011). Multiethnic studies can also be found. Both Christians and Muslims were included by Germanos (2009) in Beirut, Spolsky et al. (2000) in Bethlehem, and Abu-Haidar (1990) and Blanc (1964) in Baghdad. In terms of sectarian-based descriptions, Holes (1983, 1987) compared Shi'a and Sunni Muslims in Bahrain, while Al-Khatib & Alzoubi (2009) compared Druze and Sunni dialects in Jordan. Germanos & Miller (2015) warn that regional and/or ethnic origin can sometimes be the source of observed variation, and provide examples of absence of religious or sect-based variation.

Alshangiti (2016) worked with Mauritanian Arab settlers in Medina who came from either white or black origins, while Taqi (2010) compared the dialects of Najdi and Ajami origins. Najdi Kuwaitis originate from Najd in Saudi Arabia, and include the ruling family, while Ajami Kuwaitis came from Persia. Within the established communities in Kuwait City, ethnicity (rather than similarity to Standard Arabic) plays a major role in the establishment of the prestigious variety (Hassan 2009; Taqi 2010). The Najdi dialect of the ruling Al Sabah family drives current changes in the realization of /ɣ/ and /dʒ/ in young speakers of Ajami origin (towards [q] and [j] respectively), despite the fact that the Ajami variants for /ɣ/ and /dʒ/ happen to coincide with the Standard ([ɣ] and [dʒ]).

Age

With respect to age, researchers often sample different poles of the biological age continuum (e.g., Docherty et al. 1997), or sample the whole continuum and either treat age as a continuous variable or impose categorical divisions upon it (see Eckert 1997). These approaches may be appropriate in some Arabic-speaking communities, but not all (Horesh & Cotter 2015). Where major social changes have affected a community, it might be wise to group speakers according to their shared experience of those events (e.g., Al-Shareef 2002; Taqi 2010; Cotter 2013; Shetewi 2018). In Gaza, for example, Al-Shareef (2002) divided his refugee speakers into three age groups according to their shared experiences of mass migration into Gaza following major political events in 1948 and 1967.

Taqi (2010) chose her age groups based on three waves of migration in Kuwait following the discovery of oil, and their repercussions on jobs, lifestyles, and where migrants settled, and the resulting contact with established communities. Her youngest participants from the migrant Ajami community of interest mixed with the established Kuwaitis of Najdi origin the most, leading to the biggest changes in the Ajami dialect amongst young speakers, especially females. While innovative forms are typically found amongst teenagers in Western societies, Shetewi (2018) found a reverse effect in the degree of adoption on nonlocal features in the Palestinian refugee community she studied near Damascus. Children (aged 9–12) produced Damascene variants for /ðˤ/ and /ð/ which were prominent in the speech of adult females ([dˤ] and [d] respectively), but both male and female teenagers (aged 12–16) exhibited an affinity to Palestinian Bedouin forms that were local to the community ([ðˤ] and [ð]).

Social class and social network

Social class is sometimes defined by the occupation of a speaker (or of the speaker's parents), and sometimes by a combination of occupation, education, and housing (Milroy & Gordon 2003). Haeri's (1996) Cairo study follows Labov's general principles for defining social class via a composite consisting of parental occupation, the speaker's education, neighborhood, and the speaker's occupation, arranged in order of importance. By contrast, Al-Shareef (2002) did not include class as a variable in his Gaza study, as most residents had had limited access to education, and the particular circumstance of the refugee camp meant that no clear class structure was evident at a level that could be incorporated in a formal way to the study.

In many other studies in the Middle East, however, education has been widely used as proxy for both class and social network (Al-Wer 1997, 2002). This is because education is the key route by which speakers can access the elite form of their language, such as Classical or Modern Standard Arabic (Abd-el-Jawad 1986; Al-Wer 1997). Education is also the key to white-collar jobs which, though not necessarily well paid, elevate individuals to the middle class. However, Ibrahim (1986) makes the interesting observation that we should not assume that high levels of education automatically lead to high usage of the Standard/Classical language. This is because, at least in some Middle Eastern societies, high levels of education might be associated with multilingualism, and languages other than Arabic (especially English or French) might be associated with prestige. This is certainly the case, for example, in parts of Lebanon and Egypt. Similarly, Al-Wer (2002) points out that education may be a proxy for social mobility; she presents data from a study on phonological variation and change in Jordan which shows a confound between highly educated speakers and speakers with external social networks, leading to an increase in nonlocal features such as [t] for /θ/. In fact, highly educated speakers tend to be at the forefront of vernacular innovations (e.g., [t] for /θ/, [d] for /ð/, and [ʒ] for /dʒ/; Al-Wer 2002). This points to the importance of separating the study of the Standard from the vernacular, with most of the interesting variation happening in the latter. This issue is discussed further below.

Implications for fieldwork

Communities may be structured along lines that pose major constraints in fieldwork. In some communities, for example, it can be impossible for a fieldworker to gain access to speakers unless he or she is a member of that same community (cf. Milroy 1987 on constraints in Belfast, Northern Ireland). It may therefore be necessary to recruit a team of fieldworkers to conduct analysis in a study that seeks to sample a whole city or quarter, or to spend considerable time and effort establishing trust with the community, perhaps via local mediators. In her study of the spoken variety in Ras-Beirut, Lebanon, Naïm-Sanbar (1985) depicts the rich social, religious, and ethnic variation in the area, originally comprising established Sunni and Greek Orthodox Beirutis, and subsequently witnessing further settlements (some transient) by Catholics, Druze, Syrian Jews, Muslim Shi'as, Kurds, Egyptian migrants, and Palestinian refugees. The communities were further divided by socioeconomic status, with some professions (e.g., fishing) under threat. With her data collection taking place at the height of the civil war in Lebanon, Naïm-Sanbar had to limit her fieldwork to the Muslim community, and navigated the different social classes by adopting different personas (which these days, admittedly, might require careful ethical justification). For instance, she pretended to be a journalist interested in interviewing fishermen about their tradition in one setting, and visited, for example, hairdressers and mechanics with different guises.

Constraints on the fieldworker apply more widely when it comes to working with both male and female speakers. In some Middle Eastern societies it is socially unacceptable for a man to be left alone with women from outside his immediate family. Al-Shareef (2002) solved this access problem by training his wife to conduct the fieldwork with his female informants. He also developed different interview protocols for participants of different age and sex groups, to facilitate discussion by focusing on different topics likely to be of interest to specific groups. Similarly, Alsiraih (2013) recorded male participants in her husband's presence. Cotter (2013), on the other hand, was able to access both male and female participants in Gaza, as did Khattab (2007b) in Beirut.

One potential consequence of using different fieldworkers is that the recorded data may be affected by accommodation to the fieldworker or changes in topic, either because their strategies differ or because speakers respond in different ways to different interlocutors (e.g., via accommodation processes) or topics. This was reportedly an outcome in Haeri's (1996) Cairo study, where women dramatically increased their use of palatalized variants of /t, d/ when speaking to a male fieldworker. It is important to monitor any potential effect of the fieldworker to ensure parity of data, although how to do so represents something of a challenge. Volatile political situations may make it dangerous to travel to certain communities, and researchers may not have easy access to fieldworkers from the community or the funds to pay them. Shetewi (2018) lost complete access to her community of Palestinian Syrians near Damascus due to the civil war, and as a result trained her mother and sister to carry out the fieldwork.

More generally, sensitive political or ethnic situations may create difficulties in gaining the trust of participants in a study. In Gaza, where there was particular concern among residents over the security services, Al-Shareef (2002) and Cotter (2013) very carefully adopted a "friend of a friend" approach (Milroy 1987). They established the confidence of their subjects via a fairly lengthy process of getting to know the families before embarking on recording. For instance, after an introduction to the family via the mutual friend, Al-Shareef explained at length his own family history in the camp, including who his father and grandfather were. One advantage Al-Shareef reports of working in this way is that the strong family bond enabled him to work with whole families once trust had been gained. Fieldwork would begin with the senior generation as a matter of courtesy, and to confirm the veracity of the work. Al-Shareef also reports that older family members were usually present during recordings, out of interest or for reasons of monitoring the activity, which had the useful consequence that target speakers were more likely to speak as they would normally, thus offering some security over the potential effects of the observer's paradox (Labov 1972).

Methodological challenges and innovations: Sampling the language

Sampling the vernacular

In variationist sociolinguistics the "vernacular" is the principal object of study—that is, speech produced in everyday circumstances when speakers are least conscious of how they are speaking (Labov 1972). Techniques have therefore been developed to put speakers at ease and to deflect attention from the act of speaking, for example via using carefully planned interview protocols (Tagliamonte 2006) or interviewing informants in pairs or small groups, to minimize the role played by the researcher. Arabic may present specific challenges when attempting to elicit vernacular forms. In Arabic linguistics there has traditionally been a strong priority for the study of the Classical form of the language, that of the Qur'an, or of Modern Standard Arabic (MSA). While both are no doubt prestigious varieties, they are nobody's native dialects and are only used in restricted functions—a diglossic situation *par excellence* (Ferguson 1959). Sociophonetic research on Arabic is, by contrast, concerned primarily with the vernacular, as Classical Arabic is a more homogeneous form, shared by Arabic speakers regardless of their vernacular dialects. The rules of Tajweed (Qur'anic recitation) are more explicit in their phonetic description than one is likely to encounter in any language learning situation, due to the religious teachers' attempt to preserve the "true" or "original" pronunciation (e.g., Binte Faizal, Khattab & McKean 2015; Binte Faizal 2019). However, studies of pupils of Tajweed demonstrate how variation is pervasive even in these restricted and prescriptivist environments (Alsurf 2012). Similarly, studies of MSA, the standard variety that is used in media throughout the Arab World, show that it exhibits local variation depending on the vernacular dialect of the speaker (Embarki et al. 2007).

The overwhelming use of MSA in the written form of the language presents considerable methodological difficulties if written prompts are needed to elicit controlled material. Deflecting the attention of speakers from their speech might be more difficult than in a case like English, and there is a risk that speakers will switch from the vernacular to the Standard. Alternative techniques for eliciting careful speech in this circumstance include the use of pictures (Alsiraih 2013) and direct questions (e.g., "what is the word for …?"). The same techniques are also valuable where informants have low levels of literacy. (Researchers of Western languages also often underestimate how uncomfortable speakers might be when asked to read aloud, particularly if they are not highly educated.) More recently, and thanks to the rise in the use of the written medium on social media, it has become more acceptable to use written Arabic to represent colloquial varieties, either through the use of the normal Arabic script (Khattab & Al-Tamimi 2014) or a transliterated version using the Roman script (Haggan 2007) made popular in texting (Al-Tamimi & Gorgis 2007).

Rich variation is particularly found within the vernacular. There is a continuum of local dialects and regional standards, the former ranging from varieties referred to as "vulgar" at one end of the range and "educated spoken Arabic" at the other (Mitchell 1986), with yet others emerging due to dialect contact and the evolution of popular mainstream media outlets in the Arab World (Albirini 2016). In everyday circumstances speakers may shift from nonstandard local forms to MSA (Germanos 2018), but most systematic variation takes place within the vernaculars. It should also be borne in mind that the sociophonetic variables of interest may involve variants that are shared by Standard and vernacular varieties. So while some variants are typically associated with the Standard, it is important to evaluate whether their use by speakers is actually a shift to the Standard or whether they happen to coincide with dialect features. For instance [q] can either be a realization of the standard /q/ or a dialectal variant used in Druze dialects, Syrian Alawi and rural

Syrian dialects (Behnstedt 1997; Daher 1997), as well as Christian dialects in Iraq (Blanc 1964). Thus observing use of [q] alone cannot be interpreted straightforwardly as an index of Standard or colloquial usage. Similarly, [θ] for /θ/, [ð] for /ð/, and [dʒ] for /dʒ/ can either signal the use of the Standard variants by the speakers or be local dialectal variants as can be found in Bedouin Palestinian (Shetewi 2018), indigenous Jordanian (Al-Wer 2014), or Kuwaiti Ajami (Taqi 2010).

Choice of variables

Consonants

Analysis of phonological variables is usually possible with a recording of reasonable length, although phonemes/variables do differ in frequency and it is thus important to ensure an adequate number of tokens can be extracted from a given recording. The choice of variables that characterizes Arabic studies, however, differs in an interesting way from English. While much work on variation in English has focused on vowels, Arabic work instead concentrates rather more on consonants. It is widely assumed that vowels carry a great deal of the burden of indexical information (e.g., Wells 1982:187). Existing work on Arabic suggests the opposite, as the most widely studied social and regional variables are /q/, /k/, /θ/, /ð/, /dˤ/, /ðˤ/, /dʒ/, and pharyngealization/emphasis (Al-Essa 2019). This difference may reveal Arabic to be an exception to a more general rule, potentially linked to linguistic typology, or it may simply be that consonantal variation in Arabic has been considered easier to detect. The structure of Arabic words, based on consonantal roots, is typologically unusual and appears restricted to Semitic languages (McCarthy 1979; Boudelaa & Marslen-Wilson 2001).

Several studies have been conducted on pharyngeal and pharyngealized consonants (e.g., Hassan & Heselwood 2011) but few consider sociolinguistic patterning except for "gender" (in practice, sex) (e.g., Kahn 1975; Al-Tamimi 2002; Al-Tamimi & Barkat-Defradas 2003; Khattab, Al-Tamimi & Heselwood 2006).

Another prominent aspect of the phonology of Arabic is gemination (or contrastive consonant length). Recent experimental work on this category of sounds is unveiling interesting cross-dialectal differences in their phonetic implementation (short-to-long ratio, influence on neighboring sounds, etc.) as well as their phonological patterning (syllabic affiliation, permissible preceding vowels length, etc.) (Ham 1998; Hassan 2003; Khattab 2007b; Khattab & Al-Tamimi 2009, 2014). Hardly any work has looked at nondurational indices, which play a secondary role for Lebanese Arabic (Al-Tamimi & Khattab 2015). Work on CV co-articulation also shows a promising line of enquiry for the distinction between MSA and dialects, or within-dialect differences (Al-Tamimi 2004; Embarki et al. 2007).

Vowels

Arabic vowel inventories are smaller than those of a language like English, and mainly serve to mark grammatical functions such as gender and number. It remains an empirical question of some interest to establish whether or not these structural properties make particular segments more or less likely to carry indexical meaning. Recent work demonstrates that Arabic vowels do indeed carry indexical meaning (e.g., Al-Wer 2002; Habib 2014; Wehbe 2017). For instance, Wehbe (2017) looked at the raising of /æ/ and /æ:/ in the Lebanese variety of Mahrouna and found that, apart from phonological conditioning (the vowels only raise in nonemphatic environments) there was age-related variation in the realization of these vowels, with older speakers raising towards [i(:)] while younger speakers raised towards [e(:)]. However, very little documentation of dialectal variation in vowel production or perception is available (but see Barkat-Defradas, Al-Tamimi & Benkiran 2003; Salam & Embarki 2012).

There is also a rising number of rigorous phonetic studies of segmental patterns in Arabic, but without explicit sociophonetic interest. Descriptive studies on the vowel systems of various dialects (e.g., Al-Tamimi & Ferragne 2005; Ahmed 2008; Amir, Amir & Rosenhouse 2014) show interesting variation in vowel inventory size and makeup, and marked vowel quality differences between phonologically short and long vowels which were traditionally thought to differ only in length. Sophisticated analyses have also demonstrated the value of looking at dynamic rather than just static cues for the identification of vowels in various dialects (e.g., Al-Tamimi 2007a, 2007b, 2008; Almurashi, Al-Tamimi & Khattab 2020). Vowel variation in Arabic remains an area that is ripe for further research.

Suprasegmental features

In Arabic, as in most languages, far more research has been conducted on segmental topics than suprasegmental ones. Work by Sam Hellmuth and colleagues on intonational and prosodic patterns in several dialects of Arabic thus marks a major advance in prosodic phonology and sociophonetics. They show that there are patterns of intonational variation across Arabic varieties which are interesting for both typological and sociolinguistic research. For instance, while most varieties of Arabic typically apply tonal marking to heads, Hellmuth et al. (2015) demonstrate that Moroccan Arabic is an edge-marking variety. Similarly, most accents apply accents at phrase level, but Chahal & Hellmuth (2014) found a richer accent distribution in Egyptian Arabic. Some work on cross-dialectal comparison in contrastive focus and f0 has also started to emerge (see also Yeou 2005; Hellmuth 2007; Yeou et al. 2007).

Other suprasegmental features have received limited attention. Fagyal (2010) analyses rhythmic properties of French spoken in Paris by L1 Arabic speakers from North Africa. Her aim is to test claims that Arabic is influencing youth French, as evidenced for example in phonetic forms used in rap (including vowel reduction and trilled /r/). While the quantitative data for rhythm showed little difference between immigrant and indigenous patterns, several phonetic differences were observed at an allophonic level, including onset glottal stop, use of palatal affricates, and coda devoicing in /CVC/ syllables. Sometimes differences which originate in segmental variation develop into suprasegmental ones. For instance, Alsiraih (2013) and Khattab, Alsiraih & Al-Tamimi (2018) show how the different articulatory strategies involved in pharyngeal production in Iraqi Arabic can lead to accompanying nasalization; when the degree of nasalization in certain varieties (in this case Baghdadi) advances beyond being a by-product of laryngeal constriction, a phenomenon of phonologization takes place, and nasalization becomes a salient aspect of a particular variety. Another suprasegmental aspect of pharyngeals and pharyngealized sounds relates to the extent to which they influence neighboring sounds and syllables. This is typically referred to as emphasis spread, and has been treated in phonological (Davis 1995) and phonetic accounts (Embarki et al. 2007; Embarki et al. 2011), the latter showing co-articulatory effects which vary according to style, gender, and region).

Vocal setting is also widely reported to differ in line with gender in Arabic, an observation that is above the level of consciousness and often commented upon by lay people. That is, a fronted vocal setting (involving palatalization of /t, d/ and depharyngealization) often characterizes women's voices, whereas men are inclined to use a backed or lowered setting (less palatalization and stronger pharyngealization; Schmidt 1986). Both men and women in urban settings may sound more "feminine" to Bedouin ears, whose pharyngealization tends to be even stronger (Bellem 2007).

Choice of analytic methods

One consequence of the importance of consonants in word structure is that research on Arabic has made wide use of instrumental phonetic techniques in analysis of consonants. Acoustic analysis is particularly common, as for most languages, but in sociophonetics acoustic analysis has over-whelmingly been targeted at vowels. Acoustic and articulatory techniques have been applied widely to typologically unusual consonants in Arabic, including pharyngeal and epiglottal constrictions in emphatic and post-velar articulations (e.g., Moisik, Esling & Crevier-Buchman 2010; Zeroual, Esling & Hoole 2011; Al-Tamimi 2017), tap and trill articulation (e.g., Khattab 2002a; Heselwood, Howard & Ranjoys 2011), and gemination (Khattab & Al-Tamimi 2014; Al-Tamimi & Khattab 2015, 2018; see also Scott & Idrissi 2018 for experiments on audiovisual cues). However, these are primarily phonetic or laboratory phonology studies with little direct import for sociophonetics. There has been a recent increase in acoustic work within Arabic sociolinguistics (e.g., Alsiraih 2013; Almbark & Hellmuth 2016; Ahmed 2018), but a lot more work is needed in this area. This work would benefit from mirroring recent methodological advances, including adapting forced alignment packages like FAVE (Rosenfelder et al. 2014) or DARLA (Reddy & Stanford 2015) for the large-scale study of variation in Arabic, and the use of advanced statistical techniques (e.g., Kendall & Thomas 2018; Winter 2019). Work by Al-Tamimi and colleagues is making significant first steps in that direction (e.g., Almurashi, Al-Tamimi & Khattab 2020; Al-Tamimi et al. 2022). Similarly, Hassan & Heselwood (2011) provide excellent examples of instrumental articulatory work on Arabic using techniques such as nasoendoscopy, videofluoroscopy, laryngos-copy, electropalatography, and electromagnetic articulography, while Ntelitheos & Leung (2021) include a range of experimental techniques for all levels of language structure. There is emerging ultrasound work investigating variation in the realization of affricates in Emirati Arabic (Szreder, Derrick & Ben-Ammar 2021), and research using real-time Magnetic Resonance Imaging (rtMRI) to explore pharyngealization (Hermes et al. 2021). However, little work of the kind included in these volumes is yet being carried out with a sociolinguistic interest. Future research can certainly benefit from applying these techniques to large and heterogeneous speaker samples needed to investigate socially motivated research questions.

Sociophonetic work with children

A final comment in respect of sampling the language concerns work with children. There have been several developmental studies of Arabic (e.g., Amayreh & Dyson 1998; Ammar & Morsi 2006; Saleh et al. 2007; Ayyad 2011; Alqattan 2015; AlAjroush 2020) with a focus on documenting normal development and contrasting it with pathological features, but with relatively little interest in social or regional variation. Variationist sociolinguistics, in turn, has not dealt with the issue of children's acquisition of sociolinguistic variation with anything like the industry that has been applied to adult speakers. We have relatively limited knowledge of how variation is transmitted between generations (Foulkes & Vihman 2015) or of how input to children differs from speech between adults (Foulkes, Docherty & Watt 2005). Some informative work in this vein has been conducted on Arabic, however (e.g., Khattab 2006, 2007a, 2009; Habib 2014; Shetewi 2018).

A key problem in understanding acquisition is to establish appropriate targets which children are assumed to aim for. Work on English has often misguidedly identified citation forms as targets, and monitored how well children produce citation-like pronunciations even if citation forms are in fact rare in the everyday speech of the local community. In a study of voiceless stop consonants in Newcastle English, Docherty et al. (2006) circumvented this problem by establishing targets for children based on a detailed sociophonetic analysis of both interadult speech and child-directed speech. They used an acoustic profiling technique, in which key acoustic patterns were documented in a relatively coarse way (e.g., presence/absence of full voicing or stop bursts), as well as formal quantification of less problematic parameters such as voice onset time (VOT). Examining phonetic tokens in such detail permitted an essential degree of refinement in the consideration of whether children were mastering the acquisition of the stops. The analysis was able to take into account the full range of variant forms found in the ambient language (e.g., showing that the majority of all phonologically voiceless tokens in fact involved full voicing), and thus avoided a potentially misleading reliance on standard or citation forms as the putative targets for acquisition. It is clear that research with Arabic children should not follow the latter practice, given the fact that the classical standard is not used as a variety in ordinary conversation, nor is it acquired by children until they reach primary school age. Khattab (2006, 2007a, 2009) developed a bespoke approach in her study of Arabic-English bilingual acquisition in Yorkshire, showing the importance of establishing targets for acquisition that take account both of local spoken norms and of variation in the community's speech patterns. She recorded monolingual controls for comparison with the bilinguals, and also recorded the children's parents, friends, and the friends' parents. This enabled her to build a very detailed picture of community variation involving standard and nonstandard English and Arabic variants. At first glance the bilingual children appeared to avoid marked Yorkshire forms such as monophthongal realizations of /eɪ/ and /əʊ/. It would have been possible to interpret this finding as an effect of the parents' L2 version of English, based on RP, and/or an avoidance on the part of the children of sociolinguistic or regional variants. This would in turn suggest the children might not be participating in local sound changes, and by inference that they might be peripheral to the local social groups. However, comparison with monolingual friends and their parents showed that the local Yorkshire dialect was not the only variety being spoken in the children's immediate community. On closer inspection, the Arabic bilinguals in fact showed remarkably similar phonetic patterns in their English, at a very detailed level, to their monolingual peers (but see further below). The children's Arabic was not the subject of a detailed sociolinguistic investigation given that the only regular input they received was from their parents; unsurprisingly, the children's accent was very similar to that of their parents, which in itself is interesting given the diversion in some patterns that one would expect if interaction with Arabic peers were possible.

Theoretical challenges

In this section we review key studies which document socially structured variation in Arabic (for more extensive reviews, see Bassiouney 2009; Horesh & Cotter 2016; Al-Wer & Horesh 2019; Al-Wer et al. 2022). We draw particular attention to findings that either help us to refine generally accepted models, or that differ from those typically found in studies of European languages.

Gender

Gender has received perhaps the most attention in Arabic sociolinguistics, particularly in respect of the way gender interacts with both social class and the sometimes misconstrued standard versus nonstandard language axis (Al-Wer 2014). Two main methodological issues might lead to misinterpretation of data on gender differences in sociolinguistics.

First, it might be predicted that gender-based differences should be particularly marked in societies where gender roles are assumed to be separated (e.g., Bakir 1986, referring to traditional Arab communities in Basrah). However, gender roles in fact vary widely within and across Arab countries (Al-Wer 2014). The lifestyles of men and women and their residence play a big role in their networks and subsequent adoption of innovative forms. For instance, in a study of phonological variation and change in two settings in Damascus, Ismail (2008) found women who lived in a suburb were leading the change in (r) realization, whereas those who lived in an inner-city district were not. This was explained as due to the inner-city women being unemployed at the time of the study, while the men interacted with people from all walks of life. Similar findings have been reported by Hachimi (2005) and Barontini & Ziamari (2009), whose studies demonstrate that identity and social network play a big part in determining the adoption of traditional or innovative forms and the differences observed between men and women.

The second issue relates to the way men and women use standard or prestigious forms. Studies of English often show a difference between men and women in the way sociolinguistic variables pattern. Labov (2001) summarizes the usual pattern as a "gender paradox," whereby women tend to be the leaders of change and yet are also the most conservative in that they use more prestige or standard variants than do men. It was for some time claimed that Arabic presented an exception to this pattern, that is, that it is men who produce more variants that are associated with the standard (e.g., Chambers 2003:156ff.). However, this is because the standard was being associated with the literary form, and this was wrongly assumed to be the prestigious form (Ibrahim 1986). As noted above, a dialect might share some of the same variants as the standard, which requires a careful analysis of which form speakers are actually using. More importantly, prestige is not necessarily attached to the literary standard. Rather, spoken regional or local standards may have more currency, and need to be taken into consideration when establishing whether men and/or women are adopting prestigious or innovative forms (e.g., Ibrahim 1986; Ismail 2008; Taqi 2010; Shetewi 2018). This is demonstrated in the way young highly educated speakers might be at the forefront of a change in /θ/, from the local variant [θ], which happens to be shared with the standard, to a supralocal [t] (Al-Wer 1997). Similarly, an analysis of a variable like /q/ where [q] is not part of the local variety, shows most of the differences between men and women in terms of their varying adoption of heritage or supralocal features like [g] or [ʔ], while the standard plays no role in this variation (Al-Wer & Herin 2011).

The multiglossic situation also complicates the sociolinguistic continuum that operates in everyday situations (Ibrahim 1986; Haeri 1996, 2000; Al-Wer 1997). Classical or standard variants occur only in particular domains (e.g., religion, politics, law, literature), and women have traditionally been excluded or misrepresented in those domains (Al-Wer 2014). This has generally led to lower competence or usage of the standard by women. Once again, however, one needs to be careful about overgeneralization, and there are increasing domains where particularly urban women have been found to compare closely with men in MSA usage (e.g., Barontini & Ziamari 2009; Sadiqi 2009). Thus the situation does not parallel that of stereotypical Western societies, where the standard is one variety available in principle to all speakers via education, opportunity, and choice. Instead, it is more instructive to examine sociolinguistic variation in the vernacular separately from that which may originate from differences in MSA use or command. In so doing, most studies in fact show that gender patterns in Arabic are closely comparable to those for English and similar languages: women lead in the use of supralocal variants, while men typically prefer local and older forms (Ibrahim 1986; Al-Wer 1997; Taqi 2010). Not all studies show this pattern, however. For example, Schmidt (1986) reports no differences between the sexes for /θ/, /dˤ/ and /ðˤ/ in Cairo.

The apparent similarity of patterns in Haeri's Cairo data is cited by Labov (2001:189) to support three of his general "principles of change," namely 1) that change follows a curvilinear pattern, originating in the middle of the social hierarchy; 2) that change is led by younger women; and 3) the "gender paradox." Note, however, that the gender paradox can only be supported by Arabic studies if we set aside the strong overt prescription associated with Classical Arabic. Haeri (1996, 2000) is furthermore clear that we cannot simply infer that standard forms of language automatically convey prestige on the speaker who uses them. We must also understand the local "market value" of a given variant (in other words, its indexical value, symbolism, or the ideology behind the variant). Metalinguistic commentary is a valuable source of information about language ideology. In Haeri's Cairo study, for instance, men talked about Classical Arabic as an essential tool to construct or maintain a pan-Arab identity, resisting colonialism and other external forms of domination, whereas women did not talk about Classical Arabic in this way as much. Usage of Classical forms must therefore be understood in the context of what those forms signal to particular speakers or groups of speakers in the context of discourse.

Gender differences in Arabic studies are not, in fact, necessarily more marked or more straightforward to interpret than those of European languages. Eckert (2000) reminds us that gender is not simply about men and women being different from one another and using language to index that division. It may also be the case that different types of women and different types of men behave differently relative to other people of the same sex. Indeed, in some communities, gender is more acutely defined within rather than between sex groups (e.g., Eckert 2000; Stuart-Smith 2007). In their discussion of gender effects on change, Milroy & Gordon (2003:104–105) cite two comparable studies conducted in Tunisia (Jabeur 1987; Walters 1991) to emphasize the importance of understanding local social facts and language ideology in the maintenance and change of variables. Both studies show interesting interactions between sex and age. Jabeur studied vowel patterns in Rades, a suburb of Tunis. Variation was found between traditional diphthongs and innovative monophthongs, for example in [bajt ~ bi:t] 'room' and [nawm ~ nu:m] 'sleep.' The diphthongs were markers of older urban women, and were avoided by younger women. The variants were heavily ideologized, with the older women reportedly taking pride in using them, and evidence that they were relic features historically associated with the highest-status families in the Tunis medina. Walters (1991) reports a similar difference between women of different ages in respect of the vowel /ɛ:/ in Korba, eastern Tunisia. Stigmatized raised variants were used by older women, at the time mostly illiterate, with a social meaning associated with the isolation of the community (cf. Labov's 1963 study of Martha's Vineyard).

While not dealing with sociophonetic variation, recent work by Sadiqi (2021) presents the gender dichotomy in North Africa as pertaining not to men versus women, but rather democratic men and women versus the patriarchy. Sadiqi presents a compelling theoretical framework which considers gender side by side with religion, education, power, and dominance of public physical spaces, and argues that gender perception is largely dominated by patriarchal oppression. It is crucial to look at the linguistic manifestations of these gender divisions. Furthermore, while consideration for a nonbinary division of gender is still in its infancy even in sociolinguistic research in the West, it is important to remember that queer Arabic sociolinguistics is still embryonic and its development is contingent on the provision of safe spaces for linguists involved in this endeavor (Obeidat & Hamoudi 2019; Thompson 2019).

Social class and social networks

Interpretations of the linguistic effects of social class on Arabic are in some cases subtly different from those typically found in (for example) English studies, enhancing our understanding of the importance of social networks on linguistic variation and change. The effect of education, as noted in Milroy & Gordon (2003), is key in the Middle East. Al-Wer (1997) notes that this may not be due to education per se but the marked effect it has on a speaker's social networks. High levels of education bring speakers into contact via new networks with a wider array of other people from a wider range of backgrounds. Contact between people in wide and open social networks is the ideal condition for leveling changes to develop. In Arabic-speaking communities, educated speakers lead linguistic changes towards urban and koinéized regional standards (Johnstone 1967; Palva 1982; Bassiouney 2009; Al-Rojaie 2013). Holes (2011) notes the importance of four factors in spreading urban regional varieties to the Gulf states: migration and/or more physical communication between Gulf states, media, employment, and education. Higher respect is typically given to the varieties of the ruling elites, and areas of most frequent migration and contact tend to exert the most influence—for example, Kuwait City, Manama, Doha, and Dubai. Apart from education and the ruling elites, gathering data on other indices of socioeconomic status can be trickier than in the United States or Europe, with no easily available statistics such as neighborhoods ranked according to wealth, or number of children receiving free school meals. Researchers often rely on ad hoc ways of estimating socioeconomic status.

Several studies of Arabic communities provide further detailed insights into the dynamics of social networks and lifestyle routines on language variation and change. For example, Al-Shareef (2002) studied three generations in the Jabalia refugee camp in Gaza, Palestine. Established by the United Nations after the Arab-Israeli war of 1948, Jabalia is the largest and most densely populated camp in Gaza, home to over 135,000 people. The refugees who settled the camp came from all over Palestine, and inhabitants have, ever since, largely remained in residences and networks oriented to the cities and villages from which the refugees originated. Over time, social networks and routines have changed in line with political and economic changes. For example, prior to 2006, when it was still possible to work inside Israel, many workers (mostly male) endured a 15-hour working day, starting at 3 A.M., and thus had little leisure time or social time within Gaza. Those who worked in Gaza, by contrast, had shorter days and wider social networks within the area. Although neither networks nor routines were explicitly analyzed in the study, it is clear that contexts such as this present remarkable contrasts to those communities investigated by the likes of Kerswill & Williams (2000), Milroy (1987), and Britain (2013), the findings of which have formed the basis for much theorizing about the roles of networks and mobility on language variation and change. Nevertheless, the general claims made by these scholars appear broadly supported by the Jabalia study. The intense admixture of people in the camp presents the ideal context for leveling changes to emerge, constrained by structures of social networks and daily routines. Those speakers who were adults before 1948 were found largely to maintain their original local dialects, while those born after migration showed effects of contact with other dialects. Trudgill (2004) predicts that leveling results in the survival of the variant with the widest distribution. That was the case for the /q/ variable in Gaza: the most widely used variant among the different camp residents, [g] (the dominant variant for 33 of the 35 input dialects to the camp), won out at the expense of the supralocal [ʔ]. However, leveling to the statistically dominant form was found only for /q/, the one sociolinguistic "marker" (in the sense of Labov 2001:196) that was investigated. Sociolinguistic "indicators" such as /θ/ appeared to show different leveling patterns, with the "winning" variant being not the statistically most widespread but the socially most prestigious—in the case of Jabalia, the Jaffa (urban) form [t]. (Note, however, that [t] is also widely used in Gaza City, but Al-Shareef did not explicitly consider the influence of the city on leveling patterns.)

While there is ample research on Arabic which focuses on the rural–urban dichotomy, Hachimi's (2005) study of dialect leveling in Casablanca (due to contact with Fessi) provides an original approach within Arabic sociolinguistics by adopting Eckert's communities of practice model. Hachimi found that the degree to which speakers originating from Fez either adopted Casablancan variants of the phonological variables /r/ and /q/ or maintained Fessi ones was very much influenced by their everyday social interactions and identity construction.

Sociolinguistics of L2 and peripheral communities

L2 communities offer very interesting testing grounds for general principles of variation and change. Remarkably little sociophonetic work has been conducted on such communities. However, Arabic speakers are found in diaspora throughout the world, with notably large communities in France, Sweden, South America, Canada, Côte d'Ivoire, and major cities such as London, Paris, and Sydney. "Peripheral" Arabic-speaking communities are also found in Cyprus and several countries across Asia and Africa (Grigore 2019), and there are a number of Arabic-based pidgins and creoles (Manfredi & Bizri 2019).

Arab Americans comprise one of the fastest growing immigrant groups in the United States (Samant 2010, 2011). Samant conducted a study in a high school in Dearborn, Michigan, a suburb of Detroit, adopting a methodology similar to that of Eckert (2000). Michigan has the largest Arab American population, with over 200,000 in the suburbs of Detroit, mostly drawn from Lebanon, Iraq, Palestine, and Yemen. Dearborn itself has the highest proportion of Arab Americans (30 percent) reported for any city in the United States. The majority of the Arab population's (58 percent) identify as Christian. The community is also socially very varied, with a marked tension between the Lebanese (mostly wealthy Shi'a, forming a "cool" social elite) and those of other heritage. In particular, Samant was interested in exploring to what extent her participants, when speaking English, showed signs of the Northern Cities Shift (NCS), a vowel chain shift much discussed in North American sociophonetics. She found that her speakers did indeed manifest the NCS, with variable patterns related to speaker sex, religious practice, and regional origin.

Following Fought (2006), Samant takes issue with explanations for these patterns couched in terms of the minority group "participating" in the mainstream change. This type of interpretation can be taken to imply that the minority group in some way assimilates to the mainstream through linguistic choices. Instead, Samant argues, Dearborn Arab Americans exploit the NCS variables to express social differences that are related to local social categories and dynamics rather than anything related to mainstream white speakers. Put another way, "the social meaning of variables is not fixed but flexible and specific to the social context of the high school" (Samant 2011:22). She further notes that individual vowels in the NCS patterned in a somewhat haphazard way, unlike the apparently "well-behaved" mainstream varieties reported elsewhere. In this sense, Samant's study does for ethnicity what Eckert's study did for gender: just as Eckert showed that social differences between women or between men are significant, Samant demonstrates that what matters most in the Dearborn school is not differences between ethnic groups but within them. Samant characterizes the salient social divisions in Dearborn as "mainstream" versus "marginalized" categories, which are based on a combination of socioeconomic status, religion, region of origin, and length of residence.

CASE STUDY **Sociophonetic variation in Arabic-English child language acquisition**

Khattab (2002a,b, 2006, 2007a, 2009, 2013) studied a group of Arabic-English bilingual children growing up in Yorkshire. She conducted detailed acoustic and auditory phonetic analyses of a range of segmental variables, taking into account regional and social variation in the children's community. She shows that English-Arabic bilingual children learn and exploit a range of phonetic variants comparable to that of their monolingual peers. Moreover, phonetic interference patterns from English onto Arabic can be interpreted not as imperfect learning (bidirectional interference) but as strategic devices to achieve conversational goals. For example, the children frequently adapted English words to Arabic phonology when attempting to satisfy their parents by speaking Arabic in fieldwork sessions, for example where they were struggling to recall an Arabic word. An example from a 7-year-old child is given in (1) (Khattab 2002a:119; further examples can be found in Khattab 2009).

(1)
Mother: [miːn ˈhaɪda] *'who's that?'* (pointing to picture)
Child: [ˈweɪtə]
Mother: [laʔ bɪlˈʕarabe] *'no, in Arabic'*
Child: [ˈweɪtaʃ]

The findings from this study led Khattab to reject Chambers's (2002) claim that immigrant children develop a "sociolinguistic filter" to eliminate influences from non-native speakers such as their parents. While their speech might not show L2 effects in everyday talk, under particular circumstances they can draw upon a sophisticated battery of L2 phonetic information—presumably derived from input such as that from L2 speaking parents and stored at some level in their general phonetic/phonological knowledge—and apply it to achieve social goals in speech.

An agenda for future Arabic sociophonetics

We have outlined many issues in sociophonetics, both with a particular focus on Arabic and also to identify where Arabic studies challenge received wisdom based on North American and European traditions. We end with a brief agenda for future work.

First, there remains much to be explored in respect of the sociolinguistic effects of social diversity. Western (socio)linguistic studies still tend to treat homogeneity as the norm when defining speech communities. Of course, this is not appropriate in many places at all, but it is clearly inappropriate in highly diverse communities in the Middle East, for example in cities like Beirut which are characterized by stark contrasts in religion, culture, and lifestyle (cf. also London: Cheshire et al. 2011). The ongoing dramatic shifts in populations in the Middle East and around the world continue to present extraordinary sites for sociolinguistic research both within the L1 Arabic community and also taking into account the host society and L2 context. In multilingual contexts such as Lebanon and much of Africa, while studies have investigated code-switching patterns between Arabic and post-colonial varieties of French and/or English (e.g., Owens 2007; Ziamari 2007), little work has been carried out on the outcome of Arabic contact with these varieties.

The theoretical implications of sociophonetic work are at the forefront of work exploring the value of exemplar theory as a model of linguistic knowledge (e.g., Foulkes & Docherty 2006;

Foulkes & Hay 2015; Warren this volume). Sociophonetic research on Arabic has great potential to address some of the principles of and controversies in exemplar theory, in comparison with and in contrast to work carried out on languages such as English. For example, the root structure of Arabic words suggests that the learning, storage, and processing of exemplars from Arabic data might operate differently from English. Tokens of Arabic words vary in different ways compared to the variation found in English, since vowel variation reflects morphology as well as indexical properties relating to regional or social accent. To our knowledge, however, there is as yet no work in this domain based on Arabic research.

Beyond linguistics, sociophonetics has an array of applications, including in education, speech technology, and forensic speech analysis. Language teachers are taking an increasing interest in issues of linguistic variation in order to better tailor pedagogical techniques, and to understand learners' attitudes to language. There is huge potential in considering such issues in the context of Arabic teaching. Speech technology, in particular to develop speech/speaker recognition systems and speech synthesis systems, relies upon robust descriptive accounts of spoken language in all its natural variety. Work of this sort on Arabic lags well behind that on languages such as English, but it is emerging; Brown & Hellmuth (2022) describe a study of automatic dialect classification, Kirchhoff & Vergyri (2005) and Al-Tamimi et al. (2022) describe experiments involving automatic speech recognition, and Alsulaiman, Mahmood & Muhammad (2017) discuss automatic speaker recognition.

Forensic applications also require reliable information on the distribution of spoken forms across populations, and on within-speaker variation to be expected for individuals. Again, Arabic has made little impact thus far in this field but descriptive sociolinguistic data are of great value, especially in the context of an increasing focus on identifying Arabic speakers in surveillance related to global security issues. A number of papers discuss Arabic speakers in the context of language analysis in the asylum process (e.g., Matras 2018; Hoskin, Cambier-Langeveld & Foulkes 2019).

Sociophonetics as a field is growing and diversifying rapidly. Adding a focus on Arabic presents rich and exciting opportunities for both sociophonetics and Arabic linguistics.

Acknowledgments

We are grateful to Jamal Al-Shareef, Jalal Al-Tamimi, and Sam Hellmuth for helpful comments.

References

Abd-el-Jawad, Hassan R. 1986. The emergence of an urban dialect in the Jordanian urban centers. *International Journal of the Society of Language* 61(5). 53–63. https://doi.org/10.1515/ijsl.1986.61.53

Abu-Haidar, Farida. 1990. Are Iraqi women more prestige conscious than men? Sex differentiation in Baghdadi Arabic. *Language in Society* 18(4). 471–481. https://doi.org/10.1017/S0047404500013865

Ahmed, Albashir. 2008. *Production and perception of Libyan Arabic vowels*. PhD thesis, Newcastle University.

Ahmed, Abdulkareem. 2018. *Phonological variation and change in Mesopotamia: A study of accent levelling in the dialect of Mosul*. PhD thesis, Newcastle University.

AlAjroush, Noura A. 2020. *Phonological development in typically developing Najdi Arabic-speaking children aged 1–4 years*. PhD thesis, Newcastle University.

Albirini, Abdulkafi. 2016. *Modern Arabic Sociolinguistics: Diglossia, variation, codeswitching, attitudes and identity*. Routledge.

Al-Essa, Aziza. 2019. Phonological and morphological variation. In Al-Wer & Horesh, 117–133.

Al-Khatib, Mahmoud A. & Abdulaziz A. Alzoubi. 2009. The impact of sect-affiliation on dialect and cultural maintenance among the Druze of Jordan: An exploratory study. *Glossa* 4(2). 186–219.

Almbark, Rana & Sam Hellmuth. 2016. Variation in quantity & quality of Arabic vowels: A comparison of eight dialects. Paper presented at the Arabic Linguistics Forum, University of York.

Almurashi, Wael, Jalal Al-Tamimi & Ghada Khattab. 2020. Static and dynamic cues in vowel production in Hijazi Arabic. *Journal of the Acoustical Society of America* 147(4). 2917–2927. https://doi.org/10.1121/10.0001004

Alqattan, Shaima. 2015. *Early phonological acquisition by Kuwaiti Arabic children.* PhD thesis, Newcastle University.

Al-Rojaie, Yousef. 2013. Regional dialect leveling in Najdi Arabic: The case of the deaffrication of [k] in the Qaṣīmī dialect. *Language Variation and Change* 25(1). 43–63. https://doi.org/10.1017/S0954394512000245

Alshangiti, Amin M. 2016. *Lexical borrowings in immigrant speech: A sociolinguistic study of Ḥassāniyya Arabic speakers in Medina (Saudi Arabia).* PhD thesis, Durham University.

Al-Shareef, Jamal. 2002. *Language change and variation in Palestine: A case study of Jabalia refugee camp.* PhD thesis, University of Leeds.

Alsiraih, Wasan. 2013. *Voice quality features in the production of pharyngeal consonants by Iraqi Arabic speakers.* PhD thesis, Newcastle University.

Alsulaiman, Mansour, Awais Mahmood & Ghulam Muhammad. 2017. Speaker recognition based on Arabic phonemes. *Speech Communication* 86. 42–51. https://doi.org/10.1016/j.specom.2016.11.004

Alsurf, Saeed. 2012. *The phonetics of the Qur'anic pharyngeal sounds: Acoustic and articulatory studies.* PhD thesis, Macquarie University.

Al-Tamimi, Jalal. 2002. *Variabilité phonétique en production et en perception de la parole: Le cas de l'Arabe Jordano-Palestinien.* Masters thesis, Université de Lyon 2.

Al-Tamimi Jalal. 2004. L'équation du locus comme mesure de la coarticulation VC et CV: Étude préliminaire en Arabe Dialectal Jordanien. Paper presented at Actes des 25èmes Journées d'Études sur la Parole (JEP), Fez.

Al-Tamimi, Jalal. 2007a. Static and dynamic cues in vowel production: A cross dialectal study in Jordanian and Moroccan Arabic. In Trouvain & Barry, 541–544.

Al-Tamimi, Jalal. 2007b. *Indices dynamiques et perception des voyelles: Étude translinguistique en Arabe dialectal et en Français.* PhD thesis, Université de Lyon 2.

Al-Tamimi, Jalal. 2008. L'espace vocalique perceptif dépend de la densité des systèmes vocaliques: Étude translinguistique en arabe marocain, en arabe jordanien et en français. Paper presented at Actes des 27èmes Journées d'Études sur la Parole (JEP), Avignon.

Al-Tamimi, Jalal. 2017. Revisiting acoustic cues of pharyngealization in Jordanian and Moroccan Arabic: Implications for formal representations. *Laboratory Phonology* 8(1). 28. http://doi.org/10.5334/labphon.19

Al-Tamimi, Jalal & Melissa Barkat-Defradas. 2003. Inter-dialectal and inter-individual variability in production and perception: A preliminary study in Jordanian and Moroccan Arabic. In Ignacio Ferrando & Juan José Sanchez Sandoval (eds.), *AIDA 5th Proceedings,* 171–186. Universidad de Cadiz.

Al-Tamimi, Jalal & Emmanuel Ferragne. 2005. Does vowel space size depend on language vowel inventories? Evidence from two Arabic dialects and French. In *Proceedings of Interspeech 2005,* 2465–2468. https://doi.org/10.21437/Interspeech.2005-756

Al-Tamimi, Jalal & Ghada Khattab. 2015. Acoustic cue weighting in the singleton vs. geminate contrast in Lebanese Arabic: The case of fricative consonants. *Journal of the Acoustical Society of America* 138(1). 344–360. https://doi.org/10.1121/1.4922514

Al-Tamimi, Jalal & Ghada Khattab. 2018. Acoustic correlates of the voicing contrast in Lebanese Arabic singleton and geminate stops. *Journal of Phonetics* 71. 306–325. https://doi.org/10.1016/j.wocn.2018.09.010

Al-Tamimi, Jalal, Florian Schiel, Ghada Khattab, Navdeep Sokhey, Djegdjiga Amazouz, Abdulrahman Dallak & Hajar Moussa. 2022. A romanization system and WebMAUS aligner for Arabic varieties. *Proceedings of the 13th Conference on Language Resources and Evaluation,* 7269–7276.

Al-Tamimi, Yasser & Dinha T. Gorgis. 2007. Romanised Jordanian Arabic e-messages. *The International Journal of Language Society and Culture* 21. 1–12.

Al-Wer, Enam. 1997. Arabic between reality and ideology. *International Journal of Applied Linguistics* 7(2). 251–265. https://doi.org/10.1111/j.1473-4192.1997.tb00117.x

Al-Wer, Enam. 2002. Jordanian and Palestinian dialects in contact: Vowel raising in Amman. In Mari C. Jones & Edith Esch (eds.), *Language change: The interplay of internal, external and extra-linguistic factors,* 63–80. de Gruyter Mouton.

Al-Wer, Enam. 2007. The formation of the dialect of Amman: From chaos to order. In Miller et al., 55–76.

Al-Wer, Enam. 2014. Language and gender in the Middle East and North Africa. In Susan Ehrlich, Miriam Meyerhoff & Janet Holmes (eds.), *The handbook of language, gender, and sexuality*, 396–411. Wiley Blackwell.

Al-Wer, Enam. 2020. New-dialect formation: The Amman dialect. In Chris Lucas & Stefano Manfredi (eds.), *Arabic and contact-induced change: A handbook,* 551–566. Language Science Press.

Al-Wer, Enam & Bruno Herin. 2011. The lifecycle of Qaf in Jordan. *Langage et Société* 4. 59–76.

Al-Wer, Enam & Uri Horesh (eds.). 2019. *The Routledge handbook of Arabic sociolinguistics*. Routledge. https://doi.org/10.4324/9781315722450

Al-Wer, Enam, Uri Horesh, Bruno Herin & Rudolf de Jong. 2022. *Arabic sociolinguistics*. Cambridge University Press. https://doi.org/10.1017/9781316863060

Amayreh, Mousa M. & Alice T. Dyson. 1998. The acquisition of Arabic consonants. *Journal of Speech, Language, and Hearing Research* 41(3). 642–653. https://doi.org/10.1044/jslhr.4103.642

Amir, Noam, Ofer Amir & Judith Rosenhouse. 2014. Colloquial Arabic vowels in Israel: A comparative acoustic study of two dialects. *Journal of the Acoustical Society of America* 136(4). 1895–1907. https://doi.org/10.1121/1.4894725

Ammar, Wafaa & Ranya Morsi. 2006. Phonological development and disorders: Colloquial Egyptian Arabic. In Hua & Dodd, 204–232.

Ash, Sharon. 2002. Social class. In Chambers, Trudgill & Schilling-Estes, 402–422.

Ayyad, Hadeel S. 2011. *Phonological development of typically developing Kuwaiti Arabic-speaking preschoolers*. PhD dissertation, University of British Columbia.

Bakir, Murtadha. 1986. Sex differences in the approximation to Standard Arabic: A case study. *Anthropological Linguistics* 28(1). 3–9.

Barkat-Defradas, Melissa, Jalal Al-Tamimi & Thami Benkiran. 2003. Phonetic variation in production and perception of speech: A comparative study of two Arabic dialects. In Maria-Josep Solé, Daniel Recasens & Joaquin Romero (eds.), *Proceedings of the 15th International Congress of Phonetic Sciences*, 857–860. Causal Productions.

Barontini, Alexandrine & Karima Ziamari. 2009. Comment des (jeunes) femmes Marocaines parlent "masculine": Tentative de définition sociolinguistique. *Estudios de Dialectología Norteafricana y Andalusí* 13. 153–172.

Bassiouney, Reem. 2009. *Arabic sociolinguistics*. Edinburgh University Press.

Bauer, Leonhard. 1910. *Das Palästinische Arabisch: Die Dialekte des Städters und des Fellachen*. Hinrichs.

Behnstedt, Peter. 1997. *Sprachatlas von Syrien*. O. Harrassowitz.

Bellem, Alex. 2007. *Towards a comparative typology of emphatics: Across Semitic and into Arabic dialect phonology*. PhD thesis, SOAS, University of London. https://doi.org/10.25501/SOAS.00036011

Bergsträßer, Gotthelf. 1915. Sprachatlas von Syrien und Palastina. *Zeitschrift des Deutschen en Palastina-Vereins* 38. 169–222.

Binte Faizal, Siti S. 2019. *Phonological representation on non-Arabic-speaking Qur'anic memorizers*. PhD thesis, Newcastle University.

Binte Faizal, Siti S., Ghada Khattab & Cristina McKean. 2015. The Qur'an lexicon project: A database of lexical statistics and phonotactic probabilities for 19,286 contextually and phonetically transcribed types in Qur'anic Arabic. In Scottish Consortium for ICPhS 2015, Paper 968.

Blanc, Haim. 1953. *Studies in North Palestinian Arabic: Linguistic inquiries among the Druzes of Western Galilee and Mt. Carmel*. Israel Oriental Society.

Blanc, Haim. 1964. *Communal dialects in Baghdad*. Harvard University Press.

Boudelaa, Sami & William D. Marslen-Wilson. 2001. Morphological units in the Arabic mental lexicon. *Cognition* 81(1). 65–92. https://doi.org/10.1016/S0010-0277(01)00119-6

Britain, David. 2013. Space, diffusion and mobility. In J.K. Chambers & Natalie Schilling (eds.), *The handbook of language variation and change*, 2nd edn., 471–500. Blackwell.

Brown, Georgina & Sam Hellmuth. 2022. Computational modeling of segmental and prosodic levels of analysis for capturing variation across Arabic dialects. *Speech Communication* 141. 80–92. https://doi.org/10.1016/j.specom.2022.05.003

Buchstaller, Isabelle & Ghada Khattab. 2014. Population samples. In Robert Podesva & Devyani Sharma (eds.), *Research methods in linguistics*, 74–95. Cambridge University Press.

Chahal, Dana & Sam Hellmuth. 2014. The intonation of Lebanese and Egyptian Arabic. In Sun-Ah Jun (ed.), *Prosodic typology, vol. 2, The phonology of intonation and phrasing*, 365–404. Oxford University Press.

Chambers, J.K. 2002. Dynamics of dialect convergence. *Journal of Sociolinguistics* 6(1). 117–130. https://doi.org/10.1111/1467-9481.00180

Chambers, J.K. 2003. *Sociolinguistic theory*, 2nd edn. Blackwell.

Chambers, J.K., Peter Trudgill & Natalie Schilling-Estes (eds.). 2002. *The handbook of language variation and change*, 1st edn. Blackwell.

Cheshire, Jenny. 2002. Sex and gender in variationist research. In Chambers, Trudgill & Schilling-Estes, 423–443.

Cheshire, Jenny, Paul Kerswill, Sue Fox & Eivind Torgersen. 2011. Contact, the feature pool and the speech community: The emergence of Multicultural London English. *Journal of Sociolinguistics* 15(2). 151–196. https://doi.org/10.1111/j.1467-9841.2011.00478.x

Christie, W. 1901. Der dialect der Landbevolkerung des mittleren Galilaa. *Zeitschrift des Deutschen en Palastina-Vereins* 24. 69–112. www.jstor.org/stable/27928813

Cole, Jennifer S. & José I. Hualde (eds.). 2007. *Laboratory Phonology 9*. Mouton de Gruyter

Cotter, William M. 2013. *Dialect contact and change in Gaza City*. MA dissertation, University of Essex.

Cotter, William M. 2022. The Arabic dialect of Gaza City. *Journal of the International Phonetic Association* 52(1). 122–134. https://doi.org/10.1017/S0025100320000134

Cotter, William M. & Rudolf de Jong. 2019. Regional variation. In Al-Wer & Horesh, 47–62.

Cotter, William M. & Uri Horesh. 2015. Social integration and dialect divergence in coastal Palestine. *Journal of Sociolinguistics* 19(4). 460–483. https://doi.org/10.1111/josl.12135

Daher, Jamil. 1997. Phonological variation in Syrian Arabic: Correlation with gender, age, and education. In Mushira Eid & Robert R. Ratcliffe (eds.), *Perspectives on Arabic Linguistics X,* 239–272. John Benjamins. https://doi.org/10.1075/cilt.153.15dah

Davis, Stuart. 1995. Emphasis spread in Arabic and grounded phonology. *Linguistic Inquiry* 26(3). 465–498.

Docherty, Gerard J., Paul Foulkes, James Milroy, Lesley Milroy & David Walshaw. 1997. Descriptive adequacy in phonology: A variationist perspective. *Journal of Linguistics* 33(2). 275–310. https://doi.org/10.1017/S002222679700649X

Docherty, Gerard J., Paul Foulkes, Jennifer Tillotson & Dominic Watt. 2006. On the scope of phonological learning: Issues arising from socially structured variation. In Louis M. Goldstein, D.H. Whalen & Catherine T. Best (eds.), *Laboratory Phonology 8*, 393–421. Mouton de Gruyter. https://doi.org/10.1515/9783110197211.2.393

Eckert, Penelope. 1997. Age as a sociolinguistic variable. In Florian Coulmas (ed.), *The handbook of sociolinguistics*, 151–167. Blackwell. https://doi.org/10.1002/9781405166256.ch9

Eckert, Penelope. 2000. *Linguistic variation as social practice: The linguistic construction of identity in Belten High*. Blackwell.

Embarki, Mohamed, Mohamed Yeou, Christian Guilleminot & Sallal Al Maqtari. 2007. An acoustic study of coarticulation in modern standard Arabic and dialectal Arabic: Pharyngealized vs non-pharyngealized articulation. In Trouvain & Barry, 141–146.

Embarki, Mohamed, Slim Ouni, Mohamed Yeou, Christian Guilleminot & Sallal Al Maqtari. 2011. Acoustic and EMA study of pharyngealization: Coarticulatory effects as index of stylistic and regional distinction. In Hassan & Heselwood, 1–56.

Fagyal, Zsuzsanna. 2010. Rhythm types and the speech of working-class youth in a banlieue of Paris: The role of vowel elision and devoicing. In Dennis R. Preston & Nancy Niedzielski (eds.), *A reader in sociophonetics*, 91–132. De Gruyter Mouton.

Ferguson, Charles. 1959. Diglossia. *Word* 15. 325–340. https://doi.org/10.1080/00437956.1959.11659702

Fought, Carmen. 2006. *Language and ethnicity*. Cambridge University Press.

Foulkes, Paul & Gerard J. Docherty 2006. The social life of phonetics and phonology. *Journal of Phonetics* 34. 409–438. https://doi.org/10.1016/j.wocn.2005.08.002

Foulkes, Paul, Gerard J. Docherty & Dominic Watt. 2005. Phonological variation in child directed speech. *Language* 81(1). 177–206. https://doi.org/10.1353/lan.2005.0018

Foulkes, Paul & Jennifer Hay. 2015. The emergence of sociophonetic structure. In Brian MacWhinney & William O'Grady (eds.), *The handbook of language emergence,* 292–313. Blackwell.

Foulkes, Paul & Marilyn M. Vihman. 2015. First language acquisition and phonological change. In Patrick Honeybone & Joseph C. Salmons (eds.), *The Oxford handbook of historical phonology*, 289–312. Oxford University Press.

Germanos, Marie-Aimée. 2009. *Identification et emploi de quelques stéréotypes, traits saillants et autres variables sociolinguistiques à Beyrouth [Liban]*. PhD thesis, Université de Paris 3.

Germanos, Marie-Aimée. 2018. Fonctions de l'alternance entre arabe standard et vernaculaire libanais et connotations des deux codes dans un discours politique d'opposition. *Arabica* 65(4). 501–536. https://doi.org/10.1163/15700585-12341501

Germanos, Marie-Aimée & Catherine Miller. 2015. Is religious affiliation a key factor of language variation in Arabic-speaking countries? *Language & Communication* 42. 86–98. https://doi.org/10.1016/j.langcom.2014.12.001

Grant, Elihu. 1921. *The people of Palestine.* J.B. Lippincott Company.

Grigore, George. 2019. Peripheral varieties. In Al-Wer & Horesh, 117–133.

Habib, Rania. 2011. Frequency effects and lexical split in the use of [t] and [s] and [d] and [z] in the Syrian Arabic of Christian rural migrants. *Journal of Historical Linguistics* 1(1). 77–105. https://doi.org/10.1075/jhl.1.1.04hab

Habib, Rania. 2014. Vowel variation and reverse acquisition in rural Syrian child and adolescent language. *Language Variation and Change* 26(1). 45–75. https://doi.org/10.1017/S0954394513000239

Hachimi, Atiqa. 2005. *Dialect leveling, maintenance and urban identity in Morocco.* PhD dissertation, University of Hawai'i at Manoa.

Haeri, Niloofar. 1996. *The sociolinguistic market of Cairo: Gender, class and education.* Kegan Paul.

Haeri, Niloofar. 2000. Form and ideology: Arabic sociolinguistics and beyond. *Annual Review of Anthropology* 29. 61–87. www.jstor.org/stable/223415

Haggan, Madeline. 2007. Text messaging in Kuwait. Is the medium the message? *Multilingua* 26(4). 427–449. https://doi.org/10.1515/MULTI.2007.020

Ham, William H. 2001. *Phonetic and phonological aspects of geminate timing.* Routledge. https://doi.org/10.4324/9781315023755

Hassan, Batoul. 2009. *Ideology, identity, and linguistic capital: A sociolinguistic investigation of language shift among the Ajam of Kuwait.* PhD thesis, University of Essex.

Hassan, Zeki M. 2003. Temporal compensation between vowel and consonant in Swedish & Arabic in sequences of CV: C & CVC: and the word overall duration. *PHONUM* 9. 45–48.

Hassan, Zeki M. & Barry Heselwood (eds.). 2011. *Instrumental studies in Arabic phonetics.* John Benjamins.

Heath, Jeffrey. 2002. *Jewish and Muslim dialects of Moroccan Arabic.* Routledge.

Hellmuth, Sam. 2007. The relationship between prosodic structure and pitch accent distribution: Evidence from Egyptian Arabic. *The Linguistic Review* 24(2–3). 291–316. https://doi.org/10.1515/TLR.2007.011

Hellmuth, Sam, Rana Almbark, Basma Chlaihani & Nabila Louriz. 2015. F0 peak alignment in Moroccan Arabic polar questions. In Scottish Consortium for ICPhS 2015, Paper 825.

Hermes, Zainab, Marissa Barlaz, Ryan Shosted, Zhi-Pei Liang & Brad P. Sutton. 2021. In Ntelitheos & Leung, 23–56.

Heselwood, Barry, Sara Howard & Rawya Ranjoys. 2011. Assimilation of /l/ to /r/ in Syrian Arabic: An electropalatographic and acoustic study. In Hassan & Heselwood, 63–98.

Holes, Clive D. 1983. Patterns of communal language variation in Bahrain. *Language in Society* 12(4). 433–457. https://doi.org/10.1017/S0047404500010186

Holes, Clive D. 1987. *Language variation and change in a modernising Arab state: The case of Bahrain.* Kegan Paul International.

Holes, Clive D. 2011. Language and identity in the Arabian Gulf. *Journal of Arabian Studies* 1(2). 129–145. https://doi.org/10.1080/21534764.2011.628492

Holes, Clive D. 2019. Confessional varieties. In Al-Wer & Horesh, 63–80.

Horesh, Uri & William M. Cotter. 2015. Sociolinguistics of Palestinian Arabic. In Lutz Edzard & Rudolf de Jong (eds.), *Encyclopedia of Arabic language and linguistics.* Brill. https:// doi.org/10.1163/1570-6699_eall_SIM_001007

Horesh, Uri & William M. Cotter. 2016. Current research on linguistic variation in the Arabic-speaking world. *Language and Linguistics Compass* 10(8). 370–381. https://doi.org/10.1111/lnc3.12202

Hoskin, James, Tina Cambier-Langeveld & Paul Foulkes. 2019. Improving objectivity, balance and forensic fitness in LAAP: A response to Matras. *International Journal of Speech, Language and the Law* 26(2). 257–277. https://doi.org/10.1558/ijsll.39208

Hua, Zhu & Barbara Dodd (eds.). 2006. *Phonological development and disorders in children.* Multilingual Matters.

Ibrahim, Muhammad H. 1986. Standard and prestige language: A problem in Arabic sociolinguistics. *Anthropological Linguistics* 28(1). 115–126.

Ismail, Hanadi. 2008. Sound change in Damascus: Men, women and life-modes. In Enam Al-Wer, C. Hadjimetriou, B. Herin & Uri Horesh (eds.), *Proceedings of the 8th Conference of Association Internationale de Dialectologie Arabe (AIDA)*, 104–117. University of Essex.

Jabeur, Mohamed. 1987. *A sociolinguistic study in Tunisia: Rades*. PhD thesis, University of Reading.

Johnstone, Thomas M. 1967. *Eastern Arabian dialect studies*. Oxford University Press.

Kahn, Margaret. 1975. Arabic emphasis: The evidence for cultural determinants of phonetic sex-typing. *Phonetica* 31. 38–50. https://doi.org/10.1159/000259648

Kaye, Alan S. 1994. Formal vs. informal in Arabic: Diglossia, triglossia, tetraglossia, etc., polyglossia—multiglossia viewed as a continuum. *Zeitschrift für Arabische Linguistik* 27. 47–66.

Kendall, Tyler & Erik R. Thomas. 2010. *vowels: Vowel manipulation, normalization, and plotting*. R package ver 1.2-2. https://cran.r-project.org/web/packages/vowels/vowels.pdf

Kerswill, Paul & Ann Williams. 2000. Creating a new town koine: Children and language change in Milton Keynes. *Language in Society* 29(1). 65–115. https://doi.org/10.1017/S0047404500001020

Khattab, Ghada. 2002a. /r/ production in English and Arabic bilingual and monolingual speakers. *Leeds Working Papers in Linguistics & Phonetics* 9(1). 91–129. www.latl.leeds.ac.uk/lwplp/

Khattab, Ghada. 2002b. VOT in English and Arabic bilingual and monolingual children. In Dilworth B. Parkinson & Elabbas Benmamoun (eds.), *Perspectives on Arabic Linguistics XIII–XIV*, 1–37. John Benjamins. https://doi.org/10.1075/cilt.230.03kha

Khattab, Ghada. 2006. Phonological acquisition in Arabic-English bilingual children. In Hua & Dodd, 383–412.

Khattab, Ghada. 2007a. Variation in vowel production by English-Arabic bilinguals. In Cole & Hualde, 383–410.

Khattab, Ghada. 2007b. A phonetic study of gemination in Lebanese Arabic. In Trouvain & Barry, 153–158.

Khattab, Ghada. 2009. Phonetic accommodation in children's code-switching. In Barbara E. Bullock & Almeida Jacqueline Toribio (eds.), *The Cambridge handbook of linguistic code-switching*, 142–160. Cambridge University Press.

Khattab, Ghada. 2013. Phonetic convergence and divergence strategies in English-Arabic bilingual children. *Linguistics* 51(2). 439–472. https://doi.org/10.1515/ling-2013-0017

Khattab, Ghada, Wasan Alsiraih & Jalal Al-Tamimi. 2018. Nasalisation in the production of Iraqi Arabic pharyngeals. *Phonetica* 75. 310–348. https://doi.org/10.1159/000487806

Khattab, Ghada, Feda Al-Tamimi & Barry Heselwood. 2006. Acoustic and auditory differences in the /t-T/ opposition in male and female speakers of Jordanian Arabic. In Sami Boudelaa (ed.), *Perspectives on Arabic Linguistics XIV*, 131–160. John Benjamins. https://doi.org/10.1075/cilt.266.09kha

Khattab, Ghada & Jalal Al-Tamimi. 2009. Durational cues for gemination in Lebanese Arabic. *Language and Linguistics* 22. 39–55.

Khattab, Ghada & Jalal Al-Tamimi. 2014. Geminate timing in Lebanese Arabic. *Laboratory Phonology* 5(2). 231–270. https://doi.org/10.1515/lp-2014-0009

Kirchhoff, Katrin & Dimitra Vergyri. 2005. Cross-dialectal data sharing for acoustic modeling in Arabic speech recognition. *Speech Communication* 46(1). 37–51. https://doi.org/10.1016/j.specom.2005.01.004

Labov, William. 1963. The social motivation of a sound change. *Word* 19(3). 273–309. https://doi.org/10.1080/00437956.1963.11659799

Labov, William. 1972. *Sociolinguistic patterns*. University of Pennsylvania Press.

Labov, William. 2001. *Principles of linguistic change, vol. 2, Social factors*. Blackwell.

Manfredi, Stefano & Fida Bizri. 2019. Arabic-based pidgins and creoles. 2019. Confessional varieties. In Al-Wer & Horesh, 134–147.

Matras, Yaron. 2018. Duly verified? Language analysis in UK asylum applications of Syrian refugees. *International Journal of Speech, Language and the Law* 25(1). 53–78. https://doi.org/10.1558/ijsll.35710

McCarthy, John J. 1979. *Formal problems in Semitic phonology and morphology*. PhD dissertation, MIT.

Miller, Catherine, Enam Al-Wer, Dominique Caube & Janet C.E. Watson (eds.). 2007. *Arabic in the city: Issues in dialect contact and language variation*. Routledge.

Milroy, Lesley. 1987. *Language and social networks*, 2nd edn. Blackwell.

Milroy, Lesley & Matthew Gordon. 2003. *Sociolinguistics: Method and interpretation*. Blackwell.

Mitchell, Terence F. 1986. What is educated spoken Arabic? *International Journal of the Sociology of Language* 61. 7–32. https://doi.org/10.1515/ijsl.1986.61.7

Moisik, Scott Reid, John H. Esling & Lise Crevier-Buchman. 2010. A high-speed laryngoscopic investigation of aryepiglottic trilling. *Journal of the Acoustical Society of America* 127(3). 1548–1559. https://doi.org/10.1121/1.3299203

Naïm-Sanbar, Samia. 1985. *Le parler Arabe de Ras-Beyrouth (Liban): La diversité phonologique–Étude socio-linguistique.* Librarie Orientaliste P. Geuthner.

Ntelitheos, Dimitrios & Tommi Tsz-Cheung Leung (eds.). 2021. *Experimental Arabic linguistics.* John Benjamins.

Obeidat, Hussein & Khadidja Hammoudi. 2019. Language identity and the other gender. *Journal of Modern Education Review* 9(3). 192–202.

Owens, Jonathan. 2001. Arabic sociolinguistics. *Arabica* 48. 419–469. https://doi.org/10.1163/157005801323163816

Owens, Jonathan. 2007. Close encounters of a different kind: Two types of insertion in Nigerian Arabic codeswitching. In Miller et al., 249–274.

Palva, Heikki. 1982. Patterns of koineization in Modern Colloquial Arabic. *Acta Orientalia* 43. 13–32.

Patrick, Peter. 2002. The speech community. In Chambers, Trudgill & Schilling-Estes, 573–597. Blackwell.

Proceedings of Interspeech 2005. 2005. International Speech Communication Association.

Reddy, Sravana & James N. Stanford. 2015. A web application for automated dialect analysis. In *Proceedings of the 2015 Conference of the North American Chapter of the Association for Computational Linguistics: Demonstrations*, 71–75. Association for Computational Linguistics. https://doi.org/10.3115/v1/N15-3015

Rosenfelder, Ingrid, Josef Fruehwald, Keelan Evanini, Scott Seyfarth, Kyle Gorman, Hilary Prichard & Jiahong Yuan. 2014. *FAVE: Forced Alignment and Vowel Extraction* [computer program], ver. 1.2.2. https://doi.org/10.5281/zenodo.22281

Sadiqi, Fatima. 2009. Language, gender, and power in Morocco. In Hanna Herzog & Ann Braude (eds.), *Gendering religion and politics*, 259–275. Palgrave Macmillan. https://doi.org/10.1057/9780230623378_12

Sadiqi, Fatima. 2021. Language and gender in North Africa: Contextualising an emerging discipline. *Gender & Language* 15(4). 591–602. https://doi.org/10.1558/genl.21526

Salam, Fathi & Mohamed Embarki. 2012. Gender and acoustic variation: Cases of vowels in Arabic Libyan of Tripoli. Paper presented at the 19th Sociolinguistics Symposium, Berlin.

Saleh, Marwa, Rasha Shoeib, Mona Hegazi & P. Ali. 2007. Early phonological development in Arabic Egyptian children: 12–30 months. *Folia Phoniatrica et Logopaedica* 59(5). 234–240. https://doi.org/10.1159/000104461

Salonen, Erkki. 1979. *Remarks on the Arabic dialect of the Druzes of Lebanon.* Finnish Oriental Society.

Samant, Mukta Sai. 2010. Arab Americans and sound change in southeastern Michigan. *English Today* 26(3). 27–34. https://doi.org/10.1017/S0266078410000209

Samant, Mukta Sai. 2011. *Arab American youth and sound change in southeastern Michigan.* PhD dissertation, University of Michigan.

Schmidt, Richard W. 1986. Applied sociolinguistics: The case of Arabic as a second language. *Anthropological Linguistics* 28(1). 55–72.

Scott, Mark & Ali Idrissi. 2018. Audiovisual perception of gemination and pharyngealization in Arabic. *Speech Communication* 98. 17–27. https://doi.org/10.1016/j.specom.2018.01.009

The Scottish Consortium for ICPhS 2015 (ed.). 2015. *Proceedings of the 18th International Congress of Phonetic Sciences.* University of Glasgow.

Shetewi, Ourooba. 2018. *The role of social factors in the speech of Palestinian refugee children in Syria.* PhD thesis, Newcastle University.

Spolsky, Bernard, H. Tushyeh, M. Amara & K. de Bot. 2000. *Languages in Bethlehem: The sociolinguistic transformation of a Palestinian town.* The Final Scientific Report of Project No. 94-11-1. Netherlands-Israel Development Research Programme.

Stanford, James N. & Dennis R. Preston (eds.). 2009. *Variation in indigenous minority languages.* John Benjamins.

Stuart-Smith, Jane. 2007. Empirical evidence for gendered speech production: /s/ in Glaswegian. In Cole & Hualde, 65–86.

Szreder, Marta, Donald Derrick & Chahla Ben-Ammar. 2021. Affricate variation in Emirati Arabic: An exploratory study. In Ntelitheos & Leung, 57–82.

Tagliamonte, Sali A. 2006. *Analysing sociolinguistic variation.* Cambridge University Press.

Taqi, Hanan. 2010. *Two dialects, three generations: Dialect contact in Kuwait.* PhD thesis, Newcastle University.

Thompson, Katrina Daly. 2019. Becoming Muslims with a "Queer Voice": Indexical disjuncture in the talk of LGBT members of the progressive Muslim community. *Journal of Linguistic Anthropology* 30(1). 123–144. https://doi.org/10.1111/jola.12256

Trouvain, Jürgen & William J. Barry (eds.). 2007. *Proceedings of the 16th International Congress of the Phonetic Sciences.* Saarland University.

Trudgill, Peter. 2004. *New-dialect formation: The inevitability of colonial Englishes.* Edinburgh University Press.

UNESCO. 2012. World Arabic Language Day. Retrieved 24 March 2016. www.unesco.org/new/en/unesco/events/prizes-and-celebrations/celebrations/international-days/world-arabic-language-day/

Versteegh, Kees. 2014. *The Arabic language,* 2nd edn. Edinburgh University Press.

Walters, Keith. 1991. Women, men and linguistic variation in the Arab World. In Bernard Comrie & Mushira Eid (eds.) *Perspectives on Arabic linguistics III,* 199–229. John Benjamins.

Wehbe, Reem H. 2017. *Raising of [æ] and [æ:] in the Lebanese variety of Mahrouna, Tyre: Phonological, morphological, and lexical conditioning.* MA thesis, American University of Beirut.

Wells, John C. 1982. *Accents of English.* Cambridge University Press.

Winter, Bodo. 2019. *Statistics for linguists: An introduction using R.* Routledge.

Yeou, Mohamed. 2005. Variability of F0 alignment in Moroccan Arabic accentual focus. In *Proceedings of Interspeech 2005,* 1433–1436. https://doi.org/10.21437/Interspeech.2005-510

Yeou, Mohamed, Mohamed Embarki, Sallal Al Maqtari & Christelle Dodane. 2007. F0 alignment patterns in Arabic dialects. In Trouvain & Barry, 1493–1496.

Zeroual, Chakir, John H. Esling & Philip Hoole. 2011. EMA, endoscopic, ultrasound and acoustic study of two secondary articulations in Moroccan Arabic. In Hassan & Heselwood, 277–290.

Ziamari, Karima. 2007. Development and linguistic change in Moroccan Arabic-French codeswitching. In Miller et al., 275–290.

27

SOCIOPHONETICS AND SPANISHES

Scott Sadowsky

Introduction

This chapter surveys the sociophonetic literature on the Spanish language, a relatively small but growing body of linguistic knowledge. We operationally define this as primary quantitative studies of fluent L1 speakers of Spanish which analyze the behavior of one or more phonetic or phonological dependent variables (e.g., acoustic characteristics of a given phone, allophone selection for a certain phoneme, vowel formants) in terms of at least one social independent variable (e.g., speaker socioeconomic status, sex, age) in addition to geographic provenance, if this variable is used.

These criteria thus exclude handbooks and textbooks, works based solely on authors' impressionistic reflections, language attitude surveys which happen to include phonetic or phonological variables, studies of heritage speakers, and studies of learners of Spanish as a second language. These criteria also exclude studies which simply limit their speaker sample to people with shared values for one or more social variables without examining the effects of these variables on the linguistic ones—regardless of whether or not the studies claim to be sociolinguistic or sociophonetic in nature. Thus, an investigation of intervocalic /d̪/ lenition in upper-class women from Pelotillehue would be excluded, as it is a classic phonetic study with no sociolinguistic analysis. In contrast, a study of this same linguistic phenomenon that compares and contrasts its manifestations in upper-class men and women, or in upper- and lower-class women, for example, would be included. Finally, studies that analyze the effects of geographical provenance without considering any other social variable are not included, as this is the domain of classic dialectology.

In all, we examine 123 publications written in Spanish or English which meet the criteria outlined here. While every effort was made to be exhaustive, both space restrictions and imperfections in search strategies make it inevitable that some otherwise deserving works will be excluded.

We begin with a quantitative review of the sociophonetic literature by country. We then examine early Spanish sociophonetics (1890s–1980s) chronologically, with emphasis on its origins, influences, and methods. Subsequently, we explore what might be termed contemporary Spanish sociophonetics (1990s–present) in a thematic fashion: its central research questions, key theories and frameworks, and prominent methods and approaches are examined in turn. We then present a sociophonetic study of Chilean Spanish vowels, analyzed in terms of speaker sex and SES, as well as lexical stress, and close with some brief reflections on the future of Spanish-language sociophonetics.

DOI: 10.4324/9781003034636-30

Note that the phonetic symbols used to represent Spanish vary immensely (and often confusingly) between authors. This chapter standardizes their representation using the International Phonetic Alphabet (International Phonetic Association 2015).

Spanish sociophonetics by country

The extent to which different varieties of Spanish have been researched in sociophonetic terms varies greatly. In absolute numbers, the Spanishes of Spain and Chile lead with 28 and 20 studies, respectively. A second tier is formed by Mexico (15 studies), Argentina (14), and Puerto Rico and Venezuela (11 each). From there, the amount of research declines steeply. A third tier is made up of Peru (4 studies); Colombia and Cuba (3 each); Bolivia, Costa Rica, Dominican Republic, Ecuador, El Salvador, Panama, and the United States excluding Puerto Rico (2 each); and Nicaragua (1 study). No studies that met our inclusion criteria could be found for other countries where Spanish is a de facto or de jure official or auxiliary language, including Equatorial Guinea, Guatemala, Honduras, Paraguay, Uruguay, or the Philippines.

These absolute numbers shed a certain amount of light on the extent to which each national variety of Spanish has been studied through a sociophonetic lens. However, the number of speakers of each of these lects varies enormously, and it is not unreasonable to assume that there is, on the whole, more variation to account for in a variety of Spanish with 100 million speakers than in one with 5 million. Thus, an examination of the relative numbers is warranted. These are presented in Table 27.1, in terms of the number of studies per 10 million inhabitants, a fairly accurate proxy for the number of speakers except in the case of the United States.

Table 27.1 Sociophonetic studies by country or territory, in absolute numbers and per 10 million inhabitants

Studies

Country/territory	*n*	*Per 10 million inhabitants*	*Inhabitants*
Puerto Rico	11	38.9	2,829,812
Chile	20	10.4	19,250,195
Spain	28	6.0	46,719,142
Panama	2	4.5	4,446,964
Costa Rica	2	3.9	5,182,354
Venezuela	11	3.8	29,266,991
El Salvador	2	3.1	6,550,389
Argentina	14	3.0	46,010,234
Cuba	3	2.7	11,305,652
Dominican Republic	2	1.8	11,056,370
Bolivia	2	1.7	11,992,656
Nicaragua	1	1.5	6,779,100
Peru	4	1.2	33,684,208
Ecuador	2	1.1	18,113,361
Mexico	15	1.1	131,562,772
Colombia	3	0.6	51,512,762
United States	2	0.1	334,805,269

Note. Countries with no studies are not shown. Population data are taken from https://worldpopulationreview.com/countries.

The picture that emerges from the relative numbers is a rather different one. Puerto Rican Spanish turns out to be the most sociophonetically well-researched variety of the language by far, with 38.9 studies per 10 million inhabitants. Chilean Spanish occupies a distant second place with slightly more than a quarter as many studies (10.4 per 10 million). The third most researched variety, Peninsular Spanish, has slightly more than half as many studies as Chilean Spanish (6.0 per 10 million). From there, only five varieties have been examined in three or more sociophonetic studies per 10 million speakers: those of Panama, Costa Rica, Venezuela, El Salvador, and Argentina.

While it is clear that sociophonetics has been gaining ground in the Spanish-speaking world, its development has been highly uneven, and a number of national varieties of the language are still nearly or completely unstudied in sociophonetic terms.

Early Spanish sociophonetics (1890s–1980s)

There is a long tradition of phonetic and phonological research on Spanish, with its modern phase perhaps beginning with German-Chilean linguist Rudolf Lenz's *Chilenische Studien* (Lenz 1892, 1893a, 1893b, 1893c, 1940 [reprint in Spanish]), a series of seven studies of different aspects of Chilean Spanish phonetics and phonology, as well as his *Beiträge zur Kenntnis des Amerikanospanisch* (Lenz 1893d), which in part examines the potential influence of Mapudungun, Chile's largest indigenous language, on the Spanish spoken in the country (a Spanish translation of these works is available in Lenz 1940).

Lenz was an unflinching and militant descriptivist in an academic culture that would remain largely prescriptivist for at least another century. In part as a result of his adherence to this modern, scientific principle, these works may well also constitute the first sociophonetic studies of Spanish, as they examine language variation between upper-, middle-, and lower-class speakers, the urban and rural lower classes, and occasionally the sexes, while also exploring language contact and, to a much lesser degree, speech style. This is particularly noteworthy given that what little research on language variation was being performed at the time focused mainly on elderly rural males, in the European dialectological tradition.

Unfortunately, Lenz's early forays into sociophonetics were largely ignored by the Hispanic linguistics establishment. It would not be until the early 1970s that research of this nature would finally take off.

Perissinotto's (1971) dissertation on the speech of 110 Mexico City speakers is one of the first such investigations. It explores six different linguistic phenomena: syneresis versus hiatus, final stop neutralization, /s/ voicing before voiced consonants, /f/ allophony, and /r/ and /ɾ/ fricativization. These phenomena are analyzed in terms of speakers' age, sex, and socioeconomic status (SES; in this case based on educational level, occupation, wealth, and "consciousness of the world around them"). Perissinotto cites Labov's (1966a) *Social stratification of English in New York City* as the model for his sociolinguistic analysis—which is unsurprising in light of the fact that he did his doctoral work at Columbia, where Labov was assistant professor until 1970. The investigation of /r/ and /ɾ/ fricativization was published the next year as Perissinotto (1972), and a Spanish version of his dissertation was published several years later in book form as Perissinotto (1975).

Two years later, Cedergren's (1973) much-cited Cornell dissertation on sociophonetic variation in 79 Panamanian Spanish speakers was published. This work, carried out within the variable rule framework (Labov 1966b, 1969, 1972; Sankoff 1989[1974]), examines coda /s/ allophony in terms of speaker age, sex, SES (based on educational level, occupation, and neighborhood), and region, as well as contextual style. Methodologically, it is particularly notable for using a rigorous, census-based sampling strategy, for developing a new, multiplicative probability model for variable rule analysis, and for utilizing the Varbrul software package (Cedergren & Sankoff 1974).

In the same year, Fontanella de Weinberg's (1973) study of coda /s/ allophony in 60 speakers from Bahía Blanca, Argentina was published. This investigation, also rooted in the variable rule framework, examines variation in terms of age, sex, occupational level, and style, though without computational support or the sophisticated math of Cedergren (1973). In addition to Labov (1966a), Fontanella de Weinberg bases her work in part on Shuy, Wolfram & Riley (1967) and Wolfram (1969).

Five years later, Terrell (1978) published a new study of coda /s/ allophony in Argentina, using a sample of 24 speakers from Buenos Aires. Results are analyzed in terms of speaker sex and age, and allophone counts are tabulated with the assistance of a computer. While Terrell, who was affiliated with UC Irvine at the time of publication, cites none of the foundational sociolinguistic studies of English-language speech communities, she does cite Cedergren (1973) and Fontanella de Weinberg (1973). This may be the first evidence of the spread of the nascent Spanish-language sociophonetic tradition. It could be said, however, that Terrell's study was only coincidentally sociophonetic in nature. It is grounded principally in Spanish dialectology, with a small contribution from historical linguistics. Furthermore, it uses a speaker sample deliberately designed to reflect (and perhaps appease) prescriptivist prejudices, in which speakers were required to be exclusively upper-middle class and university educated. This class bias, which is anathema to all types of sociolinguistic research, is common in Hispanic linguistics.

Argentina's early leadership in sociophonetic research was further established by Wolf & Jiménez's (1979) study of /j/ allophony in four different samples, made up of a combined 298 speakers from Buenos Aires. Using the variationist approach, with specific reference to Labov (1972), the authors focus on the devoicing of [ʒ] to [ʃ] (a phenomenon sometimes labeled *sheísmo*; cf. *zheísmo* 'merger of /j/ and /ʎ/ to [ʒ]' and *yeísmo* 'merger of /j/ and /ʎ/ regardless of the phonetic outcome') and seek to determine the social origins of what they consider to be a change-in-progress. Results are analyzed in terms of age, sex, impressionistic SES, and speech style. Neighborhood, occupation, educational level, and birth order among siblings were also examined in specific samples. This same phenomenon would later be studied by Wolf (1984) using the both the real-time and apparent-time paradigms.

At around the same time, Bobadilla & Bobadilla (1979, 1980) published reports of a study of /t̠ɾ/, /t͡ʃ/ and /r/ allophony in 144 speakers from Rancagua, a small city just south of the Chilean capital, Santiago (see Sadowsky 2015 for additional detail on the complexity of /t̠ɾ/ in Chilean Spanish). The authors analyze the production of these phonemes in terms of age, sex, SES (based on income, educational level, occupation, and "key assets"—such as owning a telephone, car, or home, and having a maid), and speech style. Bobadilla & Bobadilla (1980) is unusual in that it includes an in-depth discussion of variation as a linguistic concept, with emphasis on Labov's variable rules paradigm, while also taking inspiration from Wolfram (1978), Trudgill (1974), and Hymes (1971). It provides a defense of sociolinguistics as a legitimate approach to studying language, especially vis-à-vis the European structuralism that dominated Hispanic linguistics and the generativism that was fast taking the discipline by storm in United States. Furthermore, it includes a discussion of sociolinguistic research methodology, including speaker stratification methods and the statistical treatment of results, which refers to two unreferenced publications by Labov (most likely Labov 1966a and Weinreich, Labov & Herzog 1968), and cites Shuy, Wolfram & Riley (1967). No mention of prior sociophonetic research on Spanish is made in this paper.

Bobadilla & Bobadilla (1980) is thus a sort of primer on the theory and method of the sociolinguistic investigation of speech, and it is cited in Chilean sociophonetic literature to this day. It is not unreasonable to think that it helped spark the current strong interest in the field in Chile.

Unfortunately, the authors report almost none of the results of their investigation. They provide only a single table with the relative frequencies of two allophones of /t̠ɾ/, three of /r/, and two of /t͡ʃ/ for the overall speaker sample, along with the results of a "linguistic insecurity test." They state that they will provide a full analysis in future publications, but this apparently did not occur.

Peninsular Spanish is examined in sociophonetic terms in Holmquist's (1985) study of word-final /o/ raising (→ [u]) in 49 speakers from the rural village of Ucieda. The author's goal in this paper is to shed light on social changes caused by the Spanish Civil War and the Franco regime. To this end, he examines not just the by-then common social variables of sex, age, and occupation, but also ownership of mountain animals (which turned out to correlate with local low-prestige variants) and political orientation. Methodologically, this paper is one of the first to perform a statistical analysis of its data, using ANOVA and the SPSS statistical package. The author draws a parallel between his results and those of Labov's (1963) study of Martha's Vineyard, arguing that in both cases certain groups signal an "independent and protective attitude" toward their locality by means of the retention of an older form of a linguistic feature that is undergoing change.

The Spanish of the Dominican Republic is examined in sociophonetic terms in Alba's (1988) study of word-final /ɾ/ and /l/ in 12 speakers from Santiago, in the region of Cibao. Speakers are grouped into two SES levels, high and low, and those belonging to the lower SES group are further divided into two age groups. No mention is made of sex, including in the description of the speaker sample. However, the fact that the eight low-SES speakers are manual laborers suggests that they are men, and the four upper-SES "professionals" likely are, too, to prevent speaker sex from becoming an uncontrolled or confounding variable. This is in line with the not uncommon practice in Hispanic linguistics of only taking into account men's speech. Alba's study is firmly rooted in the dialectological tradition of Spain, and no sociolinguistic literature is mentioned. Results are presented as percentages without token counts, and no statistical analysis of the data is performed. The author would later reexamine these linguistic variables, along with /s/, in much more sociophonetic terms, after a stint as a Fulbright Scholar at the University of Pennsylvania with Labov and Gillian Sankoff (Alba 1990).

Sanicky (1988) investigated /f/ allophony in 129 speakers from Argentina's Misiones province, where this phoneme has a series of voiced, labialized, bilabial, and velar allophones. Results are analyzed in terms of speakers' age, "cultural level" (based on educational level, occupation, "interests," and "social circle"), and region within the province. There is no indication of whether the sample is made up of men, women, or a combination of the two. Results are presented as allophone counts and percentages, with no statistical treatment. Although this investigation is predominantly based on the Spanish dialectology tradition, it does cite one work from the nascent Spanish-language sociophonetic literature, Perissinotto (1975).

Dorta (1989) examines /ɾ/ and /l/ in onset consonant clusters, between vowels and in coda in 12 speakers from La Perdoma, Spain. Speakers are stratified using three social variables: sex, age, and "sociocultural level." This study is firmly rooted in the Spanish dialectological tradition; though it does make reference to certain sociolinguistic works, including López Morales (1983) and an unreferenced publication by Cedergren, it does so only to compare overall allophone counts. The results reported include these counts and their corresponding percentages. No statistical analysis is performed.

Finally, Rissel (1989) analyzes /r/ and /ɾ/ fricativization in a sample of 56 speakers from San Luis Potosí, Mexico, with the goal of shedding light on the processes that drive language change. Note that although this paper refers only to /r/, Rissel follows Harris's (1969) analysis in which Spanish has a single rhotic phoneme, and thus the coda "/r/" she refers to is in fact /ɾ/ in most analyses. The speakers, who were between 12 and 22 years of age, were stratified by sex and "sociocultural level" (calculated using speakers' school type and parents' occupation and educational levels), plus an innovative ideological variable: speakers' attitudes toward traditional male and female roles. Two speech styles were examined. This paper is methodologically innovative due to its use of computers not just to tabulate results but also to assist in coding the data. A three-way ANOVA was used to determine if social variable interactions were significant. The author finds "striking" similarities between her results and those of Fontanella de Weinberg's (1979) study of /ʒ/ devoicing in Argentina. In both cases, an innovative change appeared first in middle- and upper-class women, and subsequently spread to lower-class women, with lower-class men largely rejecting the change. Lower educational levels favored adoption of the change. Agreement with traditional sex roles favored the change in women while disfavoring it in men. Rissel's (1989) investigation, which was published while she was affiliated with SUNY Buffalo, is firmly rooted in the sociolinguistic tradition of authors such as Labov (Labov 1966a, 1972), Labov, Yaeger & Steiner (1972), Milroy (1981), and Trudgill (1972). At the same time, she also cites Perissinotto (1972) and Fontanella de Weinberg (1973), two authors from the Spanish-language sociophonetics tradition.

This overview of some of the key early works in the field shows that Spanish sociophonetics arose independently from two different traditions: American sociolinguistics and Spanish dialectology. The sociolinguistic tradition was for the most part transmitted through both Latin American and US researchers who were trained in the United States. The Spanish dialectological tradition, on the other hand, was home-grown and arose gradually, as mostly Spanish and Latin American authors added additional variables to classic dialect research, often under the influence of the burgeoning field of sociolinguistics.

Central research questions

Spanish-language sociophonetic research has focused largely on describing the same phonological phenomena that classic Spanish dialectology has studied for over a century (see, among many others, Henríquez Ureña 1921, 1930, 1931; Wagner 1927; Alonso 1930; Navarro Tomás 1945; García de Diego 1946; Rona 1958, 1964; Zamora Vicente 1960; Canfield 1962; Lapesa 1964; Resnick 1969, 1976; Montes 1970; Zamora Munné 1980; Lope Blanch 1992; Moreno Fernández 1993). These phenomena consist mainly of consonant allophony, although some work has been done on certain aspects of vowels, and a few investigations of suprasegmental processes have been performed. The number of studies which analyze each is presented in Table 27.2. Note that the number of studies exceeds the number of publications reviewed because many publications examine more than one phenomenon.

By far the most researched topic among the 123 sociolinguistic publications we have reviewed is /s/ variation, which has been studied some 43 times (see also Chappell, García & Davidson this volume). Most studies focus on coda /s/ lenition or elision. This phoneme has been examined in Argentina in terms of age, sex, SES, and style (Fontanella de Weinberg 1973), age and sex (Terrell 1978), and age, sex, and SES (Sanicky 1996); in Chile in terms of age and sex (Cepeda 1990b), age, sex, and SES (Cepeda 1990a; Bolyanatz 2017; Rogers 2020), and sex and SES (Perdomo-Pinto & Sadowsky 2019); in Colombia in terms of age and sex (Ramírez & Almira 2016), age, sex,

Table 27.2 Number and percentage of 123 Spanish-language sociophonetic studies which analyze each linguistic variable

Linguistic variable	Studies	
	n	*%*
/s/	43	35.0
/ɾ/	23	18.7
/r/	17	13.8
/d̪/	16	13.0
vowels	14	11.4
/l/	10	8.1
/j/	8	6.5
/k/	7	5.7
/t͡ʃ/	7	5.7
/b/	6	4.9
/p/	6	4.9
/g/	4	3.3
/t̪/	4	3.3
/t͡ɾ/	4	3.3
/f/	3	2.4
seseo	3	2.4
/n/	2	1.6
suprasegmental	2	1.6
/ɲ/	1	0.8
/x/	1	0.8
/ʎ/	1	0.8
/m/	0	0.0
/θ/	0	0.0

and SES (Correa 2017), and age, sex, educational level, occupation, and region of origin (Colina 2018); in Costa Rica in terms of sex (Calvo Shadid 1997) and sex, SES, perceived educatedness, and sexual orientation (Chappell 2016); in Cuba in terms of age, sex, SES, and urban/rural provenance (Alfaraz 2000); in the Dominican Republic in terms of age, sex, SES, and educational level (Alba 1990); in Ecuador in terms of age and sex (García 2015) and age, sex, regional origin, and perceived status and pleasantness (García 2019); in El Salvador in terms of age, sex, educational level, region, and urban/rural provenance (Brogan 2018; Brogan & Bolyanatz 2018); in Mexico in terms of sex (Schmidt & Willis 2011), age and sex (Schmidt & Willis 2011), and age, sex, and SES (Perissinotto 1971); in Nicaragua in terms of age, sex, and SES (Chappell 2013); in Panama in terms of age, sex, and SES (Cedergren 1973); in Peru in terms of sex (Bernate 2016) and sex, educational level, occupation, social network, migratory origin, and migrant generation (Klee et al. 2018); in Puerto Rico in terms of sex (Holmquist 2011), age, sex and SES (Emmanuelli 2000), age, sex, educational level, and years lived in Puerto Rico (Mumin 2017), and age, sex, and level of bilingualism (Mohamed & Muntendam 2020); in Spain in terms of educational level (Fernández de Molina Ortés 2016), sex (Henriksen & Harper 2016), age and sex (Tejada Giráldez 2012), age, sex, and "sociocultural level" (Calero 1990; Pérez Martín 1995), and age, sex and educational level (Tejada Giráldez 2015; Vida-Castro 2015, 2016; Kapović 2017); in the United States in terms of sex, SES, and country and region of origin (Erker 2012); and in Venezuela in terms of sex and SES (Ruiz Sánchez 2004), age, sex, and educational level (Carrasquero 2010), and age, sex, educational level, occupation, and region of origin (Colina 2018).

The second most commonly researched phenomenon is /r/ allophony, which has been examined by 23 studies, slightly more than half as many as /s/. This line of inquiry focuses on three main topics: fricativization of word-final /ɾ/, neutralization of the contrast between /ɾ/ and /l/, and general allophony. This phoneme has been analyzed in Argentina in terms of age, sex, and SES (Sanicky 2001); in Cuba in terms of age and sex (Alfaraz 2007) and age, sex, SES, and urban/rural provenance (Alfaraz 2000); in the Dominican Republic in terms of age and SES (Alba 1988) and age, sex, SES, and educational level (Alba 1990); in Mexico in terms of age and sex (Mazzaro & González de Anda 2019), age, sex, and SES (Perissinotto 1971, 1972, 1975), age, sex, and educational level (Lastra & Martín Butragueño 2006), and age, sex, and attitudes toward traditional sex roles (Rissel 1989); in Panama in terms of age, sex, SES, and attitudes toward the capital (Broce & Torres Cacoullos 2002); in Peru in terms of age, sex, and SES (Alvord, Echávez-Solano & Klee 2005); in Puerto Rico in terms of age and sex (Beaton 2015, 2016), age, sex, and SES (Prosper-Sánchez 1995; Emmanuelli 2000), age, sex, educational level, and years lived in Puerto Rico (Mumin 2017), and age, sex, educational level, and level of bilingualism (Santiago Molina 2017); in Spain in terms of age, sex, and SES (Dorta 1989); in the United States in terms of age and sex (Mazzaro & González de Anda 2019); and in Venezuela in terms of age, sex, and educational level (Ugueto 2016) and age, sex, and SES (Ugueto 2007; Molina Boscán 2010; Díaz-Campos, Fafulas & Gradoville 2011).

Variation in /r/ follows in frequency, with 17 studies, most of which focus on allophone variation or fricativization. It has been studied in Argentina in terms of age, SES, and region (Sanicky 1992); in Chile in terms of sex and "sociocultural level" (Figueroa 2011) and age, sex, and SES (Zepeda-Pallero 2019); in Mexico in terms of age, sex, and SES (Perissinotto 1971, 1972, 1975), age, sex, and educational level (Lastra & Martín Butragueño 2006), and age, sex, and attitudes toward traditional sex roles (Rissel 1989); in Peru in terms of sex, SES, urban/rural provenance, social network, bilingualism, and various attitudes (Diez Canseco 1997) and age, sex, and SES (Alvord, Echávez-Solano & Klee 2005); in Puerto Rico in terms of age, sex, and SES (Emmanuelli 2000); in Spain in terms of sex and region (Henriksen 2014), age and region (Zahler & Daidone 2014), and age, sex, and educational level (Melero 2015); and in Venezuela in terms of age, sex, and SES (Ugueto 2007; Díaz-Campos 2008).

The allophones of /d̪/ are the fourth most researched phenomenon, with 16 studies, almost all of which analyze intervocalic lenition or elision. It has been examined in Chile in terms of sex (Verdugo 2019) and age and sex (Rogers 2016); in Mexico in terms of sex and educational level (García Ponce & Mora 2018) and age, sex, and SES (Perissinotto 1971); in Puerto Rico in terms of age, sex, and SES (Emmanuelli 2000); in Spain in terms of age and sex (Villena et al. 2011; Jiménez-Fernández 2020), sex and occupation (Cruz Ortiz 2019), age, sex, and educational level (Uruburu 1994; Samper Padilla & Samper Hernández 2020), age, sex, and "cultural level" (Uruburu 1996), and age, sex, and bilingualism (Gómez Molina & Gómez Devís 2010); and in Venezuela in terms of age, sex, and SES (Bongiovanni 2013) and age, sex, and educational level (Malaver & Perdomo-Pinto 2016).

The fifth most studied phenomenon is vowels, with 14 investigations. The research that exists in this area is mostly exploratory, having little previous work on which to build. The social stratification of vowels has been studied in Chile in terms of "sociocultural level" (Salamanca & Valverde 2009) and sex and SES (Sadowsky present volume); and in Spain in terms of sexual orientation (Osle Ezquerra 2015). Vowel raising has been studied in Mexico in terms of age, educational level, occupation, mobility, and social network (Barajas 2014); and in Puerto Rico in terms of age, occupation, and social network (Holmquist 2005), age, sex, occupation, and social network (Holmquist 2008), and age, sex, occupation, mobility, and social network (Oliver 2008). Final /o/ raising to [u] has been examined in Spain in terms of age, sex, and occupation (Holmquist 1985) and sex, educational level, occupation, bilingualism, and familiarity with interlocutors (Barnes 2016). Vowel reduction has been studied in Bolivia in terms of age and sex (Sessarego 2012, 2013); and in Mexico in terms of age, sex, and SES (Dabkowski 2018). And hiatus resolution has been examined in Mexico in terms of age and sex (Vuskovich 2006) and age, sex, and educational level (Hernández 2009).

Variation in /l/ has been examined by 10 investigations, which focus almost exclusively on the allophony of this phoneme in coda position, often in tandem with /ɾ/ for the purpose of analyzing the neutralization of the two. It has been studied in Cuba in terms of age and sex (Alfaraz 2007) and age, sex, SES, and urban/rural provenance (Alfaraz 2000); in the Dominican Republic in terms of age and SES (Alba 1988) and age, sex, SES, and educational level (Alba 1990); in Panama in terms of sex, SES, and attitude toward the capital (Broce & Torres Cacoullos 2002); in Puerto Rico in terms of age and sex (Beaton 2015, 2016) and age, sex, and SES (Prosper-Sánchez 1995); in Spain in terms of age, sex, and SES (Dorta 1989); and in Venezuela in terms of age, sex, and SES (Molina Boscán 2010).

The phoneme /j/ has been examined in eight studies, which focus on the social stratification of its allophony, and often specifically on devoicing. It has been studied in Argentina in terms of age, sex, and region (Chang 2008), age, sex, and SES (Sanicky 2008; Rohena-Madrazo 2011; Rohena-Madrazo 2015), and age, sex, SES, educational level, and occupation (Wolf & Jiménez 1979); in Chile in terms of sex and "sociocultural level" (Figueroa 2011); and in Spain in terms of age, sex, and "sociocultural level" (Calero 1990).

Variation in /k/ production is studied in seven publications, most of which focus on spirantization and/or voicing. It has been examined in Chile in terms of age, sex, and SES (Rogers & Mirisis 2018; Sadowsky & Verkijk forthcoming) and age, sex, educational level, and a series of perceptual variables (Bolyanatz & Rogers 2019); in Colombia in terms of age and SES (Correa 2017); in Mexico in terms of age, sex, and SES (Perissinotto 1971) and age, sex, and bilingualism (Michnowicz & Carpenter 2013); and in Venezuela in terms of age, sex, and SES (Bongiovanni 2013).

The phoneme /t͡ʃ/ has been examined in seven studies, all regarding fricativization. In Chile, it has been studied in terms of age and "sociocultural level" (Figueroa 2011), age, sex, SES, and educational level (Valdivieso 1998), and age, sex, SES, educational level, occupation, and urban/rural provenance (Bobadilla & Bobadilla 1980); in Mexico in terms of age and sex (Mazzaro & González de Anda 2019) and age, sex, SES, educational level, and bilingualism (Méndez 2017); and in Spain in terms of age, sex, and educational level (Melguizo 2007).

The phoneme /b/ has been examined in six publications. Most focus on lenition or elision. It has been studied in Chile in terms of sex (Verdugo 2019) and age and sex (Rogers 2016); in Mexico in terms of age, sex, and SES (Perissinotto 1971); and in Venezuela in terms of age, sex, and SES (Bongiovanni 2013; Long & Baldwin 2013). One study, however, examines the use of the voiced labiodental fricative [v] as the main allophone of /b/ in Chile, in terms of age and literacy (Vergara-Fernández 2013).

Variation in /p/ production has also been examined in six studies, most of which focus on lenition or elision. In Chile, it has been analyzed in terms of sex and SES (Sadowsky & Yáñez-Valdenegro forthcoming), age, sex, and SES (Rogers & Mirisis 2018), and sex, region, and migratory status (Sadowsky & Aninao 2019); in Mexico in terms of age, sex, and bilingualism (Michnowicz &

Carpenter 2013) and age, sex and SES (Perissinotto 1971); and in Venezuela in terms of age, sex and SES (Bongiovanni 2013).

The variation of /g/ has been analyzed by four studies, which focus on lenition or elision. It has been examined in Chile in terms of sex (Verdugo 2019) and age and sex (Rogers 2016); in Mexico in terms of age, sex, and SES (Perissinotto 1971); and in Venezuela in terms of age, sex, and SES (Bongiovanni 2013).

The phoneme /ʈ/ has been examined in four publications: in Chile, in terms of age, sex, and SES (Rogers & Mirisis 2018); in Mexico in terms of age, sex, and bilingualism (Michnowicz & Carpenter 2013) and age, sex and SES (Perissinotto 1971); and in Venezuela in terms of age, sex, and SES (Bongiovanni 2013).

The variation of /t͡ɾ/ or [t̠ɾ] has been examined in four studies: in Argentina in terms of age, SES, and region (Sanicky 1992); and in Chile in terms of sex and "sociocultural level" (Figueroa 2011) and age, sex, SES, educational level, occupation, and urban/rural provenance (Bobadilla & Bobadilla 1980). In addition, various studies of /r/ examine [t̠ɾ] separately from [ɾ] in general.

Variation in /f/ production has been studied in three publications: in Argentina in terms of age, SES, and region (Sanicky 1988) and in Mexico in terms of age, sex, and educational level (Robles-Puente & Vilches-Aguado 2019) and age, sex and SES (Perissinotto 1971).

Seseo—the merger of /s/ and /θ/ to [s] (the merger is referred to as *ceceo* when it resolves to [θ]) has been explored in three investigations in Spain: in terms of age, sex and "sociocultural level" (Uruburu 1996), age, sex, and educational level (Ruiz Sánchez 2017), and perceived sex, SES, educational level, urban/rural provenance, and some other variables (Regan 2019).

The phoneme /n/ has been studied in two investigations: in Cuba in terms of age, sex, educational level, and occupation (Darías, Ruisánchez & Dohotaru 1997); and in Spain in terms of age, sex, and SES (Martín Morales 2018).

Suprasegmental phenomena have also been examined in two studies. Prosody patterns were examined in Argentina in terms of age and sex (Enbe & Tobin 2008); and [ʔ] as a word boundary marker was explored in Nicaragua in terms of age, sex, and educational level (Chappell 2013).

Finally, the loss of the /ɲ/ phoneme (→[nj]) was studied in Argentina in terms of age and sex (Bongiovanni 2019); /x/ palatalization was studied in Chile in terms of age, sex, and audience (Flores 2016); and /ʎ/ allophony in Peru was studied in terms of sex, SES, urban/rural provenance, social network, bilingualism, and various attitudes (Diez Canseco 1997). There were no sociophonetic studies of /m/ variation, nor of /θ/ except in the context of *seseo* or its absence.

Key theories and frameworks

Early sociophonetics tended to be split between the Labovian variable rule framework and traditional Spanish dialectology, as described above. By the 1980s, the variable rule framework was giving way to a more modern quantitative variationism. Research done in this school tends to elicit speech through interviews, stratifies speakers using SES or a proxy thereof (in addition to other variables), sometimes includes a statistical analysis, and often (but by no means always) seeks to contribute to the understanding of language variation and change, in addition to describing language variation.

Sociophonetics performed in the Spanish dialectological tradition added a quantitative approach to traditional dialectology, which tended to characterize entire regions in rather absolute terms based on one or a small handful of speakers. It also added some social variables to the dialectological repertoire. Otherwise, it remained largely true to its roots. Studies done in this school frequently elicit speech through the recitation of word lists, tend to focus on speaker age and sex as social variables, rarely use any sort of statistical analysis, and often aim to shed light on the historical development and geographic spread of Spanish.

In the last two decades, sociophonetics from the sociolinguistic tradition has made great advances, and looks poised to largely replace the dialectological tradition, except perhaps in Spain, where dialectology still enjoys prestige and institutional support.

The vast majority of Spanish-language sociophonetic studies are carried out (wittingly or not) within the framework of first-wave sociolinguistics, which is characterized by the analysis of variation in terms of broad demographic categories. This trend shows no sign of abating, likely because social class in most Spanish-speaking countries continues to be rigid and largely resistant to mobility, making it a useful and powerful predictor of linguistic behavior if measured accurately.

Five of the studies examined (4.1 percent) use a second-wave social network focus (see Milroy 1980). These are Diez Canseco (1997), Holmquist (2005, 2008), Barajas (2014) and Klee et al. (2018). The small number of studies of this type indicates that this framework has not prospered.

The study of style was present from the very beginning of the field, in Cedergren (1973), Fontanella de Weinberg (1973), and Wolf & Jiménez (1979), and it continues to be examined to this day with moderate frequency. However, it is normally treated as one more social variable within the first-wave paradigm, without the focus on its social meaning that characterizes the third wave of sociolinguistics.

In phonetic terms, the overwhelming majority of sociophonetic studies of Spanish analyze speech production. However, a small handful of perception investigations have begun to appear recently, including Rohena-Madrazo (2011), García (2015), Chappell (2016), Bolyanatz & Rogers (2019), and Regan (2019). Chappell's (2019) edited volume contains many such studies.

Methods and approaches

Sample size

As Spanish-language sociophonetics has developed over time, the speaker samples used by researchers have grown steadily smaller, as shown in Table 27.3 and Figure 27.1. Mean and median sample sizes have decreased every decade, from a high of 112.8 and 69.5, respectively, in the 1970s, to just 40.4 and 30.0 in the most recent period. Minimum sample sizes have also trended downward, from 24 in the 1970s to just 4 at present, with an exceptional uptick to 11 in the 2000s. Maximum sample sizes dropped from the 1970s (288) to the 1990s (129), before the trend reversed, reaching 179 in the most recent period.

Table 27.3 Number and sample sizes of sociophonetic studies over time

Years	Studies	Sample size			
		Mean	*Median*	*Minimum*	*Maximum*
1970–1979	5	112.8	69.5	24	288
1980–1989	7	67.0	52.5	12	144
1990–1999	13	58.2	49.0	8	129
2000–2009	20	45.3	33.5	11	165
2010–present	77	40.4	30.0	4	179

Note. Lenz's works from the 1890s are not included.

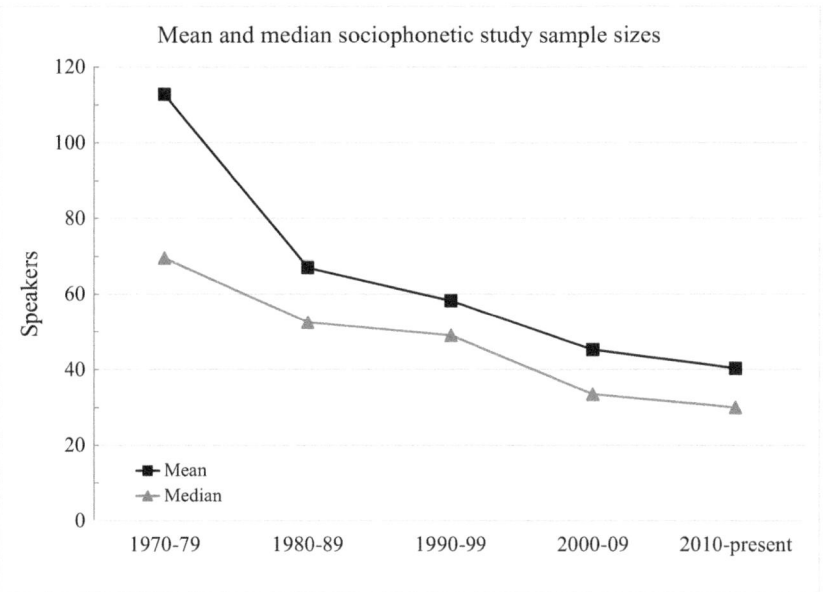

Figure 27.1   Mean and median sample sizes of sociophonetic studies over time

Considering that the reel-to-reel tape recorders, manually calculated statistics, expensive mechanical or electronic sonograph machines, and scarce mainframe computers of yore have been replaced by cheap and light digital recorders, freely available statistical and phonetic analysis software, and ubiquitous, powerful personal computers, this situation is rather counterintuitive. One would expect that the vastly increased convenience, affordability, power, and speed with which modern sociophonetic studies can be performed would lead to larger and larger sample sizes, in a quest to increase representativity, generalizability, and detail. But this is not the case. It should be noted that perception studies, which normally generate stimuli by eliciting recordings from just a small handful of speakers, are not responsible for this downward trend in sample sizes (except for the minimum sample size), as they account for only a small number of the publications examined (8.1 percent). While an exploration of the possible reasons for this phenomenon is out of the scope of this chapter, research funding levels and increasing pressure to maximize publication numbers would seem likely to play a role.

Table 27.3 also shows the number of studies published per decade. The pattern that emerges is one of very slow growth for the first 30 years of the discipline (1970–1999), followed by a 54 percent increase in publications between the 1990s and 2000s, and an impressive 285 percent jump between the 2000s and the most recent period.

Sample characteristics

On the whole, Spanish-language sociophonetic studies use a speaker sample design that is more or less balanced in terms of the social variables they analyze. However, there are two exceptions to this that deserve comment.

Firstly, in the early days of the discipline, and occasionally into more recent times, a certain proportion of studies used samples made up exclusively of men, while some others reported no information on speakers' sex, and presumably included only male speakers. These studies are mostly from the Spanish dialectological tradition. This type of sample design not only reduces new knowledge of the varieties under study but may also corrupt the scientific record by incorrectly presenting phenomena that are predominantly or exclusively present or absent in male speakers as being so in all speakers.

Secondly, a nontrivial number of studies suffer from a strong class bias. These studies limit their speaker samples to upper-middle and/or upper-class speakers, either overtly or using some sort of euphemism for these classes (e.g., "educated speakers," "professionals," "university-educated speakers," "speakers of the educated norm"), all of which refer to statuses to which access is still strongly mediated by wealth in most of the Spanish-speaking world. While the origins of this bias cannot be explored here, Lope Blanch's (1968) highly influential Project for the Coordinated Study of the Educated Linguistic Norm in the Main Cities of Ibero-America and the Iberian Peninsula, founded in 1964, doubtlessly played a significant role in normalizing it. This project, which organized and oversaw the creation of early speech corpora throughout the Spanish-speaking world, limited its speaker samples to "speakers of the educated language norm." To be considered as such, speakers were required to have a university degree, know at least one foreign language, have read "relevant literature," and (if possible) have traveled abroad (Rabanales 1992). In practice, this limited samples to members of each country's economic elite. As a result of this bias, much less is known about the speech of lower-, lower-middle-, and middle-class Spanish speakers than about the speech of the upper-middle and upper classes. Once all of society is systematically included in investigations of Spanish, it would be unsurprising if generalizations made about particular varieties of the language proved to be incorrect and new phenomena were discovered.

Elicitation

Many early Spanish-language sociophonetic studies used the reading of word lists to elicit speech, in the dialectological tradition. Although this practice is being superseded by the use of interviews, or of a series of elicitation methods aimed at obtaining different speech styles, it has not completely disappeared. This should be kept in mind when comparing otherwise similar studies.

Data coding

Impressionistic coding of speech data was predominant during the first three to four decades of Spanish-language sociophonetics. However, acoustic measurements from Praat (Boersma & Weenink 2022) have begun to dominate. One problematic practice in this area which is still fairly common is that of deciding beforehand what allophones will be analyzed, and then either forcing the allophones that are found into one of these predefined categories, or discarding unanticipated allophones entirely from the study. This can skew results and hinder the discovery of new phenomena.

Social variables

The two most common social variables in Spanish-language sociophonetics are speaker sex and age, which are used by 91.9 percent and 77.2 percent of studies, respectively (Table 27.4).

While most English-language sociophonetic studies attempt to codify speakers' socioeconomic characteristics with a single variable typically referred to as "socioeconomic status," which is largely congruent with the classic concept of social class, attempts to do the same in research on

Table 27.4 Number and percentage of 123 Spanish sociophonetic publications which analyze each listed social variable

Social variable	Publications	%
Sex	113	91.9
Age	95	77.2
Educational level	44	35.8
Socioeconomic status	35	28.5
Occupational level	16	13.0
Region/country	11	8.9
Sociocultural level	10	8.1
Other	8	6.5
Bilingualism	7	5.7
Rural/urban	6	4.9
Social network	5	4.1
Migration status	4	3.3
Other socioeconomic variables	3	2.4
Ethnicity	3	2.4
Income	3	2.4
Neighborhood	3	2.4
Sexual orientation	2	1.6
Literacy	1	0.8
Possessions	1	0.8

Spanish are highly idiosyncratic and deeply heterogeneous. The most common variable used to classify speakers in terms of social class is educational level (used in 35.8 percent of studies), despite the fact that the correlation between the two is far from certain. The second most commonly used variable, referred to by authors as "socioeconomic status" (28.5 percent), is in reality a cover term for myriad other variables, sometimes taken singly, other times used as part of an ad hoc formula, and still other times used both individually and as part of such a formula. Furthermore, many authors simply assign socioeconomic status values to speakers impressionistically. The third most utilized variable for these purposes, occupational level (13 percent), suffers from similar problems, with each author using their own ad hoc classification of economic activities. A mysterious construct known as "cultural level" or "sociocultural level" (8.1 percent) is also used in some studies, not infrequently without being defined by the authors. A handful of further variables have also been used for quantifying social class, including income (2.4 percent), neighborhood (2.4 percent), possessions (0.8 percent) and several others (2.4 percent).

This profound lack of standardization makes it doubtful that any Spanish-language sociophonetic study of a given phenomenon can be validly compared with any other in terms of socioeconomic status, except perhaps those carried out by the same author(s) using the same socioeconomic variables. This will increasingly become an issue as the discipline matures and questions about Spanish sociophonetic variation around the world and language change over time become more pressing. Sadowsky (2021) developed a standardized method for stratifying speakers of Chilean Spanish, but it is likely not transferrable to speakers of other national varieties. It would therefore be advantageous if similar efforts were undertaken in other countries.

The remaining social variables are utilized only sporadically. These include region or country of origin (used in 8.9 percent of studies); bilingualism (5.7 percent; these typically refer to

Spanish and English, but a few studies refer to Spanish and another language spoken in the Iberian Peninsula); rural or urban origin (4.9 percent); social network, usually in terms of its density (4.1 percent); migration status (3.3 percent); ethnicity (2.4 percent); sexual orientation (1.6 percent); literacy (0.8 percent); and a series of others (6.5 percent).

Statistical analysis

The statistical analysis of results was rare during the first 40 years of Spanish-language sociophonetics, but has become fairly common in the last decade. Most authors who perform a statistical analysis now do so with R (R Core Team 2022) and a series of packages, often Rbrul (Johnson 2009, 2019).

CASE STUDY   Sex, socioeconomic, and stress variation in Chilean Spanish vowels

Socially stratified consonant allophones were first observed in Chilean Spanish by Lenz (1892–1893) and have continued to be explored (e.g., Bobadilla & Bobadilla 1980; Valencia 1993; Figueroa, Soto-Barba & Ñanculeo 2010; Sadowsky 2015). Additional sociolinguistic variation has been found in the Chilean lexicon (Contardo 2008), clitic system (Silva-Corvalán 2001), and *voseo* verb forms (González 2002), among others. The rich and diverse correlations between social variables and consonant allophony suggests that similar patterns are likely to manifest themselves in the vowel system, as well.

The research presented here examines the interaction of two social variables, sex and socioeconomic status, with the vowel allophones produced by Chilean Spanish speakers. It also examines the effects of a phonological variable, lexical stress, on vowel production. Examining stress was deemed necessary because a preliminary analysis of the data showed that, contrary to the commonly held belief that Spanish vowels are stable and not particularly subject to reduction, Chilean Spanish vowels vary based on the stress of the syllable they occur in.

Methods

The speaker sample consists of 61 young adults (16–19 years of age) from the province of Concepción, a conurbation of some 1 million inhabitants located approximately 440 km south of Chile's capital, Santiago. All are native, monolingual Chilean Spanish speakers, and are life-long inhabitants of Concepción, having spent no more than one year of their lives living elsewhere. Speakers' socioeconomic status (SES) was calculated with the EMIS method (Sadowsky 2021), and a fixed-quota sample was established and filled. The final speaker sample contains 30 female and 31 male speakers belonging to one of five SES levels: Extreme Upper (A), Upper (B), Upper-Middle (Ca), Lower-Middle (Cb), and Lower + Extreme Lower (D+E; these two strata were combined due to the difficulty of recruiting participants from the Extreme Lower stratum). All cells but two contain at least five speakers; the remaining two cells contain four.

Speech was elicited by means of a 900-word reading task made up of six narrative texts. While the use of reading activities in vowel research is almost unprecedented in the English-speaking world, it is the most common method used in Spanish linguistics, likely due to the fact that most such studies seek to establish reference values rather than account for variation. This elicitation method was thus chosen, as it allows our results to be compared with those of the bulk of Spanish vowel studies.

Vowel F1 and F2 values were measured in Praat (Boersma & Weenink 2022). The central 30 ms of the stable portion of 6547 monophthong vowel tokens found in polysyllabic words were identified, segmented, and tagged for vowel phoneme, left environment, right environment, and syllable stress (pre-stressed, stressed, post-stressed). Acceptable left and right environments were any combination of /p t̪ k b d̪ g r f s x/, utterance-initial position, and utterance-final position. Devoiced and creaky-voiced vowels, vowels produced while laughing, yawning, or coughing, and vowels with any appreciable background noise were excluded. Tokens of /i/ and /e/ after /x/ were also excluded due to the possible effects of the strong palatalization that /x/ undergoes in this environment in Chilean Spanish (Tapia & Valdivieso 1997; Flores 2016).

During the vowel tagging process, the optimal "maximum formant (Hz)" and "number of formants" settings for each vowel and speaker were determined through trial and error in Praat and stored in an ad hoc metadata segment of the Praat text grid. A custom script was then used to measure the F1 and F2 values of each token and calculate their average value in the measured segments. This script made use of the optimal formant analysis settings mentioned above in order to produce maximally accurate measurements.

For the statistical analysis, vowels were normalized using the Nearey 1 formula as implemented by the vowels package (Kendall & Thomas 2014) for R (R Core Team 2022). A mixed-effects linear regression analysis was then performed for each combination of vowel phoneme and stress (hence-forth, "vowel classes") with the Rbrul package (Johnson 2019) using the Nearey-normalized F1 and F2 values as dependent variables; speaker SES, speaker sex, left phonological context, and right phono-logical context as independent variables; and speaker as a random effect.

Results

Vowel variation by lexical stress

All five vowel phonemes vary significantly by lexical stress in at least one of their formants, and most do so in both, as seen in Table 27.5. This indicates that Chilean Spanish vowels are indeed subject to reduction processes.

Table 27.5 Linear regression model *p*-values for within-sex vowel variation by lexical stress

Vowel	Females		Males	
	p (F1)	*p (F2)*	*p (F1)*	*p (F2)*
i		<0.001		<0.001
e	0.042	0.025	0.003	0.012
a	<0.001	0.039	<0.001	<0.001
o	0.008	<0.001		0.002
u	0.033	<0.001		<0.001

Note. Blank cells were not significant.

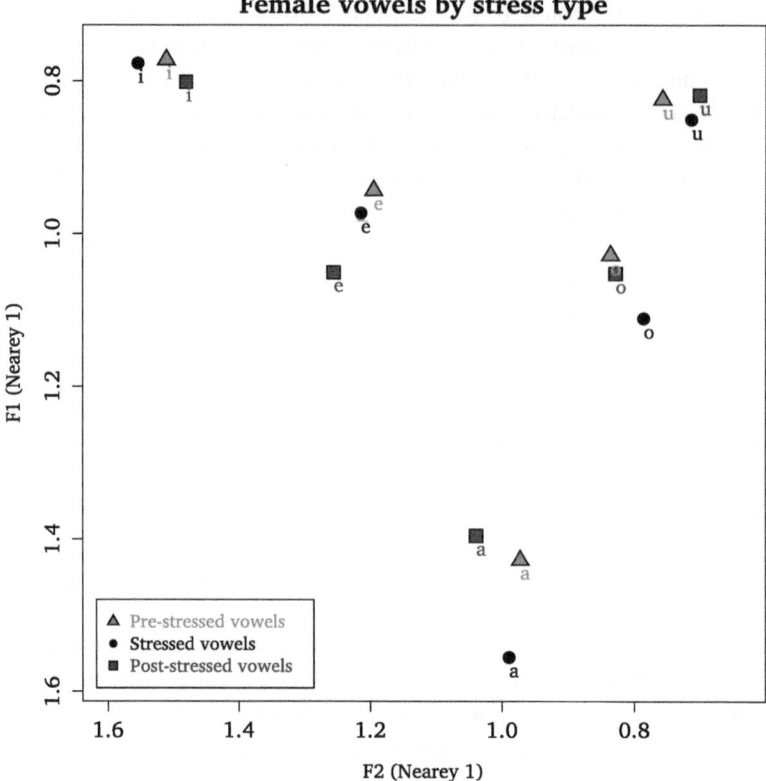

Figure 27.2 Vowels of female speakers by type of stress

The pre-stressed, stressed, and post-stressed vowels produced by female speakers are shown in Figure 27.2. Pre- and post-stressed /i/ are centralized (the slight lowering of post-stressed /i/, which corresponds to changes in F1 values, was not significant). The pre- and post-stressed allophones of /a/ are raised. Additionally, the former is slightly backed while the latter is somewhat fronted. Pre-stressed /e/, pre- and post-stressed /o/, and pre-stressed /u/ show a different pattern: they are both raised and centralized. Post-stressed /u/ is also raised, but is backed rather than centralized. Post-stressed /e/, for its part, is unique: it is lowered and fronted.

Figure 27.3 shows the pre-stressed, stressed, and post-stressed vowel allophones of male speakers. These manifest most of the same patterns found in female speakers (though often to a more moderate degree): centralization of pre- and post-stressed /i/, pre-stressed /e/, pre- and post-stressed /o/, and pre-stressed /u/; lowering and fronting of post-stressed /e/; and raising of pre- and post-stressed /a/. Male vowels differ from female ones in not undergoing statistically significant raising of pre-stressed /e/, pre- and post-stressed /o/, and pre- and post-stressed /u/.

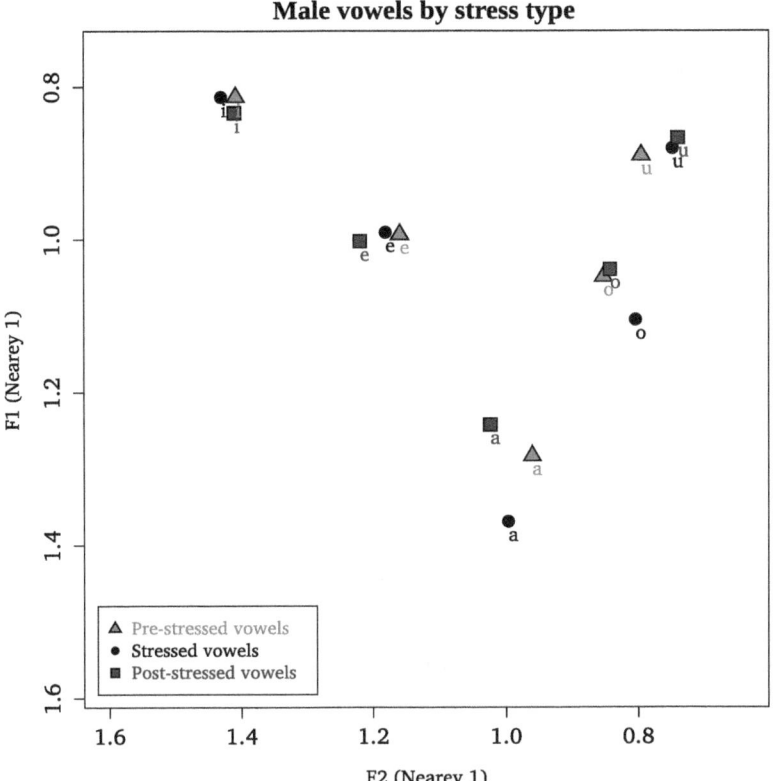

Figure 27.3 Vowels of male speakers by type of stress

Vowel variation by speaker sex

Vowel allophones differ by speaker sex in a statistically significant manner in 12 of 15 vowel classes, as indicated by the linear regression model *p*-values shown in Table 27.6. This variation occurs in F1 alone in four cases, in F2 alone in one case, and in both formants in seven cases.

As shown in Figure 27.4, male speakers' pre-stressed /i/, /e/, /a/, and /u/ are mid-centralized in comparison with the equivalent vowels of female speakers, which are consequently more peripheral. In the case of /i/, /e/, and /u/, both F1 and F2 vary significantly, while F1 alone does so in /a/. Pre-stressed /o/ does not vary significantly by speaker sex.

Male speakers' stressed vowels are likewise more mid-centralized than those of female speakers, as shown in Figure 27.5. Stressed /i/ and /u/ differ significantly in both F1 and F2, while stressed /a/ does so in F1 alone. Stressed /e/ and /o/ do not vary significantly by speaker sex.

Figure 27.6 shows the post-stressed vowel allophones of female and male speakers. The pattern of males having more mid-centralized vowels than females continues here. Post-stressed /i/ and /u/ vary significantly in both F1 and F2, and post-stressed /a/ does so in F1 alone, as is also the case when these vowels are pre-stressed and stressed.

Table 27.6 Linear regression model *p*-values for vowel class variation between the sexes

Vowel	Stress	p (F1)	p (F2)
i	Pre-stressed	<0.001	<0.001
	Stressed	0.008	<0.001
	Post-stressed	0.004	0.002
e	Pre-stressed	<0.001	0.028
	Stressed		
	Post-stressed	<0.001	
a	Pre-stressed	<0.001	
	Stressed	<0.001	
	Post-stressed	<0.001	
o	Pre-stressed		
	Stressed		
	Post-stressed		0.003
u	Pre-stressed	<0.001	<0.001
	Stressed	0.034	0.002
	Post-stressed	0.006	0.002

Note. Blank cells were not significant.

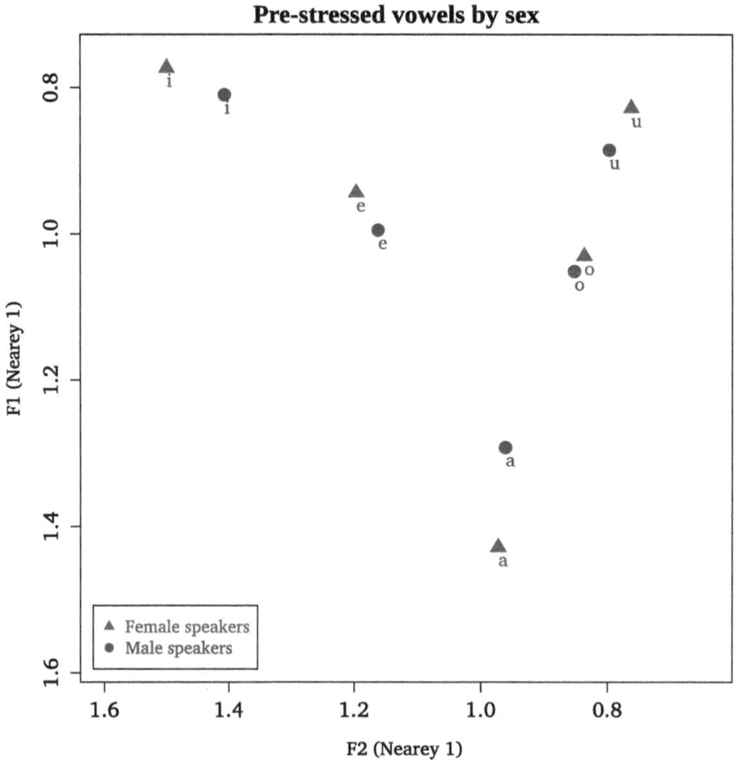

Figure 27.4 Pre-stressed vowels by speaker sex

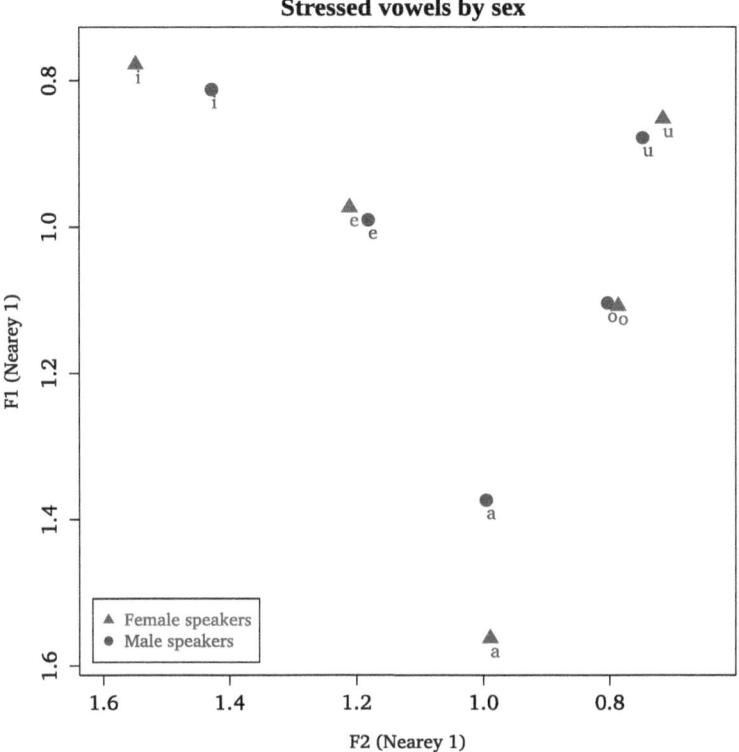

Figure 27.5   Stressed vowels by speaker sex

Post-stressed /e/ varies significantly by speaker sex in F1, and is lower in female speakers, though males' post-stressed /e/ continues to be located within the space used by the female vowel system. Finally, although post-stressed /o/ does vary significantly by speaker sex, the articulatory and acoustic distance between male and female speakers' allophones is negligible.

Vowel variation by speaker SES

Vowel allophones vary significantly by SES in three cases per sex: pre-stressed /i/, stressed /e/, and post-stressed /u/ in female speakers, and post-stressed /i/, pre-stressed /a/, and pre-stressed /u/ in male speakers. In the three female vowels, this variation occurs in F2, while in the male equivalents it occurs in F1. The *p*-values from the linear regression model are provided in Table 27.6.

Figures 27.7 and 27.8 show the values, in Nearey 1 units, of the significant formants of each of the six vowel classes whose allophones vary by SES. An underlying linear distribution is apparent in all cases (for reference, a perfectly linear distribution is marked by the dotted line in these figures). This is accompanied by movement away from the linear distribution by one or two strata in all six vowel classes.

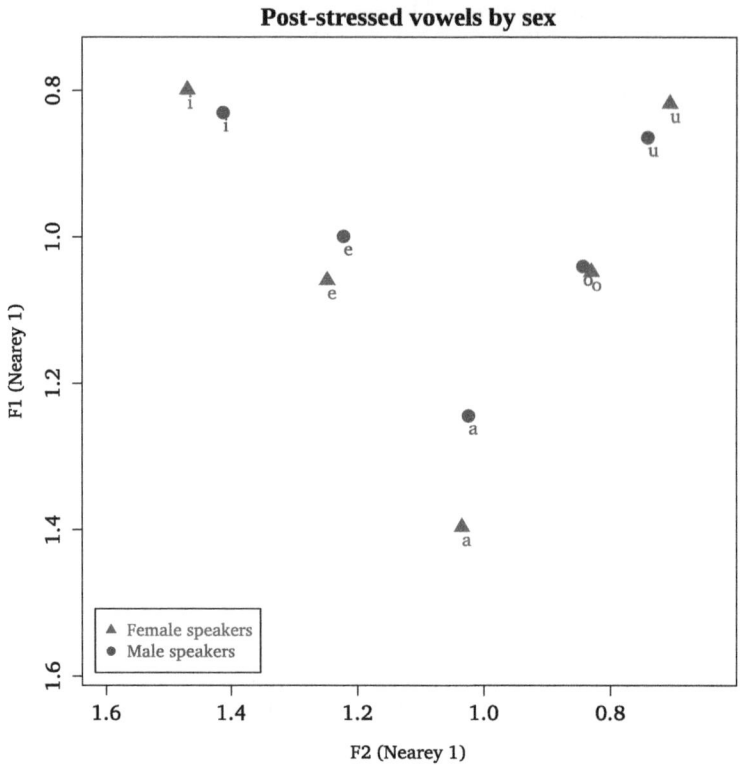

Post-stressed vowels by sex

Figure 27.6 Post-stressed vowels by speaker sex

Table 27.7 Linear regression model *p*-values for vowel class variation by speaker SES

Vowel	Stress	p-value (formant)	
		Females	Males
i	Pre-stressed	0.008 (F2)	
	Stressed		
	Post-stressed		0.018 (F1)
e	Pre-stressed		
	Stressed	0.026 (F2)	
	Post-stressed		
a	Pre-stressed		0.026 (F1)
	Stressed		
	Post-stressed		
o	Pre-stressed		
	Stressed		
	Post-stressed		
u	Pre-stressed		0.006 (F1)
	Stressed		
	Post-stressed	0.021 (F2)	

Note. The significant formant is given in parentheses. Blank cells were not significant.

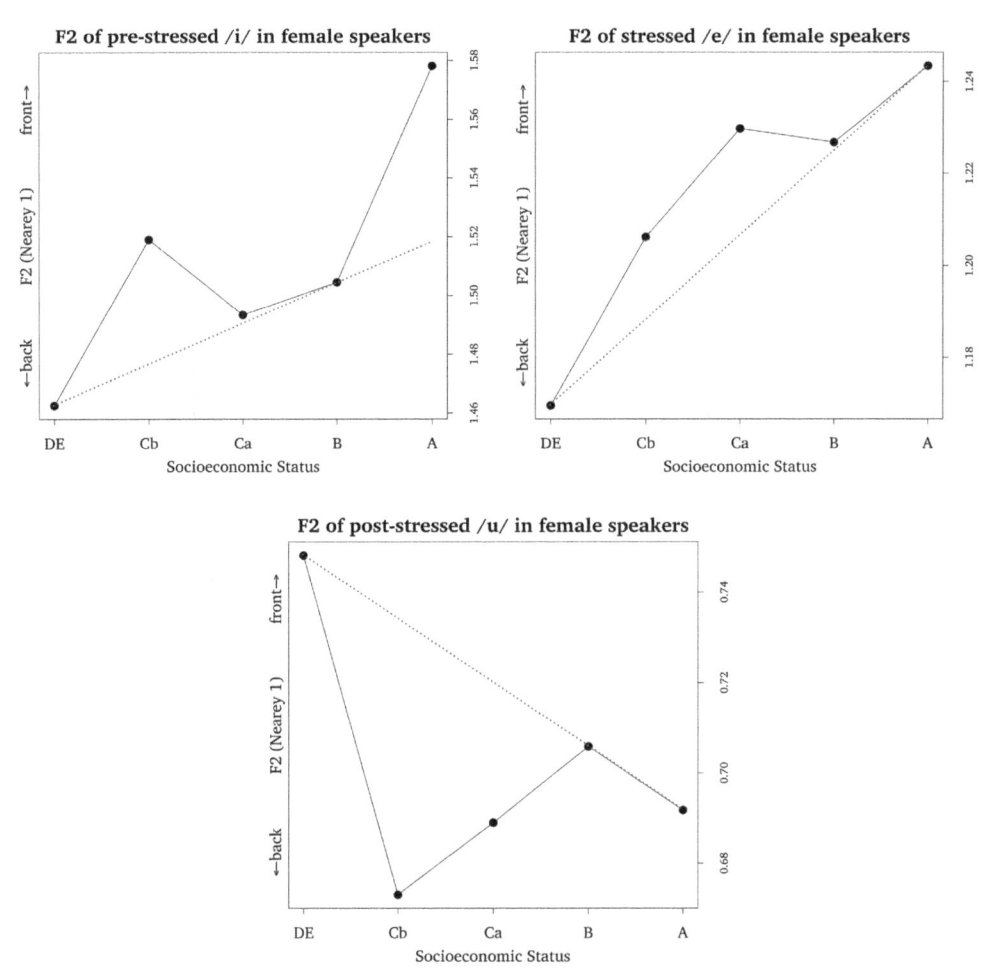

Figure 27.7   F2 of significantly varying vowels in female speakers by SES

In female speakers' pre-stressed /i/ (Figure 27.7a), the linear distribution is evidenced by the DE, Ca, and B strata. The interior Cb stratum's allophone, in contrast, is more fronted than this distribution would predict, as is the exterior A stratum's allophone.

In female speakers' stressed /e/ (Figure 27.7b) and post-stressed /u/ (Figure 27.7c), the linear distribution is manifested by the DE, B, and A strata, while the allophones of the interior Cb and Ca strata are more peripheral than this pattern would predict (stressed /e/ is more fronted; post-stressed /u/ is more backed).

With regard to male speakers, both post-stressed /i/ (Figure 27.8a) and pre-stressed /u/ (Figure 27.8b) allophones are distributed in a linear fashion in all strata except Cb. This stratum departs from the linear pattern with a more close post-stressed /i/ and a more open pre-stressed /u/.

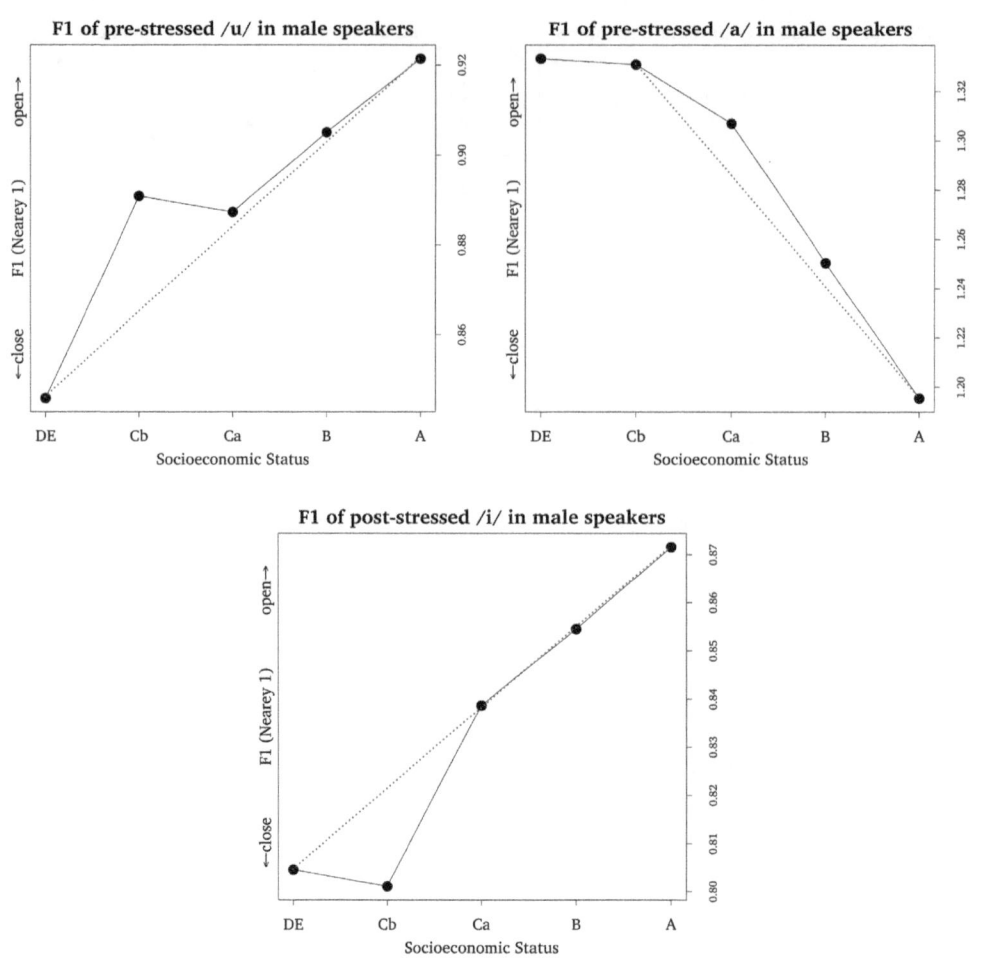

Figure 27.8 F1 of significantly varying vowels in male speakers by SES

Finally, male speakers' pre-stressed /a/ (Figure 27.8c) exhibits an essentially linear distribution between the Cb and A strata. The DE stratum deviates from the linear pattern in having a more close allophone than would be expected.

Discussion

Lexical stress

Unstressed vowels in Chilean Spanish exhibit neither the stability traditionally attributed to Spanish vowel systems nor the typologically common vowel reduction process consisting of movement toward the center of the vowel space. Instead, six of eight noncentral unstressed vowels in speakers of both sexes are centralized (/a/ cannot undergo this process, as it is already located in the approximate center of the vowel space). Likewise, seven of 10 unstressed vowels are raised in female speakers, while two are raised in male speakers. Although the movement of pre- and post-stressed /a/ allophones could be interpreted as either reduction or raising, as the location of this vowel in articulatory space means that both processes produce the same result, the predominance of raising among other Chilean Spanish vowels suggests that raising is the more plausible interpretation.

Notably, these unusual unstressed vowel centralization and raising processes also occur in Mapudungun (Sadowsky et al. 2013), the most commonly spoken indigenous language in Chile. It is thus possible that these phenomena were transferred from Mapudungun to Chilean Spanish.

In more general terms, Chilean Spanish pre-stressed and post-stressed vowels have been shown to behave quite differently from each other. This suggests that researchers of Spanish vowels of any regional variety would do well to be wary of the traditional stressed/unstressed vowel dichotomy, as the latter category may well obfuscate meaningful linguistic behavior and produce meaningless results when analyzed together.

Speaker sex

Chilean Spanish speakers exhibit statistically significant sex-based stratification in a full 80 percent of the 15 vowel classes. This suggests that signaling sex linguistically plays a meaningful role in the creation and communication of their social identities.

Additionally, female speakers' vowel allophones are without exception more peripheral than those of male speakers. The acoustic consequence of this is that their vowels use a greater proportion of the available acoustic space, and are therefore more distinct from each other, than the equivalent male vowels. This can be expected to make female vowels easier for their interlocutors to identify, which is in line with key sociolinguistic findings that indicate that women tend to adhere more closely than men do to community speech norms and expectations of "speaking well" (Labov 2001).

Socioeconomic status

The Chilean Spanish vowel system appears to reflect two different moments in this geolect's development. The underlying SES-based linear distribution of the allophones of all six significantly varying vowel classes is in line with the country's traditionally rigid, class-based social structure (see Sadowsky & Aninao 2019 for more details). Such a distribution could only have arisen after the traditional social classes developed in Chile toward the end of the nineteenth century.

The departures from the linear distribution (Table 27.8) appear to reflect a much more recent process of innovation, likely triggered by the erosion or destruction of many class-based institutions during the Pinochet dictatorship (1973–1990), and strengthened by the decreased socioeconomic segregation and increased social mobility that subsequent democratic governments achieved (see Sadowsky 2015 for a more in-depth account).

Female speakers from the interior Cb stratum participate in all three of the innovative processes that occur among women, while the adjacent Ca stratum participates in two. These speakers' vowels would seem to have moved from their expected position in the linear distribution to one that is closer to the vowels of higher-SES speakers, suggesting that this is a linguistic change motivated at some level by the quest for greater status or prestige.

Table 27.8 Participation in vowel allophone departures from the linear distribution, by sex and SES

Sex	Vowel class	Socioeconomic status					Total per sex
		A	*B*	*Ca*	*Cb*	*DE*	
Female	Pre-stressed /i/	●			●		
	Stressed /e/			●	●		
	Post-stressed /u/			●	●		
	Subtotal	*1*	*0*	*2*	*3*	*0*	*6*
Male	Post-stressed /i/				■		
	Pre-stressed /u/				●		
	Pre-stressed /a/					●	
	Subtotal	*0*	*0*	*0*	*2*	*1*	*3*
	Total per SES	**1**	**0**	**2**	**5**	**1**	**9**

Note. A circle represents movement toward higher-SES allophones; a square represents movement toward lower-prestige allophones.

In the single case in which a vowel allophone of female speakers from an exterior stratum departs from the linear distribution (pre-stressed /i/ of the A stratum), it is located where the allophone of a hypothetical SES higher than A would be positioned. This movement has the effect of increasing the articulatory and perceptual distance between this allophone and that of the next lower stratum, B, which is likely the motivation for this change. While relatively rare, this same pattern of stratum A changing its linguistic behavior to increase its distance from stratum B has also been observed in the prevalence of verbs conjugated in the *voseo* paradigm in female speakers from the cities of Arica, Concepción, and Santiago (Sadowsky 2021).

With regard to male speakers, the interior Cb stratum is the only one participating in two of the three innovative processes that occur among men. One of the affected vowel classes, pre-stressed /u/, involves movement toward a higher SES's allophone. The other, post-stressed /i/, moves in the opposite direction, toward the allophone of the lower-status DE stratum, likely motivated by covert prestige (Trudgill 1972). The third vowel which departs from the linear distribution, pre-stressed /a/, exhibits a fairly uncommon phenomenon: movement in the direction of a higher-prestige group by males of the lowest SES, the DE stratum.

The innovative departure from the linear SES distribution that is occurring in Chilean Spanish vowels appears to be a change from below, as speakers seem to be almost entirely unconscious of vowel allophony of any sort. Although we are aware of one exception to this lack of awareness, it occurs with a single vowel in a single word, and only with extreme upper-SES male speakers, who do not appear to be participating in the sound change described here (the vowel in question is the /i/ in ⟨sí⟩, which is sometimes written as ⟨sé⟩ by those imitating or mocking this group, indicating that at least some speakers are conscious of one aspect of the strong mid-centralization of this SES's vowel system). We have seen nothing to indicate that speakers are conscious of any other vowel-related phenomena.

This process of change is being led by women, who—when broken down by SES—are seen to participate in it at twice the rate as men (six cases vs. three). This is very much in line with the majority of other sociophonetic studies performed around the world, which show that female speakers tend to lead changes from below (Labov 2001:280, 283).

In terms of SES, the lower interior Cb stratum leads in the adoption of this innovation with five cases, followed by the upper interior Ca stratum with two cases. These are the socioeconomic strata which tend to lead in change from below processes, as per Labov's Curvilinear Principle (Labov 2001: 188). At the same time, the exterior A and DE strata show deviation from the underlying linear pattern in one case each. The participation in this sound change of male speakers from the lowest stratum, DE, suggests that this innovation is expanding beyond its initial socioeconomic origins, but requires further study.

The motivation for the departure from the linear pattern appears to be the obtention of greater overt prestige in four of the six cases. In the fifth, male speakers' post-stressed /i/, increasing covert prestige would seem to be the reason for the change. In the final case, the pre-stressed /i/ of female speakers, although the vowel movement is in the direction of increased overt prestige, as is the general tendency of this change, the motivation here is likely subtly different. Rather than increasing its prestige, which is already maximal withing the socioeconomic hierarchy, the A stratum seems to be attempting to make its speech more distinct from that of its only potential social competitor, the B stratum.

In closing, this study strongly suggests that the vowels of the different national varieties of Spanish, which are currently understudied in sociophonetic terms, are a potentially fruitful topic for future investigation.

The future of Spanish-language sociophonetics

Spanish-language sociophonetics is a burgeoning field with an exciting future. The fourfold increase in the number of studies published between the 2000s and 2010s indicates that the field is experiencing explosive growth, and the increasingly sophisticated technical and statistical methods being employed promise even more reliable results in the future. The trend of ever-decreasing speaker sample sizes warrants some concern, however, as does the chaotic situation of socioeconomic stratification techniques. It is to be hoped that the class and sex biases that have existed since the beginning of discipline will be definitively overcome in the near future. The abandonment of the vestiges of the Spanish dialectological approach seems all but assured, as does the continued predominance of the first-wave sociolinguistic focus.

References

Alba, Orlando. 1988. Estudio sociolingüístico de la variación de las líquidas finales de palabra en el español cibaeño. In Robert M. Hammond & Melvyn C. Resnick (eds.), *Studies in Caribbean Spanish Dialectology*, 1–12. Georgetown University Press.

Alba, Orlando. 1990. *Variación fonética y diversidad social en el español dominicano de Santiago*. PUCMM.

Alfaraz, Gabriela. 2000. *Sound change in a regional variety of Cuban Spanish*. PhD dissertation, Michigan State University.

Alfaraz, Gabriela. 2007. Effects of age and gender on liquid assimilation in Cuban Spanish. In Jonathan Holmquist, Augusto Lorenzino & Lotfi Sayahi (eds.), *Selected proceedings of the Third Workshop on Spanish Sociolinguistics*, 23–29. Cascadilla Proceedings Project.

Alonso, Amado. 1930. Problemas de dialectología hispanoamericana. In A.M. Espinoza (ed.), *Estudios sobre el español de Nuevo Méjico I: Fonética*. Imprenta de la Universidad de Buenos Aires.

Alvord, Scott M., Nelsy Echávez-Solano & Carol Klee. 2005. La (r) asibilada en el español andino: un estudio socio lingüístico. *Lexis* 29(1). 27–45. https://doi.org/10.18800/lexis.200501.002

Barajas, Jennifer. 2014. *A sociophonetic investigation of unstressed vowel raising in the Spanish of a rural Mexican community*. PhD dissertation, The Ohio State University.

Barnes, Sonia. 2016. Variable final back vowels in urban Asturian Spanish. *Spanish in Context* 13(1). 1–28. https://doi.org/10.1075/sic.13.1.01bar

Beaton, Mary Elizabeth. 2015. *Coda liquid production and perception in Puerto Rican Spanish*. PhD dissertation, The Ohio State University.

Beaton, Mary Elizabeth. 2016. Revisiting incomplete neutralization: The case of Puerto Rican Spanish. *University of Pennsylvania Working Papers in Linguistics* 22(1). 31–40. https://repository.upenn.edu/pwpl/vol22/iss1/5

Bernate, Emily. 2016. La aspiración de la /s/ en las hablas femenina y masculina de los limeños en los Estados Unidos. *Íkala, Revista de Lenguaje y Cultura* 21(3). 267–279. https://doi.org/10.17533/udea.ikala.v21n03a02

Bobadilla, Félix & Gustavo Bobadilla. 1979. El comportamiento de las variables lingüísticas /tɾ/, /r/ y /t͡ʃ/ en el área urbana de Rancagua. *Cuadernos de Lenguas Modernas* 2. 18–24.

Bobadilla, Félix & Gustavo Bobadilla. 1980. El estudio de tres variables sociolingüísticas en Rancagua: problemas preliminares. *Boletín de Filología* 31(2). 721–741.

Boersma, Paul & David Weenink. 2022. *Praat: Doing phonetics by computer* [Computer program]. www.praat.org/

Bolyanatz, Mariška. 2017. *Plural production and perception in Santiago Spanish*. PhD dissertation, University of California.

Bolyanatz, Mariška & Brandon M.A. Rogers. 2019. The social perception of intervocalic /k/ voicing in Chilean Spanish. In Chappell, 211–234.

Bongiovanni, Silvina. 2013. "¿Tomas [pepsi], [peksi] or [pesi]?": A variationist sociolinguistic analysis of Spanish syllable coda stops. *IULC Working Papers* 13(1). 43–61.

Bongiovanni, Silvina. 2019. An acoustical analysis of the merger of /ɲ/ and /nj/ in Buenos Aires Spanish. *Journal of the International Phonetic Association* 51(2). 1–25. https://doi.org/10.1017/S0025100318000440

Broce, Marlene & Rena Torres Cacoullos. 2002. "Dialectología urbana" rural: La estratificación social de (r) y (l) en Coclé, Panamá. *Hispania* 85(2). 342–353. https://doi.org/10.2307/4141096

Brogan, Franny. 2018. *Sociophonetically-based phonology: An Optimality Theoretic account of /s/ lenition in Salvadoran Spanish*. PhD dissertation, University of California.

Brogan, Franny D. & Mariška Bolyanatz. 2018. A sociophonetic account of onset /s/ weakening in Salvadoran Spanish: Instrumental and segmental analyses. *Language Variation and Change* 30(2). 203–230. https://doi.org/10.1017/S0954394518000066

Calero, María Ángeles. 1990. Distribución y estratificación de /s/ implosiva y /j/ intervocálica en el habla de la ciudad de Toledo. *Sintagma* 2. 29–44.

Calvo Shadid, Annette. 1997. El fonema fricativo /s/ en el habla culta de San José: Implicaciones teóricas en el sistema fonológico de las coronales. *Revista de Filología y Lingüística de la Universidad de Costa Rica* 23(1). 235–246. https://doi.org/10.15517/rfl.v23i1.20399

Canfield, D. Lincoln. 1962. *La pronunciación del español en América*. Instituto Caro y Cuervo.

Carrasquero, Viktor. 2010. Un caso de variación sociofonética: /-s/ posnuclear en el español actual de Caracas. *Letras* 52(81). 87–116.

Cedergren, Henrietta. 1973. *The interplay of social and linguistic factors in Panama*. PhD dissertation, Cornell University.

Cedergren, Henrietta & David Sankoff. 1974. Variable rules: Performance as a statistical reflection of competence. *Language* 50(2). 333–355. https://doi.org/10.2307/412441

Cepeda, Gladys. 1990a. La alofonía de /s/ en Valdivia (Chile). *Estudios filológicos* 25. 5–16.

Cepeda, Gladys. 1990b. La variación de /s/ en Valdivia: sexo y edad. *Hispania* 73(1). 232–237. https://doi.org/10.2307/343011

Chang, Charles. 2008. Variation in palatal production in Buenos Aires Spanish. In Westmoreland & Thomas, 54–63.

Chappell, Whitney. 2013. *Social and linguistic factors conditioning the glottal stop in Nicaraguan Spanish*. PhD dissertation, The Ohio State University.

Chappell, Whitney. 2016. On the social perception of intervocalic /s/ voicing in Costa Rican Spanish. *Language Variation and Change* 28(3). 357–378. https://doi.org/10.1017/S0954394516000107

Chappell, Whitney (ed.). 2019. *Recent advances in the study of Spanish sociophonetic perception*. John Benjamins.

Colantoni, Laura & Jeffrey Steele (eds.). 2008. *Selected proceedings of the 3rd Conference on Laboratory Approaches to Spanish Phonology*. Cascadilla Proceedings Project.

Colina, Andreina. 2018. *La elisión de la /-s/ en el español del Caribe y los Estados Unidos*. MA thesis, Louisiana State University.

Contardo, Óscar. 2008. *Siútico*. Vergara.

Correa, Leonardo. 2017. *Variación y cambio en el español de Bogotá: Análisis de dos variables sociofonéticas*. PhD dissertation, University at Albany, State University of New York.

Cruz Ortiz, Rocío. 2019. Mantenimiento y elisión de la /d/ intervocálica en los políticos andaluces en Madrid. *Tonos Digital* 37. 1–26.

Dabkowski, Meghan. 2018. *Variable vowel reduction in Mexico City Spanish*. PhD dissertation, The Ohio State University.

Darías, José Luis, María del Carmen Ruisánchez & Puica Dohotaru. 1997. El proceso de la velarización del fonema nasal distensivo en el español de Pinar del Río — Enfoque sociolingüístico. *Romanistisches Jahrbuch* 48(1). 287–295. https://doi.org/10.1515/roja-1997-0143

Díaz-Campos, Manuel. 2008. Variable production of the trill in spontaneous speech: Sociolinguistic implications. In Colantoni & Steele, 47–58.

Díaz-Campos, Manuel, Stephen Fafulas & Michael Gradoville. 2011. Going retro. An analysis of the interplay between socioeconomic class and age in Caracas Spanish. In Jim Michnowicz & Robin Dodsworth (eds.), *Selected proceedings of the 5th Workshop on Spanish Sociolinguistics*, 65–78. Cascadilla Proceedings Project.

Diez Canseco, Susana. 1997. *Language variation: The influence of speakers' attitudes and gender on sociolinguistic variables in the Spanish of Cusco, Peru*. PhD dissertation, University of Pittsburgh.

Dorta, Josefa. 1989. La variación fonética de /r/ y /l/ en La Perdoma, norte de Tenerife. *Anuario de Letras. Lingüística y Filología* 27. 81–125.

Emmanuelli, Mirna. 2000. Valoración social y actuación lingüística hacia algunas variantes fonológicas del español puertorriqueño. *Revista de Estudios Hispánicos* 27(1). 209–218.

Enbe, Claudia & Yishai Tobin. 2008. Sociolinguistic variation in the prosody of Buenos Aires Spanish according to the theory of phonology as human behavior. In Colantoni & Steele, 140–154.

Erker, Daniel. 2012. *An acoustically based sociolinguistic analysis of variable coda /s/ production in the Spanish of New York City*. PhD dissertation, New York University.

Fernández de Molina Ortés, Elena. 2016. El nivel social como indicador de la variación de -/s/ en el habla de Mérida (Badajoz). *Dialectología* 16. 93–116.

Figueroa, Mauricio A. 2011. *El eje oclusión–fricción en el sistema sociofónico del castellano chileno*. MA thesis, Universidad de Concepción.

Figueroa, Mauricio, Jaime Soto-Barba & Marco Ñanculeo. 2010. Los alófonos del grupo consonántico /tr/ en el castellano de Chile. *Onomázein* 22(2). 11–42.

Flores, Tanya. 2016. Velar palatalization in Chilean public speech. *Glossa* 1(1). 1–17. https://doi.org/10.5334/gjgl.105

Fontanella de Weinberg, María Beatriz. 1973. Comportamiento ante -s de hablantes femeninos y masculinos del español bonaerense. *Romance Philology* 27(1). 50–58.

Fontanella de Weinberg, María Beatriz. 1979. *Dinámica social de un cambio lingüístico*. Universidad Nacional Autónoma de México.

García, Christina. 2019. Regional identity in Highland Ecuador social evaluation of intervocalic /s/ voicing. In Chappell, 125–152.

García, Christina Marie. 2015. *Gradience and variability of intervocalic /s/ voicing in Highland Ecuadorian Spanish*. PhD dissertation, The Ohio State University.

García de Diego, Vicente. 1946. *Manual de dialectología española*. Ediciones Cultura Hispánica.

García Ponce, Edgar & Irasema Mora. 2018. Análisis sociolingüístico de la elisión de /d/ en español de Toluca. *Cuadernos de Lingüística de El Colegio de México* 5(2). 45–78. https://doi.org/10.24201/clecm.v5i2.114

Gómez Molina, José Ramón & María Begoña Gómez Devís. 2010. Mantenimiento y elisión de la /d/ intervocálica en el español de Valencia. *Verba: Anuario Galego de Filoloxia* 37. 89–122.

González, Carlos. 2002. La variación "eríh" / "soi" en el voseo verbal de Santiago de Chile. Un estudio exploratorio. *Onomázein* 7. 213–230.

Harris, James. 1969. *Spanish phonology*. MIT Press.

Henriksen, Nicholas. 2014. Sociophonetic analysis of phonemic trill variation in two sub-varieties of Peninsular Spanish. *Journal of Linguistic Geography* 2(1). 4–24. https://doi.org/10.1017/jlg.2014.1

Henriksen, Nicholas & Sarah Harper. 2016. Investigating lenition patterns in south-central Peninsular Spanish / sp st sk / clusters. *Journal of the International Phonetic Association* 46(3). 287–310. https://doi.org/10.1017/S0025100316000116

Henríquez Ureña, Pedro. 1921. Observaciones sobre el español de América. *Revista de Filología Española* VIII. 357–390.

Henríquez Ureña, Pedro. 1930. Observaciones sobre el español de América II. *Revista de Filología Española* XVII. 277–284.

Henríquez Ureña, Pedro. 1931. Observaciones sobre el español de América III. *Revista de Filología Española* XVIII. 120–148.

Hernández, Edith. 2009. *Resolución de hiatos en verbos–ear: un estudio sociofonético en una ciudad mexicana.* PhD dissertation, The Ohio State University.

Holmquist, Jonathan. 1985. Social correlates of a linguistic variable: A study in a Spanish village. *Language in Society* 14(2). 191–203. https://doi.org/10.1017/S004740450001112X

Holmquist, Jonathan. 2005. Social stratification in women's speech in rural Puerto Rico: A study of five phonological features. In Lotfi Sayahi & Maurice Westmoreland (eds.), *Selected proceedings of the Second Workshop on Spanish Sociolinguistics*, 109–119. Cascadilla Proceedings Project.

Holmquist, Jonathan. 2008. Gender in context: Features and factors in men's and women's speech in rural Puerto Rico. In Westmoreland & Thomas, 17–35.

Holmquist, Jonathan. 2011. Gender and variation: Word-final /s/ in men's and women's speech in Puerto Rico's western highlands. In Manuel Díaz-Campos (ed.), *The handbook of Hispanic sociolinguistics*, 230–243. Blackwell.

Hymes, Dell. 1971. On communicative competence. In J.P. Pride & J. Holmes (eds.), *Sociolinguistics*, 269–293. Penguin.

International Phonetic Association. 2015. The International Phonetic Alphabet and the IPA Chart. www.internationalphoneticassociation.org/content/ipa-chart

Jiménez-Fernández, Rafael. 2020. Variación fonológica de la /d/ intervocálica en el sociolecto alto de Sevilla. *RILCE. Revista de Filología Hispánica* 36(2). 674–707. https://doi.org/10.15581/008.36.2.674-707

Johnson, Daniel Ezra. 2009. Getting off the GoldVarb standard: Introducing Rbrul for mixed-effects variable rule analysis. *Language and Linguistics Compass* 3(1). 359–383. https://doi.org/10.1111/j.1749-818X.2008.00108.x

Johnson, Daniel Ezra. 2019. Rbrul [R package]. www.danielezrajohnson.com/rbrul.html

Kapović, Marko. 2017. Variable within variable–Simultaneous stability and change. The case of syllable-final s in Ciudad Real. *Borealis* 6(2). 249–283. https://doi.org/10.7557/1.6.2.4223

Kendall, Tyler & Erik R. Thomas. 2014. *vowels: Vowel manipulation, normalization and plotting in R* [R package]. https://cran.r-project.org/web/packages/vowels/index.html

Klee, Carol, Brandon M.A. Rogers, Rocío Caravedo & Lindsey Dietz. 2018. Measuring /s/ variation among younger generations in a migrant settlement in Lima, Peru. *Studies in Hispanic and Lusophone Linguistics* 11(1). 29–57. https://doi.org/10.1515/shll-2018-0002

Labov, William. 1963. The social motivation of a sound change. *Word* 19. 273–309. https://doi.org/10.1080/00437956.1963.11659799

Labov, William. 1966a. *The social stratification of English in New York City.* Center for Applied Linguistics.

Labov, William. 1966b. The linguistic variable as a structural unit. *Washington Linguistics Review* 3. 4–22.

Labov, William. 1969. Contraction, deletion and inherent variability of the English copula. *Language* 45. 715–762. https://doi.org/10.2307/412333

Labov, William. 1972. *Sociolinguistic patterns.* University of Pennsylvania Press.

Labov, William. 2001. *Principles of linguistic change*, vol. 2, *Social factors.* Blackwell.

Labov, William, Malcah Yaeger & Richard Steiner. 1972. *A quantitative study of sound change in progress.* US Regional Survey.

Lapesa, Rafael. 1964. El andaluz y el español de América. In *Presente y futuro de la lengua española II*, 173–182. Ediciones Cultura Hispánica.

Lastra, Yolanda & Pedro Martín Butragueño. 2006. Un posible cambio en curso: el caso de las vibrantes en la Ciudad de México. In Ana María Cestero, Isabel Molina & Florentino Paredes (eds.), *Estudios sociolingüísticos del español de España y América*, 35–68. Arco/Libros.

Lenz, Rudolf. 1892. Chilenische Studien I. *Phonetische Studien* 5. 272–292.

Lenz, Rudolf. 1893a. Chilenische Studien II, III. *Phonetische Studien* 6. 18–34.

Lenz, Rudolf. 1893b. Chilenische Studien IV, V. *Phonetische Studien* 6. 151–166.

Lenz, Rudolf. 1893c. Chilenische Studien VI, VII. *Phonetische Studien* 6. 274–301.

Lenz, Rudolf. 1893d. Beiträge zur Kenntnis des Amerikanospanisch. *Zeitschrift für romanische Philologie* 17. 188–214.

Lenz, Rodolfo [Rudolf]. 1940. Estudios Chilenos I–VII. In Amado Alonso & Raimundo Lida (eds.), *El español en Chile. Trabajos de Rodolfo Lenz, Andrés Bello y Rodolfo Oroz*, 84–208. Instituto de Filología de la Universidad de Buenos Aires.

Long, Avizia Yim & Lisa Baldwin. 2013. A sociolinguistic analysis of intervocalic /b/ in Caracas speech. *IULC Working Papers* 13(1). 1–20.

Lope Blanch, Juan M. 1968. El proyecto de estudio coordinado de la norma lingüística culta de las principales ciudades de Iberoamérica y de la Península Ibérica. In *El Simposio de México*, 222–233. Universidad Nacional Autónoma de México.

Lope Blanch, Juan M. 1992. Diferenciación dialectal y polimorfismo lingüístico. *Boletín de Filología* 33. 71–77.

López Morales, Humberto. 1983. *Estratificación social del español de San Juan de Puerto Rico*. Universidad Nacional Autónoma de México.

Malaver, Irania & Lorena Perdomo-Pinto. 2016. La elisión de /d/ en posición intervocálica en la comunidad caraqueña. *Boletín de Filología* 51(2). 147–179. https://doi.org/10.4067/S0718-93032016000200006

Martín Morales, Miriam. 2018. Factores lingüísticos y sociales en el proceso de debilitamiento de /-n/ final de palabra y el uso de formas vulgares en la ciudad de Málaga. *ELUA. Estudios de Lingüística Universidad de Alicante* 32. 237–262. https://doi.org/10.14198/ELUA2018.32.11

Mazzaro, Natalia & Raquel González de Anda. 2019. The perception-production connection /tʃ/ deaffrication and rhotic assibilation in Chihuahua Spanish. In Chappell, 287–340.

Melero, Fernando. 2015. Análisis acústico de la vibrante múltiple en el español de Valencia (España). *Studies in Hispanic and Lusophone Linguistics* 8(1). 183–206. https://doi.org/10.1515/shll-2015-0007

Melguizo, Elisabeth. 2007. La fricatización de /ĉ/ en una comunidad de hablantes granadina. *Interlingüística* 17 . 748–757.

Méndez, Luis Alberto. 2017. The variant [ʃ] in the Spanish of Ciudad Juárez. *Borealis* 6(1). 243–260. https://doi.org/10.7557/1.6.1.4102

Michnowicz, Jim & Lindsey Carpenter. 2013. Voiceless stop aspiration in Yucatan Spanish: A sociolinguistic analysis. *Spanish in Context* 10(3). 410–437. https://doi.org/10.1075/sic.10.3.05mic

Milroy, Lesley. 1980. *Language and social networks*. University Park Press.

Milroy, Lesley. 1981. The effect of two interacting extralinguistic variables on patterns of variation in urban vernacular speech. In David Sankoff & Henrietta Cedergren (eds.), *Variation omnibus*, 161–170. Linguistic Research.

Mohamed, Sherez & Antje Muntendam. 2020. The Use of the glottal stop as a variant of /s/ in Puerto Rican Spanish. *Studies in Hispanic and Lusophone Linguistics* 13(2). 391–417. https://doi.org/10.1515/shll-2020-2035

Molina Boscán, Nancy. 2010. Las consonantes líquidas posnucleares en el habla cotidiana de la ciudad de Maracay. *Revista Ciencias de la Educación* 36. 15–33.

Montes, José Joaquín. 1970. *Dialectología y geografía lingüística. Notas de orientación*. Instituto Caro y Cuervo.

Moreno Fernández, Francisco. 1993. *La división dialectal del español de América*. Universidad de Alcalá de Henares.

Mumin, Zahir. 2017. *A study of sociolinguistic variation in a small community: Puerto Rican Spanish in Amsterdam, New York*. PhD dissertation, State University of New York at Albany.

Navarro Tomás, Tomás. 1945. *Cuestionario lingüístico hispanoamericano*, 2nd edn. Instituto de Filología de la Universidad de Buenos Aires.

Oliver, Julia. 2008. *Vowel raising in Puerto Rican Spanish*. PhD dissertation, University of Illinois at Chicago.

Osle Ezquerra, Angel. 2015. The impact of sexual orientation on the pronunciation of stressed vowels in Peninsular Spanish: An acoustic analysis. *Sociolinguistic Studies* 9(1). 137–150. https://doi.org/10.1558/sols.v9i1.18395

Perdomo-Pinto, Lorena & Scott Sadowsky. 2019. The ultra-high-frequency whistled /s/ of Southern Chilean Spanish: Socioeconomic and gender stratification of its spectral moments and prevalence. In Sasha Calhoun, Paola Escudero, Marija Tabain & Paul Warren (eds.), *Proceedings of the 19th International*

Congress of Phonetic Sciences, Melbourne, Australia 2019, 48–52. Australasian Speech Science and Technology Association.

Pérez Martín, Ana María. 1995. *Estudio sociolingüístico de la /s/ implosiva en el español de El Hierro*. BA thesis, Universidad de Las Palmas de Gran Canaria.

Perissinotto, Giorgio. 1971. *The phonology of the Spanish spoken in Mexico City*. F.H. Jungemann.

Perissinotto, Giorgio. 1972. Distribución demográfica de la asibilación de vibrantes en el habla de la Ciudad de México. *Nueva Revista de Filología Hispánica* 21(1). 71–79. https://doi.org/10.24201/nrfh.v21i1.2860

Perissinotto, Giorgio. 1975. *Fonología del español hablado en la Ciudad de México. Ensayo de un método sociolingüístico*. El Colegio de México.

Prosper-Sánchez, Gloria. 1995. *Neutralización homofonética de líquidas a final de sílaba: Aspectos sociolingüísticos en el Español de Puerto Rico*. PhD dissertation, University of Massachusetts Amherst.

R Core Team. 2022. *R: A language and environment for statistical computing*. R Foundation for Statistical Computing. www.R-project.org

Rabanales, Ambrosio. 1992. Fundamentos teóricos y pragmáticos del "Proyecto de estudio coordinado de la norma lingüística culta del español hablado en las principales ciudades del mundo hispánico." *Boletín de Filología* 33. 251–272.

Ramírez, Alexánder & Alina Almira. 2016. Variación del fonema /s/ en contextos de juntura de palabra en el español caleño: una mirada sociolingüística. *Lenguaje* 44(1). 11–33. https://doi.org/10.25100/lenguaje.v44i1.4628

Regan, Brendan. 2019. Dialectology meets sociophonetics. The social evaluation of ceceo and distinción in Lepe, Spain. In Chappell, 85–121.

Resnick, Melvyn. 1969. Dialect zones and automatic dialect identification in Latin American Spanish. *Hispania* 52. 553–568.

Resnick, Melvyn. 1976. Algunos aspectos histórico-geográficos de la dialectología hispanoamericana. *Orbis* XXV. 264–276.

Rissel, Dorothy A. 1989. Sex, attitudes, and the assibilation of /r/ among young people in San Luis Potosí, Mexico. *Language Variation and Change* 1(3). 269–283. https://doi.org/10.1017/S0954394500000181

Robles-Puente, Sergio & José Jesús Vilches-Aguado. 2019. Bilabial fricatives in Mexican Spanish: A sociophonetic analysis. *Borealis* 8(1). 143–161. https://doi.org/10.7557/1.8.1.4561

Rogers, Brandon M.A. 2016. The influence of linguistic and social variables in the spirantization of intervocalic /b,d,g/ in Concepción, Chile. *Studies in Hispanic and Lusophone Linguistics* 9(1). 207–237. https://doi.org/10.1515/shll-2016-0008

Rogers, Brandon M.A. 2020. The state of Spanish /s/ variation in Concepción, Chile: Linguistic and social trends. *Open Linguistics* 6(1). 132–153. https://doi.org/10.1515/opli-2020-0010

Rogers, Brandon M.A. & Christina Mirisis. 2018. Voiceless stop lenition and reduction as linguistic and social phenomena in Concepción, Chile. *Borealis* 7(2). 187–215. https://doi.org/10.7557/1.7.2.4401

Rohena-Madrazo, Marcos. 2011. *Sociophonetic variation in the production and perception of obstruent voicing in Buenos Aires Spanish*. PhD dissertation, New York University.

Rohena-Madrazo, Marcos. 2015. Diagnosing the completion of a sound change: Phonetic and phonological evidence for /ʃ/ in Buenos Aires Spanish. *Language Variation and Change* 27(3). 287–317. https://doi.org/10.1017/S0954394515000113

Rona, José Pedro. 1958. *Aspectos metodológicos de la dialectología hispanoamericana*. Universidad de la República.

Rona, José Pedro. 1964. El problema de la división del español americano en zonas dialectales. In *Presente y futuro de la lengua española, vol. 1*, 215–226. Ofines.

Ruiz Sánchez, Carmen. 2004. El comportamiento de la /s/ implosiva en el habla de Caracas. *Boletín de Lingüística* 21. 48–65.

Ruiz Sánchez, Carmen. 2017. Seseo, ceceo, and distinción in Andalusian Spanish: Free variation or sociolinguistic variation? *Linguistics Vanguard* 3(1). https://doi.org/10.1515/lingvan-2016-0075

Sadowsky, Scott. 2015. Variación sociofonética de las consonantes del castellano chileno [Sociophonetic variation in Chilean Spanish consonants]. *Sociolinguistic Studies* 9(1). 71–92. https://doi.org/10.1558/sols.v9i1.19927

Sadowsky, Scott. 2021. EMIS: Sistema de estratificación socioeconómica para la investigación lingüística. In Brandon M.A. Rogers & Mauricio Figueroa (eds.), *Lingüística del castellano chileno: Estudios sobre variación, innovación, contacto e identidad*, 367–396. Vernon Press.

Sadowsky, Scott & María José Aninao. 2019. Internal migration and ethnicity in Santiago. In Andrew Lynch (ed.), *The Routledge handbook of Spanish in the global city*, 277–311. Routledge. https://doi.org/10.4324/9781315716350

Sadowsky, Scott & Stella Verkijk. Forthcoming. "¡Estoy en la jasa, logo!" Ethnicity and non-canonical /k/ allophones in Chilean Spanish: Evidence for language change caused by contact with Mapudungun.

Sadowsky, Scott & Beatriz Yáñez-Valdenegro. Forthcoming. "¡No vuede ser!" Mapudungun /p/ allophones in Chilean Spanish: evidence of contact-induced systemic language change.

Sadowsky, Scott, Héctor Painequeo, Gastón Salamanca & Heriberto Avelino. 2013. Illustrations of the IPA: Mapudungun. *Journal of the International Phonetic Association* 43(1). 87–96. https://doi.org/10.1017/S0025100312000369

Salamanca, Gastón & Ana Valverde. 2009. Prestigio y estigmatización en variantes anteriorizadas y posteriorizadas de las vocales del español de Chile. *Literatura y Lingüística* 20. 125–140. https://doi.org/10.4067/S0716-58112009000100007

Samper Padilla, José Antonio & Marta Samper Hernández. 2020. The weakening of intervocalic /d/ in the Spanish of Las Palmas de Gran Canaria: Comparison with other speech communities. *Spanish in Context* 17(2). 221–246. https://doi.org/10.1075/sic.00057.sam.

Sanicky, Cristina. 1988. El comportamiento de /f/ en el habla misionera. *Bulletin of Hispanic Studies* 65(3). 273–278. https://doi.org/10.1080/1475382882000365273

Sanicky, Cristina. 1992. Las manifestaciones de [r] y [tr] en el habla de Misiones, Argentina. *Hispanic Review* 60(2). 195–205. https://doi.org/10.2307/474110

Sanicky, Cristina. 1996. Las variaciones de /s/ final en el habla de mujeres y hombres en Misiones, Argentina. *Bulletin of Hispanic Studies* 73(3). 311–324. https://doi.org/10.3828/bhs.73.3.311

Sanicky, Cristina. 2001. Influencias en el comportamiento de /r/ final en el habla dialectal de Misiones, Argentina. *Bulletin of Hispanic Studies* 78(2). 137–154. https://doi.org/10.3828/bhs.78.2.137

Sanicky, Cristina. 2008. Las variantes de /j/ en Misiones, Argentina: estudio diacrónico-sincrónico. *Bulletin of Hispanic Studies* 85(5). 599–608. https://doi.org/10.3828/bhs.85.5.1

Sankoff, Gillian. 1989. A quantitative paradigm for the study of communicative competence. In Richard Bauman & Joel Sherzer (eds.), *Explorations in the ethnography of speaking*, 2nd edn., 18–49. Cambridge University Press. [1st edn., 1974.]

Santiago Molina, Gloryfé. 2017. *Variación sociofonética en el español de Puerto Rico: vibrantes, líquidas y retroflejas*. PhD dissertation, University of Puerto Rico.

Schmidt, Lauren B. & Erik W. Willis. 2011. Systematic investigation of voicing assimilation of Spanish /s/ in Mexico City. In Scott M. Alvord (ed.), *Selected proceedings of the 5th Conference on Laboratory Approaches to Romance Phonology*, 1–20. Cascadilla Proceedings Project.

Sessarego, Sandro. 2012. Unstressed vowel reduction in Cochabamba, Bolivia. *Revista Internacional de Lingüística Iberoamericana* 10(2). 213–227.

Sessarego, Sandro. 2013. On the social and linguistic implications of unstressed vowel weakening in Cochabambino Spanish. *Sintagma* 25. 19–32.

Shuy, Roger, Walt Wolfram & William K. Riley. 1967. *Linguistic correlates of social stratification in Detroit speech*. Michigan State University.

Silva-Corvalán, Carmen. 2001. *Sociolingüística y pragmática del español*. Georgetown University Press.

Tapia, Mónica & Humberto Valdivieso. 1997. La palatalización de las velares. Análisis acústico. *Onomázein* 2. 135–149. https://doi.org/10.7764/onomazein.2.06

Tejada Giráldez, María de la Sierra. 2012. Los factores lingüísticos de la /-s/ implosiva en el nivel de estudios altos de Granada. *Normas: Revista de Estudios Lingüísticos Hispánicos* 2. 185–217.

Tejada Giráldez, María de la Sierra. 2015. *Convergencia y divergencia entre comunidades de habla a propósito de la /-s/ implosiva. Contribución al estudio de los patrones sociolingüísticos del español de Granada*. PhD dissertation, Universidad de Granada.

Terrell, Tracy. 1978. La aspiración y elisión de /s/ en el español porteño. *Anuario de Letras. Lingüística y Filología* 16. 41–66.

Trudgill, Peter. 1972. Sex, covert prestige and linguistic change in the urban British English of Norwich. *Language in Society* 1(2). 179–195. https://doi.org/10.1017/S0047404500000488

Trudgill, Peter. 1974. *Sociolinguistics. An introduction*. Penguin.

Ugueto, Marluis. 2007. Estudio sociolingüístico del archifonema vibrante en el español de Caracas, 2004–2008. *Lengua y habla* 11. 91–104.

Ugueto, Marluis. 2016. La variación de /ɾ/ en posición final de palabra en el habla de Caracas: un estudio sociofonético. *Lingüística y Literatura* 37(70). 15–46. https://doi.org/10.17533/udea.lyl.n70a01

Uruburu, Agustín. 1994. El tratamiento del fonema /-d-/ en posición intervocálica en la lengua española hablada en Córdoba (España). *La Linguistique* 30(1). 85–104. https://doi.org/10.2307/30248708

Uruburu, Agustín. 1996. La lengua española hablada en Córdoba (España). *Revista Española de Lingüística Aplicada* 11. 225–250.

Valdivieso, Humberto. 1998. La variable fonológica /ĉ/ en Concepción. *Boletín de Filología* 37(2). 1199–1209.

Valencia, Alba. 1993. Realizaciones de /s/, /ĉ/ y /ĵ/ en el habla adolescente. *Nueva Revista del Pacífico* 38–39. 159–180.

Verdugo, Carlos. 2019. Deletion of voiced plosives in Chilean Spanish. *Onomázein* 46. 197–227. https://doi.org/10.7764/onomazein.46.09

Vergara-Fernández, Viviana. 2013. Relación entre alfabetización y producción de los alófonos de /b/: Estudio del habla cuidada de hablantes prealfabetizados y alfabetizados. *Onomázein* 27. 158–170.

Vida-Castro, Matilde. 2015. Resilabificación de la aspiración de /-s/ ante oclusiva dental sorda. Parámetros acústicos y variación social. In Adrián Cabedo (ed.), *Perspectivas actuales en el análisis fónico del habla. Tradición y avances en la fonética experimental*, 441–451. Departamento de Filología Española Universitat de València.

Vida-Castro, Matilde. 2016. Correlatos acústicos y factores sociales en la aspiración de /-s/ preoclusiva en la variedad de Málaga (España). Análisis de un cambio fonético en curso. *Lingua Americana* 38. 15–36.

Villena, Juan Andrés, Francisco Díaz, Antonio Ávila & María de la Cruz Lasarte. 2011. Interacción de factores fonéticos y gramaticales en la variación fonológica: la elisión de /d/ intervocálica en la variedad de los hablantes universitarios en la ciudad de Málaga. In Yolanda Congosto & Elena Méndez (eds.), *Variación lingüística y contacto de lenguas en el mundo hispánico*, 311–360. Iberoamericana Vervuert. https://doi.org/10.31819/9783865279095-015

Vuskovich, Matthew Anthony. 2006. *A sociolinguistic perspective toward hiatus resolution in Mexico City Spanish*. MA thesis, Louisiana State University.

Wagner, Max Leopold. 1927. El supuesto andalucismo de América y la teoría climatológica. *Revista de Filología Española* 14. 20–30.

Weinreich, Uriel, William Labov & Marvin Herzog. 1968. Empirical foundations for a theory of language change. In Winifred P. Lehmann & Yakov Malkiel (eds.), *Directions for historical linguistics: A symposium*, 95–195. University of Texas Press.

Westmoreland, Maurice & Juan Antonio Thomas (eds.). 2008. *Selected proceedings of the 4th Workshop on Spanish Sociolinguistics*. Cascadilla Proceedings Project.

Wolf, Clara. 1984. Tiempo real y tiempo aparente en el estudio de una variación lingüística: ensordecimiento y sonorización del yeísmo porteño. In Lía Schwarz & Isaías Lerner (eds.), *Homenaje a Ana Ma. Barrenechea*, 175–196. Castalia.

Wolf, Clara & Elena Jiménez. 1979. El ensordecimiento del yeísmo porteño: un cambio fonológico en marcha. In Ana María Barrenechea (ed.), *Estudios lingüísticos y dialectológicos*, 115–145. Hachette.

Wolfram, Walt. 1969. *A sociolinguistic description of Detroit Negro speech*. Center for Applied Linguistics.

Wolfram, Walt. 1978. Contrastive linguistics and social lectology. *Language Learning* 28(1). 1–28. https://doi.org/10.1111/j.1467-1770.1978.tb00302.x

Zahler, Sara & Danielle Daidone. 2014. A variationist account of trill /r/ usage in the Spanish of Málaga. *IULC Working Papers* 14(2). 17–42.

Zamora Munné, Juan. 1980. Las zonas dialectales del español americano. *Boletín de la Academia Norteamericana de la Lengua Española* 4–5. 57–67.

Zamora Vicente, Alonso. 1960. *Dialectología española*. Gredos.

Zepeda-Pallero, Sebastián. 2019. *Variación social de /r/ en el español hablado en Arica, Chile*. PhD dissertation, Pontificia Universidad Católica de Chile.

28

SOCIOPHONETICS AND CHINESE

Jingwei Zhang, Weijie Tan, and Christopher Strelluf

Introduction

This chapter explores the emergence of a sociophonetics of Chinese through a lens of Chinese scholarship. We especially highlight sociophonetic research by researchers working in China, available to researchers in China, and written in Chinese. In doing so, we hope to bring greater visibility to work on Chinese language by Chinese scholars to a global audience of sociophoneticians, which has traditionally been centered in North American and European institutions and languages. Readers are also pointed to Stanford & Yang (this volume) for additional review of issues, datasets, and findings relevant to Chinese sociophonetics.

In keeping with this view of sociophonetics through a Chinese lens, we follow conventions in Chinese linguistics for using the terms "Chinese," "language," and "dialect," which will differ from the usages of these terms conventional to many linguists working in Western languages and societies. Chinese scholars view "Modern Chinese" as a unified language that encompasses a standard variety and a range of dialectal varieties (Chen 1999). We adopt this definition, and use the label "Chinese" for China's national lingua franca, Putonghua (also named "Standard Chinese" or "Standard Mandarin"), as well as for regional varieties spoken in China. Putonghua is the standard form of Modern Chinese with the Beijing phonological system as its norm of pronunciation, and Northern dialects as its base dialect, and looking to exemplary modern works in *baihua* 'vernacular literary language' for its grammatical norms. Putonghua and the standard written Chinese were set as the standard language of China by the 2001 "Law of the People's Republic of China on the Standard Spoken and Written Chinese Language." Apart from the standard language Putonghua, Chinese has 10 dialect groups, Mandarin, Jin, Wu, Xiang, Hokkien, Yue, Gan, Hakka, Hui, and Ping. To unify the use of language, the government of China has promoted Putonghua since the 1950s. After more than half a century of promotion, Putonghua has become widely used with over 80 percent of the Chinese population claiming to speak it.

In order to provide this chapter's unique (and in our view, needed) emphasis on Chinese sociophonetics, the first two authors conducted a systematic literature review of Chinese sociophonetic works published since 2000. We use 2000 as a cutoff point because sociolinguistic

DOI: 10.4324/9781003034636-31

investigations were relatively rare in China in the late twentieth century. We identified 49 Chinese sociophonetic monographs and articles, with 35 written in English and 13 written in Chinese.

From these 49 studies, we offer a general retrospect on the history and development of Chinese sociophonetics. We next synthesize a set of key theories and frameworks of Chinese sociophonetics, and highlight representative studies on Chinese sociophonetics according to their units of analysis. We then present a brief illustrative case study of tonal variation based on Zhang (2019b), before concluding by suggesting future research directions for Chinese sociophonetics.

Chinese sociophonetics: A retrospective

Chinese sociophonetics has close connections with instrumental studies in Chinese phonetics and Chinese sociolinguistics. Our historicization of sociophonetics and Chinese focuses on the coming together of these two branches of inquiry.

The first instrumental phonetic work in China was Liu's (1924) *Record of experiments on the four tones* (Lu & Shen 2003). This monograph presents experimental reports on the tonal system of 12 Chinese dialects and examines fundamental frequency as the distinctive feature among them. This strand of research was interrupted by World War II and the Chinese Civil War. After the wars, Chinese instrumental phonetics developed rapidly in the 1950s. The Institute of Language in the Chinese Academy of Science paid special attention to instrumental phonetics. Researchers like Wu Zongji used X-ray photography and palatography to conduct a series of instrumental phonetic studies on Putonghua. This initial phase of interest culminated in the 1980s, when many monographs on instrumental phonetics were published, such as *Basics of instrumental phonetics* (Zhu 1986), *The speech spectrogram of Putonghua monosyllables* (Wu 1986), and *The handbook of instrumental phonetics* (Wu & Lin 1989).

Chinese dialects were also examined. *Shanghai tonetics* (Zhu 1995, 1999) is the most representative instrumental tonetic work. Different from traditional dialectological studies in China at the time which only featured one or two typical speakers, Zhu expanded the number of speakers to 11. Those speakers were of different ages and education levels. For illustrating the tonal system of the Shanghai dialect, Zhu described individual differences in tonal contours in detail. Perhaps most importantly, Zhu also compared different tonal normalization methods, providing methodological foundations for future Chinese sociophonetics.

The emergence of theories and methods from variationist sociolinguistics was also essential to the development of Chinese sociophonetics. The start of the Chinese variationist study can be traced back to the 1980s. Catherine Barale (1982) and Daming Xu (1992) were pioneers in applying variationist approaches to Chinese language. They both encountered tremendous difficulties in making audio recordings of spontaneous speech in a closed society such as China in the 1980s. China in the late twentieth century was not well positioned for sociolinguistic investigation (cf. Zhang & Xu forthcoming).

While variationist sociolinguistics faced cultural headwinds, its development in Chinese linguistics was encouraged by the opportunities for links with dialectology. The discipline of dialectology holds a strong position in China with a long-lasting productive line of research, partly due to the great diversity in the Chinese language. Some Chinese dialectologists readily accepted variationist theories and methodologies. In particular, Barale (1982) and Xu (1992) focused on nasal-final variation in terms of Chinese dialects, comparing Beijing Mandarin and Baotou Mandarin. As a result of such approaches, a good number of linguistic variables in Chinese dialects were studied as dialect variables in ways that were informed by variationist methods. Naturally, as Chinese sociophonetics emerged, scholars drew on connections between Chinese variationist studies and Chinese dialectology.

We point to Bauer, Cheung & Cheung (2003) as the first Chinese sociophonetic study. They investigated the variation and merger of Hong Kong Cantonese (HKC) high-rising and mid-low-rising tones from a sociolinguistic perspective with acoustic evidence. They conducted acoustic analysis with the Kay Elemetrics Computerized Speech Lab (CSL) 4300B system. Given limited access to such specialized systems for sound analysis in mainland China, their methods might not have been taken up by other scholars. However, the release of Praat (Boersma & Weenink 2001) removed many obstacles to researchers by facilitating acoustic analysis of speech, as well as other phonetic-related tasks like stimuli preparation and speech synthesis. Praat substantially boosted the development of Chinese sociophonetics, enabling researchers to carry out speech analysis on their personal computers. Chinese scholars also developed other sound analysis software. Mini-Speech-Lab, developed by Shi Feng of Nankai University, is particularly widely used. Because it was developed with Chinese in mind, Mini-Speech-Lab gives special emphasis to the analysis of tone. A number of Chinese sociophonetic studies were conducted with Mini-Speech-Lab, including Shi & Wang (2006), Wang (2009), Liu (2012), Liang & Meng (2013), and Liu, Shi & Lin (2013).

Accordingly, Chinese sociophonetics grew rapidly at the start of the twenty-first century. Studies concerning the changes in tones, consonants, vowels, voice quality, and other phonetic variables emerged. The coming together of Chinese sociolinguistics and the tradition of Chinese dialectology created an impetus for phonetic variables to be examined through sociolinguistic lenses. These historical developments continue to be reflected in the key theories and frameworks of Chinese sociophonetics.

Key theories and frameworks

Linguistic urbanization

Linguistic urbanization is a new theory cultivated by Chinese sociolinguistics studies. The theory describes and explains the complex linguistic consequences of China's rapid urbanization. China's urbanization rate has risen from less than 20 percent in 1980 to reach 64.7 percent at the end of 2021—a tremendous increase in just 40 years (Textor 2021). Urbanization was spurred by reforms to China's policies with regard to economic opportunity and population mobility (Wakabayashi 1990).

Population movement caused fundamental changes in speech communities, both in urban and suburban areas. With influxes of migrants and urban expansion, existing urban speech communities are transformed. Rural speech communities are also impacted by urbanization so that new sociolinguistic stratifications are formed due to social mobility. Moreover, new speech communities are formed when migrants with different linguistic backgrounds come into contact in newly created industrial centers. Chinese sociolinguists tried to respond to these new situations. Among them, Xu (2015) proposed the theory of "linguistic urbanization" to explore the linguistic consequences of urbanization—particularly from dialect contact—in these three (sometimes distinct and sometimes overlapping) realms of metropolises, rural communities, and new speech communities. Chinese sociophonetic studies have followed this schema of speech communities; we highlight one study of each type.

Metropolises

Ping Wang's (2009) project on the description of tones and vowels in Beijing Mandarin provided large-scale data to investigate the effects of immigrants on Beijing's urban dialect. This study compared tones and vowels produced by speakers whose parents were from Beijing and speakers whose parents moved to the city. A total of 2080 tonal tokens of 52 Beijing Mandarin speakers were acoustically analyzed. Differences between "local" and "immigrant" heritage were minor but systematic. In general, the tonal contours of speakers of local heritage had higher f0 than did those of speakers whose parents were not from Beijing. For vowels, the F1 and F2 values of 1144 tokens of seven cardinal vowels produced by 52 Beijing Mandarin speakers were extracted and converted to Bark. The results showed that speakers from immigrant families had larger vowel spaces. Specifically, significant differences existed in the B1 values of /i/ and /y/. The immigrant heritage speakers had lower B1 values for /i/ and /y/, as well as higher and fronter /ʅ/, /ɿ/, and /ə/. Immigrants' dialect accents also affected the language of second-generation children. The study helped to describe the tone pattern and consonant system of Beijing Mandarin by large-scale acoustic data, while also investigating relevant social factors, giving a dynamic view of the phonetic change in Beijing Mandarin.

Rural communities

Liang & Chen (2013) examined variation in /b/ in the rural Lei dialect. Twenty-four speakers from four different age groups balanced by gender were recruited. All spoke Leicheng, a Min dialect spoken in Leicheng town in the Guangdong province and its neighboring rural areas. Four variants of onset /b/—[w], [ʙ], [b], and [ɱ]—were identified auditorily and in spectrograms. The distribution of the variants showed a strong correlation with age. Before round vowels, older speakers tended to choose the bilabial trill [ʙ] while the youngest speakers only produced the approximant [w]. Before non-round vowels, the oldest group only produced the voiced bilabial plosive [b] while the younger speakers preferred labiodental nasal [ɱ]. The findings revealed a rapid apparent-time change in the selection of allophones of /b/ in rural Guangdong.

New dialects

Xuan Wang's (2017) study of the new urban areas in Hohhot is a (so far) rare example of sociophonetic work in the exciting area of new dialect formation in new Chinese industrial centers. Hohhot is the provincial capital of Inner Mongolia in China. The city officially has four administrative districts, but the local residents normally divided the city into two parts: the old town and the new town (Jankowiak 1993). Residents in the old town are mostly local-born residents speaking the Jin dialect, and residents in the new town are mostly immigrants speaking Putonghua, thus forming a contact-induced mixture of dialects. Moreover, residents in the new town are mostly immigrants whose movements were prompted by official migratory policy since the 1950s. Most immigrants have a better educational background and work in the government, schools, and locally famous factories, and are thus marked with higher overt social and economic status than residents in the old town. Wang (2017) investigated the variation of stress patterns in Hohhot. The disyllabic words with the second syllable having /l/ onset (L-words) have a weak-strong stress pattern in the Jin dialect but have a strong-weak stress pattern in Putonghua. Thirty-five speakers in the new town were recruited from three age groups. The older group was the first generation of state-sponsored migrants, who came to Hohhot in the 1950s or 1960s. The middle group was the second-generation migrants who were born in Hohhot. The younger group was the third generation born between 1985 and 1995. They completed a word-elicitation task of L-words, a questionnaire on their attitudes to speech communities and dialects, and an interview about their local social connections. The speakers' attitudes towards the local communities and dialects were measured by Attitude Analog Scale method proposed by Llamas & Watt (2014), in which participants marked a line to indicate their degree of agreement with statements. A mixed-effects model showed a directional relation between speakers' Attitude Analog Scale and their adoption of a local Jin feature. Speakers in the first- and second-generation groups with positive attitudes to the Jin dialect tended to use the weak-strong stress pattern more often. However, the social meaning of the stress pattern variable has changed from the Jin dialect feature into the newly formed urban Hohhot community feature in the third generation. Speakers who strongly emphasize their urban Hohhot identity tend to produce the weak-strong patterns more. The findings demonstrate the role of attitudes in contact-induced linguistic change. It also illustrates how a new variety like Hu Pu (the Hohhot Mandarin variety) emerges through the formation of a speech community during urbanization. Studies in this realm offer exciting possibilities for conversations between Chinese sociophonetics and relatively better-known studies of new dialect formation in European-language communities (e.g., Kerswill & Williams 2000; Trudgill 2004, 2016; Britain 2005; Cheshire et al. 2011; Wiese 2012; Cheshire 2020).

Language contact

Language contact is another important theorical space for Chinese sociophonetics. Contact-induced sociophonetic change in local vernaculars due to the pressure from the standard language Putonghua is a frequent area of exploration.

Jin et al.'s (2008) comparison of the tonal system in Guangzhou Mandarin (a Mandarin variety spoken in Guangzhou) and Putonghua is a representative study of the influence of Putonghua on the local dialect. This study described the tonal system of Guangzhou Mandarin, summarized its differences from the tonal system of Putonghua, and also showed that those differences came from the features of Cantonese. Putonghua has four citation tones: the level tone T1 /55/, the rising tone T2 /35/, the falling-rising tone T3 /214/, and the falling tone T4 /51/. Guangzhou Cantonese has 11 citation tones: high falling tone /53/, high level tone /55/, mid-rising tone /35/, mid-level tone /33/, low-falling tone /21/, low rising tone /13/, low level tone /22/, and four entering tones /5/, /3/, /2/, and /35/ (Li et al. 1995).The production data used in this study were extracted from a corpus jointly built by Nokia and the China Academy of Social Sciences. The authors used recordings of Guangzhou Mandarin and Cantonese from 10 Guangzhou Cantonese speakers, and Putonghua recordings from 10 Beijing speakers. The segments that carried tones were extracted. F0 was then measured at 10 equidistance points in each segment to draw tonal contours. Results showed that the T1 level tone in the two Mandarin varieties had similar tonal values and tonal contours. T2 in Guangzhou Mandarin had a lower onset and later inflection point both in monosyllables and in the first syllable of disyllabic words compared to Putonghua. In the second syllable of disyllabic words, Guangzhou Mandarin had a similar tonal contour to Putonghua, but its inflection point was lower, which was considered to be a similarity of Guangzhou Cantonese. T3 in Guangzhou Mandarin had two allotones: one concave allotone and one low-falling allotone. The concave allotone was similar to T3 in Putonghua, but with greater openness and less curvature. No significant differences were observed in T4 between Guangzhou Mandarin and Putonghua. Jin et al. (2008) concluded that speakers produced T2 in Guangzhou Mandarin differently from Putonghua because of the influence of Cantonese /35/, which had a later inflection point and lower onset. T3 in Guangzhou Mandarin was also affected by Cantonese. Although Cantonese does not have a T3-like falling-rising tone, Cantonese speakers tended to use the low tones in Cantonese to produce the falling-rising contour. Jin et al.'s (2008) work serves as a good example of the linguistic outcome of language contact between Putonghua and local dialects.

Some studies further discuss the factors that drive language contact. Feifan Wang (2019) studied the variation in the Shanghai dialect of initial consonants whose historic source is the Middle Chinese *Xia* (匣) initial when followed by high front vowels. The most conservative form of those words in the Shanghai dialect had no initial consonant and had a low tone. However, among younger speakers, two variants appeared: 1) a fully adapted variant with change in both the initial and tone, and 2) a partly adapted variant with a fricative initial and an unchanged low tone. A previous study concluded that the variants were results of the "adaptation" to Putonghua (Chen 1996) since those words in Putonghua always have a fricative initial. The variant with a changed initial and tone is a fully adapted variant, while the variant with a changed initial and unchanged tone is partly adapted. Twenty-two native speakers born after 1985 in urban Shanghai were recruited to produce 43 target words with *Xia* (匣) initial and high front vowels. Those target words were elicited by two tasks: first a quick-answer interview (without the effect of Chinese characters), followed one week later by a word list reading task (with the effect of Chinese characters). The comparison of the two tasks was designed to detect the influence of the Chinese written language on language variation. The results indicated that participants tended to choose the contact-induced variants in the reading task. When they produced target words in the Shanghai dialect in the quick-answer interview—that is, the task not using any Chinese characters—there was a correlation between the choice of variants and word frequency in the Shanghai dialect and Putonghua. Higher frequency in the Shanghai dialect correlated with the better preservation of the conservative variant, whereas higher frequency in Putonghua correlated with more contact-induced variants. This study illustrates that Chinese characters and word frequency are both potential driving forces of sound changes in Chinese dialects toward Putonghua, with the role of Chinese characters being more important than that of word frequency. These findings provide exciting opportunities to bring data from Chinese into conversation with studies based on Western language varieties on the effects of lexical frequency in language change and preservation (e.g., Bybee 2007), especially in phonetics and phonology (e.g., Clark & Trousdale 2009; Hay et al. 2015; Forrest 2017; Solon, Linford & Geeslin 2018).

Review of Chinese sociophonetic studies

This section reviews representative studies of the sociophonetics of vowels, consonants, voice quality, and tones in Chinese. Table 28.1 categorizes the 49 Chinese sociophonetic studies we collected, organized by research variables.

Vowels

Vowels have been examined extensively in sociophonetic studies of varieties of English and other Western languages (see Cox & Docherty this volume). However, in Chinese sociophonetic studies, issues related to vowel quality are less commonly studied. To our knowledge, only four Chinese sociophonetic studies—all focusing on Cantonese—primarily examine vowels (Lee 2009; Liu, Shi & Lin 2013; Tse 2016, 2019).

Lee (2009) reported acoustic characteristics in terms of formants for seven Cantonese vowels [i y u ε œ ɔ a]. The study was sociophonetic in the sense that Lee categorized productions of adult

Table 28.1 Chinese sociophonetic studies

Research variable	Articles in English	Articles in Chinese
Vowels	Lee 2009; Tse 2016; Tse 2019	Li, Shi & Lin 2013
Consonants	Li 2013; Yu 2016; Sloos & Lei 2018; Lin 2018; Zhang & Levis 2021; Cheng, Jongman & Sereno 2023	Liang & Chen 2013; Ran 2017; Jin & Hong 2018; Li 2018; Wang 2019
Voice quality	Callier 2013; Gao 2016; Li et al. 2020	
Tones	Bauer, Cheung & Cheung 2003; Fung & Wong 2010a; Fung & Wong 2010b; Mok & Wong 2010; Fung & Wong 2011; Ou 2012; Mok, Zuo & Wong 2013; Zhang 2014; Cheng 2017; Chen, Yao & Yu 2018; Zhao 2018; Fung & Lee 2019; Zhang 2019a; Zhang 2019b; Zhang, Zhang & Xu 2019; Lai & Kuang 2020; Singh & Wewalaarachchi 2020	Qi 2011; Jin et al. 2008; Liang 2015; Wang, Liu & Qing 2016; Liang 2017; Yu & Huang 2019
Multiple research variables	Yang et al. 2015	Wang 2009
Others	Deutsch et al. 2009; Tseng 2005; Wang 2017; Xu & Mao 2017; Kuo 2018; Shan 2019	

males and females and of preadolescent males and females, and reported formants in terms of these social predictors. Lee (2009) might be thought of as providing a baseline for understanding the acoustics of Cantonese vowels in the same way that Peterson & Barney (1952) provided a foundational acoustic benchmark for (American) Englishes.

Liu, Shi & Lin (2013) investigated the same seven vowels in HKC, but in a dramatically larger sample of 120 speakers with ages ranging from 20 to 60. They identified differences in vowel productions according to speaker age and gender. In particular, younger speakers tended to produce vowels fronter and lower, but also produced /a/ higher than older speakers. Liu, Shi & Lin interpreted this as showing that the vowel space of HKC was shrinking among young people in Hong Kong. While their study described Cantonese vowels from a very large data sample and identified variation in apparent time and by gender, like Lee (2009) they did not offer explanations for the reasons for these changes.

Tse's (2016, 2019) studies on heritage Cantonese provided a new perspective on the sociophonetic investigation of vowel changes. Tse (2016) focused on the four allophones [iː], [ɪk/ ɪŋ], [uː], and [ʊk/ʊŋ] of two contrastive vowels /iː/ and /uː/ of Toronto Heritage Cantonese (THC) across two generations. The recordings for acoustic analysis included 600 tokens from 20 speakers, extracted from the Heritage Language Documentation Corpus (Nagy 2011). Results showed that the allophonic variation of /iː/ and /uː/ were conditioned by the presence of following velars, and allophonic conditioning was maintained across the two generations. Age and sex had a significant effect on the variation of the allophones of /iː/, with second-generation female speakers produc- ing the [iː] with lower F2 than all other groups, suggesting backing. Second-generation female speakers also produced [ɪk/ɪŋ] with greater F2 than first-generation female speakers, showing multiple levels of within-gender, intergenerational differences. The first-generation male speakers showed vowel overlap between [ɪk/ɪŋ] and [ɛː] while the first-generation female speakers did not, and the second-generation female speakers adopted overlapping productions and produced the vowels with greater overlap than even the second-generation male speakers, revealing complex interactions between gender and change-in-progress. Tse (2016) discussed the factors motivating the intergenerational change and concluded that phonological influence from Toronto English was the most likely cause, particularly for Cantonese vowels that were most phonetically similar to Toronto English vowels.

Tse (2019) further expanded on this work by enlarging the dataset to examine 11 Cantonese vowels, and by adding comparative data from HKC to explore effects of language contact. The study found a generational change-in-progress in Toronto in the retraction of /y/, as well as the fronting of /i/ in apparent time in both Toronto and Hong Kong. The retraction of /y/ was considered to be a result of contact with English, whereas the fronting of /i/ was also found in HKC and thus was not considered to be contact-induced. Tse (2019) actually found more vowel shifting in Hong Kong than in Toronto, with age being a significant predictor for the lowering of /ɪ/, /ɔ/, and /ʊ/, and for the fronting of /i/ and /ɔ/.

Tse's study shed light on the application of Labov's (1994) principles of vowel chain shifting in language-contact contexts. The fronting of tense /i/ in HKC and THC satisfies Principle 1 (tense nuclei rise along a peripheral track). The lowering of lax /ɪ/ and /ʊ/ in HKC meets Principle 2 (lax nuclei fall). The fronting of back vowel /ɔ/ in HKC satisfies the Principle 3 (back nuclei move to the front). The findings provide precious empirical evidence for vowel chain shifting beyond the European languages that Labov largely built his principles from.

Consonants

Like vowels, consonants have been examined extensively in Western sociophonetic studies (from this volume, see Chappell, García & Davidson; Chodroff & Foulkes; Sebregts, van Hout & Van de Velde; Turton), but have been studied rarely in Chinese sociophonetics. Existing Chinese sociophonetic studies on consonants mostly focus on the variation of consonants in southern dialects (Liang & Chen 2013; Yu 2016; Jin & Hong 2018) and Mandarin varieties (Ran 2017; Li 2013, Li 2018; Lin 2018; Cheng, Jongman & Sereno 2023).

Jin & Hong (2018) studied the variation of the final consonant /ʔ/ in Chaozhou, a Hokkien dialect. Entering tone is a special tone type in some Chinese dialects. Syllables carrying entering tones—syllables ending with consonants /p/, /t/, or /k/, or /ʔ/—are much shorter in duration. Previous studies found [ʔ] in the Chaozhou dialect was sometimes replaced by creaky voice on the nuclear vowel, and this variation seems to be caused by tone change. Jin & Hong examined variation of /ʔ/ in productions by four Chaozhou speakers aged around 24 years old. They identified four variants: [ʔ], creaky voice, [k], and deleted. They found that 1) the young generation tended to use creaky voice; 2) the reduction and the deletion of plosive codas frequently appeared in the young generation's casual speech; and 3) the variation was not only related to the tones but also vowels. The creaky voice variant appeared more in lower tones and lower vowels. Jin & Hong (2018) did not examine social factors beyond age.

Yu (2016) revealed individual differences in Cantonese /s/. Since the sibilant /s/ in Cantonese is heavily influenced by the followed vocalic environment, transcriptions of the sibilant in previous studies varied, appearing as [s], [ʃ], or [ɕ] (Bauer & Benedict 1997). Yu used seven acoustic measures (centroid frequency, standard deviation, kurtosis, skewness, peak frequency, amplitude ratio, and sibilant duration) of syllables with initial /s/ in different vocalic contexts elicited by 105 HKC speakers, and coded speakers for sex and individual autistic-like traits. The results revealed that among the transcription choices used in previous studies, the sibilant in HKC was produced most like IPA [s]. Yu further found that sex and autistic-like traits both affected the acoustic properties of /s/, showing that females with lower autism spectrum quotient scores exhibited the most variability as a result of the vocalic environment in which /s/ occurred. Yu's findings not only inform knowledge of the characteristics of HKC /s/ and reveal social differentiation of productions, but also reveal the value of using objective metrics to assess personality traits as a factor in sociophonetic innovation. Indeed, to the extent that lower autism spectrum quotient scores might correlate with greater likelihood that an individual might engage in a wider range of social contacts, Yu's methods suggest a way to explore Labov's (2001) positing that the leaders of language change will be people who are deeply involved in multiple networks.

Ran (2017) conducted a large-scale investigation on the variation in plosives in Beijing Mandarin. He examined voice onset time (VOT) and closure duration of 50 speakers and found differences between males and females and also between native Beijingers and non-native Beijingers. For aspirated plosives, females had a shorter closure duration but longer VOT than males. Non-native Beijingers had a longer closure duration than native Beijingers. Ran's study shows subsegmental variation in consonants to be a potentially rich space to explore sociophonetic variation in Chinese as a result of social factors like sex and migratory background.

Voice quality

Although it is known that voice quality (VQ) varies in different communication functions and works as an influential factor in paralinguistic expression, relationships between VQ and phonation and aspects of speakers' social positions and identities have only recently begun to be explored extensively (see, e.g., Esling et al. 2019; Davidson this volume). We review three Chinese sociophonetic studies on VQ: Callier (2013), Li et al. (2020), and Gao (2016).

To the best of our knowledge, Callier's (2013) study of Beijing Mandarin is the earliest Chinese sociophonetic study of VQ. Previous studies (Liu et al. 2016; Li, Lai & Kuang 2022) had already illustrated the effects of pitch, tone type, and sex on the use of creaky voice but had not examined linguistic and social constraints. Callier analyzed speech by 15 speakers of Beijing Mandarin, and found that creaky voice appeared more frequently in a low tone, neutral tone, and phrase-final position. Callier then asked listeners to rate a sample of Beijing Mandarin speech on a Likert scale on dimensions related to speakers' perceived mood, economic condition, educational background, region, social class, attractiveness, and attitude to the topic. Listeners heard creaky guise or plain guise, controlled for syllable position and lexical tone. Results showed that creak in the phrase-final position indicated higher enthusiasm and interest, while creak in the phrase-medial position indicated lower enthusiasm and interest. The study revealed the interactions between tone and creaky voice in Beijing Mandarin, and the interaction between these linguistic constraints and social meanings of VQ.

Li et al. (2020) conducted experiments on VQ differences between sarcastic speech and sincere speech in Putonghua. Thirty speakers of Putonghua read target sentences with sincere and sarcastic attitudes. Contact quotient and peak increase in closure parameters were measured by electroglottograph (EGG), and seven VQ parameters were extracted from audio signals. Eight of nine parameters were shown to effectively identify sarcastic and sincere speech. Among them, creaky voice played an important role as a prosodic feature in expressing sarcasm. There were also gendered differences, as male speakers used a vocal fry voice whereas females used a non-constriction voice when expressing sarcasm.

Gao (2016) studied the ongoing disappearance of low tone breathiness in the Wu dialect of Shanghai. Breathiness in the Shanghai dialect was a retention of breathy phonation from Middle Chinese, and serves as a secondary cue to low tone. The Shanghai dialect has been described by Chinese scholars as having undergone rapid changes in the past century-and-a-half, especially through influence by Putonghua after its promotion in the 1950s. Gao investigated the evolution of low tone breathiness among 12 younger participants aged 20 to 30 and 10 elderly participants aged 60 to 80. Gao captured audio and EGG data as participants read carrier sentences with 32 target monosyllabic words bearing all five lexical tones. Participants also completed a question-naire to elicit information on personal characteristics, including degree of fluency in Wu and Putonghua. Older participants were shown to retain the low tone breathiness more than younger participants. Females were also shown to lead in the disappearance of low tone breathiness, which Gao attributed to adoption of prestigious norms. This interpretation was consistent with the results of the questionnaire, in which females reported greater use of and competence in Putonghua, which is regarded socially as the standard variety.

Gao's (2016) findings offer an example from Chinese of females leading an apparent-time sound change and leading in the adoption of relatively prestigious linguistic features, which has been found repeatedly in sociolinguistic and sociophonetic studies of Western language varieties (e.g., Labov 2001). It extends these apparent-time studies to nonsegmental levels of sociophonetics like phonation, and explores ways that apparent-time and sociolinguistically driven sound change might take place in the context of language contact—a situation that is unfamiliar to the studies of monolingual speech communities upon which much of Labovian sociolinguistic theory has been developed. Perhaps more importantly from a Chinese sociophonetic perspective, Gao addressed a key issue in Chinese dialectology: how Middle Chinese has developed into modern-day Chinese dialects. Middle Chinese breathiness has been lost from Putonghua and the majority of Mandarin varieties, while some southern dialects including Wu still have an interplay of tones and other laryngeal and supralaryngeal cues. Gao (2016) reveals the loss of breathiness as a cue to low tone as a change-in-progress and also shows how social factors might encourage this change. This illustrates the potential of sociophonetics to help answer major questions in Chinese dialectology and historical linguistics, and similar work will undoubtedly remain an important area for Chinese sociophonetics.

Tone

Tone is undoubtedly the most extensively researched feature in Chinese sociophonetics. Given the relative paucity of "sociotonetic" (see Stanford & Yang this volume) studies in the field broadly, Chinese sociophonetic studies are filling a crucial gap in knowledge of sociophonetic variation. Our literature review identified 22 studies on tonal variables.

Tonal changes in Hong Kong Cantonese have especially drawn interest. HKC has six lexical tones: high-level T1, high-rising T2, mid-level T3, low-falling T4, low-rising T5, and low-level T6. Three allotones T7, T8, and T9 occur in syllables with final stops. T2-T5, T3-T6, and T4-T6 are mostly considered to be merging or merged, with scholars disagreeing over the extent to which these tone pairs have merged and over the processes leading to tonal merger.

Mok, Zuo & Wong (2013) investigated both the production and the perception of T2-T5, T3-T6, and T4-T6 in HKC, finding asymmetry between speakers' productions and perceptions of merging tones. Unsurprisingly, participants merging T2 with T5, T3 with T6, and T4 with T6 in production had more difficulties in perception than participants who were not merging the tones, but production data revealed that these participants still had six distinct tones. Thus, they identified tonal "near-merger" in HKC (see also Yu 2007). Mok, Zuo & Wong further showed that tones with low frequency led the change overall, but that the progress of the merger differed among some words with the same tone and frequency. They attributed this to lexical diffusion, arguing that HKC tone mergers spread through the lexicon. Liang (2017) also examined the interplay of the production and perception in HKC tone merger. The study conducted a discriminant test and captured production data on 18 monosyllables carrying 6 tones with vowels [a], [i], or [u]. More than half of the speakers in the study showed tonal mergers in the perception test, but a few of these speakers still produced the six tones distinctly. There were also a few speakers who seemed to merge tones in production but accurately identified the distinctions perceptually.

Fung & Lee (2019) further examined the interplay between production and perception of tonal merger in HKC. They recruited 120 native speakers aged from 20 to 58 years and stratified for gender. Participants completed an AX discriminant task and recorded readings of test sentences. Results of the perception test show that T3-T5 was distinguished perfectly by L1 HKC speakers, but that speakers varied in their accuracy perceiving T2-T5 and T4-T6. Fung & Lee examined productive merger by Pillai score, returning low Pillai scores (indicative of productive overlap) for T3-T6, T2-T5, and T4-T6. They concluded from the combination of production and perception results that T2 and T5 have fully merged, that T3 and T6 have merged only in production, and that T4-T6 was a near-merger where the tonal contrast had collapsed in perception but was maintained in production.

Tonal variation has also been examined in Guangzhou Cantonese (GZC). Ou (2012) found that T3-T6 of GZC had merged, resulting in a new mid-level tone. T4-T6 of GZC was a near-merger. Liang (2015) also worked on the tonal mergers of GZC, finding that T2-T5 and T3-T6 were undergoing productive merger. T3-T6 were also merging perceptually, and most participants perceived T6 as T3. This study also inferred that the merger process started in perception and then expanded to production.

Studies on HKC and GZC tone mergers complement studies of near-mergers in segments in Western sociolinguistic studies. Labov (1994) reported situations where vowels were merged in perception but distinct in production, including the cases of /oh/ and /ohr/ in New York, /uw/ and /u/ in Albuquerque, and /o/ and /oh/ in Pennsylvania (see also Herold 1990, 1997; Faber, Best & Di Paolo 1994; Faber & Di Paolo 1995; Strelluf 2016). Studies of tonal mergers suggest that near-mergers and the origins of mergers in perception rather than production are cross-linguistic, universal facts about language that apply across different levels of phonology.

Apart from HKC, tonal variation in Putonghua also attracted research interest. Yu & Huang (2019) investigated the effect of dialect background on the perception of Putonghua tones in situations of contact among varieties with differing tonal inventories. They tested four groups of participants who spoke the Boshan dialect (three tones), the Beijing dialect (four tones), the Nanchang dialect (seven tones), and Guangzhou Cantonese (nine tones). Participants were required to categorize Putonghua tones from synthetized continua. Categorization differed significantly across the four groups of participants, showing that dialect experiences influenced the perceptual categorization of Putonghua tones. However, regardless of dialect background, participants showed the same patterns in categorization: all perceived the T1-T2, T1-T3, T1-T4, and T2-T4 continua categorically and perceived the T2-T3 and T3-T4 continua continually.

In addition to the four lexical tones, Putonghua has a neutral tone (T0). The neutral tone is short, unstressed, and low in intensity. Tone values of T0 vary, and it is widely accepted that T0 tone values are dependent on preceding tone (Cheng 1973; Shen 1992). Zhao (2018) used a matched-guise test to detect the social meaning of neutral tone. Participants heard "standard-use," "low-use," and "high-use" T0 stimuli (based on the frequency with which T0 was used in cases where it could be used optionally), and rated these stimuli on dimensions of standardness, solidarity (e.g., friendliness, loyalty, and sincerity), accent of the talker, status of the talker, and occupational suitability of the talker. Ratings suggested that high use of neutral tone was related to standardness, reflecting the fact that high use of neutral tone is characteristic of the prestigious Beijing dialect. Indeed, talkers in high-use stimuli were more frequently marked as people from Beijing, while talkers in low-use stimuli were identified as coming from southern cities. High-use stimuli were also rated as leader-like. However, there were limits to the social powerfulness of voices being associated with Beijing, as the standard use of neutral tones indicated better education level to raters. Occupational suitability showed an interaction between neutral tone use and gender. Men were generally judged to have better jobs than women, but men with the standard use of neutral tone were believed to have higher-status jobs than other men. Additionally, all three types of stimuli influenced solidarity ratings. In short, Zhao's (2018) study shows that the neutral tone of Putonghua is, from a sociophonetic perspective, anything but neutral.

Further afield from Putonghua and Cantonese, Liang & Meng (2013) investigated tonal variation in the Chongqing dialect from the perspective of language contact. By analyzing the monosyllables produced by 53 speakers of different ages and gender, they found that older speakers had higher tonal contours, and younger speakers had more distinctive (Chongqing-like) level tone and rising tone contours. These findings contradicted previous studies that suggested the tones in the Chongqing were disappearing under the influence of Putonghua. They show that, even in language contact situations with a dominant variety, dialects like Chongqing may resist leveling and preserve unique features through social and cultural factors. Exploring tonal contours of other dialects seems likely to yield many more nuanced patterns in varieties.

CASE STUDY   Tonal merger in Wuxi

Middle Chinese (MC) is believed to be the ancestor of most modern Chinese dialects. It possessed four tonal categories: *ping* (level tone), *shang* (falling-rising tone), *qu* (falling tone), and *ru* (a very short tone that appeared with stop consonants). Each tonal category can be subdivided into two registers by the classification of the initial consonants of the syllables: syllables with voiceless initials are classified as *yin* (upper) register and those with voiced initials are classified as *yang* (lower) register. "Register" here is a term used in Chinese historical linguistics and Chinese dialectology. Historically, tones from the *yin* (upper) register occurred on syllables with voiceless initial obstruents, and tones from the *yang* (lower) register occurred on syllables with voiced initial obstruents. Four tonal categories and two registers together resulted in eight MC tones in total.

In the following 1000 years, MC tones went through successive mergers and resulted in fewer tone shapes occurring in modern Mandarin's tonal system. Among them, the merger of *yang shang* into *yang qu* is an important tonal change that started in Mandarin in the eighth century and then spread to other Chinese dialects (Ho 1988). This merger is still in progress in the Wu dialect. Chao (1928) investigated 33 Wu varieties in the 1920s and found that this merger was incomplete in most Wu varieties. When Qian (1992) re-examined the tonal system of those 33 Wu varieties after 60 years in 1988, only 11 varieties, including that spoken in Wuxi, still kept *yang shang* distinct. However, entering the twenty-first century, *yang shang* of the Wu dialect was beginning to undergo merger, creating an opportunity in Wuxi to observe this phonological change while it is in progress and to observe the fine details of its change process. Here, we reprise Zhang's (2019b) findings for the change pathway of the *yang shang–yang qu* merger.

Methods

Forty native speakers of Wuxi from urban and suburban areas, stratified for age (young vs. old) and sex (male vs. female), were recruited. Duration and f0 of tone-bearing segments were extracted using Praat scripts. F0 measurements were converted to semitones for tonal normalization (see Stanford & Yang this volume). The pitch reference value of a given speaker is the speaker's average f0 (Zhang 2014). Inflection points were determined for contours, identified as the highest pitch point in a convex tone or the lowest pitch point in a concave tone.

Results

Based on impressionistic transcription (using Chao's 1928 tone numerals) and f0 contours, Zhang (2019b) identified three tonal variants of *yang shang*: convex, rising, and concave (see Figure 28.1).

Mixed-effect models were built to detect associations between each of the variants and social categories of speakers. Models of the rising variant (contour 2 in Figure 28.1) and concave variant (contours 3 and 4) showed that these two tonal shapes were associated with the young and the urban participants, in a pattern consistent with a change in apparent time diffusing from cities. The inflection point in the rising tone showed time-driven variability; it initially appeared closer to the beginning of the contour as the first stage of the development of the concave tone, and then gradually the inflection point shifted later in the contour as the concave tone became entrenched. Indeed, as depicted in Figure 28.1, the movement of the inflection point appears to be an essential element of tonal change in *yang shang*. From the starting point of the conservative rise-fall contour, the inflection point drifted later in the contour until it occurred at the end of the syllable, resulting in a contour that could be interpreted as a simple rise. Then, in a sense, the inflection point cycled back to the beginning of the contour, but now targeting a low inflection prior to a rise—ultimately resulting in a fall-rise contour. The resulting concave tone is the most advanced variant of *yang shang*, the tonal contour of which coincides with T6.

The above analysis reveals the change of *yang shang* to *yang qu*. The merger started from the most conservative variant, the convex tone, and resulted in a change to the concave tone. The rising tone was the transitional variant between the convex and the concave tones, and the timing of the inflection point—along with interactions between the timing of the inflection point and speech production and

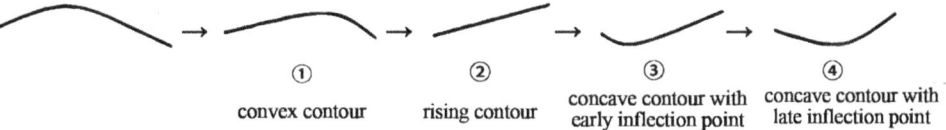

    ①   ②   ③   ④

convex contour   rising contour   concave contour with   concave contour with

early inflection point   late inflection point

Figure 28.1 The change pathway of *yang shang* in Wuxi

Source: adapted from Zhang 2019b

perception—was likely important to the advancement of the merger. The change seems to originate among urban speakers and diffuse outward from the city, and to be led by females.

Discussion

The *yang shang–yang qu* merger was well documented in historical linguistics, but the pathway by which the merger advanced was unknown. The framework of sociophonetics offered answers to the mystery. By comparing the tonal contours produced by older and younger speakers, as well as rural and urban speakers, and drawing on sociophonetic concepts of apparent time, of the diffusion of sound changes from urban centers to rural areas, and of female leadership of linguistic change, Zhang (2019b) described the sociophonetic process of tonal merger.

Wuxi tone change was similar to the T4 changes in Bangkok Thai identified by Pittayaporn (2018). This suggests a cross-linguistic trend in tone change. As T4 changes in Bangkok Thai are linguistically motivated, the cross-linguistic similarity suggests that the merger of *yang shang* to *yang qu* in the Wuxi dialect has additional linguistic motivations that remain to be explored.

Conclusion

This chapter has sketched the emergence of Chinese sociophonetic studies, especially through the first two decades of the twenty-first century. Chinese sociophonetics is deeply rooted in China's dialectological research traditions. The field is also deeply influenced by its unique context. The research questions Chinese sociophoneticians have asked have been shaped by rapid, large-scale urbanization, national promotion of Putonghua over other varieties, the centrality of tone to linguistic meaning, and even the way that lines between "languages" and "dialects" are drawn. These factors have also created spaces where Chinese sociophoneticians are uniquely positioned to contribute to linguistic theory.

While these themes will almost certainly continue to be central to Chinese sociophonetics, future research must address many gaps. More investigations of variation in segments, voice quality, and prosody are needed to map the sociophonetic diversity across the many dialects of Chinese. Such studies will reveal insights into the sociophonetic realities of more than one billion speakers, and offer potential to supplement, confirm, revise, and challenge foundational theories of sociophonetics and sociolinguistics built from datasets of major Western languages. Perceptual studies are also needed to enhance our understanding of the social meanings of sociophonetic variation in Chinese and of speakers' cognitive mechanisms for processing variation. Even some relatively well-trodden variables of first-wave sociolinguistics remain relatively under-explored in Chinese sociophonetics; while studies exploring variation as a result of gender and age are abundant, few studies refer to macro-level social categories like socioeconomic or educational attainment. Given differences between the social and economic structures of many Western speech communities and the Chinese context, discovering how speakers sociophonetically navigate such categories in China offers potentially new ways to understand interactions between traditional social variables and sociophonetic variation. Likewise, second- and third-wave sociolinguistic approaches remain rich opportunities for Chinese sociophoneticians. As this chapter makes clear, we see ourselves now as witnesses to the youth of Chinese sociophonetics, and anticipate tremendous and exciting growth ahead as the field reaches maturity.

Acknowledgments

Jingwei Zhang and Weijie Tan are the primary authors of this chapter; they completed the systematic literature review and wrote the first two complete drafts. Christopher Strelluf substantially rewrote the chapter for inclusion in this handbook. All three authors contributed to final revision.

References

Barale, Catherine Ann. 1982. *A quantitative analysis of the loss of final consonants in Beijing Mandarin.* PhD dissertation, University of Pennsylvania.

Bauer, Robert S. & Paul K. Benedict. 1997. *Modern Cantonese phonology.* De Gruyter Mouton. https://doi.org/10.1515/9783110823707

Bauer, Robert S., Cheung Kwan-hin & Cheung Pak-man. 2003. Variation and merger of the rising tones in Hong Kong Cantonese. *Language Variation and Change* 15(2). 211–225. https://doi.org/10.1017/S0954394503152039

Boersma, Paul & Vincent van Heuven. 2001. Speak and unspeak with Praat. *Glot International* 5(9–10). 341–347.

Britain, David. 2005. Where did New Zealand English come from? In Allan Bell, Ray Harlow & Donna Starks (eds.), *Languages of New Zealand*, 156–193. Victoria University Press.

Bybee, Joan. 2007. *Frequency of use and the organization of language.* Oxford University Press.

Callier, Patrick. 2013. *Linguistic context and the social meaning of voice quality variation.* PhD dissertation, Georgetown University.

Chao, Yuan R. 1928. *Xiandai Wuyu de yanjiu* [Studies in the Modern Wu-dialects]. Tsing Hua College Research Institute.

Chen, Baoya. 1996. *Lun yuyan jiechu yu yuyan lianmeng: Han Yue Dongtai yuyuan guanxi de jieshi* [Language contact and language union: Explaining the linguistic relationship between Chinese and Yue (kam-tai)]. Language and Culture Press.

Chen, Ping. 1999. *Modern Chinese: History and sociolinguistics.* Cambridge University Press.

Chen, Ziqi, Yao Yao & Alan C.L. Yu. 2018. Changing against tone merging trends in community? The case of C.Y. Leung. In *Proceedings of the 32nd Pacific Asia Conference on Language, Information and Computation.* Association for Computational Linguistics.

Cheng, Chin-chuan. (1973). *A synchronic phonology of Mandarin Chinese.* De Gruyter Mouton.

Cheng, S.K. Ken. 2017. Beginning or on-going: 2b-3a tone change in Hong Kong Cantonese revisited. *Journal of Chinese Linguistics* 45(2). 313–343.

Cheng, Ruoqian, Allard Jongman & Joan A. Sereno. 2023. Production and perception evidence of a merger: [l] and [n] in Fuzhou Min. *Language and Speech* 66(3). 533–563. https://doi.org/10.1177/00238309221114433

Cheshire, Jenny. 2020. Taking the longer view: Explaining Multicultural London English and Multicultural Paris French. *Journal of Sociolinguistics* 24(3). 307–328. https://doi.org/10.1111/josl.12385

Cheshire, Jenny, Paul Kerswill, Sue Fox & Eivind Torgersen. 2011. Contact, the feature pool and the speech com-munity: The emergence of Multicultural London English. *Journal of Sociolinguistics* 15(2). 151–196. https://doi.org/10.1111/j.1467-9841.2011.00478.x

Clark, Lynn & Graeme Trousdale. 2009. Exploring the role of token frequency in phonological change: Evidence from TH-fronting in east-central Scotland. *English Language and Linguistics* 13(1). 33–55. https://doi.org/10.1017/S1360674308002852

Deutsch, Diana, Jinghong Le, Jing Shen & Trevor Henthorn. 2009. The pitch levels of female speech in two Chinese villages. *Journal of the Acoustical Society of America* 125(5). EL208–EL213. https://doi.org/10.1121/1.3113892

Esling, John H., Scott R. Moisik, Allison Benner & Lise Crevier-Buchman. 2019. *Voice quality: The laryngeal articulator model.* Cambridge University Press.

Faber, Alice, Catherine T. Best & Marianna Di Paolo. 1994. Dialect differences in vowel production and perception. *Journal of the Acoustical Society of America* 96(5). 3283. https://doi.org/10.1121/1.410942

Faber, Alice & Marianna Di Paolo. 1995. The discriminability of nearly merged sounds. *Language Variation and Change* 7(1). 35–78. https://doi.org/10.1017/S0954394500000892

Forrest, Jon. 2017. The dynamic interaction between lexical and contextual frequency: A case study of (ING). *Language Variation and Change* 29(2). 129–156. https://doi.org/10.1017/S0954394517000072

Fung, Roxana S.Y. & Chris K.C. Lee. 2019. Tone mergers in Hong Kong Cantonese: An asymmetry of production and perception. *Journal of the Acoustical Society of America* 146(5). EL424–EL430. https://doi.org/10.1121/1.5133661

Fung, Roxana S.Y. & Cathy S.P. Wong. 2010a. Mergers and near-mergers in Hong Kong Cantonese tones. Paper presented at the 4th European Conference on Tone and Intonation, Stockholm, Sweden.

Fung, Roxana S.Y. & Cathy S.P. Wong. 2010b. The mechanisms of tone mergers in Hong Kong Cantonese. Paper presented at 15th International Conference on Yue Dialects, Macau.

Fung, Roxana S.Y. & Cathy S.P. Wong. 2011. Acoustic analysis of the new rising tone in Hong Kong Cantonese. In *Proceedings of the 17th International Congress of Phonetic Sciences*, 715–718. ICPhS.

Gao, Jiayin. 2016. Sociolinguistic motivations in sound change: On-going loss of low tone breathy voice in Shanghai Chinese. *Papers in Historical Phonology* 1. 166–186. https://doi.org/10.2218/pihph.1.2016.1698

Hay, Jennifer B., Janet B. Pierrehumbert, Abby J. Walker & Patrick LaShell. 2015. Tracking word frequency effects through 130 years of sound change. *Cognition* 139. 83–91. https://doi.org/10.1016/j.cognition.2015.02.012

Herold, Ruth. 1990. *Mechanisms of merger: The implementation and distribution of the low back merger in eastern Pennsylvania*. PhD dissertation, University of Pennsylvania.

Herold, Ruth. 1997. Solving the actuation problem: Merger and immigration in Eastern Pennsylvania. *Language Variation and Change* 9(2). 165–189. https://doi.org/10.1017/S0954394500001861

Ho, Dah-an. 1988. 'Zhuó Shǎng Guī Qù' yu xiandai fangyan ['Zhuó Shǎng Guī Qù' and the modern dialects]. *Bulletin of Chinese Phonology* 2. 267–292.

Jankowiak, William R. 1993. *Sex, death, and hierarchy in a Chinese city: An anthropological account*. Columbia University Press.

Jin, Jian & Yan Hong. 2018. Jiyu shiyan fenxi de Chaozhou fangyan housewei bianyi yanjiu [On variations of final glottal stop in Chaozhou dialect by phonetic experiments]. *Dialects* 2. 165–174.

Jin, Jian, Weixiang Hu, Xia Wang & Aijun Li. 2008. Guangzhou Putonghua he biaozhun Putonghua shengdiao duibi yanjiu [A comparative study on tone realization in Cantonese-accented Mandarin and standard Mandarin]. *Annual Phonetic Research Report* 2008. 93–98.

Kerswill, Paul & Ann Williams. 2000. Creating a new town koine: Children and language change in Milton Keynes. *Language in Society* 29(1). 65–115. https://doi.org/10.1017/S0047404500001020

Kuo, Jennifer. 2018. A large-scale smartphone-based sociophonetic study of Taiwan Mandarin. *Asia-Pacific Language Variation* 4(2). 197–230. https://doi.org/10.1075/aplv.18005.kuo

Labov, William. 1994. *Principles of linguistic change*, vol. 1, *Internal factors*. Blackwell.

Labov, William. 2001. *Principles of linguistic change*, vol. 2, *Social factors*. Blackwell.

Lai, Wei & Jianjin Kuang. 2020. The effect of speaker gender on Cantonese tone perception. *Journal of the Acoustical Society of America* 147(6). 4119–4132. https://doi.org/10.1121/10.0001411

Lee, Wai-Sum. 2009. Vowel formant frequency characteristics of adult and preadolescent males and females. *Chinese Journal of Phonetics* 2. 90–97.

Li, Aini, Wei Lai, & Jianjing Kuang. 2022. How do listeners identify creak? The effects of pitch range, prosodic position and creak locality in Mandarin. In *Proceedings of Speech Prosody* 2022, 480–484.

Li, Fangfang. 2013. The effect of speakers' sex on voice onset time in Mandarin stops. *Journal of the Acoustical Society of America* 133(2). EL142–EL147. https://doi.org/10.1121/1.4778281

Li, Shanpeng, Wentao Gu, Lei Liu, & Ping Tang. 2020. The role of voice quality in Mandarin sarcastic speech: An acoustic and electroglottographic study. *Journal of Speech, Language, and Hearing Research* 63(8). 2578–2588. https://doi.org/10.1044/2020_JSLHR-19-00166

Li, Xiaoyu. 2018. *Shandong Juxian fangyan jiantuanyin yuyin bianyi yanjiu* [A study on the phonetic variation in the dialect of jiantuan yin pronunciation in Ju country in Shandong province]. PhD dissertation, Shanghai International Studies University.

Li, Xinkui, Jiajiao Huang, Qisheng Shi, Yun Mai & Dingfang Chen. 1995. *Guangzhou fangyan yanjiu* [Study on Guangzhou dialect]. Guangdong People's Publishing House.

Liang, Lei & Xiaolin Meng. 2013. Chongqing fangyan danzidiao de gongshi bianyi [The tone variation of Chongqing dialect]. *Language and Linguistics* (14)5. 929–959.

Liang, Yuan. 2015. Yueyu shengdiao yanbiao jizhi chutan: Xiangganghua yu Guangzhouhua shengdiao huntong de bijiao [The mechanism of tonal change in Cantonese: The comparison of tone mergers in

Hong Kong Cantonese and Guangzhou Cantonese]. In Gan Yu'en (ed.), *South Chinese dialect studies*, vol. 8, 36–44. Jinan University Press.

Liang, Yuan. 2017. Shengdiao bianyi zhong de fayin yu ganzhi jizhi: Yi Xianggang Yueyu weili [The production-perception mechanism in tonal shift: The case of Hong Kong Cantonese]. *Zhongguo Yuwen* 6. 723–732+768.

Liang, Yuan & Baihua Chen. 2013. Leihua /b/ shengmu de bianyi [The variation of /b/ initial in Lei dialect]. *Zhongguo Yuwen* 4. 341–348+384.

Lin, Yuhan. 2018. The role of educational factors in the development of lexical splits. *Asia-Pacific Language Variation* 4(1). 36–72. https://doi.org/10.1075/aplv.17004.lin

Liu, Fu. 1924. *Sisheng shiyan lu* [Record of Experiments on the four tones]. Qun Yi Bookstore.

Liu, Yi. 2012. Xianggang Yueyu shegdiao de xingbie tezheng fenxi [The analysis of Hong Kong Cantonese and genders]. *Chinese Linguistics* 1. 36–43.

Liu, Yi, Feng Shi & Yuanyuan Lin. 2013. Xianggang Yueyu yiji yuanyin nianlingzu tezheng de tongji fenxi [A crossing age analysis on the basic vowels in Hong Kong Cantonese]. *Zhongguo Yuwen* 4. 349–358+384.

Liu Yi, Feng Shi, Rong Rong & Xue Sun. 2011. Xianggang Yueyu shengdiao de fenzu fenxi [The tonal analysis of Hong Kong Cantonese in age groups]. *Studies in Language and Linguistics* 31(4). 98–106.

Liu, Zhijing, Ju Lin, Jinsong Zhang & Weijia Zhang. 2016. Nianling he xingbie dui beijinghua shangshengdiao zhong galiesheng de yingxiang [The influence of age and gender on the creaky voice in Beijing Putonghua]. *Chinese Journal of Phonetics* 6. 32–27.

Llamas, Carmen & Dominic Watt. 2014. Scottish, English, British? Innovations in attitude measurement. *Language and Linguistics Compass* 8(11). 610–617. https://doi.org/10.1111/lnc3.12109

Lu, Jianming & Yang Shen. 2003. *Hanyu he hanyu yanjiu shiwu jiang* [Fifteen lectures on Chinese language and Chinese linguistics]. Peking University Press.

Mok, Peggy P.K. & Peggy W.Y. Wong. 2010. Perception of the merging tones in Hong Kong Cantonese: Preliminary data on monosyllables. Paper presented at Speech Prosody 2010, Chicago.

Mok, Peggy P.K., Donghui Zuo & Peggy W.Y. Wong. 2013. Production and perception of a sound change in progress: Tone merging in Hong Kong Cantonese. *Language Variation and Change* 25(3). 341–370. https://doi.org/10.1017/S0954394513000161

Nagy, Naomi. 2011. A multilingual corpus to explore variation in language contact situations. *Rassegna Italiana di Linguistica Applicata* 43(1–2). 65–84.

Ou, Jinghua. 2012. *Tone merger in Guangzhou Cantonese*. PhD dissertation, Hong Kong Polytechnic University.

Peterson, Gordon E. & Harold L. Barney. 1952. Control methods used in a study of vowels. *Journal of the Acoustical Society of America* 24. 175–184. https://doi.org/10.1121/1.1906875

Pittayaporn, Pittayawat. 2018. Phonetic and systemic biases in tonal contour changes in Bangkok Thai. In Haruo Kubozono & Mikio Giriko (eds.), *Tonal change and neutralization*, 249–278. De Gruyter Mouton. https://doi.org/10.1515/9783110567502-010

Qi, Haifeng. 2011. Zhaoyuan fangyan shengdiao geju de bianyi [On tone patterns changes in Zhaoyuan dialect]. *Chinese Linguistics* 2. 36–42.

Qian, Nairong. 1992. *Dangdai Wuyu yanjiu* [Studies on contemporary Wu dialects]. Shanghai Educational Press.

Ran, Qibin. 2017. Bianyi yu fenhua: Jiaoda yangben shijiao xia de Beijinghua seyin geju [Variations and differentiations: Plosive patterns of Beijing Mandarin based on a larger sample]. *Applied Linguistics* 4. 29–38.

Shan, Yunming. 2019. On intergenerational differences in code-switching among Cantonese people. *Asia-Pacific Language Variation* 5(1). 9–27. https://doi.org/10.1075/aplv.18008.sha

Shen, Xiaonan Susan. 1992. Mandarin neutral tone revisited. *Acta Linguistica Hafniensia* 24(1). 131–152. https://doi.org/10.1080/03740463.1992.10412273

Shi, Feng & Ping Wang. 2006. Beijinghua danziyin shengdiao de tongji fenxi [A statistical analysis of the tones in Beijing Mandarin]. *Zhongguo Yuwen* 1. 33–40.

Singh, Leher & Thilanga D. Wewalaarachchi. 2020. Effects of age and bilingualism on sensitivity to native and nonnative tone variation: Evidence from spoken word recognition in Mandarin Chinese earners. *Developmental Psychology* 56(9). 1642–1656. https://doi.org/10.1037/dev0001041

Sloos, Marjoleine & Lei Wang. 2018. Same stimuli, same subjects, different perception: Believed dialect bias in the perception of Chinese plosives. *Asia-Pacific Language Variation* 4(2). 231–252. https://doi.org/10.1075/aplv.17006.slo

Solon, Megan, Bret Linford & Kimberly L. Geeslin. 2018. Acquisition of sociophonetic variation. *Revista Española de Lingüística Aplicada* 31(1). 309–344. https://doi.org/10.1075/resla.16028.sol

Strelluf, Christopher. 2016. Overlap among back vowels before /l/ in Kansas City. *Language Variation and Change* 28(3). 379–407. https://doi.org/10.1017/S0954394516000144

Textor, C. 2021. Urbanization in China 1980–2021. *Statista.* www.statista.com/statistics/270162/urbanization-in-china/

Trudgill, Peter. 2004. *New-dialect formation: The inevitability of colonial Englishes.* Edinburgh University Press.

Trudgill, Peter. 2016. ELF and new-dialect formation. In Marie-Luise Pitzl & Ruth Osimk-Teasdale (eds.), *English as a Lingua Franca: Perspectives and prospects: Contributions in honour of Barbara Seidlhofer,* 115–122. De Gruyter Mouton. https://doi.org/10.1515/9781501503177-018

Tse, Holman. 2016. Variation and change in Toronto heritage Cantonese: An analysis of two monophthongs across two generations. *Asia-Pacific Language Variation* 2(2). 124–156. https://doi.org/10.1075/aplv.2.2.02tse

Tse, Holman. 2019. Vowel shifts in Cantonese? Toronto vs. Hong Kong. *Asia-Pacific Language Variation* 5(1). 67–83. https://doi.org/10.1075/aplv.19001.tse

Tseng, Shu-Chuan. 2005. Monosyllabic word merger in Mandarin. *Language Variation and Change* 17(3). 231–256. https://doi.org/10.1017/S0954394505050143

Wakabayashi Keiko. 1990. Migration from rural to urban areas in China. *The Developing Economies* 28(4). 503–523. https://doi.org/10.1111/j.1746-1049.1990.tb00195.x.

Wang, Feifan. 2019. Hanzi he zhuguan cipin dui jiechu yinfa de yuyin bianyi de yingxiang: Yi xinpai Shanghai fangyan Xamuxiyinzi weili [Effects of Chinese characters and subjective word frequency on contact-induced variation: A case study on Xia initial before high front vowels in New Shanghainese]. *Zhongguo Yuwen* 4. 418–429+510–511.

Wang, Junjia, Siwei Liu & Wei Qing. 2016. Cong fanchouganzhi kan Chongqinghua Yinping he Yangping de diaoxing: Jianlun Chongqinghua Yinping he Shangsheng yanbian de dongyin [Tonal patterns and categorical perception of Yinping and Yangping in Chongqing Mandarin: Implications to historical Chongqing of Yinping and Shangsheng]. *Chinese Journal of Phonetics* 7. 18–27.

Wang, Ping. 2009. *Beijing hua shengdiao he yuanyin de shiyan yu tongji* [Experiments and statistical analysis of tones and vowels in Beijing Mandarin]. Nankai University Press.

Wang, Xuan. 2017. Investigating the role of speaker attitudes in koinéisation in Hohhot, China. *Asia-Pacific Language Variation* 3(2). 232–270. https://doi.org/10.1075/aplv.16014.wan

Wiese, Heike. 2012. *Kiezdeutsch: Ein neuer Dialekt entsteht.* Beck.

Wu, Zongji. 1986. *Hanyu Putonghua danyinjie yutuce* [Speech spectrogram of Putonghua monosyllables]. Chinese Social Science Press.

Wu, Zongji & Maocan Lin. 1989. *Shiyan yuyinxue gaiyao* [The handbook of instrumental phonetics]. Higher Education Press.

Xu, Chenchen & Mao Lingfeng. 2017. The sociolinguistic meanings of syllable contraction in Chinese: A study using perceptual maps. *Asia-Pacific Language Variation* 3(2). 160–199. https://doi.org/10.1075/aplv.16004.xu

Xu, Daming. 1992. *A sociolinguistic study of Mandarin nasal variation.* PhD dissertation, University of Ottawa.

Xu, Daming. 2015. Speech community and linguistic urbanization: Sociolinguistic theories developed in China. In Dick Smakman & Patrick Heinrich (eds.), *Globalising sociolinguistics: Challenging and expanding theory,* 95–106. Routledge.

Xu, Chenchen & Lingfeng Mao. 2017. The sociolinguistic meanings of syllable contraction in Chinese: A study using perceptual maps. *Asia-Pacific Language Variation* 3(2). 160–199. https://doi.org/10.1075/aplv.16004.xu

Yang, Xiaohu, Yuxia Wang, Lilong Xu, Hui Zhang & Can Xu. 2015. Aging effect on Mandarin Chinese vowel and tone identification. *Journal of the Acoustical Society of America* 138(4). EL411–EL416. https://doi.org/10.1121/1.4933234

Yu, Alan C.L. 2007. Understanding near mergers: The case of morphological tone in Cantonese. *Phonology* 24(1). 187–214. https://doi.org/10.1017/S0952675707001157

Yu, Alan C.L. 2016. Vowel-dependent variation in Cantonese /s/ from an individual-difference perspective. *Journal of the Acoustical Society of America* 139(4). 1672–1690. https://doi.org/10.1121/1.4944992

Yu, Qian & Yiling Huang. 2019. Fangyanbeijing yingxiang Putonghua shengdiao fanchou ganzhi [The influence of dialect experience on categorical perception of Mandarin tones]. *Applied Linguistics* 3. 114–123.

Zhang, Jingwei. 2014. *A sociophonetic study on tonal variation of the Wúxī and Shànghǎi dialects.* Landelijke Onderzoekschool Taalwetenschap.

Zhang, Jingwei. 2019a. Tone mergers in Cantonese: Evidence from Hong Kong, Macao, and Zhuhai. *Asia-Pacific Language Variation* 5(1). 28–49. https://doi.org/10.1075/aplv.18007.zha

Zhang, Jingwei. 2019b. Gongshi yinbian lujing de shizheng fenxi: Yixiang Wuyu shengdiao bianyi de shehuiyuyinxue yanjiu [Tracing the route of a sound change in progress with empirical data: A sociophonetic study on the tonal variation in the Wu dialect]. *Linguistic Sciences* 18(6). 581–595.

Zhang, Jingwei & Daming Xu. Forthcoming. Chinese. In Yoshiyuki Asahi, Paul Kerswill & Alexandra D'Arcy (eds.), *The Routledge handbook of variationist sociolinguistics*. Routledge.

Zhang, Jingwei, Yanyong Zhang & Daming Xu. 2019. A variationist approach to tone categorization in Cantonese. *Chinese Language and Discourse* 10(1). 1–16. https://doi.org/10.1075/cld.18008.zha

Zhang, Wei & John M. Levis. 2021. The Southwestern Mandarin /n/-/l/ merger: Effects on production in Standard Mandarin and English. *Frontiers in Communication* 6. https://doi.org/10.3389/fcomm.2021.639390

Zhao, Hui. 2018. Social meaning in the perception of neutral tone variation in Putonghua. *Asia-Pacific Language Variation* 4(2). 161–196. https://doi.org/10.1075/aplv.18003.zha

Zhu, Chuan. 1986. *Shiyan yuyinxue jichu* [The basics of instrumental phonetics]. East China Normal University Press.

Zhu, Xiaonong. 1995. *Shanghai tonetics*. PhD thesis, Australian National University.

Zhu, Xiaonong. 1999. *Shanghai tonetics*. Lincom.

INDEX

Note: Page locators in **bold** and *italics* represents tables and figures, respectively.

American English (AmE) 35, 145, 224, *224*, 240, 333; General American English (GenAmE) 492; General North American English (GNAE) 299, 300; influence on South African English 498; /l/ 217; North American English 122, 155, 240, 293, 296–300, 506; *r* 199, 200; speech rate 63; stops in 146, 148; ṼNC sequences 245; vowels 127, 269

American Indian languages 395

American Sign Language (ASL) 458, 467, 468, 475; black 474, 481–2; changes in 475; *Dictionary of American Sign Language* 473; dominance reversal 479, 480, 481, *481*, 482; evolution of 478; Motivated Look at Indicating Verbs in ASL (MoLo) project 470; Signbank 471; variation 473; verb reduplication study 473

American Southern English (ASE) 61–2, 349

American Speech-Language-Hearing Association (ASHA) and website 449, 454; publication 455–6

Anglo-English *r* 202–3

anime: characters 526; voice 527–32

anti-formants 249

aphasia 449, 450

apical *r* 197, 201, 198

Applebaum, Irene 338

applied sociophonetics 14

approximants 144, 196; alveolar lateral /l/ 214; retroflex/bunched 205, 206, 207–8

Arab Americans 572

Arab communities 572

Arab countries, gender roles 569

Arab education and class 562, 571

Arab migration 560–1, 571

Arab social networks 571

Arab societies, social gendered behaviour 563

Arabic 80; Classical 562, 570; consonants 565; dialects of 564–5, 561; Emirati 567; gemination 565, 567; influence on French 566; koinéization 571; /l/ 223; Lebanese 146, 150, 221, 223, 565; Modern Standard (MSA) 562, 564, 569; multiglossic situation 560, 569; pharyngealized sounds 566–7; /q/ 154; sociolinguistics and gender 568–70; studies 562–3, 564, 567–8; suprasegmental features 566–7; vernacular 562, 564–5; vocal setting and gender 566; vowels 565–6; women's voices 566–7; words, root structure 574

Arabic-English bilingual acquisition 568, 573

Argentinian Spanish 585, 586, 587

ARPABET 491, 506, 507; adaptations to 507; symbols of transcription **506**; *see also* CMU Dictionary

articulation, place of 205, **208**

articulations, velar and alveolar 237

articulatory co-variation 239, 240, 244

articulation rate 57, *58*, 60, 61, 71; age-graded pattern 61, *61*, 63; domain of 57; model *70*; utterance lengths on 57, *58*; variability factors 63

articulatory re-analysis 244

articulatory studies 128

aryepiglottic tightening 97

Ashby accent 425

Asia Minor Greek (AMG) 39, 40, *41*, *42*

Asian speakers, bias towards 435

aspirated voiced stops 286

assibilation 148, 179

assimilation 154

Atlas of North American English (ANAE) 272, 293–4, 296

Attitude Analog Scale method 619

auditory coding 434

Australian English (AusE) 28, 95, 115, 155, 180, 335

Australian National Database of Spoken Language (ANDOSL) 335; map task corpus 30

Austrian German 222

authoritative voice 35

autocorrelation software 78

automatic speech recognition (ASR) 64, 375–6

Autosegmental-Metrical (AM) approach 26

AutoVOT 156, *157*

axiomatic principles 559–60

/b/, Spanish 590

ʙᴀɢ-raising 297

Bangkok Thai 628

Bangladeshi community 415

banlieue: accent 544, 546, 548, 552

Bantu languages 76

ʙᴀᴛʜ 16, 127, 289, 318, 418–9, 499, 507; *see also* /æh/; short-a

Battisti, Carlo 371

Beddor model 245–6

ʙᴇɢ-raising 273, *274*

behavior adaptation 332

Beijing dialect 83–4, 615, 618, 623, 625, 626

Belfast English 31, 35–6

Belgian Dutch 197, 204, 205

Belgian *r* 207

Belgium 543

Bhattacharyya's Affinity (BA) 336

bidialectal speakers 318–9

bidirectional interference 573

bilabials 154

bilingual speakers 100–1, **100**; children 421, 422, **424**, 425, 568; Māori English 332; phonetic convergence 32–4; sequential 413, 418; Turkish-German 32

bilingualism 183, 221–2

binary notation system 16, 285

biographical indexicality 319